A PEOPLE AND A NATION

A PEOPLE

A

AND A NATION
History of the United States

Second Edition   Volume II: Since 1865

MARY BETH NORTON
Cornell University

DAVID M. KATZMAN
University of Kansas

PAUL D. ESCOTT
University of North Carolina, Charlotte

HOWARD P. CHUDACOFF
Brown University

THOMAS G. PATERSON
University of Connecticut

WILLIAM M. TUTTLE, JR.
University of Kansas

HOUGHTON MIFFLIN COMPANY BOSTON
Dallas   Geneva, Illinois   Lawrenceville, New Jersey   Palo Alto

Mary Beth Norton

Now a professor of history at Cornell University, Mary Beth Norton was born in Ann Arbor, Michigan, and received her B.A. from the University of Michigan (1964). Harvard University awarded her the Ph.D. in 1969, the year her dissertation won the Allan Nevins Prize. Her writing includes *The British-Americans: The Loyalist Exiles in England, 1774–1789* (1972) and *Liberty's Daughters: The Revolutionary Experience of American Women, 1750–1800* (1980). With Carol Berkin she has edited a book of original essays, *Women of America: A History* (1979). Her many articles have appeared in such journals as the *William and Mary Quarterly*, *Signs*, and the *American Historical Review*. Mary Beth has served on the National Council on the Humanities. From 1983 to 1985 she was president of the Berkshire Conference of Women Historians, and in 1984 she was elected vice president for research of the American Historical Association. Besides holding honorary degrees from Siena College and Marymount Manhattan College, she has received research assistance from the Shelby Cullom Davis Center, Charles Warren Center, National Endowment for the Humanities, and the American Antiquarian Society.

David M. Katzman

A graduate of Queens College (B.A., 1963) and the University of Michigan (Ph.D., 1969), David M. Katzman is now a professor of history at the University of Kansas. Born in New York City, David is known for his work in labor, social and black history. His book *Seven Days a Week: Women and Domestic Service in Industrializing America* (1978) won the Philip Taft Labor History Prize. He has also written *Before the Ghetto: Black Detroit in the Nineteenth Century* (1973) and contributed to *Three Generations in Twentieth-Century America: Family, Community and the Nation* (Second Edition, 1981). With William M. Tuttle, Jr., David has edited *Plain Folk: The Life Stories of Undistinguished Americans* (1981). The Guggenheim Foundation, National Endowment for the Humanities, and Ford Foundation have awarded him research assistance. He has written articles for the *Dictionary of American Biography* and has served as the associate editor of the journal *American Studies*. For 1984–1985 he was Visiting Professor of Economic and Social History, University of Birmingham, England.

Paul D. Escott

Born and reared in the Midwest (St. Louis, Missouri), Paul D. Escott studied in New England and the South. His interest in southern history and the Civil War era probably began with southern parents, but it became conscious at Harvard College (B.A., 1969) and matured at Duke University (Ph.D., 1974). Now a professor of history at the University of North Carolina, Charlotte, Paul has written *After Secession: Jefferson Davis and the Failure of Confederate Nationalism* (1978), *Slavery Remembered: A Record of Twentieth-Century Slave Narratives* (1979), and *Many Excellent People: Power and Privilege in North Carolina, 1850–1900* (1985). Paul's articles have appeared in such journals as *Civil War History*, *Georgia Historical Quarterly*, and *Journal of Southern History*. Active in the profession, he has served on committees of the Southern Historical Association. Fellowships from the Whitney M. Young, Jr., Memorial Foundation, the American Philosophical Society, and the Rockefeller Foundation have aided his research.

Howard P. Chudacoff

A professor of history at Brown University, Howard P. Chudacoff was born in Omaha, Nebraska, and received his degrees from the University of Chicago (A.B., 1965; Ph.D., 1969). At Brown he has co-chaired the American Civilization Program. His books include *Mobile Americans: Residential and Social Mobility in Omaha, 1880–1920* (1972) and the *Evolution of American Urban Society* (Third Edition, 1986). His many articles on topics in urban and social history have appeared in such journals as the *Journal of Family History*, *Reviews in American History*, and the *Journal of American History*. Howard has lectured and presented papers at many universities and historical meetings, and has received research awards from the Rockefeller Foundation, National Endowment for the Humanities, and the Population Studies and Research Center of Brown University.

Thomas G. Paterson

Thomas G. Paterson was born in Oregon City, Oregon. He graduated from the University of New Hampshire (B.A., 1963) before earning his doctorate from the University of California, Berkeley in 1968. He is now a professor of history at the University of Connecticut. His books include *Soviet-American Confrontation* (1973), *On Every Front* (1979), and *American Foreign Policy: A History* (Second Edition, 1983). Among his edited scholarship is *Major Problems in American Foreign Policy* (Second Edition, 1984). The author of over thirty articles, Tom's work has appeared in the *American Historical Review* and the *Journal of American History*. He has served on the editorial boards of the *Journal of American History* and *Diplomatic History*, on committees of the Organization of American Historians and Society for Historians of American Foreign Relations, and on the Board of Trustees of Stonehill College. Tom has also directed National Endowment for the Humanities Summer Seminars for College Teachers. His research has been assisted by the American Philosophical Society, Institute for the Study of World Politics, National Endowment for the Humanities, and others.

William M. Tuttle, Jr.

A native of Detroit, Michigan, who graduated from Denison University (1959) and the University of Wisconsin, Madison (Ph.D., 1967), William M. Tuttle, Jr. is now a professor of history at the University of Kansas. Bill has written the award-winning *Race Riot: Chicago in the Red Summer of 1919* (1970) and has edited *W. E. B. Du Bois* (1973) and, with David M. Katzman, *Plain Folk* (1982). As an historical consultant, he has helped prepare several public television documentaries and docudramas. Bill's numerous articles have appeared in the *Journal of Negro History*, *Labor History*, *Agricultural History*, *Technology and Culture*, and the *Journal of American History*. The Guggenheim Foundation, National Endowment for the Humanities, and American Council of Learned Societies have provided him with research assistance. He has also been awarded fellowships from the Institute of Southern History at Johns Hopkins University, Charles Warren Center at Harvard, and Stanford Humanities Center. He was elected to the Nominating Board of the Organization of American Historians.

ABOUT THE COVER

Woman with Roses.   This full-length figurehead was called "Belva Lockwood" by a previous owner, although no evidence has been found to link her with a vessel of that name. Belva Lockwood (1830–1917) was a lawyer, leader in the women's suffrage movement, and twice a candidate for president. Photographs of her in the 1880s look remarkably like the Woman with Roses. The figurehead can now be seen at the Mystic Seaport Museum in Connecticut.

Printed in the U.S.A.
Library of Congress Catalog Card Number: 85-60315
ISBN: 0-395-37937-7
  BCDEFGHIJ-D-89876

CONTENTS

Chapter 22

THE QUEST FOR EMPIRE, 1865–1914

Chapter 23

AMERICA AT WAR, 1914–1920

Chapter 24

THE NEW ERA OF THE 1920s

Chapter 25

THE SHAKEN DREAM, 1929–1933

Chapter 26

THE GREAT DEPRESSION AND THE NEW DEAL, 1933–1941

Chapter 27

DIPLOMACY IN A BROKEN WORLD, 1920–1941

Chapter 28

THE SECOND WORLD WAR AT HOME AND ABROAD, 1941–1945

Chapter 29

THE COLD WAR AND AMERICAN POLITICS, 1945–1953

Chapter 30

AN AGE OF FRAGILE CONSENSUS, 1953–1961

Chapter 31

AMERICAN SOCIETY DURING THE POSTWAR BOOM, 1945–1960s

APPENDIX

MAPS/CHARTS

PREFACE

The generous reception given to the first edition of this volume by our colleagues in history, the encouragement and suggestions of the many instructors who used the book in their classrooms, and the appearance of new scholarship in the last few years have afforded us the opportunity to improve and update *A People and a Nation*. In this second edition we have retained and strengthened those characteristics of the first edition that students and faculty found attractive. As teachers and students we are always recreating our past, rediscovering the personalities and events that have shaped us, inspired us, and bedeviled us. This book is our rediscovery of America's past—its people and the nation they founded and sustained. Sometimes we find this history comforting, sometimes disturbing. As with our own personal experience, it is both triumphant and tragic, filled with injury as well as healing. As a mirror on our lives, it is always significant.

We draw on recent research as well as on seasoned, authoritative works to offer a comprehensive book that tells the whole story of American history. Presidential and party politics, congressional legislation, Supreme Court decisions, diplomacy and treaties, wars and foreign interventions, economic patterns, and state and local government have been the stuff of American history for generations. Into this traditional fabric we weave social history, broadly defined. We investigate the history of the majority of Americans—women—and of minorities. We study the history of social classes, and we illuminate the private, everyday life of the American people.

Characteristics of the Book

From the ordinary to the exceptional—the factory worker, the slave, the office secretary, the local merchant, the small farmer, the plantation owner, the ward politician, the president's wife, the film star, the scientist, the army general—Americans have had personal stories that have intersected with the public policies of their government. Whether victors or victims, all have been actors in their own right, with feelings, ideas, and aspirations that have fortified them in good times and bad. All are part of the American story; all speak here through excerpts from their letters, diaries, and other writings, and oral histories.

Several questions guided our telling of this narrative. On the official, or public, side of American history, we emphasize Americans' expectations of their governments and the everyday practice of those local, state, and federal institutions. We identify the mood and mentality of an era, in which Americans reveal what they think about themselves and their public officials. And in our discussion of foreign policy we particularly probe its domestic sources.

Major Themes

In the social and economic spheres, we emphasize patterns of change in the population, geographic mobility, and people's adaptation to new environments. We study the interactions of people of different races, ethnic backgrounds, religions, and genders, the social divisions that emerged, and the efforts made, often in reform movements, to heal them. As well, we focus on the effects of technological development on the economy, the worker and workplace, and lifestyles.

In the private, everyday life of the family and the home, we pay particular attention to sex roles, childbearing and childrearing, and diet and dress. We ask how Americans have chosen to entertain themselves, as participants or spectators, with sports, music, the graphic arts, reading, theater, film, and television. Throughout American history, of course, this private part of American life and public policy have interacted and influenced one another.

Students and instructors have liked our use of clear, concrete language, and have commented on how enjoyable the book is to read. They have also told us that we challenged them to think about the meaning of American history, not just to memorize it; to confront our own interpretations and at the same time to understand and respect the views of others; and to show how an historian's mind works to ask questions and to tease conclusions out of a mass of information.

For this revised edition, the authors met to discuss at length the themes and questions of the book. We reviewed numerous reports from instructors and worked to incorporate their suggestions. We also researched the most recent scholarship, alert to new evidence and new interpretations. As well, we examined every line of the text with an eye to conciseness, clarity, and readability. In the course of writing, the six of us read and reread one another's drafts and debated one another with a friendly spririt and mutual respect that strengthened us as scholars.

Several changes in this second edition stand out. First, that part of the book devoted to the post-1941 years has been substantially reorganized to match the way most instructors teach that period. All of the material on the Second World War—domestic and foreign—is now in Chapter 28. The Truman years are covered in Chapter 29 and the Eisenhower years in 30. They are followed by a chapter (31) on the social history of the postwar period. Chapter 32, a foreign policy segment, has been recast to emphasize the origins, experience, and aftermath of the Vietnam War. Chapter 33 then treats the domestic effects of the war and political and economic events for 1961–1973, whereas Chapter 34 does so for 1973–1981. Finally, an altogether new Chapter 35 studies the Reagan years and the interaction among social, political, economic, and diplomatic currents in the 1980s.

Changes in the Second Edition

Second, Chapter 1 has been significantly reworked to provide the stories of the three divergent cultures—Native American, African, and European—that intersected in the New World to mold the early history of the United States. Third, we have expanded our coverage of Asians and Hispanics, constitutional history, and the nuclear arms race. Fourth, throughout the book we have explained the significance of gender in employment—the sexual division of labor. Fifth, we have set out more prominently the themes of each chapter, following the opening vignette. And, finally, A People and a Nation has a new look. Not only have new illustrations and maps been added—they have also been improved through the use of full color. Full color makes the maps (all ninety of them) easier to read and understand and the illustrations (all historically accurate because they are contemporaneous with a chapter's period) truer prints of their originals.

As in the first edition, each chapter opens with the story of an American, ordinary or exceptional, whose experience was representative of the times or whose commentary facilitates our understanding of the chapter themes, which immediately follow this vignette. To help students study and review, we use bold-typed notes—like the one here—to highlight key personalities, events, concepts, and trends. Significant concepts and words are defined and italicized; important events are listed in a chart near the end of most chapters; and suggested readings for further study close each chapter. The Appendix, updated and expanded, is a unique compendium providing a historical overview of the American people and their nation.

Study Aids

To make the book as useful as possible for students and instructors, several learning and teaching ancillaries are available, including a *Study Guide* and *Computerized Study Guide*, an *Instructor's Manual*, a *Test Items* file, a *Computerized Test Items* file, and *Map Transparencies*. The *Study Guide*, which was prepared by George Warren and Cynthia Ricketson of Central Piedmont Community College, includes an introductory chapter on study techniques for history students, as well as learning objectives and a thematic guide for each chapter in the text and exercises on evaluating and using information and on finding the main idea in passages from the text, as well as test questions on the content of each chapter. The *Study Guide* is also available in a computerized version that provides the student with tutorial instruction. The *Instructor's Manual*, by Richard Rowe of Golden West College, contains chapter outlines, suggestions for lectures and discussion, and lists of audio-visual resources. The accompanying *Test Items* file, also by Professor Rowe, offers more than 1,500 multiple-choice and essay questions and more than 700 identification terms. The test items are available to adoptors on computer tape and disk. In addition, there is a set of forty full-color map transparencies available on adoption.

Ancillaries

Though each of us feels answerable for the whole, we take primary responsibility for particular chapters:

Mary Beth Norton, Chapters 1–7, David M. Katzman, Chapters 8–10, 12; Paul D. Escott, Chapters 11, 13–15; Howard P. Chudacoff, Chapters 16–21, 24; Thomas G. Paterson, Chapters 22–23, 25, 27, 30, 32, and part of 35; William M. Tuttle, Jr., Chapters 26, 28–29, 31, 33–34, and part of 35. Thomas G. Paterson also served as the coordinating author and prepared the Appendix.

Acknowledgments

Many instructors have read and criticized the successive drafts of our manuscript. Their constructive suggestions have informed and improved this second edition. We heartily thank:

John K. Alexander, *University of Cincinnati*
Roberta Alexander, *University of Dayton*
John Borden Armstrong, *Boston University*
James Barrett, *University of Illinois*
John Britton, *Francis Marion College*
Richard Burns, *California State University, Los Angeles*
Ballard Campbell, *Northeastern University*
Ron Carden, *South Plains College*
Patricia Cohen, *University of California, Santa Barbara*
Frank Costigliola, *University of Rhode Island*
Jay Coughtry, *University of Nevada, Las Vegas*
William Fleming, *Pan American University*
James Gormly, *Pan American University*
Maurine Greenwald, *University of Pittsburgh*
Linda Guerrero, *Palomar College*
James Hijiya, *Southeastern Massachusetts University*
Richard J. Hopkins, *Ohio State University*
George Juergens, *Indiana University*

Harry Lupold, *Lakeland Community College*
Bart McCash, *Middle Tennessee State University*
John Muldowny, *University of Tennessee*
Leonard Murphy, *San Antonio College*
Paul L. Murphy, *University of Minnesota*
Philip Nicholson, *Nassau Community College*
Lawrence Powell, *Tulane University*
Howard Rabinowitz, *University of New Mexico*
Roy Rosenzweig, *George Mason University*
James H. Sasser, *Central Piedmont Community College*
Constance Schulz, *University of South Carolina*
Peter Shattuck, *California State University, Sacramento*
Rebecca Shoemaker, *Indiana State University*
Harvard Sitkoff, *University of New Hampshire*
William R. Swagerty, *University of Idaho*
Emory Thomas, *University of Georgia*
James Walter, *Sinclair Community College*
Nelson Woodard, *California State University, Fullerton*

We acknowledge with thanks as well the contributions of Ruth Alexander, Nancy Fisher Chudacoff, J. Garry Clifford, Christopher Collier, Mary Ellen Erickson, Elizabeth French, William Gienapp, James L. Gormly, Frederick Hoxie, Nathan Huggins, Jacqueline Jones, Sharyn A. Katzman, Freeman Meyer, William H. Moore, Holly Izard Paterson, Shirley Rice, Barney J. Rickman, III, Janice Riley, Daniel Usner, Deborah White, David Wyllie, and Thomas Zoumaras. We also appreciate the continued guidance and generous assistance of the staff of the Houghton Mifflin Company.

T.G.P.

Reconstruction by Trial and Error

1865–1877

Chapter 15

It was a beautiful spring day in 1868. Sunlight and balmy weather bathed the nation's capital on Saturday, May 16, but few people paused to relax or enjoy their surroundings. All of Washington was tense with excitement. Professional gamblers had flooded into the city, outnumbered perhaps only by the reporters who leapt upon every rumor or scrap of information. As the morning passed, a crowd gathered around the Senate chamber. Foreign dignitaries filled the diplomatic box, and spectators packed the Senate galleries. Outside the chamber thousands milled about, choking the hallways and spilling onto the terraces and streets outside.

Precisely at noon the Chief Justice of the United States entered the Senate. Managers and counsel stood ready. Soon two senators who were seriously ill slowly made their way into the chamber, bringing the number of senators present to its full fifty-four. All principals in this solemn drama were present before the High Court of Impeachment except the accused: Andrew Johnson, President of the United States. Johnson, who never appeared to defend himself in person, waited anxiously at the White House as Chief Justice Salmon Chase ordered the calling of the roll. To each senator he put the questions, "How say you? Is the respondent, Andrew Johnson, President of the United States, guilty or not guilty of a high misdemeanor, as charged in this article?" Thirty-five senators answered, "Guilty," nineteen, "Not guilty." The total was one short of a two-thirds majority. The nation had come within one vote of removing its president from office.

How had this extraordinary event come about? What had brought the executive and legislative branches of government into such severe conflict? An unprecedented problem—the reconstruction of the Union—furnished the occasion, and deepening differences over the proper policy to pursue had led to the confrontation. Obviously, by 1868 president and Congress had reached a point of bitter antagonism, with some congressmen charging that the president was siding with traitors.

In 1865, at the end of the war, such a result seemed most unlikely. Although he was a southerner

from Tennessee, Johnson had built his career upon criticizing the wealthy planters and championing the South's small farmers. When an assassin's bullet thrust him into the presidency, many former slaveowners shared the worries of a North Carolina lady who wrote, "Think of Andy Johnson [as] the president! What will become of us—'the aristocrats of the South' as we are termed?" Northern Radicals who sounded out the new president on his views also felt confident that he would deal sternly with the South. When one of them suggested the exile or execution of ten or twelve leading rebels to set an example, Johnson had vigorously replied, "How are you going to pick out so small a number? Robbery is a crime; rape is a crime; *treason* is a crime; and *crime* must be punished."

Moreover, fundamental change was already under way in the South. During his army's last campaign, General William T. Sherman had issued Special Field Order No. 15, which set aside for Negro settlement the Sea Islands and all abandoned coastal lands thirty miles to the interior, from Charleston to the Saint John's River in northern Florida. Black refugees quickly poured into these lands; by the middle of 1865, forty thousand freed people were living in their new homes. One former slaveowner who visited his old plantation in Beaufort, South Carolina, received friendly and courteous treatment. But his ex-slaves "firmly and respectfully" informed him that "we own this land now. Put it out of your head that it will ever be yours again."

Before the end of 1865, however, these signs of change were reversed. Although Jefferson Davis was imprisoned for two years, no Confederate leaders were executed, and southern aristocrats soon came to view Andrew Johnson not as their enemy but as their friend and protector. Johnson pardoned rebel leaders liberally, allowed them to take high offices, and ordered government officials to reclaim the freedmen's land and give it back to the original owners. One man in South Carolina expressed blacks' dismay: "Why do you take away our lands? You take them from us who have always been true, always true to the Government! You give them to our all-time enemies! That is not right!"

The unexpected outcome of Johnson's program led Congress to examine his policies and design new plans for Reconstruction. Out of negotiations in Congress and clashes between the president and the legislators, there emerged first one, and then two, new plans for Reconstruction. Before the process was over, the nation had adopted the Fourteenth and Fifteenth Amendments and impeached its president.

Racism did not disappear. During the war the federal government had been reluctant to give even black troops fair treatment, and in Congress northern Democrats continued to oppose equality. Republicans were often divided among themselves, but a mixture of idealism and party purposes drove them forward. Ultimately, fear of losing the peace proved decisive with northern voters. The United States enfranchised the freedmen and gave them a role in reconstructing the South.

Blacks benefited from greater control over their personal lives and took the risks of voting and participating in politics. But they knew that the success of Reconstruction also depended on the determination and support of the North. Southern opposition to Reconstruction grew steadily. By 1869 a secret terrorist organization known as the Ku Klux Klan had added large-scale violence to southern whites' repertoire of resistance. Despite federal efforts to protect them, black people were intimidated at the polls, robbed of their earnings, beaten, or murdered. Prosecution of Klansmen rarely succeeded, and Republicans lost their offices in an increasing number of southern states. By the early 1870s the failure of Reconstruction was apparent. Republican leaders and northern voters had to decide how far they would persist in their efforts to reform the South.

As the 1870s advanced, other issues drew attention away from Reconstruction. Industrial growth accelerated, creating new opportunities and raising new problems. Interest in territorial expansion revived. Political corruption became a nationwide scandal and bribery a way of doing business. North Carolina's Jonathan Worth, an old-line Whig who had opposed secession as strongly as he now fought Reconstruction, deplored the atmosphere of greed. "Money has become the God of this country," he wrote in disgust, "and men, otherwise good men, are almost compelled to worship at her shrine." Eventually these other forces triumphed, politics moved on to new concerns, and

the courts turned their attention away from civil rights. Even northern Republicans gave up on racial reform in 1877.

Thus the nation stumbled, by trial and error, toward a policy that attempted to reconstruct the South. Congress insisted on equality before the law for black people and gave black men the right to vote. It took the unprecedented step of impeaching the president. But more far-reaching measures to advance black freedom never had much support in Congress, and when suffrage alone proved insufficient to remake the South, the nation soon lost interest. Reconstruction proclaimed anew the American principle of human equality but failed to secure it in reality.

EQUALITY:

THE UNRESOLVED ISSUE

For America's former slaves, Reconstruction had one paramount meaning: a chance to explore freedom. A southern white woman admitted in her diary that the black people "showed a natural and exultant joy at being free." Former slaves remembered rejoicing and singing far into the night after federal troops reached their plantations. The slaves on one Texas plantation jumped up and down and clapped their hands as one man shouted, "We is free—no more whippings and beatings."

A few blacks gave in to the natural desire to do what had been impossible before. One grandmother who had long resented her treatment "dropped her hoe" and ran to confront the mistress. "I'm free!" she yelled at her. "Yes, I'm free! Ain't got to work for you no more! You can't put me in your pocket [sell me] now!" Another man recalled that he and others "started on the move" and left the plantation, either to search for family members or just to exercise their new-found freedom of movement. As he traveled, one man sang about being free as a frog, " 'cause a frog had freedom to get on a log and jump off when he pleases."

Most freedmen reacted more cautiously and shrewdly, taking care to test the boundaries of their

In the changed circumstances after emancipation, former slaves and former slaveowners had to work out the terms of a new relationship. Winslow Homer suggested some of the complexity of their encounters in A Visit from the Old Mistress *(1876). National Museum of American Art, Smithsonian Institution, Washington, D.C., Gift of William T. Evans.*

new condition. "After the war was over," explained one man, "we was afraid to move. Just like tarpins or turtles after emancipation. Just stick our heads out to see how the land lay." As slaves they had learned to expect hostility from white people, and they did not presume it would instantly disappear. Life in freedom, they knew, might still be a matter of what was allowed, not what was right. "You got to say master?" asked a freedman in Georgia. "Naw," answered his fellows, but "they said it all the same. They said it for a long time."

One sign of this shrewd caution was the way freedmen evaluated potential employers. "Most all the niggers that had good owners stayed with 'em, but the others left. Some of 'em come back and some

didn't," explained one man. If a white person had been relatively considerate to blacks in bondage, blacks reasoned that he might prove a desirable employer in freedom. Other blacks left their plantation all at once, for, as one put it, "that master am sure mean and if we doesn't have to stay we shouldn't, not with that master."

Even more urgently than a fair employer, the freedmen wanted land of their own. Land represented their chance to farm for themselves, to have an independent life. It represented compensation for their generations of travail in bondage. A northern observer noted that freedmen made "plain, straight-forward" inquiries as they settled the

Blacks' Desire for Land

land set aside for them by Sherman. They wanted to be sure the land "would be theirs after they had improved it." Not just in the Sea Island region but everywhere, blacks young and old thirsted for homes of their own. One southerner noted with surprise in her diary that

> Uncle Lewis, the pious, the honored, the venerated, gets his poor old head turned with false notions of freedom and independence, runs off to the Yankees with a pack of lies against his mistress, and sets up a claim to part of her land!

Lewis simply wanted a new beginning. Like millions of other freedmen, he hoped to leave slavery behind.

But no one could say how much of a chance the whites, who were in power, would give to blacks. During the war the federal government had refused to arm black volunteers. Many whites agreed with Corporal Felix Brannigan of the Seventy-fourth New York Regiment. "We don't want to fight side and side with the nigger," he said. "We think we are a too superior race for that." In September 1862 Abraham Lincoln said, "If we were to arm [the Negroes], I fear that in a few weeks the arms would be in the hands of the rebels."

Necessity forced a change in policy; because the war was going badly the administration authorized black enlistments. By spring 1863 black troops were proving their value. One general reported that his "colored regiments" possessed "remarkable aptitude for military training," and another observer said, "They fight like fiends." Lincoln came to see "the colored population" as "the great *available* and yet *unavailed of* force for restoring the Union," and recruitment proceeded rapidly.

Black leaders hoped that military service would secure equal rights for their people. Once the black soldier had fought for the Union, wrote Frederick Douglass, "there is no power on earth which can deny that he has earned the right of citizenship in the United States." If black soldiers turned the tide, asked another man, "Would the nation refuse us our rights . . .? Would it refuse us our vote?"

Wartime experience seemed to prove it would. Despite their valor, black soldiers faced persistent discrimination. In Ohio, for example, a mob shouting "Kill the nigger" attacked an off-duty soldier; on duty, blacks did most of the "fatigue duty," or heavy labor. Moreover, black soldiers were expected to accept inferior pay as they risked their lives. The government paid white privates $13 per month plus a clothing allowance of $3.50. Black troops earned $10 per month less $3 deducted for clothing. Blacks resented this injustice so deeply that in protest two regiments refused to accept any pay, and eventually Congress remedied the discrimination.

Still, this was only a small victory over prejudice; the general attitude of northerners on racial questions was mixed. Abolitionists and many Republicans helped black Americans fight for equal rights, and they won some victories. In 1864 the federal courts accepted black testimony, and New York City desegregated its streetcars. The District of Columbia did the same in 1865, the year the Thirteenth Amendment won ratification. One state, Massachusetts, enacted a comprehensive public accommodations law. On the other hand, there were many more signs of resistance to racial equality. The Democratic party fought against equality, charging that Republicans favored race-mixing and were undermining the status of the white worker. Voters in three states—Connecticut, Minnesota, and Wisconsin—rejected black suffrage in 1865. The racial attitudes of northerners seemed mixed and uncertain.

This was a significant fact, for the history of emancipation in the British Caribbean indicated that, if equality were to be won, the North would have to take a strong and determined stand. In 1833 Great Britain had abolished slavery in its possessions, providing slaveowners with £20 million in compensation plus the benefit of a six-year apprenticeship over all former agricultural slaves. Despite such generosity to the slaveowners, the transition to free labor had not been easy.

Everywhere in the British Caribbean planters fought tenaciously to maintain control over their laborers. Retaining control of local government, the planters fashioned laws, taxes, and administrative decisions with an eye to keeping freedmen on the plantations. With equal determination, the former slaves attempted to move onto small plots of land and raise food crops instead of sugar. They wanted independence and were not interested in raising export crops for the world market. The British, even abolitionists, however,

These schoolteachers were part of Gideon's Band, volunteers sent by northern religious organizations to aid the freed people in Beaufort and Port Royal, South Carolina. Thousands followed their example during Reconstruction.   Western Reserve Historical Society, Cleveland, Ohio.

judged the success of emancipation by the volume of production for the market. Their concern for the freedmen soon faded, and before long the authorities assisted planters further by allowing the importation of indentured "coolie" labor from India.

In the United States, some of the same tendencies had appeared on the Sea Islands long before the war ended. The planters had fled and therefore were not present to try to control their former slaves. The freedmen, however, showed a strong desire to leave the plantations and establish small, self-sufficient farms of their own. Northern missionaries, soldiers, and officials brought education and aid to the freedmen but also wanted them to grow cotton. They disapproved of charity and emphasized the values of competitive capitalism. "The danger to the Negro," wrote one worker in the Sea Islands, was "too high wages."

Indeed it would be "most unwise and injurious," declared another worker, to give former slaves free land.

"The Yankees preach nothing but cotton, cotton!" complained one Sea Island black. "We wants land," wrote another, "this very land that is rich with the sweat of we face and the blood of we back." Asking only for a chance to buy land, this man complained that "they make the lots too big, and cut we out." Indeed, the government did sell thousands of acres in the Sea Islands for nonpayment of taxes, but when blacks pooled their earnings to buy almost 2,000 of the 16,749 acres sold in March 1863, 90 percent of the land went to wealthy investors from the North. Thus even among their northern supporters, the former slaves had received only partial support. How much opportunity would freedom bring? That was a major question to be answered during Reconstruction, and the answer depended on the evolution of policy in Washington.

JOHNSON'S RECONSTRUCTION PLAN

Throughout 1865 the formation of Reconstruction policy rested solely with Andrew Johnson, for shortly before he became president Congress recessed and did not reconvene until December. In the nearly eight months that intervened, Johnson devised his own plan and put it into operation. He decided to form new governments in the South by using his power to grant pardons.

Johnson had a few precedents to follow in Lincoln's wartime plans for Reconstruction. In December 1863 Lincoln has proposed a "10-percent" plan for a government being organized in captured portions of Louisiana. According to this plan, a state government could be established as soon as 10 percent of those who had voted in 1860 took an oath of future loyalty. Only high-ranking Confederate officials would be denied a chance to take the oath, and Lincoln urged that at least a few well-qualified blacks be given the ballot. Radicals bristled, however, at such a mild plan, and a majority of Congress (in the Wade-Davis bill, which Lincoln pocket-vetoed) favored stiffer requirements and stronger proof of loyalty.

Lincoln's Reconstruction Plan

Later, in 1865, Lincoln suggested but then abandoned more lenient terms. At Hampton Roads, where he raised questions about the extent of emancipation (see page 401), Lincoln discussed compensation and restoration to the Union, with full rights, of the very state governments that had tried to leave it. Then in April he considered allowing the Virginia legislature to convene in order to withdraw its support from the Confederate war effort. Faced with strong opposition in his cabinet, however, Lincoln reversed himself, denying that he had intended to confer legitimacy

Combative and inflexible, President Andrew Johnson contributed greatly to the failure and rejection of his own reconstruction program. *Library of Congress.*

on a rebel government. At the time of his death, Lincoln had given general approval to a plan drafted by Secretary of War Stanton that would have imposed military authority and provisional governors as steps toward new state governments. Beyond these general outlines, it is impossible to say what Lincoln would have done had he survived.

Johnson began with the plan Stanton had drafted for consideration by the cabinet. At a cabinet meeting on May 9, 1865, Johnson's advisors split evenly on the question of voting rights for freedmen in the South. Johnson said that he favored black suffrage, but only if the southern states adopted it voluntarily. A champion of states' rights, he regarded this decision as too important to be taken out of the hands of the states.

Such conservatism had an enduring effect on Johnson's policies, but at first it appeared that his old enmity toward the planters might produce a plan for radical changes in class relations among whites. As he appointed provisional governors in the South, Johnson also proposed rules that would keep the wealthy planter class out of power. He required every southern voter to swear an oath of loyalty as a condition of gaining amnesty or pardon. But some southerners would face special difficulties in regaining their rights.

Johnson barred certain classes of southerners from taking the oath and gaining amnesty. Former federal officials who had violated their oaths to support the United States and had aided the Confederacy could not take the oath. Nor could graduates of West Point or Annapolis who had resigned their commissions to fight for the South. The same was true for high-ranking Confederate officers and Confederate political leaders. To this list Johnson added another important group: all southerners who aided the rebellion and whose taxable property was worth more than $20,000. Such individuals had to apply personally to the president for pardon and restoration of political rights, or risk legal penalties, which included confiscation of their land.

Oaths of Amnesty and New State Governments

Thus it appeared that the South's old leadership class would be removed from power, for virtually all the rich and powerful whites of prewar days needed Johnson's special pardon. Many observers, South and North, sensed that the president meant to take his revenge on the haughty aristocrats whom he had always denounced and to raise up a new leadership of deserving yeomen.

Johnson's provisional governors began the Reconstruction process by calling constitutional conventions. The delegates chosen for these conventions had to draft new constitutions eliminating slavery and invalidating secession. After ratification of these constitutions, new governments could be elected, and the states would be restored to the Union with full congressional representation. But no southerners could participate in this process who had not taken the oath of amnesty or who had been ineligible to vote on the day the state seceded. Thus freedmen could not participate in the conventions. Although it was theoretically possible for the white delegates to enfranchise them, such action was at best unlikely.

If Johnson intended to end the power of the old elite, his plan did not work out as he had hoped. The old white leadership proved resilient and influential; prominent Confederates (a few with pardons, but many without) won elections and turned up in various appointive offices. Then, surprisingly, Johnson helped to subvert his own plan. He started pardoning aristocrats and chief rebels, who should not have been in office. By fall 1865 the clerks at the pardon office were straining under the burden, and additional staff had to be hired to churn out the necessary documents. These pardons, plus the return of planters' abandoned lands, put the old elite back in power.

Why did Johnson issue so many pardons? Perhaps vanity betrayed his judgment. Scores of gentlemen of the type who had previously scorned him now waited on him for an appointment. Too long a lonely outsider, Johnson may have succumbed to the attention and flattery of these pardon-seekers. Whether he did or not, he clearly had allowed himself too little time. It took months for the constitution-making and elections to run their course; by the time the process was complete and Confederate leaders had emerged in powerful positions, the reconvening of Congress was near. Johnson faced a choice between admitting failure and scrapping his entire effort or swallowing hard and supporting what had resulted. He decided to stand behind his new governments and declare Reconstruction completed. Thus in December 1865 many Confederate congressmen traveled to Washington to claim seats in the United States Congress, and Alexander Stephens, vice president of the Confederacy, returned to the capital as senator-elect.

Many northerners frowned on the election of such prominent rebels, and there were other results of Johnson's program that sparked negative comment in the North. Some of the state conventions were slow to repudiate secession; others only grudgingly admitted that slavery was dead. Two refused to take any action to repudiate the large Confederate debt. Northerners interpreted these actions as signs of defiance; subsequent legislation defining the status of freedmen confirmed their worst fears. Some legislatures merely revised large sections of the slave codes by substituting the word *freedman* for *slave,* and new laws written from scratch were also very restrictive. In these Black Codes, former slaves who were supposed to be free were compelled to carry passes, observe a curfew, live in housing provided by a landowner, and give up hope of entering many desirable occupations.

Black Codes

Finally, observers noted that the practice in state-supported institutions, such as schools and orphanages, was to exclude blacks altogether. To northerners, the South seemed intent on returning black people to a position of servility.

Thus it was not surprising that a majority of northern congressmen decided to take a close look at the results of Johnson's plan. On reconvening, they voted not to admit the newly elected southern representives, whose credentials were subject under the Constitution to congressional scrutiny. The House and Senate established a joint committee to examine Johnson's policies and advise on new ones. Reconstruction had entered a second phase, one in which Congress would play a strong role.

THE CONGRESSIONAL RECONSTRUCTION PLAN

Northern congressmen disagreed on what to do, but they did not doubt their right to play a role in Reconstruction. The Constitution mentioned neither secession nor reunion, but it did assign a great many major responsibilities to Congress. Among them was the injunction to guarantee to each state a republican government. Under this provision, the legislators thought, they could devise policies for Reconstruction, just as Johnson had used his power to pardon for the same purpose.

They soon found that other constitutional questions had a direct bearing on the policies they followed. What, for example, had the fact of rebellion done to the relationship between southern states and the Union? Lincoln had always insisted that the Union remained unbroken, but not even Andrew Johnson could accept the southern view that the wartime state governments of the South could merely re-enter the nation. Johnson argued that the Union had endured, though individuals had erred; thus the use of his power to grant or withhold pardons. But congressmen who favored vigorous Reconstruction measures tended to argue that war *had* broken the Union. The southern states had committed legal suicide and reverted to the status of territories, they argued, or the South was a conquered nation subject to the victor's will. Moderate congressmen held that the states had forfeited their rights through rebellion, and had thus come under congressional supervision.

These diverse theories mirrored the diversity of Congress itself. Northern legislators fell into four major categories: Democrats, conservative Republicans, moderate Republicans, and Radical Republicans. No one of these groups had decisive power. In terms of ideology the majority of congressmen were conservative. In terms of partisan politics the Republican party had a majority, but there was considerable distance between conservative Republicans, who desired a limited federal role in Reconstruction and were fairly happy with Johnson's actions, and the Radicals. These men, led by Thaddeus Stevens, Charles Sumner, and George Julian, were a minority within their party, but they had the advantage of a clearly defined goal. They believed that it was essential to democratize the South, establish public education, and ensure the rights of freedmen. They favored black suffrage, often supported land confiscation and redistribution, and were willing to exclude the South from the Union for several years if necessary to achieve their goals. Between these two factions lay the moderates, who held the balance of power.

The Radicals

One overwhelming political reality faced all the groups in Congress: the 1866 elections were approaching in the fall. Since Congress had questioned Johnson's program, its members had to develop some modification or alternative program before the elections. The northern public expected them to develop a new Reconstruction plan, and as politicians they knew better than to go before their constituents empty-handed. Thus they had to forge a majority coalition composed either of Democrats and Republicans or various elements of the Republican party. The kind of coalition that formed would determine the kind of plan that Congress developed.

Ironically, it was Johnson and the Democrats that pushed Congress toward Radical rather than conservative policies. The president and the Democrats in Congress refused to cooperate with conservative or moderate Republicans. They insisted, despite evidence of widespread concern, that Reconstruction was over, that the new state governments were legitimate, and that southern representatives should be admitted to Congress. These unrealistic, intransigent positions threw away the Democrats' potential influence and blasted any possibility of bipartisan compromise. Republicans found themselves all lumped together by Democrats; to form a new program, conservative Republicans had to work with the Radicals. Thus bargaining over changes in the Johnson program went on almost entirely within the party.

This development and subsequent events enhanced the influence of the Radicals. But in 1865, Republican congressmen were at first loath to break with the

Congress Struggles for a Compromise

president; he was, for better or worse, the titular head of their party, so they made one last effort to work with him. Early in 1866 many lawmakers thought a compromise had been reached. Under its terms Johnson would agree to two modifications of his program. The life of the Freedmen's Bureau, which fed the hungry, negotiated labor contracts, and started schools, would be extended; and a civil rights bill would be passed to counteract the black codes. This bill, drawn up by a conservative Republican, was designed to force southern courts to recognize equality before the law by giving federal judges the power to remove cases in which blacks were treated unfairly. Its provisions applied to discrimination by private persons as well as government officials. As the first major bill to enforce the Thirteenth Amendment's abolition of slavery, it was a significant piece of legislation, and it became very important in the twentieth century (see page 948).

But in spring 1866, Johnson destroyed the compromise by vetoing both bills (they were later repassed). Denouncing any change in his program, the president condemned Congress's action in inflammatory language. In so doing he questioned the legitimacy of congressional involvement in policy-making and revealed his own racism. Because the Civil Rights Bill defined United States citizens as native-born persons who were taxed, Johnson pronounced it discriminatory toward "large numbers of intelligent, worthy, and patriotic foreigners . . . in favor of the negro." The bill, he said, would "operate in favor of the colored and against the white race."

All hope of working with the president was now gone. But Republican congressmen sensed that their constituents remained dissatisfied with the results of Reconstruction. Violence in the South—notably in Memphis and New Orleans, where police aided brutal raids on black citizens—also convinced Republicans, and the northern public, that more needed to be done. The Republican lawmakers therefore pushed on, and from bargaining among their various factions there emerged a plan. It took the form of a proposed amendment to the Constitution—the fourteenth—and it represented a compromise between radical and conservative elements of the party. The Fourteenth Amendment was Congress's alternative to Johnson's program of Reconstruction.

Of four points in the amendment, there was nearly universal agreement on one: the Confederate debt was declared null and void, the war debt of the United States guaranteed. North-

Fourteenth Amendment

erners uniformly rejected the notion of paying taxes to reimburse those who had financed a rebellion; and business groups agreed on the necessity of upholding the credit of the United States government. There was also fairly general support for altering the personnel of southern governments. In language that harkened back to Johnson's Amnesty Proclamation, the Fourteenth Amendment prohibited political power for prominent Confederates. Only at the discretion of Congress, by a two-thirds vote of each house, could these political penalties be removed.

The section of the Fourteenth Amendment that would have by far the greatest legal significance in later years was the first (see Appendix). On its face, this section was an effort to strike down the black codes and guarantee basic rights to freedmen. It conferred citizenship on freedmen and prohibited states from abridging their constitutional "privileges and immunities." Similarly, the amendment barred any state from taking a person's life, liberty, or property "without due process of law" and from denying "equal protection of the laws." These clauses were phrased broadly enough to become in time powerful guarantees of black Americans' civil rights, indeed, of the rights of all citizens. They also took on added meaning with court rulings that corporations were legally "persons" (see page 487).

The second section of the amendment, which dealt with representation, clearly revealed the compromises

Chapter 15: RECONSTRUCTION BY TRIAL AND ERROR, 1865–1877

and political motives that had produced the document. Northerners, in Congress and out, disagreed whether black citizens should have the right to vote. Commenting on the ambivalent nature of northern opinion, a citizen of Indiana wrote that there was strong feeling in favor of "humane and liberal laws for the government and protection of the colored population." But he admitted to a southern relative that there was prejudice, too. "Although there is a great deal [of] profession among us for the relief of the darkey yet I think much of it is far from being cincere. I guess we want to compell you to do right by them while we are not willing ourselves to do so."

Republican congressmen shied away from confronting this ambivalence, but political reality required them to do something. Under the Constitution, representation was based on population. During slavery each black slave had counted as three-fifths of a person for purposes of congressional representation. Republicans feared that emancipation, which made every former slave five-fifths of a person, might increase the South's power in Congress. If it did, and if blacks were not allowed to vote, the former secessionists would gain seats in Congress.

What a strange result that would seem to most northerners. They had never planned to reward the South for rebellion, and Republicans in Congress were determined not to hand over power to their political enemies. So they offered the South a choice. According to the second section of the Fourteenth Amendment, states did not have to give black men the right to vote. But if they did not do so, their representation would be reduced proportionally. If they did, it would be increased proportionally—but Republicans would be able to appeal to the new black voters. This compromise protected northern interests and gave Republicans a chance to compete if freedmen gained the ballot.

The Fourteenth Amendment dealt with the voting rights of black men but ignored female citizens, black and white. For this reason it elicited a strong reaction from the women's rights movement. Advocates of equal rights for women had worked with abolitionists for decades, often subordinating their cause to that of the slaves. During the drafting of the Fourteenth Amendment, however, female activists demanded to be heard. When legislators defined them as nonvoting citizens, prominent women's leaders such as Elizabeth

Cady Stanton and Susan B. Anthony decided that it was time to end their alliance with abolitionists. Thus the independent women's rights movement grew.

In 1866, however, the major question in Reconstruction politics was how the public would respond to the amendment. Would the northern public support Congress's plan or the president's?

Southern Rejection of the Fourteenth Amendment

Johnson did his best to block the Fourteenth Amendment and to convince northerners to reject it. Condemning Congress's plan and its refusal to seat southern representatives, the president urged state legislatures in the South to vote against ratification. Every southern legislature except Tennessee's rejected the amendment by a large margin. It did best in Alabama, where it failed by a vote of 69 to 8 in the assembly and 27 to 2 in the senate. In three states the amendment received no support at all.

To present his case to northerners, Johnson arranged a National Union convention to publicize his program. The chief executive also took to the stump himself. In an age when active personal campaigning was rare for a president, Johnson boarded a special train for a "swing around the circle" that carried his message far into the Midwest and then back to Washington. In cities such as Cleveland and St. Louis, Johnson castigated the Republicans in his old stump-speaker style. But increasingly audiences rejected his views and hooted and jeered at him.

The election was a resounding victory for Republicans in Congress. Men whom Johnson had denounced won re-election by large margins, and the Republican majority increased as some new candidates defeated incumbent Democrats. Everywhere Radical and moderate Republicans gained strength. The section of the country that had won the war had spoken clearly: Johnson's policies, people feared, were giving the advantage to rebels and traitors. Thus Republican congressional leaders received a mandate to continue with their Reconstruction plan.

But, thanks largely to Johnson, that plan had reached an impasse. All but one of the southern governments created by the president had turned their backs on the Fourteenth Amendment, determined to resist. Nothing could be accomplished as long as those governments existed and as long as the southern electorate was constituted as it was. The newly elected northern Republicans were not going to ignore their constituents' wishes and surrender to the South. To break the deadlock, Republicans had little choice but to form new governments and enfranchise the freedmen. They therefore decided to do both. The unavoidable logic of the situation had forced the majority toward the Radical plan.

The Radicals hoped Congress would do much more. Thaddeus Stevens, for example, argued that economic opportunity was essential to the freedmen. "If we do not furnish them with homesteads from forfeited and rebel property, and hedge them around with protective laws; if we leave them to the legislation of their late masters, we had better left them in bondage," Stevens declared. To provide that opportunity, Stevens drew up a plan for extensive confiscation and redistribution of land. Significantly, only one-tenth of the land affected by his plan was earmarked for freedmen, in 40-acre plots. All the rest was to be sold, to generate money for veterans' pensions, compensation to loyal citizens for damaged property, and payment of the federal debt. By these means Stevens hoped to win support for a basically unpopular measure. But he failed; and in general the Radicals were not able to command the support of the majority of the public. Northerners of that era were accustomed to a limited role for government, and the business community staunchly opposed any interference in private property.

As a result, the Military Reconstruction Act that was passed in 1867 incorporated only a small part of the Radical program. The act called for new governments in the South, with a return to military authority in the interim. It barred from political office those Confederate leaders listed in the Fourteenth Amendment. It guaranteed freedmen the right to vote in elections for state constitutional conventions and for subsequent state governments. In addition, each southern state was required to ratify the Fourteenth Amendment; to ratify its new constitution; and to submit the new constitution to Congress for approval. Thus black people gained an opportunity to fight for a better life through the political process. The only weapon put into their hands was the ballot, however. The law required no redistribution of land and guaranteed no basic changes in southern social structure. It also permitted an early return to the Union.

Military Reconstruction Act of 1867

Congress's role as the architect of Reconstruction was not quite over, for its quarrels with Andrew Johnson grew more bitter. To restrict Johnson's influence and safeguard its plan, Congress passed a number of controversial laws. First it set the date for its own reconvening—an unprecedented act, since the president had traditionally summoned the legislature to Washington. Then it limited Johnson's power over the army by requiring the president to issue military orders through the General of the Army, Ulysses S. Grant, who could not be sent from Washington without the Senate's consent. Finally, Congress passed the Tenure of Office Act, which gave the Senate power to interfere with changes in the president's cabinet. Designed to protect Secretary of War Stanton, who sympathized with the Radicals, this law violated the tradition that a president controlled his own cabinet.

Johnson took several belligerent steps of his own. He issued orders to military commanders in the South limiting their powers and increasing the powers of the civil governments he had created in 1865. Then he removed army officers who conscientiously enforced Congress's new law, preferring commanders who allowed disqualified Confederates to vote. Finally, in August 1867 he tried to remove Secretary of War Stanton. With this act the confrontation reached its climax.

Twice before, the House Judiciary Committee had considered impeachment, rejecting the idea once and then recommending it by only a 5-to-4 vote. That recommendation had been decisively defeated by the House. After Johnson's last action, however, a third attempt to impeach the president carried easily. In 1868, the angry House was so determined to indict Johnson that it voted before drawing up specific charges. The indictment concentrated on Johnson's violation of the Tenure of Office Act, though modern scholars regard his systematic efforts to impede enforcement of the Military Reconstruction Act as a far more serious offense.

Impeachment of President Johnson

Johnson's trial in the Senate lasted more than three months. The prosecution, led by such Radicals as Thaddeus Stevens and Benjamin Butler, argued that Johnson was guilty of "high crimes and misdemeanors." But they also advanced the novel idea

The confrontation between Congress and Andrew Johnson culminated in the president's impeachment. Here the Senate begins his trial, which ended in acquittal by a margin of one vote. Library of Congress.

that impeachment was a political matter, not a judicial trial of guilt or innocence. The Senate ultimately rejected such reasoning, which would have transformed impeachment into a political weapon against any chief executive who disagreed with Congress. Though a majority of senators voted to convict Johnson, the prosecution fell one vote short of the necessary two-thirds majority. Johnson remained in office for the few months left in his term, and his acquittal established the precedent that only serious misdeeds merited removal from office.

In 1869, in an effort to write democratic principles and color-blindness into the Constitution, the Radicals succeeded in presenting the Fifteenth Amendment for ratification. This measure forbade states to deny the right to vote "on account of race, color, or previous condition of servitude." Ironically, the votes of four uncooperative southern states—

Fifteenth Amendment

required by Congress to approve the amendment as an added condition to rejoining the Union—proved necessary to impose this principle on parts of the North. Although several states outside the South refused to ratify, the Fifteenth Amendment became law in 1870.

RECONSTRUCTION POLITICS
IN THE SOUTH

From the start, Reconstruction encountered the resistance of white southerners. Their opposition to change appeared in the black codes and other policies of the Johnson governments as well as in

Thomas Nast, in this 1868 cartoon, pictured the combination of forces—southern opposition and northern racism and indifference—that threatened the success of Reconstruction. *Library of Congress.*

White Resistance

private attitudes. Many whites set their faces against emancipation, and—as was true in the British Caribbean—the former planter class proved especially unbending. In 1866 a Georgia newspaper frankly declared, "Most of the white citizens believe that the institution of slavery was right, and . . . they will believe that the condition, which comes nearest to slavery, that can now be established will be the best." Unwillingness to accept black freedom would have been a major problem in any circumstances; Andrew Johnson's encouragement of southern whites actively to resist Congress, only intensified the problem.

Fearing the end of their control over slaves, some planters attempted to postpone freedom by denying or misrepresenting events. Former slaves reported that

their owners "didn't tell them it was freedom" or "wouldn't let [them] go." Agents of the Freedmen's Bureau in North Carolina agreed. One agent in Georgia concluded, "I find the old system of slavery working with even more rigor than formerly at a few miles distant from any point where U.S. troops are stationed." To hold onto their workers some landowners claimed control over black children and used guardianship and apprentice laws to bind black families to the plantation.

Whites also blocked blacks from acquiring land. Though a few planters divided up plots among their slaves, most condemned the idea of making blacks landowners. One planter in South Carolina refused to sell as little as an acre and a half to each family. Even a Georgian whose family was known for its concern for the slaves was outraged that two property owners planned to "rent their lands to the Negroes!" Such action was "injurious to the best interest of the community." The son of a free black landowner in Virginia who sold nearly two hundred acres to former slaves explained, "White folks wasn't lettin' Negroes have nothing."

Such adamant resistance by propertied whites soon manifested itself in other ways, including violence. In one North Carolina town a local magistrate clubbed a black man on a public street, and bands of "Regulators" terrorized blacks in parts of that state and Kentucky. Such incidents were predictable in a society in which many planters believed, as a South Carolinian put it, that blacks "can't be governed except with the whip."

After President Johnson encouraged the South to resist congressional Reconstruction, many white conservatives worked hard to capture the new state governments. Elsewhere, large numbers of whites boycotted the polls in an attempt to defeat Congress's plans. Since the new constitutions had to be approved by a majority of registered voters, registered whites could defeat them by sitting out the elections. This tactic was tried in North Carolina and succeeded in Alabama, forcing Congress to readjust and base ratification on a majority of those voting.

Very few black men stayed away from the polls. Enthusiastically and hopefully they seized the opportunity to participate in politics, voting solidly Republican. Most agreed with one man who felt that he should "stick to the end with the party that freed me." Illiteracy did not prohibit blacks (or uneducated whites) from making intelligent choices. Although William Henry could read only "a little," he testified that he and his friends had no difficulty selecting the Republican ballot. "We stood around and watched," he explained. "We saw D. Sledge vote; he owned half the county. We knowed he voted Democratic so we voted the other ticket so it would be Republican."

Zeal for voting spread through the entire black community. Women, who could not vote, encouraged their husbands and sons, and preachers exhorted their congregations to use the franchise. Such community spirit helped to counter white pressure tactics, and the freedmen's enthusiasm showed their hunger for equal rights.

With a large black turnout, and with prominent Confederates barred from politics under the Fourteenth Amendment, a new southern Republican party came to power in the constitutional conventions. Some blacks won seats as delegates, along with northerners who had moved to the South and some native southern whites. Together they brought the South's fundamental law into line with progressive reforms that had been adopted in the rest of the nation. The new constitutions were more democratic—they eliminated property qualifications for voting and holding office, and they made state and local offices elective that had been appointive. They provided for public schools and institutions to care for the mentally ill, the blind, the deaf, the destitute, and the orphaned, and they ended imprisonment for debt and barbarous punishments such as branding.

The conventions also broadened women's rights in possession of property and divorce. Usually, the main goal was not to make women equal but to provide relief to thousands of suffering debtors. In families left poverty-stricken by the war and weighed down by debts, the husband had usually contracted the debts. Thus, giving women legal control over their own property provided some protection to their families. There were some delegates, however, whose goal was to elevate women. Blacks in particular called for women's suffrage but were ignored by their white colleagues.

Under these new constitutions the southern states elected new governments. Again the Republican party triumphed, bringing new men into positions of power.

Triumph of Republican Governments The ranks of state legislators in 1868 included black southerners for the first time in history. Congress's second plan for Reconstruction was well under way. It remained to be seen what these new governments would do and how much change they would bring to society.

There was one possibility of radical change through these new governments. That possibility depended on the disfranchisement of substantial numbers of Confederate leaders. If the Republican regimes used their new power to exclude many whites from politics, as punishment for rebellion, they would have a solid electoral majority based on black voters and their white allies. Land reform and the assurance of racial equality would be possible. But none of the Republican governments did this, or even gave it serious consideration.

Why did the new legislators shut the door on the possibility of deep and thoroughgoing reform? First, they appreciated the realities of power and the depth of racial enmity. In most states whites were the majority, and former slaveowners controlled the best land and other sources of economic power. James Lynch, a leading black politician from Mississippi, candidly explained why Negroes shunned "the folly of" disfranchisement. Unlike northerners who "can leave when it becomes too uncomfortable," former slaves "must be in friendly relations with the great body of the whites in the state. Otherwise . . . peace can be maintained only by a standing army."

Second, blacks believed in the principle of universal suffrage and the Christian goal of reconciliation. Far from being vindictive toward the race that had enslaved them, they treated leading rebels with generosity and appealed to white southerners to adopt a spirit of fairness and cooperation. Henry McNeil Turner, like other Negro ministers, urged black Georgians to "love whites . . . soon their prejudice would melt away, and with God for our father, we will all be brothers." (Years later Turner criticized his own naiveté, saying that in the constitutional convention his motto had been, "Anything to please the white folks.") Therefore southern Republicans quickly (in come cases immediately) restored the voting rights of former Confederates, as Congress steadily released more individuals from the penalties of the Fourteenth Amendment.

Thus the South's Republican party committed itself

to a strategy of winning white support. To put the matter another way, the Republican party condemned itself to defeat if white voters would not cooperate. In a few short years Republicans were reduced to the embarrassment of making futile appeals to whites while ignoring the claims of their strongest supporters, blacks.

But for a time both Republicans and their opponents, who called themselves Conservatives or Democrats, moved to the center and appealed for support from a broad range of groups. Some propertied whites accepted congressional Reconstruction as a reality and declared that they would try to compete under the new rules. As these Democrats angled for some black votes, Republicans sought to attract more white voters. Both parties found an area of agreement in economic policies.

The Reconstruction governments devoted themselves to stimulating industry. This policy reflected northern ideals, of course, but it also sprang from a growing southern interest in industrialization. Confederates had learned how vital industry was, and many postwar southerners were eager to build up the manufacturing capacity of their region. Accordingly, Reconstruction legislatures designed many tempting inducements to investment. Loans, subsidies, and exemptions from taxation for periods up to ten years helped to bring new industries into the region. The southern railroad system was rebuilt and expanded, coal and iron mining laid the basis for Birmingham's steel plants, and the number of manufacturing establishments nearly doubled between 1860 and 1880. But this emphasis on big business interests also locked Republicans into a conservative strategy. They were appealing to elite whites who never responded, and the alternate possibility of making a strong, class-based appeal to poorer whites was lost.

Industrialization

Policies appealing to black voters never went beyond equality before the law. In fact, the whites who controlled the southern Republican party were reluctant to allow blacks a share of offices proportionate to their electoral strength. Black leaders, aware of their weakness, did not push for revolutionary economic or social change. In every southern state blacks led efforts to establish public

Other Republican Policies

schools, but most did not press for integrated facilities. Having a school to attend was the most important thing at the time, for the Johnson governments had excluded blacks from schools and other state-supported institutions. As a result, virtually every public school organized during Reconstruction was racially segregated, and these separate schools established a precedent for segregation. By the 1870s segregation was becoming a common practice in theaters, trains, and other public accommodations in the South.

A few black politicians did fight for civil rights and integration. Most were mulattoes from cities such as New Orleans or Mobile, where large populations of light-skinned free blacks had existed before the war. Their experience in such communities had made them sensitive to issues of status, and they spoke out for open and equal public accommodations. But they were a minority. Most elected black officials sought instead to make more limited but essential gains in the face of enormous white hostility.

Economic progress was uppermost in the minds of many of the freed people, especially politicians from agricultural districts. Land above all else had the potential to benefit the former slave, but none of the black state legislators promoted confiscation; freedmen simply lacked the power to make that possible. South Carolina established a land commission, but its purpose was to assist in the purchase of land. Any widespread redistribution of land had to arise from Congress, which never supported such action.

Within a few years, as centrists in both parties met failure, the other side of white reaction to congressional Reconstruction began to dominate. Some conservatives had always favored fierce opposition to Reconstruction through pressure and racist propaganda. They put economic and social pressure on blacks: one black Republican complained that "my neighbors will not employ me, nor sell me a farthing's worth of anything." Charging that the South had been turned over to ignorant blacks, conservatives deplored "black domination." The cry of "Negro rule" now became constant.

Such attacks were gross distortions. Blacks participated in politics but did not dominate or control events. They were a minority in eight out of ten state conventions (northerners were a minority in nine out of ten). Of the state legislatures, only in the lower house in South Carolina did blacks ever constitute a majority; generally their numbers among officials were far inferior to their proportion in the population. Sixteen blacks won seats in Congress before Reconstruction was over, but none was ever elected governor. Freedmen were participating in government, to be sure, but there was no justification for racist denunciations of "Ethiopian minstrelsy, Ham radicalism in all its glory."

Conservatives also stepped up their propaganda against the allies of black Republicans. "Carpetbagger" was a derisive name for whites who had come from the North. It suggested an evil and greedy northern politician, recently arrived with a carpetbag into which he planned to stuff ill-gotten gains before fleeing. The stranger's carpetbag, a popular travel bag whose frame was covered with heavy carpet material, was presumably deep enough to hold all the loot stolen from southern treasuries and filched from hapless, trusting former slaves. Immigrants from the north, who held the largest share of Republican offices, were all tarred with this brush.

Carpetbaggers and Scalawags

In fact most northerners who settled in the South arrived before Congress gave blacks the right to vote. They came seeking business opportunities or a warmer climate, and most never entered politics. Those who did generally wanted to democratize the South and to introduce northern ways, such as industry, public education, and the spirit of enterprise. Hard times and ostracism by white southerners made many of these men dependent on officeholding for a living, a fact that increased Republican factionalism and damaged the party. And although carpetbaggers supported black suffrage and educational opportunities, most opposed social equality and integration.

Conservatives invented the term "scalawag" to stigmatize and discredit any native white southerner who cooperated with the Republicans. A substantial number of southerners did so, including some wealthy and prominent men. Most scalawags, however, were representatives of the yeoman class, men from mountain areas and small farming districts—average white southerners who saw that they could benefit from the education and opportunities promoted by Republicans. Banding together with freedmen, they pursued common class interests and hoped to make headway against the power of long-dominant planters.

A poster celebrating the election of blacks to Congress during Reconstruction. From left to right across the top can be seen portraits of Senator Hiram R. Revels, Representative Benjamin S. Turner, the Reverend Richard Allen, Frederick Douglass, Representatives Josiah T. Walls and Joseph H. Rainy, and the writer William Wells Brown. Library of Congress.

Yet this black-white coalition was always vulnerable to the issue of race, and scalawags shied away from support for racial equality. Except on issues of common interest, scalawags often deserted the other elements of the Republican party.

Besides propaganda, the conservatives had other weapons to use against Reconstruction. Financially the Republican governments, despite their achievements, were doomed to be unpopular. Republicans wanted to continue prewar services, repair war's destruction, and support such important new ventures as public schools. But the Civil War had destroyed much of the South's tax base. One category of valuable property—slaves—was entirely gone. Hundreds of thousands of citizens had lost much of the rest of their real and personal property—money, livestock, fences, and buildings—to the war. Thus an increase

With the rise of the Ku Klux Klan, terrorism against blacks became more organized and purposeful. Note the racist overtones even in this northern illustration of Klan violence. The Bettmann Archive.

in taxes was necessary even to maintain traditional services, and new ventures required much higher taxes.

Corruption was another powerful charge levied against the Republicans. Unfortunately, it was true. Many carpetbaggers and black politicians sold their votes, taking part in what scholars recognize was a nationwide surge of corruption (see page 526). Although white Democrats often shared in the guilt, and despite the efforts of some Republicans to stop it, Democrats convinced many voters that scandal was the inevitable result of a foolish Reconstruction program based on blacks and carpetbaggers.

All these problems damaged the Republicans, but in many southern states the deathblow came through

violence: the murders, whippings, and intimidation of the Ku Klux Klan. Terrorism **Ku Klux Klan** against blacks had occurred throughout Reconstruction, but after 1867 white violence became more organized and purposeful. The Ku Klux Klan rode to frustrate Reconstruction and keep the freedmen in subjection. Nighttime visits, whippings, beatings, and murder became common, and in some areas virtually open warfare developed despite the authorities' efforts to keep the peace.

Although the Klan persecuted blacks who stood up for their rights as laborers or people, its main purpose was political. Lawless nightriders made active Republicans the target of their attacks. Prominent

Chapter 15: RECONSTRUCTION BY TRIAL AND ERROR, 1865–1877

white Republicans and black leaders were killed in several states. After blacks who worked for a South Carolina scalawag started voting, terrorists visited the plantation and "whipped every nigger man they could lay their hands on." Klansmen also attacked Union League Clubs (Republican organizations that mobilized the black vote) and schoolteachers who were aiding the freedmen.

Klan violence was not simply spontaneous; certain social forces gave direction to racism. In North Carolina, for example, Alamance and Caswell counties were the sites of the worst Klan violence. They were in the Piedmont, where slim Republican majorities rested on cooperation between black voters and whites of the yeoman class, particularly yeomen whose Unionism or discontent with the Confederacy had turned them against local Democratic officials. Together these black and white Republicans had ousted officials long entrenched in power. But the Republican majority was a small one, and it would fail if either whites or blacks faltered in their support.

In Alamance and Caswell counties the wealthy and powerful men who had lost their accustomed political control organized the campaign of terror. They brought it into being and used it for their purposes. They were the secret organization's county officers and local chieftains; they recruited members and planned atrocities. They used the Klan to regain political power: by whipping up racism or frightening enough Republicans, the Ku Klux Klan could split the Republican coalition and restore a Democratic majority.

Thus a combination of difficult fiscal problems, Republican mistakes, racial hostility, and terror brought down the Republican regimes, and in most southern states so-called Radical **Failure of** Reconstruction was over after only **Reconstruction** a few years. But the most lasting failure of Reconstruction governments was not political—it was social. The new governments failed to alter the southern social structure or its distribution of wealth and power. Exploited as slaves, freedmen remained vulnerable to exploitation during Reconstruction. Without land of their own, they were dependent on white landowners, who could use their economic power to compromise blacks' political freedom. Armed only with the ballot, southern blacks had little chance to effect major changes.

To reform the southern social order, Congress would have had to redistribute land; and never did a majority of congressmen favor such a plan. Radical Republicans like Albion Tourgée condemned Congress's timidity. Turning the freedman out on his own without advantages, said Tourgée, constituted "cheap philanthropy." Indeed, freedmen who had to live with the consequences of Reconstruction considered it a failure. The North should have "fixed some way for us," said former slaves, but instead it "threw all the Negroes on the world without any way of getting along."

Freedom had come, but blacks knew they "still had to depend on the southern white man for work, food, and clothing," and it was clear that most whites were hostile. Unless Congress exercised careful supervision over the South, the situation of the freedmen was sure to deteriorate. Whenever the North lost interest, Reconstruction would collapse.

THE SOCIAL AND ECONOMIC MEANING OF FREEDOM

B lack southerners entered upon life after slavery hopefully, determinedly, but not naively. They had too much experience with white people to assume that all would be easy. As one man in Texas advised his son, even before the war was over, "our forever was going to be spent living among the Southerners, after they got licked." Expecting to meet with hostility, black people tried to gain as much as they could from their new circumstances. Often the most valued changes were personal ones—alterations in location, employer, or surroundings that could make an enormous difference to individuals or families.

One of the first decisions that many took was whether to leave the old plantation or remain. This meant making a judgment about where the chances of liberty and progress would be greatest. Former slaves drew upon their experiences in bondage to assess the whites with whom they had to deal. "Most all the Negroes that had good owners stayed with them," said one man, "but the others left." Not surprisingly, cruel slaveholders usually saw their former

Freed from slavery, blacks of all ages filled the schools to seek the education that had been denied them in bondage. Valentine Museum, Richmond, Virginia.

chattels walk off en masse. "And let me tell you," added one man who abandoned a harsh planter, "we sure cussed ole master out before we left there."

On new farms or old the newly freed men and women reached out for valuable things in life that had been denied them. One of these was education.

Education for Blacks Whatever their age, blacks hungered for the knowledge in books that had been permitted only to whites. With freedom they filled the schools both day and night. On "log seats" or "a dirt floor," many freedmen studied their letters in old almanacs, discarded dictionaries, or whatever was available. Young children brought infants to school with them, and adults attended at night or after "the crops was laid by." Many a teacher had "to make herself heard over three other classes reciting in concert" in a small room, but the scholars kept coming. The desire to escape slavery's ignorance was so great that many blacks paid tuition, typically $1.00 or $1.50 a month, despite their poverty. This seemingly small amount

constituted one-tenth of many people's agricultural wage.

The federal government and northern reformers assisted this search for education. In its brief life the Freedmen's Bureau founded over four thousand schools, and idealistic men and women from the North established others and staffed them ably. The Yankee schoolmarm—dedicated, selfless, and religious—became an agent of progress in many southern communities. Thus, with the aid of religious and charitable organizations throughout the north, blacks began the nation's first assault on the problems created by slavery. The results included the beginnings of a public school system in each southern state and the enrollment of over 600,000 blacks in elementary school by 1877.

Blacks and their white allies also realized that higher education was essential—colleges and universities to train teachers and equip ministers and professionals for leadership. The American Missionary Association founded seven colleges, including Fisk and Atlanta universities, between 1866 and 1869. The Freedmen's Bureau helped to establish Howard University in Washington, D.C., and northern religious groups, such as Methodists, Baptists, and Congregationalists, supported dozens of seminaries, colleges, and teachers' colleges. By the late 1870s black churches had joined in the effort, founding numerous colleges despite their smaller financial resources. Though some of the new institutions did not survive, they brought knowledge to those who would educate others and laid a foundation for progress.

Even in Reconstruction blacks were choosing many highly educated individuals as leaders. Many blacks who won public office during Reconstruction came from the prewar elite of free people of color. This group had benefited from its association with wealthy whites, who were often blood relatives. Some planters had given their mulatto children outstanding educations. Francis Cardozo, who served in South Carolina's constitutional convention and was later that state's secretary of the treasury and secretary of state, had attended universities in Scotland and England. P. B. S. Pinchback, who became lieutenant governor of Louisiana, was the son of a planter who had sent him to school in Cincinnati at age nine. And the two black senators from Mississippi, Blanche K. Bruce and Hiram Revels, were both privileged in their educations. Bruce was the son of a planter who had

Chapter 15: RECONSTRUCTION BY TRIAL AND ERROR, 1865–1877

provided tutoring on his plantation; Revels was the son of free North Carolina mulattoes who had sent him to Knox College in Illinois. These men and many self-educated former slaves brought experience as artisans, businessmen, lawyers, teachers, and preachers to political office.

While elected officials wrestled with the political tasks of Reconstruction, millions of former slaves concentrated on improving life at home, on their farms, and in their neighborhoods. A major goal of black men and women was to gain some living space for themselves and their families. Surrounded by an unfriendly white population, they sought to insulate themselves from white interference and to strengthen the bonds of their own community. Throughout the South they devoted themselves to reuniting their families, moving away from the slave quarters, and founding black churches. Given the eventual failure of Reconstruction, the practical gains that blacks made in their daily lives often proved the most enduring and significant changes of the period.

The search for long-lost family members was awe-inspiring. With only shreds of information to guide them, thousands of black people embarked on odysseys in search of a husband, wife, child, or parent. By relying on the black community for help and information, many succeeded in their quest, sometimes almost miraculously. Others walked through several states and never found their loved ones.

Reunification of Black Families

Husbands and wives who had belonged to different masters established homes together for the first time, and parents asserted the right to raise their own children. Saying "You took her away from me and didn' pay no mind to my cryin', so now I'm takin' her back home," one mother reclaimed a child whom the mistress had been raising in her own house. Another woman bristled when her old master claimed a right to whip her children, promptly informing him that "he warn't goin' to brush none of her chilluns no more." One girl recalled that her mistress had struck her soon after freedom. As if to clarify the new ground rules, this girl "grabbed her leg and would have broke her neck." The freedmen were too much at risk to act recklessly, but as one man put it, they were tired of punishment, and "they sure didn't take no more foolishness off of white folks."

Given the eventual failure of Reconstruction, many blacks, like this elderly couple, probably benefited most from small gains in their daily lives—greater freedom from white supervision, and more living space for themselves and their families. Valentine Museum, Richmond, Virginia.

Black people frequently wanted to minimize all contact with whites. "There is a prejudice against us . . . that will take years to get over," the Reverend Garrison Frazier told General Sherman in January 1865. To avoid contact with intrusive whites, who were used to supervising and controlling them, blacks abandoned the slave quarters and fanned out into distant corners of the land they worked. Some moved away to build new homes in the woods. "After the war my stepfather come," recalled Annie Young, "and got my mother and we moved out in the piney woods." Others described moving "across the creek to [themselves]" or building a "saplin house . . . back in the woods" or " 'way off in the woods." Some rural dwellers established small all-black settlements that still can be found today along the backroads of the South.

Even once-privileged slaves often shared this desire for independence and social separation. One man turned down the master's offer of the overseer's house as a residence and moved instead to a shack in "Freetown." He also declined to let the former owner grind his grain for free, because it "made him feel like a free man to pay for things just like anyone else." One couple, a carriage driver and trusted house servant during slavery, passed up the fine cooking of the "big house" so that they could move "in the colored settlement."

The other side of this distance from whites was closer communion within the black community. Freed from the restrictions and regulations of slavery, blacks could build their own institutions **Founding of** as they saw fit. The secret church **Black Churches** of slavery now came out into the open; in countless communities throughout the South, "some of the niggers started a brush arbor." A brush arbor was merely "a sort of . . . shelter with leaves for a roof," but the freedmen worshipped in it enthusiastically. "Preachin' and shouting sometimes lasted all day," ex-slaves recalled, for there were "glorious times then" when black people could worship together in freedom. Within a few years independent black branches of the Methodist and Baptist churches had attracted the great majority of black Christians in the South.

This desire to gain as much independence as possible carried over into the freedmen's economic arrangements. Since most former slaves lacked money to buy land, they preferred the next best thing—renting the land they worked. But many whites would not consider renting land to blacks; there was strong social pressure against it. And few blacks had the means to rent a farm. Therefore other alternatives had to be tried.

Northerners and officials of the Freedmen's Bureau favored contracts between owners and laborers. To northerners who believed in "free soil, free labor, free men," contracts and wages seemed the key to progress. For a few years the Freedmen's Bureau helped to draw up and enforce such contracts, but they proved unpopular with both blacks and whites. Owners often filled the contracts with detailed requirements that reminded blacks of their circumscribed lives under slavery. Disputes frequently arose over efficiency, lost time, and other matters. Besides, cash was not readily available in the early years of Reconstruction; times were hard and the failure of Confederate banks left the South with a shortage of credit facilities.

Black farmers and white landowners therefore turned to a system of sharecropping: in return for use of the land and "furnishing" (tools, mules, seed, a cabin, and food to last until harvest), the **Rise of the** farmer paid the landowner a share **Sharecropping** of his crop. The cost of food and **System** clothing was deducted from the crop before the owner took his share. Naturally, landowners tended to set their share at a high level, but blacks had some bargaining power. By holding out and refusing to make contracts at the end of the year, sharecroppers succeeded in lowering the owners' share to around one-half during Reconstruction.

The sharecropping system originated as a desirable compromise. It eased landowners' problems with cash and credit; blacks accepted it because it gave them a reasonable amount of freedom from daily supervision. Instead of working under a white overseer as in slavery, they were able to farm a plot of land on their own in family groups. But sharecropping later proved to be a disaster, both for blacks and for the South. Part of the problem lay in the fact that an unscrupulous owner in a discriminatory society had many opportunities to cheat a sharecropper. Owners and merchants frequently paid less for blacks' cotton than they paid for whites'. Greedy men could overcharge or manipulate records so that the sharecropper always stayed in debt. But the problem was even more fundamental than that.

Southern farmers were concentrating on cotton, a crop with a bright past and a dim future. During the Civil War, India, Brazil, and Egypt had begun to supply cotton to Britain; not until **Overdepen-** 1878 did the South recover its pre- **dence** war share of British cotton pur- **on Cotton** chases. This temporary loss of markets reduced per capita income, as did a decline in the amount of labor invested by the average southern farmer. Part of the exploitation of slavery had been the sending of black women and children into the fields. In freedom these people stayed at home, like their white counterparts, when possible. Black families valued human dignity more highly than the levels of production that had been achieved with the lash.

But even as southerners grew more cotton, matching and eventually surpassing prewar totals, their reward diminished. Cotton prices began a long decline whose causes merely coincided with the Civil War. From 1820 to 1860 world demand for cotton had grown at a rate of 5 percent per year; but from 1866 to 1895 the rate of growth was only 1.3 percent per year. By 1860 the English textile industry, world leader in production, had penetrated all the major new markets, and from that point on increases in demand were slight. As a result, when southern farmers planted more cotton they tended to depress the price.

In these circumstances overspecialization in cotton was a mistake. But most southern farmers had no choice. Landowners required sharecroppers to grow the prime cash crop, whose salability was sure. And due to the shortage of banks and credit in the South, white farmers often had to borrow from a local merchant, who insisted on cotton production to secure his loan. Thus southern agriculture slipped deeper and deeper into depression. Black sharecroppers struggled under a growing burden of debt that reduced their independence and bound them to landowners almost as oppressively as slavery had bound them to their masters. Many white farmers became debtors too and gradually lost their land. All these problems were serious, but few people in the North were paying attention.

THE END OF RECONSTRUCTION

The North's commitment to racial equality had never been total. And by the early 1870s it was evident that even its partial commitment was weakening. New issues were capturing people's attention, and soon voters began to look for reconciliation with southern whites. In the South Democrats won control of one state after another, and they threatened to defeat Republicans in the North as well. Before long the situation had returned to "normal" in the eyes of southern whites.

The Supreme Court, after first re-establishing its power, participated in the northern retreat from Reconstruction. During the Civil War the Court had been cautious and reluctant to assert itself. Reaction to the Dred Scott decision had been so violent, and the Union's wartime emergency so great, that the Court had refrained from blocking or interfering with government actions. The justices, for example, had breathed a collective sigh of relief when legal technicalities prevented them from reviewing the case of Clement Vallandigham, who had been convicted of aiding the enemy by a military court when regular civil courts were open (see page 407).

But in 1866 a similar case, *Ex parte Milligan,* reached the Court through proper channels. Lambdin P. Milligan of Indiana had participated in a plot to free Confederate prisoners of war and **Supreme Court** overthrow state governments; for **Decisions on** these acts a military court had sen-**Reconstruction** tenced Milligan, a civilian, to death.

In sweeping language the Court declared that military trials were illegal when civil courts were open and functioning, thus indicating that it intended to reassert itself as a major force in national affairs. This decision could have led to a direct clash with Congress, which in 1867 established military districts and military courts in the initial phase of its Reconstruction program. But Congress altered part of the Court's jurisdiction; it was constitutionally empowered to do so, but had never taken such action before (or since). By altering the Court's jurisdiction, Congress protected its Reconstruction policy and avoided a confrontation.

In 1873, however, an important group of cases, the *Slaughter-House* cases, tested the scope and meaning of the Fourteenth Amendment. In 1869 the Louisiana legislature had granted one company a monopoly on the slaughtering of livestock in New Orleans. Rival butchers in the city promptly sued. Their attorney, former Supreme Court justice John A. Campbell, argued that the Fourteenth Amendment had revolutionized the constitutional system by bringing individual rights under federal protection. Campbell expressed what had been a major Radical goal: to nationalize civil rights and guard them from state interference. Over the years his argument would win acceptance, offering shelter from government regulation to corporate "persons" in the nineteenth century and providing protection for blacks and other minorities in the twentieth.

The Court did not go that far, however, in the *Slaughter-House* decision. In a blow to the hopes of blacks, it refused to accept Campbell's argument. Neither the "privileges and immunities" clause nor the "due process" clause of the amendment guaranteed the great basic rights of the Bill of Rights against state action, the justices said. State and national citizenship remained separate, with the former more important. National citizenship involved only such things as the right to travel freely from state to state and to use the navigable waters of the nation. Thus the Court limited severely the amendment's potential for securing the rights of black citizens.

In 1876 the Court regressed even further, emasculating the enforcement clause of the Fourteenth Amendment and interpreting the Fifteenth in a narrow and negative fashion. In *United States* v. *Cruikshank* the Court dealt with Louisiana whites who were indicted for attacking a meeting of blacks and conspiring to deprive them of their rights. The justices ruled that the Fourteenth Amendment did not extend federal power to cover the misdeeds of private individuals against other citizens; only flagrant state discrimination was covered. And in *United States* v. *Reese* the Court held that the Fifteenth Amendment did not guarantee a citizen's right to vote, but merely listed certain impermissible grounds for denying suffrage. Thus a path lay open for southern states to disfranchise blacks for supposedly nonracial reasons—lack of education, lack of property, or lack of descent from a grandfather qualified to vote before the Military Reconstruction Act. ("Grandfather clauses" became a way of excluding blacks from suffrage, since most blacks were slaves before Reconstruction and hence could not vote.)

The retreat from Reconstruction continued steadily in politics as well. In 1868 Ulysses S. Grant, running as a Republican, defeated Horatio Seymour, a Democrat of New York, in a presidential campaign that revived sectional divisions. Although he was not a Radical, Grant realized that Congress's program represented the wishes of northerners, and he supported a platform that praised congressional Reconstruction and endorsed Negro suffrage in the South. (The platform stopped short of endorsing black suffrage in the North.) The Democrats went in the

Election of 1868

opposite direction; their platform vigorously denounced Reconstruction. By associating themselves with rebellion and with Johnson's repudiated program, the Democrats went down to defeat in all but eight states, though the popular vote was fairly close.

In office Grant sometimes used force to support Reconstruction, but only when he had to. He hoped to avoid confrontation with the South, to erase the image of dictatorship that his military background summoned up. In fact, neither he nor Johnson had imposed anything approaching a military occupation on the South. Rapid demobilization had reduced a federal army of more than 1 million to 57,000 within a year of surrender. Thereafter the number of troops in the South continued to fall, until in 1874 there were only 4,082 in the southern states outside Texas. Throughout Reconstruction the strongest federal units were in Texas and the West, fighting Indians, not white southerners.

In 1870 and 1871 the violent campaigns of the Ku Klux Klan moved Congress to pass two Force Acts and an anti-Klan law. These acts (important precedents for the modern enforcement of civil rights) permitted martial law and suspension of the writ of habeas corpus to combat murders, beatings, and threats by the Klan. Federal troops and prosecutors used them vigorously but unsuccessfully, for a conspiracy of silence frustrated many prosecutions. Possible witnesses were frightened or unwilling to testify and juries unwilling to convict. Thereafter the Klan disbanded officially and went underground. Paramilitary organizations known as Rifle Clubs and Red Shirts often took the Klan's place.

In 1872 a revolt within the Republican ranks foreshadowed the end of Reconstruction. A group calling itself the Liberal Republicans bolted the party and nominated Horace Greeley, the well-known editor of the *New York Tribune,* for president. The Liberal Republicans were a varied group, including civil-service reformers, foes of corruption, and advocates of a lower tariff; they often spoke of a more lenient policy toward the South. That year the Democrats too gave their nomination to Greeley. Though the combination was not enough to defeat Grant, it reinforced his desire to avoid confrontation with white southerners. Grant used troops very sparingly thereafter, and in 1875 refused

Liberal Republicans Revolt

President Grant with wife Julia and his youngest son Jessie. Photographed in 1872.   Keystone-Mast Collection, University of California, Riverside.

a desperate request for troops from the governor of Mississippi.

The Liberal Republican challenge revealed the growing dissatisfaction with Grant's administration. Strong-willed but politically naive, Grant made a series of poor appointments. His secretary of war, his private secretary, and officials in the Treasury and Navy departments were all involved in bribery or tax-cheating scandals. Instead of exposing the corruption, Grant defended some of the culprits. As the clamor against dishonesty in government grew, Grant's popularity declined. So did his party's; in the 1874 elections Democrats recaptured the House of Representatives.

Congress's resolve on southern issues weakened steadily. By joint resolution it had already removed the political disabilities of the Fourteenth Amendment from many former Confederates. Then in 1872 it adopted a sweeping Amnesty Act,

Amnesty Act   which pardoned most of the re-

maining rebels and left only five hundred excluded from political participation. A Civil Rights Act passed in 1875 purported to guarantee black people equal accommodations in public places, like inns and theaters. But it was weak and contained no effective provisions for enforcement. (The law was later struck down by the Supreme Court; see page 474.)

Democrats regained power in the South rather quickly, winning four states before 1872 and a total of eight by the start of 1876 (see map, page 444). As they did so, northern Republicans worried about their opponents' stress on the failure and scandals of Reconstruction governments. Many Republicans sensed that their constituents were tiring of the same old issues. In fact, a variety of new concerns were catching the public's eye. The Panic of 1873, which threw 3 million people out of work, focused attention on economic and monetary problems. Businessmen were disturbed by the strikes and industrial violence that accompanied the panic; debtors and unemployed

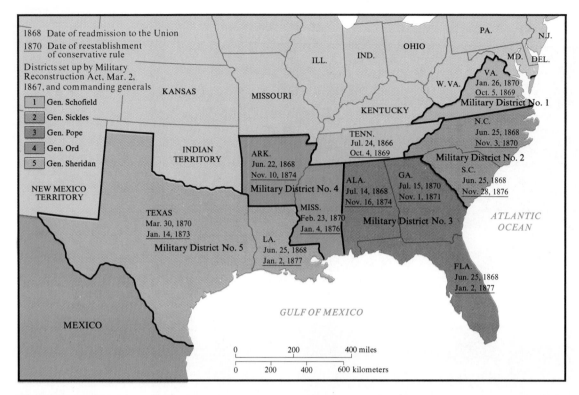

The Reconstruction

sought easy-money policies to spur economic expansion.

The monetary issue aroused strong controversy. Civil War greenbacks had the potential to expand the money supply and lift prices, if they were kept in circulation. In 1872 Democratic **Greenbacks Versus Sound Money** farmers and debtors had urged such a policy, but they were overruled by "sound money" men. Now the depression swelled the ranks of "greenbackers"—voters who favored greenbacks and easy money. In 1874 Congress voted to increase the number of greenbacks in circulation, but Grant vetoed the bill in deference to the opinions of financial leaders. The next year sound-money interests prevailed in Congress, winning passage of a law requiring that after 1878 greenbacks be convertible into gold. The law limited the inflationary impact of the greenbacks and aided creditors, not debtors.

Indeed, the government's financial policies were almost perfectly tailored to revive and support industrial growth. Soon after the war Congress had shifted some of the government's tax revenues to pay off the interest-bearing war debt. The debt fell from $2.33 billion in 1866 to only $587 million in 1893, and every dollar repaid was a dollar injected into the economy for potential reinvestment. Thus approximately 1 percent of the gross national product was pumped back into the economy from 1866 to 1872, and only slightly less than that during the rest of the 1870s. Low taxes on investment and high tariffs on manufactured goods also aided industrialists. With such help the northern economy quickly recovered the rate of growth it had enjoyed just before the war.

Another issue that claimed new attention in the 1870s was immigration. After the war the number of immigrants entering the United States began to rise again, along with the ingrained suspicions and hostilities of native Americans. The Mormon question too—how Utah's growing Mormon community, which practiced polygamy, could be reconciled to American law—became prominent.

Renewed pressure for expansion revived interest in international affairs. Secretary of State William H. Seward accomplished the only major addition of territory during these years in 1867. Through ne-

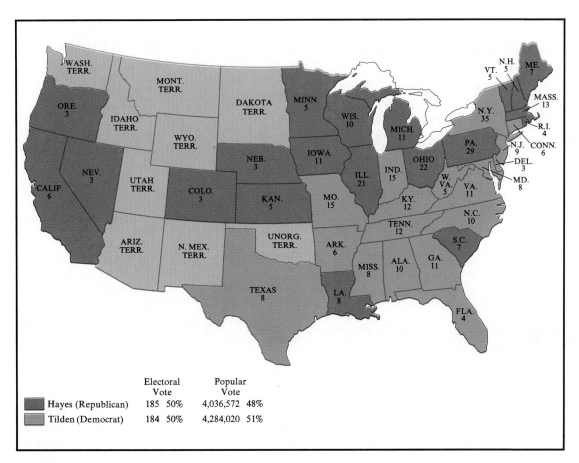

Presidential Election, 1876

	Electoral Vote		Popular Vote	
Hayes (Republican)	185	50%	4,036,572	48%
Tilden (Democrat)	184	50%	4,284,020	51%

gotiation with the Russian government, he arranged the purchase of Alaska for $7.2 million dollars. Opponents ridiculed Seward's venture, calling Alaska Frigidia, the Polar Bear Garden, or Walrussia. But Seward convinced important congressmen of Alaska's economic potential, and other lawmakers favored the dawning of friendship with Russia. In the same year the United States took control of the Midway Islands, a thousand miles from Hawaii, which were scarcely mentioned again until the Second World War. Though in 1870 President Grant tried to annex the Dominican Republic, Senator Charles Sumner blocked the attempt. Seward and his successor, Hamilton Fish, used diplomacy to arrange a financial settlement of claims against Britain for permitting the sale of the *Alabama* and other Confederate cruisers (see page 625).

By 1876 it was obvious to most political observers that the North was no longer willing to pursue the goals of Reconstruction. The results of a disputed

Election of 1876

presidential election confirmed this fact. Samuel J. Tilden, Democratic governor of New York, ran strongly in the South and took a commanding lead in both the popular vote and the electoral college over Rutherford B. Hayes, the Republican nominee. Tilden won 184 electoral votes and needed only one more for a majority. Nineteen votes from Louisiana, South Carolina, and Florida were disputed; both Democrats and Republicans claimed to have won in those states despite fraud on the part of their opponents. One vote from Oregon was undecided due to a technicality (see map).

To resolve this unprecedented situation, on which the Constitution gave no guidance, Congress established a fifteen-member electoral commission. In the interest of impartiality, membership on the commission was to be balanced between Democrats and Republicans. But one independent Republican, Supreme

All Colored People

THAT WANT TO

GO TO KANSAS,

On September 5th, 1877,

Can do so for $5.00

IMMIGRATION.

WHEREAS, We, the colored people of Lexington, Ky., knowing that there is an abundance of choice lands now belonging to the Government, have assembled ourselves together for the purpose of locating on said lands. Therefore,

BE IT RESOLVED, That we do now organize ourselves into a Colony, as follows:—Any person wishing to become a member of this Colony can do so by paying the sum of one dollar ($1.00), and this money is to be paid by the first of September, 1877, in installments of twenty-five cents at a time, or otherwise as may be desired.

RESOLVED, That this Colony has agreed to consolidate itself with the Nicodemus Towns, Solomon Valley, Graham County, Kansas, and can only do so by entering the vacant lands now in their midst, which costs $5.00.

RESOLVED, That this Colony shall consist of seven officers—President, Vice-President, Secretary, Treasurer, and three Trustees. President—M. M. Bell; Vice-President—Isaac Talbott; Secretary—W. J. Niles; Treasurer—Daniel Clarke; Trustees—Jerry Lee, William Jones, and Abner Webster.

RESOLVED, That this Colony shall have from one to two hundred militia, more or less, as the case may require, to keep peace and order, and any member failing to pay in his dues, as aforesaid, or failing to comply with the above rules in any particular, will not be recognized or protected by the Colony.

Exodusters, southern blacks dismayed by the failure of Reconstruction, left the South by the thousands for Kansas in 1877. This handbill advertised the establishment of a black colony in Graham County, Kansas. Kansas State Historical Society.

Court Justice David Davis, refused appointment in order to accept his election as a senator. A regular Republican took his place, and the Republican party prevailed 8 to 7 on every decision, a strict party vote. Hayes would then become the winner if Congress accepted the commission's findings.

Congressional acceptance, however, was not sure. Democrats controlled the House and had the power to filibuster to block action on the vote. Many citizens worried that the nation had entered a major constitutional crisis and was slipping once again into civil war. But the crisis was resolved when Democrats acquiesced in the election of Hayes. Scholars have found that negotiations went on between some of Hayes's supporters and southerners who were interested in federal aid to railroads, internal improvements, federal patronage, and removal of troops from southern states. But the most recent studies suggest that these negotiations did not have a deciding effect on the outcome. Neither party was well enough organized to implement and enforce a bargain between the sections. Northern and southern Democrats decided they could not win and failed to contest the election. Thus Hayes became president, and southerners looked forward to the withdrawal of federal troops from the South. Reconstruction was unmistakably over.

Southern Democrats rejoiced, but black Americans grieved over the betrayal of their hopes for equality. Tens of thousands of blacks pondered leaving the South, where freedom was no longer

Black Exodusters

a real possibility. "[We asked] whether it was possible we could stay under a people who had held us in bondage," said Henry Adams, who led a migration to Kansas. "[We] appealed to the President . . . and to Congress . . . to protect us in our rights and privileges," but "in 1877 we lost all hopes." Thereafter many southern blacks "wanted to go to a territory by ourselves." In South Carolina, Louisiana, Mississippi, and other southern states, thousands gathered up their possessions and migrated to Kansas. They were known as Exodusters, disappointed people still searching for their share in the American dream. Even in Kansas they met disillusionment, as the welcome extended by the state's governor soon gave way to hostile public receptions.

Thus the nation ended over fifteen years of bloody civil war and controversial reconstruction without establishing full freedom for black Americans. Their status would continue to be one of the major issues facing the nation. A host of other issues would arise from industrialization. How would the country develop its immense resources in a growing and increasingly integrated national economy? How would farmers, industrial workers, immigrants, and capitalists fit into the new social system? Industrialization promised not just a higher standard of living but also a different lifestyle in both urban and rural areas. Moreover, it augmented the nation's power and laid the foundation for an increased American role in international affairs. Again Americans turned their thoughts to expansion and the conquest of new frontiers. As the United States entered its second hundred years of existence, it confronted these serious challenges. The experience of the 1860s and 1870s suggested that the solutions, if any, might not be clear or complete.

IMPORTANT EVENTS

1865	Johnson begins Reconstruction Confederate leaders regain power Black Codes Congress refuses to seat southern representatives Thirteenth Amendment ratified	1870	Force Acts
		1871	Ku Klux Klan Act Treaty with England settles *Alabama* claims

1866	Civil Rights Act
	Congress approves Fourteenth
	  Amendment
	Freedmen's Bureau renewed
	Most southern states reject
	  Fourteenth Amendment
	Ex parte Milligan
		1872	Amnesty Act
			Liberal Republicans organize
			Debtors urge government to keep
			  greenbacks in circulation
			Grant re-elected

		1873	*Slaughter-House* cases

1867	Military Reconstruction Act; Tenure
	  of Office Act
	Purchase of Alaska
	Constitutional conventions called in
	  southern states
		1874	Grant vetoes increase in paper
			  money
			Democrats win House

		1875	Several Grant appointees indicted
			  for corruption
			Civil Rights Act
			Congress requires that after 1878
			  greenbacks be convertible into gold

1868	House impeaches Johnson; Senate acquits him Most southern states readmitted Fourteenth Amendment ratified Ulysses S. Grant elected president	1876	*U.S.* v. *Cruikshank*; *U.S.* v. *Reese* Presidential election disputed
1869	Congress approves Fifteenth Amendment (ratified 1870)	1877	Congress elects Hayes Black Exodusters migrate to Kansas

SUGGESTIONS FOR FURTHER READING

National Policy, Politics, and Constitutional Law

Richard H. Abbott, *The First Southern Strategy* (1986); Herman Belz, *Emancipation and Equal Rights* (1978); Herman Belz, *A New Birth of Freedom* (1976); Herman Belz, *Reconstructing the Union* (1969); Michael Les Benedict, *A Compromise of Principle* (1974); Michael Les Benedict, *The Impeachment and Trial of Andrew Johnson* (1973); Charles S. Campbell, *The Transformation of American Foreign Relations, 1865–1900* (1976); Adrian Cook, *The Alabama Claims* (1975); David Donald, *Charles Sumner and the Rights of Man* (1970); Harold M. Hyman, *A More Perfect Union* (1973); Ronald J. Jensen, *The Alaska Purchase and Russian-American Relations* (1975); William S. McFeely, *Grant* (1981); William S. McFeely, *Yankee Stepfather: General O. O. Howard and the Freedmen* (1968); Eric L. McKitrick, *Andrew Johnson and Reconstruction* (1966); James M. McPherson, *The Abolitionist Legacy* (1975); Kenneth M. Stampp, *Era of Reconstruction* (1965); Mark W. Summers, *Railroads, Reconstruction, and the Gospel of Prosperity* (1984); Glyndon C. Van Deusen, *William Henry Seward* (1967).

The Freed Slaves

Roberta Sue Alexander, *North Carolina Faces the Freedmen* (1985); Ira Berlin, ed., *Freedom* (1984); Edmund L. Drago, *Black Politicians and Reconstruction in Georgia* (1982); Paul D. Escott, *Slavery Remembered* (1979); Eric Foner, "Reconstruction and the Crisis of Free Labor," in *Politics and Ideology in the Age of the Civil War* (1980); Peter Kolchin, *First Freedom* (1972); Leon Litwack, *Been in the Storm So Long* (1979); Howard Rabinowitz, ed., *Southern Black Leaders in Reconstruction* (1982); C. Peter Ripley, *Slaves and Freedmen in Civil War Louisiana* (1976); Willie Lee Rose, *Rehearsal for Reconstruction* (1964); Emma Lou Thornbrough, ed., *Black Reconstructionists* (1972); Okon Uya, *From Slavery to Public Service* (1971); Clarence Walker, *A Rock in a Weary Land* (1982).

Politics and Reconstruction in the South

Jonathan Daniels, *Prince of Carpetbaggers* (1958); W. E. B. Du Bois, *Black Reconstruction* (1935); Paul D. Escott, *Many Excellent People* (1985); W. McKee Evans, *Ballots and Fence Rails* (1966); Eric Foner, *Nothing But Freedom* (1983); William C. Harris, *Day of the Carpetbagger* (1979); Thomas Holt, *Black over White* (1977); Robert Manson Myers, ed., *The Children of Pride* (1972); Elizabeth Studley Nathans, *Losing the Peace* (1968); Lillian A. Pereyra, *James Lusk Alcorn* (1966); Michael Perman, *The Road to Redemption* (1984); Michael Perman, *Reunion Without Compromise* (1973); Lawrence N. Powell, "The Politics of Livelihood," in J. Morgan Kousser and James M. McPherson, eds., *Region, Race and Reconstruction* (1982); Lawrence N. Powell, *New Masters* (1980); George C. Rable, *But There Was No Peace* (1984); James Roark, *Masters Without Slaves* (1977); James Sefton, *The United States Army and Reconstruction, 1865–1877* (1967); Mark W. Summers, *Railroads, Reconstruction, and the Gospel of Prosperity* (1984); J. Mills Thornton III, "Fiscal Policy and the Failure of Radical Reconstruction," in J. Morgan Kousser and James M. McPherson, eds., *Region, Race and Reconstruction* (1982); Albion W. Tourgée,

A Fool's Errand (1979); Allen Trelease, *White Terror* (1967); Ted Tunnell, *Crucible of Reconstruction* (1984); Sarah Woolfolk Wiggins, *The Scalawag in Alabama Politics, 1865–1881* (1977).

Women and Family History

Ellen Carol Dubois, *Feminism and Suffrage* (1978); Herbert G. Gutman, *The Black Family in Slavery & Freedom, 1750–1925* (1976); Elizabeth Jacoway, *Yankee Missionaries in the South* (1979); Jacqueline Jones, *Labor of Love, Labor of Sorrow* (1985); Jacqueline Jones, *Soldiers of Light and Love* (1980); Rebecca Scott, "The Battle over the Child," *Prologue*, 10, No. 2 (Summer 1978), 101–113.

The End of Reconstruction

Michael Les Benedict, "Southern Democrats in the Crisis of 1876–1877," *Journal of Southern History*, LXVI, No. 4 (November 1980), 489–524; William Gillette, *Retreat from Reconstruction, 1869–1879* (1980); William Gillette, *The Right to Vote* (1969); Keith Ian Polakoff, *The Politics of Inertia* (1973); C. Vann Woodward, *Reunion and Reaction* (1951).

Reconstruction's Legacy for the South

Robert G. Athearn, *In Search of Canaan* (1978); Norman L. Crockett, *The Black Towns* (1979); Stephen J. DeCanio, *Agriculture in the Postbellum South* (1974); Steven Hahn, *The Roots of Southern Populism* (1983); Susan Previant Lee and Peter Passell, *A New Economic View of American History* (1979); Jay R. Mandle, *The Roots of Black Poverty* (1978); Nell Irvin Painter, *Exodusters* (1976); Howard Rabinowitz, *Race Relations in the Urban South, 1865–1890* (1978); Roger L. Ransom and Richard Sutch, *One Kind of Freedom* (1977); Jonathan M. Wiener, *Social Origins of the New South* (1978); Joel Williamson, *After Slavery* (1966); C. Vann Woodward, *Origins of the New South* (1951).

Transformation of the West and South

1877–1892

Chapter 16

Though shaggy and dressed in buckskins, William F. "Buffalo Bill" Cody earned his nickname for his work, not his looks. Equipped with a powerful rifle, which he dubbed Lucretia Borgia after the scandalous Italian noblewoman, and riding his favorite horse, Brigham, Cody had unequaled hunting skills. Buffalo Bill had such an illustrious reputation by the 1870s that the Kansas Pacific Railroad hired him to supply meat for the company's twelve hundred track layers. For $500 a month, Cody contracted to kill twelve buffalo a day, have them butchered, and deliver them for roasting the same night. In one eight-month stretch he killed over four thousand buffalo.

The millions of buffalo (bison) that roamed the American West helped to feed railroad workers, but they also were bothersome and dangerous. Foraging herds slowed construction, the bulky animals knocked over telegraph poles, and a stampede could derail a train. Railroad operators tried to remove the nuisance and raise money at the same time by sponsoring buffalo hunts for eastern sportsmen. These were hardly sporting events: rifle-toting men sat on slow-moving trains and shot away at the huge targets. Some hunters collected the $1 to $3 offered by tanneries for hides, but others did not even stop to pick up their kill. As a result of these activities, by the 1880s only a few hundred remained of the estimated 13 million buffalo that had existed in the 1850s. Ironically, one of the remaining herds was owned and protected by Buffalo Bill Cody.

The destruction of the buffalo had a more important consequence than facilitating railroad construction: it undermined the culture of Plains Indians, who depended on the animals for almost every essential of life. For centuries natives had cooked and preserved buffalo meat; fashioned hides into clothing, shoes, and blankets; used sinew for thread and bowstrings; carved tools from bones; and made horns into implements. As buffalo became more scarce, the natives were forced to assume a different way of life, where they were more dependent on white traders and the government for their subsistence and where their hunting and territorial claims posed less of a threat to white ambitions for land and profit. Whites were fully aware of these consequences. As one army officer urged during the wars against Plains Indians, "Kill every buffalo you can. Every buffalo dead is an Indian gone."

The buffalo were victims of expansion, and their fate, along with that of the Indians, exemplifies what happened when white Americans transformed the West and South in the late nineteenth century. Settlement of the West proceeded at a furious pace. Between 1870 and 1890 the population living between the Mississippi River and the Pacific Ocean swelled from 7 million to nearly 17 million. Frontiers vanished in the South as well. Shortly after Reconstruction ended, cotton production reached pre–Civil War levels, and people were taking advantage of new opportunities afforded by the region's abundant natural resources.

By 1890 farms, ranches, mines, towns, and cities could be found in almost every region of what was to become the continental United States. That year, the superintendent of the census acknowledged that

up to and including 1880, the country had a frontier of settlement, but at present the unsettled area has been so broken into by isolated bodies of settlement that there can hardly be said to be a frontier line. In the discussion of its extent and its westward movement, etc., it can not therefore, any longer have a place in the census reports.

What had happened to the frontier and what effect did its disappearance have on the nation?

In popular American thought, the frontier—which has been defined as "the edge of the unused"—has represented the birthplace of American self-confidence and individualism. Taming the continent's vast wilderness and bringing forth foodstuffs and raw materials from it, not to mention building cities in a single generation, filled Americans with a consciousness of power and a belief that anyone eager and persistent enough could succeed. Yet that very self-confidence was easily transformed into an arrogant attitude that Americans were somehow special, and individualism often exerted itself at the expense of racial minorities and the propertyless.

As the continent filled in and the edge of the unused shifted and then faded in the late nineteenth century, Americans exhibited both their best and their worst characteristics. Development of the West was accomplished with courage, creativity, and eagerness that amazed the rest of the world. The optimistic conquerors, however, also displayed a wastefulness, violence, and greed that tarnished the American image. Recovery and growth in the South kindled new optimism, but careless exploitation exhausted the soil and left the lives of poor farmers as downtrodden as ever. Industrialization failed to lessen the dominance of southern staple-crop agriculture, and by 1900 the section was more dependent economically on the North than before the Civil War.

Americans rarely thought about conserving resources because there always seemed to be more territory to exploit. Thus the fading of the frontier, though of great symbolic importance, had little direct impact on people's behavior. Because vast stretches of land remained unsettled, millions of people continued to stream into the West, and more land in the South fell under cultivation. Compared with undeveloped regions in such other parts of the world as Siberia, South America, Africa, and Canada, the American West and South were relatively tame. If American settlers failed in one region, they did not usually perish; they could simply try again somewhere else. Even though life in the West was less romantic and comfortable than settlers might have anticipated, and the unreconstructed South failed to fulfill its potential, the various frontiers left Americans with the feeling that they would always have a second chance. This infinity of second chances, the legacy from the western and southern frontiers, left its imprint on the American character.

Exploitation of Natural Resources

John D. Archbold, an officer of the Standard Oil Corporation, once allegedly offered to drink all the oil ever found outside the state of Pennsylvania.

Luckily for him, no one ever challenged him to make good on his bravado; little did Archbold and others like him dream what vast natural resources lay waiting in the undeveloped regions of the United States. Discovery and use of these resources not only advanced settlement but also primed the revolutions in transportation, agriculture, and industry that swept the United States in the late nineteenth century. At the same time, the search for resources produced a restless, get-rich-quick mentality, reinforced the sexual division of labor, and fed habits of racial oppression.

In the years just before the Civil War, eager prospectors began to comb remote forests and mountains looking for iron, coal, timber, oil, and copper. By 1900, active exploitation of the land's riches, once confined to the Northeast and Appalachian regions, had spread across the continent. Timberlands in the Midwest, South, and Northwest were yielding more lumber than those of New York and Maine. Alabama, Michigan, and Minnesota had become leading sources of iron ore. Montana and Arizona had taken the lead in copper and silver production. And discoveries of oil fields in California and Texas gave the lie to Archbold's faith that Pennsylvania was the only oil-rich state.

The mining frontier advanced rapidly, drawing thousands of people to California, Nevada, Idaho, Montana, and Colorado in the 1850s and 1860s.

Mining and Lumbering Prospectors tended to be restless optimists, willing to tramp mountains and deserts, searching icy streams for a telltale glint of precious metal. They shot game for food and financed their explorations by convincing merchants to advance credit for equipment in return for a share of the lode yet to be discovered. When their credit ran out, unlucky prospectors took jobs and saved up for another search for riches.

Extracting minerals from the ground involved high expenses for excavation and transportation. Thus individual prospectors who did discover veins of metal seldom mined them. Instead they sold their claims to mining syndicates, lived it up off their new wealth, and then set off on another quest. The mining companies, often financed by eastern investors, had ample capital to bring in engineers, heavy machinery, railroad lines, and work crews. Although discoveries of gold and silver first drew attention to the West and its

Two women stand on a hill overlooking Helena, Montana, a typical mining town of the 1870s. In spite of their small numbers, women exerted a settling influence on frontier towns.   Montana Historical Society, Helena.

resources, such companies usually moved into the Rocky Mountain states to exploit less romantic but equally lucrative bonanzas of lead, zinc, tin, quartz, and copper. In Montana, for example, speculator William Clark's Anaconda Mine, opened in 1881, yielded more than $2 billion worth of copper over the next fifty years.

Mineral extraction concentrated intensively on a particular area or mine, but lumber production—another large-scale extractive industry—required vast stretches of land. As lumber companies moved into the thick forests of the Northwest, some not only stripped the land without regard for the future but also grabbed millions of acres fraudulently. To stimulate western settlement, Congress in 1878 passed the Timber and Stone Act; this measure, which applied to land in California, Nevada, Oregon, and Wash-

ington, allowed private citizens to buy at the low price of $2.50 per acre 160-acre plots "unfit for cultivation" and "valuable chiefly for timber." Taking advantage of the act, lumber companies hired thousands of seamen from waterfront boardinghouses to register claims to timberland and turn them over to the companies. By 1900, claimants had bought over 3.5 million acres under Timber and Stone Act provisions, and most of that land belonged to corporations.

While lumbermen were acquiring claims to timberlands in the Northwest, oilmen were beginning to sink wells in the Southwest. In 1900 most of the nation's petroleum still came from fields in the Appalachians and the Midwest, but promising developments were under way in southern California and eastern Texas. The most spectacular strike occurred in 1901 at Spindletop, Texas, where a well shot a stream of oil 160 feet into the air. Although most oil and kerosene were still used for lubrication and lighting, discoveries in the Southwest were to become a vital new source of fuel in the twentieth century.

Much of the natural-resource frontier was a man's world. Mining, general labor, and some farming were the predominant occupations. In 1880, men out-numbered women by more than two to one in Colorado, Nevada, and Arizona. Among twenty-to-forty-year-olds, men had a three-to-one majority. In the nation as a whole, by contrast, there were about 97 women for every 100 men; and in the older eastern states, women even frequently outnum-bered men.

Frontier Society

Yet many western communities had substantial numbers of women. Most women who went to the mining frontier did so for the same reasons men went: to find a fortune. But their independence, on the mining frontier, as elsewhere, was limited. They usually accompanied a husband or father and seldom pros-pected themselves. Even so, many women realized their own opportunities in the towns, where they provided cooking, laundering, and, in some cases, sexual services for the miners. Some became the family's main breadwinner when their husbands failed to strike it rich. As one wife recalled, "I began at once to figure in my mind how many men I could cook for, if there should be no better way of making money." Women's presence had a settling influence on mining communities. While they pursued new opportunities and freedoms, women also helped to bolster family life and to combat raw materialism and vice by campaigning against drinking, gambling, and whoring. According to one resident of the mining frontier, women of "honest hearts have fallen victim to the peculiar seductions [of] the place," yet "par-adoxicaly as the statement may sound, it is rigorously true that these women have improved the morals of the community."

Many of the mining and lumber communities were genuinely heterogeneous, containing small numbers of Chinese, Mexicans, Indians, and blacks. Though most Chinese migrated to work on American railroads (see pages 457–458), some were employed in the camps to do cooking and cleaning. A few blacks also held such jobs. Mexicans and Indians often had been the original settlers of land coveted by whites, and

Chinese gold miners at Auburn Ravine, California, in 1852. Chinese first came to California in the 1850s and 1860s to escape social and economic upheaval at home. They often paid for their transportation by working under a Chinese-operated contract-labor system. California State Library.

some stayed to resist white intruders. Each of these minority groups met with white prejudice, especially when it became evident that the forests and mines would not make everyone rich. California imposed a tax on foreign miners and denied blacks, Indians, and Chinese the right to testify or submit evidence in court. Throughout the West any claims Indians or Mexicans might have had to land sought by white miners were ignored or stolen. Blacks and Chinese who worked in mining camps often suffered abuse and violence. Not all harassment came from whites; in California, for example, Mexican bandits preyed on Chinese even more than on Anglos. Nonwhites defended themselves as best they could against in-timidation, but their most common tactic was to pack up and seek jobs and homes in another town or mining camp.

Development of the nation's oil, mineral, and timber resources raised serious questions about what belonged to all the people, as represented by the federal government, and what belonged to private interests whose motive was profit. Two factors worked at cross-purposes. First, most land west of the Mississippi was public domain, and some people believed the federal government, as owner of the land, should receive some return from exploitation of the land. But the government lacked both the motivation and the means to dig mines, sink wells, and cut forests, and therefore sold land to private interests who would take the initiative.

Use of Public Lands

Inevitably, developers of natural resources were more interested in what the land yielded than in the land itself. They wanted trees, not forest land that would become useless once the trees were stripped away. They wanted oil, not the scrubby plain that would be doubly worthless if—as often happened—wells were dug but no oil was found. Thus, to many companies involved in resource production, land purchased at market price was an unnecessary and sometimes prohibitive expense.

To avoid such costs, developers used several ploys, some legal and some not. One method was to purchase or rent limited rights to extract resources. Lumbermen would buy permits to fell a certain number of trees on a given forest tract and share the profits with the landowner. Oilmen and iron miners often leased property from private owners or the government and paid royalties on the minerals extracted. Other practices were corrupt or fraudulent. As they had done since colonial times, some lumbermen simply cut trees on public lands without paying a cent. And, as already noted, lumber companies used trickery to buy land cheaply under the Timber and Stone Act. Even when Congress and the U.S. Land Office tried to prevent fraud by passing tighter legislation and sending out more investigators, many communities resisted in the fear that such crackdowns would slow local economic growth.

Questions about natural resources thus caught Americans between the urge for progress and fear of spoiling the land. By the late 1870s and early 1880s, people concerned about the natural landscape began to coalesce into a conservation movement. The few scientists, artists, and government officials involved in this movement worked chiefly to preserve forests, probably because logging so visibly altered the environment. A leading figure in the conservation movement was the western naturalist John Muir, who helped establish Yosemite National Park in 1890. The next year, under pressure from Muir and others, Congress authorized the president to create forest reserves on public land, protected from cutting by private interests. Such policies met with strong objections. Lumber companies, lumber dealers, and railroads were joined in their opposition by private householders accustomed to cutting timber freely for fuel and building material. Public opinion on conservation also split along sectional lines. Most supporters came from the eastern states, where resources had become less plentiful; opposition was loudest in the West, where people were still eager to take advantage of nature's bounty.

Conquest of the mining and forest frontiers brought western territories to the threshold of statehood. Between 1876 and 1889, jockeying between Democrats and Republicans in Congress prevented the admission of any new states. But in 1889 Republicans seeking to solidify their control of Congress pushed through the Omnibus Bill, granting statehood to North Dakota, South Dakota, Washington, and Montana. Wyoming and Idaho were admitted in 1890, the same year the Census Bureau announced the disappearance of the frontier. Congress balked at granting statehood to Utah because the Mormons, who were a majority of the state's population and controlled its government, practiced polygamy. But the territory's prosperity could not be denied, and when the Mormons agreed to abandon polygamy, Congress voted Utah into the Union in 1896.

Admission of New States

The mining towns and lumber camps in these states spiced American folk culture and fostered the go-getter optimism that distinguished the American spirit. The lawlessness and hedonism of places like Deadwood, in Dakota Territory, and Tombstone, in Arizona Territory, gave the West notoriety and romance. Legends grew up about inhabitants of these towns whose lives both typified and magnified western experience. One such character was Martha Jane Canary, known as Calamity Jane, who in the 1870s worked in eastern Wyoming and the western Dakotas as a scout and wagon driver, freighting supplies to mining camps. Skilled with a rifle and dressed in men's clothes, Calamity Jane acquired a reputation for wild behavior that fiction writers later glorified. Yet she appears simply to have been seeking her place in a hard world. According to an army captain who employed her, Jane was "eccentric and wayward rather than bad and had adopted male attire more to aid her in getting a living than for any improper purpose."

Arizona mining towns, with their free-flowing cash and loose law enforcement, attracted numerous gamblers, thieves, and opportunists whose names stood for the Wild West. Near Tombstone, the infamous Clanton family and their partner John Ringgold, called Johnny Ringo, engaged in smuggling and cattle rustling to supply materials and food to mining camps. Inside the town, the legendary Earp brothers—Wyatt, Jim, Morgan, Virgil, and Warren—and their friends William Barclay "Bat" Masterson and John Henry "Doc" Holliday operated on both sides of the law as gunmen, gamblers, and politicians. A feud between Clanton and Earp factions climaxed on October 26, 1881, in the famous shoot-out at the OK Corral, where three Clantons were killed and Virgil and Morgan Earp were seriously wounded.

Characters like Wild Bill Hickok, Poker Alice, and Bedrock Tom became western folk heroes, and fiction writers like Mark Twain and Bret Harte captured for posterity some of the flavor of mining life. But violence and eccentricity were far from common. Most miners and lumbermen worked seventy hours a week and had neither time, energy, nor money for drinking, gambling, or gunfights. Women worked as long or longer as teachers, cooks, laundresses, storekeepers, and housewives; only a very few were sharpshooters or dance-hall queens. For most westerners, life was a matter of adapting and surviving.

THE AGE OF RAILROAD EXPANSION

On May 10, 1869, the whole country knew what was happening at Promontory Point in the mountains of Utah. There, the Central Pacific

Railroad construction camps were peopled by a variety of workers, from Europe and Asia as well as from the United States. Providing food, lodging, and materials for these crews required extensive organization and planning. *Library of Congress.*

Railroad, built 689 miles eastward from Sacramento, California, was to meet the Union Pacific Railroad, built 1,086 miles westward from Omaha, Nebraska, to form the nation's first transcontinental route. Work crews of six hundred Irish, Chinese, Mexicans, and white and black Americans participated in the ceremony. Though a golden railroad spike was used to commemorate the event, the last spike was actually of steel because it was wired to a telegraph line and when pounded it would signal to the world that the railroad had been completed. Governor Leland Stanford of California was given the honor of driving that final spike. As the crowd hushed, he drew back his silver hammer, swung—and missed the spike. The telegrapher sent the message anyway, and across the nation church bells rang and shouting multitudes celebrated.

Discovery and development of natural riches provided the base on which the nation's economy expanded. But raw wealth would have been of limited use without means of carrying it to factories, marketplaces, and ports. In today's world of trailer trucks,

AN EXPRESS FREIGHT SHIPMENT OF 30 COACHES, APRIL 15, 1868 BY ABBOT, DOWNING & CO., CONCORD, N.H. TO WELLS, FARGO CO., OMAHA, NEB.

Railroads hastened development of the West in many ways. Not only did they carry people to new areas of settlement; they also transported manufactured products, such as these thirty stagecoaches ordered by the Wells Fargo Company. The New Hampshire Historical Society, Concord.

cargo planes, and supertankers, a railway train seems almost an anachronism, a relic. But in the half-century following the Civil War, railroads refashioned the American economy, stitching together the nation, supporting new industries, and generating their own romance.

During these years, tens of thousands of laborers built a web of railroad track across the country. Between 1865 and 1890, total track in the United States grew from 35,000 to 200,000 miles. By 1910 the nation had a third of all railroad track in the world. In their haste to lay track, railroad managers recruited large and assorted work crews. The Central Pacific imported seven thousand Chinese to work in the Western mountains, while the Union Pacific used Irish construction gangs. Both companies also hired Civil War veterans. Workers were housed in shacks and tents that could be dismantled, loaded on flatcars, and relocated at intervals of sixty or seventy miles. At one time, the Union Pacific needed forty railcars to supply its crews with rails, ties, bridge materials, and food.

Though construction proceeded erratically, often tainted by stock fraud and mismanagement, by 1900 the country's railroad network was virtually complete (see map). The transcontinental lines were the most awe-inspiring, but regional lines, such as the New York Central in the Northeast, the Louisville and Nashville in the South, and the Burlington in the Midwest, were equally important. These railroads linked major cities and completed formation of a national market system. Henceforth the goods and raw materials of one section could be available in other sections of the country.

The economic consequences of railroads were immense. By 1890 total railroad revenues had topped $1 billion—two-and-one-half times the total revenues of the federal government. After 1880, when more-durable steel rails began to replace iron rails, railroads helped to boost the nation's steel industry to inter-

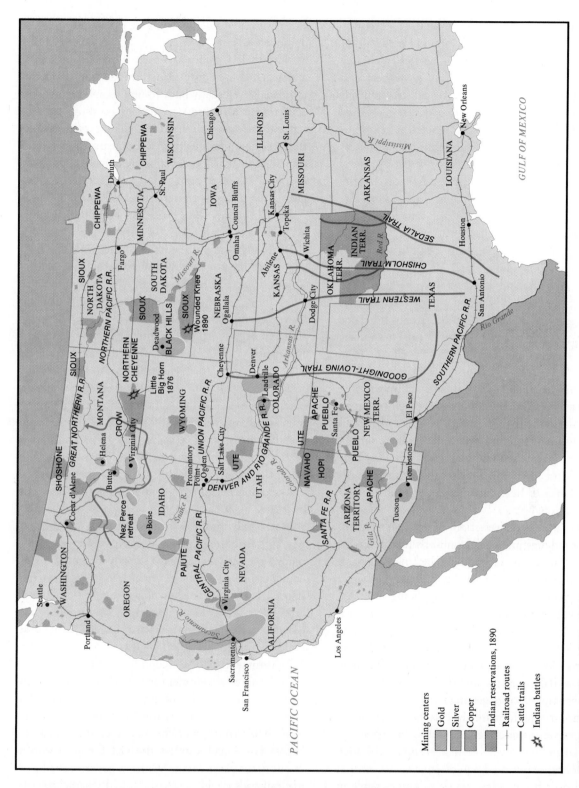

Mining centers
- Gold
- Silver
- Copper
- Indian reservations, 1890
- Railroad routes
- Cattle trails
- Indian battles

The American West, 1860–1890

Effects of Railroad Construction

national leadership. Moreover, railroad expansion spawned a number of related industries, including coal production, passenger and freight car manufacture, and depot construction. Finally, railroads altered American conceptions of time and space, and they spurred a movement for standardization. First, by overcoming barriers of distance, railroads transformed space into time. It became easier to measure the separation between places by the amount of time it took to travel from one to the other rather than by the physical distance. Second, railroad scheduling necessitated nationwide agreement on time. Before railroads, each locale had its own time. Community church bells and steeple clocks struck at noon, when the sun was overhead, and people set their own clocks and watches accordingly. But the sun was not overhead at exactly the same moment, so there were variations in time from place to place. For example, clocks in Boston differed from those in New York by almost twelve minutes. To achieve some regularity, railroads set their own time zones, but by 1880 there still were nearly fifty different standards. Finally in 1883 railroads agreed—without consulting Congress, the president, or the courts—to establish four standard time zones for the whole country. Most communities now adjusted their clocks (though Chicago held out briefly) and railroad time became national time.

Third, railroad construction brought about technological and organizational reforms. By the late 1880s, almost all lines had adopted standard narrow-gauge rails so that their tracks could connect with one another. Such devices as the Westinghouse air brake, an automatic car coupler, and standardized handholds on freight cars made rail transportation safer and more efficient. Needs for gradings, tunnels, and bridges helped the American engineering profession to grow. Organizational advances included systems for coordinating complex passenger and freight schedules and the adoption of uniform freight-classification systems.

From other perspectives, however, the effects of railroads were less favorable. For example, the high cost of construction and equipment demanded that new railroads begin operation as soon as possible in order to generate revenues to repay debts and maintain investors' confidence. As a result, many miles of track were laid hastily, without regard for safety or durability.

Nevertheless, railroads became extremely influential and acquired a uniquely American function. European railroads were usually built to link established market centers and to improve or replace existing routes of traffic. In this country, however, railroads often created the very communities they were meant to serve and carried traffic that had never before existed. Particularly in the West and South, railroads accelerated the growth of regional centers such as Omaha, Kansas City, Cheyenne, Los Angeles, Portland, Seattle, Atlanta, and Nashville.

Railroads accomplished these feats with the help of some of the largest government subsidies in American history. Railroad executives argued that their activities were benefiting the public interest and that the government should aid them by giving them land from the public domain. Congress was sympathetic. In order to encourage construction, the government gave railroad companies over 180 million acres, mostly to interstate routes chartered between 1850 and 1871. These grants usually consisted of a right of way plus alternate sections of land in a strip twenty to eighty miles wide along the right of way. Railroad corporations financed construction by using this land as security for bonds or by selling it for cash.

Government Subsidy of Railroads

States and localities heaped further subsidies on new routes. State land was frequently offered to railroads by legislators eager for the advantages railroads could bring—to them personally as well as to the state. Total state grants amounted to about 50 million acres. Counties, cities, and towns also assisted railroads, usually by offering them loans or by purchasing railroad bonds or stocks.

Government subsidies had mixed effects. Capitalists argued against government interference in one breath and accepted government aid in the next. They also pressured public agencies into meeting their needs. The Southern Pacific, for example, threatened to bypass Los Angeles unless the city came up with a bonus and built a depot. Without government help, few railroads could have established themselves sufficiently to attract private investment. Yet public aid was not always salutary. Some laborers and farmers fought subsidies, arguing that companies like the Southern Pacific would become too powerful. During the 1880s, the policy of assistance haunted some communities whose zeal for railroads had prompted them to commit too much to lines that were never built or that defaulted on loans. On the other hand, many communities boomed because they had linked their fortunes to the iron horse.

As the nation's rail network expanded, so did competition and duplication. Shippers sending raw materials or finished products across the country now had several routes to choose from, and railroad operators scrambled for new customers. Lines cut rates to attract more traffic and outmaneuver competitors. In the twenty-five years after the Civil War, freight and passenger rates between New York and Chicago fell by nearly two-thirds. But rate wars soon cut into profits, and several railroads had to reduce or omit dividends to stockholders. Moreover, wild vacillations in rates angered shippers and farmers who missed out on a saving by shipping goods just before a rate reduction or were caught awaiting a reduction when rates were raised. Stability was clearly desirable.

Competition and Discriminatory Rate Setting

Ironically, while railroad rates generally were falling, complaints about excessively high rates were increasing. Railroads often boosted rates as high as possible on noncompetitive short-distance routes in order to compensate for unprofitably low rates on competitive long-distance routes. For example, it cost twice as much to send wheat from Fargo, North Dakota, to Duluth, Minnesota, as from Minneapolis to Chicago, even though the latter distance was twice as long. Railroad managers justifiably argued that small quantities shipped over short distances involved proportionately higher transportation costs than did bulk goods carried over long distances. But farmers and other shippers continued to believe such rates were illogical and unfair. A spokesman for Michigan farmers in 1886 said he could "hardly imagine a case where it would be right or proper for a railroad to charge more for a shorter than for a longer distance for freight [similar] in kind and quantity and over the same road or roads."

Railroads also devised other forms of rate adjustment. To increase traffic they made special contracts with large shippers, offering rebates and reductions of up to 50 percent of published freight rates. They courted the favor of important shippers and politicians by offering free passenger passes. And to reduce competition, they made agreements among themselves called pools, whose participants shared traffic and earnings and set common rates. Such agreements generally discriminated against small shippers.

These practices upset farmers, retailers, bankers, reform politicians, and even some stockholders. During the 1870s, many of these groups demanded that government regulate railroads, especially their pricing practices. By 1880, fourteen states had established commissions or other agencies to limit freight and storage rates charged by state-chartered lines. Railroads bitterly fought these laws, arguing that rights of private property superseded public authority. This traditional American belief in the freedom to acquire and use property without government restraint prevented the ultimate step—public ownership of railroads—but did not halt regulation. In 1877 the Supreme Court upheld the principle of railroad regulation in *Munn* v. *Illinois*, saying, "When private property is affected with a public interest it ceases to be *juris privati* only . . . and must submit to be controlled by the public for the common good."

Government Regulation of Railroads

Although the principle of regulation had won acceptance, critics charged that state regulatory commissions were either too weak or too subservient to railroads. Moreover, state commissioners had little control over interstate lines and thus could not affect the largest, most powerful railroads. The Supreme Court affirmed this limitation in 1886 by declaring in the *Wabash* case that only Congress and not the states could regulate rates on interstate commerce. Consequently, reformers called for federal regulation.

Congress responded in 1887 by passing the Interstate Commerce Act. The act prohibited pools, rebates, and long-haul–short-haul rate discriminations; and one of its clauses directed that "all charges . . . shall be reasonable and fair." The law also created the Interstate Commerce Commission (ICC) and gave it power to investigate railroads; to issue "cease-and-desist" orders against illegal practices; and to seek court assistance to enforce compliance with the law.

The Interstate Commerce Act resulted from a political compromise between supporters of regulation and defenders of laissez faire. Its basic provisions quieted the cries of protest from farmers and other interests opposed to railroads' monopolistic practices. It affirmed the principle of regulation, forbade discriminatory practices, and gave the ICC power to investigate on its own initiative as well as in response to specific complaints. But provisions for its enforcement were blurry and left railroads much room for evasion. The ICC could issue cease-and-desist orders, but only the courts could force obedience. In a series of court cases, federal judges chipped away at ICC powers by asserting a right to review ICC orders and by interpreting the Interstate Commerce Act very narrowly. In the *Maximum Freight Rate* case in 1897, the Supreme Court ruled that the act did not grant the ICC power to set rates, and in the *Alabama Midlands* case the same year, the Court shattered prohibitions against long-haul–short-haul discriminations. Between 1887 and 1897, the judiciary overruled 90 percent of ICC rate orders; between 1887 and 1905, the Supreme Court decided against the ICC in fifteen of sixteen cases.

In spite of such setbacks, the era of railroad reform opened new paths for future generations. The right of the federal government to regulate railroads as a public enterprise did gain court support. Regulation at the state level continued, especially with regard to safety and intrastate rates. Finally, establishment of the ICC gave impetus to the movement to eliminate favoritism in society and the economy. Forces of change had begun to gather momentum, but Americans still had to decide whether they desired free competition or cooperation under government regulation.

NATIVE AMERICANS: CASUALTIES OF EXPANSION

Railroad expansion not only bound the nation together economically, it had a massive impact on previously undeveloped land. The vast domain between the Missouri and the Pacific—the Great Plains and Far West—became more accessible. But much of this land was not empty. It was the home of thousands of native American tribespeople, whose ways of life differed profoundly from those of most white people and whose presence represented a stubborn barrier to whites' exploitation of the land.

As in previous eras, the contact between white and native culture elicited a variety of responses from the Indians. Some tried to adapt to white invaders, by trading with them—usually offering hides in exchange for livestock and guns—and by accepting white alliances as a means of gaining an advantage over rival tribes. Others actively resisted white intrusion, using guerrilla tactics to harass settlers, herders, and troops. Still others alternated between alliance and enmity, depending on their leadership, material needs, and relations with other tribes. In the end, however, though they struggled to retain their culture, Indians faced insurmountable odds and an overwhelming migratory invasion.

Although there was great variety of cultures, most native tribes in the West fit into one of two cultural groups. Some were nomadic or seminomadic, subsisting on food that they hunted or gathered. These tribes included the Shoshone of the Northwest, the Apache in the Southwest, and the Cheyenne, Dakota, and Crow in the Plains. Others were more settled, depending on farming and gardening. These included the Zuni, Hopi, and Navajo tribes in the Southwest, plus Pawnee, Mandan, and Hidatsa tribes in the Plains. Tribal organization often was loose, with leadership only vaguely defined, but almost all Indians had highly formalized cultural systems and religions that regarded their relationship with nature as sacred. Black Elk, an Oglala Sioux, explained one version of this unity:

Everything an Indian does is in a circle, and that is because the Power of the World always works in circles, and everything tries to be round. . . . The sky is round, and I have heard that the earth is round like a ball, and so are all the stars. The wind, in its greatest power, whirls. Birds make their nests in circles, for theirs is the same religion as ours. The sun comes forth and goes down again in a circle. The moon does the same, and both are round. Even the seasons form a great circle in their changing, and always come back again

A Sioux camp in South Dakota, 1891. The Sioux led a no-madic life, living in harmony with the natural environment; when they packed up and moved on, they left the landscape almost undisturbed. This photograph shows the temporary situation characteristic of their camps.   Library of Congress.

to where they were. The life of a man is a circle from childhood to childhood, and so it is in everything where power moves.

Western Indians observed sexual divisions of labor, but their social organization differed greatly from that of white Americans. Generally, men took responsibility for hunting, fishing, and war, and they almost always held the most powerful positions—chief, priest, shaman (medicine man). Women raised children and crops. Often, however, the female side of kinship groups was more influential than the male side, and women had important roles in political, economic, religious, and social affairs. Zuni, Navajo, and Mandan tribes, for example, were matrilineal and matrilocal; that is, family descent was determined by the mother,

and married couples lived with or near the wife's mother. Navajo women controlled most of their family's property, and Apache and Teton Dakota women directed their tribe's most important religious ceremony, the girls' puberty rite. The Navajo and Teton Dakota also valued women for their craft skills.

When white Americans first extensively encountered western Indians in the mid-nineteenth century, they already had two centuries of experience with native tribes (see pages 53–57). Like the British before them, white Americans considered Indians as separate peoples with whom they could make treaties. Thus as white settlers began pressing into native territories, the government made treaties with various tribes, insuring peace and nominally defining boundaries of white and native lands. But the treaties seldom promised the Indians any future land rights; rather, whites assumed that eventually they could settle wherever they wished. Treaties made one week were violated the next, as more settlers streamed into the West. Some Indians acquiesced; others resisted with attacks on settlements, herds, and troops.

Between 1850 and 1877, two factors on the Great Plains accelerated the policy of concentrating Indians on reservations: military conquest and destruction of buffalo herds. Native defense of their homelands against white settlers resulted in a series of bloody battles and massacres. The most legendary battle occurred on June 25, 1876, when 2,500 Sioux, led by Chiefs Rain-in-the-Face, Sitting Bull, and Crazy Horse, annihilated white troops led by the rash Colonel George A. Custer near the Little Big Horn River in southern Montana. Though there were other Indian victories as well, shortage of supplies and relentless pursuit by white troops eventually overwhelmed armed Indian resistance and forced the Native Americans onto reservations, which were usually those parts of their previous territory least desirable to whites (see map, page 459). At the same time, extermination of the buffalo, which had been so vital to native cultures, was even more decisive than government policy in forcing Indians to change their way of life.

Reservation policy had troublesome consequences. In assigning Indians to specific territory, the United States government promised protection from white encroachment and agreed to provide food, clothing, and other necessities, in effect making Indians dependent on the government. As more reservations were created, it became evident that isolation was impossible. White farmers, miners, and herders continually sought even remote Indian lands. Moreover, Indians continued to be restive. During the 1880s violence between whites and Indians broke out on Apache, Sioux, and other reservations. As a result, whites became more intent on "civilizing" the Native Americans—making them accept whites' values, breaking up their tribal organization, and integrating them into the nation. At the same time, humanitarian concern was heightened by Helen Hunt Jackson's popular book, *A Century of Dishonor* (1881), which castigated the government for its unfair treatment of Indians.

In 1887 Congress reversed its reservation policy in the Dawes Severalty Act, which dissolved com-

Dawes Severalty Act munity-owned tribal lands and granted land allotments to individual families. To prevent Indians from selling these plots to speculators, the government retained ownership of the land for twenty-five years. The act also granted citizenship to all who accepted the allotments and authorized the government to sell unallotted land and to set aside the proceeds for the education of Indians. The Dawes Act applied to most western tribes, the major exception being Pueblo peoples who had retained land rights granted to them by the Spanish.

As a result of the Dawes Act, U.S. Indian policy as carried out by the Indian Bureau of the Department of the Interior took on three main features. First and foremost, government officials advocated allotting land to individual families because they believed Indians would become civilized by learning how to manage their own property. Ownership would make them more responsible and industrious. Second, bureau officials believed Indians would lose their "barbaric" habits more quickly if their children could be removed and educated in boarding schools away from the old reservations. Third, the bureau tried to suppress traditional religious ceremonies, such as the Sun Dance, and funded white church groups to establish religious schools among the Indians and teach them to become good Christians.

Indians had no voice in any of these policies, which were carried out by agents of the bureau. These officials lived on the reservations, spent the funds assigned by the bureau, distributed land allotments, secured pupils for the boarding schools, and supervised government farmers and teachers—all without any consultation with Indians themselves. In effect, while reservations were no longer isolated geographically, they remained isolated politically and socially. Increasingly as time went on, antagonisms developed between surrounding white populations and reservation communities, and no local means of resolving disputes existed.

Much of the new Indian policy was ineffective. Land allotment proved to be very complex. In the face of efforts by whites to acquire land titles from Indians who were to receive individual plots, the government simply abandoned the program. In the Southwest, for example, only small parts of the Navajo, Pima, and Colorado River reservations were ever allotted. The boarding school program did affect thousands of children, but rarely did they forsake their culture; most returned to their reservations rather than submit to assimilation into white society. Efforts to suppress native religious observances only forced them under cover. Moreover, whites did not give up their fears and use of violence. Late in 1890, the government sent the Seventh Cavalry, Custer's old regiment, to apprehend some Sioux who were moving north toward Pine Ridge Reservation in South Dakota and who were believed to be armed for revolt. During an encounter at a creek called Wounded Knee, the troups trained newly acquired cannons on the Indians and massacred two hundred sick and hungry men, women, and children in the snow. Although Native Americans retained their culture, the West was won at their expense, and they remained sad casualties of an aggressive age.

THE RANCHING FRONTIER

R ailroad construction and Indian removal set the stage for one of the West's most colorful and romantic industries, cattle ranching. Early in the nineteenth century, huge herds of cattle, originally introduced by the Spanish and developed by Mexican ranchers, roamed southern Texas and bred with cattle brought by American settlers. The resulting longhorn breed multiplied and became valuable by the 1860s, when the East's growing population increased demand for food and railroads made transportation of beef more feasible. By 1870 drovers were herding thousands of Texas cattle northward to railroad connections in Kansas, Missouri, and Wyoming. On these long drives, mounted cowboys (as many as 25 percent of whom were blacks) supervised the herds, which fed on open grassland along the way. At the northern terminus— usually Abilene, Dodge City, or Cheyenne—the cattle were loaded onto trains and sent eastward to Chicago and St. Louis for slaughter and distribution.

The long drive gave rise to its own romantic lore, but it was not very efficient. In trekking 1,500 miles, the cattle became sinewy and tough. Herds traveling through Indian lands and farmers' fields were sometimes shot at and later prohibited from such trespass by state laws. The ranchers' only solution was to eliminate long drives by raising herds nearer to railroad routes.

Ranchers soon discovered that crossing sturdy Texas longhorns with heavier Hereford and Angus breeds produced cattle better able to survive northern winters, and cattle raising spread across the Great Plains. Between 1860 and 1880 the cattle population of Kansas, Nebraska, Colorado, Wyoming, Montana, and Dakota increased from 130,000 to 4.5 million.

Cattle raisers were like timber cutters: they needed vast stretches of land where their herds could graze and they wanted to incur as little expense as possible to use such land. Thus they often bought a few acres bordering streams and turned their herds loose on adjacent public domain, which no one would want to own because it lacked water access. By this method, called open-range ranching, a cattle raiser could control thousands of acres by owning only a hundred or so.

Open-range Ranching

Neighboring ranchers often formed associations and allowed their herds to graze together. Herds were distinguished from each other by burning a special mark, or brand, into the hide of every animal. Each ranch had its own brand—an improvised shorthand for documenting title to movable property. Twice each year, cowboy crews rounded up the cattle, to brand new calves in the spring and to drive mature animals to market in the fall.

Roundups provided easterners with colorful images of western life: bellowing cattle, mounted rope-swinging cowboys, the smell of singed hides and smoky campfires. But the roundup was short-lived because it was too successful. By the early 1880s, the profitability of beef raising had lured scores of investors to the industry. As one publication explained:

A good sized steer when it is fit for the butcher market will bring from $45.00 to $60.00. The same animal at its birth was worth but $5.00. He has run on the plains and cropped the grass from the public domain for four or five years, and now, with scarcely any expense to its owner, is worth $40.00 more than when he started on his pilgrimage.

National and international demand for beef kept rising, and ranchers and capital flowed into the Plains. Soon cattle began to overrun the range.

The roundup was one of the most important events on the open range. In the spring, cowboys herded the cattle together and branded calves that followed cows with their owner's insignia. "The Roundup" (detail) by Charles M. Russell, 1913. MacKay Collection, Montana Historical Society.

Fearing depletion of the prairie and loss of control, ranchers began to fence in their pastures with newly invented barbed wire—even though they had no legal title to the land. Fences destroyed the open range and often provoked disputes between competing ranchers, between cattle raisers and sheep raisers, and between ranchers and farmers who claimed use of the same land. In 1885, President Cleveland ordered removal of illegal fences on public lands and Indian reservations. Enforcement was slow, but the order signaled that free use of public domain was ending.

Open-range ranching made beef a staple of the American diet and created a few fortunes, but its extralegal features could not survive the rush of history. By 1890, big businesses were taking over the cattle industry and applying scientific methods of breeding and feeding. The cowboy became just another corporate wage earner, though the myth of his freedom and individualism grew rather than faded. Most cattle ranchers now owned or leased the land they used, though some illegal fencing continued.

Meanwhile, two new groups were contending with cattle ranchers for supremacy on the Plains. From California and New Mexico, sheepherders moved into land east of the Rockies. Ranchers complained that sheep ruined grassland by eating down to the roots and that cattle refused to graze where sheep had been because the "woolly critters" left a repulsive odor. Armed conflict occasionally erupted between cowboys and sheepherders who resorted to violence rather than settle disputes in court, where the judge would discover that both were using the land illegally. More importantly, the farming frontier advanced into the West. From the Missouri to the Pacific there began an agricultural transformation whose social and political ramifications were to affect the entire nation.

Chapter 16: TRANSFORMATION OF THE WEST AND SOUTH, 1877–1892

FARMING THE PLAINS

I n an 1880 article, *Harper's New Monthly Magazine* marveled at the success of Oliver Dalrymple's farm in Dakota Territory's Red River valley. "You are in a sea of wheat," the writer rhapsodized. "The railroad train rolls through an ocean of grain. . . . We encounter a squadron of war chariots . . . doing the work of human hands. . . . There are 25 of them in this one brigade of the grand army of 115, under the marksmanship of this Dakota farmer." Dalrymple's farm exemplified two important achievements of the late nineteenth century: the taming of wide, windswept prairies so that the land would yield crops to benefit humankind; and the transformation of agriculture into big business by means of mechanization, long-distance transportation, and scientific cultivation.

These achievements did not come easily. The climate and landscape of the Plains presented formidable challenges. And overcoming these challenges did not guarantee success or even provide security. Agricultural development of the West turned the United States into the world's breadbasket, but it also scarred the lives of hundreds of thousands of men and women who made that development possible.

Migration to the Plains
Settlement of the Plains and the West involved the greatest migration in American history. Between 1870 and 1900, more acres were settled and put under cultivation than in the previous 250 years. Between 1860 and 1910, the number of farms tripled, from 2 million to over 6 million. During the 1870s and 1880s, hundreds of thousands of people streamed into states like Kansas, Nebraska, Texas, and California.

Most, though not all, migrants came from the eastern states or Europe. Several western states opened immigration bureaus in the East and in Europe to lure settlers westward. Land-grant railroads were especially aggressive, advertising cheap land, arranging credit terms, offering reduced fares, and promising instant success. Railroad agents—often former immigrants—greeted newcomers at eastern ports and traveled to Europe to recruit prospective settlers. In California, fruit and vegetable growers imported Japanese and Mexican laborers to work in the fields and canneries.

Most migrants went west because opportunities there seemed to promise a better life. Between 1870 and 1910 the nation's population rose from 40 million to 92 million, and the total urban population swelled by over 400 percent. As a result, demand for farm products grew rapidly. Meanwhile, scientific advances were enabling farmers to use the soil more efficiently. Agricultural experts developed the technique of dry farming, a system of plowing and harrowing that prevented precious moisture from evaporating. Scientists perfected varieties of "hard" wheat whose seeds could withstand northern winters, and millers invented an efficient process for grinding these tougher new wheat kernels into flour. Railroad expansion made remote farming regions more accessible, and grain-elevator construction eased problems of shipping and storage.

Hardships of Life on the Plains
In spite of such developments, life on the Plains was much harder than the advertisements suggested. Migrants often encountered scarcities of essentials they had taken for granted back home. Vast stretches of land contained little lumber for housing and fuel. Pioneer families were forced to build houses of sod and to burn manure for heat. Water was as scarce as timber. Few families were lucky or wealthy enough to buy land near a stream that did not dry up in summer and freeze in winter. Machinery for drilling wells was scarce until the 1880s, and even then it was very expensive, so that many wells were dug by hand.

Even more formidable than the terrain of the Plains was its climate. The expanse between the Missouri River and the Rocky Mountains divides climatologically along a line running from Minnesota southwest through Oklahoma, then south, bisecting Texas. East of this line, annual rainfall averages about 28 inches, enough for most crops (see map, page 469). West of the line, life-giving rain was never certain; farmers, heartened by adequate water one year, gagged on dust and broke their plows on hardened limestone soil the next.

Weather seldom followed predictable cycles on either side of the line. In summer, weeks of torrid heat and parching winds would suddenly give way to violent storms that washed away crops and property.

A family poses in front of their Kansas prairie home. The background shows the flat, treeless environment of the rural frontier. Western History Collection, University of Oklahoma Libraries.

Winter blizzards piled up mountainous snowdrifts that halted all outdoor movement. In March and April, melting snow swelled streams, and flood waters threatened millions of acres. In the fall, a week without rain could turn dry grasslands into tinder, and the slightest spark could ignite a raging prairie fire.

Even when the climate was better behaved, nature could turn vengeful. Weather that was good for crops was also good for insect breeding. Worms and flying pests ravaged corn and wheat. In the 1870s and 1880s grasshopper plagues virtually ate up entire farms. Heralded only by the rising din of buzzing wings, a cloud of insects a mile long would smother the land and devour everything in sight: plants, seeds, tree bark, and clothes. As one farmer lamented, the "hoppers left behind nothing but the mortgage."

Settlers of the Plains also had to contend with social isolation. The European pattern, whereby farmers lived together in a village and traveled each day to their nearby fields, was rare in the American West. Instead, various peculiarities of land division compelled rural dwellers to live apart from each other.

Social Isolation   The Homestead Act of 1862 and other measures adopted to facilitate western settlement offered free or cheap plots to people who would live on and improve their property. Because most homesteads and other plots acquired by small farmers were rectangular—usually encompassing 160 acres—at most four families could live near each other, but only if they congregated around the same four-corner boundary intersection. In practice, farmers usually lived back from their boundary lines, and at least a half-mile separated farmhouses. Often adjacent land was unoccupied, making neighbors even more distant.

Many observers wrote about the loneliness and monotony of life on the Plains. Men escaped the oppressiveness by working outdoors and taking occasional trips to sell crops or buy supplies. But women were more isolated, confined by domestic chores to

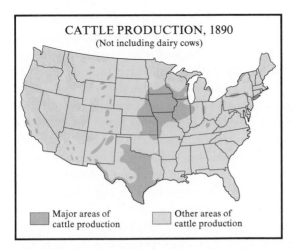

CATTLE PRODUCTION, 1890
(Not including dairy cows)

Major areas of cattle production

Other areas of cattle production

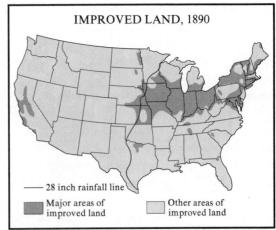

IMPROVED LAND, 1890

—— 28 inch rainfall line

Major areas of improved land

Other areas of improved land

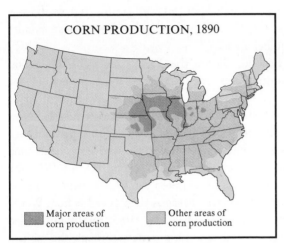

CORN PRODUCTION, 1890

Major areas of corn production

Other areas of corn production

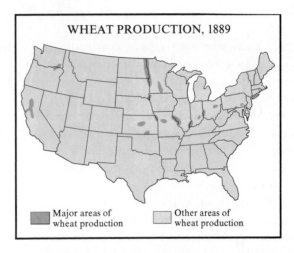

WHEAT PRODUCTION, 1889

Major areas of wheat production

Other areas of wheat production

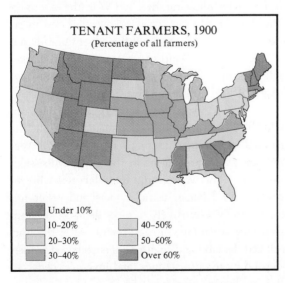

TENANT FARMERS, 1900
(Percentage of all farmers)

Under 10%

10-20%

20-30%

30-40%

40-50%

50-60%

Over 60%

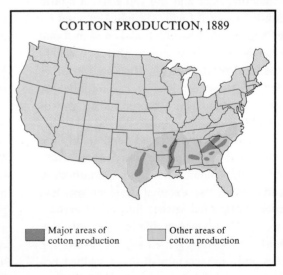

COTTON PRODUCTION, 1889

Major areas of cotton production

Other areas of cotton production

Agricultural Regions, 1889 and 1900   *Source: Charles O. Paollin,* Atlas of the Historical Geography of the United States.

the household, where, as one writer remarked, they were "not much better than slaves. It is a weary, monotonous round of cooking and washing and mending and as a result the insane asylum is ⅓d filled with wives of farmers."

The letters that Ed Donnell, a young Nebraska homesteader, wrote to his family reveal how time and circumstances could dull optimism. In fall 1885, Donnell wrote his mother in Missouri, "I like Nebr first rate. . . . I have saw a pretty tuff time a part of the time since I have been out here, but I started out to get a home and I was determined to win or die in the attempt. . . . Have got a good crop of corn, a floor in my house and got it ceiled overhead." Already, though, Donnell was lonely. He went on, "There is lots of other bachelors here but I am the only one I know who doesn't have kinfolks living handy. . . . You wanted to know when I was going to get married. Just as quick as I can get money ahead to get a cow." A year and a half later, Donnell's dreams were dissolving, and he was beginning to look for a second chance elsewhere. As he explained to his brother, "The rats eat my sod stable down. . . . I may sell out this summer, land is going up so fast. . . . If I sell I am going west and grow up with the country." By fall, things had worsened, and Donnell wrote his parents, "We have been having wet weather for 3 weeks. . . . My health has been so poor this summer and the wind and the sun hurts my head so. I think if I can sell I will . . . move to town for I can get $40 a month working in a grist mill and I would not be exposed to the weather." Donnell's doubts and hardships, shared by thousands of other people, fed the cityward migration of farm folk that characterized late-nineteenth century urban growth (see pages 512–513).

Most farm families survived by depending on their inner resolve and by organizing churches and clubs where they could socialize a few times a month. And by the early 1900s, two external developments had combined to bring rural settlers into closer contact with modern life (though people in **Mail-Order Companies and Rural Free Delivery** sparsely settled regions beyond the 28-inch rainfall line remained isolated for several more decades). First, starting in the 1870s and 1880s, mail-order houses—Montgomery Ward and Sears Roebuck—expanded and made prod-ucts of the industrial society available to almost everyone. Emphasizing personal attention to customers, Ward's and Sears Roebuck were outlets for sociability as well as material goods. Letters from customers to Mr. Ward often reported family news and sought advice on everything from birthday gifts to child care. A man from Washington State wrote, "As you advertise everything for sale that a person wants, I thought I would write you, as I am in need of a wife, and see what you could do for me." Another wrote: "I suppose you wonder why we haven't ordered anything from you since the fall. The cow kicked my arm and broke it and besides my wife was sick, and there was the doctor bill. But now, thank God, that is paid, and we are all well again, and we have a fine new baby boy, and please send plush bonnet number 29d8077. . . ."

Second, during the 1890s, scores of rural communities petitioned Congress for extension of the postal service, and in 1896 the government made Rural Free Delivery (RFD) widely available. Now farmers no longer lacked news and information; they could receive letters, newspapers, advertisements, and catalogues at home nearly every day. In 1913 the postal service inaugurated parcel post, which enabled people to receive packages, such as orders from Ward's and Sears, more easily. By 1920, rural families had access to industrializing society through the mails.

In the years following the Civil War, the extension of the farming frontier, growing national and international markets for food, and the advent of railroads **Mechanization of Agriculture** to ship goods from farm to market brought about an agricultural revolution. But that transformation would not have been possible, nor would the Plains have been conquered, without the expanded use of machinery. When the Civil War drew men away from farms in the upper Mississippi River valley, the women and male laborers who remained behind began using reapers and other implements more extensively to meet demand for grain and to take advantage of high prices. After the war, continued demand and high prices encouraged farmers to depend more on machines, and inventors perfected better implements for farm use. Seeders, combines, binders, mowers, rotary plows, and other machines were introduced to the Plains and California in the 1870s and 1880s.

A squadron of farm machines sweeps across a wheat field in Minnesota's Red River valley. Mechanization multiplied production and turned farming into a big business, enabling the United States to become the breadbasket of the world. Photographed in the 1800s.   Montana Historical Society, Helena.

For centuries the acreage of grain a farmer could plant had been limited by the amount that could be harvested by hand. Machines—first driven by animals, then by steam—increased productivity beyond imagination. Before mechanization, a single farmer could harvest about 7.5 acres of wheat. With an automatic binder that cut and tied bundles of grain, the same farmer could harvest 135 acres. Machines dramatically reduced the time and cost of farming a single acre of various other crops as well (see table).

During this period, Congress and scientists were making efforts to improve existing crops and develop new ones. The 1862 Morrill Land Grant Act (see page 395) gave each state public lands to sell in order to finance agricultural and industrial colleges. Although the act discriminated against western states by granting 30,000 acres for each senator and representative—New York thus received about 1 million acres, Kansas

Legislative and Scientific Aid to Farmers

only 90,000—it did promote the establishment of educational institutions that aided agricultural development. The Hatch Act of 1887 provided for agricultural experiment stations in every state, further encouraging the advancement of farming technology.

Farming received a great boost from science in the late nineteenth century. American agriculturists adapted hardy new varieties of wheat from Asia, alfalfa from Mongolia, corn from North Africa, and rice from the Orient. Californian Luther Burbank developed a wide range of new plants by cross-breeding. And Tuskegee Institute's chemist George Washington Carver created hundreds of new products from peanuts, soybeans, sweet potatoes, and cotton wastes and taught methods of soil improvement. Scientists also developed means of combating plant and animal diseases. Though turbulent times for farmers lay just ahead, development of the agricultural hinterland by settlement, science, and technology made America "the garden of the world."

TIME AND COST OF FARMING AN ACRE OF LAND
BY HAND AND BY MACHINE, 1890

	Hours Required		Labor Cost	
Crop	Hand	Machine	Hand	Machine
Wheat	61	3	$3.65	$ .66
Corn	39	15	$3.62	$1.51
Oats	66	7	$3.73	$1:07
Loose hay	21	4	$1.75	$ .42

Source: Ray Allan Billington, Westward Expansion: A History of the American Frontier, 2nd ed. (New York: Macmillan, 1960), p. 697.

THE SOUTH AFTER RECONSTRUCTION

In 1880 four times as many farmers lived in the South as on the Plains. Ravaged by a civil war that had killed a third of all draft animals and destroyed half the region's farm equipment, southern agriculture recovered slowly. High prices for seed and implements, declining prices for crops, taxes, and, most of all, debt trapped many white families in perpetual poverty. Conditions were even worse for blacks, who had to endure brutal racial prejudice along with economic hardship. To achieve sectional independence, some southern leaders tried to promote industrialization. Their efforts partially succeeded, but by the early 1900s many southern industries were mere subsidiaries of northern firms. Moreover, southern planters, shippers, and manufacturers depended heavily on northern banks to finance their operations. And while they were striving for progress, many southerners nurtured myths about a romantic prewar era of aristocratic grace, conflict-free race relations, and moral purity.

These fantasies sustained the South's sense of distinctiveness but warped the national image of southern culture.

During and after Reconstruction, a significant shift in the nature of agricultural labor swept the South. Between 1860 and 1880, the total number of farms in southern states more than doubled, from 450,000 to 1.1 million. But the number of landowners did not increase, and the size of the average farm decreased from 347 to 156 acres. Southern agriculture was now dominated by sharecropping and tenant farming (see page 440). Over one-third of the farmers counted in 1880 were sharecroppers and tenants, and the proportion increased to two-thirds by 1920.

This system entangled millions of southerners in a web of humiliation. At its center was the crop lien, which worked in the following way. Currency was scarce, and most farmers were too poor ever to have cash on hand. **Crop-Lien System** Forced to borrow in order to buy necessities, they could offer as collateral only what they could grow. Thus a farmer in need of supplies would deal with a nearby "furnishing merchant," who would exchange supplies for a certain portion, or lien, of the farmer's forthcoming crop. In the fall, after the crop had been harvested and brought to market, the merchant collected his debt. But all too often the farmer's debt exceeded his crop's value, and the merchant frequently took advantage of the customer's powerlessness by inflating prices to ensure that such debts could not be paid. Thus the farmer owed the merchant, had received no cash for the crop, and still needed food and supplies. His only choice was to commit the next year's crop to the merchant and sink deeper into debt.

The prices charged to credit customers averaged 30 to 40 percent higher than those charged to cash customers. Credit customers also had to pay interest of 33 to 200 percent on the advances they received. Suppose, for example, a farmer needed a 20-cent bag of seed or a 20-cent slab of bacon and had no cash to pay for it. The furnishing merchant would extend credit for the purchase but would also boost the price to 28 cents. At year's end that 28-cent loan would have accumulated interest, raising the farmer's debt to, say, 42 cents—more than double the item's original cost. The farmer, having pledged more than his crop's worth against scores of such debts, fell behind in payments and never recovered. If he fell too far behind, he could be evicted. As one writer remarked about the crop-lien system, "when one of these mortgages has been recorded against the Southern farmer, he had usually passed into a state of helpless peonage.

The lien system caused serious hardship in former plantation areas where black and white tenants and sharecroppers grew cotton for the same markets that had existed before the Civil War. But in the southern backcountry, which in the antebellum era had contained small farms, relatively few slaves, and diversified agriculture, the problems of crop liens were compounded by other economic changes.

New spending habits of backcountry farmers reflected the most important of these changes. In 1884, for example, Jephta Dickson of Jackson County in the northern Georgia hills bought $53.37 worth of flour, meal, peas, meat, corn, and syrup from one merchant and $2.53 worth of potatoes, peas, and sugar from another. Such expenditures would have been rare in the upcountry before the Civil War, when most farmers grew almost all the supplies they needed. But after the war yeoman farmers like Jephta Dickson shifted from semisubsistence agriculture to more commercialized farming—in the South that

meant cotton-raising—because debts incurred during the war and Reconstruction forced them to grow a crop that would bring in more cash and because railroad expansion enabled them to transport cotton to markets more easily than before. As backcountry yeomen put more acres under cotton cultivation, they raised less of what they needed and were forced more frequently into positions where they were at the mercy of merchants.

At the same time, backcountry farmers suffered from new laws that essentially closed the southern range. This change also resulted from the commercialization of agriculture. Before the 1870s southern farmers had always been able to let their livestock roam freely on other people's land in search of food and water. By custom, farmers who wished to protect their crops from foraging animals were supposed to build fences around those crops. But as commercial agriculture invaded the backcountry, large landowners and merchants induced county and state legislative bodies to require farmers to fence in their animals rather than their crops. Such laws hurt poor farmers who had very little land, because the laws prevented them from letting their animals feed on an open range and caused them to use more of their precious land for pasture. Though the laws accorded with the concept of individual responsibility for private property, they undermined traditional cooperative customs that yeomen cherished. As one farmer asserted, "God makes the grass . . . and corn in the valleys grow, so let's not try to deprive our poor neighbors from receiving his blessing. . . ." Increasingly, yeoman farmers developed antagonisms toward merchants, large landowners, and other supporters of commercialized agriculture. This disaffection would find political expression that eventually coalesced into populism (see Chapter 20).

Closing the Southern Range

Poor whites of the rural South not only faced economic threat from the loss of the open range; they also faced a political threat from newly enfranchised blacks. Wealthy white landowners and merchants would not bend to protests over economic distress, but they did agree with poor farmers on the issue of white supremacy and used their power to reinforce the racial order.

The majority of the nation's black people lived in

In the post-Reconstruction South, black sharecroppers such as these fared little better than under slavery. Tied to crop liens that kept them in perpetual debt, they lived in tiny shacks and struggled against white discrimination. Brown Brothers.

the South and worked in agriculture, where they found that conditions under freedom left them with the same disadvantages they had borne under slavery. As in the pre-war era, blacks adapted to racial bias by developing and controlling their own social institutions: churches, schools, and family networks. Though abolition of slavery altered their legal status, it did not improve their economic and social opportunities relative to those of whites. In 1880 some 90 percent of all southern blacks depended for a living on farming or personal and domestic service—the same occupations they had had as slaves.

Condition of Blacks

Pushed into sharecropping and burdened with crop liens, blacks also had to contend with new forms of social and political oppression. With slavery dead, white supremacists had to fashion new means of keeping blacks in a position of inferiority. Southern leaders, embittered by northern interference in race relations during Reconstruction and anxious to reassert their authority after the withdrawal of federal troops (see page 446), instituted racist measures to discourage blacks from voting and legally segregate them from whites.

The overthrow of Reconstruction had not stopped blacks from voting. Although threats and intimidation against them increased, blacks still formed the backbone of the Republican party in the South and some still won elective offices. In North Carolina, for example, forty-three black men were elected to the state house and eleven to the state senate between 1877 and 1890. Yet also, white politicians began more actively to seek ways of reducing the so-called Negro vote by establishing restrictions which appeared neutral but would actually bar blacks from the polls. Beginning with Georgia in 1877, southern states levied taxes of $1 to $2 on all citizens wishing to vote. Though seemingly trivial, these poll taxes were prohibitive to most black voters, many of whom were so deeply in debt to furnishing merchants and landlords that they never had cash for any purpose. Other schemes disfranchised black voters who could not read. For example, voters might be required to deposit ballots for different candidates in different ballot boxes. In order to do so correctly, voters had to be able to read instructions; otherwise, their votes were invalidated.

Racial discrimination also stiffened in social affairs. A widespread informal system of separation had governed race relations in the antebellum South. After the Civil War, this system was codified in law. In

Spread of Jim Crow Laws

a series of cases during the 1870s, the Supreme Court opened the door to discrimination by ruling that the Fourteenth Amendment protected citizens' rights only against infringement by state governments. The federal government, according to the Court, had no control over what individuals or organizations did. If blacks wanted protection under the law, the Court said, they must seek it from the states, which under the Tenth Amendment retained all powers not specifically assigned to Congress.

The climax to these rulings came in 1883, when in the *Civil Rights Cases* the Court struck down the 1875 Civil Rights Act, which had prohibited segregation in public facilities such as streetcars, hotels, theaters, and parks. Again the Court declared that the federal government could not regulate the behavior of private individuals in matters of race relations. Subsequent lower-court cases in the 1880s established the principle that blacks could be restricted to "separate-but-equal" facilities. The Supreme Court upheld the separate-but-equal doctrine in *Plessy v. Ferguson* (1896) and officially applied it to schools in *Cummins v. County Board of Education* (1899).

Thereafter, segregation laws—known as Jim Crow laws—spread rapidly. Discriminatory legislation piled up throughout the South, confronting black people with countless daily reminders of their inferior status. State laws and local ordinances restricted blacks to the rear of streetcars, to separate drinking and toilet facilities, and to separate sections of hospitals, asylums, and cemeteries. A Birmingham, Alabama, ordinance required that the races be "distinctly separated . . . by well defined physical barriers" in "any room, hall, theatre, picture house, auditorium, yard, court, ball

	IMPORTANT EVENTS
1862	Homestead Act
	Morrill Land Grant Act
1865–67	War with western Sioux
1869	First transcontinental railroad, the Union Pacific, completed
1873	Major silver discovery of Comstock Lode (Nevada)
1874	Barbed wire fence patented
1876	Gold rush in Black Hills
	Custer's Last Stand
1878	Timber and Stone Act
1881	Helen Hunt Jackson, *A Century of Dishonor*
1882–83	Transcontinental routes of Santa Fe, Southern Pacific, and Northern Pacific completed
1883	*Civil Rights Cases*
	Standardization of national time zones
1885–86	Disastrous winters in Plains states
1887	Dawes Severalty Act
	Interstate Commerce Act
	Hatch Act
1890	Wounded Knee massacre
1893	Great Northern Railroad completed
1896	*Plessy v. Ferguson*
1899	*Cummins v. County Board of Education*

park, or other indoor or outdoor place." Local laws defined certain districts or blocks as all-black or all-white. Mobile, Alabama, passed a curfew requiring blacks to be off the streets by 10 P.M. A New Orleans law confined black and white prostitutes to separate districts, and Atlanta required separate Bibles for black witnesses swearing before court. Thus for thousands of black southerners race relations had not changed much since Emancipation, nor would they change until the 1960s when a turbulent civil rights movement overturned many of the old restrictions (see Chapter 33).

In industry, breezes of change were being stimulated by new manufacturing initiatives, but there too a distinctively southern quality prevailed. Two of the **Industrial-** South's leading industries in the late **ization of** nineteenth century relied on the **the South** traditional staple crops, cotton and tobacco. In the 1870s, textile mills began to sprout up in the Cotton Belt-states. Powered by the region's abundant rivers and streams, manned cheaply by poor whites eager to escape crop liens, and fostered by low taxes, such mills grew rapidly. By 1900 the South had four hundred mills with a total of over 4 million spindles, and twenty years later the region was replacing New England in textile manufacturing supremacy. Proximity to raw materials and cheap labor also aided the tobacco industry, and the invention in 1880 of a cigarette-making machine immensely enhanced the marketability of tobacco.

Cigarettes were manufactured in cities by black and white workers; textile mills were concentrated in small towns, and developed their own exploitative labor system. Financed mostly by local investors, mills employed women and children from nearby poor white families and paid them 50 cents a day for twelve or more hours of work. Such wages were barely half what northern workers received. Many companies built squalid villages around their mills and controlled all housing, stores, schools, and churches. Criticism of the company was forbidden, and attempts at union organization were squelched. Mill families soon found that factory jobs changed their status very little. The company store simply replaced the furnishing merchant, and the mill owner replaced the landlord.

Several other industries were launched in the South, but mainly under the sponsorship of northern or European capitalists. Between 1890 and 1900, for example, northern lumber syndicates moved into the pine forests of the Gulf states, boosting production by 500 percent. During the 1880s, northern investors developed southern iron and steel manufacturing, much of which centered in the boom city of Birmingham. Coal mining and railroad construction also expanded rapidly, but New York and London financiers dominated the boards of directors of most companies.

Regardless of outside influence, industrialization prompted southern boosters to herald the emergence of a New South ready to compete economically with other sections. Henry Grady, editor of the *Atlanta Constitution* and the most articulate voice of southern progress, proclaimed, "We have sowed towns and cities in the place of theories, and put business in place of politics. We have challenged your spinners in Massachusetts and your iron-makers in Pennsylvania. . . . We have fallen in love with work." Yet in 1900 the South remained as rural as it had been in 1860. Staple-crop agriculture supported its economy, and white supremacy permeated its social and political relations. Furthermore, the South attracted few immigrants because of its relative lack of industrial jobs, and thus enjoyed little of their energizing influence. A New South would emerge, but not until after a world war and a massive black exodus had jostled old habits and attitudes. Until then, southern society continued to grasp at ways to escape its dependent economic status while holding on to its old racial order.

SUGGESTIONS FOR FURTHER READING

The Western Frontier

Ray A. Billington, *Westward Expansion* (1967); Odie B. Faulk, *Tombstone: Myth and Reality* (1972); William H. Goetzmann, *Exploration and Empire* (1966); William S. Greever, *Bonanza West: Western Mining Rushes* (1963); Robert V. Hine, *The American West* (1973); Julie Roy Jeffrey, *Frontier Women* (1979); Frederick Merk, *History of the Westward Movement* (1978); Ruth Moynihan, *Rebel for Rights: Abigail Scott Duniway* (1983); Rodman W. Paul, *The Frontier and the American West* (1971); Rodman W.

Paul, *Mining Frontiers of the Far West* (1963); Henry Nash Smith, *Virgin Land: The American West as Symbol and Myth* (1950); Roberta B. Sollid, *Calamity Jane* (1958); L. Steckmesser, *The Western Hero in History and Legend* (1965).

Railroads

Alfred D. Chandler, ed., *Railroads: The Nation's First Big Business* (1965); Robert W. Fogel, *Railroads and Economic Growth* (1964); Ari Hoogenboom and Olive Hoogenboom, *A History of the ICC* (1970); Edward C. Kirkland, *Men, Cities, and Transportation* (1948); Gabriel Kolko, *Railroads and Regulation* (1965); George R. Taylor and Irene Neu, *The American Railroad Network* (1956); Alan Trachtenberg, *The Incorporation of America* (1982); O. O. Winther, *The Transportation Frontier* (1964).

Indians and Ranching

Ralph K. Andrist, *The Long Death: The Last Days of the Plains Indians* (1964); Lewis Atherton, *The Cattle Kings* (1961); Joe B. Frantz and Julian Choate, Jr., *The American Cowboy* (1955); Norris Hundley, Jr., ed., *The American Indian* (1974); Francis Paul Prucha, *American Indian Policy in Crisis* (1976); Robert F. Spencer *et al.*, *The Native Americans* (1965); Edward H. Spicer, *Cycles of Conquest: The Impact of Spain, Mexico, and the United States on the Indians of the Southwest* (1962); Robert M. Utley, *The Indian Frontier of the American West, 1846–1890* (1984); Robert M. Utley, *Frontier Regulars: The United States Army and the Indian* (1973); Wilcomb E. Washburn, *Red Man's Land/White Man's Law* (1971).

Settlement of the Plains

Allan G. Bogue, *From Prairie to Corn Belt* (1963); Everett Dick, *The Sod-House Frontier* (1937); Gilbert C. Fite, *The Farmer's Frontier* (1966); Fred A. Shannon, *The Farmer's Last Frontier* (1963); Walter Prescott Webb, *The Great Plains* (1931).

The New South

Orville Vernon Burton and Robert C. McMath, Jr., eds., *Toward a New South?: Post–Civil War Southern Communities* (1982); Thomas D. Clark and Albert D. Kirwan, *The South Since Appomattox* (1967); Vincent P. DeSantis, *Republicans Face the Southern Question, 1877–1897* (1959); Paul Gaston, *The New South Creed* (1970); Dewey Grantham, Jr., *The Democratic South* (1963); Steven Hahn, *The Roots of Southern Populism: Yeoman Farmers and the Transformation of the Georgia Upcountry, 1850–1890* (1983); Stanley P. Hirshson, *Farewell to the Bloody Shirt: Northern Republicans and the Southern Negro* (1962); J. Morgan Kousser, *The Shaping of Southern Politics* (1974); Melton A. McLaurin, *Paternalism and Protest: Southern Cotton Mill Workers and Organized Labor* (1971); Howard N. Rabinowitz, *Race Relations in the Urban South, 1865–1890* (1978); Theodore Saloutos, *Farmer Movements in the South, 1865–1933* (1960); C. Vann Woodward, *The Strange Career of Jim Crow* (1966); C. Vann Woodward, *Origins of the New South* (1951).

THE MACHINE AGE
1877–1920

CHAPTER 17

Conrad Carl tried to appear calm, but he was understandably nervous. It was spring 1882, and Carl, who for nearly thirty years had been a tailor in New York City, was appearing before a group of U.S. senators in Washington, D.C. The Committee on Education and Labor was conducting an investigation into the causes of recent labor unrest, and Senator James L. Pugh, a former Confederate congressman from Alabama, was asking Carl to explain changing work conditions in the tailoring business.

Admitting that his testimony would probably cost him his job, Carl nevertheless answered candidly. When he first began tailoring, Carl explained, he and his wife and children had pieced together garments by hand. The pace of their work was relaxed, yet he was able to save a few dollars each year. Then, said Carl, "in 1854 or 1855, . . . the sewing machine was invented and introduced, and it stitched very nicely, nicer than the tailor could do; and the bosses said: 'We want you to use the sewing machine; you have to buy one.' "

Carl and his fellow tailors used their meager savings to buy machines, hoping they could earn more by producing more. But their employers cut wages instead of raising them. The tailors "found that we could earn no more than we could without the machine; but the money for the machine was gone now, and we found that the machine was only for the profit of the bosses; that they got their work quicker, and it was done nicer." Moreover, Carl, now old and discouraged, had seen that mechanization had other troubling effects on workers and those around them. "The machine," he said, "makes too much noise and the neighbors want to sleep, and we have to stop sewing earlier, so we have to work faster. We work now in excitement—in a hurry. It is hunting; it is not work at all; it is a hunt."

Conrad Carl's testimony to the Senate committee was one worker's view of the industrialization that was relentlessly overtaking American society. The forces prevailing in the new order were both inspiring and ominous. The factory and the machine broke down manufacturing into minute, routinized tasks and organized work according to dictates of the clock. Corporations merged and amassed frightening power in the quest for productivity and profits. Defenders of the new system devised new social and economic theories to justify it, while critics tried to counteract what they thought were abuses of power. Finally, workers, who had long thought of themselves as valued producers, were caught in the changing modes of production and fought to avoid becoming slaves to the machine.

Industrialization is a process whose complexities defy precise definition. Most simply it is characterized by the production of goods by machine rather than by hand. Factors either related to or resulting from industrialization in America include some of the following:

1. involvement of an increasing proportion of the work force in manufacturing
2. production concentrated in large, intricately organized factories
3. accelerated technological innovation, emphasizing new inventions and applied science
4. expanded markets, no longer merely local and regional in scope
5. growth of a nationwide transportation network based on the railroad, and an accompanying communications network based on the telegraph and telephone
6. increased capital accumulation for investment in expansion of production
7. growth of large enterprises and specialization in all forms of economic activity
8. rapid population increase
9. steady increase in the size and predominance of cities

A few numbers will help illustrate these patterns. In 1860 about a quarter of the American labor force worked in manufacturing and transportation; over half did so in 1920. The number of people gainfully employed rose from 17.4 million in 1880 to 41.6

Chapter 17: THE MACHINE AGE, 1877–1920

million in 1920. In 1870 Western Union handled over 9 million telegraph messages on 112,000 miles of wire; by 1900 it processed over 63 million messages on 933,000 miles of wire. And the value of exports increased twelvefold between 1879 and 1920. By the twentieth century, the United States was not only the world's largest producer of raw materials and food, but the most productive industrial nation as well.

Accelerated migration off farms and mass immigration from abroad swelled the industrial work force (see Chapter 18); but machines, more than people, boosted American productivity. Only by using more machines could manufacturers lower production costs and significantly raise each worker's output. Mechanization relied on the use of standardized parts and this brought about more specialization on factory assembly lines.

A spirit of nationalism infused American industrialization. Many industrialists believed that productivity was the key to national welfare. Thus John D. Rockefeller linked his business activities to a nationalistic mission, explaining, "I wanted to participate in the work of making our country great. I had an ambition to build." Yet the accomplishments of industrial expansion, like expansion into natural resources and agricultural frontiers, involved waste and greed. The vigor and creativity that marked the half-century after the end of the Civil War clearly initiated forces that could be considered both constructive and destructive.

These trends weighed most heavily on the industrial work force. Economic growth furnished jobs and income to millions of families who had left American farms and European villages in search of a better existence. But industry's emphasis on productivity and profitability often kept wages at or below subsistence levels and harnessed workers to monotonous routines. Fearful that American industrialism might create a class of helpless proletarians, laborers fought to retain independent work habits and to be paid a living wage. Although the period was not a triumphant one for labor, it did contain a strong undercurrent of worker activism in reforms, cooperatives, and unions in an effort to reconcile new economic realities with the desire to live a life characterized by comfort and dignity.

TECHNOLOGY AND THE QUEST FOR WEALTH

In 1876, Thomas A. Edison and his associates moved into a long wooden shed in Menlo Park, New Jersey, where Edison intended to turn out "a minor invention every ten days and a big thing every six months or so." Here was the brash American spirit adapting itself to a new age. If Americans wanted new products, they could not wait for discoveries; they had to organize and work purposefully to bring about progress. Edison envisioned his Menlo Park laboratory as an invention factory, a place where creative people would pool their ideas and skills to fashion marketable products. Such efforts were part of a process that enlivened American industrialization at the end of the nineteenth century.

The years between 1865 and 1900 were an age of invention. Important devices like the steam engine, dynamo (generator), and sewing machine that had existed since the early nineteenth century now were adapted more fully to the needs of industry and agriculture. Moreover, new late-nineteenth-century inventions and refinememts in electricity, internal combustion, and industrial chemistry laid the technical foundations for twentieth-century industrial development. The patent system, created by the Constitution to "promote the Progress of science and useful Arts," testified to an outburst of American inventiveness. Between 1790 and 1860 the U.S. Patent Office had granted a total of 36,000 patents. In 1897 alone, however, it granted 22,000 patents, and in the seventy years after 1860 it granted 1.5 million.

As one of the world's leading pioneers in the electrical industry, Thomas Edison came close to fulfilling the goal he set for his work at Menlo Park. He

Birth of the Electrical Industry patented over a thousand inventions, many of which used electrical power to transmit light, sound, and images. Perhaps the biggest of his "big-thing" projects began in 1878 when he formed the Edison Electric Light Company and embarked on a search for a cheap, efficient means

Thomas Alva Edison (1847–1931) at work in his laboratory around 1890. Edison developed countless inventions, including the incandescent light bulb, the phonograph, and early forms of motion picture reproduction. He also was a skilled publicist, capable of selling his ideas for commercial purposes. Library of Congress.

of indoor lighting. Gas, candles, and oil lamps had become impractical for lighting streets and large buildings. So Edison turned to light made by an electric current flowing between two carbon rods. His major contribution was perfection of an incandescent bulb, which used a filament in a vacuum. At the same time he worked out a *system* of power production and distribution—an improved dynamo and a parallel circuit of wires—that would provide cheap, convenient lighting to a large number of customers.

Aware that he had to make his ideas marketable, Edison acted as his own publicist. During the 1880

Christmas season he illuminated Menlo Park with forty incandescent bulbs, and in 1882 he built a power plant that would light eighty-five buildings in New York's Wall Street financial district. When this Pearl Street Station began service with great fanfare, a *New York Times* reporter marveled that working in his office at night "seemed almost like writing in daylight." The next year, New Yorkers celebrated Edison's achievement by staging a ballet complete with an electrically lighted model of the Brooklyn Bridge and ballerinas whose costumes were wired so they glowed.

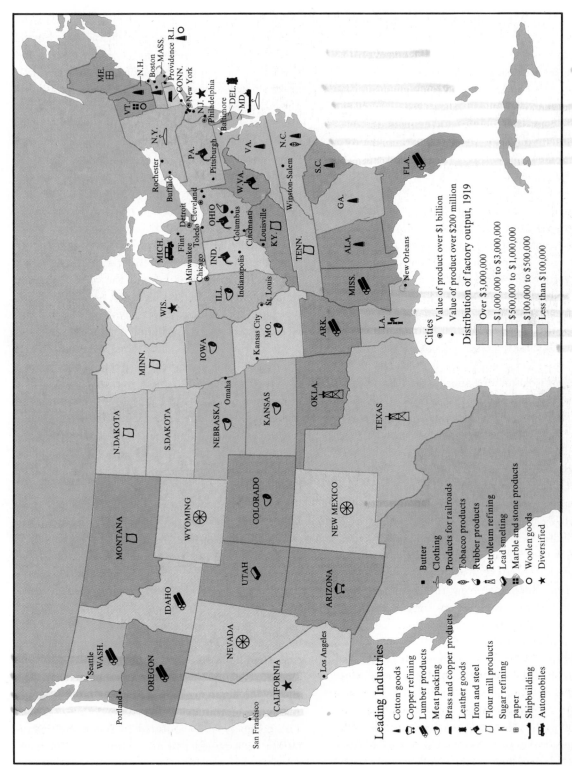

Industrial Production, 1919. *Source: © American Heritage Publishing Co., Inc., American Heritage Pictorial Atlas of United States History; data from U.S. Bureau of the Census, Fourteenth Census of the United States, 1920. Vol. IX: Manufacturing (Washington: U.S. Government Printing Office, 1921).*

Edison's system had a major limitation: it used direct current at low voltage, and could thus send electric power only a mile or two. George Westinghouse, an inventor from Schenectady, New York, who at age twenty-three had become famous for devising an air brake for railroad cars, solved the problem. Westinghouse used alternating current and transformers to reduce high-voltage power to lower voltage levels, thus making transmission over long distances cheaper.

Once Edison and Westinghouse had made their technological breakthroughs, others helped them distribute their inventions to a wide market. Samuel Insull, Edison's private secretary, who later amassed a huge electric-utility empire, deftly attracted investments and organized Edison power plants across the country. In the late 1880s and early 1890s, financiers Henry Villard and J. P. Morgan consolidated patents in electric lighting and merged equipment-manufacturing companies into the General Electric Company. Equally important, General Electric and Westinghouse Electric established research laboratories that paid practical-minded scientists to find new uses for electricity. Under talented scientist and organizer Willis M. Whitney, the General Electric lab pioneered in myriad developments ranging from vacuum tubes for radios through tungsten filaments for light bulbs to atomic theory.

Research laboratories did not eliminate individual dreamers. One such optimist was Henry Ford, who in the 1890s worked as an electrical engineer in Detroit's Edison Company and in his spare time experimented with a gasoline-burning internal combustion engine to power a vehicle. George Selden, a lawyer from Rochester, New York, had been tinkering with internal combustion engines since the 1870s. But Ford's vision and organizational genius spawned a massive industry.

Like Edison, Ford had a scheme as well as an invention. In 1909 he declared, "I am going to democratize the automobile. When I'm through everybody will be able to afford one, and about everyone will have one." The way to do so, according to Ford, was to produce millions of identical cars in exactly the same fashion. The key was mass production, and the watchword was *flow*. Adapting models from the meatpacking and metalworking industries, Ford man-

Mass Production of the Automobile

agers and engineers set up assembly lines that drastically reduced the time and cost of producing cars. Instead of a single worker being responsible for making and assembling the entire automobile, production was broken down so that each worker had responsibility for only one task, constantly repeated, and there was a continuous flow of these tasks from raw materials to finished product. When the Ford Motor Company began operation in 1903, there were only 8,000 autos on the streets of Detroit. In 1908, the first year the famous Model T was built, Ford sold 10,000 cars. By 1914, the year after the first moving assembly line was inaugurated, 248,000 Fords were sold. Many of them cost $490 apiece, only about one-fourth of what they would have cost a decade earlier.

Even this price was beyond the means of many workers, who earned at best $2 a day. In 1914, however, Ford tried to boost buying power and spur worker productivity by offering combined wages and profit sharing of $5 a day. "This is neither charity nor wages," he explained, "but profit sharing and efficiency engineering." Moreover, rising automobile production made for more jobs, higher earnings, and higher profits in such related industries as oil, paint, rubber, and glass. The value of automobiles manufactured, only $6 million in 1900, reached $420 million by 1914. The Model T was indeed replacing the family horse.

The du Ponts did for the chemical industry what Edison and Ford had done for the electrical and automobile industries. The du Pont family had been

Du Ponts and the Chemical Industry

manufacturing gunpowder and other explosives in America since the early 1800s. In 1902 three du Pont cousins, Alfred, Coleman, and Pierre, took over the family company and began to broaden production. Branching out from explosives research in 1911, the du Pont laboratories began to adapt the flammable substance cellulose to the eventual production of such materials as photographic film, rubber, lacquer, and textile fibers. The company also pioneered in systematic organization, devising efficient methods of executive management, accounting, and earnings investment.

Although the timing of mechanization varied from one industry to another, a host of other machines and processes helped to alter the nation's economy and everyday life between 1865 and 1900. The tele-

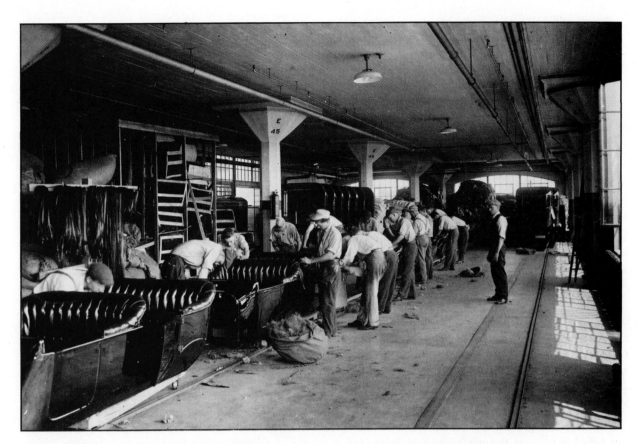

This assembly line at the Ford Motor plant shows how the process of production was broken down into simple, repetitive tasks—here, the fashioning of auto seats. Rather than building the entire product, specialized crews worked on individual parts that later were assembled into the whole automobile.   Ford Motor Company.

phone and typewriter revolutionized communications, making face-to-face conversations less important and facilitating business correspondence and record-keeping. Sewing machines made mass-produced clothing available to almost everyone. Refrigeration changed American dietary habits by making it easier to preserve meat, fruit, vegetables, and dairy products. Streetcars, elevated railroads, and subways extended city limits and enabled people to live farther from their workplaces. Cash registers and adding machines revamped accounting and created new clerical jobs.

All these developments and more thrust the United States into the vanguard of industrial nations. Other effects, however, were less positive. Industrial expansion created countless new jobs, but because most machines and inventions were labor-saving, fewer workers could produce more in less time—as Conrad Carl knew all too well. Mechanization not only destroyed time-honored crafts but subordinated men and women to rigid schedules and repetitive routines. On another level, the scramble for patents resulted in as much waste as technological advancement. Entrepreneurs spent huge sums hoping to profit from inventing something slightly different from what already existed, or purchased patents on the remote chance they might be profitable. Companies like Bell Telephone and individuals like George Selden clogged the courts with suits alleging patent infringement. To minimize uncertainty, manufacturers pooled patents and tried to monopolize new discoveries by confining research to their own labs. As in farming and mining, bigness and consolidation engulfed the individual.

THE TRIUMPH
OF INDUSTRIALISM

I n the industrial sector, profits resulted from higher production at lower costs. As railroads and technological innovations made large-scale production more economical, sizable factories began to replace small ones. Between 1850 and 1900 the average amount of capital invested in a manufacturing firm increased from $700,000 to $1.9 million. Only large factories could afford to buy new machines and operate them at full capacity. And large factories could best take advantage of discount rates for shipping products in bulk and for buying raw materials in quantity. Economists call such advantages *economies of scale.*

Machines and large factories made such efficiencies possible, but profitability was as much a matter of organization as of mechanics. In other words, running a successful factory depended on how **New Emphasis** production was *arranged* as well as **on Efficiency** on the machines that were used. Thus by the 1890s, engineers and managers were working intently to increase output economically and efficiently, putting the primary emphasis on time.

Of the many people who espoused systems of efficient production, the most influential was Frederick W. Taylor. As a foreman and engineer for the Midvale Steel Company in the 1880s, Taylor observed that the only way a company could lessen the impact of fixed costs and thus increase profits was to base production on scientific studies of "how quickly the various kinds of work . . . ought to be done." The "ought" was crucial because it signified the goal of producing more for a lower cost per unit—reducing labor costs by eliminating unnecessary workers. The "how quickly" meant that time and money were equivalent.

In 1898 Taylor took his stopwatch to the Bethlehem Steel Company to illustrate how his principles of scientific management worked. His experiments, he explained, involved identifying the "elementary operations of motions" used by specific workers, selecting better tools, and devising "a series of motions which

Huge machines dwarf workers in the Minneapolis General Electric Company's Main Street Station, symbolizing the way mechanization made many human skills outmoded by the end of the nineteenth century. *Minnesota Historical Society; Louis D. Sweet, photographer.*

can be made quickest and best." Applying the technique to the shoveling of ore, Taylor designed fifteen kinds of shovel and prescribed the proper motions for using each one. As a result he reduced a crew of 600 men to 140 and cut company costs in half. The remaining shovelers received higher wages.

Taylor's writings helped to make time studies and scientific management a national obsession. Workers' skills became less valued, and managers increasingly controlled the pace and scale of output. Time rather than quality became the measure of acceptable work, and science rather than tradition determined the right ways of doing things. As integral features of the assembly line, where work was divided into specific time-determined tasks, employees had become another kind of interchangeable part.

At the same time, large manufacturers were adding new marketing techniques to their technological and organizational innovations. Meat processor Gustavus Swift used branch slaughterhouses and refrigeration to enlarge the market for fresh meat. James B. Duke, who organized the American Tobacco Company and

New Marketing Techniques made cigarettes a big business, saturated communities with billboards and free samples and offered premium gifts to retailers for selling more cigarettes. Companies like International Harvester and Singer Sewing Machine set up systems for servicing their products and introduced financing schemes to permit customers to buy the machines more easily. In many instances marketing innovations enabled producers to sell directly to retailers, squeezing out wholesalers and eliminating the excess costs wholesaling entailed.

THE CORPORATE CONSOLIDATION MOVEMENT

Neither the wonders of industrial production nor the new techniques of market promotion could mask unsettling factors in the American economy. Competition and the resulting race for higher productivity and new markets had costs as well as benefits. New technology demanded that factories operate at near-capacity in order to produce goods most economically. But the more manufacturers produced, the more they had to sell. And in order to sell more, they had to reduce prices. In order to profit more, they expanded production further and often reduced wages. In order to expand, they had to borrow money. In order to repay the money, they had to produce and sell even more. This circular process strangled small firms that could not keep pace and thrust workers into conditions of constant uncertainty. The same cycle affected trade, banking, and transportation as well as manufacturing.

Such conditions encouraged rapid growth, but optimism could dissolve at the hint that debtors were unable to meet their obligations. In the final third of the nineteenth century, financial panics afflicted the economy at least once a decade, depressing prices, destroying businesses, and putting workers out of jobs. Depressions that began in 1873, 1884, and 1893 each hovered over the nation for several years. Business leaders failed to agree on what caused the declines.

Some blamed overproduction; others pointed to underconsumption; still others attributed downturns to lax credit and investment practices. Whatever the reasons—and there were usually several—businessmen began seeking ways to combat the uncertainty of the business cycle. In those years of boom and bust, many turned to more centralized and cooperative forms of economic power, notably corporations, pools, trusts, and holding companies. These new devices of control in turn altered traditional American beliefs in individual effort.

Industrialists, unlike laborers, never questioned the capitalist system or lost faith in entrepreneurial leadership. Instead, they built on the corporate base that had supported economic growth since the early 1800s. The corporation had been given a special American flavor by general incorporation laws passed by the states to encourage commerce and industry (see page 253). Under such laws as they developed in the middle of the nineteenth century, almost anyone could start a company and raise money by selling stock to investors. Full responsibility for company administration was left in the hands of managers. Stockholders could share in profits yet avoid most losses because the laws limited their liability for company debts. Corporations proved to be the best instruments for raising the capital needed for industrial expansion, and by 1900 they were responsible for two-thirds of all goods manufactured in the United States. Moreover, in the 1880s and 1890s corporations received broad judicial protection when the Supreme Court ruled that they, like individuals, were covered by the Fourteenth Amendment. States could not deny corporations equal protection of the laws and could not deprive them of rights or property without due process of law.

As economic disorder and the urge for profits mounted, corporation managers began to seek stability in new and larger forms of economic concentration. Between the late 1880s and early 1900s, an epidemic of consolidation swept the United States, eventually resulting in the massive conglomerates that have dominated the American economy in the twentieth century. At first, however, such efforts were tentative and informal, consisting mainly of cooperative agreements among firms that made the same product or offered the same service. Through these arrangements, called *pools*, competing companies tried to control

The corporate consolidation movement resulted in giant trusts, epitomized by John D. Rockefeller's Standard Oil, which was so powerful that critics warned it could enable Rockefeller to convert the Capitol into an oil refinery and hold the White House and Treasury Department in the palm of his hand.   Library of Congress.

the market by agreeing how much each should produce and what prices should be charged. Used by railroads (to divide up traffic), steel producers, and whiskey distillers, pools depended on their members' honesty. Such "gentlemen's agreements" worked during good times when there was enough business for all; but during slow periods, the desire for profits often tempted pool members to evade their commitments by secretly reducing prices or selling more than the agreed quota. The Interstate Commerce Act of 1887 outlawed pools, but by then their usefulness was already fading.

Pools, Trusts, and Holding Companies

John D. Rockefeller disliked pools, calling them "ropes of sand." In 1879 one of his lawyers, Samuel Dodd, devised a means to overcome the limitations of pools and still control the market. Dodd adapted an old device called a *trust* whereby companies in the same industry could be lured or forced into turning over control of their stock to a board of trustees, which then supervised all operations. This device allowed Rockefeller to integrate the management of his original Standard Oil Company of Ohio with that of other companies he controlled, thus strengthening his grip on the highly profitable petroleum industry. Then in 1888 New Jersey adopted new incorporation laws allowing corporations chartered there to own property in other states and to own stock in other corporations (trusts provided for trusteeship but not ownership). This liberalization led to the creation of the *holding company*, which controlled a partial or complete interest in other companies.

Holding companies could in turn merge their constituent companies' assets (physical plant, equipment, inventory, cash, and the like) as well as their management. Thus Rockefeller incorporated Standard Oil of New Jersey, merging the assets of forty constituent companies. By 1898, Standard Oil refined 83.7 percent of all the oil produced in the nation, controlled most pipelines, and had moved into natural-gas production and ownership of oil-producing properties.

Standard Oil's expansion into activities besides oil refining exemplified a new form of integration that accompanied the rise of trusts. In an effort to control the market, many companies took over several levels of production and distribution, including control of raw materials and transportation as well as manufacturing. The prime example of this *vertical integration* was Gustavus Swift's meat-processing operation. During the 1880s, Swift boldly invested in livestock, slaughterhouses, refrigerator cars, and a marketing organization of butchers so as to assure sale of his beef without unexpected inconvenience. The device of the holding company aided this kind of consolidation, which fused a broad range of business activities into one entity under unified management.

Originally designed as an arrangement whereby responsible individuals would manage the financial affairs of people unwilling or unable to handle them alone, the trust became the answer to industry's search for order. Between 1889 and 1903, some three hundred combinations were formed, most of them trusts and holding companies. By far the most spectacular was the U.S. Steel Corporation, financed by J. P. Morgan. This new enterprise, made up of iron-ore properties, freight carriers, wire mills, plate and tubing companies, and other firms, was capitalized at over $1.4 billion. Other mammoth combinations included the Amalgamated Copper Company, the American Sugar Refining Company, the American Tobacco Company, and the U.S. Rubber Company, each worth over $50 million.

The merger movement created a new species of businessmen, whose vocation was financial organizing rather than producing a particular good or service. Shrewd operators sought out opportunities for combination, formed corporations, and then persuaded producers to sell their firms to the new company. These businessmen usually raised money by selling stock and borrowing from banks. Unwedded to any one industry, their attention ranged widely. Thus W. H. Moore organized the American Tin Plate Company, the Diamond Match Company, and the National Biscuit Company. Elbert H. Gary aided consolidation of the barbed-wire industry and the organization of U.S. Steel. And investment bankers like J. P. Morgan and Jacob Schiff piloted the merger movement, inspiring awe with their financial power and organizational skills.

The growth of corporations in the late nineteenth century turned stock exchanges into pulsating centers of activity where investors bought and sold stocks and bonds feverishly. By the end of 1886, trading on the New York Stock Exchange had reached 1 million shares a day. By 1914 the number of industrial stocks traded had reached 511, compared with 145 in 1869. Investment could not have occurred without growth in the capital available for such purposes. Between 1870 and 1900 foreign investment in American companies rose from $1.5 billion to $3.5 billion. More important, personal savings and institutional investment mushroomed: the assets of savings banks, concentrated in the Northeast and on the West Coast, rose by $900 million between 1875 and 1897, to a total of $2.2 billion. States gradually loosened regulations to enable banks to invest in railroads and industrial enterprises. Commercial banks, insurance companies, and corporations also invested heavily. As one journal proclaimed, "Nearly the whole country (including the typical widow and orphan) is interested in the stock market." Though this statement was a gross exaggeration, it reflected what optimistic industrial capitalists wanted to believe.

THE GOSPEL OF WEALTH

To corporate investors, growth was not only desirable; it was necessary. Profits depended on it, and profits meant everything. Pursuit of wealth had become a struggle for life. As Milton H. Smith of the Louisville and Nashville Railroad put it, "Society, as created, was for the purpose of one man's getting what the other fellow has, if he can, and keep out of the penitentiary."

But the merger movement that resulted in trusts and holding companies upset this philosophical underpinning. J. P. Morgan, whose steely eyes, full mustache, and bulky frame made him a commanding figure among American capitalists, heralded the new order when he told a meeting of railroad directors, "The purpose of this meeting is to cause the members of this association to no longer take the law into their own hands . . . as has been too much the practice heretofore. This is not elsewhere customary in civilized communities, and no good reason exists why such a practice should continue among railroads." Business leaders turned to consolidation under the new corporate forms both to promote growth and to cut down wasteful competition. The monopolistic companies that resulted, however, found it necessary to justify their size and power to a public raised on the ideology of open competition.

Defenders of business thus eagerly embraced the doctrine of Social Darwinism, which seemed to justify aggression in human society. Developed by English philosopher Herbert Spencer and

Social Darwinism

preached in the United States by Yale professor William Graham Sumner, Social Darwinism loosely adapted Charles Darwin's theory of the origin of species to the principles of laissez faire. Human society had evolved naturally, the Social Darwinists reasoned, and any interference with existing institutions would only hamper progress and aid the weak. In a free society operating according to the principle of survival of the fittest, power would flow naturally to the most capable. Property holding and acquisition were therefore sacred rights, and wealth was a mark of well-deserved power and responsibility. Civilization depended on this system, explained Sumner. "If we do not like the survival of the fittest," he wrote, "we have only one possible alternative, and that is survival of the unfittest." Clergymen, journalists, and popular writers also proclaimed the doctrine of Social Darwinism, assuring the public that progress would result only from natural evolution.

This philosophy required that people be left free to accumulate and dispose of wealth. In fact, however, the new corporate forms, with their domination of production and finance, prevented most individuals who did not already have wealth from acquiring it. To compensate for this inconsistency, Social Darwinists

reasoned that humanitarian elites could provide for the needs of those less fortunate or less capable. Thus captains of industry strongly believed that their wealth carried moral responsibilities. John D. Rockefeller once stated, "I believe it is my duty to make money and still more money and to use the money I make for the good of my fellow man according to the dictates of my conscience." This belief implied a right to define what was good and necessary for society, and especially for workers. It meant that the wealthy could and should endow churches, hospitals, and schools, since such gifts promoted progress by raising the "moral culture" of all classes. But it also meant that government should not force the rich, through taxation or regulation, to become more humanitarian.

The urge for efficient organization also affected social attitudes of businessmen. Under scientific management, experts determined schedules, production quotas, techniques, and tools. Their rigid principles acquired almost religious certitude: there was only one true way to economic efficiency. Once business leaders had accepted these principles for their own companies, they were only a short step from using them on the rest of society. Scientific management could, it appeared, apply to politics and personal affairs just as easily as it did to factories.

Paradoxically, business executives who exalted individual initiative and independence also pressed for government assistance. They denounced any measures

Government Assistance to Business

that might aid unions or regulate factory conditions; such legislation, they said, thwarted natural economic laws. At the same time, though, they lobbied forcefully for subsidies, loans, and tax relief that would encourage business growth. Tariffs were by far the largest form of government assistance to industry. By putting high import duties on competing goods from abroad, such as kerosene, steel rails, worsted wools, and tin plate, Congress enabled American producers to keep the prices of their goods relatively high. Industrialists argued that tariff protection encouraged the development of new products and the founding of new enterprises. But tariffs also forced consumers to pay artificially high prices for many products.

Railroads and industrial firms also manipulated state and local governments to their own advantage (see pages 460–461). As reformer Henry Demarest Lloyd

Economic expansion in the New South included exploitation of cheap labor. The most extreme example of this exploitation was the employment of prisoners by private companies. Here, convicts are clearing a route for the New Orleans Pacific Railroad. Armed guards supervise the laborers. Culver.

remarked in 1881, Standard Oil "has done everything with the Pennsylvania legislature except refine it." In the South, railroads and mining companies often leased prisoners to work as laborers. Such companies paid the states about 10 cents per prisoner for a day's work, in preference to paying a free laborer $1 a day. Although business executives believed that natural law would lead directly to economic progress, they were not above enlisting help to ensure that natural law would work profitably for them.

Whatever their inconsistencies, business leaders took great pride in the achievements of their era. Many accepted credit for the meteoric rise of the American standard of living—national wealth rose 550 percent between 1860 and 1900, and per capita income increased 150 percent—and they scoffed at charges that only the wealthy were benefiting. Carroll D. Wright, a pioneering social statistician, denied that the rich were getting richer and the poor poorer. "To the investigator," he testified, "the phrase should be, The rich are growing richer; many more people than formerly are growing rich; and the poor are better off."

The trouble with this materialistic philosophy was that it rested on a shaky foundation. Believers first justified it by invoking natural economic law and the survival of the fittest. But mounting criticism forced them into the illogical position of defending such principles by emphasizing how fragile they were. Thus, they warned, any interference in the business system by labor unions or by government—in the form of regulation, taxation, or support for the underprivileged—would upset everything and stall or even reverse progress. Government interference in the form of tariffs and other aid, however, they considered to be quite another matter.

DISSENTING VOICES

Writers who attacked trusts rarely challenged this reasoning; instead, they based their arguments on traditional American beliefs in independence and opportunity. In doing so, they argued within the same framework of values as did corporate leaders who defended the new economic system. While defenders insisted that trusts were the natural and efficient outcome of economic development, critics charged that trusts were unnatural because they were created by greed and inefficient because they stifled opportunity. Underlying such charges was a deep-seated fear of monopoly. As Charles Francis Adams, a descendant of two presidents, put it, "In the minds of the great majority, and not without reason, the idea of any industrial combination is closely connected with that of monopoly, and monopoly with extortion." Those who feared monopoly believed that large corporations could exploit consumers by fixing prices, demean workers by cutting wages, destroy opportunity by eliminating small businesses, and threaten democracy by corrupting politicians—all of which was not only unnatural but immoral. To critics of trusts, ethics eclipsed economics.

Many believed there was a better way to achieve progress. By the mid-1880s, a number of young professors, troubled by the growing size of industrial and financial organizations, began to challenge Social Darwinism and laissez faire. Some, like pioneering sociologist Lester Ward, attacked the application of evolutionary theory to social and economic relations. In *Dynamic Sociology* (1883), Ward argued that human control of nature, not natural law, accounted for the advance of civilization. To Ward, a system that guaranteed survival only to the fittest was wasteful and brutal; instead, he reasoned, cooperative activity, fostered by planning and government intervention, was the best means to unity and happiness. Economists Richard Ely, John R. Commons, and Edward Bemis agreed that natural forces should be harnessed for the public good. In 1885 they and others of like mind formed the American Economic Association and denounced the laissez-faire system for its "unsound morals." They preferred the positive assistance of the state, which was, Ely declared, "an educational and ethical agency whose positive aid is an indispensable condition of human progress." This sentiment provided a strong rationale for government action during the Progressive era in the early twentieth century (see Chapter 21).

While academics were recommending intervention into natural economic order, others were proposing more utopian schemes for combating monopolies.

Utopian Economic Schemes

Reformer Henry George, whose early life of poverty as a printer and writer had sensitized him to the exploitative power of large enterprises, declared that inequality stemmed from the ability of a few to profit from rising land values. Land values rose, George argued, without effort on the part of owners simply because a growing population increased the demand for living and working space, especially in cities. To restore equality, George proposed to tax the "unearned increment"— the rise in land values caused by increased market demand rather than by owners' improvements—and to eliminate all other taxes. By confiscating undue profits, George insisted, this *single tax* would end monopolistic tendencies and ensure social progress. George's scheme, argued forcefully in his book *Progress and Poverty* (1879), had great popular appeal over the next quarter-century and almost won him the mayoralty of New York in 1886.

Unlike George, who approved of private ownership, novelist Edward Bellamy envisioned a socialist state where government would own and oversee the means of production and distribution and would unite all people under moral laws. Bellamy outlined his vision in the utopian *Looking Backward, 2000–1887,* published in 1888. The novel, which sold over 1 million copies within a few years, warned that catastrophe would result from the extremes of wealth and poverty that characterized American society. The remedy, said Bellamy, was a fully nationalized state free of greedy bankers, industrialists, lawyers, and politicians. A "principle of fraternal cooperation" would replace vicious competition and wasteful monopoly, and a classless society living under the Golden Rule would erase inequality and corruption. Bellamy's system, which he called *Nationalism,* rested on his belief that all people are interested in "breaking the meshes which entangle us, and struggling upward to a higher, nobler plane of existence." His ideas sparked the formation of Nationalist clubs and journals all over the country, and vitalized popular appeals for civil service reform, social welfare measures, and government ownership of railroads and utilities.

Journalist and reformer Henry Demarest Lloyd arrived at a similar conclusion by a different route. His *Wealth Against Commonwealth* (1894) was a quasi-scholarly indictment of Standard Oil and its monopolistic supremacy. Using his evidence loosely, Lloyd portrayed John D. Rockefeller as a ruthless ogre who trampled widows and invalids as well as competing oil refiners in his rush for profits. Lloyd warned that such unbridled aggression and resulting monopolistic power would lead only to public enslavement. As an alternative, he offered a cooperative commonwealth similar to Bellamy's. Government ownership and operation of the means of production, Lloyd exclaimed, would create a society in which "the organization of processes have become so far developed that the profit-hunting Captains of Industry may be replaced by the public-serving Captains of Industry. . . . We are to have a private life of new beauty. . . . We are to be commoners, travelers to Altruria."

While George, Bellamy, Lloyd, and others grappled with ways to meet what they believed to be a moral crisis of civilization, public clamor against monopolies and trusts began to prod legislators

Antitrust Legislation

into action. Before 1900, very few people advocated the kind of government ownership Bellamy and Lloyd envisioned, but several state governments did take steps to prohibit monopolies and regulate big business. By the end of the century, fifteen states had constitutional provisions outlawing trusts, and twenty-seven had laws forbidding pools. Most of these were states in the agricultural South and West, responding to antimonopolistic pressure exerted by various farm organizations. But problems of definition and enforcement mounted. State attorneys general lacked the staff and judicial support for a concerted attack on big business, and corporations always found ways to evade restrictions. Consequently, the need for national legislation became more pressing.

Throughout the 1880s both major parties moved gingerly toward such legislation, and in 1890 Congress passed the Sherman Anti-Trust Act. Introduced by Senator John Sherman of Ohio and rewritten by eastern conservatives in the Senate, the law made illegal "every contract, combination in the form of trust or otherwise, or conspiracy in the restraint of trade." People found guilty of violating the law faced fines and jail terms, and those wronged by illegal combinations could sue for triple damages. However, the law was vague—purposely so, some have said—because that was the only way it could have been passed. It did not define clearly what a restraint of trade was. Moreover, it entrusted interpretation of its provisions to the courts, which at that time were strong allies of business. As one corporate lawyer scoffed, "Legislators madly dashed to the work, threw ink upon paper, and called it a statute and legislation, and they asked the courts to enforce it—enforce a statute based upon doubt and guess and speculation and against the natural laws of trade and business."

The Sherman Anti-Trust Act was intended to encourage free competition by prohibiting unreasonable restraints of trade, but judges—particularly the Supreme Court—blurred distinctions between reasonable and unreasonable. When in 1895 the government prosecuted the so-called Sugar Trust for owning 98 percent of the nation's sugar-refining capacity, eight of nine Supreme Court judges ruled that control of manufacturing did not necessarily mean control of trade (*U.S.* v. *E. C. Knight Co.*). According to the Court, the Constitution empowered Congress to regulate interstate commerce, but manufacturing, which in the case of sugar took place entirely within the state of Pennsylvania, did not fall under congressional control. The Sugar Trust, said one justice, was attempting to increase its profits from refining, but was innocent of trying to restrain trade.

This interpretation left the antitrust act with only token power to combat industrial bigness. The law, passed to soothe public clamor, found little support among public officials, even those entrusted with enforcing it. Thus Attorney General Richard Olney was prompted to remark, "You will have observed that the Govt has been defeated in the Supreme Court on the trust question. I always supposed it would be & have taken the responsibility of not prosecuting under a law I believed to be no good." Between 1890 and 1900 the federal government prosecuted only eighteen cases under the act. The most successful of these were aimed at railroads directly involved in interstate commerce. Ironically, the Sherman Act did serve government officials as a tool for breaking up labor unions: courts that did not consider monopolistic production a restraint of trade willingly applied antitrust provisions to union strikes that affected trade.

The antimonopoly spirit did not die—in fact, "trustbusting" accelerated between 1900 and the First World War. But the problems of enforcing the Sherman Act reflected the uneven distribution of power among American interest groups. Corporate enterprises had been the first to consolidate, and they controlled great resources of economic and political power. Other groups—farmers, laborers, intellectuals, humanitarians—had numbers and ideas but lacked power. Almost all members of these groups desired the material gains that technology and large-scale production and organization were providing, but they increasingly feared that business was acquiring too much influence. How to rebalance society became the pressing dilemma of industrialism.

MECHANIZATION AND THE
CHANGING STATUS OF LABOR

By 1880, when almost 5 million Americans worked in manufacturing, construction, and transportation, the status of labor had shifted dramatically from what it had been a generation earlier when there were only 1.5 million workers in these industries. Most workers could no longer accurately be termed producers—as craftsmen and farmers had traditionally considered themselves. The enlarged working class now consisted mainly of employees—people who worked only when someone else hired them, not when or how they pleased. Whereas producers were paid by consumers according to the quality of what they produced, employees were paid wages based on time spent on the job.

As mass production subdivided manufacturing into minute tasks, workers spent their time repeating one specialized operation. One investigator who looked into the effects of specialization on a typical laborer found that

> he became a mere machine. . . . Take the proposition of a man operating a machine to nail on 40 to 60 cases of heels in a day. That is 2,400 pairs, 4,800 shoes in a day. One not accustomed to it would wonder how a man could pick up and lay down 4,800 shoes in a day, to say nothing of putting them . . . into a machine. . . . That is the driving method of the manufacture of shoes under these minute subdivisions.

No longer was it up to the worker to decide when to begin and end the work day, when to rest, and what tools and techniques to use. Especially as assembly-line production spread, employees lost their sense of independence. As a Massachusetts factory worker complained in 1879, "During working hours the men are not allowed to speak to each other, though working close together, on pain of instant discharge. Men are hired to watch and patrol the shop." And workers were now surrounded by others who, like themselves, worked at the same rate for the same pay, regardless of the quality of their work.

The men and women affected by these changes did not accept them passively. Workers reacted to industrialization by struggling to retain their independence and self-respect in the face of employers' ever-increasing power. As new groups of people encountered the industrial system, they resisted in various ways. Artisans such as cigar makers, glass workers, and coopers, caught in the transition from hand labor to machine production, fought to preserve the pace and quality of their efforts and held on to such customs as appointing a fellow worker to read aloud while they worked. When immigrants went to work in factories, they often succeeded in getting their relatives and friends hired, thus maintaining on-the-job family and village ties they had always known. Off the job, workers continued to get together for traditional leisure-time activities like social drinking and holiday celebrations.

Employers in turn took steps to establish standards that they thought would enhance efficiency and productivity. In order to make workers docile (like machines), they supported temperance and moral reform societies, dedicated to combating supposed drinking

Even as work became more routinized, workers held onto traditional customs. In this photograph a cigar maker reads the newspaper to his fellow workers, according to tradition. International Museum of Photography, George Eastman House.

and debauchery on and off the job. Managers at Ford Motors required workers to meet the company's behavior code before they could earn the profit-sharing segment of the Five-Dollar-Day plan. Other employers established piece rates, paying workers only for the number of items they produced, to encourage maximum use of new machines. And they lowered wages, forcing people to work harder and longer just to maintain the same income.

As machines and assembly-line production reduced the need for skilled workers, employers cut wage costs by hiring more women and children. Between 1880 and 1900, the numbers of employed women grew from 2.6 million to 8.6 million, and their employment patterns underwent major changes (see figure, page 496). First, the proportion of working women engaged in domestic and personal service jobs

Employment of Women

(maids, cooks, laundresses), traditionally the most common form of female employment, dropped dramatically as jobs opened in other economic sectors. Some new jobs were in manufacturing—usually menial positions in textile mills and food-processing plants that paid women as little as $1.56 a week for seventy hours of labor. But though the number of female factory hands tripled, the proportion of women workers in these jobs remained about the same.

Second and more important, a major shift was occurring that set the trend among female workers for much of the twentieth century. The numbers and percentages of women in clerical jobs—clerks, typists, bookkeepers, salespersons—skyrocketed. These workers served the new needs of retail marketing and corporate record-keeping. From the late nineteenth century onward, the invention of numerous machines, such as the typewriter, cash register, adding machine, and

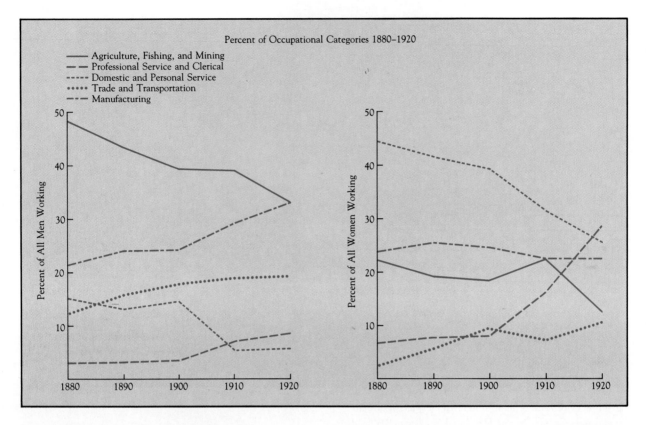

Percent of Occupational Categories, 1880–1920.
Source: U.S. Bureau of the Census, Census of the
United States, 1880, 1890, 1900, 1910, 1920
(Washington: U.S. Government Printing Office).

others, greatly simplified office and sales work. Firms could now increase efficiency by hiring more clerks to operate machines and to replace more expensive managers. An official of a sugar company observed in 1919 that "all the bookkeeping of this company . . . is done by three girls and three bookkeeping machines . . . one operator takes the place of three men."

By 1920 nearly half of all clerical workers were women; only 4 percent had been women in 1880. Analysts often explain the transformation of the clerical sector by asserting that women would work for lower wages than men would and that women's nimble fingers and toleration of boring work suited them for office and sales-floor labor. A more likely explanation, however, is that machines reduced the skills needed for clerical jobs, and companies were willing to hire large numbers of women streaming into the labor market who needed little training for these jobs.

Elementary and high schools were providing basic education in reading and writing and often included courses in typing and shorthand. Thus employers could pay low wages to female workers and not have to invest much in training them, while reserving their resources to train men for higher positions. Sex discrimination characterized the clerical sector, yet the new jobs opened employment opportunities for women.

Although most working children toiled on their parents' farms, the number in nonagricultural occupations tripled between 1870 and 1900. In 1900,

Employment of Children 13 percent of all textile workers were below age sixteen. In other industries too, mechanization created a number of light unskilled tasks (such as running errands and helping machine operators) that children could handle at a fraction of adult wages. Many parents lied about their children's ages to help

Chapter 17: THE MACHINE AGE, 1877–1920

The rise of clerical occupations was one of the most important developments in employment for women at the beginning of the twentieth century. Female typists like these in the Bureau of Chemistry found increasing job opportunities in expanding corporations and bureaucracies.   Library of Congress.

them get jobs to supplement the family income. By 1900, child labor laws and further automation had reduced the number of children working in manufacturing, but many more worked in street trades—shining shoes and peddling newspapers—and as helpers in stores.

While working conditions loomed as the major issue laborers had to face, the problem of wages was often the immediate catalyst of worker unrest. Many employers believed in the "iron law of wages," which dictated that employees be paid according to the conditions of supply and demand. Ideally, this principle meant that workers would receive the highest possible wages that would not drive the employer out of business. But in reality it meant that employers did not have to raise wages—and could even lower them—as long as there were people who would accept low pay. Employers justified the system with references to individual freedom: a worker who did not like the

wages being paid was free to quit and find a job elsewhere. Courts reinforced the principle, denying workers the right to bargain collectively and instead saying that whatever wages an employee received should be the result of an individual bargain between employee and employer. Wage earners saw things differently. They believed the wage system trapped and exploited them. As one Massachusetts worker testified in 1879, "The market is glutted, and we have seasons of dullness; advantage is taken of men's wants, and the pay is cut down; our tasks are increased, and if we remonstrate, we are told our places can be filled. I work harder now than when my pay was twice as high."

Moreover, even steady employment was insecure. Repetitive tasks using high-speed machinery dulled workers' concentration, and the slightest mistake could cause serious injury. Industrial accidents rose steadily before 1920, killing or maiming hundreds of thousands

Industrial Accidents

of people each year. Even as late as 1913, after factory owners had installed some safety devices, some 25,000 people died in industrial mishaps, and close to 1 million were injured. Each year several sensational disasters, such as explosions, mine cave-ins, and fires, aroused public clamor for better safety regulations. The most notorious of these tragedies was the fire at New York City's Triangle Shirtwaist Company in 1911, which killed 146 workers, most of them women. Equally tragic, however, were the countless accidents that resulted in mangled limbs, infected cuts, chronic illness, and death. A railroad coupler described his own accident in 1888:

> It was four or five months before I "got it." I was making a coupling one afternoon. . . . Just before the two cars were come together, the one behind me left the track. . . . Hearing the racket, I sprang to one side, but my toe caught the top of the rail. I was pinned between the corners of the cars as they came together. I heard my ribs cave in like an old box smashed with an ax.

Families stricken by such accidents suffered acutely, because disability insurance and pensions were almost nonexistent. Nineteenth-century laissez-faire attitudes prevented protective legislation for workers, and employers would not take responsibility for employees' well-being. As one railroad manager told his workers, "The regular compensation of employees covers all risk or liability to accident. If an employee is disabled by sickness or any other cause, the right to claim compensation is not recognized." The only recourse for a stricken family was to sue and prove in court that the killed or injured worker did not realize the risks involved in the job and had not caused the accident.

Reformers in several states passed laws to ease working conditions, but the Supreme Court limited their impact by making narrow interpretations of what jobs were dangerous and which

Courts Restrict Labor Reform

workers needed protection. Initially, in *Holden* v. *Hardy* (1896), the Court decided to uphold a law regulating the working hours of miners because their work was so dangerous that overly long hours would increase the threat of injury. In *Lochner* v. *New York* (1905), however, the Court struck down a law limiting bakery workers to a sixty-hour week and a ten-hour day. In response to the argument that a state had authority to protect workers' health and safety, the Court ruled that baking was not a dangerous enough occupation for the legislature to restrict the right of workers to sell their labor freely. According to the Court, interference with the right of individuals to make contracts for their labor would violate the Fourteenth Amendment's guarantee that no state could "deprive any person of life, liberty, or property without due process of law."

Then, in *Muller* v. *Oregon* (1908), the Court resorted to a different rationale to uphold a law limiting working hours for women to ten a day. In this case, heralded by liberals as a progressive decision, the Court set aside its *Lochner* argument. Labor legislation for women was necessary, the Court asserted, because a woman's health "becomes an object of public interest and care in order to preserve the strength and vigor of the race." As a result, women were barred from many occupations, such as printing and transportation, which required long or nighttime hours, and they thus were confined to the same menial jobs they had always held.

Throughout the nineteenth century, tensions rose and fell as workers confronted mechanization. Adjustments were made in different ways as different groups—rural migrants, foreign immigrants, women, and children—entered the industrial labor force. Some people bent to the demands of the factory, the machine, and the time clock. Some tried to blend old ways of working into the new system. Some never adjusted and wandered from place to place, from job to job. Others, however, turned to organized resistance.

In many ways, the year 1877 was a historical watershed. In July of that year, a series of strikes broke out among railroad workers who were protesting wage

Strikes of 1877

cuts. Violence spread across Pennsylvania and Ohio all the way to Chicago and St. Louis. Venting their anger against corporations rather than against individual employers, rioters attacked railroad property, derailing trains and burning rail yards. Militia companies organized by employers broke up picket lines and fired into threatening crowds. In several areas, factory workers, wives, and even local merchants aided the strikers, while railroads enlisted strikebreakers to replace union men. The

Strikebreaking train operators being dragged from their work in Pittsburgh during the 1877 railroad strikes. Strikers did extensive damage to railroad cars and equipment throughout the country. Library of Congress.

worst violence occurred in Pittsburgh, where on July 21 troops bayoneted and then fired on a crowd of demonstrators, killing ten and wounding many more. Infuriated, the mob drove the soldiers into a railroad roundhouse and set a fire that destroyed 39 buildings, 104 engines, and 1,245 freight and passenger cars. The next day, the troops shot their way out of the roundhouse and killed twenty more citizens before fleeing the city.

After more than a month of unprecedented carnage that reached from Maryland to Illinois, Texas, and California, President Rutherford B. Hayes sent federal troops to restore order and end the strikes. His action marked the first significant use of troops to quell labor unrest.

The immediate cause of these strikes was the squeeze of depression. In the economic slump that followed the Panic of 1873, railroad managers had cut wages, increased workloads, and laid off workers, especially those who had joined a union. Such actions drove workers to strike and riot. Laborers in other industries who suffered the same conditions sympathized with

the strikers, as did other members of their communities. A Pittsburgh militiaman, ordered out to break the 1877 strike by his fellow townsmen, recalled, "I talked to all the strikers I could get my hands on, and I could find but one spirit and one purpose among them—that they were justified in resorting to any means to break down the power of the corporations."

THE UNION MOVEMENT

Anxiety over their loss of independence drove some workers to unionize in protection of their interests. The union movement had precedents but few successes. Craft unions, composed of skilled workers in a particular trade, dated from the early nineteenth century, but their emphasis on exclusive membership left them without broad power. The National Labor Union, which flourished briefly after its founding in 1866, grew to 650,000 members but died during the depression of the 1870s. The only broad-based labor organization to survive that depression was the Knights of Labor. Founded in 1860 by Philadelphia garment cutters, the Knights opened their doors to other workers during the 1870s. In 1879, when the union still had fewer than 10,000 members, it elected Terence V. Powderly, a Catholic machinist, as grand master. Under Powderly's guidance, Knights membership mushroomed, peaking at 730,000 in 1886.

Arising at a time when the factory system was not yet firmly established, the Knights of Labor tried to avert the bleak future that they believed industrialism portended by building an alliance among all workers. Thus the organization recruited women, blacks, immigrants, and unskilled and semiskilled workers, who were excluded from craft unions. Like the farmers' alliances, with which they felt kinship, the Knights believed that all workers could stand together against the forces of monopoly—corporations, banks, and railroads—to create a more harmonious society. The goal, argued Powderly, was to "eventually make every man his own master—every man his own employer. . . . There is no good reason why labor cannot, through cooperation, own and operate mines, factories, and railroads."

Knights of Labor

Technological and economic changes were making it impossible for each worker to be his or her own employer. But like many farmers, the Knights saw producer and consumer cooperatives as preferable alternatives to the forces of greed that surrounded them. They agreed with Edward Bellamy that a society in which all groups lived cooperatively was possible. This view was the source of the organization's strength and of its weakness. The cooperative idea, while attractive in the abstract, did not give laborers much bargaining power with employers. It was simply too vague a concept, and employers held most of the economic leverage. Strikes were a means of seeking immediate goals, but Powderly and other leaders were uncertain: would strikes, which could become violent, help or hinder the long-range goal of peace and cooperation? As strikes began to fail in 1886, as Powderly began to denounce radicalism and violence, and as the more militant craft unions broke away, Knights membership dwindled. The union survived only in a few small towns, where a brief attempt was made to unite with the Populists in the 1890s. The special interests of craft unions overcame the Knights' general appeal, and dreams of labor unity faded.

As the depression of the 1870s subsided and better conditions returned in the early 1880s, a number of labor groups, including the Knights of Labor, began to campaign for an eight-hour workday. This effort by workers to regain control of their work gathered most momentum in Chicago, where radical anarchists as well as various craft unions— perhaps as many as 100,000 workers in all—agitated for the cause. On May 1, 1886, the workers' deadline for achieving their goal, city police were mobilized to prevent possible disorder, especially among striking workers at the huge McCormick reaper factory. The day passed calmly, but two days later police stormed an area near the McCormick plant and broke up a battle between striking unionists and nonunion workers hired as strikebreakers. Police shot and killed two unionists and wounded several others. The next evening, labor groups organized a rally at Haymarket Square, near downtown Chicago, to protest police brutality. As a company of police officers approached the meeting, a bomb exploded near their front ranks, killing seven and injuring sixty-seven. Mass arrests of anarchists and unionists followed. Eventually eight men, all anarchists, were tried and convicted of the bombing, though there was no evidence of their guilt. Four were executed and one committed suicide in prison. The remaining three were pardoned in 1893 by Illinois governor John P. Altgeld, who believed they had been victims of the "malicious ferocity" of the courts.

Haymarket Riot

The Haymarket bombing drew public attention to labor campaigns for better conditions but also revived middle-class fear of radicalism. The fact that strikes had erupted all over the country in 1886, not just in Chicago, and that anarchists and socialists, many of them foreign-born, had participated in some of the agitation, created a sense of crisis, a feeling that forces of law and order had to act swiftly to prevent social turmoil. To protect their city, private Chicago donors helped to establish Fort Sheridan and the Great Lakes Naval Training Station. Elsewhere police forces and armories were strengthened. And employer associations multiplied. These associations of man-

The Haymarket riot, Chicago, 1886. A bomb explodes among a police brigade trying to break up the labor demonstration. In retaliation, police fired into the crowd of strikers, killing seven men. The caption for the drawing, which appeared in Harper's Weekly, falsely identified the incident as an "anarchist riot." *Bettmann Archive.*

ufacturers in the same industry worked to counter labor militancy by agreeing to resist strikes and by purchasing strike insurance.

The newly formed American Federation of Labor was the major workers' organization to emerge after the 1886 upheavals. A combination of national craft unions, the AFL initially had about 140,000 members, most of whom were skilled native workers. As a federation, it allowed member unions independence in their own areas of interest, but tried to develop a general policy that would suit the self-interest of all members. Led by Samuel Gompers, the pragmatic and opportunistic head of the Cigar Makers' Union, AFL unions avoided

American Federation of Labor

the idealistic rhetoric of worker solidarity (they excluded unskilled industrial workers) to press for specific goals, such as higher wages, shorter hours, and the right to bargain collectively. As Gompers's associate Adolph Strasser explained, "We have no ultimate ends. We are going from day to day. We are fighting only for immediate objects—objects that can be realized in a few years." Thus the AFL, in contrast to the Knights of Labor, accepted industrialism and worked to achieve better conditions within the wage-and-hours system.

Under Gompers the AFL grew to over 1 million members by 1901 and 2.5 million by 1917, when it included 111 national unions and 27,000 local unions. The national organization required all constituent unions to hire organizers to expand membership, and it collected dues for a fund to aid members on strike. The AFL generally refrained from political activity, though it occasionally supported prolabor candidates and prolabor party platforms.

The AFL and the labor movement in general staggered in the early 1890s, when once again labor violence evoked public fears. In July 1892, Henry C. Frick, the stubborn president of the Carnegie Steel Company, closed the company plant in Homestead, Pennsylvania, when the AFL-affiliated Amalgamated Association of Iron and Steelworkers refused to accept pay cuts and went on strike. Shortly thereafter, angry workers attacked and routed three hundred Pinkerton guards hired by Frick to protect the plant. State militia were called in, and after five months the strikers gave in. By then public opinion was against the strike because a young anarchist—who was not a striker—tried to assassinate Frick.

In 1894, workers at the Pullman Palace Car Company walked out in protest over exploitative policies at the company town near Chicago. The paternalistic

Pullman Strike

company head George Pullman tried to do everything for the twelve thousand residents of his so-called model town. His company owned and controlled all land and buildings, the school, the bank, and the water and gas systems. It paid workers' wages, fixed their rents, and employed spies to report on disgruntled workers. One laborer grumbled, "We are born in a Pullman house, fed from the Pullman shop, taught in the Pullman school, catechized in the Pullman church, and when we die we shall be buried in the Pullman cemetery and go to the Pullman hell."

One thing Pullman would not do was negotiate with workers. When the depression that began in 1893 threatened his business, Pullman managed to maintain profits and pay dividends to stockholders by cutting wages 25 to 40 percent but holding firm on rents and prices in the model town. Workers, squeezed into debt and deprivation, sent a committee to Pullman in May 1894 to protest his policies. Pullman reacted by firing three of the committee. The enraged workers, most of whom had joined the American Railway Union, called a strike. Pullman retaliated by shutting down the plant. When the American Railway Union, led by the charismatic young organizer Eugene V. Debs, voted to aid the strikers by boycotting

all Pullman cars, Pullman stood firm and rejected arbitration. The railroad owners' association then enlisted the aid of U.S. Attorney General Richard Olney, who obtained a court injunction to prevent the union from "obstructing the railways and holding up the mails." President Grover Cleveland sent federal troops to Chicago, supposedly to protect the mails but in reality to crush the strike. Within a month the strike was over, and Debs was jailed for six months for contempt of court in defying the injunction. The Supreme Court upheld Debs's sentence on the grounds that the federal government had the power to remove obstacles to interstate commerce.

After the turn of the century, a number of battles occurred between workers and employers in the mining industry. The fledgling United Mine Workers led several strikes in the coal fields of Pennsylvania, Colorado, and West Virginia between 1902 and 1922. Out of the western mining struggles emerged the Industrial Workers of the World (IWW), a radical labor organization, founded in 1905, that fused the Knights of Labor vision of worker solidarity with the tactics of strikes and sabotage. In contrast with the AFL, the IWW hoped to organize workers along industrial, not craft, lines. Using the rhetoric of class conflict—"The final aim is revolution," according to an IWW organizer—the "Wobblies," as they were called, believed that workers should organize and seize the nation's industries and run them without interference from industrialists or politicians. Because of their anticapitalist goals and threatening tactics, the Wobblies attracted considerable attention in spite of their small numbers, and their activities influenced debates on labor reform during the Progressive era (see Chapter 21).

It must be emphasized that during the half-century following the Civil War, only a small fraction of American workers belonged to unions. In 1900 only about 1 million out of a total of 27.6 million workers were unionized. In 1920, total union membership had grown to 5 million—still only 13 percent of the work force. Unionization was strong among workers in the building trades, transportation, communications, and to a lesser extent manufacturing. But organizers took no interest in large segments of the industrial labor force and intentionally excluded others. Many unions, such as those of the AFL, were openly hostile toward women. Of the 6.3 million

In 1909, thousands of shirtwaist workers in New York, most of whom were women, went on strike and later formed the International Ladies Garment Workers Union. Here, their strike meeting is addressed by Samuel Gompers of the AFL.   Brown Brothers.

Women and the Labor Movement

employed women in 1910, only 125,000 were in unions. Male unionists often explained the exclusion of women by saying that women should not be employed. According to one labor leader, "I believe that woman is not qualified for the conditions of wage labor. . . . The mental and physical makeup of woman is in revolt against wage service. She is competing with the man who is her father or husband or is to become her husband." Fear of competition was crucial. Because women were paid less than men, males feared that their own wages would be lowered if women joined them in the workplace. Moreover, men feared that entry of women would transform many jobs from all-male to all-female ones, just as clerical jobs were changing. Male workers, accustomed to sex segregation in employment, could not recognize or accept the possibility of men and women working side by side. Yet female employees could organize and fight employers as bitterly as men could.

Since the early years of industrialization, female workers had organized their own unions; some, such as the Collar Laundry Union of Troy, New York, organized in the 1860s, had been successful in carrying out strikes and achieving higher wages. The first broad-based women's union was the Women's Trade Union League (WTUL), founded in 1903 and patterned after a similar union in England. The WTUL worked for protective legislation for women workers, sponsored educational activities, and joined the cause for women's suffrage. In 1909 it joined with the International Ladies Garment Workers Union in support of a massive strike against New York City sweatshops. Although the WTUL had some forceful working-class leaders—notably Agnes Nestor, a glove maker, Rose Schneiderman, a cap maker, and Mary Anderson, a shoe worker—it was dominated by middle-class women who had humane but generally non-militant purposes in helping working women. In the early 1920s, the WTUL fought a constitutional amendment guaranteeing equal rights to women, arguing that women needed protection from exploitation more than they needed equality. Such reasoning fit the assertion of males who argued that women belonged in their own sphere at home, out of the work force and out of unions. As the WTUL gradually backed away from active union organization, it lost the support of working-class women, and by 1930 it had virtually dissolved.

Organized labor also excluded most immigrant and black workers. Some trade unions welcomed skilled immigrants—in fact, foreign-born craftsmen were prominent leaders of several unions—but only the Knights of Labor and the IWW had firm policies of accepting immigrants and blacks. A few AFL unions included blacks, but the vast majority had exclusion policies. Resentments already fueled by long-held prejudices increased when blacks and immigrants worked as strikebreakers. It is likely that few strikebreakers understood the full effects of such employment when they were recruited to fill the jobs of striking workers; but even for those who did, the lure of employment was too great to resist.

Immigrants, Blacks, and the Labor Movement

The millions of men, women, and children who were not unionized tried in their own ways to cope with the pressures of the new machine age. Increasing numbers of workers, both native-born and immigrants, turned to fraternal societies. These organizations, which for small monthly or yearly contributions provided members with life insurance, sickness benefits, and funeral expenses, became widespread by the early twentieth century. For many workers, issues of wages and hours were meaningless; getting and holding a job was the first priority. Job instability and the seasonal nature of work seriously hindered organizing efforts. Few companies employed a full work force all year round; most employers hired during peak seasons and laid off workers during slack periods. Thus employment rates often fluctuated wildly. The 1880 census showed that in some communities 30 percent or more of adult males had been unemployed at some time during the previous year.

For most American workers, then, the machine age had mixed results. Industrial wages rose between 1877 and 1914, boosting purchasing power and enabling the creation of a mass market for standardized goods (see Chapter 19). Yet in 1900 most employees worked sixty hours a week at wages that averaged 20 cents an hour for skilled work and 10 cents an hour for unskilled work. Moreover, as wages rose, living costs increased even faster. The industrial

transformation had thrust the United States into international leadership in economic capability. But in factories as well as on farms, some people were beginning to question whether a system based on ever-greater profits was the best way for Americans to create a world of peace and prosperity.

IMPORTANT EVENTS

1873–78	Depression
1877	Widespread railroad strikes
1879	Henry George, *Progress and Poverty* Edison perfects the incandescent light bulb
1882	Formation of Standard Oil trust
1884–85	Depression
1886	Haymarket riot American Federation of Labor founded
1888	Edward Bellamy. *Looking Backward*
1890	Sherman Anti-Trust Act
1892	Homestead Steel strike
1893–97	Depression
1894	Pullman strike Henry Demarest Lloyd, *Wealth Against Commonwealth*
1901	United States Steel Corporation founded
1902	Reorganization of E. I. du Pont de Nemours and Company
1903	Ford Motor Company founded
1905	*Lochner v. New York*
1908	*Muller v. Oregon*
1913	First moving assembly line begins operation at Ford

Suggestions for Further Reading

General

Daniel J. Boorstin, *The Americans: The Democratic Experience* (1973); Thomas C. Cochran and William Miller, *The Age of Enterprise* (1942); Carl N. Degler, *The Age of the Economic Revolution* (1977); Sigmund Diamond, ed., *The Nation Transformed* (1963); Ray Ginger, *The Age of Excess* (1965); Samuel P. Hays, *The Response to Industrialism* (1975).

Technology and Invention

Robert W. Bruce, *Bell: Alexander Graham Bell and the Conquest of Solitude* (1973); Roger Burlingame, *Henry Ford* (1957); George H. Daniels, *Science and Society in America* (1971); Sigfried Giedion, *Mechanization Takes Command* (1948); Matthew Josephson, *Edison* (1959); Leo Marx, *The Machine in the Garden: Technology and the Pastoral Ideal* (1964); Elting E. Morison, *Men, Machines, and Modern Times* (1966); Allan Nevins and Frank E. Hill, *Ford*, 3 vols. (1954–1962); Nathan Rosenberg, *Technology and American Economic Growth* (1972); Harold I. Sharlin, *The Making of the Electrical Age* (1963); Peter Temin, *Steel in Nineteenth Century America* (1964); Frederick A. White, *American Industrial Research Laboratories* (1961).

Industrialism, Industrialists, and Corporate Growth

W. Elliot Brownlee, *Dynamics of Ascent: A History of the American Economy*, 2nd ed. (1979); Stuart Bruchey, *Growth of the Modern Economy* (1973); Alfred D. Chandler, *The Visible Hand: The Managerial Revolution in American Business* (1977); Alfred D. Chandler, *Pierre S. du Pont and the Making of the Modern Corporation* (1971); Alfred D. Chandler, *Strategy and Structure: Chapters in the History of American Industrial Enterprise* (1966); Thomas C. Cochran, *Business in American Life* (1972); Francis L. Eames, *The New York Stock Exchange* (1968); Rendigs Fels, *American Business Cycles, 1865–1897* (1959); David F. Hawkes, *John D.: The Founding Father of the Rockefellers* (1980); Robert Higgs, *The Transformation of the American Economy, 1865–1914* (1971); Matthew Josephson, *The Robber Barons* (1934); Edward C. Kirkland, *Industry Comes of Age* (1961); Harold C. Livesay, *Andrew Carnegie and the Rise of Big Business* (1975); Daniel Nelson, *Managers and Workers: Origins of the New Factory System in the United States, 1880–1920* (1975); Allan Nevins, *Study in Power: John D. Rockefeller*, 2 vols. (1953); Glen Porter, *The Rise of Big Business* (1973); Joseph Wall, *Andrew Carnegie* (1970).

Attitudes Toward Industrialism

Edward Bellamy, *Looking Backward* (1888); Sidney Fine, *Laissez Faire and the General Welfare State* (1956); Louis Galambos and Barbara Barron Spence, *The Public Image of Big Business in America* (1975); Henry George, *Progress and Poverty* (1879); Richard Hofstadter, *Social Darwinism in American Thought*, rev. ed. (1955); T. Jackson Lears, *No Place of Grace: Antimodernism and the Transformation of American Culture* (1981); Henry Demarest Lloyd, *Wealth Against Commonwealth* (1894); Robert McCloskey, *American Conservatism in the Age of Enterprise* (1951); John L. Thomas, *Alternative America: Henry George, Edward Bellamy, Henry Demarest Lloyd and the Adversary Tradition* (1983).

Work and Labor Organization

Stanley Buder, *Pullman* (1967); Alan Dawley, *Class and Community* (1977); Melvyn Dubofsky, *Industrialism and the American Worker* (1975); Melvyn Dubofsky, *We Shall Be All: A History of the Industrial Workers of the World* (1969); Leon Fink, *Workingmen's Democracy: The Knights of Labor and American Politics* (1982); Philip S. Foner, *The Great Labor Uprising of 1877* (1977); Herbert G. Gutman, *Work, Culture and Society in Industrializing America* (1976); Tamara K. Hareven, *Family Time and Industrial Time: The Relationship Between the Family and Work in a New England Industrial Community* (1982); Stuart Bruce Kaufman, *Samuel Gompers and the Origins of the American Federation of Labor* (1973); Alice Kessler-Harris, *Out to Work: A History of Wage-Earning Women in the United States* (1982); Susan Levine, *Labor's True Women: Carpet Weavers, Industrialization, and Labor Reform in the Gilded Age* (1984); Harold Livesay, *Samuel Gompers and Organized Labor in America* (1978); Milton Meltzer, *Bread and Roses: The Struggle of American Labor, 1865–1915* (1967); Stephen Meyer III, *The Five Dollar Day: Labor Management and Social Control in the Ford Motor Company, 1908–1921* (1981); David Montgomery, *Workers' Control in America: Studies in the History of Work, Technology, and Labor Struggles* (1979); Philip Taft, *Organized Labor in America* (1964); Daniel J. Walkowitz, *Worker City, Company Town* (1978); Barbara Mayer Wertheimer, *We Were There: The Story of Working Women in America* (1977); Leon J. Wolff, *Lockout: The Story of the Homestead Strike of 1892* (1965); Irwin Yellowitz, *Industrialization and the American Labor Movement* (1977).

The Fame and Shame of the Cities

1877–1920

Chapter 18

For nearly thirty years, Frank Ventrone had successfully pursued his dream until one night his world literally shattered. In the 1880s, Ventrone had emigrated from Isernia, a town in southern Italy, to Providence, Rhode Island, a bustling city in industrializing America. By saving money and buying property, Ventrone became a prominent businessman in the city's fast-growing Italian immigrant community, many of whose residents had also come from Isernia. Ventrone's biggest success was a pasta business that furnished the community's staple food. But this business was also the source of his trouble.

In the summer of 1914, food prices were rising, and Ventrone followed the trend by increasing the price of his pasta. Angered by the threat to their already overburdened incomes, people of Providence's Italian section vented their frustration against Ventrone. On a warm August weekend, they marched through the neighborhood, broke windows in a block of property owned by Ventrone, entered his business establishment, and dumped his stock of macaroni into the street. When police arrived to quell the disturbance, rioters resisted with catcalls and violence, insisting that the matter was an internal one to be resolved by the community. The next Monday, Ventrone's agent met with community members and agreed to lower his prices. Ventrone had overstepped the bounds of ethnic loyalty and had suffered as a result. "Signor Ventrone . . . owes everything to our colony," declared the neighborhood newspaper. "Our brave colony, when we all stand together, will be given justice."

The Providence "macaroni riot," with its various dimensions—the transfer of immigrant cultures from Old World to New; the mobility of some people from rags to respectability; the continued poverty of others amid economic uncertainty; the eruption of violence—was just one of millions of events that came to characterize city life in America. To be sure, a similar protest might have occurred in Italy, but the American context amplified the event's characteristics. By 1900, Providence was a rapidly growing city, and the United States was the most rapidly urbanizing nation in the western world. The hopes, frustrations, and conflicts that urban growth generated seemed both dazzling and bewildering. In 1914, the same year as the macaroni riot, a student in St. Paul, Minnesota, wrote in her diary: "There is much beauty in a city. Buildings and streets and multitudes of people, and big buildings being built, people building them, smoke, lights dripping and popping out all over; sadness, sordidness, joy, love, pain, badness, goodness all being *swept along together.*" Clanging trolleys, smoky air, crowded streets, a jumble of languages—these sensations and more contrasted with the slow, quiet pace of village and farm life. And as cities grew, they became places of both opportunity and misery.

In the middle third of the nineteenth century, the nation's urban population—those living in places with eight thousand or more people—started to grow much faster than its rural population (see pages 270–272). But not until the 1880s did the United States begin to become a truly urban nation. By 1920 the major milestone of urbanization had been passed: that year's census showed that, for the first time, a majority of Americans (51.4 percent) lived in cities. This new fact of national life was fully as significant as the disappearance of the frontier in 1890. The era of the yeoman farmer was over, and urban growth became the third major theme, along with natural resource development (Chapter 16) and industrialization (Chapter 17), of American expansion in the late nineteenth and early twentieth centuries.

The city became a dominant force by serving as a marketplace, which brought together people, resources, and ideas that were in turn responsible for many of the changes American society was experiencing. By 1900 a network of small, medium, and large cities spanned every section of the country. Only such industrializing states as Rhode Island and Massachusetts had been highly urbanized early in the nineteenth century, but other states' urban populations grew rapidly after the Civil War.

American cities attracted both exuberant admirers and sneering detractors. Some people relished the opportunities cities offered. As one editor wrote, it was "better [to] be the 1/1,000,000,000 of New York than the 1/1 of Aroostook County." Others found the crudeness of cities disquieting. "Having seen it," Rudyard Kipling wrote of Chicago, "I urgently desire never to see it again." But whatever people's personal impressions, the city had become basic to American life. To a large extent, modern American society has been shaped by the ways people built their cities and adjusted to the new urban environment.

THE BIRTH OF THE MODERN CITY

I n March 1912, a party of street-railway officials boarded a private trolley car in downtown Boston. Traveling west to Worcester and Springfield in Massachusetts, then south to Hartford, New Britain, New Haven, Bridgeport, and Stamford in Connecticut, the car carried its passengers from one set of tracks to another. The 200-mile journey ended when the car rolled into New York City, having made the entire trip on a continuous route of streetcar—not railroad—tracks. With enough patience and enough nickels for $2.40 in fares and transfers, anyone could have made the same trip. The possibility of such a journey illustrates the extraordinary connection between mass transit and urban growth that occurred at the end of the nineteenth century.

By 1900, the modern American city was reaching maturity. The compact city of the early nineteenth century—where residences were mixed in among shops, factories, and warehouses—

New Shape of the City had burst open. From Boston to San Francisco, developed areas sprawled outward several miles from the original central core. No longer did walking distance determine a city's size, and no longer did different social groups live physically close together—poor near rich, immigrant near native, black near white. Instead, cities were divided into distinct districts: working-class neighborhoods, black ghettos, a ring of suburbs, business districts. Two forces were responsible for this

new arrangement. One was centrifugal, propelling people and enterprises outward from the confines of the old walking city. The other was centripetal, drawing human and economic resources inward. Mass transportation powered the centrifugal force; economic change, the centripetal.

Mass transportation enabled people to move faster and farther. Before the 1870s, horse- and mule-drawn vehicles had been the major means of transport. But they were inefficient. They could carry relatively few riders, and purchasing, feeding, and cleaning up after the animals was costly. In 1880, for example, the 150,000 horses in New York City and Booklyn produced between 1,000 and 1,500 tons of manure daily, about 1.5 pounds per human inhabitant. Though of a different nature than it is today, pollution was a fact of urban life in the nineteenth century too.

Once the technology was developed, entrepreneurs adopted better ways to transport people. Steam-powered commuter railroads had appeared in a few cities during the 1850s and 1860s,

Mechanization of Mass Transportation but not until the late 1870s did inventors begin to mechanize mass transit. The first power-driven devices were cable cars—carriages that traveled over tracks by clamping onto a moving underground wire. Cheaper than horse cars, cable cars could also haul passengers up and down steep hills. In the 1880s cable-car lines were constructed in Chicago, San Francisco, and many other cities.

By the 1890s, however, electric-powered streetcars were replacing the early forms of mass transit. Designed almost simultaneously by Charles J. Van Doeple in Montgomery, Alabama, and Frank Sprague in Richmond, Virginia, electric trolleys spread quickly to nearly every large city. Between 1890 and 1902, total mileage of electrified track in American cities grew from 1,300 to 22,000 miles. Meanwhile horse-railway track shrank from 5,700 to 250 miles. "The long-haired mule shall no longer adorn our streets," mused one observer.

In a few cities, trolley companies raised part of their track onto stilts, enabling vehicles to travel through jammed downtown districts without interference from other traffic. And in Boston, New York, and Philadelphia, transit firms dug underground passages for their cars, also to avoid tie-ups and delays.

Sometimes the extension of mass transit preceded residential development. This trolley line in Oak Park, Illinois, a suburb of Chicago, was built in anticipation of the housing construction that eventually filled the lots on either side of the tracks. Photographed in 1903.   Oak Park Public Library.

Elevated railroads and subways were extremely expensive to construct. They thus appeared only in the few cities where companies could amass enough capital to build them and where there were enough riders to make for high profits.

Mass transit lines launched millions of urban dwellers into outlying neighborhoods and created a commuting public. Now those who could afford the fare—usually five cents a ride—could live outside the crowded, dirty central city and still return there for work, shopping, and entertainment. Working-class families, whose incomes rarely topped a dollar a day, found the fare too high and could not take advantage of the streetcars. But for the growing middle class, a home in a quiet, tree-lined neighborhood became a real possibility. Real estate development boomed around the periphery of scores of cities. Between 1890 and 1920, for example, developers in the Chicago area opened 800,000 new lots—enough to house at least three times the city's population in 1890. A

Beginnings of Urban Sprawl

home several miles from downtown was inconvenient, but the benefits seemed to outweigh the costs. As one suburbanite wrote in 1902, "It may be a little more difficult for us to attend the opera, but the robin in my elm tree struck a higher note and a sweeter one yesterday than any *prima donna* ever reached."

Urban sprawl was essentially unplanned. Eager to capitalize on new commuting possibilities, thousands of small investors who bought land in anticipation of settlement paid little attention to the need for parks, traffic control, and public services. Moreover, construction of mass transit was guided by the profit motive and thus served the urban public unevenly. Streetcar lines serviced mainly those neighborhoods that promised the most riders—whose fares, in other words, would provide dividends for stockholders.

Streetcars, elevateds, and subways altered commercial as well as residential patterns. As consumers moved outward, businesses followed. Secondary business centers sprouted at trolley-line intersections and elevated-railway stations. Branches of downtown department stores and banks joined groceries, theaters, drugstores, taverns, and specialty shops to create neighborhood shopping centers, the forerunners of today's shopping malls. Meanwhile, the urban core became the work zone, where offices, stores, warehouses, and factories hulked over streets clogged with traffic. Districts like Chicago's Loop and New York's lower Manhattan concentrated together practically every kind of business and cultural institution.

Cities also became the main arenas for industrial growth, generating and attracting concentrations of economic power. As centers of resources, labor, transportation, and communications, cities provided everything factories needed. Capital accumulated by the cities' commercial enterprises—gathering and distributing raw materials and finished goods—fed industrial investment once mass production became possible. And urban populations furnished consumers for myriad new products. Thus urban growth and industrialization wound together in a mutually beneficial spiral. The further industrialization advanced, the more opportunities it created for work and investment in cities. Increased opportunity drew more people to cities; as workers and as consumers, they in turn fueled further industrialization. By the end of the nineteenth century, urban firms were producing nine-tenths of America's industrial output.

Urban-Industrial Development

Although most cities contained a wide variety of industrial activities, specialization in a single product became common. Some cities used large numbers of workers in the mass production of clothing. The shoe industry became prominent in Philadelphia and Lynn, ready-made garments in New York City, and textiles in several New England cities. Other cities processed products from surrounding agricultural regions: flour in Minneapolis, cottonseed oil in Memphis, beer in Milwaukee. Still others processed natural resources: gold and copper in Denver, fish and lumber in Seattle, coal and iron in Pittsburgh and Birmingham, oil in Houston and Los Angeles. These and countless other activities increased the magnetic attraction of cities.

Urban and industrial growth transformed the national economy and freed the United States from dependence on European capital and manufactured goods. Imports and foreign investments still flowed

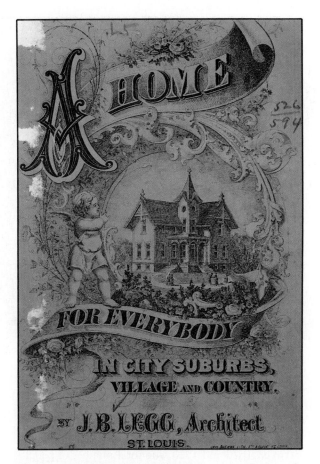

Though ads like this one exaggerated the romantic nature of living in the urban outskirts, a comfortable, detached single-family house surrounded by grass and trees became a realizable ideal in the late nineteenth century.   Library of Congress.

into the country. But by the early 1900s, cities and their factories, stores, and banks were converting the United States from a debtor agricultural nation into a major industrial, financial, and exporting power.

PEOPLING THE CITIES:
MIGRANTS AND IMMIGRANTS

E conomist Edmund J. James had good reason to assert in 1899 that the era he was living in was "not only the age of cities but the age of great cities."

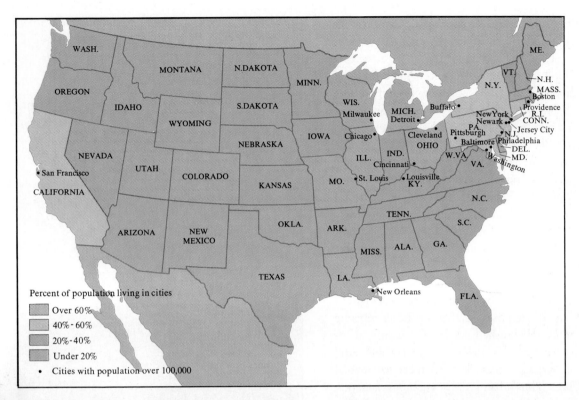

Urbanization, 1880

Percent of population living in cities

- Over 60%
- 40% - 60%
- 20% - 40%
- Under 20%
- Cities with population over 100,000

Between 1870 and 1920, the total number of people living in American cities exploded from 9.9 million to 54.3 million. During the same period, the number of cities with populations over 100,000 grew from fifteen to sixty-eight, and the number with more than 500,000 people swelled from two to twelve (see maps). These figures are dramatic enough by themselves, but they also represent millions of stories of hope and frustration, adjustment and confusion, success and failure.

How Cities Grew

The population of a given place can grow in three ways: by extension of its borders to include nearby land and people; by natural increase—an excess of births over deaths; and by migration—an excess of in-migrants over out-migrants. Between the Civil War and the early 1900s, many cities annexed nearby suburbs, thereby increasing their populations. The most notable consolidation occurred in 1898 when New York City, which had previously consisted only of Manhattan, merged with four surrounding boroughs and grew overnight from 1.5 million to over 3 million people. Everywhere the thirst for

expansion was insatiable. As one observer remarked, "Those who locate near the city limits are bound to know that the time may come when [the city] will extend the limits and take them in." Moreover, many suburbs desired annexation because they needed the services like water, fire protection, and sewer systems that cities had developed. Annexation also added vacant land where new city dwellers could live. Cities like Chicago, Minneapolis, and Cincinnati incorporated hundreds of undeveloped square miles into their borders in the 1880s, only to see them fill up in succeeding decades. Although annexation did increase urban populations, its major effect was to enlarge the physical size of cities.

As death rates declined in the late nineteenth century, the populations of most cities increased naturally. But urban birthrates also fell steadily throughout the nineteenth century. As a result, natural increase did not account for very much of any city's population growth.

Migration and immigration made by far the greatest contribution to urban population growth. In fact, migration to cities nearly matched the migration to

Chapter 18: THE FAME AND SHAME OF THE CITIES, 1877–1920

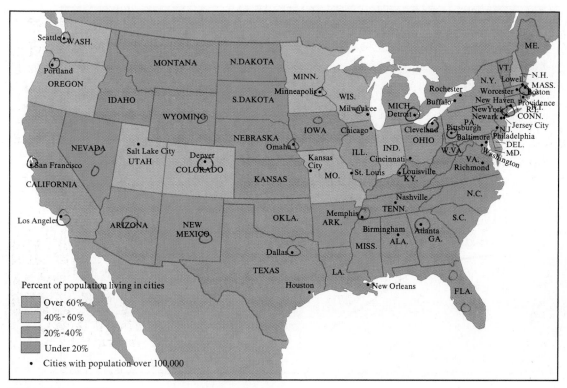

Urbanization, 1920

the West that was occurring at the same time. Each year millions of people were on the move, many of them lured by the cities' promise of opportunity. Urban newcomers arrived from two major sources: the American countryside and Europe. Asia, Canada, and Latin America also supplied immigrants, but in smaller numbers.

In all sections of the country, a variety of factors dashed farmers' hopes and drove them off the land and toward the cities. Rural populations of Vermont, New York, Ohio, Illinois, and other states declined during the 1880s as their urban populations mushroomed. Growth occurred not only in Cleveland, Detroit, and Chicago, but also in scores of secondary cities like Toledo, Indianapolis, Salt Lake City, Birmingham, and San Diego. The thrill and bustle of city life beckoned especially to young people. A character in George Fitch's play *The City* voiced the dreams of many youths when she exclaimed, "Who wants to smell new-mown hay, if he can breathe in gasoline on Fifth Avenue instead! Think of the theaters! the

Major Waves of Migration and Immigration

crowds! *Think* of being able to go out on the street and *see some one you didn't know by sight!*"

An even larger group of newcomers consisted of immigrants who had fled foreign farms and villages for American shores. Many did not intend to stay. They hoped instead to make enough money to return home and live in greater comfort and security. For every hundred foreigners who entered the country, around thirty left. Still, most of the 26 million immigrants who arrived between 1870 and 1920 stayed, and the great majority settled in cities, where they helped to shape modern American culture.

These immigrants were only part of a global movement. Population pressures and economic changes resulting from land reforms and industrialization induced millions to leave Europe and Asia for Canada, Australia, Brazil, Argentina, and other relatively unsettled places as well as the United States. Countless others migrated shorter distances, usually from a rural village or town to an industrial city. Migration always has been a key chapter in human history, but now the telegraph, railroad, and steamship made communications and travel cheaper, quicker, and safer.

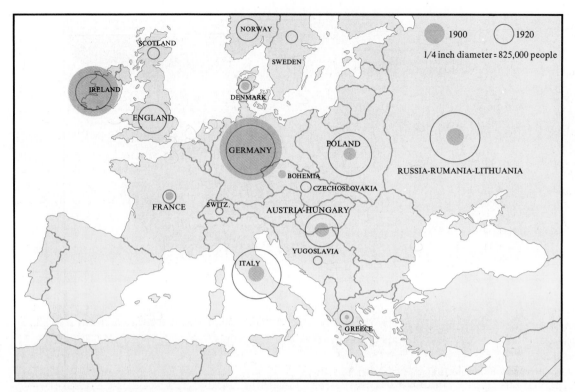

Sources of Foreign-Born Population, 1900 and 1920.

The United States had been the destination of immigrants from northern and western Europe since the 1840s (see pages 280–284), but after 1880 a second wave of mass immigration began from new sources. Though northern and western Europeans continued to arrive, the new wave contained mainly people from eastern and southern Europe, plus smaller contingents from Canada, Mexico, and Japan (see map and figure). For example, two-thirds of the immigrants who arrived in the 1880s were from Germany, England, Ireland, and Scandinavia; between 1900 and 1909, however, two-thirds were from Italy, Austria-Hungary, and Russia. By 1910 arrivals from Mexico were beginning to outnumber arrivals from Ireland; and large numbers of Japanese had moved to the West Coast and Hawaii (see Appendix).

The New Immigration

Differences between the two waves of immigrants were in many ways more imagined than real. Many Americans feared that the strange customs, non-Protestant religions, illiteracy, and poverty of the "new" immigrants made them less desirable and as-similable than the "old" immigrants, whose languages and beliefs seemed less alien. This view received sober support from authorities like future president Woodrow Wilson, who wrote in his popular *History of the American People* (1902), "The immigrant new-comers of recent years are men of the lowest class from the South of Italy, and men of the meaner sort out of Hungary and Poland, men out of the ranks where there was neither skill nor energy, nor any initiative or quick intelligence."

In reality, however, the old and new immigrants resembled each other more closely than many Americans wished to believe. The majority of both groups were young—between fifteen and forty-four years old—and male. Both groups settled chiefly in cities, and both lived initially in old districts of the central city vacated by residents who had moved to new outlying neighborhoods.

Perhaps most important, all immigrants brought with them memories of their homelands and adjusted to American life in light of those memories. In new surroundings where the language was a struggle, the workday followed the clock rather than the sun, and

Chapter 18: THE FAME AND SHAME OF THE CITIES, 1877–1920

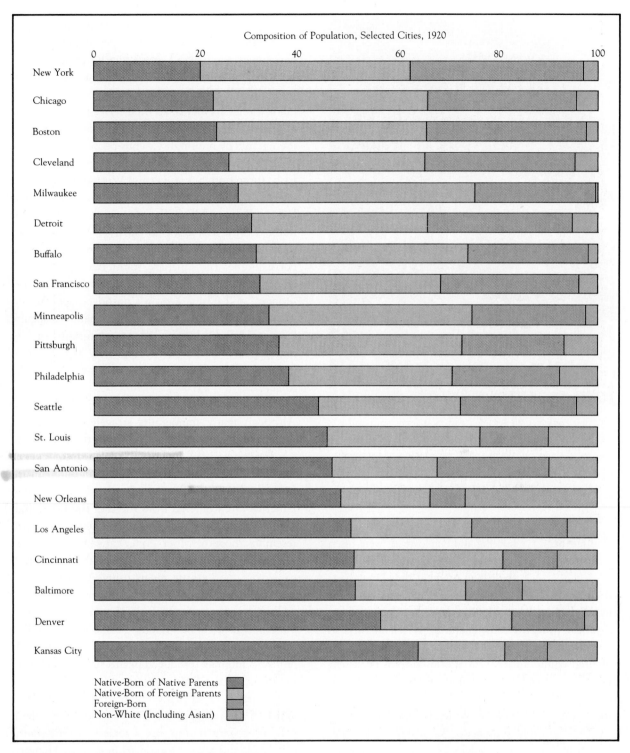

Composition of Population, Selected Cities, 1920

The first contact with America that most immigrants had was on Ellis Island, just offshore of New York City. Here they were herded into pens, registered, and examined for disease. As this photograph shows, the experience was quite dehumanizing. Library of Congress.

Immigrant Cultures housing and employment were often uncertain, immigrants anchored their lives on what they knew best: their culture. Many immigrant neighborhoods were made up of enclaves of Italians from the same province, Japanese from the same island district, and Russian Jews from the same *shtetl* (village). In these transplanted communities, Old World customs persisted. People practiced their religions as they always had, held traditional feasts and pageants, married within their group, and pursued old feuds with people from rival villages and provinces. As in eastern Europe, Jewish men grew long sidelocks, women wore wigs, and children were sent to afternoon religious training. Italians transplanted the system whereby a boss, or *padrone*, found jobs for unskilled workers by acting as a kind of broker between an employer and a labor gang.

Yet the very diversity of American cities forced immigrants to modify their attitudes and habits. Few newcomers could avoid contact with people different from themselves, and few could prevent such contacts from altering their traditional ways of life. Although many foreigners identified themselves by their village or region of birth, native-born Americans categorized immigrants by nationality. Thus people from County Cork and County Limerick were lumped together as Irish; those from Schleswig and Wurttemberg became Germans; and those from Calabria and Campobasso became Italians. Mutual benefit and fraternal societies that aided the sick and paid burial expenses continued to be organized along village and provincial lines. For example, the Japanese transferred their *ken* societies, which organized social celebrations and relief services, and Chinese from Canton brought *hui* institutions that raised money to help members acquire businesses. But other immigrant institutions, such as newspapers and churches, found they had to appeal more broadly to the entire nationality group in order to survive.

Still other forces chipped away at old loyalties. Although many immigrants struggled to maintain their native languages and to pass them down to younger generations, English was taught in the schools and needed on the job; it soon penetrated nearly every community. Because the goods available in America often differed from those of the homeland, immigrants were forced to adjust their lifestyles to resemble those of other Americans. Foreigners did not automatically adopt American habits: they continued to cook ethnic meals using American foods and fashioned American fabrics in European styles. Still, convenience and availability influenced their material culture. Thousands of immigrant families had no choice but to buy the American ready-made clothing and mass-produced furniture that were commonplace in the larger society.

The influx of so many immigrants between 1870 and 1920 transformed the United States from a basically Protestant nation into a society of Protestants, Catholics, and Jews. Newcomers from Italy, Hungary, and what would become Czechoslovakia, Yugoslavia, and Poland joined the Irish and Germans to boost the proportion of Catholics in several large cities. In places like Buffalo, Cleveland, Chicago, and Milwaukee, Catholic immigrants and their offspring ap-

An immigrant family at home in their tenement. Though immigrant families were often large and their living conditions difficult, the newcomers displayed resilience and persistence in adapting to a strange environment. The people shown here were poor but proud, with a sense of integrity that shows in their faces. Bettmann Archive.

proached a majority of the population. Catholic Mexicans comprised over half the population of El Paso. German and eastern European immigrants gave New York one of the largest Jewish populations in the world.

Partly in response to Protestant-based charges that they could not retain Old World religious beliefs and still assimilate into American society, many Catholics and Jews tried to accommodate their faiths to the new environment. A number of Catholic and Jewish leaders—usually from older, more established immigrant groups—supported liberalizing trends such as the use of English in services, the phasing-out of Old World rituals such as saints' feasts, and a preference for public over parochial schooling. As long as new immigrants continued to arrive, however, these tendencies met stiff opposition. Newcomers usually sought to retain familiar religious practices, whether the folk

Catholicism of southern Italy or the orthodox Judaism of eastern Europe; they recoiled from reforms. Catholic immigrants continued to press for ethnically separate parishes in spite of church attempts to make American Catholicism more uniform. Bishops often had to accede to pressures for Polish rather than German-born priests to serve predominantly Polish congregations. Eastern European Jews, believing that Reform Judaism accommodated their faith too much to American ways, established the Conservative branch of their faith, which retained traditional ritual, though it did abolish the segregation of women in synagogues and eased English prayers into the service.

In the 1880s, another group of migrants began to move into American cities. Thousands of rural blacks moved northward and westward, fleeing crop liens, violence, and political oppression and seeking better employment. Although numbers of black urban

Black Migration to the Cities dwellers would grow much larger after 1915, thirty-two cities contained ten thousand or more blacks by 1900, and 79 percent of all blacks outside the South lived in cities. Black migrants resembled foreign immigrants in their peasant backgrounds and economic motivations, but they differed in several important ways. Because few factories would employ blacks, most black workers found jobs in the service sector—cleaning, cooking, carting—rather than the industrial trades. Also, because the majority of jobs in domestic and personal service were traditionally female jobs, black women outnumbered black men in cities such as New York, Baltimore, and New Orleans.

Together the three major migrant groups that peopled American cities—native whites, foreigners, and native blacks—sowed the seeds of modern American culture, to which each group made important contributions. Just as the cities had grown up because they centralized the varied economic functions of commerce, finance, and production, so too they nurtured rich cultural variety: American folk music and literature, Italian and Mexican cuisine, Irish comedy, Yiddish theater, Afro-American jazz and dance, and much more. Like their predecessors, newcomers in the late nineteenth century changed their environment as much as they were changed by it.

LIVING CONDITIONS IN THE
INNER CITY

Population growth created intense pressures on the public and private sectors of the city. Masses of people jammed inner-city districts, where they were known less for their cultural contributions than for the problems they bred. American cities seemed to harbor all the afflictions that plague modern society: poverty, disease, crime, decay, and other unpleasant conditions that result when large numbers of people live close together. City dwellers generally adjusted as best as they could until technology, science, private enterprise, or public authority could alleviate their problems. Some remarkable successes were achieved. In the late nineteenth century and early twentieth, construction of buildings, homes, streets, sewers, and schools proceeded at a furious pace. American cities set world standards for fire protection and water purification. Yet hardship and other ills await solution.

One of the most persistent shortcomings of American cities has been their failure to provide adequate housing to all who need it. The failure has roots in nineteenth-century urban development. **Housing Problems** In spite of massive construction in the 1880s and early 1900s, population growth outpaced housing supplies. This condition especially affected working-class families who, because of low-paying jobs, had to rent their living quarters. As cities grew, landlords took advantage of shortages in low-cost rental housing by splitting up existing buildings to house more people, constructing multiple-unit tenements, and hiking rents. Low-income families adjusted to high costs and short supply by sharing space and expenses. Thus it became common in many big cities for a one-family apartment to be occupied by two or three families or by one family plus a number of paying boarders.

The result was unprecedented crowding. In 1893, there were 702 people per acre in the heart of New York City's immigrant-packed Lower East Side, one of the highest population densities in the world. Low-rent districts had distinctive physical appearances: block after block of six- to eight-story barrackslike buildings in New York; dilapidated row houses in Baltimore and Philadelphia; converted slave quarters in Charleston and New Orleans; and crumbling two- and three-story frame houses in Boston, Chicago, and St. Louis. Everywhere the crowding was acute.

Inside many buildings, living conditions were intolerable. The largest rooms were barely ten feet wide, and interior rooms either had no windows at all or opened onto narrow shafts that bred vermin and rotten odors. "You see," said an immigrant housekeeper describing one such shaft, "it's damp down there, and the families, they throw out garbage and dirty papers and the insides of chickens, and other unmentionable filth. . . . I just vomited when I first cleaned up the air shaft." Few buildings had indoor plumbing, and the only source of heat was coal-burning stoves.

In several places housing problems aroused concerned citizens to mount reform campaigns. New York State took the lead in 1867, 1879, and 1901 by legislating light, ventilation, and safety codes for new tenement buildings. These and similar laws in other states could not remedy the ills of existing buildings, but they did impose government regulation on landlords' property rights. A few reformers, such as Jacob Riis and Lawrence Veiller, advocated housing low-income families in model tenements, with more spacious, airier rooms and better facilities. Model tenements, however, required landlords and investors to accept lower profits—a sacrifice few were willing to make. Neither reformers nor public officials would consider government financing of better housing, fearing such a step would undermine private enterprise. Still, the codes and commissions that resulted from reform campaigns did strengthen the power of local government to regulate housing construction.

Although housing reforms had only limited success, scientific and technological advances enabled city dwellers and the nation in general to live in greater comfort and safety. By the 1890s, most doctors had accepted the germ theory of disease. As a result, cities established more efficient systems of water purification and sewage disposal. Although disease and death rates remained higher in the city than the countryside, and tuberculosis and other respiratory ills continued to plague inner-city districts, public-health regulations helped to control such dread diseases as cholera, typhoid fever, and diphtheria. Street paving, modernized firefighting equipment, and electric street-lighting spread rapidly across urban America. Steel-frame construction, which supported a building by a metal skeleton rather than masonry walls, made possible the construction of skyscrapers—and thus more efficient use of scarce, costly urban land. Electric elevators and steam-heating systems serviced these buildings. Streetcars and subways hastened the pace of urban travel, and steel-cable suspension bridges, developed by John A. Roebling and epitomized by the great Brooklyn Bridge (completed in 1883), linked metropolitan sections more closely.

But none of these improvements lightened the burden of poverty. The urban economy, though generally expanding, advanced erratically. Employment, especially for unskilled workers in manufacturing and construction, rose and fell with business cycles and

Behind the tenements that housed poor working-class families in many cities were even more squalid alley structures such as these in Chicago. In cellars and in these old wooden houses that had been moved back to make room for newer brick buildings lived the poorest of the poor. *Chicago Historical Society.*

changing seasons. Often, to make ends meet, more than one member of a working-class family had to work. But the wages other family members could earn were minuscule. Thus an ever-increasing number of urban families lived on the margins of survival, where any kind of unlucky occurrence could plunge them into destitution.

Urban Poverty

Since colonial days, Americans have never agreed on how much responsibility the general public should assume for poor relief. In the late nineteenth and early twentieth centuries, many people held to the traditional beliefs that anyone could escape poverty through hard work and clean living and that poverty was inevitable only because some people were weaker than others. Such reasoning bred fears that assistance to poor people would encourage paupers to depend on public relief rather than self-reliance. As the numbers of poverty cases increased, this attitude hardened, and many city governments discontinued direct grants of food, fuel, and clothing to needy families. Instead, cities either provided relief in return for work on public projects or sent special cases to state-run institutions such as almshouses, orphanages, and homes for the blind, deaf, mentally ill, and handicapped.

Private philanthropic agencies also concerned themselves with helping only the "worthy poor," but their efforts to organize relief more efficiently did foster some change in attitude. Between 1877 and 1892, philanthropists in ninety-two cities formed Charity Organization Societies, an attempt to put social welfare on a more scientific and systematic basis by merging disparate charity groups into a coordinated unit. Believing poverty to be the result of personal defects such as alcoholism and laziness, members of these organizations spent most of their time visiting poor families and encouraging them to be thriftier and more virtuous.

Yet close observation of the poor caused some welfare workers to conclude that people's environments, rather than personal failure, caused poverty. That is, they came to believe that the ills of poverty could be cured by improving housing, sanitation, and job opportunities rather than by admonishing the poor to be more moral. This new attitude, which had been gaining ground since the mid-nineteenth century, fueled drives for building codes, factory regulations, and public-health measures. Nevertheless, most middle- and upper-class Americans remained wedded to the belief that in a society of abundance only the unfit were poor, and that relief of poverty should be tolerated but never encouraged. As one charity worker urged, relief "should be surrounded by circumstances that shall . . . repel every one . . . from accepting it."

Even more than crowding and pauperism, crime and disorder alarmed Americans and nurtured fears that urban growth, especially the growth of slums, was corrupting the nation. The more

Crime and Violence

cities grew, it seemed, the more they shook with violence. While homicide rates in other urban-industrial nations like England and Germany declined, those in America rose at an alarming rate: 25 per million people in 1881; 107 per million in 1898. Pickpockets, swindlers, sneak thieves, and holdup men roamed every city. Native whites were quick to blame immigrants and blacks for the so-called crime waves that swept the nation.

Yet it is possible that as a greater proportion of the population was concentrated in cities, crime merely became more conspicuous and sensational rather than more prevalent. To be sure, urban wealth and the mingling of different kinds of people provided new opportunities for organized thievery, petty larceny, vice, and violent grudge-settling. But how do such activities compare to the lawlessness and brutality of backwoods mining camps and southern plantations? Moreover, in spite of distress over Irish bank-robbery gangs, German pickpockets, and Italian Black Hand murderers, there is little evidence that more immigrants than natives populated the rogues' gallery. One investigation of jails in 1900 concluded that "we have ourselves evolved as cruel and cunning criminals as any that Europe may have foisted upon us."

Whatever the extent of criminality, city life in the late nineteenth and early twentieth centuries certainly supported the thesis that there is a tradition of violence in the United States. Cities served as arenas for many of the era's worst riots. As laborers and employers tried to adjust to the uncertainties of industrialization, violence became, in the words of one observer, "a sort of natural and inevitable concomitant." And urban ethnic and racial minorities were often victims of the violent bigotry that was the underside of the American myth of equality. The cityward movement of black people roused white fears, and as the twentieth century dawned, a series of race riots spread across the nation: Wilmington, North Carolina, 1898; Atlanta, Georgia, 1906; Springfield, Illinois, 1908. In cities of the Southwest and Pacific Coast, Chinese and Mexican immigrants often felt the sting of native intolerance. In addition, thousands of minor disruptions made cities scenes of constant turbulence.

Since early in the nineteenth century, city dwellers had increasingly depended on the police to protect life and property. But by the early 1900s law enforcement had become complicated and controversial, because different groups had different interpretations of the law and how it should be enforced. Disadvantaged groups—usually ethnic and racial minorities—could not escape arrest as easily as those with economic or political influence. Individual police officers could apply the law less harshly to members of their own ethnic group (police work was a route of mobility for several immigrant groups) or to people

The burgeoning cities required large professional police forces to keep order and protect life and property. Station houses like this one became important neighborhood outposts, and the police department an avenue of upward mobility for immigrants.   Library of Congress.

who bought exemptions in the form of bribes. Moreover, political and business leaders often enlisted the government's police power to break up strikes and demonstrations, but not to end or alleviate the exploitative conditions that caused such unrest among workers.

As the public's chief law-enforcement agency, the police were often caught between conflicting pressures for swift and severe action on the one hand and leniency on the other. For when some people clamored for police crackdowns on drinking, gambling, and prostitution, other people privately supported loose law enforcement so they could indulge in these so-called customer crimes. As American society became more diversified, especially in the cities, and as different groups asserted different interests, achieving a balance between the idealistic intentions of criminal law and people's desire for individual freedom became increasingly difficult. It has remained so to this day.

The mounting problems of city life seemed to many

Americans to demand greater government action. Thus city governments passed more laws and ordinances that regulated housing, provided poverty relief, and expanded police power. Yet public responsibility always ended at the boundaries of private property. Eventually some advances in housing construction, sanitation, and medical care did reach slum dwellers. But for most people, the only hope was to look to the next generation or to move elsewhere.

PROMISES OF MOBILITY

Between the Civil War and the First World War, Baptist minister Russell Conwell delivered the same sermon more than six thousand times to untold millions across the United States. Titled "Acres of

Diamonds," his immensely popular lecture affirmed the belief that any American could achieve success. People did not have to look very far for riches, Conwell preached; acres of diamonds lay at everyone's feet. Night after night, Conwell would insist to his audience, "the opportunity to get rich, to attain unto great wealth, is here . . . within the reach of almost every man and woman who hears me speak tonight. . . . I say you ought to get rich, and it is your duty to get rich. . . . If you can honestly attain unto riches it is your Christian and Godly duty to do so." Success, then, was not only possible; it was a religious obligation. But how possible was it for people actually to improve their lot and fulfill that duty?

Basically, there were three ways a person could get ahead: occupational advancement (and the higher income that accompanied it); property acquisition (and the potential for greater wealth it represented); and migration to an area of better conditions and greater opportunity. These options were open chiefly to white men. Although many women worked, owned property, and migrated, their social standing was usually defined by the men in their lives—their husbands, fathers, or other kin. Many women did improve their economic status by marrying men with wealth or potential, but other avenues were mostly closed. Men and women who were Afro-American, American Indian, Hispanic-American, or Asian-American had even fewer opportunities for success. Pinned to the bottom of society by prejudice, these groups were expected to accept their inherited station.

To a large number of people, however, the urban and industrial expansion of the late nineteenth century should have offered broad opportunity for occupational mobility. Thousands of small businesses were needed to supply goods and services to burgeoning urban populations. As corporations grew larger and centralized their operations, they required new managerial personnel. Although capital for a large business was hard to obtain, a person could open a saloon or a small store for only $200 or $300. And knowledge of accounting or typing could qualify one for a number of white-collar jobs that sometimes paid better than manual labor. Thus nonmanual work and the higher social status that tended to accompany it were possible.

Occupational Mobility

Such advancement occurred often. To be sure,

only a very few traveled the rags-to-riches path that men like Andrew Carnegie and Henry Ford had discovered. Studies of the era's wealthiest businessmen have shown that the vast majority started their careers with distinct advantages: American birth, Protestant religion, better-than-average education, and relatively affluent parents. Yet considerable movement occurred along the path from rags to moderate success as men climbed from manual to nonmanual jobs or saw their children do so. Thus personal successes like that of Meyer Grossman, a Russian immigrant to Omaha, Nebraska, who worked as a teamster before saving enough to open a successful furniture store, were common.

Rates of occupational mobility in late-nineteenth- and early-twentieth-century American communities were slow but steady. In new, fast-growing cities such as Atlanta, Los Angeles, and Omaha, approximately one in five manual workers rose to white-collar or owner's positions within ten years—provided they stayed in the city that long. In older northeastern cities like Boston and Newburyport, upward mobility averaged closer to one in six in ten years. Some people slipped from a higher to a lower rung of the occupational ladder, but rates of upward movement were almost always double the downward rates. Although patterns were far from consistent, immigrants generally experienced lower rates of upward mobility and higher rates of downward mobility than natives did. Still, regardless of birthplace, the chances for a white male to rise occupationally over the course of his career or to have a higher-status job than his father had were relatively good.

It must be remembered, however, that what constitutes a better job depends on an individual's definition of improvement and desires. Many an immigrant artisan, such as a German carpenter or an Italian shoemaker, would have considered an accountant's job demeaning and unproductive. People with long traditions of pride in manual labor neither wanted nonmanual jobs nor enouraged their children to seek them. As one Italian tailor explained, "I learned the tailoring business in the old country. Over here, in America, I never have trouble finding a job because I know my business from the other side [Italy]. . . . I want that my oldest boy learn my trade because I tell him that you could always make at least enough for the family."

Changing one's place of residence has been one of the most universal experiences of urban dwellers throughout American history. By the end of the nineteenth century, moving companies like this one in Omaha, Nebraska, arose to assist families seeking to improve their living conditions in a new home. Bekins Industries, Inc.

Moreover, business ownership entailed risks. Rates of failure were high among shopkeepers, saloon owners, and the like because business was so uncertain. Thus many manual workers sought security rather than mobility, preferring a steady wage to the risks of ownership. A Sicilian who lived in Bridgeport, Connecticut, observed that "the people that come here they afraid to get in business because they don't know how that business goes. In Italy these people don't know much about these things because most of them work on farms or in [their] trade."

In addition to or instead of advancing occupationally, a person could achieve social mobility by acquiring property. But property was not easy to acquire in turn-of-the-century America. Banks and savings institutions were far stricter in their lending practices than they would become after the 1930s, when the

Acquisition of Property

federal government began to insure real-estate financing. Mortgage loans carried relatively high interest rates and short repayment periods. Thus renting, even of single-family houses, was common, especially in big cities. Nevertheless, a general rise in wage rates enabled many families to build savings accounts, which could be used as down payments on property. Among working-class families who stayed in Newburyport for as long as ten years, a third to a half managed to accumulate some property; two-thirds did so within twenty years. In 1900, 36.3 percent of urban American families owned their homes. That figure may not seem large; yet it was higher than the home ownership rates of all Western nations except Denmark, Norway, and Sweden.

Finally, each year millions of families tried to improve their living conditions by packing up and moving elsewhere. As early as 1847, a foreign visitor, amazed

Residential Mobility by American transiency, wrote, "If God were suddenly to call the world to judgment He would surprise two-thirds of the American population on the road like ants." Americans have always followed the maxim that movement means improvement. This urge to move affected every region, every city. From Boston to San Francisco, from Minneapolis to San Antonio, it became significant that no more than half the families residing in a city at any one time could be found there ten years later.

Some evidence shows that many people who left one place for another, particularly unskilled workers, did not improve their status; they simply floated from one low-paying job to another. Others, however, did find greener pastures. Studies of turn-of-the-century Boston, Omaha, Atlanta, and other cities have revealed that most of the men who rose occupationally had migrated from somewhere else. Thus while cities frustrated the hopes of some, they offered opportunities to others.

In addition to population movement between cities, extraordinary numbers of people moved from one residence to another within the same city. In American communities today, one in every five families moves in a given year. A hundred years ago, the proportion was closer to one in four, or even one in three. In Omaha between 1880 and 1920, for example, nearly 60 percent of those families who remained in the city for as long as fourteen years had lived at three or more addresses during that span of time. Population turnover affected almost every neighborhood, every ethnic and occupational group.

Rapid residential flux undermined the stability of even the most homogeneous neighborhoods. Rarely did a single nationality comprise a clear majority in any large area, even when that area **Ethnic Neighborhoods and Ghettos** was known as Little Italy, Jewtown, Over-the-Rhine, or Greektown. Even in as heavily ethnic a city as Chicago, a survey of one district found a kaleidoscope of immigrants packed tightly together:

Between Halsted Street and the river live about ten thousand Italians, Neapolitans, Sicilians, and Calabrians. . . . To the South on Twelfth Street are many Germans, and the side streets are given over almost entirely to Polish and Prussian Jews. Further south, three Jewish colonies merge into a huge Bohemian colony. . . . To the north-west are many Canadians . . . and to the north are many Irish.

Moreover, the families inhabiting a certain neighborhood at one point in time were not likely to be living there five or ten years later. Residential change dispersed immigrants from their original areas of settlement into many different neighborhoods. In New York, Boston, and other eastern ports, ethnically homogeneous districts did exist, and people tended to change residences within those districts rather than move away from them. Elsewhere, however, most immigrant families lived dispersed in ethnically mixed neighborhoods rather than in ghettos.

In most places an area's institutions and enterprises, more than the people who actually lived there, identified it as an ethnic neighborhood. A certain part of town, familiar and accessible to a particular group, became the location of its churches, clubs, bakeries, meat markets, and other establishments. Some members of the group lived nearby, while others lived farther away but could travel there on streetcars or on foot. Thus some of the secondary business centers that formed at the intersections of mass transit routes became locations of ethnic business and social activity. A Bohemian Town, for example, received its nickname because it was the location of Swoboda's Bakery, Cermak's Drug Store, Cecha's Jewelry, Knezacek's Meats, St. Wenceslaus Church, and the Bohemian Benevolent Association. Such institutions gave a district an ethnic identity even though the surrounding neighborhoods were mixed and unstable.

If the term *ghetto* is defined as a place of enforced residence from which escape is at best difficult, only nonwhites in this era had a true ghetto experience. Wherever Asians and Mexicans immigrated, they encountered discrimination in housing, occupations, and other areas of public life. Though these groups often preferred to remain separate in Chinatowns and *barrios*, white Americans made every effort to keep them confined. In the 1880s the city of San Francisco, for example, tried to prohibit Chinese laundries from locating in most neighborhoods, and its school board tried to isolate Japanese and Chinese children in Chinatown schools.

Prejudice and discrimination not only trapped blacks at the bottom of the occupational ladder but operated in housing markets to limit their residential opportunities. Whites organized protective associations that pledged not to sell homes in white neighborhoods to blacks, and occasionally used violence to scare away black families who did move in. Such efforts seldom worked. Whites who lived on the edge of black neighborhoods often fled, leaving their homes and apartments to be sold and rented to black occupants. In almost every city, totally black residential districts expanded while white native and ethnic neighborhoods dissolved. By 1920 ten Chicago census tracts were over 75 percent black. In Detroit, Cleveland, Los Angeles, and Washington, D.C., two-thirds or more of the total black population lived in only two or three wards. Within these districts, blacks nurtured distinct cultural institutions that helped them adjust to urban life: storefront churches, business and educational organizations, social clubs, and saloons. But the ghettos also bred frustration, the result of stunted opportunity and racial bigotry. Color, more than any other factor, made the urban experiences of blacks different from those of whites.

All groups, however, including blacks, could and did move—if not from one part of the city to another, then from one city to another. Americans were always seeking greener pastures, and the hope that things might be better somewhere else acted as a kind of safety valve, relieving some of the tensions and frustrations that simmered inside the city. At times these emotions erupted into violence; more often, people simply left. A railroad ticket from one city to another cost a few dollars; there was little to lose by moving.

Moreover, the possibilities for upward mobility, however limited, seemed to temper people's dissatisfaction. Although the gap between the very rich and the very poor widened, the expanding economies of American cities created more room in the middle of the socioeconomic scale. Few could hope to become another Rockefeller, but many could become respectable merchants, shopkeepers, foremen, clerks, or agents. If advancement was not possible in one generation, it could be possible in the next. Finally, even if migration, occupational mobility, and property acquisition offered little hope of improvement or relief, there was still one sphere to which city dwellers could turn: politics.

THE RISE OF URBAN BOSS POLITICS

Andrew D. White, the American educator and diplomat, was dismayed and disgusted. He wrote in 1890 that he could not accept "the idea that a city is a political body, and therefore that it is to be ruled . . . by a city proletarian mob . . . and . . . that men who carry their ward can control the city." Such an arrangement, White concluded, made American city government "the worst in Christendom." But others characterized the same situation much differently. Referring to Israel Durham of Philadelphia, the very kind of politician whom White despised, one journalist wrote, "Everybody likes him, hundreds love him, and almost everybody calls him 'Iz.' " What provoked such impassioned differences of opinion? It was the urban political machine, one of the most remarkable and notorious of American institutions.

The sudden growth and mounting rivalry among social and economic interest groups that occurred in the late nineteenth century mired cities in a governmental swamp. From suburbs to slums, burgeoning populations, business expansion, and technological change created urgent needs for water, sewers, police and fire protection, schools, parks, and many other services. Such needs strained government institutions beyond their capacities. Furthermore, city governments approached these needs in a disorganized fashion. Legislative and administrative functions were typically dispersed among a mayor, a city council, and independent boards that administered health regulations, public works, poverty relief, and other matters. Philadelphia at one time had thirty different boards plus a mayor and a council to tend to the city's needs. And state governments often imposed their will on city administrations, appointing board members and limiting local prerogatives to levy taxes and sell bonds to raise revenue.

Power thrives on confusion and out of this governmental chaos arose the political machine. Unlike political parties, which ideally exist for higher purposes than merely electing their candidates to office, ma-

Political Machines chines were organizations whose main goal was getting and keeping political power. In order to achieve that goal, a machine had to win popular support. Machine politicians routinely used bribery and graft to further their ends. But they could not have succeeded if they had not provided relief, security, and municipal services to large numbers of people. By doing so, machine politicians alleviated many urban problems and accomplished things that other agencies had been unable or unwilling to attempt.

Machines were also beneficiaries of the new urban conditions. As cities grew larger and economically more complex, business leaders either vied to use government to advance their own interests or withdrew from local affairs to pursue their interests in interurban or interregional economic organizations. At the same time, hordes of newcomers, often unskilled and foreign-born, crowded into the cities. Enfranchised by liberal voting qualifications, the men of these groups became a substantial political force.

These circumstances bred a new kind of leader: the political boss. Conflicting interest groups needed brokers who could bypass governmental stalemates, and urban newcomers had needs that required government attention. Bosses and machines did just that; they established power bases among new urban voters and used politics to solve urban problems. Machines made politics a full-time profession. According to George Washington Plunkett, a small-time boss in New York City who published his memoirs in 1905, "As a rule [the boss] has no business or occupation other than politics. He plays politics every day and night in the year and his headquarters bears the inscription, 'Never closed.' "

Bosses and machines were rarely as dictatorial or corrupt as their critics charged. To be sure, fraud, bribery, and thievery tainted the system. Bosses such as Philadelphia's "Duke" Vare, Kansas City's Tom Pendergast, and New York's Richard Croker lived like kings, though their official incomes were slim. A few bosses had no permanent organization; rather, they were freelance opportunists who bargained for power, sometimes winning and sometimes losing. But from the 1880s onward, most machines evolved into highly organized political structures that wedded accomplishments for the city with personal gain for politicians.

The system rested on a popular base and was held together by loyalty and service. City machines were coalitions of smaller machines that derived their power directly from the neighborhoods, particularly inner-city neighborhoods inhabited by the native and immigrant working classes. In return for votes, bosses provided jobs, built parks and bathhouses, distributed food to the needy, and helped when someone ran afoul of the law. Such personalized service cultivated mass attachment to the boss; never before had government or public leaders assumed such responsibility for people in need.

Moreover, bosses were genuinely public people. They attended weddings and wakes, joined clubs, and held open house in saloons where neighborhood people could contact them person-**Techniques of** ally. Each boss had his own style. **Bossism** Pittsburgh's Christopher Magee gave his city a zoo and a hospital. Brooklyn's Hugh McLaughlin provided free burial services. Boston's James Michael Curley would approach a haggard old woman and tell her that "a woman should have three attributes. She should have beauty, intelligence, and money." Then he would press a silver dollar into her hand, adding, "Now you have all three."

In order to finance their largesse and support their system, bosses exchanged favors for votes or money. Their power over local government enabled machines to control the letting of contracts, the granting of utility or streetcar franchises, and the distribution of city jobs. Recipients of city business and jobs were expected to repay the machine with a portion of their profits or salaries and to cast supporting votes on election day. Bosses called this process gratitude; critics called it graft. Machines constructed public buildings, sewer systems, mass transit lines, and more that otherwise might not have been built; but bribes and kickbacks made such projects costly to taxpayers. Moreover, machines dispensed favors to illegal businesses as well as legitimate ones. Payoffs from gambling, prostitution, and illegal liquor traffic were important sources of machine revenue.

Though there was great variety, between 1880 and 1920, nearly every major city experienced some kind of bossism. Hierarchical machine organization, whereby a city boss presided over neighborhood bosses, was most highly developed in New York City. There,

Political bosses won friends and courted votes through their benevolence. Timothy D. "Big Tim" Sullivan sponsored this huge free barbecue for constituents in a New York City neighborhood.   Brown Brothers.

after the downfall of Boss William M. Tweed in the early 1870s, "Honest John" Kelly took over Tweed's Tammany Hall organization and tightened its structure by combining Tammany more thoroughly with the Democratic party. In the late 1880s, Richard Croker assumed control of Tammany Hall and completed Kelly's efforts by making neighborhood bosses more dependent on the city boss for jobs and money and by allying with wealthy business leaders. By contrast, the machine system in Chicago was decentralized, with several ward bosses exercising independent power and cultivating their own special interests.

Medium-sized cities generally had a single boss who used the inner-city districts as his power base. Cincinnati's George Cox and Kansas City's Jim Pendergast (Tom's brother) were downtown saloonkeepers who became powerful political brokers. In the South,

bosses such as New Orleans's Martin Behrman and Memphis's Edward H. Crump drew strength from the region's well-established Democratic party. A few bosses, such as San Francisco's Abe Ruef and Minneapolis's "Doc" Ames, were well educated. But many, including St. Louis's Ed Butler and New York's "Big Tim" Sullivan, never finished grammar school and received their most influential training in city streets and tenements.

Bosses held onto their power because they knew people's needs firsthand and because they tended to the problems of everyday life. Martin Lomasney, boss of Boston's South End, explained, "There's got to be in every ward somebody that any bloke can come to—no matter what he's done—and get help. Help, you understand, none of your law and justice, but help." In an era when unemployment insurance and welfare were virtually unknown, machine politicians believed government existed to aid people in need and to provide services.

The boss system, however, was neither innocent nor fair. Jobs, Christmas turkeys, and funeral money were accompanied by bribery, thievery, and extortion. Moreover, bosses never distributed favors equitably. New immigrant groups such as Italians and Poles, and racial minorities like blacks and Latinos, received only token recognition, if any, from machines. Nevertheless, in an age of economic individualism, bosses were no more guilty of self-interest and discrimination than the respectable business leaders who exploited workers, spoiled the landscape, and manipulated government in pursuit of profits. Sometimes humane and sometimes criminal, bosses were brokers between various sectors of urban society and an uncertain world.

CIVIC REFORM

Machine politics brought some order to city government, met some of the needs of immigrants and other inner-city residents, and lined the pockets of some leaders and their business allies. But the boss system also alarmed the established classes inhabiting the outlying neighborhoods and sensitized many men and women to the problems of urban growth. At the same time the bosses were consolidating their power, a reform movement was organizing to destroy political machines and improve the quality of urban life. This urban reform movement, which paralleled its agrarian counterpart (see pages 572–575) and which laid the foundation for the national reforms of the Progressive era (see Chapter 21), shared the strengths and weaknesses of the American liberal tradition.

In 1885, Congregational minister Josiah Strong wrote, "The city is the nerve center of our civilization. It is also the storm center. . . . It has become a serious threat to our civilization." Strong's sentiments were shared by many middle- and upper-class Americans who feared that immigrant-based political machines menaced the republic and that unsavory alliances between bosses and business undermined municipal finances. Anxious over the mounting poverty, crowding, and disorder that seemed to accompany population expansion, and convinced that urban services were making taxes too high, civic reformers organized to oust bosses and to install more responsible leaders at the helm of urban administration.

Urban reform derived from the industrial system's emphasis on eliminating waste and inefficiency. Business-minded reformers believed government could be made more efficient by running it like a business. They believed that the only way to prevent civic decay was to elect officials who would hold down expenses and prevent corruption. Thus the major goals of reform leaders such as future president Grover Cleveland, mayor of Buffalo in 1881, were to reduce city budgets, make employees work longer, and cut taxes.

As a means of introducing sound business principles to government, civic reformers supported a number of structural changes, such as city-manager and commission forms of government and **Structural** nonpartisan, citywide election of **Reforms in** officials. Each of these reforms was **Government** aimed at removing politics from government and placing local decision-making in the hands of experienced experts. Armed with such strategies, reformers believed they could centralize administration under their control and thereby undermine bosses' ward and neighborhood power bases. They rarely realized, however, that bosses succeeded because they used government to meet people's needs. Reformers only noticed the waste and corruption that machines bred.

A few reformers did move beyond structural changes to a genuine concern for social problems. Hazen S. Pingree, mayor of Detroit from 1889 to 1896; Samuel "Golden Rule" Jones, mayor of Toledo from 1897 to 1904; and Thomas L. Johnson, mayor of Cleveland from 1901 to 1909, worked to provide jobs for poor people, to reduce charges by transit and utilities companies, and to establish greater governmental responsibility for the welfare of all citizens. Some supported public ownership of gas, electric, and telephone companies—a quasi-socialistic reform that alienated their business allies. But Pingree, Jones, and Johnson were exceptions. Most civic reformers were narrow of vision. Although they achieved temporary success, they could not match the bosses' political savvy and soon found themselves out of power.

Consumer reform originated in many cities at the end of the nineteenth century. Often instigated by reform-minded women, local governments passed laws and created agencies to inspect for adulterated milk and other tainted foods dangerous to health.   Culver.

Nevertheless, the seeds of social reform were beginning to sprout outside of politics. Convinced that laissez-faire ideology could no longer work in a complex urban-industrial world and driven by an urge to identify and address urban problems, a number of men and women—mostly young and middle-class—embarked on campaigns for social betterment. These urban social reformers operated within a variety of fields and sought solutions to a variety of problems. Housing reformers wanted local government to pass building codes to ensure safety in tenements. Protestant reformers influenced by the Social Gospel movement, which emphasized social responsibility as a means to salvation, built churches in slum neighborhoods and urged businesses to be socially responsible. Believing that service to fellow human beings was a Christian

Social Reform

duty, Social Gospel clergymen such as Washington Gladden of Columbus, Ohio, and Walter Rauschenbusch of Rochester, New York, worked to alleviate poverty and to make peace between employers and labor unions. Educational reformers such as William T. Harris of St. Louis saw public schools as a means of preparing immigrants and their children for citizenship by teaching them American values as well as the English language.

Perhaps the most ambitious and inspiring feature of the urban reform movement was the settlement house. Patterned after London's Toynbee Hall, settlements were efforts by young, educated, middle-class men and women to live in slum neighborhoods and bridge the gulf between classes, in hopes that people could learn from each other. Early settlement founders such as Jane Addams, Florence Kelley, and

Graham Taylor wanted to improve the lives of working-class people by helping them to obtain an education, an appreciation of the arts, better jobs, and better housing. Their settlement houses provided neighborhood residents with a wide array of activities, ranging from vocational classes to childcare for working mothers to ethnic art exhibits and pageants. Because of their efforts in areas such as the establishment of school nurses, the passing of building safety codes, the construction of public playgrounds, and the support for labor unions, settlement workers often became reform leaders in cities and in the nation. Though the neighborhood residents they served sometimes mistrusted them because they were outsiders to working-class and immigrant cultures, settlement workers made valuable contributions to urban life.

While settlement-house workers tried to revive neighborhoods, other reformers tried to beautify whole cities. Inspired by the World's Columbian Exposition of 1893, a dazzling world's fair held **Beautification** in the specially built White City **Campaigns** on Chicago's South Side, architects and city planners worked to redesign the urban landscape. Led by architect Daniel Burnham, the City Beautiful movement undertook to build civic centers, parks and boulevards, and transportation systems that would make cities more attractive as well as economically efficient. "Make no little plans," Burnham urged city officials. "Make big plans; aim high in hope and work." This attitude spawned beautifying projects in Chicago, San Francisco, and Washington, D.C., in the first decade of the twentieth century. Yet most big plans turned out to be only big dreams. Neither the public nor the private sector could muster enough money to undertake major projects, and planners disagreed with each other and with social reformers over whether or not beautification would really solve urban problems.

Whether they concentrated on changing government, social services, or city design, urban reformers wanted to save cities, not abandon them. The men and women of the various reform movements believed that they could improve urban life by restoring feelings of service and cooperation among all citizens. They often failed to realize, however, that cities were places of great diversity and that different people had different views of what reform actually meant. Distributing city jobs on the basis of civil service exams rather

than political patronage meant progress to governmental reformers, but to working-class men it signified reduced employment opportunities. Moral reformers tried to prohibit the sale of alcoholic beverages to prevent working-class breadwinners from wasting their wages and ruining their health, but European immigrants saw such crusades as interference in their long-held wine- and beer-drinking customs. Planners saw new civic buildings and transportation systems as modern necessities, but such structures often replaced low-cost housing units and displaced the poor. Thus early urban reform merged idealism with naiveté and insensitivity.

THE LEGACY OF URBANISM

Much of what American society has become today originated in the urbanization of the late nineteenth century. American cities may have been less orderly and beautiful than European cities, but they hummed with energy and excitement. When old-fashioned native inventiveness met the traditions of European, African, and Asian cultures, a new kind of society emerged. This new society seldom functioned functioned smoothly; in fact, there really was no coherent urban community, only a collection of sub-communities. Yet its jumble of social classes, ethnic and racial groups, political organizations, and other components left important legacies.

Martin Lomasney, the Boston ward boss, once observed that "one of the strongest human cravings is to be left alone and the uplifter is never liked." By the early 1900s, American cities **Cultural** had become so diverse socially that **Pluralism** immigrant groups were straining to protect their cultures in a changing, bewildering world. Fearful and puzzled native-born Americans tried a host of ways to Americanize and uplift immigrants, but the newcomers stubbornly clung to their religious rituals, languages, family and social organizations, and drinking habits. Optimists had envisioned the American nation as a melting pot where various nationalities would blend into a new, unified people. Instead, many ethnic groups proved

Streets clogged with people and vehicles, canyon walls of tall buildings, a hodge-podge of signs and banners, and a maze of overhead wires gave the modern American city its image of growth and bustling activity. The New York Historical Society, New York City.

to be unmeltable, and nonwhite racial minorities got burned on the bottom of the pot.

As a result of immigration and urbanization, the United States became a culturally pluralistic society—not a melting pot but a salad bowl. As one immigrant priest told a social worker, "There is no such thing as an American." He meant the same thing literary critic Randolph Bourne meant when he dubbed the United States "a cosmopolitan federation of national colonies." This kind of reasoning produced hyphenated identifications: people considered themselves Irish-American, Italo-American, Polish-American, and the like.

Pluralism and its attendant interest-group loyalties

1867	First law passed regulating tenements (New York)
1880s	"New" immigrants from eastern and southern Europe begin to arrive in large numbers
1883	Brooklyn Bridge completed
1886	First settlement house opened
1890s	Electric trolleys replace horse-driven mass transit
1893	World's Columbian Exposition, Chicago
1898	Race riot in Wilmington, North Carolina
1900– 1910	Peak years of immigration
1906	Race riot in Atlanta, Georgia
1920	Majority (51.4 percent) of Americans live in cities

made politics an important institution. If America was not a melting pot, then different groups were competing with each other for power, wealth, and status. When lack of skills, education, capital, and influence closed off paths to success, immigrants turned to politics to protect their interests and to open up new opportunities. American cities became arenas in which different groups formed coalitions to achieve their goals. But such coalitions were fragile, and their membership shifted according to the issue in question.

Adherents of different cultural traditions battled over how much control government should exercise over people's lives (see page 563). The most provocative issue was about the use of leisure time and celebration of Sunday, the Lord's day. In the Puritan tradition, natives supported blue laws (see page 284) designed to prevent the desecration

Cultural-Political Alignments

of the Sabbath by prohibiting various commercial and recreational activities. European immigrants, accustomed to feasting and playing after church, fought Sunday closings of saloons and other restrictions on the only day they had free for fun and relaxation. Thus in 1913, when the New York General Assembly proposed a law granting cities authority to end restrictions on Sunday baseball games and liquor sales, both sides argued vehemently. One rural Republican charged that such a measure amounted to "amending Moses' law," while a New York City Democrat of Irish lineage retorted that "Moses was an organization Democrat" who wrote the commandment "Don't covet your neighbor's rights." At about the same time, the Illinois and Ohio legislatures were split over whether or not to legalize boxing, which small-town Republicans opposed and urban Democrats favored. Similar splits developed elsewhere over public versus parochial schools and prohibition versus the free availability of liquor.

Such conflicts, plus the ever-growing diversity of the American population illustrate why local and state politics were so heated in the late nineteenth and early twentieth centuries. Some people carried polarization to its extreme and tried to suppress everything new and allegedly un-American. In several communities during the 1890s, the American Protective Association achieved considerable influence by attacking "the diabolical works of the Catholic Church" and demanding an end to immigration. Some of this sentiment influenced national legislation. In 1882, Congress bowed to pressure from West Coast nativists and prohibited Chinese immigration for ten years. In 1902 a new law excluded the Chinese permanently. And periodic attempts were made to prevent foreign-born citizens from voting by imposing literacy tests on them.

Efforts to enforce homogeneity generally failed, though, because too many people had a stake in the country's cultural diversity. By 1920, immigrants and their offspring outnumbered natives in many cities, and the national economy depended on the new workers and consumers. They had transformed the United States into an urban nation; they had given American culture its rich and varied texture; and they had laid the foundations for the political liberalism and sensitivity to individual liberty that would characterize American politics and society in the future.

SUGGESTIONS FOR FURTHER READING

Urban Growth

Howard P. Chudacoff, *The Evolution of American Urban Society*, rev. ed. (1981); Blake McKelvey, *The Urbanization of America* (1963); Arthur M. Schlesinger, *The Rise of the City* (1933); Jon Teaford, *City and Suburb: The Political Fragmentation of Metropolitan America, 1850–1970* (1979); Sam Bass Warner, Jr., *The Urban Wilderness* (1972); Sam Bass Warner, Jr., *Streetcar Suburbs* (1962).

Immigration, Ethnicity, and Religion

Aaron I. Abell, *American Catholicism and Social Action* (1960); Josef J. Barton, *Peasants and Strangers: Italians, Rumanians, and Slovaks in an American City* (1975); John Bodnar, *Immigration and Industrialization* (1977); John Bodnar et al., *Lives of Their Own: Blacks, Italians, and Poles in Pittsburgh, 1900–1960* (1982); John W. Briggs, *An Italian Passage* (1978); Jack Chen, *The Chinese of America* (1980); Leonard Dinnerstein and David Reimers, *Ethnic Americans* (1975); John B. Duff, *The Irish in the United States* (1971); Mario T. Garcia, *Desert Immigrants: The Mexicans of El Paso, 1880–1920* (1981); Nathan Glazer and Daniel P. Moynihan, *Beyond the Melting Pot*, rev. ed. (1970); Caroline Golab, *Immigrant Destinations* (1977); Milton Gordon, *Assimilation in American Life* (1964); Victor Greene, *For God and Country: The Rise of Polish and Lithuanian Ethnic Consciousness in America* (1975); Oscar Handlin, *The Uprooted*, 2nd ed. (1973); Marcus Lee Hansen, *The Immigrant in American History* (1940); John Higham, *Strangers in the Land: Patterns of American Nativism* (1955); Edward R. Kantowicz, *Polish-American Politics in Chicago* (1975); Harry Kitano, *Japanese Americans: The Evolution of a Subculture* (1969); Alan M. Kraut, *The Huddled Masses: The Immigrant in American Society, 1880–1921* (1982); Matt S. Maier and Feliciano Rivera, *The Chicanos: A History of Mexican Americans* (1972); Henry F. May, *Protestant Churches and Industrial America* (1949); Humbert S. Nelli, *The Italians of Chicago* (1970); Moses Rischin, *The Promised City: New York's Jews* (1962); Philip Taylor, *The Distant Magnet: European Emigration to the U.S.A.* (1971); Thomas Wheeler, ed. *The Immigrant Experience* (1972).

Urban Needs and Services

Robert H. Bremner, *From the Depths: The Discovery of Poverty* (1956); James H. Cassedy, *Charles V. Chapin and the Public Health Movement* (1962); Marvin Lazerson, *Origins of the Urban School* (1971); Thomas L. Philpott, *The Slum and the Ghetto* (1978); James F. Richardson, *The New York Police* (1970); Barbara Gutmann Rosencrantz, *Public Health and the State* (1972); Mel Scott, *American City Planning Since 1890* (1969); Selwyn K. Troen, *The Public and the Schools* (1975); Christopher Tunnard and Henry Hope Reed, *American Skyline* (1955); David B. Tyack, *The One Best System: A History of American Urban Education* (1974).

Mobility and Race Relations

Howard P. Chudacoff, *Mobile Americans* (1972); Clyde Griffen and Sally Griffen, *Natives and Newcomers* (1977); David M. Katzman, *Before the Ghetto* (1973); Thomas Kessner, *The Golden Door* (1977); Kenneth L. Kusmer, *A Ghetto Takes Shape* (1976); Gilbert Osofsky, *Harlem: The Making of a Ghetto* (1966); Howard N. Rabinowitz, *Race Relations in the Urban South* (1978); Allan H. Spear, *Black Chicago* (1967); Stephan Thernstrom, *The Other Bostonians: Poverty and Progress in the American Metropolis* (1973); Olivier Zunz, *The Changing Face of Inequality: Urbanization, Industrial Development, and Immigrants in Detroit, 1880–1920* (1982).

Boss Politics

John M. Allswang, *Bosses, Machines and Urban Voters* (1977); Blaine Brownell and Warren E. Stickle, eds., *Bosses and Reformers* (1973); Alexander B. Callow, Jr., ed., *The City Boss in America* (1976); Lyle Dorsett, *The Pendergast Machine* (1968); Zane L. Miller, *Boss Cox's Cincinnati* (1968); Bruce M. Stave, ed., *Urban Bosses, Machines, and Progressive Reformers* (1972).

Urban Reform

John D. Buenker, *Urban Liberalism and Progressive Reform* (1973); James B. Crooks, *Politics and Progress* (1968); Allen F. Davis, *American Heroine: The Life and Legend of Jane Addams* (1973); Allen F. Davis, *Spearheads for Reform* (1967); Michael Ebner and Eugene Tobin, eds., *The Age of Urban Reform* (1977); Melvin Holli, *Reform in Detroit* (1969); C. H. Hopkins, *The Rise of the Social Gospel in American Protestantism* (1940); Roy M. Lubove, *The Progressives and the Slums* (1962); Martin J. Schiesl, *The Politics of Efficiency: Municipal Administration and Reform in America* (1977); John G. Sproat, *The Best Men: Liberal Reformers in the Gilded Age* (1968).

EVERYDAY
LIFE AND CULTURE
1877–1920

CHAPTER 19

Abigail Roberson was young, sensitive, shy, and beautiful; but none of these qualities inhibited her from suing the Rochester Folding Box Company and one of its customers, the Franklin Mills Company. The Rochester company, it seems, had used Miss Roberson's photograph without her permission on the flour bags it made for Franklin Mills. Hoping that her face would induce consumers to buy the product, the company added the caption "Flour of the Family" above Abigail's image. Miss Roberson claimed that this advertisement brought her ridicule and mental distress, and she sued to prevent unauthorized use of her picture on the flour bags. In 1902 the case reached the New York Court of Appeals, which ruled against Abigail Roberson after heated debate. But public disapproval of the decision was so strong that the next year the New York General Assembly passed one of the nation's first right-to-privacy laws, stipulating that "A person, firm or corporation that uses for advertising purposes or for the purpose of trade the name, portrait or picture of any living person, without having obtained the written consent of such a person . . . is guilty of a misdemeanor."

The Roberson case represents one of many issues that resulted from the changing character of American life. Not only had goods such as Franklin Mills' "Flour of the Family" become widely available, but also companies like Rochester Folding Box strove for new ways to package and advertise their products. In earlier times, before mass markets, mass advertisement, and photography existed, personal privacy and its invasion were not matters that concerned individuals, much less the courts. Suddenly, however, economic, technological, and social changes were affecting everyday life in ways that few had anticipated.

During the half-century between the end of Reconstruction and the end of the First World War, American society began to shift its focus from production to consumption. The nation's farms and industries were producing so much that Americans could afford to reorient their attitudes toward material wants. What had once been accessible only to a few was becoming available to many; what had formerly been

dreams were becoming necessities. No trend affected everyday life more decisively than this one. And as Americans tried to adapt to the new values of consumption and its attendant conflicts, they raised questions about themselves that have not been resolved to this day.

Most Americans at the end of the nineteenth century were still relatively isolated. In 1880, seven out of every ten people lived on farms and in small towns. Life in such places was shaped by the dictates of nature and the traditional institutions of family and church. In the fields and in the household, people worked from sunup to sundown—though they could usually control their own work pace and the number of breaks they took. Most foods and clothes were made in the home or nearby. Houses were heated by wood- or coal-burning stoves and lit by oil lamps; most had no bathroom, only basins and tubs indoors and outhouses in the back yard. Families burned what little trash they had, fed their garbage to animals, and poured waste water outside. Besides church, people mingled at the general store and at such special occasions as fairs, circuses, political rallies, and evangelical revivals. Fatigue and pitch-darkness restricted nighttime activities; street lights were rare. People normally went to bed at nine or ten P.M. and rose at four or five A.M.

But such lifestyles were changing rapidly. As the nation's population became increasingly urban (by 1920 the majority lived in cities), there developed a new kind of neighborhood society in which street corners, saloons, shops, and commercial amusements replaced the village church and general store. People tended to spend more time with their peers—members of the same age group—and less with their families. The rapid spread of intercity transportation and of postal, telephone, and electrical service drew even isolated communities into the orbit of a consumer-oriented society. American inventiveness combined with technology, mass production, and mass marketing to produce and make available myriad goods that had not previously existed or had been the exclusive property of the wealthy. This new material well-being, brought about by the advent of such products

Chapter 19: EVERYDAY LIFE AND CULTURE, 1877–1920

A drugstore, complete with soda fountain and showcases of merchandise, symbolizes the new materialism of the late nineteenth century. New mass production and marketing techniques made such materialism possible. Library of Congress.

as ready-made clothes, canned foods, and home appliances had a dual effect. It enabled Americans of differing status to join communities of consumers—communities defined not by place or class but by common possession. But it also accentuated the differences between those who could afford such goods and services and those who could not.

STANDARDS OF LIVING

If the affluence of a society can be measured by how quickly it converts luxuries into commonplace articles of everyday life, the United States was indeed becoming affluent in the years between 1880 and 1920. In 1880, for example, almost no one smoked cigarettes. (That year a young Virginian named James Bonsack invented a cigarette-making machine.) Only wealthy women could afford silk stockings, and only residents of Florida, Texas, and California could enjoy fresh oranges. The sweets people ate were made at home, and few people ever bought soap. But by 1899, manufactured and perishable products were becoming increasingly common. That year Americans bought 2 billion cigarettes (an average of 27 per person) and 151,000 pairs of silk stockings, consumed oranges at the rate of 100 crates for every 1,000 people, and spent an average of $1.08 per person on store-bought candy and pastries and $.63 on soap. By 1921 the transformation was even more advanced. Americans smoked 43 billion cigarettes that year (403 per person), ate 248 crates of oranges per 1,000 people, bought 217 million pairs of silk stockings, and spent $1.66

per person on confectionery goods and $1.40 on soap. How did Americans afford these goods? How did changes in standards of living come about?

What people can afford depends largely on their resources and incomes. Data for the period from 1880 to 1920 are scattered, but there is no doubt that incomes rose. As always, the rich

Rising Personal Income

got richer. The rapidly expanding economy spawned massive fortunes and created a new industrial elite. The writer of "The Coming Billionaire," an article published in *Forum* magazine in 1891, estimated that there were already 120 Americans worth at least $10 million. By 1920, when income-tax figures made possible the first accurate tabulations of income distribution, the richest 5 percent of the population was receiving almost one-fourth of all income in the country. Returns on investments were even more skewed; the same top 5 percent was receiving almost half of all interest payments and 85 percent of all stock and bond dividends.

But incomes also rose among the middle classes. For example, the average pay for clerical workers rose 36 percent between 1890 and 1910 (see table). After the turn of the century, employees of the federal executive branch were averaging $1,072 a year, and college professors $1,100—not handsome sums, but much more than manual workers received. With these incomes, the middle class could afford relatively comfortable housing. A six- to seven-room house cost around $3,000 to buy or build and $15 to $20 per month to rent.

Wages for industrial workers increased as well, though they varied widely and income figures were deceiving. On the average, the annual wages of industrial workers rose from $486 in 1890 to $630 in 1910. Hourly rates in industries with large female work forces, such as shoe and paper manufacturing, were lower than those in industries with predominantly male work forces, such as coal mining and iron production. Also, regional variations were wide. Nevertheless, wages for all moved upward (see table). Pay for farm laborers followed the same trend, though wages remained relatively low because generally those workers received room and board along with their pay.

Pay scales for industrial and farm workers, however, ignore a vital aspect of living standards. Wage increases

Cost of Living

mean little if living costs rise as fast or faster than incomes. In fact, this is what happened in the United States around the turn of the century. According to one economic index, the weekly cost of living for a typical wage earner's family of four rose over 47 percent between 1889 and 1913. In other words, a quantity of food and other items that may have cost $6.78 in 1889 increased, after a slight dip in the mid-1890s, to $10.00 by 1913 (see table for specific food prices). Very rarely did the income for a particular working-class occupation rise at the same rate as the cost of living.

How then could working-class Americans afford the new goods and services that the industrial age offered? Obviously, many could not. The daughter of a textile worker, recalling her school days at the turn of the century, described how "some of the kids would bring bars of chocolate, others an orange. . . . I suppose they were richer than a family like ours. My father used to buy a bag of candy and a bag of peanuts every payday. . . . And that's all we'd have until the next payday. If we asked for something my mother would say, 'Well, we're too poor. We can't afford to buy that.' " Another woman explained how her family coped with high prices and low wages: "My mother made our clothes. People then wore old clothes. My mother would rip them out and make them over."

Still, a working-class family could raise its income and partake at least partially in consumer society by sending children and women into the labor market.

Supplements to Family Income

Thus in a household where the father made $600 a year, the wages of other family members might lift the total income to $800 or $900. Many families also rented household space to boarders and lodgers, a practice that could yield up to $200 a year. These means of increasing family income enabled people to spend more and save more. Between 1889 and 1901, for example, working-class families markedly increased their expenditures for such items as life insurance, amusements, alcoholic beverages, and union dues. Thus workers were able to improve their living standards, but not without sacrifices in their family and home life.

The work people did was part of a more highly developed money economy. Between 1890 and 1920, the American labor force grew from 28 million workers

AMERICAN LIVING STANDARDS, 1880–1920

	1880	1890	1900	1910	1920
Income and earnings					
Annual income:					
clerical worker		$848		$1,156	
public school teacher		$256		$492	
industrial worker		$486		$630	
farm laborer		$233		$336	
Hourly wage:					
soft-coal miner		$0.18[a]		$0.21	
iron worker		$0.17[a]		$0.23	
shoe worker		$0.14[a]		$0.19	
paper worker		$0.12[a]		$0.17	
Labor statistics					
Number of people in labor force	17.4 million	28.5 million			41.7 million
Average workweek, manufacturing		60 hours		51 hours	47.4 hours
Food costs					
10 pounds potatoes		$0.16		$0.17	
Dozen eggs		$0.21		$0.34	
1 pound bacon		$0.12½		$0.25	
Demographic data					
Life expectancy at birth:					
women			48.3 years		54.6 years
men			46.3 years		53.6 years
Death rate per 1,000 people			172		130
Birthrate per 1,000 people	39.8		32.3		27.7
Other					
Number of students in public high schools		203,000			2.3 million
Advertising expenditures	$20 million		$95 million	$500 million	
Telephones per 100 people		0.3[b]	2.1[c]	12.6[d]	

[a]1892 [b]1891 [c]1901 [d]1921

to 42 million. But these figures are somewhat misleading: in general, they represent a change in the nature of work rather than an increase in the number of available jobs relative to the number of people who could work. In the rural society that the United States was in the nineteenth century, women and children worked at tasks that were important to the family's daily existence—cooking, cleaning, planting, and harvesting. Their jobs were often hard to define, and they seldom appeared in employment figures because they earned no wages. But as the nation industrialized and the agricultural sector's share of the national income and population declined, waged and salaried employment became more common. Jobs in industry and commerce were both easier to define and easier to count. It is probable, then, that the proportion of Americans who were working was not increasing markedly—most Americans, male and female, had always worked. What was new was the increase in paid employment, which also made purchases of consumer goods and services more affordable.

Scientific developments eased some of life's struggles, and their impact on living standards increased after 1900. Advances in medical care and better living

Higher Life Expectancy conditions sharply reduced death rates and extended the life span. Between 1900 and 1920, for example, life expectancy rose six years, and the death rate dropped by 24 percent (see table, page 539). During the same period there were spectacular declines in the death rates from typhoid, diphtheria, influenza (except for a harsh epidemic in 1918 and 1919), tuberculosis, and intestinal ailments—diseases that had been the scourge of earlier generations. There were, however, significantly more deaths from cancer, diabetes, and heart disease. Americans also found more ways to kill: though the suicide rate remained about the same, homicides and automobile deaths increased dramatically between 1900 and 1920.

Not only were amenities and luxuries more readily available in the early 1900s than they had been a half-century earlier, but the means to upward mobility seemed more accessible as well. The spread of public education—particularly high schools—helped equip young people to achieve a higher standard of living than their parents. Between 1890 and 1922 the number of students enrolled in public high schools grew dramatically (see table). And more than ever before, education was becoming the key to success. The creation of new white-collar occupations in the growing service industries helped to stem the downward mobility that resulted when mechanization pushed skilled workers out of their crafts. Yet the United States was not a meritocracy—a society in which the most able individuals rise to the top. The inequality that had pervaded earlier eras remained. A caste system still prevailed: race and sex, more than any other factors, determined one's status. Religion and ethnicity also influenced social relations.

Moreover, the new material abundance and consumerism seemed to make places, things, and experiences too similar. Some people mourned for the more individualistic, self-reliant (and partly mythical) past, when Americans had had to pay more attention to summer heat and winter cold, when they had had to make things for themselves. Critics charged that the new society was creating products and demands that were unnecessary and even harmful. But it was too late to turn back. Americans had set their course toward a future that promised prosperity and comfort.

THE QUEST FOR CONVENIENCE

One of the most representative agents of the revolution in American lifestyles at the end of the nineteenth century was the toilet. The chain-pull, washdown water closet, invented in England around 1870, was adopted in the United States in the 1880s. Shortly after 1900 the flush toilet was developed; thanks to mass production of enamel-coated fixtures, it soon became common in American homes and buildings.

The indoor toilet, suddenly cheaper and easier to install, brought about a shift in habits and attitudes. In the past, people had believed there was no danger in disposing of human waste on or below the ground; only luxury hotels and estates had private bathrooms. By the 1880s, however, acceptance of the germ theory of disease had raised fears about human pollution as a source of infection and water contamination. Much more rapidly than Europeans did, Americans combined a desire for cleanliness with an urge for convenience, and water closets became common, especially in middle-class urban houses. Bodily functions took on a more unpleasant image, and the home bathroom became a place of utmost privacy. Also, the toilet plus the private bathtub gave Americans new ways to use—and waste—water. This process can be seen as part of a broader change that accompanied industrialization and mass production: the democratization of convenience.

The tin can also altered lifestyles. Before the mid-nineteenth century, Americans ate most foods only in season. Drying, smoking, and salting could preserve meat for a short time, but the availability of fresh meat, like that of fresh milk, was very limited; there

A salmon canning factory in Oregon, 1904. Canning preserved food in sealed containers enabled processors to market meats, fruits, and vegetables that formerly had spoiled easily or had been available only at limited times of the year. Factories such as this one also provided expanded employment opportunities for women.   Library of Congress.

was no way to prevent spoilage. But around 1810, a French inventor developed the cooking-and-sealing process of canning. And in the 1850s, an American named Gail Borden developed a means of condensing and preserving milk. Canned goods and condensed milk became more common during the 1860s, but supplies remained low because cans had to be made by hand. By 1880, however, inventors had fashioned stamping and soldering machines that mass-produced cans from tin plate. Suddenly all kinds of foods could be preserved and bought at all times of the year. Americans had acquired still another means of overcoming nature— and littering the landscape.

Processed and Preserved Foods

Other trends and inventions helped make it possible for Americans of all classes to vary their daily diets. Growing urban populations created the demand that encouraged fruit and vegetable farmers to raise more produce. Railroad refrigerator cars enabled growers and meatpackers to ship perishables greater distances and to preserve them for longer periods. Thus by the 1890s, northern city dwellers could enjoy southern and western strawberries, grapes, and tomatoes, previously available for a month at most, for up to six months of the year. In addition, increased use of iceboxes enabled families to store perishables. An easy means of producing ice commercially had been invented in the 1870s, and by 1900 the nation had more than two thousand commercial ice plants, most of which made home deliveries. The icebox became a fixture in the up-to-date middle-class home, and remained so until the mechanized refrigerator replaced it in the 1920s and 1930s.

Even the working class had a more diversified diet. The lowest-income people still ate what their counterparts in previous eras had eaten: the cheapest foods, heavy with starches and carbohydrates. Southern textile workers, for example, ate corn mush and fatback almost every day. Unskilled urban breadwinners seldom could afford meat. Nevertheless, many families could take advantage of previously unavailable fruits, vegetables, and dairy products, to achieve more varied fare. Workers had to spend a high percentage of their income—almost half the main breadwinner's wages—on food. But they never suffered the severe malnutrition that plagued other developing nations.

Just as tin cans and iceboxes made many foods widely available, the sewing machine brought about a revolution in clothing. In the eighteenth century, **Ready-made Clothing** almost all the clothes Americans wore were made at home, and a person's social status was indicated largely by what he or she wore. Then in the 1850s the sewing machine (invented in Europe but developed by Americans Elias Howe, Jr., and Isaac M. Singer) came into use for clothing and shoe manufacture. Demand for uniforms during the Civil War boosted the ready-made clothing business, and by 1890 annual retail sales of mass-produced garments had reached $1.5 billion. Through mass production manufacturers could turn out good-quality garments at relatively low cost and develop standard sizes that fit different body shapes. By the turn of the century, only the poorest families could not buy "ready-to-wear" clothes, and tailors and seamstresses, once the originators of fashion, had largely been relegated to repair work.

The clothing revolution had a socially leveling effect. Rich and poor alike bought their clothes "off the rack." As one merchant crowed, "We have provided not alone abundant clothing at a moderate cost for all classes of citizens, but we have given them at the same time the style and character in dress that is essential to the self-respect of a free democratic people."

By 1900 mass-produced clothing had also enabled a large segment of the population to become concerned with style. Restrictive Victorian fashions still dominated women's clothing, but some of the most bur-densome features were beginning to be abandoned. Women's dress design now placed greater emphasis on comfort. Designers used less fabric; by the 1920s a dress required three yards of material instead of ten. Long sleeves and skirt hemlines receded, and high-boned collars disappeared. Petite was still the ideal, however: the most desirable waist measurement was 18 to 20 inches. (Corsets were big sellers at 79 cents apiece, and reformers complained that women often tried to squeeze into dresses, gloves, and shoes that were a size too small.) At the turn of the century, long hair tied at the back of the neck was the most popular style. But by the First World War, when many women worked in hospitals and factories, shorter, more manageable styles had become acceptable.

Men's clothes too became lighter-weight and more stylish. Before 1900, among the middle and more affluent working classes, a man would have had no more than two suits, one for Sundays and special occasions and one for everyday wear. No distinction was made between summer and winter suits. After 1900, however, manufacturers began to produce garments from fabrics of different weights. Men began wearing soft felt hats rather than stiff derbies. Soft collars and cuffs replaced stiff ones, and plain dark-blue serge gave way to softer shades and more intricate weaves. Workingmen's clothes did not change markedly: laborers still needed the most durable, least expensive overalls, shirts, and shoes. But even for those of modest means, clothing was becoming something to be bought rather than to be made and remade at home. It too had become a feature of mass consumerism.

Department stores and chain stores helped to create and serve this new world of consumerism. The great boom in department-store growth occurred between **Department and Chain Stores** 1865 and 1900, when companies like Macy's, Wanamaker's, Jordan Marsh, and Marshall Field became fixtures of metropolitan America. With their open displays of clothing, housewares, and furniture—all available in large quantities to anyone who had the purchase price—department stores effected a merchandising revolution. Not only did they offer wide variety; they added home deliveries, liberal exchange policies, and charge accounts. The Great Atlantic Tea Company, founded in 1859, became the first chain-store system. Renamed

In just a few decades American fashions changed dramatically. Dark, heavy fabrics (left) gave way to lighter, more colorful clothing (right, worn by Governor of New York Al Smith and his wife). Keyston-Mast Collection, University of California, Riverside.

the Great Atlantic and Pacific Tea Company in 1869 and known more familiarly as A&P, the firm's stores sold groceries on a cash-and-carry basis. By buying in volume, the chain could sell to the public at low prices. By 1912 there were almost five hundred A&P stores, and more were being built in communities of all sizes across the nation. Other chains, such as Woolworth's, grew rapidly during the same period.

Though the greatest expansion of chain stores did not occur until after 1920, large-volume, broad-variety food and department stores changed the nature of shopping long before then. They offered personal conveniences (like credit and deliveries) formerly available only at specialty shops that catered to the wealthy, and they provided such services in attractive, sometimes ornate settings. Not only could anyone buy the goods for sale, but anyone who wanted to could enter and just look. No longer were clothes, furniture, and even some foods stocked merely to meet a demand. Now they were displayed in large

quantities, to entice shoppers and create demand. Shopping and consuming had become a thoroughly enjoyable American pastime.

FAMILY LIFE

Though the overwhelming majority of Americans continued to live their lives within a family, this most basic of social institutions underwent considerable strain during the industrial era. As American society became more affluent and complex, it generated new institutions—schools, social clubs, political organizations, and others—that competed with the family to provide nurture, education, companionship, and security. Many popular and scholarly writers warned that rising divorce rates, the growing separation be-

This photograph, titled "The Stork's Visit," epitomizes the new middle-class nuclear family, surrounded by consumer goods and with parents exuding devotion toward their new baby. Library of Congress.

tween home and work, the entrance of large numbers of women into the work force, and loss of parental control over children spelled peril for home and family. Yet the family retained its fundamental usefulness as a cushion in a hard, uncertain world.

Throughout modern Western history, most people have lived in two overlapping kinds of basic units: the household and the family. A *household* is a residential unit, a group of related and/or unrelated people who live in the same abode. A *family* is a group of people related by kinship, some of whom typically live together. The distinction between household and family is important in describing how Americans lived in the late nineteenth and early twentieth centuries, since the two institutions followed different patterns.

Family and Household Structures

At the most elementary level, Americans between 1877 and 1920 grouped themselves in traditional ways. As in the past, the vast majority (75 to 80 percent) of American households consisted of *nuclear families*—usually a married couple with or without children and including no other relatives. About 15 to 20 percent of households consisted of *extended families*, which might include grandparents, grandchildren, aunts and uncles, in-laws, cousins, or combinations of such relatives. About 5 percent of the population lived alone. Despite slight variations from one ethnic, racial, or socioeconomic group to another, the prevailing pattern held relatively constant among all groups.

Several factors explain this pattern. Because the United States was a nation of immigrants, who tended to be young, the country had a very young population. In 1880 the median age was under twenty-one, and by 1920 it was still only twenty-five. (Presently it is almost thirty-one.) Moreover, fewer people than now lived to old age. In 1900 the death rate among people aged forty-five to sixty-four was over twice what it is today. As a result, there were relatively few old people: in 1900 only 4 percent of the population was sixty-five or older, compared with 12 percent today. Thus few families could form extended three-generation households. Fewer children than today knew their grandparents, and the experience of being a grandparent was rarer. Upward social mobility and migration separated many families, and the ideal of a home of one's own encouraged nuclear household organization.

The relative size of nuclear families did change over time, however. In the nineteenth century almost all of Europe and North America experienced a decline in birthrates. In the United States the decline began early in the 1800s and accelerated toward the end of the century. In 1880 the birthrate was 39.8 live births per 1,000 people; by 1900 it had dropped to 32.3, by 1920 to 27.7. The reasons for this decline remain unclear. The pattern seems to have been that women in the settled eastern areas of the country were ending childbearing at an earlier age—thus limiting the span during which they bore children—than were women in western areas. Possibly the greater availability of arable land in the West encouraged larger families; differences in a child's economic productivity may also have had an effect.

Declining Birthrates

On farms, where children could work at home or in the fields at an early age, a new child contributed a new set of hands to the family work force. But in the wage-based eastern economy, children could not contribute significantly to the family income for many years; a new child therefore represented another mouth to feed. Throughout the nation, as diet and medical care improved, infant mortality fell, and families did not have to have many children just to ensure that some would survive. It also appears that decisions to limit family size—by abstaining from sex during the wife's fertile period, or by means of other forms of contraception and abortion—resulted from people's growing consciousness that they could improve the quality of life for themselves and their children if their families were smaller than their ancestors' families.

Though fertility among blacks, immigrants, and rural dwellers was consistently higher than among white native urban dwellers, the birthrates of all groups fell. As a result, families with six or eight children became less common; three or four children became more usual. Thus the nuclear family tended to reach its maximum size and then to reduce faster than in earlier eras.

In spite of the predominance of the nuclear family, the household typically expanded and contracted over the lifetime of a given family. First, the size of the family fluctuated as children were born and later left home. Though there were many variations, both male and female children, especially in working-class families, often left home before they were twenty years old, usually to work. Second, the process of leaving home made for huge numbers of young people—and some older people—who lived as boarders and lodgers, especially in cities. Middle- and working-class families commonly took in boarders to help pay the rent or to occupy unused rooms vacated by grown children. Immigrants often lodged newly arrived relatives and fellow villagers until they could establish themselves. Some historians have estimated that there was a 50-percent chance that a city dweller at the end of the nineteenth century would either have lived as a boarder or have taken in boarders at some point during his or her lifetime.

Boarding

Housing reformers charged that boarding caused overcrowding and loss of privacy. Yet for those who boarded, the practice was highly useful. As one immigrant woman recalled:

We had four boarders and I had to cook for them. When I first came here I didn't want to do this because everybody want to have their own house. Well, I change my mind because everybody was doing this thing. That time some of the people that came from the other side didn't have no place to stay and we took some of the people in the house that we knew. . . . This is the way that everybody used to do it that time.

Boarding was a transitional stage for immigrants and young people who had left home, providing them with a quasi-family environment until they set up their own households. And it gave the household flexibility, bringing in extra income to meet its needs.

Some households also included extended family members who lived as quasi-boarders. Especially in communities where economic hardship or rapid growth made housing expensive or scarce, newlyweds tended to live with the husband's or wife's parents until they could afford a place of their own. Often a family would take in a widowed parent or unmarried sister or brother who would otherwise have had to live alone. For immigrants and migrants, the family served as a refuge in a strange new place. Having moved from the Old World to the New or from one region to another, they sought out relatives who had preceded them. A Russian Jewish woman prepared for emigration to the United States by writing to relatives in New York. "When I came off the ship," she recalled, "an uncle of mine was supposed to pick me up. . . . But I didn't live with this uncle because I had my mother's sister so I stayed with her."

Kinship, then, had important functions, especially for immigrants and others in need. At a time when welfare and service agencies were rare, the family continued to be the institution to which people could turn. Even when relatives did not live together, they often lived nearby and could help each other with childcare, meals, shopping, advice, consolation, and the like. Family members also obtained jobs for each other. Factory foremen usually had responsibility for hiring, and they often recruited

Importance of Kinship

new workers recommended by their employees. According to one new arrival, "After two days my brother took me to the shop he was working in and his boss saw me and he gave me the job." A woman who worked in an optical factory recalled, "My uncle was foreman there. . . . That was my first job. I worked there with my mother. . . . My sister worked there a while too."

The obligations of kinship, however, were not always welcome or even helpful. Immigrant families often put pressure on last-born children to stay at home and care for aging parents, a practice that stifled opportunities for education, marriage, and economic independence. As an aging Italian-American father confessed, "One of our daughters is an old maid [and] causes plenty of troubles. . . . It may be my fault because I always wished her to remain at home and not to marry for she was of great financial help." Tensions also developed when one relative felt another was not helping out enough. One woman, for example, complained that her brother-in-law "resented the fact that I saved my money in a bank instead of handing it over to him." Nevertheless, kinship, for better or worse, provided people a means of coping with the many stresses caused by an urban industrial society. Social and economic change did not dissolve family ties.

While the family remained resilient and adaptable, subtle but momentous changes began to occur in individual life patterns. Before the twentieth century, the stages of life were less distinct

Stages of Life than they are today, and generations blended into each other with relatively little separation. Childhood, for instance, was regarded as a period during which young people prepared for adulthood by assuming gradually more adult roles and responsibilities. The subdivisions of childhood—toddlers, schoolchildren, adolescents, and the like—were not nearly as clear-cut as they are today. Because few people lived past sixty-five or left work voluntarily and because homes for the elderly were rare, old people were not treated as separately as in later periods. Married couples had relatively large numbers of children born over a longer time span than is common among twentieth-century couples, so active parenthood occupied most of their adult lives. And older children, who often cared for younger

sisters and brothers, might begin parenting even before reaching adulthood.

By the turn of the century, demographic and social changes had altered these patterns. Decreasing fertility rates reduced the period of parental responsibility, so more middle-aged couples experienced an "empty-nest" stage when all their children had grown up and left home. Longer life expectancy and a tendency on the part of employers, especially in manufacturing, to force the retirement of aged workers further isolated the old from the young. At the same time, work became more specialized and education more formalized—especially after the passage of compulsory-school-attendance laws. Childhood and adolescence therefore became more distinct from adulthood. As a result of these and other trends (including the lower fertility rate, which gave people fewer sisters and brothers to relate to), Americans became more age- and peer-conscious. People's roles in school, in the family, on the job, and in the community came to be defined by age as much as by any other characteristic.

At the turn of the century, family life and its functions were both changing and holding firm. New institutions were assuming tasks formerly performed by the family. Schools were making education more of a community responsibility. Employment agencies, personnel offices, labor unions, and legislatures were beginning to take responsibility for employee recruitment and job security. And age-based peer groups were exerting greater influence over people's values and activities. In addition, migration and a soaring divorce rate seemed to be splitting families apart: 19,633 divorces were granted in the United States in 1880; by 1920, that number had grown to 167,105. Yet in the face of these changes, the family remained a resilient institution. Households and families adjusted, sometimes from one year to the next, by expanding and contracting to meet temporary needs. And kinship remained a dependable, though not always appreciated, institution. In the early 1900s, popular and scholarly writers were predicting the decline of the family just as they are today. But for the majority of people, family life was vital. "As I grew up, living conditions were a bit crowded," one woman reminisced, "but no one minded because we were a family [and we were] thankful we all lived together."

The New Leisure and Mass Culture

On December 2, 1889, as hundreds of workers paraded through Worcester, Massachusetts, in support of shorter working hours, a group of carpenters hoisted a banner that proclaimed, "Eight Hours for Work, Eight Hours for Rest, Eight Hours for What We Will." That last phrase, "for What We Will," was significant, for it marked recognition of a special segment of everyday life that belonged to the individual. Increasingly, leisure activities filled this time segment, among working classes as well as middle and upper classes.

Increase in Leisure Time

For a nation nurtured on a frontier tradition of hard work and distaste for wasted time, the leisure-time revolution of the late nineteenth century marked a dramatic shift. American inventors and tinkerers had always tried to create labor-saving devices, but not until the late nineteenth century did the effects of technological development become truly time-saving. Mechanization and assembly-line production helped to reduce the average workweek for manufacturing workers from sixty-six hours in 1860 to sixty in 1890 and forty-seven in 1920. These reductions not only meant shorter workdays but also freer weekends. Middle-class white-collar workers in the cities spent eight to ten hours a day on the job and often worked only half a day or not at all on weekends. Even on farms, mechanization helped to expand free time. To be sure, many had no time for leisure; thousands still spent twelve- or fourteen-hour shifts in steel mills and sweatshops. Nevertheless, more Americans began to have time for a variety of diversions, and for the first time a substantial segment of the economy began providing for—and profiting from—leisure. By the early 1900s, many Americans were enmeshed in the business of play.

After the Civil War, amusement became an organized activity like production and consumption. The vanguard of this trend was sports. Formerly a fashionable indulgence of the genteel class, organized sports quickly became the most popular pastime of all classes, attracting huge numbers of participants and spectators. Even those who could not play or watch became involved by reading about sports in the newspapers.

Baseball

The first and most popular organized sport was baseball. Having evolved out of older bat, ball, and base-circling games, baseball was formalized in 1845 when a group of wealthy New Yorkers organized the Knickerbocker Club and codified the rules of the game. By 1860 there were at least fifty baseball clubs, and pick-up games were played on city lots and rural fields across the nation. In 1869 a professional club, the Cincinnati Red Stockings, went on a national tour, and several other clubs quickly followed suit. The National League of Professional Baseball Clubs, founded in 1876, gave the sport a more stable, businesslike structure. By the 1880s, professional baseball was a big business: in 1887, for example, over 51,000 people paid to watch a championship series between St. Louis and Detroit. In 1903, the National League and competing American League (formed in 1901) began a World Series between their championship teams (the Boston Red Socks beat the Pittsburgh Pirates in that first series), further entrenching baseball as the national pastime.

Croquet and Cycling

Baseball appealed mostly to men. But croquet, which also swept the nation after the Civil War, attracted both sexes. Across the country, middle- and upper-class people held croquet parties and even rigged wickets with candles for night games. In an era when the removal of work from the home had begun separating men and women, croquet renewed the opportunity for social contact between the sexes.

Bicycling achieved a popularity rivaling that of baseball—especially after 1885, when the cumbersome velocipede, with its huge front wheel and tall seat, gave way to the safety bicycle with pneumatic tires and wheels of identical size. By 1900 Americans owned over 10 million bicycles, and cycling clubs such as the League of American Wheelmen were pressing state and local governments to build more paved roads. One journal boasted that cycling cured dyspepsia, headaches, insomnia, and sciatica, and

In 1883, the New York Giants began playing their baseball games in a converted six-thousand-seat polo stadium. Within a few years, professional baseball had become so popular that crowds overflowed the stands and had to sit in the outfield. In 1891, a new Polo Grounds was built, enabling the Giants to set an attendance record of over a million fans three years later. Baseball had indeed become the national pastime. Library of Congress.

gave "a vigorous tone to the whole system." Like croquet, bicycling brought men and women together. Especially on the bicycle-built-for-two, it provided a combination of courtship with exercise. Moreover, the bicycle played an influential role in freeing women from the constraints of Victorian fashions. In order to ride bikes, even the dropped-frame female models, women had to wear divided skirts and simple undergarments. Gradually the freer styles of cycling costumes began to have an influence on the style of everyday fashions. As the 1900 census declared, "Few articles . . . have created so great a revolution in social conditions as the bicycle."

Tennis and golf won enthusiasts of both sexes but remained pastimes of the wealthy. Played mostly at private clubs, these sports lacked baseball's team competition and cycling's informality. American football also began as a sport for people of high social rank. At first mainly an intercollegiate sport, football attracted mostly players and spectators wealthy enough to have access to higher education. By the end of the century, however, football was attracting a broader class of supporters. The 1893 Princeton-Yale game drew fifty thousand spectators, and informal football games were being played in the yards and playgrounds of many communities throughout the country.

Football

At the same time, college football was becoming

a national scandal because of its violence and use of "tramp athletes," nonstudents whom colleges hired to play on their teams. Critics charged that football mirrored the worst features of American society. An editor of the *Nation* complained in 1890 that "the spirit of the American youth, as of the American man, is to win, to 'get there,' by fair means or foul; and the lack of moral scruple which pervades the struggles of the business world meets with temptations equally irresistible in the miniature contests of the football field." The scandals climaxed in 1905, when 18 football players were killed and over 150 seriously injured. President Theodore Roosevelt, a strong advocate of athletics, convened a White House conference to discuss ways of eliminating brutality and foul play. The conference founded the Intercollegiate Athletic Association (renamed the National College Athletic Association in 1910) to police college sports. In 1906 the association altered the rules of football to make it less violent and more open. The new rules extended the distance to be gained by the first down from 5 to 10 yards, legalized the forward pass, and tightened player eligibility requirements.

As more women attended college, they began to pursue other forms of physical activity besides croquet, riding, and bicycling. Believing that in order to succeed intellectually they needed to be active and healthy, college women participated in a variety of sports, such as rowing, track, and swimming. Eventually basketball became the most popular sport among college women. Invented in 1891 as a winter sport for men, basketball was given women's rules (that limited dribbling and running and encouraged passing) by Senda Berenson of Smith College in the 1890s, and intercollegiate games became common across the country.

The rise of American show business paralleled the rise of sports, and similarly became a mode of leisure created by and for the common people. Circuses—

Circuses

traveling shows of acrobats and animals—had existed since the 1820s. But after the Civil War, railroads enabled circuses to reach more of the country, and the popularity of the big show increased enormously.

Circuses offered two main attractions: so-called freaks of nature, both human and animal, and the temptation and conquest of death. More important, however, was the sheer astonishment aroused by the trapeze artists, lion tamers, high-wire artists, acrobats, and clowns. Writer Hamlin Garland captured the circus's effect on a thousand towns and villages:

> From the time the "advance man" flung his highly colored posters over the fence till the coming of the glorious day, we thought of little else. . . . It was our brief season of imaginative life. In one day—in a part of one day—we gained a thousand new conceptions of the world and of human nature. It was the embodiment of all that was skillful and beautiful in human action. . . . It gave us something to talk about.

Several branches of American show business matured with the growth of cities. Popular drama, musical comedy, and vaudeville all gave Americans a chance

Popular Drama and Musical Comedy

to escape from the harsh realities of urban-industrial life into melodrama, adventure, and comedy. The plots were simple, the heroes and villains instantly recognizable. For urbanized people increasingly distant from the frontier, popular plays brought to life the mythical Wild West and Old South through stories of Davy Crockett, Buffalo Bill, and Civil War romances. Virtue, honor, and justice always triumphed in melodramas such as *Uncle Tom's Cabin* and *The Old Homestead,* reinforcing the popular belief that even in an uncertain and disillusioning world, goodness would nevertheless prevail.

Musical comedies raised audiences' spirits with song, humor, and dance. American musical comedy grew out of the lavishly costumed operettas popular in Europe. By introducing American themes (often involving ethnic groups), folksy humor, and catchy tunes and dances, these shows launched the nation's most popular songs and entertainers. George M. Cohan, born into an Irish family of vaudeville entertainers, became the master of American musical comedy after the turn of the century. Drawing on urbanism, patriotism, and traditional values in songs like "Yankee Doodle Boy" and "You're a Grand Old Flag," Cohan helped to reinforce national morale during the First World War. Comic opera too became a fad, and the talented, beautiful, dignified Lillian Russell its most admired performer. The first American comic operas were weak imitations of European musicals, but by the early 1900s, composers like Victor Herbert were writing for American audiences. Shortly

Lavish musical reviews and vaudeville shows became a very popular form of American entertainment. Filled with song, dance, and comedy, these performances reflected the new scale and organization of the American economy and culture.   Culver Pictures.

thereafter Jerome Kern began to write more sophisticated musicals, and American musical comedy came into its own.

The French term *vaudeville* first referred to light drama with musical interludes, but in the United States vaudeville became a unique entertainment form.

Vaudeville Originally staged by saloonkeepers to attract customers, vaudeville variety shows were developed by skilled promoters who used the term to lend respectability to a once-disreputable entertainment. Vaudeville was probably the most popular entertainment in early-twentieth-century America because its variety made it attractive to mass audiences. Shows included magic and animal acts, juggling, stunts, comedy (especially

ethnic humor), and song and dance. Around 1900, the number of vaudeville theaters and troupes skyrocketed. Fostered by sharp promoters who did for entertainment what Edison and Ford did for technology, vaudeville quickly became big business. The most famous promoter, Florenz Ziegfeld, brilliantly packaged popular entertainment in a stylish format—the Ziegfeld follies—and gave the nation a new model of femininity, the Ziegfeld Girl, whose graceful dancing and alluring costumes were meant to suggest a haunting sensuality.

Show business provided new economic opportunities for women, blacks, and immigrants, but also indulged in stereotyping and exploitation. Lillian Russell, vaudeville singer and comedienne Fanny Brice, and burlesque queen Eva Tanguay attracted intensely loyal fans, commanded handsome fees, and won respect for their genuine talents. In contrast to the demure Victorian female, they conveyed pluck and creativity. There was something both shocking and refreshingly confident about Eva Tanguay when she sang earthy songs like "I Want Someone to Go Wild with Me," "It's All Been Done Before But Not the Way I Do It," and her theme song "I Don't Care." But lesser female performers were often exploited by male promoters and theater owners, many of whom wanted only to titillate the public with the sight of scantily clad women.

Before the 1890s, the only form of entertainment open to black performers was the minstrel show. By century's end, however, minstrel shows had given

Blacks and Immigrants in Vaudeville

way to more sophisticated musicals, and blacks had begun to break into vaudeville. As stage sets shifted from the plantation to the city, the music shifted from folk tunes to ragtime. Pandering to the prejudice of white audiences, composers and performers of both races ridiculed blacks. The popularity of songs like "He's Just a Little Nigger, But He's Mine All Mine," and "You May Be a Hawaiian on Old Broadway, But You're Just Another Nigger to Me" is evidence that blacks on the stage suffered in the same way they did elsewhere in society. Even Burt Williams, a highly paid black comedian and dancer who was one of the era's most talented performers, achieved his tormented success mainly by playing the stereotypical roles of darky and dandy.

Much of the uniqueness of American mass entertainment came from its ethnic flavor. Indeed, immigrants were the core of American show business. Vaudeville particularly drew on and embellished ethnic humor, exaggerating its characters' dialects and other national traits. Though countless skits and songs reinforced ethnic stereotypes and made fun of ethnic groups, such distortions were more self-conscious and sympathetic than those directed at blacks. Ethnic humor often focused on the difficulties immigrants faced. A typical scene involving Italians, for example, would revolve around a character's uncertain grasp of English, which caused him to confuse *mayor* with *mare, diploma* with *the plumber,* and *pallbearer* with *polar bear.* Such scenes allowed audiences to laugh at the human condition and reminded them that,

deep down, all people—at least white people—were the same. Blacks, however, were never assumed to share the same hopes and frustrations as whites.

Shortly after 1900, live entertainment began to yield to an even more accessible form of amusement: moving pictures. Perfected by Thomas Edison in the

Movies

late 1880s, movies began as slot-machine peepshows in penny arcades and billiard parlors. Eventually images were projected onto a screen so large audiences could view them, and a new medium was born. At first, the subject matter of films was unimportant; it was enough merely to awe viewers with moving pictures of speeding trains, galloping horses, and writhing belly dancers.

Producers soon discovered, however, that a film could tell a story—and tell it with flair. By 1910 motion pictures had become an art form, thanks to creative directors like D. W. Griffith. Griffith's most famous work, *The Birth of a Nation* (1915), an epic film about the Civil War and Reconstruction, fanned racial prejudice by depicting blacks as threatening white moral values; its exaltation of the Ku Klux Klan also helped to revive the hooded empire. But the film's innovative techniques—close-ups, fade-outs, and battle scenes—gave viewers heightened drama and excitement. From the beginning, movies were popular among all classes (admission usually cost a nickel), and audiences idolized such film stars as Mary Pickford, Lillian Gish, and Charlie Chaplin with a passion no stage performer ever enjoyed.

The still camera, modernized by inventor George Eastman, enabled ordinary people to make their own photographic images; and the phonograph, another of Edison's inventions, made possible musical performances at home. The spread of movies, photography, and phonograph records meant that access to live performances no longer limited people's exposure to art and entertainment. Technology had dissolved the uniqueness of experience; now it was possible to mass-produce sound and images. Entertainment had become more widely available than ever before.

To some extent, the new amusements and pastimes had a homogenizing influence, bringing together disparate ethnic and social groups into a common experience. Parks, ball fields, vaudeville shows, and movies were designed for and appealed to everyone; they were nonsectarian and apolitical. Yet various

By the end of the nineteenth century, recreation of all sorts became a value of, and attainable by, almost all classes for the first time in American history. Note the free-spirited relaxation of these bathers on a Coney Island beach; their poses contrast markedly with the stiff formality of people on city streets and the serious concentration of people at work. Library of Congress.

groups adopted leisure institutions in their own way. Even though promoters and entrepreneurs were largely responsible for the spread of amusements, consumers often used them to reinforce their own cultural habits. For example, in some communities working-class immigrant groups used parks and amusement parks as locations for traditional family and ethnic gatherings. Much to the dismay of reformers who hoped that recreation would help assimilate newcomers and teach them habits of restraint, immigrants used picnics and Fourth of July celebrations as occasions for boisterous drinking and sometimes violent behavior. Many early movies intentionally had working-class characters and settings (Charlie Chaplin's films, for instance), reflecting the tastes of their audiences. Thus as Americans learned to play, their leisure—like their work and politics—was shaped by pluralistic forces.

THE TRANSFORMATION OF MASS COMMUNICATIONS

With so many new things to do and buy, how did Americans decide what they wanted? Two new types of communication influenced consumer tastes and mass opinion. Modern advertising molded people's needs and consumption patterns; and popular journalism spread mass culture throughout the country.

A society of scarcity does not need advertising. When demand exceeds the supply of goods and ser-

vices, producers have no trouble selling what they
market. But in a society of abun-
Advertising dance such as industrial America,
supply frequently outstrips demand.
Thus a way of creating or increasing demand becomes
necessary. Advertising had existed in the United
States long before the late nineteenth century, but
it took on a new scale and function in the decades
before 1900. In 1865 about $9.5 million was spent
on advertising; by 1900 the sum had reached $95
million, and by 1919 nearly $500 million.

The American salesperson's function has traditionally been to respond to a particular need and to
convince the customer that a particular product—
an insurance policy, a suit of clothes, a home appliance—is uniquely suited to fill that need. Advertisers, on the other hand, aim to *invent* a demand
by convincing whole groups that everyone in that
group should buy a particular product—a brand of
cigarettes, a particular cosmetic, a certain company's
canned foods. Indeed, the growth in the late nineteenth century of large companies that mass-produced
consumer goods gave advertisers the task of creating
"consumption communities"—bodies of consumers
loyal to a particular brand name.

In 1881, Congress passed a federal trademark law
enabling producers to register and protect brand names.
Thousands of companies eventually did so, creating
such well-known products as Hires Root Beer, Carter's
Little Liver Pills, Uneeda Biscuits, Grape-Nuts, and
countless others. Advertising agencies—a new service
industry pioneered by N. W. Ayer & Son of Philadelphia—offered expert advice to companies that
wished to cultivate brand loyalty. By the turn of the
century, advertising techniques had been perfected
to such an extent that the French composer Jacques
Offenbach observed, "Decidedly the American advertising men play upon the human mind as a musician
plays on his piano."

The major vehicle for advertising was the newspaper.
Around the mid-nineteenth century, publishers began
to pursue greater revenues from advertising by selling
more ad space, especially to big urban department
stores. In 1879 Wanamaker's placed the first full-
page ad, and at about the same time newspapers
began to allow advertisers to print pictures of products.
Such attention-getting techniques transformed advertising into news. More than ever before, people

*As producers exerted themselves to try to lure consumers,
advertising became more elaborate, often using personal images and suggestive themes to sell a product. More than ever
before, marketing had the function of creating a demand
rather than serving a demand that already existed.   Library
of Congress.*

read the newspapers to find out what was for sale as
well as what was happening.

Just as advertising became news, news became a
form of advertising, or at least of publicity. Canny
publishers made people crave news just as they craved
amusements and consumer goods. City life and the
increase in leisure time seemed to nurture a fascination
with the sensational, and from the 1880s onward
popular newspapers increasingly whetted and catered
to that desire.

Joseph Pulitzer, a Hungarian immigrant who bought
the *New York World* in 1883, pioneered the development of journalism as a branch of mass culture.
Believing that newspapers should be "dedicated to
the cause of the people rather than
Yellow to that of the purse potentates,"
Journalism Pulitzer filled the *World* with stories

A newsstand beneath an elevated railway station displays a large variety of popular magazines and newspapers. By the early 1900s these publications were read by millions daily—for their advertisements as well as for their news and sports. Ford Archives.

of disasters, crimes, and scandals. Sensational headlines, set in large bold type like that of advertisements, screamed from every page. Pulitzer's journalists not only reported the news but sought it out—and sometimes even created it. *World* reporter Nellie Bly (real name Elizabeth Cochrane) faked her way into an insane asylum and wrote a sensational exposé of the sordid conditions she found. Other reporters staged stunts and sought out heart-rending human-interest stories. Pulitzer also popularized the comics, and the yellow ink they were printed in gave his emphasis on the sensational the nickname "yellow journalism."

Pulitzer's strategy was immensely successful. In one year he increased the *World's* daily circulation from 20,000 to 100,000, and by the late 1890s it had reached 1 million. Soon other publishers, such as William Randolph Hearst (who bought the *New York Journal* in 1895 and started an empire of mass-circulation newspapers), adopted Pulitzer's techniques. Yellow journalism became a nationwide phenomenon, enhancing interest in bizarre aspects of the human condition and kindling sentiments for reform.

Pulitzer and his rivals fanned popular interest even further by emphasizing sports and women's news. Newspapers had always reported on sporting events, but the yellow-journalism papers gave such stories far greater prominence by printing separate, expanded sports sections. Such sections did more than anything else to promote sports as a leisure-time attraction. Sports news became a new addiction, recreating a particular game's drama through narrative and statistics. And at the same time they expanded sports news, mostly for male readers, newspapers were adding more women's news. A special section devoted to household tips, fashion, decorum, and women's-club news captured the interest of female readers. Like crime and disaster stories, sports and women's sections helped to make the news a mass commodity.

By the early twentieth century, the communications media, like the mass consumption of goods, were becoming commonplace. Alongside newspapers, mass-circulation magazines were overshadowing the expensive elitist journals of earlier eras. Publications like *McClure's*, the *Saturday Evening Post*, and *Ladies' Home Journal* offered human-interest stories, muck-raking exposés (see pages 589–590), titillating fiction, and eye-catching advertisements to a growing mass market. And the total number of books published more than quadrupled between 1880 and 1917. This rising popular consumption of news and books reflected a growing literacy rate. Between 1870 and 1920, the proportion of Americans aged ten or over who could not read or write fell from 20 percent to 6 percent.

Other forms of communication were also expanding. In 1891 there were only 0.3 telephones per 100 people in this country; by 1901 the number had grown to 2.1, and by 1921 it had swelled to 12.6. In 1900 Americans used 4 billion postage stamps; in 1922 they used 14.3 billion stamps. Little wonder, then, that the term *community* took on new dimensions, as people used the media, the mail, and the telephone to extend their horizons far beyond their place of residence. More than ever before, people in different parts of the country knew about and discussed the same staples of mass culture, whether it was a sensational murder, a sex scandal, or the fortunes of a particular entertainer or athlete. America was becoming a mass society.

POPULAR LITERATURE

The same society that celebrated the machine also idolized Tarzan the Ape Man. American culture has long focused one eye on an increasingly complex technological future while casting the other at a sentimentalized, simpler past. These two dispositions shared the popular mind between 1877 and 1920. When modern wonders like telephones, high-speed printing presses, phonographs, and cameras made information and entertainment more accessible, people demanded diversions that reaffirmed the traditional values of optimism, individualism, and freedom. Thus in 1914, just when they were beginning to fully appreciate automobiles, movies, and electricity, Americans made Edgar Rice Burroughs's *Tarzan of the Apes* a best seller.

Popular fiction writers in tune with the times concentrated on the sensational. Such efforts were not exactly new; since the 1840s, low-priced, paperbound adventure novels had circulatd widely among the literate public.

Dime Novels

After the Civil War such books, called dime novels, became the most widely read variety of American literature, especially among youths. As one man recalled, "I read them at every chance; so did every normal boy of my acquaintance. . . . We swapped them on the basis of two old volumes for every new one; we maintained a clandestine circulating library system which had its branch offices in every stableloft in our part of town." The principal publisher of dime novels was the firm Beadle and Adams, which issued over thirteen hundred titles in the three decades before it went out of business in 1897. Popular magazines like *Tip Top Weekly*, which serialized adventure stories, attracted hundreds of thousands of readers.

These adventure publications offered three types of stories. The first evoked the Wild West for a population that was seeing the frontier fade into the past. Intertwining fact and fiction, writers like Zane Grey wove adventure stories around famous folk heroes like Buffalo Bill Cody, the Lone Ranger, and Wild Bill Hickok. During the 1880s, however, many authors, recognizing the lure and growing impact of city life, began to give their tales urban settings and themes. Detective thrillers became the leading type of popular urban fiction, and hard-nosed, wily characters like Old Cap Collins and Nick Carter captivated readers of various ages. Just before the end of the century, science fiction and superheroes came to the fore. Influenced by the marvels of new scientific discoveries, such works as the Tom Swift series described

Frank Merriwell, the fictional hero of hundreds of sports and adventure stories, was a popular character model for young men. In this story, first published in Tip Top Weekly, *an unscrupulous sportsman tries to bribe Frank into teaching him his secret pitch, the "double shoot." Frank not only resists the temptation but teaches a moral lesson in the process. Culver Pictures.*

spaceships, gravity nullifiers, and other inventions that surpassed even Edison's imagination.

One popular writer, Horatio Alger, moved beyond the fantasies of dime novels and offered his readers a formula for contending with new social and economic forces. A failed Unitarian clergyman, Alger began writing boys' stories in the 1860s, producing some 130 titles over the next three decades. As Alger's titles attest, each emphasizes the virtues of self-reliance and hard work: *Work and Win, Do and Dare, Struggling Upward, Rise from the Ranks.*

Moral Messages of Popular Fiction

Alger's heroes begin their lives in poverty and call on ambition, honesty, courage, thrift, and luck to overcome some obstacle and achieve success. But his message was more than an exhortation to morality and frugality. The moral of Alger's stories was that success came to those who were not only virtuous but alert enough to capitalize on a lucky break. Thus Ragged Dick, the hero of Alger's first novel, is clean, honest, and polite, but his opportunity to escape poverty arrives when he rescues the drowning child of a banker. The hero of *Bound to Rise* ministers to a lonely old man who repays him with a bundle of real estate deeds. Thus while the main theme emphasized virtue as the means to overcome poverty, Alger also made his characters models of American resourcefulness.

Just before Alger's death in 1899, one of America's most popular superheroes, Frank Merriwell, was created by Gilbert Patten (using the pen name of Burt Standish), a writer of hack fiction since his teens. Frank Merriwell's adventures had a common theme that accorded with the way many Americans liked to think of themselves and their nation: he attempted and accomplished the impossible. Merriwell's name symbolized American virtues: according to Patten, "I took the three qualities I most wanted him to represent—frank and merry in nature, well in body and mind—and made the name Frank Merriwell."

In a series of fast-paced adventures, Merriwell provided youthful readers with one of the first character models in popular fiction. Whether performing amazing athletic feats or daring rescues, he was a picture of refinement and valor who taught by example, not by preaching. In one story, Frank knocks down a thug hired to break his arm before a big game. Graciously, Frank helps him to his feet and befriends him. The thug exclaims, "Gee, I don't know w'y it is, but jes' bein' wid youse makes me want ter do de square t'ing." Patten wrote 208 Merriwell novels, with titles such as *Frank Merriwell's Trip West, Frank Merriwell at Yale, Frank Merriwell's Air Voyage,* and *Frank Merriwell on Wall Street.*

Young women found escape and inspiration in sentimental tales about growing up and about animals. One of the most widely read was Louisa May Alcott's *Little Women,* published in two parts in 1868 and 1869. This novel, which eventually sold over 2 million copies, recreated the domestic delights and moral trials of four girls based on Alcott and her sisters. A generation later, Gene Stratton-Porter's romantic novels about animals, like *Freckles* (1904) and *Laddie* (1913), became best sellers. Others in the same vein were Margaret Sidney's *Five Little Peppers* (1880), Anna Sewell's *Black Beauty* (1890), Kate Douglas Wiggins's *Rebecca of Sunnybrook Farm* (1903), and Lucy M. Montgomery's *Anne of Green Gables* (1908).

Popular literature for adults also oozed sentimentality. The best-selling titles of the late nineteenth century included Marie Corelli's *Thelma* (1887) and Charles Majors's *When Knighthood Was in Flower* (1898)—both romances about chivalry and honor— and *Ben Hur* (1880), General Lew Wallace's powerful religious melodrama set in the Roman Empire. Not since *Uncle Tom's Cabin* had a book captured as much attention as *Ben Hur*, which sold 2 million copies by 1933. Self-help and inspiration, both perennial themes in American popular literature, also burgeoned. The style pioneered by *Poor Richard's Almanac* and McGuffey's readers was developed in such works as Samuel Smiles's *Self-Help* (1860), *Character* (1871), *Thrift* (1875), and *Duty* (1880); Andrew Carnegie's *Gospel of Wealth* (1901); and Russell Conwell's published sermon "Acres of Diamonds" (see pages 521–522).

While some popular writers focused on escapism, others were trying to introduce realism into romance. During the 1870s and 1880s, a number of "local-color" writers began producing works

Local Colorists that depicted the people and environment of a particular region more realistically. This movement was largely centered in the South, whose writers felt compelled to rebuild the region's national image. Works by Joel Chandler Harris, who created the popular Uncle Remus stories; Mary Noailles Murfree, who located her tales in Appalachia; and George Washington Cable, who captured the aura of exotic New Orleans, all reproduced authentic characters and dialects. The regional writers of the Far West and Midwest included Bret Harte, who spun tales about the California mining experience; Edward Eggleston, who recreated the life of his native southern Indiana; and Constance Fenimore Woolson, who wrote about the lumbering and fur-trading districts of the Great Lakes. Each of these writers used authentic manners and ways of speech to depict a romantic, rustic past.

One local colorist, Mark Twain (the pen name of Samuel Clemens), moved beyond romance and adventure, and in doing so won recognition from both intellectuals and the masses. A

Literary Classics westerner who had grown up in Hannibal, Missouri, Twain worked as a river pilot on the Mississippi and traveled through the mining towns of the Far West. Though he wrote several works about Europe, such as *Innocents Abroad* (1869) and *A Connecticut Yankee at King Arthur's Court* (1889), he was best known for his books about the American West: *Tom Sawyer* (1876), *Life on the Mississippi* (1883), and *Huckleberry Finn* (1884). These antisentimental novels were realistic portrayals of western life and of human weakness. Twain was sensitive to both the comic and the tragic sides of life, and his writing reflected the dynamic energy and materialism of his era. He once wrote that "my books are mainly autobiographies," and his most famous character, Huck Finn, seemed to represent the daring, hypocrisy, and amiability of both Twain and his nation.

A number of Twain's contemporaries shunned the falseness of escape writing and focused instead on the moral tests life holds. Realists like William Dean Howells, Edith Wharton, and Henry James wrote chiefly about upper-class Americans (James usually wrote about Americans in Europe), but other realists examined the lives of more ordinary folk and in so doing opened new literary vistas. These writers, sometimes called naturalists, often viewed life in terms of the survival of the fittest; they portrayed ruthless struggles for life and power in frank detail. Among the naturalists were Stephen Crane, whose *Maggie: A Girl of the Streets* (1893) shocked readers with its candid description of slum life and sexual immorality; Kate Chopin, who in her novel *The Awakening* (1899) also addressed sensitive topics of sexuality and divorce; Hamlin Garland, whose *Main Traveled Roads* (1891) portrayed a depressing side of rural America, Frank Norris, whose *McTeague* (1899) graphically depicted the brutality of human greed; Jack London, whose stories of the West and Northwest portrayed violence among humans and animals; and Theodore Dreiser, whose *Sister Carrie* (1900) showed that people do not always suffer for their wrongdoings.

The escapism of popular fiction and the realism of serious fiction, though seemingly at odds, offered others had known. The obstacles to success were not simple, and making one's way in the world required technological skills, organizational know-how, and a lot of capital. More sophisticated and more familiar with the possibilities of a consumption-oriented society, readers craved more from their heroes, such as prowess in the new mass cult of sports (Merriwell), conquest of science (Tom Swift), or abilities to commune with nature (Gene Stratton-Porter's characters).

Meanwhile serious authors, striving to recreate realistically what they saw around them, examined the flaws of progress. Whereas virtue still triumphed in popular and juvenile literature, naturalist writers saw that the new demands the industrial age placed on individuals threatened traditional American values of family, practicality, and moral restraint. The challenges of adjusting to a growing emphasis on consumption would become a major theme of twentieth-century American history.

SUGGESTIONS FOR FURTHER READING

Living Standards and New Conveniences

Daniel J. Boorstin, *The Americans: The Democratic Experience* (1973); James H. Collins, *The Story of Canned Foods* (1924); Richard O. Cummings, *The American and His Food* (1940); Boris Emmet and J. E. Jeuck, *Catalogues and Counters: History of Sears, Roebuck and Company* (1950); *Historical Statistics of the United States*, 2 vols., (1976); T. J. Jackson Lears and Richard W. Fox, eds., *The Culture of Consumption* (1983); Godfrey M. Lebhar, *Chain Stores in America* (1962); Clarence D. Long, *Wages and Earnings in the United States, 1860–1890* (1960); H. Pasadermadjian, *The Department Store* (1954); Peter R. Shergold, *Working Class Life: The "American Standard" in Comparative Perspective, 1899–1913* (1982); Lawrence Wright, *Clean and Decent* (1960).

Family and Individual Life Cycles

W. Andrew Achenbaum, *Old Age in the New Land* (1979); John E. Bodnar *et al.*, *Lives of Their Own: Blacks, Italians, and Poles in Pittsburgh, 1900–1960* (1982); Carl N. Degler, *At Odds: Women and the Family in America* (1980); Michael

similar commentaries on the American society of the early twentieth century. It was no coincidence that Frank Merriwell replaced Horatio Alger's heroes in popular fiction around 1900: by then Americans knew that it took more than honesty, energy, and a timely rescue to become rich. Numberless little-noticed revolutions had transformed the world that Alger and

Gordon, ed., *The American Family in Social-Historical Perspective*, 3rd ed. (1983); Carole Haber, *Beyond Sixty-five: Dilemmas of Old Age in America's Past* (1983); Tamara K. Hareven, *Family Time and Industrial Time: The Relationship Between the Family and Work in a New England Industrial Community* (1981); Tamara K. Hareven, ed., *Transitions: The Family and Life Course in Historical Perspective* (1978); Tamara K. Hareven and Maris Vinovskis, eds., *Family and Population in Nineteenth Century America* (1978); Joseph Kett, *Rites of Passage: Adolescence in America* (1979); David J. Pivar, *Purity Crusade: Sexual Morality and Social Control, 1868–1900* (1973); Richard Sennett, *Families Against the City* (1970); Virginia Yans-McLaughlin, *Family and Community: Italian Immigrants in Buffalo* (1977).

Mass Entertainment and Leisure

Robert Clyde Allen, *Vaudeville and Film, 1895–1915: A Study in Media Interaction* (1977); Gunther Barth, *City People* (1980); Allison Danzig, *History of American Football* (1956); Foster R. Dulles, *America Learns to Play* (1966); Roland Gelatt, *The Fabulous Phonograph* (1965); John F. Kasson, *Amusing the Million: Coney Island at the Turn of the Century* (1978); John A. Lucas and Ronald Smith, *Saga of American Sport* (1978); Donald J. Mrozek, *Sport and American Mentality, 1880–1910* (1983); Joseph A. Musselman, *Music in the Cultured Generation: A Social History of Music in America, 1870–1900* (1971); Beaumont Newhall, *The History of Photography*, rev. ed. (1964); Benjamin G. Rader, *American Sports* (1983); Roy Rosenzweig, *Eight Hours for What We Will! Workers and Leisure in an Industrial City,* *1870–1920* (1983); Harold Seymour, *Baseball*, 2 vols. (1960–1971); Robert Sklar, *Movie-Made America* (1976); Sigmund Spaeth, *History of Popular Music* (1948); Robert C. Toll, *On with the Show: The First Century of Show Business in America* (1976); David Q. Voigt, *American Baseball*, 2 vols. (1966–1970).

Advertising and Journalism

George Juergens, *Joseph Pulitzer and the New York World* (1966); Frank L. Mott, *American Journalism*, 3rd ed. (1962); Frank L. Mott, *A History of American Magazines*, 5 vols. (1930–1968); Daniel Pope, *The Making of Modern Advertising* (1983); W. A. Swanberg, *Citizen Hearst* (1961); Bernard A. Weisberger, *The American Newspaperman* (1961); James P. Wood, *The Story of Advertising* (1958).

Popular Literature

Katharine Anthony, *Louisa May Alcott* (1938); John G. Cawelti, *Apostles of Success in America* (1965); John L. Cutler, *Patten and His Merriwell Saga* (1934); Theodore P. Greene, *America's Heroes: The Changing Models of Success in American Magazines* (1970); Frank L. Mott, *Golden Multitudes: The Story of Best Sellers in the United States* (1947); Edmund L. Pearson, *Dime Novels* (1929); Moses Rischin, ed., *The American Gospel of Success* (1965); Henry Nash Smith, *Mark Twain* (1962); John W. Tebbel, *From Rags to Riches: Horatio Alger, Jr. and the American Dream* (1963); Dixon Wector, *Sam Clemens of Hannibal* (1952); Irvin G. Wyllie, *The Self-Made Man in America* (1954).

GILDED AGE POLITICS
1877–1900

CHAPTER 20

The platform written by the newly organized People's party that met in Omaha, Nebraska, in July 1892 seethed with discontent. Claiming to speak "in the name and on behalf of the people of this country," the platform's preamble charged that the nation had been

> brought to the verge of moral, political, and material ruin. Corruption dominates the ballot-box, the legislatures, the Congress, and touches even . . . the bench. . . . The fruits of the toil of millions are boldly stolen to build up colossal fortunes for a few. . . . From the same prolific womb of governmental injustice we breed the two great classes— tramps and millionaires.

To a modern reader, such rhetoric may seem like the ranting of extremists. Yet to thousands of Americans in the late nineteenth century, these words represented a measured sense of reality.

The transformation of the nation by industrialization, urbanization, and the commercialization of agriculture (see Chapters 16, 17, and 18) introduced disruptive forces that threatened time-honored customs and institutions. Members of the People's party, called Populists, were mostly farmers who believed that new, large-scale modes of production undermined their rights to equality and freedom. Like other protesters, such as labor unions and socialists, the Populists concluded that the economic system was creating irresponsible concentrations of power and wealth that would crush small producers and control government. To Populists, the sense of material ruin, political corruption, and division of society into tramps and millionaires represented the loss of the American dream. Thus they gathered in Omaha to preserve a civilization of cooperation and justice against the greed of market competition and the despotism of big business.

Populists believed that politics and government, the supposed forum for the democratic spirit, had been captured by the forces of monopoly and irresponsibility. In some ways they were right. Corruption and greed tugged at the fabric of democracy, and the venality of the era prompted novelists Mark Twain and Charles Dudley Warner to dub it the Gilded Age. Officeholders used their positions to amass personal fortunes and dispense patronage appointments to their supporters. But more important were the emphases the branches of government seemed to put on cautious policymaking and preserving the status quo. Congress, though split by powerful partisan and regional rivalries, did grapple with important issues, such as the tariff and the currency, and passed some legislation initiating needed reforms. But also, many congressional accomplishments were either weak compromises or favors to special interests. Meanwhile, the judiciary became active in determining public policy. By defending vested rights of property against state and federal regulation, the courts supported the emerging power of big business. The presidency was filled by a series of honest, respectable men who seldom took legislative initiatives; and when they did, they often found themselves beaten back by Congress and the courts.

During the 1870s and 1880s, serious problems were resulting from social and economic change, but the political system seemed slow to respond. The gap between those with political influence and those who were excluded was becoming a chasm, further separating opposing interest groups: farmers versus businesspeople; debtors versus creditors; blacks versus whites; employees versus employers. Then in the 1890s, two developments brought the social and economic turmoil to a boiling point and brought about political change: the climax of rural discontent that had accompanied the transformation of the West and South; and a deep economic depression that had resulted from flaws in the industrial system. In the midst of these crises, a presidential campaign in 1896 stirred Americans as they had not been stirred for a generation. Two candidates, William Jennings Bryan and William McKinley, and three parties, Democrats, Populists, and Republicans, compressed all the symbols of the era into a single election. The nation emerged from the turbulent 1890s with new political alignments, just as it had developed new economic configurations. These alignments prepared the way for the new century and for an era of reform that would try to overcome the injustices identified in the Omaha platform of the People's party.

POLITICAL EQUILIBRIUM AND EMOTIONAL ISSUES

The historian Henry Adams, grandson and great-grandson of presidents, wrote that in American political history, the period between 1870 and 1895 "was poor in purpose and barren in results." But such a judgment overlooked important characteristics, namely, the spirited competition between major parties and the extensive popular participation in politics.

From the voters' perspective, politics appeared anything but barren. At no other time in the nation's history was public interest in elections higher. Except in the South, where blacks endured growing voting restrictions, 80 to 90 percent of eligible voters cast ballots in local and national elections. (Fewer than 50 percent typically do so today.) Politics was the prime form of mass entertainment, outdistancing even baseball, vaudeville, and circuses. Though only men could vote, campaigns were community events that excited women and children as well. Voting was only the last stage in a process that included rallies, parades, picnics, and speeches, all of which were as much public amusement as civic responsibility. As one observer remarked, "What the theatre is to the French, or the bull fight . . . to the Spanish . . . [election campaigns] and the ballot box are to *our* people." Politics was a personal as well as a community activity. In an era before advertising, polls, and the mass media influenced political choices, people formed strong loyalties to individual politicians, loyalties that often overlooked crassness and corruption.

High Voter Participation

Allegiances to parties and to individual politicians were usually so evenly distributed that no major faction or party gained lasting supremacy. Between 1877 and 1897, Republicans held the presidency for twelve years, Democrats for eight. The same party controlled the presidency and both houses of Congress for only three two-year spans: the Republicans twice, the Democrats once. Throughout the 1880s and early 1890s elections were extremely close, especially on the national level. The balance persisted despite the admission of six territories to statehood during this period (see map, page 564).

Government appeared to accomplish little in the Gilded Age because little was expected of it. Most Americans wanted an impartial government that did not interfere in social and economic matters. Also, struggles between and within parties stymied passage of effective, lasting legislation. Because the president was rarely of the same party as the majority of Congress, the two branches often blocked rather than supported each other's efforts.

In some ways, the major parties did resemble each other. Both were led by wealthy men, and both tried to appeal to farmers and wage earners as well as merchants and manufacturers. But differences in religious and ethnic values separated voters in the two parties. People who became Republicans were usually *pietistic*: Anglo-Saxon Protestants who believed that salvation was achieved through good works and encouraging others to be moral. They wanted government to legislate moral behavior, as the first Republicans had done in attempting to end slavery. After 1865 the party continued to attract people who supported moral controls such as prohibition of alcoholic beverages, restrictions on Sabbath activities (blue laws), and guidelines for school curricula.

Democrats, by contrast, attracted people whose culture was *ritualistic*: Roman Catholics, Jews, and high Protestants who believed that a person should accept the world as it is and that the way to salvation involved following the beliefs and rituals of the church. They preferred to leave questions of morality to individual conscience, rather than to government, and they preached moderation rather than interference. Thus they opposed government regulation of individual behavior.

These cultural differences—pietism versus ritualism—made for emotional conflicts over social issues, especially on the local level. But at the national level and in Congress, parties split over long-standing political and economic issues, such as sectional controversies, patronage, tariffs, and the currency.

Long after Reconstruction ended, Americans were haunted by the conflicts and disruptions that had

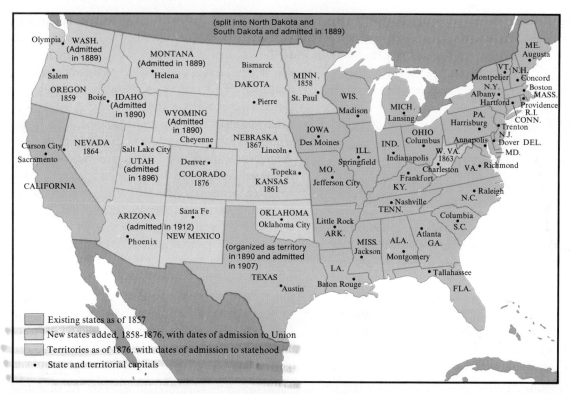

The United States, 1876–1912

followed the Civil War. Republicans capitalized on the war by "waving the bloody shirt"

Sectional Conflict

whenever they faced a Democratic challenge. As one Republican orator harangued in 1876, "Every man that tried to destroy this nation was a Democrat. . . . Soldiers, every scar you have on your heroic bodies was given you by a Democrat." In the South voters also waved the bloody shirt, calling all Republicans traitors. The use of such emotional appeals persisted well into the 1880s.

Politicians were not the only ones who attempted to profit by keeping the memory of the war alive. In the 1880s and 1890s, the Grand Army of the Republic, an organization of Union Army veterans numbering over 400,000, allied itself with the Republican party and pressured Congress into legislating generous pensions for former soldiers and their widows. The bullying tactics of veterans' lobbyists angered some legislators, but few could resist the demands of this huge interest group. "The pension agents who sit around this Capitol," griped one senator, "issue their circulars and decrees . . . and the Senators of

the United States, great and mighty as they may be, bow to the behests . . . and vote the money that they require, and they are afraid not to do it for fear that they would lose political status at home."

Many pensions were well deserved. Union soldiers had been poorly paid, and the war had widowed thousands of women. But for many veterans, the emotional wake of the war provided an opportunity to profit at the public's expense. By the end of the century the federal government was spending $157 million annually for soldiers' pensions, one of the largest welfare commitments it has ever made. No Confederate veterans received any of the largesse, though several southern states did fund small pensions and built old-age homes for ex-soldiers.

Few politicians could afford to oppose Civil War pensions, but a number of reformers attempted to dismantle the spoils system. The practice of awarding government jobs to party workers,

Civil Service Reform

regardless of their qualifications, had taken root in the antebellum years and blossomed after the Civil War in the federal government as well as states and cities.

Before the Pendleton Act of 1883, many government positions were filled by patronage: hat in hand, job seekers beseeched the president to find a place for them. Here a member of Congress presents constituents for office in return for their past political support.   Library of Congress.

As building construction, the postal service, the diplomatic corps, and other government activities expanded, so did the number of jobs on the public payroll. Between 1865 and 1891 federal government positions tripled, from 53,000 to 166,000. Elected officials scrambled to control new appointments as a means of cementing support for themselves and their parties. In return for the relatively short hours and high pay of government jobs, appointees pledged their votes and a portion of their earnings.

A system so susceptible to corruption vexed a growing number of independents, who began advocating appointments and promotions based on merit rather than connections. The movement grew during the 1870s, when scandals in the Grant administration bared the defects of the spoils system. It reached full flower in 1881 with the formation of the National Civil Service Reform League, an organization led by George W. Curtis, editor of *Harper's Weekly,* and E. L. Godkin, editor of the *Nation.* The same year, Charles Guiteau, a frustrated and demented job-seeker, assassinated President James Garfield, and the murder hastened the drive for civil service reform. Late in

1882 Congress passed the Pendleton Civil Service Act, and President Chester Arthur signed it early in 1883.

The law outlawed political contributions by officeholders and created the Civil Service Commission, which would supervise competitive examinations for government positions. The act, however, gave the commission jurisdiction over only about 10 percent of federal jobs—although the president could expand the list. The remaining jobs were subject to the old spoils system. Also, examinations were to apply only to new applicants, not to incumbents. These limitations explain why Republicans, then the majority in Congress, strongly supported the Pendleton Act, while most Democrats opposed it. As one Democratic senator complained, it was simply "a bill to perpetuate in office the Republicans who now control the patronage of the Government."

Civil service reform has often been considered one of the major accomplishments of the Gilded Age; yet its actual impact can be debated. Certainly the system of hiring government workers needed improvement. Under the spoils system, clerical jobs were given to people who could neither read nor write, and because the diplomatic corps contained so many untrained officers (many of whom could not speak the language of the country where they served), the American foreign service was one of the most incompetent in the field. But civil service reformers were not egalitarians who would give all qualified Americans a chance to participate in government. They were conservatives who wanted to restore an era when public servants were chosen from among men whose birth, wealth, and education supposedly fitted them for leadership. Moreover, no one has ever proven that the quality of government employees improved under civil service.

In the 1880s tariffs and money, not government jobs, attracted the most attention in Congress. Through the mid-nineteenth century Congress had raised tariff rates to protect American manufactured goods and some agricultural products from European competition. By the 1880s there were separate tariffs on over four thousand items, and the resulting revenues were making for an embarrassing surplus in the federal treasury. Though a few economics professors and farmers argued for free trade, most Americans still

Tariff Policy

believed high tariffs were necessary to support industry and preserve the jobs of wage earners.

The Republican party, claiming responsibility for economic growth, made protective tariffs a core feature of its policies. Democrats complained that tariffs made prices artificially high, benefiting those interests, such as woolen manufacturers, whose products were protected while hurting farmers whose crops were not protected and consumers who had to buy manufactured goods. Although Democrats generally saw a need for some protection of American goods and raw materials, they favored lower tariff rates to encourage foreign trade and to reduce the treasury surplus.

Privileged interests continued to dominate tariff policy in the 1890s. When in 1894 House Democrats supported by President Grover Cleveland passed a bill to reduce tariff rates, Senate Republicans, aided by southern Democrats eager to protect their region's infant industries, added some six hundred amendments restoring most cuts. In 1897 a new tariff bill, the Dingley Act, raised rates even further, though it greatly expanded reciprocity provisions. Introduced in the McKinley Tariff of 1890 and designed to encourage new foreign trade and to discourage foreign retaliation against high American duties, reciprocity gave the president authority to remove items from the free list if their countries of origin placed unreasonable tariffs on American goods.

The currency controversy was even more tangled than the tariff issue. In brief, it involved opposing reactions to the fall in prices caused by increased industrial and agricultural production after the Civil War (see pages 443–444). Farmers, most of whom were debtors, suffered because they had to pay fixed mortgage and interest payments even while their incomes declined because prices for their crops were dropping. Correctly perceiving that an insufficient money supply had made their debts more expensive relative to other prices, farmers favored schemes like the coinage of silver to increase the amount of currency in circulation. Creditors, on the other hand, believed that overproduction had caused the price decline. They favored a more stable, tightly controlled money supply backed only by gold as a means of maintaining the confidence of native and foreign investors in the American economy.

But the issue involved more than economics. The quantity and quality of money symbolized a whole series of conflicts—social, regional, and emotional. The creditor-versus-debtor conflict translated into haves versus have-nots. It also involved a sectional cleavage, the western silver-mining areas and agricultural regions of the South and West against the more conservative industrial Northeast. Finally, the issue had moral, almost religious, overtones. Gold, the traditional basis of money, was a durable yet malleable metal. Those qualities plus its beauty and rarity gave it a magical potency, a God-given symbol of value. But others considered the gold standard for currency too limiting for the machine age; prosperity, they felt, demanded new attitudes.

By the late 1870s, the currency controversy had become a matter of gold versus silver. Up to that time the government had coined both silver and gold dollars; a silver dollar weighed sixteen times more than a gold dollar, meaning that gold was officially worth sixteen times as much as silver. But gold discoveries since 1848 had increased the supply, lowering gold's market price relative to that of silver. Producers of silver, which was now worth more than one-sixteenth the value of gold, preferred to sell their metal on the open market rather than to the government. As a result, silver dollars disappeared from circulation—owners hoarded them rather than spend them—and in 1873 Congress officially stopped coining silver dollars. At about the same time, European nations also stopped buying silver. Thus the United States and many of its trading partners adopted the gold standard, meaning that their currency was backed chiefly by gold.

Within a few years, however, new mines in the American West began to flood the market with silver, and its price dropped. Gold was now worth more than sixteen times what silver was worth. It became profitable to spend silver dollars—and would have been worthwhile to sell silver to the government in return for gold, but the government was no longer buying it. Debtors, who were suffering from the depression of the mid-1870s in addition to falling prices, and who saw silver as a means of expanding the currency supply, now joined with silver producers to denounce the "Crime of '73" and to press for resumption of coinage at the old sixteen-to-one ratio.

Congress, split into silver and gold factions, tried to neutralize the issue with compromise legislation:

Monetary Policy

the Bland-Allison Act of 1878, which required the treasury to buy $2 to $4 million worth of silver each month; and the Sherman Silver Purchase Act of 1890, which fixed the monthly purchase of silver in weight (4.5 million ounces) rather than in dollars. But neither act satisfied the different interest groups. The Sherman Act, passed partially in response to an economic decline in the mid-1880s, failed to expand the money supply: as the price of silver dropped, the government, now required only to buy a certain weight of silver, could spend less to purchase the stipulated number of ounces. Thus the money supply was not increased as substantially as some had hoped. Not until after a depression in the 1890s and an emotion-filled presidential election would the money issue subside.

While debates over tariffs and money raged, Congress and state legislatures began to face the issue of women's suffrage more squarely than ever before.

Women's Suffrage
After the Civil War, several events mobilized women to pursue the vote. Late in 1869 a Missouri couple, Francis and Virginia Minor, drew up a resolution stating that the Constitution and its amendments had already given women the right to vote. According to the recently adopted Fourteenth Amendment, the Constitution granted citizenship to "all persons born or naturalized in the United States," and no state could abridge the "privileges or immunities" of any citizen, including his—or, said the Minors, her—right to vote. Eventually the Minors, with support from the National Woman Suffrage Association (NWSA), sued a St. Louis registrar who had refused to permit Mrs. Minor to vote. After a series of adverse decisions in lower courts, the case went to the Supreme Court in 1874. The majority opinion written by Chief Justice Morrison R. Waite upheld the lower courts, declaring that suffrage did not automatically accompany citizenship and that states could legally withhold voting rights from certain classes of citizens, such as criminals, the insane—and women.

The Minor decision did not deter the cause of women's suffrage or the NWSA. In 1878 Susan B. Anthony, the indomitable fighter for human rights who also had been rebuffed by the courts when she tried to vote in 1872, convinced Senator A. A. Sargent of California, a strong supporter of women's

suffrage, to introduce a constitutional amendment stating that "the right of citizens of the United States to vote shall not be denied or abridged by the United States or by any state on account of sex." (The Women's Suffrage Amendment finally ratified forty-two years later was identical to this "Anthony Amendment.") The bill was killed by a Senate committee, but supporters reintroduced it several times over the next eighteen years. On the few occasions when the bill reached the Senate floor, it was voted down by senators who expressed fears that suffrage would interfere with women's family responsibilities and ruin female virtue.

While the NWSA and others fought for the vote on the national level, the American Woman Suffrage Association worked for constitutional amendments at the state level. (The two suffrage groups joined in 1890 to form the National American Woman Suffrage Association.) Between 1870 and 1910, there were seventeen referenda in eleven states (all but three of which were west of the Mississippi River) to legalize women's suffrage. These attempts seldom succeeded, but they attracted attention from newly formed women's clubs and trained a corps of female leaders in organizing and public speaking. Women did attain partial victories: by 1890 nineteen states allowed women to vote on school issues, and three granted suffrage on tax and bond issues.

The thrust for women's suffrage in the Gilded Age failed because society was still not prepared to accept such reform. Even in the western states where some limited gains were made, male politicians were willing to grant the vote not because women asked for it, but because they believed female voters could help give their communities a more civilized image and thereby attract settlers. Thus in politics, as in other areas of life, women were considered neither similar nor equal to men; instead, they were different and unequal.

Throughout the Gilded Age, legislative leaders did address some of the basic issues, but they failed to agree on clear solutions to pressing economic problems. Congressmen and their constituents were so divided among factions and interest groups that the only passable legislation was the kind, like the Pendleton Civil Service Act, that was ideal to no one but acceptable to most. And while complex problems like the tariff demanded careful study, Congress, and

Sheet music for a late-nineteenth-century song about women's suffrage. Women increased their agitation for the vote until in 1878 a constitutional amendment granting them suffrage was introduced in Congress. The Senate killed the measure that year, but women's groups like the National Woman Suffrage Association continued to fight for the cause. *American Antiquarian Society.*

particularly the Senate, became an oratorical battle-ground for party and intraparty rivalry over patronage. Between late 1879 and early 1881, for example, the prevailing question was not the nation's economic or social condition, but which member of which Republican faction would be appointed to the patronage-rich post of Collector of the Port of New York. Politics has always been the art of compromise, but in the two decades after Reconstruction, compromise became equated with the postponement of major decisions.

THE DECLINE OF THE PRESIDENCY

In the years between 1877 and 1900, American presidents contrasted sharply with more headstrong predecessors like Jackson and Lincoln. Proper, honorable, and honest, Presidents Hayes, Garfield, Arthur, Cleveland, Harrison, and McKinley won public respect but seldom provoked strong positive or negative emotions. Like other politicians, they used symbols. Hayes served lemonade at the White House to emphasize that, unlike his predecessor Grant, he was no hard drinker. McKinley put aside his cigar in public so photographers would not catch him setting a bad example for youth. But none of the era's six presidents was an inspiring personality, nor could any of them dominate the factional chieftains of their parties.

Thus during the Gilded Age the presidency declined in influence relative to Congress. Until the 1890s no serious crisis threatened the nation, so no president was in a position to assume emergency powers. The nature of domestic issues coupled with the generally nonassertive personalities of the presidents created an atmosphere in which the presidency had little independence. The nation's growing involvement in foreign affairs and the wars and treaties accompanying that involvement did give Presidents Cleveland and McKinley a few opportunities to set policy, but they too had to bow to the pressures of Congress. Cleveland initiated a few pieces of legislation and used the veto to fight some congressional abuses, but he had no intention of expanding his presidential prerogatives. "I shall keep right on doing executive work," he once stated. "I did not come here to legislate."

Rutherford B. Hayes (1877 to 1881) personified the belief that the president was a caretaker elected to execute what Congress initiated. Honest and a model of self-control, Hayes had

Hayes, Garfield, and Arthur

been a Union general and an Ohio congressman and governor before his disputed election to the presidency (see pages 445–446). Once in office, he avoided such controversial issues as the tariff and sectional rivalry. He did, however, take a conservative position on currency, and ordered out troops to quell the 1877 railroad strikes. Hayes pleased civil service advocates by appointing reformer Carl Schurz to the cabinet and battling New York's patronage king, Senator Roscoe Conkling. (He fired Conkling's protégé, Chester Arthur, from the post of New York Customs House Collector.) But Hayes also demanded that his own appointees contribute to Republican coffers for the 1878 elections. He was not a beloved leader. As one reformer wrote, "I have little or no patience with Mr. Hayes. He is a victim of . . . good intentions and his contributions to the pavement of the road to the infernal regions are vast and nefarious."

When Hayes refused to run for re-election in 1880, Republicans selected another Ohio congressman and Civil War hero, James A. Garfield. A husky, serious, and cautious man, Garfield defeated the Democrats' Winfield Scott Hancock, also a Civil War hero, by just 40,000 votes out of over 9 million. By carrying the pivotal states of New York and Indiana, however, Garfield won in the electoral college by a comfortable margin, 214 to 155. Garfield spent most of his brief presidency trying to secure an independent position among party potentates. He appeared to have no relish for his responsibilities, and especially disliked dealing with the hordes of office seekers. "Once or twice," he complained, "I felt like crying out in the agony of my soul against the greed for office and its consumption of my time." He did please civil service reformers by refusing to satisfy Conkling's demands, but Garfield's opportunity to make lasting contributions ended in July 1881 when the crazed Charles Guiteau shot him in a Washington railroad station. Not seriously wounded at first, Garfield lingered for seventy-nine days while doctors tried unsuccessfully to remove a bullet lodged in his back. His condition steadily deteriorated, and he finally succumbed to infection, dying September 19.

Garfield's vice president and successor was New York politician Chester A. Arthur, the spoilsman Hayes had fired in 1878. Arthur had been nominated for vice president only to help the Republicans carry New York State; his elevation to the presidency made reformers shudder. Yet he became a dignified and temperate executive. Arthur lent some support to civil service reform and signed the Pendleton Act. He urged Congress to modify outdated tariff rates, and spoke in favor of federal regulation of railroads. Using the veto as a means to influence Congress, Arthur killed a number of bills that excessively benefited privileged interests. But like his two predecessors, Arthur had no taste for his office. Suffering from illness, he made little effort to run in 1884.

The 1884 presidential campaign magnified the political banalities of the era. The Republicans nominated Senator James G. Blaine of Maine, whose impressive leadership skills and popularity were offset by his practice of using his influence to obtain favorable financial deals for railroads, for which he was paid handsomely. The Democrats named New York's Governor Grover Cleveland, a rotund and righteous bachelor whose respectable reputation was tainted by his having once fathered an illegitimate son—a fact he admitted openly during the campaign. Both parties focused on the sordid side of the opposition, and disapproval of Blaine was so strong that a number of disaffected Republicans called Mugwumps deserted their party for Cleveland. On election day Cleveland beat Blaine by only 23,000 popular votes; his tiny margin of 1,149 votes in New York gave him that state's 36 electoral votes, enough to squeeze a 219-to-182 victory in the electoral college. Cleveland may have won New York because in the last week of the campaign a local Protestant minister publicly equated Democrats with "rum, Romanism, and rebellion" (drinking, Catholicism, and the Civil War). Democrats eagerly publicized the slur among New York's numerous Irish-Catholic population, urging voters to protest by turning out for Cleveland.

Cleveland, the first Democratic president since Buchanan, complained like his Republican predecessors of the "cursed constant grind" of his office

and the "want of rest." He did, however, exercise more vigorous leadership. Cleveland used the veto extensively against outrageous pension bills, and he extended the scope of civil service. But his most forceful action was his unsuccessful campaign for tariff reform. Worried about the growing treasury surplus, Cleveland urged Congress to cut duties on raw materials and manufactured goods. When advisers warned him that his stand might weaken his chances for re-election, the president retorted, "What is the use of being elected or re-elected, unless you stand for something?" Cleveland's firmness did not prevail, though. The Mills tariff bill of 1888, passed by the House in response to Cleveland's wishes, was killed by the Senate. Although the Democrats renominated Cleveland for the presidency in 1888, protectionists in the party were soon able to convince Cleveland to temper his attacks on high tariffs.

Cleveland and Harrison

Republicans in 1888 nominated Benjamin Harrison, an intelligent but chilly former senator from Indiana and grandson of President William Henry Harrison. The campaign was less savage than the 1884 campaign had been, but it was far from clean. Some shrewd Republicans manipulated the British minister in Washington into stating that Cleveland's re-election would be good for England. Irish Democrats took offense, as intended, and Cleveland's campaign was weakened. Perhaps more helpful to Harrison was the bribery and multiple voting that helped him to win Indiana by just 2,300 votes and New York by only 14,000. (Democrats also indulged in bribery and vote fraud, but the Republicans were more successful at it.) These crucial states assured Harrison's victory; though Cleveland outpolled Harrison by 90,000 popular votes, Harrison carried the electoral vote by 233 to 168. After the election, Harrison told Matt Quay, the Republican national chairman, "Providence has given us the victory." Quay later quipped to a friend, "Think of the man. He ought to know that Providence hadn't a damned thing to do with it. . . . [He] would never learn how close a number of men were compelled to approach the gates of the penitentiary to make him president."

Harrison was the first president since 1875 whose party controlled both houses of Congress, but he did little to take advantage of this circumstance. Several aspects of his administration were contradictory.

Gilded Age politics was a mass activity, involving both sexes and all age groups. This painting, titled "The Lost Bet," shows a parade in Chicago just after Grover Cleveland won his second term as president in 1892. A local Republican had offered to pull his Democrat friend in a cart if Cleveland won. Here, the Democrat is collecting on the bet to the great enjoyment of a throng of onlookers. Library of Congress.

Harrison was a fiscal conservative, but under his administration Congress passed the first peacetime budget to exceed $1 billion. At Harrison's urging the House passed a "force bill" to protect blacks' civil rights by allowing federal courts to investigate irregularities in voter registration and jury selection; but Republican senators filibustered and then tabled the bill, causing the president to abandon the cause. And though Harrison supported protective tariff rates and reciprocity agreements to aid business, he agreed to the Sherman Anti-Trust Act and the Sherman Silver Purchase Act (1890), both of which were considered damaging to business. Harrison professed support for civil service and appointed Theodore Roosevelt a civil service commissioner, but the president's lackluster character prompted the reform-minded and impatient Roosevelt to call him a "cold-blooded, narrow-minded, prejudiced, obstinate, timid, old psalm singing Indianapolis politician."

Cleveland and Harrison ran against each other again in 1892. This time Cleveland attracted heavy contributions from business and beat Harrison by 380,000 popular votes (3 percent of the total) and by 277 to 145 electoral votes.

In office once more, Cleveland took bolder steps to meet the problems of currency, tariffs, and labor unrest. But his actions reflected a narrow orientation to the interests of business and bespoke political weakness. In order to protect the nation's gold reserve, which was shrinking during the Panic of 1893, Cleveland enlisted aid from bankers, who bailed out the nation on terms highly favorable to themselves. During the election campaign Cleveland promised sweeping tariff reform, but he made little effort to line up support for such reform in the Senate, where protectionists undercut all efforts to reduce rates. And when 120,000 boycotting railroad workers paralyzed western trade in the 1894 Pullman strike (see page 502), Cleveland bowed to the requests for federal troops from railroad managers and Attorney General Richard Olney. Throughout Cleveland's second term, events—particularly the economic downturn and the Populist ferment—seemed too much for the president. Cleveland's party abandoned him in 1896.

STIRRINGS OF AGRARIAN UNREST

While the political system in Washington faltered, inequities in the new agricultural and industrial systems were creating the first rumblings of a mass democratic movement that was to shake American society in the late nineteenth century. The agrarian revolt—a complex mixture of strident rhetoric, nostalgic dreams, and hard-headed egalitarianism—began when farmers' alliances formed in Texas in the late 1870s, then spread across the Cotton Belt and the Plains in the 1880s. The movement caught on chiefly in areas where farm tenancy, crop liens, furnishing merchants, railroads, banks, weather, and insects threatened the ambitions of hopeful farmers. Once under way, it inspired visions of a truly cooperative, democratic society.

Agricultural expansion in the West and South exposed millions of people to the hardships of rural life (see Chapter 16). Uncertainties might have been more bearable if the rewards had been more promising, but such was not the case. As farmers put more land under cultivation, as mechanization boosted productivity, and as foreign competition increased, supplies exceeded national and worldwide demand for agricultural products. Consequently, prices for staple crops dropped steadily. A bushel of wheat that sold for $1.45 in 1866 brought only $.80 in the mid-1880s and $.49 by the mid-1890s. Meanwhile transportation, storage, and commission fees remained high relative to other prices. Costly seed, fertilizer, manufactured goods, taxes, and mortgage interest combined with social isolation to trap many farm families in disadvantageous and sometimes desperate circumstances. In order to buy necessities and pay bills, farmers had to produce more. But the spiral only wound more tightly, since the more farmers produced, the lower prices dropped.

Even before the full impact of these developments was felt, farmers had begun to organize to relieve their mounting distress. With aid from Oliver H. Kelley of the Department of Agriculture, farmers founded a network of local organizations called Granges in almost every state during the late 1860s and early 1870s. By 1875 the Grange had nearly twenty thousand local branches and over 1 million members. Strongest in the Midwest and South, Granges served chiefly as social organizations, sponsoring meetings and educational events to help relieve the loneliness of farm life. Family-oriented and open to all, local Granges made explicit provisions for women's participation.

Grange Movement

As membership flourished, Granges moved beyond social functions into economic and political action. At its 1874 national convention, the Grange proposed to avoid high retail prices by forming local cooperatives to buy equipment and supplies directly from manufacturers. Granges also encouraged the formation of sales cooperatives, whereby farmers would pool their grain and dairy products and then divide the profits. In a few instances, Grangers operated implements factories and insurance companies. Most such enterprises failed, however, because farmers lacked cash for cooperative buying and because ruthless competition from large manufacturers and dealers undercut them. In politics, Grangers used their numbers to some advantage, electing sympathetic legislators and pressing for laws to regulate transportation and storage rates.

In spite of their progressive, even radical, efforts, Granges nevertheless declined in the late 1870s. The requirement that cooperatives run on a cash-only basis excluded large numbers of farmers who never had any cash. Efforts to regulate business and transportation withered when corporations won court support against "Granger laws." Politically, Granges disavowed third parties but could not overcome the power of business interests within the established parties. Finally, the Grange's promotion of thrift and hard work was of little value to families already overburdened with both virtues. Thus, after a brief assertion of influence, the Grange reverted to an organization of farmers' social clubs. Its short-lived agrarian campaign served, however, as a precedent for future action.

Rural activism then shifted to the Farmers' Alliances, two networks of organizations—one in the Plains and one in the South—that by 1890 constituted a genuine mass movement. The first

Farmers' Alliances

alliances sprang up in Texas, where hard-pressed farmers rallied against crop liens, furnishing merchants, and railroads in particular, and against money power in general. Adopting an effective system of traveling lecturers to recruit members, alliance leaders extended the movement to other southern states. By 1889 the Southern Alliance boasted over 3 million members, including the powerful Colored Farmers' National Alliance, which claimed over 1 million black members. A similar movement flourished in the Plains, where by the late 1880s 2 million members were organized in Kansas, Nebraska, and the Dakotas.

Alliance members pushed the Grange concept of cooperation to new limits by sponsoring organizational rallies, educational meetings, and cooperative buying and selling agreements. Seeing themselves as laborers battling capitalists in a new age, some alliance members advocated unity with the Knights of Labor and other workers' groups.

Beyond urging democratic cooperation, the alliance movement proposed a scheme to alleviate the most serious rural problems: lack of cash and credit. The

Subtreasury Plan

subtreasury plan, adapted from French and Russian precedents, called for the federal government to construct warehouses in every major agricultural county. At harvest time, farmers could store their crops in these subtreasuries while awaiting higher prices, and the government would loan farmers treasury notes amounting to 80 percent of the market price the stored crops would bring. Farmers could use these subtreasury notes as legal tender to pay debts and make purchases. Once the stored crops were sold, farmers would pay back the loans plus small interest and storage fees.

The subtreasury scheme was meant to replace the crop-lien system and to give farmers greater control over their financial affairs. No longer would merchants be able to take advantage of farmers at harvest time, when market gluts depressed prices. No longer would farmers have to mortgage crops (through crop liens)

VOL 19 NO. 483   JANUARY 17 1891   PRICE 10 CENTS.

Judge

THE NEW UNCLE SAM
How the Farmers' Alliance propose to have the Government run when they get the power.

The Farmers' Alliance movement organized agrarian unrest into a cogent list of reforms. This cartoon shows how alliance members hoped to protect their mortgages and crops with a series of economic proposals that would make the currency system more flexible. Library of Congress.

at high interest. And no longer would they lack cash to buy supplies. Moreover, by issuing subtreasury notes, the government would be injecting more money into the economy and encouraging the kind of inflation agrarian reformers desired: inflation that would raise crop prices without raising the costs of supplies and rents. If government subsidized business, reasoned alliance members, why should it not help farmers earn a decent living too?

Implementation of their plans confronted alliance members with questions of political participation. If the various alliance groups, North and South, had been able to unite, they would have made for a formidable political force. But early attempts at merger were thwarted by sectional differences and personality clashes. At a meeting in St. Louis in 1889, white southerners, fearing reprisals from landowners and objecting to the participation of blacks, rejected proposals that would have ended secrecy in alliance activities and white-only membership rules. Northerners too shied away from amalgamation, fearing they would be dominated by more experienced southern leaders. Differences on issues also prevented unity. Northern farmers, who were mostly Republicans, wanted protective tariffs to keep out foreign grain; white southerners, mostly Democrats, wanted low tariffs. Nevertheless, both alliances favored government control of transportation and communications, liberal credit policies, equitable taxation, prohibition of alien land ownership, and currency reform.

Growing membership and rising confidence drew alliances more deeply into politics. By 1890, farmers had elected a number of officeholders sympathetic to their programs—especially in the

Rise of Populism

South, where alliance members controlled four governorships, eight state legislatures, forty-four seats in the U.S. House of Representatives, and three seats in the U.S. Senate. In the Midwest, alliance candidates often ran on independent third-party tickets, and achieved some success in Kansas, Nebraska, and the Dakotas. Campaigns included spirited rallies and parades that resounded with songs and orations; their banners proclaimed "We Are All Mortgaged But Our Votes." During the summer of 1890, the Kansas Alliance held a "convention of the people" and nominated candidates who swept the fall elections. Formation of this People's party, whose members were called Populists, from *populus*, the Latin word for people, gave a name to alliance political activism.

The 1890 election results energized new efforts to consolidate all alliance groups into a single Populist party. A May 1891 meeting of northern and southern alliances in Cincinnati failed when southerners chose to remain Democrats rather than risk joining a third party. But by early 1892, southern alliance members were ready for independent action. Meeting with northern counterparts in St. Louis, they issued a call for a People's party convention in Omaha on July 4, to draft a platform and nominate a presidential candidate.

The new party's platform, ratified by the 1,300 delegates who gathered in Omaha, was one of the most comprehensive reform documents in American

Mary E. Lease (1850–1933) was a fiery and controversial speaker for the Farmers' Alliance and Populist party in Kansas. Tall and intense, she had a deep, almost hypnotic voice that made her an effective publicist for the farmers' cause. She was one of the founders of the Populist party and gave a seconding speech to the nomination of James B. Weaver at the party convention in 1892. Library of Congress.

history. Declaring in its preamble that "wealth belongs to him that creates it," the Omaha platform presented a host of proposals generated by rural unrest. Most of its planks addressed three central issues: transportation, land, and money. Frustrated with weak state and federal regulation, the Populists demanded government ownership of railroad and telegraph lines. They called on the federal government to reclaim all land owned for speculative purposes by railroads and aliens. The monetary plank called for a flexible currency system based on free and unlimited coinage of silver that would increase the money supply and enable farmers to pay their debts more easily. Other planks advocated a graduated income tax, postal savings banks, the direct election of U.S. senators, and shorter hours for workers. As its presidential candidate, the party nominated James B. Weaver of Iowa, a former Union general and greenback supporter.

The Populist campaign featured colorful personalities and vivid rhetoric. The Kansas plains rumbled with the speeches of Sockless Jerry Simpson, an unschooled but canny rural reformer, and of Mary Lease, a fiery orator who urged farmers to "raise less corn and more hell." The South produced equally forceful but somewhat less flamboyant leaders, such as Charles W. Macune of Texas, Thomas Watson of Georgia, and Leonidas Polk of North Carolina. And there was Minnesota's Ignatius Donnelly, a pseudoscientist and writer of apocalyptic novels who became the chief organizer and ideologue of the northern Plains. Finally, the campaign had its opportunists, like James Hogg of Texas and "Pitchfork Ben" Tillman of South Carolina, who were not genuine Populists but used the rising agrarian fervor for their own political ambitions.

Although Weaver lost badly in 1892, he garnered over 1 million popular votes (8 percent of the total), winning majorities in four states and 22 electoral votes. Not since 1856 had a third party won so many votes in its first national effort. The party's central dilemma—whether to stand by its ideals at all costs or compromise those ideals in order to gain power—still loomed ahead (see pages 580–582). But in the early 1890s, rural dwellers in the South and West foresaw a promising future. The alliance movement had kindled an emotional faith. Although Populists were not perfectly democratic—their mistrust of blacks and foreigners gave them a reactionary vein—they sought change in order to fulfill their version of American ideals. Amid hardship and desperation, millions of people had begun to believe that they could overcome corporate power with a cooperative democracy in which government would act to ensure equal opportunity. A banner hanging above the stage at the Omaha convention summed up the movement's spirit: "We do not ask for sympathy or pity. We ask for justice."

THE DEPRESSION OF THE 1890s

Early in 1893, shortly before Grover Cleveland assumed the presidency for the second time, a seemingly minor but ominous economic event occurred: the Philadelphia and Reading Railroad, once a thriving and profitable line, went bankrupt. Like other railroads, the Philadelphia and Reading had borrowed heavily to lay track and build new stations and bridges. But overexpansion cut into revenues. Profits dwindled, and the company was unable to pay its debts.

The same problem nagged manufacturers. For example, output at the McCormick farm machinery factories was nine times greater in 1893 than it had been in 1879, but revenues had only tripled. To compensate, the company tried to boost profits by automating its plants and squeezing more work out of fewer laborers. But this strategy only enlarged the debt and increased unemployment. And it pushed unemployed workers into the same plight as their employers: they could not pay their creditors.

Banks suffered too. As primary lending agents, their problems compounded when customers defaulted. The failure of the National Cordage Company in May 1893 set off a chain reaction of business and bank closings. During the first four months of 1893, 28 banks failed. By June the number reached 128. In 1894 one adviser warned President Cleveland, "We are on the eve of a very dark night." He was right; between 1893 and 1897, the nation suffered the worst economic depression it had yet experienced.

Personal hardship arrived in the wake of business failures. Although records are sketchy, it appears that about 2.5 million people, or nearly 20 percent of the labor force, were jobless for some time during the depression. Falling demand caused the cost of living to drop between 1892 and 1895, but that decline was more than offset by layoffs and wage cuts. Many people could not afford basic necessities. New York police estimated that twenty thousand homeless and jobless people roamed the city's streets. Surveying the impact of the depression on his own city of Boston, Henry Adams wrote, "Men died like flies under the strain, and Boston grew suddenly old, haggard, and thin."

As the depression deepened, currency problems reached a critical stage. The Sherman Silver Purchase Act of 1890 had committed the government to buy 4.5 million ounces of silver each

Currency Problems

month (see page 567). Payment was to be in gold, at the ratio of one ounce of gold for every sixteen ounces of silver. But the western mining boom made silver more plentiful, and its value relative to gold fell. Thus every month the government exchanged gold, whose worth remained fairly constant, for less valuable silver. Fearful that the dollar, which was based on the treasury's holdings in silver and gold, was losing its value, merchants at home and abroad began to exchange paper money and securities for gold. As a result, the nation's gold reserves dwindled, falling below $100 million in April 1893.

The $100-million level was psychologically significant. If business leaders believed that the country's gold reserve was disappearing, they would lose confidence in its economic stability and refrain from investing. For example, British capitalists owned some $4 billion in American stocks and bonds. If the dollar were to depreciate too much, they would stop investing in American economic growth. Yet the lower the gold reserve dropped, the more people rushed to redeem their money and securities—to get their gold before it disappeared. The panic spread, causing further bankruptcies and unemployment.

President Cleveland, promising to protect the gold reserves, called a special session of Congress to repeal the Sherman Silver Purchase Act. But though the repeal was passed in October 1893, the run on the treasury continued through 1894. By early 1895 gold reserves had fallen to only $41 million. In desperation, Cleveland accepted an offer of 3.5 million ounces of gold in return for $62 million worth of federal bonds from a banking syndicate led by J. P. Morgan. When the bankers resold the bonds to the public, they profited handsomely at the nation's expense. Cleveland claimed that the gold reserves had been saved, but discontented farmers, workers, silver miners, and even some members of Cleveland's own party saw only humiliation in the president's actions. "When Judas betrayed Christ," charged South Carolina's Senator "Pitchfork Ben" Tillman, "his heart was not blacker than this scoundrel, Cleveland, in betraying the [Democratic party]."

No one knew what was really happening to the president. At about the time that Cleveland called Congress into special session, doctors discovered a malignant tumor on his palate. The cancer required immediate removal. Fearful that public knowledge of his illness would hasten the run on gold, and intent on preventing Vice President Adlai E. Stevenson, a silver supporter, from gaining influence, Cleveland kept his condition a secret. He announced that he was going sailing with a friend, and doctors removed his cancerous upper left jaw while the yacht sailed up the East River from New York City. Outfitted with a rubber jaw, Cleveland resumed a full schedule five days later, enduring terrible pain to dispel rumors that he was seriously ill. He eventually recovered, but those who knew about his operation believed it had sapped his vitality.

The deal between Cleveland and Morgan did not end the depression. After a slight improvement in 1895, the economy plunged again. Farm income, on the decline since 1887, continued to slide; factories closed; banks that remained open restricted withdrawals and refused to honor checks. Immigration in the mid-1890s dropped to almost 200,000 a year less than in the early 1890s. Economic hardship and reduced immigration depressed housing construction, drying up an important source of jobs. Each night police stations in almost every city became crowded with vagrants who had no place else to stay.

In the final years of the century, new gold discoveries, good harvests, and saner industrial growth brought better times. But the depression had hastened the crumbling of an old system and the emergence of a new one. The processes of industrial development and technological change had been under way for some time. Since the 1850s, railroads had been at the center of American economic development, opening new markets, boosting steel production, spawning numerous subsidiary industries, and expanding banking and finance. But the organizational features of the new business system—consolidation and a trend toward bigness—were just beginning to solidify when the depression hit.

Emergence of New Economic Structures

What had happened was that the national economy had reached the point of interdependence, the point at which the fortunes of a business in one part of the country or the world had repercussions elsewhere. By the 1890s railroads were overextended; their reckless investments inevitably crumbled. And when railroads collapsed, they pulled other industries down with them. In the first half of 1893, for example, thirty-two steel companies failed. In all, five hundred banks and sixteen thousand businesses toppled into bankruptcy that same year. Moreover, European economies also slumped in the 1890s, and more than ever before the fortunes of one country affected those of other countries.

To complicate matters, American farmers had to contend not only with fluctuating transportation rates and falling crop prices at home, but also with Canadian and Russian wheat growers, Argentine cattle ranchers, Indian and Egyptian cotton producers, and Australian wool producers. When farmers fell into debt and lost their purchasing power, their depressed condition in turn affected the economic health of railroads, farm-implements manufacturers, banks, and other businesses. The downward spiral reversed late in 1897, but the depression had left deep scars.

DEPRESSION-ERA PROTESTS

The depression bared a number of problems in the industrial system. For half a century technological and organizational changes had been widening the gap between employers and employees. By the 1890s workers' protests against exploitation threatened economic and political upheaval. In 1894, when the American economy plunged, there were over thirteen hundred strikes and countless riots. Violence reached an alarming pitch, and radical rhetoric escalated. Contrary to the fears of business leaders, all the protesters were not anarchists or communists from Europe come to sabotage American democracy. The disaffected included thousands of men and women who simply wanted a better chance, regardless of how the government was organized.

The era of protest began with the great railroad strikes of 1877 (see pages 498–499). The vehemence of those strikes and the support they drew from other working-class people aroused fears that the United States would repeat what had happened in France six years earlier, when a popular uprising briefly overturned the government and introduced communist principles. Such anxieties were heightened by another railroad strike in 1880, the Haymarket riot of 1886, a general strike in New Orleans in 1891, and the prolonged strike at the Homestead Steel plant in 1892. In the West, too, miners were becoming embittered; in 1892 violence broke out at a silver mine in Coeur d'Alene, Idaho. Angered by wage cuts and a lockout, strikers seized the mines and battled federal troops sent to subdue them. Such actions prompted some business owners to believe that force was the only effective response to the radical wave, apparently fomented by socialists and anarchists.

Socialists had been involved in these and other incidents, but their numbers were small. Led by Daniel DeLeon, the fiery West Indian–born lawyer and lecturer who dominated the Socialist Labor Party, they agreed with Karl Marx, the father of communism, that whoever controlled the means of production held the power to determine how well people lived. Marx had written that capitalism increased the output of goods by oppressing labor, divorcing workers from the means of production, and pitting classes against each other. No longer did workers have control over how a product would be made; mechanization and the division of labor had demeaned them. Marx predicted that workers throughout the world would become so discontented they would revolt and seize factories, farms, banks, and transportation lines. The governments resulting from this revolution would end exploitation and erase class differences, paving the way for a new order of social justice. Marx's vision appealed to some workers because it promised them independence and abundance, and to intellectuals because it promised an end to class conflict and crude materialism.

Socialism

American socialism suffered from internal disagreements and lack of strong leadership. DeLeon had an antagonistic personality and could not unite the Socialist Labor Party. But events in 1894 triggered changes within the movement. That year the government's quashing of the Pullman strike and of the newly formed American Railway Union created a new and inspiring socialist leader. Eugene V. Debs, the railway union's president, had become a socialist while serving a six-month prison term for defying an injunction against the strike. Once released, the bald, forceful Indianan became the leading spokesperson for American socialism, combining visionary Marxism with Jeffersonian and Populist antimonopolism. Though never good at organizing, Debs attracted huge audiences and captivated them with passionate eloquence. His attacks on the free enterprise system were indignant. "Many of you think you are com-

Coxey's Army. Jacob Coxey (in the foreground, in front of the flag) leads the procession of unemployed workers that became the first of many to march on the capital seeking government relief. In his hand Coxey carries a "war club of peace." Library of Congress.

peting," he would lecture. "Against whom? Against Rockefeller? About as I would if I had a wheelbarrow and competed with the Santa Fe [railroad] from here to Kansas City." Debs's major accomplishments would occur after 1900, but in the late 1890s the group soon to be called the Socialist Party of America was already beginning to unite around him.

In 1894, however, it was not the tall, animated Debs but a short, quiet, frustrated businessman from Massillon, Ohio, who captured public attention. His name was Jacob S. Coxey, and like

Coxey's Army   Debs he had a vision. Coxey had become convinced that, to help debtors, the government should issue paper money unbacked by gold—purposeful inflation, in other words. As the depression spread, Coxey recommended a federal job program financed by an issue of $500 million of this "legal tender" paper money to relieve unemployment and revive consumer spending. He planned to publicize his scheme by leading a march

from Massillon to Washington, D.C., gathering a "commonweal army" of unemployed workers along the way. Coxey was so enthusiastic about his project that he christened his newborn son Legal Tender and proposed that his eighteen-year-old daughter lead the procession in a red-white-and-blue gown on a white horse.

About two hundred strong, Coxey's army left Massillon on March 24, 1894. Moving across Ohio and into Pennsylvania, the army received food, housing, and recruits from a score of depressed industrial towns and rural villages. Many participants succumbed to boredom or the weather and dropped out of the march, but elsewhere in the country similar armies organized and began the trek toward Washington.

Coxey's troops, including women and children, entered the capital on April 30. The next day (May Day, a date that made the police nervous because of its traditional association with socialist demonstrations), the citizen army of some five hundred people marched to the Capitol, armed with "war clubs of peace." When Coxey and a few others vaulted the wall surrounding the Capitol grounds, mounted police moved in and routed the crowd. According to one witness, "Women and children were ruthlessly ridden down. A commonwealer who had in some way escaped from the ranks, stood behind a tree and struck a policeman a terrible blow in the back with his war club of peace. The next officer that came up saw the attack and clubbed the commonwealer into insensibility." Coxey tried to speak from the Capitol steps, but the police arrested him and dragged him away. As the arrests and clubbings continued, Coxey's dreams of a demonstration of 400,000 jobless workers dissolved. Like the strikes, the people's first march on Washington had yielded to police muscle.

Coxey's march was an expression of frustration by people who were seeking relief from the uncertainties of industrialization. Unlike socialists, who believed in altering the whole economic system, the Coxey commonwealers merely wanted more jobs and better living standards. Today, in an age of union contracts, regulation of business, and government-sponsored job relief in times of high unemployment, their goals do not appear radical. Yet the brutal reactions of officials reveal how threatening the dissenters, from Coxey to Debs, must have seemed.

POPULISTS AND THE SILVER CRUSADE

Populists too were part of the activist current of protest. Although they did not experience the same kinds of government suppression that unions and Coxey's army experienced, Populists suffered from problems that surfaced just when their political goals seemed attainable. In 1892 their presidential candidate had received over 1 million votes, and as late as 1894 Populist candidates were making good showings in local and state elections throughout the West and South. Nevertheless, like all third parties, the Populists were underfinanced and underorganized. They had strong and colorful candidates, but not enough of

them to wrest control from the two major parties. Many voters were reluctant to break old loyalties, and the Populists had trouble luring supporters away from the Republicans and Democrats. Moreover, the two major parties fought to destroy Populist voting strength, especially in the South.

By the 1890s, the threat of biracial political dissent posed by the farmers' alliance movement prompted southern white Democrats to take urgent action. During the 1880s southern legislatures had enacted several measures to curtail black voting, including poll taxes and literacy tests (see pages 473–475). Dissatisfied that these measures would thwart a coalition of black and white voters in the Populist party and fearful that northern Republicans might enact federal supervision of elections, southern states in the 1890s tried more directly to prevent all blacks from voting.

Disfranchisement was accomplished in clever and devious ways. In 1876 the Supreme Court had affirmed that the Fifteenth Amendment prohibited states from denying the vote to people "on account of race, color, or previous condition of servitude." But, said the court, Congress had no control over state elections beyond provisions set by the Fifteenth Amendment (*U.S.* v. *Reese*). Subsequently, state legislatures found ways to exclude black voters without ever mentioning race, color, or previous condition of servitude. In 1890, Mississippi led the way by requiring all voters to prove they could read and interpret the state constitution. Registration officials applied much stiffer standards to blacks than whites, even to the extent of declaring black college graduates ineligible on grounds of illiteracy. In 1898 Louisiana enacted the first "grandfather clause," which excluded from voting anyone whose ancestors were ineligible to vote before 1867, and other southern states soon followed suit. These and other measures proved effective. In South Carolina, for example, 70 percent of eligible blacks had voted in the presidential election of 1880; by 1896 the rate had dropped to 11 percent. By the early 1900s, blacks had effectively lost their political rights in every southern state except Tennessee.

To a large extent, white supremacist fears were unjustified, for fundamental factors impeded acceptance of blacks by white Populists. To be sure, some Populists had sought a coalition of distressed black and white farmers. Tom Watson, Georgia's most prominent

Critics of the free silver policy advocated by Populists and Democrats in 1896 tried to convince voters that such a policy would result in poverty and low wages. The message of this broadside is that free silver would make Americans as downtrodden as peasants of the most backward countries. Smithsonian Institution.

Populist, noted that "the crushing burdens which now oppress both races in the South will cause each to . . . see a similarity of cause and a similarity of remedy." But even poor white farmers could not put aside their racism. Many came from families that had supported the Ku Klux Klan during Reconstruction, some had once even owned slaves, and they considered blacks to be a permanently inferior people who would never be able to do things for themselves. They seemed to take comfort in the belief that there would always be people worse off than they were. Thus Populists seldom addressed needs of black farmers and used white supremacist rhetoric in order to avoid charges that they encouraged racial mingling.

On the national level, the Populist crusade against the "money power" settled on the issue of silver. Though the currency problem was one of the most complex facing American political leaders, many people saw silver as a simple solution to the nation's ills. To them, free silver meant the end of special privilege for the rich and the return of government to the people. William H. Harvey, author of the immensely popular *Coin's Financial School* (1894), preached that by coining silver "you increase the value of all property by adding to the number of money units in the land. You make it possible for the debtor to pay his debts; business to start anew,

Free Silver

and revivify all the industries of the country, which must remain paralyzed so long as silver as well as all other property is measured by a gold standard."

Using this kind of reasoning, Populists adopted free coinage of silver as their political battle cry. But as the elections of 1896 approached, they faced the dilemma of what strategy to use in order to translate their few previous electoral victories into much greater success. Would they lose their identity by joining with sympathetic factions of the major parties, or would they remain independent as a third party and settle for at best minor successes? Except in the Rocky Mountain states, where free coinage of silver had strong support, the Republicans were unlikely allies. Although Republican politicians could be as moralistic as the Populists, their anti-inflationist conservatism, support for the gold standard, and big-business orientation stood for everything the Populists opposed. In the North and West, alliance with Democrats was more plausible. In many areas the Democratic party retained vestiges of antimonopoly ideology as well as some sympathy for a looser currency system—although gold Democrats like President Grover Cleveland and Senator David Hill of New York did exert powerful opposition. Populists believed they also had links with traditionally Democratic urban workers, who, they assumed, suffered from the same kind of oppression that stifled farmers. In the South, fusion with Democrats seemed less likely, since there the party was the very power structure against which Populists had revolted in the late 1880s. Regardless of their options, the Populists had made certain that the political campaign of 1896 would be like none before it.

THE ELECTION OF 1896

The presidential campaign of 1896 brought the nation's political wanderings to a climax. Each party was divided. Republicans, under the direction of Marcus Alonzo Hanna, a prosperous Ohio industrialist, had the fewest problems. Since early in 1895, Hanna had been maneuvering to win the nomination for Ohio's governor, William

McKinley and Bryan

William Jennings Bryan (1860–1925) in a photograph taken in 1896 when he first ran for president. Bryan was a spellbinding orator who turned agrarian unrest and the issue of free silver into a moral crusade. Library of Congress.

McKinley. By the time the party convened in St. Louis in 1896, Hanna had corralled enough delegates to succeed. "He has advertised McKinley," quipped Theodore Roosevelt, "as if he were a patent medicine." The Republicans' only trauma occurred when the party adopted a moderate platform supporting gold, rejecting a prosilver stance proposed by Senator Henry M. Teller of Colorado. Teller, who had been among the party's founders forty years earlier, walked out of the convention in tears, taking a small group of silver Republicans with him.

At the Democratic convention, silver delegates paraded through the Chicago Amphitheatre wearing silver badges and waving silver banners. Observing their tumultuous demonstrations, one eastern delegate

William McKinley (1843–1901) ran for president in 1896 on a platform that linked business prosperity with national prestige and economic well-being. *Library of Congress.*

vention, Bryan rose to speak on its behalf. In the heat and humidity of the Chicago summer, Bryan's now-famous closing words gripped the delegates:

> Having behind us the producing masses of this nation and the world, supported by the commercial interests, the laboring interests, and the toilers everywhere, we will answer their [the wealthy classes'] demand for a gold standard by saying to them: You shall not press down upon the brow of labor this crown of thorns, you shall not crucify mankind upon a cross of gold.

The speech could not have been more timely; indeed, Bryan planned it to be so. Friends who had been pushing Bryan for the presidential nomination now had no trouble enlisting support. It took Bryan five ballots to win the nomination, but finally the magnetism of the Boy Orator proved irresistible. In bowing to the silverite will of southerners and westerners and repudiating Cleveland's policies in its platform, the party became more attractive to discontented farmers. But like the Republicans, it too drove away a dissenting minority wing. A group of gold Democrats withdrew and nominated their own candidate.

Bryan's nomination presented the Populist party with a dilemma. Should Populists join Democrats in support of Bryan, or should they nominate their own candidate? Tom Watson of Georgia, expressing strong southern sentiment against fusion with the Democrats, warned that "the Democratic idea of fusion [is] that we play Jonah while they play whale." But others reasoned that supporting a different candidate would split the anti-McKinley vote and allow the Republicans to win. In the end the convention compromised, first naming Watson as its vice-presidential nominee to preserve party identity (the Democrats had nominated Maine shipping magnate Arthur Sewall for vice president) and then nominating Bryan for the presidency.

The campaign, in the words of journalist William Allen White, "took the form of religious frenzy. . . . Far into the night, the voices rose—women's voices, children's voices, the voices of old men, of youths and of maidens, rose on the ebbing prairie breezes, as the crusaders of the revolution rode home, praising the people's will as though it were God's will and cursing wealth for its iniquity." Republicans countered Bryan's moral evangelism and attacks on privilege

wrote, "For the first time I can understand the scenes of the French Revolution!" "All the silverites need is a Moses," remarked a *New York World* reporter. They found one in William Jennings Bryan.

Bryan had arrived at the Democratic national convention in Chicago in July 1896 as a member of a contested Nebraska delegation. A former congressman whose support for free coinage of silver had annoyed President Cleveland, he was only thirty-six years old, avidly religious, and highly distressed by what the depression had done to midwestern farmers. The convention, as expected, chose to seat Bryan and his colleagues instead of a competing faction that supported the gold standard. Shortly afterward, as a member of the party's resolutions committee, Bryan helped to write a platform calling for free coinage of silver.

When the platform was presented to the full con-

Chapter 20: GILDED AGE POLITICS, 1877–1900

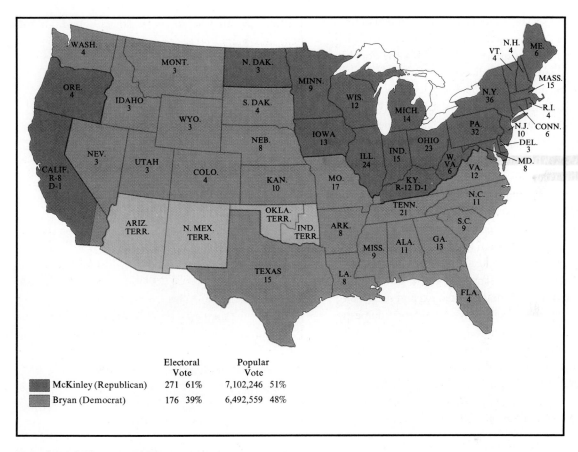

		Electoral Vote	Popular Vote
■	McKinley (Republican)	271 61%	7,102,246 51%
▨	Bryan (Democrat)	176 39%	6,492,559 48%

Presidential Election, 1896

(he repeatedly preached that "every great economic question is in reality a great moral question") by predicting chaos if he should win. While Bryan raced around the country giving as many as twenty speeches a day, Mark Hanna invited hundreds of thousands of people to McKinley's home town of Canton, Ohio, where the candidate plied them with speeches on moderation and prosperity. Leaving moralizing to the Democrats, Republican candidates adopted the pragmatic approach of promising something for everyone and a live-and-let-live philosophy for all.

The election results revealed that the political standoff had finally ended. McKinley, the symbol of Republican pragmatism and the new **Election** economic order, beat Bryan by over **Results** 600,000 popular votes and by 271 to 176 in the electoral college (see map). It was the most lopsided presidential election since 1872.

Democrats and Populists had done all they could to rally the nation. Bryan had tried to offset the huge Republican campaign chest, estimated at between $3.5 and $7 million, by traveling 18,000 miles and giving over six hundred speeches, but lean campaign finances and obsession with the silver issue undermined his effort. Silver especially prevented the Populists from building the urban-rural coalition that would have given them political breadth. Reformer Henry Demarest Lloyd summarized the matter succinctly: "Free silver," he wrote, "is the cow bird of the reform movement. It waited till the nest had been built by the sacrifices and labor of others, and then it laid its eggs in it, pushing out the others which it smashed to the ground." Farmers' demands for an expanded currency lacked broad appeal. Urban workers shied away from the silver issue because they feared that high prices would result. Labor leaders like Samuel Gompers of the AFL, though partly sympathetic, would not join with Populists because they were unconvinced that farmers were employees, like industrial workers. And socialists like Daniel DeLeon denounced Populists as "retrograde" because, unlike socialists, they still believed in free enterprise. Thus the Populist crusade for democracy collapsed in 1896. Although Populists and fusion candidates made a few gains in state and congressional elections, the Bryan-Watson ticket polled only 222,600 votes nationwide.

As president, McKinley signed the Gold Standard Act (1900), which required that all paper money be backed by gold. A seasoned politician, personable and attractive, McKinley was best

The McKinley Presidency known for his expertise in crafting high protective tariffs; as a congressman from Ohio, he had guided passage of record high rates in 1890. He accordingly supported the Dingley Tariff of 1897, which raised duties even higher—though it did expand reciprocity provisions. During McKinley's presidency domestic tensions subsided; an upward swing of the business cycle and an increased money supply from new gold discoveries in Alaska, Australia, and South Africa helped to restore prosperity. Good times enabled McKinley to beat Bryan again in 1900, using the slogan "The Full Dinner Pail." Freed from the care of the economy, McKinley spent time on foreign affairs. A strong believer in the need to open new markets abroad, he encouraged imperialistic ventures in Latin America and the Pacific (see Chapter 22).

As a result of the 1896 campaign, political parties learned that in future elections they would have to be sensitive to the pluralism of American society. They would have to satisfy a broad spectrum of interests rather than march under the banner of moral perfection. The reform spirit would survive, but its success would depend on cooperation, not on the sermons of righteous evangelists. Ironically, by 1920 many of the Populists' reform goals would be achieved, including regulation of railroads, banks, and utilities; shorter working hours; a variant of the subtreasury system; a graduated income tax; direct election of senators; the secret ballot, and more. These reforms succeeded because a number of groups united behind them. Immigration, urbanization, and industrialization had transformed the United States into a pluralistic society where compromise among interest groups had become a political fact of life. The election of 1896 and the end of the Gilded Age equilibrium confirmed that transformation.

IMPORTANT EVENTS

1873	Coinage of silver dollars ends
1873–78	Depression
1876	Hayes elected president *U.S.* v. *Reese*
1878	Bland-Allison Act Anthony Amendment defeated in Congress
1880	Garfield elected president
1881	Garfield assassinated; Arthur assumes presidency
1883	Pendleton Civil Service Act
1884–85	Depression
1884	Cleveland elected president
1887	Collapse of farm prices
1888	Harrison elected president
1890	McKinley Tariff Sherman Silver Purchase Act Sherman Anti-Trust Act
1892	Populist convention in Omaha Cleveland elected president
1893	Repeal of Sherman Silver Purchase Act
1893–97	Depression
1894	Wilson-Gorman Tariff Pullman strike; Debs arrested and turns to socialism Coxey's march
1895	Cleveland deals with bankers to save gold reserve
1896	McKinley elected president
1897	Dingley Tariff
1900	Gold Standard Act McKinley re-elected

SUGGESTIONS FOR FURTHER READING

General

Sean Denis Cashman, *America in the Gilded Age* (1984); Harold U. Faulkner, *Politics, Reform, and Expansion, 1890–1900* (1959); Ray Ginger, *The Age of Excess*, 2nd ed. (1975); H. Wayne Morgan, ed., *The Gilded Age* (1970); H. Wayne Morgan, *From Hayes to McKinley* (1969); Paul Studenski and Herman E. Krouss, *Financial History of the United States* (1952); Alan Trachtenberg, *The Incorporation of America: Culture and Society in the Gilded Age* (1982); R. Hal Williams, *Years of Decision: American Politics in the 1890s* (1978).

Parties and Political Issues

John H. Dobson, *Politics in the Gilded Age* (1972); Eleanor Flexner, *Century of Struggle: The Women's Rights Movement in the United States* (1959); Elisabeth Griffith, *In Her Own Right: The Life of Elizabeth Cady Stanton* (1984); J. Rogers Hollingsworth, *The Whirligig of Politics: The Democracy of Cleveland and Bryan* (1963); Ari A. Hoogenboom, *Outlawing the Spoils: The Civil Service Movement* (1961); Richard J. Jensen, *The Winning of the Midwest* (1971); David M. Jordan, *Roscoe Conkling of New York* (1971); Matthew Josephson, *The Politicos* (1938); Morton Keller, *Affairs of State* (1977); Paul Kleppner, *The Third Electoral System, 1853–1892* (1979); Paul Kleppner, *The Cross of Culture* (1970); Robert D. Marcus, *Grand Old Party* (1971); Samuel T. McSeveney, *The Politics of Depression* (1972); Walter T. K. Nugent, *Money and American Society* (1968); A. M. Paul, *Conservative Crisis and the Rule of Law: Attitudes of Bar and Bench, 1887–1895* (1969); David J. Rothman, *Politics and Power: The United States Senate, 1869–1901* (1966); John G. Sproat, *The Best Men: Liberal Reformers in the Gilded Age* (1968); Tom E. Terrill, *The Tariff, Politics, and American Foreign Policy, 1874–1901* (1973).

The Presidency

Kenneth E. Davison, *The Presidency of Rutherford B. Hayes* (1972); Lewis L. Gould, *The Presidency of William McKinley* (1981); Margaret Leech and Harry J. Brown, *The Garfield Orbit* (1978); Horace Samuel Merrill, *Bourbon Leader: Grover Cleveland and the Democratic Party* (1957); H. Wayne Morgan, *William McKinley and His America* (1963); Allan Peskin, *Garfield* (1978); Thomas C. Reeves, *Gentleman Boss: The Life of Chester Alan Arthur* (1975); H. J. Sievers, *Benjamin Harrison*, 3 vols. (1952–1968).

Currents of Protest

William M. Dick, *Labor and Socialism in America* (1972); John P. Diggins, *The American Left in the Twentieth Century* (1973); Ray Ginger, *Bending Cross: A Biography of Eugene Victor Debs* (1969); John Laslett, *Labor and the Left* (1970); Donald L. McMurray, *Coxey's Army* (1929); Nick Salvatore, *Eugene V. Debs: Citizen and Socialist* (1982); David Shannon, *The Socialist Party of America* (1955).

Populism and the Election of 1896

Peter H. Argersinger, *Populism and Politics: William Alfred Peffer and the People's Party* (1974); Paolo Coletta, *William Jennings Bryan: Political Evangelist* (1964); Paul W. Glad, *McKinley, Bryan, and the People* (1964); Paul W. Glad, *The Trumpet Soundeth: William Jennings Bryan and His Democracy* (1964); Lawrence Goodwyn, *Democratic Promise: The Populist Moment in America* (1976); Sheldon Hackney, *Populism to Progressivism in Alabama* (1969); Steven Hahn, *The Roots of Southern Populism* (1983); John D. Hicks, *The Populist Revolt* (1931); Richard Hofstadter, *The Age of Reform: From Bryan to FDR* (1955); Stanley L. Jones, *The Election of 1896* (1964); J. Morgan Kousser, *The Shaping of Southern Politics* (1974); Walter T. K. Nugent, *The Tolerant Populists* (1963); Norman Pollack, ed., *The Populist Mind* (1967); Norman Pollack, *The Populist Response to Industrial America* (1962); Martin Ridge, *Ignatius Donnelly* (1962); Allan Weinstein, *Prelude to Populism: Origins of the Silver Issue* (1970); Charles Morrow Wilson, *The Commoner: William Jennings Bryan* (1970); C. Vann Woodward, *Tom Watson* (1938).

THE PROGRESSIVE ERA
1895–1920

CHAPTER 21

*T*homas Edison, *of* all people, would have known if something was not working properly. He perfected and promoted so many items of modern mass technology—the light bulb, the phonograph, and the motion-picture projector, among others—that he should have had good reason to view his world optimistically. But he did not. With the perceptiveness of the good inventor he was, Edison found American society unsatisfactory and perplexing. Writing to his friend Henry Ford in 1912, Edison observed that

in a lot of respects we Americans are the rawest and crudest of all. Our production, our factory laws, our charities, our relations between capital and labor, our distribution—all wrong, out of gear. We've stumbled along for a while, trying to run a new civilization in old ways, but we've got to start to make this world over.

Americans had always been preoccupied with reforming their society, with "making it over," but between the 1890s and the end of the First World War, an intensified rush of reform swept the country. More and more people who felt as Edison did tried to address the problems of their time directly. Their efforts, inspired by a complicated mixture of calculated self-interest and unselfish benevolence, shaped what can be called the Progressive era.

During the 1890s, a severe depression, frightening labor violence, political upheaval, and foreign entanglements had shaken the nation. Although many of the promises of technology had been fulfilled, great numbers of Americans continued to suffer from poverty and disease. In the minds of many, industrialists had become the nation's new monsters, controlling markets, wages, and prices in order to maximize their profits. And government seemed corroded by bosses and their henchmen, who used politics to enrich themselves.

From this malaise emerged a broad, complex spirit of reform, so many-sided that it is hard to identify the movement's unifying characteristics. By the 1910s many reformers were calling themselves progressives, and a new political party by that name had formed to embody their principles. Since that time historians

have used the term *progressivism* to refer to the reform spirit in general, while disagreeing over the movement's meaning and its membership. It is probably most accurate to consider the era between 1895 and 1920 as characterized by a series of movements, each aimed in one way or another at renovating or restoring American society, its values, and its institutions.

The urge toward reform had many causes. Industrialization had brought unprecedented productivity, awesome technology, and a cornucopia of new consumer goods. But it had also included labor problems, wasteful use of natural resources, and abuse of corporate power. The rapidly growing network of cities facilitated the amassing and distribution of goods, services, and cultural amenities but also magnified the problems of poverty, disease, crime, and political corruption. Massive influxes of immigrants and the rise of a new class of managers and professionals shook the foundations of the old social classes. And the debilitating depression that blanketed the nation from 1893 to 1897 made many leading citizens realize what working people had known for some time: the central promise of American life was not being kept. Equality of opportunity—whether economic, political, or social—was a myth.

Progressives tried to surmount these problems by organizing their ideas and actions around three basic themes. First, they would end abuses of power. Attacks on unfair privilege, monopoly, and corruption were not new in 1900; Jacksonians and Populists are only two of many examples of such a tradition. But in the Progressive era, the attacks became more strenuous than ever before. Trustbusting, consumers' rights, and good government became important political issues. Second, progressives aimed to replace corrupt power with the power of reformed social institutions. Though they wanted to protect the individual's rights, they abandoned old individualistic assumptions such as the notion that hard work and good character automatically assured success and that the poor had only themselves to blame for their plight. Instead, progressives acknowledged that society and its institutions had power to help or harm the individual, and they believed these institutions must provide opportunity for everyone. Their revolt against unchanging categories of thought challenged entrenched attitudes toward women's role, race relations, public education, legal and scientific thought, and morality. Third, progressives wanted to apply principles of science and efficiency on a nationwide scale to all economic, social, and political institutions. Their aim was not only to minimize social and economic disorder but to establish cooperation, especially between business and government, that would end wasteful competition.

Befitting their name, progressives had strong faith in the ability of humankind to create a better world. They often used such phrases as "humanity's universal growth" and "the upward spiral of human development." Judge Ben Lindsey of Denver, who spearheaded reform in the treatment of juvenile delinquents, expressed the progressive creed when he wrote, "In the end the people are bound to do the right thing, no matter how much they fail at times." Government, purged of corruption and favoritism to make it the servant of the people, became the instrument of progress. During the Progressive era, a new activism infused the presidency, as well as Congress and state and local governments. More than ever before, Americans looked to government as an agent that could and should intervene in social and economic relations to protect the common good and substitute public interest for self-interest.

WHO WERE THE PROGRESSIVES?

The Progressive era emerged out of the new political atmosphere that formed after the tumultuous election of 1896 (see pages 581–584) and the issues raised by urban reformers in the previous half-century (see pages 528–530). As the twentieth century dawned, the loyalty that political parties had once commanded seriously eroded, and voter turnouts declined considerably. In presidential elections, voter participation dropped from Gilded Age levels of over 80 percent of the eligible electorate to almost 60 percent in northern states and under 30 percent in southern states, where blacks had been excluded from

the polls. Parties and elections, it seemed, were losing their functions of providing Americans with a means of influencing government policies.

Instead, the political system was opening up to entry by various and shifting interest groups, many of which supported reform issues related to their activities. First, voluntary associations had been a vital feature of local life since the 1790s, but after the 1890s many organizations became nationwide in scope and began to try to shape government policy. These organizations included professional associations, such as the American Bar Association; women's organizations, such as the National American Woman Suffrage Association; issue-oriented lobbies, such as the National Consumers League; civic associations; and so on. Members of these organizations hoped to advance their own interests and to educate others about their goals. They made politics much more fragmented and issue-focused than in earlier eras.

Second, although a spirit of moral regeneration, political democracy, and antimonopolism lingered from the rural-based Populist movement, the prevailing issues of the Progressive era were urban. The progressive quest for social justice, educational and legal reform, and streamlining of government was actually an extension of the urban-reform goals of the previous half-century. Indeed, between 1890 and 1920 the proportion of the nation's population living in cities rose from 35 percent to over 51 percent; the number of places with fifty thousand or more people rose from 58 to 144. Recognition of the magnitude of such changes, as well as easier communications by mail, telephone, and telegraph, stimulated urban reformers to exchange information and to consolidate their efforts. The formation of the National Municipal League in 1895 and the National Civic Federation in 1900 signaled the beginning of the new reform era. The National Municipal League served as a forum for debate on issues of civic reform, such as bossism versus civil service, revisions of tax laws, nonpartisan elections, and municipal ownership of public utilities. The National Civic Federation broadened discussion of social reforms, such as workers' compensation and arbitration of labor disputes.

Organizations and individuals who accepted the three progressive themes—opposition to abuse of power, reform of social institutions, quest for cooperation and scientific efficiency—could be found

Judge Ben Lindsey (1869–1943) of Denver was a progressive reformer who worked for better legal protection for children. Typical of many reformers of his era, Lindsey had an earnest faith in the ability of humankind to build a better world.   Library of Congress

in almost all levels of society. The new middle class, consisting of men and women in the professions of law, medicine, social work, religion, teaching, and business, formed the vanguard of the progressives. Repelled by inefficiency and immorality in business, government, and human relations, these people set out to apply scientific techniques they had learned in their professions to problems of the larger society.

Many middle-class progressive reformers were motivated by personal indignation, if not revulsion, at corruption and injustice. This feeling was expressed by journalists whom Theodore Roosevelt dubbed *muckrakers* (alluding to a character in John Bunyan's *Pilgrim's Progress* who rejected a crown for a muckrake). These writers, unlike journalists who merely reported events, fed the public taste for scandal and sensation by investigating and attacking social, economic, and political wrongs. Their fact-filled articles in *McClure's*, *Hampton's*, and other popular magazines, as well as books, exposed such offenses as the sale of tainted meat, fraudulent insurance schemes, and prostitution. Lincoln Steffens's articles in *McClure's*, later published as *The Shame of the Cities* (1904), ranked among the highlights of muckraker journalism. Steffens hoped

his surveys of misrule by bosses would inspire mass indignation and ultimately reform. Other well-known muckraking efforts included Upton Sinclair's *The Jungle* (1906), a novel that attacked the meatpacking industry, Burton J. Hendrick's *Story of Life Insurance* (1907), and David Graham Phillips's *Treason of the Senate* (1906).

Middle-class indignation also revealed itself in opposition to party politics, a reflection of the new political system that arose after 1896. Reformers had

Political Reformers

a strong distaste for the bargaining and self-serving they believed permeated boss-ridden parties. They felt, as the journalist William Allen White did, that machines and bosses should "be reduced to mere political scrap iron by the rise of the people." (When reformers referred to "the people," they all too often meant middle-class people like themselves, excluding the native working class, blacks, and immigrants.) To improve the political process, these progressives advocated such reforms as nominating candidates through direct primaries instead of party caucuses and nonpartisan elections to prevent the corruption and bribery that party loyalties seemed to breed.

To involve more people and to make legislators more responsible, they advocated three reform devices: the initiative, which would enable voters to propose new laws on their own; the referendum, which would enable voters to accept or reject a law at the ballot box; and the recall, which would allow voters to remove officials and judges from office before their terms were up. Their goal, like that of the business consolidation movement, was efficiency. The government would be reclaimed by replacing the favoritism of the boss system with rational, accountable management chosen by a responsible electorate.

Middle-class progressive reformers, then, had an aversion to party politics, not to government. They turned to government for aid in achieving most of their goals, for they became convinced that only government had the leverage they needed. Members of the new professions in which systematic investigation and efficient management were of prime importance also believed with the muckrakers that knowledge was the key to progress. Science and scientific method—system, planning, control, predictability—were central to their values. Just as corporations were applying scientific management to achieve economic efficiency, progressives used expertise and planning to achieve social and political efficiency.

The progressive spirit also stirred some elite business leaders. Successful executives like Alexander Cassatt of the Pennsylvania Railroad supported limited government regulation and political re-

Upper-class Reformers forms as means of protecting their interests from more radical political elements. Others, like E. A. Filene, founder of a Boston department store, and Thomas L. Johnson, a wealthy streetcar magnate, were humanitarians who worked unselfishly for social justice. Business leaders guided organizations like the Municipal Voters League and the U.S. Chamber of Commerce, which supported limited political and economic reform. Their aim was to stabilize society by imposing the model of corporate organization on institutions like schools, hospitals, and local government. Women of the elite classes often led reform organizations like the YWCA, which sponsored aid and education for the growing numbers of unmarried working women who had moved away from their families, and the Women's Christian Temperance Union, which was the largest women's organization of its time and which

participated in numerous causes besides those linked with drinking.

But not all progressive reformers had middle- or upper-class standing. During this era vital elements of what would become modern American liberalism

Working-class Reformers grew out of the working-class urban experience. By the close of the nineteenth century, many urban workers were pressing for government intervention to ensure safety and promote welfare. They wanted improvements in housing and health, safe factories, shorter working hours, workers' compensation, and other reforms. Often these were the very people who supported the political bosses, supposedly the enemies of reform. Workers knew that bosses needed to cultivate support among their constituents and would cater to voters' needs. And in fact bossism was not necessarily at odds with humanitarianism. Indeed, when Tammany Hall boss "Big Tim" Sullivan was asked why he supported a law requiring shorter working hours for women, he explained, "I had seen me sister go out to work when she was only fourteen and I know we ought to help these gals by giving 'em a law which will prevent 'em from being broken down while they're still young."

After 1900, voters from inner-city districts populated by migrant and immigrant working-class families elected a number of progressive legislators who had trained in the arena of machine politics. People like New York's Alfred E. Smith and Robert F. Wagner, Massachusetts's David I. Walsh, and Illinois's Edward F. Dunne—all of whom came from immigrant backgrounds—became important reform spokesmen at the state and national levels. They were most successful when they allied with other reformers, particularly those from the middle class, to pass laws aiding labor and social welfare. The chief goal of these legislators was to establish government responsibility for alleviating the hardship that had resulted from urban-industrial growth. They opposed such reforms as prohibition, Sunday closing laws, civil service, and nonpartisan elections, all of which conflicted with their constituents' interests.

Some deeply frustrated workers wanted more than progressive reform. They wanted a different society. These people turned to the socialist movement, a mixture of immigrant intellectuals, industrial workers, disaffected populists, and western miners and lum-

Though their objectives sometimes differed from those of middle-class progressive reformers, socialists also became a more active group in the early twentieth century. Socialist parades on May Day, such as this one in New York in 1910, were meant to express the solidarity of all working people. Library of Congress.

bermen. Some factions had more impact than others. The radical union known as the Industrial Workers of the World—the IWW, or "Wobblies" (see page 502)—organized strife-torn strikes in western lumber and mining camps, in the steel town of McKees Rocks, Pennsylvania (1907), and in the textile mills of Lawrence, Massachusetts (1912). Led by former miner "Big Bill" Haywood, along with the charismatic seventy-five-year-old Mother Jones and the young radical Elizabeth Gurley Flynn, the IWW reached out to unskilled laborers, promising to unite all workers by enabling them to control their own factories. IWW membership probably never exceeded 150,000, however, and the organization faded during the First World War when federal prosecution—and persecution—sent many of its leaders to jail.

Socialists

The majority of socialists united behind Eugene V. Debs (see page 577), the tall, dynamic railroad organizer who drew nearly 100,000 votes in the 1900 presidential election. Though Debs was never able to develop a consistent program beyond his opposition to war and bourgeois materialism, he was a spellbinding speaker for the radical cause. On his speaking tours, he touched increasing numbers of disenchanted workers and intellectuals. As candidate for the Socialist party, Debs won 400,000 votes in his 1904 campaign for the presidency, and in 1912, at the pinnacle of his and his party's career, he polled over 900,000.

With their stinging attacks on exploitation and unfair privilege, Debs and other socialists like Milwaukee's Victor Berger and New York's Morris Hilquit made attractive overtures to reform-minded people. Some, such as settlement-house worker and child-labor reformer Florence Kelley, identified with the socialist cause. But most progressives avoided radical attacks on free enterprise. Municipal ownership of public utilities was as far as they would go toward changing the system. Indeed, progressives had too much at stake in the capitalist system to overthrow it. Thus even in Wisconsin, where progressivism was most highly developed, progressives would not join with Berger's more radical group. California progressives even formed a temporary alliance with reactionaries to prevent socialists from gaining power in Los Angeles. And few humanitarian reformers objected when in 1918 Debs was jailed for giving an antiwar speech.

But it would be a mistake to imagine that the progressive spirit touched all of American society between 1895 and 1920. There were still large numbers of people, heavily represented in Congress, who opposed reform. They disliked government interference in economic affairs—except when it strengthened the tariff—and saw nothing wrong with existing power structures. Outside government, this outlook was represented by business leaders like J. P. Morgan, John D. Rockefeller, and E. H. Harriman, men who insisted that real progress would result from maintaining the profit incentive. Within government, this ideology was expressed by old-guard Republicans like Senator Nelson W. Aldrich of Rhode Island and House Speaker Joseph Cannon of Illinois.

Progressive reformers operated from the center of the ideological spectrum. Moderate, concerned, sometimes contradictory, they believed on the one hand that the laissez-faire system was obsolete and on the other that radical challenges to the fundamentals of capitalism were dangerous. Like the Jeffersonians, they believed in the conscience and will of the people; like the Hamiltonians, they opted for a strong central government to act in the interest of conscience.

The Progressive era, then, was a complex period of multiple, overlapping, and sometimes conflicting reform movements. The era is best characterized by its challenges to almost every aspect of conventional society: politics, social relationships, ideas, institutions, and morality. The goals of progressive reformers were both idealistic and realistic. As minister-reformer Walter Rauschenbusch wrote, "We shall demand perfection and never expect to get it."

GOVERNMENTAL AND LEGISLATIVE REFORM

What were the responsibilities of government? Answers to this question in the early twentieth century were much different from those of the nineteenth century. Traditionally, theorists had held that a democratic government should be small and unobtrusive, interfering in private affairs only in unique circumstances and withdrawing once balance had been restored. In the late nineteenth century this conception eroded. Corporations, though opposed to government regulation of their activities, nevertheless pursued government aid and protection for their enterprises. Discontented farmers organized to seek government regulation of railroads and other monopolistic businesses. City dwellers, accustomed to the favors furnished by local political machines, came to expect government to act positively on their behalf.

By the turn of the century, professionals and intellectuals were accepting the notion that government could and should exert more power to ensure justice and well-being. They were becoming convinced that a simple, inflexible government was ineffective in a complex industrial age, and that public power was needed to counteract corruption and exploitation. But before reformers could use such power in ways they believed to be necessary, they would have to recapture government from the politicians whose greed had soiled the democratic system. Thus an important thrust of progressive activity was the effort to root out corruption in government.

Reformers first attacked this problem in the cities (see pages 528–529). Between 1870 and 1900 opponents of the boss system tried to redirect government through structural reforms such as civil service, nonpartisan elections, and tighter scrutiny of public expenditures. A few reform leaders developed sympathies for poverty relief, housing improvement, and prolabor laws. But most worked chiefly for an efficient—meaning economical—government. After 1900 the momentum for reform brought into being the city manager and city commission forms of government (where urban officials were chosen for their professional expertise, not their political connections) and public ownership of utilities (so that gas, electricity, telephone, and streetcar companies would not profit at the public's expense).

Reformers discovered, however, that the city was too small an arena for the kind of changes they sought. State and federal government offered more promising opportunities for effecting reform through legislation. Because of their faith in a strong, fair-minded executive, progressives looked to governors and other elected officials to extend and protect the reforms that had been achieved at the local level. The reformers' goals varied from one region or state to another. In the Plains and Far West, reformers rallied behind railroad regulation and such governmental reforms as the initiative and referendum. In the South they continued the Populist crusade against big business and autocratic politicians. And in the urban-industrial Northeast and Midwest, reformers directed their attention to corrupt political machines and unsafe labor conditions.

The reform movement produced a number of skillful, influential, and often charismatic governors who used executive power to achieve change. Their ranks included Braxton Bragg Comer of Al-

Progressive Governors

abama and Hoke Smith of Georgia, who introduced business regulations and other reforms in the South; Albert Cummins of Iowa and Hiram Johnson of California, who battled the railroads that dominated their states; and Woodrow Wilson of New Jersey, whose administrative reforms were copied by other governors. Such men were not always saints, however. Smith supported the disfranchisement of blacks, and Johnson discriminated against Japanese-Americans.

Probably the most notable progressive governor was Wisconsin's Robert M. La Follette. A self-made small-town lawyer whose short, compact build and thick, bristling hair suited his combative personality, La Follette rose through the ranks of the state Republican party to the governorship in 1900. As governor he initiated a multipronged reform program that included direct primaries, more equitable taxes, and regulation of railroad rates. He also established regulatory commissions staffed with experts, whose investigations supplied La Follette with facts and figures that he used in fiery speeches to muster public support for his policies. After three terms as governor, La

Robert M. La Follette (1855–1925) was one of the most dynamic of progressive politicians. As governor of Wisconsin, he sponsored a program of political reform and business regulation known as the Wisconsin Plan. In 1906 he entered the U.S. Senate and continued to champion progressive reform. The National Progressive Republican League, which La Follette founded in 1911, became the core of the Progressive party. Library of Congress.

Follette was elected senator and carried his progressive ideals into national politics. "Battling Bob" had a rare ability to take a tempered, scientific approach to reform while still appealing to the people with moving rhetoric. His goal, he once asserted, "was not to 'smash' corporations, but to drive them out of politics, and then to treat them exactly the same as other people are treated."

Not all state leaders were as successful as La Follette. To be sure, the crusade against party politics and corruption did accomplish some permanent changes. By 1916 all but three states had direct primaries, and many states had adopted the initiative, referendum, and recall. And political reformers achieved a major goal in 1912 when the states ratified the Seventeenth Amendment, which provided for the direct election of U.S. senators (formerly elected by state legislatures, which often were corrupted by private interests). But political reforms did not always bring about the desired results. Party bosses, better organized and more experienced than reformers, were still able to dominate elections. The initiative, referendum, and recall often failed because special-interest groups could control outcomes by using large funds to lobby the public and organize the voting. Moreover, political reformers found that entrenched power, aided by the courts, many times could counterattack and defeat progressive campaigns.

New state laws aimed at bettering social welfare had greater impact than most political reforms, especially in factories. Broadly interpreting their powers to protect the health and safety of their citizens, many states enacted factory inspection laws, and by 1916 nearly two-thirds of the states had insurance for victims of industrial accidents. A coalition of labor and humanitarian groups supported these laws and even induced some legislatures to grant aid to mothers with dependent children. Under pressure from the National Child Labor Committee, nearly every state established a minimum age for employment (varying from twelve to sixteen), and prohibited employers from working children more than eight or ten hours a day. Such laws, however, were hard to enforce because they seldom provided for the close inspection of factories that full enforcement required. Moreover, families that needed extra income encouraged their children to work and to lie about their ages. Several groups also joined forces to limit working hours for women. After the Supreme Court upheld Oregon's ten-hour limit in 1908, many more states passed laws protecting women workers. Finally, efforts of the American Association for Old Age Security began to succeed in 1914, when Arizona established old-age pensions. Though the law was struck down by the courts, the First World War renewed interest in pensions, and in the 1920s many states enacted laws to provide for needy older people.

Progressive Legislation

These and other social reforms were strongly opposed by people who thought them detrimental to their self-interest or who believed that government interference in such matters would destroy the free enterprise system. Some business associations bitterly fought consumers' efforts to legislate milk and meat inspections. The National Association of Manufacturers coordinated the battle against regulation of business and working conditions. And legislators friendly to special interests connived to weaken the new laws by failing to fund their enforcement.

Reformers themselves were not always certain about what was progressive, especially in terms of human behavior. The main problem seemed to be whether or not it was possible to create a desirable moral climate through legislation. Some reformers, such as the members of the Social Gospel movement (see page 529), believed that only church-based inspiration and humanitarian work, rather than legislation, could transform society. But other people believed state intervention was necessary to achieve purity, especially in drinking habits and sexual behavior.

Moral Reform

The formation of the Anti-Saloon League in 1893 marked a new turn in the long campaign against drunkenness and its effects on society. This organization of reformers joined with the Women's Christian Temperance Union (founded in 1873) to publicize the connections between alcoholism and poverty, unemployment and family breakups and to show that drinking produced liver disease and other health problems. The result was that a large number of states, counties, towns, and city wards restricted the sale and consumption of liquor. By 1900 almost one-fourth of the nation's population lived in communities with such restrictions. But as consumption of alcohol, especially beer, increased after 1900, prohibitionists became convinced that a national law was the only solution. By 1917 they had converted to their cause such notables as Supreme Court Justice Louis D. Brandeis and former president William Howard Taft. And in 1918 they induced Congress to pass the Eighteenth Amendment, prohibiting the manufacture, sale, and transportation of intoxicating liquors. (The amendment was ratified in 1919 and implemented in 1920.) Not all prohibitionists were progressive reformers, and all progressives were not prohibitionists. Yet the Eighteenth Amendment can be seen as an outcome of the progressive urge to change society and elevate morality through reform legislation.

Public outrage boiled over after 1900 when muckraking journalists exposed interstate and international rings that kidnapped young women and forced them to become prostitutes, a practice called white slavery. Middle-class moralists, already alarmed by a perceived link between immigration and prostitution, prodded governments to investigate the problem and recommend corrective legislation. The Chicago Vice Commission, for example, undertook a "scientific" survey and published its findings, called *The Social*

Evil in Chicago, in 1911. The report underscored the poverty, ignorance, and desperation that drove women, especially immigrants and blacks, to prostitution. Above all, however, it asserted that

> it is a law and not a woman problem which we face today—commercialized by men—supported by men—the supply of fresh victims furnished by men. . . . So long as there is lust in the hearts of men [the Social Evil] will seek out some method of expression. Until the hearts of men are changed we can hope for no absolute annihilation of the Social Evil.

Nonetheless, reformers believed they could attack prostitution without changing "the hearts of men." By 1915 nearly every state had outlawed brothels and the soliciting of sex. And in 1910 Congress passed the Mann Act, or White Slave Traffic Act, prohibiting interstate and international transportation of women for immoral purposes.

Like prohibition, the Mann Act had reactionary as well as progressive elements. Even so, it reflected growing sentiment that state and national governments could improve human behavior. Reformers believed that the source of evil was not original sin but the social environment. If evil were human-made, then it could be human-destroyed. Thus human intervention, in the form of laws, could help create a heaven on earth.

ASSAULT ON OLD ASSUMPTIONS IN EDUCATION, LAW, AND THE SOCIAL SCIENCES

While legislation anchored the reform impulse, equally important changes were occurring in schools, courts, and settlement houses during the Progressive era. The preoccupation with efficiency and scientific management challenged educators, judges, and social scientists to seek solutions to the problems of modern mass society. Darwin's theory of evolution had upset traditional beliefs; immigration had replaced social uniformity with diverse nationalities; and economic change had shaken old habits of production and consumption. Ways of thinking and acting had to be found that would be meaningful for the new era yet preserve what was best in the past. A new flexibility was needed. Knowledge, as philosopher and educator John Dewey wrote, was "no longer an immobile solid; it has been liquefied. It is actively moving in all the currents of society itself." Such an attitude produced what historians have called a revolt against formalism.

Changing patterns of school attendance encouraged these new ways of thinking. As late as the 1870s, when rural society needed children to do farm work and schools were located far apart, Americans attended school for an average of only four years. By 1900, however, swelling cities contained multitudes of children who were removed from farm work and had more time for school. Also urban taxpayers were providing revenues to make extended mass education possible. Boosted by compulsory-attendance laws, public-school enrollments rose from 6.9 million in 1870 to 17.8 million in 1910. During the same period the number of public high schools grew from five hundred to over ten thousand.

Reformers had long envisioned education as a means of bettering society. As early as 1883, psychologist G. Stanley Hall, whose ideas strongly influenced John Dewey, had noted that the experiences of modern urban schoolchildren were much different from those of their farm-bred parents and grandparents. In the early nineteenth century, school curricula chiefly taught moralistic pieties. *McGuffey's Reader*, used by primary schools throughout the nation, contained homilies such as, "By virtue we secure happiness" and "One deed of shame is succeeded by years of penitence." Hall and Dewey, however, asserted that education had to adjust in order to prepare children for productive citizenship and self-fulfilling lives. Children, not subject matter, should be the focus of school policy, and schools should serve as community centers and instruments of social progress. Above all, said Dewey, education should relate directly to experience. Children should be encouraged to discover things for themselves. Rote memorization

Progressive Education

The objective of progressive education was to free children from the rigid classrooms of the past, where pupils had to sit quietly at attention, and enable them to learn by doing and making things. Rather than make the subject matter the major focus of the learning process, progressives made children the centers of attention.   Library of Congress.

and outdated subjects should be replaced by subjects relevant to students' lives.

Progressive education, based on theories Dewey explored in *The School and Society* (1899) and *Democracy and Education* (1916), was a uniquely American phenomenon. Like American economic theory, it emphasized growth. To Dewey, personal growth, not mastery of a given body of knowledge, was the goal of human existence. Because people grew fastest mentally in their youth, and because the family could no longer perform the educational functions it had fulfilled in an agrarian society, schools had to assume responsibility for cultivating intelligence and creativity. From kindergarten (a new development pioneered by the German educator Friedrich Froebel) through high school, children were supposed to learn through experience. In the Laboratory School that Dewey and his wife Alice directed at the University of Chicago, children were not required to recite lessons as their counterparts had done in the nineteenth

century. Instead they examined, built, and discussed things just as they would outside school.

Personal growth also became the driving principle behind college education. The purpose of American colleges and universities had traditionally been that of their European counterparts: to train a select few for the professions of law, medicine, teaching, and religion. But in the late nineteenth century, places of higher education multiplied, spurred by public aid and increases in the number of people who could afford tuition. Between 1870 and 1910 the number of colleges and universities grew from 563 to nearly 1,000. Curricula expanded as educators sought to make learning attractive to more students. Harvard University, under President Charles W. Eliot, pioneered in substituting electives for required courses and in experimenting with new teaching techniques.

Much of the expansion in college enrollments,

Growth of Colleges and Universities

ARITHMETIC.

THE NEW
EDVCATION
ILLVSTRATED
by Edith C. Westcott

Number 2

WITH PHOTOGRAPHS
FROM LIFE
by
Frances Benjamin Johnston

PVBLISHED BY
B. F. JOHNSON PVBLISHING COMPANY RICHMOND VA.

As part of the progressive impulse to make learning more meaningful to everyday life, textbooks included more illustrations, including "photographs from life." Library of Congress.

especially in the Midwest and West, was prompted by the Morrill Land Grant Act of 1862 (see pages 395 and 471). The new land-grant colleges offered a wide variety of courses that ranged from the classics and natural science to carpentry and farming. Many schools considered athletics a vital part of a student's growth, and intercollegiate sports became a central feature of student life, as well as a source of school pride and alumni contributions. Southern states, in keeping with the "separate but equal" policy, set up segregated land-grant colleges for blacks. *Separate* was more descriptive of these institutions than *equal,* however; blacks continued to be constrained by inferior educational institutions.

As colleges and universities expanded, so did their enrollment of women. Between 1890 and 1910 the number of females enrolled in institutions of higher learning swelled from 56,000 to 140,000. By the latter date, 106,000 women attended coeducational institutions (many of which were state universities

aided by the Morrill Act), while 34,000 attended women's colleges. By 1920, 283,000 women were attending college, accounting for 47.3 percent of total enrollment. Their numbers alone disproved earlier objections that women were unfit for higher learning because they were mentally and physically inferior to men, but discrimination lingered in admissions and curriculum policies. Most women were encouraged (indeed, they usually sought) to take home economics courses rather than science and mathematics, and most medical schools, including Harvard and Yale, refused to admit women.

At the same time they were developing new approaches to knowledge, American educators adopted the prevailing attitude of business: that more is better. They justifiably congratulated themselves for drawing more people into schools and for making instruction more meaningful. By 1920, fully 78 percent of all children between ages five and seventeen were enrolled in public elementary and high schools; another 8 percent were in private and parochial schools. These figures represented a huge increase over the attendance rate of 1870. And there were 600,000 college and graduate students in 1920, compared with 52,000 in 1870. Yet few people looked beyond the numbers to assess how well schools were doing their job. The faith that schools could promote equality and justice as well as personal growth and responsible citizenship underwent very little critical analysis.

The law, like education, began to exhibit new emphases on experience and scientific principles. An influential proponent of the new point of view was

Progressive Legal Thought

Harvard scholar Roscoe Pound, whose writings urged that social experience influence legal thinking. In practice, Oliver Wendell Holmes, Jr., associate justice of the Supreme Court between 1902 and 1932, led the attack on the old view of law as universal and unchanging—like the Ten Commandments. "The life of the law," said Holmes, sounding like Dewey, "has not been logic; it has been experience." The view that law should reflect society's needs challenged the judicial practice of invoking traditional beliefs and precedents in an inflexible way that often obstructed social legislation. Louis D. Brandeis, a brilliant lawyer who later joined Holmes on the Supreme Court, carried legal reform one step further by insisting that judges' opinions be based on factual, scientifically gathered information about social realities. In the landmark case *Muller* v. *Oregon* (1908), Brandeis mustered extensive scientific evidence to convince the Supreme Court to uphold Oregon's law limiting women's working hours.

New legal thought, however, met some tough resistance. Judges brought up on laissez-faire economic theory continued to strike down the kind of law progressive lawyers thought necessary for effective reform. Thus in 1905 the Supreme Court overturned a New York law limiting bakers' working hours (*Lochner* v. *New York*) in spite of Holmes's forceful dissent. As in other cases where it struck down reform, the Court's majority argued that the Fourteenth Amendment protected an individual's right to make contracts without government interference, and that this protection thus superseded reform sentiments. Also, judges weakened federal regulations by invoking the Tenth Amendment, which prohibited the federal government from interfering in matters reserved for state super-

vision. Thus the judiciary's use of constitutional principles governing freedom of contract and the division of government powers continually impeded reform.

The judiciary during the Progressive era was not entirely negative. Courts did sustain some regulatory measures, particularly those affecting the safety of the general public. A string of decisions, beginning with *Holden* v. *Hardy* in 1898 in which the Supreme Court upheld Utah's mining regulations, supported use of state police powers to protect the health, safety, and morals of their citizens. The judiciary also recognized federal police powers and Congress's authority in interstate commerce in sustaining such federal legislation as the Pure Food and Drug Act, the Meat Inspection Law (see page 607), and the Mann Act (see page 596). In these instances the welfare of citizens took precedence over the Tenth Amendment.

Still, the concept of general welfare posed thorny legal problems. Even if one agreed that law should reflect society's needs, which part of society should be represented? The United States was a mixed nation, and religion and ethnicity deeply influenced law. In many places a native white Protestant majority required Bible reading in public schools (thereby offending Catholics and Jews), stipulated that business establishments close on Sundays, restricted the religious practices of Mormons and other groups, prohibited interracial marriage, and enforced racial segregation. Though Holmes asserted that laws should be made for "people of fundamentally differing views," Americans have always had difficulty creating and applying such laws.

At about the same time, social science—the study of society and its institutions—experienced changes like those overtaking law and education. In economics,

Social Science

for example, a group of young scholars used statistics to argue that laws governing economic relationships were not immutable. Instead, they asserted, economic theory should reflect prevailing social conditions. Richard T. Ely of Johns Hopkins University and the University of Wisconsin, an early spokesman for this point of view, argued that opposition to government interference in social and economic affairs had been outmoded by industrialization. Thus, practical solutions to current problems should be derived through "the united efforts of Church, state, and

Some of the most lasting of progressive reforms were in the areas of health and welfare. Women often were in the vanguard of these movements. In this photograph, a member of the Visiting Nurses Association provides medical aid to the mother of an immigrant family. Western Heritage Museum, Omaha, with permission of Visiting Nurses Association.

science." A new breed of sociologists led by Lester Ward, Albion Small, and Edward A. Ross agreed, adding that citizens should engage in planning to cure social ills rather than passively waiting for problems to solve themselves. Meanwhile the progressive historians, Frederick Jackson Turner, Charles A. Beard, and Vernon L. Parrington, were examining the past as a means of explaining current problems in American society and motivating social change. And political scientists like Woodrow Wilson emphasized the practical over the theoretical advocating the expansion of government power as a means to ensure justice and progress.

Social scientists joined with doctors and organizations like the National Consumers League to bring about some of the most far-reaching of progessive reforms: those in the area of public health. Founded by Josephine Shaw, a socially prominent Massachusetts widow, the National Consumers League initially worked to improve wages and conditions of young

National Consumers League and Public Health Reform

women employed in department stores. After settlement worker Florence Kelley became the league's general secretary, the organization expanded its activities to include women's suffrage, protection of child laborers, and removal of potential health hazards. Local branches supported such consumer protection measures as the licensing of food vendors and inspection of dairies. They also urged city governments to fund neighborhood clinics that provided health education and medical care to the poor. Their efforts spurred a movement for consumer and health awareness that has continued to the present.

Between the end of the nineteenth century and the First World War, a new breed of men and women pressed for institutional change as well as political reform. Largely middle-class in background, trained by new professional standards, confident that new ways of thinking would bring progress, these people helped to broaden government's role in meeting the needs of a mature industrial society. Their questioning extended beyond their immediate goals and jostled conventional attitudes toward race and sex.

CHALLENGES TO RACIAL AND SEXUAL DISCRIMINATION

W. E. B. Du Bois, the forceful black scholar and teacher, ended an essay in his book *The Souls of Black Folk* (1903) with a call that heralded the twentieth-century civil rights movement: "By every civilized and peaceful method," he wrote, "we must strive for the right which the world accords to men."

By "men" Du Bois meant all human beings, not just one sex. But his statement and its context suggest the dilemma that vexed the two largest groups of underprivileged Americans in the early 1900s: women and nonwhites. Both lived in a society dominated by white males. Both suffered from disfranchisement, discrimination, and humiliation. And for centuries both groups had been striving for "the right which the world accords to men"—freedom and equality. The progressive challenge to old ideas and customs gave impetus to blacks' and women's struggles for their rights, but it posed a dilemma as well. Should women and blacks strive to become just like white men, with white men's values and power as well as their rights? Or was there something unique about racial and sexual identity that should be retained at the risk of sacrificing some gains? Both groups wavered between accepting and rejecting the culture from which they had been excluded.

The problems of blacks in white American society remained regional in scope until well into the twentieth century, though important shifts were beginning to occur. In 1900 only one in ten blacks lived in the North. The rest lived in southern states, where repressive Jim Crow measures had multiplied in the 1880s and 1890s. Southern blacks were not only denied legal and voting rights but were officially segregated in almost all walks of life. They faced constant exclusion and violence. In 1910 only 8,000 out of 970,000 high-school-age blacks in the entire South were enrolled in high schools. Between 1900 and 1914 white mobs lynched over a thousand blacks.

Blacks began to migrate northward in the 1880s, accelerating their rate of departure after 1900. But job and housing discrimination, inferior schools, and segregated neighborhoods characterized northern as well as southern cities. White humanitarians contributed to discrimination by maintaining separate and inferior institutions for blacks, rather than integrating them with whites. A half-century after the abolition of slavery, most whites still agreed with the northern historian James Ford Rhodes that blacks were "innately inferior and incapable of citizenship."

Black leaders differed over how—and whether—to achieve assimilation. In the wake of emancipation, ex-slave Frederick Douglass had urged "ultimate assimilation through self-assertion, and on no other terms." Other blacks, who favored isolation from cruel white society, supported migration back to Africa or establishment of all-black communities in Oklahoma Territory and Kansas. Still others advocated militancy. According to one extremist, "Our people must die to be saved and in dying must take as many along with them as it is possible to do with the aid of firearms and all other weapons."

Most blacks, however, could neither escape nor conquer white society. They thus had to find other routes to improvement. Self-help, a strategy articulated by educator Booker T. Washington, **Booker T. Washington** was one of the most popular alternatives. Born in 1856 to slave parents, Washington worked his way through school and in 1881 founded Tuskegee Institute in Alabama, a vocational school for blacks. There he developed the philosophy that blacks' hopes for assimilation lay in at least temporarily accommodating themselves to whites. Rather than fighting for political rights, he said, blacks should work hard, acquire property, and prove they were worthy of their rights. Washington voiced his views in a widely acclaimed speech at the Atlanta Exposition in 1895. "Dignify and glorify common labor," he urged in what became known as the Atlanta Compromise. "Agitation of questions of racial equality is the extremest folly." Envisioning a society where blacks and whites would remain apart but share the same goals, Washington observed that "in all things that are purely social we can be as separate as the fingers, yet one as the hand in all matters essential to mutual progress."

Whites, including progressives, welcomed Washington's policy of accommodation because it urged patience and seemed to remind black people to stay

Black students practicing woodwork at Hampton Institute, Hampton, Virgina. Like Tuskegee Institute, Hampton offered vocational instruction in the belief that by acquiring skills and working hard, blacks could convince whites they were worthy of equal rights. Library of Congress.

in their place. White businesspeople, reformers, and politicians chose to regard Washington as representative of all blacks, because he said what they wanted to hear. Yet though Washington endorsed the separate-but-equal policy, he projected a subtle racial pride that would find more direct expression in black nationalism later in the twentieth century, when some blacks would urge control of their own businesses and schools. Washington never argued that blacks were inferior to whites; he instead argued that their dignity could be enhanced through self-improvement.

But to some blacks Washington seemed to favor second-class citizenship, which they considered degrading. In 1905 a group of "anti-Bookerites" convened near Niagara Falls and pledged a more militant pursuit of such rights as unrestricted voting, equal access

W. E. B. Du Bois

to economic opportunity, integration, and equality before the law. Spokesperson for the Niagara movement was W. E. B. Du Bois, a vociferous critic of the Atlanta Compromise. A New Englander with a Ph.D. from Harvard, Du Bois had the background of a typical progressive. He had studied in Germany, where he learned about scientific investigation, and he was a professor on the faculty of Atlanta University. Du Bois used scientific methods to compile fact-filled sociological studies of black ghetto dwellers, and he wrote poetically for the cause of civil rights. In his essays and speeches, Du Bois treated Washington politely, but he could not accept Washington's submission to white domination. "The way for a people to gain their reasonable rights," Du Bois asserted, "is not by voluntarily throwing them away." Blacks needed, instead, to agitate for what was indeed rightfully theirs.

Du Bois showed that accommodation was an un-realistic strategy, but his own solution may have been just as fanciful. A blunt elitist, Du Bois believed that an intellectual vanguard of cultivated, highly trained blacks, which he called the Talented Tenth, would save the race by setting an example to whites and uplift other blacks. Inevitably, such sentiments had more attraction for middle-class white liberals than for black sharecroppers. Thus when Du Bois and his allies formed the National Association for the Advancement of Colored People (1909), which aimed to use legal redress in the courts to end racial discrimination, the leadership consisted chiefly of white progressives. Very few working-class black people belonged. By 1914 the NAACP had fifty branch offices and over six thousand members, but rarely did its activities touch sharecropping and laboring families.

Whatever strategy they pursued—accommodation or agitation—black Americans faced continued oppression. In fact, those who managed to acquire property and education encountered increased resentment. And the federal government only aggravated conditions. Under the administration of Woodrow Wilson, segregation within the federal government expanded; southern cabinet members supported racial separation in the rest rooms, restaurants, and offices of government buildings and balked at hiring black workers. Commenting on Wilson's racism in 1913, Booker T. Washington wrote, "I have never seen the colored people so discouraged and so bitter as they are at the present time."

Blacks still sought to fulfill the American dream of success, but many wondered whether membership in a corrupt white society should be part of their quest. Du Bois voiced these doubts poignantly, writing that "one ever feels his twoness—an American, a Negro, two souls, two thoughts, two unreconciled strivings, two warring ideals in one dark body." Somehow blacks would have to reconcile that twoness by combining racial pride with national identity. As Du Bois wrote in 1903, a black

would not Africanize America, for America has too much to teach the world and Africa. He would not bleach his Negro soul in a flood of white Americanism, for he knows that Negro blood has a message for the world. He simply wishes to make it possible for a man to be both a Negro and an American.

That simple wish would haunt the nation for decades to come.

During this time too, the progressive challenge to social relations stirred women to seek liberation from the traditional confines of hearth and home. Their struggle raised questions of identity that resembled those blacks were facing. What tactics should women use to achieve equality, and what should be their role in society? The writer Henry James summed up the dilemma inherent in such questions when he complained that women who wanted to become just like men were disregarding their own uniqueness. Could women achieve equality with men and at the same time change male-dominated society?

The Progressive era included a number of efforts by and on behalf of women to extend their influence beyond domestic bounds. Some of these efforts derived from radical impulses. Feminist Charlotte Perkins Gilman sounded a clarion call in her book *Women and Economics* (1898), declaring that domesticity and female innocence were obsolete and attacking the male monopoly on economic opportunity. This and Gilman's other writings moved some women, but even more were swept up by the women's club movement. Originated as literary and educational organizations, these groups of middle-class women began entering public affairs in the late nineteenth century. Consolidated as the General Federation of Women's Clubs in 1890, they claimed nearly one million members by 1910.

Women's Clubs

The reform activities of clubs and other women define a particularly female dimension of the Progressive era. Because women were generally excluded from the political arena before 1920 (see page 604), those with reform motivations were drawn less to movements to improve government than to movements for social betterment. Thus rather than press for such reforms as trustbusting, nonpartisan elections, and direct primaries, female reformers tended to work for social goals such as factory inspection, regulation of children's and women's labor, housing reform, and pure food and drug laws. At the same time, college-educated and professionally trained women became active in settlement houses and educational reform movements.

A number of such women joined the birth control movement led by Margaret Sanger. As a visiting

TO THE MALE CITIZEN

IF THIS IS WOMANLY—
WHY NOT THIS?

This cartoon supporting women's rights addressed the illogical attitudes of those who believed women should stay out of public affairs. "No man denies that government is public housekeeping," the caption pointed out. Were women allowed to hold office, the artist's reasoning suggested, they could keep public administration—as well as the streets—clean. The Schlesinger Library, Radcliffe College.

Birth Control nurse in New York's East Side immigrant neighborhoods, Sanger distributed information about contraception in hopes of preventing unwanted pregnancies and their tragic consequences among poor women. Her crusade, however, captured the attention of middle-class women, who wanted to limit their own families and to control the growth of immigrant masses. It also aroused the opposition of men and women who saw birth control as a threat to family and morality. In 1914 moral purists caused Sanger to be indicted for sending obscene literature (articles on contraception) through the mail, forcing her to flee the country for a year. Sanger persevered and in 1921 formed the American Birth Control League, which enlisted physicians and social workers to convince judges to allow distribution of birth control information. Most states still prohibited the sale of contraceptives, but the issue had entered the realm of public discussion.

Except for a few visionaries like Gilman, the women who participated in reform movements seldom thought about effecting a sexual revolution. Many could not decide which aspects of their identity to cultivate and which to drop. Most women opposed birth control, for example, in the belief that contraception threatened women's status as mothers. Others feared that if women became the equals of men they would lose what they considered the special virtues of the female personality.

Ambivalence about the supposed uniqueness of the feminine character pervaded the suffrage movement, which achieved victory in 1920 when enough states ratified the Nineteenth Amendment giving women the vote. The suffrage crusade dated back to the mid-nineteenth century. It had grown out of the abolitionist

Suffragists

Chapter 21: THE PROGRESSIVE ERA, 1895–1920

crusade's insistence that all Americans, regardless of race or sex, were equal and thus deserved the same rights. Confronted by male resistance, however, some women defended female suffrage by arguing that women's special, even superior, traits would humanize politics. Settlement-house founder Jane Addams, for example, supported the vote for her sex by asking, "If women have in any sense been responsible for the gentler side of life which softens and blurs some of its harsher conditions may not they have a duty to perform in our American cities?"

Suffragists achieved their first successes at the local level; by 1912 nine states, all of them in the West, allowed women to vote. After 1900 women pressed increasingly for the vote on the national level. The suffragists' tactics ranged from the moderate but persistent propaganda campaigns of the National American Women Suffrage Association, led by Carrie Chapman Catt, to the active picketing and marching of the National Women's party, led by Alice Paul. All these activities heightened public awareness of the suffragist cause. More decisive, however, was women's participation on the home front during the First World War as factory laborers, medical volunteers, and municipal workers (see pages 662–664). Their efforts convinced legislators that women could shoulder public responsibilities and gave final impetus to passage of the suffrage amendment.

Although women's clubs and the suffrage movement attracted mostly middle-class women, some efforts were made to encourage feelings of sisterhood among all classes. Since the early nineteenth century, a number of well-to-do women had recognized that all females had common grievances; that feeling gained ground in the early 1900s. Thus Alva Belmont, a wealthy supporter of the shirtwaist workers' strike, said in 1909, "It was my interest in women, in women everywhere and every class that drew my attention and sympathies first to the striking shirtwaist girls." This feeling of sisterhood formed the basis of the feminist movement, for as Mrs. Belmont urged "Women the world over need protection and it is only through the united efforts of women that they will get it."

But women's united efforts failed to create an interest group solid enough or powerful enough to dent political, economic, and social systems run by men.

Like blacks, women knew that voting rights would mean little until people's attitudes could be changed. The Progressive era had helped women to clarify the issues that concerned them, but major reforms would await the future. As the feminist Crystal Eastman, echoing Du Bois, observed in the aftermath of the suffrage crusade,

Men are saying perhaps, "Thank God, this everlasting women's fight is over!" But women, if I know them, are saying, "Now at last we can begin." . . . Now they can say what they are really after, in common with all the rest of the struggling world, is *freedom*.

Theodore Roosevelt and the Revival of the Presidency

The Progressive era's theme of reform—in politics, institutions, and social relations—directed attention to government, especially the federal government, as the ultimate agent of change. At first, however, the federal government seemed incapable of assuming such responsibility. Dominated by two political parties that resembled private clubs more than bodies of impartial statesmen, the government acted mainly for special interests when it acted at all. Then suddenly, in September 1901, the climate changed. The assassination of President William McKinley by an anarchist named Leon Czolgosz vaulted Theodore Roosevelt, the young, vigorous vice president, into the White House.

Political manager Mark Hanna had warned fellow Republicans against nominating Roosevelt for the vice presidency in 1900. "Don't any of you realize," Hanna asked after the nominating convention, "that there's only one life between that madman and the Presidency?" As governor of New York, Roosevelt had angered party bosses by showing sympathy for regulatory legislation. So Republican leaders rid themselves of their pariah by pushing him into national politics. Little did they realize that they were about to present the nation with its most forceful president since Lincoln, a man who would infuse the office with much of its twentieth-century character.

In marked contrast to his predecessors, Theodore Roosevelt lacked the dignified appearance of a president. He stood five-foot-nine but looked shorter.

Theodore Roosevelt: His Early Life Very nearsighted, he was helpless without his metal-rimmed glasses. He had big, prominent teeth and talked in a high-pitched voice. As a youth he had suffered from asthma.

Yet throughout his life he was driven by a near-obsession to overcome his physical limitations and exert what he and his contemporaries called manliness. In his teens he practiced diligently to become an expert marksman and horseman. As a Harvard student he competed on the boxing and wrestling teams. In the 1880s he went to live on a Dakota ranch, where he roped cattle and brawled with other cowboys.

A descendant of a Dutch aristocratic family, Roosevelt inherited the wealth to indulge in such pursuits. But he also inherited a sense of civic responsibility that he translated into a career in public office. He served three terms in the New York State Assembly, ran for mayor of New York City in 1886 (finishing third), and served on the federal Civil Service Commission, as New York City's police commissioner, and as assistant secretary of the navy. In this series of offices Roosevelt earned a reputation as a combative, politically crafty leader. He also distinguished himself as a historian with his *The Naval War of 1812* (1882) and *The Winning of the West* (1889).

In 1898 Roosevelt thrust himself into the Spanish-American War by organizing a volunteer cavalry brigade, the Rough Riders, to fight in Cuba (see pages 629–630). His dramatic act excited the public, though it had little impact on the war's outcome. Nevertheless, Roosevelt returned from the war a folk hero (people called him Teddy, a name he disliked) and was elected governor of New York, then vice president.

As president, Roosevelt became a progressive hero. At heart, though, he was a conservative. His impulsive patriotism, admiration for big business, and dislike of anything he considered effeminate recalled the previous era of unbridled expansion when raw power prevailed in social and economic affairs. Yet Roosevelt came to conclusions similar to those reached by pro-

President Theodore Roosevelt (1858–1919) giving one of his typically dynamic speeches. With his broad interests and energetic leadership, Roosevelt revitalized the presidency and gave it much of its twentieth-century character. Library of Congress.

gressives. His sense of history convinced him that the kind of small government Jefferson had hoped for would not suffice in the modern industrial era. Instead, economic development necessitated a Hamiltonian system of government powerful enough to guide national affairs. Like his supporters, Roosevelt believed in the wisdom and talents of a select few, whose superior backgrounds and education qualified them to coordinate public and private enterprise. "A simple and poor society," he observed, "can exist as a democracy on the basis of sheer individualism. But a rich and complex society cannot so exist."

Roosevelt's presidency inaugurated the federal regulation of economic affairs that has characterized twentieth-century American history. Roosevelt first turned his attention to big business, where the com-

Regulation of Trusts

bination movement had produced giant trusts that controlled almost every sector of the economy. Though Roosevelt has a reputation as a trustbuster, he actually believed in consolidation as the most efficient means to achieve material and technological progress. Rather than return to uncontrolled competition, he preferred to distinguish between good and bad trusts, and to prevent the bad ones from manipulating markets. Thus he instructed the Justice Department to use antitrust laws to prosecute the railroad, meatpacking, and oil trusts, which he believed had unscrupulously exploited the public. Roosevelt's policy triumphed in 1904 when the Supreme Court, convinced by the government's arguments, ordered the dissolution of the Northern Securities Company, the huge railroad combination created by J. P. Morgan and his powerful business allies. (Roosevelt chose, however, not to attack other gigantic trusts, such as U.S. Steel, another of Morgan's creations.)

When the prosecution of Northern Securities began, Morgan reportedly collared Roosevelt and offered, "If we have done anything wrong, send your man to my man and they can fix it up." The president refused. But Roosevelt was more sympathetic to such arrangements than his refusal might suggest. He preferred cooperation between business and government. Rather than prosecute, he urged the Bureau of Corporations (part of the newly created Department of Labor and Commerce) to work with companies on mergers and other forms of expansion. Thus through investigation and cooperation the administration exerted pressure on business to regulate itself.

Roosevelt also pushed for regulatory legislation, especially after 1904, when he won a resounding electoral victory by garnering the votes of progressives and businesspeople alike. After a year of wrangling with business lobbyists in Congress, he succeeded in 1906 in getting passage of the Hepburn Act, which imposed stricter control over railroads and expanded the powers of the Interstate Commerce Commission. The act gave the ICC more authority to fix railroad rates, though it did allow the courts to overturn rate decisions. Progressives like Robert La Follette deplored the fact that Roosevelt had compromised with business representatives like Senator Nelson W. Aldrich of Rhode Island to assure the bill's passage. But Roosevelt's aim was to establish at least the principle of

government regulation rather than risk defeat over more idealistic objectives.

Roosevelt showed a similar willingness to compromise on legislation to ensure pure food and drugs. For decades reformers had been urging government regulation of patent medicines and processed meat. The outcry against fraud and adulteration heightened in 1906 with the publication of Upton Sinclair's *The Jungle*, a fictionalized exposé of Chicago meatpacking plants. Sinclair, a young socialist more interested in freeing workers from oppression than in muckraking, nevertheless shocked public sensibilities by describing scandalous conditions like the following:

Pure Food and Drug Laws

> There was never the least attention paid to what was cut up for sausage; there would come all the way back from Europe old sausage that had been rejected, and that was mouldy and white—it would be dosed with borax and glycerine, and dumped into the hoppers, and made over again for home consumption. . . . There would be meat stored in great piles in rooms; and the water from the leaky roofs would drip over it, and thousands of rats would race about on it. It was too dark in these storage places to see well, but a man could run his hand over these piles of meat and sweep off handfuls of dried dung of rats. These rats were a nuisance, and the packers would put poisoned bread out for them; they would die, and then rats, bread, and meat would go into the hoppers together.

On reading Sinclair's novel, Roosevelt ordered an investigation. Finding Sinclair's descriptions accurate he supported the Pure Food and Drug Act and the Meat Inspection Act, both passed in 1906. Like the Hepburn Act, these laws reinforced the principle of government regulation. But as part of the compromise to obtain their passage, the government had to pay for inspections, and meatpackers could appeal government decisions in court.

Roosevelt's policy on labor issues resembled his stance toward business. When, for example, the United Mine Workers struck against coal-mine owners in 1902, the president intervened by using the progressive tactics of investigation and arbitration. The mine workers, led by feisty John Mitchell, wanted higher pay and an eight-hour day, but the owners stubbornly refused to recognize the union or arbitrate the grievances. As winter approached and fuel shortages threatened, Roosevelt mustered public opinion. He warned that he would use federal troops to reopen the mines, thereby forcing both sides to accept arbitration of the dispute by a special commission. The commission decided in favor of higher wages and reduced hours, but also declared that the owners did not have to recognize the union. The decision, according to Roosevelt, created a "square deal" for all. The strike settlement illustrated Roosevelt's belief that the president or his agents should have a say in which labor demands were legitimate and which were not—just as he could help to guide business regulation. In Roosevelt's mind there were good and bad labor organizations (socialists, for example, were bad), just as there were good and bad business combinations.

On the issue of conservation, Roosevelt displayed the same mix of flamboyant executive action and quiet compromise that he applied to other domestic

Conservation

matters. He built a reputation as a determined conservationist, warning Congress in 1907, "We are prone to think of the resources of this country as inexhaustible; this is not so." A lover of the outdoors, Roosevelt used presidential authority to add almost 150 million acres to the national forests and to preserve vast areas of water and coal from private plunder. He sympathized with conservationist Gifford Pinchot, who was the government's chief forester, and in 1908 called forty-four governors and five hundred natural-resource experts to a National Conservation Congress. True to the progressive spirit, Roosevelt wanted a "well-conceived plan" for resource management, a plan for ordered growth rather than mere preservation of nature as it was. But compromises and factors beyond his control weakened his scheme. Timber and mining companies shunned supervision of their wasteful practices, and Congress never authorized enough funds to enforce federal regulations.

Roosevelt also had to compromise his principles in the face of economic crisis. In 1907 a financial panic caused by overspeculation forced some New York banks to close to prevent frightened depositors from withdrawing money. J. P. Morgan helped to stem the panic by persuading other financiers to stop dumping their securities. In return for Morgan's aid, Roosevelt approved a deal allowing U.S. Steel to absorb its competitor, the Tennessee Iron and Coal Company—an act that flouted Roosevelt's trustbusting aims.

During his last year in office, Roosevelt moved further away from the Republican party's traditional alliance with big business. He lashed out at irresponsible actions of "malefactors of great wealth" and supported stronger regulation of business and heavier taxation of the rich. Having promised in 1904 that he would not seek re-election, Roosevelt backed his friend Secretary of War William Howard Taft for the nomination in 1908, hoping that Taft would continue to pursue the Roosevelt initiatives. The Democrats nominated William Jennings Bryan for the third time, but the Great Commoner lost again. Aided by Roosevelt, who still had strong popular influence, Taft won by 1.25 million popular votes and a 2 to 1 margin in the electoral college.

Early in 1909 Roosevelt went to Africa to shoot game (he saw no contradiction between hunting and conservation), leaving Taft to face the political problems his predecessor had managed

Taft Administration

to postpone. Foremost among them were tariff rates, which had risen to excessive levels. Honoring Taft's pledge to cut rates, the House passed a bill sponsored by Representative Sereno E. Payne that provided for numerous downward revisions. As they had in the past, protectionists in the Senate prepared to amend the House bill and revise rates upward. But Senate progressives, led by La Follette, organized a stinging attack on the ways the tariff benefited vested interests. Taft was caught between the reformers, who claimed they were carrying on Roosevelt's antitrust spirit, and the protectionists who still controlled the Republican party. In the end Senator Aldrich and other protectionists restored many of the cuts, and Taft, who was more reluctant than Roosevelt to interfere in the legislative process, signed what became known as the Payne-Aldrich Tariff. To many progressives, Taft had failed the test of filling Roosevelt's shoes.

The progressive and conservative wings of the Republican party were rapidly drifting apart. Soon after the tariff controversy a group of insurgents in the House, led by George Norris of Nebraska, challenged Speaker "Uncle Joe" Cannon of Illinois, whose power over committee assignments and scheduling of debate could make or break a piece of legislation. Taft first supported and then abandoned the insurgents, who nevertheless managed to liberalize procedures by enlarging the important rules committee and removing its appointments from Cannon's control. Meanwhile, Taft also angered conservationists by allowing Secretary of the Interior Richard A. Ballinger to remove 1 million acres of forest and mineral land from the reserved list and to fire Gifford Pinchot when he protested a questionable sale of coal lands in Alaska.

In reality Taft was as sympathetic to reform as Roosevelt was. He prosecuted more trusts than Roosevelt; expanded the national forest reserves; signed the Mann-Elkins Act of 1910, which bolstered regulatory powers of the ICC; and supported such labor reforms as the eight-hour day and mine safety legislation. The Sixteenth Amendment, which legalized a federal income tax, and the Seventeenth Amendment, which provided for direct election of U.S. senators, were initiated during Taft's presidency. Like Roosevelt, Taft was forced to compromise with big business, but he lacked Roosevelt's ability to maneuver and to publicize the issues he supported. Roosevelt, who had worked to expand presidential power, had also infused the office with vitality. "I believe in a strong executive," he once asserted. "I believe in power." Taft, on the other hand, believed in the strict restraint of law. He had been a successful lawyer and judge (he returned to the bench as Chief Justice of the United States between 1921 and 1930). His caution and unwillingness to offend disappointed those used to Roosevelt's impetuosity.

Thus in 1910, when Roosevelt returned from Africa boasting over three thousand animal trophies, he found his party torn and tormented. Reformers, angered by Taft's apparent insensitivity to their cause, formed the National Progressive Republican League and rallied behind Robert La Follette for president in 1912—though many hoped Roosevelt would run. Another wing of the party stood loyal to Taft. Roosevelt, disappointed by Taft's performance (particularly his refusal to back Pinchot), began to speak out and to rekindle public attention. He filled his speeches with references to "the welfare of the people" and to stronger regulation of business. When La Follette became ill early in 1912, Roosevelt, proclaiming himself fit as a "bull moose," threw his hat in the ring for the Republican presidential nomination.

Taft's supporters controlled the convention and nominated him for a second term, but Roosevelt forces formed a third party—the Progressive or Bull Moose party—and nominated the fifty-three-year-old former president. Meanwhile, the Democrats endured forty-six ballots before selecting as their candidate New Jersey's progressive governor Woodrow Wilson. The Socialists, by now an organized and growing party, nominated their perennial candidate Eugene V. Debs. The campaign exposed voters to the most thorough evaluation of the American system in nearly a generation.

WOODROW WILSON AND THE EXTENSION OF REFORM

In his acceptance speech before the Progressive party, Theodore Roosevelt had proclaimed, "We stand at Armageddon and we battle for the Lord." But on inauguration day 1913, it was Woodrow Wilson who assumed command of the forces of good. "The Nation," he exhorted,

> has been deeply stirred by a solemn passion, stirred by the knowledge of wrong, of ideals lost, of government too often debauched and made an instrument of evil. The feelings with which we face this new age of right and opportunity sweep across our heartstrings like some air out of God's own presence, where justice and mercy are reconciled and the judge and the brother are one.

The election's outcome illustrated the extent to which the electorate had been swept up by the moral fervor of these pronouncements. Wilson won with 42 percent of the popular vote—he was a minority president, though he did capture 435 out of 531 electoral votes (see map, page 610). Roosevelt received about 27 percent of the popular vote. Taft finished a poor third, polling 23 percent of the popular vote and only 8 electoral votes. Debs won 902,000 votes, 6 percent of the total, but no electoral votes. Thus fully three-quarters of the electorate supported some alternative to the restrained approach to government that Taft represented.

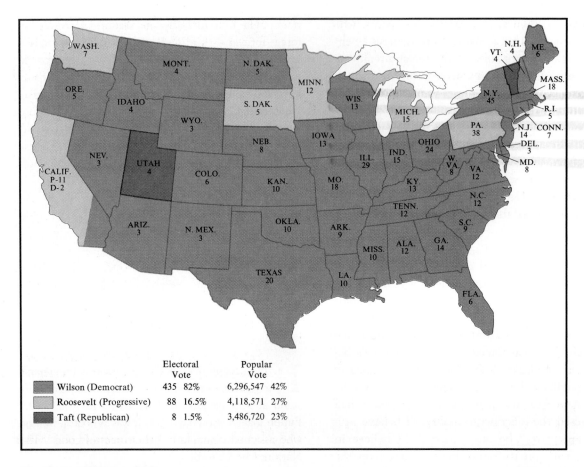

Presidential Election, 1912

		Electoral Vote		Popular Vote	
	Wilson (Democrat)	435	82%	6,296,547	42%
	Roosevelt (Progressive)	88	16.5%	4,118,571	27%
	Taft (Republican)	8	1.5%	3,486,720	23%

The campaign had featured a sharp debate over the fundamentals of progressive government. On one side stood Roosevelt with a system called the New Nationalism, a term coined by reform editor Herbert Croly. Roosevelt foresaw a new era of national unity in which governmental authority would balance and coordinate economic activity. He would not destroy big business, which he saw as an efficient way to organize production. Rather, he would establish regulatory commissions, groups of experts who would protect citizens' interests and ensure the wise use of concentrated economic power. "The effort at prohibiting all combinations has substantially failed," he claimed. "The way out lies . . . in completely controlling them."

The New Nationalism and the New Freedom

Wilson offered a more idealistic scheme in his New Freedom, based on ideas of the progressive lawyer Louis D. Brandeis. Wilson believed that concentration of economic power threatened individual liberty, that monopolies had to be broken so that the marketplace could again become open. But he did not want to restore laissez faire. Like Roosevelt, Wilson would enhance governmental authority to protect and regulate. "Freedom today," he declared, "is something more than being let alone. Without the watchful . . . resolute interference of the government, there can be no fair play between individuals and such powerful institutions as the trusts." But Wilson stopped short of the cooperation between big business and big government inherent in Roosevelt's New Nationalism. In the campaign at least, he spoke in evangelical tones of the need for economic emancipation, the need to "come out of a stifling cellar into the open . . . breathe again and see the free spaces of the heavens."

Roosevelt and Wilson stood closer together than

their rhetoric implied. In spite of his faith in experts as regulators, Roosevelt harbored sentiments for individual freedom as strong as Wilson's. And Wilson was not as hostile to concentrated power as his speeches suggested. Both men strongly supported equality of opportunity, conservation of natural resources, fair wages for workers, and social betterment for all classes. Perhaps more important, both would expand government activity through strong personal leadership and bureaucratic reform. Thus, even though he received a minority of the total vote in 1912, Wilson could interpret the results of the election as a popular mandate to subdue trusts and broaden the federal government's concern for social reform.

Though the public had often fondly referred to Roosevelt as Teddy or TR, no one ever called Thomas Woodrow Wilson Tommy or WW. The son of a Presbyterian minister, Wilson was **Woodrow** born and raised in the South. His **Wilson: His** mother, Janet Woodrow, and his **Early Career** first wife, Ellen Axson, were both daughters of Presbyterian ministers. But Wilson chose to become an academic rather than a cleric. He earned a B.A. at Princeton, studied law at Virginia, received a Ph.D. from Johns Hopkins, and became a professor of history, jurisprudence, and political economy. Between 1885 and 1908 he published a number of books on American history and government that established him as a respectable scholar. Wilson's manner and bearing reflected his religious and academic background. Tall, lean, and stiff, he seemed to stare coldly through his pince-nez glasses. He exuded none of Roosevelt's flamboyance, and often spoke self-righteously.

Yet Wilson was an effective and charismatic leader. A superb orator, he could inspire intense loyalty with religious images and an eloquent expression of American ideals. Wilson's convictions had led him early into reform. In 1902 he became president of Princeton, where he upset tradition with his curricular reforms and battles against aristocratic elements in the university. In 1910 New Jersey Democrats, eager for respectability, nominated Wilson for the governorship. After winning the election, Wilson repudiated the party bosses and directed passage of progressive legislation. He was not good at administration, often losing his temper and stubbornly refusing to compromise. But his accomplishments attracted national

Looking like a preacher, Woodrow Wilson (1856–1924) delivers a speech at a campaign rally. Wilson's forceful, carefully crafted speeches, which resembled moral lectures more than political pitches, raised citizens' expectations for the fulfillment of his idealistic promises.   Brown Brothers.

attention and won him the Democratic nomination for president in 1912.

As president, Wilson had to blend his New Freedom ideals with New Nationalism precepts, and in so doing he set the direction of federal economic policy for much of the twentieth century.
Wilson's The corporate merger movement
Policy on had proceeded so far that restoration
Business of free competition was impossible.
Regulation Thus Wilson could only acknowledge economic concentration and try to prevent its abuse by expanding the government's regulatory powers. His administration moved toward that end with passage in 1914 of the Clayton Anti-Trust Act and a bill creating the Federal Trade Commission (FTC). The Clayton Act extended the Sherman Anti-Trust Act of 1890 by outlawing quasi-monopolistic practices such as price discrimination (whereby a company might try to destroy competition by lowering prices in some regions but not others) and interlocking directorates (management of two or more competing companies by the same executives). The FTC, which replaced the Bureau of Corporations, was to investigate corporations and issue cease-and-

desist orders against unfair trade practices. As in ICC rulings, accused companies could appeal FTC orders in the courts. Nevertheless, the FTC represented a further step in the protection of consumers.

Wilson increased federal regulation of finance with the Federal Reserve Act of 1913. The law established the nation's first centralized banking system since Andrew Jackson destroyed the Second Bank of the United States (see pages 340–341). Twelve newly created district banks would hold the reserves of member banks throughout the nation. (The act created many banks rather than one to allay the agrarian fear of a monolithic eastern banking power, which had doomed the bank in Jackson's time.) The district banks would loan money to member banks at a low interest rate, called the *discount rate*. By adjusting this rate (and thus the amount of money a bank could afford to borrow), the district banks could increase or decrease the amount of money in circulation. In other words, depending on the nation's needs, the reserve bank could loosen or tighten credit. Monetary affairs would no longer depend on the supply of gold, and interest rates would be fairer, especially for small borrowers.

Perhaps the only act of Wilson's first administration that promoted free competition was the Underwood Tariff, passed in 1913. For years rising prices had thwarted consumers' desires for the material benefits of the industrial age. Some prices were unnaturally high because government tariffs had discouraged importation of cheap foreign materials and manufactured products. The Underwood Tariff encouraged imports by drastically reducing or eliminating tariff rates. To recover revenues lost due to the reductions, the act levied a graduated income tax on U.S. residents—an option made possible earlier that year when the Sixteenth Amendment was ratified. The income tax was tame by today's standards. Incomes under $4,000 were exempt; thus almost all factory workers and farmers escaped the tax. People and corporations earning $4,000 to $20,000 had to pay a 1-percent tax, and the rate for higher incomes rose gradually to a maximum of 6 percent on earnings over $500,000. Such rates made no holes in the pockets of the rich. But the income tax did become an institutional feature of American life.

Tariff and Tax Reform

The First World War and the approaching presidential campaign prompted Wilson to support stronger reforms in 1916. Concerned that food shortages might result if farmers could not borrow money to sustain production, the president backed the Federal Farm Loan Act of 1916. The measure created twelve federally supported banks (not to be confused with the Federal Reserve banks) that would lend money at moderate interest rates to farmers who belonged to credit institutions—a watered-down version of something the Populists had agitated for a generation earlier. To stave off railroad strikes that might disrupt transportation at a time of national emergency, Wilson pushed passage of the Adamson Act of 1916, which mandated an eight-hour day and time-and-a-half for overtime for railroad laborers. Early that year, he pleased progressives by appointing Louis D. Brandeis, the "people's advocate," to the Supreme Court. Finally, Wilson courted the support of social reformers by backing laws that outlawed child labor and provided workers' compensation for federal employees who suffered from injury or illness.

In selecting their candidate to oppose Wilson in 1916, the Republicans snubbed Theodore Roosevelt, who wanted the nomination, in favor of Charles Evans Hughes, former reform governor of New York and Supreme Court justice. Wilson ran on a platform of peace, progressivism, and preparedness. Many voters were attracted by the Democratic party's campaign slogan: "He Kept Us Out of War." Hughes led a fractured party, and he could not muzzle Roosevelt, whose bellicose speeches suggested that the Republicans would drag Americans into the world war. Wilson received 9.1 million votes to Hughes's 8.5 million, and the president barely won in the electoral college by a 277-to-254 count. The Socialist party, which had earned 902,000 votes four years earlier, dropped to 600,000, largely because Wilson's reforms had attracted some socialists and the ailing Eugene Debs was not the party's standardbearer.

Election of 1916

Wilson's second term and the subsequent involvement in the First World War saw a shift away from competition toward interest-group politics and government regulation. During his first term Wilson had been convinced that laws, not regulatory commissions

IMPORTANT EVENTS

1893	Anti-Saloon League founded		1909	NAACP founded
				Payne-Aldrich Tariff
1895	Booker T. Washington's Atlanta			
	Compromise speech		1910	White Slave Traffic Act
				Ballinger-Pinchot controversy
1898	*Holden* v. *Hardy*			
			1912	Roosevelt runs for president on
1900	McKinley re-elected			Progressive (Bull Moose) ticket
				Wilson elected president
1901	McKinley assassinated; Roosevelt			
	assumes presidency		1913	Sixteenth and Seventeenth
				Amendments ratified
1903	Elkins Act			Underwood Tariff
				Federal Reserve Act
1904	*Northern Securities* case			
	Roosevelt elected president		1914	Federal Trade Commission Act
				Clayton Anti-Trust Act
1905	Niagara Falls Convention			Sanger indicted
	Lochner v. *New York*			
			1916	Wilson re-elected
1906	Hepburn Act			Federal Farm Loan Act
	Pure Food and Drug Act			
			1919	Eighteenth Amendment ratified
1907	Economic panic			
			1920	Nineteenth Amendment ratified
1908	Taft elected president			
	Muller v. *Oregon*			

that could easily fall under the influence of the very interests they were meant to regulate, should govern social and economic behavior. But wartime crisis and the desire for re-election convinced him to adopt a different attitude. The war effort required government coordination of production and cooperation between the public and private sectors. The War Industries Board (see page 661) was one example of this co-operation. The private businesses that were regulated by the board submitted to its direction on the condition that their own profit motives would continue to be satisfied.

After the war the Wilson administration dropped most cooperative and regulatory measures, including farm price supports, guarantees of collective bargaining, and high taxes. This move away from regulation would stimulate a new era of business ascendancy in the 1920s (see Chapter 24).

THE PROGRESSIVE ERA IN PERSPECTIVE

In 1912 Thomas Edison had cautioned uneasily, "We've got to start to make this world over." But by 1920 not many Americans agreed. A quarter-century of reform, climaxing in the nation's participation in a brutal war, had wrought momentous changes. Government, the economy, and society as they had existed in the nineteenth century were gone forever. Public concern over poverty and injustice had been raised to new heights. But for every American who suffered some form of deprivation, three or four enjoyed material comforts unprecedented in human history. This majority simply could not sustain reform indefinitely. Though effects of the Progressive era lingered and in some cases expanded after the First World War, a mass consumer society had begun to refocus people's attention from reform to materialism.

The Progressive era was characterized by a welter of confusing and sometimes contradictory goals. Certainly there was no single progressive movement. On the national level, reform programs ranged from Roosevelt's New Nationalism, with its faith in big government as a coordinator of big business, to Wilson's New Freedom, with its promise to dissolve economic concentrations and legislate open competition. At the state and local levels, reformers pursued causes as varied as neighborhood improvement, government reorganization, public ownership of utilities, betterment of working conditions, and moral revival. Although local organizations and national associations coordinated their efforts on particular issues, reformers with different goals often worked at cross-purposes.

The failure of many progressive initiatives testifies to the strength of opposition to reform as well as ambiguities within the reform movements themselves. By asserting constitutional and liberty-of-contract maxims, the courts struck down some key progressive legislation, most notably the federal law prohibiting child labor. In states and cities, adoption of the initiative, referendum, and recall did not encourage greater participation in government; either those mechanisms were seldom used or they became the tools of special interests. On the federal level, new regulatory agencies rarely had the resources for thorough investigations; they had to obtain their information from the companies they were meant to police. Thus in many respects, progressives failed to redistribute power; in 1920, as in 1900, government remained under the influence of business and industry, a condition which many people considered quite satisfactory.

Yet in spite of all their weaknesses, the numerous reform movements that characterized the Progressive era did refashion the nation's future. Trustbusting, however faulty, had forced industrialists to become more sensitive to public opinion, and reforms initiated by insurgents in Congress had partially diluted the power of dictatorial politicians. Progressive legislation gave government important tools to protect consumers against price-fixing and dangerous products. The income tax was a first step toward building government revenues and redistributing wealth. Social reformers soothed some of the festering sores of urban life. But perhaps most important, progressives challenged old ways of thinking. They raised questions about the quality of American life which, though they remained unresolved, made the nation more aware of its principles and promises.

SUGGESTIONS FOR FURTHER READING

General

Richard Abrams, *The Burden of Progress* (1978); John W. Chambers, *The Tyranny of Change: America in the Progressive Era* (1980); Arthur Ekirch, *Progressivism in America* (1974); Louis Filler, *The Muckrakers*, rev. ed. (1980); Samuel P. Hays, *The Response to Industrialism* (1957); Richard Hofstadter, *The Age of Reform* (1955); William R. Hutchinson, *The Modernist Impulse in American Protestantism* (1976); Gabriel Kolko, *The Triumph of Conservatism* (1963); David W. Noble, *The Progressive Mind*, rev. ed. (1981); James Weinstein, *The Corporate Ideal in the Liberal State, 1900–1918* (1968); Robert Wiebe, *The Search for Order* (1968).

Regional Studies

Dewey Grantham, *Southern Progressivism: The Reconciliation of Progress and Tradition* (1983); Sheldon Hackney, *Populism to Progressivism in Alabama* (1969); Richard L. McCormick, *From Realignment to Reform: Political Change in New York State, 1893–1910* (1981); George E. Mowry, *The California Progressives* (1951); David P. Thelen, *Robert La Follette and the Insurgent Spirit* (1976); David P. Thelen, *The New Citizenship: Origins of Progressivism in Wisconsin* (1972); C. Vann Woodward, *Origins of the New South* (1951).

Legislative Issues and Reform Groups

Norman H. Clark, *Deliver Us from Evil: An Interpretation of American Prohibition* (1976); Allen F. Davis, *Spearheads for Reform: The Social Settlements and the Progressive Movement, 1890–1914* (1967); Ruth Rosen, *The Lost Sisterhood: Prostitution in America, 1900–1918* (1982); James H. Timberlake,

Prohibition and the Progressive Crusade (1963); Walter I. Trattner, Crusade for the Children (1970); Irwin Yellowitz, Labor and the Progressive Movement in New York State (1965). (For works on socialism, see listings at end of Chapter 20.)

Education, Law, and the Social Sciences

Jerold S. Auerbach, Unequal Justice: Lawyers and Social Change in Modern America (1976); Loren P. Beth, The Development of the American Constitution, 1877–1917 (1971); Lawrence Cremin, The Transformation of the School: Progressivism in American Education (1961); Martin S. Dworkin, ed., Dewey on Education (1959); Thomas L. Haskell, The Emergence of Professional Social Science (1977); David W. Marcell, Progress and Pragmatism: James, Dewey, Beard, and the American Idea of Progress (1974); Philippa Strum, Louis D. Brandeis, Justice for the People (1984); David Tyack and Elizabeth Hansot, Managers of Virtue: Public School Leadership in America, 1820–1980 (1982); Lawrence Veysey, The Emergence of the American University (1970).

Women

Lois Banner, Women in Modern America: A Brief History, 2nd ed. (1984); Ruth Borden, Women and Temperance (1980); Carl N. Degler, At Odds: Women and the Family in America (1980); Eleanor Flexner, Century of Struggle: The Women's Rights Movement in the United States (1959); Linda Gordon, Woman's Body, Woman's Right: A Social History of Birth Control in America (1976); David Kennedy, Birth Control in America: The Career of Margaret Sanger (1970); Alice Kessler-Harris, Out to Work: A History of Wage-Earning Women in the United States (1982); Aileen Kraditor, The Ideas of the Women's Suffrage Movement (1965); Ellen Condliffe Lagemann, A Generation of Women: Education in the Lives of Progressive Reformers (1979); William L.

O'Neill, Everyone Was Brave: The Rise and Fall of Feminism in America (1969); William L. O'Neill, Divorce in the Progressive Era (1967); Ross Evans Paulson, Woman's Suffrage and Prohibition (1973); Rosalind Rosenberg, Beyond Separate Spheres: Intellectual Roots of Modern Feminism (1982); Elyce J. Rotella, From Home to Office: U.S. Women and Work, 1870–1930 (1981); Sheila M. Rothman, Woman's Proper Place (1978).

Blacks

John Dittmer, Black Georgia in the Progressive Era, 1900–1920 (1977); George Frederickson, The Black Image in the White Mind (1971); Louis R. Harlan, Booker T. Washington: The Wizard of Tuskegee, 1901–1915 (1983); Louis R. Harlan, Booker T. Washington: The Making of a Black Leader, 1856–1901 (1972); Charles F. Kellogg, NAACP (1970); James M. McPherson, The Abolitionist Legacy: From Reconstruction to the NAACP (1975); August Meier, Negro Thought in America, 1880–1915 (1963); Elliot M. Rudwick, W. E. B. Du Bois (1969); Donald Spivey, Schooling for the New Slavery: Black Industrial Education (1978).

Roosevelt, Taft, and Wilson

John M. Blum, Woodrow Wilson and the Politics of Morality (1956); John M. Blum, The Republican Roosevelt, 2nd ed. (1954); Paolo E. Coletta, The Presidency of William Howard Taft (1973); John Milton Cooper, Jr., The Warrior and the Priest: Woodrow Wilson and Theodore Roosevelt (1983); William Harbaugh, The Life and Times of Theodore Roosevelt (1961); Arthur S. Link, Wilson, 5 vols (1947–1965); Arthur S. Link, Woodrow Wilson and the Progressive Era (1954); Edmund Morris, The Rise of Theodore Roosevelt (1979); George E. Mowry, The Era of Theodore Roosevelt (1958); James Penick, Jr., Progressive Politics and Conservation: The Ballinger-Pinchot Affair (1968).

THE QUEST FOR EMPIRE

1865–1914

CHAPTER 22

William H. Seward's travels through scenic Alaska in August 1869 revived his enthusiasm for the huge territory he had, as secretary of state, bought from Russia two years earlier. In the colony's abundant marine treasures—whales, sea otters, seals, salmon—Seward foresaw new opportunities for fishing and the fur trade. He remarked effusively on Alaska's thick forests and rich deposits of iron ore, coal, copper, and gold, unaware of the vast petroleum supplies that would be so eagerly tapped in the twentieth century. He told white settlers in Sitka that they were true pioneers in an Indian-populated land. And reinforcements were on the way, he reassured them, for Alaska was destined to become a prosperous "shipyard for the supply of all nations."

Seward's oratory was exaggerated, but it reflected the optimism so characteristic of nineteenth-century Americans, to whom expansion seemed natural, if not preordained. Under the banner of "manifest destiny," they had purchased Louisiana, annexed Florida, Oregon, and Texas, seized California and other western areas from Mexico, and acquired the Gadsden Purchase; and through the export of their products abroad they had developed a foreign trade important to the nation's economic health. "Their destiny is always to expand," remarked the Russian diplomat who negotiated the sale of Alaska—which, he regretted, had not "escaped the lust of Americans."

But the American "lust" for more space, more land, more markets, and more resources was tempered in the late nineteenth century. Although most Americans applauded expansionism, some were uneasy with *imperialism:* the imposition of control over other peoples, denying them the freedom to make their own decisions, undermining their sovereignty. Imperialism could take a variety of forms, both formal (annexation, colonialism, or military occupation) and informal (the threat of intervention or economic manipulation). Many Americans seemed hesitant to become full-fledged participants in the scramble among the great powers for colonies in Asia and Africa. Anti-imperialist critics feared that an overseas American empire would undermine institutions at home, invite perpetual war, and violate honored principles.

The road to trade and empire was strewn with other obstacles. The federal government did not always adequately fund the vehicles of expansion, neglecting the navy until the 1880s and maintaining a foreign service weakened by the political spoils system. Leaders also played politics with foreign policy, complicating the diplomatic process. And most business leaders actually ignored foreign commerce in favor of the bustling domestic marketplace. Still, a pattern of accelerating activity abroad culminated in the tumultuous decade of the 1890s, when the doubters' voices were drowned out by shouts for war and foreign territory, and when American power was sufficient to deliver both.

This chapter is the story of the roots and sources of American expansionism, the tremendous growth of American activity abroad in the late nineteenth century, the building of an overseas empire, and the momentous 1890s debate between imperialists and anti-imperialists over the fundamental course of American foreign policy. After 1900 it is the story of the opportunities opened and the troubles encountered in managing, protecting, and expanding an empire that stretched from Latin America to Asia and that faced threats from restless nationalists, commercial competitors, and other expansive great nations.

EXPANSIONISM REVIVED

The Civil War had temporarily interrupted the country's expansionist course. Once freed from that conflict, however, Americans North and South scouted new frontiers to conquer. Seward eyed Cuba, President Ulysses Grant coveted Santo Domingo, and others envisioned new outposts in the Pacific Ocean. Religious leaders contemplated the conversion of "natives" and "savages" to Christianity. Businesspeople and farmers talked of untapped overseas markets. Nationalists spoke of exporting America's superior political principles and practices to other peoples.

And to ensure the success of these dreams, to protect all these activities, American leaders planned for an enlarged modern navy of the first order. The humorist Finley Peter Dunne captured the American mood near the end of the nineteenth century by putting words in the mouths of his fictional Irish-American characters: " 'We're a gr-reat people,' said Mr. Hennessy, earnestly. 'We ar-re,' said Mr. Dooley. 'We ar-re that. An' th best iv it is, we know we are.' "

After the searing Civil War, American leaders tried to heal sectional wounds with soothing patriotic oratory. The 1876 centennial celebration emphasized national unity; Confederate and **American Nationalism** Union soldiers met to exchange captured flags; patriotic societies like the Daughters of the American Revolution (1890) were organized. Civic pride welled up when American machines earned top marks at world fairs. Notions of American exceptionalism and manifest destiny were revived. To the Reverend Josiah Strong, author of the influential book *Our Country* (1885), Americans were a special, God-favored Anglo-Saxon race destined to lead others. "As America goes, so goes the world," he claimed. To Social Darwinists, Americans were a superior people who would surely overcome all competition and thrive. "The rule of the survival of the fittest applies to nations as well as to the animal kingdom," claimed American diplomat John Barrett.

The argument for expansion and empire seemed all the more urgent when Americans anticipated the closing of the frontier at home. In 1893 Professor Frederick Jackson Turner postulated his frontier thesis. Turner argued that an ever-expanding continental frontier had shaped the American character. That "frontier has gone, and with its going has closed the first period of American history." Turner did not explicitly say that a new frontier had to be found overseas. But some thought that was what he meant when he wrote in his famous article "The Significance of the Frontier in American History," that he doubted that "the expansive character of American life has now entirely ceased. Movement has been its dominant fact, and, unless this training has no effect upon a people, the American energy will continually demand a wider field for its exercise."

Foreign policy has always sprung from the domestic setting of a nation—its needs, wants, moods, and

William H. Seward (1801–1872) had a vision of empire matched by few Americans. This ambitious secretary of state added Alaska and Midway Island to the United States domain, but anti-imperialists and political foes thwarted his plans for other territorial acquisitions. *Library of Congress.*

ideals. The people who guided America's expansionist foreign relations were the same **Domestic Roots of Foreign Policy** people who kindled the spirit of national growth at home, who championed the transcontinental railroad, forcefully removed Native Americans from the avenues of white settlement, extolled the wonders of the machine age, and built America's cities and giant corporations. Most Americans, caught up as they were in making a living or exploiting economic opportunities at home, paid scant attention to external issues or to the intense international rivalry of the post–Civil War era. They usually became alive to foreign policy questions only when war threatened. But America's leaders—in politics, business, labor, agriculture, religion, journalism, education, and the military—were alert to the nation's place in world affairs. They believed that the United States could prosper far better in a world in which American influence was exerted. They were aware of the interconnections between domestic developments and foreign events.

The expansionism so evident at home after the Civil War was deeply intertwined with foreign policy. The national network of railroads, for example, made it possible for Iowa farmers to transport their crops to seaboard cities and then on to foreign markets. Their livelihood was thus tied to international market conditions, to the outcomes of foreign wars, and to the time-honored American principle of freedom of the seas, which stood as a reminder to other nations that American goods on American ships should be free to cross the oceans, even in time of foreign war. American cities that burgeoned in the late nineteenth century became centers of foreign commerce and cosmopolitan culture. The products of companies like International Harvester were shipped to distant markets, and new technology was applied to the improved navy required to protect this lucrative commerce. Periodic depressions fostered the belief that the country's surplus production must be sold in foreign markets to restore and sustain economic well-being at home. By promoting economic health, these markets would also contribute to domestic social and political stability. Senator and two-time Secretary of State James G. Blaine put it this way: "With these markets secured new life would be given to our manufactories, the product of the Western farmer would be in demand, the reasons for and inducements to strikers with all their attendant evils would cease."

The tariff too was an issue in both domestic politics and world affairs. Tariff increases (see pages 566, 570, 584) designed to protect American industry and agriculture from foreign competition adversely affected those who sold to America, prompting them to enact retaliatory tariffs on American products. In Cuba and Hawaii, American tariff revisions actually induced economic crises, which fed revolutions that ultimately served American interests. The massive influx of immigrants caused diplomatic problems as well as social upheaval at home. Moreover, notions of racial superiority and Jim Crow practices at home influenced American policies toward Asian and Latin American peoples of color, who were considered inferior. And ambitious politicians were tempted to enhance their political reputations by flexing the national muscle

in the world arena. In general, then, the major domestic questions that preoccupied Americans from the Civil War to the First World War were closely linked to the nation's diplomacy. The threads of domestic and foreign policy were densely interwoven.

The spokesmen for expansion and empire belonged to what scholars have labeled the foreign policy elite or opinion leaders. Better read and better traveled than most Americans, more cosmopolitan than provincial in outlook, and politically active, they influenced the making of foreign policy. Unlike domestic policy, foreign policy is seldom shaped by the people. Most Americans simply do not follow international relations or express themselves on its issues. Indeed, studies have demonstrated that no more than 10 to 20 percent of the voting public was alert to world affairs in the late nineteenth century. It was this small group, whom Secretary of State Walter Q. Gresham called "the thoughtful men of the country," whose opinion counted. Increasingly in the late nineteenth century, and especially in the 1890s, they urged an imperialist course. Those members of the political elite who, like President Grover Cleveland, favored economic expansion and United States hegemony (that is, dominance) in South America, but not the annexation of more territory, gradually lost ground to these proempire leaders.

Foreign Policy Elite

The imperialists in Washington, D.C., were clannish. They met informally to talk about building a bigger navy, about an isthmian canal, and about the need to sell surpluses abroad. They gathered at Henry Adams's house on H Street or at the nearby home of John Hay, who became secretary of state in 1898; they dined together at the Metropolitan Club. Theodore Roosevelt, appointed assistant secretary of the navy in 1897, was among them; so was Brooks Adams, Henry's gloomy brother, a publicist for an American presence in China. Henry Cabot Lodge, who became a member of the Senate Foreign Relations Committee in 1895, often stopped by, and corporate lawyer Elihu Root, who would later serve in the cabinet, joined in as well. These luminaries kept up the drumbeat for empire, and after their elevation to high office in the 1890s they acquired by force much of the empire that earlier Americans had felt would gravitate peacefully to the United States.

With a characteristic mixture of self-interest and

idealism, United States leaders believed that imperialism benefited both Americans and those who came under American control. When they intervened in other lands or lectured weaker states, Americans defended their behavior on the grounds that they were extending the blessings of liberty and prosperity to less fortunate people. For those many imperialists who were also progressive reformers, interventions were necessary to improve foreign societies. To critics at home and abroad, however, American paternalism appeared hypocritical. They charged that the use of coercion to compel resistant foreigners to behave and think like Americans violated cherished American principles. For example, in order to impose on resentful Filipinos an American-style political system theoretically based on democratic tenets, American officials censored the press, jailed some dissidents and killed others, and designated candidates for public office. The persistent American belief that other people cannot solve their own problems and that only the American model of government will work produced what historian William Appleman Williams has called "the tragedy of American diplomacy."

FACTORY, FARM, AND FOREIGN AFFAIRS

Many business people and farmers were part of the foreign-policy public that savored expansion. There were, of course, profits to be made from foreign sales. "It is my dream," cried the governor of Georgia in 1878, to see "in every valley . . . a cotton factory to convert the raw material of the neighborhood into fabrics which shall warm the limbs of Japanese and Chinese." Fear generated foreign trade as well, for the nation's farms and factories produced more than Americans could consume. Foreign commerce, it was believed, could be a safety valve to avert or relieve economic depression, such as that of the 1890s. Surpluses could be exported.

The tremendous economic growth of the United States after the Civil War stimulated foreign trade, a larger navy to protect this lucrative commerce, a

Growth of Foreign Trade more efficient foreign service, a call for more colonies, and a more activist foreign policy. From the 1860s to 1914, in fact, foreign trade grew faster than the national income. In 1870 United States exports totaled $451 million; in 1900, $1.5 billion. By 1914, at the outbreak of the First World War, American exports had reached $2.5 billion, and European businesspeople complained of the "American export invasion." Beginning in the 1870s the United States began to enjoy a long-term favorable balance of trade (exporting more than it imported). Most of America's products went to Britain, Europe, and Canada, but increasing amounts flowed to new markets in Latin America and Asia. Although exports of manufactured items increased, agricultural goods accounted for about three-quarters of the total in 1870 and about two-thirds in 1900. Manufactured goods led export sales for the first time in 1913, when the United States ranked third behind only Britain and Germany in the export of manufactures.

Breadstuffs, cotton, meat, and dairy products topped the export list in 1900, providing farmers with needed foreign outlets. Over half the annual cotton crop was exported each year. Wisconsin cheesemakers shipped to Britain; the Swift and Armour meat companies exported refrigerated beef to Europe; and wheat farmers became Europe's largest supplier of wheat. James J. Hill of the Great Northern railroad worked hard to sell American grain in Asia. He distributed wheat cookbooks, translated into several Asian languages.

America's ambitious entrepreneurs and large businesses looked to foreign markets, especially in the 1890s, when it became clear that the output of industrial products was outdistancing consumption. Rockefeller's Standard Oil sold abroad, notably in Germany, England, Cuba, and Mexico. In the 1870s and 1880s about two-thirds of all American petroleum was exported, and in succeeding decades the figure was about one-half. Fifteen percent of America's iron and steel, 50 percent of its copper, and 16 percent of its agricultural implements were sold abroad by the turn of the century, making many workers in those industries dependent on exports.

So too with machinery. Thomas Edison and Alexander Graham Bell installed England's telephone network. George Westinghouse marketed his air brakes in Europe; Singer exported about 40 percent of its

Singer sewing machines were exported throughout the globe in the late nineteenth century. Here the King of Ou (the Caroline Islands, in the Pacific) operates the Great Civilizer. The caption for this company-sponsored photograph read: "The Herald of Civilization—Missionary Work of the Singer Manufacturing Company." But the profitable Singer business was interested in more than improving peoples' standard of living; three-quarters of the sewing machines sold in the world in 1890 were Singers.   Courtesy, Robert B. Davies, Peacefully Working to Conquer the World.

sewing machines; and Cyrus McCormick's "reaper kings" harvested the wheat of Russian fields. Photography baron George Eastman, whose business operated around the globe, remarked that the growth of foreign sales allowed Americans to "distribute our eggs and pad the basket at the same time." At the 1878 World's Fair in Paris, American exhibitors won more awards than any other country. At the Paris fair in 1889 American agricultural machinery was acclaimed, and at Chicago's Columbian Exposition in 1893 American inventive genius—especially in the application of electricity to machines—dazzled foreign visitors. And direct American investments abroad reached $3.5 billion by 1914, placing the United States among the top four investor countries.

American economic expansion in Latin America was especially impressive and aroused the nation's diplomatic interest in its neighbors to the South.

Economic Expansion in Latin America

United States exports to Latin America, which exceeded $50 million in the 1870s, climbed to over $120 million in 1900 and topped $300 million in 1914. Investments by United States citizens in Latin America amounted to a towering $1.26 billion in 1914. In 1899 two of the largest banana importers merged to form the United Fruit Company. Owning much of the land (over 1 million acres in 1913) and the railroad and steamship lines of Central America, United Fruit became a major economic and political force in the region. It developed transportation, cultivated land, and fought to eradicate yellow fever and malaria. As for Mexico, American capitalists came to own its railroads and mines. By 1910, Americans controlled 43 percent of Mexican property and produced more than half that nation's oil.

Economic expansion abroad became a mechanism for exerting political influence. Dunne's Mr. Dooley put it simply: "I tell ye, th' hand that rocks th' scales in th' grocery store is th' hand that rules th' wurruld." Indeed, by the early twentieth century American economic interests were influencing policies on taxes and natural resources in countries like Cuba and Mexico. American interests were responsible for drawing Hawaii into the American imperial net and for spreading American cultural values abroad. Religious missionaries and Singer executives, for example, joined hands in promoting the "civilizing medium" of the sewing machine. "The world is to be Christianized and civilized," declared Josiah Strong. "And what is the process of civilizing but the creating of more and higher wants. Commerce follows the missionary."

American leaders believed selling, buying, and investing in foreign marketplaces were important to the United States. Why? Because of profits, because the problems of overproduction and unemployment would be relieved at home, because a vigorous foreign trade was a symbol of national power, because economic ties permitted political influence to be exerted abroad, and because economic expansion helped spread the American way of life, creating a world more hospitable to Americans. Most nations engaged in foreign trade and investment, and they signed treaties to govern their exchanges. Most Americans championed economic expansion. But some critics, called anti-imperialists, drew the line between expansionism and imperialism: the first should not lead to the second; mutually beneficial commercial intercourse should not yield to the domination of one nation over another. Profitable and fair trade relationships, yes; exploitation, no. And, others advised, American business activity abroad should not draw the United States into unwanted diplomatic crises and wars. Few Americans sought to stop trade; rather, they wanted to make sure it did not create damaging political problems.

LOOKING OUTWARD,
1860s–1880s

The American empire was built gradually, sometimes haltingly, in the years following the Civil War. One of its chief architects was William H. Seward. As senator from New York (1849–1861) and secretary of state (1861–1869), he argued articulately for extension of the American frontier. "There is not in the history of the Roman Empire an ambition for aggrandizement so marked as that which characterized the American people," he once said. Seward envisioned a large, coordinated American empire encompassing Canada, the Caribbean, Cuba, Central America, Mexico, Hawaii, Iceland, Greenland, and certain Pacific islands. This empire would be built not by war but by a natural process of gravitation toward the attractive republican United States. Commerce would hurry the process, he thought, noting that the merchants of Venice and Britain had become "masters of the world."

William H. Seward

To ensure the unity of his American empire, Seward appealed for a canal across Central America, a transcontinental American railroad to link up with the markets of Asia, and a telegraph system to speed communications. To Seward economic expansion at home was essential to expansion abroad, and vice versa. Thus he favored an influx of immigrants to provide the labor needed for economic development, and he backed tariffs to protect youthful American factories from foreign competition.

Most of Seward's grandiose plans did not reach fruition during his own tenure as secretary of state. In 1867, for example, he signed a treaty with Denmark to buy the Danish West Indies (the Virgin Islands). Shortly afterward a hurricane and tidal wave wrecked St. Thomas, diminishing its value in the eyes of many senators. (The senators were also reluctant to hand Seward a diplomatic triumph while he was supporting Andrew Johnson during the president's impeachment proceedings.) The treaty was shelved, and the Virgin Islanders, who had voted for annexation, had to wait until 1917 to join the American empire.

Seward desired British-dominated Canada, too, and Canadians feared a United States takeover. Their alarm was intensified by the activities of the Fenian Brotherhood, an Irish-American society organized to agitate for Ireland's independence from Britain. It began raiding Canada from Vermont in 1866. Seward preferred diplomacy over such violence as a means of achieving annexation. When some Canadians petitioned London for a new confederation, and Britain agreed in 1867 to the creation of the Dominion of Canada, hopes of attaching Canada to the United States faded.

Most of Seward's plans for acquiring territory were blocked by a combination of anti-imperialists and political foes. Anti-imperialists like Senator Carl Schurz and E. L. Godkin, editor of the magazine *The Nation,* believed that the country had enough unsettled land, and that creation of a showcase of democracy and prosperity at home was the best way to persuade other peoples to adopt American institutions and principles. Some anti-imperialists, sharing the racism of the times, did not want to annex territory populated by "inferior" dark-skinned people, such as Santo Domingo or slavery-plagued Cuba. And Seward's political antagonists hoped to punish him by denying him his dreams.

Seward did enjoy some successes. When an American naval officer seized the Midway Islands in 1867, Seward laid claim to them for the United States. The same year he paid Russia $7.2 million for the 591,000 square miles of Alaska (see page 445). His

The imperial competition for Samoa pitted Britain, Germany, and the United States against one another. In this 1889 Judge magazine cover, the British "John Bull" admonishes German Chancellor Otto von Bismarck to avoid provoking the sometimes menacing American eagle. At the Berlin Conference of that year the great powers defused the crisis by dividing Samoa among themselves.   Library of Congress.

Chapter 22: THE QUEST FOR EMPIRE, 1865–1914

critics ridiculed the purchase, but the Senate voted overwhelmingly for the treaty. Seward also shepherded the Burlingame Treaty with China (1868) through the Senate. The treaty provided for free immigration between the two countries and pledged Sino-American friendship. (A new treaty in 1880 permitted Congress to suspend Chinese immigration to the United States, which it did two years later to satisfy anti-Oriental bias in the Far West.) The secretary's forceful handling of French interference in Mexico also furthered his reputation. In 1861, Napoleon III had placed Archduke Ferdinand Maximilian of Austria on the throne in Mexico. Preoccupied with the Civil War, Seward could do little to help the Mexicans dislodge the intruding Europeans. But in 1866, citing the Monroe Doctrine, he told the French to get out as American troops headed for the Mexican border. Napoleon, troubled at home and now opposed by both Mexicans and Americans, abandoned his venture.

Seward's dream of a world knit together into a giant communications system was satisfied. In 1866, through the persevering efforts of Cyrus Field, an underwater transatlantic cable linked **Impact of** European and American telegraph **the Telegraph** networks. And, backed by J. P. Morgan's capital, James A. Scrymser strung telegraph lines to Latin America, reaching Chile in 1890. Information about markets, diplomatic crises, and war flowed steadily and quickly. Whereas delivery of surface mail from Washington, D.C., to European capitals often took from ten to twenty-one days, the transatlantic cable enabled the State Department to make same-day contact. In a serious squabble with Spain in 1873 over the Cuban-owned gun-running ship *Virginius*—the Spanish executed some Americans on board—officials made good use of the telegraph system to manage the crisis. In general, drawn closer to one another by improvements in communications and transportation, nations found that far-away events became more important to their prosperity and security. Technology shrank the globe.

Seward's successor, Hamilton Fish (1869–1877), inherited the knotty and emotional problem of the *Alabama* claims. The *Alabama* and other vessels built by Great Britain for the Confederacy during the Civil War had marauded Union shipping. Senator Charles Sumner demanded that Britain pay $2 billion in damages or give up Canada, but Fish patiently took

Anglo- the question to the bargaining table. **American** In 1871 Britain and America signed **Relations** the Washington Treaty, whereby the British apologized and agreed to the creation of a tribunal, which later awarded the United States $15.5 million. Disputes over fishing rights along the North Atlantic coast and the hunting of seals in the Bering Sea near Alaska also dogged Anglo-American relations and would continue to do so for decades. Yet the two powers, however competitive, were slowly coming to the conclusion that rapprochement rather than confrontation best served their interests. American politicians still tried to "twist the lion's tail" to score political points at home, but the trend toward Anglo-American accommodation could not be reversed.

Fish also had to deal with President Grant's designs on the Dominican Republic. The president was impressed by the island's raw materials and its potential as a market for American textiles, and the navy eyed the harbor at Samaná Bay. Grant's personal secretary, Orville Babcock, negotiated a treaty of annexation. But Senator Sumner smelled a rat in Babcock, who through private intrigue stood to gain financially from the venture. Furthermore, the Dominican Republic was embroiled in civil war and was nearly at war with its neighbor Haiti. Political rivalry also colored the question. "No wild bull ever dashed more violently at a red rag than he does at anything that he thinks the President is interested in," Fish said of Sumner's political motives. The treaty was defeated in 1870.

Another venture in the Pacific succeeded. In 1878 the United States gained rights to a naval station at the strategic port of Pago Pago in Samoa, several islands four thousand miles from San Francisco on the trade route between Australia and America. The Germans and British also coveted the islands. Year by year tensions grew. To avoid war, Germany, Britain, and the United States met in Berlin in 1889 and, without consulting the Samoans, carved Samoa into three parts. A decade later the United States annexed part of the islands, including Pago Pago.

In Latin America United States interests became extensive. Trade with the region was flourishing, investments were growing, and the navy's presence was conspicuous. The convening of **Pan-American** the first Pan-American Conference **Conference** in Washington, D.C., in 1889 bore witness to growing ties. Sponsored by Secretary of State James G. Blaine, the conference was designed to improve commercial relations. The Latin American conferees toured United States factories and then negotiated several general agreements to promote trade. To improve inter-American cooperation, they founded the Pan American Union, which in 1907 moved into handsome new quarters in Washington, D.C., financed by Andrew Carnegie.

As the United States acquired new territories and markets and extended its influence abroad, the call went out for an improved and enlarged navy. Captain Alfred T. Mahan, who had served on blockade duty during the Civil War and had written a naval history of the conflict, became a major popularizer for the "New Navy." Since foreign trade was vital to the nation's well-being, he argued, the nation required an efficient navy to protect its shipping, and in turn a navy required colonies for bases. "Whether they will or no," Mahan wrote, "Americans must now begin to look outward. The growing production of the country demands it." Mahan became president of the Naval War College in Newport, Rhode Island, founded in 1884, and there gave a series of lectures that was published as *The Influence of Sea Power upon History* (1890). This widely read book sat on every good expansionist's shelf. Theodore Roosevelt and Henry Cabot Lodge consulted Mahan, sharing his belief in the links between trade, navy, and colonies.

Until its modernization the American navy was in a sorry state. Many of its wooden ships were rotting. Its shipyards were havens of political patronage; congressional appropriations were frequently wasted. But in 1883 Congress authorized construction of the first steel warships. American factories went to work to produce steel for hulls, boilers for steam engines, armor plate, high-velocity shells, powerful guns, and precision instruments. Andrew Carnegie, displaying none of the pacifism that would later distinguish him as a champion of world peace, exclaimed "there may be millions for us in armor," and signed a highly profitable naval contract. Businesspeople seeking men-of-war escorts for their commercial vessels and scouts for new trade opportunities cheered the birth of the New Navy.

Gradually, but especially in the 1880s, the navy

New Navy

shifted from sail to steam and from wood to steel. New Navy ships like the *Maine*, the *Oregon*, the *Boston*, and the *Columbia* thrust the United States into naval prominence. The *Columbia* held the naval record for average sea speed, and the other three figured in the imperialist ventures of the 1890s. Incidentally, many of these steel vessels were named for states and cities in a deliberate campaign to kindle patriotism and local support for naval expansion. The enlarged navy provided the United States with the tools to expand and build a greater empire.

CRISES IN THE 1890s: HAWAII, VENEZUELA, AND CUBA

When the United States became engaged in a number of crises in the 1890s, the New Navy warships were put to the test. For decades the Hawaiian Islands had commanded American attention. This major Pacific way station was significant for trade with Asia and had long been a site of missionary work. Its undeveloped but strategic port of Pearl Harbor tempted naval expansionists, and the vast sugar plantations of the islands attracted American entrepreneurs. In 1875 the United States signed a treaty granting Hawaiian sugar duty-free entry to the American market; the Hawaiian sugar industry boomed and became dependent on mainland business. Six years later Secretary Blaine warned other nations away from the islands, declaring them "essentially a part of the American system." In 1887 the United States gained naval rights to Pearl Harbor. When the Congress revised the tariff laws in the early 1890s, however, it eliminated the special protection for Hawaiian sugar and gave American producers a bounty of two cents a pound. Exports of Hawaiian sugar to the United States declined quickly, and American planters in Hawaii were severely hurt. To gain exemption from American tariffs, a group of planters called the Annexation Club plotted a revolution.

In January 1893 the white minority overthrew the native monarch, Queen Liliuokalani. Their success stemmed in part from the support of the chief Amer-

Annexation of Hawaii

ican diplomat in Honolulu, John L. Stevens, who saw to it that sailors from the warship *Boston* encircled the royal palace. Stevens informed Washington that the "Hawaiian pear is now fully ripe, and this is the golden hour for the United States to pluck it." Against the protests of Japan, whose nationals accounted for about 40 percent of Hawaii's population (Americans equaled only 5 percent), President Benjamin Harrison sent a treaty of annexation to the Senate. But incoming President Grover Cleveland, an expansionist who disapproved of forced annexation, withdrew it. Five years later, on July 7, 1898, during the Spanish-American-Cuban-Filipino War, President William McKinley successfully maneuvered annexation through Congress. The president, fearing that the Senate lacked the two-thirds majority necessary to pass a treaty, chose the method of a joint resolution, which required only a simple majority. Thus was Hawaii added to the American empire.

The Venezuelan crisis of 1895 also gave the United States an opportunity to express its expansive mood. For decades Venezuela and Great Britain had squabbled over the border between Venezuela and British Guiana. The disputed territory contained rich gold deposits and the mouth of the Orinoco River, the commercial gateway to northern South America. Venezuela asked for American help, charging that the imperialist British were violating the Monroe Doctrine. President Cleveland decided that the "mean and hoggish" British had to be warned away. In July 1895, Secretary of State Richard Olney sent the British a brash 12,000-word message that Cleveland compared to a twenty-inch gun—in the naval parlance of the time, a huge weapon. Olney lectured the British that the Monroe Doctrine prohibited European intervention in the Western Hemisphere, whose states "are friends and allies, commercially and politically, of the United States." The spread-eagle words that followed were clearly directed at an international audience: "To-day the United States is practically sovereign on this continent, and its fiat is law upon the subjects to which it confines its interposition."

Venezuelan Crisis

This statement of United States hegemony did not impress the British, who rejected American interference in what they considered a local issue. American jingoistic nationalists clamored for action. "Let the

"The Real British Lion," according to this 1895 American cartoon, was actually an ugly hog astride the globe. The Venezuelan crisis stimulated this Anglophobic view. *New York Evening World, 1895.*

fight come if it must; I don't care whether our sea coast cities are bombarded or not; we would take Canada," snorted Theodore Roosevelt. But neither London nor Washington wanted war. The British, seeking international friends to counter an intensifying German competition, quietly retreated from the crisis. In 1896 an Anglo-American arbitration board divided the disputed territory. Throughout the deliberations Venezuela was barely consulted. Thus the United States displayed a trait common to imperialists: a disregard for the rights and sensibilities of small nations. This trait characterized American foreign policy thereafter, as did the assertive rhetoric of 1895.

In 1895 another crisis rocked Latin America: the Cuban revolution against Spain. From 1868 to 1878 the Cubans had battled their mother country to no avail. Slavery was abolished but independence denied, and Spanish rule continued to be repressive. The Cuban rebels waited for another chance. José Martí, one of the heroes of Cuban history, collected money, arms, and men in the United States. As in the case of Hawaii, a change in American tariff policy hastened the revolution. The Wilson-Gorman Tariff (1894) imposed a duty on Cuban

Cuban Revolution

sugar, which had been entering the United States duty-free under the McKinley Tariff (1890) and a reciprocity agreement with Spain. The Cuban economy, highly dependent on exports, was thrown into turmoil.

From American soil, Martí launched a revolution that became gruesome in its human and material costs. Rebels burned cane fields and razed mills, using guerrilla tactics to avoid head-on clashes with Spanish soldiers. Under the command of Valereano Weyler, soon dubbed the Butcher, Spanish officials instituted a policy of "reconcentration": hundreds of thousands of Cubans were herded into fortified towns and camps to separate them from the insur-

Spanish Reconcentration Policy gents. Camp conditions were ghastly; hunger, starvation, and killer diseases took a heavy toll. As much as one-quarter of the total Cuban population perished in these reconcentration centers. Weyler's forces ransacked the countryside, Cuba's economy deteriorated badly, and American investments of $50 million were jeopardized. Cuban-American trade in tobacco and sugar further declined. American imports from Cuba, which had amounted to $76 million in 1894, slumped to $15 million in 1898; American exports to the island dropped by half in the same period.

As tragic stories of atrocity and destruction reached the United States—and were played up by the American yellow press (see pages 553–554)—people grew angry with the Spanish and sympathetic toward the insurrectionists. In late 1897 a new government came to power in Madrid. The Spanish modified reconcentration and promised that Cuba would be given some autonomy. Americans waited to see if the new reforms would subdue the rebellious island and restore peace.

When President McKinley came to office he was already an expansionist. He agreed that a large navy was imperative; he recognized that surplus production had to be exported; and he echoed the belief that American supremacy was essential in the Western Hemisphere. The 1896 Republican platform on which McKinley ran demanded both an enlarged American empire and Cuban independence. In his annual message of December 1897, McKinley surveyed the Cuban crisis, ruling out American intervention while Spain

was walking the path of reform. McKinley was by no means the weak leader his critics said he was (Roosevelt once remarked that McKinley did not have the backbone of a chocolate eclair). "He was a man of great power," said Elihu Root, who *"always had his way."* The president, not Congress or public opinion, made the decisions that led to war. But McKinley wanted to avoid war if at all possible.

Events in the first few months of 1898 sabotaged the Spanish reforms and exhausted American patience. Early in January, antireform pro-Spanish loyalists and army personnel rioted in Havana. The Spanish government, it seemed to Americans, could not even maintain discipline within its own ranks. After the riots, Washington officials ordered

Sinking of the *Maine* the battleship *Maine* to Havana harbor to demonstrate United States concern over the violence and to protect American citizens if need be. On February 15 an explosion ripped the *Maine*, killing 260 American officers and crew. Americans were quick to blame Spain for the disaster.

Spain's image in the United States had been undermined a week earlier when William Randolph Hearst's inflammatory *New York Journal* published a stolen private letter from Enrique Dupuy de Lôme, the Spanish minister in Washington. In the letter de Lôme scorned McKinley as "weak and a bidder for the admiration of the crowd" and revealed Spanish determination to fight on in Cuba. In March the irritated president asked for $50 million in defense funds, and Congress complied unanimously. The naval board created to investigate the sinking of the *Maine* then reported that a mine had caused the explosion. (A report by Admiral Hyman G. Rickover in 1976 refuted that conclusion, blaming the explosion on an internal accident.) The panel did not assign responsibility, but restless Americans blamed Spain—if not for the catastrophe, then at least for creating an atmosphere that permitted it to happen.

McKinley's diplomatic options were greatly reduced by the impact of these events. He decided to send Spain an ultimatum. In late March the United States insisted that Spain accept an armistice, end reconcentration altogether, and designate McKinley as arbiter. The basic American goal was Cuban independence, but the president and his diplomats never so informed Spain. Yet no Spanish government could have given up Cuba and remained in office.

The Spanish did make concessions. They abolished reconcentration and accepted an armistice on the condition that the insurgents agree first. McKinley had wanted more; he began to write a message to Congress. After completing his speech, however, he received the news that Spain had gone one step further and declared a unilateral armistice. The weary McKinley—who was taking medication in order to sleep—hesitated but chose to go to Congress with a war message nonetheless. He could no longer tolerate the chronic disorder just ninety miles off the American coast. As Senator Lodge explained, "We can not go on indefinitely with this strain, this suspense, and this uncertainty, this tottering upon the verge of war."

In his address on April 11, the president did not ask for a declaration of war against Spain but rather for an authorization to use force, as "an impartial neutral," to effect "a rational compromise between the contestants." McKinley listed American grievances and the reasons why the United States had to end the turmoil. First, the "cause of humanity." Second, the protection of American life and property. Third, the "very serious injury to the commerce, trade, and business of our people." And fourth, referring to the destruction of the *Maine,* the "constant menace to our peace." At the very end of his speech McKinley mentioned Spain's recent concession, but made little of it.

THE SPANISH-AMERICAN-CUBAN-FILIPINO WAR

Congress debated for over a week and then on April 19 declared Cuba free and independent, directing the president to use force to remove Spanish authority from the island. The legislators also passed the Teller Amendment, which disclaimed any American intention to annex Cuba. McKinley beat back a congressional amendment to recognize the rebel government, for he believed the Cubans were unready for self-government and would first need a period of tutoring by Americans.

Diplomacy had failed. By the time the Spanish concessions were forthcoming, events had already pushed the antagonists to the brink. Washington might have been more patient and Madrid might have faced the fact that its once-grand empire had disintegrated. But the Cuban insurgents would settle for nothing less than independence, which Spain could not easily grant, and which the United States could achieve only through war. What was striking in the Cuban crisis, as in the Venezuelan crisis, was the American insistence that the United States would set the rules for nations in the Western Hemisphere. Great Britain had backed down in 1895, but Spain stood firm in 1898.

The motives of those Americans who favored war were mixed and complex. McKinley's message of April 11 expressed a humanitarian impulse to stop the bloodletting; concern for commerce and property; and the psychological need to end the nightmarish anxiety once and for all. Republican politicians advised McKinley that they would lose the upcoming congressional elections unless the Cuban question was solved. And many businesspeople who had been hesitant before the crisis of early 1898, joined many farmers in the belief that removing Spain from Cuba would open new markets for surplus production—to which the depression of the 1890s had given some urgency.

Motives for War

Inveterate imperialists saw the war as an opportunity to fulfill what Senator Lodge called the "large policy." Naval enthusiasts could prove the worth of the New Navy. Religious leaders too saw merit in war. Social Gospel advocate Washington Gladden remarked that "in saving others we may save ourselves." Some conservatives, alarmed by violent labor strikes and Populism, welcomed war as a national unifier. One senator commented that "internal discord" was disappearing in the "fervent heat of patriotism. . . . You will not see another Debs riot for many years." Sensationalism also figured in the march to war. Assistant Secretary of the Navy Theodore Roosevelt and others too young to remember the inhumanity of the Civil War looked on war as adventure. The yellow press exaggerated

The garrulous Rough Rider Theodore Roosevelt in Cuba during the 1898 war. His ballyhooed role in the battle for San Juan Hill at Santiago earned him a reputation as a war hero, and he went on to become president. Library of Congress.

no outlet for their vigorous and daring energy, there was always the chance of their fighting one another." The Rough Riders were undisciplined and not always effective warriors, but largely because of Roosevelt's self-serving publicity efforts they got a good press.

The war was hardly splendid. Over 5,400 Americans died, but only 379 of them in combat. The rest fell to malaria and yellow fever. Disease-carrying mosquitos were unrelenting, food was bad, and medical care was unsophisticated. Soldiers were issued heavy woolen uniforms in a tropical climate, and the stench of body odor was sickening. For black troops there was no relief from racism and Jim Crow. Their regiments were segregated and they were constantly insulted with the epithets *coon* and *nigger*. Cafes, saloons, and other public places refused to serve them. Race riots broke out; one in Tampa in early June sent twenty-seven blacks and several whites to the hospital. In Macon, Georgia, black soldiers tore down a park sign reading "No Dogs and Niggers Allowed" and chopped down a persimmon tree famous in the region as a lynching site. Whites in the South, where most troops were stationed, resented the appearance of status the military uniform gave to blacks and used threats and violence to intimidate those who suggested that a war to free the Cubans might help to break down the color line at home. One angry black Iowan announced: "I will not go to war. I have no country to fight for. I have not been given my rights." But most volunteers, black and white, shared the attitude of a soldier who wrote to his parents back in the coal-mining country of Pennsylvania: "The boys are all in good health and spirits, and think they can whip the world."

Before Americans began to fight and die in Cuba, the first news of war came from far-away Asia. It surprised many Americans, who knew little about the steady United States push into the Pacific, the dreams of farmers and businesspeople for a huge market in China, or the foreign-policy elite's knowledge of the Spanish colony of the Philippines. On May 1 Commodore George Dewey's New Navy ship the *Olympia* steamed into Manila Bay, the Philippines, and wrecked the Spanish fleet. Dewey became an instant hero. His sailors had to be handed volumes of the *Encyclopaedia Britannica*

Commodore Dewey in the Philippines

stories of atrocities. Anglo-Saxon supremacists like politician Albert Beveridge shouted, "God's hour has struck." But underlying all explanations of American acceptance of war was the spirit and reality of expansionism, which had been moving the nation ever outward in the last half of the nineteenth century.

Author Sherwood Anderson observed that fighting Spain was "like robbing an old gypsy woman in a vacant lot at night after a fair." Indeed, Spain was a weak belligerent, and the war lasted less than four months. But for some there was glory in what John Hay called a "splendid little war." As Roosevelt said of his motley unit of Ivy Leaguers and cowboys, the Rough Riders, they were "children of the dragon's blood, and if they had no outland foe to fight and to acquaint them with this strange land, but officials in Washington knew that Manila ranked with Pearl Harbor and Pago Pago as a choice harbor.

Popular accounts still distort the historical record by crediting (or blaming) Theodore Roosevelt for having ordered Dewey to Manila. The story goes that one day in February when the secretary of the navy was away from the office, Assistant Secretary Roosevelt usurped authority and cabled Dewey to take on coal, rest at Hong Kong, and head for Manila upon the outbreak of war. Actually Roosevelt was a member of the McKinley administration following established policy; the president himself approved Roosevelt's instructions to Dewey.

Facing rebels and Americans in both Cuba and the Philippines, Spanish resistance collapsed rapidly. The Spanish Caribbean fleet, trapped in Santiago harbor, made a desperate attempt to escape but was destroyed by American warships on July 3. Several days later, the island of Puerto Rico fell to the invading Americans. Manila surrendered in August under pressure from Americans and Filipino insurgents led by Emilio Aguinaldo. Undermanned and ill-equipped, Spain sued for peace. The combatants signed an armistice on August 12, thus ending a war that should be called—to reflect where it was fought and whose interests were at stake—the Spanish-American-Cuban-Filipino War. "Let's see what we get by this," said Secretary of State William R. Day as he twirled the large globe in his office.

In Paris in December, American and Spanish negotiators agreed on the peace terms: independence for Cuba; cession of the Philippines, Puerto Rico, and Guam to the United States;

Treaty of Paris and American payment of $20 million to Spain for the new territory.

Filipino nationalists tried to persuade American officials to set their nation free, but they were rebuffed. The American empire now stretched deep into Asia; and the annexation of Wake Island (1898), Hawaii (1898), and Samoa (1899) gave American traders, missionaries, and naval promoters other steppingstones to China. Puerto Rico provided a long-desired base in the Caribbean which could help protect an American-built isthmian canal. And the United States would soon acquire another naval base at Guantánamo Bay in Cuba.

TASTE OF EMPIRE: IMPERIALISTS AND ANTI-IMPERIALISTS DEBATE

During the war the *Washington Post* detected "a new appetite, a yearning to show our strength. . . . The taste of empire is in the mouth of the people. . . ." But as the debate over the Treaty of Paris intensified in the United States, it became evident that many Americans found the taste sour. Anti-imperialists like Mark Twain, William Jennings Bryan, William Graham Sumner, Andrew Carnegie, Charles Francis Adams, Jr., and Senator George Hoar argued vigorously against annexation of the Philippines. They were disturbed that a war to free Cuba had led to an empire. Their arguments varied. Some appealed to principle, citing the Declaration of Independence and the Constitution: the conquest of people against their will violated the sacred concept of self-determination. Philosopher William James charged that the United States was losing its special place among nations; it was, he warned, about to "puke up its heritage." To those who believed the Filipinos were not yet fit for self-government, former senator and active reformer Carl Schurz mockingly replied that Manila's city council was probably less corrupt than Chicago's. Others protested that the dispatch of troops overseas by the president, as commander-in-chief, greatly increased the power of the presidency and subverted the constitutional checks-and-balances system. Other anti-imperialists argued that the United States could acquire markets without having to subjugate foreign peoples.

Reform-minded critics of the treaty emphasized domestic priorities, including the improvement of race relations. "Until our nation has settled the Negro and Indian problems," said Booker T. Washington, "I do not believe that we have a right to assume more social problems." A black politician from Massachusetts—who had just protested a lynching in Georgia watched by two thousand people, followed

Anti-Imperialist Arguments

"Declined with thanks" reads this 1900 Puck *magazine cartoon. President William McKinley measures Uncle Sam, fattened by a series of territorial meals, as a group of antiimperialists led by Carl Schurz futilely attempt to administer an antidote. The message was clear: the United States would continue to expand.   Library of Congress.*

by mutilation of the black man's body by souvenir hunters—cried that the United States was exhibiting quite a spectacle to the world: "Columbia stands offering liberty to the Cubans with one hand, cramming liberty down the throats of the Filipinos with the other, but with both feet planted upon the neck of the negro." Other anti-imperialists feared the absorption of dark-skinned peoples, who, they warned, would undermine white Anglo-Saxon purity.

Samuel Gompers and other labor leaders worried about the possible undercutting of American labor—and the union movement—by what Gompers called the "half-breeds and semi-barbaric people" of the nation's new colonies. Might not they be imported as cheap contract labor to drive down the wages of American workers? Might not this new empire require a large standing army that would take workers away from their jobs? Would not exploitation of the weak abroad become contagious and lead to further exploitation of the weak at home? Would not an overseas empire drain interest and resources from pressing domestic problems, delaying reform? Gompers charged, in fact, that imperialism was an attempt "to divert the attention of our people from the ills from which we suffer at home."

The imperialists responded with a mixture of arguments invoking patriotism, destiny, and commerce. They sketched a scenario of American greatness: merchant ships plying waters to boundless Asian markets; naval vessels cruising the Pacific to protect American interests; missionaries uplifting inferior peoples. It was America's duty, they insisted, quoting a then-popular Rudyard Kipling

The Case for Empire

The missionary Grace Roberts teaches the Bible to Chinese women in Manchuria in 1903. The prominent American flag reveals that Americanism and religious work abroad went hand in hand. And the mission force was feminized; the great majority of missionaries were women. ABCFM pictures, courtesy of Houghton Library, Harvard University.

poem, to "Take Up the White Man's Burden." Furthermore, insurgents were beginning to resist American rule, and it was cowardly to pull out under fire. Germany and Japan, two major international competitors, were snooping around the Philippine Islands, seemingly ready to seize them if the United States did not. National honor dictated that Americans keep what they had shed blood to take. Senator Beveridge asked what history would say. "Shall it say that, called by events to captain and command the proudest, ablest, purest race of history in history's noblest work, we declined that great commission?"

The anti-imperialists entered the debate with many handicaps. Possession of the Philippines was an accomplished fact; the anti-imperialists' role was thus a negative one. Then, too, they were internally divided, never able to launch an effective campaign. Although many of them belonged to the Anti-Imperialist League, they differed on so many domestic issues that it was difficult for them to speak with one voice on a foreign question. They were also inconsistent: Gompers favored the war but not the postwar annexations; Carnegie would accept colonies if they were not acquired by force; Hoar voted for the annexation of Hawaii but against that of the Philippines. The imperialists sneered that some of their critics

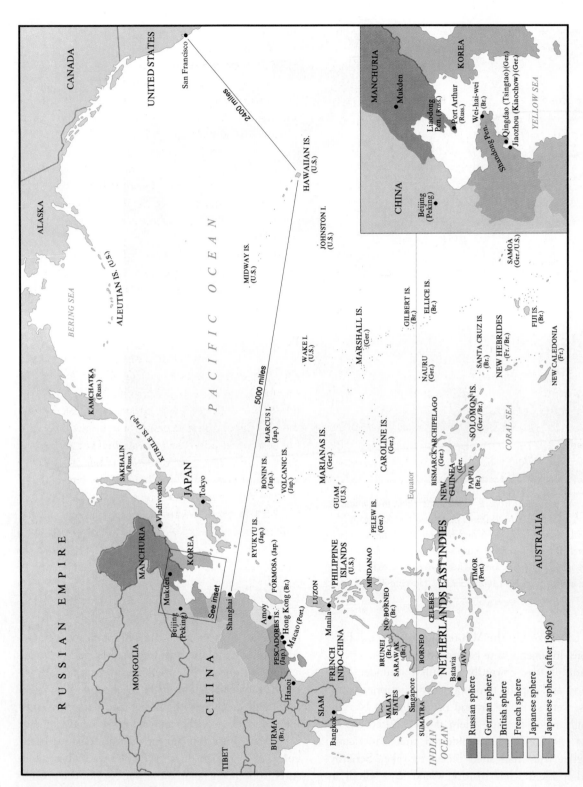

Imperialism in Asia: Turn of the Century

were hypocrites, showing more concern for Filipinos than for American Indians, blacks, unskilled workers, or destitute immigrants. John Hay commented privately that Carnegie "does not seem to reflect that the government is in a somewhat robust condition after shooting down several [striking] American citizens in his interest at Homestead."

On February 6, 1899, the Senate passed the Treaty of Paris by a 57-to-27 vote. Republicans, except for Hoar and Senator Eugene Hale of Maine, voted with

Senate Approval of Treaty of Paris

their president; 22 Democrats voted no, but 10 voted for the treaty. The latter group was probably influenced by Bryan, who had served as a colonel during the war; he urged a favorable vote in order to end the war and then push for Philippine independence. An amendment promising independence as soon as the Filipinos formed a stable government was defeated only by the tie-breaking ballot of the vice president.

The anti-imperialists lost, but Bryan carried the debate into the election of 1900 as the Democratic standard-bearer against McKinley. In that unsuccessful campaign the Nebraskan charged that imperialism benefited only American economic interests. To repudiate the principle of self-government in the Philippines would weaken it at home. "It is not necessary to own people to trade with them," Bryan protested. But McKinley would not apologize for American imperialism. "It is no longer a question of expansion with us," he told a midwestern audience. "If there is any question at all it is a question of contraction; and who is going to contract?"

TROUBLES IN ASIA

I n 1895, the same year as the advent of the Cuban revolution and the Venezuelan crisis, Japan claimed victory over China in their war of only eight months. Outsiders had been pecking away at China—known as the Sick Man of Asia—since the 1840s, but the Japanese onslaught intensified the international scramble. The Germans carved out a sphere of interest in Shandong; the Russians moved into Manchuria

and the Liaodong Peninsula; the French grabbed some provinces; and the British drove in stakes too. Japan controlled Formosa and Korea as well as parts of China proper (see map). Within their spheres, the imperial powers built fortified bases, leased territory, and claimed exclusive economic privileges. Religious leaders, whose missions in China had doubled to one thousand in the 1890s, and business interests, who saw trade opportunities threatened, petitioned Washington to halt the dismemberment before they were closed out. What good were the Philippines as steppingstones to China if there was nothing left to step into? asked some.

Secretary of State John Hay recognized that the United States could not force the imperial powers from China. But he was determined to protect American commerce. In September 1899

Open Door Policy

Hay sent the imperial nations a note asking them to offer assurances that they would respect the principle of equal trade opportunity—an Open Door—for all nations in their spheres. Germany, France, and the others sent evasive replies, privately complaining that the United States was seeking for free the trade rights the others had gained and maintained at considerable military and administrative cost. Then in 1900, a secret Chinese society called the Boxers revolted against the foreigners in their midst and laid siege to the foreign legations in Beijing (Peking). The United States joined the imperialists in sending troops to Beijing to lift the siege. And Hay, in a note dated July 3, 1900, again asked for "equal and impartial trade." He also instructed the other nations to preserve China's territorial integrity. Hay's protests notwithstanding, China continued for years to be fertile soil for foreign exploitation, especially for the expansionist Japanese.

Hay's foray into Asian politics settled little, but the Open Door policy thereafter became a central element in United States diplomacy. Actually, the Open Door had long been an American principle, for as a trading nation the United States opposed barriers to international commerce and demanded equal access to markets. After 1900, when the United States began to emerge as the premier world trader, the Open Door policy became an instrument first to pry open markets and then to dominate them, not just in China but in the rest of the world as well.

During the Philippine Insurrection, American soldiers battled Filipino nationalists bent on independence. This United States warrior sits in a Manila churchyard, anticipating action and no doubt wondering what he is doing so far from home. Library of Congress.

But the Open Door was not just a policy; it also became an ideology. The tenets of this ideology were that America's domestic well-being required exports, that foreign trade would suffer interruption unless the United States intervened abroad to implant American principles and keep markets open, and that any area closed to American products, citizens, or ideas threatened the survival of the United States itself.

In the Philippines, meanwhile, the United States antagonized its new colonials, or "wards", as McKinley labeled them. Emilio Aguinaldo, the Philippine nationalist leader, believed that Dewey had promised independence for his country. But after the victory, Aguinaldo was ordered out of Manila and isolated from decisions affecting his nation. Racial slurs like *gugu* and *nigger* infuriated the Filipinos, and they felt betrayed by the Treaty of Paris. Americans' paternalistic attitude toward their new charges grated on Filipino nationalist feelings. Once again Mr. Dooley caught the mood: "In ivry city in this unfair land we will erect schoolhouses an' packin' houses an' houses of correction; and we'll larn ye our language,

Philippine Insurrection

because 'tis aisier to larn ye ours than to larn oursilves yours. An' we'll give ye clothes, if ye pay f'r them; an' if ye don't, ye can go without."

In January 1899, an uncowed Aguinaldo proclaimed an independent Philippine Republic. Soon the Filipinos took up arms. Before the Philippine Insurrection was suppressed in 1901, over 5,000 Americans and over 200,000 Filipinos were dead. The atrocities committed by both sides were abominable. Americans burned villages, tortured people, and introduced a variant of the reconcentration policy. It was the American practice not to take prisoners. Anti-imperialists cried foul, but President Roosevelt remarked that "we haven't a single incident in the Philippines as bad as the massacre at Wounded Knee." This reference to the massacre of Native Americans in South Dakota (see page 465) was appropriate, because Americans stationed at the Philippine front often spoke of the "savage" Filipino insurgents who might "injun up" on them. One soldier from Kansas declared that the Philippines "won't be pacified until the niggers are killed off like the Indians." From 1898 through 1902, twenty-six of thirty U.S. Army generals ordered to the Philippines had had prior experience battling Indians in the American West.

After Aguinaldo's capture in 1901, the United States imposed its regime on the Philippines. Through a policy of "bread and guns," public works programs were introduced, and the architect Daniel Burnham, who led the City Beautiful movement in the United States, planned modern Manila. English was made the official language, American teachers were imported for local schoolhouses, and the University of the Philippines was founded (1908) to train a native American-oriented elite. The Americanization of the Philippines even included the introduction of basketball. Meanwhile a sedition act and political imprisonment silenced critics. The Philippine economy grew as a satellite of the United States economy. In 1916 the Jones Act promised Filipino independence, but not until thirty years later was Aguinaldo's dream realized.

Possession of the Philippines meant American participation in the turbulent politics of Asia. The major contender for influence in the area was Japan, and the Open Door policy was no deterrent to its advances. When competition for Manchuria and Korea led to the Russo-Japanese War (1904–1905), Japan scored quick victories over the stunned Russians. Roosevelt mediated the crisis at the Portsmouth Conference in New Hampshire. The peace settlement, he hoped, would preserve a balance of power in Asia. It did not. In 1905, in the Taft-Katsura Agreement, the United States conceded Japanese hegemony over Korea in return for Japan's pledge not to undermine the American position in the Philippines. (Roosevelt soon came to think of the vulnerable Philippines as America's Achilles' heel.) To alert Japan to American naval power and to persuade Congress to increase the navy's budget, Roosevelt in 1907 sent the "Great White Fleet" on a world tour, with conspicuous stops in the Pacific. The Japanese were duly impressed, and began to build a bigger navy themselves.

Japanese-American Rivalry

Troubles with Japan boiled to the surface in 1906 when the San Francisco School Board, reflecting the anti-Orientalism of the West Coast, segregated all Chinese, Koreans, and Japanese in a special school. Japan protested this discrimination against its citizens. Because there was little President Roosevelt could do to budge the insistent Californians, he struck a gentleman's agreement with Tokyo restricting Japanese immigration to the United States. Relations with Tokyo were jolted again in 1913 when the California legislature denied Japanese residents the right to own property in the state.

Despite the Root-Takahira Agreement (1908), in which the United States recognized Japan's interests in Manchuria and Japan again pledged the security of American possessions in the Pacific, Japanese-American relations deteriorated. Japan became alarmed by President Taft's ineffective attempt at dollar diplomacy, inducing American bankers to join an international consortium to build a Chinese railway. Dollar diplomacy was an effort to use private funds to serve American diplomatic goals and at the same time to garner profits for American financiers. Realizing neither purpose, Taft's venture seemed only to embolden the Japanese to solidify and extend their holdings in China. When the First World War broke out in Europe, Japan seized the opportunity to grab Shandong and some Pacific islands from the Germans. In 1915 Japan issued its Twenty-One Demands, virtually insisting on hegemony over all of China. The Chinese Revolution of 1911 had brought some unity and strength to the Chinese government, but the aggressive Japanese showed little respect for it. As parts of China passed into the hands of the Japanese, Americans could only protest feebly.

THE FRUITS AND TASKS OF EMPIRE IN LATIN AMERICA

If the United States demonstrated feebleness in Asia, it did not in its own backyard of Latin America (see map, page 638). Although the Teller Amendment (see page 629) had outlawed annexation, it did not rule out American control of postwar Cuba. American troops remained there until 1902. In Washington, officials wrote the Platt Amendment for inclusion in the new Cuban constitution: a frank avowal of United States hegemony, the Platt Amendment provided that Cuba could not make a treaty with another nation that might impair its independence. In short, all treaties had to be approved by the United States. Most important, Cuba granted the United States "the right to intervene" to preserve the island's independence and to maintain domestic order. Cuba was also required to undertake a sanitation program and to lease to the United States a naval base (Guantánamo). These violations of Cuban sovereignty, formalized in 1903, governed Cuban-American relations until 1934. The Cubans, like the Filipinos, resisted their new masters: they marched in the streets against the Platt Amendment, and a revolution in 1906 prompted Roosevelt to send in marines. The marines stayed until 1909, were ordered back for a short time in 1912, and occupied Cuba again from 1917 to 1922. José Martí had warned Cubans from the beginning that the United States posed a threat: "I know the Monster, because I have lived in its lair."

Platt Amendment

The United States presence left an imprint on Cuban life. Americans helped to improve transportation, expand the public school system, found a national army, and improve sugar production. Walter Reed's experiments, based on the theory of Cuban

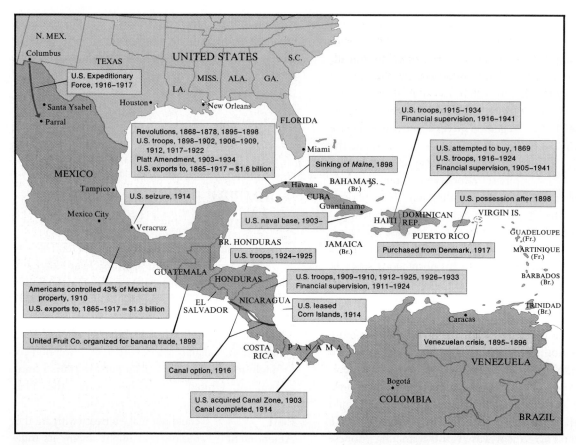

The United States and Latin America

physician Carlos Finlay, proved that the mosquito transmitted yellow fever; American sanitary engineers soon controlled the insect and eradicated the disease from the island. American investments in Cuba grew from $50 million before the revolution to $220 million by 1913, and American exports to the island rose from $26 million in 1900 to $196 million in 1917. But the Cuban nation developed with a colonial mentality, and Cuban nationalists nurtured a resentment that developed into anti-Americanism.

Panama was the site of one of Theodore Roosevelt's boldest expansionist ventures. United States fascination with an isthmian canal in Central America,

Panama Canal

to link the waters of the Pacific and Atlantic, was long-standing. With the opening of the Suez Canal in Egypt in 1869, as well as an abortive attempt by Ferdinand de Lesseps to duplicate that triumph in Panama, American attention heightened.

"A canal under American control, or no canal," snapped President Rutherford B. Hayes. In 1880, he dispatched two warships to the Panamanian coast to demonstrate United States interest. American business interests lobbied for a canal, citing better access to Asian and Latin American markets. But three obstacles had to be overcome. First, the Clayton-Bulwer Treaty with Britain (1850) provided for joint control of a Central American canal. President Theodore Roosevelt persuaded the British, who were cultivating United States friendship and who knew that their influence in the region was diminishing, to step aside (Hay-Pauncefote Treaty of 1901). Second, Colombia was driving a hard bargain in talks over a canal to be cut through its province of Panama. Roosevelt urged Panamanian rebels to declare independence from Colombia, and he sent American warships to the isthmus to ensure the success of the rebellion. In 1903 the United States signed a treaty with the new nation of Panama: the United States was awarded a canal zone and long-term rights to its control; Panama was guaranteed its independence. Colombians would not easily forget this dispoiling of their sovereignty. Third, the cost of constructing a canal was enormous. Roosevelt, having overcome the British and Colombian problems, successfully pressed an obliging Congress for substantial funds.

The completion of the Panama Canal in 1914 marked a major technological achievement. The special bearings and gears used to operate the locks were manufactured by a Wheeling, West Virginia, firm; some fifty Pittsburgh factories and shops made the various bolts and steel girders; and the General Electric Company produced the electrical apparatus. People greeted the canal's opening the way people in the 1960s hailed the landing on the moon. During the canal's first year of operation, over one thousand merchant ships squeezed through its locks. (Ten years later the annual rate was five thousand, equal to the traffic through the Suez Canal.) The United States fortified the zone with conspicuous sixteen-inch guns, the nation's largest.

As for the rest of the Caribbean, it became an American lake. "Speak softly and carry a big stick," said Roosevelt. He did wield a big stick, but he seldom curbed his bombastic rhetoric. In 1904 the president announced his Roosevelt Corollary to the Monroe Doctrine, warning Latin Americans to stabilize their politics and finances to forestall European meddling in their affairs. "Chronic wrongdoing," he lectured, might require "intervention by some civilized nation, and in the Western Hemisphere the adherence of the United States to the Monroe Doctrine may force the United States, however reluctantly, in flagrant cases of such wrongdoing or impotence, to the exercise of an international police power." Roosevelt and his successors were not bluffing. From 1900 to 1917, when the United States entered the First World War, American troops intervened in Cuba, Panama, Nicaragua, the Dominican Republic, Mexico, and Haiti. American officials took over customs houses (as in the Dominican Republic, from 1905 to 1941) to control tariff revenues and thus governmental budgets; they renegotiated foreign debts with American banks; they trained national guards and ran elections.

Roosevelt Corollary

The cruiser Brooklyn *steams out of Havana harbor, Cuba in May 1902. Aboard the warship was General Leonard Wood, the American military governor of the Caribbean island, 1899–1902. Before he departed, Wood had forced the Platt Amendment on the Cubans—a document, he admitted, that left Cuba with "little or no independence." Library of Congress.*

The United States set out to police the Caribbean in the name of order. Whether such order was achieved by the landing of marines, the development of a national guard, a managed electoral process, or a manipulated economy, it was deemed necessary to guarantee United States security and prosperity. After Roosevelt helped to slice off Panama from Colombia and initiated construction of the Panama Canal, Washington would not tolerate disturbances that might threaten the vital waterway. Order was believed essential to American commerce and investment too. Between 1900 and 1917 American exports to Latin America swelled from $132 million to $309 million, and imports from Latin America increased even more. Investments in sugar, tobacco, transportation, and banking also rose impressively. Finally, order seemed imperative to Americans eager to remake Latin American societies in the image of the United States. "When properly directed there is no people not fitted for self-government," Woodrow

The Quest for Order

Wilson remarked. Furthermore, "every nation needs to be drawn into the tutelage of America."

Roosevelt, Taft, and Wilson gave varying expression to this quest for order. The Rough Rider saw world affairs as a constant struggle for international power. The United States, in its own interest, had to lay claim to as much power as possible. The very struggle would ennoble Americans; the result would enrich them. Taft emphasized dollar diplomacy: dollars, not bullets, he predicted, would effect stability and enhance American interests. Wilson was no less a nationalist or pragmatist in desiring to safeguard and expand American prosperity and security. He ordered troops to Haiti, the Dominican Republic, and Mexico, justifying military force by proclaiming it "our peculiar duty" to teach other peoples "order and self-control" and "the drill and habit of law and obedience." Wilson became known for his missionary paternalism, his insistence on liberal capitalism and constitutional government. He spoke of regenerating a benighted world through American salvation. Whether by means of Roosevelt's big stick, Taft's dollars, or Wilson's sermons—in fact, each president used all three methods—United States behavior toward its southern neighbors was imperialistic, because it denied some of them the freedom to make their own choices and thwarted their national sovereignty. The United States possessed few colonies, but developed an empire nonetheless—an informal one largely marked by economic and political control rather than formal annexation.

One of the assumptions that governed United States policy toward Europe was that European nations should not intervene in Western Hemispheric affairs; the Monroe Doctrine, European officials now knew, had power behind it. Another assumption of American policy toward Europe was that the United States should stand outside continental embroilments. And a third was that America's best interests lay in cooperation with Great Britain. The balance of power in Europe was precarious, and seldom did an American president involve the United States directly. At Germany's request, Roosevelt helped to settle a Franco-German clash over Morocco by mediating a settlement at Algeciras, Spain (1906). But the president drew American criticism for entangling the United States in a European problem. Americans endorsed the ultimately futile Hague peace conferences (1899 and 1907) and negotiated various arbitration treaties, but on the whole they stayed outside Europe's embittered arena.

A major offshoot of the German-British rivalry was London's search for American friendship. The makings of the "great rapprochement" had been developing since the late nineteenth century. When the British supported the Americans in the war of 1898, stepped aside in the Hay-Pauncefote Treaty (1901) to permit the building of an American canal, virtually endorsed the Roosevelt Corollary, and withdrew their warships from the Caribbean, Americans warmed toward them. The British overtures paid off in 1917 when the United States threw its arms and men into the First World War on the British side.

Anglo-American Rapprochement

From the Civil War to the First World War, expansionism and empire were central to American foreign policy. By 1914 Americans held extensive interests in a world made smaller by modern technology. The outward reach of American policy from Seward to Wilson met opposition from domestic critics, congressional doubters, other nations, and nationalists in subjugated lands, but the trend was never seriously diverted. Ideas of racial supremacy, the belief that the nation needed foreign markets to absorb surplus production so the domestic economy could thrive, a mission to uplift the less fortunate, and emotional appeals to national greatness—all fed the appetite for foreign adventure and commitments. The instruments of expansion and empire were the machines produced by American entrepreneurs and inventors. The underwater cable, the new steel warships, the Panama Canal, the exportation of American products across the globe, and the rifles American soldiers toted into Philippine jungles and into the streets of Latin American capitals—all facilitated the imperial odyssey.

In 1914 Americans braced themselves for the immediate shock of full-scale war in Europe. In the long term, however, their foreign policy would be preoccupied with challenges to United States hegemony from proud and resentful nationalists victimized by American paternalism. And Americans who sincerely believed that they had been helping others to enjoy a better life would feel betrayed and baffled that their foreign clients could be so ungrateful.

IMPORTANT EVENTS

1861–69	Seward is secretary of state	1899	Senate passes Treaty of Paris United Fruit Company founded First Open Door note Outbreak of Philippine Insurrection
1866	Transatlantic cable completed France withdraws from Mexico		
1867	Alaska and Midway acquired	1900	Second Open Door note U.S. exports total $1.5 billion McKinley re-elected
1868	Burlingame Treaty with China		
1870	Senate rejects annexation of Dominican Republic	1901	Theodore Roosevelt becomes president Aguinaldo captured Hay-Pauncefote Treaty
1871	*Alabama* claims settled		
1878	U.S. products monopolize awards at Paris World's Fair	1903	Panama breaks from Colombia U.S. granted canal rights in Panama Platt Amendment
1883	Advent of New Navy		
1887	U.S. gains naval rights to Pearl Harbor	1904	Roosevelt Corollary
		1905	Taft-Katsura Agreement Portsmouth Conference U.S. imposes financial supervision on Dominican Republic
1889	First Pan-American Conference		
1890	Alfred T. Mahan, *The Influence of Sea Power upon History*		
		1906	San Francisco segregates Asian schoolchildren U.S. invades Cuba
1893	Severe depression begins Turner's frontier thesis Hawaiian revolution begins		
		1907	Great White Fleet Gentleman's agreement with Japan
1895	Crisis over Venezuela Cuban revolution begins Japan defeats China	1908	Root-Takahira Agreement
		1910	Mexican Revolution begins
1896	McKinley elected president	1912	U.S. troops enter Cuba again U.S. troops occupy Nicaragua
1898	Sinking of the *Maine* Spanish-American-Cuban-Filipino War Hawaii and Wake Island annexed Treaty of Paris	1914	U.S. troops invade Mexico First World War begins Panama Canal opens

SUGGESTIONS FOR FURTHER READING

General

"American Empire, 1898–1903," *Pacific Historical Review,* 48 (1979), entire issue; Robert L. Beisner, *From the Old Diplomacy to the New, 1865–1900* (1975); Charles S. Campbell, *The Transformation of American Foreign Relations, 1865–1900* (1976); Richard D. Challener, *Admirals, Generals, and American Foreign Policy, 1889–1914* (1973); James A. Field, Jr., "American Imperialism," *American Historical Review,* 83 (1978), 644–668; John A. S. Grenville and George B. Young, *Politics, Strategy, and American Diplomacy* (1967); David Healy, *U.S. Expansionism* (1970); Ronald J. Jensen, *The Alaska Purchase and Russian-American Relations* (1975); George F. Kennan, *American Diplomacy, 1900–1950* (1951); Walter LaFeber, *The New Empire* (1963); Ernest R. May, *American Imperialism* (1968); H. Wayne Morgan, *America's Road to Empire* (1965); Milton Plesur, *America's Outward Thrust* (1971); David M. Pletcher, *The Awkward Years* (1962); Emily Rosenberg, *Spreading the American Dream* (1982); Rubin F. Weston, *Racisim in United States Imperialism* (1972); William Appleman Williams, *The Tragedy of American Diplomacy,* rev. ed. (1962).

Theodore Roosevelt and Other Expansionists

Howard K. Beale, *Theodore Roosevelt and the Rise of America to World Power* (1956); John M. Blum, *The Republican Roosevelt* (1954); John M. Cooper, Jr., *The Warrior and the Priest: Woodrow Wilson and Theodore Roosevelt* (1983); Lewis L. Gould, *The Presidency of William McKinley* (1981); William H. Harbaugh, *The Life and Times of Theodore Roosevelt* (1975); Frederick Marks, III, *Velvet on Iron: The Diplomacy of Theodore Roosevelt* (1979); Frank Merli and Theodore A. Wilson, eds., *Makers of American Diplomacy* (1974); Edmund Morris, *The Rise of Theodore Roosevelt* (1979); Ernest N. Paolino, *The Foundations of the American Empire* (1973) (on Seward); William C. Widenor, *Henry Cabot Lodge and the Search for an American Foreign Policy* (1980). (For works on Woodrow Wilson, see Chapter 23.)

Economic Expansion

See the works by Beisner, Campbell, and LaFeber cited above; William H. Becker, *The Dynamics of Business-Government Relations* (1982); Robert B. Davies, *Peacefully Working to Conquer the World: Singer Sewing Machines in Foreign Markets, 1854–1920* (1976); David M. Pletcher, "Rhetoric and Results: A Pragmatic View of American Economic Expansionism, 1865–98," *Diplomatic History,* 5 (1981), 93–105; Tom Terrill, *The Tariff, Politics, and American Foreign Policy, 1874–1901* (1973); Mira Wilkins, *The Emergence of the Multinational Enterprise* (1970); William Appleman Williams, *The Roots of the Modern American Empire* (1969).

The American Navy

Benjamin F. Cooling, *Gray Steel and Blue Water Navy* (1979); Kenneth J. Hagan, ed., *In Peace and War,* 2nd ed. (1984); Kenneth J. Hagan, *American Gunboat Diplomacy and the Old Navy, 1877–1889* (1973); Walter R. Herrick, *The American Naval Revolution* (1966); Peter Karsten, *The Naval Aristocracy* (1972); Robert Seager, II, *Alfred Thayer Mahan* (1977); Ronald Spector, *Admiral of the New Empire* (1974) (on Dewey).

The Spanish-American-Cuban-Filipino War

Graham A. Cosmas, *An Army for Empire: The United States Army in the Spanish-American War* (1971); Willard B. Gatewood, Jr., *Black Americans and the White Man's Burden, 1898–1903* (1975); Richard Hofstadter, "Cuba, the Philippines, and Manifest Destiny," in *The Paranoid Style in American Politics,* ed., Richard Hofstadter (1967); Walter LaFeber, "That 'Splendid Little War' in Historical Perspective," *Texas Quarterly,* 11 (1968), 89–98; Gerald F. Linderman, *The Mirror of War: American Society and the Spanish-American War* (1974); Ernest R. May, *Imperial Democracy* (1961); Julius Pratt, *Expansionists of 1898* (1936); David F. Trask, *The War with Spain in 1898* (1981).

Anti-imperialism and the Peace Movement

Robert L. Beisner, *Twelve Against Empire* (1968); Peter Brock, *Pacifism in the United States* (1968); Kendrick A. Clements, *William Jennings Bryan, Missionary Isolationist* (1983); Merle E. Curti, *Peace or War* (1936); Charles DeBenedetti, *Peace Reform in American History* (1980); C. Roland Marchand, *The American Peace Movement and Social Reform, 1898–1918* (1973); Thomas J. Osborne, *"Empire Can Wait": American Opposition to Hawaiian Annexation, 1893–1898* (1981); David S. Patterson, *Toward a Warless World* (1976); E. Berkeley Tompkins, *Anti-Imperialism in the United States* (1970). (See also works in Chapter 23.)

Relations with Cuba and Latin America

Samuel F. Bemis, *The Latin American Policy of the United States* (1943); David Healy, *The United States in Cuba,*

1898–1902 (1963); Walter LaFeber, *Inevitable Revolutions: The United States in Central America* (1983); Walter LaFeber, *The Panama Canal* (1979); Lester D. Langley, *The Banana Wars* (1983); Lester D. Langley, *The United States and the Caribbean, 1900–1970* (1980); Lester D. Langley, *Struggle for the American Mediterranean* (1976); David McCullough, *The Path Between the Seas: The Creation of the Panama Canal, 1870–1914* (1977); Allan R. Millett, *The Politics of Intervention: The Military Occupation of Cuba, 1906–1909* (1968); Dana G. Munro, *Intervention and Dollar Diplomacy in the Caribbean, 1900–1921* (1964); Dexter Perkins, *The Monroe Doctrine, 1867–1907* (1937); Ramon Ruiz, *Cuba* (1968); Karl M. Schmitt, *Mexico and the United States, 1821–1973* (1974); Josefina Vazquez and Lorenzo Meyer, *The United States and Mexico* (1985).

Asia and the Pacific

Charles S. Campbell, *Special Business Interests and the Open Door Policy* (1951); Warren I. Cohen, *America's Response to China*, 2nd ed. (1980); Raymond A. Esthus, *Theodore Roosevelt and Japan* (1966); Michael Hunt, *The Making of a Special Relationship: The United States and China to 1914* (1983); Akira Iriye, *Pacific Estrangement: Japanese and American Expansion, 1897–1911* (1972); Akira Iriye, *Across the Pacific* (1967); Jerry Israel, *Progressivism and the Open Door* (1971); Paul M. Kennedy, *The Samoan Tangle* (1974); Robert McClellan, *The Heathen Chinee: A Study of American Attitudes Toward China, 1890–1905* (1971); Thomas J. McCormick, *China Market* (1967); Charles E. Neu, *The Troubled Encounter* (1975) (on Japan); Merze Tate, *The United States and the Hawaiian Kingdom* (1965); James C. Thomson, Jr., *et al.*, *Sentimental Imperialists* (1981); Paul A. Varg, *The Making of a Myth: The United States and China, 1897–1912* (1968); Paul A. Varg, *Missionaries, Chinese, and Diplomats* (1958); Marilyn Blatt Young, *The Rhetoric of Empire* (1968).

The Philippines: Insurrection and Colony

John M. Gates, *Schoolbooks and Krags: The United States Army in the Philippines, 1898–1902* (1973); Henry F. Graff, ed., *American Imperialism and the Philippine Insurrection* (1969); Glenn A. May, *Social Engineering in the Philippines* (1980); Stuart C. Miller, *"Benevolent Assimilation"* (1982); Julius Pratt, *America's Colonial Experiment* (1950); Daniel B. Schirmer, *Republic or Empire?* (1972); Peter Stanley, *A Nation in the Making: The Philippines and the United States, 1899–1921* (1974); Richard E. Welch, *Response to Imperialism: American Resistance to the Philippine War* (1972); Walter L. Williams, "United States Indian Policy and the Debate over Philippine Annexation," *Journal of American History*, 66 (1980), 810–831; Leon Wolff, *Little Brown Brother* (1961).

Britain and Canada

Kenneth Bourne, *Britain and the Balance of Power in North America, 1815–1908* (1967); Robert C. Brown, *Canada's National Policy, 1883–1900* (1964); Alexander E. Campbell, *Great Britain and the United States, 1895–1903* (1960); Charles S. Campbell, *From Revolution to Rapprochement: The United States and Great Britain, 1783–1900* (1974); Adrian Cook, *The Alabama Claims* (1975); Bradford Perkins, *The Great Rapprochement* (1968).

AMERICA AT WAR
1914–1920

CHAPTER 23

"*Oh, my God*, what am I to do?" murmured Woodrow Wilson. Just moments before he had been holding Ellen Axson Wilson's hand when she died after years of suffering kidney disease. Two days earlier, on August 4, 1914, as he kept vigil at her bedside, the president had drafted a message offering American mediation to end the menacing war the European nations had just begun. Seldom have such painful personal and official burdens fallen on a president at the same time.

In twenty-nine years of marriage Ellen Axson Wilson had been central to his well-being and success. Woodrow Wilson cherished her loyalty, intelligence, and strength in the family. She was a southern woman, born into a Presbyterian minister's family, educated at a small Georgia women's college, and dedicated to making a pleasant home for her husband and daughters. Ellen Axson Wilson was also a painter, avid reader of Shakespeare and Wordsworth, and mother who made her children's clothing, nursed them through scarlet fever, and planned the family budget. A well-managed and serene household mattered to her. "A woman's place is to keep one little spot in the world quiet," she said. She was not, in today's sense, an emancipated woman, although she once complained about having to stay home "like the fixtures." Yet she did not confine herself to the home, often entering her husband's active political world to discuss issues with decision-makers.

Now, at a time of wrenching bereavement, when the partner who had always helped him in times of crisis was gone, Woodrow Wilson faced momentous decisions about America's place in the First World War. In his private grief he found it difficult to concentrate on affairs of state. Wilson had always striven to practice self-control; nations, too, he had long believed, should demonstrate the "dignity of self-control." Yet, as the president entered the era of the First World War, both personal and national self-control, however imperative, seemed elusive. He sought to achieve both, but soon personal and national tragedy, not achievement, would mark his record.

The Great War in Europe shocked Woodrow Wilson and the American people: it seemed a throwing off of civilization. Americans had, of course, witnessed and participated in the years of international competition for colonies, markets, and weapons supremacy. Sporadic military encounters had disturbed the peace, but full-scale war was thought to be a barbarity of the past. "The nineteenth-century view of history as progress," the historian Henry F. May has written, "received a shattering blow." The battle news was gruesome. "We were not used to smelling blood from vast slaughterhouses," recalled William Allen White.

For almost three years President Wilson kept America out of the world war. He sought to protect American interests as a neutral trader and to improve the nation's military posture, all the while lecturing the belligerents to rediscover their humanity and to respect international law. But American neutrality, lives, and property fell victim to British and German naval warfare. In early 1917 the president asked Congress for a declaration of war with his characteristic crusading zeal. America joined the battle not just to win the war but to reform the world that would emerge from it.

The American people in the era of the First World War, even after over a decade of progressive reform, remained heterogeneous and fractious. In 1914 labor-capital confrontations—like the Ludlow Massacre in Colorado, in which two women and eleven children were killed when state militia attempted to break a miners' strike—still claimed headlines. Racial antagonisms were evident in Wilson's decision to segregate federal buildings in Washington, D.C., and by continued lynchings of blacks (fifty-one in 1914). Nativists protested the fast pace of immigration; 1.2 million immigrants entered the United States in 1914 alone. Ethnic groups eyed one another suspiciously. Many women articulated the case for equality among the sexes and for female suffrage, while most men restated the case for traditional subordination.

The war experience accentuated and intensified the nation's social divisiveness. Whites who did not like the migration of southern blacks to work in northern defense plants resisted their new neighbors,

The Wilson family: from left to right, Margaret, Ellen Axson Wilson (1860–1914), Eleanor, Jessie, and President Woodrow Wilson (1856–1924). After his wife's death, the president married again, in the midst of a debate over American preparedness for war. Library of Congress.

and race riots revealed once again the depth of racial prejudice. German-Americans were denounced as traitors, and war hawks harassed pacifists. The federal government itself trampled on civil liberties to silence critics. And, as communism implanted itself in Soviet Russia, America suffered a postwar Red Scare that did further damage to its reputation as a free and democratic society. In the aftermath of war, groups that sought to consolidate gains made during the war vied with those who sought to restore the prewar status quo.

America's participation in the war also wrought massive changes and accelerated trends already in motion. Wars are emergencies, and during such times the normal way of doing things surrenders to the extraordinary and exaggerated. This period witnessed greater powers for the presidency, the military draft, unprecedented centralization and integration of the economy, increased standardization of products, and unusual cooperation between government and business. Indeed, some historians date the "military-industrial complex"—a term coined years later by President Dwight D. Eisenhower—from the First World War. The war experience also helped cause the splintering and fading of the progressive movement, although reformers did put wartime effort into a few issues, such as prohibition and women's suffrage. But, Jane Addams remarked sadly, "the spirit of fighting burns away all those impulses . . . which foster the will to justice."

The United States came out of the war a major power in a disrupted and economically hobbled world.

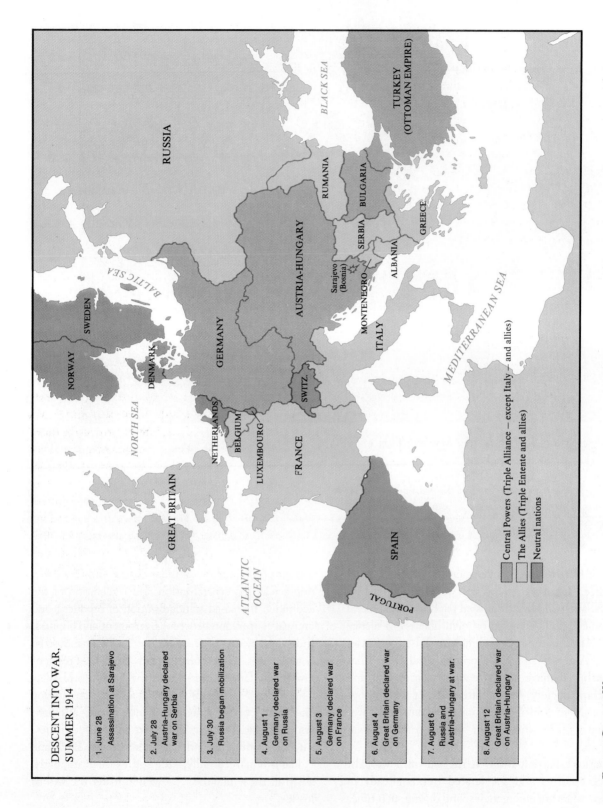

DESCENT INTO WAR,
SUMMER 1914

1. June 28
Assassination at Sarajevo

2. July 28
Austria-Hungary declared
war on Serbia

3. July 30
Russia began mobilization

4. August 1
Germany declared war
on Russia

5. August 3
Germany declared war
on France

6. August 4
Great Britain declared war
on Germany

7. August 6
Russia and
Austria-Hungary at war.

8. August 12
Great Britain declared war
on Austria-Hungary

Central Powers (Triple Alliance — except Italy — and allies)

The Allies (Triple Entente and allies)

Neutral nations

NORWAY
SWEDEN
RUSSIA
BALTIC SEA
NORTH SEA
DENMARK
GREAT BRITAIN
NETHERLANDS
BELGIUM
LUXEMBOURG
GERMANY
FRANCE
SWITZ.
ATLANTIC OCEAN
SPAIN
PORTUGAL
MEDITERRANEAN SEA
AUSTRIA-HUNGARY
ITALY
SWITZ.
RUMANIA
BULGARIA
SERBIA
Sarajevo (Bosnia)
MONTENEGRO
ALBANIA
GREECE
BLACK SEA
TURKEY (OTTOMAN EMPIRE)

Europe Goes to War

Yet Americans who had marched to battle as if on a crusade grew disillusioned. They recoiled from the spectacle of the victors squabbling over the spoils and they chided Wilson for failing to deliver his promised "peace without victory." As in the 1790s, 1840s, and 1890s, Americans engaged in a fundamental national debate about foreign policy. The president appealed for American membership in a new international organization, the League of Nations, which he touted as a vehicle for reforming world politics. But the Senate killed his diplomatic offspring, fearful that it might entangle Americans once again in Europe's problems, impede the growth of the American empire, and compromise the country's traditional unilateralism in international affairs. On many fronts, then, Americans during the era of the First World War were at war with themselves.

THE QUESTION OF NEUTRALITY

The war that erupted in August 1914 grew from tangled roots. Years of imperialist competition over trade, colonies, allies, and armaments had generated two alliance systems. The

European Origins of the First World War

Triple Alliance joined together Germany, Austria-Hungary, and Italy. The Triple Entente combined Britain, France, and Russia. All had economic and territorial ambitions, but Germany seemed particularly bold as it rivaled Britain for world leadership. A series of crises in the Balkans (southeastern Europe) started a chain of events that propelled the European nations into battle.

Slavic nationalists sought to build a Slavic state by adding territories to independent Serbia. Bosnia, part of the Austro-Hungarian Empire, was one of those coveted territories. In June 1914, at Sarajevo, Bosnia, the heir to the Austro-Hungarian throne was assassinated by a Slavic revolutionary linked to Serbia. Austria-Hungary consulted Germany, which urged toughness. Serbia called upon its Slavic friend Russia for help. Russia looked to its ally France. When Austria-Hungary declared war against Serbia in late

July, Russia began to mobilize its armies. Certain that war was coming its way, Germany struck first, declaring war against Russia on August 1 and against France two days later. What would the British do? They hesitated, but when Germany slashed into Belgium to get at France, Britain declared war against Germany on August 4. Eventually Turkey joined the Central Powers of Germany and Austria-Hungary, and Japan and Italy teamed up with the Allies of Britain, France, and Russia. The world was aflame (see map).

President Wilson at first sought to distance America from the conflagration by issuing a proclamation of neutrality. He also asked Americans to refrain from taking sides, to exhibit "fine poise" and "the dignity of self-control." Privately, the president said that "we definitely have to be neutral, since otherwise our mixed populations would wage war on each other." The United States, he fervently hoped, would stand as the pre-eminently sane, civilized nation in a deranged international environment.

Wilson's lofty appeal for American neutrality and unity at home collided with three realities. First, ethnic groups in the United States naturally took

Ethnic Ties to Europe

sides. Many German-Americans and anti-British Irish-Americans (Ireland was then trying to break free from British rule) cheered for the Central Powers. Americans of British and French ancestry applauded the Allies. Anglo-American traditions and slogans like "Remember Lafayette," as well as the sheer number of Americans with roots in the Allied nations, drew a majority to the Allied cause. To them the war was a matter of democracy against autocracy. Germany's attack on neutral Belgium at the start of the war confirmed in many minds that it was the archetype of unbridled militarism, the defiler of innocent women and children.

Second, America's economic links with the Allies also rendered neutrality difficult, if not impossible. England had long been one of the nation's best customers. New war-inspired orders flooded American

Economic Links with the Belligerents

companies and farms, pulling the economy out of its recession. In 1914 American exports to England and France were $753 million; in 1916 the figure spurted to $2.75 billion.

In the same period, however, exports to Germany dropped from $345 million to only $29 million. Much of the American-Allied trade was financed through private American loans, amounting to $2.3 billion during the period of neutrality; in stark contrast, Germany received only $27 million.

The Wilson administration, which at first frowned on the transactions, came to see them as necessary to the economic health of the United States. Without loans to help the Allies pay for American products, one of Wilson's key advisers gloomily told the president, the United States would suffer "restriction of output, industrial depression, idle capital, idle labor, numerous failures, financial demoralization, and general unrest and suffering among the laboring classes." From Germany's perspective, of course, the linkage between the American economy and the Allies meant that the United States had become the quite-unneutral Allied arsenal and bank. Americans, however, were caught in a dilemma that further highlighted the difficulty of maintaining pure neutrality: for the United States to cut its economic ties with Britain would constitute an unneutral act in favor of Germany. That is, under international law the British—who controlled the seas—could buy contraband (war-related goods) and noncontraband from neutrals at their own risk. It was Germany's responsibility, therefore, not America's, to stop the trade in ways that international law prescribed: an effective blockade of the enemy's territory or the seizure of all goods from belligerent (British) ships and contraband from neutral (American) ships.

The third reason neutrality did not work derived from the pro-Allied sympathies of Wilson administration officials. Shortly after Ellen Wilson's death,

Pro-Allied Sympathies

the president received a note from another man who had lost his wife, British Foreign Secretary Edward Grey. Wilson, moved by the thoughtful message, replied that he felt "that we are bound together by common principle and purpose." He was talking about more than shared bereavement. Indeed, for Wilson, a German victory would destroy government by law and "free industry and enterprise." If Germany won the war, he prophesied, "it would change the course of our civilization and make the United States a military nation." Wilson's chief advisers and diplomats—Colonel Edward House, Sec-

retary of State Robert Lansing, and Ambassador to London Walter Hines Page among them—also shared these sentiments and were often openly pro-Allied in their viewpoints.

Wilson and his aides also believed that Wilsonian principles stood a better chance of international acceptance if Britain, rather than the Central Powers, sat astride the postwar world. Wil-

Wilsonianism

sonianism—the name scholars have given to the body of ideas Wilson espoused—consisted of traditional American diplomatic principles, to which Wilson eloquently gave coherence and currency. His ideal world was to be open in every sense of the word: no barriers to commerce, no impediments to democratic politics, no secret diplomatic deals. Empires were to be opened up in keeping with the principle of self-determination, and armaments were to be reduced. Wilson envisioned free-market, nonexploitative capitalism and political constitutionalism for all nations, to ensure the good society and world peace. His critics complained that Wilson often violated his own tenets in his eagerness to force them upon others.

Wilson also articulated the traditional belief in American exceptionalism. America, he believed, had a mission to reform international relations and other societies. American progressivism was to be projected onto the world. "We created this Nation," he intoned, "not to serve ourselves, but to serve mankind." Wilson's missionary zeal blended with a pragmatism that bespoke his understanding of the balance of world power and the intertwining of the American economy with the economies of other countries. His inheritance was the expansionism that characterized American foreign policy before the First World War. And he shared with his predecessors the belief that even unsavory methods—such as military intervention—were sometimes necessary to protect American interests.

To say that American neutrality was never a real possibility, given ethnic loyalties, economic ties, and Wilsonian preferences, is not to say that Wilson sought to enter the war. He emphatically wanted to keep the United States out of the military conflict, and in fact did so for two and a half years. Time and again, Wilson tried to mediate the crisis; he did not wish for one power to crush the other. The president remarked in early 1917 that "we are the only one of the great white nations that is free from war today, and it would be a crime against civilization for us to go in." But go in the United States finally did.

Americans got caught in the Allied–Central Power crossfire. British naval policy was designed to sever neutral trade with Germany in order to cripple the German economy. The British,

British Naval Policy

"ruling the waves and waiving the rules," declared a loose, ineffective, and hence illegal blockade; defined a broad list of contraband (including foodstuffs) which was not supposed to be shipped to Germany by neutrals; mined the North Sea; and harassed neutral shipping by seizing cargoes. American vessels bearing goods for Germany seldom reached their destination. To counter German submarines, the British flouted international law by arming their merchant ships and flying neutral (sometimes American) flags. Wilson frequently protested British violations of neutral rights, pointing out that neutrals had the right to sell and ship noncontraband goods to belligerents without interference. But London often deftly defused American criticism by paying for confiscated cargoes. More than once provocative German actions made British behavior seem comparatively mild or inconsequential.

Germany was determined to lift the injurious blockade and to end American-Allied commerce. Unable to win the war on land, German leaders looked for victory at sea. These ambitious tasks were assigned to the submarine. In February 1915 Berlin announced that it was creating a war zone around the British Isles. All enemy ships in the area would be sunk; neutral vessels were warned to stay out so as not to be attacked by mistake; and passengers from neutral nations like the United States were warned to stay off enemy ships. Writing diplomatic messages on his own typewriter, President Wilson stiffly informed Germany that the United States was holding it to "strict accountability" for any losses of American life and property.

Wilson was interpreting existing international law in the strictest sense. Such law held that an attacker had to warn a passenger or merchant

The Submarine and International Law

ship before attacking, so that passengers and crew could disembark into lifeboats for safety. That rule predated the development of the submarine as a major weapon, but Wilson refused to adjust tradition. The Germans thought him unfair. As they saw it, the slender, frail, and sluggish *unterseebooten* could not surface to warn ships of their imminent destruction: surfacing would deny the U-boats the advantage of surprise. A surfaced submarine was also a sitting target for a British deck gun or hand grenade, and British vessels had standing orders to ram U-boats and sink them. Finally, the time required to evacuate passengers usually gave the distressed ship adequate opportunity to radio for help to a British destroyer in nearby waters. Berlin frequently complained to Wilson that he was denying the Germans the one weapon they could use to break the British economic stranglehold, disrupt the Allies' substantial connection with American producers and bankers, and win the war. To all concerned—British, Germans, and Americans—this naval warfare seemed a matter of life and death, a vital question of national survival.

FROM THE *LUSITANIA* TO WAR

Over the next few months the U-boats sank ship after ship. Then the sinking of the *Lusitania* forced the submarine issue for Wilson. The swift British passenger liner had few rivals for luxurious accommodations. When it left New York City on May 1, 1915, with over twelve hundred passengers, it was carrying a cargo of foodstuffs and contraband, including 4.2 million rounds of ammunition for Remington rifles. Before "Lucy's" departure, the newspapers carried an unusual announcement from the German embassy: travelers on British vessels were warned that a war zone existed and that Allied ships in those waters "are liable to destruction." Few passengers paid attention to the notice; few shifted to an American vessel for the transatlantic trip. On May 7, off the Irish coast, U-20 unleashed torpedoes at the four-stacked vessel. The *Lusitania* exploded, quickly capsized, and carried 1,198 people to their deaths. One hundred twenty-eight Americans died.

Even if the ship carried armaments, argued Wilson, the sinking was a brutal assault on innocent people.

Reaction to the Sinking of the *Lusitania* But he ruled out a military response. Secretary of State William Jennings Bryan advised that Americans not be permitted to travel on belligerent ships and that passenger vessels not be allowed to carry war goods. "Germany has a right to prevent contraband going to the Allies," wrote Bryan, "and a ship carrying contraband should not rely on passengers to protect her from attack—it would be like putting women and children in front of an army." Bryan also urged that simultaneous protest notes be sent to London and Berlin.

Wilson moved deliberately. He rejected Bryan's counsel, as well as that of Theodore Roosevelt and others who clamored for war. Instead he sent a note to Berlin insisting on the right of Americans to sail on belligerent ships and demanding that Germany cease its inhumane submarine warfare. "Weasel words" from "the word-lover in the White House," shouted Roosevelt. The Germans were not contrite; they asked Wilson to rethink the relationship between international law and the submarine. Wilson fumed. After a stormy White House meeting marked by Bryan's charge that the cabinet was pro-Allied, Wilson dispatched a second letter to Germany reiterating the demand that submarines be kept in port. When the president refused to ban American travelers from belligerent ships, Bryan resigned in protest—an uncommon act for secretaries of state, who usually resign quietly. The pro-Allied Robert Lansing was elevated to the top diplomatic post. For some Americans the *Lusitania* disaster became a rallying cry like the Alamo or the *Maine*. Certainly Wilson's attitude toward Germany hardened. To criticism that he was pursuing a double standard favoring the Allies, Wilson responded that the British were taking cargoes and violating property rights, but the Germans were taking lives and violating human rights.

Germany, seeking to avoid war with America, ordered its U-boat commanders to halt attacks on passenger liners. But in mid-August another British vessel, the *Arabic*, was sunk; two American lives were lost. The Germans hastened to pledge that never again would an unarmed passenger ship be attacked without warning. But the sinking of the *Arabic* fueled the debate over American passengers on belligerent vessels. Why not require Americans to sail on American craft? asked critics. From August 1914 to March 1917 only 3 Americans died on an American ship (the tanker *Gulflight* in May 1915), while about 190 were killed on belligerent ships.

In early 1916 the Gore-McLemore resolution, which would prohibit Americans from traveling on armed merchant vessels or ships carrying contraband, was introduced in Congress. The resolution, it was hoped, would prevent incidents like the *Lusitania* from hurtling the United States into war.

Gore-McLemore Resolution

But Wilson would tolerate no interference in the presidential making of foreign policy (he had just sent Colonel House to Europe to mediate) and no restrictions on American travel. The resolution, he argued, would destroy the "whole fine fabric of international law." After heavy politicking, the House defeated the resolution 276 to 142 and the Senate followed suit 68 to 14. If America's goal was to avoid entry into the First World War, Wilson's critics have pointed out, passage of the Gore-McLemore resolution would have avoided or at least delayed a German-American confrontation over the submarine without undercutting American interests or besmirching national honor.

In March 1916 an attack on the *Sussex*, a French vessel crossing the English Channel, took the United States a step closer to war. Four Americans on that ship, which the U-boat commander mistook for a minelayer, were injured. Stop the marauding submarines, Wilson lectured Berlin, or he would sever diplomatic relations. Again the Germans backed off, pledging not to attack merchant vessels without warning. About the same time, relations with Britain soured. The British crushing of the Irish Easter Rebellion and further restriction of American trade with the Central Powers aroused American ire.

Sentiment for peace remained strong, as evidenced by Wilson's victory on a peace platform in the 1916 election. After his triumph, Wilson futilely labored once again to bring the belligerents to the conference table. In early 1917 he advised them to temper their acquisitive war aims, appealing for a "peace without victory."

In early February 1917, Germany startled the Wilson administration by launching unrestricted submarine warfare. All vessels, belligerent or neutral, warship or merchant, would be attacked if sighted in the declared war zone. This bold decision, reached after extensive debate within the German government, represented a calculated risk that submarines could impede the valuable munitions shipments from America to England and thus defeat the Allies before Americans could be mobilized and ferried across the Atlantic to enter the fight. Wilson quickly broke diplomatic relations with Berlin. Everybody waited for the inevitable collision.

With this German challenge to American neutral rights and economic interests came a German threat to American security. In late February, the British intercepted, decoded, and handed

Zimmermann Telegram

to the American government a telegram addressed to the German minister in Mexico from Foreign Secretary Arthur Zimmermann. The minister was instructed to tell the Mexican government that if it joined a military alliance against the United States, Germany would help Mexico to recover the territories it was forced to give up to its northern neighbor in 1848. Zimmermann hoped, as he expressed it to other German officials, to *set new enemies on America's neck—enemies which give them plenty to take care of over there.*"

American officials took the message seriously, since at the time Mexican-American relations were extremely tense. The Mexican Revolution, a bloody civil war with strong anti-American overtones, had spilled across the Rio Grande, and the Mexican government was threatening to nationalize American properties. Wilson had twice ordered American troops onto Mexican soil: in 1914 at Veracruz, to avenge a slight to the American uniform and flag; and again in 1916 in northern Mexico, where General John J. Pershing spent months trying to capture the elusive Pancho Villa after his raid on an American border town. Lansing and Wilson agreed that Zimmermann's telegram constituted "a conspiracy against this country."

Soon after learning of Zimmermann's ploy, Wilson asked Congress for "armed neutrality" to defend American lives and commerce. Specifically he requested the authority to arm American merchant ships, and more generally the power to "employ any other instrumentalities or methods that may be nec-

The cartoonist William A. Rogers of the New York Herald *reacted to the German declaration of unrestricted submarine warfare with this drawing. Like many Americans, Rogers saw the Germans as conniving, heartless pirates of the high seas who cared little for the rights of neutrals or human life. Library of Congress.*

essary." In the midst of the debate, Wilson released Zimmermann's telegram to the press; the nation was stunned. Still, antiwar Senators Robert M. La Follette and George Norris, among others, saw the armed-ship bill as a blank check for the president to move the country to war and filibustered it to death. Wilson, angrily labeling them a "little group of willful men," proceeded to arm America's commercial vessels anyway. The action came too late to prevent the sinking of several American ships. War cries echoed across the nation. In late March, after a good deal of personal agony and seclusion, Wilson called Congress into special session.

On April 2, 1917, the president stepped before a hushed Congress. Solemnly he chided the Germans

Jeannette Rankin (1880–1973), the first woman to sit in the House of Representatives and the only member of Congress to vote against American entry into both world wars, shown shortly after her election. Elected in 1916, she was defeated in 1918, but ran successfully again in 1940. Born in Montana, Rankin became a social worker, woman's suffrage activist, and devout pacifist. UPI/Bettmann Newsphotos.

for "warfare against mankind." Passionately and eloquently Wilson explained American grievances: Germany's violation of the principle of freedom of the seas, disruption of American commerce, attempt to stir up trouble in Mexico, and violation of human rights by killing innocent Americans. The "Prussian autocracy" had to be punished by the "democracies." Russia was now among the latter, he was pleased to report, because the Russian Revolution had ousted the czar just weeks before. Wilson's most famous words rang out: "The world must be made safe for democracy." Congress quickly declared war against Germany, by a vote of 373 to 50 in the House and 82 to 6 in the Senate. The first woman ever to sit in Congress, Montana's Jeannette Rankin, elected in 1916, cast a ringing "no" vote that won her high ranking in the pantheon of American pacifism. "Peace is a woman's job," she believed, "because men have a natural fear of being classed as cowards if they oppose war" and because mothers should protect their children from death-dealing weapons.

Declaration of War

For principle, for morality, for honor, for commerce, for security—for all these reasons the United States took up arms against Germany. The submarine was certainly the culprit that drew a reluctant president and nation into the maelstrom. Yet critics like Bryan, Gore, McLemore, La Follette, and Rankin did not think that the U-boat alone was responsible for the American descent into war. They emphasized Wilson's rigid definition of international law, which did not take account of the submarine's tactics. They faulted his contention that Americans could travel anywhere, even on a belligerent ship loaded with contraband, in time of war. But they lost the debate. Although Americans might agree that Wilson's decisions were anti-German, they seemed to accept his view that the Germans had to be checked to ensure an open and orderly world in which American principles and interests would be safe.

In the most general sense, America went to war to reform world politics, not to destroy Germany. That is, by early 1917 Wilson seemed to believe that America could not claim a seat at the peace conference unless it became a combatant. At such a conference, Wilson intended to put into constitutional form the principles he thought essential to a stable world order, to promote democracy and the Open Door, and to outlaw revolution and aggression. If he remained the representative of a neutral nation, he could only "call through a crack in the door" at the postwar peace conference. In the end, Woodrow Wilson decided for war to gain an American-fashioned peace.

TAKING UP ARMS

Even before the war decision, the United States had been preparing for combat. Encouraged by such groups as the National Security League and the Navy League, and by mounting public outrage against Germany's submarine warfare, the president in 1915 began to plan a substantial military buildup. As the debate over preparedness swirled about the nation's capital, Wilson took a new bride, the widowed Edith Bolling Galt, and went on a two-week honeymoon. When the Wilsons returned in early 1916, Senator La Follette and House Majority Leader Claude Kitchin, among others, vowed to block preparedness. Some pacifist progressives, like Jane Addams, Paul Kellogg, and Lillian Wald, had organized in late 1915 an antiwar coalition, the American Union Against Militarism. Addams and suffragist Carrie Chapman Catt founded the Women's Peace party. The businessman Andrew Carnegie, who in 1910 had established the Carnegie Endowment for International Peace with $10 million in U.S. Steel bonds, helped to finance the peace groups. So did Henry Ford, who spent half a million dollars in late 1915 to send a "peace ship" to Europe to propagandize for a negotiated settlement. Socialists like Eugene Debs added their voices to the peace movement.

The various messages of these antiwar advocates were that war drained a nation of its youth, resources, and impulse for reform; that it fostered a repressive spirit at home; that it violated Christian morality; and that wartime business barons reaped huge profits at the expense of the people. Furthermore, Europe's Great War was self-serving. The

Antiwar Sentiment

very outbreak of the war, they argued, proved that an increase in armaments, such as occurred in Europe before the war, only precipitated hostilities. Militarism and conscription, Addams pointed out, were what millions of immigrants had left behind in Europe. Were they now—in the United States—to be forced into the decadent system they had escaped?

But the peace movement was splintered, some of its followers endorsing peace but not pacifism, and it could not prevent passage of the National Defense Act of 1916. This legislation provided for increases in the army and National Guard and for summer training camps modeled on the one in Plattsburg, New York, where a slice of America's social and economic elite had trained in 1915 as "citizen soldiers." The Navy Act, providing for a three-year naval expansion program, soon followed. To pay part of the huge cost of these undertakings, Congress passed the Revenue Act in 1916. Backers of the bill believed that businesspeople should pour back into the national treasury a portion of the profits they were sure to derive from the new defense contracts. The act, which antipreparedness people applauded, raised the surtax on high incomes and corporate profits, imposed a federal tax on large estates, and significantly increased the tax on the gross receipts of munitions manufacturers.

To raise an army after the declaration of war, Congress in 1917 passed the Selective Service Act, requiring the registration of all males between the ages of twenty and thirty (later changed to eighteen and forty-five). National service, proponents believed, would not only prepare the nation for battle but also promote efficiency, order, democracy, personal sacrifice, and nationalism, and, as one general put it, "heat up the melting pot." Where else but in an army tent could a Boston Brahmin, a butcher, a college student, a dairy farmer, and the son of a washerwoman be brought together? Critics, on the other hand, feared that "Prussianism," not democratization, would instead be the likely outcome.

Raising an Army

On June 5, 1917, over 9.5 million men signed up for the "great national lottery." By war's end, 24 million men had been registered by local draft boards. Over 4.8 million served in the armed forces, 2 million

Government posters became a popular medium to rally Americans to the armed forces and domestic mobilization. In this poster, the artist Howard Chandler Christy uses the traditional theme of war as masculine enterprise to recruit sailors. *National Archives.*

of whom fought in France. About 16 percent of the male labor force was drawn into military service; millions of laborers received deferments from military duty because they worked in war industries or had personal dependents. Over 300,000 men evaded the draft by failing to show up when called, and 4,000 were classified as conscientious objectors (many more applied for that classification but failed or changed their minds after induction).

Hundreds of thousands of citizens volunteered to the sound of the popular song "Johnny Get Your Gun." Asked why he joined the army, one soldier replied that he was eager "to see a little of the biggest scrap the world has ever known." Other volunteers gave different answers: "Girls like soldiers," they

wanted to become men, they were homeless, they wanted to "kick the Kaiser." The typical soldier was a draftee between twenty-one and twenty-three years old, white, single, and poorly educated (most had not attended high school). Perhaps as many as 18 percent were foreign-born, and 400,000 were black. Some women became navy clerks; others served in the U.S. Army Signal Corps and Nurse Corps. On college campuses, 150,000 students entered the Student Army Training Corps or similar navy and marine units.

Camp life sapped the fresh recruits of some of their enthusiasm for war. They put in seventeen-hour days. Calisthenics, kitchen duty, target practice, grounds maintenance ("policing the area"), and bayonet drills consumed their regimented time. They ate well but slept on straw mattresses and marched around uncomfortably in olive-drab uniforms and leggings. There were never enough weapons to go around, so some trained without. At officer training camps, the army turned out "ninety-day wonders." Although some soldiers imbibed Wilson's idealism, others were ignorant of the reasons they were going to war. This ignorance of purpose so alarmed Wilson administration officials that they put a copy of the president's war message in every knapsack.

President Wilson, Secretary of War Newton D. Baker, and General John J. "Black Jack" Pershing (head of the American Expeditionary Force) all worried that the young soldiers, once away from their home environments, would turn to vice—especially prostitutes and liquor. They were right. To protect the supposed novices with social armor, the government created the Commission on Training Camp Activities to coordinate the work of the YMCA, the Knights of Columbus, the Salvation Army, the Red Cross, and the Jewish Welfare Board, among others. These organizations dispensed food and provided movies and vaudeville. Athletic contests also kept the soldiers busy, as did the American Library Association's in-camp book depositories. The commission declared five-mile "sin-free" zones around military bases. "Short-arm" inspections became daily routine and prophylactics were distributed to combat venereal disease. Men in uniform were not permitted to drink. "Men must live straight if they would shoot straight," said Secretary of the Navy Josephus Daniels.

Like most black troops in the First World War, these soldiers were assigned to non-combat tasks—here the assembling of coffins in France. Ironically the United States sent a segregated army abroad so that the world, to use President Wilson's words, could be made "safe for democracy." National Archives.

In 1918 a worldwide flu epidemic struck the United States, killing at least 550,000 people. The flu spread quickly to the army. At one time or another during the war, at least one-quarter of the army had influenza. Soldiers had to be quarantined, and training suffered badly. A total of 62,000 soldiers and sailors died of disease during the war, about 52,000 of them from influenza and pneumonia. By comparison, 51,000 lost their lives in battle.

Jim Crow was in the army too. Fearing "arrogant, strutting representatives of black soldiery in every community," as Senator James K. Vardaman of Mississippi snarled, many southern politicians opposed the drafting of blacks. But the army needed men, white and black. The NAACP and W.E.B. Du Bois urged blacks to join the fight for "world liberty," optimistically thinking that a war to make the world safe for democracy would blur the color line at home. They were greatly disappointed. Military leaders segregated facilities, discouraged blacks from becoming officers, and assigned black recruits to menial labor. Ugly racial slurs echoed through the camps. In Houston, Texas, angry black soldiers

Segregation in the Army

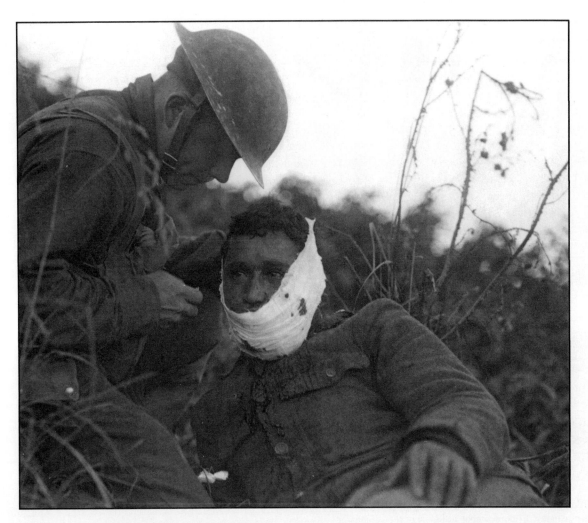

An American soldier of Company K, 110th Infantry Regiment, receives first aid during fighting at Verennes, France. National Archives.

responded to goading from whites by seizing arms and killing thirteen of them. Official white retaliation was immediate and excessive. After brief "trials," thirteen blacks were executed; another six were hanged after an unsuccessful appeal of their death sentences; others were court-martialed and given long prison terms.

In Europe, Pershing wisely refused to submerge American troops in Allied units (officially the United States declared itself an Associated power). Allied commanders had wedded themselves to unimaginative and deadly trench warfare, producing military stalemate and ghastly casualties. Zig-zag trenches fronted by barbed wire and mines stretched across France. Beyond the muddy and stinking trenches lay "no man's land," denuded by artillery fire. When ordered out, soldiers would charge the German lines, also a maze of trenches. Machine guns mowed them down; chlorine gas, first used by Germany in 1915, poisoned them. And so little was gained. At the Battle of the Somme in 1916 the British and French suffered 600,000 dead or wounded to earn only 125 square miles (the Germans lost 500,000 men). Pershing would not commit his clean, fresh "doughboys" to this death-dealing type of warfare.

Firsthand war, the soldiers soon learned, was quite

different from the abstract slogans spoken at home to glorify American participation. They came to know the muck and stink of trench warfare and the horrors of poison gas. Over 230,000 were wounded, and many suffered battle shock: violent tremors, dazed eyes, listless arms and legs. By today's standards army medicine and psychiatry were primitive. Away from the front lines, Red Cross canteens, staffed by women volunteers, served the soldiers as way stations in a strange land, offering haircuts, food, and recreation. American troops might even have met some American literary figures. Early in the war e e cummings, John Dos Passos, Ernest Hemingway, and others had volunteered for ambulance service in Allied countries because they thought it a humane thing to do. But another motive drove them, too, as Dos Passos explained candidly: "What was war like? We wanted to see with our own eyes. . . . I wanted to see the show."

For some young warriors, "the show" played in cafes and brothels—just as officials had feared. It was a common saying in Paris that the British were drunkards, the French whoremongers, and the Americans were both. Despite Pershing's lecture that "sexual intercourse is not necessary for good health, and complete continence is wholly possible," soldiers indulged. Venereal disease became a serious problem. At one point, French Prime Minister Georges Clemenceau offered licensed, supposedly health-inspected prostitutes to the American army. When the generous Gallic offer was received in Washington, Secretary Baker gasped, "For god's sake . . . don't show this to the President or he'll stop the war." Frequent health checks, prophylactics, medical attention, and the threat of court-martial for infected soldiers helped reduce the disease rate.

The influx of American men and material decided the outcome of the First World War. With both sides virtually exhausted, the Americans tipped the balance toward the Allies. Actually **Americans in Combat in France** the inexperienced Americans did not engage in much combat until after the lull of the severe winter of 1917 and 1918. Then in the spring, after knocking Russia out of the war and closing the eastern front, the Germans launched a major offensive. Kaiser Wilhelm's forces got within

fifty miles of Paris; American troops helped to blunt their advance at Château-Thierry. In June the U.S. 2nd Division recaptured Belleau Wood; then followed battles at Cantigny, the Marne, the Somme, and St. Mihiel (see map, page 660). In September over 1 million Americans joined British and French troops in the Allied offensive that pushed the Germans back. Its submarine warfare a dismal failure, its ground war a shambles, its troops and cities mutinous, abandoned by Turkey and Austria, Germany sued for peace. The armistice was signed on November 11, 1918.

The armistice was Wilsonian. That is, the president insisted that his Fourteen Points, which he had enunciated in January, be made the general terms for peace negotiations. The Allies balked, but Wilson scared them into acceptance by threatening a separate peace with Germany. The Fourteen Points were a summary of Wilsonianism. The first five called for diplomacy in the "public view," freedom of the seas, lower tariffs, reductions in armaments, and the decolonization of empires. Points 6 through 13 appealed for self-determination for national groups in Europe. For Wilson the last point was the most essential, the vehicle for achieving all the others: "a general association of nations" or League of Nations. Having won the war, the resolute Wilson set out to win the peace.

THE HOME FRONT

"It is not an army that we must shape and train for war," declared the president, "it is a nation." The United States was a belligerent for only nineteen months, but the impact of the war on domestic America was conspicuous. In that comparatively short period the national government quickly geared the economy to war needs and marshaled public opinion for the sacrifices and adjustments belligerency imposed. As never before, the state intervened in American life. An unprecedented concentration of bureaucratic power developed in Washington, D.C. To progressives

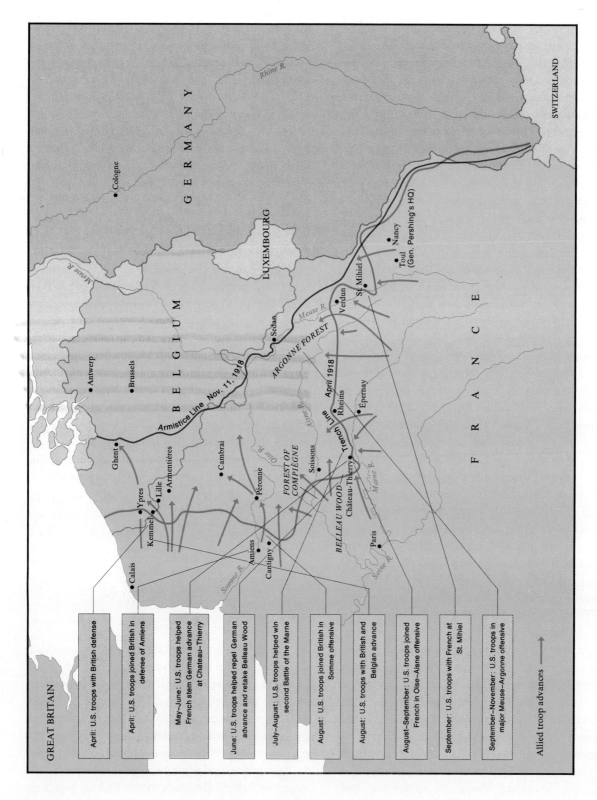

GREAT BRITAIN

April: U.S. troops with British defense

April: U.S. troops joined British in defense of Amiens

May–June: U.S. troops helped French stem German advance at Château-Thierry

June: U.S. troops helped repel German advance and retake Belleau Wood

July–August: U.S. troops helped win second Battle of the Marne

August: U.S. troops joined British in Somme offensive

August: U.S. troops with British and Belgian advance

August–September: U.S. troops joined French in Oise–Aisne offensive

September: U.S. troops with French at St. Mihiel

September–November: U.S. troops in major Meuse–Argonne offensive

Allied troop advances

American Troops at the Front, 1918

GERMANY

SWITZERLAND

Cologne

Rhine R.

Meuse R.

Antwerp

Brussels

BELGIUM

LUXEMBOURG

Ghent

Ypres

Lille

Armentières

Kemmel

Calais

Cambrai

Péronne

FOREST OF COMPIÈGNE

Oise R.

Soissons

Somme R.

Amiens

Cantigny

BELLEAU WOOD

Château-Thierry

Trench Line

Rheims

Epernay

Marne R.

Aisne R.

Paris

Seine R.

FRANCE

Armistice Line Nov. 11, 1918

Sedan

ARGONNE FOREST

Meuse R.

April 1918

Verdun

St. Mihiel

Toul

Nancy

(Gen. Pershing's HQ)

660

of the New Nationalist persuasion, the expansion and centralization of governmental power were welcome. To others they seemed an excessive and dangerous development. "War is the health of the state," said radical intellectual Randolph Bourne.

The federal government and private business became partners during the war. Dollar-a-year executives flocked to the nation's capital from major companies; they retained their corporate salaries while serving in administrative and consulting capacities. Early in the war, the government relied on several industrial committees for advice on purchases and prices. But evidence of self-interested businesspeople cashing in on the national interest aroused public protest. The chief of the aluminum advisory committee, for example, was also president of the largest aluminum company in America. The committees were disbanded in July 1917 in favor of the War Industries Board (WIB). The government continued, however, to work closely with business through trade associations, which grew significantly in number. Business-government cooperation was also stimulated by the suspension of antitrust laws; by cost-plus contracts, which guaranteed companies a healthy profit and a means to pay higher wages to head off labor strikes; by the Webb-Pomerene Act (1918), which granted immunity from antitrust legislation to companies that combined to operate in the export trade; by the virtual abandonment of competitive bidding; and by a floor placed under prices to ensure profits.

Business-Government Cooperation

Hundreds of new government agencies, staffed largely by businesspeople, came into being to wage the war. Some of the superagencies placed unprecedented controls on the economy. The Food Administration, led by Herbert Hoover, undertook programs to improve production and conserve food through voluntary action; it also set prices and regulated distribution. Americans were urged to grow "victory gardens" in their backyards and to eat meatless and wheatless meals. The Railroad Administration took over the snarled and financially troubled railway industry. When strikes threatened the telephone and telegraph companies, the federal government seized and ran them.

The largest and potentially most powerful of the wartime agencies was the War Industries Board. Designed as a clearinghouse to coordinate the national economy and headed after early 1918 by millionaire financier Bernard Baruch, the WIB faced the enormous task of satisfying both Allied and domestic needs. It made purchases, allocated supplies, and fixed prices. This usually meant satisfying business requests for price increases. The WIB ordered the standardization of goods to save materials and streamline production. The number of colors of typewriter ribbon, for example, was reduced from 150 to 5. Although the WIB seemed all-powerful, in reality it had to conciliate competing interest groups and compromise with the businesspeople whose advice it so valued.

The performance of the mobilized economy was mixed, but it delivered enough men and materiel to France to ensure the defeat of the Central Powers. About a quarter of all American production was diverted to war needs. Farmers enjoyed boom years as they put more acreage into production and watched prices go up. Induced to produce more at a faster pace, farmers mechanized as never before. From 1915 to 1920 the number of tractors in American fields jumped tenfold. Gross farm income for the period from 1914 to 1919 increased from $7.6 billion to $17.7 billion. Although manufacturing output leveled off in 1918, some industries enjoyed substantial increases because of wartime demand. Steel reached a peak production of 45 million tons in 1917, twice the prewar figure. The cigarette industry profited from the marked wartime increase in the consumption of tobacco, from 26 billion cigarettes in 1916 to 48 billion in 1918. The gross national product in 1920 was 237 percent higher than in 1914.

Massive assignments had to be completed in a hurry, and there were mistakes. Weapons deliveries fell short of demand; the bloated bureaucracy of the War Shipping Board failed to build enough ships. And the severe winter of 1917 and 1918 was a near-disaster for the nation. As the mercury dipped, millions of Americans found that they could not get coal, because the coal companies had held back on production to raise prices and railroads did not have enough coal cars. Harbors froze, closing out coal barges, and the federal government seemed immobilized. People died of pneumonia or freezing: a Brooklyn man went out in the morning to forage for coal and returned to find his two-month-old daughter frozen to death in her crib. In January, blizzards shut down midwestern railroads and factories, impeding the war effort.

If the fuel crisis could be blamed on the weather, inflation was directly attributable to governmental policy. Although inflation was partly caused by demand exceeding supply, due to increases **Inflation and** in Allied buying, the government's **Tax Policy** liberal credit policies and fixing of prices at high levels also encouraged it. As a result, the wholesale price index was 98 percent higher in 1918 than it had been in 1913. By fixing prices on raw materials rather than finished products, the government lost control of inflation. By bowing to the political pressure of southerners who wanted cotton left unregulated, the government permitted runaway cotton prices. Clothing tripled in cost and food prices more than doubled. A quart of milk that cost 9 cents in 1914 had climbed to 17 cents by 1920.

Tax policies during the war months were designed to pull some of the profits reaped from high prices back into the treasury. The Wilson administration believed that wealth as well as labor should be conscripted. Still, the government financed only one-third of the war through taxes. The other two-thirds came from loans, including Liberty Bonds sold to the American people through aggressive campaigns. The War Revenue Act of October 1917 provided for a graduated personal income tax, a corporate income tax, an excess profits tax, and increased excise taxes on alcoholic beverages, tobacco, and luxury items. Although these taxes did curb excessive corporate profiteering, they had several loopholes. Sometimes companies inflated costs to conceal profits or paid high salaries and bonuses to their executives. Four officers of Bethlehem Steel, for example, divided bonuses of $2.3 million in 1917 and $2.1 million the next year. Corporate net earnings for 1913 totaled $4 billion; in 1917 they had risen to $7 billion; and in 1918, after the tax bite and the war's end, they still stood at $4.5 billion. Patriotism and profits had to be partners, the federal government believed, in order for the United States to win the war.

Organized labor sought a partnership with government too, but its gains were far less spectacular.

For unions the war seemed to offer opportunities for recognition and better pay. Samuel **Wartime Labor** Gompers, president of the AFL, **Relations** threw his loyalty to the Wilson administration, promising to deter strikes. He and other moderate labor leaders were rewarded with appointments to high-level wartime government agencies. The National War Labor Board, created to mediate labor disputes, ruled out strikes and lockouts but fostered the eight-hour day and guaranteed workers the right to organize for collective bargaining. Unionization moved at a fast pace; from roughly 2.7 million in 1916, union membership climbed to over 4 million in 1919. The AFL could not curb strikes by the radical Industrial Workers of the World (IWW) or rebellious AFL locals, especially those with a high proportion of antiwar socialists as members. In the nineteen war months, over six thousand strikes expressed workers' discontent with their wages, working conditions, and inflation. There were some gains: the eight-hour day and forty-eight-hour week became more common, and some companies improved the workers' welfare by installing bathrooms, providing rest periods, and initiating insurance programs. Given the high cost of living, however, workers' earnings rose only slightly.

When 16 percent of the male work force trooped off to battle, and when immigration dropped off and some aliens sailed off to fight for their homelands, depriving business of much-needed labor, the call went out to women, blacks, and Mexican-Americans to fill the vacancies. Munitions makers in Bridgeport, Connecticut, for example, dropped leaflets from airplanes urging women to work in their factories. Though the number of women in the work **Women in the** force increased slightly, the real story **Work Force** was that many shifted from one job to another, sometimes into formerly male domains. Some white women left domestic service for factories, moved from clerking in department stores to stenography and typing, and departed textile mills for employment in firearms plants. Twenty percent or more of all workers in the wartime manufacture of electrical machinery, airplanes, and food were women. As white women took advantage of the new opportunities, black women took some of their places in domestic service and in textile factories. For the

Goggled women workers, hired by the Bethlehem Steel Corporation to replace men gone to war, tend their machines. Bethlehem Steel Corporation.

first time department stores employed black women as elevator operators and cafeteria waitresses, though they favored light-skinned blacks for these highly visible positions. Overall, most working women remained concentrated in sex-segregated occupations ("women's jobs") as typists, nurses, teachers, and domestic servants.

The movement of women into jobs that had been the preserve of males generated controversy. Male workers complained that women were destabilizing the work environment with their higher productivity; women answered that they were used to seasonal employment and piecework and hence worked at a faster pace. Men protested that women were undermining the wage system by working for lower pay; women pointed out that male-dominated companies discriminated against them and unions denied them membership. Finally, male employees resented the spirit of independence evident among women whose labor was now greatly valued. The female workers in a Vermont machine-tool company addressed a crude poem to their harping male cohorts:

We're independent now you see,
Your bald head don't appeal to me,
I love my overalls;

And I would rather polish steel
Than get you up a tasty meal.
Or go with you to balls.
Now, only premiums good and big,
Will tempt us maids to change our rig.
And put our aprons on;
And cook up all the dainty things,
That so delighted men and kings
In days now past and gone.[1]

When the war was over, the gains women made were largely reversed. The attitude that women's proper sphere was the home changed very little. Married working women found their family relationships growing tense; husbands and children resented the disruption of home life. Moreover, reformers complained that working mothers were neglecting their children: keeping older siblings home from school to care for younger ones; leaving their children with neighbors; failing to prepare good meals; and coming home so tired that their housework suffered. Day nurseries were scarce and beyond the means of most working-class families, and few employers provided child-care facilities. Whether married or single—and the great majority of working women were unmarried—they lost their jobs to the returning veterans. "During the war they called us heroines," cried Mary McDowell of the University of Chicago Settlement, "but they throw us on the scrapheap now."

Women who did not join the work force participated in the war effort in other ways. As volunteers they made clothing for refugees and soldiers, rolled bandages, served at Red Cross facilities, and taught French to nurses assigned to the war zone. Many joined the state-level activities of the Women's Committee of the Council of National Defense, whose leaders included Ida Tarbell and Carrie Chapman Catt. This vast network publicized government programs, encouraged home gardens, sponsored drives to sell Liberty Bonds, and continued the push for many social welfare reforms.

Wartime mobilization wrought significant changes for the black community. Wartime jobs in the North provided an escape from southern lynchings, political disenfranchisement, low wages, sharecropping, ten-

---

[1] From the *Springfield Reporter*, December 5, 1917. Reprinted by permission.

Black Migration to the North ancy, crop liens, floods, and boll-weevil-stricken cotton crops. During the war years, southern blacks undertook a great migration to northern cities to work in railroad yards, packing houses, steel mills, shipyards, and coal mines. In the decade from 1910 to 1920, Cleveland's black population swelled by over 300 percent, Detroit's by over 600 percent, and Chicago's by 150 percent, much of the increase occurring between 1916 and 1919. All told, about a half-million black Americans uprooted themselves to move north. Most were young (twenty to twenty-four years old), skilled or semiskilled, unmarried males seeking economic opportunity. One black man explained in a letter to a friend in Mississippi why he found the North attractive: "I should have been here twenty years ago. I just begin to feel like a man. It's a great deal of pleasure in knowing that you have got some privileges. My children are going to the same school with the whites and I don't have to humble to no one. I have registered. Will vote the next election."

New jobs and improved opportunities could not erase the fact that blacks, North and South, continued to be a minority in a white society. When the United States entered the First World War, there was not one black judge in the entire country and segregation was social custom. The Ku Klux Klan began to revive and racist films like D. W. Griffith's *The Birth of a Nation* (1915) further fed prejudice. Lynching statistics exposed the wide gap between American declarations of humanity in the war and the American practice of inhumanity at home: between 1914 and 1920, 382 blacks were lynched, some of them in military uniform.

Northern whites who resented the "Negro invasion" vented their anger in riots. In East St. Louis, Illinois, in 1917, whites opposed to black employment in a defense plant rampaged through the **Race Riots** streets; forty blacks and nine whites lost their lives. In the bloody "Red Summer" of 1919, race riots rocked two dozen cities and towns. The worst race war occurred in Chicago, a favorite destination for migrating blacks. In the very hot days of July 1919, a black youth swimming at a segregated white beach was hit by a thrown rock and drowned. Rumors spread, tempers flared, and soon blacks and whites were battling one another. Stabbings, burnings, and shootings went on for days until state police restored some calm. Thirty-eight people died—fifteen whites and twenty-three blacks; over five hundred others were injured.

For some white Americans, this sad record meant that the nation should direct its missionary zeal at the reform not of foreign societies but of its own. Some black leaders spoke out similarly hinting at more militancy than Booker T. Washington, who died in 1915, would have countenanced. Insisting on equality and an end to segregation, W. E. B. Du Bois vowed a struggle: "We return. We return from fighting. We return fighting." The black poet Claude McKay of New York expressed in 1919 a self-assertion and self-defense that prefigured later black protest:

If we must die—let it not be like hogs
Hunted and penned in an inglorious spot,
While round us bark the mad and hungry gods,
Making their mock at our accursed lot.

. . .

Like men we'll face the murderous, cowardly pack,
Pressed to the wall, dying but fighting back![1]

For his opposition to American participation in the First World War, Senator Robert La Follette (1855–1925) was cruelly misrepresented as a traitor. In this cartoon from Life magazine he is decorated by the German Kaiser. La Follette believed a majority of Americans, if given the opportunity in a referendum, would vote his way on the war. "The poor . . . who are the ones called upon to rot in the trenches, have no organized power," he once said. The State Historical Society of Wisconsin.

THE ATTACK ON CIVIL LIBERTIES

"Woe be to the man that seeks to stand in our way in this day of high resolution," warned President Wilson. Dissenters who questioned his war decision and the draft soon faced an official and unofficial campaign to silence them. Jingoists warped truth and incited violence, civil liberties were trampled, and an "Americanization" crusade cut a gaping wound in American democracy. The targets of abuse were the hundreds of thousands of Americans and aliens who refused to support the war: pacifists from all walks of life, conscientious objectors, socialists, the Industrial Workers of the World, the debt-ridden tenant farmers of Oklahoma who staged the Green Corn Rebellion against the draft, the Non-Partisan

League, reformers like Robert La Follette and Jane Addams, and countless others.

Shortly after the declaration of war in 1917, the president appointed George Creel, a progressive journalist, to head the Committee on Public Information. The CPI was a propaganda agency pure and simple. Employing some of the nation's most talented writers and scholars, the CPI set out to shape and mobilize public opinion by means of anti-German tracts; speeches by "four-minute men," who visited thousands of schools and churches; films like *America's Answer* (1918); and "self-censorship" of the press. The CPI encouraged people to spy on their neighbors and report any suspicious behavior. "Not a pin dropped in the home of any one with a foreign name," Creel

---

[1]From *Selected Poems of Claude McKay*, Copyright 1981 and reprinted with the permission of Twayne Publishers, a division of G.K. Hall and Co., Boston.

claimed, "but that it rang like thunder on the inner ear of some listening sleuth." Exaggeration, fear-mongering, distortion, half-truths—such were the stuff of the CPI's "mind mobilization."

The Wilson administration also guided through an obliging Congress the Espionage Act (1917) and the Sedition Act (1918). The first statute forbade "false statements" designed to impede the draft or promote military insubordination and banned from the mails materials considered treasonous. The Sedition Act made it unlawful to obstruct the sale of war bonds and to use "disloyal, profane, scurrilous, or abusive" language against the government, the Constitution, the flag, and the military uniform. These loosely worded laws gave the government wide latitude to crack down on those with whom it differed. Fair-minded people could disagree over what constituted false or abusive language, but in the feverish home-front atmosphere of the First World War and under the threat of federal prosecution, the Justice Department's definition prevailed. Over two thousand people were prosecuted under the acts and many others were intimidated into silence.

Espionage and Sedition Acts

Stories of arrests and an intellectual reign of terror began to fill the newapapers. Three Columbia University students were picked up in mid-1917 for circulating an antiwar petition. The liberal-left journal *The Masses* and Tom Watson's *The Jeffersonian* were denied use of the mails and forced to shut down. Jane Addams was put under Justice Department surveillance, causing her, by her own admission, to moderate her appeals for peace. The producer of *The Spirit of '76*, a film about the American Revolution complete with redcoats shooting minutemen, was given a ten-year prison sentence for, according to the judge, questioning the "good faith of our ally, Great Britain." In the summer of 1918, with a government stenographer present, Socialist party leader Eugene Debs delivered a ringing oration against the war and for free speech. He was given a ten-year sentence. Debs told the court what many dissenters—and later many jurists and scholars—thought of the Espionage Act: it was "a despotic enactment in flagrant conflict with democratic principles and with the spirit of free institutions." Debs remained in jail until late December 1921, when he received a pardon (see page 764).

State and local governments joined the campaign. Because towns had Liberty Bond quotas to fill, they sometimes threatened "slackers" into purchases through public humiliation. Officials banned what they considered "pro-German" books from public schools; the governor of Iowa prohibited the use of any language but English in schools and public places; and Pittsburgh banned Beethoven's music. Everywhere teachers who questioned the war faced dismissal by hostile school boards.

Across the nation, supporters of "Americanization" or "100% Americanism" exploited the emotional wartime atmosphere to urge or compel immigrants to throw off their Old World cultures. The director of the National Security League, conjuring up the image of a nation imperiled by its alien residents, declared that "in the bottom of the melting pot there lies heaps of unfused metal." To fuse a superpatriotic national unity, the CPI set up Loyalty Leagues in ethnic communities. Companies offered English-language and naturalization classes in their factories, and refused jobs and promotions to those who did not make adequate strides toward learning English. What began as education gave way to repression.

Encouraged by official behavior, groups like the American Protective League, the Sedition Slammers, and the American Defense Society took it upon themselves to cleanse the nation through vigilantism. German books were burned in Nebraska and a German-American miner in Illinois was wrapped in a flag and lynched. In Tulsa, a mob whipped IWW members and then poured tar into their bleeding sores. Nor were universities shelters for unorthodox ideas. In a celebrated case, antiwar Professor J. M. Cattell, a distinguished psychologist at Columbia University, was fired. His colleague Charles Beard, an historian with prowar views, resigned in protest: "If we have to suppress everything we don't like to hear, this country is resting on a pretty wobbly basis."

The point was just that: Wilson and his officers tried to crush what they did not like to hear. In particular, the administration concentrated on the IWW and the Socialist party. The war emergency and the frank opposition of those two radical organizations gave progressives and conservatives alike an opportunity to throttle their political rivals. Standing for revolution against cap-

Persecution of Radicals

italism and often violent in its tactics, the IWW aroused bitter opposition (see pages 502, 592). Soon after the declaration of war, government agents raided union meetings and arrested IWW leaders. The army was sent into western mining and lumbering regions to put down IWW strikes on the pretense that they were pro-German. Under the immigration acts, alien members of the IWW were deported. Town after town evicted the "Wobblies," and by the end of the war most of the union's leaders were in jail. The Socialist party fared little better: others besides Debs were imprisoned. Although the new Civil Liberties Bureau (forerunner of the American Civil Liberties Union) defended many of the dissenters, it could not stop the rampant suppression. Even the head of the Bureau, Roger Baldwin, was jailed as a conscientious objector.

The Supreme Court, itself attuned to the pulse of the times, upheld the Espionage Act. Justice Oliver Wendell Holmes, in *Schenck* v. *U.S.* (1919), expressed the Court's unanimous opinion that in time of war the First Amendment could be restricted: "Free speech would not protect a man falsely shouting fire in a theater and causing panic." If words "are of such a nature as to create a clear and present danger that they will bring about the substantial evils that Congress has a right to prevent," Holmes went on, free speech could be limited. In another case, *Abrams* v. *U.S.* (1919), the Court voted 7 to 2 (with Holmes and Brandeis in the minority) that the Sedition Act was constitutional. This time Holmes, writing the minority opinion, expressed concern that the "free trade in ideas" was being jeopardized.

THE RED SCARE

The line between wartime suppression of dissent and the postwar Red Scare is not easily drawn. Both were directed against suspected internal enemies, both put on the mask of patriotism to harass radicals and deprive them of their constitutional rights, and both had government sanction. In the last few months of the war, guardians of Americanism began to label dissenters not only pro-German, but pro-Bolshevik.

After the Bolshevik Revolution in the fall of 1917, American hatred for Kaiser Germany was readily transferred to Communist Russia. When the new Russian government under V. I. Lenin made peace with Germany in early 1918, thereby closing the eastern front, Americans felt betrayed. Many lashed out at American radicals, casually applying the term "Red" to people of varying beliefs, such as anarchists, Wobblies, Socialists, pacifists, Communists, union leaders, and reformers.

The ordeal of Victor Berger illustrates the blending of the wartime and postwar suppression of civil liberties. A Socialist of German descent and former congressman from Wisconsin, Berger was indicted under the Espionage Act for denouncing American entry into the European war. Nonetheless, in 1918 the voters of Milwaukee elected him once again to Congress. In early 1919 he was convicted and sentenced to twenty years in federal prison. The House of Representatives thereupon refused to admit him, its members absurdly charging that he was both pro-German and pro-Bolshevik. While out on bail pending an appeal of his conviction, Berger won the special election held to replace him. The House again blocked his admission. Berger's ordeal did not end until 1921 when the Supreme Court reversed his conviction. He was elected to Congress again in 1924; this time he took his seat.

Case of Victor Berger

An early sign of the Wilson administration's anti-Bolshevism was the president's ordering of five thousand American troops to northern Russia in June 1918. Then, a month later, he sent another ten thousand soldiers to Siberia, where they joined other Allied contingents. Wilson did not consult Congress; he announced that the military expeditions were intended to guard Allied supplies and Russian railroads from German seizure, and to rescue a group of Czechs who wished to return to their homeland to fight the Germans. Wilson also worried that the Japanese were building influence in Siberia and closing the Open Door. But he hoped primarily to smash the infant Bolshevik government. The Allied governments were blunter about this goal than Wilson, for they feared that Bolshevism had the potential to spread across Europe. (Indeed, there were short-lived uprisings in Germany and Hungary

Intervention in Russia

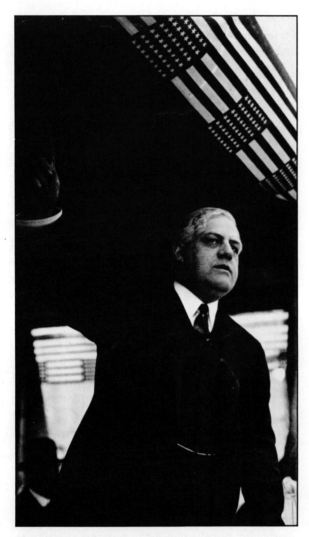

A. Mitchell Palmer (1872–1936), the ambitious attorney general who launched raids against suspected radicals during the Red Scare. Palmer ranks as one of the most notorious violators of civil liberties in American history. Library of Congress.

in early 1919). Not only did Wilson attempt to subvert Lenin's regime by military means; he participated in an economic blockade of Russia, sent arms to anti-Bolshevik forces, refused to recognize the Bolshevik government, and later blocked Russian participation in the Paris Peace Conference. American troops did not leave Siberia until spring 1920. These interventions in civil war–torn Russia immediately embittered Washington–Moscow relations—a legacy that was to persist deep into the twentieth century.

At home too, the Wilson administration moved against radicals and others imprecisely defined as Bolsheviks or Communists. After the war Americans were edgy: the war had disrupted race relations, the workplace, and the family; it had increased the cost of living; postwar unemployment loomed; and in 1919 the Russian Communists established the Comintern to promote world revolution. Already hardened by wartime violations of civil liberties, legal and illegal, Americans found it easy to blame their postwar troubles on new scapegoats.

Dramatic events sparked the Red Scare. First came a rash of labor strikes in 1919. All told, over 3,300 strikes involving 4 million laborers occurred that year, including a Seattle general strike in January that sent ripples of fear across the nation. America, said Wilson's press secretary with exaggeration, was poised between "organization and anarchy." In May, bombs were sent through the mails to prominent Americans; most of the devices were intercepted and dismantled. Police never captured the conspirators. The common and not-unreasonable assumption was that anarchists and others bent on the destruction of the American way of life were responsible. Next came the Boston police strike in September; some thought it part of a Bolshevik conspiracy. The governor of Massachusetts, Calvin Coolidge, gained fame by proclaiming that nobody had the right to strike against the public safety. State guardsmen were brought in to replace the striking police force.

The strike in the steel industry in September seemed more ominous. Over 350,000 workers walked out. Conservative steel executives, who had long resisted unionization and perpetuated terrible working conditions, were determined to roll back wartime concessions to higher wages and unions. Many workers still put in twelve-hour days seven days a week and went home to squalid living quarters. Postwar unemployment in the industry was climbing. The steel barons responded to the strike by sending agents to club strikers, hiring strikebreakers, and deliberately trying to plant in the public mind the belief that it was Bolshevik-inspired and led. When the strike collapsed in 1920, it was evident that the steelworkers' union was severely weakened.

Steel Strike

One of the leaders of the steel strike was William

Z. Foster, a radical who joined the Communist party after the strike began. His presence in a labor movement seeking legitimate bread-and-butter goals permitted political and business leaders to dismiss the steel strike as a foreign threat orchestrated by American radicals. There was actually no conspiracy, and the American left was badly splintered. After breaking away from the Socialist party, John Reed and Benjamin Gitlow founded the Communist Labor party in the summer of 1919. That September the Communist party, largely composed of aliens, was launched. Neither Communist party commanded much of a following—perhaps about seventy thousand members total—and in 1919 the harassed Socialist party could muster no more than approximately thirty thousand members.

Although divisiveness among radicals was actually symptomatic of weakness, both progressives and conservatives interpreted the advent of the new parties as a strengthening of the radical menace. That is certainly how the American Legion saw the matter. Organized in May 1919, the veterans' organization soon became a standard-bearer for the Red Scare. The editor of the *London Daily News* visited the United States in 1919 and recalled what he witnessed: the nation was "hag-ridden by the spectre of Bolshevism. . . . 'Radical' covered the most innocent departure from conventional thought with a suspicion of desperate purpose. 'America,' as a wit of the time said, 'is the land of liberty—the liberty to keep in step.' "

Attorney General A. Mitchell Palmer insisted on conformity. A progressive, a Quaker, and an aspirant to the 1920 Democratic presidential nomination, Palmer claimed that the "blaze of revolution" was "eating its way into the homes of the American workmen, its sharp tongues of revolutionary heat . . . licking the altars of the churches, leaping into the belfry of the school bell, crawling into the sacred corners of American homes, burning up the foundations of society." To stamp out the radical fire, Palmer created a new Bureau of Investigation and appointed J. Edgar Hoover to run it. Hoover organized a file of thousands of index cards bearing the names of alleged radical individuals and organizations. In 1919 agents jailed IWW members and deported alien radicals like Emma Goldman.

Titled "Moving Days," this 1919 cartoon credits the newly formed American Legion with frightening away aliens and Bolsheviks. Declaring itself an exponent of "Americanism," the Legion aroused the anti-immigrant and anti-radical feelings so common to the Red Scare. Library of Congress.

Again, state and local governments took their cue from Washington. The New York State legislature expelled five duly elected Socialist members. States passed peacetime sedition acts under which hundreds of people were arrested. Vigilante groups and mobs flourished once again, their numbers swelled by returning veterans. In November 1919, in Centralia, Washington, a town beset by emotional antiradicalism, four American Legionnaires were shot when they broke from an Armistice Day parade in an apparent attempt to storm the IWW hall. Several Wobblies were arrested and later convicted of murder; one, an exsoldier, was taken from jail by a mob, beaten, castrated, and then shot.

The Red Scare reached a climax in January 1920 when the attorney general staged his Palmer Raids. Using information gathered by Hoover, government agents in thirty-three cities broke into meeting halls, poolrooms, and

Palmer Raids

homes without search warrants. Four thousand people were thrown into overcrowded jails and denied counsel. Of this number, about 550 were deported. In Boston alone, approximately 400 people were kept in detainment on bitterly cold Deer Island; two died of pneumonia, one leaped to his death, and another went insane.

Palmer's disregard for elementary civil liberties soon drew criticism. Civil libertarians and lawyers pointed out that Palmer's blatant tactics ignored the Constitution, that many of the arrested "Communists" had committed no crimes, and that some were not even radicals. Palmer's call for a peacetime sedition act alarmed leaders of many political persuasions. His dire prediction that major violence would mar May Day 1920 proved mistaken. Palmer's exaggerations, his scenarios of Bolshevik conspiracy, simply exceeded the truth so far that he lost credibility. With the steel strike over, the threat of Bolshevism in Europe receding, and the nation settling down into a postwar routine of business as usual, Palmer could no longer count on stampeding the public. Finally, even officials in the Wilson administration refused to cooperate with him. Assistant Secretary of Labor Louis Post and immigration commissioner Frederick Howe blocked Palmer's attempts at wholesale deportations, while charging him with gross violations of human rights.

The campaign against free speech in the period from 1917 through 1920 left casualties. Critics, radical or otherwise, were afraid to speak their minds. Debate, so essential to democracy, was curbed. Reform suffered as reformers either joined in the antiradicalism or became victims of it. The radical movement was badly weakened, the IWW becoming virtually extinct and the Socialist party paralyzed. The government's war on its critics and disrespect for the Bill of Rights left an indelible blot on Wilson's political record. The president made it appear that his critics were attacking the nation itself, when in fact they were questioning the policies of the Wilson administration. Wilson's intolerance of those who disagreed with him seemed to bespeak a distrust of democracy. At the least it illustrated that some progressives would use coercion and authoritarian methods to achieve their goal of a reformed society. Senator La Follette thought the sorry experience demonstrated what was for him

the supreme issue: "the encroachment of the powerful few upon the rights of the many."

THE PEACE CONFERENCE AND LEAGUE FIGHT

As the Red Scare was threatening American democracy, Woodrow Wilson was struggling to make his Fourteen Points a reality. When the president departed for the Paris peace conference in December 1918, he faced obstacles erected by his political enemies, by the Allies, and by himself. Some observers suggested that the ambitious Wilson, confident of his own abilities and religious in his belief that destiny directed his course, underestimated his task.

In the 1918 congressional elections, Wilson had urged a vote for the Democrats as a sign of support for his peace goals. But the American people, probably voting less in response to foreign-policy issues than to domestic questions like inflation, did just the opposite. The Republicans gained control of both houses, signaling trouble for Wilson in two ways. First, any peace treaty would have to be submitted for approval to a potentially hostile Senate; second, Wilson's stature had been diminished in the eyes of foreign leaders. After this setback, Wilson aggravated his political problems by not naming any senator to the American Peace Commission, refusing to take any prominent Republican with him to the conference, and failing to consult with the Senate Foreign Relations Committee before he sailed for Paris. Analysts thought he had lost his political senses.

Another obstacle in Wilson's way was the Allies' determination to impose a harsh, vengeful peace on the Germans. Georges Clemenceau of France, David Lloyd George of Britain, and Vittorio Orlando of Italy—with Wilson, the Big Four—were formidable adversaries. They had signed secret treaties during the war and expected to enlarge their empires at Germany's expense. They scoffed at the headstrong, self-impressed president who wanted to deny them the spoils of war. Sizing up Wilson as a theologian self-consciously wielding United States power, they challenged his blueprint for peace. "God gave us the Ten Commandments, and we broke them," remarked Clemenceau. "Wilson gives us the Fourteen Points. We shall see."

The Paris Conference at the palace of Versailles was a meeting of the titans, "the clearing house of the Fates," as a contemporary put it. Much of the

Paris Conference

business of the conference was conducted by the Big Four behind closed doors: critics quickly pointed out that Wilson had thus abandoned the first of his Fourteen Points, which urged diplomacy in the "public view." The victors demanded that Germany pay a huge reparations bill. Wilson called for a small indemnity, fearing that a resentful and economically hobbled Germany might turn to Bolshevism or disrupt the postwar community in some other way. Unable to moderate the Allied position, the president reluctantly gave way, agreeing to a clause blaming the war on the Germans and to the creation of a reparations commission to determine a figure (later set at $33 billion).

As for decolonization (the breaking up of empires) and the principle of self-determination, Wilson only partially overcame the land-grabbing mood of the conference. The conferees placed former German and Turkish colonies under the control of other imperial nations in a League-administered "mandate" system. France and Britain, for example, obtained parts of the Middle East, and Japan gained authority over Germany's colonies in the Pacific. The mandate system was a halfway station between outright imperial domination and independence. In other compromises, Japan was granted influence over China's Shandong Peninsula, and France was permitted occupation rights in Germany's Rhineland. Elsewhere in Europe, however, Wilson's prescriptions fared better. Out of Austria-Hungary and Russia came the new independent states of Austria, Hungary, Yugoslavia, Czechoslovakia, and Poland. Wilson and his colleagues also built a *cordon sanitaire* of new westward-looking nations (Finland, Estonia, Latvia, and Lithuania) around Russia to quarantine the Bolshevik contagion.

Wilson worked harder on the charter for the League of Nations than on anything else. In the long run, he believed, the League would moderate the harshness of the Allied peace terms and temper imperial ambitions. He devised a League that

League of Nations

reflected the power of large nations like the United States: an influential council of five permanent members (great powers) and elected delegates from smaller states; an assembly for discussion; and a World Court. The heart of the League covenant, said Wilson, was Article 10:

> The Members of the League undertake to respect and preserve as against external aggression the territorial integrity and existing political independence of all Members of the League. In case of any such aggression or in case of any threat or danger of such aggression the Council shall advise upon the means by which this obligation shall be fulfilled.

This collective-security provision was the centerpiece of Wilson's international reform program, and with the entire League charter it became part of the peace treaty.

German representatives at first refused to accept the punitive Treaty of Paris, but then signed it in June 1919. In so doing they gave up 13 percent of Germany's territory, 10 percent of its population, all its colonies, and a huge portion of its national wealth. Secretary Lansing and others prophesied that the League could not function in the poisoned atmosphere of revenge and humiliation. But Wilson, filled with America's traditional missionary zeal, was euphoric: "The stage is set, the destiny disclosed. It has come about by no plan of our conceiving, but by the hand of God, who led us into this way."

Americans vigorously debated the merits of the treaty. In March 1919, as the conferees in Paris were hammering out the accord, thirty-nine senators

Debate over the Treaty

(enough to deny the treaty the necessary two-thirds vote) signed a petition stating that the League's structure did not adequately protect American interests. Wilson lamented the "pygmy" minds of his antagonists, but persuaded the peace conference to exempt the Monroe Doctrine and domestic matters from League jurisdiction. Having made these concessions to senatorial advice, Wilson would budge no more.

Near the end of his controversial presidency, Woodrow Wilson was a saddened man. A stroke had undercut his health, American voters had repudiated his party and some of his policies in the election of 1920, and the Senate had rejected his pet project—American membership in the League of Nations. National Archives.

Yet criticism mounted: Wilson had bastardized his own principles; he had conceded Shandong to Japan; he had personally killed a provision affirming the racial equality of all peoples. There was no mention in the treaty of freedom of the seas; there was no reduction in tariffs. Negotiations had been conducted in private, and reparations promised to be punishing. Senator La Follette joined others in complaining that the League was an imperialist assemblage that would perpetuate empire. Conservative critics like Senator Henry Cabot Lodge of Massachusetts feared that the League would limit American freedom of action in world affairs, stymie its expansion, and intrude on domestic questions. Racist nationalists wanted no part of an organization that bestowed the vote on nonwhite peoples. And Article 10 raised serious questions: Would the United States be obligated to use armed force to ensure collective security? And what about colonial rebellions, such as in Ireland or India? Would they be disturbances of the peace the League would feel compelled to crush?

Wilson pleaded for understanding and lectured his opponents. Did they not realize that compromises were necessary given the awesome, stubborn resistance of the Allies, who had threatened to jettison the conference unless Wilson made concessions? Did they not recognize that the League would rectify wrongs? Could they not see that membership in the League would give the United States "leadership in the world"? Senator Lodge was unimpressed. A Harvard-educated Ph.D. and partisan Republican, he ridiculed Wilson's charter as poor scholarship. Lodge packed the Foreign

Relations Committee with critics of the League and prolonged public hearings. He introduced reservations to the treaty: one stated that the nation's immigration acts could not be subject to League decision; another held that Congress had to approve any obligation under Article 10.

In September 1919, Wilson embarked on a speaking tour of the United States. Growing more exhausted every day, he dismissed his critics as "absolute, contemptible quitters." When he met Irish-American and German-American hecklers, he lashed out in Red Scare language: "I cannot say too often—any man who carries a hyphen about him carries a dagger which he is ready to plunge into the vitals of the Republic." In Colorado, while delivering another passionate speech, the president collapsed. A few days later, in Washington, D.C., he suffered a stroke that paralyzed his left side. Although his mind remained alert, he became grumpy and peevish, fearful of displaying weakness and unable to conduct the heavy business of the presidency. Told by advisers to placate senatorial critics so the treaty would have a chance of passing, Wilson stubbornly refused to "dip [his] colors to dishonorable compromise." From Democrats in the Senate he demanded loyalty—a vote against all reservations.

The Senate first tested the treaty's strength in November. In two votes, one on the treaty with reservations (39–55) and one without (38–53), the Senate rejected it. A group of six-

Senate Rejection of the Treaty

teen "Irreconcilables," determined to defeat any treaty, voted nay each time. Republicans either opposed the treaty altogether or favored reservations; Democrats, on the whole, voted for the treaty without reservations. Eastern and midwestern senators largely voted against an unamended treaty; senators from the South tended to vote aye; western senators were divided. Again in March 1920, the Senate fell short of the necessary two-thirds vote of approval (49–35). Had Wilson permitted Democrats to compromise, he could have achieved his fervent goal of American membership in the infant League of Nations.

Who or what was responsible for the defeat of the treaty? Wilson's stroke incapacitated the president, sapping his energy and the ability to lead effectively; yet, even a healthy Wilson would likely have set his jaw against compromise. Certainly his concessions to a harsh peace at Paris undercut his case in the United States; yet it seems that two-thirds of the Senate were willing to forgive his errors in Versailles if he would accept some reservations. And the bitter personal feud between Wilson and Lodge does not account for enough—it does not, for example, explain the determination of the Irreconcilables.

Wilson's refusal to compromise with his senatorial foes certainly doomed the treaty. Still, this begs the question: why were Wilson's critics so committed to cripple Article 10, and why was the president so adamant against its revision? Because at the core of the debate lay a basic issue of American foreign policy: whether the United States would endorse *collective security* or continue to travel the path of *unilateralism* articulated in Washington's Farewell Address and the Monroe Doctrine. In a world dominated by imperialist states unwilling to subordinate their selfish, acquisitive ambitions to an international organization, Americans preferred their traditional nonalignment and freedom of choice over binding commitments to collective action. Woodrow Wilson failed to create a new world order through reform; he promised more than he could deliver.

THE EXPERIENCE OF WAR

As the war ground to a close in Europe, the historian Albert Bushnell Hart observed that "it is easy to see that the United States is a new country." What had changed? America emerged from the war years an unsettled mix of the old and the new. Above all else the war exposed the heterogeneity of the American people and the deep divisions among them: white versus black, nativist versus immigrant, capital versus labor, dry versus wet, men versus women, radical versus progressive or conservative, pacifist versus interventionist, nationalist versus internationalist. Race riots, labor strikes, the Americanization movement, suppression of civil liberties, the Red Scare, the League fight, and male resentment of female workers—all underscored the distempers of the times. It is no wonder that after 1920 Americans would

IMPORTANT EVENTS

1914	American troops invade Mexico First World War begins	1918	Wilson announces Fourteen Points Sedition Act Eugene Debs imprisoned U.S. troops at Château-Thierry U.S. troops intervene in Russia Flu epidemic Republicans win congressional elections Armistice
1915	Germany declares war zone around British Isles German U-boat sinks *Lusitania* Bryan resigns in protest		
1916	Gore-McLemore resolution loses U.S. troops invade Mexico again *Sussex* torpedoed National Defense Act Wilson re-elected	1919	Paris Peace Conference at Versailles Eighteenth Amendment ratified May Day bombings American Legion founded Red Summer; Chicago race riot Steel strike U.S. Communist party founded President Wilson suffers stroke Treaty of Paris rejected by Senate *Schenck v. U.S.*
1917	Germany declares unrestricted submarine warfare Zimmermann telegram Russian Revolution U.S. entry into First World War Selective Service Act Espionage Act Race riot in East St. Louis, Illinois War Industries Board created Fuel crisis due to severe winter	1920	Red Scare and Palmer Raids Nineteenth Amendment ratified

seek relief in "normalcy" and escape from what John Dewey called the "cult of irrationality."

During the war the federal government intervened in the economy and influenced people's everyday lives as never before. In the period 1916 to 1919 annual federal expenditures increased 2,500 percent, and war expenses ballooned to $33.5 billion. The total cost of the war was probably triple that figure, since future generations would have to pay veterans' benefits and interest on loans. Centralization of control in Washington, D.C., and mobilization of the home front served as a model for the future. The partnership of government and business in managing the wartime economy contributed to the development of a mass society through the standardization of products and the promotion of efficiency.

Enlarged Federal Role

The wartime cooperation of government and business also encouraged the growth of trade associations, which numbered about two thousand by 1920. After the war these industry-wide groups would continue to lobby to protect their interests and to minimize competition. Wilsonian wartime policies also nourished the continued growth of big business and of oligopoly through the suspension of antitrust legislation. A 1920 Supreme Court decision not to dissolve the giant U.S. Steel Corporation symbolized the persistent trend toward bigness. After a short postwar recession, business power revived to dominate the next decade. American labor, by contrast, entered what one historian has called its lean years.

America's changed place in world affairs also held significance for later generations. By 1920 the United States was the world's leading economic power, producing 40 percent of its coal, 70 percent of its petroleum, and half its pig iron. It rose to first rank in world trade. During the war years, American companies expanded their overseas operations. Goodyear went into the Dutch East Indies for rubber; copper interests dug new mines in Chile; and Swift and Armour reached into South America. Preoccupied with the war, competitors like Britain and Germany were outdistanced by American economic expansionists, especially in Latin America. The United States also shifted from a debtor to a creditor nation, becoming the world's leading banker.

Economic Expansion Abroad

The disillusionment common to so many Americans after the disappointment of Versailles did not cause the United States to adopt a policy of isolationist withdrawal (see Chapter 27). Although the League of Nations began to operate without United States membership, Americans became curious onlookers who even occasionally participated in League activities. But in general Americans stood against intervening in European affairs until the Europeans first set their own house in order.

The carnage of the war—10 million people lost their lives—stimulated new appeals for arms control and a revitalized peace movement. At the same time, the military became more professional. The Reserve Officer Training Corps (ROTC) became permanent; military "colleges" provided upper-echelon training; and the Army Industrial College, founded in 1924, pursued business-military cooperation in the area of logistics and planning. The National Research Council, created in 1916 with governmental and Carnegie and Rockefeller funds, continued after the war as an alliance of scientists and businesspeople engaged in research relating to national defense. As before the war, the tendencies toward disarmament on the one hand and preparedness on the other continued to compete.

The international system born in these years was unstable and fragmented. The process of decolonization was set in motion at this time. Nationalist leaders like Ho Chi Minh of Indochina and Mahatma Gandhi of India, taking to heart the Wilsonian principle of self-determination, vowed to achieve independence for their peoples. Communism became a new and disruptive force in world politics, and the Russians bore a grudge against the Allies, who had futilely tried to thwart their revolution. The new states in Central and Eastern Europe proved weak, dependent on outsiders for security. Germans bitterly resented the harsh peace settlement. And the war debts and reparations problems would dog international order for years.

The war experience also changed Americans' mood. The war was grimy and ugly, far less glorious than Wilson's lofty rhetoric had it. People recoiled from the photographs of bodies dangling from barbed wire, poison-gas victims, and battle-shocked faces. American soldiers were eager to return home. Apparently tired of idealism and cynical about their ability to right wrongs, they craved the latest baseball scores. Still, for the doughboys the army years were memorable, a turning point in their lives. They shed some of their parochialism, as the title of a popular song hinted: "How 'Ya Gonna Keep 'Em Down on the Farm, After They've Seen Paree?" And they made lasting friendships that would be cemented by membership in the American Legion. A young soldier from Missouri, Harry S Truman of Battery D, would never lose touch with his wartime buddies, and when he became president in 1945 he would bring some of them into the White House as advisers.

Those progressives who had believed entry into the war would deliver the millennium now marveled at their naiveté. Many lost their enthusiasm for crusades, and many others turned away in disgust from the bickering of the victors. Randolph Bourne commented that progressives felt "like brave passengers who have set out for the Isles of the Blest only to find that the first mate has gone insane and jumped overboard." Some felt betrayed, distraught that the Great War had not proven exceptional. William Allen White angrily wrote to a friend that the Allies "have—those damned vultures—taken the heart out of the peace, taken the joy out of the great enterprise of the war, and have made it a sordid malicious miserable thing like all the other wars in the world."

Woodrow Wilson himself had remarked soon after taking office in 1913, before the Great War, that "there's no chance of progress and reform in an administration in which war plays the principal part." From the vantage point of 1920, looking back on the array of distempers at home and abroad, Wilson would have to agree with his fellow citizens that progress and reform had been dealt blows.

Suggestions for Further Reading

General

Randolph Bourne, *War and the Intellectuals,* ed. Carl Resek (1964); John W. Chambers, *The Tyranny of Change* (1980); Allen F. Davis, *American Heroine* (1974) (on Jane Addams); Otis L. Graham, Jr., *The Great Campaigns* (1971); Ellis W. Hawley, *The Great War and the Search for a Modern Order* (1979); Henry F. May, *The End of American Innocence* (1964); Emily S. Rosenberg, *Spreading the American Dream* (1982); Bernadotte Schmitt and Harold E. Vedeler, *The World in the Crucible: 1914–1919* (1984); Ronald Steel, *Walter Lippmann and the American Century* (1980); David P. Thelan, *Robert M. La Follette and the Insurgent Spirit* (1976).

Woodrow Wilson and His Diplomacy

Thomas A. Bailey and Paul B. Ryan, *The Lusitania Disaster* (1975); Edward H. Buehrig, ed., *Wilson's Foreign Policy in Perspective* (1957); John M. Cooper, Jr., *The Warrior and the Priest: Woodrow Wilson and Theodore Roosevelt* (1983); Patrick Devlin, *Too Proud to Fight* (1975); Robert H. Ferrell, *Woodrow Wilson and World War I* (1985); Lloyd C. Gardner, *Safe for Democracy: The Anglo-American Response to Revolution, 1913–1923* (1984); Ross Gregory, *The Origins of American Intervention in the First World War* (1971); Manfred Jonas, *The United States and Germany* (1984); N. Gordon Levin, Jr., *Woodrow Wilson and World Politics* (1968); Arthur S. Link, ed., *Woodrow Wilson and a Revolutionary World, 1913–1921* (1982); Arthur S. Link, *Woodrow Wilson: Revolution, War, and Peace* (1979); Arthur S. Link, *Wilson,* 5 vols. (1947–1965); Ernest R. May, *The World War and American Isolation, 1914–1917* (1959); Walter Millis, *Road to War* (1935); Robert E. Osgood, *Ideals and Self-Interest in American Foreign Relations* (1953); Jeffrey J. Safford, *Wilsonian Maritime Diplomacy* (1977); Frances W. Saunders, *Ellen Axson Wilson* (1985); Daniel M. Smith, *The Great Departure* (1965); Barbara Tuchman, *The Zimmermann Telegram* (1958); Edwin A. Weinstein, *Woodrow Wilson: A Medical and Psychological Biography* (1981).

The American Military and the First World War

Arthur E. Barbeau and Florette Henri, *The Unknown Soldiers: Black American Troops in World War I* (1974); J. Garry Clifford, *The Citizen Soldiers* (1972); Edward M. Coffman, *The War to End All Wars* (1968); Harvey A. DeWeerd, *President Wilson Fights His War* (1968); Marvin E. Fletcher, *The Black Soldier and Officer in the United States Army, 1891–1917* (1974); Thomas C. Leonard, *Above the Battle* (1978); David Trask, *The United States in the Supreme War Council* (1961); Russell F. Weigley, *The American Way of War* (1973).

The Home Front

Valerie Jean Conner, *The National War Labor Board* (1983); Alfred W. Crosby, Jr., *Epidemic and Peace, 1918* (1976); Robert D. Cuff, *The War Industries Board* (1973); Allen F. Davis, "Welfare, Reform, and World War I," *American Quarterly,* 19 (1967), 516–533; Edward R. Ellis, *Echoes of Distant Thunder* (1975); Charles Gilbert, *American Financing of World War I* (1970); Maurine W. Greenwald, *Women, War, and Work* (1980); Frank L. Grubbs, Jr., *The Struggle for Labor Loyalty* (1968); Michael T. Isenberg, *War on Film* (1981); David M. Kennedy, *Over Here* (1980); Paul A. C. Koistinen, "The 'Industrial-Military Complex' in Historical Perspective: World War I," *Business History Review,* 41 (1967), 378–403; Seward W. Livermore, *Politics Is Adjourned* (1966); Frederick C. Luebke, *Bonds of Loyalty: German-Americans and World War I* (1974); John F. McClymer, *War and Welfare: Social Engineering in America, 1890–1925* (1980); Barbara J. Steinson, *American Women's Activism in World War I* (1982); Stephen L. Vaughn, *Holding Fast the Inner Lines: Democracy, Nationalism, and the Committee on Public Information* (1979).

Black Americans

Robert V. Haynes, *A Night of Violence: The Houston Riot of 1917* (1976); Florette Henri, *Black Migration* (1975); Thomas C. Holt, "Afro-Americans," in *Harvard Encyclopedia of American Ethnic Groups,* ed. Stephan Thernstrom (1980); Elliot M. Rudwick, *Race Riot at East St. Louis, July 2, 1917* (1964); William M. Tuttle, *Race Riot: Chicago in the Red Summer of 1919* (1970).

Wartime Dissent, Civil Liberties, and the Red Scare

David Brody, *Labor in Crisis: The Steel Strike of 1919* (1965); Charles Chatfield, *For Peace and Justice: Pacifism in America, 1914–1941* (1971); Stanley Coben, *A. Mitchell Palmer* (1963); Charles DeBenedetti, *Origins of the Modern Peace Movement* (1978); Robert L. Friedheim, *The Seattle General Strike* (1965); Sondra Herman, *Eleven Against War* (1969); Donald Johnson, *The Challenge to American Freedoms* (1963); C. Roland Marchand, *The American Peace Movement and*

Social Reform, 1898–1918 (1973); Paul L. Murphy, *World War I and the Origin of Civil Liberties* (1979); Robert K. Murray, *Red Scare* (1955); H. C. Peterson and Gilbert C. Fite, *Opponents of War, 1917–1918* (1968); William Preston, *Aliens and Dissenters: Federal Suppression of Radicals, 1903–1933* (1966); Francis Russell, *A City in Terror: 1919—The Boston Police Strike* (1975); Harry N. Scheiber, *The Wilson Administration and Civil Liberties, 1917–1921* (1960); James Weinstein, *The Decline of Socialism in America, 1912–1923* (1967).

Hostility Toward Bolshevik Russia

Peter G. Filene, *Americans and the Soviet Experiment, 1917–1933* (1967); John L. Gaddis, *Russia, The Soviet Union, and the United States* (1978); George F. Kennan, *The Decision to Intervene* (1958); George F. Kennan, *Russia Leaves the War* (1956); Christopher Lasch, *The American Liberals and the Russian Revolution* (1962); John Thompson, *Russia, Bolshevism, and the Versailles Peace* (1966); Betty M. Unterberger, ed., *American Intervention in the Russian Civil War* (1969); Betty M. Unterberger, *America's Siberian Expedition, 1918–1920* (1956); William Appleman Williams, *American-Russian Relations, 1781–1947* (1952).

Versailles and the League Fight

Thomas A. Bailey, *Woodrow Wilson and the Great Betrayal* (1945); Thomas A. Bailey, *Woodrow Wilson and the Lost Peace* (1944); Inga Floto, *Colonel House in Paris* (1973); Herbert Hoover, *The Ordeal of Woodrow Wilson* (1958); Warren F. Kuehl, *Seeking World Order* (1969); Arno Mayer, *Politics and Diplomacy of Peacemaking* (1967); Keith Nelson, *Victors Divided* (1973); Ralph A. Stone, *The Irreconcilables* (1970); William C. Widenor, *Henry Cabot Lodge and the Search for an American Foreign Policy* (1980).

Aftermath

Stanley Cooperman, *World War I and the American Mind* (1970); Malcolm Cowley, *Exile's Return* (1951); Paul Fussell, *The Great War and Modern Memory* (1975); Stuart I. Rochester, *American Liberal Disillusionment in the Wake of World War I* (1977); Stephen R. Ward, ed., *The War Generation: Veterans of the First World War* (1975).

THE NEW ERA OF
THE 1920s

CHAPTER 24

At 9:39 P.M. on August 6, 1926, a young American woman trudged out of the rough sea onto the English coast. Nineteen-year-old Gertrude Ederle had left France that morning in an attempt to swim the English Channel, a feat that only five men and no women had ever accomplished. She not only succeeded but swam the treacherous thirty-mile stretch in 14 hours 31 minutes, the fastest time yet recorded.

Already known as a swimming champion—she had won a gold medal at the 1924 Olympics—Ederle now became a champion of women. Her conquest of the Channel, wrote the *Literary Digest*, "would be hailed as a battle won for feminism" and the "unanswerable refutation of the masculine dogma that woman is, in the sense of physical power and efficiency, inferior to man." According to a columnist for the *Boston Globe*, "The Channel has been the means of giving to women new physical dignity."

Yet Americans seemed to appreciate that dignity in narrow ways. Along with adulation, Ederle's feat inspired a profusion of swimsuit ads linking physical fitness to sex appeal. Newspapers and magazines not only heralded her swim but increased their coverage of bathing beauties at the Miss America Pageant, a contest begun in 1922, the year Ederle won her first long-distance race. And whatever her accomplishments, the name of Ederle was never as renowned as those of the era's most admired males: Dempsey, Ruth, Lindbergh, or even Capone.

During the 1920s the flower of consumerism reached full bloom. Spurred by advertising and new forms of credit, Americans eagerly bought automobiles, radios, real estate, and stocks. The majority of the population enjoyed an unparalleled standard of living. As in the Gilded Age of the late nineteenth century, government policies supported the interests of business. The most fundamental and perplexing trend of the 1920s was the effect of the new mass consumer culture on individuals and communities. Changes in work habits, family responsibilities, and health care fostered new uses of time and new attitudes about proper behavior.

By the end of the decade, new habits and values had altered American society. Whereas people had once identified with those who believed as they did, they now felt as much, if not more, of a sense of community with fellow consumers of Ford cars, Listerine mouthwash, and Lucky Strike cigarettes. Whereas they had once expressed their individuality in their work and family lives, now they sought vicarious identification with popular heroes like Gertrude Ederle, Charles Lindbergh, and Jack Dempsey.

The 1920s was an era when important reforms occurred at state and local levels of government, and significant advances were made in science and technology. An outburst of creativity occurred in literature, music, and art. Still, the consumer culture predominated in everyday life, causing Americans to ignore rising debts and other increasingly negative economic signs. But poverty dogged small farmers, workers in declining industries, and nonwhites living in slums.

In many ways the Ederle story illustrates the complexities and ironies of the new era of the 1920s. The decade was a time both of great accomplishments—in economic productivity as well as athletics—and of frivolous commercial stunts, contests, and fads. It was a time of swift social change, of frankness and liberation. But the winds of change also stirred up waves of reaction. The new, more liberal values repelled some groups, such as the Ku Klux Klan, immigration restrictionists, and religious fundamentalists. Such groups reacted by trying to restore a society of simpler values, where people knew their place and deviants were not tolerated. Yet in spite of their efforts, material bounty and increased leisure time enticed Americans into a variety of new mass amusements, including games, sports, and movies. In an impersonal world, Americans had turned to mass culture to personalize their lives.

POSTWAR OPTIMISM

Poor Richard's Almanac would have sold poorly in the 1920s. Few Americans of that era had much interest in the virtues of thrift and sobriety that Benjamin Franklin had preached. They saw more attraction in acquisition, amusement, and salesmanship. Instead of traditional homilies like "waste not, want not," they harkened to the advice of an advertising executive: "Make the public want what you have to sell. Make 'em pant for it." With such an attitude Americans attained the highest standard of living they had yet experienced. Though poverty and social injustice still infected the country, many people shared the belief, as journalist Joseph Wood Krutch put it, that "the future was bright and the present was good fun at least."

The decade did not begin very brightly. Besides political wrangling over membership in the League of Nations and ratification of the Treaty of Paris and the Red Scare, the nation suffered a frightening economic decline. For two years after the First World War, consumer spending drove prices up. Then in 1920 people stopped buying, and the export trade and industrial production dropped as wartime orders ended. Net farm income plunged. Unemployment, which had hovered around 2 percent in 1919, passed 12 percent in 1921. The railroad and mining industries suffered declining profits, and layoffs spread through New England as textile companies abandoned outdated factories for the raw materials and cheap labor of the South.

Recovery began in 1922 and continued unevenly until 1929. During this period, industrial output nearly doubled. Electric motors were responsible for much of the rise; by 1929 electricity

**Postwar
Economic
Recovery**

powered 70 percent of American industry, and thousands of steam engines had been relegated to the scrap heap. The new technique of manufacture by assembly line also contributed, adding countless new consumer products to the market. New metal alloys, chemicals, synthetic materials, and preserved foods became commonplace. As Americans acquired more spending money and as their leisure time expanded, service industries boomed. More people could afford department and specialty stores, restaurants, beauty and barber shops, and movie theaters. This new consumerism was fueled by refined methods of credit, especially the installment or time-payment plan ("a dollar down and a dollar forever," as one critic quipped). Of 3.5 million automobiles sold in 1923, some 80 percent were bought on credit.

Poor Richard would have thrown up his hands in disgust.

Behind the prosperity, an economic revolution was climaxing. First, the consolidation movement that had given birth to trusts and holding companies in the late nineteenth century reached a new stage. Although Progressive-era trustbusting had harnessed big business to some extent, it had not halted *oligopoly*—the control of a whole industry by a few large firms. By the 1920s oligopolies dominated not only production but marketing, distribution, and even financing. In businesses as varied as automobile manufacturing, steel production, meatprocessing, and railroads, a few sprawling integrated companies predominated. Oligopolistic firms, like General Electric, General Motors, and U.S. Steel, developed specialized management techniques to maximize profits and minimize market uncertainties.

The organizational movement that had begun around 1900 also matured in the 1920s. Myriad business and professional associations sprang up to protect their members' interests. Retailers and small manufacturers formed trade associations to pool information and coordinate planning. Farm bureaus and cooperative associations promoted scientific agriculture, lobbied for government protection, and tried to stabilize the market. Lawyers, engineers, and social scientists cooperated with business to promote economic growth.

THE BUSINESS OF GOVERNMENT, THE GOVERNMENT OF BUSINESS

In this outburst of expansion, many Americans shed their fear of big business—swayed in part by the testimonials of probusiness propagandists. "Among the nations of the earth today," one writer proclaimed in 1921, "America stands for one idea: *Business* . . . Thru business, properly conceived, managed and conducted, the human race is finally to be redeemed." Government reflected this outlook. As corporations became more national in scope, they looked increasingly to the federal government for assistance in integrating the economy. Thus during the 1920s a series of Republican administrations extended Theodore Roosevelt's notion of government-business cooperation—though they often made government a passive coordinator rather than the active director Roosevelt had advocated.

All branches of the federal government supported business interests during these years. In 1921 Congress reduced taxes on corporations and wealthy individuals, and in 1922 it raised tariff rates in the Fordney-McCumber Tariff Act. Presidents Harding, Coolidge, and Hoover appointed strong cabinet officers who pursued policies favorable to business. Regulatory agencies such as the Federal Trade Commission and the Interstate Commerce Commission cooperated with corporations more than they regulated them.

The revival of business prompted political analysts to lament the death of progressivism. They were partly right; the concern for social and economic justice that had moved the previous generation faded in the 1920s, especially as the image of big business improved. Yet many of the Progressive era's achievements were sustained and consolidated in these years. Although federal trustbusting declined, regulatory commissions and other government agencies still monitored business activities and worked to reduce wasteful practices. And in Congress a sizable corps of reformers, led by George Norris of Nebraska and Robert La Follette of Wisconsin, kept progressive causes alive by supporting labor legislation, federal aid to farmers, and government operation of a federally constructed hydroelectric dam at Muscle Shoals, Alabama. (Business-oriented politicians wanted to sell or lease the dam and its nitrate plant to private interests.) Women's reform organizations marked a major achievement in 1921 when Congress passed the Shepard-Towner Act, which provided federal funds to help set up maternity and pediatric clinics (though the measure was overturned in 1929 when Congress, under pressure from private physicians, cut off funding).

Extension of Progressive Reforms

Most reform, however, occurred at the state and local levels. Following initiatives begun before the First World War, thirty-four states instituted or expanded workers' compensation laws in the 1920s. At the same time many states established old-age pensions and other welfare programs. In hundreds of cities, trained social scientists gathered data and drew maps as part of a systematic effort to identify and solve urban problems. Planning became a common feature of urban government; by 1926 every major city and many smaller ones had planning and zoning commissions that aimed to harness physical growth to the common good. And social workers continued to strive for justice and economic relief. During the 1920s the nation's state houses, city halls, and universities trained a new generation of reformers who would eventually influence national affairs during the New Deal government of the 1930s.

Organized labor, which had gained ground during the Progressive era, suffered setbacks during the 1920s. Public opinion, influenced by prosperity and pro-business rhetoric, turned against workers who disrupted everyday life with strikes. The federal government frequently stifled union attempts to exercise power during these years. Early in the decade, for instance, the Justice Department used troops and court injunctions to end strikes by steel, mine, and railroad workers. Meanwhile, large corporations worked to counteract the appeal of unions by promising workers pensions, profit-sharing (which actually amounted to wages withheld for later distribution), and company-sponsored social and sporting events—a policy that became known as *welfare capitalism*. In such a climate, union membership fell from 5.1 million in 1920 to 3.6 million in 1929.

Suppression of Labor Unions

The Supreme Court, led by Chief Justice and former president William Howard Taft, became a powerful policy-making body, exerting its authority as aggressively as in the Gilded Age to protect private property. Its key decisions sheltered business from government regulation and undermined attempts by organized labor to achieve its ends through strikes and legislation. Thus in 1922 Taft ruled in *Coronado Coal Company* v. *United Mine Workers* that a striking union, like a trust, could be prosecuted for illegal restraint of trade. Yet in *Maple Floor Association* v. *U.S.* (1929), the Court gave support to trade associations which had formed to gather and disseminate information within particular industries, by effectively exempting them from antitrust laws. The Court also struck down labor reform in cases such as *Bailey* v. *Drexel Furniture Company* (1922), which voided re-

This photo of President Warren G. Harding (1865–1923) shows both the optimism of the years immediately after the First World War and Harding's affinity for good times with good friends. Library of Congress.

strictions on child labor, and *Adkins v. Children's Hospital* (1923), which overturned a minimum wage law for women because it infringed on liberty of contract.

A symbol of the decade's goodwill toward business was President Warren G. Harding, a Republican elected in 1920 at a time when the populace wanted to avoid national and international crusades. Democrats had nominated Governor James M. Cox of Ohio, who stood behind Woodrow Wilson's fading hopes for United States membership in the League of Nations (see pages 671–673). But the efforts of Cox and his running mate, Franklin D. Roosevelt of New York, failed to attract voters. Harding, who kept his opinion on the League vague, captured 16.1 million popular votes to only 9.1 million for Cox.

A small-town newspaper publisher and senator from Ohio, Harding selected some capable assistants, notably Secretary of State Charles Evans Hughes, Secretary of Commerce Herbert **Harding** Hoover, Secretary of the Treasury **Administration** Andrew Mellon, and Secretary of

Agriculture Henry C. Wallace. Harding also backed some important reforms. He helped streamline the budget, supported antilynching legislation, approved bills assisting farm cooperatives and liberalizing farm credit, and, unlike his predecessor Wilson, was generally tolerant on civil liberties issues.

Harding's problem was that he had too many predatory friends. His father once reputedly remarked, "Warren, it's a good thing you wasn't born a gal. You'd be in the family way all the time—you can't say no." Harding said yes too often, appointing friends to positions from which they infested government with corruption. Charles Forbes of the Veterans Bureau served time in Leavenworth prison after being convicted of fraud and bribery in connection with government contracts. Thomas W. Miller, alien property custodian, was jailed for accepting bribes. Attorney General Harry Daugherty was implicated in a scheme of accepting bribes and in other fraudulent acts; he escaped prosecution only by refusing to testify against himself. In the most notorious case of all, a congressional inquiry in 1923 and 1924 revealed that Secretary of the Interior Albert Fall had accepted bribes to lease government property to private oil companies. For his role in the affair, called the Teapot Dome scandal after a Wyoming oil reserve that had been turned over to the Mammoth Oil Company, Fall was fined $100,000 and spent a year in jail. He was the first cabinet officer to be so disgraced.

In June 1923, few Americans knew how corrupt Harding's administration had become. The president, however, had become disillusioned. Amid rumors of mismanagement and crime, he told journalist William Allen White, "My God, this is a hell of a job. I have no trouble with my enemies. . . . But my friends, my God-damned friends . . . they're the ones that keep me walking the floor nights." On a speaking tour of the West that summer, Harding became ill and died in San Francisco on August 2. Though his death preceded revelation of the Teapot Dome scandal, some people later believed that Harding had committed suicide rather than face the brewing storm. Most evidence, however, points to death from natural causes, probably a heart attack. At any rate, Harding was truly mourned. A warm, dignified-looking man who relished a good joke or an evening of poker and drinking, he seemed right for a nation that had just experienced racking upheaval at home and abroad.

Harding's successor, Vice President Calvin Coolidge, was far more solemn. A dour New Englander (Alice Roosevelt Longworth, Theodore's daughter, once quipped that Coolidge looked as if he had been weaned on a pickle), Coolidge had an undistinguished record as Republican governor of Massachusetts. He had first attracted national attention by his firm stand against striking Boston policemen in 1919, a policy that won him the vice-presidential nomination in 1920. Usually, however, he was content to let events take their course, prompting columnist Walter Lippmann to grumble, "It is a grim, determined, alert inactivity, which keeps Mr. Coolidge occupied constantly."

Coolidge had great respect for private enterprise; he once remarked, "The man who builds a factory builds a temple. The man who works there, worships there." Fortunately for him, his presidency coincided with extraordinary business prosperity. Aided by Andrew Mellon, whom he retained as secretary of the treasury, and other cabinet officers,

Coolidge Prosperity

his administration balanced the budget, reduced government debt, lowered income-tax rates (especially for the rich), and began construction of a national highway system. With his generally tightfisted fiscal policies he won business support. Congress took little initiative during these years and assented to most measures recommended by the cabinet and by business associations such as the U.S. Chamber of Commerce. The only disruptions arose over farm policy. Responding to farmers' complaints of falling prices, Congress twice passed bills to establish government-backed price supports for staple crops (the McNary-Haugen bills of 1927 and 1928). But Coolidge exercised his executive privilege and vetoed the measure both times.

"Coolidge prosperity" was the determining issue in the presidential election of 1924. That year both major parties ran candidates who accepted business supremacy. The Republicans nominated Coolidge with little dissent. At their national convention the Democrats first debated heatedly whether or not to condemn the Ku Klux Klan, voting 542 to 541 against condemnation. Then they endured 103 ballots before breaking a deadlock between southern prohibitionists who favored former Secretary of the Treasury William G. McAdoo and antiprohibition easterners who backed New York's Governor Alfred E. Smith. They finally settled on John W. Davis, a corporation lawyer from New York. Remnants of the progressive movement, along with various farm, labor, and socialist groups, formed a new Progressive party and nominated Robert M. La Follette, the aging reformer from Wisconsin. The new party revived issues unresolved in previous generations: public ownership of utilities; aid to farmers; decreased restraint on organized labor; increased regulation of business.

The election results resembled those of 1912 in reverse: the two probusiness candidates captured most of the votes. Coolidge beat Davis by 15.7 million to 8.4 million popular votes, 382 to 136 electoral votes. Like Taft in 1912, La Follette finished a poor third, receiving a respectable but ineffective 4.8 million popular votes and only 13 electoral votes. Though the trend of low voter turnout begun in the Progressive era continued (to the dismay of feminists, even newly enfranchised women voted in small numbers), those who did vote seemed satisfied with the general prosperity.

The age of electrical appliances dawned in the 1920s. Here, a family gathers around a radio, one of the most popular electrical innovations of the age. The radio not only popularized modern music and folksy drama but also created new schedules in family life.   National Archives.

MATERIALISM UNBOUND

"One day," Henry Ford recalled, "someone brought to us a slogan which read: 'Buy a Ford and Save the Difference.' I crossed out the 'save' and inserted 'spend'—'Buy a Ford and Spend the Difference.' It is the wiser thing to do. Society lives by circulation and not by congestion." Ford had a way of making new values sound like old truths. His ardent consumerism was a major theme of the 1920s, to which he contributed materially as well as philosophically. By 1925 the assembly line at Ford's Highland Park plant produced a motor car every ten seconds.

Indeed, between 1919 and 1929 the gross national product—the total value of all goods and services produced in the United States—swelled by 40 percent.

Expansion of the Consumer Society
Wages and salaries also increased (though not as much) while the cost of living remained relatively stable. The result was that people had more purchasing power. And they spent as Americans had never spent. In an article in *Survey* magazine in 1928, Eunice Fuller Barnard contrasted family expenditures in 1900 with those of 1928:

1900	
2 bicycles	$ 70
wringer and washboard	$ 5
brushes and brooms	$ 5
sewing machine (mechanical)	$ 25
Total	$105

1928	
automobile	$700
radio	$ 75
phonograph	$ 50
washing machine	$150
vacuum cleaner	$ 50
sewing machine (electric)	$ 60
other electrical equipment	$ 25
telephone (year)	$ 35
Total	$1,145[1]

[1]From Paul Carter, *Another Part of the Twenties,* © 1977, Columbia University Press. By permission.

Barnard added that certain items, such as education and medical care, had become costlier. Yet she felt the change had been worthwhile. She would rather pay more for a quart of milk knowing it was safer and purer than the product of a generation earlier. "When some of us bewail the higher cost of living we may be talking about the higher cost of *better* living," Barnard concluded.

The benefits of modern technology were reaching more people than ever before. By 1929 two-thirds of all Americans lived in dwellings that had electricity, compared with one-sixth in 1912. In 1929 one-fourth of all families owned electric vacuum cleaners and one-fifth had electric toasters. Many could afford these and other items such as radios, washing machines, and movie tickets only because more than one family member worked or because the breadwinner took a second job. Nevertheless, new products and services were available to more than just the rich.

Of all the era's technological and economic wonders, the automobile was the vanguard. During the 1920s automobile registrations soared from 8 million to 23 million. Mass production and com-

Effects of the Automobile petition had brought down prices, making cars affordable even to some working-class families. By 1926 a Ford Model T cost under $300 and a Chevrolet sold for $700—at a time when workers in manufacturing earned around $1,300 a year and clerical workers about $2,300. The car had become a source of pride as well as a means of transportation; no sacrifice was too great to obtain one. Thus when an interviewer asked a rural housewife why her family owned a car but not a bathtub, the woman retorted, "Bathtub? You can't go to town in a bathtub."

The motor car altered society as much as the railroad had seventy-five years earlier. Public officials were forced to pay more attention to safety regulations and traffic control. (In 1924 the General Electric Company responded to the needs with the first timed stop-and-go traffic light.) Changes in car design provided new opportunities for youths to escape watchful parents. By 1927, five-sixths of all autos were enclosed (in 1919 most had had open tops), making for a privacy that bred fears of "houses of prostitution on wheels." The growing choice of models (there were 108 different automobile manufacturers in 1923) and colors allowed automobile owners to suit their personal tastes in a growing mass society. But most important, the car was the ultimate symbol of social equality. As one writer observed in 1924, "It is hard to convince Steve Popovich, or Antonio Branca, or plain John Smith that he is being ground into the dust by Capital when at will he may drive the same highways, view the same scenery, and get as much enjoyment from his trip as the modern Midas."

Americans' newly acquired taste for driving necessitated extensive construction of roads and abundant supplies of fuel. Since the late 1800s farmers and bicyclists had been pressing for improved roads; after the First World War motorists joined the campaign, prompting cities and states to improve local arteries. The important advances came in 1921 when Congress passed the Federal Highway Act, which provided federal aid for state roads; and in 1923 when the Bureau of Public Roads planned a national highway system.

The oil industry, already vast and powerful, shifted its emphasis from products providing illumination and lubrication to products providing propulsion. In 1920 the United States was producing about 65 percent of the world's oil, much of it controlled by the Standard Oil trust. But already Americans were tasting a bitter future (see pages 976–979) as corporate and government officials warned of fuel shortages and shrinking reserves. Early in 1920 a U.S. Geological Survey report stated that "unless our consumption is checked, we shall by 1925 be dependent on foreign oilfields." In some parts of the country companies limited the amount of gasoline people could buy and doubled the price. But the crisis had a dubious flavor. Just after the shortages and price hikes occurred, the State Department persuaded the British to grant Standard Oil a share in British-controlled Iraqi oilfields. Immediately thereafter, the crisis abated.

More than ever, Americans' taste for automobiles and other goods and services was whetted by advertising. By 1929 total advertising earnings reached

Advertising $3.4 billion, more than was spent on all types of formal education. For many, advertising became the language of a new gospel. In his best-selling *The Man Nobody Knows* (1925), advertising executive Bruce Barton called Jesus "the founder of modern business" because he "picked up twelve men from the bottom ranks of business and forged them into an organization

"Everyone owns a car but us"~

You, too, can own an automobile without missing the money, and *now*, is the time to buy it—through the easiest and simplest method ever devised:

Ford Weekly Purchase Plan

Thousands of families, who thought a car was out of the question because of limited incomes, found that they could easily, quickly and surely buy a car of their own under this remarkable plan

You *can* own an automobile, and you *should*. It will mean so much to you. It will add much to the happiness of your family that is worth while. It will bring the most glorious pleasures into your life. It will increase your chances for success. It will give you and your family a social and business prestige that will be invaluable—and which you, and every family, should enjoy. A car is a symbol of success—a mark of achievement, and it brings opportunities to you that you would probably never secure otherwise. You should have a car of your own, and *you can.*

The Ford Plan makes it possible for anyone to own an automobile. It is so easy, simple and practical that many who could easily pay "spot cash" take advantage of it—and buy their car from weekly earnings. The plan is simply wonderful! Before you realize it, you are driving your own automobile. If you have felt that you did not make enough to buy a car, you must read The Ford Plan Book. Send for it. See how easy it is to get a car of your own, *now*, and pay for it without missing the money. It seems almost too good to be true, doesn't it? *But it is true.* Get the book—at once. Simply mail the coupon. *Mail it today!*

Give your family the advantages which others have. Get a car of your own. The Ford Plan Book tells you "how" you can buy a car and pay for it without missing the money. Get it! Read it!

Mail Coupon Now. This Book Will be Sent by Return Mail.

COUPON

FORD MOTOR COMPANY
Dept. B-3   Detroit, Michigan
Please send me your book, "The Ford Plan" which fully explains your easy plan for owning an automobile.

Name ⎯⎯⎯⎯⎯⎯⎯⎯⎯

R. F. D. Box or St. & No. ⎯⎯⎯⎯

Town ⎯⎯⎯⎯   State ⎯⎯⎯⎯

Ford Motor Company
Detroit

IT IS EASY TO OWN A CAR BY USING THIS PLAN

By the 1920s, not only was an automobile affordable, especially through installment payments such as the "Ford Weekly Purchase Plan," but also there was strong social pressure on families to own one. As this advertisement so vividly illustrates, Americans were made to feel that they needed an automobile for the pleasure and status it would bring them.   Library of Congress.

that conquered the world." About the same time, a pamphlet titled *Moses, Persuader of Men* declared, "Moses was one of the greatest salesmen and real-estate promoters that ever lived"—demonstrating that advertising could be ecumenical. Advertising theorists also adopted psychological principles and practical cynicism in asserting that, with proper environmental influences, any person's tastes could be manipulated.

Although daily newspaper circulation declined during the 1920s, other media assumed vital advertising functions. By 1929 over 10 million families owned radios, which bombarded them almost continuously with advertisements. Station KDKA in Pittsburgh pioneered in commercial radio broadcasting beginning in 1920; by 1922 there were 508 such stations. By 1929 Americans were spending $850 million a year on radio equipment, and the National Broadcasting Company, which had begun to assemble a network of radio stations three years earlier, was charging advertisers $10,000 to sponsor an hour-long show. Commercial intermissions at movie houses and highway billboards also reminded viewers to buy. Packaging and product display became sciences, with the object of creating demand.

Though poor people could not afford many of the products and services, some of the new trends touched working-class groups, especially those in the cities. Indoor plumbing and electricity became more common in private residences, and canned foods, varied diets, ready-made clothes, and mass-produced shoes became more affordable. A little cash and a lot of credit enabled many to purchase an automobile. And even if a family could not afford a radio, vacuum cleaner, or vacation, there was always hope. Spending became a national pastime. No wonder many people wanted Henry Ford to run for president in 1924.

CITIES, MIGRANTS, AND SUBURBS

The expansion of consumerism bespoke not only an economically mature nation but an urbanized one. In 1920 for the first time the federal census

Continuing Urbanization revealed that a majority of Americans, 51.4 percent, lived in urban areas (places with 2,500 or more people)—a sign that the city had become the locus of national experience. Indeed, the growth of services and industry both derived from and responded to urbanization. Industries such as steel, oil, and auto production boosted cities like Detroit, Birmingham, and Houston; service and retail trades accounted for expansion in Atlanta, Minneapolis, and Seattle. The most explosive growth occurred in areas of warm climate—Miami and San Diego—where promises of comfort and profit attracted thousands of speculators.

The trend toward urbanization continued during the 1920s, as an estimated 6 million Americans left their farms for nearby or distant cities. Midwestern migrants, particularly young single people, moved to regional centers or to California. A steady stream of southerners moved into burgeoning industrial cities of the South or followed railroad lines north.

Blacks accounted for a sizable portion of the migrants. Crushed by tenant farming and lured by industrial jobs, 1.5 million blacks moved cityward during the 1920s, accelerating a trend begun a decade earlier (see pages 517–518). The black populations of New York, Chicago, Detroit, and Houston doubled during these years. Forced by necessity and discrimination to seek the cheapest housing, the newcomers squeezed into ghettos—low-rent districts from which escape was difficult at best. For unlike white migrants, who were free to move away from inner-city districts if and when they could afford to do so, blacks found better housing closed to them. The only way they could expand their housing opportunities was to spill into nearby neighborhoods, a process that sparked resistance and violence. Fears of such expansion prompted white neighborhood associations to adopt restrictive covenants, whereby homeowners pledged not to sell their property to blacks.

In response partly to their new urban experiences and partly to race riots and threats, thousands of blacks in northern cities joined movements that glorified black independence. The most **Marcus Garvey** influential of these black nationalist groups was the Universal Negro Improvement Association (UNIA), headed by Marcus Garvey, a Jamaican immigrant who believed blacks

During and after the First World War, thousands of southern blacks migrated northward, taking railroad routes into cities like Chicago, New York, and St. Louis. In these cities blacks found new job opportunities and better housing but also racial tension and occasional violence.   The Phillips Collection, Washington.

should separate themselves from a corrupt white society. Proclaiming "I am the equal of any white man," Garvey cultivated race pride through militant mass meetings and parades. He also promoted black capitalism to demonstrate blacks' management skills. His newspaper, the *Negro World,* refused to publish ads for hair straighteners and skin-lightening cosmetics, and his Black Star shipping line was intended to help blacks emigrate to Africa.

The UNIA declined in the mid-1920s when the Black Star line went bankrupt (unscrupulous dealers had sold the line dilapidated ships) and when anti-radical fears prompted government prosecution (ten of the organization's leaders were arrested on charges of anarchism and Garvey was deported for mail fraud). Black middle-class leaders like W. E. B. Du Bois opposed the UNIA. Nevertheless, the organization had attracted a huge following (contemporaries estimated it at 500,000; Garvey claimed 6 million) in New York, Chicago, Detroit, and other cities. And Garvey's speeches had served notice that blacks had their own aspirations, which they could and would translate into action.

The newest immigrants to American cities came from Mexico and Puerto Rico. As in the nineteenth century, many Mexicans moved north to work as agricultural laborers in the Southwest, but in the 1920s a large number also flowed into growing cities like Denver, San Antonio, Los Angeles, and Tucson. Like other immigrant groups, Mexicans generally lacked resources and skills, and men greatly outnumbered women. Victims of white discrimination, Mexicans crowded

Mexican and Puerto Rican Immigrants

During the 1920s, a housing boom occurred in many suburbs. The automobile facilitated commuting to the nearby city and enabled middle-class families to live in "bedroom communities" such as Tarrytown, New York, pictured above. The Bettmann Archive.

into low-rent, inner-city districts where they often were deprived of decent city services, such as sanitation, schools, and police protection. Yet their communities, called *barrios*, provided an environment in which the immigrants could sustain customs and values of the homeland and develop institutions to help them adapt to American society.

The 1920s also saw a great influx of Puerto Ricans to the mainland (Puerto Rico had been a U.S. possession since 1898; see page 631). A shift in the island's economy from sugar to coffee production had created a surplus population willing to move and attracted by contracts from American employers seeking cheap labor. Most Puerto Rican migrants moved to New York City where they formed *barrios* in parts of Brooklyn and Manhattan. Besides manufacturing, Puerto Ricans found jobs in hotels, res-

taurants, and domestic service. As with Mexicans, Puerto Rican communities contained some educated elites—doctors, lawyers, business owners—who served as ethnic leaders. The *barrios*, which contained nearly equal numbers of women and men, also developed their own consumer institutions, such as *bodegas* (grocery stores), restaurants and boardinghouses.

As urban growth peaked, suburban growth accelerated. Although towns had existed around the edges of urban centers since the nation's earliest years, prosperity and easier transportation—mainly the automobile—made the urban fringe more accessible in the 1920s. Between 1920 and 1930, suburbs of Chicago (such as Oak Park and Evanston), Cleveland (such as Shaker Heights), and Los Angeles (such as Burbank and Inglewood) grew

Growth of the Suburbs

five to ten times as fast as the central cities. Most such suburbs were middle- and upper-class bedroom communities, though they included industrial suburbs like Highland Park (near Detroit) and East Chicago.

With their own police, fire protection, and water and gas services, many suburbs resisted annexation to core cities. Suburbanites wanted to escape big-city crime, dirt, and taxes, and they fought to preserve local control. "Under local government," one suburban editor reasoned, "we can absolutely control every objectionable thing that may try to enter our limits—but once annexed we are at the mercy of city hall." Particularly in the Northeast and Midwest, the fierce independence of growing suburbs choked off expansion by the central city and divided metropolitan areas in ways that would cause problems for future generations.

The bulging cities and suburbs fostered the new mass culture that gave the decade its character. Most of the consumers who jammed retail establishments, movie houses, and sporting arenas and who embraced fads like crossword puzzles, miniature golf, and marathon dancing were city and suburb dwellers. Cities and suburbs were the places where people flouted law and morality by patronizing speakeasies (illegal saloons), wearing outlandish clothes, and listening to jazz. They were also the places where women, ethnic and racial minorities, and religious denominations strained hardest to adjust to the new era. And yet the ideal of small-town society survived. While millions thronged cityward and intellectuals carped that small towns stifled personal growth, Americans still reminisced about the innocence and simplicity of a world gone by. This was the dilemma of a modern nation: how could one anchor oneself in a world of rampant material and social change?

NEW RHYTHMS
OF EVERYDAY LIFE

Amid all the change, Americans developed new social values and new ways of using time. Increasingly, people were splitting their daily lives into three distinct compartments: work, family, and leisure. Each type of time was altered in the 1920s. For many people, time on the job shrank. Among industrial workers the five-and-one-half-day workweek (half a day on Saturday) was becoming common. Many white-collar employees enjoyed two days off and worked a forty-hour week. Annual vacations were becoming a standard job benefit for white-collar workers, whose numbers grew by 40 percent during the decade.

Family time is harder to measure, but certain figures suggest important changes. As birth control became more widely accepted, birthrates dropped noticeably between 1920 and 1930. As a result, family size decreased. Among American women who married in the 1870s and 1880s, well over half who survived to fifty had had five or more children; of those who married in the 1920s, however, just 20 percent had five or more children. Over the same period the divorce rate rose. In 1920 there was one divorce in every 7.5 marriages; in 1929 the national ratio was 1 in 6, and in many cities it was 2 in 7. Lower birthrates, more divorce, plus longer life expectancy meant that adults were devoting a smaller portion of their lives to parental and other family tasks.

At the same time the availability of ready-to-wear clothes, preserved foods, and mass-produced furniture meant that family members spent less time producing household necessities. Wives still

Household Management spent most of their day cleaning, cooking, mending, and otherwise maintaining the home, but new machines lightened some of their tasks. Especially in middle-class households, electric irons and washing machines made the most tedious chores less burdensome. Central heating and hot-water heaters eliminated the hauling of wood, coal, and water, the upkeep of a kitchen fire, and the removal of ashes.

As a result, housewives filled their time differently from their forebears. In some ways the new technology made new demands on them. By eliminating servants, who had formerly helped with cleaning, cooking, and childcare, machines shifted the entire job of household management and childraising onto the wife herself. And instead of being a producer of food and clothing as women had been, the wife now became chief consumer, doing the shopping and making sure the family spent its money wisely.

The ready availability of washing machines, hot

$1000.00 PRIZE CONTEST—(INQUIRE WITHIN)

Life

Commuters' Number

Suburbanization and the demands of white collar work created new schedules and roles in the middle class family. Here the housewife, now the chief consumer and household manager, sews a button on the sleeve of the breadwinner husband while he gulps coffee and reads his paper before rushing to catch his commuter train.   Library of Congress.

water, and commercial soap put greater pressure on wives to keep everything clean. Advertisers tried to coax women into buying products by making them feel guilty for not giving enough attention to cleaning the home, caring for the children, and tending to personal hygiene. "Are you unpopular with your own children?" asked the makers of Listerine mouthwash. If so, the ad continued, "More often than you would imagine . . . halitosis is at fault. Children are quick to resent it. . . . Realizing this, [intelligent people] eliminate any risk of offending by the systematic use of Listerine in the mouth. Every morning. Every night." Thus, while the industrial and service sectors became more specialized as a result of technological advances, housewives retained a wide variety of responsibilites and added new ones as well.

While family time shifted and work time decreased, nonwork, nonfamily activities were expanding. More people spent more years in school. High school en-rollment quadrupled between 1910 and 1929; by 1929 over a third of all high school graduates went on to college. And as the use of electricity spread, people stayed up later at night to read or listen to the radio. They filled their expanding leisure time with automobile rides, sports events, motion pictures, shopping, and other forms of amusement.

In general, more rest and better diets were making Americans healthier. Between 1920 and 1930 life expectancy at birth increased from fifty-four to sixty years, and infant mortality decreased by two-thirds. Sanitation and medical research in bacteriology and immunology combined with better nutrition to reduce the risks of life-threatening diseases such as tuberculosis and diphtheria. Medical progress did not benefit all groups equally, however. Rates of stillbirth and infant mortality were 50 to 100 percent higher among blacks than among whites, and the incidence of tuberculosis in urban slums remained alarmingly high. Moreover, the death rate from automobile accidents rose 150 percent, and deaths from heart disease and cancer, diseases of old age, increased about 15 percent. Nevertheless, Americans in general were living longer: the total number of people age sixty-five and over grew 35 percent between 1920 and 1930, while the rest of the population increased only 15 percent.

Growing numbers and worsening economic conditions of the elderly stirred interest in old-age pensions and other forms of assistance. Old people increasingly faced poverty due to forced retirement and reduced income, for the industrial system put a premium on youth and agility. Realizing the needs of their aging citizens, most European countries had established state-supported pension systems in the early 1900s. But many Americans still believed that people should prepare for old age by saving in their youth; pensions, they felt, smacked of socialism. As late as 1923 the Pennsylvania Chamber of Commerce labeled old-age assistance "unAmerican and socialistic . . . an entering wedge of communistic propaganda."

Old Age and Retirement

Yet something had to be done. During the decade, a large majority of all inmates in state pauper institutions were old people, and almost one-third of all Americans sixty-five and older were financially dependent on someone else. Only a few companies had retirement plans; most, including the federal government, did not take care of retired employees. Noting that the government fed retired horses until they died, one postal worker complained, "For the purpose of drawing a pension, it would have been better had I been a horse than a human being." Resistance to pensions finally broke at the state level in the 1920s. Led by Isaac Max Rubinow and Abraham Epstein, reformers persuaded voluntary associations, labor unions, and legislators to accept the principle of old-age support through pensions, insurance programs, and retirement homes. By 1933 almost every state provided at least minimal assistance to the needy elderly, and the way had been opened for a national program of old-age insurance.

With more people spending time away from work and family, new values were inevitable. Especially among the middle class but among the working class too, clothes became a means to per-

Social Values sonal expression and freedom. Both men and women wore more casual and more gaily colored styles than their parents would have considered. The line between inappropriate and acceptable behavior blurred as smoking, swearing, and frankness about sex became more common. Thousands who had never read psychoanalyst Sigmund Freud's theories were certain that he prescribed an uninhibited sex life as the key to mental health. Birth-control advocate Margaret Sanger, who a decade earlier had been accused of promoting race suicide and forced to flee the country, now gained a large following in respectable circles. Newspapers, magazines, motion pictures, and popular songs (such as "Hot Lips" and "Burning Kisses") made certain that Americans did not suffer from "sex starvation." A typical movie ad announced "brilliant men, beautiful jazz babies, champagne baths, midnight revels, petting parties in the purple dawn, all ending in one terrific smashing climax that makes you gasp."

Still other trends contributed to the breakdown of traditional values. Because child-labor laws and compulsory-school-attendance laws kept children in school longer than was common in earlier generations, schools and peer groups now played a greater role in socializing children. In earlier times, different age groups had common activities; for example, children worked with older people in the fields, and young apprentices worked with older journeymen and craftsmen. Now, however, graded school classes, sports, clubs, and

By obtaining jobs, many young women of the 1920s could afford the latest fashions. These three modishly dressed black women from Harlem were part of the swelling numbers of female secretaries, store clerks, waitresses, and hairdressers.   The Schomburg Collection, New York Public Library.

other activities constantly brought together children who were the same age, separating them from the company and influence of adults. In addition, parents tended to rely less on family tradition and more on childcare manuals in raising their children. Old-age homes, public health clinics, and workers' compensation reduced the family's responsibilities even further.

Although the home remained a female domain, and in spite of the closing off of employment opportunities the First World War had created, women continued to stream into the labor

Jobs for force during the 1920s. By 1930
Women 10.8 million women worked, an increase of over 2 million since the war's end. The sex segregation that had long characterized occupations continued; most female workers could be found in jobs where few men worked. More than a million women were teachers and nurses. Some 2.2 million were typists, bookkeepers, and office

clerks, a tenfold increase since 1920; another 736,000 were salespeople in stores. Increasingly large numbers of women took jobs as waitresses and hairdressers. Almost 2 million women worked in factories, though their numbers grew very little over the decade.

Women's foray into work outside the home reflected an extension of their family roles. Although they worked for a combination of reasons, the economic

Married Women in the Labor Force needs of their families shaped the job experiences of most women. The consumerism of the 1920s prompted working-class and middle-class families to satisfy their wants either by living beyond their means or by sending women and children into the labor force. In previous eras, most of these extra wage earners were young and single. But in the 1920s, married women joined the group, a trend that has increased down to the present. Between 1920 and 1930, the proportion of the work force that contained married women rose by 30 percent, and the numbers of married women working swelled from 1.9 million to 3.1 million. Pressures of poverty gave many of these women no choice but to work; yet others did so because they wanted to increase their family's material comforts. They still justified their work on the basis of need, but this definition of need reflected the new consumer values—the family "needed" a radio and a car as well as food and clothing. The vast majority of married women remained out of the work force (only 12 percent were employed in 1930), but they did so because social pressures and demands of housework and child-care prevented them. (Black women were the exception; their proportions in the work force were twice those of white women, indicating both greater economic burdens and family arrangements that enabled them to balance housework along with their outside jobs.)

Feminists in the 1920s directed their concern to the issue of married women in the labor force, but they did not fully understand the motivations of married working women. Building on

Economic Feminism the ideas of Charlotte Perkins Gilman (see page 603), a number of female writers pushed for greater economic opportunity for women, especially married women. They believed that the separation of place of work from place of residence had left women at

home to tend household chores that few men would do. Women's earlier functions as economic producers of food and clothes, said feminists, had lapsed into passive roles as child nurturers and homemakers; the result was economic dependency. The way to restore married women's sense of worth in a money-oriented society was for them to have gainful employment. A job, asserted *Harper's* editor Dorothy Bromley, would make a married woman "a full-fledged individual who is capable of molding her own life."

But because feminists tried to separate the notion of career from domestic roles, they had little appeal to women who placed family needs, not individual needs, above all else regardless of whether or not they held jobs. Thus few women heeded the call for equal pay and equal opportunity voiced by Alice Paul, leader of the new National Women's party, who in 1922 supported an equal rights amendment to the Constitution. Indeed, after obtaining the vote in 1920, many women seemed to turn their backs on politics. The National American Women Suffrage Association disbanded, and the League of Women Voters which followed it, avoided party politics and controversial issues.

Whether they worked or not, all types of women were exposed to alternative images of femininity. Short skirts and bobbed hair, regarded as signs of

Alternative Images of Femininity sexual freedom, became common among office workers and store clerks as well as among middle-class college coeds. Several studies claimed that sexual experimentation, including premarital sex, increased among young women during the decade. The most popular models of female behavior were not chaste, sentimental heroines but movie vamps like Clara Bow, the "It Girl," and Gloria Swanson, who specialized in torrid love affairs on and off the screen. And though not everyone was a flapper, as the young independent-minded woman was called, many women were clearly asserting their equality with men. As one observer described the "new woman":

She takes a man's point of view as her mother never could. . . . She will never make you a hatband or knit you a necktie, but she'll drive you from the station . . . in her own little sports car. She'll don knickers and go skiing with you . . . she'll dive as well as you, perhaps better, she'll dance as long as you care to, and she'll take everything you say the way you mean it. . . .

These new social trends represented a sharp break with the more restrained culture of the nineteenth century. But social change, as always, did not proceed smoothly. As the decade wore on, various groups prepared to defend against the threat to older, more familiar values.

LINES OF DEFENSE

In the spring of 1920 the leader of a newly formed organization decided to hire two public-relations experts to recruit members. Using modern advertising techniques, the promoters, Edward Clarke and Elizabeth Tyler, canvassed cities and towns in the South, Southwest, and Midwest, where they found thousands of men eager to pay $10 to join and another $6 for a uniform made of white cloth. For their efforts, Clarke and Tyler pocketed $2.50 out of each membership fee. No one could argue with their success. By 1923 the organization claimed 5 million members. But this was no ordinary civic club like the Lions or Kiwanis; it cultivated a very special kind of social consciousness. It was the Ku Klux Klan, a revived version of the hooded order that had terrorized southern communities following the Civil War, and its appeal was based largely on fear. As one of the pamphlets distributed by Clarke and Tyler put it, "Every criminal, every gambler, every thug, every libertine, every girl ruiner, every home wrecker, every wife beater, every dope peddler, every moonshiner, every white slaver, every Rome-controlled newspaper, every black spider—is fighting the Klan. Think it over, which side are you on?"

The Klan was the most sinister reactionary movement of the 1920s. Founded in 1915 by William J. Simmons, an Atlanta evangelist and insurance salesman who wanted to purify southern

Ku Klux Klan culture, the new Invisible Empire revived the hoods, intimidating tactics, and mystical terms of its forerunner. (Local societies were *klaverns*, its leader the Imperial Wizard,

its book of rituals the *kloran*.) But the new Klan was broader in membership and in objectives than the old. Its chapters fanned outward from the deep South and for a time wielded frightening power in all other regions of the country. And unlike the first Klan, which terrorized mostly emancipated blacks, the new Klan directed its venom toward a variety of groups.

One brief phrase expressed the Klan's objectives: "Native, white, Protestant supremacy." *Native* meant no immigration, no "mongrelization" of white Protestant culture. According to Imperial Wizard Hiram Wesley Evans, *white* supremacy was a matter of survival. "The world," he warned, "has been so made so that each race must fight for its life, must conquer, accept slavery, or die. The Klansman believes the whites will not become slaves, and he does not intend to die before his time." Evans praised *Protestantism* for permitting "unhampered individual development." The Catholic Church, on the other hand, prevented immigrants from assimilating and suppressed free conscience by subordinating people to priests and a foreign pope.

Using threatening assemblies, violence, and political pressure, Klan members made their presence felt in many communities in the early 1920s. Assuming the role of moral protector, they meted out vigilante justice to bootleggers, wife beaters, and adulterers; forced schools to adopt Bible readings and stop teaching the theory of evolution; and campaigned against Catholic and Jewish political candidates. By the mid-1920s, however, the Invisible Empire was on the wane, outnumbered by its foreign-stock opponents and rocked by scandal. (In 1925 Indiana Grand Dragon David Stephenson allegedly kidnapped and raped a woman who later died either from taking poison or from an infection caused by bites on her body; Stephenson was convicted of second-degree murder on the grounds that he was responsible for her suicide.) The Klan's negative, exclusive brand of patriotism and purity could not compete in a pluralistic society.

The Ku Klux Klan had no monopoly on bigotry. The 1920s bared the pervasiveness of intolerance in American society. Since the 1880s a number of groups had been urging an end to free immigration. Huge influxes of Catholic and Jewish immigrants, these nativists charged, clogged inner-city slums, upset traditional norms with their drinking habits, and stubbornly held to alien religious and political beliefs.

Sacco and Vanzetti, painted by Ben Shahn. The trial and execution of the two immigrant anarchists touched the consciences of many artists and writers, prompting them to incorporate social themes in their work.   Collection, The Museum of Modern Art, New York. Gift of Abby Aldrich Rockefeller.

As self-styled expert Madison Grant wrote in *The Passing of the Great Race* (1916): "These immigrants adopt the language of the native American, they wear his clothes, they steal his name and they are beginning to take his women, but they seldom adopt his religion or understand his ideals."

Fear of radicalism, left over from the Red Scare of 1919, fueled these antiforeign sentiments. The most notorious outburst of hysteria occurred in 1921, when a court convicted Nicola Sacco and Bartolomeo Vanzetti, two immigrant anarchists, of murdering a guard and paymaster during a robbery in South Braintree, Massachusetts. But Sacco and Vanzetti's main offenses seem to have been their political beliefs and Italian origins, since evidence failed to prove their involvement in the robbery.

Sacco and Vanzetti

Judge Webster Thayer nevertheless openly sided with the prosecution, privately calling the defendants "those anarchist bastards." Appeals by protesters failed to win a new trial, and the two Italians, who remained calm and dignified throughout their ordeal, were executed in August 1927. Their deaths chilled those who had looked to the United States as the land that nurtured freedom of belief.

Meanwhile, the move to restrict immigration was gathering support. Labor leaders warned that a flood of aliens would depress wages and raise unemployment. Business executives who had formerly opposed restrictions because immigrant laborers were easy to exploit changed their minds when they discovered that mechanization and the hiring of native black workers could enable them to keep labor costs low. Drawing support from these groups as well as other

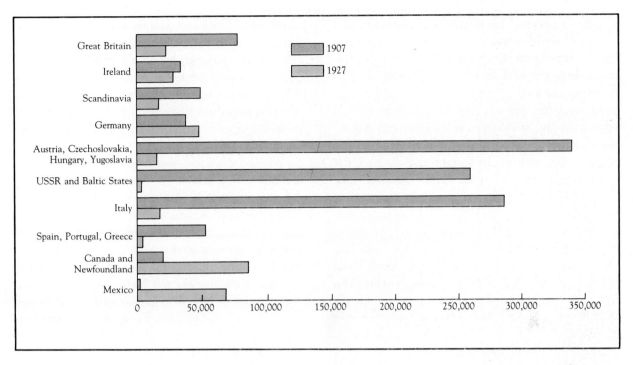

Immigration, 1907 and 1927

nativists, Congress established yearly immigration quotas for each nationality.

These quotas favored northern and western Europeans, reflecting the prejudices of natives against newer immigrant groups from southern and eastern Europe. The Emergency Quota, or Johnson, Act of 1921 provided that the annual immigration of any given nationality could not exceed 3 percent of the number of immigrants from that nation residing in the United States in 1910. But this law, meant to be temporary, did not satisfy restrictionists' aims, so Congress replaced it with the National Origins Act of 1924. The new law set the quota at 2 percent of each nationality residing in the United States in *1890*, further limiting the influx of southern and eastern Europeans, since far fewer of these groups lived in the United States in 1890 than in 1910. The National Origins Act was amended in 1927, at which time Congress moved the base year to 1920 and set a limit of 150,000 immigrants a year—including 65,721 from Great Britain and 25,957 from Germany, but only 5,802 from Italy and 2,712 from Russia. These laws virtually excluded Asians, but left the

Immigration Quotas

door open to peoples from the Western Hemisphere. Soon Canadians, Mexicans, and Puerto Ricans became the largest groups of newcomers (see figure).

The impulse to insure moral purity also stirred religious fundamentalists. Millions of Americans sought certainty in a rapidly changing world by following the evangelical branches of Protestantism that accepted a literal interpretation of the Bible. For them unquestioning faith was not only a means to salvation but a traditional and highly comforting defense against the skepticism and irreverence of a materialistic, hedonistic society.

In 1925 fundamentalist Christianity clashed with new scientific theory in a celebrated case in Dayton, Tennessee. Early that year the Tennessee legislature passed a law forbidding public school instructors to teach the theory that humans had evolved from lower forms of life rather than from Adam and Eve. Shortly thereafter, high school teacher John Thomas Scopes was arrested for violating the law (he had volunteered to serve in a test case). Scopes's trial that summer became a headline event, with William Jennings Bryan, former secretary of state and three-time pres-

Scopes Trial

idential candidate, arguing for the prosecution, and a team of civil-liberties lawyers headed by Clarence Darrow arguing for the defense. Hordes of news correspondents crowded into town, and radio stations broadcast the trial.

Although Scopes was convicted—clearly he had broken the law—modernists claimed victory; the testimony, they believed, had shown fundamentalism to be at odds with secular social trends. Indeed, the trial's climax occurred when Bryan agreed to take the witness stand as an expert on religion and science. Responding to Darrow's probing, Bryan asserted that Eve had truly been created from Adam's rib; that a big fish had swallowed Jonah; and that God had created the world in six days—though Bryan noted that a "day" might have lasted a million years. The liberal press mocked Bryan's uncritical faith; humorist Will Rogers quipped, "I see you can't say that man descended from the ape. At least that's the law in Tennessee. But do they have a law to keep a man from making a jackass of himself?" Nevertheless, fundamentalists nursed their wounds and steadfastly pursued their cause of faith and salvation.

Ku Klux Klan rallies, immigration restriction, and fundamentalist protests might be seen as last gasps of a rural society yielding to modern urban-industrial values. Yet city dwellers swelled the ranks of these defensive movements. Nearly half the Klan's members lived in cities, especially in native white working-class neighborhoods, where fear of invasion by blacks and foreigners was strong. Even urban reformers backed laws limiting immigration, seeing them as a means of controlling poverty and quickening the assimilation of foreign groups. Cities also housed hundreds of pentecostal churches, which attracted whites struggling between the middle and lower classes. Such people were swayed by the pageantry and closeness to God these churches offered. Using elaborately staged services, radio broadcasts, and modern advertising techniques, cult leaders such as Aimee Semple McPherson of Los Angeles stirred revivalist fervor. Finally, many urban dwellers supported prohibition. Middle-class Protestants and even some Catholics and Jews believed that by eliminating the temptation of drink they could win the battle against poverty, vice, and corruption.

The emotional responses Americans made to events during the 1920s were part of a larger attempt to sustain old, local values in a fast-moving, materialistic world. Occasionally Americans lashed out at minority cultures and seemingly hedonistic trends in behavior. Millions of otherwise decent Americans firmly believed that nonwhites and immigrants were inferior people who threatened existing values. And evangelists who preached against evolution were rare compared to the number of clergy and teachers of all faiths who condemned drinking, dancing, new styles of dress, and new sexual habits.

Even as they worried about losing old values, most Americans tried to adjust to the new order in one way or another. Few refrained from attending motion pictures or listening to the radio, activities that proved less corrupting than critics feared. Radio featured harmless music, news, and homey drama. And the movie industry bowed to pressure from legislatures in 1927 and instituted self-censorship, forbidding nudity, rough language, and plots that did not end with justice triumphant. More than ever, Americans sought fellowship in civic organizations. Membership swelled in Rotary, Kiwanis, Lions, Elks, and women's clubs, and the number of community chests—associations that coordinated civic and welfare projects—grew from 12 in 1919 to 361 in 1930. But perhaps most important, more and more people were finding release in a world of leisure.

THE AGE OF PLAY

During the 1920s Americans developed an almost insatiable thirst for recreation. In 1919 they spent about $2.5 billion on leisure activities; by 1929 such expenditures topped $4.3 billion, a figure that would not again be equaled until after the Second World War. Spectator amusements—movies, theater, sports, and the like—accounted for about 21 percent of the figure for 1929. Individual recreation, from participation sports to reading, hobbies, music, and travel, took up the remainder.

Entrepreneurs responded quickly. The decade marked the flowering of fads, frivolities, and what contemporaries called ballyhoo, a blitz of publicity that lent exaggerated importance to some person or event. New games and fancies were particularly attractive to middle-class families with large spendable incomes. In the early 1920s the Chinese tile game of mahjongg was the rage. Merchants could not import enough of the games, so dozens of American manufacturers began to produce them. By the mid-1920s people were turning to crossword puzzles, which mass-circulation newspapers and magazines had begun printing a decade earlier. In 1924 the new publishing firm of Simon and Schuster brought out a book of crossword puzzles with a pencil attached—anyone who did a crossword puzzle in pen was labeled a foolish optimist—and the volume became an instant best seller. A few years later fun seekers adopted miniature golf as their new craze. By 1930 some thirty thousand miniature golf courses featuring tiny castles, windmills, and waterfalls dotted cities and towns across the country. And throughout the decade dance crazes like the Charleston riveted public attention, aided by radio music and the growing popularity of jazz.

In addition to their active participation in leisure activities, Americans were avid spectators, particularly of movies and sports. In terms of total capital investment, motion pictures became one of the nation's leading industries.

Movies

Nearly every community had at least one theater, whether it was a hundred-seat Bijou on Main Street or a big-city picture palace with ornate walls, fountains in the lobby, and thousands of cushioned seats. In 1922 movies attracted 40 million viewers a week; by 1930 the number had reached 100 million—at a time when total population was just over 120 million and total weekly church attendance was under 60 million. The introduction of sound in *The Jazz Singer* in 1927 and of color a few years later made movies even more attractive and realistic. Movie producers provided the public fantasy and vicarious escape more than they did a serious new art form. The most popular films were mass spectacles such as Cecil B. DeMille's *The Ten Commandments* (1923) and *The King of Kings* (1927); lurid titles such as *Souls for Sale* (1923) and *A Woman Who Sinned* (1924); and slapstick comedies starring Fatty Arbuckle, Harold Lloyd, Buster Keaton, and Charlie Chaplin. Ironically, the comedies, with their often poignant satire of the human condition, carried the most thought-provoking messages.

Spectator sports also boomed. Each year millions packed stadiums, arenas, and parks to watch athletic events. By the late 1920s gate receipts from college football alone had surpassed $21 million. In an age when technology and mass production had robbed experiences and objects of their uniqueness, sports provided the unpredictability and drama that people craved. Newspapers and radio captured and exaggerated this drama, feeding news to an eager public and often overpromoting events with unrestrained narrative. Thus in 1920 the otherwise staid *New York Times* resorted to wild hyperbole to summarize a tennis match between William Tilden, the national champion, and challenger William Johnston:

> The Tilden-Johnston struggle will go down on the records as the most astounding exhibition of tennis, the most nervewracking battle that the courts have ever seen. . . . Tilden and Johnston played five acts of incredible melodrama, with a thrill in every scene, with horrible errors leading suddenly to glorious achievements with skill and courage and good and evil fortune. . . . Tilden's victory was a triumph for supertennis.

With reporting like this, sports promoters did not need to buy advertisements.

Baseball, with its drawn-out suspense, infinite variety of plays, and potential for statistics-keeping, attracted a huge following. After the World Series scandal of 1919, in which eight members of the Chicago White Sox were accused of taking bribes to lose games (they were acquitted in 1921), the two major professional leagues appointed Kenesaw Mountain Landis, a federal district judge, as baseball commissioner. Landis gave the game renewed respectability by rooting out alleged dishonest players. At the same time, the nature of the game changed. Discovering that home runs aroused excitement, the leagues redesigned the ball to make it livelier. Thereafter, attendance at major-league games skyrocketed. In 1921 a record 300,000 people attended the six-game World Series between the New York Giants and the New York Yankees. That same year millions more gathered regularly to watch their local teams take on nearby rivals.

Sports, movies, and the news gave Americans a galaxy of heroes. As society became more anonymous and the individual less significant, people clung to heroic personalities as a means of identifying with the unique. Though names such as Tilden in tennis,

The first million-dollar fight. Close to 90,000 people jammed an arena in Jersey City, New Jersey, on July 2, 1921, to witness heavyweight boxing champion Jack Dempsey knock out Georges Carpentier in the fourth round. The fight grossed $1.8 million, more than twice as much as any previous match. Brown Brothers.

Ederle in swimming and Bobby Jones in golf became household words, boxing, football, **Sports Heroes** and baseball produced the biggest sports heroes. Heavyweight champion Jack Dempsey, a powerful brawler from Manassa, Colorado, attracted the first of many million-dollar gates in his fight with Georges Carpentier in 1921. Harold "Red" Grange, running back for the University of Illinois football team, thrilled thousands and became the idol of sportswriters. During his senior year in 1925 Grange was offered huge contracts by real-estate and motion-picture companies, collected $42,000 for his first two games as a professional with the Chicago Bears, and received a petition from admirers who wanted him to run for Congress.

Baseball's major hero was George Herman "Babe" Ruth, who began his career as a pitcher but found

he could use his prodigious strength to better advantage hitting home runs. Ruth hit 29 of them in 1919, 54 in 1920, the year he moved from the Boston Red Sox to the New York Yankees, 59 in 1924, and 60 in 1927—each year a record. His exaggerated gestures on the field, defiant life style, and boyish grin endeared him to millions, and he became a national legend. Known for overindulgence in food, drink, and women, Ruth missed almost two months of the 1925 season when he was hospitalized with "the stomach ache that was heard round the world." But he usually made fans forget his excesses by appearing at public events and making special efforts to visit children in hospitals.

If Americans identified with the physical exploits of sports stars, they fulfilled a yearning for romance and adventure through adulation of movie stars. The films and personal lives of Douglas Fairbanks, Gloria

Rudolph Valentino in The Sheik, *his most famous movie. With flashing eyes and wanton smile, Valentino carries a swooning woman to his tent. This immensely popular movie earned a million dollars for Paramount Pictures. Museum of Modern Art Film Still Archive.*

Swanson, Charlie Chaplin, and scores of others were discussed in parlors and pool halls across the country. Perhaps the decade's most ballyhooed personality was Rudolph Valentino, whose Latin machismo made women swoon and prompted men to copy his pomaded hairdo and slick sideburns. Valentino's films exploited the era's new-found sexual liberalism and flirtation with evil. Playing a sheik who passionately snatched women into his arms and carried them into his tent, he combined the roles of seducer and abductor. When Valentino died of complications from ulcers and appendicitis at the age of thirty-one, the press turned his funeral into a public extravaganza. Crowds lined up for over a mile to file past his coffin.

News promoters created their own heroes outside the worlds of athletics and entertainment. For two weeks in 1925, newspapers kept readers on edge with reports on the plight of Floyd Collins, trapped in a Kentucky cave. Rescuers eventually found Collins dead, but not before the entire country had idolized him as a hero battling nature. Flagpole sitters, marathon dancers, and other record seekers regularly occupied the front pages. The most notable news hero was Charles A. Lindbergh, the pilot whose daring nonstop solo flight across the Atlantic in 1927 was cheered by millions. A modest, independent midwesterner whom writers dubbed the Lone Eagle, Lindbergh accepted fame but did not try to profit from it. Because his quiet personality contrasted so starkly with the ballyhoo that surrounded him, Americans honored him even more fervently. A few months after Lindbergh returned from Paris to a mammoth reception, columnist Mary B. Mullett wrote in *American Magazine:*

Movie Stars and Public Heroes

We shouted ourselves hoarse. Not because a man had flown across the Atlantic! Not even because he was an American! But because he was as clean in character as he was strong and fine in body; because he put "ethics" above any desire for wealth; because he was as modest as he was courageous; and because—as we know beyond any shadow of doubt—*these are the things which we honor most* in life.

In part the adulation of Lindbergh may have reflected guilt over betrayal of the virtues Mullett extolled. For in their quest for fun and individual

Prohibition

expression—liberties that prohibition seemed to deny—Americans became lawbreakers and supporters of crime. The constitutional amendment and federal law that prohibited the manufacture, sale, and transportation of alcoholic beverages (see page 595) worked very well at first. Per capita consumption of liquor dropped, arrests for drunkenness diminished, and the price of illegal booze rose higher than the average worker could afford. But beyond passing supportive laws, legislators saw little need to enforce prohibition. In 1922 Congress gave the Prohibition Bureau only three thousand employees and less than $7 million for nationwide enforcement.

Prohibition was especially effective in regions where temperance movements had historically been successful. In fact, some people believe that, had it applied only to hard liquor, not beer or wine, it might have succeeded more widely. But after about 1925 the noble experiment broke down in the cities, where the desire for personal freedom overwhelmed the weak means of enforcement. The law allowed the manufacture of beer for dilution into near-beer and the sale of alcohol for medicinal and sacramental purposes, but bootleggers cleverly obtained and sold such spirits for other purposes. Smuggling and home manufacture of liquor were rampant. Hundreds of thousands of people made their own wine and bathtub gin, and illegal importation along the country's long borders and shorelines was beyond the reach of the few patrols that attempted to curb it.

Local officials realized it was impractical to devote their scarce resources to strict enforcement of Prohibition. For drinking, like gambling and prostitution, was a business that had willing cus-

Al Capone

tomers. Criminal organizations were quick to recognize the possibilities of the situation. The most notorious of such mobs belonged to Al Capone, a burly tough who seized control of illegal liquor and vice organizations in Chicago and exercised his influence through bribery, intimidation, and violence. With his armed force of gangsters, Capone was able to influence local politics as well as vice operations until 1931, when the federal government convicted and imprisoned him for income-tax evasion.

It is important to recognize that Prohibition and its weak enforcement did not create organized crime. Gangs like Capone's had provided illegal goods and services long before the 1920s. As Capone explained it, "Prohibition is a business. All I do is supply a public demand. I do it in the least harmful way I can." Americans wanted their liquor and their freedom; Capone took advantage of these desires.

Thus during the 1920s Americans were caught between two value systems. On the one hand, the Puritan tradition of hard work, sobriety, and restraint—"waste not, want not"—still prevailed, especially in rural areas where new diversions were unavailable. On the other hand, a liberating age of play beckoned. At no previous time in American history had so many opportunities for recreation presented themselves. Not just mass entertainment such as nightclubs, movies, sports, and radio, but individual amusements such as stamp collecting, puzzle working, and playing and listening to music became commonplace. Most of these activities were not illegal or immoral, but many people were increasingly willing to break the law or shun moral tradition if such restrictions interfered with their personal quest for pleasure. As Walter Lippmann wrote in 1931, "The high level of lawlessness is maintained by the fact that Americans desire to do so many things which they also desire to prohibit."

CULTURAL CURRENTS

This tension between value systems pulled artists and intellectuals in new directions. Rejection of old beliefs energized an experimental movement in literature, art, and music. Fear that materialism and conformity were being fostered by mass society gave this movement a bitterly critical tinge. Yet critics seldom voiced a radical message; they had no urge to destroy modern society, only to protect the individual from dehumanizing forces.

Many of the era's leading literary figures, finding the vulgar materialism of the time hostile to their art, succumbed to disillusionment and became known as the Lost Generation. A number

Literature of Alienation

of them, including the novelist Ernest Hemingway and the poets Ezra Pound and T. S. Eliot, moved to Europe. Others, such as the novelists William Faulkner and Sinclair Lewis, remained, but assailed what they saw happening around them. Along with innovative forms of expression and the realistic portrayal of emotions, these writers also produced biting social commentary.

The dominant themes of their social criticism were middle- and upper-class materialism and the impersonality of modern society. F. Scott Fitzgerald's *This Side of Paradise* (1920) and *The Great Gatsby* (1925); Lewis's *Babbitt* (1922), *Arrowsmith* (1925), and *Elmer Gantry* (1927); and Eugene O'Neill's plays exposed Americans' overemphasis on money. The powerful antiwar sentiments of John Dos Passos's *Three Soldiers* (1921) and Hemingway's *A Farewell to Arms* (1929) were skillfully interwoven with passionate critiques of the impersonality of modern relationships.

Perhaps the most trenchant social criticism flowed from the pen of H. L. Mencken. A Baltimore newspaperman and founder of the *American Mercury*, Mencken jabbed at prevailing customs with stinging cynicism. No group, no individual was too sacred to escape his satire. He jeered at the inane quest for status of the middle-class "booboisie," labeled Woodrow Wilson a "self-bamboozled presbyterian," and scorned political reformers as "saccharine liberals" and "jitney messiahs." A man with a unique flair for language, Mencken could not stomach its misuse. He once charged that President Harding

writes the worst English I have ever encountered. It reminds me of a string of wet sponges; it reminds me of tattered wash on the line, it reminds me of stale bean soup, of college yells, of dogs barking idiotically through endless nights. . . . It drags itself out of the dark abyss . . . of pish and crawls insanely up to the topmost pinnacle of posh.

A spiritual discontent quite different from that of white writers inspired the work of a new generation of young black artists. Largely middle-class and well-educated, these writers often rejected

Harlem Renaissance

the amalgamation of black and white cultures, exalting the militantly assertive "New Negro," proud of his or her African heritage. Most of them lived in Harlem, the black section of upper Manhattan. In this "Negro Mecca" black intellectuals and artists, aided by a few white patrons, celebrated modern black culture in what became known as the Harlem Renaissance.

Harlem in the 1920s fostered a number of gifted writers, among them Langston Hughes, who wrote forceful and sometimes humorous poems, stories, and essays; Countee Cullen, a poet with moving lyrical skills; and Claude McKay, whose militant verses sounded a clarion call for rebellion against bigotry. Jean Toomer's novels and poems portrayed black life with passionate realism, and Alain Locke's essays gave direction to the artistic renaissance. Much of this group's writing addressed issues of identity. For though black intellectuals took pride in African culture, they also realized that black Americans had to assert themselves and come to terms with themselves as Americans. Thus Locke urged that the New Negro should "lay aside the status of beneficiary and ward for that of a collaborator and participant in American civilization." Simultaneously, Hughes wrote, "We younger Negro artists who create now intend to express our individual dark-skinned selves without fear or shame. If white people are pleased we are glad. If they are not, it doesn't matter. We know we are beautiful."

Although black authors did not reach many people (Jean Toomer's stirring novel *Cane* sold only five hundred copies when it was first published), black

Jazz

musicians had considerable influence. The Jazz Age, as the decade is sometimes called, owed its name to the music that grew out of black urban culture. Evolving from African and black American folk music, early jazz communicated unrestrained freedom that black people seldom knew in their public, working, or political lives. With its emotional rhythms and emphasis on improvisation, jazz blurred the distinction between composer and performer and created a new intimacy between performer and audience.

Jazz, a music form that was originated and developed by black artists such as those posing in this photograph, became America's most distinctive art form in the first half of the twentieth century. Its unrestrained improvisational qualities reflected the joys and sorrows of life and the freedom that blacks were denied in white society.   The New York Public Library.

As blacks moved north from the Mississippi Delta, they brought jazz with them. By the 1920s dance halls and bars featured jazz, sometimes popularized by white musicians such as Paul Whiteman and Bix Biederbecke. Gifted black performers like trumpeter Louis Armstrong, trombonist Kid Ory, and singer Bessie Smith enjoyed widespread fame. Phonograph records and radio, better suited than sheet music to the spontaneity of jazz, helped to popularize it. In fact, jazz boosted the recording industry immensely, and music recorded by black artists and bought by millions of black purchasers (sometimes called race records) gave black Americans a distinctive place in the new consumer culture. More important, jazz endowed America with its most distinctive art form.

In many ways the 1920s were the most creative years the nation had yet experienced. Influenced by jazz and by experimental writing, painters such as Georgia O'Keeffe and John Marin tried to forge a distinctively American style of painting. And although European composers and performers still dominated classical music, Americans such as Henry Cowell, who pioneered electronic music, and Aaron Copland, who built orchestral and vocal works around native folk motifs, began careers that later won wide acclaim. George Gershwin gave popular music increased respectability by blending jazz, classical, and folk musical forms in his serious compositions (*Rhapsody in Blue*, 1924 and *Concerto in F*, 1925), musical dramas (*Funny Face*, 1927), and numerous hit tunes. In architecture the skyscraper boom drew worldwide attention, and Frank Lloyd Wright's "prairie-style" houses, churches, and schools reflected the magnificence of the American landscape. At the beginning of the decade, essayist Harold Stearns had complained that "the most . . . pathetic fact in the social life of America today is emotional and aesthetic starvation." By 1929 such a contention was hard to support.

THE ELECTION OF 1928

Whatever doubts intellectuals may have had about materialism in the 1920s faded before the confident rhetoric of politics. Herbert Hoover epitomized that confidence in his speech accepting the Republican nomination for president in the summer of 1928. "We in America today," Hoover boasted, "are nearer to the final triumph over poverty than ever before in the history of any land. . . . We have not yet reached the goal, but, given a chance to go forward with the policies of the last eight years, we shall soon, with the help of God, be in sight of the day when poverty will be banished from this nation."

Hoover was an apt candidate for the Republicans in 1928 (Coolidge chose not to run for re-election), because he blended old values of success through individual hard work with the new emphasis on collective action. A Quaker from West Branch, Iowa, who was orphaned at the age of ten, Hoover worked his way through Stanford University and became a wealthy mining engineer. During and after the First World War, he distinguished himself as U.S. food administrator and as head of food relief for Europe. As secretary of commerce under Harding and Coolidge, Hoover expanded Theodore Roosevelt's New Nationalism. Recognizing the extent to which large nationwide associations had come to dominate commerce and industry, Hoover mounted a campaign calculated to stimulate cooperation between business and government. He took every opportunity to make his department a center for the promotion of business, encouraging formation of trade associations, holding conferences, sponsoring studies, and issuing reports, all aimed at improving production, marketing, and profitability. His active leadership prompted one observer to quip that Hoover was "Secretary of Commerce and assistant secretary of everything else."

As Hoover's opponent, the Democrats chose Governor Alfred E. Smith of New York, whose career contrasted markedly with that of Hoover. Whereas Hoover had rural, native, Protestant, business roots and had never run for public office, **Al Smith** Smith was an urbane, gregarious

Herbert Hoover

IMPORTANT EVENTS

1919	Eighteenth Amendment ratified
1920	Nineteenth Amendment ratified
	Harding elected president
	First commercial radio broadcast
1920–21	Postwar deflation and depression
1921	Federal Highway Act
	Immigration quotas established
	Sacco and Vanzetti convicted
1922	Economic recovery
1923	Harding dies; Coolidge assumes presidency
	Peak of Ku Klux Klan activity
	Equal Rights Amendment introduced
1923–24	Exposure of government scandals
1924	National Origins Act
	Coolidge elected president
1925	Scopes trial
1927	Sacco and Vanzetti executed
	Lindbergh's transatlantic flight
	Babe Ruth hits sixty home runs
	The Jazz Singer first sound movie
1928	Stock market soars
	Hoover elected president

politician of immigrant stock whose career was rooted in New York City's Tammany Hall. Smith was also the first Roman Catholic to run for president on a major party ticket. As such, he had considerable appeal among urban ethnic groups, who were voting in increasing numbers, but he lost southern and rural votes for the same reason. During his governorship, Smith had compiled a strong record as a promoter of progressive reforms and civil rights, but his campaign failed to build a reform coalition of farmers and city dwellers because he stressed issues that were not likely to unite these groups. That is, he openly opposed prohibition, and he struck back at charges that his Catholicism made him a servant of the Pope.

Though Smith waged a dynamic campaign, Hoover, who stressed the nation's prosperity, won the popular vote by 21 million to 15 million, the electoral vote by 444 to 87. But Smith's candidacy had important effects on the Democratic party. Smith carried the nation's twelve largest cities, which formerly had given majorities to Republican candidates, and lured millions of foreign-stock voters to the polls for the first time. From 1928 onward, the Democratic party would solidify this urban base, which when combined with its traditional strength in the South made the party a formidable force in national elections.

Democrats and Republicans both had reasons to be encouraged in 1928. But a few people had begun to grow uneasy over the nation's economic climate. Just before Hoover stood in front of his party and predicted the conquest of poverty, a banker surveyed the soaring stock market and observed,

> Stocks look dangerously high to me. This bull market has been going on for a long time and although prices have slipped a bit recently, they might easily slip a good deal more. Business is none too good. Of course if you buy the right stock you'll probably be all right in the long run and you may even make a profit. But if I were you I'd wait awhile and see what happens.

Little did the banker know how sound his advice was. In the next several years the era of expansion and frivolity would end, and the economy would have to be rebuilt.

SUGGESTIONS FOR FURTHER READING

Overviews of the 1920s

Frederick Lewis Allen, *Only Yesterday* (1931); John Braeman et al., eds., *Change and Continuity in Twentieth Century America: The 1920s* (1968); Paul A. Carter, *Another Part of the Twenties* (1977); Ellis Hawley, *The Great War and the Search for a Modern Order* (1979); John D. Hicks, *Republican Ascendancy* (1960); William E. Leuchtenburg, *The Perils of Prosperity* (1958); Robert Lynd and Helen Lynd, *Middletown* (1929); Donald R. McCoy, *Coming of Age* (1973); George Soule, *Prosperity Decade* (1947).

Business and the Economy

Irving L. Bernstein, *The Lean Years: A History of the American Worker, 1920–1933* (1960); Alfred D. Chandler, *Strategy and Structure* (1962); James J. Flink, *The Car Culture* (1975); Allan Nevins, *Ford*, 2 vols. (1954–1957); J. W. Prothro, *The Dollar Decade* (1954); John Rae, *The Road and the Car in American Life* (1971); Robert Zieger, *Republicans and Labor, 1919–1929* (1969).

Politics and Law

David Burner, *Herbert Hoover* (1979); David Burner, *The Politics of Provincialism* (1968); Paula Elder, *Governor Alfred E. Smith: The Politician as Reformer* (1983); J. Joseph Huthmacher, *Massachusetts People and Politics* (1959); Matthew Josephson and Hannah Josephson, *Al Smith* (1970); Allan J. Lichtman, *Prejudice and the Old Politics: The Presidential Election of 1928* (1979); Richard Lowitt, *George W. Norris* (1971); Samuel Lubell, *The Future of American Politics* (1952); Donald R. McCoy, *Calvin Coolidge* (1967); Alpheus Mason, *The Supreme Court from Taft to Warren* (1958); Robert K. Murray, *The Harding Era* (1969); Andrew Sinclair, *The Available Man* (1965); George Tindall, *The Emergence of the New South* (1967); James Weinstein, *The Decline of Socialism in America, 1912–1925* (1967); Joan Hoff Wilson, *Herbert Hoover: The Forgotten Progressive* (1975).

Blacks and Hispanics

Rodolfo Acuna, *Occupied America: A History of Chicanos* (1980); E. D. Cronon, *Black Moses: The Story of Marcus Garvey* (1955); Kenneth Kusmer, *A Ghetto Takes Shape* (1976); Matt S. Meier and Feliciano Rivera, *The Chicanos* (1972); Gilbert Osofsky, *Harlem: The Making of a Ghetto* (1965); Mark Reisler, *By the Sweat of Their Brows* (1976) (on Mexican-Americans); Alan Spear, *Black Chicago* (1967); Theodore Vincent, *Black Power and the Garvey Movement* (1971).

Women and the Family

W. Andrew Achenbaum, *Shades of Gray: Old Age, American Values, and Federal Policies Since 1920* (1983); William H. Chafe, *The American Woman: Her Changing Social, Economic, and Political Role* (1972); Ruth Schwartz Cowan, *More Work for Mother* (1983); David H. Fischer, *Growing Old in America* (1977); Linda Gordon, *Woman's Body, Woman's*

Right: A Social History of Birth Control in America (1976); J. Stanley Lemons, The Woman Citizen: Social Feminism in the 1920s (1973); Sheila Rothman, Woman's Proper Place (1978); Lois Scharf, To Work and to Wed (1980); Susan Strasser, Never Done: A History of American Housework (1982); Winifred D. Wandersee, Women's Work and Family Values, 1920–1940 (1981).

Lines of Defense

David M. Chalmers, Hooded Americanism: The History of the Ku Klux Klan (1965); Norman F. Furnis, The Fundamentalist Controversy (1954); Joseph R. Gusfeld, Symbolic Crusade (1963); John Higham, Strangers in the Land: Patterns of American Nativism (1955); Kenneth T. Jackson, The Ku Klux Klan and the City (1967); G. L. Joughin and E. M. Morgan, The Legacy of Sacco and Vanzetti (1948); William G. McLoughlin, Modern Revivalism (1959); Andrew Sinclair, Prohibition: The Age of Excess (1962).

Mass Culture

Erik Barbouw, A Tower of Babel: A History of Broadcasting in the United States to 1933 (1966); Robert Creamer, Babe (1974); Kenneth S. Davis, The Hero, Charles A. Lindbergh (1959); Paula Fass, The Damned and the Beautiful: American Youth in the 1920s (1977); Fred J. MacDonald, Don't Touch That Dial (1979); Otis Pease, The Responsibilities of American Advertising (1958); Randy Roberts, Jack Dempsey, The Manassa Mauler (1979); Philip T. Rosen, The Modern Stentors: Radio Broadcasting and the Federal Government, 1920–1933 (1980); Robert Sklar, Movie-made America (1976).

Literature and Thought

Robert Crunden, From Self to Society: Transition in American Thought, 1919–1941 (1972); George H. Douglas, H. L. Mencken (1978); Robert Elias, Entangling Alliances with None: An Essay on the Individual in the American Twenties (1973); Nathan I. Huggins, Harlem Renaissance (1971); David L. Lewis, When Harlem Was in Vogue (1981); Roderick Nash, The Nervous Generation: American Thought, 1917–1930 (1969); Marvin K. Singleton, H. L. Mencken and the American Mercury Adventure (1962); Kenneth M. Wheller and Virginia L. Lussier, eds., Women and the Arts and the 1920s in Paris and New York (1982).

THE SHAKEN DREAM
1929–1933

CHAPTER 25

"*Anything wrong with* my work for company?" asked an autoworker of Slavic descent who had just been fired by the Ford Motor Company after fourteen years of employment. No, his work had been good, but cars were not selling. "I have no money now . . . lose my home quick, what I do children, what I do doctor?" When two of his daughters went to work to support the family and their sick mother, he cried, "I ain't man now."

People like John Boris were among the three thousand men and women who gathered on March 7, 1932, for a hunger march to Ford's huge River Rouge plant in Dearborn, just outside Detroit, Michigan. Most of the marchers were unemployed Ford workers. Dearborn-Detroit authorities nonetheless blamed the march on the Communist party, which had in fact helped to plan the protest and to prepare the list of demands for jobs, food, medical aid, and the right to organize.

At the Dearborn line, the marchers, shivering from the near-zero temperature, were blocked by a phalanx of police. Ordered to disperse, they refused to retreat. When the police volleyed tear gas, the marchers hurled back rocks. Firefighters soon hosed down the demonstrators and Ford's stern-faced private police assembled. Suddenly shots rang out, killing two marchers. A policeman shouted, "Get your gats and let them have it." By the end of the skirmish, four marchers were dead, more than twenty wounded. Twenty-five police officers had to be treated for wounds from rocks and other objects.

The fundamental source of this trouble was not the Communist party, not the marchers, not the Dearborn police, not Henry Ford himself, but a nationwide disaster called the Great Depression. Detroit was especially hard hit; by fall 1932, 350,000 workers, or about half the city's wage earners, were unemployed. At the River Rouge plant, employment of hourly workers fell from 98,337 to 28,915 during Herbert Hoover's administration (1929–1933). The Ford Hunger March was just one of the many desperate American cries for relief from the pain of this very human tragedy.

Only three years earlier, optimism, not tragedy,

marked the nation's mood. Hoover administration officials knew that the economy suffered weaknesses and that society seethed with divisiveness, but they were confident men who believed they could solve or isolate the problems. What a shock the stock market crash of fall 1929 was to these leaders. Slowly but steadily cascading tremors rolled through the economy, and the nation moved from economic downturn to Great Depression. Many Americans watched their incomes dwindle or disappear and their health decline. Unemployment placed strains on relations within the family. Blacks and other minorities sank deeper into destitution. Working women, still located in sex-segregated jobs, some of which contracted less than those of men, heard renewed calls for their return to the home in order to open places for males in the labor market. Overall, the economic catastrophe aggravated old tensions: labor versus capital, white versus black, male versus female.

Americans tried to puzzle out the many interrelated causes of the depression, but to little avail. Questions of underconsumption and international trade, after all, bedeviled even the experts. Americans found it especially difficult to understand how people could be hungry when farmers' bins were overflowing or how workers could be unemployed when they remained able-bodied and eager and the factories stood in place. Only one thing was certain: too many Americans did not have enough money to buy the goods stocked in their local stores. Stunned by the magnitude of their plight, Americans' faith in themselves and in their dream of success was shaken. But they did not turn to violent revolt or political extremism. Their rootedness in the past—their traditionalism—would not let them. Instead, they improvised to survive, and they looked to their governments for help.

Although President Hoover activated the federal government more than any of his predecessors had done in an economic crisis, he opposed direct relief. When he refused to take measures strong enough to relieve their hardship, Americans peacefully resorted to a traditional method of voicing disapproval: they turned Hoover out of office in the election of 1932. They replaced the somber Hoover with smiling

Franklin D. Roosevelt, who had promised vigorous action and who projected hope in a time of despair.

THE NEW DAY

There was little sense of impending tragedy in 1928, when 62 percent of Wayne County (Detroit and Dearborn) voters cast their ballots for Republican presidential candidate Herbert Hoover. (In 1932 they would give him only 39 percent.) And in early 1929, when Hoover entered the White House, the byword was optimism. In his inaugural address the president proclaimed a New Day, telling his listeners that the future "is bright with hope."

The new president, known popularly as the Great Engineer, was a proven administrator who promised to bring efficiency to the federal government and harmony to society. He believed that America's economic growth would persist, that the country's problems were manageable. Yet privately Hoover worried that his reputation was being oversold. "They expect the impossible of me and should there arise in the land conditions with which the political machinery is unable to cope, I will be the one to suffer." Hoover's uneasiness also prompted him to sell all his common stock just a few months after taking office because "possible hard times [are] coming."

Hoover's government was a mixture of the old and the new. Sitting in the cabinet, composed largely of businessmen, were six millionaires. Andrew Mellon stayed on as secretary of the treasury. This vastly wealthy man's aluminum monopoly, petroleum and banking interests, and prized art collection marked him as one of the most successful practitioners of the American success story. With his icy and aloof personality and his heartlessness toward human suffering, Mellon contrasted sharply with Hoover, who had gained a reputation for compassion when he managed food relief for destitute Europeans during and after the First World War. On the whole, Hoover's appointees to high office were, like Mellon, smug devotees of the existing order, champions of a capitalist utopia. Innovation was not expected from them. In

Hoover Administration

Herbert Hoover (1874–1964), the wealthy mining engineer and businessman, headed a relief program during the First World War and served as Secretary of Commerce in the 1920s. His reputation for brilliance and compassion was tarnished when as president he faced the Great Depression.   Library of Congress.

the lower ranks, on the other hand, Hoover brought in the New Patriots, mostly young professionals who agreed with the president that scientific methods could be applied to government to solve its problems. The New Patriots, called such because they seemed willing to pass up opportunities for personal wealth to serve their nation, emphasized modernization of operations, collection of data, and rational decision-making. In time, Hoover and his experts believed, they could establish a stable social order based on cooperation between government and various civic groups.

If Hoover and his advisers were optimistic about the future, so were most Americans. To them American achievements seemed boundless. The new era of the 1920s had given birth to such exciting gadgets as radios and refrigerators. Americans owned 23 million automobiles, roughly three-quarters of the world's

This Judge *magazine cartoon titled "There is a Santa Claus," published in December 1929, captured well President Herbert Hoover's initial response to the Great Depression: build up business confidence. Then the economy—and the people—would enjoy once again the benefits of the American system. But confidence-building proved impossible as businesses and banks closed their doors and workers lost their jobs. Library of Congress.*

many of its offices were vacant in 1931 when Hoover pushed the button that turned on the building's innumerable lights—sad evidence that dreams could be undermined by economic realities. After walking its marbled hallways, critic Edmund Wilson remarked that it was tragic that the regal building "is advertised now as a triumph in the hour when the planless competitive society, the dehumanized urban community, of which it makes the culmination, is bankrupt."

Still, before the Great Depression sapped the national spirit, reverence for what Hoover called "the American system" ran high. The belief that individuals were responsible for their own condition, that unemployment or poverty suggested personal failing, was widespread. "It is as if we set a race," said Hoover. The individual, seizing the ever-present opportunity, had to demonstrate will power and ambition in the face of competition. The government provided the competitors with an equal start through public education and served as referee to ensure fairness. The winners were the people with the best training, ability, and character.

Prevailing thought also held that changes in the business cycle were natural and therefore not to be tampered with. Depressions were to be weathered stoically until the economy inevitably wound its way back to prosperity. As for the government, its job was limited: to ensure equal opportunity and to stimulate the economy through judicious advice and public works projects. "The spread of government," concluded Hoover, "destroys initiative and thus destroys character." He implored people to regulate themselves, to join voluntary associations (such as farm cooperatives and private charities) to right wrongs, but not to expect the federal government to bail them out of their difficulties.

Much of this thinking was, of course, shallow, self-serving, or utopian. Self-interested businesspeople had often tinkered with the system. Government had long played favorites or neglected to blow the referee's whistle. A few companies dominated each industry, squeezing out smaller firms. Equal opportunity was denied to Americans who were nonwhite or female. Educational programs were segregated and unequal. Both government and business were hostile to labor unions (in 1929 only 10 percent of the nonagricultural

total. Conquests of new frontiers seemed inevitable, and promoters strove to outdo each other in grandiose displays. As businesspeople in Chicago laid plans for the World's Fair, a huge celebration of material progress, Al Smith and Democratic party chairman John J. Raskob were organizing a company to build the tallest structure in the world, the Empire State Building. When this monument to the new era was completed, it stood 102 stories high on fashionable Fifth Avenue in New York and had through accidents cost the lives of forty-eight workers. Yet

Business Optimism

work force was unionized). Discriminatory wages for women and minorities, the stretch-out (more work for the same pay), automation, and safety hazards also plagued workers. In Waterbury, Connecticut, for example, clock workers risked death from radium poisoning. At least one-third of the nation's farmers were tenants or sharecroppers—dependent, propertyless, and unable even to join the race. Because of these conditions, income and wealth were maldistributed.

Hoover himself knew that not all was well. "The only trouble with capitalism is capitalists," he complained. "They're too damned greedy." Hoover's ideal capitalist was one who tempered his self-interest to advance the general welfare, who cooperated with others to build a progressive, nonexploitative society. He later admitted that most businesspeople did not approach this ideal.

Evidence that there was quite a difference between the optimistic spirit and rhetoric of the New Day and the reality of everyday life came in March 1929 in Elizabethton, Tennessee. In that **Elizabethton** textile town, where 40 percent of **Textile Strike** the rayon mill laborers were young women earning 16 to 18 cents an hour for a fifty-six-hour week, workers went on strike for better wages. The state militia marched in to break the strike, and employees who had joined the United Textile Workers found themselves blacklisted. By 1931, wrote one observer, what remained were a "few hundred unemployed ex-strikers, half-starved and disillusioned, cynical and justly bitter." Just a few months before the strike erupted, Hoover had addressed a large crowd in Elizabethton, extolling the progress of southern industry and its "great reserve of labor."

On the eve of the Great Depression, then, America seemed tangled in contradictions: optimism and pessimism; prosperity and hardship; individualism and mass culture; competition and cooperation; progress and deterioration; opportunity and inequality; strength and weakness. But the shortcomings of American life received far less attention than the dramatic accomplishments of the New Era. Then came the Great Depression to deflate the boom mentality, expose infirmities, prompt reanalysis, and redefine the role of the federal government.

THE GREAT CRASH AND THE GREAT DEPRESSION

The gloom and economic woe that people in mining towns, textile mills, and agricultural communities suffered at the end of the 1920s hardly penetrated the elegant offices of Wall Street. There, all seemed magical; glamour stocks such as General Electric, International Harvester, and Radio Corporation of America soared in value. By late 1928 one share of RCA cost $400, the equivalent of several months' income for many people. The bull market attracted millions of buyers, many of whom joined the speculative binge by buying their shares on margin (paying only a portion of the cost in cash and borrowing the rest) or investing their savings. By October 1929 brokers' loans to stock purchasers amounted to a staggering $8.5 billion. John J. Raskob, a member of General Motors' board of directors as well as chairman of the Democratic party, was so enthusiastic about the boom that he proclaimed that "anyone not only can be rich, but ought to be rich" by speculating in the stock market.

The get-rich-quick mentality was jolted in September and early October when stock prices dropped. Analysts attributed the dip to "shaking out the lunatic fringe." But on October 24, Black **Wall Street** Thursday, a record number of shares **Crash** was traded; many stocks sold at low prices, and some could find no takers. Stunned crowds gathered outside the frantic New York Stock Exchange, buzzing about the apparent seriousness of the decline. At noon, banking leaders met at the headquarters of J. P. Morgan and Company to halt the skid and restore confidence. They put up $20 million, told everybody about it, and ceremoniously began by buying ten thousand shares of United States Steel. The mood changed and some stocks rallied. The bankers, it seemed, had preserved the dream of success.

But the nation gradually succumbed to panic. News of Black Thursday spread across the country, and trouble ("sell!") ricocheted back to New York via

Reginald Marsh's sketch of the New York Stock Exchange on the day of the Great Crash revealed the more-than-usually hectic, noisy, and intense activity of trading in shares.   Library of Congress.

telephone. Another bolt struck on Black Tuesday (October 29) when stock prices plunged again. The market settled into a grim pattern of declines and weak rallies. Hoover, who had never approved of what he called the "fever of speculation," assured Americans that the economy was sound. He shared the popular assumption that the stock market's ills could be quarantined from a generally healthy economy. Businesspeople, schooled in the credo of progress, comforted themselves with the thought that the stock market would soon right itself. Although their boosterism seems terribly misguided or deceptive today, it was sincerely, if blindly, believed at the time. Anyway, said the secretary of labor, "one doesn't improve the condition of a sick man by constantly telling him how ill he is."

The crash ultimately helped to unleash a devastating depression. The economic downturn did not come suddenly; it was more like a leak in a punctured tire than a blowout. There were several interrelated causes of the Great Depression. The first was the increasing weakness of the economy in the 1920s. Had the economy of the new era been strong, it would have stood

Economic Weaknesses

a better chance of weathering the crash on Wall Street. In fact, some historians suggest that the stock market collapse merely moved an ongoing recession into depression. Throughout the 1920s the agricultural sector was plagued with overproduction, declining prices for farm products, mounting debts, bankruptcies, and small bank failures. Some industries, like coal, railroads, and textiles, were in distress long before 1929, and two mainstays of economic growth, autos and construction, also declined early (see pages 685–686). What all these weaknesses meant by 1929 was that major sectors of the economy were not expanding; businesspeople were not investing funds to build new plants, hire more workers, and produce more goods. Indeed, the opposite was true: unsold inventories were stacking up in warehouses, investments were shrinking, laborers were being sent home, and consumer purchases were dropping off.

Second and related, the onset and severity of the depression can be attributed to underconsumption. That is, production (supply) had outstripped consumption (demand). Wages and mass purchasing power had lagged behind the industrial surge of the 1920s; the workers who produced the new consumer products

**Under-
consumption** ultimately could not afford to buy them. Why did purchasing decline? Laborers and farmers constituted the great majority of consumers. Yet, as we have seen, farmers suffered economic distress and had to trim their purchases. And as industries like coal, autos, and construction declined, they laid off men and women who then lacked the money to sustain buying. Other laborers lost their jobs because machines displaced them. In Hartford and New Haven in 1929, for example, the installation of more efficient machinery threw 1,190 rubber workers out of their jobs. And 35,000 orchestra musicians were unemployed in mid-1929 because "machine music" had been installed in the nation's theaters. Overall, then, a sizable nonconsuming group had grown in America before the Great Depression hit.

Another important aspect of underconsumption was the unequal distribution of income. In the 1920s the rich got much richer while others made only **Unequal Distribution of Wealth** modest gains. Average per capita disposable income (income after taxes) rose about 9 percent from 1920 to 1929, but the income of the wealthiest 1 percent rose 75 percent. In 1929 experts estimated that about 60 percent of America's families lived on or below the subsistence level ($2,000 a year), despite a 29 percent increase in the number of employed married women over the decade. The Federal Trade Commission reported that 1 percent of the American people owned 59 percent of the country's wealth; 87 percent owned only 10 percent. Income and wealth, in other words, were concentrated at the top of America's economic ladder. Why did this uneven distribution contribute to underconsumption and depression? Because much of the accumulating income was put into luxuries, savings, investments, and stock-market speculation instead of being spent on consumer goods. Put another way, more money in the hands of workers and farmers and less money building up in the vaults of the wealthy would probably have meant more consumption and hence more stable economic growth.

Third, the American business system was shaky, for a few large corporations in each industry—oligopolies—unbalanced it. In 1929 **Large Corporations** the top two hundred nonfinancial corporations controlled 49 percent of corporate wealth. The old cliché "The bigger they are, the harder they fall" was literally true. Many companies speculated dangerously on the stock market and built pyramidlike businesses based on shady, if legal, manipulation of assets through holding companies. If one part of the edifice collapsed, the entire structure crumbled. Such was the case with Samuel Insull's mighty electrical empire based in Chicago. Insull built a utilities network that produced one-eighth of America's electrical power and operated in thirty-nine states. Within this vast system one company held the stock of another company, which held the stock of another company, and so on. Sometimes Insull's various companies bought stock from one another, each showing an artificially high profit from the transactions. Even Insull admitted that he was not sure how it all worked; his sixty-five chairmanships, eighty-five directorships, and seven presidencies confused him as much as anybody else. When his interlocking network collapsed in 1932, he fled to Europe to escape arrest for fraud. Found in Turkey, he returned to the United States, hired advertising agencies to improve his public image, and in 1934 was acquitted.

The depression derived, fourth, from pell-mell, largely unregulated, speculation on the stock market. Corporations and banks invested large sums in stocks; some speculated in their own issues. **Speculation on the Stock Market** Brokers sold stocks to buyers who put up little cash, borrowed in order to purchase, and then used the stocks they bought as collateral for their loans. When the stocks came tumbling down, so did brokers, bankers, and companies. Brokers called up buyers to ask for more cash. Some buyers drained their savings from banks, but when others could not come up with the money, the brokers sold the stock for the little it would command. Bankers, meanwhile, were calling up brokers and other speculators, searching for cash. The domino effect was crushing, and the whole economic system tottered as obligations went unmet. From 1930 to 1933 stock-market losses climbed to $85 billion. A new byword circulated: "Trust God, not stocks."

International economic troubles constitute a fifth explanation for the coming of the depression. As the world's leading creditor and trader, the United States was deeply involved with the world economy. Billions of dollars in loans had flowed to Europe during the

International Economic Troubles First World War and then during postwar reconstruction. Yet in the late 1920s American investors were beginning to keep their money at home, to invest it in the more exciting and lucrative stock market. Europeans, unable to borrow more funds and unable to sell their goods easily in the American market because of high tariffs, began to buy less from America and to default on their debts. Pinched at home, they raised their own tariffs, further crippling international commerce, and withdrew their investments from America. It was Hoover's view that "the European disease had contaminated the United States." He would have been more accurate had he said that the European and American illnesses were mutually infectious.

Finally, government policies and practices contributed to the crash and depression. The federal government failed to regulate the **The Failure of** wild speculation, contenting itself **Federal Policies** with occasional scoldings of bankers and businesspeople. It neither checked corporate power nor raised income taxes to encourage a more equitable distribution of income. Indeed, it lowered taxes, thus promoting the uneven distribution. And the Federal Reserve Board pursued easy-credit policies, charging low discount rates, or interest rates, on its loans to member banks, even though it knew the easy money was paying for the speculative binge. The "Fed" blundered again after the crash, in 1931. This time the board drastically raised the rate, tightening the money market at a time when just the opposite was needed: loosening to spur borrowing and spending.

Today, in an era of computerized data, daily economic forecasts, and the watchdog Council of Economic Advisers (see page 833), it is difficult to recall that in 1929 the state of economic analysis and statistics-gathering was comparatively primitive. The several explanations for the onset of depression were not easily grasped in 1929, especially while people were absorbed in a headlong rush to make as much money as possible as fast as possible. And the conventional wisdom, based on the experience of previous depressions, was that little could be done to correct economic problems. So in 1929 people waited for the deflation to bottom out.

DESPAIRING AMERICANS

As the economy limped into the 1930s, statistics began to tell the story of a human tragedy. Between 1929 and 1933 a hundred thousand businesses failed; corporate profits fell from $10 billion to $1 billion; and the gross national product was cut in half. What happened to America's banks—and savings—illustrates especially well the cascading nature of the Great Depression. Banks tied into the stock market or foreign investments were badly weakened; some failed. When nervous Americans made runs on banks to salvage their threatened savings, a powerful momentum—panic—took command. In 1929, 659 banks folded; in 1930 the number of failures climbed to 1,350. The next year proved worse, 2,293 banks shutting their doors, and another 1,453 ceased to do business in 1932. By 1933 9 million savings accounts had been lost, amounting to $2.5 billion in losses. Americans who believed that saving was a virtue, a path to material fulfillment, discovered that their deposits had disappeared with the banks.

Americans lost savings—and jobs. Although most people remained employed, day after day thousands of men and women received severance slips. At the beginning of 1930 the number of jobless had reached at least 4 million; by November it had jumped to 6 million. When President Hoover left office in 1933, about one-fourth of the labor force was idle—13 million workers—and millions more were underemployed, working only part-time. Hoover asked businesspeople not to cut wages, but labor income dropped by 40 percent during his presidency. Half the workers in Cleveland went off payrolls; in Lowell, Massachusetts, two-thirds of the labor force was unemployed.

Blacks and the unskilled lost their jobs first; whites and managerial personnel were let go last. Black women were more likely to lose jobs than white women. In Cleveland, for example, one-half of black female workers were unemployed, compared with one-sixth of white female laborers. Desperate whites proved willing to take menial jobs once held largely by blacks, and because white employers preferred to hire whites, blacks were pushed out of the labor force. Thus many whites displaced blacks as domestic servants, and Atlanta fired its black sanitation workers to replace them with whites.

In 1930 over 10.5 million women were in the work force, composing 22 percent of all workers. Despite these statistics, most Americans believed that

Women Workers

women should not work outside the home, that they should strive instead to be good wives and mothers, and that women who worked were doing so for "pin money" to buy frivolous things. Moreover, the depression invigorated the longstanding charge that women in the labor force necessarily displaced male breadwinners. One Chicago civic group protested that women "are holding jobs that rightfully belong to the God-intended providers of the household." Married women workers received the most criticism; some states even passed laws forbidding the hiring of married women for civil service positions. Such thinking missed the point, for two reasons. First, women were heavily concentrated in certain occupations or "women's jobs," including clerical positions (49 percent of all employees were women), teachers (81 percent), telephone operators (95 percent), and nurses (98 percent). Men rarely sought these "feminized" jobs and probably would not have been hired had they applied for such work. Second, most women workers (72 percent in 1930) were single, not married. Many were self-supporting or were keeping their families from slipping into poverty. Work was thus a necessity for them. Although married women, because of depression-induced hardship, entered the labor force in greater numbers, they do not seem to have displaced men.

The depression thus affected women workers in different ways from their male counterparts. Women suffered the stings of popular antagonism toward their employment. The depression retarded the movement of women into professional occupations. But the rate of unemployment for women was lower than that for men. Why? Because "men's jobs" (in manufacturing, for example) were harder hit by the depression than were women's sex-typed occupations; because, given traditional wage discrimination, women were cheaper to hire than men; and because men did not think of competing for feminized secretarial or nursing jobs.

The experience of teachers provides an example. Because women accounted for four-fifths of all teachers in 1930, the depression's damage to school systems particularly alarmed women. Some towns failed to meet payrolls. To save money, others shortened terms, released teachers, increased class loads, eliminated kindergartens and art and music classes, or shut down schools altogether. In 1931–1932, about 5,000 rural schools closed across the nation. Of the 1,500 urban school systems surveyed by the National Education Association in 1930–1931, 77 percent refused to hire married women as teachers and 63 percent fired female teachers who married while employed. Still, fewer jobs were lost in teaching than in occupations more associated with males. By fall 1933 only 8 percent of the teaching force was unemployed, whereas the figure for the entire American work force had reached 25 percent.

How could a nation of such abundance and high production, with its factories intact and its workers eager to work, find itself saddled with such utter hardship? men and women asked themselves. It was difficult for Americans raised on the philosophy of hard work and self-help to understand the contradiction of poverty amidst plenty. "Why," asked one man, "must they wear shabby clothes? Because we have too much cotton, too much wool, too many mills, and too many hands." Humorist Will Rogers quipped, "We are the first nation in the history of the world to go to the poorhouse in an automobile."

Actually people were putting their cars up on blocks and using other means to search for work. In Detroit auto workers roamed from plant to plant, only to discover padlocked gates. "A worker's got no right to have kids any more," cried one. Western apple growers sent their surplus to the cities, where a new class of street-corner entrepreneurs peddled the fruit at five cents each. A reporter portrayed a New York City unemployment office: "The room is almost silent. A slight, despairing hum from the job seekers. Patient, stretched on the rack of a social system that compels this degradation, they stand quite mute. The suspense is painful." A Minneapolis woman described her futile daily vigil at the city unemployment department: "So we sit in this room like cattle waiting for a nonexistent job, willing to work to the farthest atom of energy, unable to work, unable to get food and lodging,

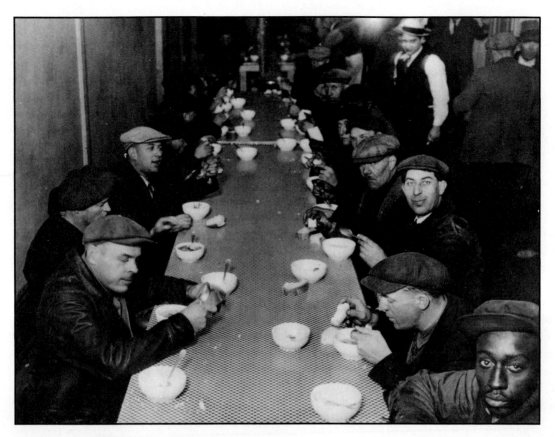

In Chicago in 1930 the gangster Al Capone's soup kitchen attracted hungry men eager for a free meal.   *Library of Congress.*

unable to bear children. Here we must sit in this shame looking at the floor, worse than beasts at a slaughter."

People's diets deteriorated, malnutrition became common, and the undernourished fell victim more easily to disease. Some people quietly lined up at Red Cross and Salvation Army soup kitchens or queued in breadlines. Others ate only potatoes, crackers, or dandelions, stole dog biscuits from the local dog pound, or scratched through garbage cans for bits of food. Milk consumption decreased to such an extent that Kentucky miners called it medicine. Pregnant women went without essential foods like eggs and vegetables. Because of inadequate diets doctors witnessed an increase in tuberculosis, typhoid, dysentery, and heart and stomach disorders. Lillian Wald of the Henry Street Settlement House in New York City saw semistarved parents trembling

Deterioration of Health

uncontrollably: what food they had they had given to their children. In that city in 1932, hospitals reported 95 deaths from starvation. The nation's suicide rate also climbed, though the overall death rate continued its long-term trend downward.

Millions of Americans were not only hungry and ill; they were cold. Unable to afford fuel, some huddled in unheated tenements and shacks. Families doubled up in crowded apartments, but some who were unable to pay the rent were evicted, furniture and all. Urban jungles sprouted up, constructed from packing boxes and other debris usually carted away as junk. Several hundred women took to sleeping in Chicago's Lincoln and Grant parks; in Oakland, California, hundreds of people lived in the leftover concrete waste ducts of Sewer-Pipe City.

In the countryside, hobbled long before the depression struck, economic hardship deepened. Between 1929 and 1933 farm income was cut in half. Though farm prices dropped 60 percent, production decreased only 6 percent as individual farmers struggled to make up for lower prices by producing more, thereby creating

Plight of the Farmers

an excess. And the surplus that so depressed agricultural prices could not be exported, since foreign demand had shrunk. Drought, foreclosure, clouds of hungry grasshoppers, and bank failures further plagued the American farmer. A Missouri man who could not pay his taxes or his mortgage, nor afford to truck his corn and barley to market, appealed for help: "I have no horses, no car am 73 yrs old, born on this farm but don't seem like I can hold it much longer." On southern cotton plantations, black sharecroppers barely subsisted on an income of less than $300 a year; whites fared little better with $400.

Native Americans descended further into malnutrition and disease. In Oklahoma, where the Choctaw, Cherokee, and Seminole lived with over

Native Americans

twenty other tribes on infertile soil, three-fourths of all Indian children were undernourished. Tuberculosis swept through the reservations. Told to grow gardens to feed themselves, the Indians lacked seed. At the heart of the problem was a 1929 ruling by the U.S. comptroller general that landless tribes were ineligible for federal aid. Not until 1931 did the Indian Bureau take steps to relieve the suffering. A federal relief program was launched to provide flour from the Red Cross, surplus clothing from the War Department, and seed from the Department of Agriculture. Yet, when Congress substantially increased the bureau's budget that year, much of the money went to raise the salaries of white employees and to hire more bureaucrats. The bureau thus had an average of about one supervisor for every thirty-six Indians.

Some Americans became transients in search of jobs or food. Desperate tenant farmers—husbands, wives, and children—walked the roads of the South. The California Unemployment Commission reported in 1932 that an "army of homeless" had trooped into the state and moved constantly from place to place, forced by one town after another to move on. Hundreds of thousands jumped aboard freight trains—"rode the rods"—or hitchhiked. Some boys and girls wandered on their own, living in hobo jungles usually populated

Going West—1933, *painted by Robinson Boardman. This stark rendering of anxious migrants searching for work and a happier life is typical of art produced during the depression era. National Museum of American Art, Smithsonian Institution, Washington, D.C.*

by adults. Congressman Maury Maverick of Texas, who wanted to find out for himself what it was like, was stunned by his hobo tour: "There was promiscuity, filth, degradation. . . . Men and families slept in jails, hot railroad urinals, cellars, dugouts, tumbledown shacks." Routes south were the most popular, for there the weather was less cruel.

During these years many Mexicans and Mexican-Americans moved south of the border, sometimes willingly, sometimes deported by immigration officials or forced out by California officials eager to purge them from the relief rolls. As an inducement, the government offered free one-way train tickets to Mexico. From 1929 through 1934, about 425,000, mostly from Texas, California, Indiana, and Illinois, returned to Mexico.

Across America economic woe and geographical mobility changed marriage patterns and family life. People postponed marriage, and married couples postponed having children. Demographers estimate

Marriage and the Family that 800,000 marriages that would normally have occurred in the years 1930 through 1933 did not occur because of the depression. The birthrate fell from 21.3 live births per 1,000 population in 1930 to 18.4 in 1933. Divorces also declined, from 206,000 in 1929 to 164,000 in 1932. Couples may not have been able to afford a divorce, or they may have decided they could face hardship better by sticking together. Families made other adjustments, too. Maybe they moved to a less expensive house or apartment; maybe they sold the car or sacrificed the telephone; maybe sons and daughters were denied a college education.

With less opportunity for outside recreation, family members were forced to spend more time together. This enforced closeness did not cause difficulty for happy, well-integrated, and stable families, but it did create unpleasantness and disorder in families suffering unemployment and crowded living quarters. Out-of-work fathers felt ashamed, resenting their diminished role. "A child who was playing irritated him," recalled the son of an unemployed Waterloo, Iowa, tool-and-die maker. "It wasn't just my own father. They all got shook up." The self-esteem of fathers and husbands was further undermined by a reversal of sex roles caused when the wage-earning work of wives and daughters supported the family. Some women made all their children's clothing and canned vegetables and fruits, becoming in essence the family's provider. Yet in most families the husband still remained the dominant partner.

Some men and women tried to massage their despair with humor. Even the president asked comedians to tell jokes to lighten people's burdens. Hoover himself bore the brunt of much of the comedy. "What? You say business is better? You mean Hoover died?" Jackrabbits shot by hungry farmers were "Hoover hogs"; makeshift shanty towns in vacant urban lots were "Hoovervilles"; and newspapers were "Hoover blankets". Even home run–hitter Babe Ruth got into the act. When he was negotiating his salary for 1930 ($80,000) with the New York Yankees, the Babe was criticized for asking for more money than the president of the United States made. He shot back: "What the hell has Hoover got to do with it? Besides, I had a better year than he did." Eddie Cantor drew laughs when he imitated a hotel clerk asking a stock-broker whether he wanted a room for sleeping or jumping. Others joked about two men who had jumped to their deaths hand in hand because they had a joint account.

Although a third of the nation's movie theaters shut down in the early years of the depression, millions of Americans still paid to see Hollywood's latest offerings. Movies were a form of escape from economic troubles. One studio put it this way: "There's a Paramount Picture probably around the corner. See it and you'll be out of yourself, living someone else's life." The "someone elses" included gangsters (played by Edward G. Robinson and James Cagney) whose lives were success stories in a disordered society, and comedians like the horseplaying Marx brothers, who in *Animal Crackers* (1930) and *Duck Soup* (1933) poked fun at convention. Seductive Mae West, who demonstrated that woman could be the hunter as well as the hunted, and whose line "Come up and see me sometime" became a legend, rose to stardom. And the role of the "fallen woman" who offered sex for personal survival (played by Tallulah Bankhead and Marlene Dietrich) became popular. There were also musicals like the popular *Gold Diggers* (1933) and horror films like *Dracula* (1932) and *Frankenstein* (1932). And then there was the giant monster in *King Kong* (1933) who scaled the Empire State Building and smashed his way through New York City. King Kong, wrote the historian Robert Sklar, "may have given the audiences precisely the proper combination of fear for the survival of their society and pleasure at seeing someone, if only a doomed gorilla, vent his rage at it."

Movies as an Escape from Hardship

THE AGGRAVATION OF RACIAL TENSIONS

The depression sank the vast majority of blacks deeper into an already precarious mire of fear, political disfranchisement, Jim Crow segregation, and privation. "It was a frightening time," Susie W. Walker of Canton, Mississippi, recalled. "A lot of people didn't know where their next meal was coming from." In 1931, when her daughter was born, "I couldn't even produce breast milk for the baby because we weren't getting enough to eat."

In 1930 about three-quarters of all blacks lived in the South. Most were not permitted to vote; were excluded from juries; could not be treated at the local hospital; were not hired except for the least desirable, most menial jobs; could not enroll at universities; and were denied access to public parks and swimming pools. Blacks living in rural areas (in 1930, 56.9 percent) were propertyless share-croppers, tenants, or wage hands caught in a cycle of poverty, disease, and illiteracy. The infant mortality rate for blacks in 1930 was double that of whites; pneumonia, tuberculosis, and venereal disease were far more prevalent among black Americans as well. In 1929 black life expectancy was more than ten years lower than white life expectancy (46.7 years versus 57.1). And the specter of the lynch mob's noose—the unspeakable torture, the crowd shouting for death, the utter lawlessness—was ever before black men. In 1929 seven blacks were lynched; in 1930, twenty; the following year, twelve. In 1932 the figure was comparatively low at six, but in 1933, when the depression was at its worst, twenty-four blacks were lynched.

Blacks in the Depression

Southern blacks continued to migrate to the cities and to the North, as they had since the First World War, but they found conditions not much better. Both employers and unions discriminated against them. Black unemployment rates ran high; in Pittsburgh, 48 percent of black workers were jobless in 1933, compared with 31 percent of white laborers. And in the movie theaters, blacks appeared on the screen only as yea-saying domestics, jungle natives, plump mammies, or gospel singers. For black Americans, then, the depression made for no dramatic shift in status. They had been stereotyped, segregated, and poor long before 1929. Now, though, they lost jobs to whites and were discriminated against even on the breadlines.

Blacks were aware that Herbert Hoover shared prevailing white racial attitudes; what was more, they knew he was attempting to push them out of the Republican party in order to attract white southern Democrats. Hoover sought, as a saying of the time put it, a lily-white GOP. He appointed few blacks to federal office, disbanded the Negro division of the Republican National Committee, rejected appeals for an antilynching law, and continued the segregation of the army and federal buildings in the nation's capital. Hoover's philosophy of individualism, opportunity, and fair play was, like the signs posted across the country, "For Whites Only."

In 1930, the president showed his insensitivity to blacks by nominating Judge John J. Parker of North Carolina to a position on the Supreme Court. Ten years earlier Parker had endorsed the disfranchisement of blacks; the NAACP remembered the speech and protested the nomination. Because Judge Parker had also decided in favor of the yellow-dog contract—a contract in which employees agree not to join a union—and the use of the injunction in labor disputes, the American Federation of Labor joined the protest. This combined pressure plus liberal votes in the Senate defeated Parker's nomination, 41 to 39. Unmoved, Hoover stood by his nominee throughout.

Then came Scottsboro, a celebrated civil-liberties case that symbolized the ugliness of race relations in the depression era. One afternoon in March 1931 a freight train pulled into the yard at Paint Rock, near Scottsboro, Alabama. Aboard were some youthful transients traveling in the boxcars. When the train stopped, armed sheriff's deputies arrested nine blacks, charging them with roughing up some white hobos and throwing them off the train earlier in the day. When two white women who were removed from the same freight claimed that the blacks had raped them, an angry white mob gathered. Within two weeks eight of the "Scottsboro boys" had been convicted of rape by all-white juries and sentenced to death. The ninth, only twelve years old, was favored by a hung jury. But because court-appointed lawyers had offered little defense for the homeless, illiterate, poorly clad, and sickly youths, the Supreme Court in 1932 overturned the convictions on the grounds that the accused had not been granted adequate legal counsel.

Scottsboro Trials

New trials opened in 1933, again with all-white juries. This time, however, the Scottsboro blacks

The nine Scottsboro youths in jail in Decatur, Alabama.
Seated with the attorney Samuel Leibowitz is Haywood
Patterson.   Brown Brothers.

were defended by Samuel Leibowitz, a talented attorney
hired by the Communist-sponsored International Labor
Defense. To a crowded courtroom, the local prosecutor
sneered at Leibowitz, announcing that "Alabama justice cannot be bought and sold with Jew money from
New York." Medical evidence showed that the women
had not had intercourse on the train. Ruby Bates
and Victoria Price had lied, perhaps because they
feared arrest as prostitutes. Nevertheless, the first
defendant up for retrial, Haywood Patterson, was
once again found guilty. Judge James Horton, who
had stated that under American law "we know neither
black nor white. . . . It is our duty to mete out even-

handed justice," was convinced that Patterson was
an innocent victim of racial hatred. The courageous
Horton overturned the jury's decision.

A new judge was found, a new trial held, and for
the third time Patterson was ordered to die. But
another Supreme Court ruling intervened, this time
because it was evident that in Alabama blacks were
systematically excluded from juries. Patterson faced a
fourth trial in 1936. Found guilty again, he was given
a seventy-five-year jail sentence. Four of the other
youths were sentenced to life imprisonment, and the
state dropped charges against the remaining four. Not
until 1950 were all five out of jail—four by parole

and Patterson by escaping from his work gang. Scottsboro's constitutional implications were important for the future: for the first time the Supreme Court used the Fourteenth Amendment as a vehicle to apply the criminal protection procedures of the Bill of Rights against the states (previously they had been applied only against the federal government).

Blacks coped with their white-circumscribed environment and fought back against racism in a variety of ways during the depression. Black Baptist and African Methodist Episcopal churches articulated black concerns; black newspapers like the *Amsterdam News* (New York), the *Chicago Defender*, and the *Pittsburgh Courier* cultivated racial consciousness. Black Renaissance poets and writers like Langston Hughes promoted civil rights. And Howard University, Tuskegee Institute, and Atlanta University, among others, trained a generation of black leaders. The NAACP, although internally divided, lobbied quietly against a long list of injustices, and A. Philip Randolph's Brotherhood of Sleeping Car Porters defended the rights of black workers. In Cleveland and New York, black doctors protested discriminatory practices at municipal hospitals. In Harlem the militant Harlem Tenants League fought rent increases and evictions, and in some cities black consumers began to boycott white merchants. But America's white leaders made few concessions. Only the Supreme Court, which declared the Texas "white primary" law unconstitutional and attempted to check the abuses in the Scottsboro trials, provided a measure of protection for black Americans in the thirties.

THE TEMPERED PROTEST

Most Americans—black or white—met the new crisis not with violence, protest, or political extremism, but with bewilderment and an inability to fix the blame. They scorned businesspeople, of course, but often they blamed themselves as well, as the traditional ideology of the self-made man had taught them to do. There were some grocery-store robberies, an increase in homicides, a few nasty strikes and protest marches, and flirtations with radicalism on the left and right, but they were usually scattered, unconnected, and spontaneous. Nothing like the extreme political convulsions that rocked Europe hit the United States. Robert Hutchins, president of the University of Chicago, thought about why Americans responded so temperately to the catastrophe: "How could there be a revolt against a system in which everybody believed, including those who were starving to death because of it?" The few protests sought immediate relief—jobs, food, housing—not long-term radical social change. In the words of a depression-era song:

I don't want your millions, mister,
I don't want your diamond ring.
All I want is the right to live, mister;
Give me back my job again.
I don't want your Rolls-Royce, mister,
I don't want your pleasure yacht.
All I want is food for my babies;
Give me my old job back.[1]

Despair, sullenness, demoralization, and shock cut deeply into the American psyche. When the novelist Sherwood Anderson picked up hitchhikers along the road, he found many of them to be apologetic about their plight. A psychiatrist describing unemployed miners wrote, "They hung around street corners and in groups. They gave each other solace. They were loath to go home because they were indicted, as if it were their fault for being jobless. A jobless man was a lazy good-for-nothing. . . . They felt despised, they were ashamed of themselves." This was the stuff not of revolution, but of self-hatred and melancholy.

Scattered protests did, however, raise the specter of popular revolt. In Iowa's Cow War of 1931, angry farmers assailed state tuberculin inspectors who condemned diseased cattle but gave farmers little compensation for their losses. Soon the National Guard was escorting veterinarians on their rounds, arresting uncooperative farmers. In Nebraska, Iowa, and Minnesota, farmers protesting low prices put up barricades, stopped trucks, and dumped milk and vegetables on the road. Some of these demonstrations were organized by the Farmers' Holiday Association. Its leader, Milo Reno, argued that the propertied farmer was the

---

[1]From "I Don't Want Your Millions Mister" by Jim Garland. © Copyright 1947 by Stormking Music, Inc. All Rights Reserved. Used by permission.

Farmers' Holiday Association

backbone of society and the economy; lift up the farmer and the nation would be lifted out of depression. Reno encouraged farmers to take a holiday—to keep their products off the market until they commanded a better price. The Sioux City milk strike in the summer of 1932 was the association's most dramatic effort, but like others it failed to improve significantly the economic position of farmers. The following year a Wisconsin dairy farmers' strike ended unsuccessfully after National Guardsmen tossed tear gas and charged with fixed bayonets into a crowd of rock-throwing farmers.

Like their forebears in Shays' Rebellion (1786), farmers were more effective in slowing foreclosures on farm properties. By harassing sheriffs, judges, and lawyers, they sometimes prevented evictions; and they conspired at auctions to bid very low on foreclosed land and then turned over the property to its relieved former owners. Their protests contributed to the passage of state laws that inhibited foreclosure.

Isolated protests also sounded in cities and in mining regions. In Chicago, Los Angeles, and Philadelphia, the unemployed marched on city halls. Chicago schoolteachers, protesting drastic budget cuts, pulled down the 1933 World's Fair flag and stormed the city hall. And in Harlan County, Kentucky, miners struck against wage reductions (1931). Mine owners responded with strikebreakers, bombs, the National Guard, the closing of relief kitchens, and evictions from company-owned housing. "The law," grumbled one woman, "is a gun thug in a big automobile." Though Theodore Dreiser, Lincoln Steffens, and other socially conscious writers traveled to the poor Kentucky county to draw national attention to the struggle, the strike failed nonetheless.

The most spectacular confrontation shook Washington, D.C., in summer 1932. Congress was considering a bill authorizing immediate issuance of bonuses of $2.4 billion already allotted to First World War veterans, but not due for payment until 1945. To lobby for the bill, fifteen thousand unemployed veterans and their families converged on the tense nation's capital, calling themselves the Bonus Expeditionary Force (BEF). They camped in crude shacks on vacant lots and in empty government buildings. Blacks mingled with

Bonus Expeditionary Force

whites; Jim Crow was "absent with leave," said Roy Wilkins of the NAACP.

Though President Hoover threw his weight against the bonus bill, the House passed it. The showdown came in the Senate, which voted "no" after much debate. One BEF member shouted: "We were heroes in 1917, but we're bums today." Many of the bonus marchers then left Washington, but several thousand stayed on. Hoover grew impatient, carelessly labeled them "insurrectionists" and Communists, and refused to meet with them.

In July General Douglas MacArthur, assisted by Majors Dwight D. Eisenhower and George S. Patton, met the veterans and their families with cavalry, tanks, and bayonet-bearing soldiers. The BEF hurled back stones and bricks. What followed shocked the nation. Men and women were chased down by horsemen; children were teargassed; shacks were set afire. As smoke wafted above the capital's stately buildings, a United Press correspondent commented on the ugly scene: "So all the misery and suffering had finally come to this—soldiers marching with their guns against American citizens." Although one might argue whether ex-servicemen deserved special legislative favor, there can be no question that the answer to their predicament was not violence but food. Hoover's image as a humanitarian was badly tarnished, even though he thought MacArthur had gone too far in using force. When presidential hopeful Franklin D. Roosevelt heard about the attack on the Bonus Army, he turned to his friend Felix Frankfurter and said: "Well, Felix, this will elect me."

With capitalism on its knees, American Communist leaders anticipated large gains for their party. Across the nation they organized "unemployed councils" to arouse class consciousness and to agitate for jobs and food. In March 1930 they conducted urban demonstrations, some of which ended in violent clashes with local police. And with the slogan "Fight—Don't Starve," they led a hunger march on Washington, D.C., in 1931. Their tangles with authority publicized the real human tragedy of the depression.

Still, the Communist party gained few followers. Workers shunned it, blacks responded without enthusiasm to its recruiting drives, and farmers, although attracted to its call for debt relief and federal aid, rejected the party's appeal that they abandon the in-

Communist Party

Their lobbying having failed, these members of the Bonus Expeditionary Force buried not only the bonus they so ardently sought from an unobliging Senate, but also President Hoover and former Secretary of the Treasury Andrew Mellon, both of whom had opposed payment of the bonus. One message was surely that the veterans intended to bury politically the Republican president in the forthcoming election of 1932. Within a month, these BEFers and others would be driven violently from their makeshift houses by American troops. Library of Congress.

dividual ownership of property for collectivization. Ordinary Americans, the journalist Gerald Johnson commented, "have no more idea of turning communistic than they have of turning Mohammedan." Some intellectuals were attracted to Marxism and saw the party as one vehicle for social change, economic planning, and antifascism. Theodore Dreiser, Lincoln Steffens, Jack Conroy, John Dos Passos, and Erskine Caldwell were among them. But many of these writers became disenchanted with the Communists' rigid discipline and dogma and attachment to the Soviet Union. The hero of Conroy's *The Disinherited* (1933) grows critical of the party's abstractions: "Why don't they talk about beans and potatoes, land and bacon instead of 'ideology,' 'agrarian crisis,' and 'rationalization.' " Total party membership in 1930 was only six thousand; by 1932 it remained small at twelve thousand.

The Socialist party, which argued with both Communists and capitalists, fared little better. More reformist than radical, more evolutionary than revolutionary, the Socialists ran well in municipal elections after the stock market crash but scored few victories. In the 1932 presidential election, Socialist candidate Norman Thomas received 884,000 votes, a mere 2 percent of the total. (Communist candidate William Z. Foster won only 103,000 votes.) Party membership consisted mostly of older Jewish trade-union leaders, Protestant pacifists, students, and teachers; workers and labor unions gave the party little support. In 1930 the membership rolls listed 9,700 persons; by 1932 the figure had grown to 17,000, fewer than in 1903. Thomas found it "amazing that the workers were so comparatively quiet." Indeed, few despairing Americans looked to left-wing parties and doctrines, protest marches, or violence for relief from their misery. They turned instead to institutions of considerable longevity and stability: their local, state, and federal governments.

HOOVER HOLDS THE LINE

When urgent daily appeals for government relief for the jobless reached the White House, Hoover at first became defensive, if not hostile. "We cannot legislate ourselves out of a world depression; we can and will work ourselves out," he replied. Hoover rejected direct relief—derisively called the dole—because he believed it would undermine character and individualism. "It is a reassuring thought, in the cold weather," the critic Edmund Wilson wrote sarcastically, "that the emaciated men in the bread lines, the men and women beggars in the streets, and the children dependent on them, are all having their fibre hardened." Indeed, to a growing number of Americans, Hoover seemed heartless and inflexible at a time when humanitarianism and activity were called for. Rather than deal with the quarter of the work force that was jobless, he emphasized the many who were still on payrolls. The president did not help his public image by brooding and conveying indifference. "This is not a showman's job," he snapped. "You can't make a Teddy Roosevelt out of me." And he made the mistake of being photographed on the White House lawn—feeding his dog.

True to his beliefs, the president urged people to help themselves and their neighbors. He applauded private voluntary relief through charitable agencies such as the Community Chest and the Red Cross. Yet when the need was greatest, donations declined. State and urban officials found their treasuries drying up too. Philadelphia, after hiring the unemployed to paint city buildings, exhausted its relief funds by 1931, leaving 57,000 families without assistance. The "demands of suffering humanity," cried the mayor, required federal action. He got no sympathy from Secretary of the Treasury Andrew Mellon, who with a mixture of conventional wisdom and callousness advised the president to "let the slump

Reliance on Private Relief

liquidate itself. Liquidate labor, liquidate stocks, liquidate the farmers, liquidate real estate. . . . It will purge the rottenness out of the system." Will Rogers cast the problem in a different light. "We got more wheat, more corn, more food, more cotton, more money in the banks, more than any nation that ever lived ever had, yet we are starving to death." "It's simply a case," Rogers advised, "of getting it fixed."

Hoover did try to fix the economy. As the depression intensified, his opposition to federal action diminished. He rejected Mellon's insensitive counsel, hesitantly and gradually energizing the White House and federal agencies to take action—more action than the government had taken before. He met with business and labor leaders, winning pledges from them to maintain wages and production and to avoid strikes. He urged state governors to increase their expenditures on public works. And he created the President's Organization on Unemployment Relief (POUR) to generate private contributions for relief of the destitute. Unfortunately, the chairman, president of the American Telephone and Telegraph Company Walter Gifford, seemed a man of limited concern and vision. Asked by a senator to specify the nation's relief requirements, Gifford said he had no precise information. The incredulous senator leaned forward: "Do you know what the relief needs are in the rural districts of the United States?" Gifford answered simply, "No."

If POUR proved ineffective, Hoover's spurring of federal public works projects (including the Boulder, or Hoover, and Grand Coulee dams) did provide some jobs. Help also came from the Federal Farm Board, created before the depression under the Agricultural Marketing Act of 1929. An outcome of Hoover's emphasis on cooperation among individuals, groups, and government, the Farm Board supported agricultural prices by lending money to cooperatives to buy products and keep them off the market. But the board soon found itself short of money, and unsold surplus commodities jammed warehouses. And though the federally sponsored and privately funded National Credit Corporation assisted faltering banks, it barely slowed the number of bank failures. To retard the collapse of the international monetary system, Hoover announced a moratorium on the payment of First World War debts and reparations (1931).

The president also reluctantly asked Congress to charter the Reconstruction Finance Corporation

In early 1931 needy children in El Paso, Arkansas, lined up for soup dispensed free by Red Cross workers. Soup lines and bread lines became conspicuous features of American life during the Great Depression, but declining contributions put restraints on the activities of voluntary, charitable associations like the Red Cross.   National Archives.

Reconstruction Finance Corporation

(RFC). Created in 1932 and eventually empowered with $2 billion, the RFC was designed to make loans to banks, insurance companies, and railroads and later to state and local governments. The theory behind the RFC was that it would lend money to large entities at the top of the economic system, and benefits would trickle down to people at the bottom through a sort of percolation process. Liberal Republican Representative Fiorello La Guardia of New York labeled the plan a "millionaires' dole." It did not work; banks continued to collapse and small companies to go into bankruptcy.

Despite warnings from prominent economists, Hoover also signed the Hawley-Smoot Tariff (1930). A congressional compromise serving special interests, the tariff raised duties by about one-third. Besides wishing to fulfill a Republican party pledge, Hoover argued that the tariff would help farmers and manufacturers by keeping foreign goods off the market. Actually, the tariff further weakened the economy by making it even more difficult for foreign nations

to sell their products and thus earn the money to buy American products and pay off their First World War debts.

Like most of his contemporaries, Hoover believed that a balanced budget was sacred, and deficit spending sinful. In 1931 he appealed for a decrease in federal expenditures and an increase in taxes. The following year he supported a sales tax on manufactured goods, which liberal Democrats charged was an attempt to avoid higher income and corporate taxes. The sales tax was defeated, but the Revenue Act of 1932 raised corporate, excise, and personal income taxes. Hoover seemed caught in a contradiction: he urged people to spend to spur recovery, but his tax policies deprived them of spending money. He never did balance the budget. Nor did he seek repeal of the legal loopholes that permitted the partners of J. P. Morgan and other wealthy Americans to escape paying any income taxes in 1931 and 1932.

Although Hoover expanded public works projects and approved loans to some institutions, he vetoed a variety of relief bills presented to him by the an ideologue who, when faced with problems of unprecedented magnitude, failed to take bold steps to meet them. Hoover once said that nobody was starving, and in late 1931 he remarked, "Our people have been protected from hunger and cold." Such a statement arose not from heartlessness but from faith in the status quo. Whatever one's interpretation, Hoover's restrained and cautious response to the depression did not mean that he was weak. "Weak Presidents are ignored or brushed aside," the historian Albert Romasco has written. "Hoover remained a formidable, effective obstacle to new ideas and innovations until he was blasted away by the presidential election returns."

Hoover's traditionalism was well demonstrated by his handling of prohibition. Despite the Eighteenth Amendment, Americans were producing and drinking liquor with grand illegality and hypocrisy. The law was not and could not be enforced. Yet Hoover resisted the mounting public pressure for repeal. Opponents argued not only that prohibition encouraged crime, but that its repeal would stimulate economic recovery in Milwaukee and St. Louis, increase demand for grain, and revive the nation's old beer, liquor, and pretzel factories. But the president would not, he said, tamper with the Constitution, and the liquor industry, having no socially redemptive value, was best left depressed. Instead, Hoover pushed for better enforcement of the Eighteenth Amendment. And during the presidential election campaign of 1932, he stood firm against repeal. As on other issues, Hoover held the line.

Democratic Congress. "Prosperity," he intoned, "cannot be restored by raids upon the public treasury." He also vetoed a multipurpose development project for the Tennessee River, arguing that its cheap electricity would compete with power from private companies. Clinging to his old viewpoints, Hoover stretched government activities as far as he thought he could without violating his cherished principles.

Because Hoover mobilized the resources of the federal government as never before, some historians have depicted him as a bridge to the New Deal of the 1930s. If nothing else, he pre-

Hoover Assessed pared the way for massive federal activity by giving private enterprise the opportunity to solve the depression—and to fail. They point out, moreover, that Hoover was a progressive trapped by unprecedented events, and that few leaders of the time were sure what to do. But others have argued that Hoover was

TRADITION IN TIME OF CRISIS: THE ELECTION OF 1932

Herbert Hoover and the Republican party faced dreary prospects in 1932. The tired and sullen president grumbled at reporters, banks continued to close, and memories of the Bonus March persisted. Hoover kept pointing to international causes for the economic crisis, when Americans were less concerned with abstract explanations than with tomorrow's meal. He grew impatient with critics who held him responsible for the depression. "Is it my fault," he asked a reporter, "that cheap politicians and selfish men over the whole world have refused to see the folly of their policies until it was too late?" His critics replied that as secretary of commerce during the 1920s Hoover shared responsibility for the depression. But what soured public opinion most was that Hoover seemed not to lead at a time when innovative generalship was required, that he refused to budge. "No president," Hoover told a friend, "must ever admit he has been wrong."

In 1932 Republicans who did not want to be associated with a loser ran independent campaigns; Progressive Republicans like Senator George Norris deserted Hoover; W. E. B. Du Bois urged blacks to vote Democratic. The president made few major speeches, rarely left Washington, and when he did venture out was frequently jeered and booed. On the final day of the campaign, when Hoover returned to California to vote, his motorcade was interrupted by stink bombs.

Franklin D. Roosevelt, on the other hand, enjoyed a different reputation. The smiling, ingratiating governor of New York appealed to the American penchant for optimism. "I figure out that if we can get rid of Old Gloom and put in a feller that can laugh and act human," a cab driver remarked, "the Depression will be half over."

Democratic Candidate Franklin D. Roosevelt

As governor of New York, Roosevelt had launched relief programs and an unemployment commission. In 1932 he outmaneuvered try-again Al Smith and Speaker of the House John Nance Garner to gain the top spot on the Democratic ticket. Accepting the nomination in person, the fifty-year-old Roosevelt called for a "new deal for the American people."

The two party platforms differed little, but the Democrats were willing to abandon prohibition and to launch federal relief. Roosevelt, playing the political game superbly, promised to help everybody—a Santa Claus campaign, one critic called it. Hoover complained that his opponent was a chameleon on plaid. Indeed, Roosevelt's speeches, pieced together by ghostwriters, seemed contradictory. He would agree with Hoover that the budget had to be balanced,

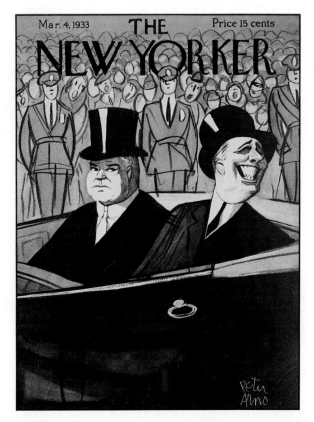

Mar. 4, 1933 THE NEW YORKER Price 15 cents

A gloomy Hoover and a buoyant Roosevelt ride to the inauguration in 1933. This magazine cover was actually never published, apparently because the editors of the New Yorker magazine thought it inappropriate after an attempted assassination of the president-elect. *Franklin D. Roosevelt Library.*

then appeal for costly new programs. When Roosevelt spoke of the forgotten man and declared himself ready to provide direct relief to individuals, Hoover boiled: "This campaign is more than a contest between two men," he said. "It is more than a contest between two parties. It is a contest between two philosophies of government." Roosevelt seemed to agree, explaining his liberalism with a metaphor:

Say that civilization is a tree which, as it grows, continually produced rot and dead wood. The radical says: "Cut it down." The conservative says: "Don't touch it." The liberal compromises: "Let's prune, so that we lose neither the old trunk nor the new branches." This campaign is waged to teach the country to march upon its appointed course . . ., avoiding alike the revolution of radicalism and the revolution of conservatism.

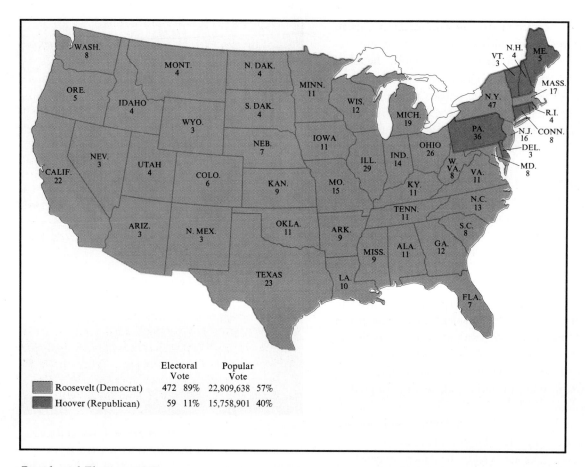

Presidential Election, 1932

	Electoral Vote		Popular Vote	
Roosevelt (Democrat)	472	89%	22,809,638	57%
Hoover (Republican)	59	11%	15,758,901	40%

More people went to the polls in 1932 than in any election since the First World War. In a crisis-ridden moment Americans quietly, calmly, even routinely followed tradition and peacefully exchanged one government for another. Roosevelt's 22.8 million popular votes far outdistanced Hoover's 15.8 million: 57 percent of the popular vote went to the Democrat, 40 percent to the Republican, and 3 percent to minor party candidates.

1932 Election Results

Hoover won only Vermont, New Hampshire, Maine, Connecticut, Delaware, and Pennsylvania, giving him a paltry 59 electoral votes to Roosevelt's 472 (see map). Cities continued the trend, begun in 1928, of voting Democratic. But although Hoover was in trouble with some black leaders, two-thirds of the black vote remained Republican in 1932. Roosevelt had appealed to southern whites as Hoover had, and he held racial views that seemed to differ little from Hoover's.

Democrats also won overwhelming control of the Senate and the House. From November to March, a lame-duck president, a lame-duck Congress (158 of whose members had been defeated), and a hesitant president-elect took little positive action, and the depression continued to cut its debilitating path. Americans wondered what would happen next. Might not radicals make gains? Some thought Roosevelt would reform the American system enough to forestall radical solutions. Others envisioned demagogues, splinter parties, or violence. Hoover feared Roosevelt would implant "collectivism" in the nation, smothering individualism and destroying the American system. But Hoover exaggerated his differences with Roosevelt, who hardly sought the destruction of capitalism. The two parted ways largely on the extent to which the federal government should intervene in economic and social affairs. And the majority of Americans had spoken for more intervention. How strikingly different from their mood four years earlier was their mood on inauguration day 1933.

SUGGESTIONS FOR FURTHER READING

Hoover and His Administration

David Burner, *Herbert Hoover* (1979); Carl N. Degler, "The Ordeal of Herbert Hoover," *Yale Review*, 52 (1963), 563–583; Martin L. Fausold, *The Presidency of Herbert C. Hoover* (1985); Martin L. Fausold and George T. Mazuzan, eds., *The Hoover Presidency* (1974); Ellis W. Hawley, *The Great War and the Search for a Modern Order* (1979); Richard Hofstadter, *The American Political Tradition* (1949); Barry D. Karl, "Presidential Planning and Social Science Research: Mr. Hoover's Experts," *Perspectives in American History*, 3 (1969), 347–409; William E. Leuchtenberg, *The Perils of Prosperity, 1914–1932* (1958); James S. Olson, *Herbert Hoover and the Reconstruction Finance Corporation, 1931–1933* (1977); Edgar E. Robinson and Vaughn D. Bornet, *Herbert Hoover* (1975); Albert V. Romasco, *The Poverty of Abundance: Hoover, The Nation, The Depression* (1965); Elliot A. Rosen, *Hoover, Roosevelt, and the Brains Trust* (1977); Jordan A. Schwarz, *Interregnum of Despair* (1970); Richard N. Smith, *An Uncommon Man* (1984); Harris G. Warren, *Herbert Hoover and the Great Depression* (1959); Joan Hoff Wilson, *Herbert Hoover: Forgotten Progressive* (1975).

The Great Depression and Its Causes

W. Elliot Brownlee, *Dynamics of Ascent*, 2nd ed. (1979); Lester V. Chandler, *America's Greatest Depression, 1929–1941* (1970); Milton Friedman and Anna Schwartz, *The Great Contraction, 1929–1933* (1965); John K. Galbraith, *The Great Crash*, 50th anniv. ed. (1979); Robert L. Heilbroner and Aaron Singer, *The Economic Transformation of America*, 2nd ed. (1984); Susan Kennedy, *The Banking Crisis of 1933* (1973); Charles Kindleberger, *The World in Depression, 1929–1939* (1973); Broadus Mitchell, *Depression Decade* (1947); Jim Potter, *The American Economy Between the Wars* (1974); George Soule, *Prosperity Decade* (1947); Peter Temin, *Did Monetary Forces Cause the Great Depression?* (1976); Gordon Thomas and Max Morgan-Witts, *The Day the Bubble Burst* (1979).

The American People in Hard Times

Francisco E. Balderrama, *In Defense of La Raza: The Los Angeles Mexican Consulate and the Mexican Community, 1929–1936* (1982); Andrew Bergman, *We're in the Money: Depression America and Its Films* (1971); Caroline Bird, *The Invisible Scar* (1965); Sidney Fine, *Frank Murphy: The Detroit Years* (1975); Milton Meltzer, *Brother, Can You Spare a Dime?* (1969); Cabel Phillips, *From the Crash to the Blitz, 1929–1939* (1969); Robert Sklar, *Movie-made America* (1975); Bernard Sternsher, ed., *Hitting Home: The Great Depression in Town and Country* (1970); Studs Terkel, *Hard Times* (1970); David Tyack et al., *Public Schools in Hard Times* (1984); Dixon Wecter, *The Age of the Great Depression, 1929–1941* (1948); Edmund Wilson, *The American Earthquake* (1958).

Workers

Irving Bernstein, *The Lean Years: A History of the American Worker, 1920–1933* (1960); John W. Hevener, *Which Side Are You On? The Harlan County Coal Miners, 1931–1939* (1978); Lois Scharf, *To Work and to Wed: Female Employment, Feminism, and the Great Depression* (1980); Winifred D. Wandersee, *Women's Work and Family Values, 1920–1940* (1981).

Farmers

Lowell K. Dyson, *Red Harvest: The Communist Party and American Farmers* (1982); Theodore Saloutos and John D. Hicks, *Twentieth Century Populism: Agricultural Discontent in the Middle West, 1900–1939* (1951); John L. Shover, *Cornbelt Rebellion: The Farmers' Holiday Association* (1965).

Protest

Roger Daniels, *The Bonus March* (1971); John P. Diggins, *The American Left in the Twentieth Century* (1973); Harvey Klehr, *The Heyday of American Communism* (1984); Donald J. Lisio, *The President and Protest: Hoover, Conspiracy, and the Bonus Riot* (1974); Mark Naison, *Communists in Harlem During the Depression* (1983); David Shannon, *The Socialist Party of America* (1955).

Race Relations

Dan T. Carter, *Scottsboro*, rev. ed. (1979); Harvard Sitkoff, *A New Deal for Blacks* (1978); Bernard Sternsher, ed., *The Negro in Depression and War* (1969); Raymond Wolters, *Negroes and the Great Depression* (1970); Robert L. Zangrando, *The NAACP Crusade Against Lynching, 1909–1950* (1980).

THE GREAT DEPRESSION
AND THE NEW DEAL
1933–1941

CHAPTER 26

*F*ranklin D. Roosevelt loved the sea. So in August 1921, when a business associate with a yacht offered a cruise to Roosevelt's summer home on Campobello Island, off the coast of New Brunswick, he happily accepted. Sailing into the frigid waters of the Bay of Fundy between New Brunswick and Nova Scotia, the two encountered rough water, and Roosevelt stood for hours at the helm until the boat was in harbor.

The next day Roosevelt went fishing and fell overboard. "I never felt anything so cold as that water!" he said later, "so cold it seemed paralyzing." Roosevelt was exhausted, but he did not slacken his pace. There was a forest fire to be fought, followed by another dip in the cold waters. Finally, he was too tired to stand up. When Roosevelt awoke the next morning, his left leg ached. He also had a fever. Soon he had no feeling in either leg. A doctor diagnosed polio. Just a year before, in 1920, he had been the robust vice-presidential candidate of the Democratic party. Now he was crippled, totally paralyzed in both legs.

What should Roosevelt do next? Should he retire from public life, a rich invalid? His answer and his wife Eleanor's was no. Throughout the 1920s Franklin and Eleanor contended with his new handicap. Rejecting self-pity even though he at times experienced intense pain, Roosevelt worked to rebuild his body. People who had known him before commented that polio had made him a "twice-born man," that his "fight against that dread disease had evidently given him new moral and physical strength." As Roosevelt explained it: "If you had spent two years in bed trying to wiggle your big toe, after that anything would seem easy."

For her part, Mrs. Roosevelt learned to do things for herself, such as driving a car; and she began to shape her own career in public life, giving speeches and participating in the activities of the League of Women Voters, the Women's Trade Union League, and the Democratic party. Two of her strongest commitments came to be equal opportunity for women and for Afro-Americans, and she especially wanted to help the poor and suffering.

In 1933 Franklin D. Roosevelt became president, and the source of strength for a nation troubled by the Great Depression. The qualities of character he and Eleanor had discovered and nurtured in the 1920s would prove invaluable assets in the years to come.

From the first days of his presidency Roosevelt displayed a buoyancy and a willingness to experiment that helped to restore public confidence in the government and the economy. He acted not only to reform such economic institutions as banks and stock exchanges, but also to provide relief to the suffering. After shoring up the banking system, Roosevelt proposed a succession of laws to aid landowning farmers, blue-collar workers, businesses and local governments facing bankruptcy, the unemployed, the elderly, and even impoverished writers and artists. This sweeping legislation was based on the unorthodox concept of "pump priming," or deficit financing, to stimulate consumer buying power, business enterprise, and ultimately employment by pouring billions of federal dollars into the economy.

Roosevelt's New Deal inspired opposition from both the left and right. Businesspeople and economic conservatives found it fiscally irresponsible; demagogues and left-wing politicians thought it too conservative. Ultimately Roosevelt prevailed, however, revitalizing the progressive movement, vastly expanding both the scope of the federal government and the popularity of the Democratic party, and in the process establishing America's welfare state.

During these years several million workers seized the chance to organize for better wages and working conditions. The new Congress of Industrial Organizations (CIO) established unions in major industries like automobiles, steel, and meatpacking. Nonwhites registered political and economic gains too, though in general they benefited less from the New Deal than did whites. Some federal agencies actually worked against blacks; on the other hand, black advisers took posts in the White House, and Native Americans discovered that New Dealers respected their culture and tribal rights.

Two-and-a-half million additional women workers joined the labor force during the 1930s. But female workers were segregated in low-income jobs, and the New Deal excluded many women from Social Security coverage and minimum-wage protection.

Roosevelt was re-elected in 1936, but soon thereafter his fortunes began to wane. In 1937 the nation sank into a severe economic recession, and Congress rejected Roosevelt's attempt to increase the number of sympathetic judges on the federal bench. In 1938 the spate of relief and reform legislation came to an end. But by that time the New Deal had transformed the United States; although the New Deal was not a revolution, its legacy is still with us today. Farmers still plant according to federal crop allotments. The elderly and disabled still collect Social Security payments. The Federal Deposit Insurance Corporation still insures bank deposits. And the Securities and Exchange Commission still monitors the stock exchange. One goal the New Deal did not accomplish—putting back to work all the people who wanted jobs. That would await the nation's entry into the Second World War.

FRANKLIN DELANO ROOSEVELT

F ranklin D. Roosevelt was born into privilege, the only child of doting parents who heaped on him all sorts of advantages. He was graduated from Harvard in 1903, and in fall 1904 he entered the School of Law at Columbia University. He soon announced his engagement to his fifth cousin once-removed, Anna Eleanor Roosevelt, the niece of President Theodore Roosevelt. The next spring they were married.

Roosevelt began the practice of law, but he had other ambitions—political ones. In 1910 he ran for the New York State Assembly and won. In 1912 he accepted President Wilson's offer of **Roosevelt's** the post of assistant secretary of the **Early Career** navy. For eight years Roosevelt supervised the navy's relations with business and labor unions. He learned lessons about the emergence of the United States as a world power and the need for decisive presidential leadership in times of crisis.

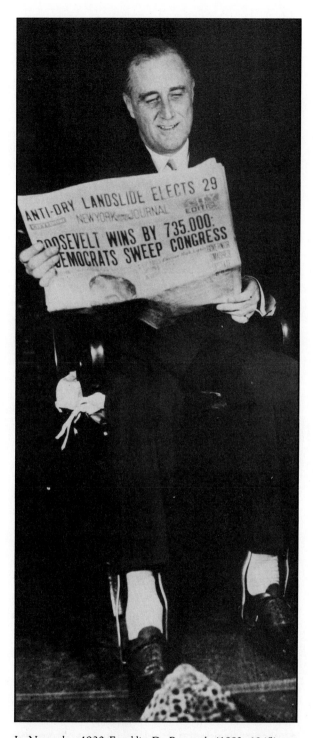

In November 1930 Franklin D. Roosevelt (1882–1945) read the good news. Re-elected governor of New York by 735,000 votes, he immediately became a leading contender for the 1932 Democratic presidential nomination. Note Roosevelt's leg braces, rarely shown in photographs because of an unwritten agreement by photographers to shoot him from the waist up. UPI/Bettmann Newsphotos.

In 1920 the Democratic party nominated Roosevelt for the vice presidency. Campaigning on the need for the League of Nations and continued domestic reform, he and Governor James M. Cox of Ohio were roundly defeated by Republicans Harding and Coolidge. But Roosevelt suffered his most devastating loss the next year, when he was struck by polio. After deciding to fight his polio rather than succumb to it, Roosevelt practiced law and pursued various business ventures. And he returned to politics, nominating New York's Governor Al Smith for president at both the 1924 and 1928 Democratic conventions and becoming a spokesperson for progressive Democrats. Also in 1928 Roosevelt agreed to run for governor of New York; in November he won by 25,000 votes. Smith, in contrast, not only lost the election, but failed to carry his home state of New York, losing it by 100,000 votes. Right away Roosevelt became an obvious prospect for the 1932 Democratic presidential nomination. "You are," Virginia's Senator Harry Byrd wrote to Roosevelt, "the hope of the Democratic party."

Roosevelt's governorship coincided with Hoover's presidency, and both coincided with the onset of the Great Depression. But whereas Hoover appeared hard-hearted and unwilling to help the jobless, Roosevelt seemed just the opposite. He urged unemployment insurance and direct relief payments for the jobless. Under his leadership New York's Temporary Emergency Relief Administration (1931) became the first state agency to mobilize on behalf of the poor. Aid to the unemployed, Roosevelt declared, "must be extended by Government, not as a matter of charity, but as a matter of social duty."

Roosevelt as Governor of New York

Roosevelt was also more willing than Hoover to experiment. As governor of New York, he advocated creating jobs in publicly funded reforestation, land reclamation, and hydroelectric power projects. He also endorsed and worked for old-age pensions and protective legislation for labor unions. Roosevelt warned people not to dismiss such experimentation "with the word radical. Remember the radical of yesterday is almost [always] the reactionary of today." After he was re-elected in 1930 by a record-setting plurality of 735,000 votes, politicians had to take a serious look at his vote-getting ability.

To prepare a national political platform, Roosevelt surrounded himself with a "brain trust" of lawyers and university professors. Foremost among these advisers were Columbia University professors Rexford G. Tugwell, Raymond Moley, and Adolf A. Berle, Jr. Bigness was unavoidable in the modern American economy, these experts reasoned; thus the cure for the nation's ills was not to go on a rampage of trustbusting, but to place large corporations, monopolies, and oligopolies under effective government regulation. "We are no longer afraid of bigness," declared Tugwell, speaking in the tradition of Theodore Roosevelt's New Nationalism. "We are resolved to recognize openly that competition in most of its forms is wasteful and costly; that larger combinations in any modern society must prevail."

Roosevelt's "Brain Trust"

Roosevelt and his brain trust agreed that it was essential for the government to restore purchasing power to farmers, blue-collar workers, and the middle classes, and that the way to do so was to cut production. If the demand for a product remained constant and the supply were cut, they reasoned, the price would rise. Producers would make higher profits, and workers would earn more money. This method of combating a depression has been called the economics of scarcity. Unlike Hoover, Roosevelt also advocated immediate and direct relief to the unemployed. Finally, Roosevelt and his advisers rejected Hoover's explanation that the depression was international, not domestic, in origin. They demanded that the federal government engage in centralized economic planning and experimentation to bring about recovery.

The presidential election of 1932 had never been much of a contest (see page 730). But once elected, Roosevelt had to wait until his inauguration on March 4 to act.[1] It was a troubled four months. Almost 13 million unemployed people walked the streets, some participating in hunger riots and job protest marches. Prices for agricultural and manufactured goods continued to plummet, forcing the bankruptcy of countless farms, small businesses, railroads, and even local governments. Industrial production sank to new depths. And while farmers in the Farm Holiday movement

---

[1] As a result of that crucial loss of time, the Twentieth Amendment to the Constitution—the Lame Duck Amendment—was ratified. It moved all future inaugurations forward to January 20.

poured milk into ditches and threatened to hang foreclosing judges, another kind of holiday was observed in some states: the bank holiday. Throughout the United States, depositors lined up in front of banks demanding their money. Banks with insufficient funds on hand to pay depositors had to close their doors and declare themselves insolvent. In February, Michigan and Maryland suspended banking operations, and by March 4, thirty-six other states, including New York, had followed suit.

On the afternoon of March 2, 1933, President-elect Roosevelt and his family and friends boarded a train for Washington, D.C., and the inauguration ceremony. Roosevelt was carrying with him rough drafts of two presidential proclamations, one summoning a special session of Congress, the other declaring a national bank holiday, suspending banking transactions throughout the nation.

RESTORING CONFIDENCE

"First of all," declared the newly inaugurated president, "let me assert my firm belief that the only thing we have to fear is fear itself—nameless, unreasoning, unjustified terror." In his inaugural address Roosevelt scored his first triumph as president, instilling hope and courage in the rank and file. Roosevelt attacked the nation's bankers, accusing them of having "fled from their high seats in the temple of our civilization." He invoked "the analogue of war," proclaiming that, as in the First World War, the American people must march forward "as a trained and loyal army willing to sacrifice for the good of a common discipline." And if need be, he asserted, "I shall ask the Congress for the one remaining instrument to meet the crisis—broad Executive power to wage a war against the emergency, as great as the power that would be given to me if we were in fact invaded by a foreign foe."

On March 5, Roosevelt declared a four-day national bank holiday and summoned Congress to an emergency session. Congress convened on March 9 to begin what observers would call the Hundred Days. Roosevelt's initial legislative requests were cautious; por-

Beginning of the Hundred Days

tions had even been drafted by Hoover's advisers before leaving office. The first measure, the Emergency Banking Relief Bill, was introduced on March 9, passed sight unseen by unanimous House vote, approved 73 to 7 in the Senate, and signed by the president that evening. The act confirmed Roosevelt's emergency actions and provided for the reopening, under Treasury Department license, of banks that were solvent and the reorganization and management of those that were not. It also prohibited gold hoarding and export. But it was a conservative law that upheld the status quo, leaving the nation's banking system essentially unchanged, with the same people in charge. This was a special disappointment to those who had taken seriously the antibanker rhetoric of Roosevelt's inaugural address. Complained one representative, "The President drove the money-changers out of the Capitol on March 4th—and they were all back on the 9th."

On the next day, March 10, another conservative New Deal bill was introduced in Congress; ten days later it became law. Called the Economy Act, its purpose was to balance the federal budget by chopping veterans' benefits and allowances by $400 million and reducing by $100 million the pay of federal employees. Under Roosevelt, the budget balancers had won a battle that could not have been won under Hoover. Despite the deflationary effects of this legislation, the important point was that Roosevelt had acted and had done so boldly.

On Sunday evening, March 12, the president broadcast the first of his fireside chats, and 60 million people heard his comforting voice on their radios.

First Fireside Chat

His message: banks were once again safe places for depositors' savings. On Monday morning the banks opened their doors, but instead of queuing up to withdraw their savings, people were waiting outside to deposit their money. "The people trust this administration," a wealthy woman jotted in her diary, "as they distrusted the other." The bank runs were over; people had regained confidence in their political leadership, their banks, even their economic system.

So far, the New Deal had embraced a drastically deflationary economic policy that decreased rather than increased the amount of money in circulation.

Roosevelt next pursued a measure, the Beer-Wine Revenue Bill, that was not only deflationary but would actually take money out of people's pockets. The bill was designed to generate revenues by legalizing the sale of low-alcohol wines and beers and levying a tax on them. (Repeal of prohibition had been proposed by Congress in the Twenty-first Amendment in February 1933; it would be ratified by the states in December 1933.) To many, levying new taxes seemed a strange way to restore purchasing power to people who could not afford to buy what they needed. Roosevelt knew that. "I realize well," he wrote a friend, "that thus far we have actually given more of deflation than of inflation. . . . It is simply inevitable that we must inflate." He added that his "banker friends may be horrified" by the large-scale federal spending that was to come. And beginning in mid-March, Roosevelt did seek congressional authorization to spend.

LAUNCHING THE NEW DEAL

The New Deal seemed to promise something for everybody—farmers, businesspeople, workers, homeowners. Roosevelt was the artful broker, weighing the claims of these competing interest groups. On March 16, he sent to Congress the Agricultural Adjustment Bill, his plan to restore farmers' purchasing power. If overproduction was the cause of farmers' problems—falling prices and mounting surpluses—then the government had to encourage farmers to grow less food. Under the domestic allotment plan, as it was called, the government would pay farmers to reduce their acreage or plow under crops already in the fields. Farmers would receive payments based on *parity*, a system of regulated prices for corn, cotton, wheat, rice, hogs, and dairy products that would allow them the same purchasing power they had had during the prosperous period of 1909 through 1914. In effect, the government was making up the difference between the actual market value of farm products and the income farmers needed to

Agricultural Adjustment Act

make a profit. The funds for the subsidies would come from taxes levied on the processors of agricultural commodities.

Roosevelt's farm plan immediately encountered vehement opposition. How, people asked, could there be crop surpluses and overproduction when some Americans were hungry and even starving? Underconsumption, they argued, was the result of a maldistribution of wealth and power as well as of goods and services. Some politicians wanted to stimulate inflation by coining silver, printing greenbacks, altering the gold content of the dollar, or taking the nation off the gold standard altogether. Cheap money, they contended, was the farmers' panacea, for it would make it easier for them to repay their debts. On May 12 Congress finally overcame opposition to the domestic allotment plan and passed the Agricultural Adjustment Act (AAA). A month later the Farm Credit Act also became law. By providing short- and medium-term loans to farmers—more than $100 million worth in seven months—the Farm Credit Act enabled many farmers to refinance their mortgages and hang on to their homes and land.

Meanwhile, other relief measures became law. On March 21 the president requested massive infusions of relief of three kinds: a job corps called the Civilian Conservation Corps (CCC); direct cash grants to the states to provide relief payments for needy citizens; and public works projects. Ten days later Congress approved the CCC. Within four months 1,300 camps were in operation and 300,000 young men between the ages of eighteen and twenty-five went to work planting trees, clearing camping areas and beaches, and building bridges, dams, reservoirs, fish ponds, and fire towers. More than 2.5 million young men eventually lived and worked in CCC camps. Then on May 12 Congress passed the Federal Emergency Relief Act, which authorized $500 million in aid to state and local governments.

Roosevelt's proposed plan for public works became Title II of the National Industrial Recovery Act (NIRA). Passed on June 16, it established in the Public Works Administration (PWA) a fund of $3.3 billion to build roads, sewage and water systems, public buildings, and a host of other projects, including

Civilian Conservation Corps (CCC)

Under the Agricultural Adjustment Act, farmers received government payments for not planting crops or for destroying crops that had already been planted. These farmers in Kaufman County, Texas, are lined up for their checks. National Archives.

ships and naval aircraft. The purpose of the PWA was to prime the economic pump to spur economic recovery.

Pump priming was an unorthodox concept in 1933, and Roosevelt resorted to it only as a last-ditch measure. He remained orthodox in his views, anxious to return to a balanced budget at the earliest opportunity. Not until 1936 was the masterwork on pump priming, John Maynard Keynes's *General Theory of Employment, Interest and Money*, published. Roosevelt met with Keynes after the book's publication, but claimed he could not make heads or tails of the British economist's advice to spend massively.

If the AAA was the agricultural cornerstone of the New Deal, the National Industrial Recovery Act was the industrial cornerstone. The NIRA was a testimony to the New Deal belief in national planning as opposed to an individualistic, intensely competitive, laissez-faire economy. It was essential, the planners argued, for

Economic Planning under the NIRA

businesses to end cutthroat competition and raise prices by limiting production. Like the War Industries Board (WIB) during the First World War (see page 661), the NIRA exempted businesses from antitrust laws through the National Recovery Administration (NRA). The NRA adopted a symbol, the Blue Eagle, and rallied popular support through motorcades and mass meetings. Also under the NRA, competing businesses met with representatives of workers and consumers to draft codes of fair competition, which limited production and established prices.

With businesses enjoying new concessions, workers wanted a share of the pie too. Congress guaranteed their right to unionize and to bargain collectively in Section 7(a) of the NIRA, which called for industrywide codes establishing minimum wages and maximum hours.

One of the boldest programs that Congress enacted during this period concerned the badly depressed Tennessee River valley, which ran through Tennessee, North Carolina, Kentucky, Virginia, Mississippi,

New Deal Achievements

	Labor	Agriculture	Business and Industrial Recovery	Relief	Reform
1933	Section 7A of NIRA	Agricultural Adjustment Act Farm Credit Act	Emergency Banking Act Economy Act Beer and Wine Revenue Act Banking Act of 1933 (guaranteed deposits) National Industrial Recovery Act	Civilian Conservation Corps Federal Emergency Relief Act Home Owners Refinancing Act Public Works Administration Civil Works Administration	TVA Federal Securities Act
1934	National Labor Relations Board				Securities Exchange Act
1935	National Labor Relations (Wagner) Act	Resettlement Administration Rural Electrification Administration		Works Progress Administration and National Youth Administration	Banking Act of 1935 Social Security Act Public Utilities Holding Company Act Revenue Act (wealth tax)
1937		Farm Security Administration			
1938	Fair Labor Standards Act	Agricultural Adjustment Act of 1938			

Source: Adapted by permission from Charles Sellers, Henry May, and Neil R. McMillen, *A Synopsis of American History*, 5th ed., pp. 296–297. Copyright © 1981 by Houghton Mifflin Company.

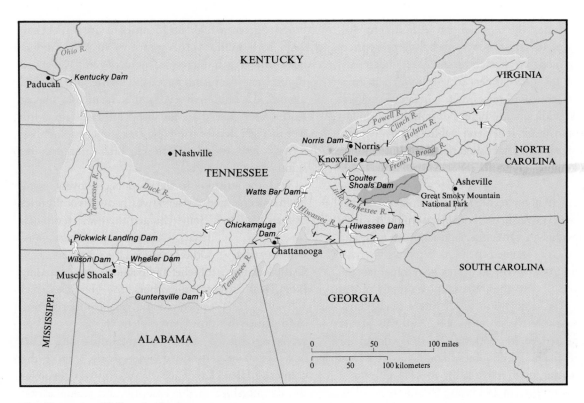

The Tennessee Valley Authority

Georgia, and Alabama. For years progressives led by Senator George Norris of Nebraska had advocated government operation of the Muscle Shoals electric power and nitrogen facilities on the Tennessee River. But Roosevelt's Tennessee Valley Authority (TVA), as finally established in May 1933, was a much broader program than the progressive plan. Its dams would not only serve to control floods, but they could also generate hydroelectric power, reclaim and reforest land, and prevent soil erosion. The TVA also would produce and sell nitrogen fertilizers to private citizens and nitrate explosives to the government; dig a 650-mile navigation channel from Knoxville to Paducah; and construct public power facilities as a yardstick for determining fair rates for privately produced electric power. The goal of the TVA was nothing less than enhancement of the economic well-being of the entire Tennessee River valley (see map).

Congress finally adjourned on June 16, its Hundred Days completed. Roosevelt had delivered fifteen messages to Congress, and fifteen significant laws had been enacted (see **End of the Hundred Days** table). Notable among these laws

were the Federal Securities Act, to compel brokers to tell the truth about new securities issues, and the Banking Act of 1933, which set up the Federal Deposit Insurance Corporation for insuring bank deposits. Finally, on April 19 the United States abandoned the gold standard by announcing that it would no longer guarantee the gold value of the dollar abroad. Freed from the gold standard, Roosevelt's monetary policy became another tool for economic recovery.

Within a few months of Roosevelt's taking office, the United States had rebounded from shock, hysteria, and near-collapse. Columnist Walter Lippmann wrote that at the time of the inauguration, the country was a collection of "disorderly panic-stricken mobs and factions. In the hundred days from March to June we became again an organized nation confident of our power to provide for our own security and to control our own destiny."

Throughout the remainder of 1933 and the spring and summer of 1934, more New Deal bills became law. The beneficiaries of many of the new recovery acts were property-owning farmers. In October 1933, for example, the Commodity Credit Corporation was organized under the Agricultural Adjustment Administration. Its purposes were to bolster crop prices by lending money to farmers against their underpriced crops, and to allow farmers to withhold their crops from the market until prices rose. Nonfarm legislation designated additional hundreds of millions of dollars for unemployment relief and public works. Finally, in 1934 legislation established the Securities and Exchange Commission and the National Labor Relations Board.

The New Deal represented interest-group democracy at work, with government benefits accruing not only to business but to agriculture and labor; to farm and homeowners; to corporations, railroads, and city governments; and to the jobless. In the midst of this coalition of all interests was President Roosevelt, the artful broker. And this broker state appeared to be working. In 1933 almost 13 million people had been jobless. Following New Deal legislation the figure fell steadily to 11.4 million in 1934, 10.6 million in 1935, and 9 million in 1936. Net farm income rose from $2.5 billion in 1932 to just over $3 billion in 1933, almost $3.5 billion in 1934, and $5.85 billion in 1935. And manufacturing salaries and wages also increased, jumping from $6.25 billion in 1933 to over $9.5 billion two years later and almost $13 billion in 1937.

Broker State Democracy

There was no doubt about the popularity of either the New Deal or Roosevelt. In the 1934 congressional elections, the Democrats gained ten seats in the House and ten in the Senate. The New Deal, according to Arthur Krock of the *New York Times,* had won "the most overwhelming victory in the history of American politics." And as for Roosevelt, "he has been all but crowned by the people," wrote William Allen White.

REACTIONS AGAINST THE NEW DEAL

Yet there was more than one way to read employment and income statistics and election returns. For example, though unemployment had dropped from a high of 13 million (25 percent) in 1933 to 9 million (16.9 percent) in 1936, it had been only 1.5 million (3.2 percent) in 1929. And though manufacturing wages and salaries had reached almost $13 billion in 1937, that figure was almost $1.5 billion less than the total for 1929. In other words, regardless of the New Deal's successes, it had a long way to go before reaching predepression standards.

With the arrival of partial economic recovery, many businesspeople and conservatives became vocal critics of the New Deal. Some charged there was too much taxation and government regulation. Others criticized the deficit financing of relief and public works. According to still others, the New Deal had subverted individual initiative and self-reliance by providing welfare payments. Conservatives hinted darkly of totalitarianism. This "maelstrom of centralized order-giving," wrote the columnist David Lawrence, "more strongly resembles the dictatorships of the Fascistic and Communistic states of Europe than it does the American system."

Conservative Critics of the New Deal

If businesspeople felt the government was their enemy, others thought the government favored business too much. Critics argued that business leaders had dominated the drafting of NRA codes, which, they claimed, favored industry's needs over those of workers and consumers. In addition, a major debate developed between the trustbusters and probusiness planners in the NRA. For a while, government propaganda urging Americans to support the NRA quieted the debate, particularly during the business recovery of 1933. In time, however, criticism grew. Farmers, labor unions, individual entrepreneurs, and antitrust critics complained that the NRA set prices too high and favored large-scale producers over small businesses. And the federal courts began to scrutinize the constitutionality of the legislation in cases brought by critics.

The AAA came under attack as well because of its encouragement of cutbacks in production. In 1933 farmers had plowed under 10.4 million acres of cotton and slaughtered 220,000 sows and 6 million pigs—at a time when people were ill-clothed and ill-fed. Though for landowning farmers the program was successful, the average person found such waste to be shocking. And what about tenant farmers and sharecroppers? They too were supposed to receive government payments for taking crops out of cultivation, but very few of them, especially if they were black, received what they were entitled to. Furthermore, the AAA's hopes that landlords would keep their tenants on the land even while cutting production were not fulfilled. In the South the number of sharecropper farms dropped from 776,278 in 1930 to 541,291 in 1940. The result was a homeless population, some of whom, known in the folklore of the times as "Okies" and "Arkies," packed up and took off for California.

As dissatisfaction mounted, so too did the appeal of various demagogues. Father Charles Coughlin, the Roman Catholic priest whose weekly radio sermons offered a curious combination of anti-Communism, anticapitalism, and anti-Semitism, was one of the more famous. According to Coughlin, the worst abuses of capitalism had been inflicted by the Jews. Such anti-Semitism also was popular among some farm leaders (for example, Milo Reno of the Farm Holiday Association, who referred to the New Deal as the "Jew Deal") and some urban Catholics. For a while Coughlin supported the New Deal, calling it "Christ's deal." But he was critical of the AAA's plowing-under of crops and slaughtering of livestock. In late 1934, declaring "these old parties are all but dead," Coughlin organized the National Union for Social Justice and began to criticize the New Deal for having "out-Hoovered Hoover."

Demagogic Attacks on the New Deal

Another challenge to the New Deal came from Dr. Francis E. Townsend, who had conceived what he called an Old Age Revolving Pensions plan. Under Townsend's scheme the government would pay monthly pensions of $200 to all citizens over age sixty, on condition that they spent the money in the same month they received it. Townsend claimed his plan would not only aid the aged but cure the depression by pumping enormous purchasing power into the economy. Though the plan was fiscally impossible, it addressed a real need. Many old people suffered extreme deprivation in the 1930s, a time when local relief for the elderly was nonexistent in many places and Social Security had not yet been established.

And then there was Huey Long, "the Kingfish," perhaps the most successful demagogue in American history. In 1928 Long was elected governor of Louisiana

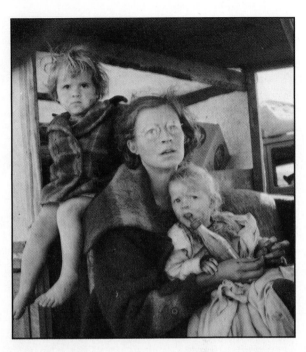

Plagued by dust storms, evictions, and the unsympathetic policies of the Agricultural Adjustment Administration, thousands of tenant farmers and sharecroppers were forced to leave their land during the Great Depression. Known as "Okies" and "Arkies," they took off for California with their few belongings. This woman and her two children were photographed by Dorothea Lange near Tulelake, California, in 1939. Library of Congress.

with the slogan "Every Man a King, But No One Wears a Crown." Highly intelligent, aggressive, and at times brutal, Long adopted the methods of a dictator, especially after defeating an effort to remove him from office in 1929. At first Long supported the New Deal; but he found the Economy Act and the NRA too conservative, and began to believe that Roosevelt had fallen captive to big business and big money. Long countered in 1934 with the Share Our Wealth Society, which advocated the seizure by taxation of all incomes over $1 million and all inheritances over $5 million. With those funds, the government would furnish each family a homestead allowance of $5,000 and an annual income of $2,000, along with free college education, government storage of crops and control of planting, and limitations on working hours. By mid-1935 Long's movement claimed 7 million members, and few doubted that Long aspired to the presidency. Though an assassin's bullet extinguished

Senator Huey Long of Louisiana (center) had a mass following in the 1930s, and he had presidential ambitions. But he was assassinated in 1935, the same evening this photograph was taken. Long fell into the arms of James O'Connor (left), a political crony, while Louisiana's Governor O. K. Allen (right) seized a pistol and dashed into a corridor after the murderer, shouting, "If there's shooting, I want to be in on it." National Archives.

his ambition in September 1935, the Share Our Wealth movement persisted under a new leader, the vitriolic anti-Semite Gerald L. K. Smith.

Some politicians of the 1930s, like Floyd Olson, governor of Minnesota, declared themselves socialists. Olson sought a third party that would "preach the gospel of government and collective ownership of the means of production and distribution." In neighboring Wisconsin the left-wing Progressive party re-elected Robert La Follette, Jr., to the Senate in 1934, sent seven of the state's ten representatives to Washington, and placed La Follette's brother Philip in the governorship. And the old muckraker Upton Sinclair almost won the Democratic gubernatorial nomination in California

Left-wing Critics of the New Deal

in 1934 on the platform End Poverty in California (EPIC).

Perhaps the most controversial alternative to the New Deal was the Communist party of the United States of America (CPUSA). In the early days of the depression Communists had organized hunger marches and helped to establish labor unions among auto and electrical workers, seamen, and longshoremen (see pages 724–725). And in 1932 a number of distinguished writers had endorsed the Communist presidential candidate, William Z. Foster. But membership in the CPUSA remained small until 1935, when the party leadership changed its strategy. Proclaiming "Communism is Twentieth Century Americanism," the CPUSA disclaimed any intention of overthrowing the United States government and began to cooperate with left-wing labor unions, student groups, and writers' organizations.

Russia's response to the Spanish Civil War also encouraged some Americans to join the CPUSA. Only Russia seemed determined to stem the tide of fascism that had washed over Germany and Italy and in 1936 threatened Spain (see Chapter 27). One convert to the CPUSA, writer and editor Whittaker Chambers, explained that Communism offered "what nothing else in the dying world had power to offer at the same intensity—faith and a vision." Still, at its high point for the decade in 1938, the CPUSA had only 55,000 members.

In addition to challenges from the right and the left, the New Deal was threatened by the Supreme Court. Many New Deal laws had been hastily drafted and enacted, and the majority of

Supreme Court Decisions Against the New Deal

the justices feared that this legislation had vested too much power in the presidency. In January 1935, in *Panama Refining Co.* v. *Ryan*, the Court struck down part of the NIRA. By granting the president power to prohibit interstate and foreign shipment of oil, the Court ruled, Congress had unconstitutionally delegated legislative power to the executive branch. Then on May 27 the Court unanimously struck down the whole NIRA (*Schechter* v. *U.S.*) on the grounds that it gave excessive legislative power to the White House, and that the commerce clause of the Constitution did not give the federal government authority to regulate intrastate businesses. Roosevelt's industrial recovery program was dead. In January 1936 his farm program met a similar fate when the Court invalidated the AAA (*U.S.* v. *Butler*), deciding that agriculture was a local problem and thus, under the Tenth Amendment, subject to state, not federal, action.

As Roosevelt looked ahead to the presidential election of 1936, he saw that he was in danger of losing his capacity to lead and to govern. His coalition of all interests was breaking up; radicals and demagogues were offering Americans alternative programs; and the Supreme Court was dismantling the New Deal. In the spring and summer of 1935, Roosevelt took the initiative once more, and the New Deal scored some of its biggest victories. So impressive was the new legislation that some historians have called it the Second New Deal.

THE SECOND NEW DEAL

There was an important difference between the First and Second New Deals. In 1933 and 1934 Roosevelt had cooperated with business. Beginning in 1935, however, he denounced business leaders for placing their selfish interests above the national welfare. Roosevelt also was being pushed left by the liberal Congress that had been elected in 1934 and by the unions' militancy and growing ranks.

The first triumph of the Second New Deal was an innocuous-sounding but momentous law called the Emergency Relief Appropriation Act, which

Emergency Relief Appropriation Act

Congress passed and Roosevelt signed in April 1935. The act authorized the president to issue executive orders establishing massive public works programs for the jobless, including the Works Progress Administration (WPA).

Later renamed the Work Projects Administration, the WPA ultimately employed more than 8.5 million people on a total of 1.4 million projects. By the time it was terminated in 1943, the WPA had built over 650,000 miles of highways, streets, and roads, 125,000 public buildings, and 8,000 parks, as well as numerous bridges, airports, and other structures. But WPA did more than lay bricks. Its Federal Theatre Project brought plays, vaudeville shows, and circuses to cities and towns across the country, and WPA artists painted murals in post offices and other public buildings. The Federal Music Project and the WPA Dance Theatre sponsored laboratories for young composers and choreographers. And the Federal Writers' Project hired writers like Conrad Aiken, John Cheever, Claude McKay, John Steinbeck, and Richard Wright to write local guidebooks and regional, ethnic, and folk histories.

Besides the WPA, the Emergency Relief Appropriation Act funded other relief and public works measures. The Resettlement Administration (RA) resettled destitute families and organized rural homestead communities and suburban greenbelt towns for low-income workers. The Rural Electrification Administration (REA) distributed electricity to isolated

During the Great Depression the Works Progress Administration (WPA) employed artists to decorate public buildings and record its public works projects for posterity. Harold Lehman's painting of a burly, determined driller was one product of the federally sponsored employment program. National Museum of American Art, Transfer from the Newark Museum.

rural areas. And the National Youth Administration (NYA) sponsored work relief programs for young adults and provided jobs for the part-time employment of students.

As significant as these achievements were, Roosevelt wanted new legislation, some of it aimed at controlling the activities of big business. The Supreme Court had condemned the government-business cooperation that had been the foundation of the First Hundred Days. And businesspeople had become increasingly critical of Roosevelt and the New Deal. Now Roosevelt

determined that if big business would not cooperate with government, government should "cut the giants down to size" through antitrust suits and heavy corporate taxes. In June he asked Congress to enact five major bills: a labor bill sponsored by Senator Robert Wagner; a Social Security bill; a banking bill; a measure to regulate public-utilities holding companies; and a "soak-the-rich" tax bill.

These were the Second Hundred Days; when they were over, the president would have everything he had requested. On July 5 the National Labor Relations

Roosevelt's Second Hundred Days

(Wagner) Act granted workers something for which they had long struggled: the right to unionize and to bargain collectively with management. When the Supreme Court struck down the NIRA, labor unions had lost their federal protection. But the new Wagner Act was stronger than its predecessor. It empowered the National Labor Relations Board to supervise the democratic election of bargaining agents and to issue cease-and-desist orders against unfair labor practices by employers, such as the firing of workers for union membership. Now employers had no legal way to resist unionization of their plants.

On August 15 Roosevelt signed the Social Security Act, which established a cooperative federal-state system of unemployment compensation and old-age

Social Security Act

and survivors' insurance. According to the law, workers who paid social security taxes out of their wages would receive retirement benefits at age sixty-five. The benefits would be paid for partially by their own contributions and partially by their employers. Social Security was a conservative measure: the government did not pay for old-age benefits; workers and their bosses did. The tax was also regressive—the more workers earned, the less they were taxed proportionately—and deflationary—it took money out of people's pockets that it did not repay for years. Finally, many people were ineligible for coverage under the law, including farm workers, domestic servants, and many hospital and restaurant workers. Large numbers of women and nonwhites were excluded from coverage. But although the act was far from inclusive, it was still a milestone in American history. It acknowledged the government's responsibility to establish a system of insurance for the aged, the dependent, the disabled, and the temporarily unemployed.

In the next two weeks Roosevelt gained the remainder of what he had asked for, including the Banking Act of 1935, the Public Utilities Holding Company (Wheeler-Rayburn) Act, and the Revenue (Wealth Tax) Act of 1935. None of these laws contained everything Roosevelt had requested. The Wealth Tax Act, which some critics saw as the president's attempt to "steal Huey's thunder," did not result in a redistribution of income, for instance, though it did increase the income taxes paid by the wealthy. It also increased taxes on inheritances, large gifts, and profits from the sale of property.

The Second Hundred Days indicated not only that the president was once again in charge, but that he was set to run for re-election. The campaign was less heated than might have been expected, however. Naturally the Republican nominee, Governor Alf Landon of Kansas, criticized Roosevelt, condemning him for threatening the free enterprise system with regulated monopolies, unconstitutional laws, and deficit spending. But Republicans conceded the need for government action, and they did not advocate wholesale repeal of the New Deal. The followers of Father Coughlin, Dr. Townsend, and the late Senator Long banded together in the Union party and nominated Representative William Lemke of North Dakota. The Socialists nominated Norman Thomas; the Communists, Earl Browder.

Election of 1936

The president and the Democratic party swept to a landslide victory. Roosevelt polled 27.8 million votes to Landon's 16.7 million; Lemke, Thomas, and Browder together received slightly over 1 million. The Democrats carried every state but Maine and Vermont and won huge majorities in the House and Senate. Some observers worried that the two-party system was about to collapse.

Political analysts have suggested that demographic shifts lay behind the Democratic triumph at the polls. In the 1920s and 1930s the sons and daughters of 13 million southern and eastern European immigrants were reaching voting age and swelling the ranks of their parents' traditional party. In addition, the 6 million Americans who had migrated from farms to cities in the 1920s looked to the government for rent control and food purity laws, regulation of working hours and conditions, and welfare for the unemployed. Before long they too had gravitated to the Democratic party. In 1920 the nation's twelve largest cities gave the Republicans 1.6 million more votes than the Democrats. In 1924 the Republican plurality dropped to 1.25 million, and in 1928 it disappeared. But that was just the beginning of the Democratic groundswell, which in 1932 jumped to 1.9 million and in 1936 to 3.6 million more big-city votes than the Republicans.

By 1936 Roosevelt and the Democrats had forged what observers have called the "New Deal coalition." The growing strength of the party in the cities, the suffering wrought by the Great Depression, and the New Deal response to social distress had converged to make Roosevelt the champion of the urban masses, as well as of farmers and the elderly. Labor, especially the new unions of the Congress of Industrial Organizations (CIO), was an indispensable member of the coalition (see pages 749–751). These unions fused the interests of millions of workers, native and foreign-born, black and white, male and female, skilled and unskilled. And black voters in northern cities, most of whom had been Republicans prior to the 1930s, now cast their lot with the Democratic party (see pages 752–753). Finally, many lifelong Socialists began to vote Democratic. In 1932 Norman Thomas, the Socialist party candidate, had polled 884,000 votes; in 1936 his total slipped to just 187,000. The Democratic party had become the dominant half of the two-party system.

New Deal Coalition

ROOSEVELT'S SECOND TERM: THE UNREALIZED PROMISE

Despite the bold and unprecedented steps of his first term, Roosevelt faced a darkening horizon during his second term. The economy faltered again between 1937 and 1939, bringing renewed unem-

ALL I SAID WAS "GIMME SIX MORE JUSTICES!"

President Roosevelt's court-packing plan provoked an outcry from Democrats as well as Republicans. Roosevelt's miscalculation resulted in a major defeat for his administration. Library of Congress.

ployment and suffering. And Europe drew closer to war, threatening to drag the United States into the conflict (see Chapter 27). To gain support for his foreign and military policies, Roosevelt began to court conservative politicians who had been long-time opponents of his domestic reforms. The eventual result was the demise of the New Deal.

In several instances Roosevelt caused his own defeat. The Supreme Court had invalidated much of the work of the First Hundred Days; now Roosevelt feared it would do the same with the fruits of the Second Hundred Days. So in February 1937 the president sent to Congress his Judiciary Reorganization Bill. What the federal judiciary needed, he claimed, was a more enlightened and progressive world view. Four of the justices steadfastly opposed the New Deal; three generally approved of it; and two were swing votes: Chief Justice Charles Evans Hughes and Associate Justice Owen J. Roberts. Although the justices had overturned some New Deal legislation on unanimous votes, they had also declared some other laws unconstitutional by such narrow margins as 5 to 4 and 6 to 3.

What Roosevelt requested was the authority to add a federal judge whenever an incumbent who had already served at least ten years failed to retire within six months of reaching age seventy. He wanted the

Roosevelt's Court-packing Plan

power to name up to fifty additional federal judges, including six to the Supreme Court. Though Roosevelt spoke of understaffed courts and aged and feeble judges, it was obvious that he envisioned using the bill to create a Supreme Court sympathetic to the New Deal.

Opposition to Roosevelt's attempt to pack the Court was widespread and vocal. Naturally, Republicans and some conservative Democrats opposed the bill, but liberals resisted as well. In many ways Roosevelt had only himself to blame. Had he made the bill an issue during the 1936 presidential election and won a great victory nevertheless, he could have sent his plan to Congress as the mandate of the people. Instead he had to concede defeat. The bill Roosevelt signed in August made pensions available to retiring judges, but it denied him the power to increase the number of judges.

This episode had an ironic final twist. During the public debate over court packing, the two swing-vote justices, Hughes and Roberts, began to vote in favor of liberal, pro-New Deal rulings. In March 1937, for example, the Court upheld a Washington State minimum-wage statute 5 to 4 (*West Coast Hotel* v. *Parrish*). Just a year before, in a case almost indistinguishable from this one, the Court had invalidated a similar New York State law. Then in April the Court upheld the Wagner Act 5 to 4 (*N.L.R.B.* v. *Jones & Laughlin Steel Corp.*), ruling that Congress's power to regulate interstate commerce involved also the power to regulate production of goods for interstate commerce. And in May the Court upheld the Social Security Act 5 to 4.

Roosevelt had lost the legislative battle but won the war for a more progressive judicial outlook. Encouraged by the new pensions, judges past the age of seventy did begin to retire, and the president was able to appoint seven new associate justices in the next four years, including such notables as Hugo Black, Felix Frankfurter, and William O. Douglas. Overwhelmingly, the new justices voted to sustain Roosevelt's policies and actions, and they continued to have a progressive influence for decades.

Another New Deal defeat, the renewed economic recession of 1937 through 1939, had no unexpected payoffs. Roosevelt had never abandoned his commitment to the balanced budget. In 1937, confident

Recession of 1937–1939 that most of the problems of the depression had been solved, he began to order drastic cutbacks in government spending. Between January and August 1937 the WPA cut its job rolls in half, from 3 million to 1.5 million people, and the government slashed other relief programs as well. To reduce the inflation rate of 3.6 percent, the Federal Reserve System increased the reserve requirements of member banks. The sudden tightening of credit sent the economy into a tailspin: unemployment soared from 14.3 percent in 1937 to 19.1 percent the next year.

In response to the new recession Roosevelt eventually revived deficit financing, and Congress appropriated billions more for the WPA, the CCC, and other programs. But even with sudden infusions of relief in 1938, unemployment still stood at 17.2 percent in 1939. Not until the end of that year did the economy return to 1937 levels. Many people wondered whether they had lived through two years of unnecessary recession and hardship.

Roosevelt's personal campaign against three conservative southern Democrats in the off-year elections of 1938 further revealed his desperation. Senators Walter George of Georgia, "Cotton Ed" Smith of South Carolina, and Millard Tydings of Maryland, all critics of the New Deal, won re-election despite Roosevelt's campaigning against them. As it turned out, Roosevelt would soon need the support of these conservatives for his programs of military rearmament and preparedness.

In spring 1938, with conflict over events in Europe commanding more and more of the nation's attention, the New Deal came to an end. The last significant laws enacted were a new Agricultural Adjustment Act and the Fair Labor Standards Act, which established minimum wages and maximum hours for many but by no means all workers.

THE RISE OF THE CIO

As governor of New York, Franklin Roosevelt had expressed his belief in the right of workers to organize and bargain with their bosses through representatives of their own choosing. Yet he arrived at the White House with no specific program for guaranteeing this right. Section 7(a) of the NIRA had not been his idea; when he signed the bill into law he did not appreciate what it meant or how it could be enforced.

On its enactment in June 1933, Section 7(a) inspired the organization of new unions and the vigorous recruitment of members. "Millions of workers throughout the nation," recalled American Federation of Labor (AFL) President William Green, "stood up for the first time in their lives to receive their charter of industrial freedom." Organizers for the United Mine Workers (UMW) told coal miners, "President Roosevelt wants you to join the union," and many thousands did. By October 1933 an additional 1.5 million workers had enlisted in unions, bringing total membership to 4 million. With passage of the Wagner Act in mid-1935, labor union recruiting received another big boost; within three years total membership surpassed 7 million.

But these gains did not always come easily. Management put up determined resistance in the 1930s, hiring armed thugs to intimidate workers and break up strikes. Violence surfaced in the **Rivalry Between Craft and Industrial Unions** steel, automobile, and textile industries and among the dock workers of the West Coast, the lumber workers of the Pacific Northwest, and the teamsters in Minneapolis. Labor confronted yet another obstacle in the AFL craft unions' traditional skepticism and hostility toward industrial unions. Craft unions typically consisted of skilled workers in a particular trade, such as carpentry, plumbing, or typography. Industrial unions, on the other hand, represented all the workers in a given industry, skilled and unskilled. The UMW, the United Brewery Workers, and the International Ladies' Garment Workers Union were all industrial rather than craft unions. Ever since its establishment in 1886, the AFL had been dominated by craft unions. But organizing gains in the 1930s were far more impressive in industrial unions than in craft unions, with hundreds of thousands of workers joining unions in such industries as autos, garments, rubber, and steel. What resulted was a struggle for control of the labor movement between craft and industrial union leaders.

Personifying this power struggle were the leaders

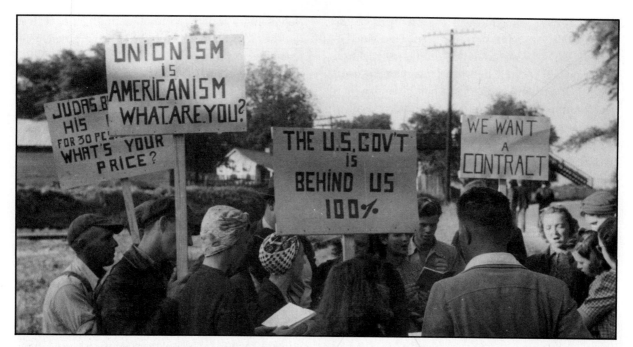

Like many pickets at this time, these men and women proclaimed their New Deal support and their "Americanism." Singing union songs and hymns, these pickets met outside of a textile mill in Greensboro, Georgia, in 1941. Library of Congress.

of the two sides, William Green, leader of the AFL, and John L. Lewis of the UMW. Lewis was probably the most colorful and tenacious labor leader in the nation's history, a fighter with a flair for the dramatic. William Green, on the other hand, was dull. But he was president of the entire AFL, whereas Lewis represented only one of the many unions within the AFL.

Attempts to reconcile the craft and industrial union movements failed, and in late 1935 Lewis resigned as vice president of the AFL. He and other industrial unionists within the AFL formed the Committee for Industrial Organization (CIO). When the AFL's Executive Council demanded that the CIO disband, Lewis replied: "The American Federation of Labor is standing still, with its face toward the dead past." In 1938 the AFL expelled the CIO unions, and the CIO reorganized itself as the Congress of Industrial Organizations. By that time CIO membership stood at 3.7 million, more than the AFL's 3.4 million.

The CIO, which in the 1930s evolved into a pragmatic, bread-and-butter labor organization, had or-

ganized millions of workers who had never before had an opportunity to join a union.

Sit-down Strikes One of these unions, the United Auto Workers (UAW), scored a major victory in late 1936. The union, thirty thousand strong, demanded recognition from General Motors, Chrysler, and Ford. When GM refused, the UAW launched a new kind of strike: the sit-down. Beginning in the Fisher Body plants in Flint, Michigan, workers refused to leave the plants. To discourage the strikers, GM managers turned off the heat; when that tactic failed, they called the police, who were met by a barrage of missiles—iron bolts, coffee mugs, and pop bottles. When the police resorted to tear gas, the strikers turned the plant's water hoses on them, and the police retreated in what the high-spirited strikers called the Battle of the Running Bulls.

The strike lasted for weeks, GM obtained a court order to evacuate the plant, but the strikers continued, risking imprisonment and fines. With the support of their families and neighborhoods, the workers stuck

On Memorial Day 1937, Chicago police used guns, clubs, and tear gas to break up a peaceful picket line at a Republic Steel plant. Ten people were killed and forty wounded in the Memorial Day Massacre.   *Wide World Photos.*

to their rigid discipline. Community women organized an "emergency brigade" to picket and deliver food and supplies to the strikers. In 1937 the UAW prevailed: GM agreed to recognize the union. Chrysler signed a similar agreement, but Ford held out for four more years, a time of bloody encounters between the UAW and union-busting hoodlums hired by the Ford Service Department.

What made the sit-down strike significant was that it spread to all kinds of workers: textile, glass, and rubber workers, dime store clerks, janitors, dressmakers, and pie bakers began using the technique. Some people condemned the sit-down as a trespass on private property; others endorsed it, including muckraker Upton Sinclair, who wrote that "for 75 years big business has been sitting down on the American people, and now I am delighted to see the process reversed."

In 1937 too the Steel Workers Organizing Committee (SWOC) signed a contract with the nation's largest steelmaker, U.S. Steel, that guaranteed an eight-hour day and a forty-hour week. Other steel companies refused to go along, however. Confrontations between these so-called little steel companies and the SWOC led to violence. On Memorial Day in Chicago, strikers and their families had joined with sympathizers in a peaceful picket line in front of the Republic Steel plant. Suddenly and without provocation the police opened fire. They continued to shoot into the crowd even as people turned away and began to run. Of the ten fatalities, none had been shot in the front of the body; of the forty gunshot wounds, only four were frontal.

Memorial Day Massacre

As senseless as the Memorial Day Massacre was, its occurrence was not surprising. During the 1930s industries had hired private police agents and accumulated large stores of arms and ammunition for use in deterring workers from organizing and joining unions. A Senate committee headed by Robert La Follette, Jr., found that companies had spent millions of dollars in the process. Republic Steel, for example, was the nation's largest single purchaser of tear and sickening gas. Youngstown Sheet and Tube owned 8 machine guns, 369 rifles, 190 shotguns, 450 revolvers, and thousands of rounds of ammunition. All told, companies had hired almost four thousand private detectives to infiltrate unions, provoke discontent, impede organization, and report on union activities.

Through it all, the CIO continued to enroll new members. By 1938 industrial unions had enlisted 600,000 miners, 375,000 steelworkers, 400,000 auto workers, 300,000 textile workers, 250,000 ladies' garment workers, and 100,000 agricultural and packinghouse workers. By the end of the decade the CIO had succeeded in organizing most of the nation's mass-production industries.

MIXED PROGRESS FOR

NONWHITES

For another segment of the New Deal coalition, black Americans, Franklin D. Roosevelt had become the most appealing president since Abraham Lincoln. Part of the reason was the courageous way he bore his physical disability. Blacks, who suffered from a handicap of their own—racism—knew what courage was. Moreover, Roosevelt seemed a decided improvement over Herbert Hoover, who had nominated a white supremacist to the Supreme Court (see page 721) and appeared hardhearted in the face of extreme suffering. Blacks suffered more than whites during the depression, and Roosevelt, in his fireside chats and through his personal magnetism and buoyancy, spoke directly to them. When they saw pictures of black visitors at the White House and read about Roosevelt's Black Cabinet, they were heartened.

The Black Cabinet, or black brain trust, was unique in United States history. Never before had there been so many black advisers at the White House, and never had they been highly trained professionals.

Black Cabinet There were black lawyers, journalists, and doctors of philosophy; black experts on housing, labor, and social welfare. William H. Hastie and Robert C. Weaver, both of whom held advanced degrees from Harvard, served in the Department of the Interior. Mary McLeod Bethune, a college president, was director of the Division of Negro Affairs of the National Youth Administration. Eugene Kinckle Jones, executive secretary of the National Urban League, and Lawrence A. Oxley, a professional social worker, served in comparable posts in the Departments of Commerce and Labor. Black social scientists, among them Ralph Bunche, Abram L. Harris, and Rayford W. Logan, acted as government consultants.

There were also among the New Dealers some whites who had committed themselves to first-class citizenship for Afro-Americans. Foremost among these people was Eleanor Roosevelt. In 1939, when the acclaimed black contralto Marian Anderson was barred from performing in Washington's Constitution Hall by its owners, the Daughters of the American Revolution, Mrs. Roosevelt arranged for Anderson to sing on Easter Sunday at the Lincoln Memorial.

The president himself, however, remained uncommitted to black civil rights. Fearful of alienating southern whites, he never endorsed two key goals of the civil rights struggle: a federal law against lynching and abolition of the poll tax. Furthermore, some New Deal programs functioned in ways that were definitely hostile to black Americans. The AAA, rather than benefiting black tenant farmers and sharecroppers, actually forced many of them off the land. The Federal Housing Administration (FHA) refused to guarantee mortgages on houses purchased by blacks in white neighborhoods. The CCC was racially segregated, as was much of the TVA, which constructed all-white towns and handed out skilled jobs to whites first. Finally, waiters, cooks, hospital orderlies, janitors, farm workers, and domestics, many of whom were black, were excluded from Social Security coverage and from the minimum-wage provisions of the Fair Labor Standards Act of 1938. In short, though blacks benefited, they did not get their fair share.

Despite these shortcomings, blacks overwhelmingly supported Roosevelt's New Deal. As Nancy J. Weiss,

Antiblack Effects of the New Deal

the historian, has written: "Meager though the Negro's share may have been, it came in the form of tangible benefits that touched the lives of millions of black Americans." And at election time, black voters showed their gratitude by giving Roosevelt large majorities.

Confronted with the mixed message of the New Deal, some blacks concluded that ultimately they could depend only on themselves and organized self-help and direct-action movements. Black tenant farmers and sharecroppers joined with poor whites to form the Southern Tenant Farmers' Union. In the North blacks boycotted stores in Don't Buy Where You Can't Work campaigns, launched Jobs for Negroes movements, and started tenants' unions to fight high rents. More and more they criticized the NAACP for ignoring the economics of second-class citizenship and for being too middle-class and legalistic in its war on racism. Although the NAACP had scored notable victories in opening up graduate and professional schools to black students, critics charged that these gains benefited only the black bourgeoisie, not the masses who above all needed jobs.

Nowhere was the trend toward direct action more evident than in the March on Washington Movement of 1941. In that year billions of federal dollars flowed into American industry as the nation

March on Washington Movement
prepared for the possibility of another world war. The government funds generated many thousands of new jobs, but discrimination deprived blacks of their fair share. One executive in the aircraft industry notified black job applicants that "the Negro will be considered only as janitors and in other similar capacities." So in early 1941, A. Philip Randolph, president of the Brotherhood of Sleeping Car Porters, proposed that blacks march on the nation's capital to demand equal access to jobs in defense industries.

The idea was a popular one, and by midsummer thousands of blacks were ready to march. Roosevelt and other government officials feared that the march might provoke riots and that Communists might infiltrate the movement. The president announced that if the march were cancelled, he would issue an executive order with "teeth in it" prohibiting discrimination in war industries and in the government. The result was Executive Order No. 8802, issued on June 25, 1941, which established the Fair Employment

In 1938 Eleanor Roosevelt presented the NAACP's Spingarn Medal to the black opera star Marian Anderson. A year later when the Daughters of the American Revolution refused to let Anderson perform in Washington's Constitution Hall, Roosevelt arranged for her to sing before a much larger crowd at the Lincoln Memorial. *Metropolitan Opera Archives.*

Practices Committee (FEPC). The March on Washington Movement anticipated future trends in the civil rights movement. It was all-black; its tactic was direct action—a threat by the masses to take to the streets; and the beneficiaries of the movement were the urban working classes, not the black bourgeoisie.

Native Americans benefited more directly than blacks from the New Deal. In recent years they had suffered from governmental neglect (see page 719),

Indian Reorganization Act
but in 1933 with the New Deal, federal policy changed. Roosevelt appointed John Collier commissioner of Indian affairs. In the 1920s, as founder of the American Indian Defense Association, Collier had crusaded for Indian landownership; now he championed the Indian Reorganization (Wheeler-Howard) Act of 1934, which

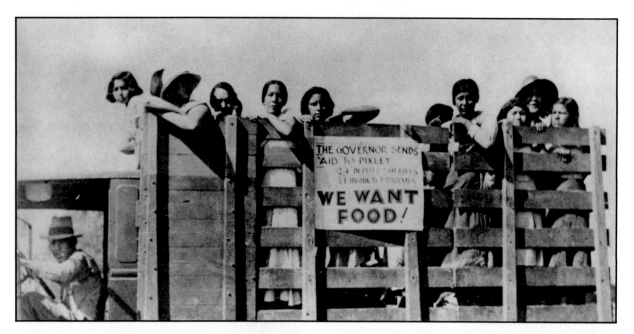

Violence erupted in October 1933 in California's San Joaquin Valley. When Mexican farm workers struck, the growers evicted them and their families. The growers also fired upon workers holding strike meetings at Pixley and Arvin, killing three. This group of Mexican women was bound for the picket line to protest for food relief for the hungry families.   Library of Congress.

ended the allotment policy of the Dawes Severalty Act of 1887 (see pages 464–465).

"The allotment act," Collier wrote in 1934, "contemplates total landlessness for the Indians of the third generation of each allotted tribe." First the tribal lands had been divided among the tribal members, many of whom then sold their holdings to white ranchers, miners, and farmers. Indeed, since 1887, Indian landholdings had dropped from 138 million acres to 48 million acres, 20 million of which were arid or semiarid. The Indian Reorganization Act sought to reverse the process by restoring lands to tribal ownership and forbidding future division of Indian lands into individual parcels. Other provisions of the act enabled tribes to obtain loans for economic development and to establish self-government. Collier also encouraged the perpetuation of Indian religions and cultures. One of his orders stated: "No interference with Indian religious life or expression will hereafter be tolerated. The cultural history of Indians is in all respects to be considered equal to that of any non-

Indian group. And it is desirable that Indians be bilingual." Collier's reforms would stand until 1953 (see page 857).

Mexican-Americans also suffered extreme hardship during the depression, but no government programs benefited them. Indeed, due to a variety of government discouragements (see page 719), many Mexican-Americans packed up their belongings and left the United States. According to the federal census, the Mexican-born population dropped from 617,000 in 1930 to 377,000 in 1940. One reason for this sharp decline was that many employers had changed their minds about the desirability of hiring Mexican-American farm workers. In the 1920s farmers had boasted that Mexican-Americans were a cheap, docile labor supply and would not join unions. But in the 1930s Mexican-Americans belied their image by engaging in prolonged and sometimes bloody strikes. During one protest in the strawberry fields of El Monte, California, workers established their own union, the Confederación de Uniones de Campesinos y Obreros

Mexicanos (CUCOM), which waged a couple of dozen strikes from 1933 to 1936. In united action in the San Joaquin valley in October 1933, eighteen thousand cotton pickers walked off their jobs and set up a "strike city" after being evicted from the growers' camps. Shortly after, their union hall was riddled with bullets and two strikers died.

The New Deal offered little help to these Mexican-Americans. The AAA was created to assist property-owning farmers, not migratory farm workers. The Wagner Act did not cover farm workers' unions, nor did the Social Security Act or the Fair Labor Standards Act cover farm laborers. One New Deal agency, the Farm Security Administration (FSA), was established in 1937 to help farm workers, in part by setting up migratory labor camps. But the FSA came too late to help Mexican-Americans, most of whom had by that time been replaced by dispossessed white farmers. Between 1935 and 1940 more than 350,000 Okies and Arkies fled to California from Oklahoma, Arkansas, Texas, and other drought-stricken "Dust Bowl" states. As early as 1936 they made up 85 to 90 percent of the state's migratory work force, compared to less than 20 percent before the depression.

In just a few years, however, Mexican-Americans would be back. With the onset of the Second World War, the United States would again need Mexican-Americans to work in the fields and on the railroads. In 1942 the United States and Mexico would agree to the *bracero* program, whereby Mexicans would be admitted to the United States on short-term work contracts, with guarantees of minimum wages, inspected housing, and return transportation.

WOMEN, WORK, AND THE DEPRESSION

During the depression women had to work overtime to maintain themselves and their families. In *It's Up to the Women* (1933), Eleanor Roosevelt wrote that during such periods, wives and mothers often had to bear a heavier responsibility than husbands and fathers. "The women know," she asserted, "that

life must go on and that the needs of life must be met. . . ."

With families experiencing severe income reductions, wives and mothers followed the maxim, "Use it up, wear it out, make it do, or do without." Making do, Eleanor Roosevelt wrote, meant

Wives and Mothers Face the Depression "endless little economies and constant anxiety for fear of some catastrophe such as accident or illness which may completely swamp the family budget." Women bought day-old bread and cheap cuts of meat; they relined old coats with blankets and saved string, rags, and broken crockery for possible future use. In short, many families with reduced incomes were able to maintain their standard of living only because of astute women shoppers or because women substituted their own labor in the home for goods and services they used to purchase. Husbands and fathers shared these financial concerns, but it was usually women's responsibility to do the family budgeting; it was estimated that wives and mothers in the 1930s allocated over 80 percent of all family income.

An irony of the 1930s was that women's assistance with family expenses did not improve their status. As the sociologists Robert and Helen Lynd observed at the time: "The men, cut adrift from their usual routine, lost much of their sense of time and dawdled helplessly and dully about the streets; while in the homes the women's world remained largely intact and the round of cooking, housecleaning, and mending became if anything more absorbing." But even while women were making increased contributions to the family, their husbands, including those without jobs, still exercised authority over the family. In her 1940 book, *The Unemployed Man and His Family*, Mirra Komarovsky found that in only 25 percent of the families she studied did unemployment undermine the man's predominant role as family decision-maker. Regardless of circumstances, the father was still in charge.

What added to this irony was that during the 1930s more women than ever left the home to become paid workers in the labor force. In 1930 over 10.5 million women were paid workers; ten years later, the female labor force topped 13 million. These women obtained and held onto their jobs despite widespread hostility to their working, particularly if they were married.

Some people in the 1930s argued that male unemployment stemmed directly from women working. Norman Cousins, the magazine editor, wrote that there was an easy solution to the depression: "Simply fire the women, who shouldn't be working anyway, and hire the men. Presto! No unemployment. No relief rolls. No depression." And when a Gallup poll in 1936 asked whether wives should work if their husbands had jobs, 82 percent of the respondents (including 75 percent of the women) answered no. Severe job discrimination resulted from these attitudes. A 1939 survey showed that most insurance companies, banks, and public utilities had policies against married women working. From 1932 to 1937 federal law prohibited more than one family member from working for the civil service, and because wives usually earned less than their husbands, they were the ones who quit their government jobs.

Still, married women constituted 35 percent of the female work force in 1940, an increase from 29 percent in 1930 and 15 percent in 1900. Many women had no choice; necessity forced them into the labor market. But how did they find work? One explanation is that the occupations in which women were concentrated, such as clerical and sales positions and nursing, shrank less than those in manufacturing, where men had held most of the jobs. Just as important, the economy had become so segregated into "men's jobs" and "women's jobs" that men rarely competed for work performed by women. The problem for women in this labor market was that, on balance, their wages lagged far behind those for men.

Women were active participants in the New Deal. Susan Ware, the historian, has written that there was in Washington a "women's network" of government and Democratic party officials **The "Women's Network"** who were united by their attitudes toward social reform and the role of women in politics and government. Many were long-time personal friends and professional allies who had worked together in the National Consumers' League, Women's Trade Union League, and other organizations. Most were "social feminists" who believed that working women needed protective laws for their health and safety on the job. At the center of the network was Eleanor Roosevelt, who was her husband's valued adviser. Frances Perkins, the secretary of labor, was the nation's first

woman cabinet officer. Other historic New Deal appointments included the first woman federal appeals judge and the first women ambassadors. Molly Dewson, head of the Democratic party's Women's Division, noted with pride: "The change from women's status in government before Roosevelt is unbelievable."

The New Deal did take into account women's needs, but only if reminded forcefully to do so. The maximum-hour and minimum-wage provisions mandated by the NRA, for example, won women's applause. Women workers in the lowest-paying jobs, many of them laboring under sweatshop conditions, had the most to gain from these standards. At the same time, some NRA codes mandated pay differentials based on gender, so that women's minimum wages were lower than those for men. Federal relief agencies, such as the Civil Works Administration and the Federal Emergency Relief Administration, put only one woman to work for every eight to ten men placed in relief jobs. A popular New Deal program, the Civilian Conservation Corps, was limited by law to young men, and women who were low-income workers, especially in agriculture and domestic service, were not protected by the 1935 Social Security Act or the 1938 Fair Labor Standards Act.

THE ELECTION OF 1940 AND THE LEGACY OF THE NEW DEAL

As the presidential election of 1940 approached, many people wondered whether Roosevelt would run for a third term (no president had ever served more than two terms). Roosevelt himself seemed undecided until May 1940, when Hitler's military advances apparently convinced him to stay on. He confided his decision to no one, however, and even sent a message to the Democratic convention that he did not want to be renominated. But at a timely moment, loudspeakers broadcast the chant "We want Roosevelt!" throughout the convention hall, and delegates began to snake dance up and down the aisles. Roosevelt wanted the nomination, but he also wanted the appearance of a draft. He was nominated

IMPORTANT EVENTS

1932	Franklin D. Roosevelt elected president
1933	13 million Americans unemployed National Bank Holiday Agricultural Adjustment Act Tennessee Valley Authority National Industrial Recovery Act Twentieth (Lame Duck) Amendment Twenty-first Amendment repeals Eighteenth (Prohibition) Amendment
1934	Townsend's Old Age Revolving Pensions plan Huey Long's Share Our Wealth Society Indian Reorganization (Wheeler-Howard) Act Democratic victories in congressional elections Coughlin's National Union for Social Justice
1935	Emergency Relief Appropriation Act Works Progress Administration *Schechter* v. *U.S.* invalidates NIRA

	National Labor Relations (Wagner) Act Social Security Act Huey Long assassinated Committee for Industrial Organization (CIO) established
1936	*U.S.* v. *Butler* invalidates AAA Roosevelt defeats Landon
1937	United Auto Workers' sit-down strikes "Court-packing" plan *N.L.R.B.* v. *Jones & Laughlin* upholds Wagner Act Memorial Day Massacre Farm Security Administration
1937–39	Business recession
1938	AFL expels CIO unions Fair Labor Standards Act 10.4 million Americans unemployed
1939	Marian Anderson's concert at the Lincoln Memorial
1940	Roosevelt defeats Willkie
1941	March on Washington Movement Fair Employment Practices Committee (FEPC) established

on the first ballot and selected Secretary of Agriculture Henry A. Wallace as his running mate.

The Republican candidate was Wendell Willkie, a utilities executive who had been an anti–New Deal Democrat throughout most of the 1930s. As president of the Commonwealth and Southern Corporation, Willkie had battled the Tennessee Valley Authority, condemning it as socialistic, but as a politician he was an unknown. As late as April 1940 he did not have a single delegate to the Republican convention, which was scheduled to open in two months. In May, however, with the Nazi invasion of the Low Countries

and France, Willkie's support mounted in public opinion polls. Other anti–New Deal Democrats joined with eastern Republicans to boost his candidacy, painting him as an internationalist who would halt the Nazi advance before it reached England. On the sixth ballot Willkie defeated the early leader at the convention, New York County's District Attorney Thomas E. Dewey.

Willkie campaigned against the New Deal, contending that its meddling in the affairs of business had failed to return the nation to prosperity. He also criticized the government's lack of military preparedness. But Roosevelt pre-empted the defense issue by beefing up military and naval contracts. And as workers streamed into the factories to fill the new orders, unemployment figures dropped as well. In his speeches Roosevelt reminded workers that it was his administration that had provided the defense jobs. When Willkie reversed his approach and accused Roosevelt of being a warmonger, the president promised, "Your boys are not going to be sent into any foreign wars."

Willkie never did come up with an effective campaign issue, and when the votes were tallied on election day, Roosevelt had received 27 million votes to Willkie's 22 million. In the electoral college, Roosevelt buried Willkie 449 to 82. Willkie did manage to win the farm and small-town vote in the Midwest, but as in 1936 Roosevelt triumphed in the cities, primarily among working-class, lower-income, and black voters. Although the New Deal was over, Roosevelt was still riding a wave of public approval.

Any analysis of the New Deal must begin with Franklin Delano Roosevelt. Assessments of his career varied widely during his presidency. In the 1930s a popularity poll among New York schoolchildren produced an easy victory for Roosevelt; God finished a distant second. Other people called Roosevelt a liar, a crook, a madman, a dictator, and a Communist. Most historians have considered him a truly great president, citing his courage, his buoyant self-confidence, his willingness to experiment, and his capacity to inspire the nation during the most somber days of the depression. But those who have criticized him have charged that he was too pragmatic, that he failed to formulate a bold and coherent strategy of economic recovery and political and economic reform.

On this last point, one of Roosevelt's biographers, James MacGregor Burns, has written in Roosevelt's defense: "Everything conspired in 1932 to make Roosevelt a pragmatist, an opportunist, an experimenter." The United States had never faced an economic disaster of the magnitude of the Great Depression. "The country needs," Roosevelt once said, "and, unless I mistake its temper, the country demands bold, persistent experimentation." Burns admits that the New Deal lacked coherence, and that at times the wary president "failed to exercise creative leadership," playing the fox—devious, crafty, and difficult

to pin down—rather than the lion—bold and assertive. Notwithstanding Roosevelt's faults, Burns prefers to see "the lineaments of greatness—courage, joyousness, responsiveness, vitality, faith and, above all, concern for his fellow man."

Though scholars have debated Roosevelt's performance, they all agree that he transformed the presidency. "Only Washington, who made the office, and Jackson, who remade it," Clinton Rossiter, the political scientist, observed, "did more than Roosevelt to raise it to its present condition of strength, dignity, and independence." Scholars in a later era would charge that Roosevelt laid the foundations of the "imperial presidency" (see page 975). But whether for good or ill, Roosevelt strengthened not only the presidency but the whole federal government. "For the first time for many Americans," the historian William Leuchtenburg has written, "the federal government became an institution that was directly experienced. More than state and local governments, it came to be *the* government." In the past, the federal government had served as a regulator of railroads, corporations, and other businesses; during the New Deal it became a guarantor and stimulater as well.

Strengthening of the Presidency

The New Deal laid the foundation of America's welfare system on which subsequent presidential administrations would build. For the first time the government acknowledged a responsibility to bring relief to the jobless and the needy, and for the first time it resorted to deficit spending in order to stimulate the economy. Millions of Americans benefited from governmental programs that are still operating today. The New Deal not only provided immediate unemployment relief during the worst days of the depression; it also reformed economic institutions for decades to come.

Yet the economy itself remained basically capitalistic under the New Deal. Though the government took on responsibility for public welfare and the vitality of the economy, the profit motive and private property remained fundamental to the system. And though some redistribution of wealth did result from the New Deal, the wealthy survived as a class. In 1929, for example, the most well-to-do 5 percent of the population received 30 percent of the total family income. By 1941, the same group's share of total income had

DISTRIBUTION OF TOTAL FAMILY INCOME[a] AMONG VARIOUS SEGMENTS OF THE POPULATION, 1929–1944 (IN PERCENTAGES)

Year	Poorest Fifth	Second Poorest Fifth	Middle Fifth	Second Wealthiest Fifth	Wealthiest Fifth	Wealthiest 5 Percent
1929	12.5		13.8	19.3	54.4	30.0
1935–1936	4.1	9.2	14.1	20.9	51.7	26.5
1941	4.1	9.5	15.3	22.3	48.8	24.0
1944	4.9	10.9	16.2	22.2	45.8	20.7

[a]Monetary and nonmonetary income.

Source: Adapted from U.S. Bureau of the Census, *Historical Statistics of the United States, Colonial Times to 1970*, Bicentennial Edition (Washington: U.S. Government Printing Office, 1975), p. 301.

shrunk, but was still a healthy 24 percent. Most of the income lost by the wealthy ended up in the pockets of the middle and upper-middle classes, not of the poor (see table).

The New Deal brought about limited change in the nation's power structure. Beginning in the 1930s, business interests had to share their political clout with others. Finally the labor movement gained influence in Washington, and farmers got more of what they wanted from Congress and the White House. But there was no real increase in the power of Afro-Americans and other minorities. And if people wanted their voices to be heard, they had to organize in labor unions, trade associations, or other special-interest lobbies.

The New Deal was a liberal, evolutionary reform program and did not represent a radical, or revolutionary, break with the past. Most New Deal ideas had been around for decades, and prominent New Dealers had been involved in various reform movements since the Progressive era. Some left-wing historians have criticized the New Deal for its conservative commitment to the status quo; a handful of right-wing scholars have argued that the New Deal was a revolution that produced socialism and political cor-

ruption and lowered national morale. But most historians view the New Deal as a reform movement that benefited middle-class Americans. William Leuchtenburg has concluded that the New Deal "swelled the ranks of the bourgeoisie but left many Americans—sharecroppers, slum dwellers, most Negroes—outside of the new equilibrium."

The New Deal failed in its fundamental purpose: to put people back to work. As late as 1938, over 10 million men and women were still jobless. That year unemployment was 19.1 percent; over the next two years it fell no lower than 14.6 percent. What plagued the nation throughout the 1930s was underconsumption: people and businesses either could not or would not purchase enough goods to sustain high levels of employment. In 1929, for example, sales of new cars totaled almost $6.5 billion; by 1933 that figure had dropped to $2.1 billion. Though New Deal pump priming helped to raise auto sales to $5.1 billion in 1936, Roosevelt's attempt to balance the budget reduced the figure to $3.9 billion in 1938. The same thing was true of capital investment in new industrial construction. In 1929 companies had invest-

New Deal Failure to Solve Unemployment

ed $546 million in new buildings, but by 1933 the total had fallen to $128 million. It climbed again to $314 million in 1937, only to plummet in 1938 to $121 million.

In the end it was not the New Deal but massive government spending during the Second World War that put people back to work. In 1941, as a result of mobilization for war, unemployment would drop to 9.9 percent, and in 1944, at the height of the war, only 1.2 percent of the labor force would be jobless.

SUGGESTIONS FOR FURTHER READING

The New Deal

Barton J. Bernstein, "The New Deal: The Conservative Achievements of Liberal Reform," in Barton J. Bernstein, ed., *Towards a New Past* (1968), 263–288; Paul K. Conkin, *The New Deal*, 2nd ed. (1975); Otis L. Graham, Jr., *Encore for Reform: The Old Progressives and the New Deal* (1967); Ellis W. Hawley, *The New Deal and the Problem of Monopoly* (1966); Peter H. Irons, *New Deal Lawyers* (1982); William E. Leuchtenburg, *Franklin D. Roosevelt and the New Deal* (1963); Katie Loucheim, ed., *The Making of the New Deal* (1983); Robert S. McElvaine, *The Great Depression* (1984); Albert U. Romasco, *The Politics of Recovery: Roosevelt's New Deal* (1983); Harvard Sitkoff, ed., *Fifty Years Later: The New Deal Evaluated* (1985).

Franklin D. Roosevelt

James MacGregor Burns, *Roosevelt: The Lion and the Fox* (1956); Frank Freidel, *Franklin D. Roosevelt*, 4 vols. (1952–1973); Joseph P. Lash, *Eleanor and Franklin* (1971); William E. Leuchtenburg, *In the Shadow of FDR* (1983); Arthur M. Schlesinger, Jr., *The Age of Roosevelt*, 3 vols. (1957–1960); Rexford G. Tugwell, *The Democratic Roosevelt* (1957).

Voices from the Depression

James Agee, *Let Us Now Praise Famous Men* (1941); Ann Banks, ed., *First-Person America* (1980); Federal Writers' Project, *These Are Our Lives* (1939); Robert S. McElvaine, ed., *Down and Out in the Great Depression: Letters from the Forgotten Man* (1983); Studs Terkel, *Hard Times: An Oral*

History of the Great Depression (1970); Tom E. Terrill and Jerrold Hirsch, eds., *Such as Us: Southern Voices of the Thirties* (1978).

Alternatives to the New Deal

David H. Bennett, *Demagogues in the Depression* (1969); Alan Brinkley, *Voices of Protest: Huey Long, Father Coughlin & the Great Depression* (1982); Harvey Klehr, *The Heyday of American Communism: The Depression Decade* (1984); R. Alan Lawson, *The Failure of Independent Liberalism, 1930–1941* (1971); Mark Naison, *Communists in Harlem During the Depression* (1983); James T. Patterson, *Congressional Conservatism and the New Deal* (1967); Leo Ribuffo, *The Old Christian Right: The Protestant Far Right from the Great Depression to the Cold War* (1983); Frank A. Warren, *An Alternative Vision: The Socialist Party in the 1930s* (1976); T. Harry Williams, *Huey Long* (1969); George Wolkskill, *The Revolt of the Conservatives: A History of the American Liberty League, 1934–1940* (1962).

Labor

Jerold S. Auerbach, *Labor and Liberty: The La Follette Committee and the New Deal* (1966); John Barnard, *Walter Reuther and the Rise of the Auto Workers* (1983); Irving Bernstein, *Turbulent Years: A History of the American Worker, 1933–1941* (1969); Cletus E. Daniel, *Bitter Harvest: A History of California Farmworkers, 1870–1941* (1981); Melvin Dubofsky and Warren Van Tine, *John L. Lewis: A Biography* (1977); Sidney Fine, *Sit-Down: The General Motors Strike of 1936–1937* (1969); August Meier and Elliott Rudwick, *Black Detroit and the Rise of the UAW* (1979); David Milton, *The Politics of U.S. Labor: From the Great Depression to the New Deal* (1980); Ronald W. Schatz, *The Electrical Workers* (1983).

Agriculture

David E. Conrad, *The Forgotten Farmers: The Story of Share-croppers in the New Deal* (1965); R. Douglas Hurt, *The Dust Bowl: An Agricultural and Social History* (1981); Richard S. Kirkendall, *Social Scientists and Farm Policies in the Age of Roosevelt* (1966); Theodore M. Saloutos, *The American Farmer and the New Deal* (1982); Walter J. Stein, *California and the Dust Bowl Migration* (1973); Donald Worster, *Dust Bowl: The Southern Plains in the 1930s* (1979).

Nonwhites

Abraham Hoffman, *Unwanted Mexican Americans in the Great Depression: Repatriation Pressures, 1929–1939* (1974); Laurence C. Kelly, *The Assault on Assimilation: John Collier and the Origins of Indian Policy Reform* (1983); John B.

Chapter 26: THE GREAT DEPRESSION AND THE NEW DEAL, 1933–1941

Kirby, *Black Americans in the Roosevelt Era: Liberalism and Race* (1980); Carey McWilliams, *North from Mexico* (1949); Donald L. Parman, *The Navajos and the New Deal* (1975); Kenneth Philp, *John Collier's Crusade for Indian Reform, 1920–1954* (1977); Mark Reisler, *By the Sweat of Their Brow: Mexican Immigrant Labor in the United States, 1900–1940* (1976); Harvard Sitkoff, *A New Deal for Blacks* (1978); Nancy J. Weiss, *Farewell to the Party of Lincoln: Black Politics in the Age of FDR* (1983); Raymond Wolters, *Negroes and the Great Depression: The Problem of Economic Recovery* (1970); Robert L. Zangrando, *The NAACP Crusade Against Lynching* (1980).

Women

Julia Kirk Blackwelder, *Women of the Depression: Caste and Culture in San Antonio, 1929–1939* (1984); Glen H. Elder, Jr., *Children of the Great Depression: Social Change in Life Experience* (1974); Joan Hoff-Wilson and Marjorie Lightman, eds., *Without Precedent: The Life and Career of Eleanor Roosevelt* (1984); Alice Kessler-Harris, *Out to Work* (1982); Lois Scharf, *To Work and To Wed: Female Employment, Feminism, and the Great Depression* (1980); Winifred Wandersee, *Women's Work and Family Values, 1920–1940* (1981); Susan Ware, *Holding Their Own: American Women in the 1930s* (1982); Susan Ware, *Beyond Suffrage: Women in the New Deal* (1981); Jeane Westin, *Making Do: How Women Survived the '30s* (1976).

Cultural and Intellectual History

Daniel Aaron, *Writers on the Left: Episodes in American Literary Communism* (1961); Andrew Bergman, *We're in the Money: Depression America and Its Films* (1971); Jerre Mangione, *The Dream and the Deal: The Federal Writers' Project, 1935–1943* (1972); Richard H. Pells, *Radical Visions and American Dreams: Culture and Social Thought in the Depression Years* (1973); Warren I. Sussman, "The Thirties," in Stanley Coben and Lorman Ratner, eds., *The Development of an American Culture*, 2nd ed. (1983), 215–260.

Diplomacy
in a Broken World
1920–1941

Chapter 27

On December 24, 1921, prisoner #9653 strode out of Atlanta's federal penitentiary. After a train ride to Washington, D.C., he entered the White House to meet the man who had just pardoned him. "Well," said the good-natured President Warren G. Harding, "I have heard so damned much about you, Mr. Debs, that I am now very glad to meet you personally." They had a good talk, and Eugene V. Debs told reporters that Harding was a "gentleman" who "possesses human impulses. We understand each other perfectly." The First World War now over for him, Debs went home to Terre Haute, Indiana.

It seemed out of character for a conservative, pro-business Republican who had supported the American effort in the First World War to pardon Eugene V. Debs—Debs the anticapitalist leader of the Socialist party, Debs the antiwar critic, Debs the convict serving a ten-year sentence for violating the wartime Sedition Act, Debs the Socialist presidential candidate in 1920 who ran against Harding from jail and won nearly a million votes. President Woodrow Wilson had snarled a firm "no" to pardoning this "traitor." But Harding was more compassionate, and he believed that Debs's continued imprisonment simply reminded Americans of a troubled past they were trying to forget.

Debs's release was one of Harding's ways of saying that the United States was liquidating the war and returning to what he called "normalcy." "I thought the spirit of clemency was quite in harmony with the things we were trying to do here in Washington." What "things?" A return to peacetime, free from missionary zeal, overseas crusades, huge military expenditures, and domestic divisiveness. Interpreting his 1920 victory as a repudiation of Wilson's League of Nations, Harding also wished to shelve that issue. Henceforth, he said, the United States would not become "entangled" in "Old World affairs."

The president took several other steps in November 1921 that further demonstrated his resolve to put the war behind him. He buried the Unknown Soldier in Arlington Cemetery to initiate, he said, "a new and lasting era of peace." He signed peace treaties with the defeated Central Powers, until then tech-nically still at war with the United States because the Senate had rejected the Treaty of Paris with its offending League provisions. Harding urged acceptance of these treaties "so that we may put aside the last remnant" of the war. That month too he opened an international conference in Washington, where the United States insisted on a major reduction in naval armaments to ensure a stable world order. Harding's pardon of Debs was thus but one element in a self-conscious attempt to chart a new American foreign policy for a warless future.

Harding's desire to shove the war into the past and his emphasis on avoiding entanglements with Europe should not be interpreted to mean that Americans cut themselves off from international affairs after the First World War. To be sure, Americans were disillusioned with their war experience. But they remained quite active in the world in the 1920s—from gunboats on Chinese rivers to negotiations in the financial centers of Europe to interventions in Latin America. The most useful description of interwar foreign policy is *independent internationalism*. That is, the United States was active on a global scale but retained its independence of action, its traditional unilateralism. Even if they had wanted to, Americans could not have escaped the tumult of international relations; their interests were too far-flung and too vast—colonies, client states, overseas naval bases, investments, trade, missionaries.

At the same time, many Americans called them-selves *isolationists*. By that label they meant that they wanted to isolate themselves from Europe's political squabbles, from military alliances and interventions, and from commitments like the League of Nations that might restrict their freedom of choice. Americans, then, were isolationists in their desire to avoid war, but independent internationalists in their behavior in foreign affairs.

The desire to avoid war led American leaders to search for nonmilitary means to exercise power. In the aftermath of the First World War, Americans had grown disenchanted with military methods of achieving order and protecting American prosperity and security. "We can never herd the world into the paths of righteousness with the dogs of war," Herbert Hoover said. American diplomats thus put increasing emphasis on conferences, moral lectures and calls for peace, nonrecognition of disapproved regimes, arms control, and economic and financial ties in accord with the principle of the Open Door. They pulled American troops out of Caribbean states, fashioning a Good Neighbor policy that would reduce hostility to United States influence in the region.

American policies and power, however, failed to create a stable world order. The debts and reparations tangle left over from the First World War bedeviled world finance and trade. More than any other event, the Great Depression of the 1930s undercut stability. The global economic cataclysm threatened America's prominence in the international marketplace. It also spawned revolutions in Latin America and political extremism, militarism, and war in Europe and Asia. The peace and disarmament agreements of the 1920s were smashed. In answer especially to the turmoil in Europe sparked by Germany's drive to restore its power, the United States passed the Neutrality Acts.

Yet in the late 1930s, Americans, along with President Franklin D. Roosevelt, changed their minds. Perceiving Germany and Japan as terrible menaces to the national interest, Roosevelt first appealed for preparedness and then begged the nation to abandon its neutrality in order to aid Britain and France. German victory in Europe, he reasoned, would imperil Western political principles, destroy traditional American economic links, threaten America's influence in the Western Hemisphere, and place at the pinnacle of European power a fanatical man—Adolf Hitler—whose ambitions and barbarities knew no limits.

At the same time Japan seemed determined to dismember America's friend China, to squelch the principle of the Open Door, and to surround and isolate the American colony of the Philippines. To deter Japanese expansion in the Pacific, Roosevelt cut off supplies of vital American products like oil. But economic warfare intensified antagonisms. Japan's surprise attack on Pearl Harbor finally brought the United States into the Second World War. Americans had wanted peace. But the relentless march of the militarists boded ill for the kind of world Americans thought necessary to their well-being. By 1941 they were convinced that remaining at peace would be more costly than going to war.

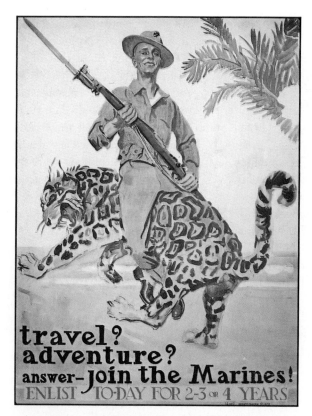

This recruiting poster reflected the postwar American mood of independent internationalism by offering exciting overseas duty to prospective marines. Library of Congress.

THE SEARCH FOR PEACE AND ORDER IN THE 1920s

In the early 1920s Secretary of State Charles Evans Hughes predicted that "there will be no permanent peace unless economic satisfactions are enjoyed." Like the nation's business leaders, Hughes expected American economic expansion to bring about world stability: out of economic prosperity would spring a world free from political extremes, revolution, aggression, and war. The government thus facilitated business activities abroad through the Webb-Pomerene Act (which excluded from antitrust prosecution those combinations set up for export trade); the Edge Act (which permitted foreign branch banks); and the overseas offices of the Department of Commerce. It also stimulated and monitored foreign loans made by American investors, discouraging those that might be used for military purposes.

United States economic influence became conspicuous after the First World War. By the late 1920s the United States produced about half the world's industrial goods, ranked first among exporters ($5.4 billion worth of shipments in 1929), and also acted as the financial capital of the world (see map). During the period from 1914 to 1930 private investments abroad grew fivefold, to over $17 billion. To cite some examples, General Electric joined international cartels and invested heavily in Germany; American companies began to exploit Venezuela's rich petroleum resources; the Radio Corporation of America built Poland's radio system; in the Middle East, American companies began to challenge the British for control of oil resources. Britain and Germany lost ground to American businesses in Latin America, where Standard Oil was active in eight nations, the United Fruit Company was a huge landowner, and International Telephone and Telegraph dominated Cuba's communication network. An American diplomat denied that this impressive economic expansionism meant that selfish private interests were running the State Department. "Any student of modern diplomacy knows," he claimed, "that in these days of competition, capital, trade, agriculture, labor and statecraft all go hand in hand if a country is to profit."

Economic Expansion

Many foreigners saw United States expansionism as imperialism. A famous Argentine critic, the writer Manuel Ugarte, asserted that the United States was a new Rome: it annexed wealth rather than territory, enjoying the "essentials of domination" without the "dead-weight of areas to administrate and multitudes to govern." To such criticisms the American ambassador to Chile replied that "American capital will be the controlling factor in public and private finance in these countries. . . . American civilization, material and cultural, is bound to impress itself upon, and I believe, benefit these peoples. If anti-American critics wish to describe this as our 'imperialism' let them make the most of it."

Other foreigners were grateful to Americans for a helping hand. Europe lay in shambles at the end of the war. From 1914 to 1921 there were 60 million casualties in Europe from world war, civil war, massacre, epidemic, and famine. Germany and France each lost 10 percent of its workers. Crops, livestock, factories, trains, forests, bridges—little had been spared. The plight of Europeans drew American sympathies and aid. The American Relief Administration delivered food to needy Europeans, including Russians who were wracked by famine in 1921 and 1922. All told, private charities and official relief programs delivered foodstuffs that were valued at over half a billion dollars.

But if Americans won praise from Europeans for their humanitarianism, they earned the nickname Uncle Shylock for their handling of war debts and reparations, an issue that dogged international relations for a decade. Twenty-eight nations were tangled in the web of inter-Allied debts which totaled $26.5 billion, about half of it owed to the United States. Europeans urged Americans to forgive the debts as a magnanimous contribution to the war. During the war, they charged, Europe had bled while America profited. But American leaders insisted on repayment. "They hired the money, didn't they?" Coolidge reportedly said. Other Americans argued that the victorious European nations had gained vast lands and resources through the war; to cancel their debts would be to increase their spoils even more. Senator George Norris, emphasizing domestic priorities, declared that the United States could build highways in "every county seat" if the Europeans would only pay their debts.

First World War Debts and Reparations

The debts question was linked to Germany's $33 billion reparations bill. Hobbled by inflation and economic disorder, Germany had begun to default on its payments. Americans grew worried that German economic troubles would spawn radicalism. To keep Germany afloat, American bankers poured millions of dollars in loans into the floundering nation. A triangular relationship developed: American investors' money flowed to Germany; German reparations payments went to the Allies; the Allies then paid some of their debts to the United States. The American-crafted Dawes Plan of 1924 greased the financial tracks by reducing Germany's annual payments, extending the repayment period, and providing still more loans. And the United States gradually scaled

Chapter 27: Diplomacy in a Broken World, 1920–1941

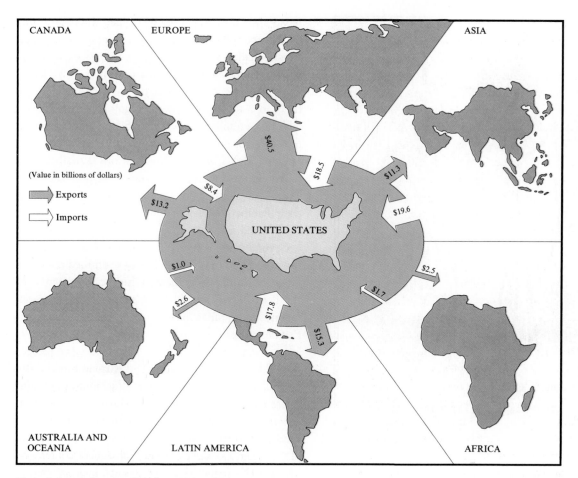

CANADA   EUROPE   ASIA

(Value in billions of dollars)

➤ Exports

▷ Imports

UNITED STATES

$40.5 $18.5 $11.3 $8.4 $19.6 $13.2 $1.0 $2.5 $2.6 $17.8 $1.7 $15.3

AUSTRALIA AND OCEANIA   LATIN AMERICA   AFRICA

United States Foreign Trade, 1920–1941

down Allied obligations, cutting the debt by half during the 1920s.

But the triangular arrangement was dependent on continued German borrowing in the United States, and in 1928 and 1929 American lending abroad declined sharply in the face of more lucrative opportunities in the stock market. The American-negotiated Young Plan of 1929, which reduced the total of Germany's reparations, salvaged little as the international economy sputtered and collapsed. That year the British rejected an ingenious offer from Hoover to trade their debt altogether for British Honduras, Bermuda, and Trinidad. By 1931, when Hoover declared a moratorium on payments, the Allies had paid back only $2.6 billion. Wracked by depression, they defaulted on the rest.

In the end, American economic power had proved unable to sustain a healthy world economy. But many nations shared responsibility for the failure. The selfish and vengeful Europeans might have trimmed Germany's huge indemnity. The Germans might have borrowed less from abroad and taxed themselves more. The Bolsheviks might have agreed to pay rather than repudiate Russia's $4 billion indebtedness. And Americans might have tried for a comprehensive, multinational settlement and lowered their tariffs, giving Europeans a market in which to earn the money to pay off their debt.

American influence also failed to curb militarism. During the 1920s and 1930s peace societies advocated numerous strategies to preserve world order: cooperation with the League of Nations; membership in the World Court; disarmament, arms reduction; curbs on exploitative business ventures; arbitration of international disputes; the outlawing of war; and strict neutrality in times of belligerency. The Fellowship

"*Come on in. I'll treat you right. I used to know your daddy.*" *Clarence D. Batchelor's haunting antiwar cartoon recalling the human tragedy of the First World War. The artist won a Pulitzer Prize for his statement.   Library of Congress.*

naval arms race, and they welcomed the opportunity to deflect it. As Secretary Hughes argued, arms competition had to stop because large military expenditures endangered economic rehabilitation. In the Five-Power Treaty the delegates set a ten-year moratorium on the construction of large, or capital, ships, and established a total tonnage ratio of 5:5:3:1.75:1.75 among the five top nations (Britain:United States:Japan: France:Italy). The first three nations actually agreed to dismantle some existing vessels to meet the ratio. They also pledged not to build new fortifications in their Pacific possessions (such as the Philippines for the United States).

Several other agreements were reached at the conference. The Nine-Power Treaty reaffirmed the Open Door in China, recognizing Chinese sovereignty. In the Four-Power Treaty, the United States, England, Japan, and France agreed to respect each other's Pacific possessions and to consult in the event of aggression in Asia. In another agreement Japan pledged to pull back from Shandong and Russian Siberia. But although the treaties signed at Washington provided a rare example of mutual disarmament, they did not, critics pointed out, limit submarines, destroyers, or cruisers, and there were no provisions for enforcement of the Open Door declaration. Subsequent conferences in the 1930s produced meager results, and rearmament rather than disarmament became the thrust of the times.

Peace advocates also placed their hopes in the Kellogg-Briand Pact of 1928, eventually signed by sixty-two nations. The signatories agreed simply to

Kellogg-Briand Pact "condemn recourse to war for the solution of international controversies, and renounce it as an instrument of national policy." The treaty's backers billed it as a first step in a long journey toward international cooperation and the outlawry of war. Though it passed the Senate 85 to 1, many senators thought the document no more than a moral statement, because it lacked provisions for enforcement. The agreement did in fact prove impotent in the 1930s. But however weak it was, the pact reflected a sincere popular belief that war was barbaric, inhumane, and wasteful; and it served a useful educational purpose in getting people to think about peace and war.

The League of Nations, also looked to as a peace-

of Reconciliation, the Women's International League for Peace and Freedom, and the National Council for Prevention of War, among others, struggled to remind Americans of the carnage of the First World War and the futility of war as a solution to international problems. Antiwar films like *What Price Glory* (1926) and *Submarine* (1928) emphasized the cruelties of military combat.

At the time, the Washington Conference (November 1921–February 1922) seemed a substantial step toward arms control. There the United States discussed with eight other nations limits on naval armaments. Britain, the United States, and Japan, the three top naval powers, were facing a costly

Washington Conference

Chapter 27: DIPLOMACY IN A BROKEN WORLD, 1920–1941

maker, exhibited a conspicuous feebleness, not only because the United States refused to join, but because members themselves usually chose not to use it to settle disputes. Starting in the mid-1920s, however, American officials did participate discreetly in League meetings on public health, prostitution, drug trafficking, and other such questions. By 1930 American "observers" had sat in on over forty League conferences. And individual jurists like Charles Evans Hughes served on the World Court in Geneva, although the United States also refused to join that institution. Neither the World Court, League of Nations, nor the Kellogg-Briand Pact proved capable of keeping the peace once the Great Depression upended an already wobbly world order.

SPHERE OF INFLUENCE
IN LATIN AMERICA

In Latin America the interwar themes of independent internationalism, isolationism, nonmilitary means, and the destabilizing impact of the Great Depression were prominent. Before the First World War the United States had thrown an imperial net over much of the region by means of the Platt Amendment, the Roosevelt Corollary, construction of the Panama Canal, military intervention, and economic domination. By the 1920s the supposed benefits of American expansionism—hospitals, schools, roads, telephones, and irrigation systems—were evident in much of Latin America. As one observer put it, America's "imperialistic temper" was "manifested in works of benevolence."

A patronizing attitude permeated United States activities in the region. A leading State Department officer told the Foreign Service School that Latins were incapable of political progress because of their temperament, the tropical climate, and their "low racial quality." They were, however, "very easy people to deal with if properly managed." And indeed managed they were. United States financial advisers supervised government budgets in the Caribbean, and in 1920 American soldiers were occupying Cuba, the Dominican Republic, Haiti, Panama, and Nicaragua.

Yet these military expeditions to Latin America were becoming unpopular and counterproductive. Critics like Senator William Borah insisted that South Americans should be granted the right of self-determination. The president was usurping constitutional power, others protested, by ordering troops to Latin America without a congressional declaration of war. Businesspeople feared that nationalists would direct their anti-Yanqui emotion against American *gringos* and their property. And there was the embarrassment of the double standard. Secretary of State Henry L. Stimson outlined the problem in 1932 when he was protesting Japanese incursions in China: "If we landed a single soldier among those South Americans now . . . it would put me absolutely in the wrong in China, where Japan has done all this monstrous work under the guise of protecting her nationals with a landing force."

Turning away pragmatically from military intervention, then, the United States sought less controversial methods of maintaining its influence in Latin America: Pan-Americanism; support for strong native leaders; the training of national guards; economic penetration; Export-Import Bank loans; and when necessary, political subversion. Although the process began before his presidency, Roosevelt gave it a name in 1933: the Good Neighbor policy. It meant that the United States would be less blatant in its domination—less willing to defend exploitative business practices, less eager to send in military expeditions, and less wary of consultation with Latin Americans. "Give them a share," FDR recommended. In 1936 he approved a treaty that restored some sovereignty to Panama and increased that nation's income from the canal. Roosevelt's popularity in Latin America grew enormously for this and other such acts.

Good Neighbor Policy

So did American interests. From 1914 to 1929, direct American investments in Latin America (excluding bonds and securities) jumped from almost $1.3 billion to $3.5 billion. In the same period American exports to the area tripled in value. In country after country Latin Americans felt the repercussions of American economic and political decisions. The price Americans set for Chilean copper

*Often at loggerheads, William E. Borah (1865–1940),
chairman of the Senate Foreign Relations Committee
(left), and Henry L. Stimson (1867–1950), secretary
of state (right), here confer in 1929 on Cuba. The
Idaho senator became a passionate anti-imperialist and
isolationist who protested United States interventions in
Latin America. Because of critics like Borah, Secretary
Stimson was eager to find nonmilitary means to maintain
United States hegemony in the Western Hemisphere.
Library of Congress.*

determined whether Chile was up or down in the business cycle. American oil executives bribed Venezuelan politicians for tax breaks. In Honduras, where United Fruit and Standard Fruit accounted for most of the nation's revenue, American interests so manipulated and disrupted politics that American troops were sent there in 1924 to restore calm and protect property. What was more, American businesses drew substantially greater sums out of Latin America in profits than they put in as investments. Latin American nationalists complained that their resources were being drained away, and that many of their own businesspeople put their profits not into investments at home but into New Orleans and New York banks.

The training of national guards went hand in hand with support of dictators: many Latin American dictators rose to power through the ranks of a national guard trained by the United States.

Training of National Guards For example, before the United States withdrew its troops from the Dominican Republic in 1924, American personnel created a constabulary. One of its first officers was Rafael Leonidas Trujillo, who became head of the National Army in 1928. Trujillo became president in 1930 through fraud and intimidation and ruled the Dominican Republic with an iron fist until his assassination in 1961. "He may be an S.O.B.," Roosevelt remarked candidly, "but he is our S.O.B."

In Nicaragua the experience was similar. The United

States occupied Nicaragua from 1912 to 1925 and returned in late 1926 during a civil war. The justification for United States involvement was the need to clean up and stabilize Nicaragua's politics. Anti-Yanqui resistance, led by the rebel Augusto Sandino, and noisy opposition at home and abroad finally prompted Washington to end the occupation, and in 1933 the U.S. Marines departed. But they left behind a powerful national guard headed by General Anastasio Somoza, who "always played the game fairly with us," according to the top-ranked American military officer there. With American backing, the Somoza family ruled Nicaragua from 1936 to 1979 through corruption, political suppression, and torture.

The long Marine Corps occupation of black, French-speaking Haiti from 1915 to 1934 had similarly negative results. Even the most charitable historian must

Occupation of Haiti

point out that American intervention did not establish democracy or improve Haitian life. American officials censored the Haitian press; manipulated elections; wrote the constitution; jailed or killed thousands of protesters; managed government finances; and created a national guard. Under American supervision, the National City Bank of New York became the owner of the Haitian Banque Nationale and the United States became Haiti's largest trading partner. The American High Commissioner, General John H. Russell of Georgia, boasted that the Haitian president "has never taken a step without first consulting me."

American black leaders were particularly alert to Haitian issues. Just before his death, Booker T. Washington spoke of the "benevolence" of American intentions and relished the prospect of establishing another Tuskegee Institute in the island nation. But W. E. B. Du Bois angrily criticized the "rape" of Haiti. And James Weldon Johnson of the National Association for the Advancement of Colored People reported after an investigative trip that Haitians forced to work without pay (the *corvée* system) to build roads "were in the same category with the convicts in the Negro chain gangs" of the American South. Indeed, Jim Crow had cut deeply into Haiti.

When Haitians resorted to violent protest against American rule in 1929, President Hoover vetoed a further military build-up and began plans to withdraw American soldiers. His investigative commission

From the leftist magazine New Masses *came this critique of United States intervention in Nicaragua, a nation occupied by American troops, 1912–1925 and 1926–1933. Library of Congress.*

concluded: "The failure of the Occupation to understand the social problems of Haiti, its brusque attempt to implant democracy by drill and harrow, its determination to set up a middle class—however wise and necessary it may seem to Americans—all these explain why, in part, the high hopes of our good works in this land have not been realized." Indeed, the American occupation brought very few benefits to the Haitian people, who continued to suffer Latin America's highest illiteracy rate, lowest per capita income, and poorest health. Speaking for many of his compatriots, one Haitian called Americans "exploiters" and asked, "How can they teach us when they have so much to learn themselves?"

The Cubans too grew restless under American domination. By 1929 American investments in the

Domination of Cuba

Caribbean nation totaled $1.5 billion, up from $220 million in 1913. Most of this money was bound up in the profitable Cuban sugar industry, about two-thirds of which was in American

Early in the long United States occupation of the black island nation of Haiti (1915–1934), marines stand guard over captured Haitians they called "bandits." National Archives.

hands. And the American military uniform was conspicuous at the naval base at Guantánamo Bay. But during the Cuban revolution of 1933, in open defiance of the American warships cruising offshore, rebels made Professor Ramon Grau San Martín president. Grau declared the Platt Amendment, which accorded the United States the right to intervene in Cuban affairs, null and void, seized some American-owned mills, failed to repay American bank loans, and talked of land reform. A startled United States refused to recognize the new government and encouraged a coup by army sergeant Fulgencio Batista in 1934. During the dictatorial Batista era that lasted until 1959, Cuba protected American investments and granted the United States military sites. In return it received military aid, Export-Import Bank loans, abrogation of the Platt Amendment, and a favorable sugar tariff.

The pattern was different in Mexico. Woodrow Wilson had sent troops to Mexico in 1914 and 1916 in an attempt to rearrange politics in that border state bloodied by revolution and civil **Confrontation** war. But the military expeditions **with Mexico** only united the Mexican people against the United States. In 1917 the Mexicans adopted a new constitution specifying that all "land and waters" and all subsoil raw materials (like oil) belonged to the Mexican nation—a clear threat to American landholdings and petroleum interests. Here was a unique case: a weak, undeveloped Latin American nation issuing a direct challenge to the powerful United States.

Washington and Mexico City wrangled for years over the rights of American economic interests. Then, in 1938, Mexico boldly expropriated the property of all foreign-owned petroleum companies. The United

States countered by reducing purchases of Mexican silver and encouraging a business boycott of the upstart nation. But President Roosevelt decided to compromise, because he feared the Mexicans would sell their oil to the aggressors Germany and Japan. In 1941 the United States conceded that Mexico owned its raw materials and could treat them as it saw fit; and Mexico compensated American companies for their lost property. Although American investments and trade continued to claim an important share of Mexican business, American power had been diminished, setting a precedent to which Latin American nationalists would refer in the future.

Roosevelt's movement toward nonmilitary methods—the Good Neighbor policy—can be seen also in Pan-Americanism. Throughout the 1920s the United States had refused to abandon its right of intervention in Latin America. But in 1936, at the Pan American Conference in Buenos Aires, Americans endorsed nonintervention. Though American interventionism of a nonmilitary sort was still conspicuous in Latin America, the new policy marked a distinct change from the days of the Roosevelt Corollary and sending in the marines. One payoff was the Declaration of Panama (1939), wherein the Latin American governments drew a security line around the hemisphere and warned aggressors away. In exchange for more trade and foreign aid, Latin American governments also reduced their sales of raw materials to Germany, Japan, and Italy and increased shipments to the United States. On the eve of the war, then, the United States' sphere of influence was virtually intact, ready to back American military and diplomatic policies.

THE GREAT DEPRESSION AND GROWING ISOLATIONISM

Cordell Hull, secretary of state from 1933 to 1944, liked to say that the character of international relations derived from economic conditions. In the 1930s the effect of economics was particularly apparent as the Great Depression swept through both hemispheres, shattering international order. Hull pointed in 1935 to political extremism, border squabbles, resurgent militarism, increased military expenditures, and new weapons development as products of maimed economies. "We cannot have a peaceful world, we cannot have a prosperous world," he advised, "until we rebuild the international economic structure." Hull was right; the depression so disoriented the international community that it ranks as one of the main causes of the Second World War.

The depression wrecked international finance and trade. In the late 1920s, when First World War debts and reparations proved too much for the shattered European economies to bear, international finance collapsed. Banks failed as wary investors drained gold and foreign currency reserves. World trade, heavily dependent on an easy and safe exchange of currencies, also faltered: from 1929 to mid-1933, it declined in value by 40 percent. American exports alone slumped from $5.4 billion to $2.2 billion over roughly the same period.

The United States actually added to the burdens of the world economy with the Hawley-Smoot Tariff (1930), a selfish move that shut off the American market to European nations struggling to earn cash to pay off their war debts. President Hoover's moratorium on debts payments in 1931 came too late. By 1932 about twenty-five nations had retaliated against the American tariff by imposing similar restrictions on American imports. In short, economic nationalism gained momentum.

Referring to the world economic emergency in his first inaugural address in 1933, President Franklin D. Roosevelt said that he favored a "practical policy of putting first things first." In other words, he would work to restore world trade, but he would attend first to the emergency at home. Roosevelt thereupon barred American cooperation in international monetary stabilization at the London Conference (1933).

Cordell Hull was beside himself over the world's conspicuous nose-dive into economic nationalism. A start-up of world trade, he insisted, would not only help the United States to pull itself

Cordell Hull's Economic Foreign Policy out of the economic doldrums, but would boost the chances for global peace. Calling the protective tariff the "king of evils," Hull successfully pressed Congress to pass the Reciprocal Trade Agreements Act in 1934. This important piece of legislation, which would guide American economic foreign policy thereafter, empowered the president to reduce American tariffs by as much as 50 percent through special agreements with foreign countries. The central feature of the act was the *most-favored-nation principle,* whereby the United States was entitled to the lowest tariff rate set by a nation with which it had an agreement. For example, if Belgium and the United States granted each other most-favored-nation status, and if Belgium negotiated an agreement with Germany that reduced the Belgian tariff on German typewriters, American typewriters would receive the same low rate.

In 1934 Hull also sponsored the creation of the Export-Import Bank, a government agency that provided loans to foreigners for the purchase of American goods. The bank not only stimulated trade but became a formidable diplomatic weapon, allowing the United States to exact concessions through the approval or denial of loans. Though Hull's ambitious programs brought only mixed results in the short term, they stood as rare examples of internationalism in an era of rampant nationalism.

As depression-induced authoritarianism, racial hatred, and military expansion descended upon Europe and Asia, Americans reasserted their isolationist beliefs. And they remembered the First

Isolationist Thought World War largely in negative terms: the shelving of reform; civil liberties abuses; unusual federal and presidential power; race riots; inflation; windfalls for business; government propaganda; and postwar labor strikes (see Chapter 23). A 1937 Gallup poll found that nearly two-thirds of the people asked about the war thought American participation had been a mistake. Conservative isolationists feared higher taxes and increased federal power if the nation went to war again. Liberal isolationists spoke of the need to give domestic problems priority. Senator Gerald P. Nye, for example, complained that the federal government appropriated more for the care of National Guard horses than for the Children's Bureau. And critics of many persuasions predicted that in attempting to spread democracy abroad, Americans would lose it at home.

Although isolationist thought was strongest in the Midwest and among anti-British ethnic groups, especially German- and Irish-Americans, it was a truly national phenomenon that cut across socioeconomic,

ethnic, party, and sectional lines and attracted a majority of the American people. Isolationist leadership in the 1930s included Republicans like Congressman Hamilton Fish of New York, Senator William Borah of Idaho, Senator George Norris of Nebraska, and former president Herbert Hoover; Democrats like Congressman Maury Maverick of Texas; Socialists like Norman Thomas; Communists and Nazi sympathizers; and pacifists like Congresswoman Jeannette Rankin. It also included the publisher Robert R. McCormick of the *Chicago Tribune*; the historian Charles Beard; the scientist Albert Einstein; and anti-Semite Father Charles E. Coughlin. What united these people was the opinion that there were alternatives to American involvement in another futile Old World war. Only when events grew uglier and more menacing toward the end of the depression decade did many, like President Roosevelt, change their minds.

Some liberal isolationists, critical of business practices at home, charged that corporate "merchants of death" were undermining the national interest by assisting the aggressors. From 1934 to 1936 a congressional committee chaired by Senator Nye held hearings on the role of business interests in the American decision to enter the First World War. The hearings did not prove that businesspeople and financiers had dragged reluctant Americans into the war, but they did uncover evidence that corporations had bribed foreign politicians to improve arms sales in the 1920s and 1930s, and had lobbied against arms control. And records show that isolationists were correct to suspect American business ties with

Business Ties with the Aggressors Nazi Germany and fascist Italy. Twenty-six of the top one hundred American corporations in 1937 had contractual agreements with Germany. And after Italy attacked Ethiopia in 1935, American petroleum, copper, and iron and steel scrap exports to Italy increased substantially, despite Roosevelt's call for a moral embargo on those items. Du Pont, Standard Oil, General Motors, and Union Carbide executives apparently agreed with a Dow Chemical Company officer, who stated, "We do not inquire into the uses of the products. We are interested in selling them." (One exception was the Wall Street firm of Sullivan and Cromwell, which severed lucrative ties with Germany to protest the persecution of Jews.)

Chapter 27: DIPLOMACY IN A BROKEN WORLD, 1920–1941

European Upheaval and American Neutrality

I n depression-wracked Germany, where 6 million workers were unemployed in the early 1930s, Adolf Hitler came to power. Like Benito Mussolini, who had gained control of Italy in 1922, Hitler was a fascist. Fascism (called Nazism, or National Socialism, in Germany) was a collection of ideas and prejudices that included supremacy of the state over the individual; of dictatorship over democracy; of authoritarianism over freedom of speech; and of militarism and war over peace. The Nazis vowed not only to revive German economic and military strength, but to "purify" the German "race" of Jewish influence, for which they blamed Germany's problems.

Hitler's Germany

In 1933, resentful of the punitive terms of the 1919 Treaty of Paris, Hitler pulled Germany out of the League of Nations, ended reparations payments, and began to rearm. Secretly laying plans for the conquest of neighboring states, he watched admiringly as Mussolini's troops invaded the African nation of Ethiopia in 1935. The next year Hitler ordered his goose-stepping troopers into the Rhineland, an area the Treaty of Paris had declared demilitarized. Germany's timid neighbor France did not resist this aggressive action. "The world belongs to the man with guts!" crowed Hitler.

Soon the aggressors began to join hands. In fall 1936 Italy and Germany formed an alliance called the Rome-Berlin Axis. Shortly thereafter Germany and Japan united against Russia in the Anti-Comintern Pact. To these events Britain and France responded with a policy of appeasement, hoping to curb Hitler's expansionist appetite by permitting him a few nibbles. But the policy eventually proved disastrous; taking advantage of European caution, the German leader continually raised his demands.

In those hair-trigger times, a civil war in Spain turned into an international struggle. From 1936 to 1939 the Loyalist Republicans battled the fascist-backed insurgents under Francisco Franco. Hitler and

The Nazi leader Adolf Hitler (1889–1945) in a propagandistic German painting. Hitler is surrounded by the images that came to symbolize hate, genocide, and war: Nazi flags with emblems of the swastika; iron cross on the dictator's pocket; saluting Nazi troops. Hitler denounced the United States as a "Jewish rubbish heap" of "inferiority and decadence" that was "incapable of conducting war." This soon proved to be a gross misperception that ultimately caused the downfall of Hitler and forced defeat upon the Germans. U.S. Army.

Mussolini sent military aid to Franco; Russia assisted the Loyalists. France and Britain held to the fiction of a nonintervention pledge that even Italy and Germany had signed. And about three thousand American volunteers known as the Lincoln Battalion joined the fight on the side of the Republicans. When Franco won in 1939, his victory tightened the grip of fascism on the European continent.

Early in 1938 Hitler once again tested the limits of European patience when he sent his soldiers into Austria to annex that nation. In September of the same year he seized the Sudeten region of Czechoslovakia. Appeasement reached its peak that month at the Munich Conference when France and Britain, without consulting the helpless Czechs, agreed to allow Hitler this one last territorial bite. British Prime Minister Neville Chamberlain returned home to proclaim "peace in our time," confident he had satiated the dictator. But in March 1939 Hitler swallowed the rest of Czechoslovakia. Poland was next on his list. Scuttling appeasement, London and Paris announced they would stand by their ally. Undaunted, Germany neutralized Russia by signing the Nazi-Soviet Pact and with Russia struck Poland on September 1. Britain and France declared war on Germany two days later. The Second World War had begun.

President Franklin D. Roosevelt witnessed these events with sadness and anxiety. Like his famous older cousin Theodore, Franklin as a young man believed that the United States

Franklin D. Roosevelt

should exert leadership in the world community and flex its military muscle to ensure American security and prosperity. He was an expansionist and interventionist who had imbibed the belief that Americans knew what was best for other societies. "Sooner or later . . . the United States must go down there and clean up the Mexican political mess," he had remarked in 1914. Later, as assistant secretary of the navy under Wilson, Roosevelt helped write the constitution the United States imposed on Haiti. FDR's later statements, however, would not have pleased his cousin (who died in 1919). Like most Americans during the interwar period, Roosevelt talked less about preparedness and more about disarmament and the horrors of war. Alert to public criticism of American military intervention in Latin America, he moved toward a Good Neighbor policy and stressed economic rather than military ties. When Europe and Asia were torn by economic and political crisis and war in the 1930s, Roosevelt at first declared that the United States should avoid foreign squabbles and he signed the Neutrality Acts.

However much they opposed fascism and disapproved aggression, Roosevelt and his fellow Americans tried to stay clear of the recurrent crises of the 1930s. Americans resented the fact that some Europeans looked to the United States to do what they themselves refused to do: block Hitler. With each crisis isolationist sentiment rose. In a series of acts Congress sought to protect the nation by stopping contacts that had compromised American neutrality

Neutrality Acts

two decades earlier. The Neutrality Act of 1935 prohibited arms shipments to either side in a war once the president had declared the existence of belligerency. Roosevelt had wanted the authority to name the aggressor and apply an arms embargo against it alone, but Congress was reluctant to leave such matters to the president's discretion. The Neutrality Act of 1936 forbade loans to belligerents. A joint resolution in 1937 declared the United States neutral in the Spanish Civil War; Roosevelt then embargoed arms shipments to both sides. And finally, the Neutrality Act of 1937 introduced the cash-and-carry principle: warring nations wishing to trade with the United States would have to pay cash for their purchases and carry the goods away in their own ships. The act also forbade Americans from traveling on vessels of belligerent nations—something Woodrow Wilson had been unwilling to do in the First World War.

Sharing the isolationist sentiment of the times and making a pitch for the pacifist vote in the upcoming election, Roosevelt gave a stirring speech in August 1936 at Chautauqua, New York: "I have seen war. . . . I have seen blood running from the wounded. I have seen men coughing out their gassed lungs. . . . I have seen the agony of mothers and wives. I hate war." He promised that the United States would remain distant from European conflict. During the Czech crisis of 1938 Roosevelt actually endorsed appeasement. The United States, he wrote to Hitler, had "no political involvements in Europe." The results of the Munich Conference, he commented on another occasion, elicited a "universal sense of relief."

But Roosevelt was deeply troubled by the arrogant behavior of the "three bandit nations," Germany, Italy, and Japan. He was disgusted by Nazi persecution of the Jews and by Japanese slaughter of Chinese civilians. Privately he snarled against the refusal of the British and French to collar Hitler in their own backyards. And he worried that the United States was militarily ill-prepared to confront the aggressors.

The United States had not been neglecting its military. Roosevelt's New Deal public works programs included millions for the construction of new ships. In 1935 the president requested the largest peacetime defense budget in American history; three years later,

Chapter 27: DIPLOMACY IN A BROKEN WORLD, 1920–1941

in the wake of Munich, he asked Congress for funds to build up the air force. "Had we had this summer 5,000 planes and the capacity immediately to produce 10,000 per year," he told his chief civilian and military advisers, "Hitler would not have dared to take the stand he did." (Whether Hitler would have been deterred by a militarily superior United States is questionable, given the Führer's view of Americans as a mongrel race incapable of playing an important role in foreign affairs.) The president also began to cast about for ways to encourage the British and French to show more backbone. One result was his agreement in January 1939 to sell bombers to France.

In his annual message early in 1939, the president lashed out at the international lawbreakers. Soon afterward he urged Congress to repeal the arms embargo and permit the sale of munitions to belligerents on a cash-and-carry basis. Roosevelt saw repeal as an aid to Britain, which dominated the seas. When the Senate Foreign Relations Committee balked, voting down repeal by a 12-to-11 vote, Roosevelt exploded: "I think we ought to introduce a bill for statues of [Senators] Austin, Vandenberg, Lodge and Taft . . . to be erected in Berlin and put the swastika on them." Although he did not yet have the votes to win repeal, he stepped up his public condemnation of the aggressors, warning them that "we, too, have a stake in world affairs." Hitler shot back that the president was a "contemptible . . . creature."

Roosevelt Proposes Repeal of Arms Embargo

When Europe fell into the abyss of war in September 1939, Roosevelt declared neutrality. But unlike Woodrow Wilson, he did not ask Americans to be neutral in thought, and he pressed again for repeal of the arms embargo. Senator Arthur Vandenberg, an isolationist from Michigan, roared back that the United States could not be "an arsenal for one belligerent without becoming a target for the other." After much lobbying, debate, and bipartisan consultation, however, Congress revised the neutrality legislation. In November 1939 it lifted the embargo on contraband and approved cash-and-carry exports of arms. Now Roosevelt was ready to aid the Allies—short of war—and to challenge the isolationists more boldly and openly than before.

Soviet Russia was a special problem in American foreign relations. Following Wilsonian precedent, the Republican administrations of the 1920s had not recognized the Soviet government, arguing that the Bolsheviks had refused to pay over $600 million for the confiscation of American-owned property and the repudiation of Russian debts. To Americans the Communists were also godless, radical malcontents bent on destroying the American way of life through world revolution. Yet American businesses began to enter the Soviet marketplace, offering technology and machinery. International Harvester and General Electric, among others, struck deals with the Soviets. Henry Ford himself signed a contract in 1929 to build a huge automobile plant using mass-production methods (*Fordizatsia*). By 1930 Russia was the largest buyer of American agricultural and industrial equipment.

Relations with Russia

In the early 1930s, however, trade began to slump. To stimulate business and help the United States pull out of the depression, some businesspeople began to lobby for diplomatic recognition of Russia. "We would recognize the Devil with a false face if he would contract for some pitchforks," quipped Will Rogers. President Roosevelt agreed that a change in policy was necessary, not only to improve trade. He believed it foolish not to recognize a major country like Russia; nonrecognition had failed to alter the Soviet system; and closer Russian-American relations might deter the Japanese and stabilize Asia.

Roosevelt began negotiations in 1933 with the Soviet Commissar for Foreign Affairs, Maxim Litvinov. In a classic example of personal, one-on-one diplomacy, Roosevelt hammered out a number of agreements, some of them vague in language: United States recognition of Soviet Russia; future discussion of the debts question; a Soviet promise to forgo propagandistic or subversive activities in the United States; and religious freedom and legal rights for Americans in Russia. Although the first American embassy in Moscow opened in 1934, within a few years Soviet-American relations had once again become embittered. Especially upsetting to Americans was Russia's pact with Nazi Germany, its grabbing half of Poland in 1939, and its attack against Finland in 1940, marking Russia as yet another aggressor.

Jiang Jieshi (1887–1976) and his wife Song Meiling were Time *magazine's Man and Wife of the Year in 1937. Their anticommunism and resistance to Japanese aggression earned Jiang's regime favor in the United States. Reprinted by permission from* Time, *the Weekly Newsmagazine; Copyright Time Inc. 1938.*

A NEW ORDER IN ASIA

I f United States power was massive in Latin America and limited in Europe, it was minuscule in Asia. Still, there were American interests in that region that official Washington believed it needed to defend: the Philippines and Pacific islands; religious missions; trade and investments; and the Open Door in China. Americans increasingly saw the Japanese as a threat to these interests, and specifically as strong-willed expansionists bent on subjugating China and unhinging the Open Door doctrine of equal trade and investment opportunity. Pearl Buck's best-selling novel *The Good Earth* (1931), made into a widely distributed film six years later, confirmed their opinion with its image of the noble, persevering Chinese peasant. In traditional missionary fashion, Americans came to believe they were China's special friend, its protector and uplifter. "With God's help," Senator Kenneth Wherry proclaimed, "we will lift Shanghai up and up, ever up, until it is just like Kansas City."

But the Chinese were always uneasy about the American presence in Asia, and the Japanese were forthrightly hostile. Both wished to exclude white foreigners from Asia. The highly nationalistic Chinese Revolution of 1911 still rumbled in the 1920s; anti-foreign riots increased, visiting damage on American property and harassment and violence on American missionaries, business representatives, and sailors. And Chinese nationalists demanded an end to the imperialistic practice of extraterritoriality (the exemption of foreigners accused of crimes from Chinese legal jurisdiction). When nationalist leader Sun Zhongshan (Sun Yat-sen) invited Soviet agent Michael Borodin to help him reorganize the governing Guomindong party, some Americans concluded that the Chinese were going Bolshevik.

In the late 1920s Jiang Jieshi (Chiang Kai-shek) emerged as the pre-eminent leader of this convulsed nation. Jiang ousted Communists from the Guomindong, forcing Mao Zedong and

Rise of Jiang Jieshi in China his followers to flee to the hills, and sent Borodin back to Russia. Americans applauded his anti-Bolshevik measures and his conversion in 1930 to Christianity. Jiang's new wife, Song Meiling, also won their hearts. The American-educated daughter of a Chinese businessman, Madame Jiang spoke flawless English, dressed in western fashion, and cultivated close social and political ties with prominent Americans. Warming to Jiang, United States officials signed a treaty in 1928 restoring control of tariffs to the Chinese. American gunboats and marines remained, however.

The Japanese were suspicious of United States–Chinese ties. In the early twentieth century Japanese-American relations were seldom cordial. Japan intruded more and more into China, driving economic and political stakes into Manchuria, Shandong, and

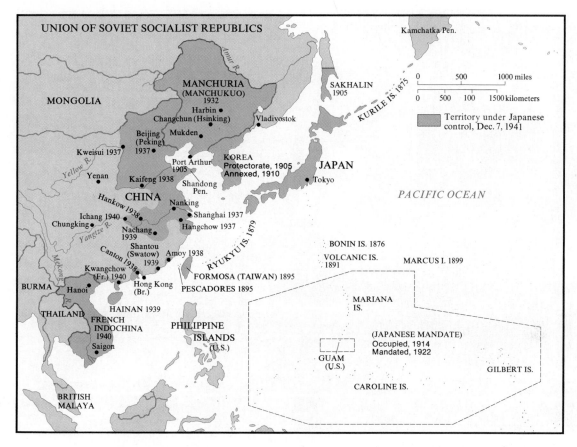

Japanese Expansion Before Pearl Harbor

neighboring Korea. Anti-imperialist only in the sense that they wished to oust Western imperialists from Asia, the Japanese were determined to claim Asian territories that produced the raw materials their island nation depended on. When Americans protested blatant Japanese expansionism, Tokyo reminded Washington of its own sphere of influence in Latin America. The proud Japanese also resented the immigration statute of 1924, which excluded Japanese from entry into the United States. And despite the Washington Conference treaty of 1922, naval competition continued; in fact, American naval officers, betting on a future war with Japan, used that country as the imaginary enemy on the war-game board at the Naval War College. Finally, although the volume of Japanese-American trade was twice that of Chinese-American trade, commercial rivalry strained relations between the two nations. American producers and workers whose profits and jobs were threatened by the im-

portation of inexpensive Japanese goods, especially textiles, organized Buy America campaigns and boycotts.

Relations deterioriated further after the Japanese military seized Manchuria in September 1931 (see map). Only nominally a Chinese region, Manchuria was important to the Japanese both

Japanese Seizure of Manchuria

as a buffer against the Russians and as a vital source of coal, iron, timber, and food. More than half of Japan's foreign investments were in Manchuria; the South Manchurian Railway, which the Chinese had threatened to take over, linked the extensive Japanese holdings. "We are seeking room that will let us breathe," said a Japanese politician, arguing that his tiny, heavily populated nation (65 million people in an area smaller than Texas) needed to expand in order to survive. Though the seizure of Manchuria violated the Nine-Power Treaty and

Victorious soldiers celebrate in the port of Hankow, China, which fell to the Japanese in October 1938.   Paul Dorsey, Life Magazine © 1938 Time Inc.

the Kellogg-Briand Pact, the United States did not have the power to compel Japanese withdrawal. The American response therefore went no further than a moral lecture called the Stimson Doctrine (1932): the United States would not recognize any impairment of China's sovereignty or of the Open Door policy, Secretary of State Henry L. Stimson declared.

Hardly cowed by protests from Western capitals, Japan continued to harry China. In mid-1937 full-scale Sino-Japanese war erupted, although Tokyo preferred to call it the "China incident" to maintain the fiction that it had not violated Kellogg-Briand. The Japanese seized cities and bombed innocent civilians. Senator Norris, an isolationist who moved further away from his isolationism with each new Japanese thrust, condemned the Japanese as "disgraceful, ignoble, barbarous, and cruel, even beyond the power of language to describe." In an effort to

help China, Roosevelt refused to declare the existence of war, thus not invoking the Neutrality Acts and thereby allowing the Chinese to buy weapons in the United States. In a stirring speech denouncing the aggressors in October 1937, he called for a "quarantine" to curb the "epidemic of world lawlessness." People who thought Washington had been too gentle with Japan cheered; confirmed isolationists warned that the president was edging toward war. Actually, Roosevelt had formulated no program to halt the Japanese. When Japanese aircraft sank the American gunboat *Panay*, an escort for Standard Oil Company tankers on the Chang Jiang Zangbo (Yangtze River), in late 1937, Roosevelt demanded an apology but stopped short of retaliation. He was much relieved when Tokyo apologized and offered to pay for damages.

Japan's declaration of a "New Order" in Asia "banged, barred, and bolted" the Open Door, as one

American official observed. Alarmed, the Roosevelt administration found small ways to assist China and thwart Japan in 1938 and 1939. Military equipment flowed to the Chinese, as did a $25 million loan. Secretary of State Hull declared a moral embargo against the shipment of airplanes to Japan. The navy continued to grow, helped by a billion-dollar congressional appropriation in 1938. And in mid-1939 the United States abrogated the 1911 Japanese-American trade treaty. Yet America continued to ship oil, cotton, and machinery to Japan. The administration hesitated to initiate economic sanctions for fear they would spark an Asian war at a time when the more serious threat was emanating from Berlin. When war broke out in Europe in 1939, Japanese-American relations were stalemated.

ON THE BRINK, 1939 TO 1941

"What worries me, especially," President Roosevelt told interventionist William Allen White in late 1939, "is that public opinion over here is patting itself on the back every morning and thanking God for the Atlantic Ocean [and the Pacific]." The European war, he went on, seriously jeopardized American security, and the American people had better recognize their precarious place in world affairs. Polls showed that Americans strongly favored the Allies, and that most supported aid to Britain and France; but the great majority emphatically wanted the United States to remain at peace. Troubled by this conflicting advice—defeat Hitler, aid the Allies, but stay out of war—the president between 1939 and 1941 gradually moved the United States from neutrality to undeclared war and then to war itself.

During those tense months of inching toward belligerency, isolationist sentiment declined. Alarmed by the swift defeat of one European nation after another, some liberals left the iso-

Decline of Isolationism lationist fold, which became more and more the province of conservatives. Die-hard isolationists organized the America First Committee in fall 1940; interventionists, meanwhile, joined the Committee

to Defend America by Aiding the Allies (formed in mid-1940). Roosevelt, who now called the isolationists "ostriches," even hinted they were pro-Nazi subversives—"conscious disorganizers or unwitting dupes." The White House began to turn over to the Federal Bureau of Investigation letters criticizing Roosevelt's foreign policy.

In September 1939 Poland succumbed to German stormtroopers in two weeks (see map, page 782). In November Soviet Russia marched into Finland, prompting Roosevelt to denounce "this dreadful rape"; by March 1940 Finland had been defeated. The following month Germany invaded Denmark and Norway, a month later the Netherlands and Belgium. "The small countries are smashed up, one by one, like matchwood," sighed the new British Prime Minister Winston Churchill. In July 1940 France collapsed, frightening Americans even more. Would England be next? After the failure of a peace mission led by his close associate Sumner Welles, Roosevelt told his advisers that though he was "not willing to fire the first shot," he was waiting for some incident to push the United States into war.

In the meantime, assuring people that New Deal reforms would not have to be sacrificed to achieve military preparedness, Roosevelt began to aid the faltering Allies. In May 1940 he ordered the sale of surplus First World War equipment to Britain and France. In July he cultivated bipartisan support for the war by naming Republicans Henry L. Stimson and Frank Knox, ardent backers of aid to the Allies, secretaries of war and navy respectively. In September he announced that by executive agreement he was trading fifty old American destroyers for leases to eight British bases, including Newfoundland, Bermuda, and Jamaica. Two weeks later he signed into law the Selective Training and Service Act, the first peacetime military draft in American history. The act called for the registration of all men between the ages of twenty-one and thirty-five. Soon over 16 million men had been signed up and draft notices were beginning to be delivered. Ironically, Roosevelt won re-election that fall with promises of peace: "Your boys are not going to be sent into foreign wars." Republican candidate Wendell Willkie, who in the emerging spirit of bipartisanship had not made an issue of foreign policy, snapped: "That hypocritical son of a bitch! This is going to beat me!"

The German Advance, 1939–1942

Through the fall Roosevelt spoke of the need for a huge foreign aid program to save England from the Nazis. The United States, he implored, must become the "great arsenal of democracy."

Lend-Lease Act He justified his pro-Allied stance as a way to keep the United States out of war (by enabling the British to win). In January 1941 the controversial Lend-Lease bill was introduced in Congress. Britain was broke, the president reported. The United States should thus lend military weapons, much as a neighbor lends a garden hose to fight a fire. Roosevelt's analogy did not convince strict isolationist Senator Burton K. Wheeler, who shouted out another comparison: Lend-Lease was "the New Deal's triple A foreign policy; it will plow under every fourth American boy." But in March 1941, with pro-British sentiment running high, the House passed the Lend-Lease Act 317 to 71; the Senate followed suit 60 to 31. The initial appropriation was $7 billion,

but by the end of the war the amount had reached $50 billion, over $31 billion of it for England.

To ensure the safe delivery of Lend-Lease goods, Roosevelt ordered the navy to patrol halfway across the Atlantic and sent American troops to Greenland. Then a stunning turn of events in Europe spurred a new decision. In June 1941 Hitler struck his erstwhile ally Russia, and news from the quiet western front was soon eclipsed by the vicious warfare in the east. Fearing a German attack on Iceland and arguing that the North Atlantic nation was essential to the defense of the Western Hemisphere, Roosevelt sent American troops one step closer to the continent. He talked up the importance of aid to Russia; if the Soviets could hold off the more than two hundred German divisions engaged in the east, Britain would gain some breathing time. By November Lend-Lease aid was flowing to appreciative Russians. Churchill, who had thundered loudly against the Communists for

President Franklin D. Roosevelt reviews the fleet with Admiral Claude Bloch aboard the U.S.S. Houston on July 14, 1938, a time when the United States was expanding its military power. Library of Congress.

years, now applauded the aid: "If Hitler invaded Hell I would make at least a favorable reference to the Devil in the House of Commons," he said.

In August 1941 Churchill and Roosevelt met for four days off Newfoundland. They got along well, trading naval stories, paying deference to one another, and taking pleasure in the fact that Churchill was half American. "It is fun to be in the same decade with you," Roosevelt later wrote to his new friend. At this conference the two leaders wrote the Atlantic Charter, a set of war aims reminiscent of Wilsonianism: collective security, disarmament, self-determination, economic cooperation, and freedom of the seas. Later, on January 1, 1942, twenty-six nations signed the Declaration of the United

Atlantic Charter

Nations, pledging themselves to fulfill the charter. According to Churchill, the president told him in Newfoundland that although he could not ask Congress for a declaration of war against Germany, "he would wage war, but not declare it, and that he would become more and more provocative."

In September 1941, there occurred the incident Roosevelt had been waiting for: the American destroyer *Greer* was fired on (but not hit) by a German submarine. In a special national radio broadcast the president protested the "piracy" and announced a policy he had privately promised to Churchill. American naval vessels would convoy British merchant ships all the way to Iceland and shoot German submarines, the "rattlesnakes of the Atlantic," on sight. Roosevelt practiced deliberate deception in the *Greer*

IMPORTANT EVENTS

1921	Washington Conference opens		Outbreak of Spanish Civil War
1922	Mussolini comes to power in Italy		Neutrality Act
1924	Dawes Plan for German reparations U.S. departs Dominican Republic	1937	Neutrality Act "China incident" Roosevelt's quarantine speech
1926	American troops occupy Nicaragua		
1927	Jiang Jieshi attacks Communists in China	1938	Mexico nationalizes American-owned oil companies Munich Conference
1928	Kellogg-Briand Pact		
1929	Onset of the Great Depression Young Plan for German reparations	1939	Nazi-Soviet pact Germany invades Poland Second World War begins U.S. repeals arms embargo
1930	Hawley-Smoot Tariff		
1931	Japan seizes Manchuria	1940	Soviets invade Finland Committee to Defend America by Aiding the Allies formed Tripartite Pact Destroyer-bases deal America First Committee formed Selective Service Act
1932	Stimson Doctrine		
1933	Hitler comes to power in Germany U.S. recognition of Soviet Russia Good Neighbor policy announced U.S. subverts Cuban revolution		
1934	Reciprocal Trade Agreements Act Export-Import Bank founded		
1935	Italy invades Ethiopia Neutrality Act	1941	Lend-Lease Act Germany attacks Russia U.S. freezes Japanese assets Atlantic Charter *Greer* incident Japan attacks Pearl Harbor
1936	U.S. votes for nonintervention at Pan American Conference		

case, for he did not mention that the *Greer* had been tailing the German U-boat for hours, radioing the submarine's location to British airplanes hunting the ship with depth charges. He and his advisers thought it necessary to manipulate public opinion in order to scare Americans into defending Britain.

The United States had in essence entered into an undeclared war with Germany. When in early October a German submarine torpedoed the American destroyer *Kearny* off the coast of Iceland, the president announced that "the shooting has started. And history has recorded who fired the first shot." When later that month the destroyer *Reuben James* went down with the loss of over one hundred American lives, Congress scrapped the cash-and-carry policy and further revised the Neutrality Acts to permit the transport of munitions to England on armed American merchant ships. When would war be declared? tense observers asked themselves.

In retrospect it seems ironic that the Second World War came to the United States via Asia, where Roosevelt so wanted to avoid it in order to concentrate

Chapter 27: DIPLOMACY IN A BROKEN WORLD, 1920–1941

This Japanese photograph of December 7, 1941, was taken soon after an air assault force bombed American ships in Pearl Harbor, Hawaii, making several direct hits. "The wretched enemy's capital ships," read the Japanese caption, "were converted into a sea hell." National Archives.

American resources on the defeat of Germany. In September 1940 Americans read the unwelcomed news of the Tripartite Pact, an alliance between Germany, Italy, and Japan. Roosevelt slapped an embargo on shipments of aviation fuel and scrap metal to

Cutoff of Trade with Japan

Japan. Because the president believed the petroleum-thirsty Japanese would consider a cutoff of oil a life-or-death matter, he did not stop that vital commodity. But after Japanese troops occupied French Indochina in July 1941, Washington froze Japanese assets in the United States, virtually ending trade (including oil) with Japan.

Tokyo recommended a high-level meeting between President Roosevelt and Prime Minister Prince Konoye, but the United States rejected the idea. American officials insisted that the Japanese first agree to respect China's sovereignty and territorial integrity, and to honor the Open Door policy—in short, to get out of China. Roosevelt also told the Japanese ambassador that his nation would have to withdraw from the Tripartite Pact. Although the American public, according to polls in fall 1941, seemed willing

to risk war with Japan to thwart further aggression, Roosevelt was not ready for an Asian war; Europe still claimed first priority. Yet he would not back down in Asia either. Nor would Japan, now eyeing the oil-rich East Indies, abandon its plans for hegemony in Asia—the Greater East Asia Co-Prosperity Sphere.

Roosevelt told his advisers to string out Japanese-American talks to gain time—time to fortify the Philippines, and time to check the fascists in Europe. "Let us do nothing to precipitate a crisis," he told the cabinet in November 1941. But by breaking the Japanese code through "Operation Magic," Americans learned that Tokyo had committed itself to war with the United States if the oil embargo was not lifted. In late November the Japanese rejected American proposals that they withdraw from Indochina. On December 1 decoding experts informed the president that Japanese task forces were being ordered into battle. Why not attack first? asked aide Harry Hopkins. No, said Roosevelt, "we would have to wait until it came." Secretary Stimson explained later that the United States let Japan fire the first shot so as "to have the full support of the American people" and "so that there should remain no doubt in anyone's mind as to who were the aggressors."

Fearing that they could not win a prolonged war, the Japanese plotted a daring raid on Pearl Harbor in Hawaii. A flotilla of Japanese aircraft carriers crossed 3,000 miles of ocean undetected. On the morning of December 7, 350 planes stamped with the Rising Sun swept down on the unsuspecting American naval base and nearby airfields, killing more than 2,400 people, sinking or damaging eight battleships, and smashing aircraft. Three American Pacific aircraft carriers, at sea, escaped the disaster.

Attack on Pearl Harbor

Though Roosevelt was distressed that his proud navy had been caught by surprise, like many Americans he felt relief after the weeks of tension. But how could Pearl Harbor have happened? Americans asked. Roosevelt did not, as his critics later charged, conspire to leave the fleet vulnerable to attack, so the United States could enter the Second World War through the "back door" of Asia. The base was not ready—not on red alert—because a message of warning from Washington had been sent by Western Union telegraph rather than by navy cable and arrived too late. Base commanders were relaxed, thinking Hawaii, so far from Japan, an unlikely target for all-out attack. They expected the assault to come at British Malaya, Thailand, or the Philippines. Mistakes there were, but not conspiracy.

On December 8, referring to the previous day as a "date which will live in infamy," Roosevelt asked Congress for a declaration of war against Japan. A unanimous vote in the Senate and a 388 to 1 vote in the House thrust America into war. (Representative Jeannette Rankin of Montana alone voted no, matching her vote against entry into the First World War.) Three days later Germany and Italy declared war against the United States. Winston Churchill was pleased that America was now fully at war. "Hitler's fate was sealed," he wrote in his memoirs. "Mussolini's fate was sealed. As for the Japanese, they would be ground to powder. . . . I went to bed and slept the sleep of the saved and thankful."

The war was now a global conflict. The old emphasis on independent internationalism, on economic and nonmilitary means to peace, seemed archaic at that stirring moment. And the Great Depression, which had brought on so much of the international havoc—it too faded in memory as the economy geared up for war. The Neutrality Acts that had been designed to insulate the United States from European troubles had been gradually revised and retired. President Roosevelt had wanted to avoid American entry into a second world war, yet he sought also to aid the Allies and thwart Japanese aggression. What he tried to avoid he could not, because he ultimately believed that the United States, deeply involved in international affairs and with economic and strategic interests to protect, had to defend itself overseas. Moreover, he warned, the Axis nations loomed as threats to Western civilization itself. And there was the perennial American desire to set things right. As the publisher Henry Luce put it in his best-selling book *American Century* (1941), the United States must "exert upon the world the full impact of our influence, for such purposes as we see fit and by such means as we see fit."

As they had so many times before, Americans flocked to the colors. Isolationists now joined the president in spirited calls for victory. "We are going to win the war, and we are going to win the peace that follows," Roosevelt predicted.

SUGGESTIONS FOR FURTHER READING

General and 1920s Foreign Policy

Thomas H. Buckley, *The United States and the Washington Conference, 1921–1922* (1970); Frank Costigliola, *Awkward Dominion: American Political, Economic, and Cultural Relations with Europe, 1919–1933* (1984); L. Ethan Ellis, *Republican Foreign Policy, 1921–1933* (1968); Robert H. Ferrell, *American Diplomacy in the Great Depression* (1957); Peter G. Filene, *Americans and the Soviet Experiment, 1917–1933* (1967); Melvyn P. Leffler, *The Elusive Quest* (1979); Elting E. Morison, *Turmoil and Tradition* (1964) (on Stimson); Arnold A. Offner, *The Origins of the Second World War* (1975); Emily S. Rosenberg, *Spreading the American Dream*

(1982); Raymond Sontag, *A Broken World, 1919–1939* (1971); Joan Hoff Wilson, *Herbert Hoover* (1975).

The Peace Movement and Kellogg-Briand Pact

Charles Chatfield, *For Peace and Justice: Pacifism in America, 1914–1941* (1971); Charles DeBenedetti, *The Peace Reform in American History* (1980); Charles DeBenedetti, *Origins of the Modern American Peace Movement, 1915–1929* (1978); Robert H. Ferrell, *Peace in Their Time* (1952); Harold Josephson, *James T. Shotwell and the Rise of Internationalism in America* (1976).

The United States in the World Economy

Frederick Adams, *Economic Diplomacy* (1976); Derek H. Aldcroft, *From Versailles to Wall Street, 1919–1929* (1977); Herbert Feis, *The Diplomacy of the Dollar, 1919–1932* (1950); Lloyd C. Gardner, *Economic Aspects of New Deal Diplomacy* (1964); Michael J. Hogan, *Informal Entente: The Private Structure of Cooperation in Anglo-American Economic Diplomacy, 1918–1928* (1977); Charles Kindleberger, *The World in Depression* (1973); Carl Parrini, *Heir to Empire* (1969); Mira Wilkins, *The Maturing of Multinational Enterprise* (1974); Joan Hoff Wilson, *American Business and Foreign Policy, 1920–1933* (1971).

Latin America

Jules R. Benjamin, *The United States and Cuba* (1978); Bruce J. Calder, *The Impact of Intervention* (1984) (on Dominican Republic); Alton Frye, *Nazi Germany and the American Hemisphere, 1933–1941* (1967); Irwin F. Gellman, *Good Neighbor Diplomacy* (1979); David Green, *The Containment of Latin America* (1971); Walter LaFeber, *Inevitable Revolutions: The United States in Central America* (1983); Lester D. Langley, *The United States and the Caribbean, 1900–1970* (1980); Neil Macaulay, *The Sandino Affair* (1967); Lorenzo Meyer, *Mexico and the United States in the Oil Controversy, 1917–1942* (1977); Richard Millett, *Guardians of the Dynasty* (1977) (on Nicaragua); Stephen G. Rabe, *The Road to OPEC* (1982) (on Venezuela); Robert I. Rotberg, *Haiti* (1971); Ramon Ruiz, *Cuba* (1968); Karl M. Schmitt, *Mexico and the United States, 1821–1973* (1974); Robert F. Smith, *The United States and Revolutionary Nationalism in Mexico, 1916–1932* (1972); Bryce Wood, *The Making of the Good Neighbor Policy* (1961).

Isolationism and Isolationists

Warren I. Cohen, *The American Revisionists* (1967); Wayne S. Cole, *Roosevelt and the Isolationists, 1932–1945* (1983); Wayne S. Cole, *America First* (1953); Manfred Jonas, *Isolationism in America, 1935–1941* (1966); Thomas C. Kennedy, *Charles A. Beard and American Foreign Policy* (1975); Richard Lowitt, *George W. Norris*, 3 vols. (1963–1978); John Wiltz, *In Search of Peace: The Senate Munitions Inquiry, 1934–1936* (1963).

Franklin D. Roosevelt and Europe

Thomas A. Bailey and Paul B. Ryan, *Hitler vs. Roosevelt* (1979); Edward Bennett, *Recognition of Russia* (1970); James MacGregor Burns, *Roosevelt: The Lion and the Fox* (1956); Mark Chadwin, *The Hawks of World War II* (1968); James V. Compton, *The Swastika and the Eagle* (1967); David H. Culbert, *News for Everyman: Radio and Foreign Affairs in Thirties America* (1976); Robert Dallek, *Franklin D. Roosevelt and American Foreign Policy, 1932–1945* (1979); Robert A. Divine, *The Reluctant Belligerent*, 2nd ed. (1979); Robert A. Divine, *Roosevelt and World War II* (1969); Manfred Jonas, *The United States and Germany* (1984); Warren F. Kimball, *The Most Unsordid Act: Lend-Lease, 1939–1941* (1969); William L. Langer and S. Everett Gleason, *The Undeclared War, 1940–1941* (1953); William L. Langer and S. Everett Gleason, *The Challenge to Isolation, 1937–1940* (1952); Thomas R. Maddux, *Years of Estrangement: American Relations with the Soviet Union, 1933–1941* (1980); Arnold A. Offner, *American Appeasement* (1969); Julius W. Pratt, *Cordell Hull*, 2 vols. (1964); David Reynolds, *The Creation of the Anglo-American Alliance, 1937–1941* (1982); Bruce Russett, *No Clear and Present Danger* (1972).

China, Japan, and the Coming of War in Asia

Charles A. Beard, *President Roosevelt and the Coming of the War, 1941* (1948); Dorothy Borg and Shumpei Okomoto, eds., *Pearl Harbor as History* (1973); R. J. C. Butow, *Tojo and the Coming of the War* (1961); Warren I. Cohen, *America's Response to China*, 2nd ed. (1980); Roger Dingman, *Power in the Pacific* (1976); Herbert Feis, *The Road to Pearl Harbor* (1950); Waldo H. Heinrichs, Jr., *American Ambassador* (1966) (on Joseph Grew); Akira Iriye, *Across the Pacific* (1967); Akira Iriye, *After Imperialism: The Search for a New Order in the Far East, 1921–1931* (1965); Charles Neu, *The Troubled Encounter: The United States and Japan* (1975); Paul W. Schroeder, *The Axis Alliance and Japanese-American Relations, 1941* (1958).

Pearl Harbor

Martin V. Melosi, *The Shadow of Pearl Harbor* (1977); Gordon W. Prange, *At Dawn We Slept* (1981); John Toland, *Infamy* (1982); Roberta Wohlstetter, *Pearl Harbor* (1962).

The Second World War at Home and Abroad

1941–1945

Chapter 28

"*We are going* on a mission to drop a bomb different from any you have ever seen or heard about," Colonel Paul Tibbets informed his crew on the small Pacific island of Tinian. Silent and incredulous, they listened to "Old Bull" describe the strange new weapon, which packed the destructive power of twenty thousand tons of TNT. Resting in the bay of a converted B-29 named the *Enola Gay*, after Tibbets's mother, was "Little Boy"—a ten-thousand-pound uranium bomb on which the airmen had scribbled anti-Japanese graffiti.

On August 6, 1945, the *Enola Gay* lumbered down the runway at Tinian. Once airborne, crew members assembled the firing mechanism. "Knock wood," muttered one of them. Several hours later they received a radio message that the weather over Hiroshima was clear. Cruising at over 30,000 feet, they put on welder's goggles and made their run on the unsuspecting city of a quarter-million people.

At 8:15 A.M. the atomic bomb dropped from the aircraft. It exploded in less than a minute over the target. A flash of dazzling light shot across the sky. "Everything just turned white in front of me," Tibbets recalled. Then two violent slaps rocked the ship. "My God!" gasped co-pilot Captain Robert Lewis as he watched a huge purplish mushroom cloud boil 40,000 feet into the atmosphere. Dense smoke, swirling fires, and suffocating dust soon engulfed the ground for miles. Much of the city was leveled almost instantly. "Even though we had expected something terrific," Lewis remembered, "what we saw made us feel that we were Buck Rogers twenty-fifth century warriors."

Approximately 130,000 people were killed at Hiroshima; tens of thousands more suffered painful burns and nuclear poisoning. As Hiroshima suffered its unique nightmare, Washington, D.C., celebrated its military and scientific triumph. "This is the greatest thing in history," exclaimed President Harry S Truman on hearing of the successful mission.

For forty-five months Americans had fought abroad to subdue the Nazi and Japanese aggressors. After military engagements against the fascists in North Africa and Italy, in June 1944 American troops had joined the dramatic crossing of the English Channel on D-Day. The massive invasion forced the Germans to retreat through France to Germany. Battered by merciless bombing raids, leaderless after Adolf Hitler's suicide, and pressed by a Russian advance from the east, the Nazis capitulated in May 1945. In the Pacific, Americans drove the Japanese from one island after another before turning to the just-tested atomic bombs that demolished Hiroshima and Nagasaki and helped spur a Japanese surrender in August.

Throughout the war the Allies—Britain, Russia, and the United States—were held together by their common goal of defeating Germany. But they squabbled over many issues: when the second, or western, front would be opened; how a new international organization would be structured; how Eastern Europe, liberated from the Germans, would be reconstructed; how Germany itself would be governed after defeat. At the end of the war Allied leaders seemed more intent on keeping and expanding their own nations' spheres of influence than on building a community of mutual interest. The United States and the Soviet Union emerged from the war as major competitors in a world facing the task of reconstruction. The prospects for postwar international cooperation seemed bleak, and the advent of an atomic age with nuclear weapons frightened people everywhere.

The atomic bomb was a milestone in world affairs, but events on the home front transformed American life in different ways. The nation united behind the war effort, collecting scrap iron, rubber, and old newspapers and planting victory gardens. But more than national unity and enthusiasm were required to win the war. Essential to victory was the successful mobilization of all sectors of the economy—industry, finance, agriculture, and labor. The federal government had the monumental task of coordinating these several elements, as well as a couple of new ones: higher education and science. For this was a scientific and technological war, supported by the development of new weapons like radar and the atomic bomb.

For millions of Americans the war was a time to relocate in other parts of the country. Between 1941 and 1945, over 16 million men and women served in the armed forces. They traveled to new duty stations in the United States and abroad, acquired new skills, and broadened their horizons. But at war's end they were older, both physically and emotionally, and many felt they had sacrificed the best years of their lives. Also on the move during the Second World War were blacks, Mexican-Americans, and whites who migrated to war-production centers in the North and the West. For numerous Afro-Americans, the war offered new economic and political opportunities, encouraging them to demand their full rights as citizens. But it also provided the ingredients of racial violence; in 1943 race riots erupted across the country.

Employers' negative attitudes toward women workers eased during the Second World War, and millions of married middle-class women, many of them over thirty-five, took jobs in war industries. For some, work was an economic necessity; for others it was a patriotic obligation. Whatever the motivation, paying jobs brought women benefits—financial independence and enhanced self-esteem—that many were unwilling to give up at war's end.

The United States underwent profound change during the course of the war. Its big businesses got even bigger, while hundreds of thousands of neighborhood enterprises and family farms ceased to function. Membership in the nation's labor unions increased dramatically, and the federal government experienced tremendous growth in both its budget and its bureaucracy. Furthermore, the experiences of the First World War and the New Deal proved an inadequate guide in this longer, more demanding conflict. For all of these reasons the Second World War was a turning point in American history.

WINNING THE SECOND WORLD WAR

"We are now in the midst of a war, not for conquest, not for vengeance, but for a world in which this Nation, and all that this Nation represents, will be safe for our children." President Roosevelt was speaking just two days after the surprise attack on Pearl Harbor. Americans believed with Roosevelt that they were defending their homes and families against aggressive and satanic Nazis and Japanese. Few of them, however, knew much about the principles of the Atlantic Charter (see page 783) or about United States war aims. To most Americans the Second World War was simply a grimy job. Like cartoonist Bill Mauldin's popular GI characters Willy and Joe, who were more interested in tasty food and dry socks than in abstractions, they were eager to get it over with. Americans also seemed wary of lofty rhetoric about the future, remembering how Woodrow Wilson had promised so much and delivered too little during the era of the First World War. The army's Morale Branch, worried that the average American was ignorant or cynical about the reasons for war, hired prominent Hollywood director Frank Capra to produce a series of propaganda films called *Why We Fight*.

In these widely distributed films and in the popular mind, the Allies were heroic partners in a common effort against evil. Actually, wartime relations among the United States, Great Britain, and the Soviet Union ran hot and cold. Although winning the war claimed top priority, Allied leaders knew that military decisions had political consequences. Should one ally become desperate, for instance, it might sue for a separate peace. And the position of troops at the end of the war might determine the politics of the region they occupied. Thus an undercurrent of suspicion ran beneath the surface of Allied cooperation.

Roosevelt, British Prime Minister Winston Churchill, and Soviet Premier Josef Stalin differed vigorously over the opening of a second, or western, front. After Germany conquered France in 1940 and invaded Russia in 1941, the Russians bore the brunt of the war until mid-1944, suffering heavy casualties. By late 1941, before the fierce Russian winter stalled their onslaught, German troops had reached the edge of Moscow and Leningrad and had slashed deeply into the Ukraine, taking Kiev. Stalin pressed for a British-American landing on the northern coast of Europe to draw German troops away from the eastern front, but Churchill would not agree. The Russians therefore did most of the fighting and dying on land, while the British and Americans concentrated on getting Lend-Lease supplies across the Atlantic and harassing the Germans from the air

Second Front Controversy

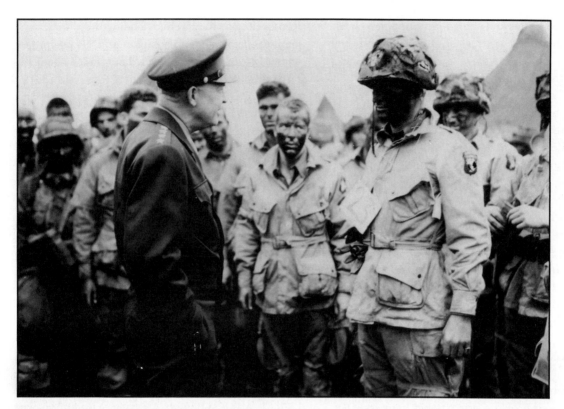

In January 1944 General Dwight D. Eisenhower arrived in England to assume his duties as Supreme Commander, Allied Expeditionary Forces. His mission was to organize the D-Day invasion of Europe by Allied forces. Here Eisenhower talks with members of the spearhead assault forces. U.S. Army.

with attacks on factories and civilians alike. When Secretary of State Cordell Hull bemoaned the 200,000 American casualties suffered from 1941 to 1943, a Russian official replied, "We lose that many each day before lunch. You haven't got your teeth in the war yet."

Roosevelt was particularly sensitive to the suggestion that Americans were shirking their responsibility by avoiding an invasion of Europe. He feared that Russia might be knocked out of the war, leaving Hitler free to send his goose-stepping soldiers into England. In 1942 Roosevelt told the Russians they could expect the Allies to open a second front later that year. The move across the English Channel, later tagged Operation OVERLORD, was exactly what Stalin sought to take pressure off his wracked country. But Churchill balked. "To postpone that evil day, all his arts, all his eloquence, all his great experience was spent," the prime minister's chief military adviser

later wrote. Churchill feared heavy losses in a premature cross-channel invasion. Though American Generals George C. Marshall and Dwight D. Eisenhower argued for a direct attack on the heart of German power, Churchill held out for a series of small jabs at the enemy's Mediterranean forces. American officials suspected that Churchill's strategy derived from his desire to recover British imperial power in the Mediterranean.

Churchill won the debate. Instead of attacking France, the western Allies invaded North Africa in November 1942. To reduce resistance to the invasion, the Americans agreed to recognize the pro-Nazi Vichy French regime in North Africa—a "deal" many critics denounced as unsavory. Roosevelt deemed it justified in order to get Americans into combat. "We are striking back," the cheered president declared. News from Russia also buoyed Roosevelt. In the battle for Stalingrad (September 1942 to January 1943), probably the turning point of the war, the Red Army defeated the Germans in bloody block-by-block fighting, forcing Hitler's divisions to retreat. But shortly after Stalingrad, the president once again angered the Russians by declaring another delay in launching the second front. Marshal Stalin was not mollified in the summer of 1943 by the Allied invasion of Italy. When Italy surrendered in September, it capitulated to American and British officers; Russian officials were not invited to participate. Stalin grumbled that the arrangement smacked of a separate peace and wondered if Roosevelt and Churchill's policy of unconditional surrender for the Axis, announced that January at the Anglo-American conference at Casablanca, had been violated.

With the Grand Alliance badly strained, Roosevelt sought reconciliation through personal diplomacy. The three Allied leaders met in Teheran, Iran, in December 1943. Stalin dismissed Churchill's repetitious justifications for further delaying the second front. Roosevelt had had enough too; with Stalin he rejected Churchill's proposal for another peripheral attack, this time through the Balkans to Vienna. The three finally agreed to launch OVERLORD in early 1944. An appreciative Russia promised to aid the Allies against Japan once Germany was defeated.

Like a coiled spring bursting free, the second front opened in the dark morning hours of June 6, 1944: D-Day. Two hundred thousand Allied troops under the command of General Eisen-

D-Day hower scrambled ashore in Normandy, France, in the largest amphibious landing in history. Thousands of ships ferried the men within a hundred yards of the sandy beaches. Craft and soldiers became entangled in sharp obstacles and triggered mines, and were pinned down by fire from cliffside pillboxes. Meanwhile, airborne troops .dropped behind German lines. Although heavy aerial and naval bombardment and the clandestine work of underground saboteurs had softened up German defenses, the fighting was still ferocious. One soldier felt like a "pigeon at a trap shoot."

After digging in at now-famous places like Utah and Omaha beaches and gaining reinforcements, Allied forces broke through disorderly German lines and gradually ground inland, reaching Paris in August. That same month another force invaded southern France and threw the stunned Germans back. Allied

As the Second World War drew to a close in Europe, American and Russian troops linked up in Germany. These Americans from the 82nd Airborne Division met up with Russian soldiers at Grabow, Germany, on May 3, 1945. Five days later, Germany surrendered. U.S. Army.

troops soon spread across the countryside, liberating France and Belgium and entering Germany itself in September. In December German panzer divisions counterattacked in Belgium's Ardennes Forest, hoping to push on to Antwerp to halt the flow of Allied supplies through that major Belgian port. After weeks of heavy fighting in what has come to be called the Battle of the Bulge—because of the noticeable dent in the Allied line—the Allies pushed the enemy back once again. Meanwhile, battle-hardened Russian troops streamed through Poland and cut a path to the German capital, Berlin. American forces crossed the Rhine in March 1945 and captured the heavily industrial Ruhr valley. Some units peeled off to enter Austria and Czechoslovakia, where they met up with Russian soldiers. In bomb-ravaged Berlin, defended largely by teenage boys and old men, Adolf Hitler killed himself in his bunker. On May 8 Germany surrendered.

Allied strategists had devised a "Europe first" for-

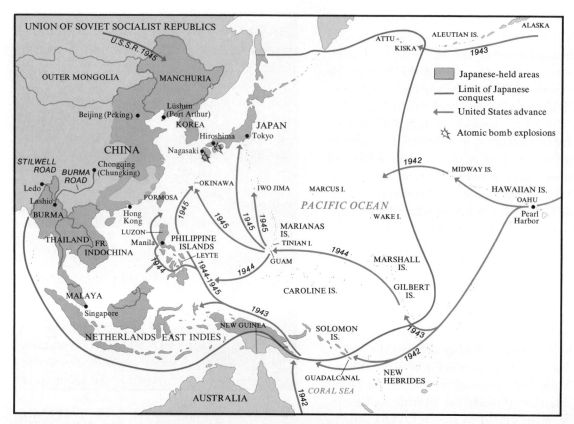

The Pacific War *Source: By permission of the publisher, from American Foreign Policy: A History by Paterson et al., p. 474. (Lexington, Mass.: D.C. Heath and Company, 1977).*

mula: knock out Germany first and then concentrate on an isolated Japan. Nevertheless, the Pacific theater claimed headlines throughout the war, for the American people regarded Japan as the United States' chief enemy. The treacherous Japanese—"monkeys" and "bastards," boomed Admiral William Halsey—had to be repaid for Pearl Harbor. By mid-1942 Japan had seized the Philippines, Guam, Wake, Hong Kong, Singapore, Malaya, and the Dutch East Indies. In the Philippines in 1942 Japanese soldiers forced American prisoners, weak from insufficient rations, to walk sixty-five miles, clubbing, shooting, or starving to death about ten thousand of them. The Bataan Death March intensified the American hatred of the Japanese.

In April 1942 Americans began to hit back. They bombed Tokyo, and in May, in the momentous Battle of the Coral Sea, carrier-based U.S. planes halted a Japanese advance toward Australia (see map). The next month American forces defeated the Japanese at Midway, sinking four of the enemy's valuable aircraft carriers. Thanks to the success of Operation Magic—the work of American experts who deciphered the secret code used by the Japanese to transmit messages—American naval officers knew ahead of time the approximate date and direction of the Japanese assault. The Battle of Midway broke the Japanese momentum and relieved the threat to Hawaii. Thereafter, Japan was never able to match American manpower, sea power, air power, or economic power. Still, the war in Asia was contested until the very end. "There are no breathers in this schedule," exclaimed General H. H. Arnold in the football jargon of the time. "You take on Notre Dame every time you play!"

American strategy was to "island-hop" toward Japan itself, skipping the most strongly fortified points whenever possible and taking weaker ones. Americans also set out to sink the Japanese merchant marine,

American Offensive in the Pacific in an effort to strand the Japanese armies in their island outposts and to cut off raw materials from the factories of the home islands. The first American offensive—at Guadalcanal in the Solomon Islands in summer and fall 1942—gave troops their first taste of jungle warfare: thick vegetation, mosquitos, scorpions, tropical heat, and rotting gear. From the Solomons the U.S. military pushed relentlessly on, colliding with the entrenched enemy in the Gilberts, Marshalls, and Marianas in 1943 and 1944. In June 1944 the navy smashed Japanese forces in the Battle of the Philippine Sea. In October General Douglas MacArthur landed at Leyte to reclaim the Philippines for the United States. Then in early 1945 both sides took heavy losses at Iwo Jima and Okinawa. In desperation, Japanese pilots began suicide (*kamikaze*) attacks, flying their planes directly into American ships.

Hoping to avoid a humiliating unconditional surrender (and to preserve the emperor's sovereignty), Japanese leaders refused to admit defeat. They hung on while American bombers leveled their cities. In one staggering attack on Tokyo on May 23, 1945, American planes dropped napalm-filled bombs that engulfed the city in a firestorm. Eighty-three thousand people died; observers described the ghastly scene as a mass burning.

Impatient for victory, American leaders began to plan a fall invasion of the Japanese islands, an expedition that was sure to bring high casualties. But the successful development of an atomic bomb by American scientists provided another route to victory. The secret atomic program, known as the Manhattan Project, began in August 1942 and cost $2 billion. The first atomic bomb was exploded in the desert near Alamogordo, New Mexico, on July 16, 1945. On August 6 the Japanese city of Hiroshima was destroyed by an atomic blast, killing half of the city's inhabitants at a stroke.

American planes continued their devastating conventional bombing and scattered leaflets over other Japanese cities warning that they too would face atomic terror unless the Japanese empire surrendered. On August 9 another atomic attack flattened Nagasaki, killing at least sixty thousand people. The next day a sobered President Truman suspended the further atomic bombing of Japan. He had belated qualms about killing "all those kids." Four days later the Japanese, who had sent out peace feelers since June, surrendered. The victors promised that the Japanese emperor could remain as the nation's titular head. Formal ceremonies were held September 2 aboard the battleship *Missouri*. The Second World War was over.

Most Americans agreed with President Truman that the atomic bombing of two Japanese cities had been necessary, to end the war as quickly as possible and to save American lives. Use of **Why the Atomic Bomb Was Used** the bomb to achieve victory had, in fact, been the primary assumption of the Manhattan Project. At the highest governmental levels and among atomic scientists, alternatives had been discussed: detonate the bomb on an unpopulated Pacific island, with international observers as witnesses; blockade and bomb Japan conventionally; follow up Tokyo's peace feelers; encourage a Russian declaration of war. But Truman's aides had rejected these options on the grounds that they would take too long and would not convince the tenacious Japanese they had been beaten. Then, too, memories of Pearl Harbor played a part. "When you have to deal with a beast you have to treat him as a beast," Truman said.

Diplomatic considerations also sped the decision to use the bomb. Leaders envisioned the real and psychological power the bomb would bestow on the United States. It might serve as a deterrent against aggression; it might intimidate Russia into making concessions in Eastern Europe; it might end the war in the Pacific before Russia could claim a role in the management of Asia. "If it explodes, as I think it will," Truman remarked, "I'll certainly have a hammer on those boys" (the Russians).

ECONOMIC EFFECTS OF THE WAR AT HOME

The Second World War had been won at great cost not only abroad, but also on the American home front. While the guns boomed in Europe and

The federal government used a variety of methods to exhort home-front Americans to obey wartime regulations. This Office of War Information poster suggested that the gas cheat was betraying his patriotic duty to support American troops. National Archives.

Asia, the war changed American lives and institutions. One month after Pearl Harbor, President Roosevelt had established the War Production Board (WPB). First on the WPB's list of tasks was the conversion from civilian to military production. Factories that had manufactured silk ribbons began to turn out silk parachutes; automobile companies switched to the production of tanks and airplanes; adding-machine companies converted to make automatic pistols. Factories had to be expanded and new ones built. The WPB was so successful that the production of durable goods more than tripled. For example, manufacture of military aircraft, which had totaled 6,000 in 1940, jumped to over 47,000 in 1942 and 85,000 in 1943.

The wartime emergency spurred the establishment of totally new industries, the best known of which was synthetic rubber. The Japanese, in their conquest of the South Pacific in the weeks following Pearl Harbor, had captured 90 percent of the world's supply of crude rubber. Though the government resorted to conservation measures, including a national speed limit and gasoline rationing to save wear and tear on tires, neither conservation nor recycling could meet wartime needs. So with an investment of $700 million, the government underwrote the creation of a synthetic-rubber industry based on petroleum. By war's end the nation that had been the world's largest importer of rubber had become the world's largest exporter of rubber—all of it synthetic. New industries, of course, introduced new pollutants: smog (first detected in Los Angeles in 1943); artificially made radioactive elements; and petrochemical wastes from such new products as plastics, detergents, and DDT.

To gain the cooperation of business, the WPB and other government agencies met it more than halfway. The government guaranteed profits in the form of cost-plus-fixed-fee contracts, generous tax writeoffs, and exemption from antitrust prosecution. And it allowed prime contractors to distribute subcontracts as they saw fit, including those involving scarce war-related materials. These rewards made sense for a government—and a nation—that wanted the most possible war goods manufactured in the shortest possible time.

Government Incentives to Business

From mid-1940 through September 1944 the government awarded contracts totaling $175 billion, no less than two-thirds of which went to the top one hundred corporations. General Motors received 8 percent of the total; big awards also went to other automobile companies, as well as to aircraft, steel, electrical, and chemical companies. Almost all these industries had been dominated by big corporations at the beginning of the war; the billions of dollars they received in government contracts only accentuated their dominance. Though no one had yet thought to call it the "military-industrial complex," as President Dwight Eisenhower would in 1961 (see page 875), the web of government-business interdependence had begun to be woven.

The big also got bigger in science and higher education. To develop radar and do other research, the Massachusetts Institute of Technology received contracts valued at $117 million. The California Institute of Technology came next with contracts totaling $83 million, followed by Harvard, Columbia, the University of California, Johns Hopkins, and the University of Chicago. The most spectacular result of a government contract with a university was, of course, the atomic bomb; its testing was run by the University of California at Berkeley.

Big labor also grew bigger during the war. Union membership ballooned from 8.5 million in 1940 to 14.75 million in 1945. Less than a week after Pearl Harbor, a White House labor-management conference produced a no-strike–no-lockout pledge to guarantee uninterrupted war production. "When the nation is attacked," declared John L. Lewis, the gruff president of the United Mine Workers union, "every American must rally to its defense. All other considerations become insignificant." In 1942, to minimize labor-management conflict, President Roosevelt created the National War Labor Board (NWLB), sometimes referred to as the Supreme Court for labor disputes. Unions were permitted to enroll as many new members as possible, but workers were not required to join a union. Thus the NWLB forged a compromise between the unions' demand for a closed shop, in which only union members could be hired, and management's interest in open shops.

When the NWLB attempted to limit wage increases to increases in the cost of living, there were wildcat strikes and other work stoppages that tripled the production time lost in 1943. "Strikes are spreading at an alarming rate," bemoaned a member of the NWLB, "and unless they are checked immediately, the 'no strike–no lockout' agreement will become meaningless." But the worst labor disruptions of 1943 came in the coal fields, where 450,000 soft-coal miners and 80,000 anthracite miners struck. "When the mine workers' children cry for bread, they cannot be satisfied [with words];" declared John L. Lewis, who seemed to forget his earlier patriotic commitment to sacrifice.

Public hostility grew toward organized labor in general and John L. Lewis in particular. To discourage further work stoppages, Congress passed the War Labor Disputes, or Smith-Connally, Act of June 1943. The act conferred on the president the authority to seize and operate any strike-bound plant deemed necessary to the national security, and established a mandatory thirty-day cooling-off period before any new strike

could be called. The Smith-Connally Act also gave the NWLB the legal authority to settle labor disputes for the duration of the war. Over the course of the war the NWLB handled close to eighteen thousand disputes, reducing time lost due to strikes to one-third the peacetime level.

Although the war demanded sacrifices from Americans, it also brought new highs in personal income. Savings deposits jumped from $32.4 billion in 1942 to $51.4 billion in 1945. It was an even more bountiful time both for corporations, which doubled their net profits between 1939 and 1943, and for employees, whose wages and salaries rose more than 135 percent from 1940 to 1945. The government did not tax this extra income as heavily as it might have. Instead it resorted to deficit financing and borrowed approximately 60 percent of the cost of the war, about half of it in the form of war bonds sold to patriotic citizens; the national debt skyrocketed from $49 billion in 1941 to $259 billion in 1945.

Agriculture also made an impressive contribution to the war effort, not only through hard work but through the introduction of labor-saving machinery

Increased Mechanization of Agriculture

to replace the men and women who had gone to the front or migrated to war-production centers. Farming was in the midst of a transition from the family-owned and operated farm to the large-scale, mechanized agribusiness dominated by banks, insurance companies, and farm co-ops. The Second World War accelerated the trend, for wealthy financial institutions were better able than family farmers to pay for expensive new machinery. From 1940 to 1945 the value of American agricultural machinery rose from $3.1 billion to $6.5 billion, and the average acreage per farm jumped from 175 to 195. The use of the new machines and fertilizers boosted farm output per man-hour by 25 percent. At the same time the farm population fell from 30.5 million to 24.4 million. Like business and labor, agriculture was becoming more consolidated as it contributed to the war effort.

At the head of the burgeoning national economy stood the federal government, whose size and importance, like that of business and labor, was mushrooming: from 1940 to 1945 the federal bureaucracy expanded from 1.1 million workers to 3.4 million. The executive branch, which included the Office of the Commander-in-Chief and bore the responsibility for directing the war effort, grew the most. Besides raising the armed forces, mobilizing industrial production, pacifying labor and management, and controlling inflation, the executive also had to manage the labor supply. Through the War Manpower Commission (WMC), composed of representatives of various agencies, the government determined where labor was most needed, allocated labor between industry and the armed forces, and recruited new workers.

Although the WMC was far from successful in accomplishing its goals, another government agency, the Office of Price Administration (OPA), did succeed in combating inflation by fixing price ceilings on commodities and introducing rationing programs. Consumers became skilled in handling ration stamps, each worth ten points—red for meats and cheese, blue for canned goods—and car windows displayed "A" stamp decals for gasoline. In addition, the OPA issued a series of proclamations and rules that governed the behavior of landlords, employers, rationing boards, wholesalers, retailers, and consumers. In May 1943, as economic mobilization became increasingly bogged down in red tape, President Roosevelt created the Office of War Mobilization which became, in effect, a court of appeal in disputes between conflicting civilian and military claims.

Although government-business-labor relations were sometimes bitter and slowed production, Americans were generally ready to make personal sacrifices. They knew the war would be costly and long. In previous conflicts Americans had flocked to the colors with flags, wild rallies, and militaristic songs, but in the Second World War they fought with a grim, realistic determination. To elicit the people's enthusiasm, the Office of War Administration took charge of domestic propaganda and hired Hollywood filmmakers and New York advertising copywriters to sell the war. But as historian Allan Nevins observed, "In this war there was . . . no such straw fire of frothy enthusiasm." Most Americans wanted to leave behind their concerns about the war, so the motion pictures produced and books published during this war were typically light, fluffy, sentimental escapes from the harsh realities of life. In 1861, 1898, and 1917, Nevins wrote, Americans had thought that "the war would be easy. They knew full well in 1941 that it wouldn't."

THE MILITARY LIFE

In America's forty-five months at war, a total of 16.4 million of its citizens responded to the colors. Some served for the war's duration, others for shorter periods. At the war's conclusion in 1945, over 12 million men and women were serving in the U.S. armed forces. The army topped the list with 8.3 million, including 100,000 WACS (Women's Army Corps). Though women were prohibited from engaging in combat duty, they worked at a variety of noncombat jobs, not only in the WACS but as WAVES (Women Accepted for Volunteer Emergency Service) in the navy, as pilots in the WASPS (Women Air Service Pilots), and as members of the Coast Guard and the Marine Corps Women's Reserve. The WASPS taught basic flying, towed aerial targets for gunnery practice, and flight-tested military aircraft.

American troops served overseas for an average of about sixteen months. Some, of course, never returned: total deaths exceeded 405,000; total wounded, 670,000. In terms of human life, the cost of the war was second only to that of the Civil War. Still, compared with losses suffered by other nations, U.S. figures were low. Less than 1 percent of the population was killed or wounded in the war; the Soviet Union lost 8 percent of its population—about 20 million people.

Many soldiers and sailors, who had never been more than a few miles from home, became homesick. GIs joked, somewhat bitterly, about having found a home in the army. But this loneliness was minor compared with the intense fear that soldiers admitted to feeling in battle. Combat veterans told a group of psychologists that a man who burst out weeping was "not regarded as a coward unless he made no apparent effort to stick to his job." Some Americans became looters. One veteran explained that when soldiers took a town, they "wanted something to drink. Then they wanted a woman. And then they wanted to go out and see what they could loot. And brother, when I say loot, I mean some of them looted."

But if combat's cruelties robbed many GIs of their innocence, military service itself broadened the ho-

B-17 pilots return from a training flight in their Flying Fortress Pistol Packin' Mama. *WAF pilots ferried the planes for the Air Corps.   U.S. Air Force Photo.*

rizons of millions of men and women. "Take these kids from the hills," noted one GI,

Broadening of GIs' Horizons

"the service opened their eyes some. . . . And some of these guys from Chicago, why they'd never been outside of Chicago. They talked about fellows 'from the sticks' and they'd never been out in the 'sticks'— they'd never even known what the 'sticks' were."

Wartime service not only broadened horizons but stimulated soldiers' ambitions. A soldier from the Midwest, who reported that he found himself "living among fellows from all over the country," said, "I picked up a lot of ideas from them, not only [about] what the United States was really like—I mean the whole country—but about how to live my own life and to get more out of it. . . . I came out a lot more ambitious than I was before I went in." Finally, many GIs returned to civilian life with new skills they had learned in the military's technical schools. Some became fluent in foreign languages; others became medical technicians, electronics experts, and aircraft mechanics. Still others took advantage of the educational benefits offered in the GI Bill of Rights (1944) to study for a college degree (see page 895).

Still, after two or three years abroad, men and women in the service returned to the United States not knowing what to expect from civilian life. Earlier in the war, troops had been given orientation lectures and booklets introducing them to the historical backgrounds and social customs of the foreign nations where they would serve. Now they were coming home, and yet, as one observer wrote, they were "to a surprising degree, foreigners in their own land." Returning soldiers also feared a postwar economic depression. A B-17 crew chief complained that people were "spending too much money and . . . not saving up for what's coming—you know, unemployment after the war."

But what might have been most disturbing to GIs was the feeling that life at home had passed them by. For one thing, returning GIs were much older in experience and in exposure to brutality; they had lost their innocence. Many came back to the United States convinced that they had sacrificed their youth.

"Just gimme a coupla aspirin. I already got a Purple Heart." The cartoonist Bill Mauldin became famous through his GI characters Willie and Joe, two battle-hardened veterans who hated officers almost as much as they hated the army. *By permission of Bill Mauldin and Wil-Jo Associates, Inc.*

Still worse, they found that home had changed as well. "Our friends are gone," one GI lamented. "The family and the town naturally had to go on even if we weren't there, and somehow it seems things have sort of closed in and filled that space we used to occupy."

CIVIL LIBERTIES AND THE INTERNMENT OF JAPANESE-AMERICANS

Once the United States entered the war, its leaders had to consider whether enemy agents were operating within its borders and threatening the war effort. It was clear that not all Americans were en-

thusiastic supporters of the nation's involvement in the war. Following Pearl Harbor, several thousand "enemy aliens" were arrested and taken into custody, some of them Nazi agents who had accumulated firearms, shortwave radios, and codes in the course of their work. Other people had conscientious objections to the war, particularly Quakers, Mennonites, and members of the Church of the Brethren. During the Second World War conscientious objectors (COs) had to have a religious (as opposed to moral or ethical) reason for refusing military service. About 25,000 qualified COs accepted noncombat service, most of them as medical corpsmen. An additional 12,000 were placed in civilian public-service camps, where they worked at forestry or conservation or as orderlies in public health hospitals. Some—5,500 in all, three-fourths of whom were Jehovah's Witnesses—refused to participate in any way; they were imprisoned.

The one enormous exception to the nation's generally creditable wartime civil liberties record was the internment in "relocation centers" of more than

Internment in "Relocation Centers"

110,000 Japanese-Americans. Of these people, 70,000 were Nisei, or native-born citizens of the United States. Their imprisonment was based not on suspicion or evidence of treason; their crime was their ethnic origin—the fact that they were of Japanese descent. As General John L. DeWitt, chief of the Western Defense Command, expressed it:

> The Japanese race is an enemy race and while many second and third generation Japanese born on United States soil, possessed of United States citizenship, have become "Americanized," the racial strains are undiluted. . . . It, therefore, follows that along the vital Pacific Coast over 112,000 potential enemies, of Japanese extraction, are at large today.

With strained illogic he declared: "The very fact that no sabotage [by Japanese-Americans] has taken place to date is a disturbing and confirming indication that such action will be taken." DeWitt was not alone in his paranoia.

Charges of criminal behavior were never brought against Japanese-Americans; none were ever indicted or tried for espionage, treason, or sedition. Even their alleged crime, disloyalty to the United States, was

Branded members of an enemy race by the government, more than 110,000 Japanese-Americans were rounded up and shipped to internment camps. Included among the evacuees were children and the elderly.   National Archives.

not against the law. Nevertheless in 1942 more than 110,000 people were rounded up and imprisoned. "It was really cruel and harsh," recalled Joseph Y. Kurihara, a citizen and a veteran of the First World War. "To pack and evacuate in forty-eight hours was an impossibility. Seeing mothers completely bewildered with children crying from want and peddlers taking advantage and offering prices next to robbery made me feel like murdering those responsible." After the war, Kurihara, along with 8,000 other Japanese-Americans, did the next best thing: he emigrated to Japan, a country he had never seen.

The internees were sent to flood-damaged lands at Relocation, Arkansas; to the intermountain terrain of Wyoming and the desert of western Arizona; and to other arid and desolate spots in the West. Although the names were evocative—Topaz, Utah; Rivers, Arizona; Heart Mountain, Wyoming; Manzanar, California—the camps themselves were bleak and demoralizing. Behind barbed wire stood tarpapered

wooden barracks where entire families lived in a single room furnished only with cots, blankets, and a bare light bulb. Toilets and dining and bathing facilities were communal; privacy was almost nonexistent. Besides their freedom, the Japanese-Americans lost property valued at $500 million, along with their positions in the truck-garden, floral, and fishing industries. Indeed, their economic competitors were among the most vocal proponents of their relocation.

The Supreme Court upheld the government's policy of internment. In wartime, the Court said in the *Hirabayashi* ruling (1943), "residents having ethnic affiliations with an invading enemy may be a greater source of danger than those of different ancestry." And in the *Korematsu* case (1944), the Court, with three justices dissenting, approved the removal of the Nisei from the West Coast. One dissenter, Justice Frank Murphy, denounced the decision as the "legalization of racism," and Justice Robert Jackson warned that the precedent established by the cases "lies about like a loaded weapon ready for the hand of any authority that can bring forward a plausible claim of an urgent need." But the most damning appraisal of all came from Circuit Court Judge William Denman, who in an earlier ruling wrote that "the identity of this doctrine with that of the Hitler generals . . . justifying the gas chambers of Dachau is unmistakable."

In 1983, forty-one years after he had been placed in a government camp, Fred Korematsu had the satisfaction of hearing a federal judge rule that he—and by implication all the detainees—had been the victim of "unsubstantiated facts, distortions and misrepresentations of at least one military commander whose views were affected by racism." In 1982 the government's special Commission on Wartime Relocation and Internment of Civilians had recommended compensating the victims of this policy. Because of "race prejudice, war hysteria and a failure of political leadership," the commission concluded, the U.S. government had committed "a grave injustice" to more than 110,000 people.

JOBS AND RACISM ON THE HOME FRONT

F or other nonwhite groups in America, the Second World War would prove to be a mixed blessing, providing both the benefits of employment and the insults of racism. For many black Americans, the war was a watershed, the point at which they determined to make a stand against racial discrimination. Several factors highlighted Afro-American involvement in the war: the presence of nearly 1 million black men and women in the armed services; the mass migration of blacks, particularly from the rural South to the urban North and West, to work in war industries; and the participation of black people in all kinds of wartime activities—buying war bonds, serving as air-raid wardens, and volunteering for the Red Cross.

At peak enrollment the army had over 700,000 black troops. An additional 187,000 had enlisted in the navy, the Coast Guard, and the once all-white Marine Corps. In response to the March on Washington Movement of 1941 (see page 753), the Selective Service System and the War Department agreed to draft black Americans in proportion to their presence in the population: about 10 percent.

Though blacks in the service were still segregated, they made some real advances in the direction of racial equality during these years. For the first time

Black Troops

the War Department sanctioned the training of blacks as pilots. After instruction at Tuskegee Institute in Alabama, pilots saw heroic service in such all-black units as the Ninety-ninth Pursuit Squadron, winner of eighty Distinguished Flying Crosses. And some blacks reached positions of leadership. In 1940 Colonel Benjamin O. Davis became the first black brigadier general. Wherever black people were offered opportunities to distinguish themselves, they proved they were just as capable as whites. The performance of black marines in the Pacific theater was such that the Corps Commandant proclaimed: "Negro Marines are no longer on trial. They are Marines, period."

Set against these accomplishments, however, were serious failures in race relations. Race riots instigated by whites occurred on military bases, and white civilians assaulted black soldiers and sailors throughout the South. In North Carolina a white bus driver murdered a black soldier in full view of the passengers, but was found not guilty. When the War Department issued an order in mid-1944 forbidding racial segregation in military recreation and transportation, the *Montgomery Advertiser* replied, "Army orders, even armies, even bayonets, cannot force impossible and unnatural social relations upon us."

Of course, experiences such as these caused black soldiers and sailors to wonder what, in fact, they were fighting for. They recalled the remark of the governor of Tennessee, when blacks urged him to appoint Afro-Americans to local draft boards: "This is a white man's country. . . . The Negro had nothing to do with the settling of America." They noted that the Red Cross separated blood taken from whites and blacks, as if there were some difference. And many considered black participation in the First World War a mistake, for it had resulted not in social advances but in race riots and lynchings. Some even argued that the Second World War was a white man's war. But most telling was the charge that American racism was little different from German racism.

At the same time, there were positive reasons for blacks to participate in the war effort. Perhaps this was an opportunity, as the NAACP believed, "to persuade, embarrass, compel and shame our government and our nation . . . into a more enlightened attitude toward a tenth of its people." Proclaiming that in the Second World War they were waging a "Double V" campaign (for victory at home and abroad), blacks were more militant than before, and readier than ever to protest. Membership in civil rights organizations soared. The NAACP, whose membership had stood at 50,000 in 1940, had 450,000 members by 1946. And in 1942 civil rights activists founded the Congress of Racial Equality (CORE).

Because of the war, blacks found new opportunities in industry. Roosevelt's Executive Order 8802, issued in 1941, required employers in defense industries to make jobs available "without dis-

Black War Workers
crimination because of race, creed, color or national origin." To secure defense jobs, 1.2 million blacks migrated from the South to the industrial cities of the North and West in the 1940s. Almost three-fourths settled in the urban-industrial states of California, Illinois, Michigan, New York, Ohio, and Pennsylvania. More than half a million became active members of CIO unions such as the United Auto Workers, the United Steel Workers, and the United Rubber Workers. Finally, black voters in northern cities were beginning to constitute a vital swing vote not only in presidential contests, but in local and state elections.

But along with the benefits of urban life came liabilities. The migrants had to make enormous emotional and cultural adjustments, and white hostility and ignorance made their task particularly difficult. Southern whites who had migrated north brought with them the racial prejudices of the Deep South. Blacks competed with these whites for housing, jobs, and seats on buses; they rubbed elbows with them in city schools and parks and at the beaches. But just as significant was the ignorance of northern whites, more than half of whom believed in 1942 that blacks should be segregated in separate schools and neighborhoods; that black people were receiving all the

opportunities they deserved; and that if blacks suffered economically, politically, or socially, it was their own fault. These attitudes encouraged racial violence.

Many people, black and white, feared that the summer of 1943 would be like 1919, another Red Summer. And indeed, almost 250 racial conflicts exploded in forty-seven cities that

Race Riots of 1943
year. The worst of the 1943 race riots bloodied the streets of Detroit in June. At the end of thirty hours of rioting, twenty-five blacks and nine whites lay dead. White mobs, undeterred by police, had roamed the city attacking blacks. Blacks had hurled rocks at police and hauled white passengers off streetcars. This was outright racial warfare. In response to the riot a city councilman suggested that the city build a bigger ghetto and pen blacks up in it. Surveying the damage, an elderly black woman said, "There ain't no North any more. Everything now is South."

The federal government did practically nothing to prevent further racial violence. From Roosevelt on down, most federal officials put the war first, domestic reform second. Unquestionably many government leaders were racists themselves; Secretary of War Henry L. Stimson claimed that the riots were "the deliberate effort . . . on the part of certain radical leaders of the colored race to use the war for obtaining . . . racial equality and interracial marriages." But this time governmental neglect could not discourage Afro-Americans and their century-old civil rights movement. By war's end they were ready—politically, economically, and emotionally—to wage the struggle for voting rights and for equal access to public accommodations and institutions.

Not all racial violence was directed against blacks. In the 1943 Los Angeles zoot suit riot, the victims were Mexican-Americans. In the eyes of the rioters, most of whom were sailors and soldiers, people of Mexican origin were as despicable as those whose roots were African. In 1942, American farms and war industries needed workers, and the United States and Mexico had agreed to the *bracero* program, whereby Mexicans were admitted to the United States on short-term work contracts. Although the newcomers suffered racial discrimination and segregation, they seized the economic opportunities that had become available. In Los Angeles, 17,000 people of Mexican descent found shipyard jobs where before

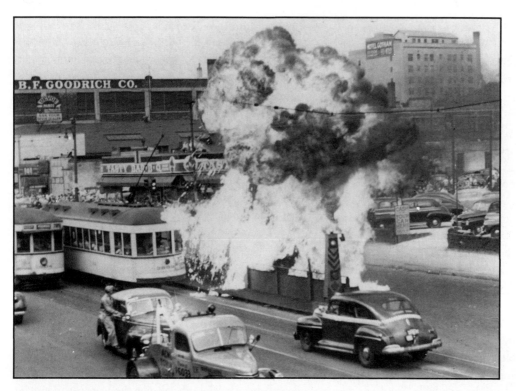

The bloodiest race riot of 1943 struck Detroit, where 34 people, 25 black and 9 white, were killed. At the peak of the rioting a white mob overturned a black person's car, showering trolley passengers with burning gasoline. *UPI/ Bettmann Newsphotos.*

the war there had been none available. Mexican-American teenagers in that city joined street gangs (*pachucos*), adopted ducktail haircuts, and donned "zoot suits": long coats (called "drapes") with wide, padded shoulders, pegged pants, wide-brimmed hats, and long watch chains. Whites' racial hatred boiled over in June, and for four days mobs invaded Mexican-American neighborhoods. According to one report: "Procedure was standard: grab a zooter. Take off his pants and frock coat and tear them up or burn them. Trim the '. . . ducktail' haircut that goes with the screwy costume." Not only did white policemen look the other way during these assaults, but the city of Los Angeles even passed an ordinance that made it a crime to wear a zoot suit within city limits.

Such experiences made life difficult for people of Mexican descent within the United States. Although the war opened up brief economic opportunities for Mexican-Americans, these years were not the watershed experience that they were for Afro-Americans.

A MILESTONE FOR WOMEN

If the Second World War was a turning point for Afro-Americans, it was equally or even more so for the women of America. During the Great Depression, when millions of men were unemployed, public opinion had been hostile to the hiring of women, but the war brought about a rapid increase in employment. Just when men were going off to war, industry had to recruit millions of new workers to supply the rapidly expanding need for military equipment. Afro-Americans, southern whites, teenage boys and girls, Mexicans and Mexican-Americans, and, above all, women filled these new jobs.

Well over 6 million women entered the labor force during the war years, increasing the number of working women 57 percent in less than five years. Two million

Over six million women entered the labor force during the war, many of them taking skilled jobs that had once been reserved for men. These women on the assembly line at a Douglas Aircraft plant are making bombardier noses for bombers.   National Archives.

took clerical jobs; another 2.5 million worked in manufacturing. The significance of the trend lay not only in the numbers, but in the kinds of women who were entering the work force. Seventy-five percent of the new women workers were married, and 3.7 million were not only married but mothers. Before the war the average woman wage earner had been young, single, and largely self-supporting; by 1945 more working women were married than single, and more were over thirty-five than under.

But statistics, no matter how impressive, tell only part of the story. There was a change in attitude toward heavy labor for women. Up to the early months of the war employers had insisted **Women in War** that women were not suited for in- **Production** dustrial jobs. If women were allowed to work in factories they would begin to wear overalls instead of dresses; their muscles would bulge; they might even drink whiskey and swear like men. As labor shortages began to threaten the war

effort, employers did an about-face. "Almost overnight," said Mary Anderson, head of the Women's Bureau of the Department of Labor, "women were reclassified by industrialists from a marginal to a basic labor supply for munitions making." Women became riveters, lumberjacks ("lumberjills"), welders, crane operators, keel benders, tool makers, shell loaders, cowgirls, blast-furnace cleaners, locomotive greasers, police officers, taxi drivers, and football coaches.

The new employment opportunities increased women's geographic and occupational mobility. Especially noteworthy were the gains made by black women; over 400,000 quit work as domestic servants to enjoy the better working conditions, higher pay, and union benefits of industrial employment. Hundreds of thousands of others, black and white, abandoned menial jobs in dime stores, restaurants, laundries, and hospitals for higher-status, higher-paying jobs. To take these jobs, women uprooted themselves. Over 7 million women moved from their original counties of residence to new locations during the war. Many sought jobs in the rapidly expanding aircraft industry, which increased its employment of women from 4,000 in December 1941 to 310,000 two years later.

Public opinion quickly changed from hostility to support of women's war work. Posters and billboards urging women to "Do the Job HE Left Behind" soon began to appear. Newspapers and magazines, radio and movies proclaimed Rosie the Riveter a war hero. But very few people asserted that women's war work should bring about a permanent shift in sex roles. This was merely a response to a national emergency. Once the victory was won, women should go back to nurturing their husbands and children, leaving their jobs to returning GIs. From "a humanitarian point of view," stated the president of the National Association of Manufacturers, "too many women should not stay in the labor force. The home is the basic American institution." Wartime surveys showed, however, that many of the women wanted to remain in their jobs. Eighty percent of New York's women workers felt that way, as did 75 percent of Detroit's female laborers. "War jobs have uncovered unsuspected abilities in American women," explained one woman. "Why lose all these abilities because of a belief that 'a woman's place is in the home.' For some it is," she added, "for others not."

Though women increased their wages when they acquired better jobs, they still received lower pay than men, even for the same work. In 1945 women in manufacturing earned only 65 percent of what men were paid. An important reason for this inequality was the sex-segregated labor market. **"Women's Work"** Although the wartime emergency caused some traditionally male jobs to be reclassified for women, most jobs were defined as either "women's work" or "men's work." Even in factories, most women worked in all-female shops. And working women, particularly working mothers, suffered in other ways as well. Perhaps the most persistent problem was the near-absence of supportive services such as childcare centers and communal kitchens. Some of the most serious wartime social problems were a direct result of the lack of such services. During the war there were increases in juvenile delinquency, venereal disease, teenage pregnancy, and the incidence of "eight-hour orphans,"

Latchkey Children or "latchkey children," left alone while their mothers worked eight-hour shifts in war plants. In 1940 Congress passed the Lanham Act to provide federal aid to communities that had to absorb large war-related populations. Benefits included funds for daycare centers, hospitals, sewer systems, police and fire-fighting facilities, and recreation centers. But provision was made for the care of only 107,000 children. Many of the remaining children roamed the streets or were locked in cars or sent to all-day or even all-night movies. In an area of concentrated war industry in Los Angeles, one social worker counted forty-five infants locked in cars in a single lot.

Crime was another problem: juvenile arrests jumped 20 percent nationwide in 1943. The increase was greater for girls than for boys; in San Diego, arrests increased 55 percent for boys and 355 percent for girls. Many girls became prostitutes: in 1943, arrests for that crime climbed 68 percent. Among boys the most common crime was theft, but vandalism and violence were also problems.

Perhaps because of such statistics, the massive contributions children made to the war effort were often overlooked. Children contributed their own nickels and dimes to buy war stamps and bonds, and they pulled their wagons from house to house collecting old newspapers and tin cans. The Boy Scouts collected 109 million pounds of rubber and 370 million pounds of scrap metal. Even more significant was that thousands of young people went to work during the war. In 1940, for example, 900,000 boys and girls between the ages of fourteen and eighteen were employed. By spring 1944 their number had climbed to 3 million—one-third of their age group. Indeed, some observers felt that the most pressing social problem afflicting teenagers was not juvenile delinquency but failure to finish school. High school enrollments hit new lows during the war, prompting a back-to-school drive in 1944.

At the same time that millions of women and youths were entering the work force, hundreds of thousands of women were getting married. From 1939 to 1942 the marriage rate rose from **Increase in Marriage, Divorce, and Birth Rates** 73 marriages per 1,000 unmarried women to 93 per 1,000. Some couples scrambled to get married so they could spend time together before

In June 1942 Boy Scouts in Stevens Point, Wisconsin, led a parade of trucks carrying more than 80 tons of old automobile and bicycle tires collected in scrap drives. Throughout the nation children aided the war effort by selling bonds and gathering materials for recycling.   Wide World Photos.

the man was sent overseas. Some doubtless married and had children to qualify for military deferments. But the rush to get married was also fueled by prosperity. A justice of the peace in Yuma, Arizona, explained that the marriage rate "began going up as soon as those boys were given employment in those plants at San Diego and Los Angeles and were taken off WPA." He was not exaggerating; 90 percent of the marriage licenses in Yuma went to aircraft workers.

These hasty marriages often did not survive long military separations. As a result, divorces soared too, from 25,000 in 1939 to 359,000 in 1943 and 485,000 in 1945. And as might be expected, the birthrate also climbed: total births rose from over 2.4 million in 1939 to 3.1 million in 1943. Many of these births were "good-bye babies," conceived as a hedge against

the future before the father left for the war, a guarantee that the family would be perpetuated should he die in battle overseas.

Ironically, women's efforts to hold their families together during the war posed problems for returning fathers. Women war workers had brought home the wages; they had taken over the budgeting of expenses and the writing of checks. In countless ways they had proved they could hold the reins in their husbands' absence. When the husbands began returning home in the waning months of the war, many found that the pattern of life for their wives and children seemed to be complete without them. For some men, it was not just a case of appearances; they knew their families could survive and even prosper without them.

And what of the women who wanted to remain in the labor market? Many were forced by employers, or by their husbands, to quit. Others chose to leave their jobs for a year or two, but then returned to work. And throughout the rest of the 1940s and 1950s, millions more who had never worked took jobs.

THE DECLINE OF LIBERALISM AND THE ELECTION OF 1944

Another wartime trend was the decline of political liberalism. Even before Pearl Harbor, liberals had suffered major defeats. Some Democrats hoped to revive the reform movement during the war, but Republicans and conservative Democrats were on guard against such a move. New Dealers, warned Republican Senator Robert Taft early in 1942, "are determined to make the country over under the cover of war if they can." Taft and his fellow conservatives successfully blocked reform.

Aided by a small turnout in November 1942, the Republicans scored impressive gains, winning forty-four new seats in the House and nine in the Senate and defeating Democratic governors in New York, California, and Michigan. Part of the Democrats' problem was that, unlike the 1930s, the war years were a time of full employment. Once people had acquired jobs and gained some economic security, they began to be more critical of New Deal policies. The New Deal coalition had always had the potential for fragmentation. Southern white farmers had little in common with northern blacks or white factory workers. And in northern cities, blacks and whites who had voted for Roosevelt in 1940 were competing for jobs and housing and would soon collide in race riots.

With Republican victories in 1942, the alliance of conservative southern Democrats and Republicans became a formidable threat to New Deal programs. In 1942 and 1943 the conservative coalition actually abolished several New Deal relief and social-welfare agencies, among them the Civilian Conservation Corps and the Work Projects Administration.

But though liberalism was enfeebled, it was far from dead. The liberal agenda began with a pledge to secure full employment. Roosevelt emphasized the concept in his Economic Bill of Rights, delivered as part of his 1944 State of the Union address. Every American had a right, the president declared, to a decent job; sufficient food, shelter, and clothing; and financial security in unemployment, illness, and old age. If to accomplish those goals the government had to operate at a deficit, Roosevelt was willing to do so. But first he had to be re-elected.

In 1944 Franklin D. Roosevelt looked like an exhausted old man. His eyes were tired and puffy; he was almost bald; and the loose flesh that hung on his large frame made him appear emaciated. Though the president's personal physician pronounced "nothing organically wrong with him at all—he's perfectly O.K.," rumors of his ill health persisted. Because Roosevelt expected to survive his fourth term, he believed he could select a running mate who was inexperienced in international affairs. His choice was Senator Harry S Truman of Missouri. During the war Truman had gained favorable publicity for chairing a senatorial watchdog committee on favoritism and waste in the awarding of defense contracts. A representative of both a border state and a big-city machine (the Pendergast machine in Kansas City), Truman was satisfactory both to southerners and to the bosses. As an ardent and loyal New Dealer, the senator was also approved by liberals. But there was little evidence that he possessed the qualities of national and world leadership that he would need as president. And Roosevelt did not take Truman into his confidence; he even failed to inform his running mate about the atomic bomb project.

The Republicans were optimistic about their prospects for regaining the presidency. New York Governor Thomas E. Dewey, who won the nomination on the first ballot, was a moderate who did not advocate repeal of the essentials of the New Deal—social security, unemployment relief, collective bargaining, and price supports for farmers. And he was cautious in his criticism of Roosevelt's foreign policy. But Dewey had one great liability, his public image. Short of stature and dull of personality, Dewey looked, as Alice Longworth, Theodore Roosevelt's daughter, described him, "like the bridegroom on a wedding cake."

Although Roosevelt won a fourth term, the margin

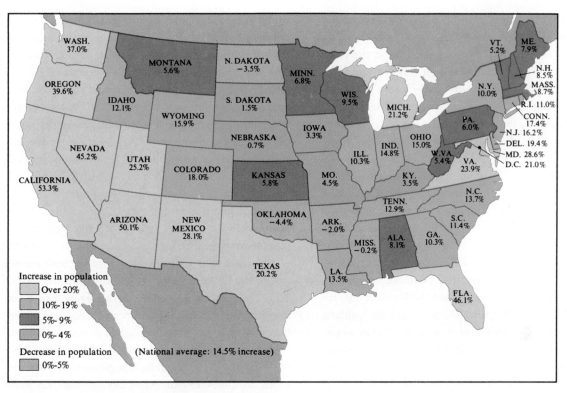

A Nation on the Move, 1940–1950 *Source: U.S. Bureau of the Census,* Portfolio of United States Census Maps, 1950 *(Washington: U.S. Government Printing Office, 1953), p. 4.*

of victory in the popular vote was his narrowest ever; it was the closest presidential election since 1916. Nevertheless, he won 53.4 percent of the popular vote and 432 electoral votes to Dewey's 99. It was the urban vote that returned Roosevelt to the White House. Wartime population shifts had much to do with the cities' new political clout. New workers—notably southern whites who had been lifelong Democrats and southern blacks who had never before voted—had migrated to the urban industrial centers (see map). Added to the urban vote was a less obvious factor. Many voters seemed to be exhibiting what has been called "depression psychosis." Fearful that hard times would return once war contracts were terminated, they remembered New Deal relief programs and voted for Roosevelt. Finally, as Senator Taft conceded, the Republicans had "underestimated the difficulty of changing a President at the very height of a victorious war." With victory within grasp, many Americans wanted Roosevelt's experienced hand to guide the nation, and the world, to a lasting peace.

WARTIME DIPLOMACY

The lessons of the post–First World War period weighed heavily on the minds of American diplomats throughout the war. Americans vowed to make a peace that would ensure a postwar world free from depression, totalitarianism, and war. The Atlantic Charter, so reminiscent of Woodrow Wilson's vision of an open world, was their general guide, tempered and compromised by the interests of the great powers. Thus American goals included the Open Door and lower tariffs; self-determination for liberated peoples; avoidance of the debts-reparations tangle that had plagued Europe after the First World War; expansion of the United States sphere of influence; and management of world affairs by what Roosevelt once called the Four Policemen: Russia, China, Great Britain, and the United States.

Although the major Allies concentrated on defeating the aggressors, their suspicions of one another undermined cooperation. More dogged them than the timing of the second front and the **Allied Disagreement over Eastern Europe** Italian surrender. Eastern European questions proved the most difficult. The Russians sought to fix their boundaries where they had stood before Hitler attacked in 1941. In the case of Poland, this meant that the part of the country the Soviets had invaded and captured in 1939 would become Russian territory. The British and Americans hesitated, preferring to deal with Eastern Europe at the end of the war. But the sustained drive of the Russian armies through the region on the heels of the retreating Germans persuaded Churchill to act. In an October 1944 agreement, he and Stalin struck a bargain: Russia would gain Rumania and Bulgaria as a sphere of influence; Britain would have the upper hand in Greece; and the two would share authority in Yugoslavia and Hungary. The two leaders did not, however, agree on Poland.

Poland was a special case. In 1943 Moscow had broken off diplomatic relations with the conservative Polish government-in-exile in London. The Poles had angered Moscow when they asked the International Red Cross to investigate German charges that the Russians had massacred thousands of Polish army officers in the Katyn Forest in 1940. Then an uprising in Warsaw in July 1944 complicated matters still further. Taking advantage of the nearness of Soviet troops, the Warsaw underground rose against the occupying Germans. To the dismay of the world community, Soviet armies stood aside as German troops slaughtered 166,000 people and devastated the city. Finally, in late 1944 and early 1945 the Soviets spawned a pro-Communist government in Lublin. Thus near the end of the war Poland had two competing governments, one in London, recognized by America and Britain, and another in Lublin.

Early in the war the Allies had begun talking about a new international organization. At Teheran in 1943 Roosevelt called for an institution **Creation of the United Nations Organization** controlled by the Four Policemen. The next year, in a Washington, D.C., mansion called Dumbarton Oaks, American, British, Russian, and Chinese representatives conferred on the details.

Since American participation had been endorsed in public opinion polls and congressional resolutions, United States diplomats proceeded with some assurance that their handiwork would not meet the legislative fate of Wilson's League of Nations. The conferees approved a preliminary charter for a United Nations Organization, providing for a supreme Security Council dominated by the great powers and a weak General Assembly (Roosevelt called it "an investigatory body only"). The Security Council would have five permanent members, each with veto power.

Disagreement surfaced when the United States pushed China forward as a great power entitled to permanent membership on the council: Churchill complained that China was a captive vote on the side of the United States. To mollify him, the United States reluctantly agreed to elevate France to a permanent seat. Russia accepted both France and China, believing that its veto power would protect its national interest against unfriendly decisions. But noting that the United States would have a group of sympathetic votes in the General Assembly among the Latin American states, and that Britain could muster support from members of its Commonwealth, the Soviets asked for a balancing of power. They wanted separate membership in the General Assembly for the sixteen Soviet republics. This issue was not resolved at Dumbarton Oaks, but the meeting proved a success nevertheless. The conferees had achieved 90 percent of their goals, Roosevelt pointed out. "Well, that is what we used to call in the old days a darn good batting average."

The diplomatic batting average on another problem, Nazi treatment of the Jews, was considerably lower. Even before the war Nazi officials had targeted Jews throughout Europe for extermination. By war's end, about 6 million Jews had been forced into concentration camps and systematically killed by firing squads, unspeakable tortures, and gas chambers. Many others who survived the Holocaust could never forget the terror. During the depression the United States and other nations had refused to relax their immigration restrictions to save Jews fleeing persecution. The **Jewish Refugees from the Holocaust** American Federation of Labor and Senator William Borah, among others, argued that new immigrants would compete with American workers for scarce jobs, and public opinion polls supported their position. The fear of economic competition was, of course, fed by anti-Semitism. Bureaucrats applied the rules so strictly—requiring legal documents fleeing Jews could not possibly provide—that otherwise qualified refugees were kept out of the country. From 1933 to 1945 less than 40 percent of the German-Austrian quota was filled.

Even the tragic voyage of the *St. Louis* did not change government policy. The vessel left Hamburg in mid-1939 with 930 desperate Jewish refugees who lacked proper immigration documents. Denied entry to Havana, the *St. Louis* headed for Miami, where Coast Guard cutters prevented it from docking. Aroused American citizens appealed to Washington, but the ship was forced to return to Europe. Some of those refugees took shelter in countries that were later overrun by Hitler's legions. "The cruise of the *St. Louis*," wrote the *New York Times*, "cries to high heaven of man's inhumanity to man."

As news of the Nazi atrocities filled government files during the war years, American officials futilely attempted to persuade Latin American countries to accept refugees. They also approached the British, who proved unhelpful as well: they would not open Palestine. Some American leaders were themselves lax in their attention to the problem. The State Department officer in charge was Breckinridge Long, a Democratic politician who actually hindered private citizens' efforts to save victims.

When evidence mounted that Hitler intended to exterminate the Jews, British and American representatives met in Bermuda (1943) but came up with no plans. Secretary Hull made a discouraging report to the president, emphasizing "the unknown cost of moving an undetermined number of persons from an undisclosed place to an unknown destination." Appalled, Secretary of the Treasury Henry Morgenthau, Jr., charged that the State Department's foot-dragging made the United States an accessory to murder. "It takes months and months to grant the visa and then it usually applies to a corpse," he wrote bitterly. Early in 1944, stirred by Morgenthau's well-documented plea, Roosevelt created the War Refugee Board, which set up refugee camps in Europe and saved thousands from death.

But American officials waited too long to act, and they missed a chance to destroy the gas chambers and ovens at the extermination camp at Auschwitz in occupied Poland. They had aerial photographs and diagrams of the camp, but they argued that bombing it would detract from the war effort or prompt the Germans to step up the anti-Jewish terror. In 1944 American planes bombed synthetic oil and rubber plants in the industrial sector of Auschwitz, only five miles from the gas chambers and crematoria. "How could it be," historian David S. Wyman has asked, "that Government officials knew that a place existed where 2,000 helpless human beings could be killed in less than an hour, knew that this occurred over and over again, and yet did not feel driven to search for some way to wipe such a scourge from the earth?"

THE YALTA CONFERENCE AND A FLAWED PEACE

With the war in Europe nearing an end, and a host of political questions—including what to do with Germany—yet to be settled, President Roosevelt urged another summit meeting. The three Allied leaders met at Yalta, on the Russian Crimea, in early February 1945. Controversy has surrounded the conference ever since. Roosevelt was obviously ill. "His appearance could change in a couple of hours from looking like a ghost to looking okay," remarked the new Secretary of State Edward Stettinius, Jr. The sixty-two-year-old president suffered from hypertension, heart disease, and hardening of the arteries. His doctors prescribed rest, a reduction in cigarette smoking, and medication, but the president maintained a busy schedule. Critics of the Yalta agreements later charged that Roosevelt was too weak to resist the demands of a guileful Stalin, that he struck a poor bargain. The evidence suggests, however, that Roosevelt was mentally alert and that he managed to sustain his strength during negotiations.

The Yalta meeting has also been criticized because some of its agreements were secret (suggesting the Allies had something to hide) and because it decided the fate of weak nations like Poland and China without their consent. The truth is that some agreements were secret because they contained military information

The three Allied leaders—Winston Churchill, Franklin D. Roosevelt, and Josef Stalin—met at Yalta in February 1945. Having been president for twelve years, Roosevelt showed signs of age and fatigue.   Franklin D. Roosevelt Library.

that had to be kept from the still undefeated Japanese and Germans. But the criticism that the Allies paid scant attention to small nations was well deserved. It exposed a general pattern of wartime diplomacy, which assumed that the most powerful of the Allies would dominate international relations after the war.

Each of the Allies entered into the conference with definite goals. Britain sought a place for France in occupied Germany; a curb on Soviet influence in Poland; and protection for the vulnerable British Empire. Russia wanted reparations from Germany, to assist in the massive task of rebuilding at home; possessions in Asia; continued influence in Poland; and a permanently weakened Germany, so that Russia would never again suffer a German attack. The United States lobbied for the United Nations Organization, where it believed it

Allied Goals at Yalta

could exercise influence; for a Soviet declaration of war against Japan; for recognition of China as a major power; and for compromise between rival factions in Poland.

Military positions at the time of the conference helped to shape the final agreements. Soviet troops had occupied much of Eastern Europe, including Poland, while the Western Allies were emerging from the Battle of the Bulge. In Asia the Japanese were still resisting the American advance. Millions of Japanese troops in China, Manchuria, Korea, and the home islands seemed ready to die to the last man for the empire. As near as victory was, Britain and the United States still needed the Soviets to win the war.

The unsettled issue of Poland preoccupied the conferees. Stalin repeatedly pointed out that twice in the century German armies had marched through Poland into Russian territory, killing millions. He insisted on a government friendly to Moscow—the Lublin regime—in order to prevent another German onslaught. And he demanded boundaries that would give Poland part of Germany in the west and Russia part of Poland in the east. Churchill boiled over in protest; he wanted the London regime to return to Poland. A compromise was reached under Roosevelt's leadership: a boundary favorable to Russia in the east; postponement of the western boundary issue; and the creation of a "more broadly based" coalition government that would include members of the London government-in-exile. Free elections would be held sometime in the future. The agreement was vague, but given Soviet occupation of Poland, Roosevelt considered it "the best I can do."

As for Germany, the Big Three agreed that it would be divided into four zones, the fourth to go to France. On the question of reparations, Russia wanted a precise figure, but Churchill and Roosevelt said they would first have to determine Germany's ability to pay. Without the British, the Americans and Russians agreed that an Allied committee would consider the sum of $20 billion as a basis for discussion in the future, with half the amount to go to the Soviet Union.

Other issues found trade-offs. Stalin promised to declare war on Japan two or three months after Hitler's defeat. Since the atomic bomb was still on the drawing boards, American military leaders applauded the commitment. The Soviet premier also consented to sign a treaty of friendship and alliance with Jiang Jieshi (Chiang Kai-shek), America's ally in China, rather than with the Communist Mao Zedong. In return the United States agreed to Russia's taking the southern part of Sakhalin Island and Lüshun (Port Arthur). To the Russians these concessions amounted to a recovery of holdings lost after the Russo-Japanese War in 1905. Regarding the new world organization, Roosevelt and Churchill granted the Soviets three votes in the General Assembly. (Fifty nations officially launched the United Nations Organization in May.) Finally, the conferees accepted the Declaration of Liberated Europe, pledging to establish order and to rebuild economies by democratic methods.

Yalta marked the high point of the Grand Alliance; each of the Allies came away with something, in the tradition of diplomatic give-and-take. But as the great powers jockeyed for influence at the close of the war, neither the spirit nor the letter of Yalta held firm.

Potsdam Conference

The crumbling of the alliance became evident at the Potsdam Conference, which took place between July 17 and August 2, 1945. Roosevelt had died in April, and Harry S Truman had replaced him. Truman was a novice at international diplomacy and less patient with the Russians. Stalin "seems to like it when I hit him with a hammer," he bragged in a letter to his beloved wife Bess. "We had a tough meeting," he also wrote. "I reared up on my hind legs and told 'em where to get off and they got off." Truman seemed especially emboldened after he learned during the conference that the atomic test in New Mexico was successful. "Now I know what happened to Truman," said Churchill. "When he got to the meeting after having read this report he was a changed man. He told the Russians just where they got off and generally bossed the whole meeting."

Despite the "brawl" at Potsdam, as Truman called it, the Big Three did agree on general policies toward Germany: complete disarmament; elimination of industry used for military production; and dissolution of Nazi institutions and laws. In a compromise over reparations, they decided that each occupying nation should take reparations from its own zone; but they could not agree on a total figure. To resolve other issues, such as peace treaties with Italy, Finland, and Hungary, the Big Three created the Council of Foreign Ministers.

Potsdam left much undone. As the war drew to a close, there was little that bound the Allies together. Roosevelt's cooperative style was gone; the spirit of Yalta was evaporating; the common enemy, Hitler, was defeated. And America, with the awesome atomic bomb in the offing to force defeat upon Japan, no longer needed, or even wanted, Russia in the Pacific war. Moreover, the victors were seeking to preserve and enlarge their spheres of influence. The British claimed authority in Greece and parts of the Middle East; the Russians already dominated much of Eastern Europe; and Americans continued their hegemony in Latin America. The United States also seized several Pacific islands as strategic outposts and laid

IMPORTANT EVENTS

1941   Japan attacks Pearl Harbor; U.S. enters Second World War

1942   National War Labor Board established
War Production Board established
Internment of 110,000 Japanese-Americans in "relocation camps"
War Manpower Commission established
Bataan Death March
Battles of Coral Sea and Midway
Office of War Information established
Manhattan Project established
Allied invasion of North Africa
Republican gains in Congress
Synthetic-rubber program begins

1943   Russian victory at Stalingrad
Strikes by soft-coal and anthracite miners
Office of War Mobilization established
War Labor Disputes (Smith-Connally) Act
Race riots in Detroit, Harlem, and 45 other cities

Allied invasion of Italy
Teheran Conference

1944   Roosevelt requests Economic Bill of Rights
War Refugee Board established
Supreme Court upholds Japanese-American internment
GI Bill of Rights
Normandy landings (D-Day)
Dumbarton Oaks Conference
Roosevelt re-elected
U.S. retakes Philippines

1945   Yalta Conference
Battles of Iwo Jima and Okinawa
Roosevelt dies; Truman assumes presidency
United Nations founded
Germany surrenders
Potsdam Conference
First atomic bomb exploded in test at Alamogordo, New Mexico
Atomic bombs devastate Hiroshima and Nagasaki
Japan surrenders

---

plans to dominate a defeated Japan. Let the Americans have their Pacific bases, responded Churchill, "but 'Hands off the British Empire' is our maxim." Furthermore, American interests increased their stake in Middle Eastern oil during the war. By 1944 American petroleum companies controlled 42 percent of the proved oil reserves of the Middle East—a nineteenfold increase since 1936. Both the British and Russians complained about this new evidence of American expansionism.

Hitler once said, "We may be destroyed, but if we are, we shall drag a world with us—a world in flames." Indeed, *rubble* became the word most commonly invoked to describe the global landscape at the end of the war. Hamburg, Stuttgart, and Dresden had been laid waste; three-quarters of Berlin was in ruins. In England, Coventry and parts of London were bombed out. Across the continent transportation systems had been disrupted and water supplies contaminated. Everywhere ghostlike people wandered about searching desperately for food, and mourning those who would never come home. Russia had lost 20 million people; Poland 5.8 million; Germany 4.5 million. In all, about 35 million Europeans died as a result of the war. In Asia untold millions of Chinese and 2 million Japanese died.

Only one major combatant escaped these grisly statistics: the United States. Its cities were not burned and its fields were not trampled. American deaths from the war—about 400,000—were **Postwar Supremacy of the United States** few compared with the losses of other nations. In fact, Americans came out of the Second World War more powerful than they had gone in. They alone had the atomic bomb. The American air force and navy were the largest anywhere. And though the United States demobilized the major part of its regular army after the war, it still had 2 million men in arms in 1946, 1.6 million in 1949. What is more, only the United States had the capital and economic resources to spur international recovery. America was, gloated Truman, a "giant." In the coming struggle to fashion a new world out of the ashes of the old, soon called the Cold War (see Chapter 29), the United States held a commanding position.

Events at home and abroad during the Second World War had transformed the United States. For many Americans in 1945, life was fundamentally different from what it had been before Pearl Harbor. The Academy Award–winning film for 1946 was *The Best Years of Our Lives,* the painful story of the postwar readjustments of three veterans and their families and friends. Not only veterans' lives had been changed by the experiences of war; with the advent of the Cold War, millions of younger men would be inducted into the armed forces over the next thirty years. War and the expectation of war would become part of American life.

Though the gains made during the war by blacks and women were overdue, other changes were less welcome. The war had stimulated the trend toward bigness in business, labor, and government. In the next few years, government agencies that had been conceived as temporary would become permanent and would grow in size and influence. The results are well known—a Department of Defense (consolidating the War and Navy Departments), the Central Intelligence Agency (succeeding the Office of Strategic Services), the Atomic Energy Commission. The seeds of the military-industrial complex were sown in these years. For better or worse—and clearly there were elements of both—the Second World War was a turning point in the nation's history.

SUGGESTIONS FOR FURTHER READING

Fighting the War

Stephen A. Ambrose, *Eisenhower,* vol. 1 (1983); Stephen A. Ambrose, *The Supreme Commander* (1970); Hanson Baldwin, *Battles Lost and Won* (1966); A. Russell Buchanan, *The United States in World War II,* 2 vols. (1964); Peter Calvocoressi and Guy Wint, *Total War* (1972); R. Ernest Dupuy, *World War II* (1969); Dwight D. Eisenhower, *Crusade in Europe* (1948); Kent R. Greenfield, *American Strategy in World War II* (1963); B. H. Liddell Hart, *History of the Second World War* (1970); Max Hastings, *OVERLORD: D-Day and the Battle of Normandy* (1984); Clayton D. James, *The Years of MacArthur, 1941–1945* (1975); David Kahn, *The Codebreakers* (1967); Richard M. Leighton and Robert W. Coakley, *Global Logistics and Strategy, 1940–1945,* 2 vols. (1955–1968); Douglas MacArthur, *Reminiscences* (1964); Samuel Eliot Morison, *The Two-Ocean War* (1963); Samuel Eliot Morison, *Strategy and Compromise* (1958); Forrest C. Pogue, *George C. Marshall,* 3 vols. (1963–1973); Bradley F. Smith, *The Shadow Warriors: O.S.S. and the Origins of the C.I.A.* (1983); R. Harris Smith, *OSS* (1972); Ronald H. Spector, *Fighting Against the Sun: The American War with Japan* (1984); Russell F. Weigley, *The American Way of War* (1973); Gordon Wright, *The Ordeal of Total War, 1939–1945* (1968).

Diplomatic Issues

Robert Beitzell, *The Uneasy Alliance* (1972); James MacGregor Burns, *Roosevelt: The Soldier of Freedom* (1970); Thomas Campbell, *Masquerade Peace: America's UN Policy, 1944–1945* (1973); Winston S. Churchill, *The Second World War,* 6 vols. (1948–1953); Diane Clemens, *Yalta* (1970); Robert Dallek, *Franklin D. Roosevelt and American Foreign Policy, 1932–1945* (1979); Robert A. Divine, *Roosevelt and World War II* (1969); Robert A. Divine, *Second Chance: The Triumph of Internationalism in America During World War II* (1967); Henry L. Feingold, *Politics of Rescue* (1970); Herbert Feis, *Churchill, Roosevelt, and Stalin* (1957); George C. Herring, *Aid to Russia, 1941–1946* (1973); Akira Iriye, *Power and Culture: The Japanese-American War, 1941–1945* (1981); Gabriel Kolko, *The Politics of War* (1968); William R. Louis, *Imperialism at Bay: The United States and the Decolonization of the British Empire* (1978); William H. McNeill, *America, Britain, and Russia* (1953); Vojtech

Mastny, *Russia's Road to the Cold War* (1979); Arthur D. Morse, *While Six Million Died* (1968); Gaddis Smith, *Diplomacy During the Second World War, 1941–1945*, 2nd ed. (1985); Michael Stoff, *Oil, War, and American Security* (1980); Mark Stoler, *The Politics of the Second Front* (1977); Christopher Thorne, *Allies of a Kind* (1977); David S. Wyman, *The Abandonment of the Jews: America and the Holocaust, 1941–1945* (1984).

The Home Front

John Morton Blum, *V Was for Victory: Politics and American Culture During World War II* (1976); Alan Clive, *State of War: Michigan in World War II* (1979); Philip J. Funigiello, *The Challenge to Urban Liberalism: Federal-City Relations During World War II* (1978); Jack Goodman, ed., *While You Were Gone: A Report on Wartime Life in the United States* (1946); Mark Jonathan Harris et al., *The Homefront* (1984); John W. Jeffries, *Testing the Roosevelt Coalition: Connecticut Society and Politics in the Era of World War II* (1979); Richard R. Lingeman, *Don't You Know There's a War On? The American Home Front, 1941–1945* (1970); Francis E. Merrill, *Social Problems on the Home Front: A Study of War-time Influences* (1948); Geoffrey Perrett, *Days of Sadness, Years of Triumph: The American People 1939–1945* (1973); Richard Polenberg, *War and Society: The United States, 1941–1945* (1972); Studs Terkel, ed., *"The Good War": An Oral History of World War Two* (1984).

Mobilizing for War

John Morton Blum, ed., *From the Morgenthau Diaries: Years of War* (1967); Bureau of the Budget, *The United States at War* (1946); Bruce Catton, *The War Lords of Washington* (1948); George Q. Flynn, *The Mess in Washington: Manpower Mobilization in World War II* (1979); Eliot Janeway, *The Struggle for Survival* (1951); Paul A. C. Koistinen, *The Hammer and the Sword: Labor, the Military, and Industrial Mobilization, 1920–1945* (1979); Donald Nelson, *Arsenal of Democracy* (1946); Smaller War Plants Corporation, *Economic Concentration and World War II* (1946); William M. Tuttle, Jr., "The Birth of an Industry: The Synthetic Rubber 'Mess' in World War II," *Technology and Culture*, 22 (1981), 35–67; Gerald T. White, *Billions for Defense: Government Finance by the Defense Plant Corporation During World War II* (1980); Allen M. Winkler, *The Politics of Propaganda: The Office of War Information, 1942–1945* (1978).

Farmers and Workers, Soldiers and Sailors

John L. Blackman, Jr., *Presidential Seizure in Labor Disputes* (1967); Melvyn Dubofsky and Warren H. Van Tine, *John L. Lewis: A Biography* (1977); Nelson Lichtenstein, *Labor's War at Home: The CIO in World War II* (1983); Bill Mauldin, *Up Front* (1968 ed.); Davis R. B. Ross, *Preparing for Ulysses: Politics and Veterans During World War II* (1969); Joel Seidman, *American Labor from Defense to Reconversion* (1953); Samuel A. Stouffer et al., *The American Soldier*, 2 vols. (1949); Walter W. Wilcox, *The Farmer in the Second World War* (1947).

Japanese-American Internment

Commission on Wartime Relocation and Internment of Civilians, *Personal Justice Denied* (1982); Roger Daniels, *Concentration Camps U.S.A.* (1971); Morton Grodzins, *Americans Betrayed: Politics and the Japanese Evacuation* (1949); Bill Hosokawa, *Nisei: The Quiet Americans* (1969); Peter Irons, *Justice at War: The Story of the Japanese American Internment Cases* (1983); Jacobus tenBroek et al., *Prejudice, War and the Constitution: Causes and Consequences of the Evacuation of the Japanese Americans in World War II* (1954); Michi Weglyn, *Years of Infamy: The Untold Story of America's Concentration Camps* (1976).

Science and Education

James Phinney Baxter, *Scientists Against Time* (1946); Isaac Kandel, *The Impact of War upon American Education* (1948); Daniel J. Kevles, *The Physicists* (1977).

Politics

James C. Foster, *The Union Politic: The CIO Political Action Committee* (1975); Alonzo J. Hamby, "Sixty Million Jobs and the People's Revolution: The Liberals, the New Deal, and World War II," *The Historian*, 30 (1968), 578–598; Maurice Isserman, *Which Side Were You On? The American Communist Party During the Second World War* (1982); Donald R. McCoy, "Republican Opposition in Wartime, 1941–1945," *Mid-America*, 49 (1967), 174–189; Roland Young, *Congressional Politics in the Second World War* (1956).

Afro-Americans and Wartime Violence

A. Russell Buchanan, *Black Americans in World War II* (1977); Dominic J. Capeci, Jr., *Race Relations in Wartime Detroit* (1984); Dominic J. Capeci, Jr., *The Harlem Riot of 1943* (1977); Richard M. Dalfiume, *Desegregation of the U.S. Armed Forces: Fighting on Two Fronts, 1939–1953* (1969); Lee Finkle, *Forum for Protest: The Black Press During World War II* (1975); Phillip McGuire, ed., *Taps for a Jim Crow Army: Letters from Black Soldiers in World War II* (1982); Mauricio Mazon, *The Zoot-Suit Riots* (1984); Harvard Sitkoff, "Racial Militancy and Interracial Violence in the

Second World War," *Journal of American History*, 58 (1971), 661–681; Neil A. Wynn, *The Afro-American and the Second World War* (1976).

Women

Karen T. Anderson, "Last Hired, First Fired: Black Women Workers During World War II," *Journal of American History*, 69 (1982), 82–97; Karen T. Anderson, *Wartime Women: Sex Roles, Family Relations, and the Status of Women During World War II* (1981); M. Joyce Baker, *Images of Women in Film: The War Years, 1941–1945* (1981); William H. Chafe, *The American Woman: Her Changing Social, Economic, and Political Roles, 1920–1970* (1972); Sherna Berger Gluck, "Interlude or Change: Women and the World War II Work Experience," *International Journal of Oral History*, 3 (1982), 92–113; Chester W. Gregory, *Women in Defense Work During World War II: An Analysis of the Labor Problem and Women's Rights* (1974); Susan M. Hartmann, *The Home Front and Beyond: American Women in the 1940s* (1982);

Sally Van Wagenen Keil, *Those Wonderful Women in Their Flying Machines: The Unknown Heroes of World War II* (1979); Ruth Milkman, "Redefining 'Women's Work': The Sexual Division of Labor in the Auto Industry During World War II," *Feminist Studies*, 8 (1982), 337–372; Leila J. Rupp, *Mobilizing Women for War: German and American Propaganda, 1939–1945* (1978).

The Atomic Bomb

Gar Alperovitz, *Atomic Diplomacy* (1965); Barton J. Bernstein, ed., *The Atomic Bomb* (1976); Robert J. C. Butow, *Japan's Decision to Surrender* (1954); Committee for the Compilation of Materials on Damage Caused by the Atomic Bombs in Hiroshima and Nagasaki, *Hiroshima and Nagasaki* (1981); Herbert Feis, *The Atomic Bomb and the End of World War II* (1966); Gregg Herken, *The Winning Weapon* (1981); Richard G. Hewlett and Oscar E. Anderson, *The New World* (1962); Chalmers M. Roberts, *The Nuclear Years* (1970); Martin J. Sherwin, *A World Destroyed* (1975).

The Cold War
and American Politics
1945–1953

Chapter 29

*P*resident Harry S Truman was exhausted on March 13, 1947, as his official plane flew him from Washington to his Florida vacation spot in Key West. "This terrible decision I had to make," he wrote his daughter Margaret that day, "had been over my head for about six weeks." He had known since the Potsdam Conference of 1945 "that there is no difference in totalitarian or police states, call them what you will, Nazi, Fascist, Communist. . . . The attempt of Lenin, Trotsky, Stalin, et al., to fool the world and the American Crackpots Association . . . is just like Hitler's and Mussolini's so-called socialist states. Your Pop had to tell the world just that in polite language."

The day before, in a controversial speech to a joint session of Congress, the president had announced the Truman Doctrine. Without mentioning the Soviet Union by name, he equated its policies with the former "totalitarian regimes" of Germany and Japan. "I believe," he said, "that it must be the policy of the United States to support free peoples who are resisting attempted subjugation by armed minorities or by outside pressures." These words became the backbone of containment, a doctrine that in the coming years would not only lead the United States into armed conflict in Asia, the Middle East, and Latin America but also heighten fears at home that a Communist conspiracy had gained control of the federal government.

The central theme of Truman's presidency was anti-Communism at home and abroad. A week later, on March 21, Truman made another momentous decision. Through an executive order, he announced the Employee Loyalty Program for the executive branch of the government. Henceforth, all agency heads had to ensure that each employee under their jurisdictions was a loyal American. In doubtful cases, the boss had to appoint a loyalty board to hear the evidence and make recommendations. For the first time, government officials had the authority to pass judgment on a job applicant's personal beliefs and past associations. People already on the job who were accused of disloyalty were presumed to be guilty, not innocent. Although some critics argued that Truman's anti-Communist actions were bellicose and a threat to

civil liberties and that he shot from the hip, his decisiveness initially won him many followers across the country.

When Franklin D. Roosevelt died in office in April 1945, Truman had acceded to the presidency. Contrary to his later "Give 'em hell, Harry" image, Truman's initial response to this challenge was a deep feeling of inadequacy. "I'm not big enough for this job," he confided to a friend. Even an experienced, well-respected president would have faced an enormous task in guiding the nation's transition from war to peace. But the new president was little more than an obscure politician. "Who is Harry Truman?" Americans asked themselves when they heard the news of Roosevelt's death. As a senator from Missouri, Truman had been a New Deal liberal. He was intelligent, warm, hard-working, and honest, a loving husband and father. But he was also short-tempered, impulsive, headstrong, and quick to call people names ("son of a bitch" was one of his favorites). Neither his virtues nor his defects, however, were well known at the time. People knew Truman mainly from his wartime chairmanship of a special Senate committee on awarding defense contracts. And of course he had received some publicity as his party's vice-presidential nominee in 1944.

Although Roosevelt had chosen Truman as his running mate in 1944, he had left the vice president in the dark about crucial foreign and military policies, even including the development of the atomic bomb. "They didn't tell me anything about what was going on," Truman fretted after a month in the presidency. With the deterioration of Soviet-American relations, however, the new president got a quick education.

In foreign affairs the theme of anti-Communism revealed itself in Cold War policies that protected and expanded American overseas interests, challenged the Soviet Union, created alliance systems, rebuilt Western Europe and Japan, drew the United States into civil wars, and favored a military build-up over diplomacy. The United States emerged from the Second World War the most powerful nation on earth, but the world it faced seemed uninviting to the exercise of that power. Much of Asia and Europe lay in ruins, requiring a huge reconstruction task, and civil wars and colonial rebellions rocked political stability. The United States and the Soviet Union scrambled to win friends and to drive in economic and strategic stakes. The two nations clashed constantly, "like two big dogs chewing on a bone," remarked Senator J. William Fulbright. Truman saw the Soviet threat as global and decided to project American power on a worldwide scale. This new globalism, with the containment doctrine as its guide, brought the United States into crisis after crisis. As Secretary of State Dean Acheson said, the United States was "playing for keeps" in a global contest with the Soviet Union and would go around the world creating "situations of strength."

Just five years after the Second World War, the Cold War turned hot on the peninsula of Korea. Although the threat of world war did not materialize, the Korean conflict significantly accelerated the process toward globalism. The United States began to enlarge its military power and to develop new nuclear weapons.

As in foreign policy, the new president got a crash course in the intricacies of governing the United States. At home in 1945, the nation's reconversion from war to peace was not smooth, and Truman managed to anger liberals, conservatives, farmers, consumers, and union members during his first year as president. In 1946 voters responded to inflation and a wave of strikes by electing a Republican Eightieth Congress. But just two years later, partly because of public approval of his decisive foreign policy, Truman confounded political experts by winning the presidency in his own right. Truman had continued to be loyal to the welfare state fashioned in the 1930s. And his upset victory in 1948 was proof that the New Deal coalition was alive and well.

As Truman's victory indicated, however, Cold War politics were volatile. And the key domestic issues of the period—black civil rights and the anti-Communist witch hunt called McCarthyism—were the most highly charged of all. The outbreak of the Korean War in June 1950 intensified domestic discontent. The military stalemate frustrated war-weary citizens; inflation began another upward climb; and evidence of corruption surfaced in the White House. Truman's popularity plummeted. In 1952 Americans cast their presidential votes for a legitimate hero, General Dwight D. Eisenhower.

THE SOURCES OF THE COLD WAR

After overseeing the defeat of Germany and Japan, President Truman participated in the rapid deterioration of Soviet-American relations—the Cold War. In this new conflict, competitive ideologies, propaganda, reconstruction programs, military alliances, atomic arms development, and spheres of influence condemned the world once

Unsettled International Environment

again to instability and fear. Some conflict was inevitable after the Second World War, because the international environment was so unsettled. First, the world was in serious economic trouble. Across Europe and Asia, factories, bridges, transportation and communications systems, and houses had been reduced to rubble. Agricultural production was low, and displaced persons wandered around in search of food and family members. How would this devastated world be pieced back together? America and Russia each offered a different model. Second, the collapse of Germany and Japan created power vacuums that drew the two major powers into collision as they sought to claim influence in countries where the Axis had once held sway. Third, political turmoil within nations spurred Soviet-American competition. In Greece and China, for example, where civil wars were waged between leftists and conservative regimes, the two powers favored different sides. Fourth, empires were disintegrating. In this process of decolonization, the European imperial nations were forced to withdraw by nationalist rebels and by their own financial constraints. New nations were born in the Middle East and Asia, and America and Russia competed to win them as friends who might provide military bases, resources, and markets. Finally, conflict seemed inevitable because of the shrinkage of the globe. That is, because of the triumph of the airplane and the advent of the "air age," the world became more compact. Nations were brought closer together by faster travel; at the same time, they became more vulnerable to surprise attack from the air. The Americans and Soviets once again collided

People and governments in the postwar period faced the awesome job of rebuilding. Berlin, which had been reduced to rubble, was an example.   National Archives.

as they strove to establish defensive positions, sometimes far from home.

Conflict may have been inevitable because of these international conditions, but the Cold War may not have been. That is, the national policies of the United States and the Soviet Union and their leaders' conduct of diplomacy exacerbated rather than resolved postwar issues. Both nations marched into this new Cold War with a sense of righteousness that gave the contest an almost religious character. Each country saw the other as the world's bully. If Americans feared "communist aggression," Russians feared "capitalist encirclement." In mirror image, each side saw the other as the obstacle to peace.

"We are in this thing all over the world to the extent few people realize," Secretary of State James F. Byrnes (1945–1947) told Truman's cabinet. Why were Americans "all over the world"? For one reason, they had determined never to repeat the experience of the 1930s. They vowed no more depressions that would spawn political extremism and in turn produce war; no more Munichs, no more appeasement. It seemed to Americans in the 1940s that Nazi Germany had merely been replaced by Soviet Russia, that communism was simply the flip side of the totalitarian coin. The popular term "Red fascism" captured this sentiment.

American officials also knew that the nation's economic well-being depended on an activist foreign policy. In the postwar years the United States was the largest supplier of goods to world markets: in 1947 its exports amounted to $14 billion. That trade was jeopardized by the postwar economic paralysis of Europe, traditionally America's major customer, and by discriminatory trade practices that violated the Open Door doctrine. "Any serious failure to maintain this flow," declared an assistant secretary of state, "would put millions of American businessmen, farmers, and workers out of business." Indeed, exports constituted about 10 percent of the gross national product; the automobile, steel, and machine-tool industries, among others, relied heavily on foreign trade. About half of America's wheat was shipped abroad, and surpluses of cotton and tobacco also required foreign outlets. Finally, the United States needed to export in order to pay for imports such as zinc, tin, and manganese. Economic expansionism, so much a part of pre–Cold War history, thus remained a central feature of postwar foreign relations.

New strategic theory also propelled the United

States toward an activist, expansionist, globalist diplomacy. "As top dog, America becomes target No. 1," warned Air Force General Carl Spaatz. To be ready for a military challenge in the postwar air age, American strategists believed that the nation's defenses had to begin far beyond its own borders. Thus the United States felt compelled to acquire overseas bases to guard the approaches to the Western Hemisphere. Overseas bases would also permit the United States to launch offensive attacks with might and speed. When asked where the American navy would float, Navy Secretary James Forrestal declared: "Wherever there is a sea."

American Strategic Thinking

President Truman, who shared these assumptions, had a personality that tended to increase international tensions. Whereas Franklin D. Roosevelt had been ingratiating, patient, and evasive, Truman was brash, impatient, and direct. He seldom displayed the appreciation of subtleties so essential to successful diplomacy; for him issues were sketched in black and white, not shades of gray. As a friendly Winston Churchill said of him, Truman "takes no notice of delicate ground, he just plants his foot firmly on it."

Shortly after Roosevelt's death, Truman met Soviet Commissar of Foreign Affairs V. M. Molotov at the White House. The president sharply berated Russia for violating the Yalta accords, a charge Molotov denied. When Truman shot back that the Soviets should honor their agreements, Molotov stormed out of the room. The president was pleased with his "tough method": "I gave it to him straight 'one-two to the jaw.'" But the Yalta agreements were vague; although Soviet actions in Poland had been heavy-handed, whether they were in violation of the agreements was a matter of interpretation. Nonetheless, Truman's simplistic display of toughness would become a trademark of American Cold War diplomacy.

As for the Soviets, they were not easy to get along with either. Dean Acheson, a high-ranking diplomat from 1945 to 1947 and secretary of state from 1949 to 1953, found them rude and abusive. This conservative graduate of Yale and Harvard Law School could, he said, talk with "everybody who was housebroken." The Russians, he asserted, were not: "I think it is a mistake to

American Anti-Soviet Views

believe that you can, at any time, sit down with the Russians and solve problems." Indeed, Premier Josef Stalin's blunt *nyets* stung American ears. But more than Soviet style bothered Americans. Soviet territorial ambitions—and successes—included a portion of eastern Poland, the Baltic states of Lithuania, Latvia, and Estonia, and parts of Finland and Rumania. In Eastern Europe Russian officials began to suppress non-Communists.

For their part, the Russians remembered how the hostile West had attempted to ostracize them before: "We were always outsiders," complained one Soviet diplomat. Driven by memories of the past, by fear of a revived Germany, by the huge task of reconstruction, and by Marxist-Leninist doctrine, the Soviets suspected capitalist nations of plotting once again to extinguish the Communist flame. They protested that the Americans were surrounding them with hostile bases and practicing atomic and dollar diplomacy.

"After World War II," Senator J. William Fulbright remembered, "we were sold on the idea that Stalin was out to dominate the world." This view pitted a generous United States ready to rebuild a peaceful world against a selfish, uncooperative Soviet Union; Americans were forced to react defensively against expansionist Russians. But Fulbright came to believe that the Soviets probably never intended to dominate the world and they certainly lacked the capability to do so. Russia emerged from the war with a weak military establishment, a hobbled economy, and obsolete technology. Knowing this, American leaders did not expect the Soviets to attack Western Europe or to start a war they obviously could not sustain. The Soviet Union was a regional power in Eastern Europe, but not a global menace.

American officials nonetheless exaggerated the Soviet threat. There are several reasons why, and they sum up the American global perspective in the early Cold War. First, President Truman liked things in black and white, as his aide Clark Clifford remarked. Nuances, ambiguities, and counterevidence were often glossed over to satisfy Truman's penchant for the simple answer. Second, military officers often overplayed the Soviet threat to persuade Congress to pass larger defense budgets. Third, some Americans fixed their attention, as they had since the Bolshevik Revolution of 1917,

Question of the Soviet Threat

on the utopian communist goal of world revolution rather than on actual Soviet behavior, which was limited largely to regions along the Russian border and to bombastic rhetoric. Fourth, American leaders feared that the terrible postwar conditions of poverty and social unrest abroad would leave United States strategic and economic interests vulnerable to political disorders which the Soviets might exploit. In other words, Americans feared less a direct Soviet attack and more the Soviets' potential seizing of opportunities to challenge American interests, perhaps through subversion. Last and overall, the United States, flushed with its own strength, took advantage of the postwar power vacuum to expand its overseas interests and shape a peace on American terms. The American pursuit of nuclear superiority, outlying bases, raw materials and markets, supremacy in Latin America, control of the Atlantic and Pacific Oceans, and air transit rights across other nations aroused a growing number of opponents, in particular the Soviet Union. Americans overreacted to the criticism, unable to understand it except as further evidence of wicked Soviet obstructionism on a worldwide scale. George F. Kennan, one of the chief architects of Cold War policy, later regretted that Americans had created the image of the Soviet Union as "the totally inhuman and malevolent adversary," because this distorted view contributed to the American abandonment of diplomacy during the rash of crises that bedeviled the global community.

COLD WAR CRISES AND THE CONTAINMENT DOCTRINE

One of the first Soviet-American clashes came in Poland in 1945, when the Russians refused to admit conservative Poles from London to the Communist government in Lublin, as agreed at Yalta.

Soviet Domination of Eastern Europe

A visit to Stalin by former Roosevelt aide Harry Hopkins in May of that year brought about some broadening of the Lublin regime, but did not change Poland's status as a subser-vient, Soviet-directed state where the Communists could not claim majority support. The Russians also snuffed out civil liberties in the former Nazi satellite of Rumania. Though they allowed free elections to be held in Hungary and Czechoslovakia, as the Cold War progressed and they came to fear American power more and more, they encouraged Communist coups. First Hungary (1947) and then Czechoslovakia (1948) succumbed to Soviet subversion. Yugoslavia was a unique case: its independent Communist government, led by Josip Broz Tito, successfully broke with Stalin in 1948.

To justify their actions the Soviets complained that the United States was reviving Russia's traditional enemy, Germany. Citing radio broadcasts that encouraged resistance, clandestine meetings with anti-Soviet groups, repeated calls for elections, and the extension or withholding of loans to gain political influence ("dollar diplomacy"), the Soviets protested that the United States was meddling in Eastern Europe. Russia also charged that the United States was pursuing a double standard in intervening in the affairs of Eastern Europe but expecting Russia to stay out of Latin America and Asia. They pointed to the lack of free elections in United States–backed Latin American dictatorships. Americans insisted that their spheres of influence were far more open, their methods far less repressive than the Russians'. But protest as Washington did, it was unable to roll back Soviet influence in Eastern Europe.

Another issue that divided America and Russia was the atomic bomb. The Soviets believed that the Americans were practicing "atomic diplomacy"—

Atomic Diplomacy

maintaining a frightening nuclear monopoly and bragging about it to scare the Soviets into diplomatic concessions. At a stormy foreign ministers' conference in London in fall 1945, Soviet Commissar of Foreign Affairs V. M. Molotov asked Secretary of State James F. Byrnes if he had an atomic bomb in his side pocket. Byrnes replied that southerners "carry our artillery in our hip pocket. If you don't cut out all this stalling and let us get down to work, I am going to pull an atomic bomb out of my hip pocket and let you have it." Retiring Secretary of War Henry L. Stimson was one among the few who opposed the use of the bomb as a diplomatic lever. As he told the president in September 1945,

A Soviet tank in Gdansk, Poland, April 1945. After driving the Germans from Poland, the Red Army stayed on to ensure the power of the Communist regime in that war-weary nation. Sovfoto.

if Americans continued to have "this weapon rather ostentatiously on our hip, their [the Russians'] suspicions and their distrust of our purposes and motives will increase."

In this atmosphere of suspicion and distrust, the United States and the Soviet Union could not agree on the international control of atomic energy. The American proposal, called the Baruch Plan, provided for America's abandoning its monopoly after the world's fissionable materials had been brought under the authority of an international agency. The Soviets retorted that this plan denied them the right to develop their own bomb while the United States continued its supremacy. Secretary of Commerce Henry A. Wallace understood why Moscow rejected the Baruch Plan: "We are telling the Russians that if they are 'good boys' we may eventually turn over our knowledge of atomic energy. . . ."

The two adversaries also collided in Iran. By wartime agreement, British, American, and Russian troops occupied Iran. The Russians had some influence in the north, near the Russian-Iranian border, and the British dominated the country's rich oil industry. When American petroleum companies asked the Iranian government for an oil concession, Moscow sniffed a capitalist plot on its border. In March 1946, the date agreed on for troop withdrawal, the Russians stayed on in violation of the wartime treaty. Americans angrily accused the U.S.S.R. of intending to take over Iran. The Russians countered that American military advisers remained in Iran, and that British oil interests ensured Anglo-American political influence in the Teheran government. When the American-dominated United Nations investigated only Soviet actions in Iran, Moscow ordered its delegation to boycott the international body.

Crisis in Iran

Still, Iranian and Soviet diplomats managed to negotiate a settlement in April: Soviet soldiers would leave Iran in exchange for an oil concession. Americans claimed a Cold War victory, believing their tough words had forced the Soviets to withdraw. (In

1947 they turned the tables by persuading the Iranians to go back on their promise of a Russian oil concession. Moscow cried that it had been double-crossed.)

Soviets and Americans clashed on every front in 1946. They could not agree on the unification of Germany, so they built up their zones independently. The new World Bank and International Monetary Fund, created at the 1944 Bretton Woods Conference to stabilize trade and finance, also became tangled in the Cold War struggle. The Soviets refused to join because the United States so dominated both institutions. In early 1946 Washington extended a $3.5 billion loan to Great Britain but turned down a similar Soviet request. Already smarting from an abrupt cutoff of Lend-Lease aid in mid-1945, the Soviets denounced the United States for using its reconstruction dollars in order to manipulate foreign governments.

When in early February 1946 Stalin gave a pre-election speech depicting a world threatened by capitalist acquisitiveness, the American chargé d'affaires in Moscow, George F. Kennan, concluded that Russian fanaticism made even a temporary understanding impossible. Kennan's pessimistic "long telegram" to Washington fed the growing belief that only toughness would work with the Russians. On March 5, Winston Churchill made his stirring Iron Curtain speech, warning that Eastern European countries were being cut off from the West by Russia. With the approving Truman sitting on the stage, the former prime minister called for an Anglo-American partnership to resist the Russian menace. Stalin protested that "Russia was not attacking, she was being attacked."

Secretary of Commerce Henry A. Wallace, a critic of Truman's get-tough policy, feared the United States was substituting atomic and economic coercion for diplomacy. " 'Getting tough,' " he told a Madison Square Garden audience in September 1946, "never brought anything real and lasting—whether for schoolyard bullies or businessmen or world powers. The tougher we get, the tougher the Russians will get." Truman fired Wallace from the cabinet, blasting him privately as "a real Commy and a dangerous man." The president crowed that he had now "run the crackpots out of the Democratic Party."

The Cold War escalated further on March 12, 1947, when in response to a request from the British, who could no longer afford to fund their Greek client government, the president asked Congress for $400 million in aid to Greece and Turkey, both of which were threatened by economic dislocation and Communist political pressure. To repeat Truman's famous words: "It must be the policy of the United States to support free peoples who are resisting attempted subjugation by armed minorities or by outside pressures." It was time to draw the line, to contain the Communist menace. The president's statement quickly became known as the Truman Doctrine. Critics correctly pointed out that there was no evidence that the Soviet Union was involved in the civil war in Greece; that the rebel National Liberation Front had good reason to resent the repressive and corrupt regime supported by the British; and that the resistance movement included non-Communists as well as Communists. Others suggested that aid should be channeled through the United Nations. But after much debate the Senate approved Truman's request 67 to 23. Using American dollars and military advisers, the Greek government defeated the insurgents in 1949.

Truman Doctrine

In July 1947 George F. Kennan, now director of the State Department's policy planning staff, offered another statement of what became known as the containment doctrine. Writing under the name "Mr. X" in the magazine *Foreign Affairs,* this expert on Soviet affairs advocated a "policy of firm containment, designed to confront the Russians with unalterable counterforce at every point where they show signs of encroaching upon the interests of a peaceful and stable world." Such a counterforce, Kennan argued, would check Soviet expansion and eventually foster a "mellowing" of Soviet behavior. Together with the Truman Doctrine, Kennan's article became the chief manifesto of Cold War foreign policy.

The highly regarded journalist Walter Lippmann was critical of the containment doctrine. In *The Cold War* (1947), Lippmann called containment a "strategic monstrosity" that did not distinguish between areas vital and peripheral to American security. If American leaders thought every place on earth was of strategic importance, he reasoned, the nation's patience and resources would soon be drained. Nor did Lippmann share Truman's view that Russia was

Debate over Containment

plotting to take over the world. Truman, he asserted, put too little emphasis on diplomacy.

Lippmann was happier with the Marshall Plan for the reconstruction of Western Europe. In 1946 and 1947 an unusually harsh winter swept over Europe. Coal supplies dwindled; meager food stores were exhausted. European nations, still reeling from the war, lacked the dollars to buy American goods. Especially in France and Italy, leftists and Communists gained in political influence. Americans, who had already spent billions of dollars on European relief and recovery by 1947, recalled the troubles of the 1930s: global depression; political extremism; war born of economic discontent. It could not be allowed to happen again. Western Europe, Dean Acheson emphasized, was the "keystone in the arch which supports the kind of a world which we have to have in order to conduct our lives."

On June 5, 1947, Secretary of State George C. Marshall (1947–1949) announced that the United States would finance a massive European recovery program. Though Marshall did not

Marshall Plan exclude Eastern Europe or the Soviet Union, few American leaders believed that Russia and its allies would want to join an American-dominated project. And indeed, they did not join. Launched in 1948, the Marshall Plan sent $12.4 billion (or 1.2 percent of the United States gross national product) to Western Europe before the program ended in late 1951 (see map, page 828). To stimulate business at home, the legislation provided that the foreign aid dollars must be spent in the United States. The Marshall Plan was a mixed success. In Europe, it caused inflation, failed to solve a serious balance-of-payments problem, and took only tentative steps toward economic integration. But it also sparked impressive Western European industrial production and investment and started the region toward self-sustaining economic growth. By 1952 the recovery program had given way to military assistance. From the beginning the Soviets blasted the Marshall Plan as the enslavement of Europe. They created a special propaganda agency—the Cominform—to harangue against it and the feeble Molotov Plan for Eastern Europe to imitate it.

To strengthen the nation's defenses, Truman worked with Congress to streamline the government's administrative structure under the National Security

At Edgewater, New Jersey, in 1949, Ford trucks are being loaded for a shipment to Israel. As America's trade with its allies boomed, so too did business profits at home. Some of the United States's foreign-aid packages required the receiving countries to buy only American goods with the money. National Archives.

Act (July 1947). The act created the Department of Defense, the National Security Council (NSC) to advise the president, and the Central Intelligence Agency (CIA) to conduct spying and information gathering. By the early 1950s the CIA had expanded its functions to include covert (secret) operations aimed at overthrowing unfriendly foreign leaders and, as a high-ranking American official put it, stirring up economic trouble in "the camp of the enemy" through a "Department of Dirty Tricks." In 1953 the United States Information Agency was created to counter Soviet propaganda.

American officials also reached out to find new foreign friends and build new bases. In 1946, when the United States granted the Philippines independence, it maintained its old military, economic, and political ties. And in 1947 American diplomats created

Divided Europe

Moscow •

UNION OF SOVIET SOCIALIST REPUBLICS

Exploded first atomic bomb, 1949

BLACK SEA

Ankara •

TURKEY
$

Truman Doctrine, 1947
Joined NATO, 1952

FINLAND
Helsinki •

Stockholm •

BALTIC SEA

SWEDEN
$

Copenhagen •

Warsaw •

POLAND

RUMANIA

Bucharest •

BULGARIA
Sofia •

Communist coup, 1948
U.S.S.R. invasion, 1968

Berlin blockade, 1948–1949

West Berlin ○ East Berlin

Prague •
CZECHOSLOVAKIA

Budapest •
HUNGARY

Belgrade •
YUGOSLAVIA

Tito–Stalin schism, 1948

Athens •

GREECE

Truman Doctrine, 1947
Joined NATO, 1952
Joined Common Market, 1981

NORWAY
$
Oslo •

DENMARK

EAST
GERMANY

Vienna •
AUSTRIA
$

Revolution, 1956

Tiranë •
ALBANIA

Left COMECON, 1961
Withdrew from WP, 1968

NORTH SEA

Joined Common
Market, 1973

Amsterdam •
NETHERLANDS
$

Bonn •

WEST
GERMANY

Bern •
SWITZ.

Joined NATO, 1955

Zones of occupation ended, 1955

Rome •

ITALY
$

MEDITERRANEAN SEA

U.S. 6th Fleet

U.S. loan of $3.5 billion, 1946
Exploded first atomic bomb, 1952
Joined Common Market, 1973

GREAT
BRITAIN
$

London •

Brussels •
BELGIUM
$

LUX.
$

Paris •

FRANCE
$

Dublin •
IRELAND
$

Joined Common Market, 1973

Exploded first atomic bomb, 1960
Withdrew from NATO, 1966

*ATLANTIC
OCEAN*

Reykjavik •
ICELAND
$

Joined Common Market, 1973

Madrid •

SPAIN

PORTUGAL
$
Lisbon •

$ Participants in the Marshall Plan

Member of NATO,*
formed in 1949

Member of COMECON,** formed in
1949, and the Warsaw Pact,
organized in 1955

Member of the European
Common Market, formed in 1958

*North Atlantic Treaty Organization
**Council for Mutual Economic Assistance

the Rio Pact—a military alliance with Latin American countries. To enforce the Rio Pact, the United States helped found the Organization of American States (OAS) the following year. Under this and other agreements the Truman administration sent several military advisory missions to Latin America, and others to Greece, Turkey, Iran, China, and Saudi Arabia. In 1948 Americans activated an air base in Libya. And in May of that year Truman quickly recognized the new state of Israel, which had been carved out of the British-held territory of Palestine after years of Arab-Jewish dispute. America's perceived need for international allies joined the president's desire for Jewish-American votes in the upcoming election to hurry the decision.

One of the most electric moments in the Cold War came a month later. In June 1948 the Russians cut off Western access to the jointly occupied city

Berlin Blockade and Airlift

of Berlin, located well inside the Soviet zone of Germany. Before the Soviets' bold move, the Americans, French, and British had agreed to fuse their zones into what became known as West Germany. The three allies planned to integrate West Germany, including the three Western sectors of Berlin, into the Western European economy, complete with a reformed German currency. The Soviets, fearing a resurgent Germany tied to the American Cold War camp, may have sparked the Berlin crisis to stimulate negotiations. But if they thought Truman would compromise, they guessed wrong. Instead the president ordered a massive airlift of food, fuel, and other supplies to the isolated city— a plane almost every minute. Finally, in May 1949, their image badly damaged, the Soviets lifted the blockade. They had spurred the very result they feared: the creation of the Federal Republic of Germany (West Germany) that month. In retaliation they founded the People's Republic of Germany (East Germany).

On April 4, 1949, believing that a military shield should be added to the economic shield of the Marshall Plan, the United States, Canada, and much of Western

Creation of NATO

Europe founded the North Atlantic Treaty Organization (NATO). The treaty aroused considerable debate at home, for not since 1778 had the United States entered a formal European military

alliance. Senator Robert A. Taft protested that NATO would provoke an arms race with Russia or cause American soldiers to be stationed in Europe. Others complained that the scheme gave the president power to send troops into combat without a congressional declaration of war, and that it would cost too much, ultimately weakening the nation. Truman responded that NATO would give Europeans the will to resist, the confidence to thwart Communism in their midst. And it would function as a "tripwire," bringing the full force of the United States to bear on the Soviet Union if it dared to cross the East-West line with troops—which it was not expected to do, with or without a NATO. Quietly, administration spokesmen also indicated that NATO was designed to knit Western Europe together, to discourage some nations' tendency toward neutrality. The Senate ratified the treaty in July, 82 to 13. Truman then asked for a $1.5 billion Mutual Defense Assistance Act, to which Congress also consented, as it did to all Truman's major foreign policy requests.

Just before passage of the military aid bill (September 1949), an American aircraft carrying sensitive equipment detected unusually high radioactivity in the atmosphere: the Soviets had exploded an atomic bomb. "This is now a different world," commented Senator Arthur Vandenberg. The American nuclear monopoly was no more, and Western Europe now seemed more vulnerable. The Communists were also winning the civil war in China (see pages 830–831) and Moscow was scoring propaganda points by advocating "peaceful coexistence" with the West. American leaders could have responded to this changed state of affairs with diplomatic negotiations. But Secretary of State Dean Acheson announced that there would be no "appeasement." The United States would instead build "situations of strength" around the world. In early 1950 Truman ordered production of the hydrogen bomb. And in May Congress finally endorsed funds for technical assistance to developing nations, to draw them into the American sphere of influence (a plan called the Point Four Program, after point 4 of Truman's 1949 inaugural address).

A month earlier, the National Security Council had delivered to the president a top-secret document numbered NSC-68. Predicting continued tension with the Communists and describing a "shrinking world of polarized power," the report appealed for an enlarged

NSC-68 military budget to counter the Soviet global design American strategists perceived. The authors advised that public opinion would have to be mobilized behind huge defense expenditures. Administration officials worried about how to sell this strong prescription to the voters and budget-conscious congressional representatives. "We were sweating over it, and then—with regard to NSC-68—thank God Korea came along," recalled one of Dean Acheson's aides.

THE COLD WAR IN ASIA

When the Korean War erupted in mid-1950, it came in the wake of vast changes in Asia. The Second World War had accelerated the process of decolonization begun during the First World War. Occupied with defending themselves and then with rebuilding after the war, imperial countries were no longer able to resist their colonies' demands for independence. Britain gave up India and what are now Pakistan and Bangladesh in 1947, Burma and Ceylon in 1948. The Dutch reluctantly let go of Indonesia in 1949. Only the French fought on in Indochina, finally retiring from that outpost in 1954.

The defeat of Japan brought about the division of its empire among the victors. Korea was divided between the United States and the Soviet Union. The Pacific islands (the Marshalls, Marianas, and Carolines) came under American control. Half of Sakhalin went to Russia as agreed at Yalta, and Formosa (Taiwan) was returned to the Chinese. As for Japan itself, the United States monopolized its reconstruction. Though the British and Russians asserted that they too had fought in the Asian theater and deserved a say in the occupation, **Reconstruction of Japan** Ambassador W. Averell Harriman answered that Washington was "very firm on the matter of keeping the power in American hands." Stalin wondered what the difference was between American domination of Japan and Russian domination of Rumania. But General Douglas MacArthur, who envisioned turning the Pacific Ocean into "an Anglo-Saxon lake," had the last word in Japan. As director of the American occupation, MacArthur wrote a democratic constitution for Japan, revitalized its economy, and destroyed the weapons of the Japanese military.

Though United States supremacy in Japan was an established fact, the Russians would not recognize it. Thus, after squabbling with Russia for years over a peace treaty with Japan, the United States finally signed a separate peace in 1951. The treaty restored Japan's sovereignty, ended the occupation, granted the United States a military base at Okinawa, and permitted American troops to be stationed in Japan. Tokyo and Washington also initialed a defense pact. The people who had been called beasts after their surprise attack on Pearl Harbor were now American allies in the Cold War. Along with Germany, Japan was, as Kennan noted, one of "our most important pawns on the chessboard of world politics."

Meanwhile, America's Chinese ally was faltering. The United States was feeding and fueling Jiang Jieshi's (Chiang Kai-shek's) Nationalist army in its battle against Mao Zedong and Zhou **Chinese Civil War** Enlai's Communists. Immediately after the Second World War American troops had occupied northern China, flown Nationalist soldiers to Manchuria, and stayed on to advise Generalissimo Jiang. From 1945 to 1949 the United States sent China $3 billion in aid. But it soon became evident that Jiang was an unreliable friend. His government was corrupt and inefficient; he was out of touch with the rebellious peasants, whom the Communists enlisted with promises of land redistribution; and he tolerated a grossly unfair tax system. Journalist Theodore White thought the Nationalists combined "some of the worst features of Tammany Hall and the Spanish Inquisition," and Truman privately denounced them as "grafters and crooks." Jiang ignored American advice to root out corruption, halt inflation, and begin land reform. He also worked to disrupt the efforts of the Marshall mission (1945–1947) to negotiate a cease-fire and a coalition government. And he rejected American military advice. "We picked a bad horse," Truman admitted. Still, seeing Jiang as the only viable alternative to Mao, Truman backed him to the end.

American officials were divided on the question of whether Mao was a puppet of the Soviet Union. Some diplomats considered him an Asian Tito—

In this 1945 photograph taken at the Chinese Communists' headquarters at Yenan, Mao Zedong (1893–1976) stands with Lin
Biao (at right), a war hero whom Mao had designated his
"closest comrade in arms and successor." Four years later,
the Communists were victorious over Jiang Jieshi's Nationalists and proclaimed the People's Republic of China. In 1971,
Biao betrayed Mao and was shot down in a jet airplane
while trying to escape from China.   Wide World Photos.

Communist but independent—but most believed he
was part of an international Communist movement
and would thus give the Soviets a springboard into
Asia. In the *White Paper* of 1949—a government
report written to explain America's efforts to contain
Communism through aid to Jiang—Secretary Acheson
overstated his case in saying that the "Communist
leaders have foresworn their Chinese heritage and
have publicly announced their subservience to a foreign
power." Thus when the Chinese Communists made
secret overtures to begin diplomatic talks in 1945
and again in 1949, American officials rebuffed them.
Mao soon decided that he was "leaning to one side"
in the Cold War—the Soviet side.

Actually, Americans had overestimated Mao's dependence on the Soviet Union. The Russians gave
Mao little support, rejecting his interpretation of

Marxism-Leninism and resenting his determination
to resist their influence. For its own purposes Russia
preferred a weak China under Jiang to a strong China
under Mao, an attitude that derived from a long
history of Sino-Russian rivalry.

In fall 1949, after numerous military setbacks, Jiang
fled to the island of Formosa, and Mao proclaimed
the People's Republic of China. Would the United
States extend diplomatic recognition
Nonrecogni- to Mao's new government? Truman
tion of the hesitated; he tried unsuccessfully to
People's persuade the British to wait. "Are
Republic we to refuse to recognize facts,
of China however unpleasant they may be?"
asked the British prime mini-
ster. "Are we to cut ourselves off from all contact
with one-sixth of the inhabitants of the world?" But

for several reasons Washington did just that. First, American officials were alarmed by a Sino-Soviet treaty of friendship signed in February 1950. Second, Mao's followers had harassed Americans and seized American-owned property in China. Third, Mao was now openly hostile to the United States, blaming it for prolonging the bloody civil war. Fourth, Secretary Dean Acheson simply wanted to "wait until the dust settles." He predicted that Mao would conquer Formosa, thus eliminating Jiang, and that frictions between Beijing and Moscow would ultimately convince Mao to sever his ties with the Soviets.

Still another reason lay behind the policy of nonrecognition. A noisy group of Republican critics called the China lobby, shattering the postwar spirit of bipartisanship, was seeking to blame Jiang's defeat on Truman. Publisher Henry Luce, Senator William Knowland of California, and Congressman Walter Judd of Minnesota won headlines by charging that the United States had "lost" China. Senator Joseph McCarthy of Wisconsin snorted that "egg-sucking liberals" and "queers" had sold China into "atheistic slavery."

Truman and Acheson answered that the United States had never had China to lose, that Jiang was not willing to help himself, and that large-scale military intervention in the Chinese civil war would have been costly and probably interminable. Moreover, major involvement in China would have drained valuable resources from Europe, the primary front in the Cold War. "The United States cannot furnish determination, it cannot furnish the will, and it cannot furnish the loyalty of a people to its government," Acheson insisted—adding, "China lost itself." For reasons of both domestic politics and international relations, the United States did not open formal diplomatic relations with the People's Republic of China until 1979—thirty years after Mao's government came to power.

Reaching for some way to offset Jiang's collapse, the National Security Council urged the president to fortify "friendly and independent" states in Asia as a bulwark against Communist expansion. In February 1950 the United States recognized the French puppet regime of Bao Dai in Vietnam, and a few months later decided to extend aid to the beleaguered French there. In April the National Security Council sent the president its alarming report NSC-68. And in May more funds went to Jiang Jieshi in Formosa. It is in this context of globalist thought and action that America's response to war in Korea must be seen (see pages 843–845).

A ROUGH TRANSITION AT HOME

Truman's crises abroad were matched by several challenges at home. The atomic bombs that fell on Hiroshima and Nagasaki brought about victory much sooner than the economic planners had anticipated. Mid-1946 was the target date for victory, and administrators had planned a gradual conversion from a wartime to a peacetime economy. But in 1945 the war was over, and important questions remained unanswered. What would be the effect of reconversion—the cancellation of war contracts, the termination of wage and price controls, and the end of wartime labor agreements? Would depression recur once the artificial stimulus of the war was withdrawn, throwing people out of work and sending prices downward? Or would Americans go on a buying spree, driving prices up to record highs? After all, during the Great Depression penny-pinched Americans could not afford to buy autos, houses, appliances, and other consumer durables. During the prosperity of the Second World War civilian items such as these were not manufactured. Therefore, by 1945 Americans had bulging bank accounts, and they wanted to treat themselves.

Most Americans were pessimistic about the future. Even before the war's end, cutbacks in production had caused layoffs. Workers at the Ford Motor Company's massive Willow Run plant outside Detroit, where nine thousand Liberator bombers had been produced, were let go in spring 1945. Ten days after the victory over Japan, 1.8 million people received pink slips and 640,000 filed for unemployment compensation. The peak of postwar unemployment came in March 1946, when 2.7 million people were seeking work.

Postwar Job Layoffs

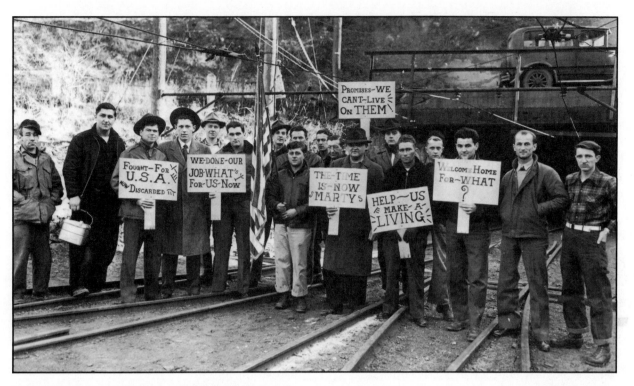

In 1946 ex-servicemen picketed coal mines in Panther Valley, Pennsylvania, complaining that mine owners had hired outside help during the war and then had refused to lay these workers off in favor of the returning veterans, former coalminers themselves.   Wide World Photos.

Swelling the ranks of those seeking jobs were the millions of soldiers and sailors who received their discharges from the armed services in 1945 and 1946. As with the cancellations of government contracts, the demobilization of the armed forces was rapid. The army had expected to muster out 1.1 million people in the eighteen months between V-E and V-J days, but the atomic bombings of Hiroshima and Nagasaki had cut that period to four months. The army's demobilization rate was increased fivefold, with a target of 5.5 million by July 1946. The navy hurriedly converted landing and cargo ships to troop carriers and returned 4 million GIs from abroad in the first year of peace. In mid-1945 the nation's armed forces stood at over 12 million. A year later, the figure had fallen to just over 3 million; in 1947 it hit 1.5 million. "The program we were following," Truman recalled, "was no longer demobilization—it was disintegration of our armed forces."

Truman declared his determination not only to combat unemployment, but also to expand on New Deal programs begun in the 1930s. On September 6, 1945, he delivered to Congress a twenty-one-point message urging extension of unemployment compensation, an increase in the minimum wage, adoption of permanent farm-price supports, and new public works projects. Truman revived Roosevelt's Economic Bill of Rights: every able-bodied American had a right to a job. Should the economy fail to provide one, the government should create it. Congress responded to Truman's message with the Employment Act of 1946, which announced that the government would use its resources, including deficit spending if necessary, to achieve "maximum employment, production, and purchasing power." The act established the Council of Economic Advisers to assist the president. But it fell short of Truman's hopes: Congress had deleted a commitment to absolute full employment.

Truman's Reconversion Plan

Despite high unemployment in the immediate post-war period, the United States was not teetering on the brink of depression; in fact, after a brief period of readjustment, the economy would blast off into a quarter-century of unprecedented boom. People had plenty of savings to spend in 1945 and 1946, and suddenly there were new houses and cars for them to buy. Easy credit and new war-inspired industries like synthetic rubber and electronics promoted the buying spree. As a result, though war production began to wind down in 1944, the gross national product (GNP) continued to rise in 1945. And though there was a slight dip in economic activity in 1946, the GNP jumped from $209 billion to $231 billion the next year. In 1948 it rose to $258 billion (see Chapter 31).

So the nation's postwar economic problem was not depression; it was inflation, fueled by maddening shortages of consumer goods like meat and housing. Throughout 1945 and 1946 prices skyrocketed; the inflation rate for 1946 was 18.2 percent.

Meanwhile, though prices were spiraling upward, many people were earning less than they had during the war. Industrial workers complained that the National War Labor Board had limited them to cost-of-living pay increases, thus preventing them from improving their status. To complicate matters, workers who had put in long hours of overtime during the war were returning to the forty-hour paycheck. Although employers claimed they could not afford to guarantee workers the same take-home pay for fewer hours, most workers believed it was possible. The result was an impasse between management and labor and a spate of strikes. During fall and early winter 1945, daily absences due to strikes ballooned to 28.4 million, more than double the 1943 figure. But although such strikes were massive and frequent, they were peaceful compared with the fiery confrontations that had followed the First World War.

Throughout the period of reconversion the government hesitated to act in the face of competing special-interest groups. Big business and small business, management and labor, farmers and consumers, liberals and conservatives offered conflicting prescriptions, and to serve one interest was to risk offending others. For all these groups, Truman was the perfect scapegoat. "Sherman was *wrong*," Truman told a Gridiron Dinner

audience in December 1945. "I'm telling you I find peace is hell."

As severe as was the discontent of farmers, factory workers, and consumers in 1945, in 1946 it became worse. As volatile as labor-management relations were in 1945, the next year they exploded. And as unpopular as President Truman was in 1945, in 1946 his rating hit new lows.

Over 4.5 million men and women left their jobs to strike in 1946, more even than in 1919. Daily absences due to strikes totaled 113 million—four times as many as in 1945. One reason for **Upsurge in** workers' discontent was that while **Labor Strikes** wages and salaries had declined slightly in 1946, net profits had reached all-time highs, jumping more than 50 percent from 1945 to 1946. Indignant that they were not sharing in the increased prosperity, workers forced nationwide shutdowns in the coal, automobile, steel, and electric industries and halted railroad and maritime transportation.

John L. Lewis's United Mine Workers was among the most powerful unions to walk off the job. Coal was the nation's primary source of energy in 1946; when soft-coal production stopped on April 1, steel and automobile output plummeted, railroad service was canceled, thousands of people were laid off, and twenty-two states reinstituted wartime "dim-outs" to conserve coal. Though the miners' demands were legitimate—higher wages, a federal safety code, and a royalty of ten cents per ton to finance health services and welfare and pension funds—a two-week truce in May failed to produce a solution. On May 21, with time running out and the country still desperate for coal, Truman ordered the seizure of the mines. Lewis and the government reached an accord a week later and the miners returned to work. But within six months the agreement had collapsed, and once again the government seized the mines.

There was no doubt in 1946 about the growing unpopularity of labor unions and their leadership. Many Americans believed that the **Truman's** unions were responsible for strikes **Attack on** that not only restricted the output **the Unions** of consumer goods and inflated prices, but also threatened the national security. In May, when a nationwide railroad

Chapter 29: THE COLD WAR AND AMERICAN POLITICS, 1945–1953

strike was threatened, Truman hopped aboard the antiunion bandwagon. A special board appointed to mediate the dispute had managed to satisfy eighteen of the disgruntled unions, but two held out for a better settlement. In exasperation, Truman made a dramatic appearance before a joint session of Congress. If the government seized a strike-bound industry, he said, and the workers in that industry refused to honor a presidential order to return to work, "I [would] request the Congress immediately to authorize the President to draft into the Armed Forces of the United States all workers who are on strike against their government." He also requested authority to strip strikers of seniority benefits, to take legal action against union leaders, and to fine and even imprison them for contempt. Truman's speech alienated not only railroad workers but union members in general. Many dedicated themselves to defeating him in the upcoming presidential election.

Truman fared little better in his direction of the Office of Price Administration. Now that the war was over, powerful interests wanted OPA controls **Consumer Discontent** lifted. Consumers were impatient with shortages and black-market prices, and manufacturers and farmers wanted to jack up prices legally. Yet when most controls expired in mid-1946 and inflation rose higher, people became angry. When the OPA price ceilings on beef expired in June, for example, the cost of beef soared, cattle ranchers beamed, and consumers grumbled. When the OPA reimposed ceilings in August, however, producers retaliated by withholding beef from the market. Soon consumers were standing in long lines at the butcher shop and buying beef through the black market. In an election year, they blamed the Democrats. "This is going to be a damn *beefsteak* election," groused Speaker of the House Sam Rayburn.

Truman's popularity rating plunged from 87 percent in late 1945 to 32 percent in 1946. Even liberals were unhappy with the president's performance. Truman had prompted the resignation of Harold Ickes, one of the two New Dealers left in the cabinet, by appointing a California oil and real estate baron (who also happened to be a Democratic fundraiser) as undersecretary of the navy. Fearing another Teapot Dome scandal, Ickes angrily denounced Truman's policy of "government by crony." Seven months later Truman fired Henry A. Wallace, the only remaining New Dealer, for making a speech critical of his containment policy (see page 826). By election time the president was out of favor with labor, consumers, farmers, liberals, and—because of his advocacy of welfare programs—conservative Democrats as well.

Republicans made the most of public discontent. "Got enough meat?" asked Republican Congressman John M. Vorys of Ohio. "Got enough houses? Got enough OPA? . . . Got enough inflation? . . . Got enough debt? . . . Got enough strikes?" When the votes were tabulated, the Republicans had won a majority in both houses of the Eightieth Congress and captured twenty-five of thirty-two nonsouthern governorships. The White House in 1948 seemed within their grasp.

THE EIGHTIETH CONGRESS AND THE ELECTION OF 1948

The politicians who ruled the Eightieth Congress, both Republicans and southern Democrats, were committed conservatives. Although they supported Truman's foreign policy, they perceived the Republican landslide as a mandate to reverse the New Deal, to curb the power of government and of labor. Truman had had little success with the Seventy-ninth Congress; he would have even less success with this one. Ironically, however, it would be the Eightieth Congress that would help him to win the presidency in 1948. For if Truman had alienated labor, farmers, and liberals, the Eightieth Congress made them livid.

One extremely unpopular measure was the Taft-Hartley Act, which Congress adopted over Truman's veto in 1947. A revision of the Wagner Act of 1935, **Taft-Hartley Act** the bill prohibited the closed shop, in which only union members could be hired. The framework of the Wagner Act still governed labor-management relations, and workers could still organize, elect a union to represent them, enroll new union members, bargain collectively, and strike. But the Taft-Hartley Act forbade union contributions to political funds in federal elections; required union leaders to sign non-Communist affidavits; and mandated an eighty-day cooling-off period in strikes that imperiled the national security. Although it was not the slave-labor act labor spokespersons said it was, responses to the act quickly distinguished supporters of labor from opponents. Truman's veto therefore vindicated him in the eyes of labor. Just a year earlier, labor leaders had pledged all-out war against the president; now they threw their resources behind him.

Throughout 1947 and into 1948 the Eightieth Congress offended numerous interest groups, which in turn swung back to Truman. For example, the president asked Congress for continued price supports for farmers; the Eightieth Congress responded with weakened price supports. The president requested nationwide health insurance; the Eightieth Congress refused. It was the same with federal funding of public housing and aid to public education; with broadened and increased unemployment compensation, old-age and survivors' benefits, and the minimum wage; with funds for land reclamation, irrigation, and public power; and with antilynching, anti-poll tax, and fair-employment legislation. Truman proposed; Congress rejected or ignored his requests.

But Republicans seemed oblivious to public opinion. Not since 1928 had they been so confident of capturing the presidency, and most political experts agreed. "Only a political miracle," stated **Campaign of 1948** *Time*, "or extraordinary stupidity on the part of the Republicans can save the Democratic party." At their national convention, Republicans strengthened their position by nominating for president and vice president the governors of the nation's two most populous states: Thomas E. Dewey of New York and Earl Warren of California.

Democrats revealed how fragmented they were when they convened to nominate a candidate and adopt a platform. A curious alliance of big-city bosses and liberals, reasoning that Truman was a loser, tried to dump him in favor of General Dwight D. Eisenhower. But Eisenhower declined the overtures of both Democrats and Republicans, declaring that "life-long professional soldiers should abstain from seeking high political office." In the end, Truman received the nomination.

Democrats were fighting against more than Republicans in 1948. After his dismissal from the cabinet, Henry Wallace decided to run for president on a third-party ticket. Wallace's Progressive party advocated friendship and negotiation with the Soviet Union and condemned the Truman Doctrine as a "global Monroe Doctrine." Wallace also argued for desegregation and for the nationalization of oil companies, railroads, and other basic industries. Experts predicted that the Progressives would poll at least 5 million and perhaps as many as 8 million votes, thus dashing the Democratic party's hopes for victory. To complicate matters, a fourth party, the Dixiecrats (States Rights Democratic party), nominated Governor Strom Thurmond of South Carolina. The Dixiecrats had bolted the Democratic party when the 1948 national convention adopted a pro–civil rights plank; waving Confederate flags, they had won control of the Democratic party in four southern states. If Wallace's candidacy did not destroy Truman's chances, experts said, the Dixiecrats certainly would.

But Truman had ideas of his own. He called the Eightieth Congress into special session and demanded that it enact all the planks in the Republican platform. If Republicans really wanted to transform their ideals into law, said Truman, this was the time to do it. After Congress had met for two weeks and accomplished nothing of significance, Truman took to the road. Traveling more than 30,000 miles by train, he delivered scores of whistle-stop speeches denouncing the "do-nothing" Eightieth Congress. Still, no amount of furious campaigning on Truman's part seemed likely to change the predicted outcome. Hours before the returns were in, the *Chicago Tribune* had printed a headline announcing "DEWEY DEFEATS TRUMAN."

Yet as the votes were counted early into the morning, it became clear that Truman had confounded the experts. The final tally was 24.1 million popular votes, 304 electoral votes, for Truman; 21.9 million popular votes, 189 electoral votes, for Dewey (see map, page 838). Not only had Truman won four more years in the White House, but the Democrats had regained control of Congress—in the House by a majority of ninety-three, in the Senate by twelve.

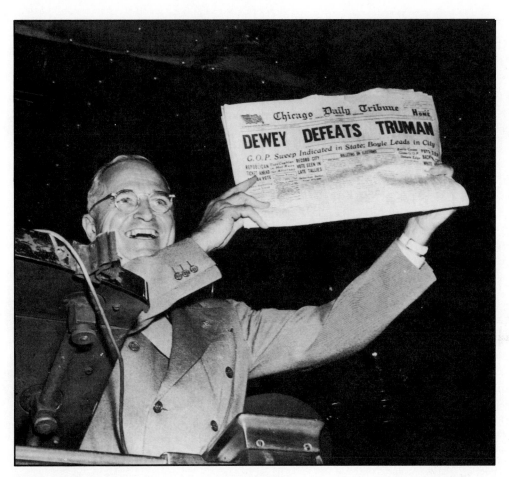

So few pollsters predicted that President Harry S Truman (1884–1972) would win in 1948 that the Chicago Tribune announced his defeat before all the returns were in. Here a victorious Truman pokes fun at the newspaper for its premature headline.   UPI.

How and why had the upset occurred? First, no matter how troubled Truman's presidency had been, the United States was prosperous, at peace, and essentially united on foreign policy. Moreover, the Roosevelt legacy—the New Deal coalition—had endured; the big cities, Afro-Americans, and labor unions had rallied to Truman's support. Many Jewish and Catholic voters also supported Truman, as did voters of Eastern European ancestry who approved of his hard line toward the Soviet Union. Ironically, the Progressive and Dixiecrat parties helped him, for their extremist images made the Democratic party look moderate by comparison. The Democrats, for their part, did not hesitate to distort the facts by denouncing

the Progressives as a pack of Communists. Truman himself was adept at redbaiting; he once declared, "I do not want . . . the political support of Henry Wallace and his Communists." Rather than the predicted 5 million votes apiece, Wallace and Thurmond polled just a little over 1 million each.

There were still other reasons for Truman's victory. Some formidable Democrats also ran for offices that year—Adlai E. Stevenson, Hubert H. Humphrey—and their presence on the ticket helped Truman. Without doubt, too, Dewey's smug campaign did not stand up well to Truman's aggressive effort. But in the end it was the farmers whose votes made the difference. Truman advocated continued high price

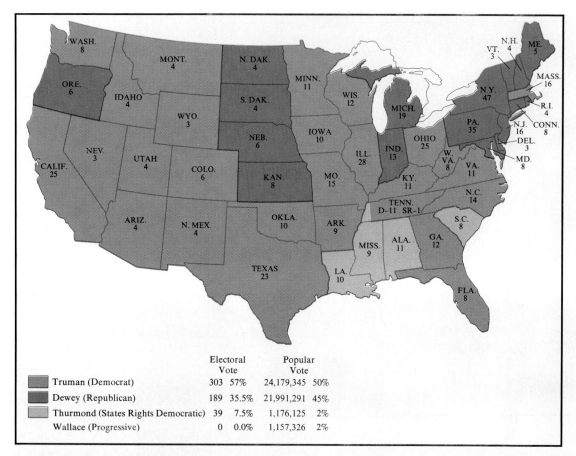

	Electoral Vote		Popular Vote	
Truman (Democrat)	303	57%	24,179,345	50%
Dewey (Republican)	189	35.5%	21,991,291	45%
Thurmond (States Rights Democratic)	39	7.5%	1,176,125	2%
Wallace (Progressive)	0	0.0%	1,157,326	2%

Presidential Election, 1948

supports for farmers; Republicans wanted to decrease supports. In the bumper-crop year of 1948, Republicans actually wanted to cut back on grain storage. As the harvest mounted, prices began to fall; corn dropped from $1.78 a bushel in September to $1.38 in mid-October. Ever ready, Truman told farmers that the Eightieth Congress had "stuck a pitchfork in the farmer's back." Practically all the midwestern and border states went for Truman.

Truman entered his new term brimming with confidence. He believed that it was time for government to fulfill its responsibility to provide economic security for the poor and the elderly. As he worked on his 1949 State of the Union message, he penciled in an expression of his intentions: "I expect to give every segment of our population a fair deal." Little did Truman know that he had selected the label that historians would hereafter associate with his presidency: Fair Deal.

TRUMAN ON CIVIL RIGHTS

The postwar years were a period of gathering strength for Afro-Americans. Truman and other politicians knew they would have to compete for the growing black vote in urban-industrial states like California, Illinois, Michigan, Ohio, Pennsylvania, and New York. Many Republicans now cultivated the black vote. Thomas Dewey, who as governor of New York had pushed successfully for the establishment of a fair employment practices commission, was particularly popular with blacks. In Harlem, which had gone Democratic by a 4-to-1 margin in 1938, Dewey won by large margins in 1942 and 1946.

Certainly, then, Truman had political reasons for supporting black civil rights. But he also felt a moral obligation to blacks. For one thing, he believed that it was only fair that each American, regardless of race, should enjoy the full rights of citizenship. More than that, Truman was disturbed by the resurgence of racial terrorism. The Ku Klux Klan had taken to the road again, burning crosses and murdering blacks who had had the audacity to vote. Senator Theodore G. Bilbo of Mississippi had exhorted every "red-blooded Anglo-Saxon man in Mississippi to resort to any means to keep . . . Negroes from the polls," and Eugene Talmadge had won the governorship of Georgia with the promise that "no Negro will vote in Georgia for the next four years." But what really horrified Truman was the report that police in Aiken, South Carolina, had gouged out the eyes of a black sergeant just three hours after he had been discharged from the army. Several weeks later, on December 5, 1946, Truman signed an executive order establishing the President's Committee on Civil Rights.

A year later the committee delivered its report, *To Secure These Rights.* Among the committee's recommendations, which would become the agenda for the civil rights movement for the next twenty years, were the enactment of federal antilynching, antisegregation, antibrutality, and anti-poll-tax laws. *To Secure These Rights* also called for laws guaranteeing voting rights and equal employment opportunity, and for the establishment of a permanent commission on civil rights and a civil rights division within the Department of Justice. In February 1948 Truman sent a special message to Congress. The protection of citizens' rights, Truman said, was "the duty of every government which derives its powers from the consent of the governed." Congress made no formal response. Some southerners told Truman that with such a civil rights program, "You won't be elected dogcatcher in 1948." There is evidence that the president did not expect congressional action, and that his real goal was the black vote in 1948. But whatever his motive, this was the first time since Reconstruction that a president had acknowledged the federal government's responsibility to protect Afro-Americans.

Truman also used the power of the executive to proclaim a policy of "fair employment throughout the federal establishment," and he created the Employment Board of the Civil Service Commission to

President's Committee on Civil Rights

hear charges of discrimination. His Committee on Equality of Treatment and Opportunity in the Armed Services issued a report, *Freedom to Serve,* in 1950 stating that racial desegregation would "make for a better Army, Navy, and Air Force." Though strong, at times even fierce, opposition to desegregation existed within the military, by the outbreak of the Korean War segregated units were being phased out.

Blacks also benefited from a series of Supreme Court decisions. The trend toward judicial support of civil rights had begun in the late 1930s, when the NAACP established its Legal Defense Fund led by Thurgood Marshall, who in 1967 became the first black Supreme Court justice. Marshall and his staff were trying to destroy the separate-but-equal doctrine established in *Plessy* v. *Ferguson* (1896) by insisting on its literal interpretation. In higher education, the NAACP figured, the cost of racially separate schools was prohibitive. "You can't build a cyclotron for one [black] student," the president of the University of Oklahoma acknowledged. As a result, in the 1940s black students won admission to professional and graduate schools at a number of state universities. The NAACP also scored notable victories in two other cases. In 1944, in *Smith* v. *Allwright*, the Supreme Court outlawed the whites-only primaries held by the Democratic party in some southern states, branding them a violation of the Fifteenth Amendment. Two years later the Court declared segregation in interstate bus transportation unconstitutional (*Morgan* v. *Virginia*).

In 1947 the Department of Justice began to submit friend-of-the-court briefs on behalf of the civil rights movement, most notably in cases involving higher education and restrictive covenants, which were private agreements among white homeowners not to sell to blacks. In the *Thompson Restaurant* case, a Justice Department brief helped to bring about the desegregation of restaurants and eventually hotels in the District of Columbia. But most important was the attorney general's brief supporting the NAACP's effort to desegregate the nation's public schools. Although the Supreme Court did not decide the landmark *Brown* v. *Board of Education of Topeka* until 1954, the Truman administration's legal efforts helped overturn the separate-but-equal doctrine that had been the law of the land since *Plessy* v. *Ferguson* (see page 475).

Supreme Court Decisions on Civil Rights

Jackie Robinson cracked the color line in major league baseball when he joined the Brooklyn Dodgers for the 1947 season. Robinson won rookie-of-the-year honors and was later elected to the Baseball Hall of Fame. In this game against the Philadelphia Phillies, Robinson stole home. Wide World Photos.

A change in social attitudes accompanied these gains in black political and legal power. Books such as Gunnar Myrdal's *An American Dilemma* (1944) and Richard Wright's *Native Son* (1940) and *Black Boy* (1945) had increased white awareness of the social injustice that plagued blacks. A new black middle class had emerged, composed of college-educated activists, veterans, and union workers. Blacks and whites were working together in CIO unions and with service organizations such as the National Council of Churches, the Anti-Defamation League, the National Urban League, and the American Friends Service Committee. And in 1947 a black baseball player, Jackie Robinson, cracked the major-league color barrier and electrified crowds with his spectacular hitting and base running.

Cold War pressures also benefited blacks. As the Soviet Union was quick to point out, the United States could not pose as the leader of the free world, or condemn the denial of human rights behind the Iron Curtain, so long as it condoned racism at home. Nor could it convince new African and Asian nations of its dedication to human rights if Afro-Americans were subjected to segregation, disfranchisement, and racial violence. To win the support of nonaligned nations, the United States would have to live up to its own ideals. That the nation was not doing so was evident. Segregation was still an accepted practice in the 1950s, even if it was no longer the law of the land. Blacks continued to suffer job discrimination and disfranchisement. Nevertheless, in the ten years following the Second World War, Afro-Americans had made considerable progress, more than in any period since Reconstruction.

MCCARTHYISM

A common misconception about the postwar era is that anti-Communist hysteria began in 1950 with the furious speeches of Senator Joseph R. McCarthy. Actually, anti-Communism had been part of the American political temper ever since the First

World War and the Red Scare of 1919 and 1920. The Cold War heightened anti-Communist fears at home, and by 1950 they reached hysterical proportions. McCarthy did not create this hysteria; he manipulated it to his own advantage. He was, though, undeniably the most successful and frightening redbaiter the country had ever seen.

What reason was there to fear Communist influence in the 1940s and 1950s? The party had never been strong, even during the hard times of the depression. When news of the trial and execution of large numbers of anti-Stalinists in the Soviet Union reached America in 1937 and 1938, followed shortly by the signing of the Nazi-Soviet Pact in August 1939, the party had quickly lost much of its following. With the German invasion of Russia in summer 1941, however, American attitudes toward the Soviet Union became more favorable. Suddenly the United States and Russia were allies in the war against Hitler.

Communist Party Membership

At the same time anti-Communism persisted in the United States. In 1940 Congress enacted the Alien Registration, or Smith, Act, which made it unlawful to advocate the overthrow of the U.S. government by force or violence or to join any organization that did so. And politicians began playing on anti-Communist paranoia again. In the 1944 presidential campaign Dewey warned that the Democratic party was about to be captured by the Communists.

Then in March 1945 an incident occurred that tended to confirm anti-Communists' worst fears. In a raid on the offices of *Amerasia,* a little-known magazine whose editors sympathized with the Chinese Communists, the Office of Strategic Services confiscated classified government documents. Who had supplied the documents to the magazine, and why? people asked. Concern was also mounting north of the Canadian border, where in 1946 a royal commission issued a report claiming that Soviet spies were operating in Canada. Among them, the report said, were a member of Parliament and a scientist who had transmitted atomic secrets to a Soviet agent.

Spurred by these revelations, Truman in March 1947 ordered investigations into the loyalty of the more than 3 million employees of the U.S. government. In 1950 the government began discharging people deemed "security risks," among them alcoholics,

Truman's Loyalty Probe

homosexuals, and debtors thought to be susceptible to blackmail. In most cases there was no question of these people's loyalty. Without the right to confront their accusers and demand evidence, however, many were ruined for life. Still others became victims of guilt by association—they knew people considered to be subversive, disloyal, or dangerous.

The wellspring of this fear of Communism was, of course, the Cold War. Fear of internal subversion was intertwined with fear of external attack. It was no coincidence that Truman ordered the loyalty probe the same week he appeared before a joint session of Congress to announce his containment policy (see pages 820, 826–827). His alarmist rhetoric only heightened public anxiety.

Truman was not alone in peddling fear; conservatives and liberal Democrats joined him. Republicans used the same technique to attack the Democratic candidates for president in 1948 and 1952; liberal Democrats used it to discredit the far-left, pro-Wallace wing of their party. In many ways, then, the anti-Communist hysteria of the late 1940s was a phenomenon created by professional politicians and promoted by labor union officials, religious leaders, Hollywood moguls, and other influential figures.

People began to point accusing fingers at each other. "Reds, phonies, and 'parlor pinks,' " in Truman's words, seemed to lurk everywhere. Hollywood film personalities who had been ardent left-wingers were blacklisted; some writers and directors were sentenced to prison for contempt of Congress when they refused to answer questions and name names. Schoolteachers and college professors were fired for expressing dissenting viewpoints, and in some communities "pro-Communist" books were removed from school libraries. In labor-union elections and in struggles to dominate local parent-teacher associations, redbaiting became a convenient tactic for discrediting the opposition. The hysteria was particularly damaging to the labor movement, which forsook its class-conscious militancy in favor of patriotism and anti-Communism. In the United Auto Workers, Walter Reuther used redbaiting to destroy his opposition and win the union's presidency. Union bulletin boards that had once bristled with strike notices and photographs of police clubbing strikers were now adorned with such slogans as "UAW Americanism for Us." At its 1949 convention, the

CIO expelled eleven unions with a combined membership of over 1 million for alleged Communist domination. And all this occurred at a time when membership in the Communist party was rapidly declining, from a high of about 83,000 in 1947 to 55,000 in 1950 and 25,000 in 1954.

Despite the false accusations, there was cause for alarm—especially in 1949, which dramatist Arthur Miller called "the year it came apart." Throughout

Hiss Trial

that year a former State Department official, Alger Hiss, was on trial for perjury for denying in congressional testimony that he had passed to the Russians "numerous secret, confidential and restricted documents." When Truman and Secretary of State Dean Acheson came to his defense, charging that the Republicans were publicizing the case to divert attention from their own failures, some people began to suspect the worst. The Democrats, they decided, had something to hide. Republican Congressman Richard M. Nixon of California, a member of the House Committee on Un-American Activities, which had led the investigation of the Hiss case, harped constantly on that theme. Then in September two events shoved the Hiss trial off the front page. The Russians exploded their first atomic bomb, and the Chinese Communists, finally victorious in the civil war, proclaimed the People's Republic of China (see page 831). A howl of indignation arose from the China lobby; Truman and Acheson were now on the defensive.

The dawn of a new decade brought no end to the hysteria; indeed, 1950 saw more disquieting news. Hiss was convicted. Scotland Yard arrested Klaus Fuchs, a nuclear scientist, for turning over to Soviet agents secrets from the atomic-bomb project at Los Alamos, New Mexico. And President Truman announced that in response to the Russian atomic bomb, the United States would embark on a crash project to develop a hydrogen bomb. "How much more are we going to have to take?" wailed one right-wing Republican. "Fuchs and Acheson and Hiss and hydrogen bombs threatening outside and New Dealism eating away at the vitals of the nation. In the name of Heaven, is this the best America can do?" The ingredients of the situation were ripe for a demagogue: an irrational blurring of enemies; simplistic conspiracy theories; awareness that the Second World War had not ended the threat of war, but brought a new threat of nuclear holocaust. It was in this atmosphere that on February 9, 1950, Senator Joseph McCarthy mounted a rostrum in Wheeling, West Virginia, and gave a name to the hysteria: McCarthyism.

That day in Wheeling, McCarthy proclaimed, "The reason we find ourselves in a position of impotency is . . . because of the traitorous actions of those who

McCarthy's Attack on the State Department

have been treated so well by this nation." The State Department, he asserted, was "thoroughly infested with Communists," and the most dangerous person in the State Department was Dean Acheson. Reporters wrote that the senator claimed to have a list of 205 Communists working in the State Department; later McCarthy lowered the figure to "57 card-carrying members," then raised it to 81. No matter the number. What McCarthy needed was a winning campaign issue, and he had found it. Republicans, distraught over losing what had appeared to be a sure victory in 1948, were eager to support his attack. Here was a chance to discredit both Roosevelt's New Deal and Truman's Fair Deal. "A generation was on trial," wrote journalist Alistair Cooke.

McCarthy and McCarthyism gained momentum throughout 1950. Nothing seemed to slow the senator down, not even attacks by other Republicans. Seven Republican senators broke with their colleagues and publicly condemned McCarthy for his "selfish political exploitation of fear, bigotry, ignorance, and intolerance." A Senate committee reported that his charges against the State Department were "a fraud and a hoax." But McCarthy had much to sustain him, including Julius and Ethel Rosenberg's 1950 arrest for espionage; they allegedly had recruited and supervised a spy at the Los Alamos atomic laboratory.

The widespread support for anti-Communist measures was also apparent in the adoption, over Truman's veto, of the Internal Security, or McCarran, Act of 1950. The act made it unlawful for anyone to "contribute to the establishment . . . of a totalitarian dictatorship," required members of "Communist-front" organizations to register with the government, and prohibited such people from holding defense jobs or traveling abroad. And in a telling decision in 1951 (*Dennis et al.* v. *U.S.*), the Supreme Court upheld the Smith Act, under which eleven Communist leaders had been convicted and imprisoned.

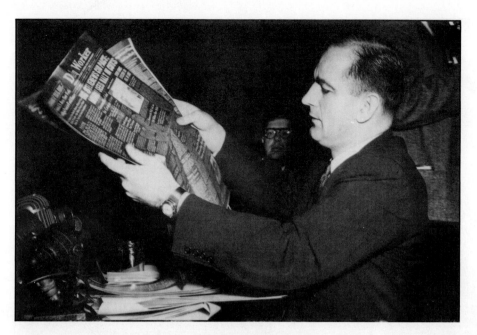

Senator Joseph R. McCarthy gave his name to the anti-Communist hysteria that infected many people. Testifying in March 1950, he waved a copy of the Daily Worker *published by the Communist Party. National Archives.*

Meanwhile, McCarthy continued to display his unparalleled talent for demagoguery, making unsubstantiated charges, implying guilt by association, interpreting writings out of context, and telling outright lies. "It would seem easy to pin down the preposterous utterances," a reporter covering the Senate observed. "But no; McCarthy is as hard to catch as a mist—a mist that carries lethal contagion." And there is no doubt that the outbreak of the Korean War in June 1950 made McCarthyism even more virulent than before.

THE KOREAN WAR AND ITS GLOBAL CONSEQUENCES

In the early morning hours of June 25, 1950, thousands of troops under the banner of the Democratic People's Republic of Korea (North Korea) moved across the 38th parallel into the Republic of Korea (South Korea). They "struck like a cobra," recalled General Douglas MacArthur. For years the two Koreas had skirmished along the border the great powers had drawn for them in 1945. Both regimes sought reunification of the divided country, but each on its own terms. Now it appeared that the North Koreans, heavily armed by the Russians, would realize their goal by force, for the South Koreans, armed by the Americans, soon disintegrated. When the news reached Washington, D.C., people recalled Pearl Harbor and braced themselves for a third world war.

For the thirty-third president, it was the 1930s all over again. "Communism was acting in Korea just as Hitler, Mussolini, and the Japanese had acted," Truman recalled. After huddling with his advisers, the president decided to intervene; he ordered MacArthur to send arms to South Korea and to attack North Korean forces from the air. Thinking beyond Korea, he directed the Seventh Fleet to patrol the waters between the Chinese mainland and Jiang's sanctuary, Formosa, thus inserting the United States once again into Chinese politics. Finally, on June 30, Truman ordered American troops into battle. "If Washington only will not hobble me," boasted

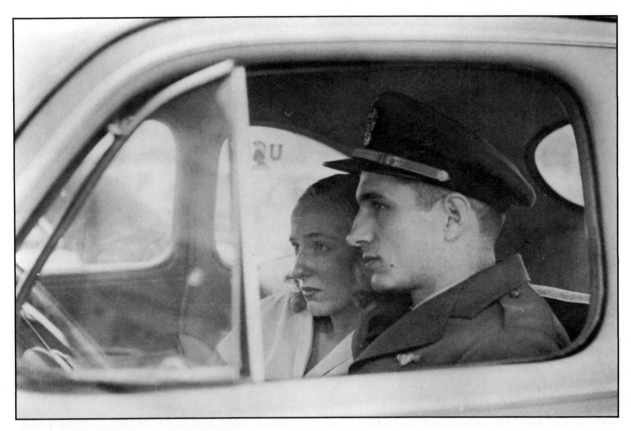

In 1950, after only five years of peace, the United States intervened in a war in Korea. In San Diego this officer and his wife stare at a waiting aircraft carrier before he departs for Korea. National Archives.

MacArthur, "I can handle it with one arm tied behind my back." After the Security Council, in the Soviet delegate's absence, voted to assist South Korea, MacArthur became United Nations Commander.

Truman acted decisively for war because he believed, in the Cold War mentality of the time, that the Soviets had masterminded the North Korean attack.

Origins of the Korean War

As an assistant secretary of state put it, the relationship between the Soviet Union and North Korea was "the same as that between Walt Disney and Donald Duck." Though there is little evidence that the Soviets began the Korean War, at the time there was reason to believe that the Soviets were exploiting an opportunity to expand their influence. When most American troops withdrew from Korea in mid-1949, the Joint Chiefs of Staff had secretly declared South Korea nonvital to American security. And in a public speech in January 1950, Secretary Acheson had drawn the American defense line in Asia through the Aleutians, Japan, and Okinawa to the Philippines. Although Formosa and Korea were clearly beyond that line, Acheson did say that those areas could expect United Nations (and hence American) assistance in the event of attack. Still, Stalin might have read Acheson's speech as an abandonment of South Korea. Russia may also have been willing to risk war to challenge China for leadership of the Communist world or to disrupt American peace negotiations with its long-time rival Japan.

But unanswered questions dog the thesis that Russia started the Korean War. The Soviet delegate was absent from the Security Council when it voted to aid South Korea because he was protesting the United Nations' refusal to seat the People's Republic of China. If the Soviets had fomented the war in Korea, it is surprising that their delegate was not present to veto aid to South Korea. Were they caught off-guard? And other questions are puzzling. Why did the Soviets give so little aid to the North Koreans once the war broke out? And why, when they were scoring important propaganda points by advocating peaceful coexistence, would they destroy their gains by igniting a war? Some scholars believe that the North Koreans began the war, for their own nationalistic reasons. To suggest this is to emphasize the *Korean* rather than international origins of the conflict—to focus on the civil war between the North Korean Communists led by Kim Il-sung and the South Korean government ruled by Syngman Rhee.

In June 1950 such questions were not being asked. Truman and his aides never doubted that Russia or international Communism was testing their policy of containment; that American prestige was at stake; and that failure to act in Korea would prompt Russian aggression in Iran or Berlin. And having bragged about toughness against Communism before, Truman could not now refrain from acting against North Korea.

At first the war (Truman called it a "police action") went badly. The North Koreans, utilizing tanks and superior firepower, sent the South Korean army into chaotic retreat. The first American troops sent into battle tried to buy time for General MacArthur's effort to amass larger forces. Taking heavy casualties, American soldiers slowed but could not stop the North Korean advance. Within weeks the South Koreans and Americans found themselves pushed into the tiny Pusan perimeter at the base of South Korea. There they dug in.

MacArthur began to plan a daring operation: an amphibious landing at Inchon, several hundred miles behind North Korean lines (see map). Inchon seemed an inhospitable place for such an **Inchon** attack, with high tides, narrow approach channels, mud flats, and heavy enemy fortifications. The Joint Chiefs of Staff balked, but MacArthur insisted. After American naval guns and bombs pounded Inchon, U.S. Marines sprinted ashore on September 15, 1950. By nightfall, 18,000 American troops were inland, ready with tanks and vehicles to move against the South Korean capital of Seoul. Soon they had liberated Seoul and pushed the North Koreans back to the 38th parallel. Even

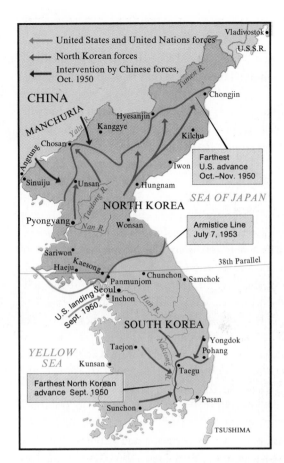

The Korean War, 1950–1953 *Source: By permission of the publisher, from* American Foreign Policy: A History *by Paterson et al., p. 378. (Lexington, Mass.: D.C. Heath and Company, 1977).*

before Inchon, Truman had decided to redefine the American war goal from the containment of North Korea to the reunification of Korea by force. Communism would not only be stopped; it would be rolled back. On September 27 Truman authorized United Nations forces (90 percent of them American) to cross the 38th parallel.

Within several weeks American troops had driven deeply into North Korea. In early November American aircraft began strikes against bridges on the Yalu River, the border between North Korea and the People's Republic of China. The Chinese watched warily, wondering if the Americans who had supported Jiang Jieshi would soon stab at the People's Republic. Mao issued public warnings that China could not permit the continued bombing of its transportation links with Korea or the annihilation of North Korea itself. MacArthur shrugged off the warnings, telling Truman that the Chinese would face the "greatest slaughter" if they entered the war. Officials in Washington agreed.

Chinese Entry into the Korean War
But they were dead wrong. In late October Americans had tangled with some Chinese soldiers, who pulled back quickly after the encounter. This may have been one of many signals to the United States that American advances to the Chinese border should halt, or China would enter the war. A month later an unmoved MacArthur sent his Eighth Army northward in a new offensive. On November 26, tens of thousands of Chinese troops counterattacked, surprising the general's forces and driving them pell-mell southward. Embarrassed, MacArthur demanded that Washington order a massive air attack on China. Truman hesitated, reflecting on the costs and consequences of a wider war. He hinted that he might use the atomic bomb, but he seemed chastened, uneager for a war that might drag on for years.

By March 1951 the military lines had stabilized around the 38th parallel. Truman contemplated negotiations, and the Soviets stated publicly that they favored a political settlement. But MacArthur had other ideas. The theatrical general was making reckless public statements, calling for an attack on China or for Jiang's return to the mainland. Now was the time, he insisted, to smash Communism by destroying its Asian flank. MacArthur also hinted that the president was practicing appeasement. Denouncing the concept of limited war (war without nuclear weapons, confined to one place), he told one member of Congress: "There is no substitute for victory."

Truman Fires MacArthur
On April 10 Truman fired the general for insubordination. MacArthur, who had not set foot in the United States for over a decade, returned home to a ticker-tape parade, and made a televised address to Congress that moved many in the audience to tears. One congressman was so spellbound that he murmured, "We saw a great hunk of God in the flesh."

Although Truman's popularity sagged, he withstood calls for his impeachment. The chairman of the Joint Chiefs of Staff, General Omar Bradley, spoke against MacArthur's provocative ideas. Escalation could bring Russia into battle, Bradley pointed out—American

bombs had already fallen close to the Siberian port of Vladivostok. And it was unwise to exhaust America's resources in an Asian war that promised no victory when there were allies in Europe to be protected. Indeed, a showdown with Asian Communists, Bradley told a Senate committee, would be "the wrong war, at the wrong place, at the wrong time, and with the wrong enemy." MacArthur had overestimated his popularity and soon faded from the public eye.

Armistice talks began in July 1951, but the fighting and dying went on for two more years. Though the new president, Dwight D. Eisenhower, went to Korea personally in December 1952 to fulfill a campaign pledge, his post-election visit brought no settlement.

The POW Question
Once he became president, Eisenhower let it be known privately that he was considering using atomic weapons in Korea. He hoped the Chinese would be frightened into an agreement. The sticking point in the negotiations was the fate of the prisoners of war (POWs): thousands of North Korean and Chinese captives did not want to return home. In violation of international custom, American officials honored their wishes and refused to ship them back against their will. The price for this position proved high: an extended war and 32,000 more American casualties. On July 23, 1953, an armistice was finally signed. The combatants agreed to hand the POW question over to a special panel of neutral nations (which later gave prisoners their choice of staying or leaving). The North Korean–South Korean line was set close to the 38th parallel, the prewar boundary. Thus ended a frustrating war—a limited war that Americans, accustomed to victory, had not won. No celebrations greeted news of the end of the war. The experience was indeed sobering, as was the casualty list of 34,000 Americans dead and 103,000 wounded. Total killed and wounded for all combatants in the Korean War was 1.9 million.

The Korean War had major political consequences. The failure to achieve victory and the public's impatience with a limited war undoubtedly helped to elect Eisenhower (see pages 847–849). Bipartisanship in foreign policy eroded further, and the powers of the presidency grew as Congress deferred to Truman time and again. Truman had never gone to Congress for a declaration of war, for he believed that as commander-in-chief he had the authority to send troops to Korea. A few dissenters like Senator Robert Taft disagreed, but Truman saw no need to debate the matter. Had he asked for a declaration, he would have had majorities in both houses. But as Dean Acheson later explained, Truman did not wish to invite hearings and "ponderous questions" that might have "muddled up" presidential decisions.

The Korean War also set off a great national debate. Conservative critics of globalism, like Taft, former ambassador to England Joseph P. Kennedy, and ex-president Herbert Hoover, suggested

Debate over Globalist Policy that America should reduce its overseas commitments and draw its defense line in the Western Hemisphere. If foreign nations were not willing to commit their own resources to defending themselves, the United States had no obligation to help them, they reasoned. But Republican John Foster Dulles countered that "a defense that accepts encirclement quickly decomposes." Truman himself joined the debate with bloated rhetoric exaggerating the Communist threat: "We are fighting in Korea so we won't have to fight in Wichita, or in Chicago, or in New Orleans, or on San Francisco Bay."

The advocates of global defense won the debate. Increased aid flowed to the French for their die-hard stand in Indochina; by 1954, when the French effort finally collapsed, the United States was paying three-quarters of the war's cost (see Chapter 32). South Korea and Formosa also became major recipients of American foreign aid. And Australia and New Zealand joined the United States in a mutual defense agreement, the ANZUS Treaty (1951), which provided that an attack on any of the three countries would be considered an attack on all.

The Korean War, Acheson noted happily, removed "the recommendations of NSC-68 from the realm of theory and made them immediate budget issues." Indeed, the military budget shot up to $44 billion in 1953 (it had been $14 billion in 1949) and remained at $35 to $44 billion a year throughout the 1950s. The American military acquired new bases in Morocco (1951) and Spain (1953), among other places; developed the hydrogen bomb; and introduced a new long-range bomber, the B-52. The army sent six divisions to Europe, and the administration initiated plans to rearm West Germany. Proponents claimed that the logic of the containment doctrine required

this global military watch, for if the threat was worldwide, the response had to be worldwide as well. "If you don't pay attention to the periphery," diplomat Dean Rusk warned, "the periphery changes. And the first thing you know the periphery is the center."

But the periphery did not in fact always become the center. Some areas were vital and others were not. Nor did a global watch ensure security. One member of Congress compared containment to "sending three policemen to surround a building that has 25 exits." And as Walter Lippmann had warned, blind allegiance to the containment doctrine did lead to repeated overseas ventures and alliances with questionable clients and dictators. Officials also assumed wrongly that threats to world peace always sprang from international Communist intrigue. They overlooked the local, non-Communist roots of many rebellions against the status quo, and they underestimated the independence of non-Russian Communists. In the future, Americans would struggle in a revolutionary world where nationalism rather than Communism was the driving force in international affairs—a force that would be subordinated neither to the United States nor to the Soviet Union.

WARTIME DISCONTENT AND THE ELECTION OF 1952

As Senator Joseph McCarthy raged on and Americans mobilized for the war in Korea, they remembered shortages in the last war and flocked

Korean War on the Home Front to their grocery stores for sugar, shortening, razor blades, and canned goods. And fearing that Detroit would have to convert to the manufacture of military vehicles, Americans bought cars in a hurry. Orders for military supplies flooded factories. Ford built engines for B-36 bombers; the American Locomotive Company contracted for medium-size tanks; other companies filled requests for boots, sandbags, bandages, and jackets. By the end of 1950 U.S. Steel was enjoying its greatest profits since 1917.

Fueled by panic buying and these huge federal expenditures, inflation, which had not been a problem since 1948, began to eat away at the economy again: prices rose 8 percent in the first eight months of the war. In January 1951, after six months of inflation, the government froze wages and prices. Although administering the controls proved to be a nightmare—especially after Truman's unconstitutional seizure of the steel industry in 1952, when it rejected a government-recommended wage increase—inflation had been brought under control by mid-1951. Meanwhile, factories hummed, the gross national product grew, disposable personal income increased, and unemployment fell. Reform-minded Democrats were not altogether pleased, however, for defense mobilization was taking precedence over Fair Deal programs. "Every liberal movement has been stopped cold at the time of national emergency," groaned Senator Hubert Humphrey.

Draft boards registered men between the ages of eighteen and twenty-five and began to call them up. National Guardsmen and reservists were elevated to active duty. There was no rush to join. "Everybody wants out; no one wants in," complained the director of the draft. Husbands and fathers thought single men should go first; parents wrote protest letters when in 1951 the military began to draft eighteen-and-a-half-year-olds. When the government announced that college students would be granted deferments, young people enrolled in universities. Other students hoped that the war would end before their graduation. But the war did not end quickly, and by mid-1952 American military personnel numbered 3.6 million, up from 1.5 million two years earlier.

As the 1952 presidential election approached, the Democrats foundered. Added to frustration with the war and hysteria over Communism was the revelation of influence-peddling by some of Truman's cronies. Known as "five-percenters," these presidential appointees had offered government contracts in return for 5-percent kickbacks. In exchange for help in expediting the importation of perfume ingredients, Truman's military aide and friend Major General Harry Vaughn had accepted a freezer. An employee of the executive branch admitted under oath, "I have only one thing to sell and that is influence." In 1951 Truman's public-approval rating slumped to an all-time low of 23 percent and hovered at that level for

the next year. Once again the Democratic party seemed doomed along with its leader—only this time the prediction was correct. Voters agreed with the 1952 Republican campaign slogan, "It's Time for a Change."

What sealed the fate of the Democratic party was the Republican candidate, General Dwight D. Eisenhower, who had changed his mind about the appropriateness of a military man running for office. "Ike" was a bona fide war hero with a winning smile, a man who seemed to embody the virtues Americans most admired: integrity, decency, lack of pretense, and the ability to rise from humble beginnings. His running mate, Senator Richard M. Nixon, was less likable. Accused during the campaign of having been the beneficiary of a secret slush fund raised by wealthy Californians, Nixon went on television to deny the charge. The only gift his family had received, he explained, was a puppy named Checkers. His daughters loved the little dog, and "we're gonna keep it."

The Republican Ticket

Eisenhower's unlucky Democratic opponent was Adlai Stevenson, the thoughtful, literate, and witty governor of Illinois. From the outset it was never much of a contest. Eisenhower promised to end the Korean War, and though he remained cautiously silent on the subject of McCarthyism, his running mate did not. Nixon scored political points by referring to Stevenson as "Adlai the appeaser . . . who got a Ph.D. from Dean Acheson's College of Cowardly Communist Containment." The result was a landslide: Eisenhower won almost 34 million popular votes and 442 electoral votes, compared with the Democrats' 27 million popular and 89 electoral votes.

Dwight D. Eisenhower's 1952 presidential election victory was a great personal triumph. Several issues, including the Korean War, stirred the voters. By election day, armistice negotiations in Korea had been dragging on for almost one and a half years. There was still sporadic and heavy fighting, and Eisenhower had promised to visit Korea and end the war. Americans were also upset by White House corruption and alleged Communism in the State Department. All these factors coalesced to produce a record turnout of 61.5 million voters, 13 million more than in 1948. Many wanted to express their enthusiasm for Eisenhower, war hero and trusted statesman, who won the votes of Americans from a

IMPORTANT EVENTS

1945	Yalta Conference
	Roosevelt dies; Truman assumes presidency
	United Nations founded
	Germany surrenders
	Potsdam Conference
	Atomic bombs devastate Hiroshima and Nagasaki
	Japan surrenders
	Truman's 21-point economic message to Congress

1946	Crisis over Iran
	Employment Act of 1946
	Churchill's Iron Curtain speech
	Strikes by coal miners
	Paris Peace Conference
	Baruch Plan
	Truman fires Secretary of Commerce Wallace
	Inflation reaches 18.2 percent
	Republicans win both houses of Congress

1947	Truman Doctrine
	Truman's Employee Loyalty Program
	Communist takeover in Hungary
	Taft-Hartley Act
	Kennan's "Mr. X" article
	Marshall Plan announced
	To Secure These Rights
	National Security Act
	Rio Pact

1948	Communist coup in Czechoslovakia
	State of Israel founded
	Berlin blockade and airlift
	Truman elected president

1949	North Atlantic Treaty Organization founded
	Russia explodes atomic bomb
	Communist victory in China

1950	Klaus Fuchs arrested as atomic spy
	Alger Hiss convicted of perjury
	Hydrogen bomb project announced
	McCarthy alleges Communists in government
	Freedom to Serve
	NSC-68
	Point Four Program launched
	Korean War begins
	Julius and Ethel Rosenberg arrested
	Inchon
	Internal Security (McCarran) Act
	U.S. troops cross the 38th parallel
	China enters the Korean War

| 1951 | Armistice talks begin in Korea |
| | *Dennis et al. v. U.S.* |

1952	Hydrogen bomb exploded
	Eisenhower elected president
	Republicans win both houses of Congress

| 1953 | Korean War ends |

diversity of socioeconomic groups, educational levels, and religious faiths. He even captured four states in the once-solid Democratic South. Moreover, Eisenhower's coattails were long enough to carry other Republicans to victory; the party gained control of both houses of Congress, though with only a one-seat margin in the Senate (forty-eight Republicans, forty-seven Democrats, one Independent).

Although Truman was highly unpopular when he left office in 1953, historians now rate him among the nation's ten best presidents. He came to office

Truman's Presidential Legacy

suddenly and with little experience, but in eight years he greatly strengthened the powers of the presidency. At the onset of the Cold War he had announced policies to contain any presumed threat of Soviet expansion. During his presidency the Central Intelligence Agency,

National Security Council, Council of Economic Advisers, and a unified Department of Defense were all created. Truman's main problems stemmed from his overreaction to the alleged threat of Communist subversion in government. His loyalty program ruined innocent people's lives and careers. In drumming up support for his foreign and military policies, Truman presented a frightening picture to the American people of the Communists' aims and with his rhetoric he helped prepare the way for McCarthyism. Finally, he sent American troops to fight in Korea without a declaration of war from Congress.

At the same time, Truman was still a New Dealer who fought for social welfare programs and legislation for farmers and workers. His Fair Deal, most of which was enacted during subsequent presidential administrations, included first-class citizenship for Afro-Americans. He showed his spunk and courage in 1948, when he pulled the biggest upset in American political history. When he left office in 1953, he had set the United States on a course from which it would not veer in the future and had cast a long shadow across the country's twentieth-century history.

SUGGESTIONS FOR FURTHER READING

Origins of the Cold War and Policy Toward Europe

Stephen Ambrose, *Rise to Globalism*, 3rd ed. (1983); Richard J. Barnet, *The Alliance* (1983); Seyom Brown, *The Faces of Power* (1983); Leonard Dinnerstein, *America and the Survivors of the Holocaust* (1982); John L. Gaddis, *The United States and the Origins of the Cold War, 1941–1947* (1972); Louis Halle, *The Cold War as History* (1967); Laurence S. Kaplan, *The United States and NATO* (1984); Gabriel Kolko and Joyce Kolko, *The Limits of Power* (1972); Bruce Kuklick, *American Policy and the Division of Germany* (1972); Walter LaFeber, *America, Russia, and the Cold War, 1945–1980*, 4th ed. (1980); Melvyn Leffler, "The American Concept of National Security and the Beginnings of the Cold War, 1945–1948," *American Historical Review*, 89 (1984), 346–381; David McLellan, *Dean Acheson* (1976); Thomas G. Paterson, *On Every Front: The Making of the Cold War* (1979); Thomas G. Paterson, *Soviet-American Confrontation* (1973); Thomas G. Paterson, ed., *Cold War Critics* (1971); Gaddis Smith, *Dean Acheson* (1972); William Taubman, *Stalin's American Policy* (1982); Adam Ulam, *The Rivals* (1971); Bernard A. Weisberger, *Cold War, Cold Peace* (1984); Imanuel Wexler, *The Marshall Plan Revisited* (1983); Daniel Yergin, *Shattered Peace* (1977). (Also see works cited in Chapter 28 on the diplomacy of the Second World War and the atomic bomb.)

Truman Doctrine, Containment, and the Middle East

Thomas H. Etzold and John L. Gaddis, eds., *Containment* (1978); Richard M. Freeland, *The Truman Doctrine and the Origins of McCarthyism* (1972); John L. Gaddis, *Strategies of Containment* (1982); Charles Gati, ed., *Caging the Bear* (1974); John D. Iatrides, *Revolt in Athens* (1972); George F. Kennan, *Memoirs, 1925–1950* (1967); Bruce R. Kuniholm, *The Origins of the Cold War in the Near East* (1980); Walter Lippmann, *The Cold War* (1947); William R. Louis, *The British Empire in the Middle East, 1945–1951* (1984); Aaron D. Miller, *Search for Security* (1980); Thomas G. Paterson, ed., *Containment and the Cold War* (1973); Michael B. Stoff, *Oil, War, and American Security* (1980); Samuel F. Wells, Jr., "Sounding the Tocsin: NSC-68 and the Soviet Threat," *International Security*, 4 (1979), 116–158; Lawrence S. Wittner, *American Intervention in Greece, 1943–1949* (1982); C. Ben Wright, "Mr. 'X' and Containment," *Slavic Review*, 35 (1976), 1–31.

China and Asia

Robert M. Blum, *Drawing the Line* (1982); Dorothy Borg and Waldo Heinrichs, eds., *Uncertain Years* (1980); Russell Buhite, *Soviet-American Relations in Asia, 1945–1954* (1982); Warren I. Cohen, *America's Response to China*, 2nd ed. (1980); Herbert Feis, *Contest over Japan* (1967); Herbert Feis, *The China Tangle* (1953); Akira Iriye, *The Cold War in Asia* (1974); E. J. Kahn, Jr., *The China Hands* (1975); William R. Louis, *Imperialism at Bay: The United States and the Decolonization of the British Empire* (1978); Gary May, *China Scapegoat: The Diplomatic Ordeal of John Carter Vincent* (1979); Charles E. Neu, *The Troubled Encounter: The United States and Japan* (1975); Michael Schaller, *The United States and China in the Twentieth Century* (1979); Michael Schaller, *The U.S. Crusade in China, 1938–1945* (1978); William W. Stueck, Jr., *The Road to Confrontation: American Policy Toward China and Korea, 1947–1950* (1981); Christopher Thorne, *Allies of a Kind* (1978); Tang Tsou, *America's Failure in China, 1941–1950* (1963); Nancy B. Tucker, *Patterns in the Dust: Chinese-American Relations and the Recognition Controversy, 1949–1950* (1983).

Politics of the Truman Administration

Barton J. Bernstein, ed., *Politics and Policies of the Truman Administration* (1970); Bert Cochran, *Harry Truman and the Crisis Presidency* (1973); Robert J. Donovan, *Tumultuous Years: The Presidency of Harry S Truman, 1949–1953* (1982); Robert J. Donovan, *Conflict and Crisis: The Presidency of Harry S Truman, 1945–1948* (1977); Andrew J. Dunar, *The Truman Scandals and the Politics of Morality* (1984); Robert H. Ferrell, *Harry S Truman and the Modern American Presidency* (1983); Alonzo L. Hamby, *Beyond the New Deal: Harry S Truman and American Liberalism* (1973); Susan Hartmann, *Truman and the 80th Congress* (1971); Donald R. McCoy, *The Presidency of Harry S Truman* (1984).

Truman and the Economy

Stephen K. Bailey, *Congress Makes a Law: The Story Behind the Employment Act of 1946* (1950); Jack Stokes Ballard, *The Shock of Peace: Military and Economic Demobilization After World War II* (1983); Richard O. Davies, *Housing Reform During the Truman Administration* (1966); R. Alton Lee, *Truman and Taft-Hartley* (1966); Maeva Marcus, *Truman and the Steel Seizure Case* (1977); Allen J. Matusow, *Farm Policies and Politics in the Truman Years* (1967); Arthur F. McClure, *The Truman Administration and the Problems of Postwar Labor* (1969).

The Election of 1948

V. O. Key, *Southern Politics in State and Nation* (1949); Norman D. Markowitz, *The Rise and Fall of the People's Century: Henry A. Wallace and American Liberalism, 1941–1948* (1973); Richard Norton-Smith, *Thomas E. Dewey and His Times* (1982); Irwin Ross, *The Loneliest Campaign: The Truman Victory of 1948* (1968); Allen Yarnell, *Democrats and Progressives: The 1948 Presidential Election as a Test of Postwar Liberalism* (1974).

Civil Rights

William C. Berman, *The Politics of Civil Rights in the Truman Administration* (1970); Richard M. Dalfiume, *Desegregation of the U.S. Armed Forces* (1969); Richard Kluger, *Simple Justice: The History of* Brown *v.* Board of Education *and* Black America's Struggle for Equality (1975); Donald R. McCoy and Richard T. Ruetten, *Quest and Response: Minority Rights and the Truman Administration* (1973); Harvard Sitkoff, "Harry Truman and the Election of 1948: The Coming of Age of Civil Rights in American Politics," *Journal of Southern History*, 37 (1971), 597–616; Jules Tygiel, *Baseball's Great Experiment: Jackie Robinson and His Legacy* (1983).

McCarthyism

Michael R. Belknap, *Cold War Political Justice: The Smith Act, the Communist Party, and American Civil Liberties* (1977); David Caute, *The Great Fear* (1978); Larry Ceplair and Steven Englund, *The Inquisition in Hollywood* (1983); Robert Griffith, *The Politics of Fear: Joseph R. McCarthy and the Senate* (1970); Stanley I. Kutler, *The American Inquisition: Justice and Injustice in the Cold War* (1982); Harvey Levenstein, *Communism, Anticommunism, and the CIO* (1981); Mary Sperling McAuliffe, *Crisis on the Left: Cold War Politics and American Liberals, 1947–1954* (1978); Victor Navasky, *Naming Names* (1980); William L. O'Neill, *A Better World: Stalinism and the American Intellectuals* (1983); David M. Oshinsky, *A Conspiracy So Immense: The World of Joe McCarthy* (1983); Ronald Radosh and Joyce Milton, *The Rosenberg File* (1983); Thomas C. Reeves, *The Life and Times of Joe McCarthy* (1982); Michael Paul Rogin, *The Intellectuals and McCarthy* (1967); Walter and Miriam Schneir, *Invitation to an Inquest* (1983 ed.); Athan Theoharis, *Seeds of Repression: Harry S Truman and the Origins of McCarthyism* (1971); Allen Weinstein, *Perjury: The Hiss-Chambers Case* (1978).

The Korean War and Korean-American Relations

Ronald J. Caridi, *The Korean War and American Politics* (1969); Bruce Cumings, ed., *Child of Conflict* (1983); Bruce Cumings, *The Origins of the Korean War* (1980); Charles Dobbs, *The Unwanted Symbol* (1981); Joseph C. Goulden, *Korea* (1982); Glenn D. Paige, *The Korean Decision* (1968); David Rees, *Korea: The Limited War* (1964); Robert R. Simmons, *The Strained Alliance* (1975); John W. Spanier, *The Truman-MacArthur Controversy and the Korean War* (1959); I. F. Stone, *The Hidden History of the Korean War* (1952); Allen Whiting, *China Crosses the Yalu* (1960).

An Age of
Fragile Consensus
1953–1961

Chapter 30

The signs of patriotism were everywhere. Whether beating Russian athletes at the Olympics, bragging about new records in automobile ownership, or marveling at the nation's powerful military machine, Americans celebrated their country as the best place on earth. Certainly it was better than the Soviet Union. And to trumpet that difference, sermonized the Presbyterian minister George M. Docherty on February 7, 1954, religion should be enlisted. "One nation, indivisible, with liberty and justice for all"— American schoolchildren recited those famous words every morning in pledges of allegiance to the flag. With President Dwight D. Eisenhower sitting in his congregation that day, the Reverend Docherty implored political leaders to insert "under God" after "one nation" in the flag pledge. Nobody could utter *those* words in the Soviet Union, where atheistic Communists ruled. The president agreed, and Congress hastened to make the change.

This small episode conjoining religion, patriotism, and politics befitted the 1950s, an age of consensus. In that decade Americans generally shared a belief in anti-Communism and economic progress. Republican President Eisenhower, hardly the passive, ill-informed chief executive the Democrats tried to depict, was active in articulating the two beliefs and devising programs to satisfy them. But he moved cautiously and preferred a hidden-hand style to conspicuous displays of political arm-twisting.

Believing that Communists posed a mortal danger to the American system, the Eisenhower administration expanded Truman's loyalty program, endorsed restrictive legislation, and purged the State Department. The president was reluctant to confront directly Senator Joseph McCarthy, whose anti-Communist tactics proved reckless. McCarthy eventually destroyed himself with his excesses, but not before he had damaged many people and the nation itself. To maintain economic growth, Eisenhower pursued staunchly Republican goals: a balanced budget, reduced government spending, lower taxes, low inflation, private enterprise, a return of power to the states, and modest federal efforts to stimulate economic development. The Eisenhower officials did not attempt to roll back the New Deal and Fair Deal. In fact, however reluctantly, they expanded the welfare state.

Holding to their consensus thinking, white Americans celebrated their economic system for providing a high standard of living. But recurrent recessions and continued poverty in the midst of plenty raised doubts that economic progress had bestowed its benefits on all. An infant civil rights movement especially challenged the consensus view. Not only were most blacks at the bottom of the economic ladder; they were being denied their constitutional rights. How would blacks be brought into the consensus? The president, Congress, southern whites, black civil rights activists—all gave different answers as they debated the Supreme Court's 1954 *Brown* decision.

In foreign affairs, too, Eisenhower's low-key style and the two features of the consensus were evident. Eisenhower essentially continued Truman's Cold War policies, applying the containment doctrine worldwide. To wage the Cold War, the administration relied on nuclear weapons and interventions, some of them by a major new instrument of foreign policy, the Central Intelligence Agency (CIA). Many of the CIA's covert operations were directed against governments in the Third World, where new states were emerging from colonialism to nationhood. Americans feared that revolutionary nationalism and unrest in Third World countries was or would be exploited by Communists linked to a Soviet-led international conspiracy. Serious obstacles impeded the projection of United States influence into the Third World. And in Latin America the United States faced several revolutionary challenges to its hegemony. Those challenges often took the form of an economic nationalism that threatened American companies. The United States, then, intervened abroad not just to stop communism, but also to protect American economic overseas interests, which traditionally had contributed to economic growth at home.

President Eisenhower left office a disappointed man. The nuclear arms race had accelerated, race relations had deteriorated, and his vice president, Richard M. Nixon, had lost the 1960 presidential election to Senator John F. Kennedy. The young Kennedy had criticized Eisenhower's domestic policies as inadequate to sustain economic progress for all Americans. And he had faulted Eisenhower's foreign policy for not winning the Cold War and for not aligning the Third World with the United States. Yet the consensus, however fragile, remained basically intact, for Kennedy too shared its premises. Scholars largely agree that for all the political rhetoric of the 1960 campaign the Eisenhower presidency was the kind most Americans desired in the 1950s age of consensus. Americans liked "Ike's" traditionalism, caution, and moderation. He reassured them, and they trusted him.

CONSENSUS AND THE POLITICS OF EISENHOWER'S FIRST TERM

Smiling Ike, with his folksy style, displays of confusion, garbled syntax, and frequent escapes from the Oval Office to the golf course, fueled Democratic charges that he failed to lead—"the bland leading the bland." But it was not that simple. Dwight D. Eisenhower was no stranger to hard work. His low-key, hidden-hand style was his way of playing down his political role and highlighting his role as chief of state. He was also timid about tangling directly with the vocal right wing of the Republican party. Eisenhower relied considerably upon staff work, delegated authority to departments, and shied away from close involvement in the legislative process. Sometimes this meant that he was not well informed on details, giving the impression that he was out of touch with his own government. He was not, and he remained a very popular president.

During Eisenhower's presidency, with few exceptions, Americans clung to the status quo. It was a time of both national self-congratulation and worry.

The Consensus Mood The British journalist Godfrey Hodgson, describing the "consensus mood," wrote that Americans were "confident to the verge of complacency about the perfectibility of American society, anxious to the point of paranoia about the threat of communism." Much as they might bicker about how the Cold War should be waged or about how the economy should be managed, they were one when it came to anti-Communism and a faith in economic progress. Most white Americans believed not only that the United States was the greatest nation in the world, but that its potential was boundless. For middle-class Americans who surrounded themselves with the symbols of economic success—automobiles, televisions, and houses in suburbia—the American dream seemed a reality (see Chapter 31).

Demand for reform at such a time was deemed not only unnecessary but downright unpatriotic. The country was engaged in a moral struggle with Communism, people believed, and during such a crusade one should support, not criticize, the government. Almost everywhere he looked, the historian Henry Steele Commager saw conformity: "the uncritical and unquestioning acceptance of America as it is." College students shunned passionate political convictions, liking instead to be "cool." A weak minority on the left advocated checks on the political power of corporations and a noisy minority on the right vilified the government for a supposed wishy-washy campaign against Communism, but both liberal Democrats and moderate Republicans avoided extremism of any variety, satisfied to be occupying "the vital center."

Along with this attitude of conformity went trust in and respect for established authority. In government, business, labor, the military, religion, and education, Americans let those at the top bargain on their behalf. And they chose to pursue economic goals more than moral ones, believing that the latter were not merely unimportant but also unattainable. Like their leaders, Americans feared mass movements, even those with democratic goals like the civil rights movement, as threats to stability. It seemed preferable for people to spend their time earning a living, raising a family of togetherness, and contributing their tax dollars toward a stronger America than to become involved in an idealistic crusade. "The fifties under Ike," Richard Lingeman of the New York Times observed, "represented a sort of national prefrontal lobotomy: tail-finned, we Sunday-drove down the superhighways of life while tensions that later bubbled up in the sixties seethed beneath the placid surface."

Scholars of the 1950s who subscribed to the consensus proclaimed the "end of ideology" in America.

On July 4, 1961, patriotic residents of a Chicago neighborhood posed in front of their flag-draped homes. Patriotism was a prominent characteristic of the age of consensus. National Archives.

Since the early twentieth century, historians had told

Consensus Historiography

the American story as one of conflict—rich against poor, North against South, farmer against industrialist and banker. They focused on rebellions, strikes, moral crusades, and wars. But the historians of the 1950s wrote about stability, continuity, and cultural wholeness; they spoke of *the* American experience and *the* national character.

Important books were published on these themes, among them Daniel Boorstin's *The Americans: The Colonial Experience* (1958); Louis Hartz's *The Liberal Tradition in America* (1955); Richard Hofstadter's *The Age of Reform* (1955); and David Potter's *People of Plenty* (1954). Historians did not deny the existence of conflict in the American past, but they ascribed it less to flaws in society than to psychologically disturbed personalities. Among the people historians identified as maladjusted were abolitionists, feminists,

Populists, and progressive reformers. The consensus interpretation thus shifted the focus away from society's faults—slavery, sexism, or political corruption—and placed it on the critics who demanded reform. As the historian John Higham has noted, "A psychological approach to conflict enables historians to substitute a schism in the soul for a schism in society."

In this age of consensus, President Eisenhower approached his duties with a philosophy of "dynamic conservatism," explaining that he would be "con-

"Dynamic Conservatism"

servative when it comes to money and liberal when it comes to human beings." Eisenhower's was "an Administration representing business and industry," admitted Interior Secretary Douglas McKay. One journalist referred to the cabinet as "eight millionaires and a plumber"—an accurate description until the plumber resigned within a year. Eisenhower and his appointees thus gave priority to reducing the federal budget. Eisenhower officials recognized that they could not dismantle New Deal and Fair Deal programs, because this would have been politically impossible. They knew as well that most government expenditures consisted of fixed, built-in costs such as veterans' pensions, social security benefits, and interest payments on the national debt. Soon the Republican right wing complained that Ike was a "fifth-column Democrat" for not moving more forthrightly against the welfare state and slashing the budget more. In turn, Eisenhower grew impatient with those he privately scorned as "hidebound reactionaries." For the president, "progressive moderates" were more sensible.

True to the principles of the free marketplace and a balanced budget, Eisenhower tried in his first term to get the federal government out of agriculture. Since the 1930s the government had **Farm Program** made payments to farmers based upon the difference between the market price and the higher parity price for farm goods. (The parity price was equivalent in value to the price farmers enjoyed in the good years of 1909–1910.) After paying farmers this price support, the government took and stored their surplus products. Farmers received huge support payments, and government bins bulged with surplus wheat and other commodities. And farm production increased through the accelerated use of chemical fertilizers and machinery. Prices still fell, and farmers' purchasing power declined. Millions of farmers—most of them small landowners—abandoned farming altogether. Eisenhower officials concluded that lower, flexible price supports would discourage production. But the Agricultural Act of 1954 only lowered them to 75 to 90 percent of parity. Two years later the Soil Bank Act provided for federal payments to farmers who agreed to take cropland out of production. Another farm bill in 1958 reduced the price support for some crops to 65 percent of parity. None of this worked; the government spent more and the surpluses grew. All of this was very distasteful to President Eisenhower. He remarked later that the federal farm program was a "national disgrace."

Eisenhower made better headway with other issues. In 1954 Congress approved the St. Lawrence Seaway project to construct a canal between Montreal and Lake Erie. This inland waterway was intended to spur the economic development of the Midwest by linking the Great Lakes to the Atlantic Ocean. The president also made a Cold War case for the joint Canadian-American project: it would strengthen the security of both nations. That year, too, Eisenhower signed into law amendments to the Social Security Act that raised benefits and added 7.5 million workers, largely self-employed farmers, to the program's coverage. In the first of many such measures during the decade, the Housing Act of 1954 provided federal funds for the construction of houses for low-income families displaced by urban renewal's destruction of their neighborhoods. Congress also obliged the president in 1954 with tax reform that increased deductions and raised business depreciation allowances and the Atomic Energy Act, which granted private companies the right to own reactors and nuclear materials for the production of electric power. But there was a legislative setback for the president: his inability to persuade Congress to promote private rather than public development of hydroelectric power (the Dixon-Yates controversy).

The Eisenhower administration also presided over a dramatic change in the lives of Native Americans. In 1953, Congress adopted *termination,* whose purpose it was to liquidate Indian reservations and end federal services. **Termination Policy for Native Americans** Eisenhower officials seemed disposed toward the new policy because it would reduce federal costs and serve states rights by eliminating federal trusteeship, making Indians subject to state laws. Critics—including most Indians—denounced termination as another white attempt to grab Indian lands. Between 1954 and 1960, the federal government withdrew its benefits from sixty-one tribes, and about one in eight Indians abandoned their reservations in return for small relocation payments. Under the new policies many Indians joined the urban poor. A Senate committee reported in 1969 that members of the terminated tribe of the Klamath in Oregon suffered "extreme social disorganization" and "many of them can be found in state mental and penal institutions." By the time termination was halted in the 1960s, so much human tragedy had visited Native Americans that observers compared their modern plight to their distress in the late nineteenth century.

In the 1954 congressional elections, voters revealed

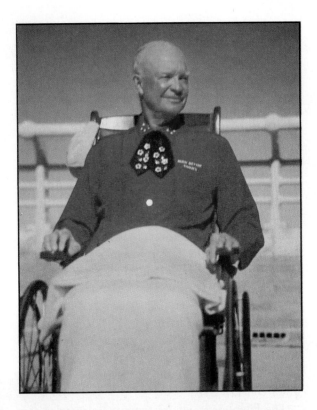

Recovering from a heart attack in 1955, President Dwight D. Eisenhower (1890–1969) registers his famous smile from a hospital wheelchair. He went on to win re-election decisively in 1956. Wide World Photos.

the already ailing railroads, and spurred the growth of the suburbs, which were built farther and farther from the central cities (see pages 890–893).

Although Eisenhower suffered a heart attack in September 1955, he regained his strength in months and soon declared his intention to run again. With

Election of 1956

much relief the Republicans nominated the popular president for a second term. The Democrats ran Adlai E. Stevenson once more (see page 848). The campaigns lacked spirit, and the party platforms differed little. With recent crises over Hungary and Suez much on their minds, Americans decided to stick with an experienced military man and statesman at a time of world unrest. Eisenhower won a landslide victory in 1956: 35.6 million votes and 457 electoral votes to Stevenson's 26 million and 73. Still, his personal victory did not aid the Republicans in Congress, where the Democrats continued to dominate.

that while they still liked Ike, at heart they remained loyal to the Democratic party. With a recession just winding down and the controversy over Joseph McCarthy as a backdrop, the voters gave the Democrats control of both houses of Congress. Lyndon B. Johnson became the new Senate majority leader. An energetic, pragmatic politician from Texas, he tried to work with the Republican White House to achieve legislation. A notable ac-

Interstate Highway System

complishment was the Highway Act of 1956. This law authorized the spending of $31 billion over the next thirteen years to build a 41,000-mile interstate highway system, intended to permit the military to move around the nation more easily and to assist commerce. The Highway Trust Fund, fed by new taxes on gasoline, would finance much of the construction. As the largest public works program in American history, the interstate highways invigorated the tourist industry, further weakened

THE DECLINE OF MCCARTHYISM

During Eisenhower's first term, one of the most vexing problems for the administration was the conduct of Senator Joseph R. McCarthy (see

Eisenhower on McCarthy

pages 842–843). His no-holds-barred search for subversives in government turned up none, but it did affront political fair play, decency, and civil liberties. The president privately labeled the senator a "pimple on the path of progress," but he avoided directly confronting him, saying he would not "get into the gutter with that guy." Eisenhower also feared that a showdown would splinter the Republican party. Instead the president spoke against unnamed "demagogues thirsty for personal power," and hoped the media and Congress would bring McCarthy down. "You know," Eisenhower told his press secretary, "what we ought to do is get a word to put ahead of Republican. Something like 'new' or 'modern' " so that McCarthy and his ilk would bolt and form a third party. But the president made no such move, even when the senator began to accuse the administration of permitting "treason" to persist in the government.

While Eisenhower tried his quiet strategy to undermine the senator, his administration practiced its own brand of anti-Communism. A new executive order in 1953 broadened Truman's loyalty program (see pages 840–841). The administration periodically announced the number of "security risks" it had dismissed from their government jobs, including State Department officials (see page 863). One of Eisenhower's most controversial decisions came in June 1953 when he denied clemency to Julius and Ethel Rosenberg, who had been convicted of treason (see page 842). They were executed. Late that year, at the urging of the chairman of the Atomic Energy Commission, the president sus-

Oppenheimer Case pended the security clearance of J. Robert Oppenheimer, the celebrated physicist who had directed the atomic bomb project at Los Alamos during the Second World War. Oppenheimer's "crimes" were not that he was either disloyal to his nation or a risk to its security, but rather that he had apparently later misrepresented a 1943 conversation with a friend on Soviet interest in atomic secrets and that he had opposed the government's crash program to develop the hydrogen bomb.

In 1954 the Communist Control Act demonstrated that both liberals and conservatives shared the consensus of anti-Communism. In effect making membership in the Communist party illegal, the measure passed the Senate unanimously and the House 265 to 2. The chief sponsor of the bill, liberal Democratic Senator Hubert H. Humphrey of Minnesota, told his colleagues just before he cast his vote: "We have closed all of the doors. These rats [Communists] will not get out of the trap." Years later Humphrey said of his role in the legislation that "it's not one of the things I'm proudest of."

As for Senator McCarthy, he finally undercut himself. He transgressed the limits of what the Senate and the public would tolerate. His crucial mistake was not merely taking on the U.S. Army, but doing so in front of millions of television viewers. At issue was the senator's wild accusation that the army was shielding and promoting Communists; he cited the case of one army dentist. The Army-McCarthy hearings, held by a Senate subcommittee in 1954, became

A falling Senator Joseph McCarthy hands the mud-slinging brush of McCarthyism to fellow McCarthyites Vice President Richard M. Nixon and Indiana Senator William Jenner. "Carry on, lads" says the Wisconsin senator in this cartoon by Herblock. From Herblock's Here and Now (Simon & Schuster, 1955).

a showcase for his abusive treatment of witnesses. At one general, whose loyalty was never in doubt, McCarthy shouted, "You are a disgrace to the uniform. You're shielding Communist conspirators. . . . You're not fit to be an officer. You're ignorant." McCarthy alternately ranted and, appearing drunk, slurred his words. Finally, after he had attacked a young lawyer who was not even involved in the hearings, Joseph Welch, counsel for the army, asked, "Have you no sense of decency, sir?" The gallery erupted in applause, and McCarthy's career as a witch-hunter rapidly came

Senate Condemnation of McCarthy to a close. In December 1954, in a 67 to 22 vote, the Senate condemned McCarthy, not for defiling the Bill of Rights but for sullying the dignity of the Senate with his contemptuous behavior. He remained a senator, but exhaustion and alcohol took their toll. He died in 1957 at the age of forty-eight.

President Eisenhower's reluctance publicly to discredit McCarthy gave the senator, other right-wing members of Congress, and some private and public institutions enough rein to damage the nation and destroy the careers of many innocent people. The City University of New York, for example, fired eighteen professors—and did not apologize to them until 1980. Eisenhower's own government-sponsored McCarthyism demoralized and frightened federal workers, some of whom were driven from public service. The anti-Communist campaigns of the 1950s also discouraged people from freely expressing themselves and hence from debating critical issues of the time. Fear and a contempt for the Bill of Rights, then, helped sustain the consensus.

AN AWAKENED CIVIL RIGHTS MOVEMENT

If Eisenhower was pleased to be rid of McCarthy, he did not welcome the invigorated civil rights movement. Although the president completed the desegregation of the armed forces started under Truman, he did not seem to want to go further. But black leaders, more and more outspoken against their people's second-class citizenship and poverty in white America, insisted on more. The NAACP challenged segregation in the courts, and young blacks turned to more direct action such as boycotts, sit-ins, and demonstrations.

In 1954 the NAACP won a historic victory against segregation. The Supreme Court's decision in *Brown v. Board of Education of Topeka* involved cases from Kansas, Delaware, South Carolina, Virginia, and the District of Columbia, which were grouped under one unanimous ruling. Written by Chief Justice Earl Warren, the Court's ruling concluded that "in the field of public education the doctrine of 'separate but equal' has no place. Separate educational facilities are inherently unequal." Such facilities, Warren wrote, generated in black children "a feeling of inferiority . . . that may affect their hearts and minds in a way unlikely ever to be undone." A year later the Court

Brown v. Board of Education of Topeka

demanded the desegregation of schools "with all deliberate speed."

Though some border states quietly implemented the order, a majority of southern communities defied the Court, at times violently. Business and professional people formed White Citizens' Councils for the express purpose of resisting the order. Known familiarly as "uptown Ku Klux Klans," the councils used their economic power against black civil rights activists, foreclosing on their mortgages and seeing to it that they were fired from their jobs or denied credit at local stores. The Klan itself experienced a resurgence, and new groups, such as the National Association for the Advancement of White People, surfaced. But the most effective resistance tactic was the enactment of state laws that paid tuition for white children attending private schools. In some cases, desegregated public schools were ordered closed.

Eisenhower, who had named Earl Warren chief justice in 1953, now pronounced that appointment "the biggest damn fool mistake I ever made." The president had hoped to avoid a confrontation over desegregation, for he tended to side with white southerners and he hoped to continue making Republican inroads in the South. Eisenhower had even approached the chief justice at a White House dinner while the Court was considering the *Brown* case. Referring to the white South, Eisenhower had said, "These are not bad people. All they are concerned about is to see that their sweet little girls are not required to sit in school alongside some big overgrown Negroes."

The president's desire to sidestep the issue was thwarted in September 1957 when the governor of Arkansas, Orval E. Faubus, intervened to halt a local plan for the gradual desegregation of Little Rock's Central High School. Faubus mobilized troops of the Arkansas National Guard to block the entry of black students. Eisenhower made no effort to stop Faubus's actions, and he seemed to agree with the sentiment behind them when he told a press conference that week, "You cannot change people's hearts merely by laws." In late September, after bowing to a federal judge's order, Faubus withdrew the guardsmen. Eight black children slipped inside Central High, as hundreds of jeering whites threatened to storm the school. The next day, fearing violence, Eisenhower federalized

Little Rock, Arkansas, Crisis

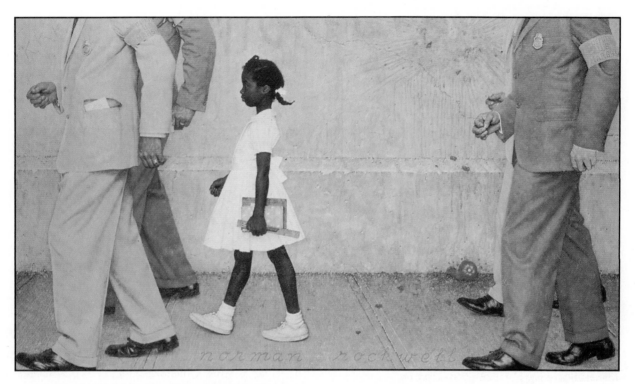

Escorted to school by federal marshals in Little Rock, Arkansas, in 1957, this black student and others had to endure shouted racial slurs, spittings, and thrown objects—this three years after the Supreme Court's Brown decision ordering the desegregation of public schools. By the noted illustrator Norman Rockwell. The Norman Rockwell Museum at the Old Corner House, Stockbridge, MA.

the Arkansas National Guard and ordered 1,100 paratroopers flown in to ensure the children's safety. Troops patrolled the school for the rest of the year, but Little Rock officials closed all public high schools in 1958 and 1959 rather than desegregate them.

Meanwhile, the civil rights movement was gaining momentum elsewhere. In December 1955 Rosa Parks refused to give up her seat to a white passenger on a public bus in Montgomery, Alabama. Jim Crow practices required that blacks sit at the back of the bus and, when asked, surrender their seats to whites. Mrs. Parks's arrest ignited a year-long black boycott of the city's bus system. Blacks walked or carpooled. "My feets is tired," remarked an elderly black woman, "but my soul is rested." With the bus company near bankruptcy and downtown merchants hurt by declining sales, city officials began harassing tactics to frighten blacks into abandoning the boycott. But the black

community's leader, Martin Luther King, Jr., urged them to persevere. "This is not a war between the white and the Negro," he said, "but a conflict between justice and injustice."

King was an Atlanta-born, twenty-seven-year-old Baptist minister who had recently earned a Ph.D. at Boston University. He insisted on nonviolent peaceful protest in the spirit of India's leader **Martin Luther** Gandhi. Although he was jailed and **King, Jr.** a bomb blew the front from his house, King persisted. What King gave to blacks was the "absence of fear," remembered black leader Bayard Rustin. "So Dr. King had this tremendous facility for giving people the feeling that they could be bigger and stronger and more courageous and more loving than they thought they could be." With the aid of a 1956 Supreme Court decision that declared Alabama's Jim Crow laws unconstitutional,

Martin Luther King, Jr. (1929–1968) helped organize the Montgomery, Alabama, bus boycott which led to the desegregation of public transportation. Here, in 1956, he is surrounded by reporters on the first integrated bus run.   Ebony Magazine.

the face of angry white mobs, SNCC members challenged the status quo, all the while singing the anthem of the civil rights movement, "We Shall Overcome." One line goes: "We are not afraid."

EISENHOWER-DULLES FOREIGN POLICY AND THE COLD WAR

Dwight D. Eisenhower had had more experience in foreign affairs than domestic affairs before he became president. He had lived and traveled in Europe, Asia, and Latin America. During the Second World War General Eisenhower came to know Europe well, negotiated with world leaders, and made tough decisions of international consequence. After the war he served as Army Chief of Staff and NATO Supreme Commander and learned the essentials of nuclear weapons development and secret intelligence operations. Like most Americans, Eisenhower accepted the Cold War consensus assumptions about the threat of Communism and the need for a global watch by the United States. As president he controlled the making of foreign policy and enjoyed comfortable vote margins in Congress on key resolutions and programs.

The image of the bumbling, aging hero that partisan Democrats helped create was in part shaped by Eisenhower himself, because he deliberately counted heavily upon his secretary of state, the strong-willed John Foster Dulles. Polished and articulate, Dulles seemed to have lived his whole life in preparation for the nation's chief diplomatic post. He had studied at Princeton and trained in law at George Washington University before, at age thirty, assisting Woodrow Wilson at Versailles. As a senior partner in a prestigious Wall Street law firm Dulles had handled international cases, and as an officer of the Federal Council of Churches he had participated in programs on behalf of world peace. He had also helped the Truman administration negotiate a peace treaty with Japan. Although experienced, Dulles impressed people as arrogant, stubborn, and preachy—

John Foster Dulles

Montgomery blacks triumphed. They won again in 1957 when Congress passed the Civil Rights Act, which created the U.S. Commission on Civil Rights. Three years later Congress strengthened voting rights.

Martin Luther King, Jr., became president of the Southern Christian Leadership Conference, organized in 1957 to coordinate civil rights activities. He criticized the White House for being "too silent and apathetic" on the issue of race relations. But Eisenhower remained reluctant to move desegregation forward. Blacks tried new tactics. In early 1960 four black students from North Carolina Agricultural and Technical College in Greensboro sat down at a segregated lunch counter and ordered coffee. Though they were refused service and were physically and verbally abused, they would not budge. Thus began the sit-in movement, which spread from the South to the North, rolling back segregation in many public accommodations (see map). Inspired by the sit-ins, some participants organized the Student Nonviolent Coordinating Committee (SNCC) in fall 1960. In

The Sit-ins

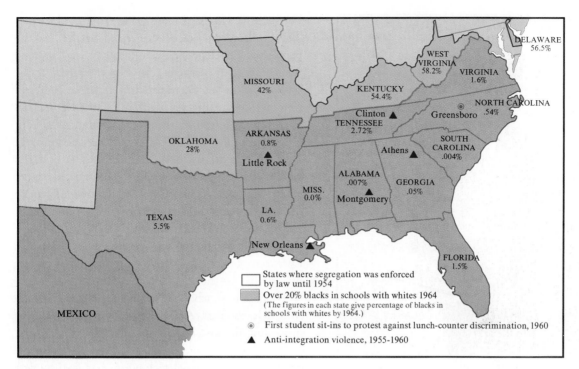

Desegregation in the South, 1954–1964 *Source: Redrawn by permission of Macmillan Publishing Company, Inc. by Peter Kingsland. Copyright © 1968 by Martin Gilbert.*

the "conscience and straightjacket of the free world," complained one European newspaper. The Eisenhower-Dulles relationship was mutually cooperative, for they agreed on basic policies, and the president delegated authority to Dulles with confidence.

Like his president, Dulles conceded much to the McCarthyites. He appointed one of Senator McCarthy's henchmen, Scott McLeod, as chief security officer of the State Department. McLeod went about trying to prove McCarthy's charge that the department was infested with Communists. Making few distinctions between New Dealers and Communists, he and Dulles forced many innocent, talented officers out of the foreign service. They included Asian specialists whose expertise was later denied to American decision-makers when they sent the United States to war in Indochina (see pages 913–915).

For the most part, Eisenhower and Dulles continued Truman's containment policy, but introduced some memorable phrases to distinguish their administration from Truman's. Thinking containment too defensive a concept, Dulles invented *liberation.* (He did not,

however, explain precisely how the countries of Eastern Europe could be freed from Soviet control.) *Massive retaliation* was the administration's phrase for the nuclear obliteration of the Soviet state or its assumed client, the People's Republic of China, if they took aggressive actions. Eisenhower said it "simply means the ability to blow hell out of them in a hurry if they start anything." The ability of the United States to make such a threat was thought to provide *deterrence,* or the prevention of hostile Soviet behavior.

Eisenhower-Dulles Policies

Related to both massive retaliation and deterrence was the *New Look* of the American military. Eisenhower and Dulles emphasized air power and nuclear weaponry and de-emphasized conventional forces. The president's preference for heavy weapons stemmed in part from his desire to trim the federal budget ("more bang for the buck" in the words of the time). With this huge military arsenal, the United States in the 1950s practiced *brinkmanship:* not backing down in a crisis, even if it meant taking the nation to the

Secretary of State John Foster Dulles (1888–1959) became a formidable debater in diplomatic negotiations. Foreigners often complained that he was too rigid, passing up chances for compromise. Although President Eisenhower admired him, he questioned Dulles's "practice of becoming a sort of international prosecuting attorney." Dulles seemed more eager to denounce the Soviets than to negotiate with them. The Reporter, 1956. *Copyright 1956 by The Reporter Magazine Company, Inc.*

brink of war. Eisenhower also popularized the *domino theory*, according to which small, weak nations would fall to Communism like a row of dominoes if they were not propped up by the United States. Adopting a globalist perspective on wrenching changes in the Third World, the Eisenhower administration conducted a diplomacy of holding the line—against Soviet Russia, Communist China, neutralism, Communism, socialism, nationalism, and revolution everywhere.

After the death of Stalin in 1953, Eisenhower hoped for a relaxation of Soviet-American relations,

but instead witnessed alternating thaws and freezes. The nuclear arms race accelerated as the two superpowers developed new military technology and nuclear delivery systems. In November 1952 the United States detonated the first hydrogen bomb. In March 1954 the biggest bomb the United States has ever tested destroyed the Pacific island of Bikini. This fifteen-megaton H-Bomb packing the power of 15 million tons of TNT, or 750 times as powerful as the atomic bomb that leveled Hiroshima, produced a fallout of radioactive dust that showered a Japanese fishing boat in the area. The crew of the *Lucky Dragon* suffered nausea, fever, and blisters. One of them died, becoming the world's first victim of a hydrogen bomb and setting off international protest in response to the incident.

The Soviets, who had tested their first H-bomb in 1953, shocked Americans in October 1957 by propelling the first man-made satellite, *Sputnik,* into outer space. Just two months earlier,

Sputnik and the Missile Race

Soviet technicians had fired the first intercontinental ballistic missile (ICBM). Americans now felt vulnerable to air attack and inferior to the Russians in rocket technology. But the United States soon tested its own ICBMs. It also enlarged its fleet of long-range bombers (the B-52s) and deployed intermediate-range missiles in Europe targeted against the Soviet Union. By the end of 1960 Americans had as well produced Polaris-missile-bearing submarines. To ensure future technological advancement, the National Aeronautics and Space Agency (NASA) was created in 1958.

Through flights by the CIA's U-2 spy planes, American officials knew that the Soviets had deployed very few ICBMs. Yet critics charged that Eisenhower had allowed the United States to fall behind in the missile race. The much-publicized "missile gap" was actually a false notion inspired in part by political partisanship. "Everyone knows," Air Force General Nathan Twining privately told the president, "we already have a [nuclear] stockpile large enough to obliterate the Soviet Union." As the 1950s closed, then, the United States enjoyed overwhelming strategic dominance because of its "triad" of long-range bombers, submarine-launched ballistic missiles (SLBMs), and ICBMs.

Still, President Eisenhower was uneasy about the

arms race. He feared nuclear war, and the cost of the new weapons made it difficult to balance the budget. In his 1953 Chance for Peace speech, the president had noted that "every gun that is made, every warship launched, every rocket fired signifies, in the final sense, a theft from those who hunger and are not fed. . . . The cost of one modern heavy bomber is this: a modern brick school in more than 30 cities." He also doubted the need for more and bigger nuclear weapons. How many times, he once asked, "could [you] kill the same man?" Spurred by such thoughts, by citizens' groups like the Committee for a Sane Nuclear Policy (founded in 1957 and popularly known as SANE), and by neutralist and Soviet appeals, the president cautiously initiated arms control proposals. But because he did not trust the Soviets, arms control talks never became a top priority. Indeed, he intended to preserve the American advantage and, in the propaganda duel with the Soviets, to put them on the defensive.

Eisenhower's 1953 "atoms for peace" initiative called upon the nuclear nations to contribute fissionable materials for use in industrial projects under the auspices of the United Nations. Two years later he issued his "open skies" proposal: aerial surveillance of both Soviet and American military sites to reduce the chances of surprise attacks. Despite numerous attempts at Geneva disarmament talks, neither side could agree on suitable inspection systems to ensure compliance with arms control treaties or bans on nuclear testing. To satisfy world opinion about radioactive fallout, however, the two powers unilaterally suspended atmospheric testing from late 1958 to fall 1961, when the Soviets resumed it. The United States began testing again at the same time, but underground.

While the nuclear arms race gained momentum, Russia and the United States waged the Cold War. The year 1955 provided a brief respite from the intensity of the competition. First, the superpowers agreed to end their ten-year joint occupation of Austria, making it an independent neutral state. And, second, Eisenhower and Soviet leader Nikita Khrushchev journeyed to Geneva for high-level talks. This first summit meeting in ten years produced no important resolutions, but the conferees "disagreed so nicely," as one reporter put it.

Events in Eastern Europe soon returned the Cold War to the more familiar fierce acrimony. In 1956

"So Russia Launched a Satellite, but Has It Made Cars With Fins Yet?"

While American genius was being applied to fancy consumer goods like the tail-finned automobiles of the 1950s, the Soviets were demonstrating their technological abilities by launching the satellite Sputnik—or so Uncle Sam seems to be thinking in this Ross Lewis cartoon. Democratic Senator Lyndon B. Johnson complained that "the Soviets have beaten us at our own game—daring scientific advances in the atomic age." Milwaukee Public Library.

Eastern Europe

Khrushchev called for "peaceful coexistence" between capitalists and Communists, denounced Stalin, and suggested that Moscow would tolerate different brands of Communism. Soon revolts against Soviet power erupted in Poland and Hungary, testing this new permissiveness. Moscow saw its new military alliance, the Warsaw Pact (1955), endangered and quickly crushed the rebellions. The Eisenhower administration, on record as favoring the liberation of Eastern Europe, found itself unable to aid the rebels without igniting a third world war. All the United States could do was to welcome Hungarian immigrants in greater numbers than American quota laws allowed.

Hardly had the turmoil in Eastern Europe subsided when the divided city of Berlin, in East Germany, once again became a Cold War flash point. The Soviets were angry about the placement in West Germany of American bombers capable of carrying nuclear warheads. And they were upset that West Berlin had become an escape route for disaffected

East Germans. In 1958 Khrushchev boldly announced that the Soviet Union would recognize East German control of all of Berlin unless East and West began talks on German reunification and rearmament. The Americans, unwilling to give up their hold on West Berlin, sought to strengthen West German ties with NATO. The two sides talked of war; finally Khrushchev backed away from his ultimatum, resolving to take up the issue at future conferences.

Berlin and Germany were on the agenda of a summit meeting planned for Paris in May 1960. But two weeks before the conference, an American U-2 spy plane carrying high-powered cameras crashed 1,200 miles inside the Soviet Union. Moscow announced that it had been shot down. At first Washington denied that its planes flew over Soviet territory, but Russian officials blasted that story by displaying the captured CIA pilot, Francis Gary Powers, his aircraft, and the pictures he had been snapping of Soviet military installations. Moscow demanded an apology, Washington refused, and the Russians walked out of the Paris summit.

U-2 Incident

While West and East sparred over Europe, both kept a wary eye on the People's Republic of China (PRC). Despite growing evidence of a Sino-Soviet split, most American officials continued to think of Communism as a unified world movement. The United States refused to open diplomatic relations with the Chinese government and continued to give aid to Jiang Jieshi (Chiang Kai-shek) on Formosa, which the Chinese claimed as part of the PRC. Washington worried about PRC calls for colonial rebellion and its support for the revolutionaries in Indochina (see pages 913–915). In 1954 China and the United States negotiated face to face in Geneva to settle the Indochinese crisis, but their relations were marked more by hostility than conciliation.

In 1954 and 1955 a crisis brought the two nations to the brink of war. Just a few miles off the Chinese coast sat the tiny islands of Quemoy and Matsu. Jiang's forces used them as bases for commando raids against the PRC. In fall 1954 China bombarded the islands. Eisenhower decided to defend the outposts, and he let it be known he was considering the use of nuclear weapons. Massive re-

Quemoy and Matsu

taliation over such an insignificant issue? "Let's keep the Reds guessing," advised John Foster Dulles. But what if they guessed wrong? asked critics. Congress passed the Formosa Resolution (1955), which authorized the president to send troops to Formosa and adjoining islands. Two years later the United States installed on Formosa missiles capable of carrying nuclear warheads. Chinese and American diplomats talked in secret meetings in Geneva and Warsaw, but again in 1958 war loomed over Quemoy and Matsu. The crisis passed, but defense of the islands became an issue in the election of 1960 at home.

INTERVENTIONS IN THE THIRD WORLD

If Eisenhower believed that he had contained the Sino-Soviet threat, he was very much less confident about challenges from the Third World. In the 1940s, as a result of changes wrought by the Second World War, a cavalcade of new nations began to alter the international community. In the period from 1943 to 1983 no fewer than ninety countries cast off their colonial bonds. The march to independence was unrelenting: Lebanon (1943), Syria (1944), the Philippines (1946), India (1947), Indonesia (1949), Libya (1951), Morocco (1956), Ghana (1957). In 1960 alone, eighteen colonies became nations (see map, page 868).

These profound stirrings arose in what is now known as the Third World, a general term applied to those parts of the global community belonging to neither of the other two "worlds": the United States and its allies in the capitalist "West" and the Soviet Union and its allies in the Communist "East." Sometimes called developing countries, Third World nations on the whole are nonwhite, nonindustrialized, and located in the southern half of the globe—Asia, Africa, the Middle East, and Latin America. With Cold War lines drawn fairly tightly in Europe by the early 1950s, Soviet-American rivalry shifted increasingly to the Third World. Much was at stake. Third World nations possessed strategic raw materials such as manganese, oil, and tin. They also attracted foreign investment—in 1959 over a third of America's private foreign investments were in Third World countries. Third World nations provided markets, especially for American products and technology. Finally, the great powers looked to these new states for support in the United Nations and for sites to be used as military and intelligence bases.

But many Third World states, like India, Ghana, Egypt, and Indonesia, did not wish to take sides in the contest between the great powers. To the dismay of both Washington and Moscow,

Neutralism

they proudly declared themselves neutral, or nonaligned, in the Cold War. Eisenhower and Dulles considered 'neutralism an immoral stance, a first step along the road to Communism. Nations, they insisted, should take sides in the life-and-death Cold War struggle.

If this negative view of neutralism inhibited United States efforts to strengthen relations with the Third World, so did America's domestic race relations. In August 1955, the ambassador from

American Racism as Handicap

India, G.L. Mehta, walked into a restaurant at the Houston International Airport, sat down, and waited to order. But Texas law required that whites and blacks be served in separate dining facilities. The dark-skinned diplomat, who had seated himself in a white-only area, was told to move. The insult stung deeply and was not soon forgotten. From Washington, Secretary Dulles telegraphed his apologies for this blatant display of racism, fearing that the incident would injure relations with a nation whose allegiance the United States was seeking in the Cold War.

Such embarrassments were not uncommon in the 1950s. Burma's minister of education was denied a meal in a Columbus, Ohio, restaurant; and the finance minister of Ghana was turned away from a Howard Johnson's just outside the nation's capital. Secretary Dulles complained that segregationist practices were becoming a "major international hazard," a threat to United States efforts to gain the friendship of Third World countries. Americans stood publicly condemned as a people who did not honor the ideal of equality.

Thus when the attorney general appealed to the Supreme Court to strike down segregation in public schools, his introductory remarks took note of the international implications. "It is in the context of the present world struggle between freedom and tyranny that the problem of racial discrimination must be viewed," he warned. The humiliation of dark-skinned diplomats in Washington, D.C., "the window through which the world looks into our house," was damaging to American interests. Racism "furnished grist for the Communist propaganda mills."

United States hostility toward revolution also obstructed the American quest for influence in the Third World. Despite its own history, the United

American Intolerance of Revolution

States has been uncomfortable with significant twentieth-century revolutions—Mexican, Chinese, Russian, Cuban, Vietnamese, and Iranian. Although Americans paid lip service to the Spirit of '76, they were intolerant of revolutionary disorder—in part because Third World revolutions were directed against their Cold War allies, but also because such upheavals threatened American investments, markets, and military bases. Indeed, by mid-century the United States had become an established power in world affairs, eager for the stability and order that seemed to ensure its own prosperity and security. During revolutionary crises, therefore, the United States usually threw its support to its European allies or to the conservative propertied classes in the Third World. When forty-three African and Asian states sponsored a United Nations resolution appealing for decolonization in 1960, the United States abstained from the vote, signaling that it stood with the white imperialists.

Still another obstacle in America's relations with the rising Third World was the country's great wealth. Foreigners both envied and resented the "people of plenty," who had so much and

America's Wealth as a Problem

wasted so much while poorer peoples went without. American movies offered enticing glimpses of middle-class materialism; American products drew attention at international trade fairs and were coveted items at native marketplaces. And Americans stationed overseas often flaunted their superior standard of living. The popular novel

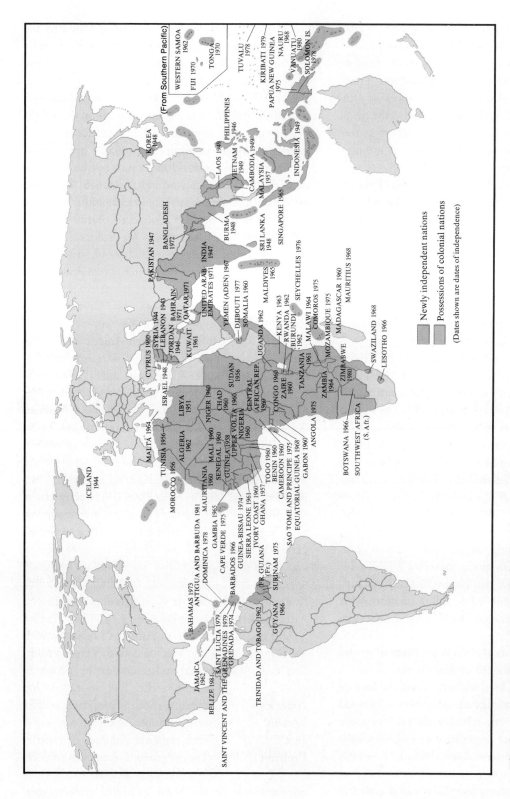

The Rise of the Third World: Decolonization Since 1943

The Ugly American (1958) drew attention to the problem by describing the "golden ghettoes" of American diplomats, separated from their poorer surroundings by high compound walls. Finally, many foreign peoples resented the ample profits that American corporations extracted from them. For all these reasons, the United States found itself often not the model of revolution but the target. Americans were blamed for the persistent poverty of the Third World, although the leaders of those nations made decisions that sometimes hindered their progress. Underfed India, for example, poured millions of dollars into the production of a nuclear bomb when it might have spent those funds improving agricultural production.

The Soviet Union enjoyed only a slight edge, if any, in the race to win friends in the Third World. It was true that Communist ideology encouraged anticolonialism, and that the Soviet

Obstacles to Soviet Influence

Union was free of association with the long years of Western European imperialism. But though Moscow kept up a heavy drumbeat of propaganda, it could not easily explain away its subjugation of Eastern European countries. The Soviet invasion of Hungary in 1956 earned Russia international condemnation. Though Khrushchev toured India and Burma in the mid-1950s, those nations refused to become Soviet clients. They were not about to replace one imperial master with another, and Russian aid was minuscule compared with American offers. Even Communist China drifted away from Soviet influence, much as Yugoslavia had in 1948. Ultimately the Soviets, like the Americans, concluded that Third World nations were playing the two superpowers against each other in order to garner larger amounts of aid and arms, and that neutralism was anathema.

Nonetheless, the United States often interpreted Third World anti-imperialism, political instability, and attacks on foreign-owned property as Soviet-inspired, rather than as expressions of nationalism or internal racial, religious, and ethnic divisiveness. Americans too simply labeled radicals, nationalists, reformers, and neutralists as Communists. To thwart these presumed enemies, the United States resorted to alignments with unrepresentative but friendly regimes and large programs of economic assistance (by 1961 over 90 percent of American foreign aid went to the Third World).

The United States also utilized the CIA to meet Third World challenges. President Eisenhower believed that secret operations were as necessary as espionage and the gathering of information,

CIA Covert Operations

which had been defined as the CIA's primary functions at its birth in 1947. In the 1950s and later, the CIA bribed foreign politicians, subsidized foreign newspapers, hired mercenaries, conducted sabotage, sponsored labor unions, dispensed "disinformation" (circulation of false information), plotted the assassination of foreign leaders like Cuba's Fidel Castro, and staged coups. These and other spoiling operations were designed to influence foreign governments toward pro-American positions. The CIA helped overthrow the governments of Iran (1953) and Guatemala (1954), but failed in attempts to topple regimes in Indonesia (1958) and Cuba (1961). The CIA and other parts of the American intelligence community followed the principle of "plausible deniability." That is, covert operations should be conducted and the decisions that launched them concealed so that the president could deny any knowledge of them. Thus President Eisenhower denied the United States role in Guatemala, even though he ordered the operation; he also denied that he had ordered the CIA to assassinate Castro, whose government after 1959 became noisily anti-American (see pages 908–912).

In Latin America, long a United States sphere of influence, where poverty, overpopulation, illiteracy, economic sluggishness, and foreign exploitation fed discontent, anti-American feelings

CIA in Guatemala

grew. In 1951 the leftist Jacobo Arbenz Guzmán was elected president of Guatemala, a poor country whose largest landowner was the American-owned United Fruit Company. United Fruit was a major force throughout Latin America. Its total assets in 1954 equaled $580 million; it owned three million acres of land and operated railroads, ports, ships, and extensive telecommunications facilities. To fulfill his promise of land reform, Arbenz expropriated United Fruit's uncultivated land and offered compensation. United Fruit dismissed the offer and began an

"It seems the C.I.A. has not been inactive in this area."

Although the Central Intelligence Agency (CIA) became active in far-away, exotic places and enjoyed considerable influence through both conspicuous and covert operations, its effect on foreign peoples probably did not go as far as depicted in this New Yorker *cartoon. Drawing by Dana Fradon; © 1970 The New Yorker Magazine, Inc.*

advertising campaign in the United States to rally official Washington against what the company called a Communist threat to Guatemala. Lacking evidence of actual Communist control of Arbenz's government, United States officials nevertheless cut off aid to Guatemala, and the CIA began a secret plot to subvert its government. When Arbenz learned that the CIA was working against him, he turned to Russia, thus reinforcing American suspicions. The CIA airlifted arms into Guatemala, dropping them at United Fruit facilities, and in June 1954 CIA-supported Guatemalans struck from Honduras. American planes bombed the capital, the invaders drove Arbenz from power, and the new pro-American regime returned United Fruit's land. But Latin Americans wondered

what had happened to the Good Neighbor policy (see page 769). Their growing hostility toward the United States surfaced in 1958, when rioters interrupted Vice President Richard M. Nixon's goodwill trip to South America.

In the boiling Middle East the Eisenhower administration also confronted challenges to United States influence. American stakes there included the survival of the Jewish state of Israel, carved out of the British mandate of Palestine in 1948, and extensive oil holdings (in the 1950s American companies produced about half the region's petroleum). Oil-rich Iran was a special friend, for the ruling shah had granted American oil companies a 40 percent interest in a new petroleum consortium in return for CIA

On a "goodwill tour" of Latin America in spring 1958, Vice President Richard M. Nixon met an angry crowd in Caracas, Venezuela. Shouting anti-American slogans, protestors threatened Nixon in his automobile. This mob's expression of bitterness represented increasing Third World discontent with the United States. UPI/Bettmann Newsphotos.

help in the overthrow of his rival, Mohammed Mossadegh (1953). Mossadegh had attempted the unpardonable sin, nationalization of foreign oil interests.

The major threat to American interests in the Middle East came from Egypt, where the fervent Arab nationalist Gamal Abdel Nasser rose to power determined to push the British out of the Suez Canal Zone and the Israelis out of Palestine. The United States was caught in a double bind. It did not wish to anger the Arabs, for fear of losing its oil holdings. Nor did it wish to lose its staunch ally Israel, which was supported by a vocal Jewish-American lobby in American politics. But when Nasser declared neutrality in the Cold War, Dulles lost patience with him. "Do nations which play both sides get better treatment than nations which are stalwart and work with us?" he asked angrily. Eisenhower was not convinced of Nasser's neutrality. "If he was not a Communist," the president wrote later, "he certainly succeeded in making us suspicious of him." In July 1956 American officials withdrew their offer to help finance the Aswan Dam, a project to provide inexpensive electricity and water for thirsty Egyptian farmlands. Nasser quickly nationalized the British-owned Suez Canal, intending to use its profits to build the dam.

Suez Crisis

Western Europe received 75 percent of its oil from the Middle East, much of it transported through the Suez Canal. Fearing an interruption in this vital trade, the British and French conspired with Israel "to knock Nasser off his perch." On October 29, 1956, the Israelis invaded the Suez, joined two days later by Britain and France. Eisenhower fumed that his allies had not consulted him, and that the attack had shifted attention from the Soviet invasion of Hungary. He feared the move might cause Nasser to seek help from the Soviets, inviting the dread enemy into the Middle East. In early November Eisenhower bluntly told London, Paris, and Tel Aviv to pull out. The troops withdrew, Egypt paid $81 million for the canal, and the Russians built the Aswan Dam.

In early 1957, in an effort to improve the Western position in the Middle East and protect American interests there, the president proclaimed what became known as the Eisenhower Doctrine.

Eisenhower Doctrine The United States would intervene in the Middle East, he said, if any government threatened by a Communist takeover asked for help. Fourteen thousand American troops scrambled ashore in Lebanon the next year to quell an internal political dispute that Washington feared might be exploited by pro-Nasser groups or Communists. American critics protested that the United States was wrongfully acting as the world's policeman. But others complained that such a drastic resort to military intervention demonstrated that Eisenhower had failed miserably to thwart challenges to American power in the Third World and to convert the emerging nations to American friends in the Cold War.

As his presidency neared its end Eisenhower was beleaguered by accumulating foreign crises. In 1959 he had had a friendly meeting with Khrushchev at the presidential retreat at Camp David, Maryland; but it was soon followed by renewed Soviet-American tensions, especially over the U-2 incident. In Laos and Vietnam inconclusive yet escalating American intervention threatened a wider war; and Cuba's Castro moved closer to the Soviets (see Chapter 32). And the president suffered the humiliating cancellation of his trip to Japan because of anti-American riots against the United States military presence there. He became short-tempered with critics who charged that America had to regain world leadership, and he blamed everything on the Soviets. When in September 1960 Khrushchev ranted at United Nations sessions—even taking off a shoe to pound it on the table—Eisenhower angrily commented that were he a dictator he would "launch an attack on Russia while Khrushchev is in New York." Eisenhower was no dictator, and he always tamed such impulses. Americans admired his caution, but they began to wonder if it was time for a younger, more energetic man to carry the anti-Communist torch.

THE SECOND TERM AND THE ELECTION OF 1960

In part because of the demands of overseas activism, Eisenhower faced rising federal expenditures in his second term. In the first three years of his presidency he had managed to trim the budget,

Deficit Spending largely by controlling defense spending. But he discovered that he had to tolerate deficit spending to achieve his goals. In 1959 federal expenditures climbed to $92.1 billion, about half of the amount going to the military. This budget produced the largest peacetime deficit to that point in American history. In all, Eisenhower balanced only three of his eight budgets. One reason for the administration's resort to deficit spending was the need to cushion the impact of three recessions—in the years 1953-1954, 1957-1958, and 1960-1961. A sluggish economy and unemployment (it peaked in 1958 at 7.6 percent) also reduced the tax dollars the federal government collected. But most Americans remained prosperous, and the administration succeeded in keeping inflation down to about 1 percent through the 1950s.

In 1958, a year after *Sputnik,* Eisenhower signed the National Defense Education Act. It created a multimillion-dollar loan fund for college students and granted money to the states for upgrading teaching in the sciences and foreign languages. After this legislative success, the administration was rocked by the resignation of the president's chief aide, Sherman Adams, for influence-peddling and by large Republican losses in the 1958 congressional elections. The Democrats, helped by the public outcry against Adams, the economic slump, and discontent among farmers, took the Senate 64 to 34 and the House 282 to 154. Some Republicans grumbled that Eisenhower had not given his party enough leadership, while others realized that the Democrats were just too great in number to be beaten in the best of times. For the last two years of his presidency, then, Eisenhower had to confront congressional "spenders" who proposed "every sort of foolish proposal" in the name of "national security and the 'poor' fellow." Often at odds with Congress, Eisenhower cast vetoes against bills he thought would plunge the nation into even greater debt, which stood at $286 billion at the end of 1960.

The election of 1960 was one of the closest and most spirited in the twentieth century. Although Democratic candidate John F. Kennedy shared the tenets of the consensus, he asserted **John F. Kennedy** that he could expand the benefits of economic progress and win foreign disputes through more vigorous leadership. People often contrasted his youth (forty-three years old) with Eisenhower's age (seventy years old). Handsome and intelligent, Kennedy was born to wealth, graduated from Harvard, and served as a congressman before joining the Senate in 1953. His running mate in 1960 was Senator Lyndon B. Johnson of Texas, who was added to the ticket to hold white southerners in the Democratic party as the civil rights issue heated up. Republican candidate Richard M. Nixon, the forty-seven-year-old vice president from California, and his running mate, Ambassador Henry Cabot Lodge of Massachusetts, expected a rugged campaign.

Kennedy, exploiting the media to great advantage, ran a risky, yet ultimately brilliant, race. Knowing his major liability was his Roman Catholicism, he addressed that issue head-on. He traveled to the Bible Belt to tell a group of Houston ministers that he respected the separation of church and state and would take his orders from the American people, not the Pope. Seeing a major opportunity in the black vote, and calculating that Johnson could keep the white South loyal to the Democrats, Kennedy appealed to black voters. He responded to an appeal to help Martin Luther King, Jr., gain release from a Georgia county jail; he promised to sign an executive order forbidding segregation in federally subsidized housing.

Foreign policy became a major issue. Nixon claimed that he knew how to deal with Communists; and he charged that because Kennedy lacked experience in foreign affairs he could not stand up to Khrushchev. Kennedy shot back, "I was not the Vice President of the United States who presided over the Communization of Cuba." Kennedy hit hard on Cuba, while Nixon played on the senator's statement that Quemoy and Matsu were not worth defending. Kennedy's most effective theme was that Eisenhower and Nixon had let American prestige and power slip. The Democratic candidate offered Cold War victory instead of stalemate; and he vowed to secure Third World countries as allies.

As Kennedy gained momentum by stressing the anti-Communist theme, Nixon continued to suffer handicaps from the recession of 1960 and the U-2 incident. Nixon also presented an **Nixon's Handicaps** unsavory TV image, because he came across as surly and heavy-jowled in the televised debates with Kennedy. Perhaps worse, Eisenhower gave him only a tepid endorsement. Asked to list Nixon's significant decisions as vice president, the president replied: "If you give me a week, I might think of one."

In an election that saw the highest voter participation (62.8 percent) in half a century, Kennedy defeated Nixon by the razor-slim margin of 118,000 votes. The electoral college margin, 303 to 219, was much closer than the numbers suggest (see map, page 874). Slight shifts in the popular vote in Illinois and Texas would have made Nixon the victor. Kennedy carried most of the large industrial states and most of the South. Black votes were important in providing him with triumphs in North Carolina, South Carolina, and Texas, and blacks in the inner cities turned out in large numbers for him. Electoral fraud in Illinois and Texas may also have figured in Kennedy's narrow victory. Although his Catholicism lost him votes, especially in the Midwest, it also gained him about 80 percent of Catholic voters. Religious bigotry, then, did not decide this election, and Kennedy became the first Roman Catholic president.

Assessments of the Eisenhower administration used to emphasize its conservatism, passive style, limited achievements, and hesitancy to confront difficult issues. And they pointed to Eisenhower's reluctance

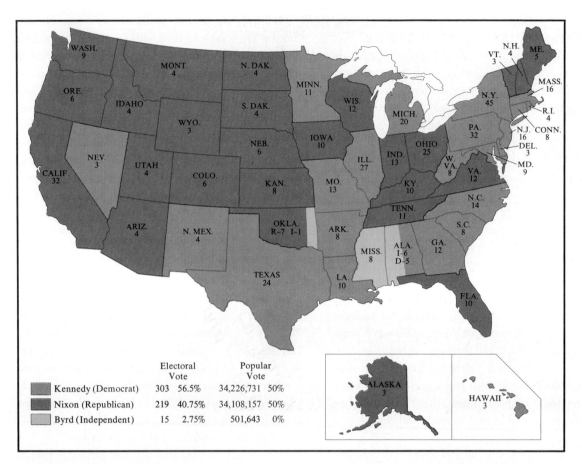

		Electoral Vote		Popular Vote	
	Kennedy (Democrat)	303	56.5%	34,226,731	50%
	Nixon (Republican)	219	40.75%	34,108,157	50%
	Byrd (Independent)	15	2.75%	501,643	0%

Presidential Election, 1960

to take strong stands, keep abreast of events, or inspire needed reforms. In recent years scholars have

Eisenhower Assessed

been researching in the now declassified documents of the consensus era, and interpretations are changing. Many have begun to stress Eisenhower's influential style, command of policymaking, sensibly moderate approach to most problems, political savvy, and great popularity. He was, in short, not an aging bystander in the 1950s, but a competent, pragmatic, compassionate leader who gave the American people what they wanted—economic growth and unrelenting anti-Communism. Most historians would agree that the record of the Eisenhower presidency is mixed. At home he failed to deal with the problems that would wrack the country in the next decade: racism, poverty, urban decay. He exacerbated the damage done by McCarthyism by refusing to come down hard on the reckless senator, and

the president's own loyalty program was excessive. Eisenhower never solved the farm problem, and he never reorganized his party to reflect the "modern Republicanism" that he championed. In foreign policy, he found no way to relax Cold War tensions, and in the end he accelerated the nuclear arms race that he so disliked. He unleashed the CIA upon the Third World and failed to adjust American diplomacy to the immense changes there.

On the other hand, when compared with his successors, Eisenhower was cautious. He kept military budgets under control and managed crises so that the United States avoided major military ventures abroad. At home he curbed inflation, kept the nation prosperous (GNP rose from $365 billion in 1953 to $504 billion in 1961), and strengthened the infrastructure by building an interstate highway system and expanding social security coverage. He brought dignity to the presidency, and the American people

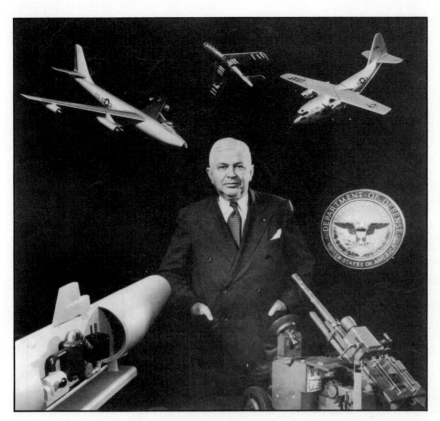

Secretary of Defense Charles E. Wilson (1890–1961) left the presidency of General Motors to join Eisenhower's cabinet. A symbol of the military-industrial complex that the president came to criticize, Wilson gained a reputation for ill-considered utterances. He once remarked that "what was good for our country was good for General Motors, and vice versa." Eisenhower frequently had to press Wilson to reduce his large defense budget requests—which Wilson's apparent fascination with the weapons of America's military might helped stimulate. Wilson resigned in 1956, much to the president's relief.   Hank Walker, © Time, Inc.

respected him. Historians now rank Eisenhower among the top third of American presidents—ahead of his successor John F. Kennedy.

In Eisenhower's final radio and television address before leaving office in early 1961, he issued a warning. Because of the Cold War, he observed, the United States had been "compelled to create a permanent industry of vast proportions," as well as a standing army of 3.5 million. "Now this conjunction of an immense military establishment and a large arms industry is new in the American experience." In it, he went on, resides the "potential for the disastrous rise of misplaced power." The demands of national security, then, had created a powerful interest group that threatened the very existence of liberty. No doubt he was thinking about the 1960 congressional report, which showed that there were 1,400 retired military officers above the rank of major, including 261 generals and admirals, employed by the one hundred leading defense contractors. Eisenhower urged Americans to guard against the "military-industrial complex." They did not.

Eisenhower's Warning Against "Military-Industrial Complex"

1952	Eisenhower elected president First U.S. H-bomb exploded	1957	Eisenhower Doctrine Little Rock desegregation crisis Civil Rights Act *Sputnik*
1953	Stalin dies Korean War ends Oppenheimer case Termination policy for Native Americans	1958	U.S. intervention in Lebanon National Defense Education Act Berlin crisis
1954	*Brown* decision CIA intervention in Guatemala Quemoy-Matsu crisis Senate condemns Senator McCarthy	1959	Castro takes power in Cuba
1955	Montgomery bus boycott begins	1960	Eighteen colonies became independent nations Greensboro, North Carolina, sit-in U-2 incident Kennedy elected president
1956	Highway Act Soviets invade Hungary Suez crisis Eisenhower re-elected	1961	Eisenhower warns against "military- industrial complex"

SUGGESTIONS FOR FURTHER READING

An Age of Consensus

Daniel Bell, *The End of Ideology* (1960); Paul A. Carter, *Another Part of the Fifties* (1983); Job L. Dittberner, *The End of Ideology and American Social Thought: 1930–1960* (1979); Marty Jezer, *The Dark Ages: Life in the U.S. 1945–1960* (1982); George Lipsitz, *Class & Culture in Cold War America* (1981); Ronald Lora, *Conservative Minds in America* (1971); Douglas T. Miller and Marion Novak, *The Fifties* (1977); George H. Nash, *The Conservative Intellectual Movement in America: Since 1945* (1976); David M. Potter, *People of Plenty* (1954); David Riesman with Nathan Glazer and Reuel Denney, *The Lonely Crowd* (1950); William H. Whyte, *The Organization Man* (1956).

Dwight D. Eisenhower

Stephen E. Ambrose, *Eisenhower*, 2 vols. (1983–1984); Robert H. Ferrell, ed., *The Eisenhower Diaries* (1981); Peter Lyon, *Eisenhower* (1974); Herbert Parmet, *Eisenhower and the American Crusades* (1972).

Eisenhower and the Politics of the 1950s

Charles C. Alexander, *Holding the Line* (1975); Larry W. Burt, *Tribalism in Crisis: Federal Indian Policy, 1953–1961* (1982); Barbara B. Clowse, *Brainpower for the Cold War: The Sputnik Crisis and the National Defense Education Act of 1958* (1981); David A. Frier, *Conflict of Interest in the Eisenhower Administration* (1969); Fred I. Greenstein, *The Hidden-Hand Presidency* (1982); Emmet John Hughes, *The Ordeal of Power* (1963); Gary W. Reichard, *The Reaffirmation of Republicanism: Eisenhower and the Eighty-third Congress* (1975); David W. Reinhard, *The Republican Right since 1945* (1983); Elmo Richardson, *The Presidency of Dwight D. Eisenhower* (1979); Mark H. Rose, *Interstate: Express Highway Politics, 1941–1956* (1979); Bernard Schwartz,

Super Chief: Earl Warren and His Supreme Court (1983). (See also works cited in Chapter 29 on McCarthyism and in Chapter 31 on social and economic questions.)

Civil Rights

John W. Anderson, *Eisenhower, Brownell, and the Congress: The Tangled Origins of the Civil Rights Bill of 1956–1957* (1964); Numan V. Bartley, *The Rise of Massive Resistance: Race and Politics in the South During the 1950s* (1969); Robert F. Burk, *The Eisenhower Administration and Black Civil Rights* (1984); William H. Chafe, *Civilities and Civil Rights* (1980) (on Greensboro sit-in); Elizabeth Huckaby, *Crisis at Central High, Little Rock, 1957–1958* (1980); Martin Luther King, Jr., *Stride Toward Freedom: The Montgomery Boycott* (1958); Richard Kluger, *Simple Justice: The History of* Brown v. Board of Education *and Black America's Struggle for Equality* (1975); Paul Murphy, *The Constitution in Crisis Times, 1918–1969* (1972); Stephen B. Oates, *Let the Trumpet Sound: The Life of Martin Luther King, Jr.* (1982); Howell Raines, *My Soul Is Rested* (1977); Harvard Sitkoff, *The Struggle for Black Equality, 1954–1980* (1981).

Eisenhower-Dulles Foreign Policy

Blanche W. Cook, *The Declassified Eisenhower* (1981); Robert A. Divine, *Eisenhower and the Cold War* (1981); Louis Gerson, *John Foster Dulles* (1968); Michael Guhin, *John Foster Dulles* (1972); Townsend Hoopes, *The Devil and John Foster Dulles* (1973); Burton I. Kaufman, *Trade and Aid: Eisenhower's Foreign Economic Policy* (1982); Douglas Kinnard, *President Eisenhower and Strategic Management* (1977); Jack M. Schick, *The Berlin Crisis* (1971). (Also see works cited in Chapter 29.)

Nuclear Arms Race

Robert A. Divine, *Blowing in the Wind: The Nuclear Test Ban Debate, 1954–1960* (1978); Lawrence Freedman, *The Evolution of Nuclear Strategy* (1981); Gregg Herken, *Counsels of War* (1985); Jerome Kahan, *Security in the Nuclear Age* (1975); Herman Kahn, *On Thermonuclear War* (1960); Henry A. Kissinger, *Nuclear Weapons and Foreign Policy* (1957); Walter A. McDougall, . . . *The Heavens and the Earth: A Political History of the Space Age* (1985); Michael Mandelbaum, *The Nuclear Question* (1979); George Quester, *Nuclear Diplomacy* (1970); Chalmers M. Roberts, *The Nuclear Years: The Arms Race and Arms Control, 1945–1970* (1970); Herbert York, *The Advisors* (1976).

The United States and the Third World

Stephen E. Ambrose, *Ike's Spies: Eisenhower and the Espionage Establishment* (1981); Richard J. Barnet, *Intervention and Revolution*, rev. ed. (1972); Chester L. Cooper, *The Lion's Last Roar: Suez, 1956* (1978); Richard Immerman, *The CIA in Guatemala* (1982); Donald Neff, *Warriors at Suez* (1981); Robert W. Stookey, *America and the Arab States* (1975). (Also see the works on Vietnam and Southeast Asia cited in Chapter 32.)

American Society During the Postwar Boom

1945–1960s

Chapter 31

Five mornings a week through the 1950s and 1960s, the same scene was played out at the bus stop at Pennsylvania Avenue and 12th Street in the District of Columbia. This was the final destination for the Red Line buses traveling from Virginia's northern suburbs to the nation's capital. Eight or nine of every ten people who debarked at that intersection were men dressed in business suits and carrying briefcases. Most were government civil servants. All were white. From shortly after seven in the morning until about ten, the buses unloaded passengers from Alexandria, Falls Church, and other rapidly growing bedroom communities across the Potomac River from Washington. The incoming passengers barely noticed the line of people waiting behind a railing to catch the return trip to the suburbs.

The difference between the busloads could hardly have been more extreme. Practically without exception, every rider on the outbound journey was a black woman from Washington's inner-city neighborhoods. Tidily dressed, many carrying shopping bags with work clothes folded inside, these women were domestic servants in the affluent homes of Washington's lawyers, bankers, politicians, lobbyists, and high-ranking bureaucrats and military officers. Next to the poverty or near-poverty to which these maids, cooks, and laundresses returned at night, the opulent white world stood in sharp contrast and raised gnawing questions. Why should these white people live in such comfort while their black servants lived precariously, wondering not what to have for dinner at night, but knowing there might not be much to eat at all?

The contrast was heightened by the fact that in 1945 the United States had entered a twenty-five-year economic boom, whose cornerstones were the automobile, housing, and defense industries. As the gross national product grew, income levels rose and property ownership spread. Automobiles rolled from assembly lines; houses and schools sprang up throughout the country. More and more Americans, including many unionized blue-collar workers, bought homes in the suburbs and consumed a seemingly endless supply of goods and services.

But while three of every four Americans were enjoying the economy of abundance, the fourth American was poor. Although poverty levels varied regionally, as well as among the cities, suburbs, small towns, and farms, it became clear by the 1960s that the American poor comprised a much larger group than people in the complacent 1950s had imagined (see pages 888–890). As calculated in 1960 by the Bureau of Labor Statistics, a "minimum comfort" budget for an urban family of four varied from $5,370 a year in Houston to $6,567 in Chicago. A widely accepted national average for the poverty line was $3,000, but the five least generous states defined subsistence as $1,600.

With the publication of Michael Harrington's *The Other America*, in 1962, people became aware of this contradiction in their midst. America's poor, wrote Harrington, were "the strangest poor in the history of mankind": they "exist within the most powerful and rich society the world has ever known. Their misery has continued while the majority of the nation talked of itself as being 'affluent.' " Crowded into the cities or living in rural isolation, the poor had "dropped out of sight and out of mind," particularly to comfortable residents in the suburbs.

Just as deprivation and pessimism defined the poor, so material comfort and optimism were the hallmarks of the middle class. Whether considered in terms of income levels or lifestyles, more Americans were better off than ever before. The most obvious expression of postwar optimism was the baby boom. From 1946 to 1961 births hit record highs. And as parents were rearing these millions of children, "family togetherness" took on almost religious significance. Landon Y. Jones, the author of a book on the baby boom, makes the analogy that this generation was like "the pig in the python." As this age group has grown older, it has had a successive impact on housing, elementary and secondary education, fads and popular music, higher education, and now the adult job market.

Postwar Americans benefited from the increase in leisure time that resulted from a return to the forty-hour week. People wanted to be entertained, and entertained they were. Sales of televisions, long-playing records, paperbacks, and comic books ballooned.

Families took to the road on expensive vacations. And, of course, there were the fads. From hula hoops to 3-D movies, the American rush to consume took new and sometimes peculiar forms.

To many people, it seemed that the American dream had come true. Whatever the nation's faults, it was the world's foremost land of opportunity. Americans boasted that they enjoyed political self-determination through the vote and social mobility through the melting pot. And public education, "the engine of democracy," guaranteed a better life to all who were willing to study and work hard. The exceptions to the dream went unnoticed by most Americans. And the lack of equal opportunities for women was concealed by an emphasis on femininity, piety, and family togetherness.

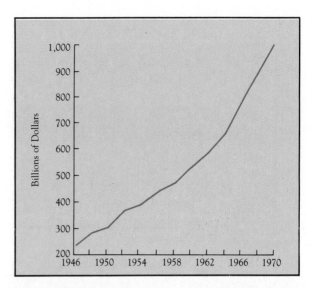

Gross National Product, 1946–1970 Source: Adapted from U.S. Bureau of the Census, Historical Statistics of the United States, Colonial Times to 1970, Bicentennial Edition (Washington: U.S. Government Printing Office, 1975), p. 224.

THE POSTWAR ECONOMIC BOOM

As Americans entered the postwar era, many wondered whether it would resemble another postwar epoch, the 1920s. In spring 1946 a *New York Times* writer predicted a return of the Roaring Twenties. Not everyone agreed. Reminding readers that the 1920s had culminated in economic depression and world war, another writer responded, "There are too many people who, knowing the results which flowed from the attitudes of 1920, are going to see to it that history does not repeat itself." Indeed, most Americans expected a replay of the 1930s. After all, it was the war that had created jobs and prosperity; surely the end of war would bring a slump.

As it turned out, neither prediction was correct. The United States in 1945 entered one of its longest, steadiest periods of growth and prosperity. The keys to this success were increasing output and increasing demand. In the twenty-five years after 1945 the American economy grew at an average rate of 3.5 percent per year. Even with occasional recessions the gross national product seldom faltered, rising from just over $200 billion in 1946 to close to $1 trillion in 1970 (see figure).

The United States was not alone in establishing new standards for economic growth and stability. Japan and the nations of Western Europe were also booming during the postwar years. "In the 'Golden Age' of the 1950's and 1960's," stated Angus Maddison, a British economist, "economic growth in the advanced capitalist countries surpassed virtually all historical records."

When the economy produced more, Americans generally brought home bigger paychecks and had more money to spend. Between 1946 and 1960 real purchasing power rose 22 percent—but that was only the beginning. In the next decade it jumped another 38 percent. Suddenly many Americans could afford goods and services that had been beyond their means in earlier decades. The result was a noticeable increase in the standard of living. To the vast majority of Americans, this nearly continuous prosperity was a vindication of the American system of free enterprise. Sociologist Seymour Martin Lipset went so far as to announce, "The fundamental problems of the industrial revolution have been solved."

Increased Purchasing Power

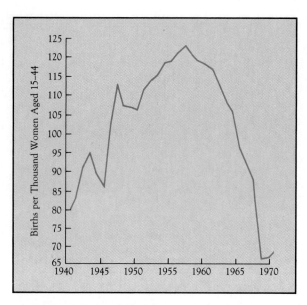

Birth Rate, 1940–1970 *Source: Adapted from U.S. Bureau of the Census,* Historical Statistics of the United States, Colonial Times to 1970, *Bicentennial Edition (Washington: U.S. Government Printing Office, 1975), p. 49.*

Crucial to the postwar economic boom was the baby boom, which was both a cause and an effect of prosperity. In 1950, 3.5 million babies were born, a sizable jump from the 2.5 million born in 1940. It was natural for the birthrate to soar immediately following the Second World War. What was confounding was that it continued to do so throughout the late 1940s and 1950s. During the 1950s the annual total exceeded 4 million (see figure), reversing the downward trend in birthrates that had prevailed for one hundred fifty years. Between 1946 and 1961, more than 63.5 million babies were born in the United States (compared with 41.5 million born in the fifteen-year period from 1930 to 1945), making the baby-boom generation the largest by far in the nation's history.

Baby Boom

What the baby boom meant was that many women who gave birth to a first child in 1946 or 1947 had second, third, fourth, and even fifth children in the years ahead. According to the Census Bureau, 83 percent of the increase in births from 1940 to 1950 were first children. Of the increased births between 1950 and 1954, however, 84 percent occurred in families that already had at least one child. The

popular belief that an only child was likely to grow up poorly adjusted had something to do with the continued increase. But *Business Week* was closer to the mark in crediting the boom to confidence in America's economic future. Professionals, white-collar workers, and college graduates contributed disproportionately to the baby boom. These were people who knew how to practice birth control and had done so in the past. (During the depression and the war the birthrate had declined most sharply among the urban middle class.) And these were people who were now having children by choice.

The baby boom spelled business for builders, manufacturers, and school systems. "Take the 3,548,000 babies born in 1950," wrote Sylvia F. Porter in her syndicated newspaper column. "Bundle them into a batch, bounce them all over the bountiful land that is America. What do you get?" Porter's answer: "Boom. The biggest, boomiest boom ever known in history. Just imagine how much these extra people, these new markets, will absorb—in food, in clothing, in gadgets, in housing, in services. Our factories must expand just to keep pace."

Of the three cornerstones of the postwar economic boom, two were related to the upsurge in births. The first was a construction boom to provide houses and schools for all these children. Office buildings, shopping centers, factories, airports, and stadiums also sprang up across the country. Much of this construction took place in the suburbs (see pages 890–893). But the postwar suburbanization of America would have been impossible without the second cornerstone, automobile manufacturing, for in the sprawling new communities a car was a necessity. Auto sales had plummeted during the Second World War, when manufacturers shifted to produce tanks and bombers, but from 1946 on sales began to climb. In 1950 they hit 6.7 million, as Americans seized the chance to get back on the road again. The number of registered automobiles climbed from 25.8 million in 1945 to 89.3 million in 1970, and total miles traveled jumped from 250 billion in 1945 to 1.1 trillion in 1970.

Auto Sales

The third cornerstone of the postwar economic boom was military spending. When the Defense Department was finally established in 1949, the nation was spending just over $13 billion a year on defense.

Military Spending

Babies meant big business for companies that produced baby foods, clothing, toys, and diapers. "In its first year as a consumer," read the caption for this 1958 Life photo, "baby is a potential market for $800 worth of products." Yale Joel, Life Magazine © 1958 Time Inc.

But beginning with the Korean War in the early 1950s, defense spending began to eclipse private domestic investment. By 1951, the Defense Department's budget was over $22 billion. Two years later it was over $50 billion. Except for a short dip from 1954 to 1958 (see page 863), it has been going up ever since. Much of the money spent on defense went into weapons research. And from 1949 to 1960 funds spent on space research alone jumped from $49 million to $401 million; by 1966 the expenditures had zoomed to almost $6 billion.

The invention of the transistor in 1948 inaugurated the computer revolution and stunning advances in electronics. Businesses and governments were so eager to buy electronic data-processing machines that sales zoomed from $25 million in 1953 to $1 billion in 1960. By the early 1960s thousands of computers had been produced and sold, marking what economist Herbert A. Simon called "an advance in man's thinking processes as radical as the invention of writing."

The evolution of electronics was a tradeoff for the American people. Computers brought about a rapid rise in productivity through the automation of numerous industries. But in doing so they stimulated technological unemployment: fewer workers were needed to accomplish the same amount of work. Computerized technology caused a decline in the demand for machinists; from 1950 to 1970 their numbers dropped from 535,000 to 390,000.

The spread of electronic technology also promoted the concentration of ownership in industry. Sophis-

Rising automobile sales not only fueled America's postwar economic boom, but also made possible the growth of the suburbs. These Cadillacs rolled off the assembly line in 1949. National Archives.

ticated technology was expensive to develop or purchase. Often only large corporations could afford it; small corporations were shut out of the market. People who believed that competition was the lifeblood of the American economy saw this tendency toward bigness as a dangerous development.

As the need for large amounts of capital increased, companies that were already established in high-technology fields expanded into related industries. General Electric was one example of a large corporation that diversified following the war. Although GE had manufactured a variety of electrical products prior to the 1940s, during the Second World War and the Cold War it expanded further, undertaking the manufacture of jet engines, nuclear-powered generators, computers, and industrial automation systems.

But not all expansion was a matter of diversification into related fields. Beginning in the early 1950s a third great merger wave swept American business. But unlike the first two waves in the 1890s and 1920s, which tended toward vertical **Conglomerate** and horizontal integration respec- **Mergers** tively (see pages 487–489, 681),

this new wave was distinguished by conglomerate mergers. A *conglomerate* merged companies in totally unrelated fields as a hedge against instability in a particular market or industry. International Telephone and Telegraph, for instance, bought up companies in the fields of car rental (Avis), baking (Continental Baking), suburban development and home construction (Levitt and Sons), food sales (Canteen Corporation), hotels and motels (Sheraton Corporation), and insurance (Hartford Fire Insurance).

This new wave of mergers resulted in unprecedented concentration of industry. The Federal Trade Commission observed that in 1968 the two hundred largest manufacturing corporations held the same proportion of total manufacturing assets as had the one thousand largest in 1941. Reflecting the directions of America's postwar boom, the country's ten largest corporations at this time were in automobiles (GM, Ford, Chrysler), oil (Exxon, Mobil, Texaco), and electronics and communications (GE, IBM, ITT, Western Electric).

Even the labor movement experienced a merger. In 1955 the American Federation of Labor and the Congress of Industrial Organizations put aside their differences and established the AFL-CIO. Union membership remained fairly constant, however, increasing from just under 18 million at the time of the merger to only 20.7 million fifteen years later. Most new jobs were opening up not in the heavy industries that hired blue-collar workers, but in the union-resistant white-collar service trades. And some observers complained that union leaders had become comfortable and lost the organizing zeal that had won over so many workers in the 1930s and 1940s. Revelations of corrupt union practices also tainted the labor movement. The nation's biggest union, the International Brotherhood of Teamsters, had ties to organized crime. When the Teamsters failed to clean their house, the AFL-CIO officially expelled the union in 1957. Two Teamsters' presidents, Dave Beck and James R. Hoffa, served federal prison sentences for offenses ranging from tax evasion to jury tampering.

The postwar economic boom was a good time for unionized blue-collar workers, many of whom not only benefited from real increases in wages, but also enjoyed a middle-class lifestyle that heretofore had been the exclusive province of white-collar workers, businesspeople, and professionals. Because most union jobs paid well, these workers could obtain mortgages for suburban homes, especially if their spouses were also working. Many enjoyed job security, including a paid two-week vacation. With Social Security and union and company pension plans, they could look forward to retirement. They aspired to college educations for their children. And they were more secure against inflation. In 1948 General Motors and the United Auto Workers Union agreed on automatic cost-of-living adjustments (COLAS) in workers' wages, a practice that spread to other industries.

The trend toward economic consolidation brought changes in agriculture as well as business and labor. While new machines such as mechanical cotton-, tobacco-, and grape-pickers and crop-dusting planes revolutionized farming methods, increased use of fertilizers and pesticides raised the cash value of farm output by 120 percent (in constant dollars) between 1945 and 1970. Meanwhile labor productivity tripled. The resulting improvement in profitability drew large investors into agriculture. Average acreage per farm almost doubled, from 195 in 1945 to 374 in 1970. Simultaneously the value of

Agricultural Consolidation

farmland skyrocketed from $69 billion in 1945 to $266 billion in 1970. By the 1960s it took money—big money—to become a farmer. In many cases only banks, insurance companies, and other large businesses could afford the necessary land, machinery, and fertilizer.

By no means did all the effects of economic growth benefit the average American. In agriculture the movement toward consolidation threatened survival of the family farm. From 1945 to 1970 the nation's farm population declined from 24.4 million to just under 10 million, or from 17.5 percent of the population to 4.8 percent. When the harvesting of cotton in the South was mechanized in the 1940s and 1950s, more than 4 million people were displaced. One result was a shift of this poverty to the North and the cities. As one farmer lamented, "We lost country life when we moved to tractors." What was more, many of the people who stayed on did so, not because they could still make a good living, but because they were too old to leave their lifelong homes and follow their children and grandchildren to the cities. Living in relative isolation on limited incomes, the rural aged were among the hidden victims of mechanization.

The significant changes that postwar growth produced in industry and agriculture were matched by changes in Americans' buying habits and lifestyles. For many Americans the postwar economic boom brought what the economist John Kenneth Galbraith called the affluent society.

THE AFFLUENT SOCIETY

As America's productivity grew by leaps and bounds in the postwar years, so did its appetite for goods and services. During the depression and the Second World War, many Americans had dreamed about buying a home or a car. In the affluent postwar years they could satisfy their deferred desires. Families purchased not one but sometimes two cars and equipped their new homes with the latest appliances and amusements—dishwashers, television, and stereophonic sound systems. When they lacked cash to buy what they wanted, they borrowed money. Credit

In 1955 the Salk polio vaccine was approved by the government for general use, and millions of children like this one received the vaccine. By 1962 the incidence of reported polio cases had dropped 97 percent.   UPI/Bettmann Newsphotos.

to support the nation's shopping spree grew from over $8 billion worth of short- and intermediate-term loans in 1946 to $127 billion in 1970. Here was the economic basis of the consumer culture.

As Americans consumed goods and services, they were using up the world's resources. Consumption of crude petroleum soared 118 percent from 1946 to 1970, but domestic production increased only 97 percent. The extra oil had to be imported. Electricity use jumped too, from 270 billion kilowatt-hours to 1.6 trillion. By the mid-1960s the United States, with only 5 percent of the world's population, produced and consumed over one-third of the world's goods and services.

Advances in public health were a particularly happy effect of postwar prosperity. The average life span increased from 65.9 years in 1945 to 70.9 in 1970, due especially to a dramatic decline in the death rate among the young. **Improvements in Public Health** Affluent Americans could afford regular prenatal and pediatric care, and they benefited from increased federal funding for medical research. As a result the

infant mortality rate dropped from over 38 deaths per 1,000 live births in 1945 to 20 per 1,000 in 1970. At the same time the discovery of wonder drugs such as streptomycin (1945) and aureomycin (1948) reduced deaths from influenza and postsurgical infection. And the Salk polio vaccine, approved for public use in 1955, reduced the number of reported cases of polio 97 percent by 1962. Other diseases, like tuberculosis, whooping cough, and diphtheria, became little more than bad memories.

Millions of Americans began their search for the affluent society by migrating to the Sunbelt. This mass migration had started during the Second World **Growth of the Sunbelt** War, when GIs and their families were ordered to new duty stations and war workers moved to the shipyards and aircraft factories of San Diego and other cities of the West and South. Soon the Sunbelt encompassed most of America's southern rim, the area running from southern California across the Southwest and South all the way to the Atlantic Coast. Between 1940 and 1950 Houston's population jumped from 385,000 to 596,000. Other Sunbelt

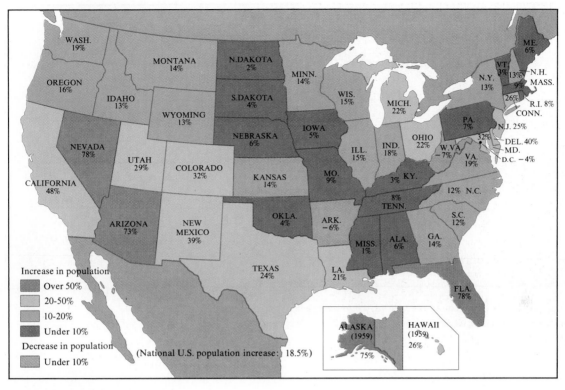

Rise of the Sunbelt, 1950–1960

Map legend:

Increase in population
- Over 50%
- 20–50%
- 10–20%
- Under 10%

Decrease in population
- Under 10%

(National U.S. population increase: 18.5%)

State population changes:
WASH. 19%, OREGON 16%, IDAHO 13%, MONTANA 14%, N.DAKOTA 2%, MINN. 14%, WIS. 15%, MICH. 22%, ME. 6%, VT. 3%, N.H. 13%, MASS. 9%, N.Y. 13%, R.I. 8%, CONN. 26%, PA. 7%, N.J. 25%, OHIO 22%, W.VA. −7%, DEL. 40%, MD. 32%, D.C. −4%, NEVADA 78%, UTAH 29%, WYOMING 13%, S.DAKOTA 4%, NEBRASKA 6%, IOWA 5%, ILL. 15%, IND. 18%, VA. 19%, KY. 3%, N.C. 12%, CALIFORNIA 48%, COLORADO 32%, KANSAS 14%, MO. 9%, TENN. 8%, S.C. 12%, ARIZONA 73%, NEW MEXICO 39%, OKLA. 4%, ARK. −6%, MISS. 1%, ALA. 6%, GA. 14%, TEXAS 24%, LA. 21%, FLA. 78%, ALASKA (1959) 75%, HAWAII (1959) 26%

cities that boomed in the 1940s were Baton Rouge, Long Beach, Miami, Mobile, and Phoenix.

The southward and westward migration continued to swell in the 1950s and 1960s (see map). Houston became a center not only of the aerospace industry but of oil and petrochemical production. Tucson, which had been scarcely more than a watering hole in the desert in 1950, grew to a city of 213,000 ten years later. California absorbed no less than one-fifth of the nation's entire population increase in the 1950s—enough, by 1963, to make the Golden State the most populous state in the union.

The economic bases of the Sunbelt's spectacular growth were easy to identify: agribusiness, the aerospace industry, the oil industry, real estate development, recreation, and, of course, defense spending. Government policies—such as large tax breaks given to oil companies and decisions about where to build military bases and award defense and aerospace contracts—were crucial to the Sunbelt's development. Industry was also drawn to the southern rim by right-to-work laws, which outlawed the closed union shop, and by low taxes and heating bills.

The millions of people who left the chilly industrial cities of the North and East for sunnier climes strengthened the political clout of the Sunbelt. In a book published in 1969, Kevin Phillips, a conservative Republican, predicted an emerging Republican majority based on the votes of the South and West. Richard Nixon's triumph in the presidential election of 1968 seemed to support Phillips's thesis. So did the tendency of political parties to nominate Sunbelt candidates for national office. (The nation's four most recently elected presidents have hailed from the Sunbelt—one from Texas, two from California, and one from Georgia. And in 1980 the Census Bureau made it official: for the first time in the nation's history, voters in the South and West accounted for a majority of those eligible to cast ballots.)

The economic boom that made for the political pre-eminence of the Sunbelt also brought increased security for whole classes of Americans. And the expanding economy combined with federal welfare legislation to reduce poverty (see Chapter 33). But even with the reduction in poverty, there was little redistribution of income. The portions of total national

DISTRIBUTION OF TOTAL PERSONAL INCOME[a] AMONG VARIOUS SEGMENTS OF THE POPULATION, 1947–1970 (IN PERCENTAGES)

Year	Poorest Fifth	Second Poorest Fifth	Middle Fifth	Second Wealthiest Fifth	Wealthiest Fifth	Wealthiest 5 Percent
1947	3.5	10.6	16.7	23.6	45.6	18.7
1950	3.1	10.5	17.3	24.1	45.0	18.2
1960	3.2	10.6	17.6	24.7	44.0	17.0
1970	3.6	10.3	17.2	24.7	44.1	16.9

[a]Monetary income only.

Source: Adapted from U.S. Bureau of the Census, *Historical Statistics of the United States, Colonial Times to 1970*, Bicentennial Edition (Washington: U.S. Government Printing Office, 1975), p. 292.

income taken home by the rich, the middle classes, and the poor remained about the same from 1947 to 1970 (see table).

THE OTHER AMERICA

In the postwar age of abundance, most Americans found it especially hard to acknowledge the presence of poverty in their midst. But according to the Bureau of Labor Statistics, in 1962 about 42.5 million Americans (nearly one out of every four people) were poor. These Americans earned less than $4,000 per year for a family of four, or $2,000 per year for a single person living alone. Age, race, sex, education, and marital status were all factors in their poverty. One-fourth of the poor were over sixty-five; many lived alone on fixed incomes, their meager purchasing power continually reduced by inflation. More than a third of the poor were under eighteen. One-fifth were nonwhite, including almost half the nation's black population and more than half the Native

American population. Two-thirds lived in households headed by a person with an eighth-grade education or less, and one-fourth lived in households headed by a single woman. For all these people, there was little reason for hope. The bureau constructed a budget to show what a poor family of four could afford: one book a year; a new car every twelve to eighteen years; no telephone; a movie once every three weeks; a wool suit every two or three years for the husband. It is clear from this meager budget that no matter how much the economy might boom, there was a limit to the money that would trickle down to the poor.

In the years after 1945, while millions of Americans, most of them white, were settling in the suburbs, the poor were congregating in the inner cities. Starting with the wartime industrial boom of the early 1940s and continuing through the 1960s, almost 4.5 million blacks, many of whom were unskilled and illiterate, trekked to the cities from the rural South. By 1970 the black population, which had been 48.6 percent urban in 1940, had become 81.4 percent urban. Joining Afro-Americans in the exodus to the cities were poor whites from the southern Appalachians, who moved to Cincinnati, Baltimore, St. Louis, Columbus, Detroit, and Chicago. Latin Americans were arriving

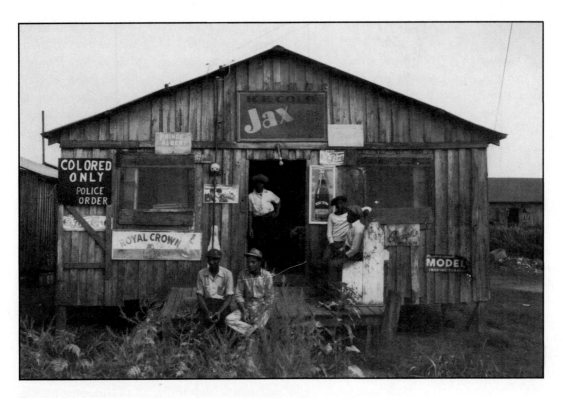

Despite America's postwar economic boom, many people still lived in poverty. In 1945, these black farm workers in Belleglade, Florida, had little hope for the future. Fifteen years later their plight was unchanged, as the historic television documentary "A Harvest of Shame" made clear in 1960. National Archives/Photo Researchers.

in growing numbers from Mexico, Puerto Rico, the Dominican Republic, Colombia, Ecuador, and Cuba. New York City's Puerto Rican population spurted from 70,000 to over 600,000 in just twenty years.

Next to Afro-Americans, the largest group of urban newcomers were the Mexican-Americans, or Chicanos. Millions came during and after the war as farm workers, and increasingly they remained to make their lives in the United States. Despite the initiation in 1953 of Operation Wetback, a program to find and deport illegal aliens, Mexicans continued to enter the country in large numbers, many of them illegally. Many settled in cities. According to the 1960 census, over 500,000 Mexican-Americans had migrated to the *barrios* of the Los Angeles–Long Beach area since 1940. If estimates of uncounted illegal aliens were added to the census figure, the total was far higher. The same was true of the *barrios* of El Paso, Phoenix, and other southwestern cities, as well as Chicano

communities in Denver, Kansas City, Chicago, Detroit, and other northern cities.

Native Americans made up the country's poorest group with an average annual income that was half the amount of the poverty level. Indians moved to the cities in the 1950s and 1960s, particularly after Congress in 1953 adopted the policy of termination that ended the status of certain tribes as wards of the United States (see page 857). Accustomed to the rural, semicommunal life of the reservation, many had difficulty adjusting to the city. Indeed, the tragedy of many groups who migrated to cities was that, instead of finding a place to prosper, they found only a dumping ground for the poor.

Not all the poor, however, lived in cities. By 1960, 30 percent lived in small towns and 15 percent on farms. Tenant farmers and sharecroppers, both black and white, suffered economic hardship. Migratory farm workers lived in abject poverty. And elderly people tended to be poor regardless of where they lived.

These Americans were poor partially because they had been shortchanged by New Deal and Fair Deal legislation. Postwar housing laws primarily helped the middle class (see page 893). The Wagner Act and federal farm programs established during the New Deal chiefly helped unionized workers and big farmers (see pages 741 and 746). Neither Social Security nor the minimum wage covered hospital janitors and orderlies, bus boys, dishwashers, and other restaurant employees, or migratory farm workers. The programs available to the poor were generally designed to give them direct relief, not to better their chances of maintaining an independent income.

Naturally, the number of people living in poverty fluctuated with the economy. During the postwar years, poverty was most widespread during the 1950 recession, when 36 percent of Americans were classified as poor. By 1962 poverty had fallen to about 25 percent; economic growth was clearly reducing the ranks of the poor. President Lyndon B. Johnson's war on poverty cut the figure further, and it fell to 13 percent by 1969. Still, it was evident that many people slipped into poverty for a variety of reasons.

A large share of the poor were women. Well-paying employment opportunities were limited and there was extensive occupational segregation, with low-paying positions being labelled women's work and better-paying positions being reserved for men. Although in 1945 many women had wanted to remain in the factories and shipyards, they were pushed out to make way for returning veterans. And those who tried later to return to industrial work were discouraged. "Rosie [the Riveter] feels something like Typhoid Mary when she applies for a factory job," stated the *Detroit Free Press*. In 1960 the median annual earnings for full-time women workers stood at 60 percent of men's earnings. Moreover, many women's jobs were not covered by either the minimum wage or Social Security. Finally, if divorce, desertion, or death did rend a family, it was usually the woman who was left to bear responsibility for the health and welfare of children. Many ex-husbands did not make their child-support payments. And on welfare, or a salary that paid women sixty cents for each dollar a man got, many single mothers and their children slipped into poverty.

One of the least-known effects of economic hardship on the poor has been physical and emotional illness. A study done in the late 1950s in New Haven, Connecticut, found that the rate of treated psychiatric illness was three times as high for the lowest fifth of income earners as it was for the upper-middle and upper classes. Psychiatrists at Cornell University's Medical School described the "low social economic status individual" as "rigid, suspicious," and having "a fatalistic outlook on life. . . . They are prone to depression, have feelings of futility, lack of belongingness . . . and a lack of trust in others."

Graphic evidence of the emotional costs of poverty came during the economic recession of 1960, when the National Federation of Settlements and Neighborhood Centers assembled reports from around the country on the effects of the downturn. A social worker from Rochester, New York, bemoaned a sharp rise in "marital discord and desertions of families by the father, increased welfare dependency, increased crime, especially robberies, burglaries and muggings, and alcoholism." Ironically, all of this suffering was occurring in a nation that was being heralded as the affluent society.

THE GROWTH OF SUBURBS

Suburban growth was closely associated with the affluent society. During the first six decades of the twentieth century, cityward migration steadily increased. But in the 1940s another migration—from the city to the suburbs—began to swell. By 1970 more Americans resided in suburbs than in central cities (see table).

A combination of motives drew people to the suburbs. Many wanted to leave behind the sounds and smells of the city and be closer to nature. They also wanted homes with yards so that, as one suburbanite put it, "every kid [would have] an opportunity to grow up with grass stains on his pants." Or they wanted the privacy and quiet that detached homes provided, as well as family rooms, extra closets, and utility rooms. Many were also looking for a community of like-minded people, a place where they could have

GEOGRAPHIC DISTRIBUTION OF U.S. POPULATION, 1930–1970 (IN PERCENTAGES)

Year	Central Cities	Suburbs	Rural Areas and Small Towns
1930	31.8	18.0	50.2
1940	31.6	19.5	48.9
1950	32.3	23.8	43.9
1960	32.6	30.7	36.7
1970	31.4	37.6	31.0

Source: Adapted from U.S. Bureau of the Census, *Decennial Censuses, 1930–1970* (Washington, U.S. Government Printing Office).

a measure of political influence. Big-city government was dense and impenetrable. In the suburbs citizens could become involved in government and have an impact, particularly on the education their children received. "The American suburb," mused a Pittsburgh building executive in 1960, "is the last outpost of democracy, the only level on which the individual citizen can make his wishes felt, directly and immediately."

Judging from the massive numbers of three- and four-bedroom houses built in the suburbs, there was no question that suburbanites' major concern was their children. "This is a paradise for children," observed a newspaper writer in 1950, referring to the new suburb where he lived. "There are so many babies here," commented one of his neighbors, "you would think everybody would be blasé about them. Still, when a new one is coming, all the neighbors make a fuss over you."

Another allure of the suburbs was closeness in age and shared experience. In many suburbs most adults were young parents between the ages of twenty-five and thirty-five, and almost all the children were toddlers. In one suburb of nine thousand homes there were eight thousand children, only about one hundred of whom were old enough for high school; most of the rest were still in playpens. "People could not outdo each other," one resident of this community reported, "because they almost all have the same income. . . . Nobody talks about the [Second World] war much, because they've all been in it. And most of the men have the same . . . commuting problem—which many have solved by car pools. All this helps to cement neighbors into friends."

Government funding and policies helped these new families to settle in the suburbs. Low-interest GI mortgages and Federal Housing Administration mortgage insurance made the difference

Housing Boom for people who would otherwise have been unable to afford a home. Such easy credit combined with postwar prosperity to produce a construction boom. In 1944 there had been only 142,000 housing starts, many of which represented temporary housing for soldiers and war workers. From 1945 to 1946 housing starts climbed from 326,000 to over 1 million, and in 1950 they approached 2 million. Never before had new starts exceeded 1 million; not until the early 1980s would they dip below that level.

To produce so much new housing so fast, contractors had to operate on a massive scale. Arthur Levitt and Sons, a firm that built planned communities (Levittowns) in New York, New Jersey, and Pennsylvania, developed the pattern adopted by other companies: using interchangeable materials and designs, Levitt erected rows of nearly identical houses on uniform

The suburbs promised a haven for the families of the baby boom. In this housing project in Lakewood Park, California, new families moved in at a rate of 25 per day during the last three months of 1950.   National Archives.

treeless lots. As suburbia spread, pasture lands yielded to whole neighborhoods with astounding rapidity. To supply the new communities, supermarkets, gas stations, shopping centers, and malls—all of them surrounded by vast parking lots—soon dotted the countryside.

At the same time highway construction opened up rural lands for the development of suburban communities. In 1947 Congress authorized the construction of a 37,000-mile chain of highways, and in 1956 President Eisenhower signed the Highway Act, which launched a 41,000-mile nationwide network. Federal funds spent on highways swelled from $79 million in 1946 to $429 million in 1950, $2.9 billion in 1960, and a huge $4.6 billion in 1970. State and local highway expenditures also mushroomed.

Highway Construction

By the 1970s most of the interstate system had been completed, and some towns along the way had prospered. Route I-70, for example, gave Junction City, Kansas, six new motels, several restaurants, and an economic boost. But the new road also siphoned traffic away from older roads. Small towns along two-lane highways withered as residents left to seek a better living in the city. "They [the towns] didn't dry up and blow away," observed the editor of Junction City's daily newspaper, "but they are much like the towns left off the railroad [lines] 100 years ago."

The spurt in highway construction combined with the mushrooming of suburbia to produce the *megalopolis*, a term first used by urban experts in the early 1960s to refer to the almost uninterrupted metropolitan complex stretching along the northeastern seaboard of the United States. Beginning in Boston and extending 600 miles south through New York, Philadelphia, Baltimore, and Washington, "Boswash" encompassed parts of eleven states and a population of 49 million people, all tied together by interstate highways. Although the suburbs within the megalopolis

Chapter 31: AMERICAN SOCIETY DURING THE POSTWAR BOOM, 1945–1960s were politically independent, they were economically dependent on the cities and connecting highways. Other megalopolises that took shape following the Second World War were "Chipitts," a band of heavy industry and dense population stretching from Chicago to Pittsburgh, and "San-San"—San Francisco to San Diego.

Middle-class whites benefited more than other Americans from the government-supported housing and highway boom. In 1948 the government cut mortgage subsidies for rental-unit construction and increased subsidies for privately owned single-family houses, a policy that worked against the poorest Americans. Moreover, the FHA refused to guarantee suburban home loans to the poor, nonwhites, Jews, and other "inharmonious racial and ethnic groups." Some federal programs actually worsened conditions for the poor. The National Housing Act of 1949, passed to make available "a decent home and a suitable living environment for every American family," failed in several respects. The primary features of the act were "urban redevelopment," or slum clearance; the construction of public housing for low-income people (810,000 units in four years); and FHA mortgages for home buyers. But the program was poorly coordinated, and slums were replaced not with low-income housing but with parking lots, shopping centers, luxury high-rise buildings, highways, and factories. The planned 810,000 housing units for the poor were constructed not in four years but in twenty.

Socially, the suburban emphasis on family togetherness tended to isolate families. Writing in 1957, sociologist David Riesman criticized "the decentralization of leisure in the suburbs . . .

Critics of Suburban Life as the home itself, rather than the neighborhood, becomes the chief gathering place for the family— either in the 'family room' with its games, its TV, its informality, or outdoors around the barbecue." The floor plan of the ranch-style home, at whose center was the TV set enthroned on a swivel, was suited to the stay-at-home lifestyle. Even when families traveled, they were isolated in the family car.

Riesman was only one of many critics of suburban living. Other observers denounced the suburbs for breeding conformity. Some writers criticized suburbanites for trying to keep up with the Joneses by buying new cars and appliances. The word *suburbia*,

These commuters from their jobs in Chicago departed the train at their suburban destination in Park Forest, Illinois. The novel The Man in the Gray Flannel Suit (1955) was the best-selling account of one such commuter. Dan Weiner photo, courtesy Sandra Weiner.

Scott Donaldson wrote in *The Suburban Myth* (1969), had "unpleasant overtones, suggesting nothing so much as some kind of scruffy disease." The titles of magazine articles and books echoed his diagnosis: "Trouble in the Suburbs," "The Crabgrass Roots of Suburbia," *The Split Level Trap.* In Sloan Wilson's novel *The Man in the Gray Flannel Suit* (1955), the main character led a treadmill existence commuting to his white-collar job in the city. And C. Wright Mills, a sociologist, castigated white-collar suburbanites, who "sell not only their time and energy but their personalities as well. They sell . . . their smiles and their kindly gestures."

When all the pluses and minuses were tallied, however, most residents of suburbia seemed to prefer family togetherness to any other lifestyle of which they were aware. Of the college students interviewed by Riesman in the 1950s, the vast majority looked forward to living in the suburbs.

IDEALS OF MOTHERHOOD AND THE FAMILY

I n the early twentieth century, Sunday dinner had been an exasperating occasion for the youngest child in a large family, for the youngest was traditionally served last. If the dinner was chicken, the little one often got the back or the neck. "I was the youngest of five children" recalled one young father shortly after the Second World War, "and by the time I was served, all the white meat was gone. . . . I swore to myself that when I grew up I would eat all the white meat I could. So I'm grown up and a father—and my children get first choice!" Times had changed, and so had the ways of the American family.

A good deal of the change was due to the publication in 1946 of Dr. Benjamin Spock's *Baby and Child Care*. The book, which quickly became a bible for new parents, answered many com-

Dr. Spock on Childrearing

mon questions about childrearing. But unlike earlier manuals, *Baby and Child Care* urged mothers (but not fathers, because Spock assigned them little formal role in childrearing) to think of their children first, even at the expense of their own mental and physical health. Dr. Spock's predecessors during the previous thirty years had advised mothers to consider their own needs as well as their children's. They had recommended early and strict toilet training; "putting away your children at six o'clock" in order to enjoy "the quiet comfort of a still household in the evening"; and ignoring a baby's crying except at feeding time. Now Dr. Spock urged the mother to be constantly available to feed and communicate with her baby, and to remember that "feeding is learning." Spock encouraged the baby's "self-realization," self-discovery," and "self-motivated behavior."

Though no mother could be all things to her baby, women who embraced Dr. Spock's teachings tended to believe they had failed if they were not. Guilt was the inevitable result of the effort to be not only mother but teacher, psychologist, and buddy. The mother of an epileptic son wrote to Dr. Spock: "I

try to give him a great deal of affection, although I am a working woman. . . . Sometimes it is so difficult to maintain my control that my hands shake. . . . Does he need the help or do I?" Another mother wrote, "We like to read and listen to music. Maybe we have neglected some aspects of A's development in our own selfishness."

At the same time Philip Wylie, author of the book *Generation of Vipers*, denounced such selfless behavior as Momism. In the guise of sacrificing for her children,

Momism

Wylie wrote, Mom was pursuing "love of herself." She smothered her children with affection so they would become emotionally dependent on her and would not want to leave home. Other experts agreed. Army psychiatrists blamed recruits' nervous disorders on mothers who, as a psychiatric adviser to the Secretary of War wrote, had "failed in the elementary mother function of weaning [their] offspring emotionally as well as physically."

But women were caught in a double bind, for if they pursued a life outside the home they were accused of being "imitation men" or "neurotic" feminists. Echoing the psychoanalyst Sigmund Freud, critics of working mothers contended that a woman could be happy and fulfilled only through domesticity. "Anatomy is destiny" was their catch phrase; a woman's gender determined her role in life. Reflecting on the contradictory expectations of women, anthropologist Margaret Mead wrote in 1946, "Choose any set of criteria you like, and the answer is the same: women—and men—are confused, uncertain, and discontented with the present definition of women's place in America."

A reason for woman's dilemma was the conflicting roles she was expected to fulfill. On the one hand, the home was premised on a full-time housewife who, with little regard for her own needs, provided her husband and children a haven from the outside world. In 1963 Betty Friedan gave this situation a name— *The Feminine Mystique*. On the other hand, women continued the wartime trend toward work outside the home. The female labor force rose from 16.8 million in 1946 to 23.3 million in 1960 and 31.6 million in 1970. These women entered the labor force lacking the support of an organized women's movement and refraining from challenging sex-role stereotypes. But because of the rough division of the labor market into "men's jobs" and "women's jobs," many women found themselves segregated in low-paying work as clerks, secretaries, and nurses, while men commanded comfortable incomes as tradesmen, business managers, and doctors.

Many women, of course, were their families' sole source of income; they had to work. Still others took jobs not to challenge male dominance but to earn additional family income, enjoy adult company, or bolster their self-esteem. Despite the cult of motherhood, most new entrants to the job market were married, a trend that had begun during the Second World War (see figure), and most were mothers.

Immediately after the Second World War, many American families moved into Quonset huts on college campuses. Accompanied by wives and babies, former GIs were getting an education. The **GI Bill** legislation making it possible was the Servicemen's Readjustment Act of 1944, or GI Bill of Rights, which provided living allowances and tuition payments to college-bound veterans. Over 1 million enrolled in 1946—almost one out of every two students. Despite dire predictions to the contrary, the veterans succeeded as students. Benjamin Fine, education editor of the *New York Times*, called it "the most astonishing fact in the history of American higher education. . . . The G.I.'s are hogging the honor rolls and the Dean's lists. . . . Far from being an educational problem, the veteran has become an asset to higher education." But there was nothing astonishing about it. Veterans saw higher education as the key to upward mobility.

These veterans were determined to succeed so they and their families could prosper, so their children could grow up in grassy suburban yards and attend good public schools. Men and **Family Togetherness** women of their generation had been children and adolescents during the economic deprivation of the 1930s. They had experienced young adulthood during the Second World War, when many had been physically separated from their families and friends. Glen H. Elder, the sociologist, has written that men and women who had grown up in the 1930s "in Depression-marked homes were most likely to anchor their lives around family and children, perhaps reflecting the

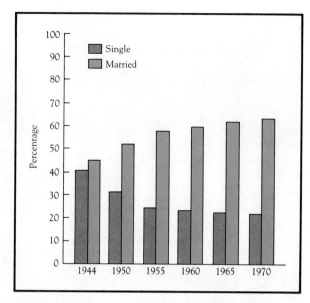

Marital Distribution of Female Labor Force, 1944–1970 Source: Adapted from U.S. Bureau of the Census, Historical Statistics of the United States, Colonial Times to 1970, *Bicentennial Edition (Washington: U.S. Government Printing Office, 1975), p. 133.*

notion of home as a refuge in an unpredictable world." These men and women became parents of the baby boom and exponents of "family togetherness." Such togetherness included family TV-watching, outings to parks and beaches, and Little League games. The destination of many family vacations was Disneyland, which opened in Anaheim, California, in 1955.

Popular periodicals echoed the importance that these parents attached to togetherness. "Ed and His Family Live Together and Love It" was the title of a typical article in a 1954 *McCall's*. "Caring for three lively children makes tremendous demands on Carol. . . . But Ed is a cheerful working partner to her, helps with the children and housework whenever he can, gives everything he has to make his family happy." In return, Ed's wife and children "give him all the love and affection a husband and father could hope for." Carol even took over some household tasks traditionally performed by men: "Paneling that extra room in the cellar used to be the man's job. But Ed and Carol do it together." Despite *McCall's* advocacy of shared tasks, the magazine stopped short of advocating complete equality. "For the sake of every

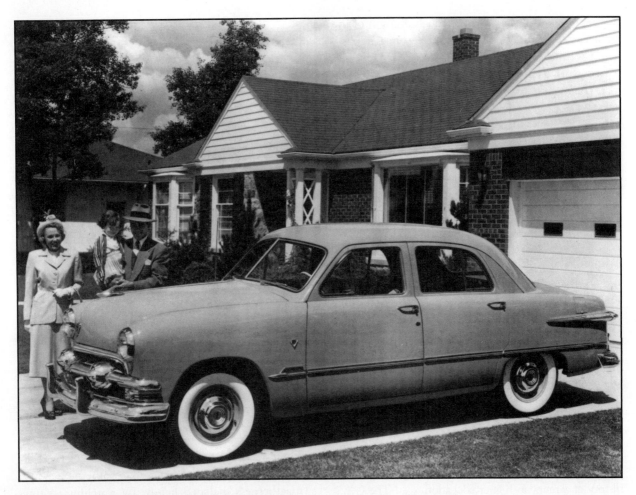

Complete with their addition to the baby boom generation, these smiling parents stand proudly in front of their suburban home and new automobile. After a dozen years of economic depression and world war, many young couples enjoyed the togetherness afforded by life in the suburbs. UPI/Bettmann Newsphotos.

member of the family, the family needs a head. This means Father, not Mother."

Most American families were preoccupied with education. As the baby boom became a grade-school boom, parents rushed to join the parent-teacher association so they would have a voice in the educational process. They expressed concern that schools were overcrowded, understaffed, and aimless, or that teachers were using obsolete methods. Educators encouraged their participation. "Just as war is 'too serious a matter to be

Education of the Baby Boom Generation

left to the generals,' so, I think, the teaching of reading is too important to be left to the educators," wrote Dr. Rudolf Flesch in 1955, in his best-selling book *Why Johnny Can't Read.*

Two years later when the Russians launched *Sputnik,* the first earth-orbiting satellite, education became a matter of national security. The Russian success challenged American military and technological superiority, based ultimately on the nation's school system. James B. Conant, Hyman G. Rickover, and other critics argued that what the United States needed to regain its technological leadership was new emphasis on mathematics, foreign languages, and the sciences. In 1958 Congress responded with the National Defense Education Act (NDEA), which funded elementary and high school programs in those disciplines and offered fellowships and loans to college students. Parents were quick to endorse the new programs. After all, public education was the engine of democracy, a guarantee of both upward social mobility and military superiority.

Just as education became intertwined with national security, religion became synonymous with patriotism. As President Eisenhower put it, "recognition of the Supreme Being is the first, the most basic expression of Americanism." After all, the United States was locked in mortal combat with an atheistic enemy. In America's Cold War with the godless Soviet Union, ministers, priests, and rabbis became foot soldiers in the battle for souls. Religious leaders emphasized family togetherness in their appeals for new converts. "The family that prays together stays together" was a famous slogan used during the 1950s and 1960s. The Bible topped the best-seller lists, and books with religious themes, such as the Reverend Norman Vincent Peale's *The Power of Positive Thinking* (1952), sold in the millions. Meanwhile evangelist Billy Graham exhorted television viewers and stadium audiences throughout the country. From 1945 to 1970 church membership nearly doubled.

Although Americans were eager to improve their minds and souls, they were not ready until the 1960s to liberate themselves sexually. When Dr. Alfred Kinsey, director of the Institute for Sex Research at Indiana University, published his pioneering book *Sexual Behavior in the Human Male* (1948), the American public was shocked. On the basis of interviews with numerous men, Kinsey estimated that 95 percent of American men had engaged in masturbation, premarital or extramarital intercourse, or homosexual behavior. Princeton's President Harold Dodds denounced the volume as "the work of small boys writing dirty words on fences." Five years later Kinsey caused even more of a disturbance with *Sexual Behavior in the Human Female*, which revealed that 62 percent of women masturbated and 50 percent had intercourse before marriage. Some angry Americans condemned the report as a slanderous attack not only on women, but on motherhood and the family as well. A

congressional representative from New York, who tried to bar the report from the mails, charged Kinsey with "hurling the insult of the century against our mothers, wives, daughters and sisters." Sex was nothing new, of course, but its existence was seldom acknowledged in polite conversation or respectable publications—and most Americans preferred that situation.

AMERICA AT PLAY

The prosperity that marked the postwar era was reflected in the materialistic values and pleasures of the period. Having satisfied their basic needs for food, clothing, and shelter, growing numbers of Americans turned their attention to luxury items. "More appliances make mom's work easier," read a typical advertisement. As families strove to acquire the latest conveniences, shopping became a form of recreation.

Of the new luxuries, television was the most revolutionary in its effects. One man who grew up in the postwar era recalled the purchase of the first family TV set in 1950. "And so the monumental change began in our lives and those of millions of other Americans. More than a year passed before we again visited a movie theater. Money which previously would have been spent for books was saved for the TV payments. Social evenings with friends became fewer and fewer still because we discovered we did not share the same TV program interests." By 1950 television had broken radio's grip on the American public. The number of households with TVs climbed from 8,000 in 1946 to 3.9 million in 1950 and 60.6 million in 1970.

TV Enters the American Home

Entertainment was TV's number one product. Situation comedies and action series were among the most popular shows. Topping these categories in the 1950s were *I Love Lucy*, starring Lucille Ball, and *Dragnet*, a detective series. Family togetherness was a theme of *Father Knows Best* and *Leave It to Beaver*. There were programs for all age groups, ranging from

The Howdy Doody Show was one of the most popular children's television shows. The show's stars were Clarabelle the clown, Howdy Doody (sitting on the back of Flubadub), and Bob Smith.   National Archives.

Ding Dong School, quiz shows, and westerns to the roller derby. As daily average TV viewing in the United States reached five hours in 1956 and six hours in 1971, the danger presented itself that television would become more than just entertainment. Some critics worried that with this much viewing, TV's distorted presentation of the world would significantly define people's sense of reality.

Advertising was the foundation of the television industry, as it had also been for radio. The first TV commerical, made by the Bulova Watch Company in 1941, was a one-minute effort that cost nine dollars. By the end of the decade, American families were spending several hours a day before the television set, and bargain rates had vanished; annual expenditures for TV advertising totaled $50 million. By 1970 the figure had soared to $3.6 billion.

Critics of the television industry have often wondered why American viewers put up with advertising. The answer is that, far from being an unwanted interruption, television advertising was a valuable service to consumers. Because keeping up with the Joneses was a goal of some suburbanites, television advertising provided visual evidence of just what the Joneses were buying. In the comfort of their living rooms Americans could study how to elevate their status through the purchase of a particular automobile, cigarette, or electric appliance. Indeed, it was not only commercials but programs themselves that tantalized viewers with glimpses of the sumptuous life. Situation comedies and dramas were nearly always set in well-furnished suburban homes; the characters dressed in the latest styles and drove the newest cars.

As television brought the world into their living

1945	Demobilization of 12 million GIs
1946	Beginning of the baby boom Spock, *Baby and Child Care* Over 1 million GIs enroll in colleges
1947	Gross national product ($231.3 billion) begins postwar rise Levittown, New York, begun 8,000 families own TVs
1948	Kinsey, *Sexual Behavior in the Human Male*
1949	National Housing Act
1952	Peale, *The Power of Positive Thinking* Ellison, *Invisible Man*
1953	*The Wild One* Kinsey, *Sexual Behavior in the Human Female*
1955	Salk polio vaccine approved for use AFL-CIO merger *Rebel Without a Cause*
1956	Highway Act Ginsberg, *Howl*
1957	Peak of baby boom (4.3 million births) Soviet Union launches *Sputnik I* Kerouac, *On the Road*
1958	National Defense Education Act
1960	Gross national product reaches $503.7 billion
1962	Harrington, *The Other America*
1963	Friedan, *The Feminine Mystique*
1970	Gross national product reaches $977.1 billion Suburbs surpass central cities in population

rooms, Americans began to read newspapers and news magazines a little less carefully, and to listen to radio a lot less frequently. But despite the

Paperback Books

lure of the tube, book readership went up. One reason for the increased consumption of literature was the mass marketing of the inexpensive paperbound book. Pocket Books hit the market in 1939; soon westerns, detective stories, and science fiction filled the newsstands, supermarkets, and drug stores. "The paperback democratized reading in America," Kenneth C. Davis has written in his history of "the paperbacking of America." The comic book, which had become popular in 1939 with the introduction of Superman, became another drug store standard. Reprints of hardcover books and condensed books also did well. All in all, funds spent for books increased by 220 percent between 1946 and 1960 and by another 265 percent between 1960 and 1970.

One obvious casualty of the stay-at-home suburban culture was the motion picture. While Americans continued to buy paperbacks and comic books in large numbers, many of them stopped visiting movie theaters. Why fight traffic to go to a movie when you could watch TV in the comfort of your living room? Why pay a babysitter? From 1946 to 1948 Americans had attended movies at the rate of nearly 90 million a week. By 1950 the figure had dropped to 60 million a week; by 1960, 40 million. Thus the postwar years saw the steady closing of movie theaters—with the notable exception of the drive-in, which appealed to car-oriented suburban families.

There was one crucial exception to the downturn in moviegoing. By the late 1950s the first children of the postwar baby boom had become adolescents, and though their parents preferred to stay home and watch television, they themselves flocked to the theaters. No less than 72 percent of moviegoers during

The most popular rock-and-roll star of the 1950s was Elvis Presley. Presley's records sold millions of copies, but so freely did he bump and grind that Ed Sullivan, the host of a popular weekly television variety show, pronounced him "unfit for a family audience." Leviton-Atlanta/Black Star.

the 1950s were under age thirty. Hollywood responded to this youthful new audience with films portraying young people as sensitive and intelligent, adults as boorish and hostile: *The Wild One, Rebel Without a Cause, Blackboard Jungle*. The cult of youth had been born.

Rise of the Youth Subculture

Soon the music industry was catering to teens with cheap 45 rpm records. Bored with the era's syrupy music, young Americans welcomed the driving energy and hard beat of rock-and-roll. Bill Haley, the Everly Brothers, and Buddy Holly thrilled teenagers with their music. Elvis Presley horrified their parents with his suggestive gyrations. Before long, Presley's ducktail haircut and leather jacket had become the uniform for rebellious teenage males. Although the roots of the new music lay in black rhythm-and-blues, most white stars did not acknowledge the debt. Presley's hit tune "Hound Dog," for example, had originally been performed by the black singer Big Mama Thornton, but Thornton received little credit for her contribution. Among the black rock-and-roll stars of the 1950s were Chuck Berry and Little Richard.

While white performers copied black rhythm-and-blues, serious black jazz artists like Charlie Parker and Dizzy Gillespie were experimenting with "bebop." In the 1950s jazz became increasingly fused with classical themes, compositions, and instrumentation.

Intellectuals began to study this art form, which had once been looked down on as vulgar.

In the arts Martha Graham was lauded in international dance circles, and Jackson Pollock became the pivotal figure of the abstract expressionist movement, which in the 1950s established New York City as a center of the art world. Rather than work with the traditional painter's easel, Pollock spread his canvas on the floor, where he was free to walk around it, "work from the four sides and literally be *in* the painting." He and other "action painters" worked with sticks, trowels, and knives, and they played with new materials like heavy impasto with "sand, broken glass and other foreign matter added." In the 1960s artists of the Pop Art movement satirized the consumer society, using commercial techniques to depict everyday objects. Andy Warhol painted Campbell soup cans; other artists did blowups of ice-cream sundaes, hamburgers, and comic-strip panels.

Every era has its fads. Slinky, selling for a dollar, began loping down people's stairs in 1947; silly putty was introduced in 1950. The 1950s also had 3-D movies and hula hoops. Within **Fads** months of the hula hoop's introduction in 1958, over 30 million had been sold. And then there were signature items such as Hoppy watches, emblazoned with pictures of cowboy star Hopalong Cassidy. Although most crazes were short-lived, they created multimillion-dollar industries and effectively promoted dozens of movies and TV shows. Other postwar crazes are still with us—Scrabble, paint-by-number sets, and Barbie dolls, to name just a few. Between 1959 and 1980 more than 120 million Barbie and Barbie family dolls were sold. Frisbee-throwing has not only survived but has prevailed over similar outdoor games. Many of these toys and games succeeded because they brought the whole family together.

Some prewar activities flourished in the 1950s and 1960s, notably golf and bowling. But though Americans still hunted and fished, they no longer did so at the farm pond or in the woods down the road; they had to travel to get to the country. And travel they did. With more money and leisure time and a much-improved highway system, middle-class families took vacations that had formerly been restricted to the rich. They visited national monuments and parks, went camping, and even ventured abroad.

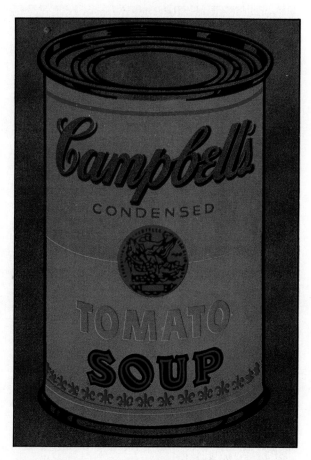

Andy Warhol's Campbell's Soup *(1965), a Pop Art satire of the consumer culture.   The Museum of Modern Art, New York, Elizabeth Bliss Parkinson Fund.*

Needless to say, the consensus society of the 1950s and early 1960s was not receptive to social criticism. The filmgoing public preferred noncontroversial doses of Doris Day and Rock Hudson, and Dean Martin and Jerry Lewis. Readers bought novels and retreated into the criminal underworld, the wild West, or science-fiction fantasy. Even serious artists tended to ignore the country's social problems.

There were exceptions. Ralph Ellison's *Invisible Man* (1952) gave white Americans a glimpse of the psychic costs to black Americans of exclusion from the white American dream. **Beat** Two films—*Gentleman's Agreement* **Generation** (1947) and *Home of the Brave* (1949)—examined anti-Semitism and white racism. And in the 1950s, one group of writers repudiated the conventional world of the middle class and the suburbs. Rejecting the same social niceties Kinsey had challenged, the writers of the Beat (for "beatific") Generation flaunted their freewheeling sexuality and consumption of drugs. The Beats produced some memorable prose and poetry, including Allen Ginsberg's long poem *Howl* (1956) and Jack Kerouac's *On the Road* (1957), and they offered American youth an alternative to their parents' materialism and righteous self-congratulation. Though the Beats were mostly ignored during the fifties, millions of young Americans discovered their writings and lifestyle in the late 1960s.

One of the most influential books of postwar years was the best-selling *The Affluent Society* (1958), by economist John Kenneth Galbraith. Galbraith's thesis dovetailed with the prevalent belief that economic growth would bring prosperity to everyone. Some would have more than others, of course, but in time everybody would have enough. "Production has eliminated the more acute tensions associated with [economic] inequality," Galbraith wrote. Not until Chapter 23 did the author mention poverty; when he did, he dismissed it as not "a universal or massive affliction," but "more nearly an afterthought."

Only in the 1960s would comfortable Americans of the middle class discover that millions of poor people lived in America (see Chapter 33). Politically and culturally, the later 1960s would be vastly different from the consensus years that preceded them. Ironically, it would be the products of suburbia—the children of the baby boom—who formed the vanguard of the assault not only on poverty, but on the whole value system of the American middle class.

SUGGESTIONS FOR FURTHER READING

The Affluent Society

Carl Abbott, *The New Urban America* (1981); Robert H. Bremner and Gary W. Reichard, eds., *Reshaping America: Society and Institutions* (1982); David P. Calleo, *The Imperious Economy* (1982); John Kenneth Galbraith, *The Affluent Society* (1958); John Kenneth Galbraith, *American Capitalism* (1952); Robert Heilbroner, *The Limits of American Capitalism* (1966).

Farmers and Workers

Willard W. Cochrane and Mary E. Ryan, *American Farm Policy, 1948–1973* (1976); Gilbert C. Fite, *American Farmers* (1981); James R. Green, *The World of the Worker* (1980); Howell John Harris, *The Right to Manage: Industrial Relations in the 1940s* (1982); John L. Shover, *First Majority—Last Minority: The Transforming of Rural Life in America* (1976).

The Baby Boom

Richard A. Easterlin, *Birth and Fortune* (1980); Landon Y. Jones, *Great Expectations: America & The Baby Boom Generation* (1980); Diane Ravitch, *The Troubled Crusade: American Education, 1945–1980* (1983).

The Other America

Joseph H. Cash and Herbert T. Hoover, eds., *To Be an Indian: An Oral History* (1971); Harry M. Caudill, *Night Comes to the Cumberland* (1963); J. Wayne Flynt, *Dixie's Forgotten People: The South's Poor Whites* (1979); Leo Grebler et al., *Mexican-American People* (1970); Michael Harrington, *The Other America* (1981 ed.); August B. Hollingshead and Frederick C. Redlich, *Social Class and Mental Illness* (1958); Oscar Lewis, *La Vida* (1966); Herman P. Miller, *Rich Man, Poor Man* (1971); Dorothy K. Newman et al., *Politics and Prosperity: Black Americans and White Institutions, 1940–75* (1978); James T. Patterson, *America's Struggle Against Poverty, 1900–1980* (1981); David S. Walls and John B. Stephenson, eds., *Appalachia in the Sixties* (1972).

Suburbia

Bennett M. Berger, *Working-Class Suburb* (1960); William B. Dobriner, *Class in Suburbia* (1963); Herbert J. Gans, *The Levittowners* (1967); Mark I. Gelfand, *A Nation of Cities* (1975); Dolores Hayden, *Redesigning the American Dream* (1984); Kenneth T. Jackson, "The Crabgrass Frontier: 150 Years of Suburban Growth in the United States," in R.A. Mohl and J.F. Richardson, eds., *The Urban Experience* (1973), 196–221; Zane L. Miller, *Suburb* (1982); John B. Rae, *The American Automobile* (1965); Robert C. Wood, *Suburbia* (1959); Gwendolyn Wright, *Building the Dream: A Social History of Housing in America* (1981).

Women, Motherhood, and the Family

William H. Chafe, *The American Woman: Her Changing Social, Economic, and Political Role, 1920–1970* (1972); Ruth Schwartz Cowan, *More Work for Mother* (1983); Carl Degler, *At Odds: Woman and the Family in America from the Revolution to the Present* (1980); Betty Friedan, *The Feminine Mystique* (1963); Susan M. Hartmann, *The Homefront and Beyond: American Women in the 1940s* (1982); Susan Estabrook Kennedy, *If All We Did Was to Weep at Home: A History of White Working-Class Women in America* (1979); Alice Kessler-Harris, *Out to Work: A History of Wage-Earning Women in the United States* (1982); Mirra Komarovsky, *Blue-Collar Marriage* (1962); Susan Strasser, *Never Done: A History of American Housework* (1982); Nancy Pottisham Weiss, "Mother, the Invention of Necessity: Dr. Spock's *Baby and Child Care*," *American Quarterly*, 29 (1977), 519–546.

Popular Culture

John W. Aldridge, *In Search of Heresy: American Literature in an Age of Conformity* (1956); Peter Biskind, *Seeing Is Believing: How Hollywood Taught Us to Stop Worrying and Love the Fifties* (1983); Paul A. Carter, *Another Part of the Fifties* (1983); Ann Charters, *Kerouac* (1973); Kenneth C. Davis, *Two-Bit Culture: The Paperbacking of America* (1984); Andrew Dowdy, *The Films of the Fifties* (1973); Maxwell Geismar, *American Moderns* (1958); Charlie Gillett, *The Sound of the City: The Rise of Rock 'N' Roll*, rev. ed. (1983); Serge Guilbaut, *How New York Stole the Idea of Modern Art* (1983); Jeffrey Hart, *When the Going Was Good: American Life in the Fifties* (1982); Douglas T. Miller and Marion Novak, *The Fifties* (1977); Gerald Nicosia, *Memory Babe: A Critical Biography of Jack Kerouac* (1983); Nora Sayre, *Running Time: Films of the Cold War* (1982).

Television

Erik Barnouw, *Tube of Plenty*, rev. ed. (1982); Leo Bogart, *Age of Television* (1958); George Comstock et al., *Television and Human Behavior* (1978); Jerry Mander, *Four Arguments for the Elimination of Television* (1978); Frank Mankiewicz and Joel Swerdlow, *Remote Control: Television and the Manipulation of American Life* (1978).

Vietnam
and the Cold War:
American Foreign Policy
1961–1981

Chapter 32

*T*he *Joint Chiefs* of Staff (JCS) memorandum lay on the table. Its recommendation: add another 100,000 to the 80,000 American troops already in Vietnam, because the war was not going well. "Is there anyone here of the opinion we should not do what the memorandum says?" asked President Lyndon B. Johnson of his advisers, assembled for a tense meeting on the morning of July 21, 1965. Only Undersecretary of State George W. Ball spoke up: "Mr. President, I can foresee a perilous voyage, very dangerous." Johnson asked, "What other road can I go?" Ball answered directly, "Take our losses, let their government fall apart, negotiate, discuss, knowing full well there will be a probable take-over by the Communists." The president, who had actually already made up his mind to escalate the American intervention in Vietnam but was willing to listen to Ball's oft-stated objections again so that he could always say he had carefully weighed all alternatives, did not like that answer. The hard-driving Texan recoiled from thoughts of losing. He simply could not accept that a small, primitive country like Vietnam could deny the United States victory.

At an afternoon session, Ball again forthrightly argued a case he knew few of his colleagues endorsed. "The war will be long and protracted. The most we can hope for is a messy conclusion." Not only did dangers arise from possible Chinese intervention, negative world opinion, and domestic politics, but "the enemy cannot be seen in Vietnam. He is indigenous to the country." Ball seriously doubted that "an army of Westerners can successfully fight Orientals in an Asian jungle." He pressed on, "It is like giving cobalt treatment to a terminal cancer case." In the long run, then, the war "will disclose our weakness, not our strength." Johnson jumped in: "But George, wouldn't all these countries say that Uncle Sam was a paper tiger," with America losing its credibility? "No sir," Ball retorted. "The worse blow would be that the mightiest power on earth is unable to defeat a handful of guerrillas."

The next day Johnson huddled with the military brass. The generals told him that more men, more bombings, and more money were needed to keep America's South Vietnamese ally in power against the North Vietnamese and Vietcong. "But if we put in 100,000 men won't they put in an equal number, and then where will we be?" Johnson asked. He became excited, asking tough questions. When an admiral claimed that if the United States did not back the faltering South Vietnamese regime, allies around the world would lose faith in America's word, Johnson knew better: "We have few allies really helping us now." And have the bombing raids hurt the enemy? Not really, the generals answered, but if more sites were added to the target list, they would. Johnson grew worried: "Isn't this going off the diving board?" The secretary of defense argued that the United States had a "commitment" to South Vietnam. Johnson shot back, "But, if you make a commitment to jump off a building and you find out how high it is, you may want to withdraw that commitment."

In late July a troubled President Johnson nonetheless decided to keep that "commitment" by giving the JCS what it wanted. A major decision of the Vietnam War, it meant that the United States was assuming, for the first time, primary responsibility for fighting the war. Fearing a national debate, Johnson muted his decision's importance when he announced it. By the end of 1965 nearly 200,000 American combat troops were at war in Vietnam. Yet Congress had not passed a declaration of war, and the American people remained largely ignorant of the government's massive venture in Southeast Asia. Ball later concluded that Johnson's July decision was "the greatest single error that America had made in its national history." Measured by the wrenching impact of the war on the United States, he was probably correct.

Vietnam, either because of the searing war experience itself or because of the lessons Americans later drew from that experience, bedeviled the Kennedy, Johnson, Nixon, and Carter presidencies. Other themes crowded the international agenda in the 1960s and 1970s: continued Soviet-American competition for global influence with dramatic swings from conciliation to confrontation in the Cold War, an accelerating nuclear arms race, turmoil in the Third World, much of it anti-American, eruptions in the Middle East, mean-spirited Cuban-American hostilities, and disorder in the world economy. But Vietnam, where Cold War and Third World issues seemed to merge, at least in American thinking, dominated American foreign policy. Kennedy enlarged a United States presence in Southeast Asia, Johnson Americanized the war, Nixon spent considerable energy trying to end the war without losing it, and Carter struggled with the postwar consequences of defeat. As he wound down the American combat role in Vietnam, Nixon also inched toward détente with the Soviet Union and China and intervened in Third World disputes to protect American interests he thought threatened. Carter sought to reverse the deterioration of American influence in the Third World and to continue détente, but the Iranian hostage crisis and a flare-up in Soviet-American relations dashed most of his hopes and returned the world to frigid Cold War.

Throughout the 1960s and 1970s Americans became uneasy not only about the troubled position of the United States in world affairs, but also about the disorder wrought at home by foreign entanglements. Foreign policy and domestic developments had been traditionally interconnected, and foreign policy had always sprung from the domestic setting of the nation—its needs, wants, moods, and ideals. Yet the experience of the Vietnam War called into question those needs, wants, moods, and ideals, because a majority of Americans came to see the effects of the war as a threat to their economic well-being, social stability, and political system (see Chapters 33 and 34). By 1981 Americans had not reached a consensus about the lessons of Vietnam; but, fearing America's slippage from its high world rank, they were eager to restore its pre-eminence and repair their own frayed society.

KENNEDY AND THE QUEST FOR COLD WAR VICTORY

John F. Kennedy's diplomacy owed much to the past. He remembered the tragedy of appeasement in the 1930s as well as the triumph of containment

Kennedy as Cold War Activist

in the 1940s. Just as Nazism had been turned back and Communism contained, now in the 1960s Communism would be routed. Kennedy's dynamic personal style suggested a new departure in foreign policy; actually it meant a bolder, more vigorous prosecution of the Cold War. An eloquent speaker, energetic worker, and fierce competitor, Kennedy was an "incandescent man. He was on fire, and he set people around him on fire," recalled Secretary of State Dean Rusk. As a diplomat, Kennedy was eager to prove his toughness. His administration kept box scores on the missile race, the arms race, the space race, and the race for influence in the Third World. When the young president prepared for his first meeting with Russian Premier Nikita Khrushchev, he seemed poised for a contest rather than a talk: "I have to show him that we can be as tough as he is," remarked Kennedy. "I'll have to sit down with him and let him see who he's dealing with."

Kennedy appointed a staff of bright, often arrogant, people who were determined to score Cold War victories. Journalist Theodore White called them "action intellectuals." A disenchanted Undersecretary of State Chester Bowles complained later that the Kennedy team was "full of belligerence." And Adlai Stevenson told a friend privately that "they've got the damnedest bunch of boy commandos running around down there [in Washington] you ever saw." That there would be no halfway measures was apparent in Kennedy's inaugural address: "Let every nation know that we shall pay any price, bear any burden, meet any hardship, support any friend, oppose any foe to assure the survival and the success of liberty."

Khrushchev matched Kennedy's rhetoric with an endorsement of "wars of national liberation" in the Third World. And in fall 1961 the Soviet Union ended a moratorium on above-ground nuclear testing by exploding a giant 50-megaton bomb. Khrushchev also bragged about Russian ICBMs, raising American anxiety over Soviet capabilities. Intelligence data soon proved the premier's claim false. Kennedy nonetheless sought to fulfill his campaign commitment to a military buildup based on the principle of *flexible response*. Junking Eisenhower's concept of massive retaliation, which emphasized nuclear weapons, Kennedy sought ways to meet any kind of warfare, from guerrilla combat in the jungles to a nuclear

When the ugly Berlin wall first went up in 1961 along the border between East and West Berlin, it was hastily constructed of barbed wire. Later East German troops added heavy concrete slabs to the barricade, as they are doing here. President John F. Kennedy drew criticism from West Germans for not stopping construction of the wall; some students even sent him an umbrella—symbol of appeasement in the 1930s. Two years later, however, West Berliners gave the president a warm reception. UPI/Bettmann Newsphotos.

showdown. In this way, he reasoned, he could contain both the Soviet Union and Third World revolutionary movements. In 1961 the military budget shot up 15 percent, ICBM arsenals swelled further, and plans were laid to increase NATO's nuclear firing power. The government even encouraged citizens to build fallout shelters in their backyards. By mid-1964 strategists measured a 150 percent increase in the number of American nuclear weapons. Though Kennedy could claim credit for the Arms Control and Disarmament Agency and a test-ban treaty with Russia (1963), which banned nuclear testing in the atmosphere, in outer space, and under water, his real legacy was an accelerated arms race.

During this time Berlin continued to claim headlines. The Russians again demanded negotiations to end the Western occupation of Berlin. But Kennedy saw the historic city as "the great testing place of Western courage and will." Instead of negotiating, he asked Congress in 1961 for an additional $3.2 billion for defense and the authority to call up reservists. Events took an ugly turn in August 1961 when the Soviets erected the Berlin Wall, a concrete-and-barbed-wire barricade designed to halt the exodus of East Germans into the more prosperous and politically free West Berlin. Yet another example of Soviet repression, the wall inspired protests all over the non-Communist world. When Kennedy visited the wall in 1963 he stirred a mass rally of West Berliners with the words "Ich bin ein Berliner" ("I am a Berliner").

Berlin Wall

But it was over Cuba, a nation whose allegiance the United States had taken for granted since the turn of the century, that Kennedy had his most serious confrontation with the Soviet Union (see map). Cuba became an obsession of American policymakers in

The *United States in the Caribbean and Central America*

909

1959, when the bearded Fidel Castro emerged from his mountain-based guerrilla camp to oust America's long-time ally Fulgencio Batista. President Eisenhower had made a last-minute attempt to install a friendly military regime there and to deny Castro his hard-fought revolutionary triumph. From the start Castro determined to break the influence of American business, which owned 3 million acres of Cuban land, controlled 40 percent of its sugar production and 90 percent of its telephone and electric service, and sold Cuba 70 percent of its imports. Indeed, American investments in the island at the time of Castro's victory totaled about $1 billion. The Cuban leader nationalized some American-owned property, suspended promised elections, indulged in a barrage of anti-American rhetoric, and in early 1960 signed a trade treaty with Russia.

In mid-1960 President Eisenhower grew impatient with Castro and reduced American purchases of Cuban sugar. Castro's response was large-scale seizures of American-owned companies. Soon the Cuban premier began to appeal to Russia for support. Historians disagree on whether Castro was always a Communist, or whether Washington's vehement opposition pushed him into Russia's arms. In any case, the Soviet Union gradually came to Cuba's assistance with loans and trade. The Monroe Doctrine, Moscow declared, was dead.

In March 1960, Eisenhower had ordered the CIA to train Cuban exiles for an invasion of their homeland. Just before he left office Eisenhower broke diplomatic relations with Castro and advised Kennedy to advance plans for the invasion. The picture sketched by the CIA appealed to Kennedy: Cuban exiles would land at the Bay of Pigs and secure a beachhead; the Cuban people would rise up against Castro; a Revolutionary Council organized in the United States would enter Havana in triumph. Kennedy was nonetheless uneasy over such a blatant attempt to topple a sovereign government; he ordered that no Americans be directly involved in the invasion so that the United States could maintain the fiction that the operation was solely a Cuban affair. The president never attempted to negotiate with Castro over Cuban-American troubles; Kennedy preferred victory over compromise.

Bay of Pigs

The CIA-directed expedition departed Nicaragua in April 1961. Escorted by American warships, the fourteen hundred commandos scrambled ashore at the Bay of Pigs. Actually, the first man to hit the beaches was an American CIA operative. The Cuban people did not rise up against Castro and within two days most of the commandos had been captured. Many of them later blamed Kennedy for the disaster, citing his refusal to permit a second air strike. But the operation, with or without more air support, had little chance of success. Boats went aground on coral reefs that the CIA had dismissed as seaweed; equipment malfunctioned; the Bay of Pigs was Castro's favorite fishing spot and he knew the details of its landscape; had the exiles of Brigade 2506 managed to move inland they would have encountered swamps; and the mountains that might have served as a sanctuary were eighty miles away. Before it was over, four Americans had died. "How could I have been so stupid to let them go ahead?" Kennedy asked himself.

Kennedy did not suffer defeat easily. Soon he and his advisers set about finding other means to unseat Castro. "My idea," Attorney General Robert Kennedy said, "is to stir things up on the island with espionage, sabotage, [and] general disorder." The president's brother instructed the CIA to let "no time, money, effort—or manpower—be spared" in a project that came to be known as Operation Mongoose. Government agents worked to disrupt the island's trade; they continued to aid anti-Castro groups in Miami; and they plotted with organized crime leaders to assassinate Castro.

Cuba soon became the site of one of the scariest crises of the Cold War. Had there been no Bay of Pigs and no Operation Mongoose, Fidel Castro has said, there would have been no missile crisis. For Castro, American hostility represented a real threat to Cuba's independence. And for the Russians, American actions were a challenge to the only pro-Communist regime in Latin America. "We had to think up some way of confronting America with more than words," recalled the Soviet premier. So Castro and Khrushchev devised a daring plan to deter any new American intervention: installation of Soviet missiles and nuclear bombers in Cuba.

Although the Kennedy administration was aware of a Soviet military buildup on the island, it was not until October 14, 1962, that a U-2 plane photographed medium-range missile sites. Whether the Soviets had

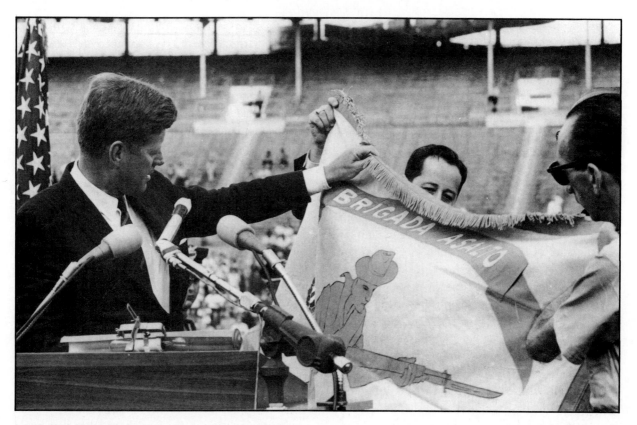

In December 1962, in Miami's Orange Bowl, President John F. Kennedy (1917–1963) welcomed home the newly released members of the CIA-sponsored landing force captured by the Cuban militia at the Bay of Pigs. Still determined to unseat Castro, Kennedy received the troops' combat banner, promising, "This flag will be returned to this Brigade in a free Havana." Wide World Photos.

acted to protect Cuba, to improve their own nuclear capability, to trigger negotiations over Berlin, or to force the United States to pull its missiles out of Turkey was not clear. In any case, the president organized an executive committee and ordered it to find a way to remove the missiles from Cuba. Some members advised a surprise air strike, likely to kill both Russian technicians and Cubans. But Robert Kennedy scotched that idea; he wanted no Pearl Harbors on his brother's record. The JCS recommended a full-scale military invasion—a Bay of Pigs with American soldiers. But that approach risked a prolonged war with Cuba, a Soviet attack against Berlin, or even nuclear holocaust. Soviet expert Charles Bohlen unsuccessfully urged quiet, direct ne-

Cuban Missile Crisis

gotiations with Soviet officials. It was Secretary of Defense Robert S. McNamara who proposed the most acceptable formula: a naval quarantine of Cuba, to prevent further military shipments. Halfway between armed warfare and doing nothing, it left the administration free to attack or negotiate, depending on the Russian response.

Over national television on October 22, Kennedy informed the Soviets of American policy and demanded their retreat. American warships headed for the Caribbean, B-52s loaded with nuclear bombs took to the skies, and American military forces around the globe went on alert. Khrushchev first replied that the missiles would be withdrawn if Washington pledged never to attack Cuba again. Then he demanded the removal of American missiles from Turkey. Kennedy accepted the first condition but rejected the second. (Privately the administration made an informal promise to the Russians to withdraw the missiles from Turkey in the future.) On October 28 Khrushchev accepted the American pledge to respect Cuban sovereignty and promised to ship the missiles back to the Soviet Union. Americans breathed a collective sigh of relief; this was, said many, Kennedy's finest hour.

But critics then and now have asked whether the crisis was really necessary. Why, they have asked, did the president attempt to solve the crisis with public brinkmanship instead of private negotiations? Television addresses and public confrontations are not the stuff of statesmanship, but of politics—and the congressional elections were just weeks away. They have noted too that Kennedy passed up a chance to protest the presence of the missiles when he met privately with Foreign Minister Andrei Gromyko in the White House on October 18. Finally, critics have claimed that the strategic balance of power was not seriously altered by the placement of Soviet missiles in Cuba. The United States had about four hundred missiles capable of reaching Russia, the Soviets only less than one hundred capable of hitting North America. Kennedy went to the nuclear brink when he did not need to, his critics have said.

The Cuban missile crisis humiliated the Soviets. (In the world of diplomacy, it is wise to give the enemy a chance to save face.) Exposed as nuclear inferiors, the Soviets vowed to catch up—and they managed to do so by the late 1960s. The crisis did produce some relaxation in Soviet-American relations. The superpower leaders installed a teletype "hot line" between Washington and Moscow staffed round the clock by translators and technicians, signed a test-ban treaty, and refrained from further confrontation in Berlin.

Elsewhere in the Third World, Kennedy called for "peaceful revolution" based on the concept of *nation building*. Drawing on the ideas of the economist Walt W. Rostow, who joined the Kennedy administration, the president determined to build goodwill in Third World countries by helping them through the infant stages of nationhood. One method would be programs aimed at improving agriculture, transportation, and communications. Kennedy thus created the multibillion-dollar Alliance

Nation Building

for Progress in Latin America. And for the same purpose, the Peace Corps, founded in 1961, sent teachers, agricultural specialists, and health workers into developing nations throughout the world. Within three years ten thousand idealistic young men and women had volunteered for service. But the Peace Corps' humanitarian purpose competed with the administration's political needs. Periodic conflicts arose between corps members in the field, who identified with Third World peoples and their desire for neutralism, and headquarters in Washington, where the goal was aligning those peoples with American foreign policy.

Besides such special development programs, Kennedy relied on *counterinsurgency*: the training of native police forces by American military and technical advisers. The assumption was that American soldiers—especially the Special Forces units, or Green Berets—would provide a protective shield against insurgents while American civilian personnel worked on economic projects.

Nation building and its methods did not work. Americans assumed, as they had for much of the twentieth century in the Caribbean, that they could simply transfer their own model of capitalism and democracy to foreign cultures. But many foreigners resented American meddling in their affairs. And because monetary aid was usually funneled through a self-interested elite, it often did not reach the very poor. And to people who preferred the relatively quick solutions of a managed economy, the American emphasis on private enterprise seemed inappropriate. "In the end," the presidential adviser Arthur M. Schlesinger, Jr., later wrote, counterinsurgency proved "a ghastly illusion. Its primary consequence was to keep alive the American belief in their capacity and right to intervene in foreign lands."

The CIA became one of the primary instruments of counterinsurgency (see pages 869–870). In the Congo (now Zaire) in 1960–1961 the CIA plotted to poison Premier Patrice Lumumba through the lethal injection of a virus; before that could be done, a CIA-backed Congolese political faction murdered Lumumba, who had turned to Russia for help after the Belgians and United Nations sent troops to protect white Europeans during a civil war. In Brazil, the CIA spent $20 million to influence

CIA Interventions

the 1962 elections against President Joao Goulart, who had earned American disapproval by expropriating the property of the American firm International Telephone and Telegraph and refusing to vote to oust Cuba from the Organization of American States. When Goulart's followers nonetheless won, the CIA then helped organize opposition groups. In 1964, with United States complicity, the Brazilian military overthrew Goulart. After failure at the Bay of Pigs, the CIA could claim the outcomes in the Congo and Brazil as Cold War successes.

DESCENT INTO THE LONGEST WAR: VIETNAM

The belief in the right to influence the internal affairs of other countries led to disaster in Southeast Asia. How Vietnam became the site of America's longest war (it lasted a quarter-century, from 1950 to 1975); how the world's most powerful nation spent itself in a futile attempt to subdue a peasant people; how those people suffered enormous losses of life and property and yet persisted, is one of the tragic stories of modern history.

The story begins with the French takeover of Vietnam during the late nineteenth century (see Vietnam Chronology). For decades the **History of Imperialism in Vietnam** French exploited the colony for its rice, rubber, tin, and tungsten, beating back peasant rebellions. Not until the Second World War, when the Japanese moved into Indochina, did French authority collapse.

Seizing their chance, the Vietminh, an anti-imperialist coalition led by Communists, began guerrilla warfare against the Japanese. Led by the nationalist Ho Chi Minh, they collaborated with American Office of Strategic Services (OSS) agents to harass the Japanese. OSS officers who worked with Ho in Vietnam were impressed by his determination to free his country of outsiders, and by his frequent references to the United States as a revolutionary model. When Ho declared Vietnam's independence in September 1945,

his words sounded familiar: "We hold these truths to be self-evident. That all men are created equal." But though Ho wrote to the Truman administration requesting support for his new government, his letters were never answered. When the Second World War ended, the French returned, and Ho and the Vietminh took up arms to defend their independence.

The United States did not recognize Vietnamese independence (and in fact attempted to undermine it) for several reasons. First, France was a valued ally in the emerging Cold War. Second, Southeast Asia was important as the world's largest producer of natural rubber and a rich source of other commodities. Third, the area seemed strategically vital to the defense of Japan and the Philippines. Finally, Ho Chi Minh was a Communist who had lived for a time in Russia. Thus Vietnam became another test in the containment of Communism—the Berlin of Asia. Overlooking the native roots of the revolution and the tenacity of a people fighting on and for their own land, American leaders from Truman through Nixon took a globalist view, interpreting events through a Cold War lens.

In the 1940s Vietnam was a French problem that few Americans watched with keen interest. More dramatic crises in Europe commanded their attention. But when Jiang Jieshi went down to defeat in China, the United States was aroused to action. The Truman administration made two crucial decisions in early 1950. First, it recognized the French puppet government of Bao Dai. Thus in Vietnamese eyes the United States became in essence a colonial power, an ally of the hated French. Second, the administration agreed to send weapons, and ultimately military advisers, to the French. By 1954 the United States had invested over $2 billion in the war and was bearing 78 percent of its cost.

Despite American aid, the French lost steadily to the Vietminh. Finally, in 1954 Ho's forces surrounded the French fortress at Dienbienphu. What would the United States do? Could the French be saved? President Eisenhower huddled with his advisers. The Chairman of the Joint Chiefs of Staff urged the president to unleash a massive air strike, using nuclear weapons if necessary. Secretary Dulles recommended that he seek help from Great Britain. Other advisers suggested sending American troops. But Eisenhower was cautious. If American forces became directly involved in the war—as distinct from merely advising

Vietnam Chronology, 1861–1961

1861–87	French consolidate colonial rule in Indochina
1890	Ho Chi Minh born
1920	Ho Chi Minh joins Communist party
1940	Japan occupies Indochina
1941	Vietminh organized
	OSS cooperates with Vietminh
1945	Ho declares independence
1946	Anticolonial war against France begins
1950	U.S. recognizes government of Bao Dai
	U.S. sends military aid to French for war in Vietnam
1954	Dienbienphu crisis
	Geneva conference and accords
	Temporary partition of Vietnam
	U.S. backs government of Diem
1955	Diem, with U.S. support, rejects Geneva accords
1956	Diem begins crackdown on opponents
1957	Anti-Diem insurgents begin terrorist attacks
1959	North Vietnam begins sending aid to Communists in the South
1960	National Liberation Front (Vietcong) organized in the South
1961	President Kennedy decides to increase U.S. military role in Vietnam

Note: For Vietnam events after 1961, see Important Events, page 934.

the French—he might not be able to limit the nation's involvement. As one high-level doubter remarked, "One cannot go over Niagara Falls in a barrel only slightly." Army Chief of Staff Matthew Ridgway was also wary. He warned the president that American troops would be fighting in hostile terrain, that air power could not guarantee victory. And American soldiers would have to be moved from elsewhere in Asia and Europe, a shift that might leave other regions vulnerable.

Nevertheless, Eisenhower worried aloud at the prospect of a Communist victory, comparing the weak nations of the world to a row of dominoes, all of which would topple if just one fell. He asked the British to help, but they would make no commitment.

At home, members of Congress refused to support military action unless the British went along.

To add to the administration's problems, the French wanted out. They agreed to peace talks at Geneva, where France, the United States, Russia, Britain, China, Laos, and Cambodia joined the two competing Vietnamese regimes of Bao Dai and Ho Chi Minh.

Geneva Conference

It was an unpleasant job for Dulles, who conducted himself, according to one biographer, like a "puritan in a house of ill repute." The 1954 Geneva accords, signed by France and Ho's Democratic Republic of Vietnam, temporarily divided Vietnam at the 17th parallel, with Ho's government confined to the North. National elections would be held in

1956, and the country would thereupon be unified. Neither North nor South was to join a military alliance or permit foreign military bases on its soil.

Certain that the Geneva agreements would ultimately mean Communist victory, the United States and Bao Dai refused to accept them and set about their sabotage. Soon after the conference a CIA team entered Vietnam and began secret operations against the North, including commando raids across the parallel. In the South, the United States cultivated the friendship of Ngo Dinh Diem. A Catholic in a Buddhist nation, Diem had no mass support and many enemies. But with American aid he outmaneuvered his opponents, including Bao Dai, and staged a fraudulent election that gave him a remarkable 98 percent of the vote. When Ho called for national elections in keeping with the Geneva agreements, Diem and Eisenhower refused, fearing the charismatic Vietminh leader would win. In September 1954 the United States joined Britain, France, Australia, New Zealand, the Philippines, Thailand, and Pakistan in an anti-Communist pact called the Southeast Asia Treaty Organization (SEATO). In a special protocol SEATO extended protection to South Vietnam.

From 1955 to 1961 Diem received more than $1 billion worth of American aid, most of it military. American advisers organized and trained the South Vietnamese army. Michigan State University police experts helped to create a national guard. And American agriculturalists worked to improve crops. As American consumer products flowed into a land of peasant villages, Diem's Saigon regime became dependent on the United States for its very existence.

Meanwhile, Diem became bent on dictatorial leadership. He abolished village elections and appointed people beholden to him to public office. He threw dissenters into jail and shut down **Civil War in** newspapers that criticized his regime. **South Vietnam** In the South non-Communists and Communists alike began to strike back at Diem's corrupt and repressive government. The Vietminh embarked on a program of terror, assassinating hundreds of Diem's village officials. In late 1960 the Vietminh organized the National Liberation Front. Called the Vietcong (Vietnamese Communists) by Diem and Americans to discredit them as tools of Moscow and Beijing, they attracted Communists and other anti-Diem groups in the South.

It became clear that the war against imperialism had become a civil war.

In the United States, the newly elected President Kennedy decided to stand firm against the Vietcong. He had suffered the humiliations of the Bay of Pigs and the Berlin Wall; he feared further criticism should the United States back down in Asia. But more important, he sought a Cold War victory. "How do we get moving?" he asked his advisers in his first meeting on Vietnam. Soon he ordered more military advisers and Special Forces units to South Vietnam, and millions of dollars worth of additional aid. Yet Diem showed no signs of using the assistance effectively, and his enemies grew in number. Fearing Diem would drag the United States down to defeat, Kennedy pressed him to reform. Meanwhile, Project Beefup was sending more Americans to South Vietnam; by late 1963 16,700 American "advisers" were stationed there. That year 489 Americans were killed, and an American project called the strategic hamlet program actually strengthened resistance to Diem. That program, which aimed to isolate peasants from the Vietcong by uprooting them into barbed-wire compounds, simply alienated villagers. When Diem's troops attacked Buddhists who opposed his religious repression, the country sank further into civil war. Protesting monks poured gasoline over their robes and ignited themselves in the streets of Saigon.

American officials began to think that if Diem could not be reformed, he should be removed. "We could not sit still and be puppets of Diem's anti-Buddhist policies," recalled a high-**Removal** ranking State Department officer. **of Diem** Moreover, Diem, who knew that American officials were preparing to dump him, was apparently trying to make peace with the North—"a possible basic incompatibility with U.S. objectives," worried General Maxwell Taylor. Through the CIA, the United States quietly encouraged disaffected South Vietnamese generals to stage a coup. With the ill-concealed backing of Ambassador Henry Cabot Lodge, the generals struck in early November 1963. Diem was captured and murdered—only a few weeks before Kennedy himself met death by an assassin's bullet.

With new governments in Saigon and Washington, some analysts thought it an appropriate time for reassessment. The Vietcong, United Nations General

Secretary U Thant, France, and others called for a coalition government in South Vietnam. But the new American president, Lyndon B. Johnson, would have none of it. He declared that America's purpose was victory, for anything less "would only be another name for a Communist take-over."

JOHNSON AND THE WAR WITHOUT VICTORY

Lyndon B. Johnson was a Texan who liked to say that he lived by the lessons of the Alamo—fight to the end. An old New Dealer, he talked about building Tennessee Valley Authorities around the world. "I want to leave the footprints of America there [in Vietnam]. I want them to say, 'This is what Americans left—schools and hospitals and dams.'" But Johnson's drive to become a global social worker—some commentators called it welfare imperialism—proved a tragic mistake, especially in Vietnam, where America's footprints were those of over 500,000 soldiers, and where bombs and chemical defoliants destroyed instead of built.

Johnson saw the world in simple terms—them against us—and privately disparaged both his allies and his enemies. Vietnam was a "raggedy-ass fourth-rate country," his critics at home "rattlebrains" or "nervous nellies." Johnson sometimes lied or exaggerated, creating what reporters referred to as a credibility gap. His public speeches, larded with trite metaphors and delivered in a belabored drawl, led some to suggest that he was unintelligent. They were wrong, for Johnson had a quick mind; his limitation was that he held firmly to fixed ideas about American superiority, the menace of Communism, and the necessity of global intervention. The problem, said Senator J. William Fulbright, chairman of the Foreign Relations Committee, was that both Johnson and the American people suffered from an "arrogance of power."

By early 1964 the Vietcong controlled nearly half of South Vietnam. Because the new Saigon government was shaky and seemed to be leaning toward neutralism, United States officials cooperated in a second coup. In neighboring Laos, American bombers hit supply routes connecting the Vietcong with the North Vietnamese. Laos, where the CIA had manipulated politics for years and where in 1962 non-Communists and Communists agreed to a neutralist government, was increasingly drawn into a wider Southeast Asian war. The bombings were kept secret from the American Congress and people; yet, as Ambassador William H. Sullivan admitted, "we ran Laos."

In August 1964 an incident in the Gulf of Tonkin, off the coast of North Vietnam, led to accelerated American warmaking (see map). On August 2, 1964, the U.S.S. *Maddox*, while monitoring South Vietnamese commando raids against North Vietnam, came under attack from northern patrol boats, which suffered heavy damage. The unharmed *Maddox* sailed away. "If they do it again," said Secretary of State Dean Rusk, "they'll get another sting." On August 4, now joined by another destroyer, the *Maddox* moved again toward the North Vietnamese shore as if to bait the Communists. During bad weather, sonar technicians reported what they thought were enemy torpedoes; the two destroyers began firing ferociously. Yet when the captain of the *Maddox* asked his crew members what had happened, not one had seen or heard hostile gunfire.

Tonkin Gulf Incident

President Johnson, although knowing that the evidence was very questionable, and unwilling to acknowledge that American ships were participating in covert raids against North Vietnam, went on television to announce that the United States was retaliating against an "unprovoked" attack: American planes would bomb North Vietnam. On August 7 Congress gave him the Tonkin Gulf resolution, passed 466 to 0 in the House and 88 to 2 in the Senate after brief debate. Only Wayne Morse of Oregon and Ernest Gruening of Alaska dissented from the resolution's sweeping language that authorized the president to "take all necessary measures to repel any armed attack against the forces of the United States and to prevent further aggression." Over time the Tonkin Gulf resolution would come to serve as the declaration of war Congress never voted on. Only in 1970 would senators repeal it, realizing too late

CHINA

Black R.

Red R.

• Dienbienphu

BURMA

Hanoi

Haiphong

Harbor mined, 1972

Gulf of Tonkin

Communist–Pathet Lao victory, 1975

PLAIN OF JARS

Maddox
incident, 1964

NORTH VIETNAM

L A O S

• Vinh
Mu Gia Pass

Vientiane

U.S. Seventh Fleet
operations during the war

Udon Thani   Nakhon Phanom

Ca R.

Demilitarized Zone

Khe Sanh   Quang Tri   Demarcation Line, July 1954
Sépone•   A Chau
Lang Vei   • Hue   **SOUTH
CHINA SEA**

Khon Kaen

Kham Duc   Da Nang

T H A I L A N D   • My Lai

Chu Lai

Ta Khli   *Ubon Ratchathani*   Quang Ngai

Rachasima   Mekong R.   Dak To
Kontum
Pleiku   *An Khe*
Don Muang   • Duc Co   Qui Nhon

•Bangkok   **CENTRAL
HIGHLANDS**   • Tuy Hoa

Ban Me Thuot

K A M P U C H E A
(CAMBODIA)

Sattahip   Nha Trang
Dalat   Can Ranh Bay

U.S. invasion, 1970   Bu Dop

Communist–Khmer Rouge victory, 1975   **Vietnamese invasion, 1978**
Phnom Penh•   **SOUTH VIETNAM**

Gulf of Siam   Vietcong and
North Vietnamese victory
and U.S. withdrawal, 1975

Cholon   Bien Hoa
Chau Duc   *Tan Son Nhut*   Long Binh
Saigon•
My Tho   *Vung Tau*
Vinh Long
Ben Tre
Can Tho   *Mekong Delta*

Mayaguez incident, 1975   Ca Mau

CA MAU PENINSULA   ——► Ho Chi Minh Trail

0   100   200 miles   ⇨ Boat-People Refugees after 1975

0   100   200   300 kilometers   ✦ Major battles of the Tet Offensive,
January 1968

■ Major U.S. bases during the war

Southeast Asia and the Vietnam War

An American marine tries to revive a wounded GI in the inhospitable terrain of Khe Sanh Valley, near the Demilitarized Zone in South Vietnam in 1967. The fallen marine soon died, as did over 57,000 other Americans in their nation's longest war.   Wide World Photos.

that they had surrendered their powers in the foreign policy process by giving the president wide latitude to conduct the war as he saw fit.

His popularity buoyed by his forceful response to the Tonkin Gulf incident, Johnson won the presidency in his own right in the fall of 1964. At his direction the military mapped plans for stepped-up bombing of North Vietnam and Laos. Undersecretary of State George Ball urged caution: "Once on the tiger's back we cannot be sure of picking the place to dismount." Nonetheless, when a Vietcong attack on an American airfield at Pleiku took nine American lives in February 1965, Johnson ordered carrier jets to ravage the North. Soon Operation Rolling Thunder—a sustained bombing program above the 17th parallel—was under way. Before the longest war was over, more bombs would fall on Vietnam than American aircraft had dropped in all of the Second World War. But the North Vietnamese would not give up. They hid in shelters and rebuilt roads and bridges with a perseverance that frustrated and awed American decision-makers.

The president, in his momentous decision of July 1965, also sent more troops to the South. By the end of 1965 184,000 Americans were assigned to Vietnam; in 1966 the figure reached 385,000; in 1969 it peaked at 543,400. But Ho only increased the flow of arms and men to the rebels in the South; in this seemingly endless war of attrition, each American escalation begot a new Vietnamese escalation. "I feel like a hitchhiker caught in a hailstorm on a Texas highway," groaned Johnson. "I can't run, I can't hide, and I can't make

Americanization of the War

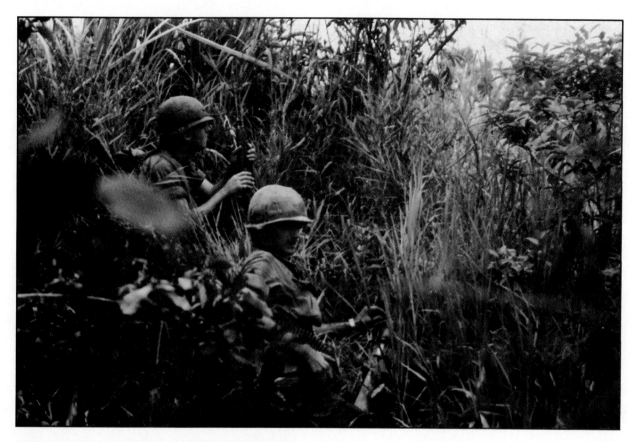

American troops in the field faced thick jungle growth—and well-hidden Vietcong and North Vietnamese opponents more familiar than Americans with an environment suited to guerrilla warfare. This photograph was taken in 1969.   U.S. Army.

it stop." He and his aides just could not believe that the Vietnamese could tangle successfully with the greatest power on the face of the earth—at least not for very long.

The "Americanization" of the war in Vietnam under Johnson bothered growing numbers of Americans, especially as increased television coverage brought the ugliness of combat into their homes every night. The pictures and stories were not pretty. Innocent civilians were caught in the line of fire; refugees flooded "pacification" camps; villages considered friendly to the enemy were burned to the ground. To destroy Vietcong hiding places, pilots whose motto was "Only You Can Prevent Forests" sprayed chemical defoliants like Agent Orange over the landscape. The Vietcong and North Vietnamese added to the carnage, but American guns, bombs, and chemicals took by far the greatest toll, and the Vietnamese people knew it. Indeed, America's search-and-destroy missions were counterproductive; rather than winning the war, they were molding an ever-growing population of anti-American peasants who gave secret aid to the Vietcong. An American official later admitted, "It was as if we were trying to build a house with a bulldozer and wrecking crane."

Stories of atrocities made their way home. Most gruesome was the My Lai massacre in March 1968 (not made public until twenty months later because of a military cover-up). An American unit, frustrated by its inability to pin down an elusive enemy and eager to revenge the loss of some buddies, shot to death scores of unarmed women and children. Private Paul Meadlo, the father of two children himself, was there. "We huddled them up. We made them squat down. . . . I poured about four clips into the group. . . . The mothers was hugging their children. . . . Well, we kept right on firing. They was waving their arms and begging. . . . I still dream about it. About the women and children in my sleep. Some days . . . some nights, I can't even sleep."

Although many incidents of the deliberate shooting of civilians, torturing and killing of prisoners, taking of Vietnamese ears as trophies, and burning of villages have been recorded, most American soldiers were not committing atrocities. They were trying instead to save their young lives (their av-

American Troops in Vietnam

erage age was only nineteen) and serve the United States mission by killing enemy troops, whom they usually called "gooks." Many of these Americans made up the rear-echelon forces that supported the "grunts" or "boonierats" in the field. Wherever they were, soldiers met an inhospitable environment, for no place in Vietnam was secure. Well-hidden booby traps blasted away parts of the body. The enemy was everywhere yet nowhere, often burrowed into elaborate underground bunkers or melded into the population, where every Vietnamese might be a Vietcong terrorist.

Infantrymen on maneuvers humped heavy rucksacks into thick jungle growth, their every step precarious. "In places the bamboo was over fifteen feet high," wrote the veteran John M. DelVecchio in his novel *The 13th Valley* (1982). "The point man felt as if he were breaking trail through knife blades of spring steel. His arms were soon slashed and bloody and his face had multiple tiny lacerations." Leeches sucked at weary bodies. Boots and human skin rotted from the rains, which alternated with withering suns. "It was as if the sun and the land itself were in league with the Vietcong," recalled the marine officer Philip Caputo in his book *A Rumor of War* (1977), "wearing us down, driving us mad, killing us." Wounded GIs shouted for a medic, who in turn might call in a "medevac" (medical evacuation helicopter), praying that it would not be shot down, knowing that a successful departure could carry the wounded to operating tables within minutes. "What I saw were young men coming in, eighteen or nineteen years old . . . and they would be without a leg," remembered Gayle Smith, a nurse at the 3rd Surgical Hospital.

As the war ground on to no discernible conclusion, the army grew troubled, and morale sagged. Racial tensions intensified as "black power" militants tangled with whites muttering racial slurs. Drug abuse became serious. Many soldiers smoked plentiful, cheap marijuana; about one-third of the troops were addicts to opium and heroin, according to a 1971 official report. "Fragging," the murder of an officer by soldiers using hand grenades or other weapons, also increased. "Grenades leave no fingerprints. Nobody's going to jail," recalled a helicopter pilot. The military elite in Washington grew alarmed as well by numerous reports of disobedience—and peace symbols scratched on helmets.

Such antiwar sentiment drew strength from dissent in the United States. In early 1966 Senator J. William Fulbright began to hold public hearings on whether the national interest was being served by pursuing the war in Asia. What exactly was the threat? senators asked. To the surprise of some, the father of the containment doctrine, George F. Kennan, testified before television cameras that his theory was meant for Europe, not the volatile environment of Southeast Asia. Within the administration, too, disenchantment rose. Secretary of Defense Robert McNamara and Undersecretary Ball resigned, unable to justify further escalation of the war. And in a direct challenge to Johnson's policies, antiwar Senator Eugene McCarthy of Minnesota announced his candidacy for the Democratic presidential nomination.

Johnson dug in, snapping at his critics and vowing to continue the battle, cheered by opinion polls that showed Americans actually favoring escalation over withdrawal. "We are not going to shimmy," he insisted. At times he halted the bombing to encourage Ho Chi Minh to negotiate. Such pauses, however, were often accompanied by increases in American troop strength. And in some cases the United States resumed or accelerated the bombing just when a diplomatic breakthrough seemed imminent—such as in late 1966, when a Polish diplomat's efforts were inexplicably cut short by a resumption of the bombing. Unpersuaded, the North demanded a stop to the bombing raids before sitting down at the conference table. And American terms were unacceptable to the Communists: nonrecognition of the Vietcong; withdrawal of northern soldiers from the South; and an end to North Vietnamese military aid to the Vietcong.

In July 1968, a war-weary President Johnson. Just months before, stunned by the Tet offensive, Johnson had decided to drop out of politics and initiate peace talks.   Lyndon Baines Johnson Library.

THE PAINFUL WITHDRAWAL FROM VIETNAM

I n January 1968 a shocking event forced Johnson to reappraise his position. During Tet, the Vietnamese lunar new year, Vietcong and North Vietnamese forces struck all across **Tet Offensive**   South Vietnam, hitting and capturing provincial capitals. In Saigon raiders actually occupied the American embassy for several hours. American and South Vietnamese units eventually regained much lost ground, inflicting heavy casualties on the enemy. But the destruction of the village of Ben Tre revealed the cost of driving the Vietcong out. "It became necessary to destroy the town to save it," reported a sober-faced American officer.

The Tet offensive jolted Americans. Hadn't the Vietcong and North Vietnamese demonstrated that they could strike when and where they wished? Didn't they have the advantage of fighting on home territory? Why did "their Vietnamese" fight harder than "our Vietnamese"? If all of America's firepower and dollars and half a million troops couldn't defeat the Vietcong, could anything? Had the American public been lied to? One television reporter asked, "Isn't there something Orwellian about it, that the more we kill, the stronger they get?"

The Tet offensive and its impact on public opinion hit the White House like a thunderclap. The new secretary of defense, Clark Clifford, told Johnson the war could not be won, even if the 206,000 more soldiers requested by the army were sent to Vietnam. The Cold Warrior of Cold Warriors, Dean Acheson, bluntly told a surprised president that the military brass did not know what they were talking about. Strained by exhausting sessions with advisers, realizing that further escalation would not bring victory, and faced with serious opposition within his own party, Johnson changed course. In an appearance on television (March 31) he announced that he had stopped the bombing of most of North Vietnam and asked Hanoi to begin negotiations. Then he surprised the nation by dropping out of the presidential race.

The United States, knowing it could not win, would at least try not to lose. As the diplomats talked in Paris, the war ground on. Late in 1968 president-elect Richard M. Nixon met with Johnson and his key advisers to discuss the war. "The travail of the long war was etched on the faces around me," Nixon recalled. "They had no new approaches to recommend to me. I sensed that, despite the disappointment of defeat, they were relieved to be able to turn this morass over to someone else."

Nixon initiated a policy of "Vietnamization"—building up South Vietnamese forces to replace American troops. And he announced the Nixon Doctrine: that the United States would help those Asian nations that helped themselves. Slowly he began to withdraw American troops from Vietnam, decreasing their number to 139,000 by the end of 1971. But he also increased the bombing in the North, hoping to pound Hanoi into making concessions. Nixon's national security adviser, Henry A. Kissinger, called it jugular diplomacy.

In April 1970 American and South Vietnamese troops invaded Cambodia in search of arms depots and enemy forces that used it as a sanctuary. The

Invasion of Cambodia

escalation sparked renewed protest at home. Demonstrations swept college campuses; the Senate forbade the expenditure of funds on the new war. But Nixon and Kissinger were unmoved. They continued to escalate the war, ordering "protective reaction strikes" against the North; acceleration of the CIA's Operation Phoenix (the assassination of thousands of enemy civilians in the South); the secret bombing of Cambodia; the mining of Haiphong harbor, near the northern capital, Hanoi; and in December 1972, a massive air strike called the Christmas bombing, or as one of Kissinger's aides put it, "calculated barbarism."

Meanwhile the peace talks seemed to be going nowhere. The South Vietnamese delegate saw defeat coming and purposely stalled the negotiations. But Kissinger was meeting privately with Le Duc Tho, the chief delegate from North Vietnam. Finally the administration, impatient to improve relations with Russia and China, win back the allegiance of its allies, and restore stability at home, made concessions. On January 27, 1973, Kissinger and Le signed a cease-fire agreement. The United States promised to withdraw its remaining troops within sixty days. Other

Cease-fire Agreement

troops would stay in place, and a coalition government that included the Vietcong would eventually be formed in the South. Pleased that a peace had been made, critics nonetheless noted that the terms of the agreement could have been accepted in 1969, and over twenty thousand American lives could have been spared.

Leaving behind some advisers, the United States pulled its troops out of Vietnam and reduced its aid program. Both North and South soon violated the cease-fire, and full-scale war erupted once more. As many had predicted, the feeble South Vietnamese government, for so long an American puppet, could not hold out. Just before its surrender, hundreds of Americans and Vietnamese who had worked for them were hastily evacuated by helicopter from the roof of the American embassy in Saigon. In those desperate last moments, crying South Vietnamese surged toward the embassy and the departing aircraft, only to be shoved violently back. On April 29, 1975, South Vietnam collapsed, and shortly after Saigon was renamed Ho Chi Minh City.

The next month a bizarre episode compounded the tragic American failure in Southeast Asia. The Communist Khmer Rouge had triumphed in Cambodia. That May Cambodian patrol boats seized the American cargo ship *Mayaguez* along with its crew. President Gerald Ford, who had taken over the presidency following Nixon's resignation (see page 975), ordered the marines to attack. Patience would have brought the news that the crew members had been released unharmed. Instead, forty Americans died in the needless venture, many of them in a helicopter accident. Nonetheless, Americans applauded the show of force at a time when the United States appeared to be on the retreat.

After twenty-five years, American intervention in Southeast Asia had come to this panicky end. The overall costs of the war were immense. Over 57,000 Americans and hundreds of thousands of Asians died in the struggle. In monetary terms the war cost the United States more than $150 billion, and as was inevitable, billions more would be paid in future veterans' benefits. At home the war brought inflation, political schism, attacks on civil liberties, and retrenchment from reform programs (see Chapter 33). The war also had negative consequences internationally: delay in moving toward better relations with the Soviet Union and the People's Republic of China, friction with allies, and the alienation of Third World nations.

Meanwhile, in South Vietnam, Cambodia, and Laos, Communists assumed power and instituted repressive governments. Acute hunger afflicted the people of those devastated lands. Soon refugees were crowding aboard unsafe vessels in an attempt to escape their battered homelands. Many of these "boat people" immigrated to the United States, where Americans, reluctant to be reminded of their defeat in Asia, received them with mixed feelings. But thoughtful Americans realized that the United States, which had relentlessly bombed, burned, and defoliated once-rich agricultural lands, bore more than a slight responsibility for the plight of the Southeast Asian peoples.

This sad conclusion prompted an American ambassador to ask the central question about the American defeat: "how so many with so much could achieve so little for so long against so few"? Rather than seek the answer to that question, most Americans preferred to put the disaster out of mind. But the Vietnam veterans were unable to forget. In the words of one veteran,

The longest war is over
Or so they say
Again
But I can still hear the gunfire
Every night
From
My bed.

The longest nightmare
Never seems to
Ever
Quite come
To
An end. [1]

---

[1] Jan Barry, "The Longest War," from *Winning Hearts & Minds: War Poems by Vietnam Veterans.* Copyright © 1972 by 1st Casualty Press. Reprinted by permission of the author.

NIXON, KISSINGER, AND DÉTENTE

For President Nixon, Vietnam was a "short-term problem"; for Kissinger it was a mere historical "footnote." Both considered the central question of international affairs to be the relationship between the United States and the Soviet Union. As a congressman, senator, and vice president, Nixon had been an ardent cold warrior. As one Soviet official commented, "We very well know with whom we have to deal." Kissinger was a German-born political scientist teaching at Harvard and a noted writer on diplomatic topics. Nixon appointed him national security adviser, a post he held until 1973, when he became secretary of state. Ambitious, witty, knowledgeable, and deliberate, Kissinger was a formidable negotiator. Critics, however, thought he adhered too callously to the principle that the end justifies the means. They cited his willingness to unseat foreign governments through secret operations, as in Chile (see page 927), and to sell massive amounts of arms to dictators like the shah of Iran. Kissinger also had his own staff wiretapped.

Together Nixon and Kissinger pursued a grand strategy designed to promote a global balance of power, or "equilibrium." The first part of the strategy was

Détente

détente, meaning limited cooperation with the Soviets through negotiations within a general environment of rivalry. Its purpose, like the containment doctrine it resembled, was to check Soviet expansion and limit a Soviet arms buildup. The second part of the strategy was the curbing of revolution and radicalism in the Third World so as to resist threats to American interests. The grand design seemed attractive to its architects, for the Cold War and limited wars like Vietnam were costing too much. And increased trade with a friendlier Russia might reduce the huge balance-of-payments deficit. Critics, even those who endorsed détente, faulted the Nixon-Kissinger posture for its arrogant assumption that the United States had the ability and the right to manipulate a disorderly world.

The architects of détente, Soviet party boss Leonid Brezhnev (1906–1982) and President Richard M. Nixon (1913–), enjoy a light moment during the 1972 Moscow summit meeting that produced the Strategic Arms Limitation Treaty (SALT-I). Photo J. P. Laffont/Sygma.

They complained that the administration paid too much attention to archaic Cold War thinking and too little to the force of nationalism, which in the Third World generated instability deriving not from Soviet intrigue but from local conditions. Rather than decreasing the need for intervention, said critics, the new design actually increased it.

Nixon and Kissinger nonetheless pursued détente with extraordinary energy and fanfare. They expanded trade relations with Russia; a 1972 deal sent $1 billion worth of American grain to the Soviets at bargain

SALT Talks   prices. To slow the costly arms race, the Nixon administration initiated Strategic Arms Limitations Talks (SALT) with the Soviets. In 1972 the talks produced a SALT treaty that limited antiballistic missile (ABM) systems. ABM systems were defensive systems that made offensive missiles less vulnerable to attack—and hence encouraged the other side to build more missiles to overcome ABM protection. Limiting ABMs was thus a step toward halting a spiraling arms race. A second agreement placed a five-year freeze on the number of offensive nuclear missiles each side could have. At the time of the agreement the Soviets held an advantage in total missiles, but the United States had more warheads per missile (see table, p. 931) because of its MIRVs (multiple independently targeted re-entry vehicles). One missile loaded with MIRVs could send several nuclear warheads to different targets. In short, the United States had a 2-to-1 advantage in deliverable warheads. Because SALT did not restrict MIRVs, the nuclear arms buildup continued.

Nixon and Kissinger also cultivated détente with the People's Republic of China, ending almost three decades of Sino-American hostility. In February 1972 the president made an historic trip

Opening to China   to what he used to call "Red" China. The Chinese Communists welcomed him because they sought to improve trade and they hoped friendlier Chinese-American relations would make the Soviets—the new Chinese enemy—more cautious. Nixon reasoned the same way. In China the president visited the Great Wall and exchanged 150-proof rice-liquor toasts with Mao Zedong and Zhou Enlai. In the end, the conferees agreed to disagree on a number of issues, except one: Russia should not be permitted to make gains in Asia. The opening of this Chinese-American dialogue ended one of the Cold War's most troublesome contests. Official diplomatic recognition and exchange of ambassadors was effected in 1979.

Tortuous events in the Middle East, however, revealed how fragile the Nixon-Kissinger grand strategy was. When Nixon took office in 1969 the Middle East was, in the president's words, a "powder keg."

Arab-Israeli Hostilities   In the Six-Day War (1967) Israel had used American weapons to score victories against Egypt and Syria.

Zhou Enlai (1898–1976) and Henry A. Kissinger (1923–   ) toast better Sino-American relations during President Richard M. Nixon's celebrated trip to China in 1972. As Nixon's assistant for national security affairs, Kissinger had secretly negotiated with the Chinese to arrange the visit—symbol of the new détente between Washington and Beijing. Foreign Minister Zhou had long sought the normalization of diplomatic relations, broken since 1949 when the Communists assumed power and the Truman administration refused to recognize the new People's Republic of China. National Archives, Nixon Project.

The Israelis had seized the West Bank and the ancient city of Jerusalem from Jordan, the Golan Heights from Syria, and the Sinai Peninsula from Egypt (see map, page 926). Soviet arms had backed the Arab nations that Israel fought. To further complicate matters, Palestinian Arabs, many of them expelled from their homeland in 1948 when the nation of Israel was created, had organized the Palestine Liberation Organization (PLO) and pledged to destroy Israel. PLO sympathizers made hit-and-run raids on Jewish settlements, hijacked jetliners, and murdered Israeli athletes at the 1972 Olympic Games in Munich, West Germany.

On October 6, 1973, Egypt and Syria attacked Israel. In spite of détente, Moscow, backing Egypt, and Washington headed for a confrontation; both superpowers put their armed forces—including nuclear—on alert. At the same time, in an attempt to pressure Americans into taking a pro-Arab stance, the Organization of Petroleum Exporting Countries

The Middle East

(OPEC) imposed an embargo on shipments of oil to the United States and a dramatic increase in oil prices occurred.

Faced with an energy crisis at home, the Nixon administration had to find a way to end Middle Eastern hostilities. Kissinger arranged a cease-fire and undertook "shuttle diplomacy," flying back and forth repeatedly between Middle Eastern capitals in an exhausting search for a settlement. In March 1974 OPEC lifted the oil embargo. The next year Kissinger persuaded Egypt and Israel to accept a United Nations peace-keeping force in the Sinai. But other problems remained: the homeless Palestinian Arabs; Israeli occupation of Jerusalem and the West Bank; Israel's insistence on building settlements in occupied lands; and Arab threats to destroy the Jewish state. Furthermore, Soviet-American rivalry was still very much alive in the Middle East, especially after the exclusion of the Soviets from the peace negotiations and after Egypt moved closer to the United States, snubbing the Soviet Union.

In Latin America, Nixon continued President Johnson's interventionist policies. Johnson had dispatched twenty thousand American troops to the Dominican Republic in 1965 to prevent a leftist government from coming to power. And in the Johnson Doctrine—the United States would prevent Communists from coming to office in the Western Hemisphere—the president had reiterated the Roosevelt Corollary's insistence on United States policing powers in the region. Thus in 1970, when the people of Chile elected a Marxist president, Salvador Allende, it was all too easy for Nixon to see him as a Communist threat who had to be removed. The CIA began secret operations to disrupt the Chilean economy; funneled money to newspapers critical of Allende; and apparently encouraged military officers to stage a coup. In 1973 a military junta ousted and killed Allende and installed an authoritarian regime in his place. Nixon and Kissinger privately pronounced their policy of "destabilization" successful, while publicly denying their role in the affair.

Intervention in Latin America

In Africa, Nixon-Kissinger maneuvers proved less successful. During the 1960s and early 1970s the CIA channeled funds to some of the groups fighting for the liberation of

Angola

Angola from Portuguese colonial rule—at the same time that Washington publicly supported Portugal. After Angola won its independence in 1975, civil war erupted. The United States, which stepped up covert aid, and South Africa, which sent troops, backed one faction while the Soviets helped another. When Congress learned about the secret aid, it voted to cut all funds. Kissinger complained that the Soviets would gain a foothold in Africa. But many members of Congress argued that Americans could not decide the outcome of an African civil war; that the United States should not be aligned with the white racist regime of South Africa; that it was very unlikely that Angola would become a Soviet puppet; and that diplomacy should have been tried. After a leftist government came to power in Angola, Washington took a keener interest in the rest of Africa, building economic ties, sending arms to friendly black nations, and putting more distance between the United States and the white minority governments in Rhodesia (now Zimbabwe) and South Africa. It was important, Kissinger said, to "prevent the radicalization of Africa."

Like other Americans before him, Kissinger clung to the belief that the United States had the answers to most international problems. In his view the Third World was a mere sideshow to the Soviet-American confrontation; and the United States had to defend its interests there against nationalist challenges. Thus in the mid-1970s about 686,000 American military personnel were stationed abroad; the United States had military links with ninety-two nations; and American arms sales overseas climbed to about $10 billion. These so-called commitments were maintained not only to impress Moscow with American might and will, but to serve as a counterrevolutionary force against nationalist stirrings that threatened American economic and strategic interests. Nixon and Kissinger stood, then, in a long line of leaders who counterpoised American power against foreign peoples determined to decide their own fate. Even American allies thought the United States too meddlesome. "Living next to you is in some ways like sleeping with an elephant," said Canadian Prime Minister Pierre Trudeau. "No matter how friendly and even-tempered is the beast, if I can call it that, one is affected by every twitch and grunt."

RICH NATIONS, POOR NATIONS: THE NORTH-SOUTH DIALOGUE

If disputes in the Middle East, Latin America, and Africa bedeviled the Nixon-Kissinger grand design for world order, global economic issues also heightened political disorder. Kissinger explained that "international political stability requires international economic stability." But in the 1970s there was little economic stability; troubles could be seen everywhere. The worldwide recession in the early part of the decade was the worst since the 1930s. Inflation and high oil prices pinched rich and poor nations alike. Protectionist tendencies raised tariffs and impeded world trade. Very poor Third World countries suffered massive famines and built up huge international debts to meet internal needs. The North-South dialogue became acrimonious when Third World countries (the "South") insisted that the wealthier, industrial "North" share economic resources and the power to exploit them. The gulf between rich and poor nations threatened world peace.

The United States could not escape these problems because it was a major participant in the world economy. Although America's economic standing had declined since the olympian days of the 1940s and 1950s as other nations, such as Japan and West Germany, had recovered from the devastation of the Second World War and as Third World countries had gained more control over their raw materials, Americans remained the richest people in the world. The United States produced about one-third of the world's goods and services. Many American companies, like Coca-Cola and Exxon, earned over half their profits abroad. One-fourth of agricultural sales came from exports; one out of every nine manufacturing jobs depended upon exports. The American economy also depended upon imports of strategic raw materials: three-quarters of the tin, over 95 percent of the manganese, and over half of the zinc consumed in the United States came from abroad. Such ties, as well as American investments abroad totaling over $133 billion in the mid-1970s, explain in part why the United States was an interventionist power; threats to markets, investments, and raw materials were read as deadly stabs at the high American standard of living. American economic holdings did in fact become targets. Venezuela nationalized American oil properties in 1976, and terrorists around the world destroyed American facilities and kidnapped and sometimes murdered American business executives.

Multinational Corporations

Multinational corporations became a symbol and a target of the conspicuous American economic position overseas. American-based multinationals like Exxon and General Motors actually enjoyed budgets and incomes larger than most countries. These giant firms brought home profits and exported American culture. But they aroused criticism. American workers protested that these global oligopolies stole their jobs by moving their plants abroad in search of cheaper labor. People of the "South" also complained that multinationals exploited poor countries, robbing them of their natural resources; that they corrupted politics, as when International Telephone and Telegraph tried to undermine President Allende in Chile and Lockheed Aircraft bribed foreign leaders to promote sales; that they sometimes provided "cover" for CIA agents; and that they evaded taxes by clever manipulations of their books.

Multinational officers and government officials defended these enterprises, pointing out that they invested in risky ventures that brought economic progress, including the transfer of technology. Multinationals, they insisted, helped rationalize a chaotic world economy, and privately owned multinationals made more rational economic choices—hence benefiting the consumer—than government-owned companies. Nonetheless, many countries passed laws requiring a certain percentage of native ownership; India, for example, legislated that its nationals own a majority of voting shares in industrial firms. Other states simply nationalized multinational properties.

Besides placing restraints on multinationals, the Third World of the South pressed for lower prices on technology and manufactured goods, low-interest loans, and higher prices for raw materials. In 1974 the United Nations issued the "New International Economic Order" encompassing many of these points, but the North made few concessions. Food was another divisive issue in the North-South dialogue. Droughts, meager harvests, high birthrates, and swelling populations condemned millions to hunger. In Africa in the early 1970s famine killed 10,000 people a day. The United States sent food aid, especially to those nations considered political friends, but it preferred to sell its surplus food for profit, as evidenced by the large grain sales to the dollar-paying Russians. Although total American foreign aid rose from $6.6 billion in 1970 to $7.8 billion in 1977, the aid dollars actually bought less because of rampant inflation.

Another question that pitted North against South was the Law of the Sea treaty, patiently composed in the 1970s through extended negotiations. Developing nations argued that the rich

Law of the Sea

seabed resources of petroleum and minerals should be shared among all nations as a "common heritage of mankind." The industrial states, alone having the capital and equipment to conduct the excavating and drilling, tended to prefer private enterprise or national exploitation, reaping the profits and raw materials for themselves. In the early 1980s the global community hammered out a compromise between international and national controls and rights, but the United States rejected the treaty in 1983. Angry Third World nations railed against what they perceived as selfish economic imperialism, whereas many American allies who supported the compromise predicted a chaotic future of competing claims of ownership, territorial disputes, and threats to freedom of navigation similar to the colonial powers' scramble for advantage in Africa and Asia in the late nineteenth century. Like other international economic issues, this one promised a future of political instability—and perhaps war.

CARTER AND A REINVIGORATED COLD WAR

President Jimmy Carter was "deeply troubled by the lies our people had been told" during the Vietnam War, and he asked Americans to put their "inordinate fear of Communism" behind them. His secretary of state, Cyrus R. Vance, said that he had learned from the Vietnam War that the United States could not "prop up a series of regimes that lacked popular support" and that "there can be no going back to a time when we thought there could be American solutions to every problem." If Carter, the first post-Vietnam president, and Vance, once an architect of the war, drew lessons from the Vietnam experience, many tried to forget the nightmare. "Coming back to America," recalled a Vietnam veteran, "I was shocked . . . that no one even talked about it." But debate about the causes and consequences of the war did develop, making the Carter administration forge its foreign policy in an unsteady setting: the old Cold War consensus seemed fractured, and Americans were both angry and confused. The historian William Appleman Williams observed that for the first time in their history Americans were suffering from a serious case of "empire shock."

Hawkish leaders who debated the meaning of the war claimed that America's ignoble failure in Vietnam undermined the nation's credibility and tempted enemies to exploit opportunities at the

Lessons of Vietnam

expense of United States interests. They pointed to a Vietnam syndrome—a mood suspicious of foreign entanglements—which would inhibit the United States from exercising its power. They advised that next time the military should be permitted to do its job, free from the constraints of whimsical public opinion and timid politicians. America lost in Vietnam, they asserted, because the American people lost their guts and will at home. They urged Carter to stop at no expense to expand the military and face down America's many adversaries.

Others drew different lessons. Some people blamed the war on strong-willed presidents like Johnson and pusillanimous Congresses that had conceded too much power to the executive branch, as evident in the Tonkin Gulf resolution. Trim the powers of the imperial presidency, they counseled, and America would become less interventionist. Others took a more hardheaded, even fatalistic, view: as long as the United States remained an industrial giant, with strong ideological, strategic, economic, and political needs that could only be satisfied through activism abroad, then the nation would continue to be expansionist and interventionist. Still others found fault with the containment doctrine: it failed to make distinctions between areas peripheral and areas vital to the national security and relied too heavily upon military means. The widely read journalist Walter Lippmann endorsed "neo-isolationism." "Compared to people who thought they could run the universe," he remarked, "I *am* a neo-isolationist and proud of it." Many of these critics thus advised Carter: not more, but less, bluster; not more, but less, military; not more, but less, interventionism.

During Carter's presidency public discussion of the Vietnam War intensified. Some of the war's 2.8 million veterans called for better benefits, especially asking for help to deal with "post-traumatic stress disorder." This illness of nightmares and extreme nervousness was different from the shell shock of the First World War or the battle fatigue of the Second. Doctors reported that the disorder stemmed largely from the fact that soldiers saw so many women, children, and elderly killed in Vietnam. Many returning veterans were also stung by the unsympathetic glances of Americans who did not want to be reminded of the unpleasant war or who blamed them for losing a war that could not be won. Films like *Coming Home* (1978), *The Deer Hunter* (1978), and *Apocalypse Now* (1979), personal accounts like Philip Caputo's *A Rumor of War* (1977), and novels like James Webb's *Fields of Fire* (1978) focused attention on the soldier's Vietnam, stimulating questions about whether defeat was inevitable given the jungle conditions and elusive enemy.

In this environment of conflicting answers and lessons Carter vowed to chart a new course. When he took office in 1977 he pledged to give as much attention to North-South as to East-West issues, to reduce the American military presence overseas, to cut back arms sales, which had reached unprecedented heights under Nixon, and to slow the nuclear arms race. "The soul of our foreign policy," he intoned, would be the championing of individual human rights abroad—the freedom to vote, worship, travel, speak out, and get a fair trial. A deeply religious man, Carter intended to infuse international relations with moral force.

Carter's Goals

From the start Carter's statements were inconsistent, and administration officials squabbled among themselves. One source of the problem was Zbigniew Brzezinski, a Polish-born political scientist who became Carter's national security adviser. The stern-faced Brzezinski was an old-fashioned Cold Warrior, a critic of détente who tended to view foreign crises in globalist terms—that is, he blamed them on the Soviet Union. One State Department official likened him to a rat terrier constantly nipping at Secretary Vance's ankles. More and more Carter listened to Brzezinski; Vance resigned in April 1980, deploring the American drift toward military power as a substitute for diplomacy.

Despite Carter's goals, détente deteriorated and the Cold War revived. The president first angered the Soviets by calling on them to respect their citizens' human rights and tolerate dissent. Moscow told him to mind his own business. Then American officials denounced Russia for sponsoring Cuban troops in Africa. And as Sino-American relations improved following the Nixon visit, Soviet leaders worried that the United States was playing its "China card"— building up their rival in order to threaten them.

A thaw came in 1979 when negotiations produced a new treaty, SALT-II, that acknowledged Soviet-American nuclear parity (see table). The agreement placed a ceiling of 2,250 delivery vehicles (long-range bombers, ICBMs, and submarine-based missiles) on each side and imposed limits on the number of warheads and the development of new kinds of nuclear weapons. Critics from the right charged that the treaty favored the Soviets; critics from the left protested that it did not go far enough toward quelling the arms race. As if to prove both sides correct, Carter soon announced that the United States would construct an expensive new MX missile system that would shuttle ICBMs back and forth along a vast maze of underground tunnels designed to confuse attackers. The president was gambling that the MX system would win votes for the SALT-II treaty from skeptical senators without alarming Moscow. He did not get the votes, but he did alarm the Soviets.

SALT-II

As doubts about Senate ratification of SALT-II mounted and Moscow fumed over the MX, events in Afghanistan led to a Soviet-American confrontation. In December 1979 the Red Army bludgeoned its way into the Soviets' southern neighbor to shore up the faltering Communist government, under siege

STRATEGIC NUCLEAR FORCES AT THE TIME OF SALT-I, 1972

	U.S.	U.S.S.R.
Intercontinental ballistic missiles (ICBMs)	1054	1607
Submarine-launched ballistic missiles (SLBMs)	656	740
Strategic bombers	450	200
Nuclear warheads	5700	2500

STRATEGIC NUCLEAR FORCES AT THE TIME OF SALT-II, 1979

	U.S.	U.S.S.R.
Intercontinental ballistic missiles (ICBMs)	1054	1400
Submarine-launched ballistic missiles (SLBMs)	656	950
Strategic bombers	350	150
Nuclear warheads	9200	5000

Sources: U.S. Department of Defense; U.S. Department of State

by Moslem rebels. But the rebels persisted, with some aid from the CIA, and analysts predicted that the Soviet Union had sunk into its own Vietnam. Determined to make the U.S.S.R. "pay a concrete price for their aggression," an embittered Carter shelved SALT-II, suspended shipments of grain and high-technology equipment to Russia, and launched an international boycott of the 1980 Summer Olympics in Moscow. In the United Nations the United States pressed for a resolution condemning the Soviet Union and was heartened by the positive response of many Third World nations. But all these efforts proved fruitless: the Soviets refused to withdraw their forces from Afghanistan.

The president also announced what was quickly dubbed the Carter Doctrine: the United States would intervene, unilaterally and militarily if necessary, against further Soviet aggression in the petroleum-rich Persian Gulf. Prominent critics spoke out against the declaration. Senator Edward M. Kennedy declared that Americans would rather ration gas than spill the blood of their children for Middle Eastern oil. And George F. Kennan, the father of containment, who like Kennedy was critical of Soviet opportunism, called Carter's reaction exaggerated. It was wrong to assume that the Soviets would attack elsewhere in the Middle East, said Kennan. He faulted Carter for not trying diplomacy first, and for playing all his nonmilitary cards prematurely. "Was this really mature statesmanship on our part?" Kennan asked.

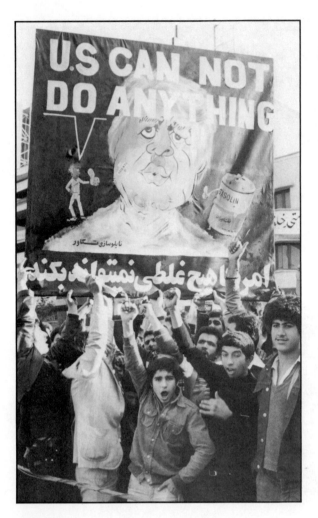

On November 4, 1979, an Iranian mob encouraged by government officials seized the American embassy in Teheran and took American personnel prisoner. For more than a year, shouting Iranians taunted the United States to do something about it. The crisis, which had its roots in close American ties to the unpopular government of the fallen shah, frustrated President Jimmy Carter, who remarked that he felt "the same kind of impotence that a powerful person feels when his child is kidnapped." Wide World Photos.

Carter met his toughest test in Iran, where in early 1979 the shah was toppled from his throne by revolutionaries under the leadership of Ayatollah Ruhollah Khomeini, a wrathfully anti-American Moslem cleric. Khomeini remembered that the United States had restored the shah to power in 1953 through a CIA-staged coup and that the CIA had trained and supplied the shah's ruthless secret police. Iranian rebels also resented the huge infusion of American arms into their country—$19 billion worth in 1973 through 1978 alone. In November, after the exiled shah was admitted to the United States for medical treatment, mobs stormed the American embassy in Teheran and took American personnel as hostages, demanding the return of the shah for trial, along with his wealth.

Hostage Crisis in Iran

Although the Iranians eventually released a few of the prisoners, fifty-two others languished over a year under Iranian guard. Frequently blindfolded or bound, they were subjected to solitary confinement, beatings, and terrifying mock executions. All the while the theocratic Khomeini regime hurled insults at Washington.

Carter would not return the shah to Iran or apologize for past American involvement there. Unable to gain the hostages' freedom through public appeals, foreign emissaries, or United Nations delegations, the president took steps to isolate Iran economically. He froze Iranian assets in the United States and appealed to American allies, largely unsuccessfully, to reduce trade with the Moslem state. In April 1980, frustrated and at low ebb in the public opinion polls, Carter broke diplomatic relations with Iran and ordered a daring rescue mission. Colonel Charles A. Beckwith eagerly led the operation, saying "America needs a win. We need one real, real bad." But the rescue effort miscarried after an equipment failure in the sandy Iranian desert. During the hasty withdrawal two aircraft collided, killing eight American soldiers. The hostages were not freed until January 1981, 444 days after their capture. In the agreement that led to their release, the United States unfroze Iranian assets and promised not to intervene again in Iran's internal affairs.

Elsewhere in the Middle East, Carter enjoyed some success. Through his tenacious personal diplomacy at a Camp David meeting in 1979, the president persuaded Egypt and Israel to agree to Israel's phased withdrawal from the Sinai, which had been occupied since 1967. Other Arab states denounced the agreement for not requiring Israel to relinquish other occupied territories. But the treaty at least ended warfare along one boundary in this troubled area of the world.

Carter also had some success elsewhere in the Third World. His appointment of Andrew Young, a black

Egypt's President Anwar al-Sadat (1918–1981), President Jimmy Carter (1924–   ), and Israeli Prime Minister Menachem Begin (1913–   ), left to right, clasp hands to celebrate the historic signing, on March 26, 1979, of the Egyptian-Israeli Peace Treaty. A triumph of American diplomacy by the president in intense negotiations with the two Mideast leaders at Camp David, Maryland, the document provided only a brief respite from the violent politics of the region.   National Archives, Carter Project.

civil rights activist and member of Congress, as ambassador to the United Nations earned goodwill among developing nations. Young believed that the United States should stay out of local disputes, even if Communists were involved. Thus when warfare broke out in 1979 between Zaire and Angola, where Cuban troops and Soviet advisers were stationed, Young persuaded the president to stand back until the fighting subsided, and no American interests were sacrificed. Third World leaders were shocked, however, when Young was forced to resign in 1979 after meeting privately with representatives of the Palestine Liberation Organization, which the United States had refused to recognize as a legitimate group.

In Latin America, Carter concluded two treaties with Panama that provided for gradual return of the

IMPORTANT EVENTS

1960	Kennedy elected president	1971	*Pentagon Papers* released
1961	Peace Corps founded Alliance for Progress Bay of Pigs invasion Berlin crisis U.S. military buildup	1972	Nixon visits China SALT-I treaty Nixon re-elected
1962	Cuban missile crisis	1973	Vietnam cease-fire agreement Allende ousted in Chile Arab-Israeli War Arab oil embargo

1963	Test-ban treaty
	Diem assassinated in Vietnam
	Kennedy assassinated; Johnson
	  assumes presidency
		1974	Nixon resigns; Ford becomes
			  president
			New International Economic Order

1964	Tonkin Gulf incident and resolution Johnson elected president	1975	Egyptian-Israeli peace agreement Communists take power in South Vietnam Civil war in Angola
1965	U.S. invasion of Dominican Republic Johnson Americanizes Vietnam War	1976	Carter elected president
1965–66	Antiwar teach-ins	1977	Human rights policy launched
1967	Peace rallies across the nation Six-Day War in the Middle East	1978	Panama Canal treaties

1968	Tet offensive in Vietnam
	My Lai massacre
	Vietnam peace talks open in Paris
	Nixon elected president
		1979	Egyptian-Israeli peace accord (Camp
			  David)
			Hostages taken in Iran
			SALT-II treaty
			Soviets invade Afghanistan
			Grain embargo and boycott of
			  Olympic Games against Soviets

1969	543,400 U.S. troops in Vietnam Nixon begins withdrawal Détente policy announced	1980	Secretary Vance resigns Reagan elected president
1970	Invasion of Cambodia	1981	American hostages in Iran released

Canal Zone to that Central American country. The treaties, endorsed by the Senate in 1978, aroused heated debate. Former governor of California Ronald

Panama Canal Treaties

Reagan, running hard for the presidency, went so far as to claim that the Canal Zone was sovereign American territory. But others saw that without the treaty the United States might have to fight the Panamanians, who longed for the restoration of territory they believed had been wrongfully severed from their nation in 1903 (see pages 638–639).

In Nicaragua in 1979 leftist revolutionaries overthrew Anastasio Somoza, a graduate of West Point, long-time ally of the United States, and member of the dictatorial Somoza family that had ruled the Central American nation since 1936. The revolutionaries called themselves Sandinistas after the Nicaraguan who had fought American marines in the early 1930s (see page 771). President Carter at first tried to tame their radicalism, but, failing, he recognized the new government. In early 1981 he shut off aid to Nicaragua to demonstrate disapproval of the Sandinistas' curbing of civil liberties, growing ties with Castro's Cuba, and alleged assistance to rebels in El Salvador, where another regime friendly to the United States was threatened by internal upheaval (see Chapter 35).

Carter's diplomatic record never met his aspirations. More American military personnel were stationed overseas in 1980 (489,000) than in 1976 (460,000);

Debate on Carter's Record

the defense budget climbed; foreign arms sales grew from $8.3 billion in 1977 to $15.3 billion in 1980; and the United States and NATO agreed to install cruise and Pershing-II missiles in Western Europe. Carter's human rights policy also proved inconsistent. In four years the president did gain the release of hundreds of political prisoners, but he left himself vulnerable to the charge that he followed a double standard. That is, he applied the human rights test to some nations (the Soviet Union, Argentina, and Chile), but not to American allies (South Korea, the shah's Iran, and the Philippines). Carter's successes in the Middle East, Latin America, and Africa became overshadowed by the shrillness of an invigorated Cold War.

Carter's performance did not satisfy Americans who wanted superiority in foreign affairs—a reinstatement of the considerable military edge the United States had had in the early days of the Cold War. As one Tennessee woman mused: "Growing up we learned in history that America was the best in everything. We had the respect of the whole world. But where can you go today and be respected for being American?" Her bluntly chauvinistic attitude reflected a broad segment of American public opinion. An Oklahoma couple urged Carter to take up once again Teddy Roosevelt's big stick. "And club the hell out of them if you need to," grumbled the husband.

This nostalgia for old-fashioned American militancy found a ringing voice in President Ronald Reagan,

elected in 1980 after a campaign in which he charged that the United States was falling behind the Soviets in the arms race and retreating under fire from the Third World. Reagan promised to abandon détente and SALT-II, dramatically increase the military budget, and support right-wing governments that stood by American foreign policy. About the Vietnam War, Reagan said, "It is time we recognized that ours was, in truth, a noble cause." The United States, it appeared, had come full circle—back to 1961 when John F. Kennedy had decided to win the Vietnam War.

SUGGESTIONS FOR FURTHER READING

General and Soviet-American Relations

Stephen Ambrose, *Rise to Globalism*, 3rd ed. (1983); Richard J. Barnet, *The Alliance* (1983); John L. Gaddis, *Strategies of Containment* (1982); John L. Gaddis, *Russia, the Soviet Union, and the United States* (1978); Alexander L. George and Richard Smoke, *Deterrence in American Foreign Policy* (1974); Raymond L. Garthoff, *Détente and Confrontation: American-Soviet Relations from Nixon to Reagan* (1985); Robert C. Johansen, *The National Interest and the Human Interest* (1980); Walter LaFeber, *America, Russia, and the Cold War, 1945–1985*, 5th ed. (1985); James A. Nathan and James K. Oliver, *United States Foreign Policy and World Order*, 2nd ed. (1981); Alvin Z. Rubenstein and Donald E. Smith, eds., *Anti-Americanism in the Third World* (1985); Adam B. Ulam, *Dangerous Relations* (1983).

Kennedy and Johnson Diplomacy

George W. Ball, *The Past Has Another Pattern* (1982); Warren I. Cohen, *Dean Rusk* (1980); Philip Geyelin, *Lyndon B. Johnson and the World* (1966); David Halberstam, *The Best and the Brightest* (1972); Jim Heath, *Decade of Disillusionment* (1975); Lyndon B. Johnson, *The Vantage Point* (1971); Madeleine G. Kalb, *The Congo Cables* (1982); Doris Kearns, *Lyndon Johnson and the American Dream* (1976); Montague Kern et al., *The Kennedy Crises* (1984); Richard D. Mahoney, *JFK: Ordeal in Africa* (1983); Herbert S.

Parmet, *JFK* (1983); Walt W. Rostow, *Diffusion of Power* (1972); Arthur M. Schlesinger, Jr., *Robert Kennedy and His Times* (1978); Arthur M. Schlesinger, Jr., *A Thousand Days* (1965); Richard Walton, *Cold War and Counter-revolution* (1972).

Latin America and Cuba

Graham Allison, *Essence of Decision: Explaining the Cuban Missile Crisis* (1971); Samuel Baily, *The United States and the Development of South America, 1945–1975* (1977); Cole Blasier, *Hovering Giant* (1974); Herbert Dinerstein, *The Making of a Missile Crisis* (1976); Walter LaFeber, *Inevitable Revolutions: The United States in Central America* (1983); Walter LaFeber, *The Panama Canal* (1979); Stephen G. Rabe, *The Road to OPEC: United States Relations with Venezuela* (1982); Peter Wyden, *Bay of Pigs* (1979).

Middle East

George Lenczowski, *The Middle East in World Affairs*, 4th ed. (1980); William B. Quandt, *Decade of Decision: American Policy Toward the Arab-Israeli Conflict, 1967–1976* (1977); Bernard Reich, *Quest for Peace: United States–Israel Relations and the Arab-Israeli Conflict* (1977); Barry Rubin, *Paved with Good Intentions: The American Experience and Iran* (1980); Robert W. Stookey, *America and the Arab States* (1975).

The Vietnam War and Southeast Asia

Larry Berman, *Planning a Tragedy* (1982); Frances FitzGerald, *Fire in the Lake* (1972); Leslie H. Gelb and Richard K. Betts, *The Irony of Vietnam* (1979); George C. Herring, *America's Longest War* (1979); Arnold R. Isaacs, *Without Honor: Defeat in Vietnam and Cambodia* (1983); Stanley Karnow, *Vietnam* (1983); Guenter Lewy, *America in Vietnam* (1978); Archimedes L.A. Patti, *Why Viet Nam?* (1980); John C. Pratt, ed., *Vietnam Voices* (1984); Al Santoli, *Everything We Had* (1981); Herbert Y. Schandler, *The Unmaking of a President: Lyndon Johnson and Vietnam* (1977); William Shawcross, *Sideshow: Kissinger, Nixon, and the Destruction of Cambodia* (1979); Ronald H. Spector, *United States Army in Vietnam* (1983); Wallace Terry, *Bloods: An Oral History of the Vietnam War by Black Veterans* (1984); Nancy Zaroulis and Gerald Sullivan, *Who Spoke Up? American Protest Against the War in Vietnam, 1963–1975* (1984).

The Lessons of Vietnam

Walter H. Capps, *The Unfinished War* (1982); Michael Charlton and Anthony Moncrieff, eds., *Many Reasons Why* (1978); Herbert Hendin and Ann P. Haas, *Wounds of War: The Psychological Aftermath of Combat in Vietnam* (1984); Myra MacPherson, *Long Time Passing: Vietnam and the Haunted Generation* (1984); Robert E. Osgood, *Limited War Revisited* (1979); Norman Podhoretz, *Why We Were in Vietnam* (1982); Earl C. Ravenal, *Never Again* (1978); Harrison E. Salisbury, ed., *Vietnam Reconsidered* (1984); Harry G. Summers, Jr., *On Strategy: A Critical Analysis of the Vietnam War* (1982); W. Scott Thompson and Donaldson D. Frizzill, eds., *The Lessons of Vietnam* (1977).

Nixon, Kissinger, and Détente

Richard J. Barnet, *The Giants: Russia and America* (1977); Seymour M. Hersh, *The Price of Power: Kissinger in the Nixon White House* (1983); Stanley Hoffmann, *Primacy or World Order* (1978); Stanley Hoffmann, "The Case of Dr. Kissinger," *New York Review of Books*, 26 (December 6, 1979), 14ff.; Bernard Kalb and Marvin Kalb, *Kissinger* (1974); Henry Kissinger, *Years of Upheaval* (1982); Henry Kissinger, *White House Years* (1979); Roger Morris, *Uncertain Greatness: Henry Kissinger and American Foreign Policy* (1977); Richard Nixon, *RN* (1978); Andrew J. Pierre, *The Global Politics of Arms Sales* (1982); Tad Szulc, *The Illusion of Peace* (1978).

Carter's Foreign Policy

Zbigniew Brzezinski, *Power and Principle* (1983); Jimmy Carter, *Keeping Faith* (1982); Warren Christopher et al., *American Hostages in Iran* (1985); James Fallows, *National Defense* (1981); Kenneth A. Oye et al., *Eagle Entangled* (1979); Gaddis Smith, *Morality, Reason, and Power* (1986); Cyrus Vance, *Hard Choices* (1983); Sandy Vogelgesang, *American Dream, Global Nightmare* (1980).

The CIA and Counterinsurgency

Philip Agee, *Inside the Company* (1975); Douglas S. Blaufarb, *The Counterinsurgency Era* (1977); Ray Cline, *Secrets, Spies and Scholars* (1976); Victor Marchetti and John D. Marks, *The CIA and the Cult of Intelligence* (1974); Thomas Powers, *The Man Who Kept the Secrets* (1979); John Stockwell, *In Search of Enemies* (1978); David Wise, *The American Police State* (1976); David Wise, *The Invisible Government* (1964); David Wise and Thomas B. Ross, *The Espionage Establishment* (1967).

Nuclear Arms Race and SALT

Desmond Ball, *Politics and Force Levels: The Strategic Missile Program of the Kennedy Administration* (1980); John Newhouse, *Cold Dawn: The Story of SALT* (1973); Samuel B. Payne, Jr., *The Soviet Union and SALT* (1980); Glenn T.

Seaborg, *Kennedy, Khrushchev, and the Test Ban* (1981); David N. Schwartz, *NATO's Nuclear Dilemmas* (1983); Stanford Arms Control Group, *International Arms Control,* 2nd ed. (1984). (See also works listed in Chapter 30 under "Nuclear arms race.")

The World Economy and North-South Issues

Richard J. Barnet, *The Lean Years* (1980); Richard J. Barnet and Ronald Müller, *The Global Reach: The Power of the* *Multinational Corporations* (1974); David P. Calleo, *The Imperious Economy* (1982); Alfred E. Eckes, *The U.S. and the Global Struggle for Minerals* (1979); Charles A. Jones, *The North-South Dialogue* (1983); Stephen D. Krasner, *Defending the National Interest* (1978); Robert K. Olson, *U.S. Foreign Policy and the New International Economic Order* (1981); William Paddock and Paul Paddock, *Time of Famines* (1976); Joan E. Spero, *The Politics of International Economic Relations,* 2nd ed. (1981).

REFORM, RADICALISM, AND DISAPPOINTED EXPECTATIONS

1961–1973

CHAPTER 33

The first dreadful flash from Dallas clattered over newsroom teletype machines across the country at 1:34 P.M., Eastern Standard Time. Carried immediately over radio and television, the news was soon on the streets. People still remember precisely where they were and what they were doing when they heard that President John F. Kennedy had been shot and killed. For them, time stopped at that moment in what psychologists call flashbulb memory, the freeze-framing of an exceptionally emotional event down to the most incidental detail. For an earlier American generation, the indelible memory was of December 7, 1941, when radio reports of the Japanese attack at Pearl Harbor had stunned the nation into silence. But now, it was November 22, 1963, the day John Kennedy's promise was snuffed out.

In New York City that afternoon, a man braked his car to a halt in the middle of a busy intersection and ran over to a sidewalk luncheonette. "Is it true?" he asked. Without looking up, the counterman replied, "Yes, he's dead." The man returned to his car and slumped behind the wheel, oblivious to the impatient honking around him. In Detroit, Sister Kate Seidenwand was the co-principal of a parochial grade school. Upon hearing that the president had been shot, she took the children into chapel and "started the Rosary, praying that it wasn't serious. And when we were in the midst of the Rosary, the secretary came in and said that he had died. And I was personally so overwhelmed . . . I had to wait a few minutes to compose myself in order to tell the students. When I finally could announce it, you could hear the children's sighs and groans, and some of them were crying." Ken Kesey's play *One Flew Over the Cuckoo's Nest* had just opened on Broadway, and he and a couple of friends were driving triumphantly back to the West Coast. They were in Pennsylvania when "the news came in over that car radio, and [as] we stopped in at service stations and Howard Johnson's and little fast-food places across the United States, a really profound thing happened to us. We felt like we were seeing the real soul of America with its shirt torn open in grief."

For four days in late November 1963, Americans wept, prayed, and stared at their television sets, numbed by the unbelievable. Throughout the afternoon and night before the funeral, 250,000 people trod silently past the coffin in the Capitol Rotunda. Jacqueline Kennedy and her daughter Caroline paid a last visit to kneel and kiss the coffin. On the fourth day, a million people lined the streets of Washington and millions more watched on television as the president's body was borne by horse-drawn caisson from the Capitol to St. Matthew's Cathedral to Arlington Cemetery. Throughout the country, people mourned. "He was our man," sobbed an elderly black man in Harlem, "and now he's gone."

Some of America's postwar confidence was riding on the caisson that carried Kennedy's body to the grave. "In retrospect," the British journalist Godfrey Hodgson has written, "people looked back to Friday, November 22, 1963, as the end of a time of hope, the beginning of a time of troubles." What was ironic about America's outpouring of grief was that the Kennedy administration had failed in many of its goals. In the final months of his presidency Kennedy had been criticized for being ineffectual in domestic affairs and reckless in foreign affairs. Few successes distinguished his legislative record, and there was already opposition to America's deepening involvement in Vietnam. But John Kennedy's assassination was a national tragedy. In their grief Americans remembered how handsome and eloquent he had been and how he had inspired their hopes for peace, prosperity, and social justice.

In the early 1960s, hope had run high among millions of Americans, including the nation's poor. Kennedy's call for a New Frontier had inspired liberal Democrats and young idealists to work to eliminate poverty, segregation, and voting rights abuses. Americans also supported Kennedy's desire to court the Third World and prevail in the Cold War. Lyndon B. Johnson, Kennedy's successor in the White House, presided over the Great Society, and Congress responded to his urgings with a flood of legislation. The 1960s saw more economic, political, and social reform than any period since the New Deal. But even during these years of liberal triumphs, anger occasionally flared into violence. Beginning with the assassination in 1963, ten years of events ensued—including bloody race riots, the murders of other political and civil rights leaders, and the war in Vietnam—that shattered the Kennedy and Johnson optimism.

In the cities, many Afro-Americans were angry that they still lived in poverty and segregation despite the civil rights movement and the passage of landmark civil rights laws. Their discontent exploded during the 1960s' "long hot summers." In July 1967, for example, twenty-six people were killed in Newark, New Jersey, in warfare between blacks, the police, and army troops. This event was followed a week later by the Detroit race riot, which led to the deaths of forty-three persons. The next year the National Advisory Commission on Civil Disorders, chaired by Governor Otto Kerner of Illinois, released its report on the causes of the race riots. "The nation is rapidly moving toward two increasingly separate Americas . . . a white society principally located in suburbs, in smaller central cities, and in peripheral parts of large central cities; and a Negro society largely concentrated within large central cities."

This social turbulence along with the growing movement opposing the Vietnam War brought down the presidency of Lyndon Johnson and gave rise to Black Power, the radical politics of the New Left, and a revived women's movement. But Johnson's departure from office did not produce calm. Richard Nixon, who was elected president in 1968, polarized the nation still further. Nixon's two immediate predecessors had been destroyed in office: both Dallas and Vietnam evoked those tragedies. A third place, Watergate, was to signify Richard Nixon's downfall. Battered by these events, by 1973 many Americans had ceased to believe in the American dream.

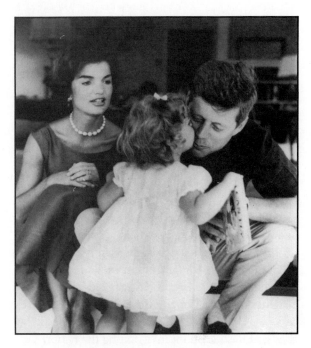

Caroline Kennedy kisses her father as her mother watches. President John F. Kennedy (1917–1963) and his wife, Jacqueline, seemed to symbolize youthful energy and idealism. Kennedy's New Frontier gave hope to nonwhites and the poor. *National Archives.*

KENNEDY AND THE NEW FRONTIER

He was, as Norman Mailer wrote of President John F. Kennedy, "our leading man." The handsome, vigorous new chief executive was young, the first president born in the twentieth century. Perceived by the public as an intellectual, he had a genuinely inquiring mind, and as a patron of the arts, he brought wit and sophistication to the White House.

Kennedy had been born to wealth and politics. His Irish-American grandfather had been mayor of Boston; his millionaire father, Joseph P. Kennedy, served as ambassador to Great Britain. In 1946 the young Kennedy, home from the Second World War a hero, continued the family tradition by campaigning in Boston for a seat in the House of Representatives. He won easily.

As a Democratic politician, Kennedy inherited the New Deal commitment to the welfare state. He generally cast liberal votes in line with the prolabor sentiments of his low-income, blue-collar constituents. But on issues of no direct concern to his district—flood control, farm price supports, the Tennessee Valley Authority—he cast his votes with some of the most conservative members of Congress. Kennedy avoided controversial issues such as civil rights and the censure of Joseph McCarthy. Though he won a Pulitzer Prize for a book *Profiles in Courage* (1956), a study of politicians who had acted on principle, some critics complained that he himself showed too much profile and not enough courage. And he shaded the truth when he claimed sole authorship of this book, which had been largely written by others. Kennedy nevertheless enjoyed an enthusiastic following, especially after his landslide re-election to the Senate in 1958.

Although he was elected president in 1960 by a razor-slim margin (see page 873), Kennedy's vitality and style captured the imagination of many Americans.

"The Best and the Brightest" In a departure from the Eisenhower administration's staid, conservative image, the new president surrounded himself with young men of intellectual verve who proclaimed that they had fresh ideas for invigorating the nation. (On the other hand, Kennedy appointed no women to significant posts.) The writer David Halberstam called these men "the best and the brightest." Secretary of Defense Robert McNamara, forty-four, had been an assistant professor at Harvard at age twenty-four and later the whiz-kid president of the Ford Motor Company. Kennedy's special assistant for national security affairs, McGeorge Bundy, forty-one, had become a dean at Harvard at age thirty-four with only a bachelor's degree. Kennedy himself was only forty-three, and his brother Robert, the attorney general, was thirty-five.

Kennedy's program, the New Frontier, was immensely ambitious, and he promised more than he could deliver: an end to racial discrimination, federal aid to farmers and to education, medical care for the elderly, and government action to halt the recession the country was suffering. But long-time members of Congress saw him and his administration as publicity hungry. Some also feared the president would seek federal aid to parochial schools. The result was the defeat of federal aid to education and of a Kennedy-sponsored boost in the minimum wage. By August 1961, eight months into his first year, it was evident that Kennedy lacked the ability to move Congress, which was largely ruled by a conservative coalition of Republicans and southern Democrats.

Still struggling to work with these conservatives, the new president pursued civil rights with a lack of vigor. On the one hand, Kennedy established the President's Committee on Equal Employment Opportunity to eliminate racial discrimination in government hiring. But on the other hand, he waited until November 1962 before finally honoring a 1960 campaign pledge to issue an executive order forbidding segregation in federally subsidized housing. Meanwhile he appointed five diehard segregationists to the federal bench in the Deep South, one of whom in open courtroom referred to blacks as "chimpanzees." Kennedy's performance disheartened civil rights advocates.

Despite the White House's lack of interest, black civil rights activists continued their struggle through the tactic of nonviolent civil disobedience. Volunteers organized by the Southern Christian Leadership Conference (SCLC), headed by Martin Luther King, Jr., deliberately violated segregation laws by sitting in at whites-only lunch counters, libraries, and bus stations throughout the South. When arrested they went to jail as an act of conscience. In May 1961 "Freedom Riders" with the racially integrated Congress of Racial Equality (CORE) boarded buses and braved attacks by southern white mobs for daring to desegregate interstate transportation. Meanwhile black students in the South were joining the Student Non-Violent Coordinating Committee (SNCC). More than any other volunteers, it was these field workers who walked the dusty back roads of Mississippi and Georgia, encouraging blacks to resist segregation and register to vote. Some SNCC volunteers were white, but most were black and many were from low-income families. These volunteers understood from experience how racism, powerlessness, and poverty intersected in the lives of Afro-Americans.

As the civil rights movement gained momentum in the early 1960s, President Kennedy gradually made a commitment to first-class citizenship for blacks. In September 1962 he ordered U.S. marshals to protect and assist James Meredith, the first black student to attend the University of Mississippi. Under court order the following spring, federal officials ignored the defiant governor of Alabama, George C. Wallace, and forced desegregation of the University of Alabama. In June 1963 Kennedy finally requested legislation to outlaw segregation in public accommodations.

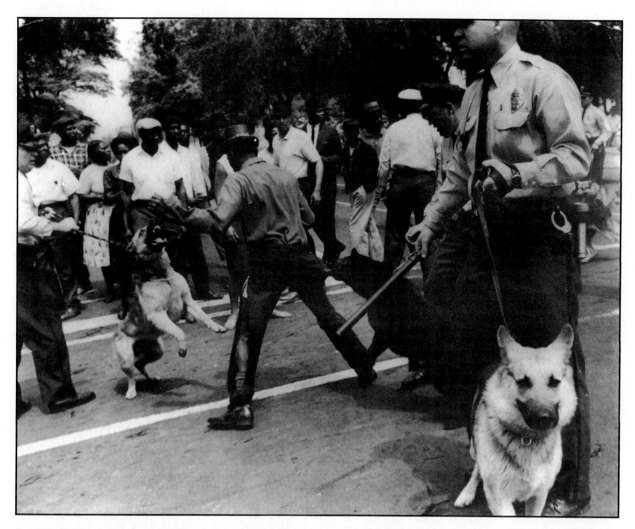

In 1963 the center of white resistance to the civil rights movement was Birmingham, Alabama. And every evening on the television news millions of Americans watched the violence. From many sides pressure mounted on the Congress to pass civil rights legislation. Charles Moore/Black Star.

When more than 250,000 people, black and white, gathered at the Lincoln Memorial for a March on Washington that August, they did so with the knowledge that President Kennedy was at last on their side. Those congregated also heard Martin Luther King, Jr., speak. "I have a dream," he told the crowd, "that my four little children will one day live in a nation where they will not be judged by the color of their skin but by the content of their character."

Meanwhile, television news programs brought civil rights struggles into Americans' homes. The story was sometimes grisly. In 1963 Medgar Evers, director of the NAACP in Mississippi, was murdered in his own driveway. That same year police under the command of Sheriff "Bull" Connor of Birmingham, Alabama, attacked civil rights demonstrators with snarling dogs, firehoses, and cattle prods. And William Moore, a white postman who attempted his own freedom march from Baltimore to Mississippi carrying a sandwich board that read "Eat at Joe's, Both Black and White" and "Equal Rights for All," was shot and killed just after entering Alabama.

Then, while Kennedy's public accommodations bill was being held up by a Senate filibuster, two horrifying events helped to convince reluctant politicians that action on civil rights was long overdue. In September white terrorists exploded a bomb during Sunday-morning services at Birmingham's Sixteenth Street Baptist Church. Sunday school was in session, and four black girls were killed. A little more that two months later, on November 22, 1963, John Kennedy was assassinated in Dallas.

Kennedy's murder still baffles many Americans. Was the accused assassin, Lee Harvey Oswald, acting alone or as part of a conspiracy, possibly involving organized crime, pro-Castro or anti-**Assassination** Castro groups, or even the Central **of President** Intelligence Agency? Was he the **Kennedy** only gunman, or were there more? What was Oswald's motive? Whatever the answers, Kennedy's death traumatized the entire nation. Then two days later, in full view of millions of TV viewers, Oswald himself was shot dead by Jack Ruby, a nightclub owner and small-time Mafia figure. The same question was asked: what was Ruby's motive?

Historians have wondered what John Kennedy would have accomplished had he lived. Although his legislative achievements were meager, he inspired idealism in Americans. When Kennedy said in his inaugural address, "Ask not what your country can do for you. Ask what you can do for your country," tens of thousands of Americans volunteered to spend two years of their lives in the Peace Corps. "We had such faith in what Kennedy was doing," recalled one volunteer, "and we all wanted to be a part of it." And the new president created a sense of national purpose through his vigorous support of the space program. Americans beamed when on February 20, 1962, Marine Lieutenant Colonel John Glenn orbited the globe in a space capsule, and they embraced Kennedy's challenge to put a man on the moon by the end of the decade.

In recent years, however, some writers have described not Kennedy's idealism, but his recklessness in world events, such as authorizing CIA assassination attempts on the life of Cuba's Pre-**Kennedy in** mier Fidel Castro. To counteract **Retrospect** that assessment, it is clear that

Kennedy had begun to grow as president during his last few months in office. He made a moving appeal for racial equality, and he called for reductions in Cold War tensions. Then there was the Kennedy aura. James Reston of the *New York Times* called Kennedy "a story-book President," handsome, graceful, "with poetry on his tongue and a radiant young woman at his side." Jacqueline Kennedy said that for her the Kennedy era evoked the image of Camelot. Partly because of this aura, John Kennedy came to have a higher reputation in death than he enjoyed in life. Although he had been elected in 1960 with only 49.7 percent of the popular vote, by June 1963, even before his assassination, 59 percent of those polled claimed to have voted for him. Immediately after the assassination, his retrospective landslide swelled to 65 percent. And in a bizarre way he accomplished more in death than in life. In the post-assassination atmosphere of grief and remorse, Lyndon Johnson pushed through Congress practically the entire New Frontier agenda. Johnson had done, Walter Lippmann wrote, "what President Kennedy could not have done had he lived."

JOHNSON AND THE GREAT SOCIETY

The new president, Lyndon Johnson, was a big man and a passionate one. The Senate majority leader from 1954 to 1960, he knew how to manipulate people and power to achieve his ends. "This ponderous . . . Texan knows more about the sources of power in the political world of Washington than any President in this century," wrote columnists Rowland Evans and Robert Novak. "He can be gentle and solicitous as a nurse, but as ruthless and deceptive as a riverboat gambler." In the aftermath of the assassination, Johnson determined to unite the country behind the unfulfilled legislative program of the martyred president. But more than that, he wanted to realize Roosevelt's and Truman's unmet goals. He called his new program the Great Society.

Shortly after the assassination of President Kennedy, Vice President Lyndon B. Johnson (1908–1973) was sworn in as the thirty-sixth president of the United States. The ceremony took place on the presidential plane as it returned to Washington from Dallas. Standing on Johnson's right is his wife, Lady Bird; on his left, a stunned Jacqueline Kennedy. AP/ Wide World Photos.

Johnson made civil rights his top legislative priority. "No memorial oration or eulogy," he told a joint session of Congress five days after the assassination,

Civil Rights Act of 1964

"could more eloquently honor President Kennedy's memory than the earliest passage of the civil rights bill." It was a happy coincidence for the civil rights movement that Johnson, a southerner, had become president. According to Clarence Mitchell, chief lobbyist for the NAACP, Johnson "made a greater contribution to giving a dignified and hopeful status to Negroes in the United States than any other President, including Lincoln, Roosevelt and Kennedy." Within months Johnson had signed into law the Civil Rights Act of 1964, which outlawed

discrimination not only in public accommodations but also in employment on the basis of race, color, religion, sex, or national origin. An Equal Employment Opportunity Commission was established the same year to investigate and judge complaints of job discrimination. The act also authorized the government to withhold funds from public agencies that discriminated on the basis of race, and it gave the attorney general powers to guarantee voting rights and end school segregation.

Johnson enunciated another priority in January 1964, in his first State of the Union address: "The administration today, here and now, declares unconditional war on poverty." Eight months later, he signed into law the Economic Opportunity Act of

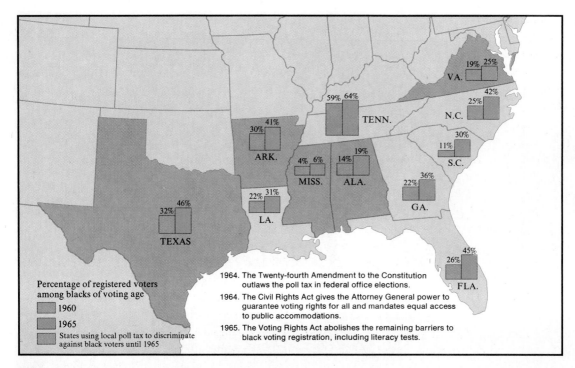

Black Voting Rights, 1960–1965

Map legend:

Percentage of registered voters among blacks of voting age
- 1960
- 1965
- States using local poll tax to discriminate against black voters until 1965

State data (1960 / 1965):
- VA. 19% / 25%
- TENN. 59% / 64%
- N.C. 25% / 42%
- ARK. 30% / 41%
- S.C. 11% / 30%
- MISS. 4% / 6%
- ALA. 14% / 19%
- GA. 22% / 36%
- LA. 22% / 31%
- TEXAS 32% / 46%
- FLA. 26% / 45%

1964. The Twenty-fourth Amendment to the Constitution outlaws the poll tax in federal office elections.

1964. The Civil Rights Act gives the Attorney General power to guarantee voting rights for all and mandates equal access to public accommodations.

1965. The Voting Rights Act abolishes the remaining barriers to black voting registration, including literacy tests.

1964, which allocated almost $1 billion to fight poverty. The act, which became the opening salvo in Johnson's War on Poverty, promised "to eliminate the paradox of poverty in the nation by opening to everyone the opportunity to live in decency and dignity." Finally, Johnson secured the $13.5 billion tax cut for which Kennedy had labored unsuccessfully.

In the year following Kennedy's death, Johnson sought to govern by consensus, appealing to the shared values and aspirations of the majority of the nation.

Election of 1964

Judging by his lopsided victory over his Republican opponent in 1964, Senator Barry Goldwater of Arizona, he succeeded. Johnson garnered 61 percent of the popular vote and the electoral votes of all but six states. Goldwater's narrowness certainly enhanced Johnson's appeal. The Republican candidate alienated voters by suggesting that Social Security be voluntary and the Tennessee Valley Authority be abolished, and he appeared reckless and provocative when he advocated using nuclear weapons in Vietnam. Republican leaders from the liberal eastern wing of the party either refused to support Goldwater or gave him half-hearted endorsements. He seemed to have solid support in only a few states in the Southwest and South.

Riding on Johnson's coattails, the Democrats won staggering majorities in both the House (295 to 140) and the Senate (68 to 32). Johnson knew that the moment for further reform had arrived. "Hurry, boys, hurry," Johnson told his staff just after the election. "Get that legislation up to the Hill and out. Eighteen months from now ol' Landslide Lyndon will be Lame-Duck Lyndon." Congress responded in 1965 and 1966 with the most sweeping reform legislation since 1935. Skillfully guided by Johnson, the liberal Democratic majorities passed a remarkable 69 percent of the president's legislative proposals. The powerful conservative coalition of Republicans and southern Democrats, which had had its way on 74 percent of House roll-call votes in 1961 and 63 percent in 1963, was victorious on only 25 percent of the votes in 1965.

Three bills enacted in 1965 were legislative milestones. The Medicare program insured the elderly against medical and hospital bills. The Elementary and Secondary Education Act became the first general program of federal aid to education. And the Voting Rights Act of 1965 empowered the attorney general to supervise voter registration in areas where fewer than half the minority residents of voting age were registered (see map). When Johnson became president, only one-fourth of the South's black population was registered to vote; when he left office in 1969 the proportion was approaching two-thirds. Even in the most resistant states, that trend has continued. Only 6.7 percent of Mississippi's black citizens were registered to vote in 1964; in 1981 the figure was 70 percent.

Other accomplishments during Johnson's presidency included establishment of the Department of Housing and Urban Development and the National Foundation on the Arts and Humanities; water and air quality improvement acts; the Teacher Corps to work in impoverished school districts; college scholarships and loans; liberalization of immigration laws; and appropriations for the most ambitious federal housing program since 1949, including rent supplements to low-income families. And in 1968 Johnson signed his third civil rights act, banning racial and religious discrimination in the sale and rental of housing. Another provision of this legislation, known as the Indian Bill of Rights, extended those constitutional protections to reservation Indians living under tribal self-government.

Even more ambitious was Johnson's War on Poverty. Because the gross national product had increased, Johnson and his advisers reasoned that the government could expect a "fiscal dividend" of several billion dollars in additional tax revenues. They decided to spend the extra money to wipe out poverty through education and job training programs. As the War on Poverty evolved in 1965 and 1966, it included the Job Corps and Neighborhood Youth Corps, to provide marketable skills, work experience, remedial education, and counseling for young people; the Work-Experience Program for unemployed fathers and mothers; Project Head Start, to prepare low-income preschoolers for grade school; and Upward Bound, for high school students from low-income families who aspired to a college education. In an innovation that was to arouse the ire of mayors and city councils, these programs encouraged "maximum feasible participation" by the poor in the administration of community action programs. Other antipoverty programs were Legal Services for the Poor; Volunteers in Service to America (VISTA); and the Model Cities program,

War on Poverty

which directed federal funds toward upgrading employment, housing, education, and health in targeted neighborhoods.

Confusion abounded in this ambitious program. Not even R. Sargent Shriver, who as head of the Office of Economic Opportunity (OEO) administered the War on Poverty, could deny this. "It's like we went down to Cape Kennedy and launched a half dozen rockets at once," he later conceded. Another serious criticism was that the War on Poverty did little to reduce suffering in the countryside or to check the South-to-North migration that exacerbated the already overwhelming northern urban problems. In a Brookings Institution study, James Sundquist noted that "when it comes to the solution of the poverty problem, a good many of the urban poverty thinkers have written off the rural areas and have concluded that the only way to deal with rural poverty is to let the people move and then handle them in the cities." Another group that remained poor despite the government's antipoverty efforts included those—mostly children—living in female-headed families, who comprised 40 percent of the poor in the United States. While the booming economy from 1963 to 1969 lifted 12 million people in male-headed families out of poverty, it stranded there 11 million in families headed by women, the same number as in 1963.

Still, the War on Poverty, in tandem with a rising gross national product, substantially alleviated hunger and suffering in the United States. The tax cut and fresh infusions of federal funds for defense ended the recession of 1960 and 1961, and beginning in the mid-1960s, the social welfare budget soared. Between 1965 and 1970 federal spending for Social Security, health, welfare, and education more than doubled. During the same years, the GNP leapt from $685 billion to $977 billion. Some of this prosperity trickled down to the poor, but of more direct importance in eradicating poverty was the government's funding of specific welfare programs. The result was a startling reduction in the number of poor people, from 25 percent of the population in 1962 to 11 percent in 1973. Particularly fortunate were the elderly, who benefited from large increases in Social Security benefits; poverty among the elderly dropped from about 40 percent in 1960 to 16 percent in 1974.

Successes in Reducing Poverty

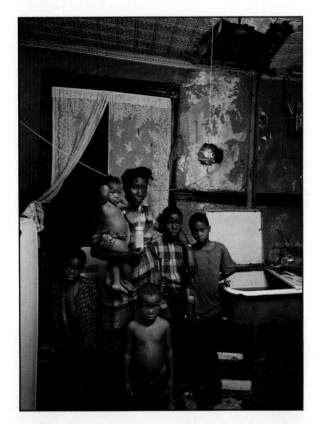

The War on Poverty lifted many people out of suffering. But this Harlem woman, photographed with her children in 1966, had a bleak future. Being black, a woman, and a single mother all contributed to her poverty.   John Launois/ Black Star.

Despite the War on Poverty's successes, the period of liberal ascendancy it represented was short lived, with its legislative achievements occurring from 1964 to 1966. Disillusioned with America's deepening involvement in Vietnam (see Chapter 32), many of Johnson's allies began to reject both him and his liberal consensus. But one branch of government continued the liberal tradition—the Supreme Court.

THE WARREN COURT

I n the volatile 1960s, the Supreme Court was disposed by political sentiment and a belief in judicial activism to play a major role in the resurgence of liberalism. Its liberal majority included Justices Hugo Black, William Brennan, and William O. Douglas in addition to Chief Justice Earl Warren. After the 1954 and 1955 school desegregation cases (see page 860), the Warren Court did not roil the political waters for the remainder of the 1950s. But the next decade was to be markedly different. According to one constitutional historian, in the 1960s the United States "changed irrevocably," and the Warren Court was "midwife to that change—if not its sire."

In 1962 the Court began handing down a series of liberal decisions. In *Baker v. Carr* (1962) and subsequent rulings, it declared that the principle of "one person, one vote" must prevail at both state and national levels. This decision required the reapportionment of state legislatures so that each representative would serve the same number of constituents. Prior to this decision, some legislators from sparsely settled rural areas represented only half as many people as their counterparts from populous urban areas. The Court also outlawed required prayers in public schools, explaining that such practices placed an "indirect coercive pressure upon religious minorities" (1962). In 1963 it struck down a Pennsylvania law requiring daily Bible readings in all public schools. Some religious groups denounced these decisions, and a few communities, feeling they were losing their freedoms, announced their refusal to comply.

The Court also attacked the constitutional basis of McCarthyism, ruling in 1965 that a person need not register with the government as a member of a subversive organization, for to do **Civil Rights** so would violate constitutional **Rulings** safeguards against self-incrimination. It also ruled on birth control, holding in *Griswold v. Connecticut* (1965) that a state law prohibiting the use of contraceptives by married persons violated "a marital right of privacy" and was unconstitutional. The Court upheld the Civil Rights Act of 1964 and the Voting Rights Act of 1965, and it broadened the interpretation of the Fourteenth Amendment by outlawing segregation in private businesses. In *Jones v. Mayer* (1968) it decided that private discrimination in the rental or sale of housing was prohibited by the Civil Rights Act of 1866. In ruling the 1866 act constitutional under the Thirteenth Amendment, the Court opened new avenues for the pursuit of legal battles for equal rights. With its decisions on prayer and contraception, the Court had deeply affected people's personal lives. And in other rulings that particularly upset conservatives, the Court decreed that books, magazines, and films could not be banned as obscene unless they were "found to be utterly without redeeming social value."

Perhaps most controversial was the Court's transformation of the criminal justice system. Beginning with *Gideon* v. *Wainwright* (1963), the Court ruled that a poor person charged with a felony had the right to a state-appointed lawyer. In *Escobedo* v. *Illinois* (1964), it decreed that the accused had the right to counsel during interrogation and could remain silent. And in *Miranda* v. *Arizona* (1966), it added that police had to inform criminal suspects that they could see a lawyer and remain silent and that any statements they made could be used against them. Critics denounced the decisions as victories for criminals, and the John Birch Society, a right-wing organization, began a campaign to impeach Earl Warren.

Despite demands for Warren's removal, most constitutional historians judge him to have been perhaps the most influential chief justice in the nation's history. Whether or not one approved of the Warren Court, which ended with his retirement in 1969, there was no denying its impact on the American people. In 1983 Bernard Schwartz, constitutional law professor at New York University, made this appraisal: "In expanding civil liberties, broadening political freedom, extending the franchise, reinforcing freedoms of speech, assembly, and religion, limiting the power of the politicians in smoke-filled rooms, [and] defining the limits of police power, the Warren Court had no equal in American history."

RACE RIOTS AND THE
MOVEMENT TOWARD BLACK
POWER

Even as the civil rights movement registered legal and constitutional victories, some activists began to grumble that the federal government was not to be trusted. During the Mississippi Summer Project of 1964, hundreds of college-age volunteers from the North had joined SNCC and CORE field workers to establish "freedom schools" for black children. Many of these volunteers believed that the Federal Bureau of Investigation was hostile to the civil rights movement. They alleged that FBI Director J. Edgar Hoover was a racist, and they were disturbed by rumors, later confirmed, that Hoover had wiretapped and bugged Martin Luther King, Jr.'s rooms and planted stories in the newspapers about his sexual improprieties. Why, activists asked themselves, had Johnson allowed Hoover to remain in office?

Indeed, some FBI informants had not only joined the Ku Klux Klan; they had reportedly become leaders of the terrorist group. One of them had organized several atrocities, including the bombing of Birmingham's Sixteenth Street Baptist Church in 1963. Small wonder that during summer 1964 there was an upsurge in racist violence in the South, particularly in Mississippi. White vigilantes bombed and burned two dozen black churches there between June and October, and three civil rights workers were murdered in Philadelphia, Mississippi, by a group including sheriff's deputies. Instead of protecting the civil rights workers, southern police had assaulted and arrested them.

Violent Attacks on Civil Rights Workers

Amid the terror, SNCC volunteers joined with black Mississippians to establish the Mississippi Freedom Democratic party (MFDP) and sent an opposition delegation to the Democratic national convention. Arguing that the MFDP supported civil rights, while the state's regular Democratic organization was vehemently segregationist, the MFDP demanded that the convention honor its credentials. But Johnson, fearful of alienating southern whites and more committed to consensus than to civil rights, offered the MFDP only two token at-large seats. Johnson's offer was inconsistent with his earlier civil rights actions, and Democratic commitment to racial equality was thrown into question.

The year 1964 also brought the first of the "long hot summers" of race riots in northern cities. In Harlem and Rochester, New York, and in several New Jersey cities, black anger exploded. A cleaning woman in Harlem expressed her rage. When the riot

Explosion of Black Anger began, "something happened to me. I felt like something was crawling in me, like the whole damn world was no good, and the little kids and the big ones and all of us was going to get killed. . . . And I see the cops are white and I was crying. . . . And I took this pop bottle . . . and I threw it down on the cops and I was crying and laughing."

Whites wondered why blacks were venting their frustration in violence at at time when real progress was being made in the civil rights struggle. Part of the reason was that the movement had been largely southern in focus, geared to abolishing Jim Crow and black disfranchisement. In the North public accommodations and the vote had been available to Afro-Americans for decades, but blacks were still living in deep poverty. The black median income was little more than half that of whites: for every dollar the white worker took home in 1964, the black worker earned 54 cents. Black unemployment in the mid-1960s was twice that of whites, and for black males between eighteen and twenty-five it was five times as high. Many black families, particularly those headed solely by women, lived in perpetual poverty, and their numbers were increasing rapidly. One reason was that Aid to Families with Dependent Children (AFDC), part of the 1935 Social Security Act that had been expanded in 1950 to include payments to the mothers as well as their dependent children, would provide these payments only if there were no able-bodied man in the household. As a result, some unemployed men left home rather than make their families ineligible for AFDC. But more important, the payments themselves were inadequate to cover a family's rent, utility bills, and household expenses, let alone its food. On the basis of food budgets in 1970, it was estimated that over 60 percent of America's black children were being raised in poverty.

As northern blacks learned of the economic and civil rights gains of the 1960s, they wondered when they would benefit from the Great Society. Unlike southern blacks, northern blacks made up a small percentage of the population and tended to be concentrated in the inner cities. When blacks looked around the ghettos in which they lived, they knew their circumstances were deteriorating. Their neighborhoods were more segregated than ever, for whites had responded to the black migration from the South by fleeing to the suburbs. And as inner-city neighborhoods became all black, so did the neighborhood schools. As one writer commented, "It doesn't cost anything to move a few feet along a hamburger counter to make room for a Negro. But the cost—economic, social, psychological—of abolishing forever a Negro ghetto of half a million souls is only now becoming apparent."

If 1964 was fiery and violent, 1965 was even more so. In August blacks gutted the Los Angeles neighborhood of Watts; thirty-four people were killed (see map). Unlike the race riots of 1919 **Watts Race Riot** and 1943, white mobs did not provoke the violence; instead, blacks exploded in anger over their joblessness and lack of opportunity, looting white-owned stores, setting fires, and throwing rocks. "Get Whitey!" they screamed. "Burn, Baby, Burn!" "What white Americans have never fully understood," stated the Kerner Commission in its report several years later, "but what the Negro can never forget—is that white society is deeply implicated in the ghetto. White institutions created it, white institutions maintain it, and white society condones it."

Other cities exploded in riots between 1966 and 1968. Besides expressing their rage, rioters increasingly sought the material wealth on display in store windows. "On Twelfth Street," a black resident of Detroit explained during the 1967 riot, "everybody was out, Mama, Papa, the kids, it was like an outing. . . . The rebellion—it was all caused by the [TV] commercials. I mean you saw all those things you'd never be able to get. . . . Men's clothing, furniture, appliances, color TV,"

It was obvious that many blacks, especially in the North, had begun to question whether the nonviolent civil rights movement had ever addressed their needs. In 1963 Martin Luther King, Jr., had appealed to whites' humanitarian instincts in his "I have a dream" speech. But another voice was beginning to be heard, one that urged blacks to seize their freedom "by any means necessary." It was the voice of Malcolm X, a one-time pimp and street hustler who, while in prison, had converted to the Nation of Islam religion, commonly known as the Black Muslims.

The Black Muslims, a small sect that espoused

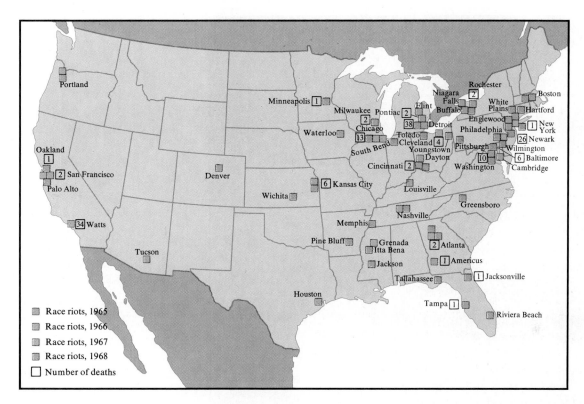

Race Riots, 1965–1968

Legend:
- Race riots, 1965
- Race riots, 1966
- Race riots, 1967
- Race riots, 1968
- Number of deaths

separatism from white society, condemned the "white devil" as the chief source of evil in the world. They attempted to dissociate themselves from white society and exhorted blacks to lead sober lives and practice thrift. Unlike Martin Luther King, Jr., they advocated violence in self-defense. By the early 1960s Malcolm X had become their chief spokesperson, and his advice was straightforward: "If someone puts a hand on you, send him to the cemetery."

Malcolm X

Malcolm X was murdered in a hail of bullets in February 1965; his assassins were Black Muslims who believed he had betrayed their cause. It was true that he had modified some of his ideas just before his death. He had met whites who were not devils, he said, and he had expressed cautious support for the nonviolent civil rights movement. Still, for both blacks and whites, Malcolm X symbolized black defiance and self-respect. A powerful figure in life, in death he would become even more of a hero to increasing numbers of black nationalists and proponents of Black Power.

Although Martin Luther King, Jr., continued to be the most admired leader of the civil rights movement, many younger blacks began to question not only his tactic of nonviolence but his dream of racial integration. In 1966 Stokely Carmichael, chairman of SNCC, called on blacks to assert Black Power. Carmichael believed that in order to be truly free from white oppression, blacks had to control their own institutions—businesses, politics, schools. They had to elect black candidates and teach black students in black schools. Soon organizations that had been committed to racial integration and nonviolence began to embrace Black Power. SNCC and CORE purged white members and repudiated integration, arguing that black people needed power, not white friendship.

Black Power

The wellspring of this new militance was black nationalism, the concept that black peoples everywhere in the world shared a unique history and cultural heritage that set them apart from whites. College students pressed for black studies programs, and blacks began to call themselves black or Afro-American

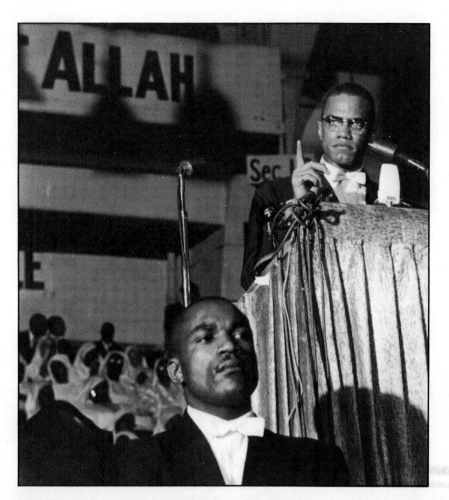

Malcolm X (1925–1965), a one-time pimp and street hustler, became the leading spokesman not only for the Black Muslims but also for many black nationalists and separatists. His autobiography, published after his death, became a classic statement of black pride.   Eve Arnold/Magnum Photos.

rather than Negro. More than at any time since the 1920s, Afro-Americans saw themselves as a nation within a nation.

To white America, one of the most fearsome of the new black groups was the Black Panther Party. Armed and wearing leather jackets, Panther leaders Bobby Seale and Huey Newton dedicated themselves to destroying capitalism. What worried white parents was that some of their own children agreed with the Panthers. Denouncing the major political parties, big business and big labor, middle-class affluence and the suburban lifestyle, even the American dream itself, this vocal minority of the baby-boom generation set out to "change the system."

THE NEW LEFT AND THE
COUNTERCULTURE

"I'm tired of reading history," a philosophy student at the University of California complained in a letter to a friend in early 1964. "I want to make it." By autumn of that year, Mario Savio would realize his ambition as the leader of the Free Speech Movement (FSM), and Berkeley would become a synonym for the campus unrest of the 1960s.

In many ways the University of California in 1964 was a model university, with a worldwide reputation for excellence. Its chancellor, the economist Clark

Free Speech Movement

Kerr, had written *The Uses of the University*, in which he likened the university to a big business. But that was what bothered some students. Berkeley, a "multiversity" with tens of thousands of students, had become hopelessly impersonal. "I am a student," rang one lament of the FSM. "Do not fold, spindle, or mutilate."

After teaching in SNCC's Mississippi Summer Project, Savio and other students had returned to Berkeley suspecting that the same power structure that dominated blacks' lives also controlled the bureaucratic machinery of the university. "Last summer I went to Mississippi to join the struggle there for civil rights. This fall I am engaged in another phase of the same struggle, this time in Berkeley. . . . The same rights are at stake in both places," Savio wrote. The struggle began in September 1964, when the university administration banned political recruitment in Sproul Plaza, the students' traditional gathering place. Savio and other students defied Kerr's ban; the administration suspended them or had them arrested. On October 1 several thousand students surrounded a police car in which a militant was being held, immobilizing it for thirty-two hours. Then in December the FSM seized and occupied the main administration building. Governor Pat Brown dispatched state police to Berkeley, and over eight hundred people were arrested. Angry students shut down classes for several days in protest. By the end of the decade, the activism born at Berkeley would spread to hundreds of other campuses.

Over two years before the confrontation in Berkeley, another group of students had met in Port Huron, Michigan, to form Students for a Democratic Society

Students for a Democratic Society (SDS)

(SDS). Like their leaders, Tom Hayden and Al Haber, most SDS members were white college students, the children of middle-class Americans. In their platform, the Port Huron Statement, they condemned racism, poverty amidst plenty, the antidemocratic tendencies of powerful corporations, and "the enclosing fact of the Cold War," symbolized by the hydrogen bomb. Above all, SDS called upon America to practice its democratic ideals, not just pay them lip service. SDS sought nothing less than the revitalization of democracy through the return of power to the people.

Inspired by the Free Speech Movement and SDS, a minority of students joined the New Left. Although the people in the New Left were united in their

New Left

hatred of racism and the Vietnam War, they were divided in other ways. Indeed, the New Left was not a single organization or even a single movement. Some people were Marxists, others black nationalists, anarchists, or pacifists. Some believed in pursuing social change through negotiation; others were revolutionaries who regarded compromise as impossible.

In the wake of the New Left appeared a phenomenon that observers called the counterculture. Revolu-

Counter-cultural Revolution

tionary figures like Mao Zedong and Fidel Castro became campus idols, "Mao caps" a cult uniform, and "right on" an all-purpose greeting. Led by Timothy Leary, the LSD prophet, millions of students experimented with marijuana, amphetamines, and hallucinogenic drugs.

But it was music more than anything else that reflected the new attitudes. In 1962, the year the founders of SDS gathered at Port Huron, four young musicians from Liverpool, England, recorded "Love Me Do." Long before the Beatles sang "you say you want a revolution," it was evident that their music had inspired one. Soon music was the chief vehicle for the countercultural assault on the status quo. Barry McGuire warned of nuclear holocaust in "Eve of Destruction," and Bob Dylan promised revolutionary answers "blowing in the wind." Young people cheered Jimi Hendrix, who sang of life in a drug-induced "purple haze"; Janis Joplin, who brought black blues to white Americans; and the Buffalo Springfield, who urged youth to stop and "look what's goin' down." Unlike the 1950s counterparts, the rock superstars of the 1960s acknowledged their roots in black rhythm-and-blues. Joplin, who moved crowds with her version of "Ball and Chain," was quick to credit its composer, Big Mama Thornton.

Rock festivals became cultural happenings, the most famous of which was Woodstock (1969), an upstate New York festival that attracted 400,000 people. The huge crowd endured several days of rain and mud together, without shelter and without violence. Some

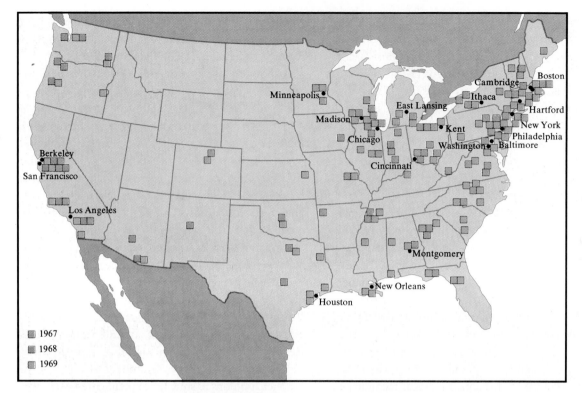

Disturbances on College and University Campuses, 1967–1969

among them began to dream of a peaceful "Woodstock nation" based on love, drugs, and rock music. Beatle John Lennon expressed it best: "All we are saying is give peace a chance."

While some youths sought alternative experiences through drugs and music, others tried to construct alternative ways of life. Among the most conspicuous were the hippies. In the Haight-Ashbury section of San Francisco, "flower children" created an urban subculture as distinctive as that of any Chinatown or Little Italy. "Hashbury" inspired numerous other communal living experiments. Throughout the country, hitchhikers hit the road in search of communes, America, and themselves.

Just as the New Left attracted a minority of students, so the counterculture represented only a small proportion of American youth. But to disconcerted middle-class parents, hippies seemed to be everywhere. Parents carped about long hair, love beads, and patched jeans. They complained that "acid rock" was loud, discordant, even savage. And they feared their chil-

Drugs and Sex

dren would suffer lifelong damage from drugs. Perhaps most disturbing were the casual sexual mores their children adopted, partly as a result of the availability of birth-control pills. For many young people, living together no longer equaled living in sin. And as attitudes toward premarital sex changed, so did notions about pornography, homosexuality, sex roles, and familial relationships.

For both cultural and political reasons, the slogan "Make Love, Not War" became popular at mid-decade. As the war in Vietnam escalated, the New Left and the counterculture discovered a common cause. Students held teach-ins on the war—open forums for discussion among students, professors, and guest speakers.

Thousands of young men also expressed their opposition to the war by fleeing the draft. By the end of 1972 more than 30,000 draft resisters were living in Canada, an additional 10,000 had fled to Sweden, Mexico, and other countries, and 10,000 more were living under false identities in the United States. During the war half a million men committed draft violations, including an estimated quarter-million who

Chapter 33: REFORM, RADICALISM, AND DISAPPOINTED EXPECTATIONS, 1961–1973

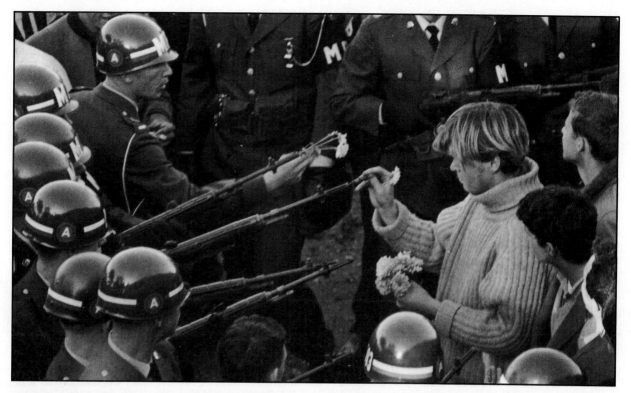

During the March on Washington in 1967, this demonstrator attempted to disarm the troops by placing flowers in their rifle barrels.   Bernie Boston.

never registered and another 110,000 who burned their draft cards in protest.

Marches and demonstrations against the war became a popular protest tactic (see map). In April 1965, 25,000 people marched on the White House, and in October the National Committee **Antiwar** to End the War in Vietnam mo- **Protests** bilized over 80,000 in demonstrations across the country. During the next two years SDS-led groups organized antiwar marches of several hundred thousand people in New York and San Francisco. And in October 1967, the March on the Pentagon of 100,000 people confirmed government officials' fears that the convergence of student activists, the New Left, and the counterculture threatened the nation's warmaking powers.

By this time growing numbers of Americans, young and old, had quit believing their elected leaders. Though President Johnson claimed the United States was fighting for honorable reasons, people wondered what goal could justify the murder of Vietnamese

women and children. As troop levels increased, many recalled ruefully that they had voted for Johnson as the more cautious of the two candidates in 1964. By 1968 almost half a million American soldiers were stationed in Vietnam, and Johnson's credibility had vanished.

1968: A YEAR OF PROTEST, VIOLENCE, AND LOSS

As stormy and violent as the years from 1963 through 1967 had been, many Americans were still trying to downplay the nation's distress in hopes it would go away. "We were in a kind of national sleepwalk," the novelist John Hersey wrote, "aware, on a dream level, of black rage; of the undertow of

Vietnam . . . of the way Lyndon Johnson's credibility gap was beginning to show." But in 1968 the sleepers awoke to a series of violent quakes.

The first shock hit in late January 1968, when the U.S.S. *Pueblo*, a navy intelligence ship, was captured by the North Koreans near the port of Wonsan; not until Christmas of that year would the crew of eighty-two be released. On January 30 came the Tet offensive in Vietnam (see page 921). For the first time many Americans believed they might lose the war. Meanwhile, American casualties had been climbing. In a two-week period in May more than eleven hundred U.S. soldiers died, more by far than in any previous two weeks. In fact, more Americans died in the first six months of 1968 than in all of 1967; on July 4, 1968, total American fatalities surpassed thirty thousand.

Controversy over the war deepened. Within the Democratic party, two men rose to challenge Johnson for the 1968 presidential nomination. One of them, the war hawk Governor George C. Wallace of Alabama, exhorted Americans to "stand up for America." The other, Senator Eugene McCarthy of Minnesota, entered the New Hampshire primary solely to contest Johnson's war policies. On March 12 McCarthy won 42 percent of the popular vote and 20 of 24 convention delegates. Yet another Democrat, Senator Robert F. Kennedy of New York, would soon enter the fray.

On March 31, President Johnson went on national television and announced a scaling-down of the bombing in North Vietnam. Then he hurled a political thunderbolt—he would not be a candidate for re-election.

Less than a week later a white assassin named James Earl Ray shot and killed Martin Luther King, Jr., in Memphis. People still wonder whether Ray was a deranged racist acting alone **Assassination** or a pawn in an organized conspir-**of Martin** acy. Whatever his motive, his crime **Luther King,** aroused instant rage in the nation's **Jr.** ghettos. Blacks rioted in 168 cities and towns, looting and burning white businesses and properties. Thirty-four blacks and five whites died in the violence. Tough talk flared from Maryland Governor Spiro Agnew, who denounced Baltimore's black leaders for not controlling "your people," and from Chicago's Mayor Richard

Daley, who ordered police to shoot to kill arsonists. The terror provoked a white backlash against blacks, and hatred mounted on both sides. "When white America killed Dr. King last night, she declared war on us," charged Stokely Carmichael.

Student protests multiplied that spring not only in the United States but in Paris, Mexico City, and elsewhere in the world. Between January and June 1968 over two hundred demonstrations rocked colleges and universities across the country. Students protested university involvement in the military-industrial complex. In New York students at Columbia University occupied the president's office and other buildings for ten days. On April 30, at the request of Columbia's president, one thousand club-swinging city policemen stormed the occupied buildings, injuring 150 protesters and onlookers.

Most Americans, of course, were not personally threatened by the violence. But nearly all owned TV sets and watched the evening news. As two scholars wrote in the *Columbia Journalism Review*, it was the nightly news that "made social disorganization a realistic threat to the comfortably-off middle-class urbanites, to suburbanites, to rural residents—to all those, in short, who have seldom faced robbery, mugging, protest marching . . . black power salutes, or perhaps even hostile questions about their values."

In April and May Gallup polls reported Robert Kennedy the front-running presidential candidate among Democrats. Kennedy had lost to McCarthy **Assassination** in the Oregon primary but won in **of Robert** California that June. While cele-**Kennedy** brating his victory in Los Angeles's Ambassador Hotel, he decided to take a short cut through the kitchen to a press conference. Suddenly a young man named Sirhan Sirhan stepped forward with a .22-caliber revolver and fired repeatedly at Kennedy. The assassin, it turned out, was an Arab nationalist who despised Kennedy for his unwavering support of Israel. But the cumulative effect of so many assassinations made some Americans wonder and worry. Whenever a charismatic, progressive leader rose to prominence, it seemed, he was mowed down.

The poor were especially grief-stricken by the assassination, because Kennedy had befriended blacks and Mexican Americans. When Cesar Chavez led

Americans mourned when Robert F. Kennedy was assassinated. Earlier in 1968, Kennedy had joined Cesar Chavez as the Mexican-American leader of the United Farm Workers ended a fast.   UPI/Bettmann Newsphotos.

the United Farm Workers' strike against growers in 1965, Kennedy had traveled to California to stand with them. Antiwar liberals also felt they had lost a friend in Kennedy.

Violence erupted again in August at the Democratic national convention in Chicago. The Democrats were divided among supporters of Vice President Hubert Humphrey (Lyndon Johnson's candidate), peace candidate Eugene McCarthy, and Senator George McGovern of South Dakota, who had inherited some of Kennedy's support. Adding to the dissension were several mule-drawn wagons driven by blacks from the Poor People's Campaign; thousands of antiwar protesters; and the Youth International Party, or Yippies, who had traveled to Chicago for a Festival of Life, which they contrasted pointedly to "Lyndon and Hubert's celebration of death."

Violence at the Democratic Convention

The Chicago police force was still in the psychological grip of Mayor Daley's shoot-to-kill directive. Twelve thousand police were assigned to twelve-hour shifts and another twelve thousand army troops and National Guardsmen were on call with rifles, bazookas, and flamethrowers. On Michigan Avenue, in front of the Conrad Hilton Hotel, they attacked, wading into ranks of demonstrators, reporters, and TV camera operators. Throughout the nation viewers watched as club-swinging police beat protesters to the ground. When onlookers rushed to shield the injured, they too were clubbed. Inside the convention hall, Senator Abraham Ribicoff of Connecticut put aside his prepared speech to denounce "those Gestapo tactics in the streets of Chicago."

The Democratic convention nominated Humphrey for president and Senator Edmund Muskie of Maine for vice president. Like Johnson and Kennedy before him, Humphrey was a political descendant of the New Deal, committed to the welfare state and supported by a coalition of northern liberals, big-city bosses, blacks, and union members. First elected to the Senate from Minnesota in 1948, Humphrey was known not just as a champion of civil rights, but as a supporter of the Cold War doctrine of containment that had led to Vietnam. Humphrey's unstinting public support of the war angered some and saddened others, who repudiated him as the candidate of Johnson, Daley, and the war.

The Republicans selected Richard M. Nixon as their presidential nominee. After his defeat by Kennedy in 1960 and his loss in the California gubernatorial race in 1962, Nixon's political career had seemed to be over. But he spent much of the decade campaigning for fellow Republicans and had built up credits with party regulars and officeholders around the country. In 1968 Nixon cashed in his credits and defeated Governors Nelson Rockefeller of New York and Ronald Reagan of California for the nomination. For his running mate, Nixon chose Governor Spiro Agnew of Maryland.

There was little voter enthusiasm for either Humphrey or Nixon. A Gallup poll taken at the time of the convention showed that 66 percent of Americans

Election of 1968

believed the United States should turn over more of the fighting to the South Vietnamese and begin withdrawing its troops. Not only independents and McCarthy followers favored an end to hostilities: large majorities of Humphrey and Nixon supporters agreed. Yet both major candidates endorsed the continuation of the war while negotiations stalled in Paris. In 1968, the nation was deeply divided between the "doves" and the "hawks" (who favored escalation of the war). The Gallup Poll reported that 41 percent of the people described themselves as doves and 41 percent as hawks, with 18 percent holding no opinion.

The candidate with the most appeal for conservatives was George Wallace, the nominee of the American Independent party, who argued that the United States should bomb North Vietnam to rubble

with nuclear weapons. Wallace also appealed to people concerned about law and order, code words for the suppression of protest. If a civil rights protester ever lay down in front of his car, Wallace declared, he would drive over the person.

When the votes were tabulated, Nixon emerged the winner. Just four years after the Goldwater debacle, the Republicans had captured the White House, though by the slimmest of margins. Wallace collected almost 10 million votes, or 13.5 percent of the total, the best performance by a third party since 1924. His strong showing made Nixon a minority president, elected with only 43 percent of the popular vote (see map). Moreover, the Democrats maintained control of the House (243 to 192) and the Senate (58 to 42). Soon there would be a new president and a new decade, but Americans doubted whether they could heal the wounds of war, poverty, racism, sexism, black rage, youthful disaffection, and the shattered promise of the American dream.

THE REBIRTH OF FEMINISM

During the turbulence of the 1960s, another liberation movement gained momentum, at first quietly and then on the picket line. Following the adoption of the Nineteenth Amendment in 1920, the women's rights movement had languished.

The Feminine Mystique

But in the 1960s feminism was reborn. In *The Feminine Mystique* (1963), Betty Friedan wrote that the American home had become a "comfortable concentration camp." TV advertisers, magazine writers, beauticians, and psychiatrists had conspired to create the image of a woman "gaily content in a world of bedroom, kitchen, sex, babies and home." Any woman who was dissatisfied with such surroundings was considered neurotic. But as Friedan pointed out, the woman who spent her life in a world of children sacrificed her adult frame of reference and sometimes her very identity. Friedan quoted a young mother: "I've tried everything women are supposed to do—hobbies, gardening, pickling, canning, and

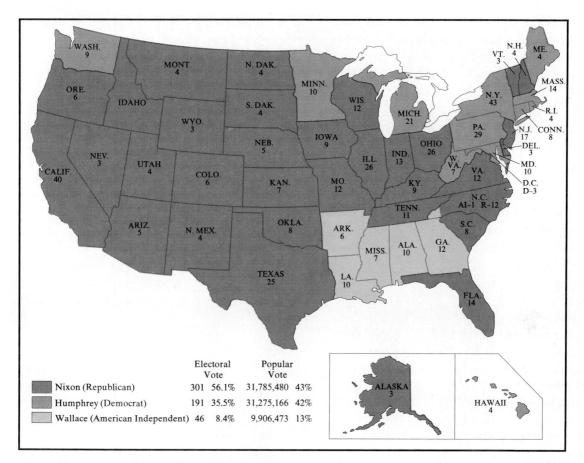

	Electoral Vote		Popular Vote	
Nixon (Republican)	301	56.1%	31,785,480	43%
Humphrey (Democrat)	191	35.5%	31,275,166	42%
Wallace (American Independent)	46	8.4%	9,906,473	13%

Presidential Election, 1968

being very social with my neighbors. . . . I love the kids and Bob and my home. . . . But I'm desperate. I begin to feel that I have no personality. . . . Who am I?" Friedan's book inspired the founding in 1966 of the National Organization for Women (NOW). A reform organization, NOW battled for "equal rights in partnership with men" by lobbying for legislation and testing laws in the courts.

Not long after NOW's formation, a new generation of radical feminists emerged—once again, the baby boom was making an impact on American life. Most were white and well educated; many **Radical** were the daughters of working **Feminism** mothers. Most had been raised in the era of sexual liberation, in which birth-control pills and other contraceptives were taken for granted. The intellectual ferment of their movement produced a new feminist literature: Shulamith Firestone's *The Dialectic of Sex*; Kate Millett's *Sexual Politics*; Robin Morgan's *Sisterhood Is Powerful*. Feminists challenged everything from women's economic, political, and legal inequality to sexual double standards and sex-role stereotypes. And unlike the members of NOW, the radical feminists practiced direct action, as when they picketed the 1968 Miss America contest in Atlantic City. One woman auctioned off an effigy of Miss America: "Gentlemen, I offer you the 1969 model. . . . She walks. She talks. She smiles on cue. *And* she does the housework." Into the "freedom trash can" the pickets dumped false eyelashes, curlers, girdles, and *Playboy*. These feminists were protesting the view of women as servants and sex objects who were pressured to conform to male-imposed "beauty standards." They were also practicing "personal politics." "There is no private domain of a person's life that is not political," explained Charlotte Bunch, a

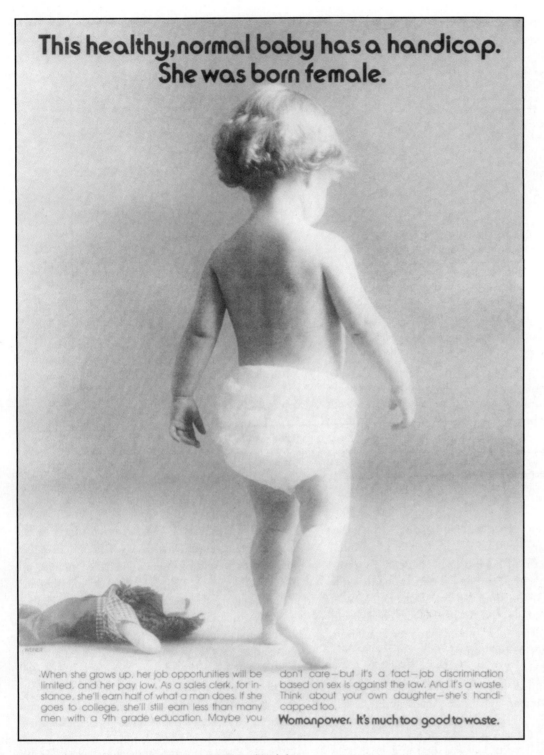

This healthy, normal baby has a handicap. She was born female.

When she grows up, her job opportunities will be limited, and her pay low. As a sales clerk, for instance, she'll earn half of what a man does. If she goes to college, she'll still earn less than many men with a 9th grade education. Maybe you don't care—but it's a fact—job discrimination based on sex is against the law. And it's a waste. Think about your own daughter—she's handicapped too.

Womanpower. It's much too good to waste.

The National Organization for Women (NOW), founded in 1966, went from 1,000 members in 1967 to 40,000 members in 1974. NOW's advertisements about sexual inequality were simple and to the point. NOW Legal Defense and Education Fund, Inc.

feminist, "and there is no political issue that is not ultimately personal."

Many radical feminists had struggled earlier for black civil rights, but they had discovered they were second-class citizens even in movements dedicated to equality. Instead of making policy, they were expected to make coffee, take minutes, and even provide sexual favors. During a staff retreat in 1964 Stokely Carmichael was challenged by women who asked for a discussion of the SNCC position paper on "women in the movement." To male laughter he replied: "The only position for women in SNCC is prone."

Radical feminists joined in consciousness-raising groups where they discussed sensitive issues such as homosexuality. In 1969 and 1970 NOW had forced lesbians to resign from membership and offices in the organization. This rift was healed in 1971, largely because homosexuals had begun to fight back. Examples of militancy—by blacks, radical feminists, and antiwar protesters—helped inspire the gay rights movement. Throughout the 1950s and most of the 1960s, many homosexuals had feared that disclosing their sexual preference would cause them to lose not only their jobs, but even their friends and families. But in June 1969 that began to change. In New York City's Greenwich Village, a riot erupted between police and the patrons of the Stonewall Inn, a gay bar on Christopher Street. Police who raided the bar were not prepared for the volley of beer bottles that greeted them. Rioting continued well into the night, and graffiti calling for "Gay Power" appeared along Christopher Street. As John D'Emilio has written in *Sexual Politics, Sexual Communities: The Making of a Homosexual Minority in the United States, 1940–1970* (1983), "Stonewall thus marked a critical divide in the politics and consciousness of homosexuals and lesbians. A small, thinly spread reform effort suddenly grew into a large, grass-roots movement for liberation. The quality of gay life in America was permanently altered as a furtive subculture moved aggressively into the open."

Gay Rights Movement

For working women in the 1960s, the problems were sex discrimination in employment, lack of professional opportunities, unequal pay for equal work, lack of adequate day care for children, and prohibitions against abortion. In 1963 the average woman earned 63 cents for every dollar a man earned. Ten years later the figure had fallen to 57 cents. What this gender-based discrimination meant for many women was less food on the table and no new shoes for the kids.

Another harsh reality women encountered was "occupational segregation," which became even more pronounced as women flooded entry-level jobs in female-dominated fields like secretarial and clerical work. Women complained of occupational ghettos in which work was broken down into men's jobs and women's jobs and where women were concentrated in the lower-paying positions. The number of women workers jumped from 23.2 million in 1960 to 31.5 million in 1970 and 34.1 million in 1972, but "men's jobs" still paid higher wages. Many women with college educations earned less than men with eighth-grade educations. It was natural that two feminist goals of the 1960s were equal job opportunity and equal pay for equal work.

Occupational Segregation

Opposition to feminist goals was widespread and intense. In December 1971 President Nixon vetoed a bill that would have set up a national system of day-care facilities for the children of working mothers. The bill, Nixon asserted, would have committed government to "communal approaches to child-rearing over against the family-centered approach," thus imperiling "the keystone of our civilization," the American family.

Despite such opposition, women made impressive gains. They entered professional schools in record numbers: from 1969 to 1973, the numbers of women law students almost quadrupled and of women medical students more than doubled. Under Title IX of the Educational Amendments of 1972, female college athletes gained the right to the same financial support as male athletes. In the same year Congress approved the Equal Rights Amendment (ERA) and sent it to the states for ratification. (The Equal Rights Amendment states, "Equality of rights under the law shall not be denied or abridged by the United States or by any State on account of sex.") In two 1973 cases (*Roe* v. *Wade* and *Doe* v. *Bolton*), the Supreme Court struck down state laws that made abortion a

Educational and Legal Advances for Women

crime. Ruling that such laws violated a woman's right of privacy, it held that the Constitution protected a woman's decision as to whether or not to end her pregnancy. Only in the last three months of pregnancy could a state absolutely bar abortion; otherwise, the state's power to regulate abortion was either non-existent or subordinate to the issue of maternal health. As a result of these victories the women's movement gained new confidence. "If the 1960s belonged to the blacks, the next ten years are ours," remarked one feminist.

Nixon and the Persistence of Chaos

Richard Nixon's presidency was born in chaos. In 1969 a hundred black students armed with rifles and shotguns seized the student union at Cornell University and occupied the building for thirty-six hours. Harvard students took over the president's office before being evicted by police. Bloody confrontations occurred at Berkeley, San Francisco State, Wisconsin, and scores of other colleges and universities. And in October 1969, three hundred Weathermen, members of an SDS splinter group, raced through Chicago's downtown district, smashing windows and attacking police officers in an attempt to incite armed class struggle. A month later half a million people assembled peacefully at the Washington Monument on Moratorium Day to call for an end to the Vietnam War. While they appealed to the nation's leaders, President Nixon watched football on TV.

One bright spot for Nixon in 1969 was the flight of *Apollo 11*, a manned spaceship, to the moon. After separating in space from the *Apollo* craft, the lunar module reached its destination in mid-July, and on July 21 astronaut Neil Armstrong made history by taking the first step onto the moon's surface. After taking rock and soil samples, Armstrong and his flightmate Edwin Aldrin successfully rendezvoused

Moon Landing

with the *Apollo* command ship, docked, and returned to earth, splashing down 950 miles southwest of Hawaii on July 24. Led by the president, the nation cheered this accomplishment.

But this was a momentary respite. Back on earth, 1970 would prove to be even bloodier and more turbulent than 1969 had been. On April 30, 1970, President Nixon appeared on television to announce that the United States had launched an "incursion" into Cambodia (see page 922), a neutral country. The war at home escalated in response. On May 4, Ohio National Guardsmen fired into a group of protesting students at Kent State University, killing four and wounding eleven. Enraged students elsewhere went on strike, shutting down 250 campuses and pouring into the nation's capital to lobby against the war. Nixon referred to the protesters contemptuously as "these bums, you know, blowing up the campuses." Ten days after the Kent State killings, police and state highway patrolmen armed with automatic weapons blasted a women's dormitory at Jackson State, an all-black university in Mississippi, killing two students and wounding nine others. No evidence of student sniping could be found; the police fired no tear gas or warning shots.

Kent State and Jackson State

While police and soldiers waged official violence in 1970, revolutionaries conducted an unofficial campaign of terror. They bombed the New York offices of Mobil Oil, IBM, General Telephone and Electronics, and various banks. In March a bomb factory exploded in Greenwich Village, blowing up at least three young revolutionaries. And there were scores of politically motivated skyjackings.

Worst of all, as far as many Americans were concerned, was street crime. "Fortress America: A nation behind locked doors," proclaimed the heading of a *Newsweek* article on crime. Sales of pistols, burglar alarms, and bullet-proof vests soared, as did the demand for private guards and special police. Conservatives accused liberals of causing the crime wave by coddling criminals. "You know what a conservative is?" asked Frank Rizzo, the hard-line police-chief-turned-mayor of Philadelphia. "That's a liberal who got mugged the night before."

Fear of Crime

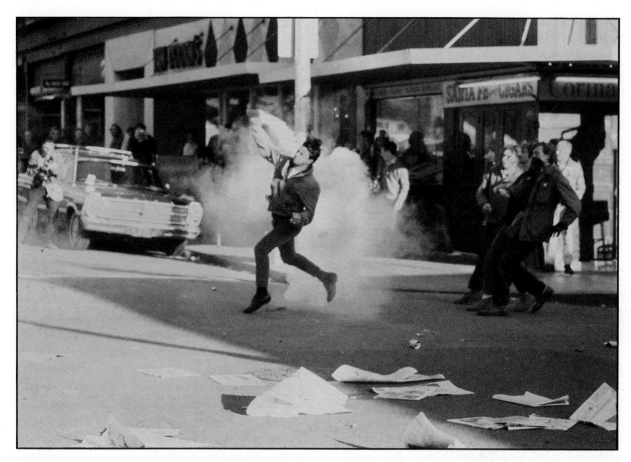

Campus protests and confrontations between students and police escalated. In 1969, these Berkeley protesters picked up tear gas cannisters and hurled them back at the police. Copeland/Black Star.

In the tense atmosphere, government officials sometimes overreacted. Governor Nelson Rockefeller of New York did so in September 1971, when more than a thousand inmates of the Attica State Correctional Facility seized thirty-eight guards and took over a cellblock. Rather than give in to the prisoners' demand that he visit Attica to negotiate, Rockefeller ordered state troopers, sheriff's deputies, and guards to storm the prison. Under a pall of tear gas Rockefeller's army regained control, but at a horrifying cost: twenty-nine inmates and ten hostages dead.

In the wake of this new wave of riots and violent crime, Nixon became convinced that the nation was plunging into anarchy. And he worried, as had Lyndon Johnson before him, that the antiwar movement was Communist-inspired. In June 1970 he ordered the FBI, the CIA, the National Security Agency, and the Defense Intelligence Agency to formulate a coordinated attack on "internal threats." "Everything is valid," a Nixon aide told the group, "everything is possible." Had it not been for FBI Director J. Edgar Hoover's refusal to cooperate in the illegal plot, the group would have had free rein to open mail, tap telephones, and break into citizens' homes and offices.

The administration also worked to put the Democratic party on the defensive. Vice President Agnew took to the road in September to warn the country of threats to its internal security and exhort people to vote Republican in the upcoming congressional

Politics of Divisiveness

elections. "Will America be led by a President elected by . . . the American people," he asked, "or will we be intimidated and blackmailed into following the path dictated by a disruptive, radical, and militant minority?" The same month Jeb Stuart Magruder, an assistant to White House Chief of Staff H.R. Haldeman, defined the theme of the upcoming congressional elections in a memorandum. "The Democrats should be portrayed as being on the fringes: radical liberals who . . . excuse disorder, tolerate crime, apologize for our wealth, and undercut the President's foreign policy," Magruder wrote. But Republican attempts to discredit the Democrats failed. In the election the Democrats gained nine seats in the House and dropped only two in the Senate. The Republicans lost eleven state governorships.

Nixon's fortunes declined further in 1971. On June 13 the *New York Times* began to publish the Pentagon Papers, a top-secret study of the Vietnam War ordered in 1967 by then Secretary of Defense McNamara. The *Times* had obtained the papers from Daniel Ellsberg, a disillusioned defense analyst with the RAND Corporation, a think tank for analyzing national defense policies. The study revealed that the government had consistently lied to the American people about the war. For instance, in August 1964, when President Johnson announced that North Vietnamese patrol boats had attacked the U.S.S. *Maddox* and *C. Turner Joy* (see page 916), he did not reveal that the destroyers had been supporting a South Vietnamese raiding party. And the emergency resolution Johnson introduced in Congress as a result of the attack turned out to have been drafted several months before. Some analysts concluded that the attacks themselves might have been a lie, invented to rally public opinion in favor of the war.

Pentagon Papers

In 1971 Nixon also had to contend with inflation, a problem not entirely of his making. Rather, it was Lyndon Johnson's policy of guns and butter—massive deficit financing to support both the Vietnam War and the Great Society—that had fueled inflation. Not until 1967 had Johnson proposed tax increases to reduce the government deficit and dampen inflation, and not until June 1968 had Congress responded with a 10-percent tax surcharge. Johnson had also trimmed federal spending by

Skyrocketing Inflation

$6 billion, but the cut was too little too late. Nixon's policies, including a $2.5-billion tax cut in late 1969, only boosted rising prices. By January 1971 the United States was suffering from a 5.3-percent inflation rate and a 6-percent unemployment rate. Soon the word *stagflation* would be coined to describe this coexistence of economic recession (stagnation) and inflation.

That January Nixon shocked both critics and allies by declaring, "I am now a Keynesian." Like his Democratic predecessors, he would try to stimulate the economy through government spending. The budget for fiscal 1971 would have a built-in deficit of $23 billion, just slightly under the all-time high of $25 billion (1968 to 1969). Then in August, in an effort to correct the nation's balance-of-payments deficit, Nixon announced he would devalue the dollar by allowing it to "float" in international money markets. He also requested a tax on imports, the repeal of certain excise taxes, and tax concessions to industry for new capital investments. Finally, to curb inflation, the president froze prices, wages, and rents for ninety days, then set limits on their increase. Nixon's commitment to the controversial wage and price controls buckled the next year under pressure from businesses and unions. Though some economists, businesspeople, and politicians argued that the controls were bound to fail, others contended that they would have been successful had they been allowed more time to work.

The wage and price controls were just one sign of what surprised observers called Nixon's "great turnabout." Another was his announcement in July 1971 that he would travel to the People's Republic of China, an enemy Nixon had denounced for years. It was clear that the president was preparing for the 1972 presidential election.

THE SOUTHERN STRATEGY AND THE ELECTION OF 1972

Political observers believed that Nixon would have a hard time running for re-election on his first-term record. Having urged Americans to use "cool" words and "lower our voices," he had ordered

Chapter 33: REFORM, RADICALISM, AND DISAPPOINTED EXPECTATIONS, 1961–1973

Vice President Agnew to denounce the press and student protesters. Having espoused unity, he had practiced the politics of polarization. Having campaigned as a fiscal conservative, he had authorized near-record budget deficits. And having promised peace, he had widened the war in Southeast Asia.

Moreover, congressional accomplishments had been made more in spite of Nixon than because of him. The Democrats dominated both houses of Congress during his first term, and they continued to follow a liberal agenda. Eighteen-year-olds gained the vote, Social Security payments and food-stamp funding were increased, and the Occupational Safety and Health Administration was established. Congress responded to the growing environmental movement by passing the Clean Air Act, the Water Quality Improvement Act, and the Resource Recovery Act. (Nixon opposed most of these social welfare, environmental, and voting rights bills.)

Democratic Legislative Victories

One Nixon innovation that bore fruit in 1972 was revenue sharing, a program that returned federal funds to the states to use as they saw fit. Nixon's effort to shift responsibility to state and local governments was known as the New Federalism. A less popular program was the Family Assistance Plan (FAP), under which a family of four would receive a guaranteed income of $1,600 per year plus $860 in food stamps. (Welfare payments fell below that level in twenty states.) Michael Harrington, the author of *The Other America*, called the plan "the most radical idea since the New Deal"; most conservatives denounced it. But a handful of conservatives, among them the economist Milton Friedman, supported the FAP, arguing that simple cash payments to the poor would do away with the mammoth welfare bureaucracy. The program did not pass Congress, in part because Democrats considered the benefit payments too low.

In his campaign for re-election, Nixon was less interested in running on his record than in employing a "southern strategy" of political conservatism. A product of the Sunbelt himself, Nixon was attuned to the growing political power of that conservative region. Thus he appealed to "the silent majority," the white suburbanites, blue-collar workers, Catholics, and ethnic

Nixon's Southern Strategy

groups of "middle America." As in the 1970 congressional elections, Nixon equated the Republican party with law and order and the Democratic party with permissiveness, crime, drugs, pornography, the hippie lifestyle, student radicalism, black militancy, feminism, homosexuality, and the dissolution of the family.

Actually, Nixon had been pursuing a southern strategy all along. A furor had arisen in February 1970 when the press published a memorandum written by Daniel Moynihan, Nixon's adviser on urban affairs and social welfare. While insisting that blacks should continue to make progress, Moynihan had recommended that "the issue of race could benefit from a period of benign neglect." Moreover, Attorney General John Mitchell had courted southern white votes by trying to delay school desegregation in Mississippi and to prevent extension of the 1965 Voting Rights Act. Mitchell sought vigorous prosecution of antiwar activists as well.

The southern strategy had also guided Nixon's nomination of Supreme Court justices. After appointing Warren Burger, a conservative federal judge, to succeed Earl Warren as chief justice, Nixon had selected two southerners to serve as associate justices. One of them, Judge G. Harrold Carswell of Florida, was a segregationist. When the Senate declined to confirm either nominee, Nixon protested angrily, "I understand the bitter feelings of millions of Americans who live in the South." By 1972, however, the president had managed to appoint three more conservatives to the Supreme Court: Justices Harry Blackmun, Lewis F. Powell, and William Rehnquist. Ironically, the new appointees did not always vote as Nixon would have wished. The Court's decisions on abortion, publication of the Pentagon Papers, the death sentence, wiretapping, and busing for school desegregation all ran counter to Nixon's politics.

The Court was at the center of one of the most emotional issues of the 1972 election: busing. In 1971, in *Swann* v. *Charlotte-Mecklenburg*, the justices had upheld a desegregation plan that required a school system in North Carolina to work toward racial integration through massive crosstown busing. The decision generated widespread protest. In March 1972 Governor George Wallace of Alabama won the Democratic primary in Florida after taking a strong antibusing stand. Three days later Nixon proposed that Congress pass a busing moratorium, and he appeared

President Nixon and Vice President Spiro T. Agnew (1918–) celebrate their re-election in 1972. Both resigned in disgrace before completing the second term. National Archives, Nixon Project.

on television to denounce busing as a reckless and extreme remedy for segregation. Though Nixon's response to busing was a well-planned part of his southern strategy, his stand clearly appealed to northern whites as well.

Besides Wallace, Democratic candidates for the 1972 presidential nomination included Senators Hubert Humphrey, Edward Kennedy, George McGovern, and Edmund Muskie. After his de-

Election of 1972

feat by Nixon in 1968, Humphrey inspired little enthusiasm. And for many Americans, Kennedy had ceased to be a contender in 1969, when he left the scene of an accident at Chappaquiddick, on Martha's Vineyard, in which a woman passenger in his car drowned. Senator Muskie fell victim to a dirty trick, a forged letter published during the New Hampshire primary that accused the senator of laughing at disparaging remarks about Canadian-Americans. When the letter and other slurs brought Muskie to the point

of tears in public, he too ceased to be a serious candidate. Governor Wallace was shot by a disturbed young man named Arthur H. Bremer and began a long convalescence. After his shooting the right-wing law-and-order vote had no place to turn but to Nixon. Meanwhile, Senator McGovern won several primaries and arrived at the Democratic convention with enough votes for the nomination.

Nixon campaigned by assuming the elevated role of world statesman: in February 1972 he traveled to China and in May to the Soviet Union. Both trips were elaborately staged and televised for maximum political effect. But it was the campaign waged by George McGovern that handed victory to the Republicans. When McGovern committed himself to a $30-billion cut in the defense budget, people began to fear he was a neo-isolationist who would reduce the United States to a second-rate power. McGovern's proposals split the Democrats between his supporters—blacks, feminists, antiwar activists, young militants—

IMPORTANT EVENTS

1960	Kennedy elected president	1968	U.S.S. *Pueblo* captured by North Korea
1961	Freedom Ride		Tet offensive
1962	John Glenn orbits globe		Martin Luther King, Jr., assassinated
	SDS's Port Huron Statement		Race riots in 168 cities and towns
1963	Friedan, *The Feminine Mystique*		Civil Rights Act of 1968
	March on Washington		Antiwar protests escalate
	Birmingham, Alabama, Baptist church bombed		Robert F. Kennedy assassinated
	Kennedy assassinated; Johnson assumes the presidency		Violence at Democratic convention
			Nixon elected president
1964	Beatles perform in the United States	1969	Stonewall riot
	Economic Opportunity Act		*Apollo II* moon landing
	Civil Rights Act of 1964		Woodstock festival
	First of the "long hot summers"		Moratorium Day
	Free Speech Movement	1970	U.S. invades Cambodia
	Johnson elected president		Students killed at Kent State University and Jackson State University
1965	Malcolm X assassinated		
	March from Selma to Montgomery		
	Antiwar demonstrations	1971	Pentagon Papers
	Voting Rights Act of 1965		Nixon's New Economic Policy
	Watts race riot		Attica prison revolt
1966	National Organization for Women (NOW) established	1972	Nixon visits China and Russia
			Equal Rights Amendment (ERA) approved by Congress
1967	Race riots in Newark, Detroit, and other cities		George Wallace shot
	March on the Pentagon		Break-in at Watergate
			Revenue-sharing adopted
			Nixon re-elected

and old-guard urban bosses, labor and ethnic leaders, and southerners.

Much to Nixon's advantage was the rumor that the Vietnam War was near its end. Troops were being pulled out; by September 1972 the death rate was almost zero. Then in late October, less than two weeks before the election, Henry Kissinger announced a breakthrough in the peace negotiations. "Peace is at hand," he proclaimed. The announcement proved inaccurate, but it helped persuade some people to vote for Nixon.

Nixon's victory in November was overwhelming. He polled 47 million votes, 60.7 percent of the votes cast. McGovern received only 29 million and won in just one state, Massachusetts, and the District of Columbia. Nixon's southern strategy was supremely successful: he carried all of the Deep South, which had once been solidly Democratic. He also gained a majority of the urban vote, wining over such long-time Democrats as blue-collar workers, Catholics, and ethnics. Only blacks,

Nixon's Landslide Victory

Jews, and low-income voters stuck by the Democrats. Remarkably, the Democrats retained control of both houses of Congress and won two additional seats in the Senate. Democratic voters were becoming independent, resorting to ticket-splitting when they perceived a Democratic candidate to be unacceptable.

When John F. Kennedy delivered his inaugural address in 1961, he had challenged Americans to "pay any price, bear any burden, meet any hardship" to defend freedom and inspire the world. Twelve years later, Richard M. Nixon echoed that rhetoric: "Let us pledge to make these four years the best four years in America's history, so that on its 200th birthday America will be as young and vital as when it began, and as bright a beacon of hope for all the world." Largely because of the president's own actions, however, the next four years would be among the most dismal in the nation's history. As for Nixon, he would resign well before the nation celebrated its bicentennial in 1976.

SUGGESTIONS FOR FURTHER READING

General

Godfrey Hodgson, *America in Our Time* (1976); Peter Joseph, *Good Times: An Oral History of America in the Nineteen Sixties* (1973); Allen J. Matusow, *The Unraveling of America: A History of Liberalism in the 1960's* (1984); Charles R. Morris, *A Time of Passion: America 1960–1980* (1984); William O'Neill, *Coming Apart: An Informal History of America in the 1960s* (1971); Milton Viorst, *Fire in the Streets: America in the 1960s* (1979).

The Kennedy Administration

Henry Fairlie, *The Kennedy Promise* (1973); David Halberstam, *The Best and the Brightest* (1972); Jim F. Heath, *Decade of Disillusionment: The Kennedy-Johnson Years* (1975); Ralph G. Martin, *A Hero for Our Time* (1983); Bruce Miroff, *Pragmatic Illusions: The Presidential Politics of John F. Kennedy* (1976); Herbert S. Parmet, *J.F.K.—The Presidency of John F. Kennedy* (1983); Herbert S. Parmet, *Jack* (1980); Arthur M. Schlesinger, Jr., *A Thousand Days: John F. Kennedy in the White House* (1965); Theodore C. Sor-

enson, *Kennedy* (1965); Theodore H. White, *The Making of the President* (1961); Garry Wills, *The Kennedy Imprisonment* (1982).

The Kennedy Assassination

Edward Jay Epstein, *Legend: The Secret World of Lee Harvey Oswald* (1978); Edward Jay Epstein, *Inquest* (1966); Michael L. Kurtz, *Crime of the Century* (1982); William Manchester, *The Death of a President* (1967); President's Commission on the Assassination of President John F. Kennedy, *The Warren Report* (1964); Anthony Summers, *Conspiracy* (1980).

The Johnson Administration

Carl M. Brauer, "Kennedy, Johnson, and the War on Poverty," *Journal of American History*, 69 (1982), 98–119; Robert A. Divine, ed., *Exploring the Johnson Years* (1981); Ronnie Dugger, *The Politician* (1982); Hugh Davis Graham, *The Uncertain Triumph: Federal Education Policy in the Kennedy and Johnson Years* (1984); Lyndon B. Johnson, *The Vantage Point* (1971); Doris Kearns, *Lyndon Johnson and the American Dream* (1976); Sar A. Levitan, *The Great Society's Poor Law* (1969); Sar A. Levitan and Robert Taggart, *The Promise of Greatness* (1976); Charles Murray, *Losing Ground: American Social Policy 1950–1980* (1983); James T. Patterson, *America's Struggle Against Poverty 1900–1980* (1981); Frances Fox Piven and Richard A. Cloward, *Regulating the Poor* (1971); Hugh Sidey, *A Very Personal Presidency* (1968); Carl Solberg, *Hubert Humphrey* (1984); Theodore H. White, *The Making of the President 1964* (1965).

Civil Rights and Black Power

Carl M. Brauer, *John F. Kennedy and the Second Reconstruction* (1977); Clayborne Carson, *In Struggle: SNCC and the Black Awakening of the 1960s* (1981); William H. Chafe, *Civilities and Civil Rights: Greensboro, North Carolina, and the Black Struggle for Freedom* (1980); David J. Garrow, *The FBI and Martin Luther King, Jr.* (1981); David J. Garrow, *Protest at Selma* (1978); David L. Lewis, *King* (1970); August Meier and Elliott Rudwick, *CORE* (1973); Malcolm X and Alex Haley, *The Autobiography of Malcolm X* (1965); Stephen B. Oates, *Let the Trumpet Sound: The Life of Martin Luther King, Jr.* (1982); Frances Fox Piven and Richard A. Cloward, *Poor People's Movements* (1977).

Warren Court

William O. Douglas, *The Court Years 1939–1975* (1980); Gerald Dunne, *Hugo Black and the Judicial Revolution* (1977); Anthony Lewis, *Gideon's Trumpet* (1964); Charles Morgan, Jr., *One Man, One Voice* (1979); Bernard Schwartz, *Super*

Chief: Earl Warren and His Supreme Court (1983); Earl Warren, *The Memoirs of Earl Warren* (1977).

The New Left and the Antiwar Movement

Wini Breines, *Community and Organization in the New Left* (1983); Todd Gitlin, *The Whole World Is Watching: Mass Media in the Making and Unmaking of the New Left* (1980); Kenneth Keniston, *Young Radicals* (1968); Thomas Powers, *Vietnam, the War at Home* (1984); Stanley Rothman and S. Robert Lichter, *Roots of Radicalism: Jews, Christians, and the New Left* (1982); Kirkpatrick Sale, *SDS* (1973); Sohnya Sayres *et al.*, eds., *The 60s, Without Apology* (1984); Jon Wiener, *Come Together: John Lennon in His Time* (1984); Nancy Zaroulis and Gerald Sullivan, *Who Spoke Up? American Protest Against the War in Vietnam 1963–1975* (1984).

The Counterculture

Stanley Booth, *Dance with the Devil: The Rolling Stones and Their Times* (1984); Morris Dickstein, *Gates of Eden: American Culture in the Sixties* (1977); Michael Medved and David Wallechinsky, *What Really Happened to the Class of '65* (1976); Philip Norman, *Shout! The Beatles in Their Generation* (1981); Charles Reich, *The Greening of America* (1970); Theodore Roszak, *The Making of a Counter Culture* (1968); Philip Slater, *The Pursuit of Loneliness*, rev. ed. (1976); Tom Wolfe, *The Electric Kool-Aid Acid Test* (1968).

The Nixon Administration

John Ehrlichman, *Witness to Power* (1982); Daniel P. Moynihan, *The Politics of a Guaranteed Income* (1973); Richard M. Nixon, *RN: The Memoirs of Richard Nixon* (1978); Leon E. Panetta and Peter Gall, *Bring Us Together: The Nixon Team and the Civil Rights Retreat* (1971); Kevin Phillips, *The Emerging Republican Majority* (1969); Raymond Price, *With Nixon* (1977); Jonathan Schell, *The Time of Illusion* (1975); Leonard Silk, *Nixonomics* (1972); Theodore H. White, *The Making of the President 1972* (1973); Theodore H. White, *The Making of the President 1968* (1969); Garry Wills, *Nixon Agonistes* (1970).

The Rebirth of Feminism

William H. Chafe, *The American Woman: Her Changing Social, Economic, and Political Role, 1920–1970* (1972); Sara Evans, *Personal Politics* (1978); Jo Freeman, *The Politics of Women's Liberation* (1975); Betty Friedan, *The Feminine Mystique* (1963); Judith Hole and Ellen Levine, *Rebirth of Feminism* (1971); Alice Kessler-Harris, *Out to Work: A History of Wage-Earning Women in the United States* (1982); Kate Millett, *Sexual Politics* (1970); Robin Morgan, ed., *Sisterhood Is Powerful* (1970); Sheila M. Rothman, *Women's Proper Place* (1978); Gayle Graham Yates, *What Women Want: The Ideas of the Movement* (1975).

DISILLUSIONMENT AND ECONOMIC UNCERTAINTY

1973–1981

CHAPTER 34

*N*ight watchman Frank Wills was making his rounds at the Watergate aparment-office complex in Washington, D.C., on June 17, 1972, when he noticed that two doors connecting the building to an underground garage had been taped to keep them from locking. Wills removed the tape, but when he returned thirty minutes later he found it had been replaced. He promptly telephoned the police to report the illegal entry. At 2:30 A.M., police arrested five men who were attaching listening devices to telephones in the sixth-floor offices of the Democratic National Committee. The men had cameras, and they had been rifling through files.

One of the men arrested was James W. McCord, a former CIA employee who had become security coordinator of the Committee to Re-elect the President (CREEP). The other four were anti-Castro Cubans from Miami. Unknown to the police, two other men had been in the Watergate building illegally at the time of the break-in. One was E. Howard Hunt, a one-time CIA agent who had become CREEP's security chief. The other was G. Gordon Liddy, a former FBI agent serving on the staff of the White House Domestic Council. What were these men trying to find in the Democrats' offices? What did they hope to overhear on the telephones? Most important, who had ordered the break-in?

In the next twenty-two months the American people would learn the answers to some but not all of these questions. What had at first appeared to be a third-rate burglary would turn out to be part of an official plot to destroy a free presidential election. As the shoddy story of Watergate unfolded, Americans' disillusion would grow. Most had grown up believing their country was the most powerful, the most righteous, the most democratic, and the most bountiful in the history of humankind. By the early 1980s, far fewer Americans clung to such beliefs, and many wondered why they had not shed their innocence earlier.

The Watergate scandal came to light at a time when Americans were still recovering from their country's defeat in the Vietnam War. Perhaps for that reason it was more traumatic than earlier national scandals; in 1974 it caused the first presidential resignation in American history.

While Americans worried about morality in government, economic events touched their lives even more deeply. The years between 1973 and 1981 were filled with uncertainty as the American people reeled under the assault of stagflation (see page 964). The first blow was dealt by the 1973 Arab oil embargo, which led to the realization that the United States was not a fortress that could stand alone; it was dependent for its survival on imported oil. Long gasoline lines, the declining value of the dollar, and persistent stagflation dogged Americans; the postwar economic boom was over.

Politicians seemed unable to cope with the floundering economy. President Gerald Ford's weak WIN program to *Whip Inflation Now* did not impress voters, who turned him out of office in 1976. Jimmy Carter, who defeated Ford by arguing that the nation needed an outsider to bring integrity, efficiency, and fiscal responsibility to Washington, fared just as badly. Under Carter inflation reached new heights and unemployment remained high.

Women and nonwhites were particularly hard hit by inflation and unemployment, for they were usually the last hired and the first to be laid off. Even when they had jobs, women and Afro-Americans were paid less than white men, and experts pointed to the growing "feminization" and "blackening" of poverty. Minorities did achieve some victories in the 1970s, though. Women made educational gains and won legislative seats in Washington and in various state houses. Many Afro-Americans attended college and joined the middle class or were elected to political office. But opposition to the aspirations of both groups mounted steadily. The feminist movement was confronted by an increasingly vocal and effective anti-feminist, or "profamily," movement. And blacks had to contend with antibusing agitation and a resurgent Ku Klux Klan.

Some Americans decided that if they could not reform society, they could at least develop their own individual potential. For them, the 1970s were the Me Decade. Millions of people took to jogging; others meditated, ate health food, or developed their assertiveness skills. But some observers thought they detected an undercurrent of desperation. By 1980 public opinion polls disclosed that most Americans found the present worse than the past and believed the future would be worse yet. "We've gone almost overnight from a nation of optimists to a nation of pessimists," reported pollster Daniel Yankelovich.

As the 1980 presidential election approached, Americans looked back on a decade of economic difficulties. With the purchasing power of their paychecks eroded by inflation, many people had raided their savings, sacrificing future security to present needs. They had seen once-proud automobile and steel plants age and close. "It's an open question," one steel company president lamented in 1980, "whether this industry will survive." As a result of "deindustrialization," many jobs were jeopardized and some disappeared forever. Increases in foreign imports on store shelves became constant reminders that the competition was gaining.

It was in this grim context that Ronald Reagan rode a wave of conservatism into office. Reagan promised a return to old-fashioned morality and a balanced budget. He blamed government for fettering American economic creativity. America could again be what it once was, he declared, and Americans believed him.

NIXON AND THE WATERGATE SCANDAL

Watergate actually began in 1971, when the White House established not only CREEP but the overlapping Special Investigations Unit, known familiarly as the Plumbers, to stop the leaking of confidential information to the press. Following publication of the Pentagon Papers (see page 964), the Plumbers burglarized the office of Daniel Ellsberg's psychiatrist in an attempt to find information to discredit Ellsberg. It was the Plumbers who broke into the Democratic National Committee's headquarters to photograph documents and install wiretaps. And it was CREEP that raised money to pay the Plumbers' expenses both before and after the break-in. CREEP's official duty was to solicit campaign contributions. The committee had managed to collect $60 million, much of it donated illegally by corporations.

The arrest of the Watergate burglars generated furious activity in the White House. Incriminating documents were shredded, E. Howard Hunt's name was expunged from the White House

White House Cover-up telephone directory, and Nixon ordered his chief of staff, H. R. Halderman, to discourage the FBI's investigation into the burglary on the pretext that it might compromise national security.

Soon after the break-in, the Democrats filed a damage suit against CREEP and the five burglars for invasion of privacy. John Mitchell, who had resigned as attorney general to chair Nixon's re-election campaign, called the suit "another example of sheer demagoguery." CREEP "did not authorize and does not condone the alleged actions of the five men apprehended there," Mitchell said. Later, Nixon announced to the press that his White House counsel, John W. Dean III, had conducted a "complete investigation," and that no one in the administration "was involved in this very bizarre incident." At the same time, Nixon privately authorized CREEP payments in excess of $460,000 to keep Hunt and others from implicating the White House in the crime.

Thanks to White House efforts to cover up the scandal, the break-in went practically unnoticed by the electorate. Had it not been for the diligent efforts of reporters, government special

Watergate Hearings and Investigations prosecutors, federal judges, and congressional representatives, Nixon might have succeeded in disguising his involvement in Watergate. Slowly, however, the ball of lies and distortions began to unravel. In early 1973, U.S. District Court Judge John Sirica tried the burglars, one of whom, James McCord, implicated his superiors in CREEP and at the White House. From May until November, the Senate Select Committee on Campaign Practices, chaired by Senator Sam Ervin, heard testimony from White House aides. John Dean acknowledged not only that there had been a cover-up, but that the president had directed it. Another aide, Alexander Butterfield, shocked the committee and the nation

During testimony before a Senate committee investigating Watergate, a White House aide revealed that President Nixon had had tape recorders installed in the White House. This cartoon, which needs no caption, suggests the public's reaction to the electronic surveillance. Reprinted by permission of the Chicago Tribune–New York News Syndicate, Inc.

by disclosing that Nixon had had a taping system installed in the White House, and that conversations about Watergate had been recorded.

Nixon feigned innocence, but on April 30, 1973, he announced the resignations of his two chief White House aides, John Ehrlichman and H. R. Haldeman. Speaking to a national television audience, the president pledged that he would find the facts and act on them. "There can be no whitewash at the White House," he intoned.

As if to give meaning to his words, the president appointed Elliot Richardson, the secretary of defense, to the post of attorney general. Richardson in turn selected Archibald Cox, a Harvard law professor, for the new position of special Watergate prosecutor. But when Cox, supported by Richardson, sought to

Saturday Night Massacre obtain the White House tapes by means of a court order, Nixon forced Richardson and Deputy Attorney General William Ruckelshaus to resign and ordered the next-ranking official in the Department of Justice to send Cox back to Harvard. The public outcry provoked by the so-called Saturday Night Massacre (October 20, 1973) compelled the president to agree to the appointment of a new special prosecutor, Leon Jaworski. When Nixon still refused to surrender the tapes, Jaworski took him to court.

In the same month as the Saturday Night Massacre, the Nixon administration was stung by another scandal. Vice President Spiro Agnew resigned after pleading no contest to charges of income-tax evasion and

Agnew's Resignation acceptance of bribes. Under the provisions of the Twenty-fifth Amendment, ratified in 1964 after President Kennedy's assassination, Nixon nominated Gerald R. Ford, congressman from Michigan and the House minority leader, to replace Agnew. Ford's voting record showed him to be a conservative; he had opposed most of the 1960s reform legislation. But Ford was congenial and popular on Capitol Hill, and his nomination was confirmed promptly by both houses of Congress. Once he had taken the oath of office, the new vice president staunchly maintained that Nixon was innocent of involvement in the Watergate cover-up.

Throughout 1973 and 1974, enterprising reporters uncovered details of the break-in, the hush money, and the various people from Nixon on down who had taken part in the cover-up. White House aides and CREEP subordinates began to go on trial, with Nixon cited as their "unindicted co-conspirator." *Washington Post* reporters Carl Bernstein and Bob Woodward found an informant in the White House known as Deep Throat, who provided damning evidence against Nixon and his aides. As Nixon's story became less credible, his hold on the tapes became more tenuous. In late April 1974 the president finally released an edited version of the tapes, which, he explained, would "at last, once and for all, show that what I knew and what I did with regard to the Watergate cover-up were just as I described them to you from the very beginning."

The tapes, however, were replete with gaps. They swayed neither the public nor the House Judiciary Committee, which had begun to draft articles of impeachment against the president. Nixon was still trying to hang onto the tapes when on July 24 the Supreme Court, in *U.S. v. Nixon*, unanimously ordered him to surrender the recordings to Judge Sirica. At about the same time, the Judiciary Committee began to conduct nationally televised hearings. After several days of testimony the committee voted for impeachment on three of five counts: obstruction of justice through the payment of hush money to witnesses, lying, and withholding of evidence; defiance of a congressional subpoena of the tapes; and the use of the CIA, the FBI, and the Internal Revenue Service to deprive Americans of their constitutional rights of privacy and free speech.

On August 5 the president finally handed over the complete tapes, which he knew would condemn him. Four days later he resigned.

Nixon's successor was Gerald R. Ford. His congressional colleagues hailed the new president as a "decent" and "good" man, respected by both Republicans and Democrats, who would bind up the wounds of Watergate. But Ford's first substantive act was to pardon Nixon, though he had said he would not do so. When the pardon was announced, some people concluded that Ford and Nixon had struck a deal.

The Watergate scandal prompted the reform of abuses that had existed before the Nixon administration. The development of what the historian Arthur M. Schlesinger, Jr., called "the imperial presidency" dated from Franklin D. Roosevelt's administration. Roosevelt had signed executive agreements with foreign nations that were in effect treaties, but had never sent them to the Senate for its advice and consent. President Johnson had led the nation into the Vietnam War without securing a congressional declaration of war as required by the Constitution, and Nixon had authorized secret bombing of Cambodia. Finally, Nixon also had impounded (refused to spend) $15 billion in funds appropriated by Congress for social programs.

Post-Watergate Restrictions on Executive Power

To remedy many of these abuses, Congress in 1973 passed the War Powers Act, which mandated that "in every possible instance" the president must consult with Congress before sending American troops into foreign wars. The law required the president to withdraw troops after sixty days unless Congress specifically directed otherwise. But the act did not specify what Congress could do if the president refused to comply. In 1974 Congress produced the Congressional Budget and Impoundment Control Act, which prohibited impounding federal money. In actions directly related to Watergate, Congress attacked campaign fund-raising abuses and the misuse of government agencies. The Federal Election Campaign Act of 1972 had restricted campaign spending to no more than ten cents per constituent, and required candidates to report individual contributions of more than $100. In 1974 Congress enacted additional legislation that set ceilings on campaign contributions and expenditures for House, Senate, and presidential elections. Finally, to aid citizens who were victims of dirty-tricks campaigns, Congress strengthened the Freedom of Information

Act, originally passed in 1966. The new legislation permitted access to "reasonably" described government documents and provided penalties if the government "arbitrarily or capriciously" withheld such information.

THE ENERGY CRISIS AND THE END OF THE POSTWAR ECONOMIC BOOM

The fallout from Watergate was not the only problem confronting the nation in the early 1970s. More disruptive in the long run was the Arab oil embargo of 1973 (see page 925), which Americans denounced as an "energy Pearl Harbor." Even before the embargo the United States had suffered occasional shortages of natural gas, heating oil, and gasoline. But the American people, who had grown up on cheap, abundant energy, made no effort to conserve; they drove big cars and lived in poorly insulated homes. By fall 1973 the country had to import one-third of its oil supplies.

Price increases ordered by the Organization of Petroleum Exporting Countries (OPEC) struck the United States another blow. From January 1973 to January 1974 oil prices rose 350 **OPEC Price** percent. In March 1974 the majority **Increases and** of OPEC members lifted the five-**Rising** month-old oil embargo, but prices **Inflation** remained high. Government officials began to fear that the price of home air conditioning and heating would soar beyond the reach of even middle-class Americans. As people grappled with the social and political costs of the price hikes, multinational oil companies prospered. Profits jumped 70 percent in 1973 and another 40 percent in 1974. Public resentment of oil companies mounted; many citizens suspected company officers were in league with the Arabs.

The boost in the price of imported oil reverberated through the entire economy. High-cost oil drove up both inflation and unemployment and considerably slowed overall economic growth. Inflation jumped from 3.3 percent in 1972 to 6.2 percent in 1973 and a frightening 11 percent in 1974. At the same time recession hit the auto industry. In Detroit General Motors laid off thirty-eight thousand workers—6 percent of its domestic work force—indefinitely and put another forty-eight thousand on leave for up to ten days at a time. The reason was obvious: sales of gas-guzzling American autos had plummeted as consumers rushed to purchase energy-efficient foreign subcompacts. Like Ford and Chrysler, GM was stuck with mostly large-car assembly plants. First-quarter 1974 profits fell 85 percent at GM, 66 percent at Ford, and 98 percent at Chrysler.

For years the American automobile industry had based production on the presumption that large autos were more profitable to manufacture than small ones.

Recession They had ignored the steady shift **in the Auto** to smaller cars, which accelerated **Industry** suddenly in late 1973. In December compact-car sales exceeded standard-size sales, a turnaround that auto makers, with the exception of American Motors, had not expected to occur before 1977. Buyers rushed to showrooms displaying Japanese, German, and other foreign cars. Moreover, the ailing American auto companies that were not selling cars were not buying steel, glass, rubber, or tool-and-die products either. Soon the recession in the auto industry spread to other manufacturers, who not only quit hiring new workers, but also began laying off experienced employees with seniority.

Unlike earlier postwar recessions, this one did not fade away in a year or two. Part of the reason was the coexistence of inflation. In the earlier recessions, Democrats, as well as many Republicans, had held to a policy of neo-Keynesianism. That is, they had manipulated federal policies to minimize the swings in the business cycle—both fiscal policies, covering taxes and government spending, and monetary policies, including interest rates and the money supply. Thus they hoped to keep employment up and inflation down. The federal government could heat up, or stimulate, the economy by increasing spending, cutting taxes, increasing the money supply, and decreasing the interest rates charged to banks that borrowed from the Federal Reserve System. And it could lower the flame by reversing these policies. Beginning in the 1970s, however, joblessness and prices both began to rise sharply. Policies to correct one problem seemed only to exacerbate the other. In 1974, as unemployment mounted, so too did inflation, but government officials hesitated to fuel it further through massive federal spending.

Even in the best of times, the economy would have been hard pressed to produce jobs for the millions of baby boomers who would join the labor market in the 1970s. As it was, economic

The Shifting Occupational Structure

activity created 26.5 million additional jobs during the decade, a remarkable increase of 32.3 percent. (By contrast, during the 1960s, total jobs increased by 12.2 million, or 17.4 percent.) But because of deindustrialization, there was a shift in the occupational structure. In Youngstown and Pittsburgh, steel mills sat idle, and in Detroit weeds grew in the empty parking lots next to abandoned automobile factories. As these heavy industries collapsed, laid-off workers took jobs in fast-food restaurants, all-night gas stations, and convenience stores, but at half their former wages. Workers who had held high-paying blue-collar jobs saw their middle-class standard of living slipping away.

There were other problems too. One was a slowing of growth in productivity, or the average output of goods per hour of labor. Between 1947 and 1965

Decreased Productivity

American industrial productivity had increased an average of 3.3 percent a year, raising manufacturers' profits and decreasing the cost of products to consumers. But from 1966 to 1970 the annual productivity increase averaged only 1.5 percent; it fell further to 1.4 percent between 1971 and 1975 and to a mere 0.2 percent between 1976 and 1980. Economists blamed the lack of business investment in state-of-the-art technology, the shift from an industrial to a service economy, and an alleged erosion of the work ethic. Whatever the causes, American goods cost more than those of foreign competitors. During the 1970s, Japanese productivity, stimulated by heavy automation, grew at four times the American rate. In 1979, for example, Toyota produced fifty cars per production worker, five times the American average. The savings to Japanese manufacturers made

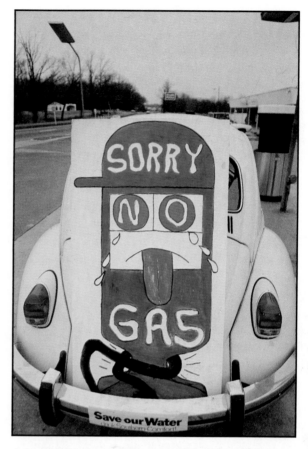

A homemade gas-station sign graphically illustrates the discomfort Americans felt when Arab oil-producing nations cut back fuel shipments in 1973. *Dennis Brack/Black Star.*

their products more competitive in the American market, and cut into American manufacturers' sales.

The lag in productivity was not matched by a decrease in workers' expectations. Wage increases regularly exceeded production increases, and some economists blamed the raises for inflation. Indeed, wages and prices that went up seldom came down again, regardless of market conditions. Managers of the nation's basic industries—steel, autos, rubber—complained that the automatic cost-of-living adjustments in their labor contracts left them little margin to restrain price hikes. Congress's Joint Economic Committee warned, "The average American is likely to see his standard of living drastically decline in the 1980s unless the United States accelerates its rate of productivity growth."

Another spur to inflation was easy credit, particularly

between 1975 and 1979. Fearing an era of scarcity, many people went on a buying spree. Household and business borrowing more than tripled (from $94 billion to $328 billion). More people had credit cards; Master Charge cardholders jumped from 32 million in 1974 to 57 million five years later. This credit explosion helped bid up the price of everything, from houses to gold. What also encouraged borrowing was that interest expenses were tax deductible and that interest-rate increases lagged behind the soaring inflation rate. But some people borrowed more than they could afford. Farmers bought new farm land and expensive machinery and irrigation equipment. The nation's farm debt in 1971 was $54.5 billion; by 1977 it was $122.7 billion, and by 1980 it had reached $165.8 billion. Overburdened with debts, many farmers would face bankruptcy in the 1980s.

Easy Credit and Inflation

Every expert had a scapegoat to blame for the nation's economic doldrums. Labor leaders cited foreign competition and called for tariffs to protect American goods. Some businesspeople and economists said the cost of obeying federal health and safety laws and pollution controls added to the price of goods. Critics estimated that regulations not only discouraged business investments, but also cost industry tens of billions of dollars annually, much of this borne by industries already hurt by recession. They urged officials to abolish the Environmental Protection Agency and the Occupational Safety and Health Administration, and pressed for deregulation of the oil, airline, and trucking industries on the theory that competition would bring prices down.

Above all, critics attacked the federal government's massive spending programs; the mounting national debt, they said, was the sad result. Since the New Deal, both Republican and Democratic administrations had resorted to pump priming to cure recessions. But the Johnson administration's attempt to finance both the War on Poverty and the Vietnam War evidently had backfired. To pay for these costly programs and to service interest on the national debt, the government needed to compete with private businesses for investment funds. This competition forced up interest rates, further fueling inflation and making it more difficult for businesses to expand. Critics of neo-Keynesian pump priming pointed to the resulting stagflation as evidence of the failure of New Deal and Great Society economics.

Inflation was certainly getting out of hand. It had begun to climb in 1966 and 1967; when it reached 5.9 percent in 1970, President Nixon had reacted by trying to restrain federal spending, and the Federal Reserve Board had tightened credit (see page 964). The results had been a stock market collapse, the bankruptcy of the Penn Central Railroad, and a national recession. By the time Gerald Ford became president in 1974, OPEC price increases had pushed the rate to 11 percent. Appalled, Ford created WIN, a voluntary program that encouraged businesses, consumers, and workers to save energy and form grassroots anti-inflation organizations. In the 1974 congressional elections, voters responded to WIN, Watergate, and the Nixon pardon by giving the Democrats forty-three additional seats in the House and four in the Senate.

Government Response to the Economic Crisis

Ford's ultimate response to inflation, like Nixon's, was to curb federal spending and encourage the Federal Reserve Board to tighten credit. As before, these actions prompted a recession—only this time it was the worst in forty years. Unemployment jumped to 8.5 percent in 1975, and because the economy had stagnated, the federal deficit for the fiscal year 1976 and 1977 hit a record $60 billion.

Neither Nixon nor Ford devised lasting solutions to the energy crisis. In 1973, in response to the oil embargo, Congress did consider gasoline rationing, higher fuel taxes to encourage conservation, and a windfall-profits tax on oil companies. Encouraged by rising prices, coal companies began to increase production. President Nixon outlined an energy program that called for lowering thermostats in government buildings, cancelling 10 percent of airline flights, and expediting the construction of nuclear power plants. For a few months the government even banned Sunday gasoline sales. But when OPEC ended the embargo, the crisis seemed to pass, and with it the incentive to prevent future shortages.

The energy crisis intensified public debate over nuclear power. For the sake of energy independence, advocates asserted, the United States had to rely more on nuclear energy. Environmental activists

Three Mile Island, the site of a major nuclear accident in March 1979. When the fail-safe system of one of the reactors failed, 800,000 gallons of radioactive water spurted from a defective valve.   UPI/Bettmann Newsphotos.

countered that the risk of nuclear accident was too great and there was no safe way to store nuclear waste. In March 1975 an accident in one of the world's largest nuclear reactors at Brown's Ferry, Alabama, gave credence to the activists' cause. And in March 1979, in a plant at Three Mile Island, Pennsylvania, a stuck valve overheated the reactor core and raised fears of meltdown and radiation poisoning; it forced the evacuation of a hundred thousand nearby residents. By that time ninety-six reactors were under construction throughout the nation, and thirty more were on order.

Nuclear Power

Meanwhile, the combined effects of the energy crisis, stagflation, and the flight of industry and the middle class to the suburbs and the South were producing fiscal disaster in the nation's cities. Not since 1933, when Detroit defaulted on its debts, had an American city gone bankrupt. But in November 1975 New York City was near financial collapse, unable to meet its payroll and make payments on bonds.

Ford vowed "to veto any bill that has as its purpose a federal bail-out of New York City," but after the Senate and House Banking Committees approved loan guarantees, he relented, and the city was saved. New York was not alone in its financial problems; other Frostbelt cities in the North and East were in trouble, saddled with growing welfare rolls, deindustrialization, and a declining tax base. In December 1978 Cleveland became the first American city to default since the Great Depression.

Throughout Ford's term Congress enjoyed new power. Though Ford almost routinely vetoed its bills, Congress in most cases overrode his vetoes. Watergate and the new criticism of the imperial presidency accounted for Congress's new self-confidence. There was also the fact that, for the first time in the nation's history, both the president and the vice president lacked the popular mandate of having been elected to office. One of Ford's first acts as president was to select former Governor Nelson Rockefeller of New York to be his vice president.

THE FAILED PROMISE OF THE CARTER PRESIDENCY

W hile Ford struggled with a Democratic Congress, the Democratic party prepared for the presidential election of 1976. Frontrunners included

Election of 1976

Senators Birch Bayh of Indiana, Lloyd Bentsen of Texas, and Henry Jackson of Washington. But against the background of Watergate secrecy and corruption, one candidate in particular promised honesty and openness. "I will never lie to you," pledged Jimmy Carter, an obscure former one-term governor of Georgia. A graduate of the U.S. Naval Academy, Carter had served aboard nuclear submarines before returning to Georgia to follow his father as a peanut farmer and politician. When this born-again Christian promised voters efficiency and decency in government, they believed him.

Carter was as ambitious as he was sincere. For two years he and his advisers plotted his campaign strategy. When the 1976 Democratic primaries began, they were ready to canvass the country state by state, primary by primary. Carter worked harder and longer than the other candidates, and he arrived at the national convention with more than enough delegates to win the nomination. His selection of Senator Walter Mondale of Minnesota as his running mate strengthened his candidacy by cementing relations with northern liberals, blacks, union members, and political bosses.

Carter presented himself as a fiscal conservative who would restrain government spending and a social liberal who would fight for the poor, the aged, nonwhites, workers, urban dwellers, and farmers. He stressed that in foreign affairs the United States should work for human rights, arms control, and nonintervention (see page 930). But most of all he emphasized his character: a simple, down-home farmer and family man; a white southerner who had won the support of blacks and northern liberals; an honest politician.

President Ford won his party's nomination after a bitter struggle with Ronald Reagan, former governor of California and champion of the party's right wing.

Ford had grown in the public's estimation since his pardon of Nixon, and the economy had improved while he was in office: inflation had dropped to 5.8 percent. But neither Ford nor Carter inspired much interest, and on election day only 53.5 percent of the electorate stirred itself to vote. Nevertheless, an analysis of the turnout was instructive. One political commentator concluded that the vote was "fractured to a marked degree along the fault line separating the haves and have-nots." Carter gained nearly 90 percent of the black and Mexican-American vote and squeaked to victory by a slim 1.7 million votes out of 80 million. Ford's appeal was strongest among middle- and upper-middle-class voters.

Carter's major domestic accomplishments were in energy, transportation, and conservation policy. To encourage domestic production of oil he instituted

Carter Administration

phased decontrol of oil prices. To moderate the social effects of the energy crisis he called for a windfall-profits tax on excessive profits resulting from decontrol, and grants to the poor and elderly for the purchase of heating fuel. Carter also reformed the civil service and created separate Departments of Energy and Education. He deregulated the airline, trucking, and railroad industries and persuaded Congress to ease federal control of banks. His administration established a $1.6 billion "superfund" to clean up abandoned chemical-waste sites. And finally, in what Carter called "the most important decision on conservation matters that the Congress will face in this century," he placed over 100 million acres of Alaskan land under the federal government's protection as national parks, national forests, and wildlife refuges.

Despite these accomplishments, Jimmy Carter's popularity flagged early. He seemed cold and uncommanding, and he lacked leadership qualities. He

Carter's Flagging Popularity

never established a close working relationship with congressional leaders, nor did he forge friendly relations with other power bases, such as the AFL-CIO. Elected as an outsider, he remained one throughout his presidency.

Carter's conservative policies alienated Democrats who had grown up in the party's New Deal liberal tradition. His support of deregulation and his opposition to wage and price controls and gasoline rationing ran counter to the liberal Democratic position. Seeing inflation as more of a threat to the nation's health than either recession or unemployment, Carter announced that his top priority would be to cut federal spending, even though doing so would add to the jobless rolls. But inflation continued to rise. Liberals grumbled that Carter was a closet Republican, the most conservative Democratic president since Grover Cleveland. In November 1979 Senator Edward Kennedy announced that he would contest the president's renomination.

Carter's problems were not entirely of his own making. In 1979, the shah of Iran's government fell to revolutionary forces; the new government then cut off oil supplies to the United States. And in November Iranian militants stormed the United States embassy in Teheran, taking sixty-six Americans hostage (see page 932). OPEC also raised its prices in 1979, and the cost of crude oil nearly doubled. During the summer, as Americans waited in long lines at gasoline pumps, public approval of the president reached new lows. The Carter administration did respond to the economic woes of the Chrysler Corporation, which had reported losses of $466 million in the first six months of 1979. In the Chrysler "bailout" of January 1980, Congress authorized loan guarantees of $1.5 billion on condition that Chrysler obtain wage reductions from employees, concessions from banks, and state and local aid.

Carter also inherited certain political problems. Not since Eisenhower's eight-year presidency had a president served two full terms; some observers worried

Decline of Presidential Authority

that America had invented the "disposable president," to be discarded every four years. And in the wake of Vietnam and Watergate, Congress had put the president in what Nixon's secretary of state, William Rogers, called "a straitjacket of legislation": campaign laws, the impoundment act, and the War Powers Act. Power had clearly shifted from the White House to Capitol Hill. At the same time Congress was filling up with political newcomers, men and women unused to blind obedience to established leadership. Party discipline seemed a thing of the past.

To complicate matters, Capitol Hill was crawling with lobbyists from a multitude of special-interest

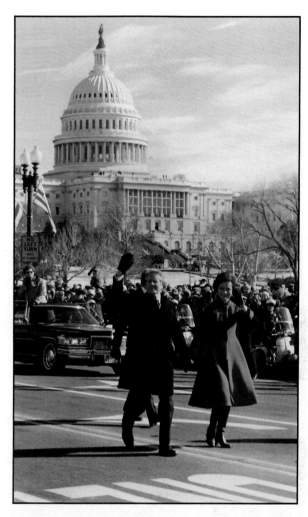

On inauguration day, President Jimmy Carter (1924–   ) and his wife, Rosalynn, caught the public's fancy by walking from the Capitol to the White House. Despite this symbolic beginning, Carter became increasingly isolated both from the American people and from Congress.   National Archives, Carter Project.

groups: trade associations, corporations, labor unions, and single-issue groups like the National Rifle Association. Carter complained that the nation had become "fragmented, Balkanized." In 1980, there were 2,765 political action committees (PACs), more than four times as many as in 1974. Partly responsible for this proliferation was the Campaign Finance Law of 1974, which put a lid of $5,000 on PAC contributions to each candidate, but weakened this provision's impact by placing no limit on the number of PACs from which politicians could accept money.

With party discipline in tatters and each group

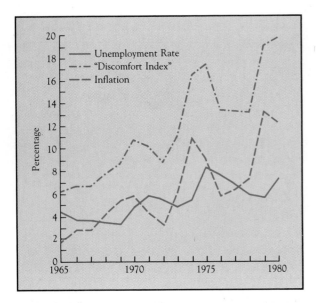

Discomfort Index (Unemployment plus Inflation), 1965–1980 Source: Economic Report of the President: 1980 (Washington: U.S. Government Printing Office, 1981), pp. 238, 263.

clamoring for its own program, the president was forced to form what one White House aide called a "roll-your-own majority" for each proposal. The task called for skills Carter did not possess—trading pork-barrel projects for votes, mobilizing public opinion, and massaging politicians' egos.

By 1980 the economy was a shambles. Inflation had jumped in 1979 to 13.4 percent, and buyers around the world had lost confidence in the dollar, causing unprecedented increases in the price of gold. To steady the dollar and curb inflation, the Federal Reserve Board had taken drastic measures in late 1979: it had raised the rates at which it loaned money to banks. As a result auto loans became more difficult to obtain, mortgage interest rates leaped beyond 15 percent, and the prime lending rate (the rate charged to businesses) hit an all-time high of 20 percent.

Worse still, by 1980 the nation was in a full-fledged recession, with an unemployment rate of 7.5 percent. For two consecutive quarters it had experienced no growth in the gross na-

Economic Discomfort in 1980

tional product. The combined high inflation and high unemployment rates had produced a staggeringly high discomfort index of just under 20 percent (see figure). Moreover, the Iranian hostage

crisis made Carter and the United States appear ineffectual. In 1976 Carter had gibed at the incumbent, President Ford, by saying, "Anything you don't like about Washington, I suggest you blame on him." In 1980 Carter was the incumbent, and many Americans blamed him for the problems that beset the country.

NONWHITES AND NEW
IMMIGRANTS

Carter and his predecessors in the 1970s, Nixon and Ford, presided over a nation in which many nonwhites saw their economic fortunes decline. Joblessness plagued blacks, Native Americans, and Hispanics, as well as the new immigrants who arrived during the decade. As a result of the sluggish economy, poverty was still a national problem in 1980, and blacks made up a disproportionate share of the poor. In the 1970s inner-city blacks experienced a 21 percent increase in poverty. By 1978, though the overall poverty rate had decreased to 11.4 percent, the rate for black families was 27.5, compared with 6.9 percent for white families.

The weight of poverty fell heavily on black children. A 1981 Children's Defense Fund survey reported that black children in the United States were four times more likely than whites to be born in poverty, twice as likely to drop out of school before twelfth grade, five times as likely as white teenagers to be murdered, and three times as likely to be unemployed. "Millions of black children lack self-confidence, feel discouragement, despair, numbness or rage as they try to grow up on islands of poverty, ill health, inadequate education . . . crime and rampant unemployment in a nation of boastful affluence," the report concluded. Indeed, in 1980 the unemployment rate for black male teenagers in the inner cities hovered around 50 percent. For each single percentage-point increase in the nation's overall unemployment rate, the increase for young black men was 6.3 percent.

Tied to the high unemployment rate was the increase in the number of young black families headed by single women. Between 1960 and 1975 the number of fatherless black families rose 130 percent. Many of these families were headed by unmarried teenagers who were forced to rely on welfare to support their children. Other mothers earned meager incomes as domestic servants, laundresses, or kitchen helpers. Like young black males, welfare mothers suffered from a sense of futility. Many were children of the welfare system; it was the only life they knew.

Some whites and even other blacks grumbled that poor blacks were responsible for their own poverty. Their own forebears had seized the opportunities at hand and raised themselves up by **Declining Job** their bootstraps, whites insisted; why **Opportunities** couldn't today's blacks do the same? **for Blacks** But the job market was far different in the 1980s from what it had been twenty-five, fifty, or seventy-five years before. In the past, unskilled European immigrants and black migrants from the South had been able to obtain blue-collar jobs during periods of rapid industrialization. But in the 1970s few such jobs were available; the auto, steel, rubber, and coal industries were contracting, not expanding. Blue-collar jobs in the inner cities were disappearing or moving to the suburbs. New York City alone had 234,000 fewer blue-collar workers in 1980 than it had at the beginning of the decade. This loss of jobs added to inner-city poverty. In 1970, the median household income in the cities was 80 percent of that in the suburbs. By 1980, it had fallen to 74 percent.

In the 1970s, the labor demand was for skilled workers such as computer operators, bank tellers, secretaries, and bookkeepers. Most jobless blacks could not qualify. During these years, too, the labor movement was no longer committed to unionizing the unskilled and the semiskilled. Instead, unions were devoting much of their energy to organizing white-collar workers. As a result the portion of the nonfarm labor force belonging to unions dropped from 33 percent in 1958 to 24 percent in 1978. The situation was tragic for young black men and women who lacked marketable skills. As the black psychiatrist Alvin Poussaint has observed, "A lot of black kids simply feel they don't count. . . . In terms of what makes this society run, they're expendable."

But even as the plight of the black poor worsened, the black middle class expanded. Black college students increased from 282,000 in 1966 to over 1 million in

Black Middle 1976. During this period an esti-
Class mated 30 percent of the urban black population joined the middle class, and many moved to the suburbs or to better housing in the cities. By 1980 about one-third of all black high school graduates were going on to college, the same proportion as among white youths. At least at the upper levels of black society, the dream of equality was being realized.

In his provocative book *The Declining Significance of Race* (1978), William Julius Wilson, the University of Chicago sociologist, spoke of the emergence of two black Americas, one very poor, the other affluent. Blacks living in inner cities and possessed of few job skills found themselves "locked in the low-wage sector . . . where there is little opportunity for advancement and rates of job turnover are high." Meanwhile middle-class blacks, better educated than poor blacks, were able to obtain jobs in government and business, in part because of the pressures of affirmative action. Wilson concluded that "the life chances of blacks" were "based far more on their present economic class position than on their status as black Americans."

Some scholars criticized Wilson's thesis, but other observers supported it. As early as 1970 Andrew F. Brimmer, a black governor of the Federal Reserve System, had warned about "the deepening schism" between poor and middle-class blacks. "There is growing estrangement," Alfred Smith, a black social worker in Boston, admitted in 1978. "The empathy is there, but there's less contact between the middle class and poor blacks."

As middle-class blacks were making gains, resentful whites complained that they were being victimized by "reverse discrimination." To meet federal affirmative-action requirements, some **White** schools and companies had estab-**Backlash** lished quotas for minorities and women. In some cases the requirements for quota groups were lower than those for whites. In a 5-to-4 ruling in 1978 the Supreme Court outlawed quotas but upheld the principle of affirmative action (*Bakke* v. *University of California*).

Anger over a special standard for blacks combined with the effects of stagflation and opposition to busing to produce an upsurge in racism in the 1970s. In Louisville in 1975, bumper stickers urged people to "Honk if you oppose busing." The Ku Klux Klan

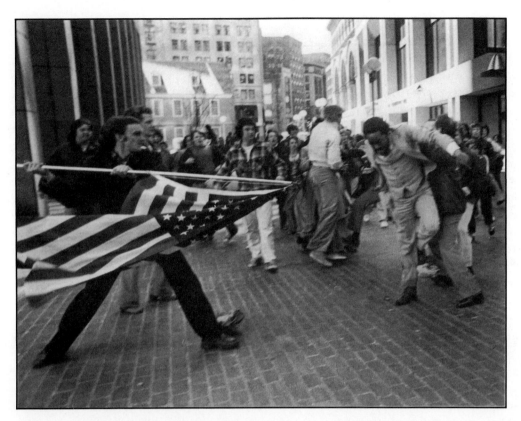

In Boston in 1976, antibusing protesters tried to impale a black man with a flagstaff. This photograph of the ugly incident won a Pulitzer Prize.   Stanley Forman/Boston Herald-American.

stepped up its recruiting in Louisville, and violence soon erupted: over two days, one hundred people were injured and two hundred arrested. In Boston, where busing caused numerous riots, a group of white students protesting busing attacked a black passer-by outside City Hall. "Get the nigger; kill him," one shouted, and they ran at him with the sharp end of a flagstaff flying an American flag. Tension rose not only in Boston and Louisville, but all across the nation. Membership in the Ku Klux Klan grew from about five thousand in 1978 to ten thousand just two years later.

Blacks were tense, too, and they showed it more openly than in the past. "After 350 years of fearing whites," Charles Silberman wrote in *Criminal Violence, Criminal Justice* (1978), "black

Black Anger Americans have discovered that fear runs the other way, that whites are intimidated by their very presence. . . . The taboo

against expression of anti-white anger is breaking down, and 350 years of festering hatred has come spilling out." That hatred erupted several times in summer 1980, most notably in Miami and Chattanooga, after all-white juries acquitted whites of the murder of blacks. (In Miami the defendants were white policemen; in Chattanooga, Ku Klux Klansmen.) Miami's three days of rioting left eighteen dead, four hundred injured, and $100 million worth of property damage. Surveying the wreckage, Vernon Jordan of the National Urban League remarked, "The ingredients that caused the explosion in Miami are present in every city in this country." Just a few days later, Jordan was seriously wounded in Fort Wayne, Indiana, by an unidentified gunman.

Every bit as angry as blacks were American Indians. Their new militancy had burst into the headlines in November 1969, when a small group of Indians seized Alcatraz Island in San Francisco Bay. Arguing that

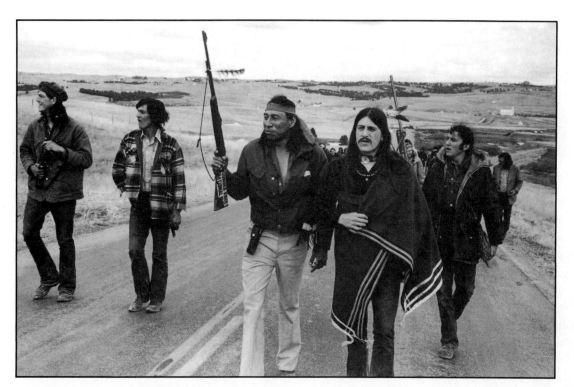

In February 1973, angered by federal government policies and by the actions of conservative Indian leaders, militant members of the American Indian Movement seized hostages at Wounded Knee, South Dakota. The militants exchanged gunfire with federal marshals and their Indian allies, whom the militants disdained as "Uncle Tomahawks." Michael Abramson/Black Star.

an 1868 Sioux treaty entitled them to possession of unused federal lands, the Indians occupied the island until summer 1971. But more was at stake than an abandoned federal penitentiary. "Not just on Alcatraz," explained Richard Oakes, a spokesperson for the Indians, "but every place else, the Indian is in his last stand for cultural survival." Two years later, members of the American Indian Movement (AIM) seized eleven hostages and a trading post on the Pine Ridge Reservation at Wounded Knee, South Dakota, the place where troops of the 7th Cavalry had massacred the Sioux in 1890 (see page 465). Their seventy-one-day confrontation with federal marshals ended with a government agreement to examine the treaty rights of the Oglala Sioux.

Indian Militancy

White society posed more than a cultural threat to Indians, however. The unemployment rate among Indians was 40 percent in the late 1970s. The average per capita income on large reservations was $974, well below the poverty line. Nine out of ten Indians lived in substandard housing, and the high school dropout rate averaged 53 percent. Being an Indian was also unhealthy: Native Americans suffered the highest incidence of alcoholism, tuberculosis, and suicide of any ethnic group in the United States. Though their population had risen since the Second World War to about 1 million (650,000 on or near reservations and 350,000 in the "red ghettos" of the cities), that was only a fraction of their number when the first Europeans arrived in North America.

Since 1924 Indians have had dual legal status as United States citizens and as members of tribal nations subject to special treaty agreements with the United States. But their dual status has proved a curse, in large part because the government has not honored its treaty commitments—especially

Indian Suits for Lost Lands

when Indian lands contained valuable minerals. In 1946 Congress established the Indian Claims Commission to compensate Indians for lands stolen from them. Under the legislation lawyers for the Native American Rights Fund and other groups scored notable victories in the 1970s. The Chippewa in the upper Midwest, Indians in the Puget Sound area of Washington, and the Cheyenne-Arapaho tribes in Oklahoma won protection of their hunting and fishing rights and restitution of their land and water. In 1971 President Nixon signed a bill returning to the Taos Pueblo their sacred forest of Blue Lake in New Mexico. And in 1980 the Supreme Court ordered the government to pay $117 million plus interest to the Sioux Indian Nation for the Black Hills of South Dakota, stolen from them when gold was discovered there in the 1870s.

Compared with earlier treatment, the court decisions, land settlements, and legislation of the 1960s and 1970s were heartening. At the same time, though, corporations and government agencies still coveted Indian lands and disregarded Indian religious beliefs. In the 1960s a coal company strip-mined a portion of the Hopi Sacred Circle, which according to tribal religion is the source of all life. And once again the Black Hills of South Dakota were being mined, this time for uranium.

As Indians fought to regain old rights, Hispanics struggled to make a place for themselves in the United States. An influx of immigrants unequaled since the turn of the century coupled with a high birthrate had made Hispanic peoples America's fastest-growing minority by the 1970s. Of the more than 20 million Hispanics living in the United States in the 1970s, 8 million were Mexican-Americans concentrated in Arizona, California, Colorado, New Mexico, and Texas. Several million Puerto Ricans and perhaps 1 million Cubans clustered principally on the East Coast. In 1980 New York City's Planning Commission estimated that the city had almost 2 million Hispanic residents, over half of Puerto Rican descent and the rest Dominicans, Colombians, Ecuadorans, and Cubans.

Hispanic-Americans

Besides these officially acknowledged Hispanics, between 8 million and 12 million more undocumented workers, or illegal aliens, lived in the United States. Beginning in the mid-1960s, large numbers of poverty-stricken Mexicans began to cross the poorly guarded 2,000-mile border between Mexico and the United States. The movement north continued in the 1970s; in the last eight years of that decade the Chicano population increased 60 percent. Pressure mounted on Congress to curtail this flow and perhaps to provide amnesty for those aliens already living illegally in the United States. In 1979 a congressional commission undertook a two-year re-examination of America's immigration policies. By 1980, one out of every four Texans and one out of every five Californians was Mexican-American. Many newcomers settled in East Los Angeles, the nation's largest barrio. As David Lizarraga, director of the East Los Angeles Community Union, explained: "If I were in Mexico now, I'd be running across that wire as fast as I could. This is the land of opportunity."

But poverty awaited these new immigrants, as it had previous groups of newcomers. The median family income for Mexican-Americans in 1979 was $11,421, as compared with $16,284 for non-Hispanic families. Nineteen percent of Mexican-Americans lived below the poverty line. Puerto Ricans were worse off, with a median family income of about $8,300, and 30 percent of their number living in poverty. Though the problems with which Hispanics contended were similar to those confronting other nonwhites, they also faced a language barrier. Most inner-city schools were ill equipped to serve the needs of bilingual students. As a result, only 30 percent of Hispanic high school students graduated, and fewer than 7 percent finished college. Finally, the larger the Hispanic population has become, the more widespread has been the discrimination against them. "Anglos are afraid," said California Assemblyman Richard Alatorre. "They think they will get to be the minorities and we'll be opposing them."

Most Hispanics preferred their family-centered culture to Anglo culture, and for that reason they resisted assimilation. "What we are saying," explained Daniel Villanueva, a TV executive, "is that we want to be here, but without losing our language and our culture. They are a richness, a treasure that we don't care to lose." A Puerto Rican woman in New York added, "We have been trying to become American for too long, and we are forgetting our roots, culture and the values of our nationality."

Hispanic Cultural Pride

The 1970s were a decade of massive immigration to the United States. These Vietnam refugees were among twenty-eight "boat people" who were rescued in the South China Sea by American sailors.   U.S. Navy.

Instead, like other minorities, Hispanics wanted power—"brown power." Cesar Chavez's United Farm Workers had been the first Hispanic interest group to gain national attention. Another group, the militant Brown Berets, attracted notice for their efforts to provide meals to preschoolers and courses in Chicano studies and consciousness-raising to older students. And throughout the 1970s the Mexican-American political party La Raza Unida was a potent force in the Southwest and East Los Angeles. Still, for a group soon to become the nation's largest minority, Hispanics exercised a disproportionately small share of political power. One reason was that Hispanic America was a tremendously diverse community. Although they shared a language and a religion, Mexican-Americans, Puerto Ricans, Cubans, and other groups differed in countless ways. "We need a Spanish Bobby Kennedy or Martin Luther King," observed Daniel Villanueva. "Right now he's just not there."

During the late 1970s and early 1980s, still other new immigrants joined America's nonwhite population. Between 1970 and 1980 the United States absorbed more than 4 million immigrants and refugees and perhaps twice that number of illegal aliens—more new residents than in any one decade in American history. Refugees of the Vietnam War arrived from Indochina, and other immigrants came from the Philippines, Korea, Taiwan, India, the Dominican Republic, and Jamaica. In 1980, 160,000 boat people poured in from the islands of Cuba and Haiti. Although well-wishers were on hand to greet these people, the history of the nation's treatment of nonwhites, along with the severe recession that began in 1979, did not augur well for them. "Clearly, some people derive great benefit from the present situation," explained Leon Castillo, former commissioner of immigration, in referring to the low wages paid to aliens. The new residents faced a long struggle.

New Influx of Immigrants

WOMEN'S STRUGGLES

In the 1970s, while civil rights struggles were engaging the energies of various racial and ethnic groups, increasing numbers of women were committing themselves to the struggle for equality with men. Feminists had scored some impressive legislative victories. In 1974 Congress passed the Equal Credit Opportunity Act, which enabled women to get bank loans and obtain credit cards on the same terms as men. Many states revised their statutes on rape, prohibiting lawyers from stressing the previous sexual experience of rape victims.

Women also made gains in education: between 1970 and 1975 the number of women enrolled in college rose 45 percent. And they campaigned for and were elected to various political offices. In 1976 Ella Grasso was elected governor of Connecticut, and two years later Nancy Kassebaum of Kansas was elected to the Senate. Perhaps most significant were women's gains, along with blacks and other minorities, from affirmative action in hiring. As mandated by the Civil Rights Act of 1964 and the establishment of the Equal Employment Opportunity Commission, women and minorities had to receive the same consideration as white males when applying for a job. To take advantage of new opportunities, many women delayed having children until they were in their thirties and had established themselves in their careers.

Still, women continued to encounter barriers in their quest for equality. One of the most formidable was the antifeminist, or "profamily," movement, which contended that men should lead and women should follow, particularly within the family. The backlash against feminism became an increasingly powerful political force in the 1970s. In defense of the family—especially the patriarchal, or father-led, family—antifeminists campaigned against the Equal Rights Amendment (ERA), the gay rights movement, and abortion on demand. Anita Bryant and Phyllis Schlafly gained fame by arguing that all these issues were interrelated and that they endangered traditional American values.

Antifeminist Movement

For one thing, antifeminists blamed the women's movement for the country's spiraling divorce rate; they charged that feminists would jettison their husbands and even their children in their quests for job fulfillment and sexual equality. Although the number of divorces almost tripled from 1960 to 1976, the decision to terminate marriages and dissolve families was often made, not by the wives, but by their husbands. According to Barbara Ehrenreich, a feminist scholar, men first started walking out on their families in large numbers in the 1950s, well before the rebirth of feminism. Tired of fulfilling their male role as financial provider and final arbiter of family disputes, many men also responded to the image of bachelorhood presented in the pages of *Playboy.* Some felt trapped emotionally, as well as financially and sexually. Beginning in the 1950s, *Playboy* and other magazines attacked wives as parasites who gobbled up their husbands' salaries but were too sexually repressed to give much in return. Increasingly, many men came to see their wives as the source of their entrapment and in their "flight from commitment," they chose divorce.

In the political arena antifeminists successfully stalled ratification of the Equal Rights Amendment, which after quickly passing through thirty-five state legislatures fell three states short of success in the late 1970s. Schlafly's STOP ERA campaign falsely claimed that the ERA would abolish alimony and legalize homosexual marriage. The ERA debate was vicious at times. Refusing to acknowledge the gender-based discrimination that was so injurious to women's welfare, morale, and aspirations, Schlafly derided ERA advocates as "a bunch of bitter women seeking a constitutional cure for their personal problems."

Equal Rights Amendment

Many antifeminists also participated in the antiabortion, or "prolife," movement, which sprang up almost overnight in the wake of the Supreme Court's 1973 decisions in *Roe* v. *Wade* and *Doe* v. *Bolton* (see page 961). People whose opposition to abortion was heartfelt and uncompromising denounced those rulings and called for an amendment to the Constitution that would define human life as beginning at conception. The battle between the prolife and prochoice forces had been joined. Along with Catholics, Mormons, and other religious opponents of abortion, the prolife movement also supported the

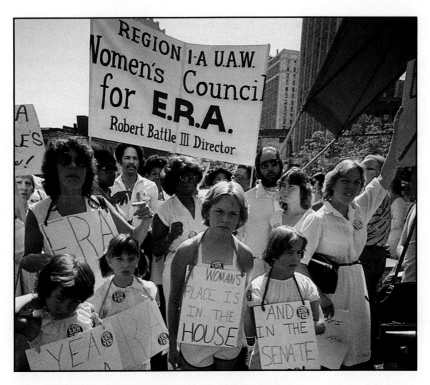

The struggle over the Equal Rights Amendment was heated on both sides. It pitted these ERA supporters against the antifeminist campaign led by, among others, Phyllis Schlafly's STOP ERA organization.   Diana Walker/Gamma Liason.

successful legislative efforts of Representative Henry Hyde of Illinois in 1976 to cut off most Medicaid funds for abortions. In summer 1980 the Supreme Court upheld the Hyde amendment, deciding that the government had no obligation to make even medically necessary abortions available to the poor (*Harris* v. *McRae*).

As activists in the women's struggle looked to the future, they had to acknowledge certain harsh realities. One was the impact of the economic recessions of the 1970s and early 1980s. In a tight job market, it was difficult for most outsiders—women and non-whites—to become insiders. Though affirmative action had certainly helped women to gain employment and receive promotions, jobs had to be available in the first place for women to benefit. "The economic environment," predicted one analyst, "may prove to be the major determinant of women's role in 1980. . . . Scarcity of jobs in the next decade [will] produce a greater

Effects of a Glutted Job Market

competition in the labor market and a tremendous backlash against women." Added to job scarcity was the continuing problem of occupational segregation in which women were concentrated in lower-paying positions while most men enjoyed much higher incomes (see page 961). By the end of the 1970s, female workers still took home only 59 cents to every male worker's dollar.

Perhaps the most disturbing trend was what *Newsweek* called "the Superwoman Squeeze." According to a report by the Worldwatch Institute in 1980, most working wives and mothers, even those with full-time jobs, "retained an unwilling monopoly on unpaid labor at home." Husbands were generally less than eager to do household tasks, and there were few readily available marketplace substitutes for loving, caring, and responsiveness to emergencies. Predictions were that by 1990 only one in four wives would be a full-time housewife and mother. The rest would be trying to

Increased Burdens on Women

balance the more-than-full-time demands of work and homemaking.

It appeared, too, that the feminist ferment of the 1970s had dwindled by the early 1980s. Some women seemed to take for granted the gains of that decade, believing that equality of opportunity had been secured for all time. Others were concentrating on planning their lives so they could have both a career and a family without shortchanging either—or themselves—in the process.

THE ME DECADE

At the beginning of 1980, the editors of *Time* magazine observed that the 1970s had been "erected upon the smoldering wreckage of the '60s. Now and then, someone's shovel blade would strike an unexploded bomb; mostly the air in the '70s was thick with a sense of aftermath, of public passions spent and consciences bewildered."

The nation had turned apathetic, and perhaps nowhere was this new attitude more evident than among youth. In the 1960s American youths had worked for change in the nation's social, political, and cultural life. But by the mid-1970s the aspirations of young Americans had been transformed. A student at Vassar commented: "We saw it all. We were freshmen in high school when our older brothers and sisters were going off to war or to exile or to revolution. . . . We saw the waste of lives and I think that determined that we would not ruin our own for lost causes." Older Americans took refuge, too, from a lost war, political scandal, and economic distress. As a theologian put it, Americans "have a beleaguered sense in their bones that the old order is dying. Very few want a radical alternative, but few also are working to develop a rationale for the system we've got."

Instead, in the 1970s Americans turned inward and concentrated on self-expression and personal improvement. As a popular beer commercial proclaimed, "You only go 'round once in life and you've got to grab for all the gusto you can get." That gusto ranged from recreational vehicles to roller skates, disco to punk rock, *The Godfather* to *Star Wars*. Social commentator Tom Wolfe branded the 1970s the Me Decade, a time of diversion and material consumption designed to make Americans' private worlds, in the midst of public confusion, at least tolerable.

In the self-centered new decade, suggestions for realizing one's full potential were consumed as readily as jogging shoes and health foods. Transactional Analysis (TA), a form of psychotherapy emphasizing interpersonal relationships, was popularized in Eric Berne's *Games People Play* (1969) and Thomas Harris's *I'm OK—You're OK* (1969). Transcendental Meditation (TM), a yogic discipline, drew 350,000 adherents and spawned over two hundred teaching centers. Est (Erhard Seminars Training), a system of encounters meant to enable people to "get in touch with themselves," was grossing $10 million a year in 1975. In addition to these fads, other new therapies and exotic religions flourished, as did such eastern religions and practices of longstanding as Zen and yoga.

Human Potential Movement

As millions of Americans sought to fill spiritual and emotional voids through esoteric movements, millions more were drawn to traditional Christian beliefs. According to a 1977 survey, about 70 million Americans defined themselves as born-again Christians, and 10 million claimed to have had the experience since 1975. President Jimmy Carter, singers Pat Boone and Johnny Cash, professional football player Roger Staubach, former Black Panther Eldridge Cleaver, and Watergate felons Jeb Stuart Magruder and Charles Colson all counted themselves among the saved. Religious revivals and evangelical sects were not new, of course, but by the mid-1970s they were a growth industry. In the latter years of the decade evangelicals were grossing $200 million annually in sales of religious books, and the Virginia-based Christian Broadcast Network was earning nearly $60 million from its four stations and 130 affiliates.

Spiritual Revival

Besides the relatively harmless human potential movements and the traditional religious enthusiasms, a dark undercurrent of cult-like adherence to charismatic leaders ran through the 1970s. In 1973 and 1974, the Reverend Sun Myung Moon, Korean

Messianic Cults

founder of the Unification Church, converted young Americans to his religion, a curious blend of Christianity, anti-Communism, and worship of Moon as a messiah. "Moonies" disposed of their possessions, moved into communes, and raised funds for the church by selling ginseng tea, candles, flowers, and peanuts. Critics charged that Moon and his disciples had brainwashed their converts. Soon worried parents were attempting to kidnap their children from the Unification Church and its influence.

For most of those who followed the Reverend Jim Jones to Guyana, attempts at rescue came too late. Jones's California cult, the People's Temple, had begun as a church committed to social reform and civil rights. But in 1977 stories began to surface alleging that Jones had made death threats and had committed extortion. Jones moved the cult to Guyana, in South America, where he established a colony named Jonestown. In November 1978, convinced that the United States was about to destroy the colony and embark on an apocalyptic race war, the crazed leader ordered his followers to poison their children and then kill themselves with a mixture of Kool-Aid and cyanide. The mass murder and suicide of 911 people at Jonestown added a satanic headline to the history of cults in the United States.

Many Americans in the 1970s were in quest not only of the "ideal self," but also of their personal identity. For this reason, another facet of "me-ness" was the phenomenon called "Roots." The 1977 television series, based on a best-selling book by Alex Haley, dramatized the author's family history beginning with his ancestor, Kunta Kinte, a Gambian boy sold into slavery. "Roots" spawned an interest in family trees that touched all races and ethnic groups. More important, the sheer numbers of Americans exposed to the book and television series (130 million watched the eight-part series) helped to sensitize the public to the agonies of slavery and racism.

When Americans went running to libraries to research their family trees during the 1970s, they usually did so in an expensive pair of Nikes, Pumas, or Adidas, for this was the decade of the jogger. James Fixx's *Complete Book of Running* (1977) enjoyed tremendous popularity, and literature on running, physical fitness, diet, and health jammed

Physical Fitness Craze

New York *magazine announces the Me Decade. The writer Tom Wolfe, who gave the label to the seventies, sensed that Americans had become self-indulgent and apolitical. © 1976 by News Group Publications, Inc. Reprinted with the permission of* New York Magazine.

bookshelves and magazine racks. Perhaps America was no longer the best nation it could be, but Americans were determined to make themselves the healthiest individuals they could be. Saunas, hot tubs, and Jacuzzis became popular, and membership in tennis and racquetball clubs, health centers, and diet clinics boomed. At the supermarket, consumers kept a careful eye out for products marked "no preservatives" or "all natural."

The dominant sound of the later 1970s was disco. One writer called disco "the affirmation of the 'unreal' seventies, the fantasies, fashions, gossip, frivolity and fun. . . . Disco emphasizes surfaces over substance, mood over meaning." Millions of Americans of various ages and backgrounds flocked to clubs to dance, display their latest fashions, and watch each other.

As the decade drew to a close, Christopher Lasch, a history professor at the University of Rochester, condemned the nation's behavior as self-indulgent and apolitical. In *The Culture of Narcissism* (1979), Lasch branded Americans an emotionally shallow, anxiety-ridden people desperately trying to ignore the waning of their nation's power. He cited advertising and the human potential movement as causes of the nation's malaise. But there was little evidence that the trend was changing. In a decade of exhausted public passions, private passions reigned supreme.

RONALD REAGAN AND THE ELECTION OF 1980

The year President Carter ran for re-election the federal government published its decennial census of the population. The figures released by the Bureau of the Census revealed significant growth in the elderly population—24 percent— and a two-year rise in the median age. By 1980 there were as many people over thirty as under, and the number of retired persons had increased by more than 50 percent since 1972. Translated into political terms, the census figures meant that the American population was becoming more conservative.

The census also documented the continuing movement of large numbers of people from the politically liberal Frostbelt states of the Northeast and Midwest to the more conservative Sunbelt states of the South and West (see map). The census findings meant that seventeen seats in the House of Representatives would shift from the Frostbelt to the Sunbelt by the 1982 elections. Florida would gain four seats and New York would lose five; Texas would gain three, California two.

Besides gaining political power, the Sunbelt enjoyed abundant energy resources and a wider tax base than the North. In 1980 Louisiana produced over four times its energy needs, New Mexico over three, and Texas over two. By contrast, Michigan and New York had to import most of their energy, at a price jacked up by export taxes imposed by producing states. Taxes were lower in the Sunbelt, too; Texas families paid less than half as much of their incomes for state and local taxes as New York families did.

The census only confirmed what had already become obvious to politicians: conservatism was the dominant mood of the nation in the late 1970s. Americans doubted government's capacity to serve the people. In 1977 Senator Gary Hart, a Colorado Democrat, characterized this mood as "a non-ideological skepticism about the old, Rooseveltian solutions to social problems." But there were hard-working conservatives whose goal was to repeal the welfare state. In 1978 California voters approved a tax-cutting referendum called Proposition 13, which reduced property taxes and put stringent limits on state spending for social programs. On the national level conservatives lobbied for a constitutional amendment to prohibit federal budget deficits and organized for the 1980 elections. One conservative campaign group, the National Conservative Political Action Committee (NCPAC), targeted a number of liberal senators for defeat.

Resurgence of Conservatism

Conservative politicians were joined by evangelical Christians, who believed they had a moral obligation to enter politics on the side of righteousness, which they defined as "a pro-life, pro-traditional family, pro-moral position." In summer 1979 the Reverend Jerry Falwell, a radio-TV minister from Lynchburg, Virginia, helped to found the Moral Majority, which in the next fourteen months registered beween 2 and 3 million new voters, raised $1.5 million, started a newspaper, and bought daily time on 140 radio stations. Together with conservative think tanks like the Hoover Institution and conservative magazines like the *National Review*, these church groups formed a flourishing network of potential supporters for conservative candidates.

In 1980 several conservative Republican politicians ran for the White House, but the champion of them all was Ronald Reagan, former Hollywood movie star and two-term governor of California.

Ronald Reagan's Early Career

A small-town boy from Dixon, Illinois, Reagan had been a radio sportscaster before moving to Hollywood in the mid-1930s. As president of the Screen Actors Guild, his politics had been those of a New Deal Democrat. But in the

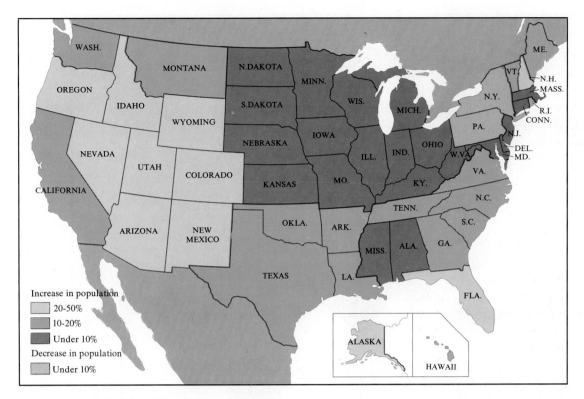

The Continued Shift to the Sunbelt.

1950s, as he toured the country as host of the television program "General Electric Theatre," Reagan became increasingly conservative. In 1964 he made a televised appeal for Senator Barry Goldwater, the conservative Republican presidential candidate. His persuasive speech not only catapulted him to the forefront of conservative politics; it became his personal platform for the presidency. America, Reagan said, had come to "a time for choosing" between free enterprise and big government, between individual liberty and "the ant heap of totalitarianism." Two years later he was elected governor of California.

During his two four-year terms as governor Reagan maintained his conservatism, but also displayed a pragmatic approach to governing. While denouncing welfare, he presided over reform of the state's welfare bureaucracy. While demanding that student radicals at the University of California either obey the rules or face the prospect of a "bloodbath," he worked to fund most of the university's budget requests. And he signed one of the nation's most liberal abortion laws.

In 1980 Reagan triumphed easily over moderate Republicans Representative John Anderson of Illinois and former CIA director George Bush of Texas. And

Election of 1980

his appeal to the voters in the presidential campaign was much more widespread than observers had predicted. He promised economy in government and a balanced budget, and he committed himself to "supply-side" economics, or tax reductions to businesses to encourage capital investment. But while he planned to slash federal spending, Reagan also pledged to cut income taxes and boost the defense budget—a prescription that George Bush dismissed as "voodoo economics." Reagan declared that he now opposed legalized abortion, and his stand against the ERA recommended him to the profamily movement. Indeed, his candidacy united the old right wing with the new. The old right, explained one fundraiser, had never been very interested in social issues. "But when political conservative leaders began to reach out and strike an alliance with social conservatives—the pro-life people, the anti-ERA people,

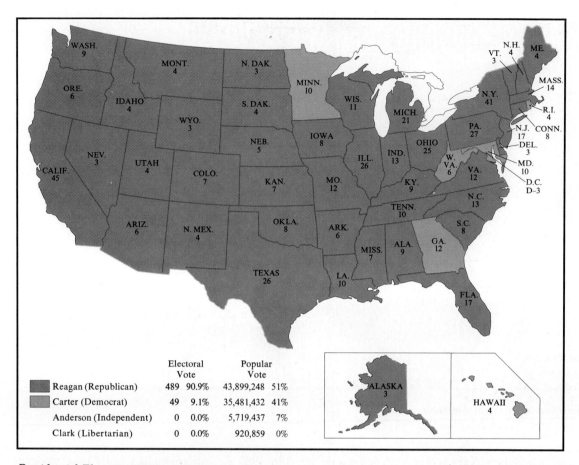

	Electoral Vote		Popular Vote	
Reagan (Republican)	489	90.9%	43,899,248	51%
Carter (Democrat)	49	9.1%	35,481,432	41%
Anderson (Independent)	0	0.0%	5,719,437	7%
Clark (Libertarian)	0	0.0%	920,859	0%

Presidential Election, 1980

the evangelical and born-again Christians, the people concerned about gay rights, prayer in the schools, sex in the movies or whatever—that's when this whole movement began to come alive. It's happened in a big way just in the last two years, and its just exploding."

For his part, President Carter had little difficulty beating back Senator Edward Kennedy's challenge. Kennedy's New Deal liberalism seemed out of place in the 1980s, and memories of Chappaquiddick lingered in voters' minds. The president had more formidable problems. American hostages were still held captive in Iran, and stagflation beset the economy. Carter retreated into the White House, contending that the nation's problems were too serious to allow him time to campaign. His supporters worried about the independent candidate, John Anderson, who had bolted the Republican party in the primaries.

As election day approached, some political analysts thought they detected a resurgence of support for Carter. Polls predicted a Reagan victory by 3 to 5 percent, a small margin given the country's problems. But on election day voters gave Reagan and his running mate, George Bush, 51 percent of the vote to 41 percent for Carter and 6.6 percent for Anderson (see map). Reagan's sweep was nationwide; Carter carried only six states and the District of Columbia. Although the vote was partially an affirmation of Reagan's conservatism, it also signified deep dissatisfaction with Carter. In addition, the Republicans were better organized and had more campaign money to spend. And Reagan espoused ideas that most Americans found relevant and sensible.

More startling than Reagan's sweep was the capture of eleven Senate seats by Republican candidates, a victory that gave the party a majority in that house.

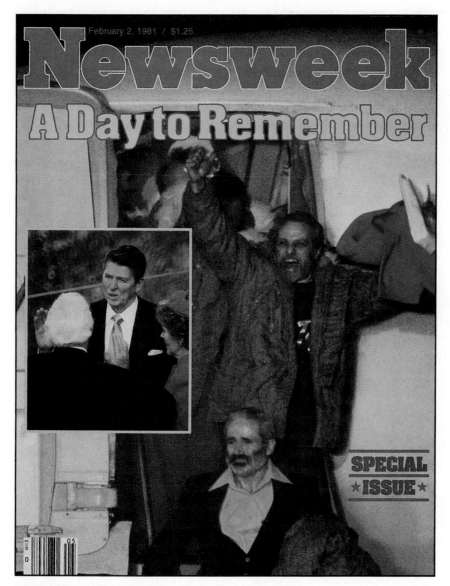

February 2, 1981 / $1.25

Newsweek

A Day to Remember

SPECIAL
★ISSUE★

Ronald Reagan began his presidency auspiciously. On his inauguration day, the American hostages were released from Iran. Borrel/SIPA–Special Features and Susan T. McElhenney, Newsweek Magazine.

Conservative advertising campaigns had succeeded in defeating most of the targeted liberals, including Senators George McGovern and Frank Church. Republicans also gained thirty-three seats in the House and four state governorships. It seemed clear that Democrats would be running scared in the 1980s.

On January 20, 1981, Ronald Reagan was inaugurated as president. He pledged to work for "an era of national renewal," for "a healthy, vigorous, growing economy that provides equal opportunities for all Americans." On the same day, after 444 days in captivity, the American hostages boarded an airplane that flew them from Teheran to freedom. Yellow ribbons welcomed the freed Americans, and the nation rejoiced. Seldom had a new administration had a more auspicious beginning.

IMPORTANT EVENTS

1973	Trials of Watergate burglars
	Ervin Watergate hearings
	White House aides Ehrlichman and
	  Haldeman resign
	Wounded Knee confrontation
	War Powers Act
	Arab oil embargo
	Agnew resigns; Ford appointed as
	  vice president
	Saturday Night Massacre
		1976	Hyde amendment on abortions
			Carter elected president

		1977	"Roots" serialized on television
		1978	*Bakke* v. *University of California* California voters approve Proposition 13 Mass suicides in Guyana

1974	OPEC oil price increases
	Supreme Court orders Nixon to
	  release White House tapes
	House Judiciary Committee votes to
	  impeach Nixon
	Nixon resigns the presidency; Ford
	  becomes president
	Rockefeller appointed as vice
	  president
	Ford pardons Nixon
	Ford's WIN program
		1979	Three Mile Island nuclear accident
			Moral Majority established
			Federal Reserve Board tightens
			  money supply
			American hostages seized in Iran

		1980	Economic recession
			Phased decontrol of oil prices and
			  deregulation of transportation
			  industries
			Race riots
			Reagan elected president

1975	Brown's Ferry nuclear accident Antibusing agitation	1981	American hostages in Iran released after 444 days

SUGGESTIONS FOR FURTHER READING

Watergate

Richard Ben-Veniste and George Frampton, *Stonewall* (1978); John W. Dean, *Blind Ambition* (1976); Seymour M. Hersh, "The Pardon: Nixon, Ford, Haig, and the Transfer of Power," *Atlantic Monthly*, 252 (1983), 55–78; Jim Hougan, *Secret Agenda* (1984); Leon Jaworski, *The Right and the Power* (1976); J. Anthony Lukas, *Nightmare: The Underside of the Nixon Years* (1976); Arthur M. Schlesinger, Jr., *The Imperial Presidency* (1973); John J. Sirica, *To Set the Record Straight* (1979); Theodore White, *Breach of Faith* (1975); Bob Woodward and Carl Bernstein, *The Final Days* (1976);

Bob Woodward and Carl Bernstein, *All the President's Men* (1974). (For works on the Nixon administration, see Chapter 33.)

Energy Shortages, Economic Woes

Richard J. Barnet, *The Lean Years: Politics in the Age of Scarcity* (1980); Daniel Bell, *The Coming of the Post-Industrial Society* (1973); John M. Blair, *The Control of Oil* (1976); Barry Bluestone and Bennett Harrison, *The Deindustrialization of America* (1982); David P. Calleo, *The Imperious Economy* (1982); Barry Commoner, *The Politics of Energy* (1979); Robert L. Heilbroner, *An Inquiry into the Human Prospect* (1974); Harry Mauer, *Not Working: An Oral History of the Unemployed* (1979); Emma Rothschild, *Paradise Lost: The Decline of the Auto-Industrial Age* (1973); John E. Schwarz, *America's Hidden Success* (1983); Robert Sherrill, *The Oil Follies of 1970–1980* (1983); Robert Stobaugh and Daniel

Yergin, eds., *Energy Future* (1979); Lester C. Thurow, *The Zero-Sum Society* (1980).

The Ford Administration

Gerald R. Ford, *A Time to Heal* (1979); Robert T. Hartmann, *Palace Politics* (1980); Ron Nessen, *It Sure Looks Different from the Inside* (1978); A. James Reichley, *Conservatives in an Age of Change: The Nixon and Ford Administrations* (1981); James L. Sundquist, *The Decline and Resurgence of Congress* (1981).

The Carter Administration

Griffin Bell, *Taking Care of the Law* (1982); Joseph A. Califano, *Governing America* (1981); Jimmy Carter, *Keeping Faith* (1982); Rosalynn Carter, *First Lady from Plains* (1984); Betty Glad, *Jimmy Carter: From Plains to the White House* (1980); Haynes Johnson, *In the Absence of Power* (1980); Hamilton Jordan, *Crisis* (1982); Jody Powell, *The Other Side of the Story* (1984); Laurence H. Shoup, *The Carter Presidency & Beyond* (1980).

Women and the Family

Susan Brownmiller, *Against Our Will: Men, Women and Rape* (1975); Andrea Dworkin, *Right-Wing Women* (1983); Barbara Ehrenreich, *The Hearts of Men: American Dreams and the Flight from Commitment* (1983); Kenneth Keniston, *All Our Children: The American Family Under Pressure* (1977); Christopher Lasch, *Haven in a Heartless World: The Family Besieged* (1977); Kristin Luker, *Abortion and the Politics of Motherhood* (1984); Maggie Scarf, *Unfinished Business: Pressure Points in the Lives of Women* (1980).

Nonwhites and New Immigrants

Thomas J. Archdeacon, *Becoming American* (1983); John Crewden, *The Tarnished Door: The New Immigrants and the Transformation of America* (1983); Vine Deloria, *Behind the Trail of Broken Treaties* (1974); Dorothy K. Newman et al., *Protest, Politics, and Prosperity: Black Americans and White Institutions, 1940–1974* (1978); Carol B. Stack, *All Our Kin: Strategies for Survival in a Black Community* (1975); Arnulfo D. Trejo, ed., *The Chicanos: As We See Ourselves* (1979); J. Harris Wilkinson III, *From Brown to Bakke: The Supreme Court and School Integration, 1954–1978* (1979); William Julius Wilson, *The Declining Significance of Race: Blacks and Changing American Institutions,* 2nd ed. (1980).

The Me Decade

Peter Clecak, *America's Quest for the Ideal Self: Dissent and Fulfillment in the Sixties and Seventies* (1983); Jim Hougan, *Decadence: Radical Nostalgia, Narcissism, and Decline in the Seventies* (1975); Christopher Lasch, *The Culture of Narcissism* (1978); Edwin Schur, *The Awareness Trap: Self-Absorption Instead of Social Change* (1976); Gail Sheehy, *Passages: Predictable Crises in Adult Life* (1976); Tom Wolfe, "The 'Me' Decade and the Third Great Awakening," *New York*, 9 (1976), 26–40; Daniel Yankelovich, *New Rules: Searching for Self-Fulfillment in a World Turned Upside Down* (1981).

The New Conservatism and the Election of Ronald Reagan

Peter N. Carroll, *It Seemed Like Nothing Happened: The Tragedy and Promise of America in the 1970s* (1982); Alan Crawford, *Thunder on the Right* (1980); Elizabeth Drew, *Portrait of an Election* (1981); Jack W. Germond and Jules Witcover, *Blue Smoke and Mirrors: How Reagan Won and Why Carter Lost the Election of 1980* (1981); Jeff Greenfield, *The Real Campaign* (1982); David W. Reinhard, *The Republican Right Since 1945* (1983); Kirkpatrick Sale, *Power Shift: The Rise of the Southern Rim and Its Challenge to the Eastern Establishment* (1975); Peter Steinfels, *The Neo-conservatives* (1979); F. Clifton White, *Why Reagan Won* (1981).

A SHARP TURN TO THE RIGHT
AMERICA SINCE 1981

CHAPTER 35

It was a political first. The vice-presidential candidate for the Democratic party was a woman. And that woman, Geraldine Ferraro, had decided to confront union members. Campaigning in October 1984, Ferraro toured a Chrysler assembly plant in Rockford, Illinois, and told a group of workers, "When I read the polls that one third of the United Auto Workers are going to vote for Ronald Reagan, I'm absolutely floored. I want to know why." Her listeners stared back in uncomfortable silence. Finally a man spoke up, "They blame Jimmy Carter for a lot of our problems. Record high interest rates. Iran. A weak foreign policy."

"I don't know how in the hell to explain it," moaned a UAW official. "We've got Chrysler workers saying they're going to vote for Reagan when he opposed the Chrysler recovery program [see page 981]. . . . Do these people know their roots?"

Ferraro knew that the Democratic percentage of the union vote had dropped from 64 percent in the 1976 presidential election to 47 percent in 1980, but she believed that the 1980 vote had signified a rejection of President Jimmy Carter, not an endorsement of Reagan's conservatism. However, in 1984 the economy was on the upswing, and Reagan's policies appeared to have conquered inflation and high interest rates, and dealt a blow to unemployment as well. Many Americans also applauded Reagan's foreign policy; they said they were proud that their country would stand up to the Russians again. Patriotism was back in style.

Yet there was a further explanation for the president's popularity. A proponent of prayer in the public schools and an opponent of abortion, Reagan argued for a return to the morality that had dominated American culture prior to the 1960s. Many Americans, including Catholics and born-again Christians, agreed. A soft-spoken woman standing near Geraldine Ferraro touched on the campaign's most volatile moral and cultural issue when she told the candidate, "My Christian friends don't like the ticket because of how you feel about abortion." "I can't change my views on abortion," Ferraro replied. "I would never have an abortion. But if I were raped I'm not sure I would

be that self-righteous. And that decision would be mine. I wouldn't leave it to you to make," she told the woman, "or you to make," pointing to a man who had just praised President Reagan's morality. There was no bridging the gulf between their position and Ferraro's.

Voters in 1984 had a clear choice, and in forty-nine states they chose the Republican ticket. Only Minnesota—the home state of Walter Mondale, the Democratic candidate—kept it from being unanimous. The election returns were the most convincing evidence yet that by 1984 the nation had taken a sharp turn to the right.

Reagan had, nonetheless, suffered severe criticism during his first term. Opponents lambasted his economic policies ("Reaganomics"), particularly the massive cuts in income taxes accompanied by large social welfare cuts, as favoring the rich and penalizing the poor. From 1981 to 1983, Reaganomics became synonymous with human suffering. In October 1982, unemployment reached 10.1 percent, the highest rate since 1940. So depressed had the economy become by January 1983 that the *New York Times* declared: "The stench of failure hangs over Ronald Reagan's White House;" the president's "loss of authority only halfway through his term should alarm all Americans." Although Reagan's policies failed for three years to produce the promised results, he urged Americans to "stay the course" and stick with his conservative agenda.

Reagan's conservatism also shaped his foreign policy. He surrounded himself with people who believed that previous administrations had shown weakness toward the Soviet Union, Cuba, Third World countries, and terrorists. The Reagan administration set out to swell the American military arsenal, denounce and intimidate the Soviets, unseat leftist governments through military intervention or covert operations, and settle civil wars in the Middle East and Latin America. Reagan was hesitant to engage in arms control talks or in negotiations to quiet regional conflict in Central America. His administration virtually ended the North-South dialogue, lecturing Third World nations that they should practice free-enterprise economics. Although many Americans and foreigners grew alarmed at the rapid acceleration of the nuclear arms race and at the application of military power to political problems, most Americans approved Reagan's harsh anti-Sovietism and emphasis on military strength. Indeed, a vibrant patriotism swept through the American people, buoyed in part by the successful invasion of the Caribbean island of Grenada.

As Reagan geared up for the 1984 election, he was alert to the mounting criticism not only of his policies, but also of his appointees for their insensitivity to ethical standards for officeholders. Despite several scandals, however, Reagan's re-election prospects seemed to improve, not deteriorate, in 1983 and 1984. For one thing, the president was a master at distancing himself not only from controversies within his administration, but even from problems in foreign and domestic policy. Representative Patricia Schroeder, a Colorado Democrat, gave this phenomenon a memorable label, saying that Reagan was "perfecting the Teflon-coated presidency. . . . He sees to it that nothing sticks to him."

Even more helpful to Reagan's campaign was that the economy showed unmistakable signs of recovery; during the first quarter of 1984, it grew at an annual rate of 8.8 percent. People were spending their tax cuts on video recorders, new cars, and other goods. Lower interest rates boosted housing sales, and renewed activity meant more jobs. Reagan's re-election bid was spurred also by the Democrats' lack of a winning candidate. Walter Mondale did not inspire Americans; most people identified him with the ineffectuality of the Carter administration. And he lost votes early when he announced in his acceptance speech that if elected he would raise taxes.

Reagan's victory was never in doubt, but his immense margin made political observers speculate that he had fashioned a new right coalition that could dominate national politics for years to come. By 1984 the New Deal coalition was in shambles. The only groups still voting for the Democratic ticket were blacks, Hispanics, Jews, the poor, and the unemployed. Reagan scored solid victories with all other voting groups, including young people, white men and women, high school and college graduates, Protestants and Catholics, and families with incomes exceeding $12,500. Whether or not Reagan had forged a lasting

coalition, there was no doubt that he had secured his place in history. After reviewing Reagan's first-term successes, a Columbia University history professor proclaimed, "He has a chance to make somebody move over on Mt. Rushmore." Still, the president confronted unsolved problems that would bedevil his second term. Heading the list were the federal budget deficit and the need to halt the nuclear arms race. Sober analysts revealed too that the United States was facing a depressing agenda of international problems—including economic instability, famine, terrorism, weakening alliances, and religious and racial tensions—that were not susceptible to military solutions and that promised a future of global disorder and threats to American tranquility.

"REAGANOMICS"

Upon taking office, President Reagan wasted little time in announcing his plans for what he called "a new beginning." In February 1981 he launched a double-barreled attack on problems in the economy. First, he asked Congress for $43.5 billion in spending cuts from domestic programs, including urban aid, Medicare and Medicaid, food stamps, welfare subsidies for the working poor, and school meals. In July Congress met most of Reagan's demands by paring $35.2 billion from social and cultural programs. Veteran agencies of the War on Poverty, such as the Community Services Administration, were gutted or dismantled. Some 300,000 public service jobs under the Comprehensive Employment and Training Act were eliminated. Reagan initiated a second round of budget cuts totaling $13 billion in September, resulting, among other things, in the trimming of 1 million food-stamp recipients from government rolls.

Massive tax cuts constituted the second part of Reagan's economic plan. Reagan was a fervent believer in supply-side economics, which called for reductions in the income taxes of the affluent
Tax Cuts and of corporations in order to stimulate savings and investments. New capital would be invested, the argument went, and would produce new plants, new jobs, and new products, and as prosperity returned, the profits at

Ronald Reagan assumed the presidency confident that his policies and leadership would restore both prosperity and national pride. In the manner of Franklin D. Roosevelt fifty years earlier, Reagan's confidence was infectious.   Bill Pierce/Time Magazine.

the top would trickle down to the middle classes and even to the poor at the bottom. Economic growth and expanding opportunities would again be the hallmarks of American society. Reagan thus proposed slashing income taxes by 30 percent over three years. And with cross-over votes given to the Republicans by conservative southern Democrats, Congress responded in August with a five-year, $750-billion tax cut, the largest ever in American history. The act's major feature was a 25-percent reduction in personal income taxes over the next three years. Other provisions increased business investment tax credits and depreciation allowances and lowered the maximum tax on all income from 70 to 50 percent. Wealthy people gained the most from these tax cuts. In an unguarded moment, budget director David Stockman acknowledged that Reagan's supply-side doctrines were a "Trojan horse" for tax relief to the rich. "It's kind of hard to sell 'trickle down,'" Stockman explained, "so the supply-side formula was the only way to get a tax policy that was really 'trickle down.'"

A third item occupied Reagan's agenda: a vigorous assault on federal environmental, health, and safety regulations that, Reagan believed, unnecessarily and excessively reduced business profits and discouraged economic growth. A lightning rod for this effort was Secretary of the Interior James Watt, who said that

his objective was to "mine more, drill more, cut more timber, to use our resources rather than simply keep them locked up." Watt began by opening up federal lands and coastal waters to rapid exploitation of oil, gas, and coal. He also proposed that 80 million acres of wilderness be turned over to developers by the year 2000. And Watt had Reagan's support. Even the business-oriented *Wall Street Journal* observed that the president was "naming regulators who by virtue of attitude or inexperience are more likely to be nonregulators."

Some critics said this approach to presidential appointments resulted in the proverbial foxes guarding the chicken coops. An example was Anne Gorsuch

Weakened Environmental Enforcement

Burford, administrator of the Environmental Protection Agency, who delayed implementing a groundwater protection program, weakened enforcement of the Clean Air Act, and resigned in March 1983 because of her controversial handling of the $1.6-billion "Superfund" for cleaning up toxic waste. Reagan's appointee to head the Occupational Safety and Health Administration was Thomas Auchter, president of a Florida construction company that had amassed forty-eight OSHA violations since 1972. ("Nobody is perfect," Auchter explained.) In Reagan's first six months, OSHA inspections were down 16 percent and penalties were down 40 percent. Reagan officials announced that slackened enforcement was necessary to reduce business costs and make American goods competitive in world markets, but environmentalists countered that such policies invited human disaster, such as toxic-waste poisoning or nuclear reactor accidents.

Reagan scored two notable economic successes during his first two years in office: the inflation rate plummeted, as did the cost of borrowing money. With the Federal Reserve Board leading the way by lowering its discount rate (see page 982), the prime rate for bank loans, which had stood at a record high of 21.5 percent in early 1981, dropped to 10.5 percent by early 1983. Inflation fell from 12.4 percent in 1980 to less than 7 percent in 1982. Oil led the way in price declines. In 1981 the United States was awash with oil, as world production exceeded demand by 2 million barrels a day; after eight years the Organization of Petroleum Exporting Countries (OPEC) at last had to put a lid on its oil prices. Americans

The "smokestack industries" were hard hit economically in the 1980s. At Christmastime 1982, workers left Bethlehem Steel's plant in Lackawana, New York, forever. Once the largest steel plant in the world, the Lackawana facility had closed. © 1983 Jamey Stillings/Black Star.

had also become conservation-minded. Homeowners by the millions turned down their thermostats and installed insulation. Partly because of declining energy costs, in 1981 food prices rose only 4.3 percent, less than half the 10.1 percent increase of 1980.

But there was also a sobering explanation for the decline in inflation. "It wasn't just luck on food and oil," said an economist with Data Resources, a leading economic-forecasting firm. "It was very much the result of the stagnant economy that brought the prices down." By mid-1981 the nation was mired in a recession that not only persisted, but deepened. During the last three months of the year, the gross national product fell 5.3 percent, and there was a sharp drop in sales of cars and houses; housing starts were down more than half from 1978. With declining economic activity, unemployment went up, soaring in October to 8 percent, the highest level in almost six years. But the worst economic news was still to come.

A year later, in October 1982, unemployment had reached 10.1 percent. On top of the 11.3 million people who were out of work, a record 6.6 million

Rising Unemployment

Americans were forced to work part-time because they could not find full-time jobs. Most of the jobless were adult men, particularly black men who suffered an unemployment rate of 19.8 percent. Many of the unemployed were blue-collar workers in such ailing "smokestack industries" as autos, steel, and rubber. Unemployment was 15.6 percent for industrial workers and over 20 percent for construction workers, compared with white-collar unemployment, which stood at just 4.8 percent.

Reagan and his advisers had hoped that his supply-side economics would produce demand-side results and that consumers would lift the economy out of the recession by spending their tax cuts. But as late as April 1983, unemployment stood at 10.2 percent, and people were angry. Jobless steelworkers paraded through McKeesport, Pennsylvania, carrying a coffin that bore the epitaph "American Dream." "I used to have big plans for myself," said one laid-off steelworker. "But not anymore. It's like I've fallen into hell and there isn't anyone who's going to pull me out." Unemployment in some West Virginia coal-mining towns hovered at 90 percent, while the state's overall rate was 20.4 percent. Michigan ranked second with 17 percent. Facing a bleak future, people took to the road; most headed to the South and Southwest.

Just as heavy industry was in shambles, so too agriculture was faltering and near collapse. Farmers suffered not only from floods and droughts, but also from burdensome debts they had incurred at high interest rates. Many lost their property through mortgage foreclosures and farm auctions. Others filed for bankruptcy. "Only in the last couple years," observed Judge Richard Stageman, a veteran of twenty-two years on the federal bankruptcy bench in Des Moines, Iowa, "have I seen grown men cry on the witness stand, and always it's the farmers. Some want reorganization when there's nothing left to reorganize. They're on the ragged edge of nowhere."

As the recession deepened in 1982, poverty rose to its highest level since 1965. (An urban family of four was classified as poor if its annual cash income was under $10,178.) The Bureau of the Census reported that the number of Americans living in poverty increased from 26.1 million (11.7 percent) in 1979 to 34.4 million (15 percent) in 1982. Poverty increased most among blacks (35.6 percent of whom were poor) and Hispanics (29.9 percent). Predictably, the largest single category of poor families consisted of households headed by women (36.3 percent). In 1983 poverty continued its rise, to 35.3 million Americans (15.2 percent). With one exception, poverty had returned to the levels that existed before the enactment of President Lyndon B. Johnson's Great Society. That exception was the elderly. For the first time in the history of federally defined need, the poverty rate among Americans over sixty-five (14.6 percent) was lower than that for the population at large, revealing that politicians had been paying attention to the needs of this rapidly growing group.

Poverty was literally painful. Federal officials announced in October 1982 that more than 16 million Americans had lost health insurance coverage as a

In 1982 and 1983, unemployment rose to the highest levels in forty years. At the same time, Reagan cut welfare benefits for the poor. Paul Conrad, cartoonist of the Los Angeles Times, suggested that Herbert Hoover's dour face lived behind the smiling Ronald Reagan mask. Paul Conrad, Los Angeles Times Syndicate.

result of unemployment, and many appeared to be deferring necessary medical care just when they most needed it. A sociologist who studied unemployed aircraft workers near Hartford, Connecticut, found evidence of "serious physical or emotional strain," including alcoholism, increased smoking, high blood pressure, insomnia, and nervous exhaustion. A few said they suffered from "recession depression" or had a bad case of the "pink slip blues." In 1982 M. Harvey Brenner, a sociologist at Johns Hopkins University, reported that for each 1 percent rise in unemployment, suicides increased 4.1 percent, homicides 5.7 percent, and mental hospital admissions 2.3 percent for women and 4.3 percent for men.

Poverty's Effects

President Reagan had announced that while his administration would reduce the rate of expansion of social and health programs, it would retain a "safety net" that would catch the "truly needy" before they hit bottom. But he reneged on his promise. Facing a budget deficit in excess of $200 billion in mid-1982, Reagan had three choices, and in each case he made a conservative decision. First, he could cut back on his rearmament plans to spend $1.7 trillion over five years, but this he refused to do. In fact, the budget signed by Reagan raised defense spending another 13 percent. Second, he could suspend or reduce the second installment of his tax cut, but this too he found unacceptable. Third, he could—and did—cut welfare and social programs. Reagan chose to push through Congress further cuts of $27.2 billion over three years in Medicare and Medicaid, food stamps, federal pensions, and government-guaranteed home mortgages. Still, in the absence of other budget cuts, the deficit continued to grow.

A *Los Angeles Times* poll in August 1982 showed that despite Reagan's personal popularity, more than a third of the people who had voted for him in 1980 said they would not support him again, largely because they lacked confidence in his economic policies. "People see little or no reason for optimism," explained a Los Angeles businessman. "I think we're headed for the bread lines," said a retired domestic worker in Miami. With the 1982 elections nearing, Democrats predicted big victories for their party.

Just a week before the 1982 elections, however, a *New York Times*/CBS News poll reported that the American public was being tugged sharply in different directions: toward the Democrats by unemployment, but toward the Republicans by declining inflation and the president's popularity. There was no denying Reagan's winning style. Nothing revealed this better than his courageous response to the attempt made on his life in March 1981. Although John W. Hinckley, Jr., failed to kill his target, he shot the president in the left side and wounded Reagan's press secretary, a Secret Service agent, and a police officer. Reagan's grace on that day caused his popularity ratings to soar. He walked into the George Washington University Hospital on his own with his blood oozing away, an undetonated explosive bullet in his chest, and his fighting spirit and sense of humor very much intact. "Honey, I forgot to duck," he told his wife.

In the 1982 elections, twenty-six House seats swung to the Democrats, giving them a lead of 267 to 166. Even with massive campaign funding, the Republicans came close to losing their majority in the Senate; four incumbents survived only narrowly. But with a continued Republican majority of 54 to 46, the Senate remained pro-Reagan. In another two years, there would be a presidential election. By

1982 Elections

then, the president had to prove that he could restore prosperity. Additionally, in order to be re-elected, Reagan had to demonstrate that his Cold War crusade would not lead to American participation in war in Central America, the Middle East, or, worst of all, against the Soviet Union.

REAGAN'S FOREIGN POLICY: THE SOVIETS AND THE NUCLEAR ARMS RACE

Ronald Reagan's foreign policy was driven by four beliefs rooted in America's past. "His is a kind of 1952 world," remarked one of Reagan's former aides. First, Reagan and the conservatives he selected to advise him believed that a malevolent Soviet Union was the source of the world's troubles. They saw almost everything through an East-West lens. If détente was already dead when Reagan became president, he buried it in an avalanche of strident anti-Soviet rhetoric. Barely settled into the White House, Reagan charged that the Soviets were prepared "to commit any crime, to lie, to cheat" to achieve a Communist world. He attributed Third World disorders to Soviet intrigue, rejecting analyses that argued, for example, that the civil wars in Central America derived not from Soviet meddling, but from deep-seated local sources of economic instability, poverty, and class oppression.

Reagan's Foreign Policy Views

Second, the Reagan administration believed that a major American military build-up would thwart the Soviet threat and intimidate the Soviets into negotiating on terms favorable to the United States. Reagan launched an eight-year, $2.3-trillion defense budget, most of which Congress approved. He pushed plans for the B-1 bomber, a much enlarged navy, production of poison gas, beefed-up special forces units for counterinsurgency, the MX missile, and an antimissile defense system in space (titled the Strategic Defense Initiative but quickly dubbed "Star Wars"). "They're screaming like they're sitting on a sharp nail," crowed Reagan when the Soviets protested the largest peacetime arms build-up in American history. In 1985 the Pentagon was spending an average of $28 million an hour, twenty-four hours a day, seven days a week. A warmongering image soon settled around the Reagan administration, especially when it became clear that the new president assigned low priority to arms control talks. Veteran diplomat George W. Ball lamented that once again "we shiver in the icy winds of the Cold War. Diplomacy is for sissies."

Third, Reagan and his advisers believed that nations must embrace private capitalism and reject managed economies. They frequently lectured Third World countries on the virtues of private enterprise. The United States even voted against—it was the only "no" vote—a United Nations resolution to restrict the marketing of baby formula in developing nations. Medical authorities had complained that the baby formula companies were marketing their product so aggressively that many mothers were foregoing healthy breast-feeding in favor of the artificial liquid, which they mixed with polluted water (all that was available to them), thus spreading disease. Regardless, Reagan officials would tolerate no interference with private business. The United States also refused to sign the Law of the Sea Treaty, protesting that it did not adequately protect private American deep-sea mining companies. Overall, the Reagan administration silenced the North-South dialogue (see pages 928–929).

Fourth, Ronald Reagan believed Americans must abandon their post-Vietnam "self-doubt" and renew their mission of converting foreign peoples to the American model. Most Americans shared Reagan's feeling that the United States had been ignobly retreating from global power and leadership—witness the treaty to return the canal to Panama, the Iranian hostage crisis, and Soviet achievement of nuclear parity. Besides talking tough and enlarging the military to reverse this trend, Reagan revitalized the Central Intelligence Agency and expanded its covert operations abroad. "America is back, standing tall," bragged the president in 1984 during a revival of passionate American patriotism.

In this atmosphere, Soviet-American relations became "white hot, thoroughly white hot," noted a Soviet leader. Actually, Reagan's first decision affecting the Soviets was to lift the grain embargo that President Carter had imposed after the Soviet invasion of Afghanistan. A grain deal worth about $3 billion was soon negotiated. Reagan thereby fulfilled a campaign promise to American farmers eager to sell wheat and corn in foreign markets. But this decision was followed in late 1981 by hostility when the Soviets cracked down on the Solidarity labor movement in Poland. In response, Washington restricted some Russian-American trade and hurled angry words at Moscow. As Soviet troops struggled to subdue Afghanistan, the CIA channeled aid to the Afghan rebels.

Reagan's expansion of the military, his coolness toward arms control, his utterances about winning a limited nuclear war, his quest for nuclear supremacy, and his insistence on placing new

Nuclear Arms Race cruise and Pershing-II missiles in Western Europe stimulated a lively international debate. In fall 1981 hundreds of thousands of marchers in London, Rome, Bonn, and other European cities demanded Soviet-American negotiations to prevent a nuclear holocaust. Talks on limiting intermediate-range nuclear forces (INF) based in Europe—such as the Soviet SS-20 missiles targeted against Western Europe and the American cruise and Pershings aimed at Russia—did get under way in late November 1981. The American proposal was called the zero option: the United States would not deploy its missiles in Western Europe if the Soviet Union would dismantle all of its SS-20s. Moscow replied that the plan did not take into account that, already, American long-range bombers and submarine-based missiles could reach the Soviet Union. Moreover, the Soviets said, Reagan's scheme did not count British and French nuclear forces aimed at the Soviet Union. Critics believed that Reagan's plan was more a propaganda ploy to quiet a worried public than a serious step toward arms control. The INF talks collapsed in November 1983 after the first American cruise and Pershing-II missiles were installed in Western Europe.

Reagan's substitute for the SALT talks, the Strategic Arms Reduction Talks (START), began in June 1982. But in December of the next year they too faltered. These difficult negotiations attracted intense American public interest. Evangelist Billy Graham and the National Council of Churches joined peace groups and prominent politicians such as Senator Edward Kennedy in appeals for a freeze in the nuclear arms race. In

In this 1983 test, the United States Army launched a Pershing-II missile on a long-range flight from Cape Canaveral, Florida. The plan to install these missiles in Western Europe provoked antinuclear weapons demonstrations in the United States and other parts of the world.   Official U.S. Navy photo.

the largest peaceful protest in American history in June 1982, 1 million people marched through New York City to support a freeze. The Roman Catholic bishops of the United States issued a long pastoral letter that said, "We are the first generation since Genesis with the power to virtually destroy God's creation." They condemned nuclear weapons as "immoral" and urged an end to the arms race, "which robs the poor and the vulnerable."

Doctors in Boston pointed out that if their city were hit by nuclear warheads, half a million people would die, thousands would suffer serious burns and fatal radiation poisoning, and hospitals would be so wrecked that they could not treat the wounded. Scientists predicted a "nuclear winter" after a nuclear war: the earth, cut off from the sun's rays, would turn cold, and food sources would disappear. An

ABC television dramatization titled "The Day After" stunned Americans in fall 1983 with its vivid depiction of the human costs of nuclear war. Even before this movie, towns across the nation had passed resolutions to freeze either the development, production, or deployment of new weapons. Despite opposition from the Reagan administration, the House of Representatives in 1983 also passed a freeze resolution. Because of such public opinion, pressure from NATO allies, worry that a more expensive and more dangerous nuclear arms race loomed, and the belief that reinvigorated American military power gave the United States a strong bargaining position, Reagan officials resumed discussions on arms control with the Soviets in early 1985.

While concern over nuclear war escalated, so did American-Soviet tensions. In early September 1983

Shooting Down of South Korean Airliner a Soviet fighter pilot tailed a South Korean commercial jet that had strayed over Soviet territory. When the airliner did not change course after having been warned, it was blasted out of the sky, killing 269 people. The world was shocked. Reagan went on television to denounce this "act of barbarism." Russian leaders claimed that the passenger plane was mistaken for an American spy aircraft. Although American spy planes did regularly travel a route close to that flown by Korean Air Lines Flight 007, few Americans accepted the Soviet explanation. Reagan halted commercial flights between the United States and the Soviet Union, but did little more. He seemed content to let the tragedy confirm in the American mind his dark view of the Soviets.

INTERVENTIONS IN THE THIRD WORLD AND FOREBODING FORECASTS

Reagan's dark view included the belief that the Soviets and their clients the Cubans were fomenting disorder in the Third World, especially in Central America. The region of Guatemala, Honduras, El Salvador, Nicaragua, and Costa Rica was a traditional sphere of influence for the United States, characterized by large economic holdings, political influence, and repeated interventions. Americans had long called Central America their backyard. For Reagan officials, El Salvador appeared to be a textbook case of Communist aggression. In that very poor country, revolutionaries challenged the government, which was dominated by the military and a small, landed elite. The regime used (or could not control) right-wing "death squads" that killed thousands of dissidents and other citizens, as well as some American missionaries who worked with landless peasants. Believing that the war against the rebels could be successfully concluded in a short time, Reagan eschewed negotiations and instead increased military assistance to the Salvadoran regime.

The controversial intervention in the Salvadoran civil war sparked a debate that sounded much like that which had erupted over Vietnam years before. Those who urged negotiations thought Reagan wrong to interpret the conflict as an East-West contest. Oppression and poverty, not Communist plots, caused people to pick up guns to fight the regime, they argued. "The region will continue to seethe with revolution—with or without the Soviets," said Connecticut Senator Christopher Dodd. Resurrecting the discredited domino theory, Reagan warned that if the "Communists" were not stopped in El Salvador they would soon be at the Mexican-American border. When that exaggerated argument convinced few, Reagan turned to a strategic case. Central America, he said, hugs the Caribbean Sea—"our lifeline to the outside world." In time of war, the Soviets could cripple American shipping from Caribbean bases. All of this assumed, of course, that the Soviets were in fact trying to take over El Salvador; critics rejected that assumption.

Although Congress voted funds for the American involvement in El Salvador, it stipulated that the United States government would have to certify every six months that the Salvadoran government was making improvements in human rights or the funds would be cut off. To keep the aid flowing, American officials made strained yet positive statements every six months that left many human rights observers incredulous. The Reagan administration's case was helped somewhat in May 1984 when a United States–influenced election produced a government under the popular José Napoleon Duarte. Still, civilian deaths mounted and land reform languished. And the guerrillas fought on and grew in numbers, showing no signs of being deterred by the continued infusion of substantial American arms, economic assistance, and CIA operatives.

Elsewhere in Central America the Reagan administration intervened, threatening a regional war. Nicaragua was ruled by a leftist government, the Sandinistas (see page 935). To succeed with their plans for improvements in health and education, they had invited several thousand Cubans into their hospitals and schools. Cuban military advisers helped them reorganize their army, and Soviet arms were ordered. Reagan early denounced the government, charging that it was becoming a Soviet puppet and was sending

The Russians (bear) and Americans (Uncle Sam) often explained their meddling in the affairs of other nations by claiming that they had to intervene in order to halt the expansion of the other. To the unhappy people whose sovereignty was violated, however, such an explanation was not convincing because it ignored the conspicuous, self-interested drive of the two great powers for control of small countries. By Auth for the Philadelphia Inquirer.

arms to the rebels in El Salvador. The Reagan administration soon strove to topple the Nicaraguan

Actions Against Nicaragua

government. The United States conducted military maneuvers off the coast and staged war games in neighboring Honduras, where major American bases were built. The CIA also began, in 1982, to train, arm, and direct over ten thousand counterrevolutionaries, called *contras*. Many of these anti-Sandinista rebels were former supporters of the Somoza dictatorship, which the Sandinistas had overthrown in 1979. From Honduras the *contras* killed Nicaraguan officials and innocent civilians and destroyed oil refineries, transportation facilities, medical clinics, and day-care centers.

In the spring of 1984 it became known that the CIA had mined the harbors of Nicaragua with explosives, causing merchant ships to be blown up.

Negative international and American opinion cascaded down on Washington. The French helped clear the harbors; the World Court ruled that Nicaragua had the right to sue the United States for damages. Conservative Republican Senator Barry Goldwater of Arizona boomed, "This is an act violating international law. It is an act of war. For the life of me, I don't know how we are going to explain it." Both houses of Congress passed a nonbinding resolution to halt the mining operations. In mid-1984 Congress voted to stop American aid to the *contras*. Then, in the fall, American journalists revealed that a CIA manual prepared for the *contras* told them not only how to conduct sabotage and incite mob violence, but also how to "neutralize" (that is, assassinate) Nicaraguan leaders. But the undeclared war against well-armed Nicaragua continued, prompting critics to assert that the United States was forcing Nicaragua into the

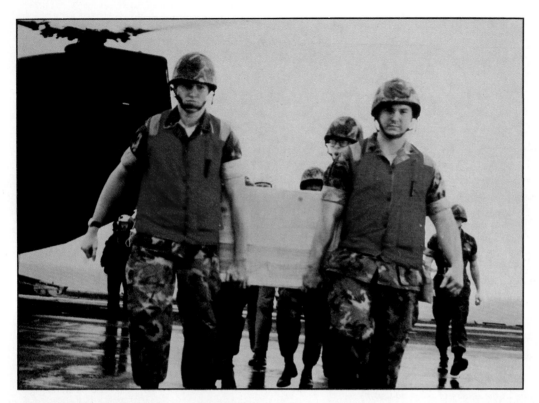

Americans mourned their war dead in Lebanon. These marines carried the body of a navy pilot from a helicopter after its arrival aboard the USS John F. Kennedy, an aircraft carrier. The pilot's aircraft had been shot down during a bombing raid over Lebanon. Official U.S. Air Force photo.

Communist camp. Moreover, they protested, the United States was bypassing opportunities to negotiate. The Nicaraguans, for example, accepted the objectives of the Contadora group (Mexico, Venezuela, Colombia, and Panama), which included the reduction of foreign military bases and advisers in Central America. But by 1985 the Reagan administration had refused to endorse the Contadora peace plan. As in El Salvador, the Reaganites preferred a military solution. His goal, the president declared in early 1985, was to remove the Sandinista government—to force it to say "uncle." And he soon imposed an economic blockade against Nicaragua.

In the Middle East too Reagan tried to use military power. Sophisticated airplanes worth $8.5 billion were sold to Saudi Arabia. United States relations with Israel cooled because of this deal, but also because the Israelis repeatedly bombed suspected Palestine Liberation Organization (PLO) camps inside Lebanon,

killing hundreds of civilians. In December 1981, without warning, Israel annexed the Syrian territory of the Golan Heights. Secretary of Defense Caspar Weinberger, like many Americans impatient with Israel's provocative acts toward its neighbors, stormed: "How long do we have to go on bribing Israel [with American aid]? If there is no real cost to the Israelis, we'll never be able to stop any of their actions." When, after the annexation, Reagan suspended an American-Israeli agreement on strategic cooperation in an attempt to punish Israel, Israeli Prime Minister Menachem Begin castigated Washington for treating his nation like a "banana republic."

Then, in June 1982, Israeli troops invaded civil war–torn Lebanon, cutting their way to the capital Beirut and inflicting massive damage. The beleaguered PLO and various Lebanese factions **Crisis in** called upon Syria to contain the **Lebanon** Israelis. Civilian deaths rose to at least ten thousand, and a million people became refugees. In August, as part of a peace-keeping force, U.S. Marines entered Lebanon and eventually dug in around Beirut. "Too few to fight and too many to die," protested one member of Congress. Their mission ill-defined, the American troops soon became allied with the faction that controlled the Lebanese government and exchanged fire with other factions and with Syrians. In October 1983, terrorist bombs demolished a marine barracks, killing 240 American servicemen. In February of the next year, with Lebanon reeling from civil war and Syrian and Israeli occupation, Reagan recognized failure and pulled the marines out. In the wake of the Lebanese tragedy, American leaders grew wary of Mideast ventures. Secretary of State George P. Schultz, upset that moderate Arab states like Jordan and Saudi Arabia were doing little to stabilize the region, muttered that "somehow or other we have to get over the notion that every time things don't go just to everybody's satisfaction in the Middle East, it's the U.S. fault or it's up to the U.S. to do something about it." Still, the United States had commitments (defense of Israel), political friends (Saudi Arabia), enemies (Iran and Libya), and oil supplies that would continue to draw it into the area.

Just before the terrorist bombing of the barracks in Lebanon, a Reagan aide remarked that "we need a major victory somewhere to show we can manage foreign policy." On October 25, 1983, just after the terrorist attack, the president ordered marines to invade Grenada. This tiny Caribbean island was troubled by political strife and ruled by a leftist government friendly with Cuba. Announcing that the invasion was necessary in order to protect several hundred Americans studying medicine there and once again trumpeting the Soviet threat, the United States implanted a new government and deported Cubans. The casualty list included about a hundred dead; the expedition cost the United States $75 million. The United Nations passed a resolution condemning this revival of gunboat diplomacy, but most Americans cheered Reagan's action. It was, said one senator, America's "Grenada high."

Invasion of Grenada

The euphoria was short-lived, for Americans faced bewildering international problems that seemed immune to military solutions. First, global economic issues were threatening world order and American prosperity. Third World nations were sinking more and more deeply into debt, less able to repay loans or to purchase goods. Between 1980 and 1983, American exports to developing nations declined by over $18 billion; that meant the loss of over 1 million jobs in the United States. In 1984 alone, America's trade deficit (more imports than exports) stood at a staggering $102 billion. Second, hunger and famine were not only taking a ghastly human toll, but also contributing to political instability. In the early 1980s population experts estimated that annual hunger-related deaths numbered between 13 and 18 million people—twenty-four people per minute. Drought-ravaged Africa was hardest hit; Ethiopia, wracked as well by civil war, counted over 6 million people on the verge of starvation in 1984.

A third major, long-term international problem was the deterioration of the global environment. Soil erosion hurt food production at a time when the world's population was growing rapidly. Toxic wastes, acid rain, shortages of clean water, and the overcutting of forests escalated environmental decline, which, in turn, burdened governments that seemed unable to respond. Fourth, international drug traffic was causing health problems for millions, enriching criminals who sometimes gained political influence (as in Bolivia and Colombia), and financing the activities of terrorists (as in Peru). American programs to eradicate crops of opium poppies (used to make heroin) in Asia and Mexico and coca (used to make cocaine) in Latin America cost a great deal, but were failing. Fifth, terrorism was increasing at an alarming rate. Terrorists struck at will without warning. Forty percent of terrorist attacks in 1983 were directed against the United States; 271 Americans were killed. In June 1985, Shiite Moslem terrorists from Lebanon hijacked an American jetliner, killed one passenger, beat others, and held 39 Americans hostage for seventeen days. Sixth, America was facing a future of uneasy relations with allies. NATO was splintering, and once-valuable allies like the Philippines were rocked by political unrest. At stake were military bases and intelligence-gathering stations. Seventh, religious and racial tensions undermined stability and spawned war. Sikhs and Hindus fought one another in India, where in 1984 Prime Minister Indira Gandhi was assassinated; Christians and Moslems battled in Lebanon; the Shiite

Moslems governing Iran were at war with the Sunni Moslems of Iraq; Roman Catholics and Protestants bloodied each other in Northern Ireland.

Finally, South Africa represented a special problem. There a blatantly racist white minority ruled a predominantly nonwhite people (85 percent) through **South Africa** the segregationist policy of *apartheid* and political repression. The Reagan administration refrained from criticizing South Africa, preferring instead what it called "constructive engagement." To many Americans it seemed necessary to pressure South Africa by cutting imports or by urging the 350 American companies operating there—led by Texaco, General Motors, Ford, and Goodyear—to stop doing business with the racist government. By early 1985 eleven cities and five states had passed divestment laws; that is, they were withdrawing dollars (such as pension funds used to buy stocks) from American companies active in South Africa. Many analysts were predicting that revolution was inevitable in South Africa. Wherever Americans turned, then, they faced unattractive questions and seemingly intractable problems that spelled global disorder and threats to American well-being both at home and abroad far into the future.

REAGAN'S OPPOSITION:
WOMEN, NONWHITES,
ORGANIZED LABOR

As the American people entered 1984, it was evident that several important groups desperately opposed Ronald Reagan's re-election. His most vocal critics were women, nonwhites, and labor leaders. In late 1983 the *New York Times* reported a "gender gap" between men's and women's opinions of Reagan's performance: far fewer women (38 percent) than men (53 percent) believed Reagan deserved re-election. The poll also found that 49 percent of women, but only 33 percent of men, feared that he would get the United States into a war. Reagan's opposition to the Equal Rights Amendment and

abortion on demand had already won him the enmity of many feminists. But what really caused the gender gap to yawn widely were Reagan's social welfare, health, and education cuts. Eleanor Holmes Norton, speaking for the Coalition on Women and the Budget, said in early 1984: "For three years we have seen unwarranted cuts in domestic survival programs that have weakened, not strengthened, families; that have made children hungrier, not healthier." Kathy Wilson, a Republican and president of the National Women's Political Caucus, was more direct: "Ronald Reagan is quite simply the most anti-woman president in history."

In May 1983, the Labor Department announced that for the first time in United States history, more than half (50.5 percent) of all women aged twenty and older held jobs. Some were blue-**Working** collar workers, including 9,000 new **Women** female carpenters and 29,000 new female truck drivers who had joined the work force since 1970. Nevertheless, in 1985 half of all working women still occupied only 20 of the 441 job categories of the United States census, mostly at the low end of the pay scale. Eighty percent worked in such "female" occupations as clerking, selling, teaching, nursing, and waitressing.

Many working women were also mothers shocked by the Reagan administration's insensitivity to child welfare. Edwin Meese, counselor to the president, lacked the facts when he said that people went to soup kitchens "because the food is free," and added that he had seen no "authoritative evidence" that children in America went hungry. That evidence appeared in 1984 when the House Select Committee on Children, Youth and Families reported: "The number of poor children increased by two million between 1980 and 1982. Today, one out of five children and one out of two black children live in poverty."

Women still earned only 60 percent as much as men, and partly for this reason an additional 2 million women fell into poverty between 1981 and 1983. Reagan's critics assailed him not only for failing to stop this "feminization of poverty," but also for approving policies, such as cuts in food stamps and school meals, that added to the woes of poor women and their children. The Reagan administration was also hostile to the feminist goal of "equal pay for jobs of comparable worth." Why, women asked, should a grade-school teacher earn less than an electrician, if the two jobs required comparable skills and involved comparable responsibilities? But "comparable worth" was only one of many feminist goals opposed by Reagan. In response, for the first time in its history, the National Organization for Women (NOW) endorsed a presidential candidate before the primaries. NOW's choice was Walter Mondale, former Minnesota senator, vice president under Jimmy Carter, and the frontrunner for the Democratic nomination.

Black civil rights leaders also opposed Reagan's re-election; they joined feminists in assailing the president's appointments. Whereas 12 percent of President Carter's high-level jobholders were black and 12.1 percent women, Reagan's comparable totals were 4.1 percent black and 8 percent women. Reagan had appointed three women to his cabinet, and he had made history by appointing Sandra Day O'Connor the first woman associate justice of the Supreme Court, but blacks could find little to applaud in Reagan's performance. After the U.S. Commission on Civil Rights issued a report expressing its concern that Reagan had not appointed more blacks, women, and Hispanic Americans to full-time, high-level positions, the president fired the commission's outspoken liberals and replaced them with opponents of affirmative action in hiring and in education.

Reagan announced in early 1982 that his administration favored tax exemptions for fundamentalist Christian schools that cited the Bible to justify racial segregation and whites-only admissions policies. (In mid-1983, the **Retreat in Civil Rights** Supreme Court ruled against Reagan 8 to 1 and ordered the Internal Revenue Service to deny tax exemptions to Bob Jones University in South Carolina and the Goldsboro Christian Institute in North Carolina.) Although Reagan denounced as "plain baloney" the allegation that "we are taking a less active approach to protecting the civil rights of all Americans," his record proved otherwise. William Bradford Reynolds, Reagan's civil rights chief in the Justice Department, fought against renewing intact the Voting Rights Act of 1965, expressed opposition to busing and affirmative action, and was criticized for lax enforcement of fair-housing laws and laws banning sexual and racial discrimination in federally funded education programs.

Hispanic and Native Americans joined Afro-Americans in blasting the Reagan administration. The League of United Latin American Citizens censured Reagan for his "very, very dismal record" in dealing with their problems, and the National Tribal Chairman's Association charged that within two years of Reagan's election, "the delivery of services by federal agencies to Indians was in a shambles."

Joining women and nonwhites in the anti-Reagan camp was the AFL-CIO. Even without Reagan in the White House, hard times would have hit the labor unions. Faced with the recession and unemployment, union negotiators had to settle for less than they were accustomed to receiving. American workers who ratified contracts during the first three months of Reagan's term settled for pay increases averaging only 2.2 percent in the first year, a stunning decline from the 9.8-percent hikes that had prevailed the year before. The drop in wage settlements was the biggest since the government began collecting such data in 1954. Unions had suffered large membership losses as unemployment hit the "smokestack industries," and their efforts to unionize the high-growth electronics and service sectors of the economy were failing. In February 1984 the Supreme Court ruled that companies declaring bankruptcy could unilaterally cancel union contracts to which they had agreed earlier, without even having a hearing.

Reagan made the unions' hard times worse. He presided over the government's busting of the Professional Air Traffic Controllers Organization (PATCO) during the union's 1981 strike. His appointees to the National Labor Relations Board consistently voted against labor and for management. Although it seemed that Reagan was clearly labor's enemy, union leaders could not rally their members to oppose his re-election. An estimated 44 percent of union families had voted for Reagan in 1980; many still responded positively to his genial personality, his espousal of old-fashioned values, and his anti-Communism. Wanting to use its political muscle against Reagan as soon as possible, the AFL-CIO followed NOW's lead and endorsed Mondale for president.

Reagan's opponents decried the "country club ethics" of his appointees, several of whom resigned after accusations that they had behaved illegally or

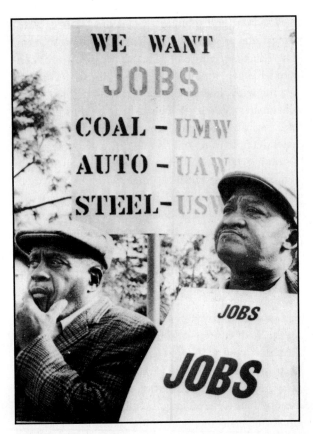

During the high unemployment of 1982 and 1983, jobless Americans came to Washington, D.C., to protest their situation. In October 1982, these demonstrators stood in a row in Lafayette Park, opposite the White House, and called attention to the loss of jobs in basic industries. AP/Wide World Photos.

improperly. The number-two administrators in both the CIA and the Department of Defense left office after newspaper reports that they had taken part in questionable stock transactions. The deputy secretary of defense, W. Paul Thayer, pleaded guilty to criminal charges of obstruction of justice and giving false information to the Securities and Exchange Commission and was sentenced to four years in a federal prison. Another resignation was that of Richard Allen, the national security adviser, after the disclosure that he had accepted gifts, including money and watches, from Japanese journalists for arranging interviews with Nancy Reagan, the president's wife. Rita Lavelle, an assistant administrator of the Environmental Protection Agency, was convicted of perjury and obstructing a congressional investigation for covering up her role in halting an EPA crack-

down on her former employer, Aerojet-General Corporation. And in 1984 when Reagan nominated his close friend Edwin Meese to be attorney general of the United States, allegations arose that Meese had accepted "sweetheart loans" from individuals who were later appointed to positions in the Reagan administration.

In ordinary political times, the Democrats would have profited from the Republicans' misfortunes. Added to the nation's economic woes, the issue of corruption in government ("the sleaze factor") should have bolstered the Democrats in 1984. But 1984 produced a stunning victory for the Republican incumbent, Ronald Reagan, whose Teflon coating protected him from personal responsibility for his administration's failings.

REAGAN'S 1984 RE-ELECTION LANDSLIDE

As the political parties mounted their 1984 presidential campaigns, it became evident early that Reagan could defeat any Democratic nominee.

Reagan's Re-election Assets

Topping the list of Reagan's re-election credentials was the rebound in the economy. The gross national product rose 6.8 percent in 1984, the sharpest increase since 1951, and mid-year unemployment fell to a four-year low of 7.1 percent. And while the economy was heating up, it did so without causing inflation to boil. Indeed, inflation (4 percent in 1984) fell to its lowest level since 1967. A second factor in Reagan's favor was people's perception of him as a strong leader in foreign as well as national affairs. In contrast, Walter Mondale had to struggle to prove that he was not a "wimp" and that he too would stand up to the Soviet Union and to terrorists. Third, Reagan was the enthusiastic choice of the political right as well as of social, cultural, and religious conservatives across the country. And he won the approval of millions of other Americans who agreed with his television ads that "America is back" after two decades of turmoil and self-doubt.

Finally, the Democrats did not pose a convincing alternative. The party was in disarray, its policies seemed timeworn, and its presidential candidate aroused little excitement, even within his own party.

Nor did the Democratic party have an appealing platform to present to the American voters in 1984. The party was fragmented into numerous caucuses **Democratic Divisions** for union members, blacks, women, Jews, homosexuals, Hispanics, and other groups. Each group had its own agenda, and at the 1984 Democratic national convention, each threatened to walk out if its demands were not met. One divisive issue was the Simpson-Mazzoli bill to change immigration laws. Organized labor supported the bill because it promised to curtail the illegal flow of undocumented Mexican-born workers to the United States. But the bill was denounced by Hispanics, an increasingly important voice in the Democratic party, who argued that punishing employers who hired undocumented workers would increase job discrimination against all Hispanics. Many Americans gained the impression that the Democratic party was not concerned with the national welfare, but rather with dividing up the spoils among its special-interest groups.

Still worse for the party's prospects, the leading contenders for the Democratic presidential nomination fought a bitter contest throughout the primaries. Walter Mondale spoke for the New Deal tradition of the welfare state and received preconvention endorsements from NOW, the AFL-CIO, and various civil rights organizations. Senator Gary Hart of Colorado evoked the image of John F. Kennedy: the tousled hair, the appearance of youthful vigor, the talk about "new ideas" and a "new generation." Hart denounced Mondale as the tool of the unions and other special interests and aimed his campaign at "Yuppies" (young urban professionals) and members of the baby boom, those 63.5 million Americans born between 1946 and 1961. When polled, Yuppies generally said they would vote for Reagan if Hart did not win the Democratic nomination. The third Democratic contender was Jesse Jackson, a former co-worker of Martin Luther King, Jr., in the southern civil rights struggle. Jackson had moved to Chicago to organize economic and educational programs for the poor, and in 1984 inspired a massive voter-registration drive among blacks. An eloquent preacher,

The Democratic party nominated Congresswoman Geraldine Ferraro to be its vice-presidential candidate in 1984. Her choice was a historic first.   Photograph for Time *by P. F. Bentley/Time Magazine.*

Jackson campaigned on his dream of forming a "Rainbow Coalition" of the "rejected"—blacks, women, Hispanics, the physically handicapped. Jackson was the first black candidate in history to win mass support in a bid for the presidential nomination of a major party.

What enthusiasm there was for the Democratic ticket arose from Mondale's historic selection of Congresswoman Geraldine Ferraro as his vice-presidential **Geraldine Ferraro** running mate. Feminists hailed this choice, as did numerous women and men throughout the country. Ferraro showed herself to be an intelligent, indefatigable campaigner who won the respect of even her opponents.

But the Democratic party was out of step with the nation's social and cultural conservatism. During the 1930s the New Deal coalition had gained the allegiance of economic liberals who subscribed to the welfare state. In 1984, however, many Democrats held conservative views on such issues as abortion and homosexuality, and they switched their votes to Ronald Reagan. The Democratic party was badly split, its confidence shaken, and it would need to redefine what it had to offer the American voter.

Reagan's personality, on the other hand, seemed to fit the public mood. In the summer of 1984, Americans carrying the Olympic torch ran from one coast of the United States to the other, through hundreds of cities, by night and day. This public relations pageantry was in harmony with a new optimism. In 1980 the pollster Daniel Yankelovich had reported that the United States had gone "almost overnight from a nation of optimists to a nation of pessimists." Four years later Yankelovich's polls told him that "the defeatism is gone. There is a reassertion of the familiar kinds of American optimism and can-do spirit—in many ways more realistic than in the 1960s." The invasion of Grenada brought not demonstrations, but a surge of new enrollments in ROTC programs. As shown in the moral and cultural conservatism of the antiabortion and profamily movements, a deep reaction also was occurring against the sexual liberalization that had begun in the 1960s. The cycle had turned sharply to the right once again, as it had in the 1920s and 1950s.

During the campaign Mondale attempted to debate what he defined as the issues, but Reagan preferred to invoke the theme of leadership and communicate traditional values to his audience. Rather than discuss the federal deficit, tax policy, and the nuclear arms race, Reagan relied on slogans and on his unofficial campaign song, "I'm Proud to Be an American." Mondale chastised Reagan for the federal deficit, which had run at $175 billion in fiscal year 1984 and was projected to jump to $210 billion in fiscal year 1985. But when Mondale announced that he would raise taxes to cut the deficit, he lost votes.

Religion became an unexpectedly hot issue. Mondale predicted that if Reagan were re-elected, he would nominate only conservative, prolife justices to the Supreme Court and thus **Religious Issues** overturn the Warren Court's liberal legacy (see page 949). Mondale even hinted that Reagan's Supreme Court appointments would be approved in advance by Jerry Falwell, the radio-TV minister and founder of the Moral Majority. Falwell's benediction delivered at the 1984 Republican national convention described Reagan and Vice President George Bush as "God's instruments in rebuilding America." Reagan responded that "religion and politics are necessarily related" and called opponents of school prayer "intolerant of religion." Mondale then denounced the Moral Majority's role in Reagan's campaign and declared, "Most Americans would be surprised to learn that God is a Republican." Still, millions of religious conservatives saw a vote for Reagan as an extension of their moral commitments; an expression of their "personal politics," just as walking an antiabortion picket line would be.

Mondale also attacked Reagan's foreign policy, but to little avail. "Mr. Reagan's approach could be summarized this way," Mondale asserted. "If there's an arms agreement, oppose it. If there's a dangerous weapon, buy it. . . . If there's a diplomatic problem, militarize it. If there's a regional conflict, Americanize it. If your policies fail, blame someone else." The Democratic candidate favored a mutual freeze in nuclear testing, arms control talks, an end to the covert war against Nicaragua, and negotiations over Central America. Reagan dismissed Mondale's suggestions as "policies of weakness." But Mondale agreed with the president that military aid should go to El Salvador and that missiles should be deployed in Western Europe. Despite Reagan's minimal success in world affairs, Mondale was unable to make political gains on foreign policy issues largely because Reagan had generated a flag-waving patriotism that supported the president's military build-up and sharp anti-Soviet utterances.

Reagan's victory in 1984 was never in doubt, but his forty-nine-state total led observers to conclude that he had transformed American politics. Columnists and scholars wrote that he had **Reagan's Victory** forged a new right coalition that could dominate national politics for years to come. Some compared this election to Franklin D. Roosevelt's comparable sweep in 1936 (he took forty-six of forty-eight states) that had put the final stamp on the New Deal coalition (see page 747). But Reagan's triumph had reduced Roosevelt's coalition to rubble.

Reagan and Roosevelt were alike in several ways. Both were skillful performers; both projected warm

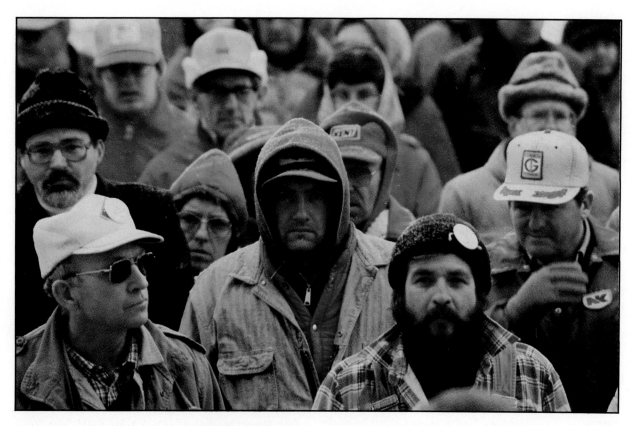

In 1985, these farmers protested the foreclosure auction of a 300-acre farm in Toledo, Iowa, by standing silent and refusing to bid. Burdened by debts and low prices, few family farmers looked forward to the future.   Max Winter/Picture Group.

images that inspired confidence. Reagan had never hidden his admiration of Roosevelt's style. The writer David McCullough, after interviewing Reagan in the White House, concluded that he "sees Roosevelt as his 'kind of guy'—confident, cheerful, theatrical, larger than life." The irony, of course, was that Reagan's goal was to repeal Roosevelt's New Deal, not to champion it. Indeed, in his second inaugural address in 1985, Reagan announced that his "new American Emancipation" would "tear down economic barriers and liberate the spirit of enterprise" by eradicating the excesses of fifty years of Democratic liberalism.

Whether Reagan had put together a lasting new right coalition was debatable. What was not debatable was that he had succeeded in his principal aims during his first term and had restored the presidency to its central role in politics and the government. Columnist David Broder wrote in 1985 that "with the nation

prosperous and at peace and his personal popularity high," Reagan could already lay claim to being "a historically significant president." Still, as Broder also noted, Reagan had "given many hostages to fortune." Although personally popular, Reagan presided over a polarized people. In the second half of the 1980s, the gap was growing between affluent whites and poor nonwhites, between Frostbelt and Sunbelt states, between the country's social and defense needs, and between liberal lifestyles and religious conservatism. Uncertainties in the economy threatened its continuing rebound. While many businesspeople made money in the mid-1980s, farmers were burdened by debts they could not possibly repay. Around them, banks collapsed and small towns died. The budget deficit during Reagan's second term was projected to add more than $700 billion to the national debt. At stake too were Reagan's commitment and ability to achieve

IMPORTANT EVENTS

1981 Prime interest rate at 21.5 percent
Congress approves Reagan's budget cuts
Economic Recovery Tax Act
Soviet crackdown in Poland
Unemployment at 8 percent
U.S. steps up role in El Salvador
INF talks begin

1982 Prime interest rate falls to 14 percent
START negotiations begin
U.S. troops ordered to Lebanon
Unemployment climbs to 10.1 percent
U.S. aid to *contras* revealed
Voting Rights Act of 1965 renewed

1983 Prime interest rate at 10.5 percent
U.S. Roman Catholic bishops' pastoral letter on nuclear war
Unemployment at 10.2 percent
Over half of women over twenty hold jobs

Soviets shoot down Korean airliner
Terrorists kill U.S. Marines in Lebanon
Invasion of Grenada
The Day After
U.S. missiles deployed in Western Europe

1984 American troops leave Lebanon
CIA mines Nicaraguan harbors
Unemployment drops to 7.1 percent
Ferraro becomes first woman vice-presidential candidate of a major party
Reagan re-elected
Inflation falls to 4 percent

1985 Reagan inaugurated
U.S. economic blockage of Nicaragua
Terrorists seize Americans from highjacked airplane and hold them as hostages

---

arms control and peace in the Middle East, Africa, and Central America. By taking the oath for a second term, President Ronald Reagan had put his place in history on the line.

SUGGESTIONS FOR FURTHER READING

The Conservative Politics of Ronald Reagan

Ronald Brownstein and Nina Easton, *Reagan's Ruling Class* (1983); Lou Cannon, *Reagan* (1982); Joan Claybrook, *Retreat from Safety: Reagan's Attack on America's Health* (1984); Robert Dallek, *Ronald Reagan: The Politics of Symbolism* (1984); Ronnie Dugger, *On Reagan* (1983); Fred Greenstein, ed., *The Reagan Presidency* (1983); Jonathan Lash, *A Season of Spoils: The Story of the Reagan Administration's Attack on the Environment* (1984); John L. Palmer and Isabel V. Sawhill, eds., *The Reagan Experiment* (1982); Gillian Peele, *Revival and Reaction: The Right in Contemporary America* (1984); Kevin Phillips, *Post-Conservative America* (1982).

Reaganomics

Frank Ackerman, *Reaganomics* (1982); Michael Harrington, *The New American Poverty* (1984); Robert Lekachman, *Greed Is Not Enough* (1983); Frances Fox Piven and Richard Cloward, *The New Class War* (1982); Sidney Weintraub and Marvin Goodstein, eds., *Reaganomics in the Stagflation Economy* (1983).

Reagan's Foreign Policy and the Nuclear Arms Race

Ruth Adams and Susan Cullen, eds., *The Final Epidemic: Physicians and Scientists on Nuclear War* (1981); William M. Arkin and Richard Fieldhouse, *Nuclear Battlefields* (1985); Richard J. Barnet, *The Alliance: America, Europe, Japan* (1983); Alexander Haig, *Caveat: Realism, Reagan, and Foreign Policy* (1984); Harvard Nuclear Study Group, *Living with Nuclear Weapons* (1983); Ole R. Holsti and James R. Rosenau, *American Leadership in World Affairs: Vietnam and the Breakdown of Consensus* (1984); George F. Kennan, *The Nuclear Delusion* (1982); National Academy of Sciences, *Nuclear Arms Control* (1985); Kenneth A. Oye *et al.*, eds., *Eagle Defiant* (1983); Strobe Talbott, *Deadly Gambits: The Reagan Administration and the Stalemate in Nuclear Arms Control* (1984); Strobe Talbott, *The Russians and Reagan* (1984). (Also see the *America and the World* series published by *Foreign Affairs* magazine and the *Great Decisions* series published by the Foreign Policy Association.)

Central America

Raymond Bonner, *Weakness and Deceit: U.S. Policy and El Salvador* (1984); Tom Buckley, *Violent Neighbors* (1984); Charles Clements, *Witness to War* (1984); Kenneth M. Coleman and George C. Herring, eds., *The Central America Crisis* (1985); Martin Diskin, ed., *Trouble in Our Backyard* (1984); Walter LaFeber, *Inevitable Revolutions*, rev. ed. (1984); Robert S. Leiken, ed., *Central America* (1984); Richard A. White, *The Morass* (1984).

APPENDIX

HISTORICAL REFERENCE

BOOKS BY SUBJECT

Encyclopedias, Dictionaries, Atlases, Chronologies, and Statistics

General

Geoffrey Barraclough, ed., *The Times Atlas of World History* (1979); *Concise Dictionary of American Biography* (1980); *Concise Dictionary of American History* (1983); *Dictionary of American Biography* (1928–); *Dictionary of American History* (1976–1978); Robert H. Ferrell and John S. Bowman, eds., *The Twentieth Century: An Almanac* (1984); Edward W. Fox, *Atlas of American History* (1964); George H. Gallup, *The Gallup Poll: Public Opinion, 1935–1971* (1972) and *1972–1977* (1978); John A. Garraty, ed., *Encyclopedia of American Biography* (1974); Bernard Grun, *The Timetables of History* (1975); Stanley Hochman, *Yesterday and Today* (1979); *International Encyclopedia of the Social Sciences* (1968–); Kenneth T. Jackson and James T. Adams, *Atlas of American History* (1978); R. Alton Lee, ed., *Encyclopedia USA* (1983–); Michael Martin and Leonard Gelber, *Dictionary of American History* (1981); Richard B. Morris, *Encyclopedia of American History* (1982); *National Cyclopedia of American Biography* (1898–); Arthur M. Schlesinger, Jr., ed., *The Almanac of American History* (1983); *Scribner Desk Dictionary of American History* (1984); U.S. Bureau of the Census, *Historical Statistics of the United States* (1975); U.S. Department of the Interior, *National Atlas of the United States* (1970).

The American Revolution

Mark M. Boatner, III, *Encyclopedia of the American Revolution* (1974); Lester J. Cappon, ed., *Atlas of Early American History: The Revolutionary Era, 1760–1790* (1976); Douglas W. Marshall and Howard H. Peckham, *Campaigns of the American Revolution* (1976); Gregory Palmer, ed., *Biographical Sketches of Loyalists of the American Revolution* (1984); *Rand-McNally Atlas of the American Revolution* (1974).

Architecture

William D. Hunt, Jr., ed., *Encyclopedia of American Architecture* (1980).

Blacks

Peter M. Bergman, *The Chronological History of the Negro in America* (1969); Rayford W. Logan and Michael R. Winston, eds., *The Dictionary of American Negro Biography* (1983); W. A. Low and Virgil A. Clift, eds., *Encyclopedia of Black America* (1981); Harry A. Ploski and James Williams, eds., *The Negro Almanac* (1983); Erwin A. Salk, ed., *A Layman's Guide to Negro History* (1967); Mabel M. Smythe, ed., *The Black American Reference Book* (1976); Edgar A. Toppin, *A Biographical History of Blacks in America* (1971).

Cities and Towns

Charles Abrams, *The Language of Cities: A Glossary of Terms* (1971); John L. Androit, ed., *Township Atlas of the United States* (1979); Ory M. Nergal, ed., *The Encyclopedia of American Cities* (1980). *See also* "Politics and Government."

The Civil War

Mark M. Boatner, III, *The Civil War Dictionary* (1959); *The Civil War Almanac* (1983); E. B. Long, *The Civil War Day by Day* (1971); Mark E. Neely, Jr., *The Abraham Lincoln Encyclopedia* (1982); Craig L. Symonds, *A Battlefield Atlas of the Civil War* (1983); U.S. War Department, *The Official Atlas of the Civil War* (1958); Jon L. Wakelyn, ed., *Biographical Dictionary of the Confederacy* (1977); Ezra J. Warner and W. Buck Yearns, *Biographical Register of the Confederate Congress* (1975). *See also* "The South."

Conservation

Forest History Society, *Encyclopedia of American Forest and Conservation History* (1983).

The Constitution and Supreme Court

Congressional Quarterly, *Guide to the Supreme Court* (1979); Leon Friedman and Fred I. Israel, eds., *The Justices of the United States Supreme Court, 1789–1978* (1980); *Judges of the United States* (1980).

Crime

Sanford H. Kadish, ed., *Encyclopedia of Crime and Justice* (1983); Carl Sifakis, *The Encyclopedia of American Crime* (1982).

Culture and Folklore

M. Thomas Inge, ed., *Handbook of American Popular Culture* (1979–1981); Marjorie Tallman, *Dictionary of American Folklore* (1959); Justin Wintle, ed., *Makers of Nineteenth Century Culture, 1800–1914* (1982). *See also* "Entertainment," "Music," and "Sports."

The Economy and Business

Christine Ammer and Dean S. Ammer, *Dictionary of Business and Economics* (1983); Douglas Auld and Graham Bannock, *The American Dictionary of Economics* (1983); Douglas Greenwald, *Encyclopedia of Economics* (1982); John N. Ingham, *Biographical Dictionary of American Business Leaders* (1983); Glenn G. Munn, *Encyclopedia of Banking and Finance* (1973); David W. Pearce, *Dictionary of Modern Economics* (1983); Glenn Porter, *Encyclopedia of American Economic History* (1980).

Education

Lee C. Deighton, ed., *The Encyclopedia of Education* (1971); Joseph C. Kiger, ed., *Research Institutions and Learned Societies* (1982); John F. Ohles, ed., *Biographical Dictionary of American Educators* (1978).

Entertainment

Tim Brooks and Earle Marsh, *The Complete Directory to Prime Time Network TV Shows, 1946–present* (1979); Barbara N. Cohen-Stratyner, *Biographical Dictionary of Dance* (1982); John Dunning, *Tune in Yesterday* [radio] (1967); Stanley Green, *Encyclopedia of the Musical Film* (1981); *Notable Names in the American Theater* (1976); *New York Times Encyclopedia of Television* (1977); Andrew Sarris, *The American Cinema: Directors and Directions, 1929–1968* (1968); Evelyn M. Truitt, *Who Was Who on Screen* (1977). *See also* "Culture and Folklore," "Music," and "Sports."

Foreign Policy

Alexander DeConde, ed., *Encyclopedia of American Foreign Policy* (1978); John E. Findling, *Dictionary of American Diplomatic History* (1980); *International Geographic Encyclopedia and Atlas* (1979); Warren F. Kuehl, ed., *Biographical Dictionary of Internationalists* (1983); George T. Kurian, *Encyclopedia of the Third World* (1981); Richard B. Morris and Graham W. Irwin, eds., *Harper Encyclopedia of the Modern World* (1970); Jack C. Plano, ed., *The International Relations Dictionary* (1982); Jack E. Vincent, *A Handbook of International Relations* (1969).

Immigration and Ethnic Groups

American Jewish Biographies (1982); Stephanie Bernardo, *The Ethnic Almanac* (1981); Matt S. Meier and Feliciano Rivera, *Dictionary of Mexican American History* (1981); Stephan Thernstrom, ed., *Harvard Encyclopedia of American Ethnic Groups* (1980).

Indians

Frederick J. Dockstader, *Great North American Indians* (1977); *Handbook of North American Indians* (1978–   ); Barry Klein, ed., *Reference Encyclopedia of the American Indian* (1978).

Labor

Gary M. Fink, ed., *Biographical Dictionary of American Labor Leaders* (1974); Gary M. Fink, ed., *Labor Unions* (1977); Philip S. Foner, *First Facts of American Labor* (1984).

Literature

James T. Callow and Robert J. Reilly, *Guide to American Literature* (1976–1977); *Dictionary of Literary Biography* (1978–   ); Eugene Ehrlich and Gorton Carruth, *The Oxford Illustrated Literary Guide to the United States* (1982); Jon Tuska and Vicki Piekarski, *Encyclopedia of Frontier and Western Fiction* (1983). *See also* "Culture and Folklore," "The South," and "Women."

Medicine

Martin Kaufman, *et al.*, eds., *Dictionary of American Medical Biography* (1984).

Music

John Chilton, *Who's Who of Jazz* (1972); Edward Jablonski, *The Encyclopedia of American Music* (1981); Roger Lax and

Frederick Smith, *The Great Song Thesaurus* (1984). *See also* "Culture and Folklore" and "Entertainment."

Politics and Government: General and Elections

Congressional Quarterly, *Congress and the Nation, 1945–1976* (1965–1977); Congressional Quarterly, *Guide to U.S. Elections* (1975); Jack P. Greene, ed., *Encyclopedia of American Political History* (1984); Kenneth C. Martis, *The Historical Atlas of United States Congressional Districts, 1789–1983* (1982); Edwin V. Mitchell, *An Encyclopedia of American Politics* (1968); Svend Peterson, *A Statistical History of the American Presidential Elections* (1963); William Safire, *Safire's Political Dictionary* (1978); Richard M. Scammon, ed., *America at the Polls* (1965); Edward L. and Frederick H. Schapsmeier, eds., *Political Parties and Civic Action Groups* (1981); Arthur M. Schlesinger, Jr., and Fred I. Israel, eds., *History of American Presidential Elections, 1789–1968* (1971); Robert Scruton, *A Dictionary of Political Thought* (1982); Hans Sperber and Travis Trittschuh, *American Political Terms* (1962). *See also* "The Constitution and Supreme Court," "States and the West," and the following section.

Politics and Government: Leaders

Roy R. Glashan, comp., *American Governors and Gubernatorial Elections, 1775–1978* (1979); Otis L. Graham, Jr., and Meghan R. Wander, eds., *Franklin D. Roosevelt: His Life and Times* (1985); Melvin G. Holli and Peter d'A. Jones, eds., *Biographical Dictionary of American Mayors, 1820–1980: Big City Mayors* (1981); Joseph E. Kallenbach and Jessamine S. Kallenbach, *American State Governors, 1776–1976* (1977); Thomas A. McMullin and David Walker, *Biographical Directory of American Territorial Governors* (1984); *Political Profiles, Truman Years to . . .* (1978); John W. Raimo, ed., *Biographical Directory of American Colonial and Revolutionary Governors, 1607–1789* (1980); John W. Raimo, ed., *Biographical Directory of the Governors of the United States, 1789–1978* (1978); John W. Raimo, ed., *Biographical Directory of the Governors of the United States, 1978–1983* (1984); Robert Sobel, ed., *Biographical Directory of the United States Executive Branch, 1774–1977* (1977); U.S. Congress, Senate, *Biographical Directory of the American Congress, 1774–1971* (1971); Robert Vexler, *The Vice-Presidents and Cabinet Members* (1975). *See also* the previous section.

Religion

Henry Bowden, *Dictionary of American Religious Biography* (1977); John T. Ellis and Robert Trisco, *A Guide to American Catholic History* (1982); Edwin S. Gaustad, *Historical Atlas of Religion in America* (1976); Samuel S. Hill, Jr., ed., *Encyclopedia of Religion in the South* (1984); J. Gordon Melton, *The Encyclopedia of American Religions* (1978); Mark A. Noll and Nathan O. Hatch, eds., *Eerdmans Handbook to Christianity in America* (1983); Arthur C. Piepkorn, *Profiles in Brief: The Religious Bodies of the United States and Canada* (1977–1979).

Science

Charles C. Gillispie, ed., *Dictionary of Scientific Biography* (1970–   ); National Academy of Sciences, *Biographical Memoirs* (1877–   ).

Social Issues

Louis Filler, *A Dictionary of American Social Reform* (1963); Louis Filler, *Dictionary of American Social Change* (1982); Robert S. Fogarty, *Dictionary of American Communal and Utopian History* (1980); Mark E. Lender, *Dictionary of American Temperance Biography* (1984); Alvin J. Schmidt, *Fraternal Organizations* (1980). *See also* "Crime."

The South

Robert Bain, *et al.*, eds., *Southern Writers: A Biographical Dictionary* (1979); Kenneth Coleman and Charles S. Gurr, eds., *Dictionary of Georgia Biography* (1983); William C. Ferris and Charles R. Wilson, eds., *Encyclopedia of Southern Culture* (1986); David C. Roller and Robert W. Twyman, eds., *The Encyclopedia of Southern History* (1979); Walter P. Webb, *et al.*, eds., *The Handbook of Texas* (1952, 1976). *See also* "Politics and Government" and "States and the West."

Sports

Ralph Hickok, *New Encyclopedia of Sports* (1977); Ralph Hickok, *Who Was Who in American Sports* (1971); Zander Hollander, *The NBA's Official Encyclopedia of Pro Basketball* (1981); Frank G. Menke and Suzanne Treat, *The Encyclopedia of Sports* (1977); *The NFL's Official Encyclopedic History of Professional Football* (1977); Paul Soderberg, *et al.*, *The Big Book of Halls of Fame in the United States and Canada* (1977). *See also* "Culture and Folklore."

States and the West

John Clayton, ed., *The Illinois Fact Book and Historical Almanac, 1673–1968* (1970); Doris O. Dawdy, *Artists of the American West* (1974–1984); Howard R. Lamar, ed., *The Reader's Encyclopedia of the American West* (1977);

Mose Y. Sachs, ed., *The Worldmark Encyclopedia of the States* (1981). *See also* "Politics and Government" and "The South."

Wars and the Military

R. Ernest Dupuy and Trevor N. Dupuy, *The Encyclopedia of Military History* (1977); Holger H. Herwig and Neil M. Heyman, *Biographical Dictionary of World War I* (1982); Michael Kidrow and Dan Smith, *The War Atlas: Armed Conflict, Armed Peace* (1983); Roger J. Spiller and Joseph G. Dawson, III, eds., *Dictionary of American Military Biography* (1984); U.S. Military Academy, *The West Point Atlas of American Wars, 1689–1953* (1959); *Webster's American Military Biographies* (1978). *See also* "The American Revolution," "The Civil War," and "World War II."

Women

Edward T. James, *et al.*, *Notable American Women, 1607–1950* (1971); Lina Mainiero, ed., *American Women Writers* (1979–1982); Barbara Sicherman and Carol H. Green, eds., *Notable American Women, The Modern Period* (1980).

World War II

Marcel Baudot, *et al.*, eds., *The Historical Encyclopedia of World War II* (1980); Simon Goodenough, *War Maps: Great Land Battles of World War II* (1983); Robert Goralski, *World War II Almanac, 1931–1945* (1981); John Keegan, ed., *The Rand-McNally Encyclopedia of World War II* (1977); Thomas Parrish, ed., *The Simon and Schuster Encyclopedia of World War II* (1978); Louis L. Snyder, *Louis L. Snyder's Historical Guide to World War II* (1982); U.S. Military Academy, *Campaign Atlas to the Second World War: Europe and the Mediterranean* (1980); Peter Young, ed., *The World Almanac Book of World War II* (1981). *See also* "Wars and the Military."

DECLARATION OF INDEPENDENCE IN CONGRESS, JULY 4, 1776

The unanimous declaration of the thirteen United States of America

When, in the course of human events, it becomes necessary for one people to dissolve the political bonds which have connected them with another, and to assume, among the powers of the earth, the separate and equal station to which the laws of nature and of nature's God entitle them, a decent respect to the opinions of mankind requires that they should declare the causes which impel them to the separation.

We hold these truths to be self-evident: That all men are created equal; that they are endowed by their Creator with certain unalienable rights; that among these are life, liberty, and the pursuit of happiness; that, to secure these rights, governments are instituted among men, deriving their just powers from the consent of the governed; that whenever any form of government becomes destructive of these ends, it is the right of the people to alter or to abolish it, and to institute new government, laying its foundation on such principles, and organizing its powers in such form, as to them shall seem most likely to effect their safety and happiness. Prudence, indeed, will dictate that governments long established should not be changed for light and transient causes; and accordingly all experience hath shown that mankind are more disposed to suffer, while evils are sufferable, than to right themselves by abolishing the forms to which they are accustomed. But when a long train of abuses and usurpations, pursuing invariably the same object, evinces a design to reduce them under absolute despotism, it is their right, it is their duty, to throw off such government, and to provide new guards for their future security. Such has been the patient sufferance of these colonies; and such is now the necessity which constrains them to alter their former systems of government. The history of the present King of Great Britain is a history of repeated injuries and usurpations, all having in direct object the establishment of an absolute tyranny over these states. To prove this, let facts be submitted to a candid world.

He has refused his assent to laws, the most wholesome and necessary for the public good.

He has forbidden his governors to pass laws of immediate and pressing importance, unless suspended in their operation till his assent should be obtained; and, when so suspended, he has utterly neglected to attend to them.

He has refused to pass other laws for the accommodation of large districts of people, unless those people would relinquish the right of representation in the legislature, a right inestimable to them, and formidable to tyrants only.

He has called together legislative bodies at places unusual, uncomfortable, and distant from the depository of their public records, for the sole purpose of fatiguing them into compliance with his measures.

He has dissolved representative houses repeatedly, for opposing, with manly firmness, his invasions on the rights of the people.

He has refused for a long time, after such dissolutions, to cause others to be elected; whereby the legislative powers, incapable of annihilation, have returned to the people at large for their exercise; the state remaining, in the mean time, exposed to all the dangers of invasions from without and convulsions within.

He has endeavored to prevent the population of these states; for that purpose obstructing the laws for naturalization of foreigners; refusing to pass others to encourage their migration hither, and raising the conditions of new appropriations of lands.

He has obstructed the administration of justice, by refusing his assent to laws for establishing judiciary powers.

He has made judges dependent on his will alone, for the tenure of their offices, and the amount and payment of their salaries.

He has erected a multitude of new offices, and sent hither swarms of officers to harass our people and eat out their substance.

He has kept among us, in times of peace, standing armies, without the consent of our legislatures.

He has affected to render the military independent of, and superior to, the civil power.

He has combined with others to subject us to a jurisdiction foreign to our constitution, and unacknowledged by our laws, giving his assent to their acts of pretended legislation:

For quartering large bodies of armed troops among us;

For protecting them, by a mock trial, from punishment for any murders which they should commit on the inhabitants of these states;

For cutting off our trade with all parts of the world;

For imposing taxes on us without our consent;

For depriving us, in many cases, of the benefits of trial by jury;

For transporting us beyond seas, to be tried for pretended offenses;

For abolishing the free system of English laws in a neighboring province, establishing therein an arbitrary government, and enlarging its boundaries, so as to render it at once an example and fit instrument for introducing the same absolute rule into these colonies;

For taking away our charters, abolishing our most valuable laws, and altering fundamentally the forms of our governments;

For suspending our own legislatures, and declaring themselves invested with power to legislate for us in all cases whatsoever.

He has abdicated government here, by declaring us out of his protection and waging war against us.

He has plundered our seas, ravaged our coasts, burned our towns, and destroyed the lives of our people.

He is at this time transporting large armies of foreign mercenaries to complete the works of death, desolation, and tyranny already begun with circumstances of cruelty and perfidy scarcely paralleled in the most barbarous ages, and totally unworthy the head of a civilized nation.

He has constrained our fellow-citizens, taken captive on the high seas, to bear arms against their country, to become the executioners of their friends and brethren, or to fall themselves by their hands.

He has excited domestic insurrection among us, and has endeavored to bring on the inhabitants of our frontiers the merciless Indian savages, whose known rule of warfare is an undistinguished destruction of all ages, sexes, and conditions.

In every stage of these oppressions we have petitioned for redress in the most humble terms; our repeated petitions have been answered only by repeated injury. A prince, whose character is thus marked by every act which may define a tyrant, is unfit to be the ruler of a free people.

Nor have we been wanting in our attentions to our British brethren. We have warned them, from time to time, of attempts by their legislature to extend an unwarrantable jurisdiction over us. We have reminded them of the circumstances of our emigration and settlement here. We have appealed to their native justice and magnanimity; and we have conjured them, by the ties of our common kindred, to disavow these usurpations, which would inevitably interrupt our connections and correspondence. They, too, have been deaf to the voice of justice and of consanguinity. We must, therefore, acquiesce in the necessity which denounces our separation, and hold them, as we hold the rest of mankind, enemies in war, in peace friends.

We, therefore, the representatives of the United States of America, in General Congress assembled, appealing to the Supreme Judge of the world for the rectitude of our intentions, do, in the name and by the authority of the good people of these colonies, solemnly publish and declare, that these United Colonies are, and of right ought to be, FREE AND INDEPENDENT STATES; that they are absolved from all allegiance to the British crown, and that all political connection between them and the state of Great Britain is, and ought to be, totally dissolved; and that, as free and independent states, they have full power to levy war, conclude peace, contract alliances, establish commerce, and do all other acts and things which independent states may of right do. And for the support of this declaration, with a firm reliance on the protection of Divine Providence, we mutually pledge to each other our lives, our fortunes, and our sacred honor.

JOHN HANCOCK
and fifty-five others

CONSTITUTION OF THE UNITED STATES OF AMERICA AND AMENDMENTS

Preamble

We the people of the United States, in order to form a more perfect union, establish justice, insure domestic tranquillity, provide for the common defense, promote the general welfare, and secure the blessings of liberty to ourselves and our posterity, do ordain and establish this Constitution for the United States of America.

Article I

Section 1   All legislative powers herein granted shall be vested in a Congress of the United States, which shall consist of a Senate and a House of Representatives.

Section 2   The House of Representatives shall be composed of members chosen every second year by the people of the several States, and the electors in each State shall have the qualifications requisite for electors of the most numerous branch of the State Legislature.

No person shall be a Representative who shall not have attained to the age of twenty-five years, and been seven years a citizen of the United States, and who shall not,

---

Passages no longer in effect are printed in italic type.

when elected, be an inhabitant of that State in which he shall be chosen.

Representatives and direct taxes shall be apportioned among the several States which may be included within this Union, according to their respective numbers, *which shall be determined by adding to the whole number of free persons, including those bound to service for a term of years and excluding Indians not taxed, three-fifths of all other persons.* The actual enumeration shall be made within three years after the first meeting of the Congress of the United States, and within every subsequent term of ten years, in such manner as they shall by law direct. The number of Representatives shall not exceed one for every thirty thousand, but each State shall have at least one Representative; *and until such enumeration shall be made, the State of New Hampshire shall be entitled to choose three, Massachusetts eight, Rhode Island and Providence Plantations one, Connecticut five, New York six, New Jersey four, Pennsylvania eight, Delaware one, Maryland six, Virginia ten, North Carolina five, South Carolina five, and Georgia three.*

When vacancies happen in the representation from any State, the Executive authority thereof shall issue writs of election to fill such vacancies.

The House of Representatives shall choose their Speaker and other officers; and shall have the sole power of impeachment.

Section 3   The Senate of the United States shall be composed of two Senators from each State, *chosen by the legislature thereof*, for six years; and each Senator shall have one vote.

Immediately after they shall be assembled in consequence of the first election, they shall be divided as equally as may be into three classes. The seats of the Senators of the first class shall be vacated at the expiration of the second year, of the second class at the expiration of the fourth year, and of the third class at the expiration of the sixth year, so that one-third may be chosen every second year; *and if vacancies happen by resignation or otherwise, during the recess of the legislature of any State, the Executive thereof may make temporary appointments until the next meeting of the legislature, which shall then fill such vacancies.*

No person shall be a Senator who shall not have attained to the age of thirty years, and been nine years a citizen of the United States, and who shall not, when elected, be an inhabitant of that State for which he shall be chosen.

The Vice-President of the United States shall be President of the Senate, but shall have no vote, unless they be equally divided.

The Senate shall choose their other officers, and also a President *pro tempore*, in the absence of the Vice-President, or when he shall exercise the office of President of the United States.

The Senate shall have the sole power to try all impeachments. When sitting for that purpose, they shall be on oath or affirmation. When the President of the United States is tried, the Chief Justice shall preside: and no person shall be convicted without the concurrence of two-thirds of the members present.

Judgment in cases of impeachment shall not extend further than to removal from the office, and disqualification to hold and enjoy any office of honor, trust or profit under the United States: but the party convicted shall nevertheless be liable and subject to indictment, trial, judgment and punishment, according to law.

Section 4 The times, places and manner of holding elections for Senators and Representatives shall be prescribed in each State by the legislature thereof; but the Congress may at any time by law make or alter such regulations, except as to the places of choosing Senators.

The Congress shall assemble at least once in every year, and such meeting *shall be on the first Monday in December, unless they shall by law appoint a different day.*

Section 5 Each house shall be the judge of the elections, returns and qualifications of its own members, and a majority of each shall constitute a quorum to do business; but a smaller number may adjourn from day to day, and may be authorized to compel the attendance of absent members, in such manner, and under such penalties, as each house may provide.

Each house may determine the rules of its proceedings, punish its members for disorderly behavior, and with the concurrence of two-thirds, expel a member.

Each house shall keep a journal of its proceedings, and from time to time publish the same, excepting such parts as may in their judgment require secrecy; and the yeas and nays of the members of either house on any question shall, at the desire of one-fifth of those present, be entered on the journal.

Neither house, during the session of Congress, shall, without the consent of the other, adjourn for more than three days, nor to any other place than that in which the two houses shall be sitting.

Section 6 The Senators and Representatives shall receive a compensation for their services, to be ascertained by law and paid out of the treasury of the United States. They shall in all cases except treason, felony and breach of the peace, be privileged from arrest during their attendance at the session of their respective houses, and in going to and returning from the same; and for any speech or debate in either house, they shall not be questioned in any other place.

No Senator or Representative shall, during the time for which he was elected, be appointed to any civil office under the authority of the United States, which shall have been created, or the emoluments whereof shall have been increased, during such time; and no person holding any office under the United States shall be a member of either house during his continuance in office.

Section 7 All bills for raising revenue shall originate in the House of Representatives; but the Senate may propose or concur with amendments as on other bills.

Every bill which shall have passed the House of Representatives and the Senate, shall, before it become a law, be presented to the President of the United States; if he approve he shall sign it, but if not he shall return it with objections to that house in which it originated, who shall enter the objections at large on their journal, and proceed to reconsider it. If after such reconsideration two-thirds of that house shall agree to pass the bill, it shall be sent, together with the objections, to the other house, by which it shall likewise be reconsidered, and, if approved by two-thirds of that house, it shall become a law. But in all such cases the votes of both houses shall be determined by yeas and nays, and the names of the persons voting for and against the bill shall be entered on the journal of each house respectively. If any bill shall not be returned by the President within ten days (Sundays excepted) after it shall have been presented to him, the same shall be a law, in like manner as if he had signed it, unless the Congress by their adjournment prevent its return, in which case it shall not be a law.

Every order, resolution, or vote to which the concurrence of the Senate and House of Representatives may be necessary (except on a question of adjournment) shall be presented to the President of the United States; and before the same shall take effect, shall be approved by him, or being disapproved by him, shall be repassed by two-thirds of the Senate and House of Representatives, according to the rules and limitations prescribed in the case of a bill.

Section 8 The Congress shall have power

To lay and collect taxes, duties, imposts, and excises, to pay the debts and provide for the common defense and general welfare of the United States; but all duties, imposts and excises shall be uniform throughout the United States;

To borrow money on the credit of the United States;

To regulate commerce with foreign nations, and among the several States, and with the Indian tribes;

To establish an uniform rule of naturalization, and uniform laws on the subject of bankruptcies throughout the United States;

To coin money, regulate the value thereof, and of foreign coin, and fix the standard of weights and measures;

To provide for the punishment of counterfeiting the securities and current coin of the United States;

To establish post offices and post roads;

To promote the progress of science and useful arts by securing for limited times to authors and inventors the exclusive right to their respective writings and discoveries;

To constitute tribunals inferior to the Supreme Court;

To define and punish piracies and felonies committed on the high seas and offenses against the law of nations;

To declare war, grant letters of marque and reprisal, and make rules concerning captures on land and water;

To raise and support armies, but no appropriation of money to that use shall be for a longer term than two years;

To provide and maintain a navy;

To make rules for the government and regulation of the land and naval forces;

To provide for calling forth the militia to execute the laws of the Union, suppress insurrections, and repel invasions;

To provide for organizing, arming, and disciplining the militia, and for governing such part of them as may be employed in the service of the United States, reserving to the States respectively the appointment of the officers, and the authority of training the militia according to the discipline prescribed by Congress;

To exercise exclusive legislation in all cases whatsoever, over such district (not exceeding ten miles square) as may, by cession of particular States, and the acceptance of Congress, become the seat of government of the United States, and to exercise like authority over all places purchased by the consent of the legislature of the State, in which the same shall be, for erection of forts, magazines, arsenals, dock-yards, and other needful buildings;—and

To make all laws which shall be necessary and proper for carrying into execution the foregoing powers, and all other powers vested by this Constitution in the government of the United States, or in any department or officer thereof.

Section 9   The migration or importation of such persons as any of the States now existing shall think proper to admit shall not be prohibited by the Congress prior to the year 1808; but a tax or duty may be imposed on such importation, not exceeding $10 for each person.

The privilege of the writ of habeas corpus shall not be suspended, unless when in cases of rebellion or invasion the public safety may require it.

No bill of attainder or ex post facto law shall be passed.

No capitation, or other direct, tax shall be laid, unless in proportion to the census or enumeration herein before directed to be taken.

No tax or duty shall be laid on articles exported from any State.

No preference shall be given by any regulation of commerce or revenue to the ports of one State over those of another; nor shall vessels bound to, or from, one State, be obliged to enter, clear, or pay duties in another.

No money shall be drawn from the treasury, but in consequence of appropriations made by law; and a regular statement and account of the receipts and expenditures of all public money shall be published from time to time.

No title of nobility shall be granted by the United States: and no person holding any office of profit or trust under them, shall, without the consent of the Congress, accept of any present, emolument, office, or title, of any kind whatever, from any king, prince, or foreign state.

Section 10   No State shall enter into any treaty, alliance, or confederation; grant letters of marque and reprisal; coin money; emit bills of credit; make anything but gold and silver coin a tender in payment of debts; pass any bill of attainder, ex post facto law, or law impairing the obligation of contracts, or grant any title of nobility.

No State shall, without the consent of Congress, lay any imposts or duties on imports or exports, except what may be absolutely necessary for executing its inspection laws: and the net produce of all duties and imposts, laid by any State on imports or exports, shall be for the use of the treasury of the United States; and all such laws shall be subject to the revision and control of the Congress.

No State shall, without the consent of Congress, lay any duty of tonnage, keep troops or ships of war in time of peace, enter into any agreement or compact with another State, or with a foreign power, or engage in war, unless actually invaded, or in such imminent danger as will not admit of delay.

Article II

Section 1   The executive power shall be vested in a President of the United States of America. He shall hold his office during the term of four years, and, together with the Vice-President, chosen for the same term, be elected as follows:

Each State shall appoint, in such manner as the legislature thereof may direct, a number of electors, equal to the whole number of Senators and Representatives to which the State may be entitled in the Congress; but no Senator or Representative, or person holding an office of trust or profit under the United States, shall be appointed an elector.

The electors shall meet in their respective States, and vote by ballot for two persons, of whom one at least shall not be an inhabitant of the same State with themselves. And they shall make a list of all the persons voted for, and of the number of votes for each; which list they shall sign and certify, and transmit sealed to the seat of government of the United States, directed to the President of the Senate. The President of the Senate shall, in the presence of the Senate and House of Representatives, open all the certificates, and the votes shall then be counted. The person having the greatest number of votes shall be the President, if such number be a majority of the whole number of electors appointed; and if there be more than one who have such majority, and have an equal number of votes, then the House of Representatives shall immediately choose by ballot one of them for President; and if no person have a majority, then from the five highest on the list said house shall in like manner choose the President. But in choosing the President the votes shall be taken by States, the representation from each State having one vote; a quorum for this purpose shall consist of a member or members from two-thirds of the States, and a majority of all the States shall be necessary to a choice. In every case, after the choice of the President, the person having the greatest number of votes of the electors shall be the Vice-President. But if there should remain two or more who have equal votes, the Senate shall choose from them by ballot the Vice-President.

The Congress may determine the time of choosing the electors and the day on which they shall give their votes; which day shall be the same throughout the United States.

No person except a natural-born citizen, *or a citizen of the United States at the time of the adoption of this Constitution,* shall be eligible to the office of President; neither shall any person be eligible to that office who shall not have attained to the age of thirty-five years, and been fourteen years a resident within the United States.

In case of the removal of the President from office or of his death, resignation, or inability to discharge the powers and duties of the said office, the same shall devolve on the Vice-President, and the Congress may by law provide for the case of removal, death, resignation, or inability, both of the President and Vice-President, declaring what officer shall then act as President, and such officer shall act accordingly, until the disability be removed, or a President shall be elected.

The President shall, at stated times, receive for his services a compensation, which shall neither be increased nor diminished during the period for which he shall have been elected, and he shall not receive within that period any other emolument from the United States, or any of them.

Before he enter on the execution of his office, he shall take the following oath or affirmation:—"I do solemnly swear (or affirm) that I will faithfully execute the office of the President of the United States, and will to the best of my ability preserve, protect and defend the Constitution of the United States."

Section 2   The President shall be commander in chief of the army and navy of the United States, and of the militia of the several States, when called into the actual service of the United States; he may require the opinion, in writing, of the principal officer in each of the executive departments, upon any subject relating to the duties of their respective offices, and he shall have power to grant reprieves and pardons for offenses against the United States, except in cases of impeachment.

He shall have power, by and with the advice and consent of the Senate, to make treaties, provided two-thirds of the Senators present concur; and he shall nominate, and by and with the advice and consent of the Senate, shall appoint ambassadors, other public ministers and consuls, judges of the Supreme Court, and all other officers of the United States, whose appointments are not herein otherwise provided for, and which shall be established by law: but Congress may by law vest the appointment of such inferior officers, as they think proper, in the President alone, in the courts of law, or in the heads of departments.

The President shall have power to fill up all vacancies that may happen during the recess of the Senate, by granting commissions which shall expire at the end of their next session.

Section 3   He shall from time to time give to the Congress information of the state of the Union, and recommend to their consideration such measures as he shall judge necessary and expedient; he may, on extraordinary occasions, convene both houses, or either of them, and in case of disagreement between them, with respect to the time of adjournment, he may adjourn them to such time as he shall think proper; he shall receive ambassadors and other public ministers; he shall take care that the laws be faithfully executed, and shall commission all the officers of the United States.

Section 4   The President, Vice-President and all civil officers of the United States shall be removed from office on impeachment for, and on conviction of, treason, bribery, or other high crimes and misdemeanors.

Article III

Section 1   The judicial power of the United States shall be vested in one Supreme Court, and in such inferior courts as the Congress may from time to time ordain and establish. The judges, both of the Supreme and inferior courts, shall hold their offices during good behavior, and shall, at stated times, receive for their services a compensation which shall not be diminished during their continuance in office.

Section 2   The judicial power shall extend to all cases, in law and equity, arising under this Constitution, the laws of the United States, and treaties made, or which shall be made, under their authority;—to all cases affecting ambassadors, other public ministers and consuls;—to all cases of admiralty and maritime jurisdiction;—to controversies to which the United States shall be a party;—to controversies between two or more States;—*between a State and citizens of another State*;—between citizens of different States;—between citizens of the same State claiming lands under grants of different States, and between a State, or the citizens thereof, and foreign states, citizens or subjects.

In all cases affecting ambassadors, other public ministers and consuls, and those in which a State shall be party, the Supreme Court shall have original jurisdiction. In all the other cases before mentioned, the Supreme Court shall have appellate jurisdiction, both as to law and fact, with such exceptions, and under such regulations, as the Congress shall make.

The trial of all crimes, except in cases of impeachment, shall be by jury; and such trial shall be held in the State where said crimes shall have been committed; but when not committed within any State, the trial shall be at such place or places as the Congress may by law have directed.

Section 3   Treason against the United States shall consist only in levying war against them, or in adhering to their enemies, giving them aid and comfort. No person shall be convicted of treason unless on the testimony of two witnesses to the same overt act, or on confession in open court.

The Congress shall have power to declare the punishment of treason, but no attainder of treason shall work corruption of blood, or forfeiture except during the life of the person attainted.

Article IV

Section 1   Full faith and credit shall be given in each State to the public acts, records, and judicial proceedings of every other State. And the Congress may by general laws prescribe the manner in which such acts, records, and proceedings shall be proved, and the effect thereof.

Section 2   The citizens of each State shall be entitled to all privileges and immunities of citizens in the several States.

A person charged in any State with treason, felony, or other crime, who shall flee from justice, and be found in another State, shall on demand of the executive authority of the State from which he fled, be delivered up, to be removed to the State having jurisdiction of the crime.

No person held to service or labor in one State, under the laws thereof, escaping into another, shall, in consequence of any law or regulation therein, be discharged from such service or labor, but shall be delivered up on claim of the party to whom such service or labor may be due.

Section 3   New States may be admitted by the Congress into this Union; but no new State shall be formed or erected within the jurisdiction of any other State; nor any State be formed by the junction of two or more States, or parts of States, without the consent of the legislatures of the States concerned as well as of the Congress.

The Congress shall have power to dispose of and make all needful rules and regulations respecting the territory or other property belonging to the United States; and nothing in this Constitution shall be so construed as to prejudice any claims of the United States, or of any particular State.

Section 4   The United States shall guarantee to every State in this Union a republican form of government, and shall protect each of them against invasion; and on application of the legislature, or of the executive (when the legislature cannot be convened), against domestic violence.

Article V

The Congress, whenever two-thirds of both houses shall deem it necessary, shall propose amendments to this Constitution, or, on the application of the legislatures of two-thirds of the several States, shall call a convention for proposing amendments, which, in either case, shall be valid to all intents and purposes, as part of this Constitution, when ratified by the legislatures of three-fourths of the several States, or by conventions in three-fourths thereof, as the one or the other mode of ratification may be proposed by the Congress; provided *that no amendments which may be made prior to the year one thousand eight hundred and eight shall in any manner affect the first and fourth clauses in the ninth section of the first article*; and that no State, without its consent, shall be deprived of its equal suffrage in the Senate.

Article VI

All debts contracted and engagements entered into, before the adoption of this Constitution, shall be as valid against the United States under this Constitution, as under the Confederation.

This Constitution, and the laws of the United States which shall be made in pursuance thereof; and all treaties made, or which shall be made, under the authority of the United States, shall be the supreme law of the land; and the judges in every State shall be bound thereby, anything in the Constitution or laws of any State to the contrary notwithstanding.

The Senators and Representatives before mentioned, and the members of the several State legislatures, and all executive and judicial officers, both of the United States and of the several States, shall be bound by oath or affirmation to support this Constitution; but no religious test shall ever be required as a qualification to any office or public trust under the United States.

Article VII

The ratification of the conventions of nine States shall be sufficient for the establishment of this Constitution between the States so ratifying the same.

Done in Convention by the unanimous consent of the States present, the seventeenth day of September in the year of our Lord one thousand seven hundred and eighty-seven and of the Independence of the United States of America the twelfth. In witness whereof we have hereunto subscribed our names.

GEORGE WASHINGTON
and thirty-seven others

*Amendments to the Constitution**

Amendment I

Congress shall make no law respecting an establishment of religion, or prohibiting the free exercise thereof; or abridging the freedom of speech, or of the press; or the right of the people peaceably to assemble, and to petition the government for a redress of grievances.

Amendment II

A well-regulated militia being necessary to the security of a free State, the right of the people to keep and bear arms shall not be infringed.

Amendment III

No soldier shall, in time of peace, be quartered in any house without the consent of the owner, nor in time of war, but in a manner to be prescribed by law.

Amendment IV

The right of the people to be secure in their persons, houses, papers, and effects, against unreasonable searches and seizures, shall not be violated, and no warrants shall issue but upon probable cause, supported by oath or affirmation, and particularly describing the place to be searched, and the persons or things to be seized.

---

*The first ten Amendments (the Bill of Rights) were adopted in 1791.

Amendment V

No person shall be held to answer for a capital, or otherwise infamous crime, unless on a presentment or indictment of a grand jury, except in cases arising in the land or naval forces, or in the militia, when in actual service in time of war or public danger; nor shall any person be subject for the same offense to be twice put in jeopardy of life or limb; nor shall be compelled in any criminal case to be a witness against himself, nor be deprived of life, liberty, or property, without due process of law; nor shall private property be taken for public use without just compensation.

Amendment VI

In all criminal prosecutions, the accused shall enjoy the right to a speedy and public trial, by an impartial jury of the State and district wherein the crime shall have been committed, which district shall have been previously ascertained by law, and to be informed of the nature and cause of the accusation; to be confronted with the witnesses against him; to have compulsory process for obtaining witnesses in his favor, and to have the assistance of counsel for his defense.

Amendment VII

In suits at common law, where the value in controversy shall exceed twenty dollars, the right of trial by jury shall be preserved, and no fact tried by a jury shall be otherwise reexamined in any court of the United States, than according to the rules of the common law.

Amendment VIII

Excessive bail shall not be required, nor excessive fines imposed, nor cruel and unusual punishments inflicted.

Amendment IX

The enumeration in the Constitution, of certain rights, shall not be construed to deny or disparage others retained by the people.

Amendment X

The powers not delegated to the United States by the Constitution, nor prohibited by it to the States, are reserved to the States respectively, or to the people.

Amendment XI
[Adopted 1798]

The judicial power of the United States shall not be construed to extend to any suit in law or equity, commenced or prosecuted against one of the United States by citizens of another State, or by citizens or subjects of any foreign state.

Amendment XII
[Adopted 1804]

The electors shall meet in their respective States, and vote by ballot for President and Vice-President, one of whom, at least, shall not be an inhabitant of the same State with themselves; they shall name in their ballots the person voted for as President, and in distinct ballots the person voted for as Vice-President, and they shall make distinct lists of all persons voted for as President, and of all persons voted for as Vice-President, and of the number of votes for each, which lists they shall sign and certify, and transmit sealed to the seat of government of the United States, directed to the President of the Senate;—the President of the Senate shall, in the presence of the Senate and House of Representatives, open all the certificates and the votes shall then be counted;—the person having the greatest number of votes for President shall be the President, if such number be a majority of the whole number of electors appointed; and if no person have such majority, then from the persons having the highest numbers not exceeding three on the list of those voted for as President, the House of Representatives shall choose immediately, by ballot, the President. But in choosing the President, the votes shall be taken by States, the representation from each State having one vote; a quorum for this purpose shall consist of a member or members from two-thirds of the States, and a majority of all the States shall be necessary to a choice. And if the House of Representatives shall not choose a President whenever the right of choice shall devolve upon them, before *the fourth day of March* next following, then the Vice-President shall act as President, as in the case of the death or other constitutional disability of the President.

The person having the greatest number of votes as Vice-President shall be the Vice-President, if such number be a majority of the whole number of electors appointed; and if no person have a majority, then from the two highest numbers on the list the Senate shall choose the Vice-President; a quorum for the purpose shall consist of two-thirds of the whole number of Senators, and a majority of the whole number shall be necessary to a choice. But no person constitutionally ineligible to the office of President shall be eligible to that of Vice-President of the United States.

Amendment XIII
[Adopted 1865]

Section 1   Neither slavery nor involuntary servitude, except as a punishment for crime whereof the party shall have been duly convicted, shall exist within the United States, or any place subject to their jurisdiction.

Section 2   Congress shall have power to enforce this article by appropriate legislation.

Amendment XIV
[Adopted 1868]

Section 1   All persons born or naturalized in the United States, and subject to the jurisdiction thereof, are citizens of the United States and of the State wherein they reside. No State shall make or enforce any law which shall abridge the privileges or immunities of citizens of the United States; nor shall any State deprive any person of life, liberty, or property, without due process of law; nor deny to any person within its jurisdiction the equal protection of the laws.

Section 2   Representatives shall be apportioned among the several States according to their respective numbers, counting the whole number of persons in each State, excluding Indians not taxed. But when the right to vote at any election for the choice of Electors for President and Vice-President of the United States, Representatives in Congress, the executive and judicial officers of a State, or the members of the legislature thereof, is denied to any of the male inhabitants of such State, being twenty-one years of age and citizens of the United States, or in any way abridged, except for participation in rebellion, or other crime, the basis of representation therein shall be reduced in the proportion which the number of such male citizens shall bear to the whole number of male citizens twenty-one years of age in such State.

Section 3   No person shall be a Senator or Representative in Congress, or Elector of President and Vice-President, or hold any office, civil or military, under the United States, or under any State, who, having previously taken an oath, as a member of Congress, or as an officer of the United States, or as a member of any State legislature, or as an executive or judicial officer of any State, to support the Constitution of the United States, shall have engaged in insurrection or rebellion against the same, or given aid or comfort to the enemies thereof. Congress may, by a vote of two-thirds of each house, remove such disability.

Section 4   The validity of the public debt of the United States, authorized by law, including debts incurred for payment of pensions and bounties for services in suppressing insurrection or rebellion, shall not be questioned. But neither the United States nor any State shall assume or pay any debt or obligation incurred in aid of insurrection or rebellion against the United States, or any claim for the loss or emancipation of any slave; but all such debts, obligations, and claims shall be held illegal and void.

Section 5 The Congress shall have power to enforce, by appropriate legislation, the provisions of this article.

Amendment XV
[Adopted 1870]

Section 1 The right of citizens of the United States to vote shall not be denied or abridged by the United States or by any State on account of race, color, or previous condition of servitude.

Section 2 The Congress shall have power to enforce this article by appropriate legislation.

Amendment XVI
[Adopted 1913]

The Congress shall have power to lay and collect taxes on incomes, from whatever source derived, without apportionment among the several States, and without regard to any census or enumeration.

Amendment XVII
[Adopted 1913]

Section 1 The Senate of the United States shall be composed of two Senators from each State, elected by the people thereof, for six years; and each Senator shall have one vote. The electors in each State shall have the qualifications requisite for electors of [voters for] the most numerous branch of the State legislatures.

Section 2 When vacancies happen in the representation of any State in the Senate, the executive authority of such State shall issue writs of election to fill such vacancies: Provided, that the Legislature of any State may empower the executive thereof to make temporary appointments until the people fill the vacancies by election as the Legislature may direct.

Section 3 This amendment shall not be so construed as to affect the election or term of any Senator chosen before it becomes valid as part of the Constitution.

Amendment XVIII
[Adopted 1919; Repealed 1933]

Section 1 After one year from the ratification of this article the manufacture, sale, or transportation of intoxicating liquors within, the importation thereof into, or the exportation thereof from the United States and all territory subject to the jurisdiction thereof, for beverage purposes, is hereby prohibited.

Section 2 The Congress and the several States shall have concurrent power to enforce this article by appropriate legislation.

Section 3 This article shall be inoperative unless it shall have been ratified as an amendment to the Constitution by the legislatures of the several States, as provided by the Constitution, within seven years from the date of the submission thereof to the States by the Congress.

Amendment XIX
[Adopted 1920]

Section 1 The right of citizens of the United States to vote shall not be denied or abridged by the United States or by any State on account of sex.

Section 2 The Congress shall have power to enforce this article by appropriate legislation.

Amendment XX
[Adopted 1933]

Section 1 The terms of the President and Vice-President shall end at noon on the 20th day of January, and the terms of Senators and Representatives at noon on the 3d day of January, of the years in which such terms would have ended if this article had not been ratified; and the terms of their successors shall then begin.

Section 2 The Congress shall assemble at least once in every year, and such meeting shall begin at noon on the 3d day of January, unless they shall by law appoint a different day.

Section 3 If, at the time fixed for the beginning of the term of the President, the President-elect shall have died, the Vice-President-elect shall become President. If a President shall not have been chosen before the time fixed for the beginning of his term, or if the President-elect shall have failed to qualify, then the Vice-President-elect shall act as President until a President shall have qualified; and the Congress may by law provide for the case wherein neither a President-elect nor a Vice-President-elect shall have qualified, declaring who shall then act as President, or the manner in which one who is to act shall be selected, and such persons shall act accordingly until a President or Vice-President shall have qualified.

Section 4 The Congress may by law provide for the case of the death of any of the persons from whom the House of Representatives may choose a President whenever the right of choice shall have devolved upon them, and for the case of the death of any of the persons from whom the Senate may choose a Vice-President whenever the right of choice shall have devolved upon them.

Section 5 Sections 1 and 2 shall take effect on the 15th day of October following the ratification of this article.

Section 6 This article shall be inoperative unless it shall have been ratified as an amendment to the Constitution by the Legislatures of three-fourths of the several States within seven years from the date of its submission.

Amendment XXI
[Adopted 1933]

Section 1 The eighteenth article of amendment to the Constitution of the United States is hereby repealed.

Section 2 The transportation or importation into any State, Territory, or Possession of the United States for delivery or use therein of intoxicating liquors, in violation of the laws thereof, is hereby prohibited.

Section 3 This article shall be inoperative unless it shall have been ratified as an amendment to the Constitution by conventions in the several States, as provided in the Constitution, within seven years from the date of submission thereof to the States by the Congress.

Amendment XXII
[Adopted 1951]

Section 1 No person shall be elected to the office of President more than twice, and no person who has held the office of President, or acted as President, for more than two years of a term to which some other person was elected President shall be elected to the office of President more than once. But this article shall not apply to any person holding the office of President when this article was proposed by the Congress, and shall not prevent any person who may be holding the office of President, or acting as President, during the term within which this article becomes operative from holding the office of President or acting as President during the remainder of such term.

Section 2 This article shall be inoperative unless it shall have been ratified as an amendment to the Constitution by the legislatures of three-fourths of the several States within seven years from the date of its submission to the States by the Congress.

Amendment XXIII
[Adopted 1961]

Section 1 The District constituting the seat of Government

of the United States shall appoint in such manner as the Congress may direct:

A number of electors of President and Vice-President equal to the whole number of Senators and Representatives in Congress to which the District would be entitled if it were a State, but in no event more than the least populous State; they shall be in addition to those appointed by the States, but they shall be considered for the purposes of the election of President and Vice-President, to be electors appointed by a State; and they shall meet in the District and perform such duties as provided by the twelfth article of amendment.

Section 2 The Congress shall have the power to enforce this article by appropriate legislation.

Amendment XXIV
[Adopted 1964]

Section 1 The right of citizens of the United States to vote in any primary or other election for President or Vice-President, for electors for President or Vice-President, or for Senator or Representative in Congress, shall not be denied or abridged by the United States or any State by reason of failure to pay any poll tax or other tax.

Section 2 The Congress shall have the power to enforce this article by appropriate legislation.

Amendment XXV
[Adopted 1967]

Section 1 In case of the removal of the President from office or of his death or resignation, the Vice President shall become President.

Section 2 Whenever there is a vacancy in the office of the Vice President, the President shall nominate a Vice President who shall take office upon confirmation by a majority vote of both Houses of Congress.

Section 3 Whenever the President transmits to the President pro tempore of the Senate and the Speaker of the House of Representatives his written declaration that he is unable to discharge the powers and duties of his office, and until he transmits to them a written declaration to the contrary, such powers and duties shall be discharged by the Vice President as Acting President.

Section 4 Whenever the Vice President and a majority of either the principal officers of the executive departments or of such other body as Congress may by law provide, transmit to the President pro tempore of the Senate and the Speaker of the House of Representatives their written declaration that the President is unable to discharge the powers and duties of his office, the Vice President shall immediately assume the powers and duties of the office as Acting President.

Thereafter, when the President transmits to the President pro tempore of the Senate and the Speaker of the House of Representatives his written declaration that no inability exists, he shall resume the powers and duties of his office unless the Vice President and a majority of either the principal officers of the executive department[s] or of such other body as Congress may by law provide, transmit within four days to the President pro tempore of the Senate and the Speaker of the House of Representatives their written declaration that the President is unable to discharge the powers and duties of his office. Thereupon Congress shall decide the issue, assembling within forty-eight hours for that purpose if not in session. If the Congress, within twenty-one days after receipt of the latter written declaration, or, if Congress is not in session, within twenty-one days after Congress is required to assemble, determines by two-thirds vote of both Houses that the President is unable to discharge the powers and duties of his office, the Vice President shall continue to discharge the same as Acting President; otherwise, the President shall resume the powers and duties of his office.

Amendment XXVI
[Adopted 1971]

Section 1 The right of citizens of the United States, who are eighteen years of age or older, to vote shall not be denied or abridged by the United States or by any State on account of age.

Section 2 The Congress shall have power to enforce this article by appropriate legislation.

Population of the United States

Year	Number of States	Population	Percent Increase	Population Per Square Mile	Percent Urban/ Rural	Percent Male/ Female	Percent White/ Nonwhite	Persons Per Household	Median Age
1790	13	3,929,214		4.5	5.1/94.9	NA/NA	80.7/19.3	5.79	NA
1800	16	5,308,483	35.1	6.1	6.1/93.9	NA/NA	81.1/18.9	NA	NA
1810	17	7,239,881	36.4	4.3	7.3/92.7	NA/NA	81.0/19.0	NA	NA
1820	23	9,638,453	33.1	5.5	7.2/92.8	50.8/49.2	81.6/18.4	NA	16.7
1830	24	12,866,020	33.5	7.4	8.8/91.2	50.8/49.2	81.9/18.1	NA	17.2
1840	26	17,069,453	32.7	9.8	10.8/89.2	50.9/49.1	83.2/16.8	NA	17.8
1850	31	23,191,876	35.9	7.9	15.3/84.7	51.0/49.0	84.3/15.7	5.55	18.9
1860	33	31,443,321	35.6	10.6	19.8/80.2	51.2/48.8	85.6/14.4	5.28	19.4
1870	37	39,818,449	26.6	13.4	25.7/74.3	50.6/49.4	86.2/13.8	5.09	20.2
1880	38	50,155,783	26.0	16.9	28.2/71.8	50.9/49.1	86.5/13.5	5.04	20.9
1890	44	62,947,714	25.5	21.2	35.1/64.9	51.2/48.8	87.5/12.5	4.93	22.0
1900	45	75,994,575	20.7	25.6	39.6/60.4	51.1/48.9	87.9/12.1	4.76	22.9
1910	46	91,972,266	21.0	31.0	45.6/54.4	51.5/48.5	88.9/11.1	4.54	24.1
1920	48	105,710,620	14.9	35.6	51.2/48.8	51.0/49.0	89.7/10.3	4.34	25.3
1930	48	122,775,046	16.1	41.2	56.1/43.9	50.6/49.4	89.8/10.2	4.11	26.4
1940	48	131,669,275	7.2	44.2	56.5/43.5	50.2/49.8	89.8/10.2	3.67	29.0
1950	48	150,697,361	14.5	50.7	64.0/36.0	49.7/50.3	89.5/10.5	3.37	30.2
1960	50	179,323,175	18.5	50.6	69.9/30.1	49.3/50.7	88.6/11.4	3.33	29.5
1970	50	203,302,031	13.4	57.4	73.5/26.5	48.7/51.3	87.6/12.4	3.14	28.0
1980	50	226,545,805	11.4	64.0	73.7/26.3	48.6/51.4	86.0/14.0	2.76	30.0
1983	50	236,600,000*	4.4	64.0	NA/NA	48.7/51.3	85.3/14.7	2.73	30.9

*1984 figure.
NA = Not available.

Vital Statistics

Year	Birth Rate*	Death Rate*	Life Expectancy in Years					Marriage Rate	Divorce Rate
			Total Population	White Females	Nonwhite Females	White Males	Nonwhite Males		
1790	NA	NA	NA	NA	NA	NA	NA	NA	NA
1800	55.0	NA	NA	NA	NA	NA	NA	NA	NA
1810	54.3	NA	NA	NA	NA	NA	NA	NA	NA
1820	55.2	NA	NA	NA	NA	NA	NA	NA	NA
1830	51.4	NA	NA	NA	NA	NA	NA	NA	NA
1840	51.8	NA	NA	NA	NA	NA	NA	NA	NA
1850	43.3	NA	NA	NA	NA	NA	NA	NA	NA
1860	44.3	NA	NA	NA	NA	NA	NA	NA	NA
1870	38.3	NA	NA	NA	NA	NA	NA	NA	NA
1880	39.8	NA	NA	NA	NA	NA	NA	NA	NA
1890	31.5	NA	NA	NA	NA	NA	NA	NA	NA
1900	32.3	17.2	47.3	48.7	33.5	46.6	32.5	NA	NA
1910	30.1	14.7	50.0	52.0	37.5	48.6	33.8	NA	NA
1920	27.7	13.0	54.1	55.6	45.2	54.4	45.5	12.0	1.6
1930	21.3	11.3	59.7	63.5	49.2	59.7	47.3	9.2	1.6
1940	19.4	10.8	62.9	66.6	54.9	62.1	51.5	12.1	2.0
1950	24.1	9.6	68.2	72.2	62.9	66.5	59.1	11.1	2.6
1960	23.7	9.5	69.7	74.1	66.3	67.4	61.1	8.5	2.2
1970	18.4	9.5	70.9	75.6	69.4	68.0	61.3	10.6	3.5
1980	15.9	8.8	73.7	78.1	73.6	70.7	65.3	10.6	5.2
1983	15.5	8.6	74.7	78.8	75.3	71.6	67.1	10.5	5.0

Data per one thousand for Birth, Death, Marriage, and Divorce rates.

NA = Not available.

*Data for 1800, 1810, 1830, 1850, 1870, and 1890 for whites only.

Immigrants to the United States

Immigration Totals by Decade

Years	Number	Years	Number
1820–1830	151,824	1911–1920	5,735,811
1831–1840	599,125	1921–1930	4,107,209
1841–1850	1,713,251	1931–1940	528,431
1851–1860	2,598,214	1941–1950	1,035,039
1861–1870	2,314,824	1951–1960	2,515,479
1871–1880	2,812,191	1961–1970	3,321,677
1881–1890	5,246,613	1971–1980	4,493,000
1891–1900	3,687,546	**Total**	49,655,620
1901–1910	8,795,386		

Source: U.S. Bureau of the Census, *Historical Statistics of the United States, Colonial Times to 1970* (1975), Part I, pp. 105–106; U.S. Bureau of the Census, *Statistical Abstract of the United States, 1984* (1983), p. 88.

Regional Origins of Immigrants (in percentages)

Period	Europe				Western Hemisphere	Asia	All Other
	Total Europe	North and West[a]	East and Central[b]	South and Other[c]			
1821–1830	69.2	67.1	—	2.1	8.4	—	22.4
1831–1840	82.8	81.8	—	1.0	5.5	—	11.7
1841–1850	93.3	92.9	0.1	0.3	3.6	—	3.1
1851–1860	94.4	93.6	0.1	0.8	2.9	1.6	1.1
1861–1870	89.2	87.8	0.5	0.9	7.2	2.8	0.8
1871–1880	80.8	73.6	4.5	2.7	14.4	4.4	0.4
1881–1890	90.3	72.0	11.9	6.3	8.1	1.3	0.3
1891–1900	96.5	44.5	32.8	19.1	1.1	1.9	0.5
1901–1910	92.5	21.7	44.5	26.3	4.1	2.8	0.6
1911–1920	76.3	17.4	33.4	25.5	19.9	3.4	0.4
1921–1930	60.3	31.7	14.4	14.3	36.9	2.4	0.4
1931–1940	65.9	38.8	11.0	16.1	30.3	2.8	0.9
1941–1950	60.1	47.5	4.6	7.9	34.3	3.1	2.5
1951–1960	52.8	17.7	24.3	10.8	39.6	6.0	1.6
1961–1970	33.8	11.7	9.4	12.9	51.7	12.9	1.7
1971–1979	18.4	4.8	4.4	9.2	44.9	34.1	2.6

Note: dash indicates less than 0.1 percent.

[a]Great Britain, Ireland, Norway, Sweden, Denmark, Iceland, Netherlands, Belgium, Luxembourg, Switzerland, France.

[b]Germany (Austria included, 1938–1945), Poland, Czechoslovakia (since 1920), Yugoslavia (since 1920), Hungary (since 1861), Austria (since 1861, except 1938–1945), U.S.S.R. (excludes Asian U.S.S.R. between 1931 and 1963), Latvia, Estonia, Lithuania, Finland, Romania, Bulgaria, Turkey (in Europe).

[c]Italy, Spain, Portugal, Greece, and other European countries not classified elsewhere.

Source: Stephan Thernstrom, ed., *Harvard Encyclopedia of American Ethnic Groups* (1980), p. 480; and U.S. Bureau of the Census, *Statistical Abstract of the United States, 1984* (1983), p. 9. Reprinted by permission of Harvard University Press.

Major Sources of Immigrants by Country (in thousands)

Period	Germany	Italy	Britain	Ireland	Austria-Hungary	Russia[a]	Canada	Denmark, Norway, Sweden[b]	Mexico	West Indies
1820–1830	8	—	27	54	—	—	2	—	5	4
1831–1840	152	2	76	207	—	—	14	2	7	12
1841–1850	435	2	267	781	—	—	42	14	3	14
1851–1860	952	9	424	914	—	—	59	25	3	11
1861–1870	787	12	607	436	8	3	154	126	2	9
1871–1880	718	56	548	437	73	39	384	243	5	14
1881–1890	1,453	307	807	655	354	213	393	656	2[c]	29
1891–1900	505	652	272	388	593	505	3	372	—	—[d]
1901–1910	341	2,046	526	339	2,145	1,597	179	505	50	108
1911–1920	144	1,110	341	146	896	922	742	203	219	123
1921–1930	412	455	330	221	64	89	925	198	459	75
1931–1940	114	68	29	13	11	7	109	11	22	16
1941–1950	227	58	132	28	28	4	172	27	61	50
1951–1960	478	185	192	57	104	6	378	57	300	123
1961–1970	191	214	206	40	26	7	413	43	454	470
1971–1979	68	124	122	11	15	31	156	13	584	668
Total	6,985	5,300	4,906	4,727	4,317	3,423	4,125	2,495	2,176	1,726

Notes: Numbers are rounded. Dash indicates less than one thousand.

[a]Includes Finland, Latvia, Estonia, and Lithuania.

[b]Includes Iceland.

[c]Figure for 1881–1885 only.

[d]Figure for 1894–1900 only.

Source: U.S. Bureau of the Census, *Historical Statistics of the United States: Colonial Times to 1970* (1975), Part I, pp. 105–108; U.S. Bureau of the Census, *Statistical Abstract of the United States, 1984* (1983), p. 91.

The American Farm

Year	Farm Population (in thousands)	Percent of Total Population	Number of Farms (in thousands)	Total Acres (in thousands)	Average Acreage Per Farm	Corn Production (millions of bushels)	Wheat Production (millions of bushels)
1850	NA	NA	1,449	293,561	203	592[a]	100[a]
1860	NA	NA	2,044	407,213	199	839[b]	173[b]
1870	NA	NA	2,660	407,735	153	1,125	254
1880	21,973	43.8	4,009	536,082	134	1,707	502
1890	24,771	42.3	4,565	623,219	137	1,650	449
1900	29,875	41.9	5,740	841,202	147	2,662	599
1910	32,077	34.9	6,366	881,431	139	2,853	625
1920	31,974	30.1	6,454	958,677	149	3,071	843
1930	30,529	24.9	6,295	990,112	157	2,080	887
1940	30,547	23.2	6,102	1,065,114	175	2,457	815
1950	23,048	15.3	5,388	1,161,420	216	3,075	1,019
1960	15,635	8.7	3,962	1,176,946	297	4,314	1,355
1970	9,712	4.8	2,949	1,102,769	374	4,200	1,370
1980	6,051	2.7	2,428	1,042,000	427	6,600	2,400
1983	5,787	2.5	2,370	1,024,000	432	4,200	2,400

[a]Figure for 1849.
[b]Figure for 1859.
NA = Not available.

The American Worker

Year	Total Number of Workers	Males as Percent of Total Workers	Females as Percent of Total Workers	Married Women as Percent of Female Workers	Female Workers as Percent of Female Population	Percent of Labor Force Unemployed	Percent of Workers in Labor Unions
1870	12,506,000	85	15	NA	NA	NA	NA
1880	17,392,000	85	15	NA	NA	NA	NA
1890	23,318,000	83	17	13.9	18.9	4 (1894 = 18%)	NA
1900	29,073,000	82	18	15.4	20.6	5	3
1910	38,167,000	79	21	24.7	25.4	6	6
1920	41,614,000	79	21	23.0	23.7	5 (1921 = 12%)	12
1930	48,830,000	78	22	28.9	24.8	9 (1933 = 25%)	7
1940	53,011,000	76	24	36.4	27.4	15 (1944 = 1%)	27
1950	59,643,000	72	28	52.1	31.4	5	25
1960	69,877,000	68	32	59.9	37.7	5.4	26
1970	82,049,000	63	37	63.4	43.3	4.8	25
1980	108,544,000	58	42	59.7	51.5	7.0	23
1983	113,226,000	57	43	58.9	52.9	9.5	19[a]

[a]1984 figure.
NA = Not available.

Year	Gross National Product (GNP) (in $ billions)	Steel Production (in short tons)	Automobiles Registered	New Housing Starts	Foreign Trade Exports (in millions of dollars)	Imports
1790	NA	NA	NA	NA	20	23
1800	NA	NA	NA	NA	71	91
1810	NA	NA	NA	NA	67	85
1820	NA	NA	NA	NA	70	74
1830	NA	NA	NA	NA	74	71
1840	NA	NA	NA	NA	132	107
1850	NA	NA	NA	NA	152	178
1860	NA	13,000	NA	NA	400	362
1870	7.4[a]	77,000	NA	NA	451	462
1880	11.2[b]	1,397,000	NA	NA	853	761
1890	13.1	4,779,000	NA	328,000	910	823
1900	18.7	11,227,000	8,000	189,000	1,499	930
1910	35.3	28,330,000	458,300	387,000 (1918 = 118,000)	1,919	1,646
1920	91.5	46,183,000	8,131,500	247,000 (1925 = 937,000)	8,664	5,784
1930	90.7	44,591,000	23,034,700	330,000 (1933 = 93,000)	4,013	3,500
1940	100.0	66,983,000	27,465,800	603,000 (1944 = 142,000)	4,030	7,433
1950	286.5	96,836,000	40,339,000	1,952,000	10,816	9,125
1960	506.5	99,282,000	61,682,300	1,365,000	19,600	15,046
1970	992.7	131,514,000	89,279,800	1,469,000	42,700	40,189
1980	2,631.7	111,800,000	121,600,000	1,313,000	220,783	244,871
1983	3,304.8	84,600,000	125,382,000	1,712,000	200,538	258,048

[a]Figure is average for 1869–1878.
[b]Figure is average for 1879–1888.
NA = Not available.

Federal Spending and Debt

Year	Defense[a]	Interest on Public Debt[a]	Veterans Benefits and Services[a]	Income Security[ad]	Health[a]	Education and Manpower[a]	Federal Debt (dollars)
1790	14.9	55.0	4.1[b]	NA	NA	NA	75,463,000[c]
1800	55.7	31.3	.6	NA	NA	NA	82,976,000
1810	48.4 (1814 = 79.7)	34.9	1.0	NA	NA	NA	53,173,000
1820	38.4	28.1	17.6	NA	NA	NA	91,016,000
1830	52.9	12.6	9.0	NA	NA	NA	48,565,000
1840	54.3 (1847 = 80.7)	.7	10.7	NA	NA	NA	3,573,000
1850	43.8	1.0	4.7	NA	NA	NA	63,453,000
1860	44.2 (1865 = 88.9)	5.0	1.7	NA	NA	NA	64,844,000
1870	25.7	41.7	9.2	NA	NA	NA	2,436,453,000
1880	19.3	35.8	21.2	NA	NA	NA	2,090,909,000
1890	20.9 (1899 = 48.6)	11.4	33.6	NA	NA	NA	1,222,397,000
1900	36.6	7.7	27.0	NA	NA	NA	1,263,417,000
1910	45.1 (1919 = 59.5)	3.1	23.2	NA	NA	NA	1,146,940,000
1920	37.1	16.0	3.4	NA	NA	NA	24,299,321,000
1930	25.3	19.9	6.6	NA	NA	NA	16,185,310,000
1940	15.7 (1945 = 85.7)	10.9	6.5	15.2	.5	.8	42,967,531,000
1950	30.4 (1953 = 59.4)	13.3	20.5	10.9	.6	.5	257,357,352,000
1960	49.0	7.5	5.9	20.6	.9	1.1	286,330,761,000
1970	40.1	7.3	4.4	26.6	3.0	4.4	370,918,707,000
1980	23.6	9.1	3.7	41.1	4.0	5.3	914,300,000,000
1983	26.4	11.3	3.1	43.4	3.6	3.3	1,381,900,000,000

[a]Figures represent percentage of total federal spending for each category.
[b]1789–1791 figure.
[c]1791 figure.
[d]Includes Social Security and Medicare.
NA = Not available.

TERRITORIAL EXPANSION OF THE UNITED STATES

Territory	Date Acquired	Square Miles	How Acquired
Original states and territories	1783	888,685	Treaty with Great Britain
Louisiana Purchase	1803	827,192	Purchase from France
Florida	1819	72,003	Treaty with Spain
Texas	1845	390,143	Annexation of independent nation
Oregon	1846	285,580	Treaty with Great Britain
Mexican Cession	1848	529,017	Conquest from Mexico
Gadsden Purchase	1853	29,640	Purchase from Mexico
Alaska	1867	589,757	Purchase from Russia
Hawaii	1898	6,450	Annexation of independent nation
The Philippines	1899	115,600	Conquest from Spain (granted independence in 1946)
Puerto Rico	1899	3,435	Conquest from Spain
Guam	1899	212	Conquest from Spain
American Samoa	1900	76	Treaty with Germany and Great Britain
Panama Canal Zone	1904	553	Treaty with Panama (returned to Panama by treaty in 1978)
Corn Islands	1914	4	Treaty with Nicaragua (returned to Nicaragua by treaty in 1971)
Virgin Islands	1917	133	Purchase from Denmark
Pacific Islands Trust (Micronesia)	1947	8,489	Trusteeship under United Nations (some granted independence)
All others (Midway, Wake, and other islands)		42	

ADMISSION OF STATES INTO THE UNION

State	Date of Admission	State	Date of Admission
1. Delaware	December 7, 1787	26. Michigan	January 26, 1837
2. Pennsylvania	December 12, 1787	27. Florida	March 3, 1845
3. New Jersey	December 18, 1787	28. Texas	December 29, 1845
4. Georgia	January 2, 1788	29. Iowa	December 28, 1846
5. Connecticut	January 9, 1788	30. Wisconsin	May 29, 1848
6. Massachusetts	February 6, 1788	31. California	September 9, 1850
7. Maryland	April 28, 1788	32. Minnesota	May 11, 1858
8. South Carolina	May 23, 1788	33. Oregon	February 14, 1859
9. New Hampshire	June 21, 1788	34. Kansas	January 29, 1861
10. Virginia	June 25, 1788	35. West Virginia	June 20, 1863
11. New York	July 26, 1788	36. Nevada	October 31, 1864
12. North Carolina	November 21, 1789	37. Nebraska	March 1, 1867
13. Rhode Island	May 29, 1790	38. Colorado	August 1, 1876
14. Vermont	March 4, 1791	39. North Dakota	November 2, 1889
15. Kentucky	June 1, 1792	40. South Dakota	November 2, 1889
16. Tennessee	June 1, 1796	41. Montana	November 8, 1889
17. Ohio	March 1, 1803	42. Washington	November 11, 1889
18. Louisiana	April 30, 1812	43. Idaho	July 3, 1890
19. Indiana	December 11, 1816	44. Wyoming	July 10, 1890
20. Mississippi	December 10, 1817	45. Utah	January 4, 1896
21. Illinois	December 3, 1818	46. Oklahoma	November 16, 1907
22. Alabama	December 14, 1819	47. New Mexico	January 6, 1912
23. Maine	March 15, 1820	48. Arizona	February 14, 1912
24. Missouri	August 10, 1821	49. Alaska	January 3, 1959
25. Arkansas	June 15, 1836	50. Hawaii	August 21, 1959

PRESIDENTIAL ELECTIONS

Year	Number of States	Candidates	Parties	Popular Vote	% of Popular Vote	Electoral Vote	% Voter Participation[b]
1789	11	**George Washington**	No party			69	
		John Adams	designations			34	
		Other candidates				35	
1792	15	**George Washington**	No party			132	
		John Adams	designations			77	
		George Clinton				50	
		Other candidates				5	
1796	16	**John Adams**	Federalist			71	
		Thomas Jefferson	Democratic-Republican			68	
		Thomas Pinckney	Federalist			59	
		Aaron Burr	Democratic-Republican			30	
		Other candidates				48	
1800	16	**Thomas Jefferson**	Democratic-Republican			73	
		Aaron Burr	Democratic-Republican			73	
		John Adams	Federalist			65	
		Charles C. Pinckney	Federalist			64	
		John Jay	Federalist			1	
1804	17	**Thomas Jefferson**	Democratic-Republican			162	
		Charles C. Pinckney	Federalist			14	
1808	17	**James Madison**	Democratic-Republican			122	
		Charles C. Pinckney	Federalist			47	
		George Clinton	Democratic-Republican			6	
1812	18	**James Madison**	Democratic-Republican			128	
		DeWitt Clinton	Federalist			89	
1816	19	**James Monroe**	Democratic-Republican			183	
		Rufus King	Federalist			34	
1820	24	**James Monroe**	Democratic-Republican			231	
		John Quincy Adams	Independent Republican			1	

Year	Number of States	Candidates	Parties	Popular Vote	% of Popular Vote	Electoral Vote	% Voter Participation[b]
1824	24	**John Quincy Adams**	Democratic-Republican	108,740	30.5	84	26.9
		Andrew Jackson	Democratic-Republican	153,544	43.1	99	
		Henry Clay	Democratic-Republican	47,136	13.2	37	
		William H. Crawford	Democratic-Republican	46,618	13.1	41	
1828	24	**Andrew Jackson**	Democratic	647,286	56.0	178	57.6
		John Quincy Adams	National Republican	508,064	44.0	83	
1832	24	**Andrew Jackson**	Democratic	688,242	54.5	219	55.4
		Henry Clay	National Republican	473,462	37.5	49	
		William Wirt	Anti-Masonic	101,051	8.0	7	
		John Floyd	Democratic			11	
1836	26	**Martin Van Buren**	Democratic	765,483	50.9	170	57.8
		William H. Harrison	Whig			73	
		Hugh L. White	Whig	739,795	49.1	26	
		Daniel Webster	Whig			14	
		W. P. Mangum	Whig			11	
1840	26	**William H. Harrison**	Whig	1,274,624	53.1	234	80.2
		Martin Van Buren	Democratic	1,127,781	46.9	60	
1844	26	**James K. Polk**	Democratic	1,338,464	49.6	170	78.9
		Henry Clay	Whig	1,300,097	48.1	105	
		James G. Birney	Liberty	62,300	2.3		
1848	30	**Zachary Taylor**	Whig	1,360,967	47.4	163	72.7
		Lewis Cass	Democratic	1,222,342	42.5	127	
		Martin Van Buren	Free Soil	291,263	10.1		
1852	31	**Franklin Pierce**	Democratic	1,601,117	50.9	254	69.6
		Winfield Scott	Whig	1,385,453	44.1	42	
		John P. Hale	Free Soil	155,825	5.0		
1856	31	**James Buchanan**	Democratic	1,832,955	45.3	174	78.9
		John C. Frémont	Republican	1,339,932	33.1	114	
		Millard Fillmore	American	871,731	21.6	8	
1860	33	**Abraham Lincoln**	Republican	1,865,593	39.8	180	81.2
		Stephen A. Douglas	Democratic	1,382,713	29.5	12	
		John C. Breckinridge	Democratic	848,356	18.1	72	
		John Bell	Constitutional Union	592,906	12.6	39	
1864	36	**Abraham Lincoln**	Republican	2,206,938	55.0	212	73.8
		George B. McClellan	Democratic	1,803,787	45.0	21	
1868	37	**Ulysses S. Grant**	Republican	3,013,421	52.7	214	78.1
		Horatio Seymour	Democratic	2,706,829	47.3	80	
1872	37	**Ulysses S. Grant**	Republican	3,596,745	55.6	286	71.3
		Horace Greeley	Democratic	2,843,446	43.9	[a]	
1876	38	**Rutherford B. Hayes**	Republican	4,036,572	48.0	185	81.8
		Samuel J. Tilden	Democratic	4,284,020	51.0	184	

Year	Number of States	Candidates	Parties	Popular Vote	% of Popular Vote	Electoral Vote	% Voter Participation[b]
1880	38	**James A. Garfield**	Republican	4,453,295	48.5	214	79.4
		Winfield S. Hancock	Democratic	4,414,082	48.1	155	
		James B. Weaver	Greenback-Labor	308,578	3.4		
1884	38	**Grover Cleveland**	Democratic	4,879,507	48.5	219	77.5
		James G. Blaine	Republican	4,850,293	48.2	182	
		Benjamin F. Butler	Greenback-Labor	175,370	1.8		
		John P. St. John	Prohibition	150,369	1.5		
1888	38	**Benjamin Harrison**	Republican	5,477,129	47.9	233	79.3
		Grover Cleveland	Democratic	5,537,857	48.6	168	
		Clinton B. Fisk	Prohibition	249,506	2.2		
		Anson J. Streeter	Union Labor	146,935	1.3		
1892	44	**Grover Cleveland**	Democratic	5,555,426	46.1	277	74.7
		Benjamin Harrison	Republican	5,182,690	43.0	145	
		James B. Weaver	People's	1,029,846	8.5	22	
		John Bidwell	Prohibition	264,133	2.2		
1896	45	**William McKinley**	Republican	7,102,246	51.1	271	79.3
		William J. Bryan	Democratic	6,492,559	47.7	176	
1900	45	**William McKinley**	Republican	7,218,491	51.7	292	73.2
		William J. Bryan	Democratic; Populist	6,356,734	45.5	155	
		John C. Wooley	Prohibition	208,914	1.5		
1904	45	**Theodore Roosevelt**	Republican	7,628,461	57.4	336	65.2
		Alton B. Parker	Democratic	5,084,223	37.6	140	
		Eugene V. Debs	Socialist	402,283	3.0		
		Silas C. Swallow	Prohibition	258,536	1.9		
1908	46	**William H. Taft**	Republican	7,675,320	51.6	321	65.4
		William J. Bryan	Democratic	6,412,294	43.1	162	
		Eugene V. Debs	Socialist	420,793	2.8		
		Eugene W. Chafin	Prohibition	253,840	1.7		
1912	48	**Woodrow Wilson**	Democratic	6,296,547	41.9	435	58.8
		Theodore Roosevelt	Progressive	4,118,571	27.4	88	
		William H. Taft	Republican	3,486,720	23.2	8	
		Eugene V. Debs	Socialist	900,672	6.0		
		Eugene W. Chafin	Prohibition	206,275	1.4		
1916	48	**Woodrow Wilson**	Democratic	9,127,695	49.4	277	61.6
		Charles E. Hughes	Republican	8,533,507	46.2	254	
		A. L. Benson	Socialist	585,113	3.2		
		J. Frank Hanly	Prohibition	220,506	1.2		
1920	48	**Warren G. Harding**	Republican	16,143,407	60.4	404	49.2
		James M. Cox	Democratic	9,130,328	34.2	127	
		Eugene V. Debs	Socialist	919,799	3.4		
		P. P. Christensen	Farmer-Labor	265,411	1.0		
1924	48	**Calvin Coolidge**	Republican	15,718,211	54.0	382	48.9
		John W. Davis	Democratic	8,385,283	28.8	136	
		Robert M. La Follette	Progressive	4,831,289	16.6	13	

Year	Number of States	Candidates	Parties	Popular Vote	% of Popular Vote	Electoral Vote	% Voter Participation[b]
1928	48	**Herbert C. Hoover**	Republican	21,391,993	58.2	444	56.9
		Alfred E. Smith	Democratic	15,016,169	40.9	87	
1932	48	**Franklin D. Roosevelt**	Democratic	22,809,638	57.4	472	56.9
		Herbert C. Hoover	Republican	15,758,901	39.7	59	
		Norman Thomas	Socialist	881,951	2.2		
1936	48	**Franklin D. Roosevelt**	Democratic	27,752,869	60.8	523	61.0
		Alfred M. Landon	Republican	16,674,665	36.5	8	
		William Lemke	Union	882,479	1.9		
1940	48	**Franklin D. Roosevelt**	Democratic	27,307,819	54.8	449	62.5
		Wendell L. Wilkie	Republican	22,321,018	44.8	82	
1944	48	**Franklin D. Roosevelt**	Democratic	25,606,585	53.5	432	55.9
		Thomas E. Dewey	Republican	22,014,745	46.0	99	
1948	48	**Harry S Truman**	Democratic	24,179,345	49.6	303	53.0
		Thomas E. Dewey	Republican	21,991,291	45.1	189	
		J. Strom Thurmond	States' Rights	1,176,125	2.4	39	
		Henry A. Wallace	Progressive	1,157,326	2.4		
1952	48	**Dwight D. Eisenhower**	Republican	33,936,234	55.1	442	63.3
		Adlai E. Stevenson	Democratic	27,314,992	44.4	89	
1956	48	**Dwight D. Eisenhower**	Republican	35,590,472	57.6	457	60.6
		Adlai E. Stevenson	Democratic	26,022,752	42.1	73	
1960	50	**John F. Kennedy**	Democratic	34,226,731	49.7	303	62.8
		Richard M. Nixon	Republican	34,108,157	49.5	219	
1964	50	**Lyndon B. Johnson**	Democratic	43,129,566	61.1	486	61.7
		Barry M. Goldwater	Republican	27,178,188	38.5	52	
1968	50	**Richard M. Nixon**	Republican	31,785,480	43.4	301	60.6
		Hubert H. Humphrey	Democratic	31,275,166	42.7	191	
		George C. Wallace	American Independent	9,906,473	13.5	46	
1972	50	**Richard M. Nixon**	Republican	47,169,911	60.7	520	55.2
		George S. McGovern	Democratic	29,170,383	37.5	17	
		John G. Schmitz	American	1,099,482	1.4		
1976	50	**Jimmy Carter**	Democratic	40,830,763	50.1	297	53.5
		Gerald R. Ford	Republican	39,147,793	48.0	240	
1980	50	**Ronald Reagan**	Republican	43,899,248	50.8	489	52.6
		Jimmy Carter	Democratic	35,481,432	41.0	49	
		John B. Anderson	Independent	5,719,437	6.6	0	
		Ed Clark	Libertarian	920,859	1.1	0	
1984	50	**Ronald Reagan**	Republican	54,451,521	58.8	525	53.3
		Walter Mondale	Democratic	37,565,334	40.5	13	

Candidates receiving less than 1 percent of the popular vote have been omitted. Thus the percentage of popular vote given for any election year may not total 100 percent.

Before the passage of the Twelfth Amendment in 1804, the Electoral College voted for two presidential candidates; the runner-up became vice president.

Before 1824, most presidential electors were chosen by state legislatures, not by popular vote.

[a]Greeley died shortly after the election; the electors supporting him then divided their votes among minor candidates.

[b]Percent of voting-age population casting ballots.

PRESIDENTS, VICE PRESIDENTS, AND CABINET MEMBERS

The Washington Administration

President	George Washington	1789–1797
Vice President	John Adams	1789–1797
Secretary of State	Thomas Jefferson	1789–1793
	Edmund Randolph	1794–1795
	Timothy Pickering	1795–1797
Secretary of Treasury	Alexander Hamilton	1789–1795
	Oliver Wolcott	1795–1797
Secretary of War	Henry Knox	1789–1794
	Timothy Pickering	1795–1796
	James McHenry	1796–1797
Attorney General	Edmund Randolph	1789–1793
	William Bradford	1794–1795
	Charles Lee	1795–1797
Postmaster General	Samuel Osgood	1789–1791
	Timothy Pickering	1791–1794
	Joseph Habersham	1795–1797

The John Adams Administration

President	John Adams	1797–1801
Vice President	Thomas Jefferson	1797–1801
Secretary of State	Timothy Pickering	1797–1800
	John Marshall	1800–1801
Secretary of Treasury	Oliver Wolcott	1797–1800
	Samuel Dexter	1800–1801
Secretary of War	James McHenry	1797–1800
	Samuel Dexter	1800–1801
Attorney General	Charles Lee	1797–1801
Postmaster General	Joseph Habersham	1797–1801
Secretary of Navy	Benjamin Stoddert	1798–1801

The Jefferson Administration

President	Thomas Jefferson	1801–1809
Vice President	Aaron Burr	1801–1805
	George Clinton	1805–1809
Secretary of State	James Madison	1801–1809
Secretary of Treasury	Samuel Dexter	1801
	Albert Gallatin	1801–1809
Secretary of War	Henry Dearborn	1801–1809
Attorney General	Levi Lincoln	1801–1805
	Robert Smith	1805
	John Breckinridge	1805–1806
	Caesar Rodney	1807–1809

Postmaster General	Joseph Habersham	1801
	Gideon Granger	1801–1809
Secretary of Navy	Robert Smith	1801–1809

The Madison Administration

President	James Madison	1809–1817
Vice President	George Clinton	1809–1813
	Elbridge Gerry	1813–1817
Secretary of State	Robert Smith	1809–1811
	James Monroe	1811–1817
Secretary of Treasury	Albert Gallatin	1809–1813
	George Campbell	1814
	Alexander Dallas	1814–1816
	William Crawford	1816–1817
Secretary of War	William Eustis	1809–1812
	John Armstrong	1813–1814
	James Monroe	1814–1815
	William Crawford	1815–1817
Attorney General	Caesar Rodney	1809–1811
	William Pinkney	1811–1814
	Richard Rush	1814–1817
Postmaster General	Gideon Granger	1809–1814
	Return Meigs	1814–1817
Secretary of Navy	Paul Hamilton	1809–1813
	William Jones	1813–1814
	Benjamin Crowninshield	1814–1817

The Monroe Administration

President	James Monroe	1817–1825
Vice President	Daniel Tompkins	1817–1825
Secretary of State	John Quincy Adams	1817–1825
Secretary of Treasury	William Crawford	1817–1825
Secretary of War	George Graham	1817
	John C. Calhoun	1817–1825
Attorney General	Richard Rush	1817
	William Wirt	1817–1825
Postmaster General	Return Meigs	1817–1823
	John McLean	1823–1825
Secretary of Navy	Benjamin Crowninshield	1817–1818
	Smith Thompson	1818–1823
	Samuel Southard	1823–1825

The John Quincy Adams Administration

President	John Quincy Adams	1825–1829
Vice President	John C. Calhoun	1825–1829
Secretary of State	Henry Clay	1825–1829
Secretary of Treasury	Richard Rush	1825–1829
Secretary of War	James Barbour	1825–1828
	Peter Porter	1828–1829
Attorney General	William Wirt	1825–1829
Postmaster General	John McLean	1825–1829
Secretary of Navy	Samuel Southard	1825–1829

The Jackson Administration

President	Andrew Jackson	1829–1837
Vice President	John C. Calhoun	1829–1833
	Martin Van Buren	1833–1837
Secretary of State	Martin Van Buren	1829–1831
	Edward Livingston	1831–1833
	Louis McLane	1833–1834
	John Forsyth	1834–1837
Secretary of Treasury	Samuel Ingham	1829–1831
	Louis McLane	1831–1833
	William Duane	1833
	Roger B. Taney	1833–1834
	Levi Woodbury	1834–1837
Secretary of War	John H. Eaton	1829–1831
	Lewis Cass	1831–1837
	Benjamin Butler	1837
Attorney General	John M. Berrien	1829–1831
	Roger B. Taney	1831–1833
	Benjamin Butler	1833–1837
Postmaster General	William Barry	1829–1835
	Amos Kendall	1835–1837
Secretary of Navy	John Branch	1829–1831
	Levi Woodbury	1831–1834
	Mahlon Dickerson	1834–1837

The Van Buren Administration

President	Martin Van Buren	1837–1841
Vice President	Richard M. Johnson	1837–1841
Secretary of State	John Forsyth	1837–1841
Secretary of Treasury	Levi Woodbury	1837–1841
Secretary of War	Joel Poinsett	1837–1841
Attorney General	Benjamin Butler	1837–1838
	Felix Grundy	1838–1840
	Henry D. Gilpin	1840–1841
Postmaster General	Amos Kendall	1837–1840
	John M. Niles	1840–1841
Secretary of Navy	Mahlon Dickerson	1837–1838
	James Paulding	1838–1841

The William Harrison Administration

President	William H. Harrison	1841
Vice President	John Tyler	1841
Secretary of State	Daniel Webster	1841
Secretary of Treasury	Thomas Ewing	1841
Secretary of War	John Bell	1841
Attorney General	John J. Crittenden	1841
Postmaster General	Francis Granger	1841
Secretary of Navy	George Badger	1841

The Tyler Administration

President	John Tyler	1841–1845
Vice President	None	
Secretary of State	Daniel Webster	1841–1843
	Hugh S. Legaré	1843
	Abel P. Upshur	1843–1844
	John C. Calhoun	1844–1845
Secretary of Treasury	Thomas Ewing	1841
	Walter Forward	1841–1843
	John C. Spencer	1843–1844
	George Bibb	1844–1845
Secretary of War	John Bell	1841
	John C. Spencer	1841–1843
	James M. Porter	1843–1844
	William Wilkins	1844–1845
Attorney General	John J. Crittenden	1841
	Hugh S. Legaré	1841–1843
	John Nelson	1843–1845
Postmaster General	Francis Granger	1841
	Charles Wickliffe	1841
Secretary of Navy	George Badger	1841
	Abel P. Upshur	1841
	David Henshaw	1843–1844
	Thomas Gilmer	1844
	John Y. Mason	1844–1845

The Polk Administration

President	James K. Polk	1845–1849
Vice President	George M. Dallas	1845–1849
Secretary of State	James Buchanan	1845–1849
Secretary of Treasury	Robert J. Walker	1845–1849
Secretary of War	William L. Marcy	1845–1849
Attorney General	John Y. Mason	1845–1846
	Nathan Clifford	1846–1848
	Isaac Toucey	1848–1849
Postmaster General	Cave Johnson	1845–1849
Secretary of Navy	George Bancroft	1845–1846
	John Y. Mason	1846–1849

The Taylor Administration

President	Zachary Taylor	1849–1850
Vice President	Millard Fillmore	1849–1850
Secretary of State	John M. Clayton	1849–1850
Secretary of Treasury	William Meredith	1849–1850
Secretary of War	George Crawford	1849–1850
Attorney General	Reverdy Johnson	1849–1850
Postmaster General	Jacob Collamer	1849–1850
Secretary of Navy	William Preston	1849–1850
Secretary of Interior	Thomas Ewing	1849–1850

The Fillmore Administration

President	Millard Fillmore	1850–1853
Vice President	None	
Secretary of State	Daniel Webster	1850–1852
	Edward Everett	1852–1853
Secretary of Treasury	Thomas Corwin	1850–1853
Secretary of War	Charles Conrad	1850–1853
Attorney General	John J. Crittenden	1850–1853
Postmaster General	Nathan Hall	1850–1852
	Sam D. Hubbard	1852–1853
Secretary of Navy	William A. Graham	1850–1852
	John P. Kennedy	1852–1853
Secretary of Interior	Thomas McKennan	1850
	Alexander Stuart	1850–1853

The Pierce Administration

President	Franklin Pierce	1853–1857
Vice President	William R. King	1853–1857
Secretary of State	William L. Marcy	1853–1857
Secretary of Treasury	James Guthrie	1853–1857
Secretary of War	Jefferson Davis	1853–1857
Attorney General	Caleb Cushing	1853–1857
Postmaster General	James Campbell	1853–1857
Secretary of Navy	James C. Dobbin	1853–1857
Secretary of Interior	Robert McClelland	1853–1857

The Buchanan Administration

President	James Buchanan	1857–1861
Vice President	John C. Breckinridge	1857–1861
Secretary of State	Lewis Cass	1857–1860
	Jeremiah S. Black	1860–1861
Secretary of Treasury	Howell Cobb	1857–1860
	Philip Thomas	1860–1861
	John A. Dix	1861
Secretary of War	John B. Floyd	1857–1861
	Joseph Holt	1861
Attorney General	Jeremiah S. Black	1857–1860
	Edwin M. Stanton	1860–1861
Postmaster General	Aaron V. Brown	1857–1859
	Joseph Holt	1859–1861
	Horatio King	1861
Secretary of Navy	Isaac Toucey	1857–1861
Secretary of Interior	Jacob Thompson	1857–1861

The Lincoln Administration

President	Abraham Lincoln	1861–1865
Vice President	Hannibal Hamlin	1861–1865
	Andrew Johnson	1865
Secretary of State	William H. Seward	1861–1865
Secretary of Treasury	Samuel P. Chase	1861–1864
	William P. Fessenden	1864–1865
	Hugh McCulloch	1865
Secretary of War	Simon Cameron	1861–1862
	Edwin M. Stanton	1862–1865
Attorney General	Edward Bates	1861–1864
	James Speed	1864–1865

Postmaster General	Horatio King	1861
	Montgomery Blair	1861–1864
	William Dennison	1864–1865
Secretary of Navy	Gideon Welles	1861–1865
Secretary of Interior	Caleb B. Smith	1861–1863
	John P. Usher	1863–1865

The Andrew Johnson Administration

President	Andrew Johnson	1865–1869
Vice President	None	
Secretary of State	William H. Seward	1865–1869
Secretary of Treasury	Hugh McCulloch	1865–1869
Secretary of War	Edwin M. Stanton	1865–1867
	Ulysses S. Grant	1867–1868
	Lorenzo Thomas	1868
	John M. Schofield	1868–1869
Attorney General	James Speed	1865–1866
	Henry Stanbery	1866–1868
	William M. Evarts	1868–1869
Postmaster General	William Dennison	1865–1866
	Alexander Randall	1866–1869
Secretary of Navy	Gideon Welles	1865–1869
Secretary of Interior	John P. Usher	1865
	James Harlan	1865–1866
	Orville H. Browning	1866–1869

The Grant Administration

President	Ulysses S. Grant	1869–1877
Vice President	Schuyler Colfax	1869–1873
	Henry Wilson	1873–1877
Secretary of State	Elihu B. Washburne	1869
	Hamilton Fish	1869–1877
Secretary of Treasury	George S. Boutwell	1869–1873
	William Richardson	1873–1874
	Benjamin Bristow	1874–1876
	Lot M. Morrill	1876–1877
Secretary of War	John A. Rawlins	1869
	William T. Sherman	1869
	William W. Belknap	1869–1876
	Alphonso Taft	1876
	James D. Cameron	1876–1877
Attorney General	Ebenezer Hoar	1869–1870
	Amos T. Ackerman	1870–1871
	G. H. Williams	1871–1875
	Edwards Pierrepont	1875–1876
	Alphonso Taft	1876–1877

Postmaster General	John A. J. Creswell	1869–1874
	James W. Marshall	1874
	Marshall Jewell	1874–1876
	James N. Tyner	1876–1877
Secretary of Navy	Adolph E. Borie	1869
	George M. Robeson	1869–1877
Secretary of Interior	Jacob D. Cox	1869–1870
	Columbus Delano	1870–1875
	Zachariah Chandler	1875–1877

The Hayes Administration

President	Rutherford B. Hayes	1877–1881
Vice President	William A. Wheeler	1877–1881
Secretary of State	William B. Evarts	1877–1881
Secretary of Treasury	John Sherman	1877–1881
Secretary of War	George W. McCrary	1877–1879
	Alex Ramsey	1879–1881
Attorney General	Charles Devens	1877–1881
Postmaster General	David M. Key	1877–1880
	Horace Maynard	1880–1881
Secretary of Navy	Richard W. Thompson	1877–1880
	Nathan Goff, Jr.	1881
Secretary of Interior	Carl Schurz	1877–1881

The Garfield Administration

President	James A. Garfield	1881
Vice President	Chester A. Arthur	1881
Secretary of State	James G. Blaine	1881
Secretary of Treasury	William Windom	1881
Secretary of War	Robert T. Lincoln	1881
Attorney General	Wayne MacVeagh	1881
Postmaster General	Thomas L. James	1881
Secretary of Navy	William H. Hunt	1881
Secretary of Interior	Samuel J. Kirkwood	1881

The Arthur Administration

President	Chester A. Arthur	1881–1885
Vice President	None	
Secretary of State	F. T. Frelinghuysen	1881–1885

Secretary of Treasury	Charles J. Folger	1881–1884
	Walter Q. Gresham	1884
	Hugh McCulloch	1884–1885
Secretary of War	Robert T. Lincoln	1881–1885
Attorney General	Benjamin H. Brewster	1881–1885
Postmaster General	Timothy O. Howe	1881–1883
	Walter Q. Gresham	1883–1884
	Frank Hatton	1884–1885
Secretary of Navy	William H. Hunt	1881–1882
	William E. Chandler	1882–1885
Secretary of Interior	Samuel J. Kirkwood	1881–1882
	Henry M. Teller	1882–1885

The Cleveland Administration

President	Grover Cleveland	1885–1889
Vice President	Thomas A. Hendricks	1885–1889
Secretary of State	Thomas F. Bayard	1885–1889
Secretary of Treasury	Daniel Manning	1885–1887
	Charles S. Fairchild	1887–1889
Secretary of War	William C. Endicott	1885–1889
Attorney General	Augustus H. Garland	1885–1889
Postmaster General	William F. Vilas	1885–1888
	Don M. Dickinson	1888–1889
Secretary of Navy	William C. Whitney	1885–1889
Secretary of Interior	Lucius Q. C. Lamar	1885–1888
	William F. Vilas	1888–1889
Secretary of Agriculture	Norman J. Colman	1889

The Benjamin Harrison Administration

President	Benjamin Harrison	1889–1893
Vice President	Levi P. Morton	1889–1893
Secretary of State	James G. Blaine	1889–1892
	John W. Foster	1892–1893
Secretary of Treasury	William Windom	1889–1891
	Charles Foster	1891–1893
Secretary of War	Redfield Proctor	1889–1891
	Stephen B. Elkins	1891–1893
Attorney General	William H. H. Miller	1889–1891
Postmaster General	John Wanamaker	1889–1893
Secretary of Navy	Benjamin F. Tracy	1889–1893
Secretary of Interior	John W. Noble	1889–1893
Secretary of Agriculture	Jeremiah M. Rusk	1889–1893

The Cleveland Administration

President	Grover Cleveland	1893–1897
Vice President	Adlai E. Stevenson	1893–1897
Secretary of State	Walter Q. Gresham	1893–1895
	Richard Olney	1895–1897
Secretary of Treasury	John G. Carlisle	1893–1897
Secretary of War	Daniel S. Lamont	1893–1897
Attorney General	Richard Olney	1893–1895
	James Harmon	1895–1897
Postmaster General	Wilson S. Bissell	1893–1895
	William L. Wilson	1895–1897
Secretary of Navy	Hilary A. Herbert	1893–1897
Secretary of Interior	Hoke Smith	1893–1896
	David R. Francis	1896–1897
Secretary of Agriculture	Julius S. Morton	1893–1897

The McKinley Administration

President	William McKinley	1897–1901
Vice President	Garret A. Hobart	1897–1901
	Theodore Roosevelt	1901
Secretary of State	John Sherman	1897–1898
	William R. Day	1898
	John Hay	1898–1901
Secretary of Treasury	Lyman J. Gage	1897–1901
Secretary of War	Russell A. Alger	1897–1899
	Elihu Root	1899–1901
Attorney General	Joseph McKenna	1897–1898
	John W. Griggs	1898–1901
	Philander C. Knox	1901
Postmaster General	James A. Gary	1897–1898
	Charles E. Smith	1898–1901
Secretary of Navy	John D. Long	1897–1901
Secretary of Interior	Cornelius N. Bliss	1897–1899
	Ethan A. Hitchcock	1899–1901
Secretary of Agriculture	James Wilson	1897–1901

The Theodore Roosevelt Administration

President	Theodore Roosevelt	1901–1909
Vice President	Charles Fairbanks	1905–1909
Secretary of State	John Hay	1901–1905
	Elihu Root	1905–1909
	Robert Bacon	1909

Secretary of Treasury	Lyman J. Gage	1901–1902
	Leslie M. Shaw	1902–1907
	George B. Cortelyou	1907–1909
Secretary of War	Elihu Root	1901–1904
	William H. Taft	1904–1908
	Luke E. Wright	1908–1909
Attorney General	Philander C. Knox	1901–1904
	William H. Moody	1904–1906
	Charles J. Bonaparte	1906–1909
Postmaster General	Charles E. Smith	1901–1902
	Henry C. Payne	1902–1904
	Robert J. Wynne	1904–1905
	George B. Cortelyou	1905–1907
	George von L. Meyer	1907–1909
Secretary of Navy	John D. Long	1901–1902
	William H. Moody	1902–1904
	Paul Morton	1904–1905
	Charles J. Bonaparte	1905–1906
	Victor H. Metcalf	1906–1908
	Truman H. Newberry	1908–1909
Secretary of Interior	Ethan A. Hitchcock	1901–1907
	James R. Garfield	1907–1909
Secretary of Agriculture	James Wilson	1901–1909
Secretary of Labor and Commerce	George B. Cortelyou	1903–1904
	Victor H. Metcalf	1904–1906
	Oscar S. Straus	1906–1909
	Charles Nagel	1909

The Taft Administration

President	William H. Taft	1909–1913
Vice President	James S. Sherman	1909–1913
Secretary of State	Philander C. Knox	1909–1913
Secretary of Treasury	Franklin MacVeagh	1909–1913
Secretary of War	Jacob M. Dickinson	1909–1911
	Henry L. Stimson	1911–1913
Attorney General	George W. Wickersham	1909–1913
Postmaster General	Frank H. Hitchcock	1909–1913
Secretary of Navy	George von L. Meyer	1909–1913
Secretary of Interior	Richard A. Ballinger	1909–1911
	Walter L. Fisher	1911–1913
Secretary of Agriculture	James Wilson	1909–1913
Secretary of Labor and Commerce	Charles Nagel	1909–1913

The Wilson Administration

President	Woodrow Wilson	1913–1921
Vice President	Thomas R. Marshall	1913–1921
Secretary of State	William J. Bryan	1913–1915
	Robert Lansing	1915–1920
	Bainbridge Colby	1920–1921
Secretary of Treasury	William G. McAdoo	1913–1918
	Carter Glass	1918–1920
	David F. Houston	1920–1921
Secretary of War	Lindley M. Garrison	1913–1916
	Newton D. Baker	1916–1921
Attorney General	James C. McReynolds	1913–1914
	Thomas W. Gregory	1914–1919
	A. Mitchell Palmer	1919–1921
Postmaster General	Albert S. Burleson	1913–1921
Secretary of Navy	Josephus Daniels	1913–1921
Secretary of Interior	Franklin K. Lane	1913–1920
	John B. Payne	1920–1921
Secretary of Agriculture	David F. Houston	1913–1920
	Edwin T. Meredith	1920–1921
Secretary of Commerce	William C. Redfield	1913–1919
	Joshua W. Alexander	1919–1921
Secretary of Labor	William B. Wilson	1913–1921

The Harding Administration

President	Warren G. Harding	1921–1923
Vice President	Calvin Coolidge	1921–1923
Secretary of State	Charles E. Hughes	1921–1923
Secretary of Treasury	Andrew Mellon	1921–1923
Secretary of War	John W. Weeks	1921–1923
Attorney General	Harry M. Daugherty	1921–1923
Postmaster General	Will H. Hays	1921–1922
	Hubert Work	1922–1923
	Harry S. New	1923
Secretary of Navy	Edwin Denby	1921–1923
Secretary of Interior	Albert B. Fall	1921–1923
	Hubert Work	1923
Secretary of Agriculture	Henry C. Wallace	1921–1923
Secretary of Commerce	Herbert C. Hoover	1921–1923
Secretary of Labor	James J. Davis	1921–1923

The Coolidge Administration

President	Calvin Coolidge	1923–1929
Vice President	Charles G. Dawes	1925–1929
Secretary of State	Charles E. Hughes	1923–1925
	Frank B. Kellogg	1925–1929
Secretary of Treasury	Andrew Mellon	1923–1929
Secretary of War	John W. Weeks	1923–1925
	Dwight F. Davis	1925–1929
Attorney General	Henry M. Daugherty	1923–1924
	Harlan F. Stone	1924–1925
	John G. Sargent	1925–1929
Postmaster General	Harry S. New	1923–1929
Secretary of Navy	Edwin Derby	1923–1924
	Curtis D. Wilbur	1924–1929
Secretary of Interior	Hubert Work	1923–1928
	Roy O. West	1928–1929
Secretary of Agriculture	Henry C. Wallace	1923–1924
	Howard M. Gore	1924–1925
	William M. Jardine	1925–1929
Secretary of Commerce	Herbert C. Hoover	1923–1928
	William F. Whiting	1928–1929
Secretary of Labor	James J. Davis	1923–1929

The Hoover Administration

President	Herbert C. Hoover	1929–1933
Vice President	Charles Curtis	1929–1933
Secretary of State	Henry L. Stimson	1929–1933
Secretary of Treasury	Andrew Mellon	1929–1932
	Ogden L. Mills	1932–1933
Secretary of War	James W. Good	1929
	Patrick J. Hurley	1929–1933
Attorney General	William D. Mitchell	1929–1933
Postmaster General	Walter F. Brown	1929–1933
Secretary of Navy	Charles F. Adams	1929–1933
Secretary of Interior	Ray L. Wilbur	1929–1933
Secretary of Agriculture	Arthur M. Hyde	1929–1933
Secretary of Commerce	Robert P. Lamont	1929–1932
	Roy D. Chapin	1932–1933
Secretary of Labor	James J. Davis	1929–1930
	William N. Doak	1930–1933

The Franklin D. Roosevelt Administration

President	Franklin D. Roosevelt	1933–1945
Vice President	John Nance Garner	1933–1941
	Henry A. Wallace	1941–1945
	Harry S Truman	1945
Secretary of State	Cordell Hull	1933–1944
	Edward R. Stettinius, Jr.	1944–1945
Secretary of Treasury	William H. Woodin	1933–1934
	Henry Morgenthau, Jr.	1934–1945
Secretary of War	George H. Dern	1933–1936
	Henry A. Woodring	1936–1940
	Henry L. Stimson	1940–1945
Attorney General	Homer S. Cummings	1933–1939
	Frank Murphy	1939–1940
	Robert H. Jackson	1940–1941
	Francis Biddle	1941–1945
Postmaster General	James A. Farley	1933–1940
	Frank C. Walker	1940–1945
Secretary of Navy	Claude A. Swanson	1933–1940
	Charles Edison	1940
	Frank Knox	1940–1944
	James V. Forrestal	1944–1945
Secretary of Interior	Harold L. Ickes	1933–1945
Secretary of Agriculture	Henry A. Wallace	1933–1940
	Claude R. Wickard	1940–1945
Secretary of Commerce	Daniel C. Roper	1933–1939
	Harry L. Hopkins	1939–1940
	Jesse Jones	1940–1945
	Henry A. Wallace	1945
Secretary of Labor	Frances Perkins	1933–1945

The Truman Administration

President	Harry S Truman	1945–1953
Vice President	Alben W. Barkley	1949–1953
Secretary of State	Edward R. Stettinius, Jr.	1945
	James F. Byrnes	1945–1947
	George C. Marshall	1947–1949
	Dean G. Acheson	1949–1953
Secretary of Treasury	Fred M. Vinson	1945–1946
	John W. Snyder	1946–1953
Secretary of War	Robert P. Patterson	1945–1947
	Kenneth C. Royall	1947
Attorney General	Tom C. Clark	1945–1949
	J. Howard McGrath	1949–1952
	James P. McGranery	1952–1953

Postmaster General	Frank C. Walker	1945
	Robert E. Hannegan	1945–1947
	Jesse M. Donaldson	1947–1953
Secretary of Navy	James V. Forrestal	1945–1947
Secretary of Interior	Harold L. Ickes	1945–1946
	Julius A. Krug	1946–1949
	Oscar L. Chapman	1949–1953
Secretary of Agriculture	Clinton P. Anderson	1945–1948
	Charles F. Brannan	1948–1953
Secretary of Commerce	Henry A. Wallace	1945–1946
	W. Averell Harriman	1946–1948
	Charles W. Sawyer	1948–1953
Secretary of Labor	Lewis B. Schwellenbach	1945–1948
	Maurice J. Tobin	1948–1953
Secretary of Defense	James V. Forrestal	1947–1949
	Louis A. Johnson	1949–1950
	George C. Marshall	1950–1951
	Robert A. Lovett	1951–1953

The Eisenhower Administration

President	Dwight D. Eisenhower	1953–1961
Vice President	Richard M. Nixon	1953–1961
Secretary of State	John Foster Dulles	1953–1959
	Christian A. Herter	1959–1961
Secretary of Treasury	George M. Humphrey	1953–1957
	Robert B. Anderson	1957–1961
Attorney General	Herbert Brownell, Jr.	1953–1958
	William P. Rogers	1958–1961
Postmaster General	Arthur E. Summerfield	1953–1961
Secretary of Interior	Douglas McKay	1953–1956
	Fred A. Seaton	1956–1961
Secretary of Agriculture	Ezra T. Benson	1953–1961
Secretary of Commerce	Sinclair Weeks	1953–1958
	Lewis L. Strauss	1958–1959
	Frederick H. Mueller	1959–1961
Secretary of Labor	Martin P. Durkin	1953
	James P. Mitchell	1953–1961
Secretary of Defense	Charles E. Wilson	1953–1957
	Neil H. McElroy	1957–1959
	Thomas S. Gates, Jr.	1959–1961
Secretary of Health, Education, and Welfare	Oveta Culp Hobby	1953–1955
	Marion B. Folsom	1955–1958
	Arthur S. Flemming	1958–1961

The Kennedy Administration

President	John F. Kennedy	1961–1963
Vice President	Lyndon B. Johnson	1961–1963
Secretary of State	Dean Rusk	1961–1963
Secretary of Treasury	C. Douglas Dillon	1961–1963
Attorney General	Robert F. Kennedy	1961–1963
Postmaster General	J. Edward Day	1961–1963
	John A. Gronouski	1963
Secretary of Interior	Stewart L. Udall	1961–1963
Secretary of Agriculture	Orville L. Freeman	1961–1963
Secretary of Commerce	Luther H. Hodges	1961–1963
Secretary of Labor	Arthur J. Goldberg	1961–1962
	W. Willard Wirtz	1962–1963
Secretary of Defense	Robert S. McNamara	1961–1963
Secretary of Health, Education, and Welfare	Abraham A. Ribicoff	1961–1962
	Anthony J. Celebrezze	1962–1963

The Lyndon Johnson Administration

President	Lyndon B. Johnson	1963–1969
Vice President	Hubert H. Humphrey	1965–1969
Secretary of State	Dean Rusk	1963–1969
Secretary of Treasury	C. Douglas Dillon	1963–1965
	Henry H. Fowler	1965–1969
Attorney General	Robert F. Kennedy	1963–1964
	Nicholas Katzenbach	1965–1966
	Ramsey Clark	1967–1969
Postmaster General	John A. Gronouski	1963–1965
	Lawrence F. O'Brien	1965–1968
	Marvin Watson	1968–1969
Secretary of Interior	Stewart L. Udall	1963–1969
Secretary of Agriculture	Orville L. Freeman	1963–1969
Secretary of Commerce	Luther H. Hodges	1963–1964
	John T. Connor	1964–1967
	Alexander B. Trowbridge	1967–1968
	Cyrus R. Smith	1968–1969
Secretary of Labor	W. Willard Wirtz	1963–1969
Secretary of Defense	Robert F. McNamara	1963–1968
	Clark Clifford	1968–1969

Secretary of Health, Education, and Welfare	Anthony J. Celebrezze	1963–1965
	John W. Gardner	1965–1968
	Wilbur J. Cohen	1968–1969
Secretary of Housing and Urban Development	Robert C. Weaver	1966–1969
	Robert C. Wood	1969
Secretary of Transportation	Alan S. Boyd	1967–1969

The Nixon Administration

President	Richard M. Nixon	1969–1974
Vice President	Spiro T. Agnew	1969–1973
	Gerald R. Ford	1973–1974
Secretary of State	William P. Rogers	1969–1973
	Henry A. Kissinger	1973–1974
Secretary of Treasury	David M. Kennedy	1969–1970
	John B. Connally	1971–1972
	George P. Shultz	1972–1974
	William E. Simon	1974
Attorney General	John N. Mitchell	1969–1972
	Richard G. Kleindienst	1972–1973
	Elliot L. Richardson	1973
	William B. Saxbe	1973–1974
Postmaster General	Winton M. Blount	1969–1971
Secretary of Interior	Walter J. Hickel	1969–1970
	Rogers Morton	1971–1974
Secretary of Agriculture	Clifford M. Hardin	1969–1971
	Earl L. Butz	1971–1974
Secretary of Commerce	Maurice H. Stans	1969–1972
	Peter G. Peterson	1972–1973
	Frederick B. Dent	1973–1974
Secretary of Labor	George P. Shultz	1969–1970
	James D. Hodgson	1970–1973
	Peter J. Brennan	1973–1974
Secretary of Defense	Melvin R. Laird	1969–1973
	Elliot L. Richardson	1973
	James R. Schlesinger	1973–1974
Secretary of Health, Education, and Welfare	Robert H. Finch	1969–1970
	Elliot L. Richardson	1970–1973
	Casper W. Weinberger	1973–1974
Secretary of Housing and Urban Development	George Romney	1969–1973
	James T. Lynn	1973–1974

Secretary of Transportation	John A. Volpe	1969–1973
	Claude S. Brinegar	1973–1974

The Ford Administration

President	Gerald R. Ford	1974–1977
Vice President	Nelson A. Rockefeller	1974–1977
Secretary of State	Henry A. Kissinger	1974–1977
Secretary of Treasury	William E. Simon	1974–1977
Attorney General	William Saxbe	1974–1975
	Edward Levi	1975–1977
Secretary of Interior	Rogers Morton	1974–1975
	Stanley K. Hathaway	1975
	Thomas Kleppe	1975–1977
Secretary of Agriculture	Earl L. Butz	1974–1976
	John A. Knebel	1976–1977
Secretary of Commerce	Frederick B. Dent	1974–1975
	Rogers Morton	1975–1976
	Elliot L. Richardson	1976–1977
Secretary of Labor	Peter J. Brennan	1974–1975
	John T. Dunlop	1975–1976
	W. J. Usery	1976–1977
Secretary of Defense	James R. Schlesinger	1974–1975
	Donald Rumsfeld	1975–1977
Secretary of Health, Education, and Welfare	Casper Weinberger	1974–1975
	Forrest D. Mathews	1975–1977
Secretary of Housing and Urban Development	James T. Lynn	1974–1975
	Carla A. Hills	1975–1977
Secretary of Transportation	Claude Brinegar	1974–1975
	William T. Coleman	1975–1977

The Carter Administration

President	Jimmy Carter	1977–1981
Vice President	Walter F. Mondale	1977–1981
Secretary of State	Cyrus R. Vance	1977–1980
	Edmund Muskie	1980–1981
Secretary of Treasury	W. Michael Blumenthal	1977–1979
	G. William Miller	1979–1981
Attorney General	Griffin Bell	1977–1979
	Benjamin R. Civiletti	1979–1981
Secretary of Interior	Cecil D. Andrus	1977–1981

Secretary of Agriculture	Robert Bergland	1977–1981
Secretary of Commerce	Juanita M. Kreps	1977–1979
	Philip M. Klutznick	1979–1981
Secretary of Labor	F. Ray Marshall	1977–1981
Secretary of Defense	Harold Brown	1977–1981
Secretary of Health, Education, and Welfare	Joseph A. Califano	1977–1979
	Patricia R. Harris	1979
Secretary of Health and Human Services	Patricia R. Harris	1979–1981
Secretary of Education	Shirley M. Hufstedler	1979–1981
Secretary of Housing and Urban Development	Patricia R. Harris	1977–1979
	Moon Landrieu	1979–1981
Secretary of Transportation	Brock Adams	1977–1979
	Neil E. Goldschmidt	1979–1981
Secretary of Energy	James R. Schlesinger	1977–1979
	Charles W. Duncan	1979–1981

The Reagan Administration

President	Ronald Reagan	1981–
Vice President	George Bush	1981–
Secretary of State	Alexander M. Haig	1981–1982
	George P. Shultz	1982–

Secretary of Treasury	Donald Regan	1981–1985
	James A. Baker, III	1985–
Attorney General	William F. Smith	1981–1985
	Edwin A. Meese, III	1985–
Secretary of Interior	James Watt	1981–1983
	William P. Clark, Jr.	1983–1985
	Donald P. Hodel	1985–
Secretary of Agriculture	John Block	1981–
Secretary of Commerce	Malcolm Baldridge	1981–
Secretary of Labor	Raymond Donovan	1981–1985
	William E. Brock	1985–
Secretary of Defense	Casper Weinberger	1981–
Secretary of Health and Human Services	Richard Schweiker	1981–1983
	Margaret Heckler	1983–1985
Secretary of Education	Terrel H. Bell	1981–1985
	William J. Bennett	1985–
Secretary of Housing and Urban Development	Samuel Pierce	1981–
Secretary of Transportation	Drew Lewis	1981–1983
	Elizabeth Dole	1983–
Secretary of Energy	James Edwards	1981–1982
	Donald P. Hodel	1982–1985
	John S. Herrington	1985–

PARTY STRENGTH IN CONGRESS

Period	Congress	House			Senate				Party of President
		Majority Party	Minority Party	Others	Majority Party	Minority Party	Others		
1789–91	1st	Ad 38	Op 26		Ad 17	Op 9		F	Washington
1791–93	2nd	F 37	DR 33		F 16	DR 13		F	Washington
1793–95	3rd	DR 57	F 48		F 17	DR 13		F	Washington
1795–97	4th	F 54	DR 52		F 19	DR 13		F	Washington
1797–99	5th	F 58	DR 48		F 20	DR 12		F	J. Adams
1799–1801	6th	F 64	DR 42		F 19	DR 13		F	J. Adams
1801–03	7th	DR 69	F 36		DR 18	F 13		DR	Jefferson

Period	Congress	House Majority Party		House Minority Party		Others	Senate Majority Party		Senate Minority Party		Others	Party of President	
1803–05	8th	DR	102	F	39		DR	25	F	9		DR	Jefferson
1805–07	9th	DR	116	F	25		DR	27	F	7		DR	Jefferson
1807–09	10th	DR	118	F	24		DR	28	F	6		DR	Jefferson
1809–11	11th	DR	94	F	48		DR	28	F	6		DR	Madison
1811–13	12th	DR	108	F	36		DR	30	F	6		DR	Madison
1813–15	13th	DR	112	F	68		DR	27	F	9		DR	Madison
1815–17	14th	DR	117	F	65		DR	25	F	11		DR	Madison
1817–19	15th	DR	141	F	42		DR	34	F	10		DR	Monroe
1819–21	16th	DR	156	F	27		DR	35	F	7		DR	Monroe
1821–23	17th	DR	158	F	25		DR	44	F	4		DR	Monroe
1823–25	18th	DR	187	F	26		DR	44	F	4		DR	Monroe
1825–27	19th	Ad	105	J	97		Ad	26	J	20		C	J. Q. Adams
1827–29	20th	J	119	Ad	94		J	28	Ad	20		C	J. Q. Adams
1829–31	21st	D	139	NR	74		D	26	NR	22		D	Jackson
1831–33	22nd	D	141	NR	58	14	D	25	NR	21	2	D	Jackson
1833–35	23rd	D	147	AM	53	60	D	20	NR	20	8	D	Jackson
1835–37	24th	D	145	W	98		D	27	W	25		D	Jackson
1837–39	25th	D	108	W	107	24	D	30	W	18	4	D	Van Buren
1839–41	26th	D	124	W	118		D	28	W	22		D	Van Buren
1841–43	27th	W	133	D	102	6	W	28	D	22	2	W	W. Harrison
												W	Tyler
1843–45	28th	D	142	W	79	1	W	28	D	25	1	W	Tyler
1845–47	29th	D	143	W	77	6	D	31	W	25		D	Polk
1847–49	30th	W	115	D	108	4	D	36	W	21	1	D	Polk
1849–51	31st	D	112	W	109	9	D	35	W	25	2	W	Taylor
												W	Fillmore
1851–53	32nd	D	140	W	88	5	D	35	W	24	3	W	Fillmore
1853–55	33rd	D	159	W	71	4	D	38	W	22	2	D	Pierce
1855–57	34th	R	108	D	83	43	D	40	R	15	5	D	Pierce
1857–59	35th	D	118	R	92	26	D	36	R	20	8	D	Buchanan
1859–61	36th	R	114	D	92	31	D	36	R	26	4	D	Buchanan
1861–63	37th	R	105	D	43	30	R	31	D	10	8	R	Lincoln
1863–65	38th	R	102	D	75	9	R	36	D	9	5	R	Lincoln
1865–67	39th	U	149	D	42		U	42	D	10		R	Lincoln
												R	Johnson
1867–69	40th	R	143	D	49		R	42	D	11		R	Johnson
1869–71	41st	R	149	D	63		R	56	D	11		R	Grant
1871–73	42nd	R	134	D	104	5	R	52	D	17	5	R	Grant
1873–75	43rd	R	194	D	92	14	R	49	D	19	5	R	Grant
1875–77	44th	D	169	R	109	14	R	45	D	29	2	R	Grant
1877–79	45th	D	153	R	140		R	39	D	36	1	R	Hayes
1879–81	46th	D	149	R	130	14	D	42	R	33	1	R	Hayes

Period	Congress	House Majority Party		House Minority Party		Others	Senate Majority Party		Senate Minority Party		Others	Party of President	
1881–83	47th	D	147	R	135	11	R	37	D	37	1	R	Garfield
												R	Arthur
1883–85	48th	D	197	R	118	10	R	38	D	36	2	R	Arthur
1885–87	49th	D	183	R	140	2	R	43	D	34		D	Cleveland
1887–89	50th	D	169	R	152	4	R	39	D	37		D	Cleveland
1889–91	51st	R	166	D	159		R	39	D	37		R	B. Harrison
1891–93	52nd	D	235	R	88	9	R	47	D	39	2	R	B. Harrison
1893–95	53rd	D	218	R	127	11	D	44	R	38	3	D	Cleveland
1895–97	54th	R	244	D	105	7	R	43	D	39	6	D	Cleveland
1897–99	55th	R	204	D	113	40	R	47	D	34	7	R	McKinley
1899–1901	56th	R	185	D	163	9	R	53	D	26	8	R	McKinley
1901–03	57th	R	197	D	151	9	R	55	D	31	4	R	McKinley
												R	T. Roosevelt
1903–05	58th	R	208	D	178		R	57	D	33		R	T. Roosevelt
1905–07	59th	R	250	D	136		R	57	D	33		R	T. Roosevelt
1907–09	60th	R	222	D	164		R	61	D	31		R	T. Roosevelt
1909–11	61st	R	219	D	172		R	61	D	32		R	Taft
1911–13	62nd	D	228	R	161	1	R	51	D	41		R	Taft
1913–15	63rd	D	291	R	127	17	D	51	R	44	1	D	Wilson
1915–17	64th	D	230	R	196	9	D	56	R	40		D	Wilson
1917–19	65th	D	216	R	210	6	D	53	R	42		D	Wilson
1919–21	66th	R	240	D	190	3	R	49	D	47		D	Wilson
1921–23	67th	R	301	D	131	1	R	59	D	37		R	Harding
1923–25	68th	R	225	D	205	5	R	51	D	43	2	R	Coolidge
1925–27	69th	R	247	D	183	4	R	56	D	39	1	R	Coolidge
1927–29	70th	R	237	D	195	3	R	49	D	46	1	R	Coolidge
1929–31	71st	R	267	D	167	1	R	56	D	39	1	R	Hoover
1931–33	72nd	D	220	R	214	1	R	48	D	47	1	R	Hoover
1933–35	73rd	D	310	R	117	5	D	60	R	35	1	D	F. Roosevelt
1935–37	74th	D	319	R	103	10	D	69	R	25	2	D	F. Roosevelt
1937–39	75th	D	331	R	89	13	D	76	R	16	4	D	F. Roosevelt
1939–41	76th	D	261	R	164	4	D	69	R	23	4	D	F. Roosevelt
1941–43	77th	D	268	R	162	5	D	66	R	28	2	D	F. Roosevelt
1943–45	78th	D	218	R	208	4	D	58	R	37	1	D	F. Roosevelt
1945–47	79th	D	242	R	190	2	D	56	R	38	1	D	Truman
1947–49	80th	R	245	D	188	1	R	51	D	45		D	Truman
1949–51	81st	D	263	R	171	1	D	54	R	42		D	Truman
1951–53	82nd	D	234	R	199	1	D	49	R	47		D	Truman
1953–55	83rd	R	221	D	211	1	R	48	D	47	1	R	Eisenhower
1955–57	84th	D	232	R	203		D	48	R	47	1	R	Eisenhower
1957–59	85th	D	233	R	200		D	49	R	47		R	Eisenhower

Period	Congress	House Majority Party		House Minority Party		Others	Senate Majority Party		Senate Minority Party		Others	Party of President	
1959–61	86th	D	284	R	153		D	65	R	35		R	Eisenhower
1961–63	87th	D	263	R	174		D	65	R	35		D	Kennedy
1963–65	88th	D	258	R	177		D	67	R	33		D	Kennedy
												D	Johnson
1965–67	89th	D	295	R	140		D	68	R	32		D	Johnson
1967–69	90th	D	246	R	187		D	64	R	36		D	Johnson
1969–71	91st	D	245	R	189		D	57	R	43		R	Nixon
1971–73	92nd	D	254	R	180		D	54	R	44	2	R	Nixon
1973–75	93rd	D	239	R	192	1	D	56	R	42	2	R	Nixon
1975–77	94th	D	291	R	144		D	60	R	37	3	R	Ford
1977–79	95th	D	292	R	143		D	61	R	38	1	D	Carter
1979–81	96th	D	276	R	157		D	58	R	41	1	D	Carter
1981–83	97th	D	243	R	192		R	53	D	46	1	R	Reagan
1983–85	98th	D	267	R	168		R	55	D	45		R	Reagan
1985–87	99th	D	253	R	182		R	53	D	47		R	Reagan

AD = Administration; AM = Anti-Masonic; C = Coalition; D = Democratic; DR = Democratic-Republican; F = Federalist; J = Jacksonian; NR = National Republican; Op = Opposition; R = Republican; U = Unionist; W = Whig. Figures are for the beginning of first session of each Congress, except the 93rd, which are for the beginning of the second session.

JUSTICES OF THE SUPREME COURT

	Term of Service	Years of Service	Life Span		Term of Service	Years of Service	Life Span
John Jay	1789–1795	5	1745–1829	Henry B. Brown	1890–1906	16	1836–1913
John Rutledge	1789–1791	1	1739–1800	George Shiras, Jr.	1892–1903	10	1832–1924
William Cushing	1789–1810	20	1732–1810	Howell E. Jackson	1893–1895	2	1832–1895
James Wilson	1789–1798	8	1742–1798	Edward D. White	1894–1910	16	1845–1921
John Blair	1789–1796	6	1732–1800	Rufus W. Peckham	1895–1909	14	1838–1909
Robert H. Harrison	1789–1790	—	1745–1790	Joseph McKenna	1898–1925	26	1843–1926
James Iredell	1790–1799	9	1751–1799	Oliver W. Holmes	1902–1932	30	1841–1935
Thomas Johnson	1791–1793	1	1732–1819	William R. Day	1903–1922	19	1849–1923
William Paterson	1793–1806	13	1745–1806	William H. Moody	1906–1910	3	1853–1917
*John Rutledge**	1795	—	1739–1800	Horace H. Lurton	1910–1914	4	1844–1914
Samuel Chase	1796–1811	15	1741–1811	Charles E. Hughes	1910–1916	5	1862–1948
Oliver Ellsworth	1796–1800	4	1745–1807	Willis Van Devanter	1911–1937	26	1859–1941
Bushrod Washington	1798–1829	31	1762–1829	Joseph R. Lamar	1911–1916	5	1857–1916

	Term of Service	Years of Service	Life Span		Term of Service	Years of Service	Life Span
Alfred Moore	1799–1804	4	1755–1810	Edward D. White	1910–1921	11	1845–1921
John Marshall	1801–1835	34	1755–1835	Mahlon Pitney	1912–1922	10	1858–1924
William Johnson	1804–1834	30	1771–1834	James C. McReynolds	1914–1941	26	1862–1946
H. Brockholst				Louis D. Brandeis	1916–1939	22	1856–1941
Livingston	1806–1823	16	1757–1823	John H. Clarke	1916–1922	6	1857–1945
Thomas Todd	1807–1826	18	1765–1826	William H. Taft	1921–1930	8	1857–1930
Joseph Story	1811–1845	33	1779–1845	George Sutherland	1922–1938	15	1862–1942
Gabriel Duval	1811–1835	24	1752–1844	Pierce Butler	1922–1939	16	1866–1939
Smith Thompson	1823–1843	20	1768–1843	Edward T. Sanford	1923–1930	7	1865–1930
Robert Trimble	1826–1828	2	1777–1828	Harlan F. Stone	1925–1941	16	1872–1946
John McLean	1829–1861	32	1785–1861	Charles E. Hughes	1930–1941	11	1862–1948
Henry Baldwin	1830–1844	14	1780–1844	Owen J. Roberts	1930–1945	15	1875–1955
James M. Wayne	1835–1867	32	1790–1867	Benjamin N. Cardozo	1932–1938	6	1870–1938
Roger B. Taney	1836–1864	28	1777–1864	Hugo L. Black	1937–1971	34	1886–1971
Philip P. Barbour	1836–1841	4	1783–1841	Stanley F. Reed	1938–1957	19	1884–1980
John Catron	1837–1865	28	1786–1865	Felix Frankfurter	1939–1962	23	1882–1965
John McKinley	1837–1852	15	1780–1852	William O. Douglas	1939–1975	36	1898–1980
Peter V. Daniel	1841–1860	19	1784–1860	Frank Murphy	1940–1949	9	1890–1949
Samuel Nelson	1845–1872	27	1792–1873	Harlan F. Stone	1941–1946	5	1872–1946
Levi Woodbury	1845–1851	5	1789–1851	James F. Byrnes	1941–1942	1	1879–1972
Robert C. Grier	1846–1870	23	1794–1870	Robert H. Jackson	1941–1954	13	1892–1954
Benjamin R. Curtis	1851–1857	6	1809–1874	Wiley B. Rutledge	1943–1949	6	1894–1949
John A. Campbell	1853–1861	8	1811–1889	Harold H. Burton	1945–1958	13	1888–1964
Nathan Clifford	1858–1881	23	1803–1881	Fred M. Vinson	1946–1953	7	1890–1953
Noah H. Swayne	1862–1881	18	1804–1884	Tom C. Clark	1949–1967	18	1899–1977
Samuel F. Miller	1862–1890	28	1816–1890	Sherman Minton	1949–1956	7	1890–1965
David Davis	1862–1877	14	1815–1886	Earl Warren	1953–1969	16	1891–1974
Stephen J. Field	1863–1897	34	1816–1899	John Marshall Harlan	1955–1971	16	1899–1971
Salmon P. Chase	1864–1873	8	1808–1873	William J. Brennan, Jr.	1956–	—	1906–
William Strong	1870–1880	10	1808–1895	Charles E. Whittaker	1957–1962	5	1901–1973
Joseph P. Bradley	1870–1892	22	1813–1892	Potter Stewart	1958–1981	23	1915–
Ward Hunt	1873–1882	9	1810–1886	Byron R. White	1962–	—	1917–
Morrison R. Waite	1874–1888	14	1816–1888	Arthur J. Goldberg	1962–1965	3	1908–
John M. Harlan	1877–1911	34	1833–1911	Abe Fortas	1965–1969	4	1910–
William B. Woods	1880–1887	7	1824–1887	Thurgood Marshall	1967–	—	1908–
Stanley Matthews	1881–1889	7	1824–1889	Warren C. Burger	1969–	—	1907–
Horace Gray	1882–1902	20	1828–1902	Harry A. Blackmun	1970–	—	1908–
Samuel Blatchford	1882–1893	11	1820–1893	Lewis F. Powell, Jr.	1971–	—	1907–
Lucius Q. C. Lamar	1888–1893	5	1825–1893	William H. Rehnquist	1971–	—	1924–
Melville W. Fuller	1888–1910	21	1833–1910	John P. Stevens, III	1975–	—	1920–
David J. Brewer	1890–1910	20	1837–1910	Sandra Day O'Connor	1981–	—	1930–

*Appointed and served one term, but not confirmed by the Senate.

Note: Chief justices are in italics.

CHAPTER OPENER CREDITS

Chapter 15
The First Vote. Colored engraving, 1867. The Granger Collection.

Chapter 16
Emigrant waiting room of the Union Pacific railroad depot, Omaha, Nebraska. Colored engraving, 1877. The Granger Collection.

Chapter 17
Bessemer steel manufacturing at Carnegie's Pittsburgh Steelworks, 1886. Contemporary colored engraving. The Granger Collection.

Chapter 18
Intersection of Orchard and Hester Streets on Lower East Side, New York City. Oil over photograph, 1905. The Granger Collection.

Chapter 19
Columbia Bicycles and Tricycles. Poster, ca. 1900. The New-York Historical Society.

Chapter 20
The Lost Bet. Library of Congress.

Chapter 21
Teddy Roosevelt campaigning for president, summer of 1912. Oil over photograph. The Granger Collection.

Chapter 22
Battle before Caloocan, Philippines. Free Public Library of Philadelphia/Joseph Martin/Scala/Art Resource.

Chapter 23
Rock of the Marne: 30th and 38th U.S. Infantry Regiments in action near Mézy, France, July 1918. Painting by Mal Thompson. The Granger Collection.

Chapter 24
Fisk Tire Advertisement. Free Library of Philadelphia/Joseph Martin/Scala/Art Resource.

Chapter 25
The Bowery, Reginald Marsh. Oil on canvas, 1930.

The Metropolitan Museum of Art, Arthur Hoppock Hearn Fund, 1932.

Chapter 26
City Lights. Victor Arnautoff. Left panel of 36′ mural in Coit Tower, San Francisco. WPA/San Francisco Art Commission.

Chapter 27
Secretary of the Navy Claude Swanson, President Roosevelt, and former Secretary of the Navy Josephus Daniels reviewing the fleet, 31 May 1934. Oil over photograph. UPI/Bettmann Newsphotos.

Chapter 28
The Big Three at Yalta. U.S. Army Photo.

Chapter 29
Homecoming Marine. Norman Rockwell, for *The Saturday Evening Post*, 13 October 1945. Printed by Permission of the Estate of Norman Rockwell. Copyright © 1945 Estate of Norman Rockwell.

Chapter 30
Ike visits the Far East. Wayne Miller/Magnum.

Chapter 31
Hawaiian vacation. Wayne Miller/Magnum.

Chapter 32
Soldiers in foxhole, Khe Sanh, Vietnam. Robert Ellison © 1968 Empirenews/Black Star.

Chapter 33
Protest, November 1963. Bob Adelman, Magnum.

Chapter 34
Richard Nixon leaving the White House. © 1979 Dennis Brack/Black Star.

Chapter 35
"Reagan in Illinois" campaign. Dennis Brack/Black Star.

INDEX

Blacks (*cont.*)
603; black nationalism, 602, 688–689, 951–952, 953; and *1960s*, 941; race riots, 949–950, 951, 956, 967, 984; Black Muslims, 950–951; Black Power, 951–952; white backlash against, 956, 983–984; and black anger, 984. *See also* Civil rights movement

IN MILITARY: in Spanish-American War, 630; in World War I, 656, 657–658; in World War II, 791, 802

AND POLITICAL TRENDS: Populism, 575, 579–580; political reforms, 590; New Deal, 734, 743, 752–753, 837, 1001; and Truman, 838–839; and *1950s* consensus, 854; and Reagan, 1013; and Democratic party, 1015

POPULATION: North/urban, 518, 520

VOTE FOR: in Reconstruction, 429, 432–433, 473–474; in post-Reconstruction South, 563, 721; in 1960 election, 873; *1960–1965*, 946; and Voting Rights Act, 946–947; in *1976*, 980

See also Racism; Slavery
Black Star shipping line, 689
Black Thursday, 713
Black Tuesday, 714
Blaine, James G., 570, 620, 626
Bland-Allison Act of *1878*, 566–567
Bloch, Claude, 783
Blockade, *see* Trade, BLOCKADE
Blue Lake forest, 986
Blue laws, 532, 563, 591, 599
Bly, Nellie (Elizabeth Cochrane), 554
Boarding, 538, 545
Boardman, Robinson, 719
"Boat People," 923, 987
Bob Jones University, 1013
Bohlen, Charles, 911
Bolivia, 1011
Bonsack, James, 537
Bonus Expeditionary Force (BEF), 724, 725, 728
Book readership, 555–558
Boone, Pat, 990
Boorstin, Daniel: *The Americans*, 856
Borah, William, 769, 770, 774, 810
Borden, Gail, 541
Boris, John, 710
Born-again Christians, 993–994
Borodin, Michael, 778
Bosnia, 649
"Boss politics," 525–528, 591, 595
Boston (warship), 626, 627
Boston, Massachusetts: subways in, 509; upward mobility in, 522; machine politics in, 526, 527; police strike in, 668, 684; in Palmer raids, 670; in megalopolis, 892–893; racial violence in, 984
"Boswash," 892
Boulder Dam, 726
Bourne, Randolph, 531, 661, 675
Bow, Clara, 694

Bowles, Chester, 907
Boxer Rebellion, 635
Boycott(s), *see* Trade
Boy Scouts, 806
Bracero program, 755, 803
Bradley, Gen. Omar, 846
"Brain trust" in New Deal, 736
Brandeis, Louis D., 595, 599, 610, 612, 667
Brannigan, Corp. Felix, 423
Brazil: cotton from, 440; immigrants to, 513. *See also* Latin America
Bremer, Arthur H., 966
Brennan, William, 948
Brenner, M. Harvey, 1004
Bretton Woods Conference, 826
Brezhnev, Leonid, 924
Brice, Fanny, 550
Brimmer, Andrew F., 983
Brinkmanship, 863–864, 912
Britain, *see* England
British Empire, 812, 814
British Guiana, 627
British Honduras, 767
Broder, David, 1017
Bromley, Dorothy, 694
Brotherhood of Sleeping Car Porters, 723, 753
Browder, Earl, 747
Brown, Pat (Edmund), 953
Brown, William Wells, 435
Brown Berets, 987
"Brown power," 987
Brown's Ferry nuclear accident, 979
Brown v. Board of Education of Topeka, 839, 854, 860
Bruce, Blanche K., 438–439
Bryan, William Jennings, 562, 582–584, 608, 631, 635; World War I stand of, 652, 654; in Scopes trial, 697–698
Bryant, Anita, 988
Brzezinski, Zbigniew, 930
Buchanan, James, 570
Buck, Pearl: *The Good Earth*, 778
Buffalo, destruction of, 452, 464
Buffalo, New York, 516, 528
Buffalo Springfield group, 953
Buford, Anne Gorsuch, 1002
Bulgaria, 810
Bulge, battle of the, 793, 812
Bull Moose party, 609
Bunch, Charlotte, 959, 961
Bunche, Ralph, 752
Bundy, McGeorge, 942
Bunyan, John: *Pilgrim's Progress*, 590
Burbank, Luther, 471
Bureau of Investigation, 669. *See also* Federal Bureau of Investigation
Burger, Warren, 965
Burlingame Treaty, 625
Burlington Railroad, 458
Burma, 830, 869
Burnham, Daniel, 530, 636
Burns, James MacGregor, 758
Burnside, Gen. Ambrose, 387
Burroughs, Edgar Rice: *Tarzan of the Apes*, 555
Bush, George, 993, 994, 1016

Business: new emphasis on, 421; and corporate "persons," 428, 441–442; marketing in, 486–487; concentration of, 487–489, 681, 715, 736, 883–884; opposition to, 492–494; and urban reform, 528; mass marketing by, 536; advertising in, 552–553 (*see also* Advertising); interdependence in, 576; in World War I, 661, 662, 674; trade associations in, 674; optimism of, 711–712; *1920s* weakness of, 714; and New Deal(s), 736, 739, 745, 746; aggressor-nation ties of, 774; and Soviets, 777; in World War II, 796, 802–803; military-industrial complex in, 647, 796, 815, 875, 956; Cuban investments by, 910

AND GOVERNMENT: patent system, 481, 485; aid and support, 490–491, 680, 681–684, 705–706; trademark law, 553; and Progressives, 595; and TR, 606–607, 610–611; and Wilson, 610–611, 612–613; and New Deal, 736 (*see also* New Deal); Eisenhower as president of, 856–857; deregulation, 978, 980; and Reagan, 1002

TYPES OF: department and chain stores, 542–543, 600; mail-order houses, 470; tailoring, 480; cooperatives, 500. *See also* Banking and finance; Economic conditions; Industry

Business cycle, 487, 519, 712, 976
Busing, desegregation and, 965–966
Butler, Benjamin, 430
Butler, Ed, 527
Butterfield, Alexander, 973–974
Byrd, Harry, 736
Byrnes, James F., 822, 824

Cable, George Washington, 557
Cable, transatlantic, 625
Cagney, James, 720
Calamity Jane (Martha Jane Canary), 456–457
Caldwell, Erskine, 725
California: oil discovered in, 453; immigrants and racism in, 455, 637, 719; population increase, 467, 688; migration to, 743, 755, 887; migrant workers in, 754–755; University of (Berkeley), 952–953, 962, 963, 993; and Proposition 13, 992
California Institute of Technology, 796–797
Cambodia, 914, 922, 923, 962, 975
Camelot, 944
Campaign Finance Law, 981
Campbell, John A., 441–442
Canada: U.S. expansionism and, 623, 625; immigrants to, 513; immigrants from, 514, 697; Soviet spies in, 841; draft resisters to, 954
Canals, *see* Transportation, river and canal
Canary, Martha Jane (Calamity Jane), 456–457

Cannon, Joseph ("Uncle Joe"), 593, 608
Cantigny, battle at, 659
Canton, Ohio, 583
Cantor, Eddie, 720
Capitalism, see Economic conditions, CAPITALISM
Capone, Al, 680, 702, 718
Capra, Frank, 791
Caputo, Philip, *A Rumor of War*, 920, 930
Cardozo, Francis, 438
Caribbean islands, see West Indies
Carl, Conrad, 480, 485
Carmichael, Stokely, 951, 956, 961
Carnegie, Andrew, 522, 626, 631, 633; *Gospel of Wealth*, 557; and Carnegie Endowment for International Peace, 655
Carpentier, George, 700
Carpetbaggers, 435
Carswell, G. Harrold, 965
Carter, Jimmy, 906, 907, 929–935, 972, 980–982, 990, 994, 1000, 1001, 1013; Doctrine, 931
Carver, George Washington, 471–472
Cash, Johnny, 990
Cassatt, Alexander, 591
Caste system, race and sex as, 540
Castillo, Leon, 987
Castro, Fidel, 869, 872, 910, 944, 953
Catholicism: and anti-Catholicism in U.S., 532; immigrants and, 516–517; and Al Smith, 706; and Kennedy, 873; and abortion, 988–989, 1000. See also Religion
Catt, Carrie Chapman, 605, 655, 664
Cattell, J. M., 666
Censorship: of the mails, 666; and "self-censorship" (World War I), 665–666
Central America, U.S. in, 909 (map), 1008–1009, 1016. See also Latin America; *specific countries*
Central Intelligence Agency (CIA), 815, 827, 849–850, 854, 869, 870, 874, 912–913, 927, 928, 944, 963, 1006, 1014; in Latin America, 869–870, 910, 912–913, 927, 944, 1008, 1009; in Middle East, 931, 932; in Vietnam, 915, 916, 922. See also Office of Strategic Services (OSS)
Central Pacific Railroad, 457, 458
Central Powers, 649
Ceylon, 830
Chamberlain, Neville, 776
Chambers, Whittaker, 745
Chamber of Commerce, U.S., 591, 684
Chance for Peace speech, 865
Chaplin, Charlie, 551, 552, 699, 701
Chappaquiddick, 966, 994
Charity: by industrial leaders, 490; and urban poverty, 520; and urban poverty, 520; in Great Depression, 726. See also Public welfare and relief

Charity Organization Societies, 520
Chase, Salmon P., 420
Château-Thierry, battle of, 659
Chattanooga race riots, 984
Chavez, Cesar, 956–957, 987
Cheever, John, 745
Chemicals industry, 484
Cherokees, 719. See also Indians
Cheyenne/Arapaho tribes, 462, 986. See also Indians
Chiang Kai-shek, see Jiang Jieshi
Chicago, Illinois, 465, 509, 511, 893; Haymarket Riot in, 500; cable cars in, 509; Catholic immigrants in, 516; Columbian Exposition (1893) in, 530, 622; beautifying projects in, 530; *Social Evil in* (1911 report), 595–596; University of, 597, 723; race war, 664; Al Capone in, 702; World's Fair (1933), 712, 724; Memorial Day Massacre in, 751; migration to, 888, 889; *1968* Democratic convention in, 957–958; Weathermen in, 962; Jackson in, 1015
Chicanos, see Mexico, AND MEXICAN-AMERICANS
Children, see Family life, CHILDREN; Labor, CHILD
Children's Defense Fund, 982
Chile, 614; -U.S. relations, 769–770, 935; U.S. intervention in, 923, 927, 928
China, 778; immigrants from, 455, 457, 458, 516, 520, 625; excluded, 532, 625; segregated, 637; treaties with, 625; Japan and, 635, 637, 671, 672, 765, 769, 778–779, 780, 781, 785; Boxer Rebellion, 635; Revolution of *1911*, 637, 778; rise of Jiang Jieshi, 778; and postwar, 809, 811, 812, 813; World War II losses of, 814; civil war, 821, 829, 830–831; Formosa returned to, 830. See also Jiang Jieshi
PEOPLE'S REPUBLIC OF, 831–832, 842; civil war, 821, 829, 830–831; "loss" of, 832; and Soviet Union, 844, 863, 866, 869, 930; and Korea, 845–846; recognition of, 866; and U.S., 866, 913; Quemoy-Matsu crisis, 866; and Vietnam, 906, 914, 922, 923; and nuclear weapons, 863; Nixon visits, 924, 930, 964, 966. See also Mao Zedong
U.S. POLICY TOWARD, 907; Open Door, 635 (see also Open Door Policy)
China Lobby, 832, 842
"Chipitts," 893
Choctaws, 719. See also Indians
Chopin, Kate, *The Awakening*, 557
Christian Broadcast Network, 990
Christianity: Indians converted to, 464; and expansionism, 618. See also Religion
Christy, Howard Chandler, 656

Chrysler Corporation, 884, 976, 981, 1000
Church, Frank, 995
Church of the Brethren, 800
Churches: black, 440, 723; membership in, 897. See also Religion
Churchill, Winston, 781, 782–783, 786, 791–792, 793, 810, 812, 813, 814, 823, 826
Cigarettes, consumption of, 537, 661
Cincinnati, Ohio, 574; growth and population of, 888
Circus, 549
Cities: growth of, 508, 512–513, 688; crime in, 520–521, 962; immigrants in, 513, 516–517; and industrialization, 480, 511; urban sprawl and urban core in, 509, 510–511, 512; mass transit in, 509–510, 524; and suburbs, 510, 690–691, 882, 890–893, 950; blacks in, 517–518, 520, 525, 688, 721, 802, 803, 809, 873, 888, 950; problems of, 518–521, 525; electric lighting in, 519; skyscrapers in, 519; reform in, 519, 528–530, 545, 593–594, 698; ethnic neighborhoods in, 524; machine politics in, 525–528; cultural pluralism of, 530–532; population increase for, 589; planning in, 682; Democratic strength in, 747; wartime population shifts to, 809; fiscal disasters in, 979. See also Lifestyle, URBAN
Citizenship, 425, 517; Indian, 448, 973. See also Immigrants
City beautiful movement, 530, 636
City University of New York, 860
Civilian Conservation Corps (CCC), 738, 749, 756, 808
Civil liberties: World War I and postwar, 647, 665–667, 667–670, 673, 683; World War II, 800–802; and loyalty program, 820; and McCarthyism, 858 (see also McCarthy, Joseph R., and McCarthyism); Sandinistas' curbing of, 935; and Nixon internal security program, 963
Civil Liberties Union, 667
Civil rights: habeas corpus, 442; and Reconstruction, 421, 428; and 14th Amendment, 441–442; to privacy, 536; and Scottsboro case, 721–723; and FDR, 752; and Dixiecrats, 836; Truman's program for, 838–839; change in attitudes toward, 840; and Kennedy, 941, 942; Warren Court rulings on, 948–949; and affirmative action, 983; and Reagan, 1013
FREEDOM: of speech, 666, 667, 670; of belief, 696
LEGISLATION: of *1866*, 428, 948; anti-Klan, 442; of *1875*, 443, 474; *Civil Rights Cases* and, 474; "force bill," 571; of *1957*, 861–862; of *1964*, 945, 948, 988
Civil rights movement, 942–943, 949;

Demographic factors (*cont.*)
War II, 807; postwar baby boom, 880, 882
DIVORCE: *1880–1920*, 546; *1920–29*, 691; *1930s*, 720; World War II, 807; *1960s–70s*, 988
LIFE EXPECTANCY: in *1900–20*, 539, 540, 546; in *1920–30*, 692; in *1945–70*, 886
MARRIAGE: in World War II, 806–807. *See also* DIVORCE, *above*; Family life
MORTALITY RATE: infant, 721; suicide, 540, 718, 985, 1004. *See also* Health factors
See also Environment; Immigrants; Migration; Population
Dempsey, Jack, 680, 700
Denman, William, 802
Denmark, 623, 781
Dennis et al. v. *U.S.*, 842
Denver, Colorado, 511, 889
Depression/recession, *see* Economic conditions, DEPRESSION
Depression, Great, 714–721; and Great Crash, 710, 713–714; causes of, 710, 714–716; protest during, 723–726; Hoover's policies in, 726–728; and 1932 election, 728–731; Roosevelt's program for, 734, 737–747 (*see also* New Deal); and Roosevelt as governor, 736; and women, 755–756, 804; and international affairs, 765, 773; and World War II, 786; and consumer purchasing, 832
Desegregation, *see* Racism, AND SEGREGATION AND DESEGREGATION
Détente, 923–924, 930, 935, 1005
Deterrence, 863
Detroit, Michigan, 688, 888, 889; race riots, 803, 804; default by, 979
Developing countries, *see* Third World
Dewey, Adm. George, 630–631, 636
Dewey, John, 596–597, 599, 674
Dewey, Thomas E., 757, 808, 836, 837, 838, 841
DeWitt, Gen. John L., 800
Dewson, Molly, 756
Dickson, Jephta, 473
Diem, Ngo Dinh, 915
Dienbienphu, 913
Diet, *see* Health factors, DIET AND NUTRITION
Dietrich, Marlene, 720
Dime novels, 555
Ding Dong School, 897–898
Dingley Act, 566
Direct primaries, 590
Disarmament; and Eisenhower, 865; Washington Conference on (1921–22), 768, 779; arms race vs., 865; and arms limitation (SALT), 924, 930, 931, 935
Disco, 991
Discount rate, 612
Discrimination, *see* Blacks; Racism; Women
Disease, *see* Health factors, DISEASE
Disneyland, 895

District of Columbia, *see* Washington, D.C.
Divorce, *see* Demographic factors, DIVORCE
Dixiecrats, 836, 837
Dixon-Yates controversy, 857
Docherty, George M., 854
Dodd, Christopher, 1008
Dodd, Samuel, 488
Dodds, Harold, 897
Doe v. *Bolton*, 961, 988
Dollar Diplomacy, 637, 640, 823, 824
Dominican Republic, 445, 625; U.S. intervention in, 639, 640, 769, 770, 927; immigrants from, 889, 986, 987
Domino theory, 864, 914, 1008
Donaldson, Scott: *The Suburban Myth*, 893
Donnell, Ed, 469
Donnelly, Ignatius, 575
Dooley, Mr. (Finley Peter Dunne), 619, 622, 636
Dos Passos, John, 659, 703, 725
Douglas, William O., 748, 948
Douglass, Frederick, 423, 435, 601
Dow Chemical Company, 774
Draft, the, *see* Conscriptions and recruitment
Dragnet, 897
Dred Scott case, 441
Dreiser, Theodore, 724, 725; *Sister Carrie*, 557
Drug traffic, 1011
Duarte, José Napoleon, 1008
Du Bois, W. E. B., 601, 602–603, 605, 657, 665, 689, 729, 771; *The Souls of Black Folk*, 601
Duke, James B., 486–487
Dulles, Allen, 866
Dulles, John Foster, 847, 862–863, 864, 867, 871, 914
Dumbarton Oaks Conference, 810
Dunne, Edward F., 591
Dunne, Finley Peter, 619, 622
du Pont de Nemours, E. I., & Company, 484, 504, 774
Dupuy de Lôme, Enrique, 628
Durham, Israel, 525
Dutch, the, *see* Netherlands
Dylan, Bob, 953

Earp brothers, 457
Eastern Europe, 795, 810, 812, 813, 823, 824–825, 827, 837, 865, 869
East Germany, 829. *See also* Germany
East Indies, 785, 794
Eastman, Crystal, 605
Eastman, George, 551, 622
Economic Bill of Rights, 808, 833
Economic conditions: public/national debt, 428, 444, 797, 857, 872, 1004, 1016, 1017; interdependence, 576–577; Gross National Product, 685, 716, 827, 834, 848, 874, 881, 947, 1014; economic expansionism, 343, 508, 622–623, 674–675, 765–

766, 822; deficit spending ("pump priming"), 734, 739, 749, 759, 797, 833, 872, 964, 978; postwar reconversion, 832–835; and New International Economic Order, 928; wage-price controls, 964; revenue-sharing, 965; "supply-side," 1002, 1003; American economy, A-21
CAPITALISM: and government, 487; opposition to, 492–494, 499, 577, 713; and Progressives, 593; welfare, 682; and New Deal, 758–759
DEPRESSION: in southern cotton economy, 441; of *1873–78*, 443, 487, 499, 500, 566–567, 575–579; of *1884–85*, 487; of *1893–97*, 487, 502, 571, 575–579, 588, 629; and expansionism, 620; of *1920–21*, 681; Great (*1930s*), 706, 710, 713–721, 723–728; of *1937–39*, 747–748, 748–749; of *1970s–80s*, 928, 978, 982
GOVERNMENT INVOLVEMENT WITH, and housing, 519, 857, 893, 947; and social science, 599–600; and TR, 606–607, 610–611; and Wilson, 610–611, 612–613; in World War I, 661; Hoover on, 712, 726–728; Council of Economic Advisers, 716, 833, 850; and New Deal, 736, 739, 758 (*see also* New Deal); in World War II, 796, 797, 798; and Truman, 833–834; wage/price controls, 848, 964; minimum wage, 890. *See also* Business, AND GOVERNMENT; Fair Deal; Great Society
INCOME: per capita, 491; *1880–1920*, 538, 539; *1919–29*, 715; Great Depression, 719; *1919–1944*, 759; World War II, 797; postwar through *1960s*, 881, 887–888; guaranteed (FAP), 965; in cities vs. suburbs, 983; *1970s* (nonwhites), 985, 986
INFLATION, from *1889* to *1913*, 538; in Coxey's plan, 578; World War I, 662, 670; *1930s*, 738, 749; World War II, 798; postwar, 827, 834; Korean War, 848; in 1950s, 872, 874; COLA clauses and, 885, 977; *1960s–70s* (stagflation), 928, 964, 972, 976–978, 979, 980, 981, 982, 994; in *1980s*, 1000, 1002–1003, 1014
MARKET ECONOMY, consumerism, 536–537, 540, 542–543, 552–553, 614, 680–681, 685–688, 694, 835, 886, 898, 901, 950, 990; Populists against, 562; and Eisenhower era, 857
POVERTY: urban, 519, 857; crop-lien system and, 472–473; of blacks, 474, 721, 854, 880, 888, 889, 948, 950, 972, 982–983, 1004; of elderly, 692, 743; in *1928*, 705; in *1950s*, 854, 880, 885, 887–890, 902; and illness, 890; legislation against and war on, 890, 946, 947; of women, 890, 947, 972, 1004,

Hydrogen bomb, 829, 842, 847, 859, 864. *See also* Nuclear weapons

IBM Corporation, 884, 962
ICBMs (intercontinental ballistic missiles), 864, 907, 908, 930, 931
Icebox, use of, 541–542
Iceland, 782, 783
Ickes, Harold, 835
Idaho, 456
Ideology: "end of," 855–856. *See also* Communism
Illinois, 719
I Love Lucy, 897
Immigrants: numbers of, 646; and western settlement, 467; and South, 476; in factories, 494; and labor unions, 500, 504; institutions of, 516; and crime, 520; and police, 520; and occupational mobility, 522; and family pattern, 544; as boarders, 545; fertility among, 545; in show business, 550, 551; diplomatic problems from, 620; in Seward's plans, 623; and World War I, 655, 666, 673; blacks contrasted with, 983; economic prospects for, 986, 987
  MAJOR WAVES OF: *1870–1920*, 514–517; newest influx, 987
  NATIONALITIES: Jews, 516, 517; Irish, 458, 514, 649; Germans, 514, 647, 648; Puerto Rican, 689–690, 986; Mexican, 689–690, 889 (*see also* Mexico, MEXICAN-AMERICANS); Japanese, 779; Jews refused as, 810–811; of Indochinese, 923; Hispanic, 986–987. *See also other countries of emigration*
  AND POLITICS, 532; and machine politics, 528; and populism, 575; and political reformers, 590
Immigration: after Civil War, 444; and industrialization, 481, 508; and city growth, 513; and *1890s* depression, 576; opposition to, 695–696, 696–697, 698; and Simpson-Mazzoli bill, 1015
Impeachment, 420, 430–431, 975
Imperialism, 618, 620–621, 623, 627; vs. anti-imperialism, 631–635; in China, 635; toward South America, 640; economic expansionism as, 766, 929; and Japan, 779; in Vietnam, 913, 915; welfare, 916. *See also* Expansion and expansionism
"Imperial" presidency, 758
Inchon landing, 845
Income, *see* Economic conditions, INCOME
Income tax, 612, 614, 662
Independent internationalism, 764
India, 440, 672, 830, 866, 867, 869, 928, 987, 1011
Indiana, 570, 719
Indian Affairs, Bureau of, 464
Indian Bill of Rights, 947

Indian Claims Commission, 986
Indian Reorganization Act, 753–754
Indian Rights Association, 448
Indians, American, population of, 985; assimilation of, 464; and buffalo, 452, 464; on western frontier, 455; and Philippine Insurrection, 636; in Great Depression, 719; in cities, 889; militancy of, 984–985; illnesses among, 985. *See also other specific tribes or groups*
  GOVERNMENT POLICY TOWARD: and westward expansion, 462–465; reservations, 464–465; and New Deal, 734, 753–754; allotment policy, 754; termination policy, 857, 889; dual legal status, 985–986; and Reagan administration, 1013
  MASSACRES OF: at Wounded Knee, 465
  TREATIES WITH, 463–464; and Alcatraz takeover, 985; and dual legal status, 985–986
Indian wars: against Plains Indians, 464
Individualism: and frontier, 452; economic, 528, 588; vs. consumerism, 540; FDR on, 606; prior to Great Depression, 712, 713; of Hoover, 712, 721
Indochina, 785, 830, 847, 863, 866, 913, 987. *See also* Vietnam
Indonesia, 830, 866, 867, 869
Industrialization and industrialism, 480–481; during Reconstruction, 434; and Civil War debt, 444; in South, 453, 472, 475–476; and labor conditions, 480; and invention, 481–485; and efficiency study, 486; social imbalance from, 494; mechanization of labor in, 494; and unions, 500, 501; results of, 504; and cities, 511; and violence, 520; problems seen solved for, 881; and employment opportunities, 983; Industrial Workers of the World (IWW), 502, 504, 592, 662, 666–667, 669
Industrial Workers of the World (IWW), 502, 504, 592, 662, 665, 666–667, 669
Industry: specialization in, 481; and railroad expansion, 459–460; *1919* production from, 483; mass production, 483, 681; mechanization of, 494–495, 497–498; in World War I, 661; U.S. leadership in, 766; in World War II, 796, 834; and deindustrialization, 973, 977, 979; decreased productivity in, 977
  TYPES OF: textile, 475–476, 495, 681, 713; steel, 458, 661, 848, 983, 1003; electrical, 481–484; chemical, 484; automobile, 484, 485, 685, 686, 882, 976, 983; tobacco, 487; armaments, 626, 774; iron and steel, 668; oil, 686; synthetic-rubber, 796, 834; electronics, 834, 883; housing, 891–892; music, 900; coal, 983; rubber, 983

Inflation, *see* Economic conditions, INFLATION
Initiative, 591, 594–595
Insull, Samuel, 484, 715
Intermediate-range nuclear forces (INF) talks, 1006, 1018
Internal Security Act, 842
International Brotherhood of Teamsters, 885
International Harvester Company, 487, 620, 713, 777
International Labor Defense, 722
International Ladies' Garment Workers Union (ILGWU), 503, 749
International Law, and WWI blockades, 649, 651, 652, 654
International Monetary Fund, 826
International Telephone and Telegraph, 766, 884, 913, 928
Interstate commerce, *see* Trade
Interstate Commerce Commission (ICC), 461–462, 607, 609, 682; and Act (1887), 461–462, 488
Interstate highway system, 858, 892
Inventions: reaper, 622; age of, 481, 484–485; of Edison, 481–484; air brakes, 484, 621; indoor toilet, 540; can-producing machines, 541; sewing machine, 542, 621–622; movies, 551; telephone, 555, 621; and overseas expansion, 640; transistor, 883
Iowa Cow War, 723
Iran, 845, 1011–1012; postwar occupation of, 825; U.S. involvement in, 829, 869, 870–871, 935, 1011; hostage crisis, 907, 932, 981, 994, 995, 1006
Ireland: -England relations, 623, 652, 672; Northern Ireland, 1012
  IMMIGRANTS FROM, 458; in World War I, 648
Iron Curtain speech, 826
Iron industry, 668
Islam, *see* Muslims
Isolationism, 764, 774, 776, 781; neo-isolationism, 930, 966
Israel, 870, 871–872; U.S. recognizes, 829; -Arab conflicts, 924–925, 927, 932, 1010–1011
Italy: immigrants from, 514, 516; in World War I, 648; at peace conference, 670; treaties and trade with, 768, 773, 774; attacks Ethiopia, 774, 775; in World War II, 786, 793
Iwo Jima, 795

Jackson, Andrew: presidency of, 569, 612, 758; policies, 588
Jackson, Helen Hunt: *A Century of Dishonor*, 464
Jackson, Henry, 980
Jackson, Jesse, 1015
Jackson, Robert H., 801–802
Jackson State College, 962
Jamaica, 781, 987. *See also* West Indies
James, Edmund J., 511
James, Henry, 557, 603

James, William, 631

Japan: immigrants from, 514, 779; racism against, 637, 800–802; and China, 635, 637, 671, 672, 765, 769, 778–779, 780, 785; and Hawaiian annexation, 627; and Philippines, 633; -Russia War, 636–637, 813; -U.S. relations, 636–637, 778–779, 780–781, 785; in World War I, 667, 671; in inter-war treaties, 768; and Latin America, 773; in anti-Comintern Pact, 775; New Order of, 778–781; in World War II, 785–786, 790, 793, 794–795, 796, 812, 814, 820; postwar, 814, 821, 830, 881, 913, 928, 977; anti-Americanism, 872

Jaworski, Leon, 974

Jazz, 691, 703–704, 900–901

Jazz Singer, The, 699

Jefferson, Thomas, 593, 606

Jeffersonian, The, 666

Jehovah's Witnesses, 800

Jenner, William, 859

Jerusalem, 925, 927

Jews: as immigrants, 516, 517; Coughlin on, 743; Nazi persecution of, 776, 810–811; and Democratic party, 1015

Jiang Jieshi (Chiang Kai-shek), 778, 813, 830, 831, 832, 843, 845, 846, 866, 913

Jim Crow laws and practices, 474–475, 601, 620, 630, 657, 720, 724, 771, 861, 950

Job Corps, 947

Jogging, 972, 991

John Birch Society, 949

Johns Hopkins University, 797

Johnson, Andrew, 420, 425–432, 434, 442, 623

Johnson, Gerald, 725

Johnson, Hiram, 594

Johnson, James Weldon, 771

Johnson, Lyndon Baines, 858, 865, 873, 916, 949, 957; presidency of, 890, 918, 927, 940, 941, 944–948, 955, 958, 963, 978; Doctrine, 927; and Vietnam, 906, 907, 916–919, 920–922, 964, 975; and Great Society, 940, 944–948, 950, 964, 1004

Johnson, Thomas L., 528, 591

Johnson Act, 697

Johnston, William, 699

Joint Chiefs of Staff (JCS), 906, 911, 913

Jones, Bobby, 700

Jones, Eugene Kinckle, 752

Jones, Rev. Jim, 991

Jones, Landon Y., 880

Jones, Mother, 592

Jones, Samuel "Golden Rule," 528

Jones Act, 636

Jones v. Mayer, 948

Joplin, Janis, 953

Jordan, Vernon, 984

Jordan, Israel vs., 925, 1011

Jordan Marsh department store, 542

Journalism, *see* News media

Judd, Walter, 832

Judiciary Reorganization Bill, 748

Julian, George, 427

Kamikaze attacks, 795

Kansas, 468; settlement of, 467; black migration to (Exodusters), 446, 601; cattle population of, 465; farmers' alliances in, 573, 574

Kansas City, as model, 778

Kansas City machine politics, 526, 527, 808

Kansas Pacific Railroad, 452

Kassebaum, Nancy, 988

Katyn Forest massacre, 810

KDKA, Pittsburgh, 688

Kearney incident, 784

Keaton, Buster, 699

Kelley, Florence, 529–530, 592–593, 600

Kelley, Oliver H., 572

Kellogg, Paul, 655

Kellogg-Briand Pact, 768, 769, 779–780

Kelly, "Honest John," 527

Kennan, George F., 824, 826, 920, 931

Kennedy, Edward M., 931, 966, 981, 994, 1006

Kennedy, Jacqueline, 940, 941, 944, 945

Kennedy, John F.: presidency of, 854–855, 873, 875, 907–912, 915, 940–944, 945, 958, 968, 1015; and Vietnam, 906, 907, 935; assassinated, 915, 940, 944, 945; *Profiles in Courage,* 942

Kennedy, Joseph P., 847, 941

Kennedy, Robert, 910, 911, 942, 956–957

Kent State University, 962

Kern, Jerome, 549–550

Kerner, Otto, and Kerner Commission, 941, 950

Kerouac, Jack: *On the Road,* 902

Kesey, Ken, 940

Keynes, John Maynard, 739

Khmer Rouge, 922

Khomeini, Ayatollah Ruhollah, 932

Khrushchev, Nikita, 865–866, 869, 872, 873, 907, 911–912

Kim Il-sung, 845

King, Martin Luther, Jr., 861–862, 873, 943, 949, 950, 951, 956, 1015

King Kong (film), 720

Kinsey, Dr. Alfred, 897, 902

Kiowas, 446. *See also* Indians

Kipling, Rudyard, 509, 632–633

Kissinger, Henry A., 922, 923–928, 967

Kitchen, Claude, 655

Klamath tribe, 857

Knights of Labor, 500, 501, 502, 504, 573

Knowland, William, 832

Knox, Frank, 781

Komarovsky, Mirra, 755

Konoye, Prince Fumimaro, 785

Korea: Japan and, 635, 636–637, 778–779, 830, 847; immigrants from, 637, 987; and *Pueblo,* 956

Korean Air Lines incident, 1008

Korean War, 821, 830, 832, 843–847; and Eisenhower, 848; and military spending, 882–883

Korematsu, Fred, 802

Korematsu case, 801

Krock, Arthur, 742

Krutch, Joseph Wood, 681

Ku Klux Klan: during Reconstruction, 421, 436–437, 442, 580; revivals of, 551, 664, 680, 684, 695, 698, 839, 860, 972, 983–984; and FBI, 949

Kurihara, Joseph Y., 801

Labor: free, 423, 440; industrialization and, 480–481, 494–495, 497–498, 538–539, 547; and scientific management, 486; of women, 495–496, 498, 503 (*see also* Women, WORKING); legislation on, 498; foreign competition for, 632; migrant, 754–755; in World War II, 806; 1960s–1970s labor market, 977

BLACK, 518; wartime, 662–663, 803; in Great Depression, 716–717, 721

CHILD, 496–497, 538; regulations on, 497, 595, 612, 614, 682–683, 693

UNEMPLOYMENT: industrialization and automation and, 504; and urban economy, 519; post-World War I, 681; 1930s, 710, 716–717, 717–718, 720, 721, 724; among blacks, 721, 735, 742, 749, 759, 1003; World War II and postwar, 760, 832, 833–834, 872; technological, 883; 1960s–80s, 964, 976–977, 978, 982, 1000, 1003–1004, 1014, 1018; among Indians, 985; effects of, 1004

Labor strikes: of 1877, 498–499, 569, 577; and Knights of Labor, 500; Haymarket riot, 500, 577; employers' associations against, 500–501; Pullman, 502, 571–572; Homestead, 502, 577; mineworkers', 502, 577, 607–608, 646, 724, 797, 834; garment workers', 503; New Orleans general strike, 577; World War I, 662; of 1919, 668; Seattle general strike, 668; police, 668, 684; steelworkers', 668–669; textile workers', 713; farmers', 723–724; sit-down, 750–751; Mexican-American, 754–755; World War II, 797; postwar, 834

Labor unions, 499–504; antitrust provisions and, 494; membership in, 500, 502–503, 682, 885, 983; women in, 500, 502–504; blacks in, 500, 504; and non-union workers, 504; World War I and, 662, 674; in 1920s, 682, 712–713; and yellow-dog contracts, 721; and New Deal, 739, 746, 749–752; craft vs. industrial, 749; struggle within, 749–750; Mexican-American, 754–755; and World War II, 791, 797; and politics, 834–835; and Taft-Hartley Act, 835–836; and right-

Lomasney, Martin, 527, 530
London, Jack, 557
London Conference (1933), 773
Lone Ranger, 555
Long, Breckenridge, 811
Long, Huey, 743–744, 747
Long Beach, California, 887, 889
Longworth, Alice Roosevelt, 684, 808
Los Angeles: and railroads, 460; and oil, 511; upward mobility in, 522; and socialists, 593; smog in, 796; zoot suit riot in, 803–804; Mexican-Americans in, 889, 986
Lost Generation, 703
Louisiana, 579; Long in, 743–746
Louisville and Nashville Railroad, 458
Lowell, Massachusetts, 716
Lower East Side, 518
Loyalty Leagues, 666
Loyalty program, in federal government, 820, 841, 850, 854, 859, 874
Luce, Henry, 832; *American Century*, 786
Lucky Dragon, 864
Ludlow Massacre (1914), 646
Lumbering, 454, 456, 608
Lumumba, Patrice, 912
Lusitania, sinking of, 651–652
Lynch, James, 433
Lynchings, 601, 630, 631–632, 646, 664, 666, 669, 721, 752, 802–803
Lynd, Robert and Helen, 755
Lynn, Massachusetts, 511

McAdoo, William G., 684
MacArthur, Gen. Douglas, 724, 795, 830, 843–844, 845, 846
McCarran Act, 842
McCarthy, Eugene, 920, 956, 957, 958
McCarthy, Joseph R., and Mc-Carthyism, 821, 832, 840–843, 847, 848, 850, 854, 858–859, 863, 874, 941–942, 948
McClure's magazine, 590
McCord, James W., 972, 973
McCormick, Cyrus, and McCormick reaper, 622
McCormick, Robert R., 774
McCullough, David, 1017
McDowell, Mary, 664
McGovern, George, 957, 966–967, 995
McGuffey's Reader, 557, 596
McGuire, Barry, 953
Machinery, *see* Industrialization and industrialism; Technology
"Machine" politics, 525–528, 591, 595
McKay, Claude, 665, 703, 745
McKay, Douglas, 856
McKinley, William, 562, 569, 581, 583, 584, 627, 628–629, 631, 632, 635; assassinated, 605
McKinley Tariff, 566
McLaughlin, Hugh, 526
McLeod, Scott, 863
McNamara, Robert S., 911, 920, 942
McNary-Haugen bills, 684
McPherson, Aimee Semple, 698

Macune, Charles W., 575
Macy's department store, 542
Maddison, Angus, 881
Maddox incident, 916, 964
Magee, Christopher, 526
Magruder, Jeb Stuart, 964, 990
Mahan, Capt. Alfred T., 626; *The Influence of Seapower . . .* , 626
Mailer, Norman, 941
Mail-order companies, 470
Maine (warship), 626, 628, 629, 652
Major, Charles: *When Knighthood Was in Flower*, 557
"Make love, not war," 954
Malaya, 794
Malcolm X, 950–951, 952
Manchuria, 635, 636, 637, 778, 779–780, 830
Mandan tribe, 462, 463
Mandate system, 671
Manhattan Project, 795
Manila Bay, battle of, 630–631
Mann Act, 596, 599
Mann-Elkins Act of 1910, 609
Manufacturing, *see* Industry
Mao Zedong, 778, 813, 830–832, 845–846, 924, 953. *See also* China, PEOPLE'S REPUBLIC OF
Maple Floor Association v. *U.S.*, 682
March on the Pentagon, 955
March on Washington (1963), 943
March on Washington Movement (1941), 753, 802
Marin, John, 704
Marine Corps, *see* Military, U.S., MARINE CORPS
Marine Corps Women's Reserve, 798
Marne, battle at, 659
Marriage, *see* Demographic factors, MARRIAGE
Marsh, Reginald, 714
Marshall, Gen. George C., 792, 827; and Marshall Plan, 827; and Marshall mission, 830
Marshall, Thurgood, 839
Marshall Field department store, 542
Marti, José, 627, 628, 637
Martin, Dean, 901
Marx, Karl, and Marxism, 577, 725, 953
Massachusetts: public accommodations law in, 423; urbanization in, 508; and 1972 election, 967
Massachusetts Institute of Technology, 796
Masses, The, 666
Massillon, Ohio, 578
Massive retaliation, 863, 866, 907
Mass transit, 509–510, 524
Masterson, William Barclay ("Bat"), 457
Matsu-Quemoy crisis, 866, 873
Mauldin, Bill, 791, 800
Maverick, Maury, 719, 774
Maximilian, emperor of Mexico, 625
Maximum Freight Rate case, 462
May, Henry F., 646
Mayaguez incident, 922

Mead, Margaret, 894
Meadlo, Pfc. Paul, 919–920
Meat Inspection Act, 599, 607
Me Decade, 972, 990, 991–992
Medicaid, 1001, 1005
Medical care, *see* Health factors, MEDICAL CARE
Medicare, 946, 1001, 1005
Meese, Edwin, 1012, 1014
Megalopolis, 892–893
Mehta, G. L., 867
Mellon, Andrew, 683, 684, 725, 726
Melting pot, American nation as, 530–531
Memorial Day Massacre, 751
Mencken, H. L., 703
Menlo Park, New Jersey, 481, 482
Mennonite sect, 800
Meredith, James, 942
Mergers, *see* Business, consolidation of; Monopoly
Meritocracy, 540
Merriwell, Frank, 556, 558
Messianic cults, 990–991
Methodists: and slavery and blacks, 438, 440. *See also* Religion
Mexico: Revolution in, 653; France withdraws from, 625; in Contadora group, 1010
AND MEXICAN-AMERICANS, 514, 517, 689–690, 697, 719, 889, 986; in labor force, 455; racism against, 520, 803–804; and New Deal, 754–755; *bracero* program, 755, 803; and Robert Kennedy, 956–957
-U.S. RELATIONS, 622, 772–773, 776; U.S. intervention in, 639, 640; world wars and, 653, 773; draft resisters to, 954
Miami, Florida, 688, 887
Miami race riots, 984
Michigan, 453
Michigan State University, 915
"Middle America," 965
Middle East, 813, 821, 906–907, 926 (map), 932; U.S. oil interests in, 766, 814, 931; U.S. intervention in, 870–871, 924–927, 1000, 1010–1011, 1018. *See also individual countries*
Midway, battle of, 794
Midway Islands, 445, 623
Migrant labor, 754–755
Migration: to the Plains, 467; off farms, 481; to cities, 512–513, 888–889; and nuclear household, 544; to Sunbelt, 886–887, 965, 992, 993; South-to-North, 947. *See also* Immigration; Westward expansion
Migratory farm workers, 755
Military, U.S.: state militia, 646, 713; segregation and desegregation of, 630; FDR's buildup of, 776; women in, 798; demobilization of, 833; Korean War buildup of, 848; "New Look" of, 863
ARMY: blacks in, 630, 656, 657–658, 802; post-World War I, 675; -McCarthy hearings, 859. *See also*

Military (*cont.*)
Conscription and recruitment; *specific wars*
MARINE CORPS: in Latin America, 637, 771; blacks in, 802; at Inchon, 845; and *Mayaguez*, 922
NATIONAL GUARD, 723, 848; and violence, 724, 860–861, 957
NAVY: enlargement of, 619, 626, 629, 655, 776; as "Great White Fleet," 637
TROOPS ABROAD: Cuba, 630; Philippines, 630, 636; Siberia, 667; Vietnam, 906, 918–922, 923; *1970s,* 927. *See also* Korean War; World War I; World War II
See also Defense, U.S. Department of; Foreign affairs; War(s); War veterans
Military-industrial complex, 647, 796, 815, 875, 956
Military Reconstruction Act (1867), 430
Military spending, 882–883, 1004–1005, 1005–1006
Miller, Arthur, 842
Miller, Thomas W., 683
Millett, Kate: *Sexual Politics*, 959
Milligan, Lambdin P., 441
Mills, C. Wright, 893
Milwaukee, Wisconsin, 511, 516
Miniature golf, 691, 699
Mining, 453–454, 456, 608
Minnesota, 423, 453
Minor, Frances and Virginia, and women suffrage case, 567
Minority groups: on western frontier, 455; and police, 520; and machine politics, 528; in Great Depression, 710. *See also* Blacks; Hispanics; Women
Minstrel shows, 551
Miranda v. *Arizona*, 949
MIRVs (missiles), 924
Miss America Pageant, 680, 959
Missiles, 864, 907, 908, 924, 930, 931
Mississippi, 579; black voters in, 947; and civil rights movement, 943, 949, 953, 965; Jackson State killings, 962
Mississippi Freedom Democratic Party (MFDP), 949
Mississippi Summer Project (1964), 949, 953
Mitchell, Clarence, 945
Mitchell, John (labor leader), 607
Mitchell, John, 965, 973
Mobil Oil, 884, 962
Mobile, Alabama, 887
Mobility: promise of, 521–522, 525; through property acquisition, 522, 523; occupational, 522–523; residential, 523–524; and education, 540, 895; and nuclear household, 544; for women, 805
Model cities program, 947
Moley, Raymond, 736
Molotov, V. M., 823, 824
Molotov Plan, 827
Momism, 894

Mondale, Walter, 980, 1000, 1001, 1013, 1014–1015, 1016
Monetary policy, 566, 976
Money, *see* Banking and finance
Monopoly, 490, 611; fears of, 493, 500, 562, 588; Sugar Trust, 493; and trust-busting, 607, 614, 682, 736. *See also* Antitrust laws
Monroe Doctrine, 625, 627, 671, 673, 910; Roosevelt Corollary to, 639, 769, 773, 927
Montana, 453, 456, 465
Montgomery, Alabama, 861
Montgomery, Lucy M.: *Anne of Green Gables*, 557
Montgomery Ward, 470
Moon landing, 639, 962
Moon, Rev. Sun Myung, 990–991
Moore, W. H., 489
Moore, William, 943
Moral Majority, 992, 1016
Morgan, J. P., 484, 489, 490, 576, 593, 607, 608, 625, 727; and Company, 713
Morgan, Robin: *Sisterhood Is Powerful*, 959
Morgan v. *Virginia*, 839
Morgenthau, Henry, Jr., 811
Mormons, the, 444, 456, 599, 988
Morocco, 640, 847, 866
Morrill Land Grant Act, 471, 598
Morse, Wayne, 916
Mortality rate, *see* Demographic factors, MORTALITY RATE
Moscow Olympics, 931
Mossadegh, Mohammed, 871
Most-favored-nation principle, 774
Motherhood, cult of, 895
Moving pictures, *see* Entertainment, MOVIES
Moynihan, Daniel, 965
Muckrakers, 555, 590, 591, 595, 607
Mugwumps, 570
Muir, John, 456
Muller v. *Oregon*, 498, 599
Mullett, Mary B., 701–702
Multinational corporations, 928, 976
Multiversity, 953
Munich Conference, 775–776, 777, 822
Munich Olympic Games, 925
Municipal Voters League, 591
Munn v. *Illinois*, 461
Murfee, Mary Noailles, 557
Murphy, Frank, 801
Muscle Shoals dam, 682, 741
Music and dance, *see* Arts, the, MUSIC AND DANCE
Musical comedy, 549–550
Muskie, Edmund, 958, 966
Mussolini, Benito, 775
Mutual Defense Assistance Act, 829
MX missiles, 930, 1005
My Lai massacre, 919–920
Myrdal, Gunnar: *An American Dilemma*, 840

Nagasaki, 790, 795, 832
Napoleon III, 625
Nasser, Gamal Abdel, 871, 872

Nast, Thomas, 432
National Advisory (Kerner) Commission on Civil Disorders, 941
National Aeronautics and Space Administration (NASA), 864
National American Women Suffrage Association, 567, 589, 605, 694
National Association for the Advancement of Colored People (NAACP), 603, 657, 721, 723, 753, 803; membership, 803; Legal Defense Fund, 839
National Association for the Advancement of White People, 860
National Association of Manufacturers, 595, 806
National Broadcasting Company (NBC), 688
National Child Labor Committee, 595
National City Bank of New York, 771
National Civic Federation, 589
National Civil Service Reform League, 565
National College Athletic Association, 549
National Committee to End the War in Vietnam, 955
National Conservation Congress, 608
National Conservative Political Action Committee (NCPAC), 992
National Consumers League, 589, 600, 756
National Council of Churches, 840, 1006
National Council for Prevention of War, 768
National Credit Corporation, 726
National Defense Act (1916), 655
National Defense Education Act, 872, 897
National Education Association, 717
National Federation of Settlements and Neighborhood Centers, 890
National Foundation on the Arts and Humanities, 947
National Guard, *see* Military, U.S., NATIONAL GUARD
National Housing Act, 893
National Industrial Recovery Act (NIRA), National Recovery Administration (NRA), 738–739, 742, 743, 745, 749, 756
Nationalism, 618, 619; black, 602, 688–689, 951–952, 953; industrialization and, 481; of Bellamy, 492; and World War I, 655; economic, 773; Third World, 847, 854, 869, 924, 927
National Labor Relations Board, 742, 1013. *See also* Wagner Act
National Labor Union, 499
National Liberation Front, 915
National Municipal League, 589
National Organization for Women (NOW), 959, 960, 961, 1013, 1015
National Origins Act, 697
National Progressive Republican League, 594, 609

Post, Louis, 670
Post Office, U.S., 555; and censorship and seizure of the mails, 666; RFD, 470
Potsdam Conference (1945), 813, 820
Potter, David, *People of Plenty*, 856
Pound, Ezra, 703
Pound, Roscoe, 599
Poussaint, Alvin, 983
Poverty, *see* Economic conditions, POVERTY
Powderly, Terence V., 500
Powell, Lewis F., 965
Powers, Francis Gary, 866
Pregnancy, *see* Demographic factors, BIRTHS AND BIRTH RATE
Presidency: in Gilded Age, 562, 569–572; revival of, 605; Roosevelt's transformation of, 758; "imperial," 758, 975; and Eisenhower, 874; resignation from, 922, 975; "disposable," 981; decline of, 981; Teflon-coated, 1001, 1014; Reagan's restoration of, 1017
AND PRESIDENTIAL POWERS: to call up and send abroad troops, 846–847, 850; and Truman, 849
See also Executive branch
President's Committee on Civil Rights, 839
President's Committee on Equal Employment Opportunity, 942
President's Organization on Unemployment Relief (POUR), 726
Presley, Elvis, 900
Press, *see* News media
Price, Victoria, 722
Princeton University, 611
Prisoners of War (POWs), in Korean War, 846
Prison uprising at Attica, 963
"Profamily" movement, 988, 1016
Professional Air Traffic Controllers Organization (PATCO), 1013
Progressive era and progressivism, 502, 528, 588–593, 600, 613–614; governmental reform in, 593–596; and education, 596–599; and legal thought, 599; and social sciences, 599–600; and racial equality, 601–603; women in, 603–605; and Roosevelt, 605–608; and Wilson, 609–613; and imperialism, 621; and 1920s, 682; and New Deal, 734, 759; in consensus history, 856
Prohibition, 698, 702; opposition to, 530, 532, 591; temperance movements, 494–495; and Republican party, 563; 18th amendment, 595, 728; in military, 656; and crime, 702; Hoover on, 728; and economic recovery, 728; Democrats on, 729; repealed, 738. *See also* Alcohol
Project Beefup, 915
"Prolife" movement, 988, 993–994
Promontory Point, Utah, 457
Property, *see* Land and property ownership

Proposition *13*, 992
Protective tariff, *see* Tariff, PROTECTIVE
Protestantism, evangelical, 697; vs. new immigration, 516, 517; and Social Gospel, 529; and Klan, 695; fundamentalism, 697–698. *See also* Catholicism; Religion; *individual denominations, sects*
Providence, Rhode Island, 508
Public debt, *see* Economic conditions, public/national debt
Public education, *see* Education, PUBLIC
Public housing, 893
Public lands, 456
Public Utility Holding Company Act, 747
Public welfare and relief, 520; charities, 490, 519–520, 726; soup kitchens and breadlines, 718; and unmarried mothers, 983
PROGRAMS FOR: old-age pensions, 595, 692, 736, 743; state, 682, 736; New Deal, 738–742, 745–746, 890; in postwar Europe, 766; AFDC, 950; food stamps, 965; Family Assistance Plan (FAP), 965; nonwhites and, 983; Reagan cuts in, 1001
Public Works Administration (PWA), 738–739
Pueblo, U.S.S., 956
Pueblo peoples, 464, 986
Puerto Rico: acquisition of, 631; immigrants from, 689–690, 697, 889, 986
Pugh, James L., 480
Pulitzer, Joseph, 553–554
Pullman, George, and Pullman strike, 502, 571–572, 577
"Pump priming," *see* Economic conditions, deficit spending
Pure Food and Drug Act, 599, 607
Pure food and drug laws, 607

Quakers, 800. *See also* Religion
Quay, Matt, 570
Quemoy-Matsu crisis, 866, 873

Racism, against freed blacks, 421, 428, 437; and expansionism, 631–632, 640; among Populists, 579–580; and foreign policy, 620, 840, 867; against Japanese-Americans, 637, 800–802; against Latin Americans, 620, 986; and anti-imperialism, 623; against Filipinos, 636; and League of Nations, 672; in Great Depression, 720–723; and FHA, 893; film treatment of, 901; protests against, 953; and "reverse discrimination," 983; and Vietnam forces, 920; of South Africa, 1012
AND SEGREGATION AND DESEGREGATION, 423, 434, 475, 525, 601, 630, 664, 688, 721, 941; Jim Crow laws, 474–475, 601, 620, 630, 657, 720, 724, 771, 861, 950; in federal government, 603, 646, 721;

in military, 657, 802, 839; and Bonus Expeditionary Force, 724; and sit-in movement, 862; of foreign visitors, 867; and Kennedy, 942; legislation on, 945, 947; busing issue, 965–966. *See also* Education
AND VIOLENCE, 601, 943–944, 949; race riots, 520, 630, 646–647, 664–665, 791, 802, 803, 941, 949–950, 951, 956, 967, 983, 984; lynchings, 601, 630, 631–632, 646, 664, 666, 669, 721, 752, 802–803
See also Blacks; Immigrants; Indians; Ku Klux Klan; Slavery
Radical Republicans, 427–428, 429, 430, 431
Radicals and radicalism: fear of, 500; in *1890s*, 577; persecution of, 666–667, 696–697; divisiveness among, 669; and Garvey, 689; and Great Depression, 723, 730; Roosevelt on, 729; and New Deal, 759; race riots blamed on, 803; Africa policy as preventing, 927; of New Left, 952–953, 954; in feminism, 959, 961
Radio, 685, 688, 711
Radio Corporation of America (RCA), 713, 766
Railroad Administration, 661
Railroads, *see* Transportation, RAILROADS
Rainbow Coalition, 1015
Rain-in-the-Face, Chief, 464
Rainy, Joseph H., 435
Ranching frontier, 465–466
Randolph, A. Philip, 723, 753
Rankin, Jeannette, 654, 774, 786
Raskob, John J., 712, 713
Rauschenbusch, Walter, 529, 593
Ray, James Earl, 956
Rayburn, Sam, 835
Raza Unida, La (political party), 987
Reagan, Nancy, 1014
Reagan, Ronald, 934, 958, 980, 992–993; presidency of, 935, 973, 994–995, 1000–1006, 1007, 1008–1014, 1016–1018
Reaganomics, 1000, 1001–1005
Rebel Without a Cause, 900
Recall, 591, 594–595
Reciprocal Trade Agreement Act, 773–774
Reconstruction, 420, 421; failure of, 421, 437; Lincoln's plan for, 425; and Johnson, 425–426; Congressional plan for, 427–428; deadlock in, 429–430; Military Reconstruction Act, 430; and southern politics, 431–437; carpetbaggers and scalawags in, 435–436; and Ku Klux Klan, 436–437; blacks' lives under, 437–441; end of, 441–443, 445–446; and military occupation, 442
Reconstruction Finance Corporation (RFC), 726–727
Recreation, *see* Entertainment; Lifestyle, SOCIAL LIFE AND RECREATION

Recruitment, *see* Conscription and recruitment

Redbaiting, 837, 841. *See also* McCarthy, Joseph R., and McCarthyism

Red Cross, 656, 659, 718, 719, 726, 727, 810

Red Fascism, 822

Red River Valley, 470

Red Scare, 647, 667–670, 673, 696, 840–841

Red Shirts, 442

"Red Summer," 664, 803

Reed, John, 669

Reed, Walter, 637–638

Referendum, 591, 594–595

Reform: and Reconstruction, 421; settlement houses, 529–530; after *1896*, 584; of Progressive era, 588 (*see also* Progressive era and progressivism); working-class, 591; activities by women's organizations, 603–605; opposition to, 614; and Red Scare, 670; and World War I, 675; in *1920s*, 682; of Harding, 683; and 1950s consensus, 855; in consensus history, 856

TYPES OF: political, 590–591; railroad, 462; labor, 498, 502; urban, 519, 528–530; 593–594, 698; civic, 528–530, 589, 593–594; civil service, 564–565, 570, 591; tariff, 570, 571; moral, 595–596, 599; tax, 857

Regionalization: in farmers' alliances, 573–574. *See also* Reconstruction

Rehnquist, William, 965

Relief programs, *see* Public welfare and relief

Religion: of Indians, 462–463, 464; black churches, 440, 723; of freed blacks, 440; and social relations, 540; pietistic vs. ritualistic, 563; as advertising, 686, 688; and social change, 697, 698; pentecostal, 698; and patriotism, 854, 897; in *1950s*, and *1960s*, 897; *1970s* revival of, 990; messianic cults, 990–991

EVANGELICAL, 697; resurgence of, 990; in conservative coalition, 992, 993–994

AND POLITICS AND GOVERNMENT: and formation of law, 599; and conscientious objection, 800; and new conservatism, 992, 993–994; in 1984 election, 1016

See also Churches; Civil rights, FREEDOM, of religion; *individual denominations and sects*

Reno, Milo, 724, 743

Representative government, *see* Self-government

Republican party (newer), in Reconstruction, 421, 427, 433–434, 435–436, 437, 441, 442, 443; and blacks, 423, 432–433, 473, 721, 730; Liberal group in, 442; and 1896 election, 562; in Gilded Age, 563; and Civil War memory, 564;

and tariffs, 566; Mugwumps from, 570; and Populists, 581; "old right" and "new right" in, 993–994

Republic of Korea (South Korea), 843

Research: in electricity, 484; World War II contracts for, 796–797; space, 883; and military spending, 883. *See also* Inventions; Science; Technology

Reserve Officer Training Corps (ROTC), 675, 1016

Resettlement Administration (RA), 745

Resource Recovery Act, 965

Reston, James, 944

Reuben James incident, 784

Reuther, Walter, 841

Revels, Hiram, 435, 438–439

Revenue Act (1916), 655

Revenue Act (1932), 727

Revenue (Wealth Tax) Act (1935), 747

Revenue-sharing, 965

"Reverse discrimination," 983

Reynolds, William Bradford, 1013

Rhee, Syngman, 845

Rhineland, 775

Rhode Island: urbanization in, 508

Rhodes, James Ford, 601

Rhodesia, 927

Ribicoff, Abraham, 957

Richardson, Elliott, 974

Rickover, Adm. Hyman G., 628, 896

Ridgway, Gen. Matthew, 914

Riesman, David, 893

Rifle Clubs, 442

Riis, Jacob, 519

Ringgold, John (Johnny Ringo), 457

Rio Pact, 829

Riots, *see* Violence

Rizzo, Frank, 962

Roads and highways, *see* Transportation, ROADS AND HIGHWAYS

Roaring Twenties, 881

Roberson, Abigail, 536

Roberts, Grace, 633

Roberts, Owen J., 748

Robinson, Edgar Eugene, 747

Robinson, Edward G., 720

Robinson, Jackie, 840

Rockefeller, John D., 481, 488, 489, 490, 493, 525, 578, 593, 621

Rockefeller, Nelson, 958, 963, 979

Rock and roll, 900, 953–954

Rockwell, Norman, 837, 861

Roebling, John A., 519

Roe v. Wade, 961, 988

Rogers, Will, 698, 717, 726, 777

Rogers, William, 981

Romansco, Albert, 728

Rome-Berlin Axis, 775

Rooney, Mickey, 822

Roosevelt, Eleanor (Mrs. Franklin D.), 734, 735, 752, 753, 755, 756

Roosevelt, Franklin D., 734–735, 758–759; fireside chats of, 737; New Deal of, 738–747; second term of, 747–749; and unions, 749; and blacks, 752; third term of, 756–759; and World War II preparedness, 765; and Latin America, 769;

770, 773; and world finances, 773; and isolationism, 774; and World War II, 776–777, 780, 781–786, 791, 792, 793, 811, 812; Soviet Russia recognized by, 777; on full employment, 808; in *1944* election, 808–809; at Yalta, 811, 813; death of, 813, 820; personality of, 823; and Johnson, 944; and imperial presidency, 975; and Reagan, 1016–1017

Roosevelt, Theodore, 549, 571, 581, 590, 605–606, 611, 620, 626, 627, 628, 629, 630, 631, 637, 640, 652, 682, 726, 776, 935; presidency of, 605, 606–608, 620, 636, 638–639, 705, 736; as presidential candidate, 609, 610–611, 612

Roosevelt Corollary, 639–640, 769, 773, 927

Root, Elihu, 620, 628; and Root-Takahira Agreement, 637

"Roots," 991

Rosenberg, Julius and Ethel, 842, 859

Rosie the Riveter, 806, 890

Ross, Edward A., 600

Rossiter, Clinton, 758

Rostow, Walt W., 912

Rough Riders, 606, 630

Roundup, 465, 466

Rubber, synthetic, 796, 834

Rubinow, Isaac Max, 693

Ruby, Jack, 944

Ruckelshaus, William, 974

Ruef, Abe, 527

"Rum, Romanism, and rebellion," 570

Rumania, 810, 823, 824, 830

Running Bulls, battle of the, 750

Rural Electrification Administration (REA), 745–746

Rural Free Delivery (RFD), 470

Rural life, *see* Lifestyle, RURAL

Rusk, Dean, 847, 907, 916

Russell, John H., 771

Russell, Lillian, 549, 550–551

Russia: and Alaska, 444–445, 623; immigrants from, 514; and Manchuria, 635; in World War I, 649, 671; Revolution in, 667. *See also* Soviet Union

Russo-Japanese War, 636–637, 813

Rustin, Bayard, 861

Ruth, George Herman ("Babe"), 680, 700, 720

Sacco, Nicola, and Sacco-Vanzetti case, 696

Sadat, Anwar, 933

St. Lawrence Seaway, 857

St. Louis (refugee ship), 811

St. Louis, Missouri, 465, 574, 888

St. Mihiel, battle at, 659

Sakhalin Island, 813, 830

Salk polio vaccine, 886

Salvation Army, 656, 718

Samoa, 624, 625, 631

San Diego, California, 688, 886, 893

Sandinistas, 935, 1009

Sandino, Augusto, 771, 935

Soviet Union, 667; and *cordon sanitaire*, 671; and Spanish Civil War, 745; and World War I debt, 767; and Germany, 775, 776; and Japan, 775, 779; and Finland, 777, 781; in World War II, 782, 790, 791–792, 793, 798; in Eastern Europe, 795, 809, 810, 812–813, 821, 822, 865–866; and Truman Doctrine, 820; as "Red Fascism," 822; and nuclear weapons, 829, 842, 864, 907, 912, 1007; and China, 831, 866, 869, 924; and Sputnik, ICBM, 864; and Vietnam, 914; and Middle East, 925, 927

-U.S. RELATIONS: World War I and, 667–668; diplomatic recognition, 777; trade, 777, 923, 924, 929, 1006; World War II and, 782, 791–792, 795, 813, 814, 841; Cold War, 821, 822, 823–824, 827, 841, 854, 863, 864, 872, 908; Korea, 830, 844–845; as political issue, 837, 873; and Third World, 854, 866–867, 869, 870, 927; and deterrence, 863; U-2 incident, 866; and Cuba, 910–912; Vietnam War and, 906, 913, 914, 922, 923; detente, 907, 923–924, 930; Nixon–Kissinger on, 923; and human rights, 935; under Reagan, 1006, 1007–1008; and Korean airliner incident, 1007–1008; and Central America, 1008–1010, 1011

Spaatz, Gen. Carl, 823

Space research, and program, 883, 944, 962

Spain: Cuban revolt against, 627–629

IN NORTH AMERICA: Florida, 464

-U.S. RELATIONS: *Virginius* crisis, 625; U.S. base in, 847

Spanish-American-Cuban-Filipino War, 629–631

Spanish Civil War, 745, 775, 776

Special Field Order No. *15*, 420

Special Forces, 912, 915

Special Investigations Unit (of Nixon White House), 973

Speech, freedom of, 666, 667, 670

Spencer, Herbert, 490

Spock, Dr. Benjamin: *Baby and Child Care*, 894

Spoils system, 530, 562, 564–565, 569, 618, 626

Sports, *see* Entertainment, SPORTS

Sprague, Frank, 509

Sputnik, 864, 896

Stageman, Richard, 1004

Stagflation, 964, 972, 976–978, 979, 994

Stalin, Josef, 791, 792, 793, 810, 811, 812, 813, 820, 823, 826, 830, 844, 864

Stalingrad, battle of, 792–793

Standard Fruit, 770

Standard Oil Corporation, 488; expansion and influence of, 489, 490–491, 493, 686; abroad, 766, 774, 780

Stanford, Leland, 457

Stanton, Edwin M., 425, 430

Stanton, Elizabeth Cady, 429

State, U.S. Department of, McCarthy's charges against, 842, 863; and Eisenhower, 854, 859

State government, *see* Government, state

States' rights: and Johnson, 425

Staubach, Roger, 990

Stearns, Harold, 704

Steel industry, *see* Industry, IRON AND STEEL

Steel Workers Organizing Committee (SWOC), 751. *See also* Labor unions

Steffens, Lincoln, 590, 724, 725; *The Shame of the Cities*, 590

Steinbeck, John, 745

Stephens, Alexander H., 426

Stephenson, David, 695

Stettinius, Edward, Jr., 811

Stevens, John L., 627

Stevens, Thaddeus, 427, 430

Stevenson, Adlai E., 576, 848

Stevenson, Adlai E. (II), 837, 858, 907

Stimson, Henry L., 769, 770, 780, 781, 785, 803, 824; and Stimson Doctrine, 780

Stockman, David, 1002

Stock market, 489; Great Crash in, 710, 713–714; speculation in, 713, 714, 715

Strasser, Adolph, 501

Strategic Arms Limitation Talks (SALT), 924, 930, 931, 935

Strategic Arms Reduction Talks (START), 1006

Strategic Defense Initiative ("Star Wars"), 1005

Stratification, *see* Social class

Stratton-Porter, Gene, 557, 558

Strikes, *see* Labor strikes

Strong, Josiah, 528, 619, 622

Student Non-Violent Coordinating Committee (SNCC), 862, 942, 949, 951, 953, 961

Student protest, 922, 952–953, 954–955

Students for a Democratic Society (SDS), 953, 955, 962

Submarine (film), 768

Subtreasury plan, 573, 584, 612

Suburbs, 509, 510, 512, 690–691, 882, 890–893, 896, 950, 983

Suez Canal, 638, 639, 858, 871–872

Suffragists, *see* Vote, the, FOR WOMEN

Sugar, 910

Sugar Trust, 493

Sullivan, Ed, 900

Sullivan, "Big Tim," 527, 591

Sullivan, William H., 916

Sullivan and Cromwell law firm, 774

Summit conference(s): Geneva (1953), 865; Paris (1960), 866; Kennedy-Khrushchev, 907

Sumner, Charles, 427, 445, 625

Sumner, William Graham, 490, 631

Sunbelt, migration to, 886–887, 965, 992, 993

Sundquist, James, 947

Sun Zhongshan (Sun Yatsen), 778

"Superfund" for environmental cleanup, 1002

"Supply-side" economics, 1002, 1003

Supreme Court, U.S.: and Reconstruction, 441; and Sherman Act, 493; and court-packing plan, 748; Warren Court, 948–949, 1016; first woman on, 1013

DECISIONS: on constitutionality, 723; on rights of contract, 599, 683; on Indians, 986; Slaughter-House cases, 441–442; and retreat from Reconstruction, 441–442; on interstate commerce, 461–462, 493; on civil rights, 474–475; on working hours and conditions, 498, 595, 599, 682–683; on Debs' sentence, 502; on suffrage, 567; on *15th* Amendment, 579; on states' power, 599; antitrust, 607, 674; and progressivism, 614; on freedom of speech, 667; Scottsboro case, 721, 722; on New Deal, 745, 746, 748; on Japanese internment, 801; on civil rights and desegregation, 839, 854, 860, 948–949; on alien registration, 842; on voting rights, 948; on church and state, 948; on criminal justice, 949; on school busing, 965–966; on Watergate tapes, 975; on abortion, 988–989; on labor practices, 1013; on tax-exempt fundamentalist schools, 1013

Sussex (French vessel), 652

Swann v. Charlotte-Mecklenburg, 965

Swanson, Gloria, 694, 701

Sweden, 954

Swift, Gustavus, 486, 489

Swift, Tom, 555–556, 558

Syria, 866, 924–925, 1010–1011

Taft, Robert A., 777, 808, 809, 829, 847

Taft, William Howard, 595, 608–609, 640, 682, 684

Taft-Hartley Act, 835–836

Taft-Katsura Agreement, 637

Taiwan (Formosa), 830, 832, 843, 987; as Jiang's headquarters, 831; U.S. aid to, treaty with, 847, 866

Talmadge, Eugene, 839

Tammany Hall, 527, 591, 705

Tanguay, Eva, 550–551

Tarbell, Ida, 664

Tariff: reciprocity in, 566; *1890* (McKinley), 566, 584, 628; *1894* (Wilson-Gorman), 566, 627–628; *1897* (Dingley), 566, 584; Mills bill (1888), 570; *1909* (Payne-Aldrich), 608; *1913* (Underwood), 612; *1922* (Fordney-McCumber), 682; *1930* (Hawley-Smoot), 727, 773; most-favored-notion principle for, 774

PROTECTIVE: 565–566, 584, 620, 978; opposition to, 565, 773; as business